# WileyPLUS

# Introduction to Corporate Finance

## Managing Canadian Firms in a Global Environment

Fifth Edition

**LAURENCE BOOTH**

University of Toronto

**SEAN CLEARY**

Queen's University

**IAN RAKITA**

Concordia University

WILEY

| | |
|---|---|
| DIRECTOR, BUSINESS, ACCOUNTING, AND FINANCE | Michael McDonald |
| EDITORS | Alden Farrar and Emily Marcoux |
| EDITORIAL ASSISTANT | Kirsten Loose |
| ASSOCIATE INSTRUCTIONAL DESIGNER | Daleara Hirjikaka |
| INSTRUCTIONAL DESIGN LEAD | Karen Staudinger |
| MARKETING MANAGER | Jenny Geiler |
| SENIOR CONTENT MANAGER | Dorothy Sinclair |
| PRODUCTION EDITOR | Meaghan MacDonald |
| DESIGN | Wiley |
| COVER DESIGN | Joanna Vieira/Wiley |
| COVER PHOTOGRAPHS | World map © PASHA18, Getty Images; Currency © Maria Toutoudaki, Getty Images; Canadian currency © Wiley. |

This book was set in 9.5/12pt STIX Two Text by Lumina Datamatics, Ltd. Printed and bound by Quad Graphics.

Founded in 1807, John Wiley & Sons, Inc. has been a valued source of knowledge and understanding for more than 200 years, helping people around the world meet their needs and fulfill their aspirations. Our company is built on a foundation of principles that include responsibility to the communities we serve and where we live and work. In 2008, we launched a Corporate Citizenship Initiative, a global effort to address the environmental, social, economic, and ethical challenges we face in our business. Among the issues we are addressing are carbon impact, paper specifications and procurement, ethical conduct within our business and among our vendors, and community and charitable support. For more information, please visit our website: www.wiley.com/go/citizenship.

ISBN (E-Pub) 978-1-119-56162-0

The inside back cover will contain printing identification and country of origin if omitted from this page. In addition, if the ISBN on the cover differs from the ISBN on this page, the one on the cover is correct.

Printed and bound in the United States.
V10017182_012820

90 Eglinton Avenue East, Suite 300
Toronto, Ontario, M4P 2Y3 Canada
Visit our website at: www.wiley.ca

We are very much aware that the target audience for this finance course is made up of bright students who seek careers in business management predominantly in Canada. This has dictated both the content that we have covered and how we have tried to cover it.

A finance textbook designed for business students of necessity means that it should take a managerial focus. In this respect, it is important to note that finance is built on three "legs": accounting, law, and economics.

*Accounting* is the language of business, and financial analysts must be able to understand a firm's financial statements. This is a prerequisite to understanding anything in finance. In fact, for most non-financial companies, the terms "finance" and "accounting" are interchangeable. This is reflected in chapters 3 and 4, where we review the basic features of financial statements and financial analysis. We do this by studying a real Canadian company, Canadian Pacific Railway Limited (CP), and using its financial statements to illustrate and develop basic financial concepts. We chose the financial statements of CP because its statements are relatively uncomplicated and easy for beginning students to understand.

However, if you go back 50 years, you will discover that introductory finance textbooks were heavily based on *corporate* and *securities laws*. This is because financial securities are contracts and the terms of these contracts are partly determined by statute, while the ability to sell them to the general public and trade them in a market is determined by securities laws. Understanding the basics of the legal system is critical for understanding how finance works in practice. Here it is important to understand that there are differences between the United States and Canada that flow from differences in their legal systems. Coercive tender offers, for example, occur in the United States but not in Canada, while bought deal underwritings are common in Canada but not in the United States.

Behind most corporate and securities law, there has been an action that has enriched one person at someone else's expense. While economists politely refer to these actions as "wealth transfers," more commonly they are referred to as "fraud." The legal system is simply the entrenchment of society's ethical or value system. For this reason, the text includes a series of ethical issues for analysis and discussion. If accounting provides the data, and the legal system provides the constraints on what can be done, *economics* provides most of the principles on how to get things done. Understanding the workings of the economy—where we are in the business cycle, industry market structure, and the response of competitors—is all critical to understanding how financial markets behave and how firms manage their finances. However, this is not a financial economics course. We are not proving the existence of equilibrium, but rather we are providing a framework to solve real problems. In this, we develop and use relevant accounting, legal, and economic skills that are used to solve financial problems faced by Canadians every day.

## New to this Edition

*Introduction to Corporate Finance*, Fifth Edition, has been revised and updated to present the most current and relevant data and coverage of topics in the world of finance. This includes updates to examples, tables, financial statements, and ratios. Notable content and chapter-specific enhancements are as follows:

- Chapters 3 and 4 contain an analysis of the updated financial statements for Canadian Pacific Railway Limited.
- Chapter 3 contains a thorough discussion of the impact on capital cost allowance (CCA) charges as a result of the Canada Revenue Agency's introduction in November 2018 of the Accelerated Investment Incentive program, which was designed to encourage additional investment by Canadian firms. This program changes the CCA rules over the November 2018–23 period, as well as over the "phase-out" period of 2024–27. These changes are discussed in Chapter 3.
- Chapter 6 includes a new table displaying global sovereign debt ratings by region.
- Chapter 8 contains a new section dealing with the coefficient of variation, whereby the standard deviation and the arithmetic mean are combined to produce a measure that can assist in the selection of securities. An example that explains this measure has been added at the end of this section.
- Chapter 14 discusses the important tax change that occurred due to the November 2018 government introduction of the Accelerated Investment Incentive program. An explanation of the new CCA tax shield is offered along with several related end-of-chapter problems.
- Chapter 16 provides a comprehensive discussion of changes in the rules for accounting for leases under both IFRS and U.S. GAAP.

We have also added more recent *Finance in the News* features to reflect current thinking in the field of finance and to help students put the material and topics being discussed into context.

# Organization of the Content

There are underlying financial principles that every student of finance needs to know. This course develops these principles first, and then applies them to business finance. However, some instructors may prefer to cover the material in a different manner. To add flexibility, we have designed the material into "parts" or themes that encompass the following chapters:

## Part 1  The Financial Environment (chapters 1 and 2)

In these opening chapters, we examine the Canadian financial system, including the major players in the system, the major securities issued, and the types of problems solved. We also discuss how Canadian markets are linked to international markets and how corporate finance is affected by shocks elsewhere in the financial system. We then discuss the different ways a business can be organized and financed, and the impact of government policy. Finally, the role of management in diverse firms is explored, with a discussion of key careers available to finance majors.

## Part 2  Financial Analysis Tools (chapters 3 and 4)

Understanding how financial statements are prepared and what they mean to external investors is a skill that is necessary for any student of finance. The tools of financial analysis are developed so that external investors can better understand and interpret financial statements. In Part 2, we discuss these skills in a detailed analysis of a real Canadian company.

## Part 3  Valuation Basics (chapters 5 through 7)

The three iron laws of finance include the time value, the risk value, and the tax value of money. In this section we develop the basic discounted cash flow model that is the workhorse of modern finance. We start with the time value of money and apply a simple discounting framework to valuing bonds and equities. In the process, we examine the widely used Gordon growth model for valuing equities and discuss basic approaches to equity valuation.

## Part 4  Portfolio and Capital Market Theory (chapters 8 through 10)

This section of the text discusses the key topics of risk, return, and portfolio theory. We discuss various measures of risk and methods for estimating the required rate of return for securities and portfolios. In Chapter 10, we discuss market efficiency and the importance of this issue for both investors and corporations.

## Part 5  Derivative Securities (chapters 11 and 12)

In Part 4, we discussed how to value stocks and bonds, and build portfolios. These are all basic securities issued by corporations. In this section, we consider derivative securities—that is, securities that are derived from these basic underlying securities. This has been one of the most dynamic areas of finance over the past 20 years, with a mushrooming derivatives market and the Nobel Prize–winning option pricing model developed by Fischer Black and Myron Scholes.

## Part 6  Long-Term Investment Decisions (chapters 13 through 16)

In chapters 13 and 14, we look at the internal acquisition of assets through capital budgeting and apply the workhorse of finance—discounting future cash flows—to evaluate capital expenditures. In chapters 15 and 16, we consider special cases: buying another firm's assets (commonly referred to as mergers and acquisitions) and leasing, which combines the asset-acquisition and financing decisions into one.

## Part 7  Long-Term Financing (chapters 17 through 20)

In chapters 17, 18, and 19, we develop an overview of corporate financing, and in Chapter 20 an understanding of the cost of capital as the overall cost of the funds invested in a firm. To understand how this cost of capital is determined, we need to understand why certain types of securities exist and the basic reasons firms issue debt rather than equity securities and vice versa.

In chapters 6 and 7, we discussed the basics of bonds and equities and how to value them. However, between traditional common equity and straight debt securities there are a range of hybrids involving a mix of both. As well, there are important differences between various types of debt. Just as important, in those earlier chapters we did not discuss why these securities exist or what the difference is between private and public markets—that is, why some securities are traded while others aren't. However, before discussing these different types of securities, we need to discuss the basics of securities law, because the process of obtaining funds from the public is heavily regulated. As discussed in Chapter 1, intermediation involves the issue of pieces of paper—i.e., securities and loans—in return for cash. This requires an understanding of how these pieces of paper are issued, what information is divulged, and how to minimize the possibility of misrepresentation and outright fraud. Paramount in this discussion is the role of provincial securities commissions and the ways in which securities laws are designed to protect the public and the integrity of Canada's financial markets.

## Part 8  Financial Policies (chapters 21 and 22)

Having discussed the range of financial securities available to the firm in the previous section, we now consider the critical aspects of financial policy: how the firm combines its outstanding securities to find an optimal financing policy and how it decides its dividend policy. These are two of the most contentious areas of corporate finance and lead to Franco Modigliani and Merton Miller, Nobel Prize winners in economics, who surprisingly showed that there is no optimal financial policy.

## Part 9  Working Capital Management (chapters 23 and 24)

This topic is critically important for two reasons. First, most new financial recruits in non-financial companies start their careers managing working capital. These new finance professionals will need to learn whether to extend credit to a trade customer, whether to invest surplus cash balances in marketable securities, and how to decide how much inventory a firm really needs. Second, if a firm is having financial problems, they will show up in the firm's short-term cash flow. The ultimate test of a firm's financial health is whether or not it has enough cash or cash equivalents to cover cash expenditures. These decisions involve interacting with a Canadian chartered bank, which frequently lends against working capital assets and actively monitors the financial health of the firm to make sure that its loans are sound.

# How to Use the Content

The division of the text into "parts" offers the instructor flexibility in how to cover the material in class. Parts 1 and 2 are traditional. We start with an overview of the financial system and business finance, before reviewing basic financial statements and financial analysis. In parts 3 to 5, we deviate from the traditional structure by developing a general understanding of discounted cash flow models, modern portfolio theory, and options and futures. In our view, this is necessary to avoid undue duplication when discussing capital budgeting, corporate financing, and cost of capital. In particular, a general introduction to options and futures is useful for discussing real options in capital budgeting, as well as hybrid securities in corporate financing.

In Part 6, we then apply these ideas to the acquisition of long-lived assets (capital budgeting), in Part 7 to corporate financing, in Part 8 to financial policy, and in Part 9 to working capital management. Furthermore, topics relating to international issues and ethics are integrated throughout the text. In this way, none of the topics are "add ons," pushed to the end, to be rarely covered.

For those instructors who prefer a more traditional structure, the content is flexible enough that Part 6 on capital budgeting may easily be moved forward to follow Part 3 and the discussion of discounted cash flow models. The discussion of modern portfolio theory and Part 4 may then be developed in conjunction with risk analysis in capital budgeting. However, the disadvantage of this structure would be that Part 5, on futures and options, would be relegated to a special topic when in reality it is too important to be left to the end of the course.

# Orientation

Many textbooks used in Canada are U.S. textbooks adapted for a Canadian market. In contrast, this text has been written from the ground up based on Canadian content and applications (such as the examples using Canadian Pacific Railway Limited, our featured company). Issues such as the day count, how to quote interest rates, takeover rules, and securities law continue to be different between Canada and the United States. Canadians working for Canadian firms are expected to know what happens in Canada, as well as what happens in the United States.

However, Canadian content includes more than just describing different rules; it must also relate to current practice. We include news articles in the *Finance in the News* features to bring to life the finance issues and topics covered in the course. Relating basic issues to Canadian examples makes the material more relevant to students. For example, it is more relevant to understand the specific issues facing Canadian pension plans and investors, than those faced by U.S. or international investors, even though many of the general issues are the same.

On the other hand, in today's global business environment, what happens around the world impacts Canadians. Therefore, it is important to consider how global factors influence the Canadian environment, and hence the decisions made by Canadian managers and investors. In fact, global influences are so great in Canada that all Canadian financial managers have to be aware of these issues. We address this by integrating international issues on a topic-by-topic basis, as they arise, rather than in a separate chapter where they are just "lumped together." In this way, awareness of international issues develops naturally.

Finally, finance is a how-to subject. Students learn how to do things in a finance course; for example, how to evaluate securities, how to manage short-term cash, how to evaluate a plant expansion, and how to build a portfolio. In helping students develop these skills, there is an extensive set of examples and problems worked out to show how to solve these problems using a financial calculator. Great care has been taken in an effort to specify calculator keystrokes that solve the examples in a simple, straightforward manner. This approach is particularly important in the foundational Part 3, which deals with discounted cash flow valuation. This section develops the basics in a cumulative manner, thus permitting the analysis of complex financial securities, while building students' confidence in their ability to solve real problems.

We believe that this content will stimulate students to understand finance, as well as to apply it. We believe that after working through this material, students will be able to solve basic financial problems, have the basic skills necessary to do more advanced work in finance, and go on to add value to the firms for whom they will eventually work. We hope that reading these chapters will lead students to a greater understanding of finance and that they will then share our enthusiasm for finance. These are our reasons for writing this textbook. We know that these are high standards for a finance textbook; if you feel we have not met these objectives, we welcome your feedback.

# Hallmark Features

Because students are motivated to learn finance if they are shown how it is relevant to their world, each chapter of *Introduction to Corporate Finance* is written with engaging real-world examples and a wealth of detail. The following features are included to further enhance this presentation.

- **Finance in the News:** Most chapters include at least one article or item from the financial press that is integrated into the main discussion of the chapter to help students draw the connection between theory and application, and to highlight the relevance of the topic being discussed.
- **Chapter Openers:** These introduce students to the main focus of the chapter through an interesting and relevant discussion, showing its real-world application.

- **Lessons to Be Learned:** These illustrate an important concept in the chapter, and how that basic tenet of finance was either ignored and thus fuelled the financial crisis, or was adhered to and helped to mitigate the effects of the crisis.
- **Ethics and Corporate Governance:** Found in various parts of the text, this feature discusses how issues of ethics and corporate governance affect corporations today. These features include questions to help launch in-class analysis and discussion.
- **Financial Calculator Keystrokes:** All relevant demonstration problems include actual keystrokes for the TI BA II Plus calculator.

# Pedagogical Features

- **Learning Objectives:** These are listed at the start of each chapter and then integrated throughout the chapter to reinforce key concepts and help guide students' learning.
- **Running Glossary:** Key terms are highlighted throughout each chapter and defined in the text margin.
- **Concept Review Questions:** At the end of each major section, questions are provided to help students check their understanding before moving on.
- **Examples:** All examples in the text are numbered and labelled for easy reference, and include fully worked-out solutions. Keystrokes for the TI BA II Plus financial calculator are included for each relevant example.
- **Chapter Summary:** Each chapter concludes with a summary of the key concepts covered in that chapter, as well as a summary of the learning objectives.
- **Equations Summary:** Equations are numbered, titled, and listed with page references at the end of each chapter.
- **Questions and Practice Problems:** These are provided at the end of each chapter and allow students to practise and enhance their understanding and learning. Questions and practice problems are identified according to the relevant chapter learning objective and practice problems are organized by level of difficulty.

# Digital Resources for Students and Instructors

*Introduction to Corporate Finance*, Fifth Edition, is completely integrated with *WileyPLUS*, featuring a suite of teaching and learning resources. *WileyPLUS* allows students to create a personalized study plan, assess their progress along the way, and access the content and resources needed to master the material. *WileyPLUS* provides immediate insight into students' strengths and problem areas with visual reports that highlight what's most important for both the instructor and student. Many dynamic resources are integrated into the course to help students build knowledge and understanding, stay motivated, and prepare for decision making in a real-world context. *WileyPLUS* also includes integrated adaptive practice that helps students build proficiency and use study time most effectively. Additional features of the *WileyPLUS* course include resources for instructors and students.

# For Instructors

- **Solutions Manual:** The solutions manual includes complete solutions to all end-of-chapter questions and practice problems, as well as answers to the concept review questions. Excel© solutions templates are also available for relevant problems in each chapter.
- **Test Bank:** The test bank includes a rich selection of multiple choice, short answer, and practice problems, with full solutions. These are coded by difficulty and knowledge level, with references to the relevant sections in the text. The test bank is available as Word files and as a computerized test bank, in an easy-to-use test-generating program.
- **PowerPoint© Presentations:** A full series of PowerPoint© slides have been prepared for each learning objective and each chapter and includes key points from each chapter and worked-out demonstration problems where applicable.
- **Data Analytics & Decision-Making Module:** With the emergence of data analytics transforming the business environment, Wiley has partnered with business leaders in the Business-Higher Education Forum (BHEF) to identify the competencies graduates need to be successful in their careers. As a result, *WileyPLUS* includes a new data analytics module with interactive lessons, case studies, and videos. This industry-validated content will help prepare finance students for the changing workforce.
- **Bloomberg Video Activities:** A new feature in *WileyPLUS* offers part-level graded analysis activities on cutting-edge business video content from Bloomberg. The corresponding video activities challenge students to tie content directly to real-world business scenarios, offering an applied, engaging learning experience to supplement their operations management course.
- **Adaptive Practice:** *WileyPLUS* also includes integrated adaptive practice that is proven to help students build proficiency, manage study time, and gain mastery.

# For Students

*WileyPLUS* provides students with a variety of interactive and media-rich study and learning tools, including:

- **Corner Suite Videos:** These videos feature the text's authors' interviews with prominent leading professionals, providing insight into the world of finance and connecting theory to the real world.

- **Office Hour Videos:** These videos feature the authors providing guided, step-by-step instructions for solving sample problems from the text.

- **Mini-Cases with Excel©:** Enhanced problems that test students' conceptual and applied knowledge using real-life scenarios, such as saving for retirement. These cases test students' understanding over multiple concepts in a chapter or across multiple chapters, and are solved using Excel©.

- **Prerequisite Course Reviews:** Brief concept reviews with exercises and problems, which allow students to refresh their knowledge of basic topics in algebra, statistics, financial accounting, and microeconomics.

- **Financial Calculator Keystrokes:** These are included for all relevant worked-out examples.

# About the Authors

**LAURENCE BOOTH**, DBA, MBA, MA (Indiana University); BS (London School of Economics), is Professor of Finance and holds the CIT chair in structured finance at the Rotman School of Management, University of Toronto, where he was the finance area co-ordinator for almost 21 years. His major research interests are in capital markets, corporate finance, and the behaviour of regulated industries. He has published over 100 articles in various outlets and journals including major journals like *Journal of Finance* and *Journal of Financial and Quantitative Analysis*. He has also co-authored a textbook on international business and two on corporate finance. Currently he is on the editorial boards of several academic journals and is a past president of the Midwest Finance Association and the Multinational Finance Society.

At the University of Toronto since 1978, Professor Booth has taught graduate courses in business finance, international financial management, corporate financing, mergers and acquisitions, financial management, financial markets, applied asset management, and financial theory. He has been the primary doctoral supervisor for 16 students at the University of Toronto. His advice is frequently sought by the media and he has appeared as an expert financial witness in both civil cases and before regulatory tribunals across Canada.

**SEAN CLEARY**, CFA, is the BMO Professor of Finance and the Executive Director of the Institute for Sustainable Finance at the Smith School of Business, Queen's University. Dr. Cleary holds a PhD in finance from the University of Toronto and an MBA, is a Chartered Financial Analyst (CFA) charterholder, and is a former board member of both the Atlantic Canada and Toronto CFA societies. He has also completed the Professional Financial Planning Course (PFPC), the Canadian Securities Course (CSC), and the Investment Funds Institute of Canada (IFIC) Mutual Fund Course.

Dr. Cleary has taught numerous university finance courses as well as courses and seminars in many programs designed to prepare students to write exams for all three levels of the CFA program and the CSC. He is the Canadian author of the first three editions of *Investments: Analysis and Management* and the co-author of the sixth edition of *Finance in a Canadian Setting*, both published by John Wiley & Sons Canada, Ltd. He is also the author of the first four editions of *The Canadian Securities Exam Fast Track Study Guide*, also published by Wiley.

Dr. Cleary has published numerous research articles in various journals, including *Journal of Finance, Journal of Financial and Quantitative Analysis, Financial Management, Journal of Banking and Finance*, and *Journal of Financial Research*. He has received several major research grants from the Social Sciences and Humanities Research Council of Canada (SSHRC). He currently serves as Associate Editor for *Managerial Finance* and *European Journal of Finance*.

Dr. Cleary frequently appears in the media on television, on the radio, and in newspapers.

**IAN RAKITA**, CFA, started teaching in the Department of Finance at Concordia University's John Molson School of Business in 1993 after extensive industry experience. He received his Bachelor of Science degree from McGill University, where he majored in mathematics, and his MBA from Concordia University. He earned his PhD from Concordia in 2000. From 1997–1998 he taught at Wilfrid Laurier University in Waterloo, Ontario, where he received a commendation for teaching excellence. Dr. Rakita teaches courses at the undergraduate and graduate level in corporate finance, fixed income securities, and derivatives. He has also taught courses in operations research and business statistics. His research interests are in the microstructure of new and secondary equity offerings as well as the efficiency of Canadian capital markets and sustainable investing.

Dr. Rakita has published articles in *Journal of Banking and Finance, Multinational Finance Journal, The Engineering Economist, Canadian Investment Review*, and *Journal of the Operational Research Society*. He is the only two-time winner of the Gold Prize for outstanding paper awarded in an annual contest sponsored by the Montreal Society of Financial Analysts, where he has also served on the board of directors. Dr. Rakita completed the requirements for the Chartered Financial Analyst designation in 2001. He currently teaches in a specialized MBA program at Concordia University's Goodman Institute of Investment Management. This program links the requirements of the CFA curriculum with the academic requirements of a traditional MBA degree. Dr. Rakita is currently the President of the Concordia University Faculty Association.

# Acknowledgements

A large-scale project such as this one is not the work of single authors; rather it is the combined effort of many people whom we wish to acknowledge. We thank the following reviewers who took the time to read and evaluate the draft manuscripts for various editions:

**Ashraf Al Zaman**, St. Mary's University

**Ben Amoako-Adu**, Wilfrid Laurier University

**Yunbi An**, University of Windsor

**Ata Assaf**, University of Windsor

**Reena Atanasiadis**, Concordia University

**Mohamed Ayadi**, Brock University

**Larry Bauer**, Memorial University of Newfoundland

**Ernest Biktimirov**, Brock University

**David Birkett**, University of Guelph

**Edward Blinder**, Ryerson University

**Trevor W. Chamberlain**, McMaster University

**Suzanne Cottreau**, Saint Mary's University

**Chris Duff**, Royal Roads University

**Alex Faseruk**, Memorial University of Newfoundland

**Bill Fletcher**, Saint Mary's University

**Louis Florence**, University of Toronto

**Merlyn Foo**, Athabasca University

**Cameron Gall**, Mount Royal University

**Myron Gordon**, University of Lethbridge

**Larbi Hammami**, McGill University

**Ken Hartviksen**, Lakehead University

**Margery Heuser**, Okanagan College

**Robert Ironside**, University of Lethbridge

**Raad Jassim**, Concordia University

**Lew Johnson**, Queen's University

**Paul Komiak,** Memorial University of Newfoundland

**Kurt Loescher**, University of Saskatchewan

**András Marosi**, University of Alberta

**Mike McIntyre**, Carleton University

**Florian Muenkel**, Saint Mary's University

**Bhavik Parikh** St. Francis Xavier University

**Lukasz Pomorski**, University of Toronto

**Lynnette Purda**, Queen's University

**William Rentz**, University of Ottawa

**Michael W. Reynolds**, Carleton University

**Wilf Roesler**, University of Lethbridge

**Raina Rudko**, MacEwan University

**Shahbaz Sheikh**, University of Western Ontario

**David A. Stangeland**, University of Manitoba

**Vijay Vishwakarma**, St. Francis Xavier University

**Thomas Walker**, Concordia University

**Eric Wang**, Athabasca University

**Sherry Wang**, Lakehead University

**Jun Yang**, Acadia University

**Jie Zhang**, Trent University

We thank the team at John Wiley & Sons Canada, Ltd., who, as always, provided us with unparalleled support on so many levels. We also thank Ross Meacher, Lana Okerlund, and Ward Jardine for their invaluable editorial and proofreading contributions.

We also thank the following for all their contributions to the end-of-chapter questions and problems and ancillaries: Shiraz Charania (Lanagara College), Adam Kadar, Jaime Morales (Trent University), Julie Slater (Concordia University), and Sorin Rizneau (University of Victoria) and Gabriela Schneider (Northern Alberta Institute of Technology).

We are also particularly grateful to the following individuals for taking the time to be interviewed for the textbook's Corner Suite Videos, and for providing invaluable insight into the world of finance: Dean Colling, First Vice-President, Portfolio Manager, CIBC Wood Gundy, The Colling Group; John Hull, Maple Financial Professor of Derivatives and Risk Management, Joseph L. Rotman School of Management, University of Toronto; Richard W. Nesbit; Marlene K. Puffer, President and CEO, CN Investment Division; and Vlad Volodarski, CFO and CIO, Chartwell Retirement Residences.

**From Laurence Booth:** My thanks to all my former students—you are the reason that faculty write books; your questions and challenges motivate us to do better. Special thanks to my wife Shiva and to my family and friends who provide the support when it is needed.

**From Sean Cleary:** Thanks to my colleagues and my students (past and present) for their inspiration. Special thanks to my wife Grace, my children (Jason [Kristy], Brennan, Brigid, Siobhan, and Rose), my grandchildren (Madden and Amelia), and my parents (Bill and Beryl) for all of their support.

**From Ian Rakita:** Without students, universities and colleges could not hope to survive. We should never fail to emphasize this point in writing textbooks that we believe will help impart some additional knowledge in a world that is being increasingly overwhelmed by enormous amounts of new information. Sincere thanks go out to my dearest Lurdes for her love, devotion, and patience. I would also like to thank my children Shawn (Lindsay), Robyn (Jesse), and grandson Jake for their ongoing support and for providing the motivation that inspired me to complete this project.

**Laurence Booth**      **Sean Cleary**      **Ian Rakita**
Toronto, Ontario      Kingston, Ontario      Montreal, Quebec

# Brief Contents

# Contents

# 19 Equity and Hybrid Instruments 19-1

# 20 Cost of Capital 20-1

# PART 8 FINANCIAL POLICIES

# 21 Capital Structure Decisions 21-1

# 22 Dividend Policy 22-1

# An Introduction to Finance

**LEARNING OBJECTIVES**

After studying this chapter, you should be able to:

**1.1** Define finance and explain what is involved in the study of finance.

**1.2** List the major financial and real assets held by Canadians.

**1.3** Explain how money is transferred from lenders to borrowers and the role played by market and financial intermediaries.

**1.4** Identify the basic types of financial instruments that are available and explain how they are traded.

**1.5** Explain the importance of the global financial system and how Canada is impacted by global events.

Often, the first finance course business students take is a business finance course. Yet business finance cannot be taught in isolation. It is simply one part of finance, which includes personal or household finance, government finance, and international finance. Recent financial crises have confirmed unequivocally that all parts of the financial system are interrelated. Financial crises in the United States and the Eurozone forced governments to raise debt and lower interest rates to stimulate their economies. The resulting low interest rates led consumers to borrow at a rapid pace. By the first quarter of 2018, total global debt (which includes government, household, and business debt) totalled US$247 trillion—up from $178 trillion in 2008, and $99 trillion in 2003—while the global debt-to-GDP ratio increased to 318 percent.[1] Canada's net federal debt at the time stood at C$650 billion, up almost C$200 billion from pre-crisis levels. Obviously, in such an environment, business finance is more heavily affected by household, government, and international finance than ever before.

## 1.1 Finance Defined

**LEARNING OBJECTIVE 1.1**

Define finance and explain what is involved in the study of finance.

So what is finance? In its broadest terms, **finance** is the study of how and under what terms savings (money) are allocated between lenders and borrowers. Here, the terms "lenders" and "borrowers" are also used in their broadest sense—as people and institutions that either have excess money to invest or need money for some reason. However, the key term in the

**finance** the study of how and under what terms savings (money) are allocated between lenders and borrowers

---

[1]Parkinson, David, and McKenna, Barrie, "The 10-Year Hangover." *The Globe and Mail Report on Business*, September 15, 2018, pp. B6, B7.

definition is "allocated," and you may recognize the similarity between finance and economics, which studies how scarce resources are allocated in an economy. In many ways, finance is closely related to economics. However, finance is distinct from economics in that finance is not just about how resources are allocated; it also examines under what terms and through what channels the allocations are made.

Whenever funds are transferred, a financial contract comes into existence. These contracts are called financial securities. As we will discuss in depth in later chapters, exchanging funds (money) for pieces of paper (securities) opens up an enormous number of opportunities for fraud. As a result, the study of finance requires a basic understanding of securities and corporate law and the institutions that facilitate and monitor this exchange of funds. This may seem dull, but it can be dramatic. For example, on December 11, 2008, Bernard Madoff was arrested for securities fraud in the United States, and on March 12, 2009, he pleaded guilty to defrauding his clients of an unbelievable $65 billion.

In this chapter, we will briefly review the structure of the Canadian financial system, considering how it links to the rest of the world and who the major agents are. Our objective is to help you understand the place of business finance in the financial system and how it is buffeted by events occurring elsewhere in "the markets."

---

### Concept Review Question

1. What is finance?

---

## 1.2 | Real versus Financial Assets

---

**LEARNING OBJECTIVE 1.2**

List the major financial and real assets held by Canadians.

---

### Canada's Balance Sheet

We begin by looking at Canada's balance sheet, which is simply a snapshot of what is owned (assets) and what is owed (liabilities) at a particular time. The difference between the value of what is owned and what is owed is "net worth" or equity—as, for example, the equity someone has in a house. We can estimate balance sheets for individuals and for institutions (both businesses and governments). In Chapter 3, we will discuss the role of assets and liabilities in financial statements.

Table 1.1 aggregates the market value of the assets and liabilities of the three major domestic groups in our economy as of the third quarter of 2018: (1) individuals, referred to as the household sector by Statistics Canada (StatsCan), (2) businesses, and (3) government. The Canadian assets and liabilities that are held by non-resident individuals, businesses, and governments compose the balance sheet of the non-resident sector, which we generally "net" out to determine what the country owes to or is owed by non-residents.

Table 1.1 shows that, as of the third quarter of 2018, Canadians had total real assets with a market value of $11,415 billion. Non-residents had net financial assets of –$648 billion—that is, we owed less to non-residents than we owned as foreign assets. So from Canada's balance sheet perspective we had net foreign financial assets of $648 billion. This means the country had a net worth of $12,063 billion (i.e., $11,415 + $648) or approximately $326,000 for every Canadian based on a population of 37 million. Thus, Canada's balance sheet is very simple—as of the third quarter of 2018, we had $11,415 billion in assets with a small net asset balance of $648 billion with non-residents. Within Canada we had lots of debts, but these were simply to other Canadians. When we add everything up, these debts to ourselves net out to zero because one person's debt is another person's asset, as we will discuss shortly.

**TABLE 1.1**   Canada's Balance Sheet ($Billion), 2018, Third Quarter

| | |
|---|---|
| Residential structures | 2,641 |
| Non-residential structures | 1,930 |
| Machinery and equipment | 401 |
| Consumer durables | 695 |
| Inventories | 335 |
| Land | 4,183 |
| Other | 1,230 |
| Net foreign assets | 648 |
| Net worth or equity | 12,063 |

**Source:** Data from Statistics Canada, "Table 36," in *National Balance Sheet Accounts, Q3, 2018*, https://www150.statcan.gc.ca/t1/tbl1/en/tv.action?pid=3610058001&pickMembers%5B0%5D=2.2&pickMembers%5B1%5D=3.1

## Real Assets

The balance sheet shows all real assets according to seven major classifications. The assets included under these headings are **real assets**, representing the tangible things that compose personal and business assets. Personal assets are the value of houses (residential structures), the land the houses are on, the major appliances in the houses (televisions, washing machines, etc.), and cars. Major appliances and cars are referred to as consumer durables because they last many years. For businesses, the major assets are office buildings, factories, mines, and so on (non-residential structures); the machinery and equipment in those structures; the land they are on; and the stock or inventories of things waiting to be used or sold.[2]

**real assets**   the tangible things that compose personal and business assets

We have introduced Canada's national balance sheet because finance is essentially the management of an entity's balance sheet. This management involves the real asset side and the liability side of the balance sheet. When we look at business finance, we will discuss how firms arrive at the decision to build a new factory, increase the level of their inventory holdings, and make strategic asset acquisition decisions, such as buying another firm (mergers and acquisitions). These are all examples of asset acquisitions, which we will generically refer to as capital expenditure (capex) decisions. On the liability side are ways to finance these expenditures, which we will refer to as corporate financing decisions. However, these same decisions are made by individuals when deciding to buy a house or a new car, and by the government, because all entities have a balance sheet.

However, there is a danger in looking only at Canada's balance sheet because it focuses attention on things that we can measure. Based on a 2008 United Nations report directed by Sir Partha Dasgupta at Cambridge University in England, researchers calculated a more inclusive definition of wealth by including both human capital—based on the skills and education of the citizens of a country—and its natural capital, based on its land, forests, fossil fuels, and minerals. In contrast, StatsCan estimates only a part of this value. According to this measure, Canada came out as the seventh wealthiest country studied, with total wealth of US$502,972 per person in 2010.[3] You are wealthier than you think.

## Financial Assets

Although the national balance sheet presented in Table 1.1 is useful for understanding wealth and the different types of real assets, it removes most of the things that are of interest to

[2]These assets also include some owned by the different levels of government in Canada.
[3]UNU-IHDP and UNEP, *Inclusive Wealth Report 2014: Measuring Progress Toward Sustainability* (Cambridge: Cambridge University Press, 2014).

**financial assets** a claim that
one individual or institution has
on another

students of finance. This is because it nets out all the debts we Canadians owe to other Canadians, which is almost all of our debts! To understand these **financial assets** and how the
financial system works, we need to disaggregate the data—that is, look at it in greater detail.
This is what StatsCan does when it prepares the National Balance Sheet Accounts (NBSA).

The basic idea behind the NBSA is to collect financial data on the major agents in the
financial system and then track the borrowing and lending between these agents. For example, StatsCan collects data on all persons and unincorporated businesses in Canada and
groups them into the household sector.[4] This is because individuals as a group tend to lend
to the other major agents in the system, thereby creating financial assets. However, within
the household sector, what one person lends to another is offset by what that person owes. In
this way, a positive financial asset is offset by a negative financial asset or a financial liability,
so the numbers are the net real assets and the net financial assets of Canadian households.
**Figure 1.1** provides the overall breakdown of both the real and the net financial assets in
Canada as of the third quarter of 2018.

Figure 1.1 shows who owns and owes what in the Canadian economy. If we start with
Canadian households and add up all the real (tangible) assets, such as homes and cars, in
aggregate, Canadian households owned real assets with a market value of $6,310 billion as
of the third quarter of 2018. In addition to these real assets, Canadian households owned
net financial assets issued by the government, corporations, and non-residents with a market
value of $4,910 billion. So, in aggregate, if we add the two together, Canadian households had
total net assets with a 2018 market value of $11,220 billion, which is slightly smaller than
Canada's total net assets of $12,063 billion, as shown in Table 1.1.

In the third quarter of 2018, all layers of Canadian government, in aggregate, had real
assets worth $1,034 billion. The bulk of these assets are government office buildings and
the machinery and equipment in them, but $151 billion represents the market value of
government-owned land. That's the good news. The bad news is that all layers of government,
in aggregate, had net financial assets of *negative* $786 billion—that is, a net financial liability
of $786 billion, which is the market value of all government debt outstanding. Similarly,
Canadian corporations and government Crown corporations had real assets with a market
value of $4,072 billion in the third quarter of 2018, representing the factories, mines, office
buildings, and so on, needed to produce the goods and services that we buy. The market value
of the net financial assets issued by the business sector to finance those real assets, or what
we call corporate financing, was −$3,476 billion. Notice that if we add up the value of real
assets owned by the three domestic sectors, we end up with a total market value of real assets
of $11,416 billion. However, when we add up the total net financial assets of these three sec-
tors, we end up with financial assets of $648 billion, which equals exactly the net financial
assets owed by Canadians to non-residents. Therefore, the value of the net assets owned by
Canadian residents, or our net worth, is the sum of these two, or $12,064 billion, which but

**FIGURE 1.1** **Borrowing and
Lending: The Big Picture,
Third Quarter, 2018**

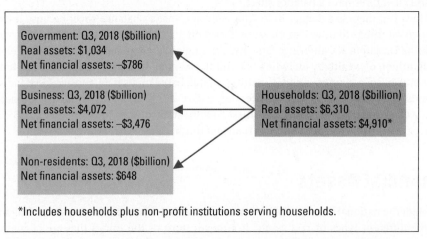

Government: Q3, 2018 ($billion)
Real assets: $1,034
Net financial assets: −$786

Business: Q3, 2018 ($billion)
Real assets: $4,072
Net financial assets: −$3,476

Households: Q3, 2018 ($billion)
Real assets: $6,310
Net financial assets: $4,910*

Non-residents: Q3, 2018 ($billion)
Net financial assets: $648

*Includes households plus non-profit institutions serving households.

**Source:** Data from Statistics Canada, *National Balance Sheet Accounts, Q3 2018*, https://www150.statcan.
gc.ca/t1/tbl1/en/tv.action?pid=3610058001&pickMembers%5B0%5D=2.2&pickMembers%5B1%5D=3.1

[4]We will discuss business organization in Chapter 2, but unincorporated businesses are basically individuals
operating a business that, for tax purposes, is indistinguishable from themselves.

for rounding errors would equal the $12,063 billion in Table 1.1. Also, notice in Figure 1.1 that the net financial assets figure for the household sector equals *positive* $4,910 billion, while the total net financial assets of the combined government and business sectors equals *negative* $4,262 billion. Again, the difference reflects the net foreign assets figure of $648 billion. Overall, the NBSA data indicate that, as Canadians, we are in pretty good shape.

Although Figure 1.1 shows the flow of savings from households to governments and business, with some money flowing in from non-residents, it does not show the flows within each sector. However, it does highlight the importance of the four major areas of finance: personal finance, government finance, corporate finance, and international finance. Although the main focus of this text is corporate finance, it is important to realize that all these sectors are part of the financial system and are affected by the same types of phenomena; a shock in the government or international sectors can quickly work through the system to affect personal and corporate finance and vice versa. Since households represent the primary source of savings, this sector will be discussed first.

## Households

**Table 1.2** provides a comprehensive listing of the assets and liabilities of Canadian households as of the third quarter of 2018.

In aggregate, the household sector looks much as we would expect from our own experiences. The major real assets are houses, worth $2,382 billion; consumer durables, such as washing machines and cars (plus some other miscellaneous assets), worth $695 billion; and the land on which our houses are built, worth $3,091 billion. Our major financial assets are money on deposit, mainly with the banks, worth $1,453 billion; debt securities, worth $134 billion; the value of pension and insurance assets, worth $2,640 billion; and the market value of the shares in corporations, worth $2,750 billion.

Offsetting these financial assets are $651 billion in consumer credit (mainly credit-card debt), $113 billion in loans (mainly bank loans), and $1,428 billion in mortgage debt taken out to buy our houses. So, in aggregate, Canadian households have $2,220 billion in financial liabilities to offset against the $7,056 billion in financial assets. This leaves net financial assets of $4,836 billion, which is $74 billion less than the $4,910 billion reported in Figure 1.1, which also includes $74 billion in net financial assets of non-profit institutions serving households. However, the household sector's liabilities are all different forms of debt, which can be netted

**TABLE 1.2   Assets and Liabilities of Households, Third Quarter, 2018**

| Assets | $Billion | Liabilities | $Billion |
|---|---|---|---|
| Houses | 2,382 | Consumer credit | 651 |
| Consumer durables | 695 | Loans | 113 |
| Land | 3,091 | Mortgages | 1,428 |
| Other | 106 | Other | 28 |
| **Real Assets** | **6,274** | **Total Liabilities** | **2,220** |
| Deposits | 1,453 | | |
| Debt | 134 | | |
| Pensions and insurance | 2,640 | | |
| Equity and investment funds | 2,750 | | |
| Other | 79 | | |
| **Financial Assets** | **7,056** | | |
| **Total Assets** | **13,330** | | |

**Source:** Data from Statistics Canada, *National Balance Sheet Accounts,* Q3 2018, https://www150.statcan.gc.ca/t1/tbl1/en/tv.action?pid=3610058001&pickMembers%5B0%5D=2.2&pickMembers%5B1% 5D=3.1

out against the debt-like financial assets—namely, deposits at banks and loans. What is left constitutes the two major financial assets of the household sector: the market value of investments in shares and the market value of investments in insurance and pensions.

It's one thing to tell people that, on average, each Canadian has almost $330,000 in wealth, but many of them will respond, "I don't have that!" So who does have all that money? Understanding wealth distribution within a country is a complex issue. However, a good starting point is to consider how borrowing and lending changes throughout the life cycle of individuals as they get older. The key decisions most people make are saving to buy a house and saving for retirement. The basic problem in retirement planning is determining how to finance our non-working or retirement years, when we will be consuming but not earning. The basic problem when we want a house is figuring out how to save to buy it and then pay down the mortgage so we are mortgage free as we age and begin to think about retirement.

When considering these problems, think about the financial assets and liabilities in Table 1.2. We can expect, for example, to observe significant differences between people in the household sector, with younger individuals borrowing to buy houses and consumer durables and having a net negative financial asset position (i.e., they are in debt). Conversely, as they age, they pay down their mortgage and build up their financial assets, so older, higher-income individuals tend to save and be wealthier. Thus, within the household sector, we see older individuals lending and younger ones borrowing. However, by aggregating across everyone within the household sector, this dynamic is lost.

Table 1.2 shows that a large part of household wealth consists of life insurance and pension claims, with the latter being promises made by a government or private company to pay money to individuals after they retire. But just how good are these promises? If the promises are made by a private company, its ability to fulfill them can be severely compromised if its own future is in doubt; as a result, pensions can be a major issue in salary and benefit negotiations.

In the third quarter of 2018, mortgage debt was $1,428 billion, and the value of the housing stock was $2,382 billion. So, on average, mortgages were worth 60 percent of the value of a house. However, some people were mortgage free, whereas many others had only recently taken out a mortgage and were heavily indebted. Therefore, a shock to the financial system, such as a recession and job loss or a collapse in house prices, can have a huge impact on the mortgage market and, through it, the whole financial system. So the key questions are: How does money flow from those who have it to those who want it? Who are the agents in the financial system? What are the types of securities issued?

---

### Concept Review Questions

1. Distinguish between real and financial assets.
2. Which sector or sectors of the economy are net providers of financing and which are the net users of financing?

---

## 1.3 | The Financial System

**LEARNING OBJECTIVE 1.3**
Explain how money is transferred from lenders to borrowers and the role played by market and financial intermediaries.

### Overview

**Figure 1.2** provides an overview of the financial system of any economy, be it Canada, the United States, or the global economy. In Canada, as we have discussed, the household sector

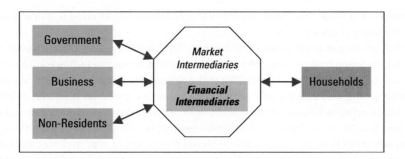

**FIGURE 1.2** **The Financial System**

is the primary provider of funds to business and government. The basic financial flow is "inter-mediated" through the financial system, which comprises (1) **financial intermediaries** that transform the nature of the securities they issue and invest in, and (2) **market intermediaries** that simply make the markets work better. The whole package of institutions is the Canadian financial system. We discuss the various facets of this system in the following sections.

## Channels of Intermediation

**Figure 1.3** demonstrates that the financial system transfers money from those with a surplus (lenders) to those who need it (borrowers). This transfer occurs through **intermediation**, which is the process of bringing these parties together. If we think about how this intermedi-ation can occur, one obvious way is for individuals to borrow directly from friends, relatives, and acquaintances. Another is to borrow from a specialized financial institution, such as the Royal Bank of Canada (RBC Financial Group). These are two extremes in terms of the transfer of money from lenders to borrowers. In the first case, borrowers obtain funds *directly* from individuals; in the second, they borrow *indirectly* from individuals who have first loaned their savings to (deposited them into) a financial institution, which in turn lends to the ultimate borrowers.

These two patterns of intermediation are illustrated in Figure 1.3, with the three basic channels represented. In the first channel is *direct* intermediation, where the lender provides money directly to the ultimate borrower without any help from a specialist. This is a non-market transaction because the exchange is negotiated directly between the borrower and lender. An example would be a relative lending money to buy a car or helping to finance a degree program. The second channel also represents direct intermediation between the lender and borrower, but in this case some help is needed, either because no one individual can lend the full amount needed or because the borrower is not aware of the available lenders. As a result, the borrower needs help to find suitable lenders, which is what market intermediaries

**financial intermediaries** entities that invest funds on behalf of others and change the nature of the transactions

**market intermediaries** entities that facilitate the working of markets and help provide direct intermediation but do not change the nature of the transaction; also called brokers

**intermediation** the transfer of funds from lenders to borrowers

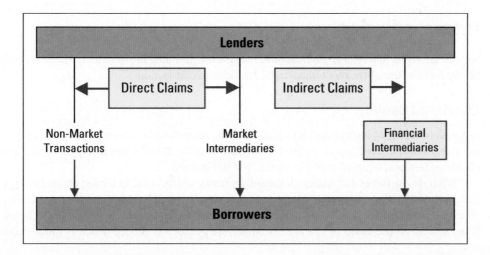

**FIGURE 1.3** **Channels of Money Transfer**

do. A market intermediary is simply an entity that facilitates the working of markets and helps the direct intermediation process.

Typically, market intermediaries are called "brokers." The real estate market has real estate and mortgage brokers, who help with the sale and financing of houses. The insurance market has insurance brokers, who facilitate the sale of insurance, and the stock market has stockbrokers, who facilitate the sale of financial securities, particularly shares. In each case, market intermediaries help make the market work. Their responsibilities are to assist with the transaction and bring borrowers and lenders together, but they do not change the nature of the transaction itself. In this way, market intermediaries are agents, and we call these types of transactions "agency transactions." The most important financial market in Canada is the stock market, or the Toronto Stock Exchange (TSX), which supports a variety of market intermediaries, from stockbrokers who advise clients, through traders who buy and sell securities, to investment bankers who help companies raise capital. In each case, their raison d'être is to make markets work; in doing so, they effect agency transactions.

The third channel is completely different. It represents financial intermediation, a situation in which the financial institution or financial intermediary lends the money to the ultimate borrowers but raises the money itself by borrowing directly from other individuals. In this case, the ultimate lenders have only an *indirect* claim on the ultimate borrowers; their direct claim is on the financial institution. In Figure 1.3, the financial intermediary is in a rectangular box to indicate that it changes the nature of the transaction, whereas the market intermediary does not. We call these types of transactions "principal transactions" because the financial intermediary acts as a principal on its own behalf rather than as an agent on behalf of its clients. However, in the end, both individuals and financial intermediaries are involved in lending to the ultimate borrowers; it is just that the route to these ultimate borrowers differs. Additionally, market intermediaries help financial intermediaries, as well as individuals, in their dealings with the ultimate borrowers. Commonly, we refer to these two market segments as the "retail" and "institutional" markets. When market intermediaries help individuals, it is retail; when they help financial intermediaries, it is institutional.

Before we move on, it's important to note that financial intermediaries rely on the willingness of individuals to lend to them; otherwise, they cannot lend to the ultimate borrowers, who are the ones who really need the money. When people are not willing to lend to financial intermediaries, and those intermediaries, in turn, have to restrict whom they can lend to, we have a **credit crunch**. In 2008–9, Canada and the world experienced the worst credit crunch in over 75 years because major financial intermediaries in the United States and Europe purchased direct claims from issuers who could not repay them. Consequently, other lenders were unwilling to lend to major financial intermediaries, causing, in September 2008, both the biggest-ever bankruptcy in the United States (Lehman Brothers Holdings Inc.) and the biggest-ever bank failure in the United States (Washington Mutual, Inc.). The failures in the U.S. banking system generated a panic that quickly spread around the world, as the financial health of otherwise sound financial intermediaries was called into question. As credit dried up, the world experienced a full-blown credit crunch that rippled through the whole financial system and pushed the world into its first-ever global recession.

**credit crunch**   a situation in which financial intermediaries have to raise the cost of their loans by a significant amount due to their own inability to raise financing on reasonable terms

## Intermediaries

So who are these market and financial intermediaries, and how important are they? We will briefly discuss four of the most important categories in this section.

### Chartered Banks

In terms of financial institutions, let's start with the most familiar and important category—the Canadian chartered banks. **Table 1.3** provides data for 2018 for the six biggest Canadian chartered banks in terms of revenue, assets, and net income.

What do the banks do? Although Canadian banks are involved in almost all areas of the financial system, their core activity is to act as deposit takers and lenders. This means that they take in deposits from individuals and institutions and then lend the money to others as loans. If we add up all the assets of the Big Six banks, we get $5,302 billion, which is much more

**TABLE 1.3   Chartered Banks—Financial Statistics, 2018**

| Bank | Revenue ($Million) | Assets ($Million) | Net Income ($Million) |
|------|-----|-----|-----|
| Royal Bank of Canada | 42,576 | 1,334,734 | 12,431 |
| Toronto-Dominion Bank | 38,834 | 1,334,903 | 11,334 |
| Bank of Nova Scotia | 28,775 | 998,493 | 8,724 |
| Bank of Montreal | 23,037 | 774,048 | 5,450 |
| Canadian Imperial Bank of Commerce | 17,834 | 597,099 | 5,284 |
| National Bank of Canada | 7,166 | 262,471 | 2,232 |

**Source:** Data retrieved from the respective companies' 2018 annual reports, February 19, 2019

than the net liabilities of the household sector, given in Table 1.2, of $651 billion in consumer credit, $113 billion in loans, and $1,428 billion in mortgage debt. The $5,302-billion figure reflects all of the lending within the household sector that StatsCan netted out, plus the corporate financing and foreign activities of the banks. You may not have a good benchmark for these numbers, but the Big Six banks are extremely large, whether they are judged by revenue, total assets, or profits.

The Canadian banks are among the soundest banks in the world and recently have become paragons of prudence. But with assets of $1,334.7 billion and net income of *only* $12.4 billion, all the Royal Bank has to lose on its assets is 0.931 percent after tax (i.e., $12,431/$1,334,734), and it will have no profits at all. In terms of a business model, banking is a low-margin, high-turnover business, which means a bank makes lots of "sales"—that is, loans—but each one in and of itself is not highly profitable. After a couple of years of losses, investors may start to worry about whether the bank can survive, and a full-scale credit crunch will erupt. This is exactly what happened throughout the U.S. banking system during 2008, when the largest bank in the world, Citigroup Inc., saw its overall market value drop from US$260 billion in 2006 to US$5 billion. Citigroup recorded a series of losses that peaked in 2010 at a pre-tax loss of US$140 billion. Global losses in banking rose to $1.24 trillion.

## Insurance Companies

Although the banks are overwhelmingly the most important financial intermediaries, the major insurance companies are also very large. **Table 1.4** provides financial data on the major insurance companies in Canada. The big three, Great-West Lifeco Inc., Manulife Financial Corporation, and Sun Life Financial Inc. each had over $270 billion in assets at the end of 2018.

Technically, life insurance is not insurance—we are all going to die, so we can't insure against it—but it is often a form of savings.[5] Insurance companies are classified as contractual savers, because in most cases the premiums on a policy are paid every month, so the insurers receive a steady flow of money: you buy life insurance and pay premiums; then you die and

**TABLE 1.4   Insurance Companies—Financial Statistics, 2018**

| Insurer | Revenue ($Million) | Assets ($Million) | Net Income ($Million) |
|---------|-----|-----|-----|
| Great-West Lifeco | 44,032 | 427,689 | 3,094 |
| Manulife Financial | 38,972 | 750,271 | 4,887 |
| Sun Life Financial | 26,997 | 271,827 | 2,914 |

**Source:** Data retrieved from the respective companies' 2018 annual reports, February 19, 2019

---

[5]Term insurance is insurance in the sense that it pays off only if you die during the life of the policy.

the policy pays off to your survivors. Before you die, the insurance company has all the premiums to invest, which is why many view selling insurance as simply a way of getting "free" money to invest.

As long as the insurance company can invest the proceeds from the premiums to earn a good return, things are fine. However, from 2006 to 2008, the world's biggest insurance company, American International Group (AIG), invested in exotic financial securities issued by major U.S. banks.[6] These risky investments forced the U.S. government to inject over US$170 billion into AIG to "rescue" it; otherwise, its collapse would have dwarfed that of Washington Mutual and Lehman Brothers.

## Pension Funds

When we looked at the major financial assets of the household sector in Table 1.2, the two largest components were insurance and pension assets, and direct investments in equity and investment funds. The funds in pension plans are held directly for their pensioners, and they substitute for having individuals save for themselves for their retirement. Not surprisingly, the data provided in **Table 1.5** on the major Canadian pension plans show that they are very large. Like the insurance companies, the pension plans are contractual savers and get a steady flow of money each month. The Canada Pension Plan Investment Board (CPPIB) is now the largest pension fund manager in Canada, with close to $370 billion in assets under management as of the end of 2018. The Caisse de dépôt et placement du Québec is the second largest; it manages the assets of several Quebec-based pension funds.

The three types of financial intermediaries discussed above are financial institutions that change the nature of the financial contract. Chartered banks take in deposits and make loans; insurance companies take in insurance premiums and pay off when an incident, such as a death or a fire, occurs; pension funds take in contributions and provide pension payments after plan members retire. These have traditionally been the three most important types of financial intermediaries.

## Mutual Funds

In contrast to the three intermediary categories discussed above, mutual funds simply act as a "pass-through" for individuals, providing them with a convenient way to invest in the equity and debt markets. Like insurance and pension plans, many mutual funds receive their monies through monthly savings plans, but this is not always the case. Unlike other financial intermediaries, mutual funds do not transform the nature of the underlying financial security. Mutual funds perform two major functions: (1) they pool small sums of money so they can make investments that would not be possible for smaller investors, and (2) they offer professional expertise in the management of those funds. We will discuss later the relative advantages of paying for professional money management through mutual funds versus simply investing directly in the stock and bond markets.

**TABLE 1.5**    **Pension Plan Assets, December 31, 2018**

| Pension Plan Managers | Net Assets ($Billion) |
|---|---|
| Canada Pension Plan Investment Board (CPPIB) | 368.5 |
| Caisse de dépôt et placement du Québec* | 309.5 |
| Ontario Teachers Pension Fund (Teachers) | 191.1 |
| Ontario Municipal Employees (OMERS) | 97.4 |

*The Caisse manages the investments of several pension plans.
**Sources:** Compiled using data from pension websites, annual and quarterly reports, April 2, 2019.

---

[6]We discuss these credit default swaps in Chapter 11.

The mutual fund business has enormous amounts of money under management. The dollar amount of mutual fund assets under management has grown dramatically, particularly since 1993, as demonstrated in **Figure 1.4**. As of December 2018, mutual fund assets totalled $1,423 billion, compared with $114.6 billion in 1993, only $24.9 billion in 1990, and a mere $1 billion at the end of 1963. Notice that the total assets under management fell dramatically in 2008 (by $190 billion), due to the severe financial and economic crisis that developed in the second half of the year and the associated stock market crash. The last time this happened was in 2002 when, again, the economy went into a slowdown and the stock market declined. Also notice that in both cases growth rebounded in the years following the decline.

This brief look at the major players in the Canadian financial system should help you understand how the system works. At the core of the system are ordinary Canadians who want to buy houses and televisions, save for retirement, and protect themselves from the impact of accidents. They then channel their savings to the ultimate borrowers—that is, governments and business—either directly, as retail investors, or indirectly, through the major financial intermediaries, where the money is invested by institutional investors. So who are the major borrowers or issuers of financial securities?

## The Major Borrowers

The previous sections introduced the central idea of intermediation—that is, money is transferred from lenders to borrowers either directly, through market intermediaries, or indirectly, through financial intermediaries. Governments are important in this process. For example, the Canada Pension Plan (CPP) and the Quebec Pension Plan (QPP) play large roles in channelling funds from lenders to borrowers. In addition, governments provide many services to Canadians, some of which are paid for out of taxes and some of which are paid for by borrowing. Indeed, the total expenditures of all governments in Canada (federal, provincial, and municipal) was $849.4 billion in 2017, with the federal government obviously being the largest spender.[7]

In addition to the governments themselves, government-owned **Crown corporations** provide goods and services needed by Canadians. Two of the largest, in terms of company assets, are Hydro-Québec and Ontario Power Generation Inc. (OPG). Hydro-Québec had 2018 total assets of $77.0 billion, while OPG had 2018 total assets of $52.3 billion. Both these

**Crown corporations** government-owned companies that provide goods and services needed by Canadians

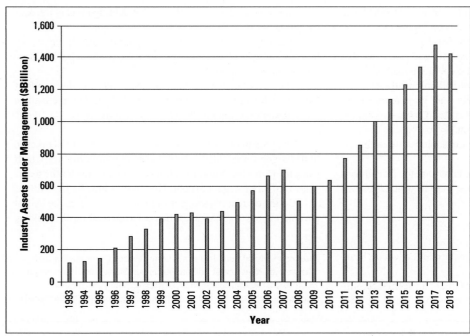

**Source:** Data from the Investment Funds Institute of Canada website at www.ific.ca

 **Canadian Mutual Fund Assets, 1993–2018 ($Billion)**

---

[7]Data are from Statistics Canada, Government Table 36-10-0450-01 (formerly CANSIM0047), March 11, 2019, https://www150.statcan.gc.ca/t1/tbl1/en/tv.action.

and many other Crown corporations issue debt to finance company growth and expenditures, and hence represent important borrowers in the financial system.

We will talk about debt markets later, but note here that the government debt market plays a very important role in the financial system. Even though the federal government produced a surplus every year from 1997 to 2009, the financial crisis and recession of 2008–9 caused the federal government to return to a deficit, which amounted to $19.0 billion by 2017–18.[8] The amount of Canadian federal debt outstanding had increased to $671.3 billion by March 31, 2018. In other words, the federal government is a net debtor and a significant borrower.

In terms of assessing how much debt this is, we normally divide the amount of debt by a country's gross domestic product (GDP). This standardizes the amount of debt by a country's income in the same way that we assess the burden of an individual's debt by dividing the amount of debt by their income. According to this measure, the federal government's debt-to-GDP ratio was 31.3 percent in 2017–18, down from 32.0 percent in 2016–17, and nowhere near peak levels of 67 percent in 1995–96.[9]

Finance in the News 1.1 provides an alternative perspective on government debt and suggests that the reported measure of total government debt of $671.3 billion for 2017–18 noted above understates the total value of "market debt" outstanding, which topped $1 trillion in 2018. This is because "federal budget data are presented under an accrual accounting method, which records transactions differently, spreads out the financial obligation and includes assets, such as cash-on-hand." The article goes on to point out that at $1.029 trillion, government debt is about half of Canada's $2-trillion economy, and the government is approaching the federal debt ceiling figure of $1.168 trillion.

## 1.1 Finance in the News    Federal Government's Total "Market Debt" Now Tops $1 Trillion, Documents Show

The federal government's market debt—the debt on which Ottawa pays interest—has topped $1 trillion for the first time, Department of Finance documents show.

It is a milestone, says former parliamentary budget officer Kevin Page.

...

Officials at Finance say the country's total "debt stock" will be $1.029 trillion when the fiscal year ends on Saturday.

It will go even higher in the coming fiscal year.

Finance Minister Bill Morneau's recent fiscal plan noted that "outstanding government and Crown corporation market debt is projected to reach $1,066 billion ($1.066 trillion) in 2018–19."

The estimate includes $755 billion in "projected year-end government market debt and an anticipated Crown corporation debt stock of approximately $311 billion."

Page said crossing the $1 trillion threshold is extraordinarily important.

"We're a $2-trillion economy. So, to have at the federal level more than a trillion dollars of liabilities, most of which is market debt, it's significant," he said.

### A Different Calculation

Why are these figures much higher than the ones Canadians heard from Morneau on budget day?

Federal budget data are presented under an accrual accounting method, which records transactions differently, spreads out the financial obligation and includes assets, such as cash-on-hand.

When assets and cash reserves are counted in, the federal government's total liabilities, including Crown corporations, are projected to be only $651.5 billion in the current fiscal year.

...

One way to understand the market debt figure is to think of the public accounts in terms of household finances.

A family that owes $400,000 on the mortgage for its home, but has equity and assets worth $150,000, could be said to have total liabilities of $250,000.

The same family's market debt, however, actually stands at $400,000—because that is how much their loan with the bank is for, and that's the amount they make payments on.

...

The growth of the market debt is also consequential because of the largely unheralded federal Borrowing Authority Act, which came into force last November. It sets a limit on how far the federal government can go into debt. That limit is now $1.168 trillion.

On the current trajectory, it will not be long before the federal government has to go back to Parliament to increase the debt ceiling.

...

[8]Government of Canada, "Annual Financial Report of the Government of Canada Fiscal Year 2017–2018," https://www.fin.gc.ca/afr-rfa/2018/report-rapport-eng.asp, retrieved February 13, 2019.
[9]Ibid.

Governments have huge power to raise money from their citizens, either through direct taxation or by monopolizing and charging higher fees for things that we want, such as gambling, alcohol, and cigarettes (these fees are often called "sin taxes"). Because of this power, government debt is generally regarded as "default free," in the sense that it is the only debt people can invest in and know for sure that they will get the promised payments.[10] When we look at various financial securities, we will see that the interest rates paid on different types of Government of Canada debt serve as benchmarks for the Canadian financial system. However, this is not always the case, as the sovereign (euro) debt crisis indicates.

Of all the monopolies that governments normally reserve for themselves, the most important is that of printing the national currency. Among the countries of the European Community, 17 gave up this monopoly when they joined together to use a common currency. However, some of these countries continued to borrow money to finance government expenditures, ignoring the fact that there were limits to how much they could tax and also how much they could cut their expenditures before the cuts caused civil unrest. Without the ability to simply print money, these countries relied on others to lend to them, like any other borrower. This has created continual issues since 2010 as lenders have refused to lend to the most indebted European countries. First Greece, then Ireland, then Portugal and Spain were all but cut off from normal lenders and sought bailouts from the richer members of the European Community (mainly Germany). For these countries, sovereign debt was regarded as anything but risk free, as they became increasingly reliant on funding from fellow Eurozone members and the International Monetary Fund! In response to receiving "aid," they have had to implement austerity measures that pushed Europe back into recession.

Although government debt is very important as a benchmark, and personal debt is important for financing houses and consumer credit, arguably the most important borrowing sector is business. The business sector makes the goods and services we consume, and it borrows to finance growth in this capacity. Indeed, when we look at Figure 1.1, we can see that the Canadian business sector as a whole had net financial liabilities outstanding with a market value of $3,476 billion, more than four times the market value of net government liabilities outstanding.

We conclude this section with a look at the 12 largest non-financial companies in Canada, based on 2017 revenues, as shown in **Table 1.6**. Although revenue is an indicator of size, in

**TABLE 1.6**    **Top 12 Non-Financial Companies Ranked by Revenue, 2017 ($Million)**

| Rank | Company | Profit | Revenue |
|------|---------|--------|---------|
| 2 | Brookfield Asset Management Inc. | 1,898 | 55,061 |
| 3 | Power Corp. of Canada | 1,338 | 51,253 |
| 4 | Magna International Inc. | 2,863 | 50,552 |
| 6 | Alimentation Couche-Tard Inc. | 1,592 | 49,920 |
| 7 | George Weston Ltd. | 759 | 48,292 |
| 9 | Enbridge Inc. | 2,859 | 44,378 |
| 11 | Suncor Energy Inc. | 4,458 | 31,975 |
| 14 | Imperial Oil Ltd. | 490 | 29,125 |
| 17 | Costco Wholesale Canada Ltd. | N/A | 24,783 |
| 18 | Walmart Canada Corp. | N/A | 24,000 |
| 19 | Empire Co. Ltd. | 158 | 23,806 |
| 20 | BCE Inc. | 2,914 | 22,719 |

**Source:** Compiled using data from "FP 500: 2017," retrieved from the *Financial Post* website on February 20, 2019, http://business.financialpost.com/features/fp500-the-premier-ranking-of-corporate-canada

[10] Deposits in banks are also default free up to certain limits because they are, in turn, insured by the government.

that it places a value on what we buy from a company, assets need to be financed and will be reflected in the firm's capital expenditure and corporate financing decisions, topics you will be studying in business finance. Typically, the profits of non-financial corporations are significantly less than those of the big five chartered banks, which reiterates the important role played by the banks in our financial system. Note, for example, that the profits for any of these firms do not exceed those of any of the big five banks, while only four of the companies' profits exceed those of the National Bank of Canada in 2018. It is also worth noting that the two largest firms in Table 1.6 that are classified as "non-financial companies" both have significant components of their operations in the financial industry.

---

### Concept Review Questions

1. Identify and briefly describe the three main channels of savings.
2. Distinguish between market and financial intermediaries.
3. Discuss how the four most important types of financial intermediaries operate.

---

## 1.4 Financial Instruments and Markets

### LEARNING OBJECTIVE 1.4
Identify the basic types of financial instruments that are available and explain how they are traded.

We have discussed the biggest borrowers and lenders in Canada, and seen how financial intermediaries coexist alongside market intermediaries to help the intermediation process. The next step is to look at the instruments and institutional arrangements that are used to transfer these funds.

## Financial Instruments

**debt instruments** legal obligations to repay borrowed funds at a specified maturity date and to provide interim interest payments

**equity instruments** ownership stakes in a company

**common share** an equity instrument that represents part ownership in a company and usually gives voting rights on major decisions affecting the company

**preferred shares** equity instruments that usually entitle the owner to fixed dividend payments that must be made before any dividends are paid to common shareholders

**non-marketable financial assets** invested funds that are available on demand in instruments that are not tradable

Financial assets are formal legal documents that set out the rights and obligations of all the parties involved. Since we discuss the various types of securities in depth at several points later on, we will provide only a brief overview here.

There are two major categories of financial securities.

1. **Debt instruments**: These represent legal obligations to repay borrowed funds at a specified maturity date and provide interim interest payments as specified in the agreement. We will discuss these instruments in more detail in Chapter 6, but note here that some of the most common examples are bank loans, commercial paper, bankers' acceptances (BAs), treasury bills (T-bills), mortgage loans, bonds, and debentures.

2. **Equity instruments**: These represent an ownership stake in a company. The most common form of equity is the **common share**, which we will discuss at length in Chapter 7 and in later chapters. Companies may also issue **preferred shares**, which usually entitle the owner to fixed dividend payments that must be made before any dividends are paid to common shareholders.

Aside from the debt-versus-equity distinction, financial instruments can be categorized in several additional ways. One way is to distinguish between **non-marketable financial** assets and **marketable financial assets.** The most familiar forms of non-marketable assets are savings accounts or demand deposits with financial institutions, such as chartered banks. The funds invested here are available on demand, which guarantees the liquidity of these investments, but you can't sell them to someone else: you have to first withdraw the funds and then transfer the cash. For several decades, another widely used type of non-marketable financial asset in Canada was the Canada Savings Bond (CSB) and its provincial counterparts, which were issued by the federal or provincial governments. These bonds are called non-marketable, because unlike traditional bonds, they are not tradable—though CSBs can still be cashed out by the owner at full par value plus eligible accrued interest at any bank in Canada at any time. While many CSBs are still held by investors, they are no longer being issued as of November 2017.

> **marketable financial assets**   those assets that can be traded among market participants

Marketable securities are those that can be traded among market participants. They are typically categorized not only according to whether they are debt or equity securities but also by their "term to maturity," or time until the obligation must be repaid. **Money market securities** include short-term (i.e., maturities less than one year) debt instruments, such as T-bills, commercial paper, and BAs. **Capital market securities** include debt securities with maturities greater than one year, such as bonds, debentures, and so on. They also include equity securities, which represent ownership in a company and generally have no maturity date.

> **money market securities**   short-term debt instruments
>
> **capital market securities**   debt securities with maturities greater than one year, and equity securities

Governments raise new financing via the debt markets. They issue T-bills as a source of short-term financing (i.e., less than one year), and they issue traditional bonds and CSBs for long-term financing. Businesses raise short-term financing in the form of debt through loans, or by issuing commercial paper, BAs, and so on (all of which will be discussed in greater detail in later chapters). They raise long-term financing in the form of debt (i.e., through loans, by issuing bonds, or by using other long-term debt instruments) or in the form of equity (i.e., by issuing common shares or preferred shares).

## Financial Markets

We have provided a brief overview of the financial instruments that are available to transfer funds from lenders to borrowers. Now we provide a brief description of the financial markets that permit the issue and trading of these instruments. It is important to recognize that financial markets play a critical role in any open economy by facilitating the transfer of funds from lenders to borrowers. In addition, if markets are efficient (which is the topic of Chapter 10), these funds will be allocated to those who have the most productive use for them.

### Primary and Secondary Markets

For discussion purposes, we will begin by distinguishing between primary and secondary markets. **Primary markets** involve the issue of new securities by the borrower in return for cash from investors (or lenders). For example, when the government sells new issues of T-bills or bonds, or when a company sells new common shares to the public, these are primary market transactions; new securities are created, and the borrowing entity raises monies it can spend. Chapters 17 and 19 deal extensively with the primary markets.

> **primary markets**   markets that involve the issue of new securities by the borrower in return for cash from investors (or lenders)

Primary markets are the key to the wealth creation process, since they enable money to be transferred to those who can make best use of it in terms of developing new real assets, such as houses and factories. However, primary markets will not work properly without well-functioning **secondary markets.** Secondary markets provide trading (or market) environments that permit investors to buy and sell existing securities. This service is critical to the functioning of the primary markets because governments and companies would not be able to raise financing if investors were unable to sell their investments when necessary. Consider how reluctant investors would be to buy a 20-year corporate bond worth $1,000, or $1,000 worth of a company's common shares, if they knew they would be unable to sell these securities when they needed to raise money quickly or when they became nervous about the company's future prospects.

> **secondary markets**   trading (or market) environments that permit investors to buy and sell existing securities

**exchanges** or **auction markets**  secondary markets that involve a bidding process that takes place in a specific location

**dealer** or **over-the-counter (OTC) markets**  secondary markets that do not have a physical location and consist of a network of dealers who trade directly with one another

**brokers**  market intermediaries who facilitate the sale of financial securities and help to make the market work

There are two major types of secondary markets: (1) **exchanges** or **auction markets**; and (2) **dealer** or **over-the-counter (OTC) markets**. Exchanges have been referred to as auction markets because they involve a bidding process that takes place in a specific location (i.e., similar to an auction). Investors (both buyers and sellers) can be represented at these markets by **brokers**. In contrast, OTC or dealer markets do not have a physical location, but rather consist of a network of dealers who trade directly with one another. The distinction has become blurred in recent years because trading on most of the major exchanges in the world is now fully computerized, making the physical location of the exchanges of little consequence. At the same time, OTC markets have become increasingly automated, reducing the amount of direct haggling between dealers.

Money market instruments trade in dealer markets. They tend to be very large and are typically issued in sizes of $100,000 or more. As a result, money market trading is dominated by governments, financial institutions, and large corporations. Long-term debt instruments, such as bonds, are also traded primarily through dealer markets, although some are traded on exchanges.

Equity securities generally, and common shares in particular, are the major financial securities issued by corporations, and they represent a proportionate ownership (share) in a firm. Unlike debt securities, which are normally paid back and result in constant refinancing activity, common shares are generally issued once and then stay outstanding indefinitely.[11] As a result, secondary market trading in equity securities is many times the size of the primary market, whereas it is the opposite for debt securities. The overwhelming majority of equity market transactions take place through a stock exchange, although there is a small OTC equity market in Canada.

## Stock Exchanges

**Toronto Stock Exchange** or **TSX**  the major stock exchange in Canada, where most equity security transactions take place; it is the official exchange for trading Canadian senior securities

**TSX Venture Exchange (TSVX)**  the stock exchange for trading the securities of emerging companies not listed on the TSX

**TMX Group Limited**  the company that owns the TSX, the TSXV, the ME, CDS, and Alpha, as well as several other related subsidiaries

**Montreal Exchange (ME)**  the exchange that acts as the Canadian national derivatives market and carries on all trading in financial futures and options

**market capitalization**  the total market value of the common equity of an entity

Dramatic changes have taken place in the major stock exchanges over the past two decades, both at home and abroad. At the start of 1999, Canada had five stock exchanges: the **Toronto Stock Exchange** or **TSX** (formerly called the TSE), the Montreal Exchange (ME), and three others in Vancouver, Winnipeg, and Alberta. An overhaul of that structure occurred during 1999 and 2000, resulting in only two Canadian stock exchanges: the TSX and the newly created **TSX Venture Exchange (TSVX)**. Both of these exchanges were owned by a newly formed company, the TSX Group Inc., which was publicly listed in 2002. In September 2007, the Winnipeg Commodity Exchange was acquired by the Intercontinental Exchange (ICE), as ICE expanded its trading to include agricultural contracts and is now called ICE Futures Canada. On December 10, 2007, the Montreal Exchange and the TSX Group announced an agreement to combine both institutions to form the TMX Group Inc., which was completed on May 1, 2008. In 2012, a new company called **TMX Group Limited** was formed with the acquisition of Canadian Depository for Securities Limited (CDS), Alpha Trading Systems Inc., and Alpha Trading Systems Limited Partnership (collectively Alpha) in August, and the TMX Group Inc. in September.

Since March 2000, the **Montreal Exchange (ME)** has functioned as the Canadian national derivatives market, and it now carries on all trading in financial futures and options in Canada. Equity trading is now concentrated on the TSX and TSVX, where oversight and regulation can be more uniformly implemented.

On April 23, 1997, the TSX closed its trading floor, and trading is now mostly computerized. Brokers enter orders to either buy or sell securities based on their client orders, and the computer matches buyers with sellers. At the end of 2018, there were 3,470 issuers listed in Canada on the TSX and the TSVX, with a **market capitalization** (that is, the total market value of all the listed firms) of approximately C$2.99 trillion; many of the larger firms were also listed on U.S. markets.[12] The barometer that measures the state of the Canadian equity market is the Standard & Poor's/Toronto Stock Exchange (S&P/TSX) Composite Index (formerly known as the TSE 300 Composite Index), which currently comprises approximately 250 companies. The S&P/TSX Composite Index is the TSX's major stock

---

[11]There are occasional share repurchases, but the amounts are small relative to the continuous retirement of debt.

[12]"The MiG Report—Toronto Stock Exchange and TSX Venture Exchange—January 2019," TSX Inc., retrieved February 20, 2019.

market index and is maintained by Standard & Poor's (S&P), a major U.S. company that also maintains the S&P 500 Index, which is one of the major indexes of the U.S. stock market. **Figure 1.5** gives the value of the S&P/TSX Composite from May 1995 to February 2019.

Notice from Figure 1.5 that the S&P/TSX Composite Index reached a month-end high (at the time) of 14,714.73 in May 2008. Then it was caught in the worldwide decline in equity markets as the U.S. banking system verged on collapse. By month-end February 2009, the TSX had declined to 8,123.02, over 45 percent down from its month-end high less than a year earlier. Globally, almost US$15 trillion in market capitalization had disappeared with the decline in stock markets around the world. By the end of April 2015, most stock markets around the globe had exceeded their pre-crisis levels, and Canada was no exception, with the S&P/TSX Index exceeding 15,000. As of February 2, 2019, the TSX Index stood at 15,937.

How big is Canada's stock market relative to other global stock exchanges? **Figure 1.6** shows the market capitalization of the major stock markets around the world as of December 2018. With a total value of just under US$2 trillion, the Canadian market ranked eleventh. Until recently it was the sixth largest, but there has been a dramatic increase in the size of the Chinese markets, with both the traditional Hong Kong markets (#5) and the newer mainland China market in Shanghai (#4) becoming larger than the TMX, as have mainland China's second-largest stock market, Shenzhen (#8), and, more recently, the two markets in India. Of course, the world's biggest market is the New York Stock Exchange, which, together with the Nasdaq, had total market capitalization of over US$30.4 trillion, so the normal rule of thumb that Canada is one-tenth the size of the United States suggests that Canada's stock market is pretty significant, even if it is presently slightly below this figure.

## Other Markets

As mentioned above, in addition to listing on an organized stock exchange, common shares also trade in the OTC or unlisted markets. Canadian OTC equities trade on the **Canadian Securities Exchange (CSE)**, which is operated by CNSX Markets Inc. This market has grown steadily and listed over 460 securities as of December 2018. The requirements to trade on this market are less stringent than those for the TSX Venture Exchange.

**Canadian Securities Exchange (CSE)** an alternative market for small emerging companies

In addition to the primary and secondary markets, there are also the third and fourth markets. The **third market** refers to the trading of securities that are listed on organized exchanges in the OTC market. Historically, this market has been particularly important for "block trades," which are extremely large transactions involving at least 10,000 shares or $100,000. The **fourth market** refers to trades that are made directly between investors (usually large institutions), without the involvement of brokers or dealers. The fourth market operates through privately owned automated systems. Two of the most widely recognized systems are Instinet (Institutional Network), which is owned by Reuters, and Alpha, which is now part of the TMX Group Limited.

**third market** the trading of securities that are listed on organized exchanges in the OTC market

**fourth market** the trading of securities directly between investors without the involvement of brokers or dealers

**FIGURE 1.5** S&P/TSX Composite Index, May 1995–February 2, 2019

**Source:** Data from Statistics Canada, Table 10-10-0125-01, retrieved February 20, 2019

**FIGURE 1.6** World Stock Markets, Market Capitalization, 2018 ($US Billion)

**Source:** Retrieved from the World Federation of Exchanges website on February 20, 2019, https://www.world-exchanges.org/ourwork/statistics

---

### Concept Review Questions

1. Distinguish among the various types of financial assets.
2. Identify the major sources of financing used by (a) governments and (b) businesses.
3. Distinguish between primary and secondary markets.

---

## 1.5 The Global Financial Community

### LEARNING OBJECTIVE 1.5

Explain the importance of the global financial system and how Canada is impacted by global events.

In addition to the domestic financial markets discussed above, global financial markets represent important sources of funds for borrowers and provide investors with important alternatives. Indeed, Canadian debt and equity markets represent only a small proportion of the total global marketplace. Therefore, it makes sense for Canadians to borrow and invest abroad, which has become easier to do in today's global business environment as investment barriers are relaxed.

Table 1.7 demonstrates the importance of global markets to Canadians, and vice versa. In particular, in the third quarter of 2018 Canadians had foreign investments totalling about $5.14 trillion (i.e., all the assets in the table). Approximately $2,203 billion of this figure represented investments in financial assets, such as foreign stocks, bonds, and so on (i.e., it excluded the $2,083 billion in direct investments). At the same time, foreign investment in Canadian assets exceeded $4.49 trillion (i.e., the liabilities), with over $2.2 trillion of this amount being in the form of financial securities and another $1.45 trillion in foreign direct investment—that is, direct ownership of Canadian firms. Combining Total Assets of $5,141 billion and Total Liabilities of $4,493 billion, we get a net investment position of $648 billion in the third quarter of 2018, which is also the figure reported in Table 1.1.

The magnitude of Canadian investment abroad and foreign investment in Canada should come as no surprise. In today's financial markets, it is easier for Canadian companies and governments to issue securities in foreign markets. At the same time, it is easier for Canadian investors to invest in foreign markets and for foreign companies to raise funds in Canadian markets. The United States represents an important market for Canadians because of its size and proximity. In fact, as discussed, a large number of Canadian companies are listed on more than one stock market, primarily markets in the United States, such as Nasdaq or the New York Stock Exchange (NYSE), which are both discussed below.

| TABLE 1.7 | Canada's International Investments, Third Quarter, 2018 | |
|---|---|---|
| | | **$Billion** |
| **Total Assets** | | **5,141.3** |
| Canadian direct investments | | 2,083.2 |
| Canadian portfolio investments | | 2,203.3 |
| Portfolio debt securities | 469.8 | |
| Portfolio equity and investment fund securities | 1,733.5 | |
| Official international reserves | | 104.5 |
| Other assets | | 750.3 |
| **Total Liabilities** | | **4,493.4** |
| Foreign direct investments | | 1,454.4 |
| Foreign portfolio investments | | 2,222.1 |
| Portfolio debt securities | 1,502.1 | |
| Portfolio equity and investment fund securities | 720.0 | |
| Other liabilities | | 816.9 |
| **Canada's Net International Investments** | | **647.9** |

**Source:** Data from Statistics Canada, "International Investment Position," https://www150.statcan.gc.ca/t1/tbl1/en/tv.action?pid=3610048501, retrieved March 9, 2019

## Global Financial Markets

The world's money markets and bond markets are very global in nature, with U.S. markets representing the largest and most active debt markets in the world. As in Canada, global debt markets are primarily dealer markets. The United States also possesses the largest equity markets in the world, which is convenient for Canadians who want to raise money or invest by using these markets. The **New York Stock Exchange (NYSE)** is the world's largest stock market. The market capitalization of the firms traded on the NYSE was US$20.7 trillion at the end of 2018. However, the NYSE, like other exchanges, has steadily been losing ground in the trading of its listed securities to alternative trading mechanisms (ATMs).

**New York Stock Exchange (NYSE)** the world's largest stock market

The second most important stock market in the United States is the Nasdaq Stock Market, or Nasdaq, which is the second-largest stock market in the world, based on its market capitalization of US$9.8 trillion in December 2018. In fact, Nasdaq has more listed companies than the NYSE; however, larger firms tend to list on the NYSE, which is why its market capitalization far exceeds that of Nasdaq.

Like the Canadian exchanges, U.S. and global stock markets have been consolidating. In 2007, the NYSE and Euronext merged, creating the first truly global securities exchange, NYSE Euronext. On January 16, 2009, the American Stock Exchange was phased out after it was acquired by the NYSE and became the NYSE's trading platform for options, closed-end funds, and exchange-traded funds (ETFs). We will discuss these types of securities in more detail in later chapters, but as trading becomes computerized, the barriers between markets get smaller. The main constraint becomes the capacity and sophistication of the computer program that manages the trading. Consequently, even though there are almost 200 stock exchanges around the world, the industry is rapidly amalgamating, and many exchanges have various sorts of partnerships. The globalization of the equity markets means that linkages between the markets are extremely tight.

### Concept Review Questions

1. Explain why global financial markets are so important to Canadians.
2. Identify and briefly describe the two major stock markets in the United States.

# Review

## Summary

This chapter provides an overview of financial systems in general and the Canadian financial system in particular. We identify the major participants and discuss the different types of financial securities and financial markets. In doing so, we provide an overview of finance in general.

In the next chapter, and for the balance of the text, we will focus on business (or corporate) finance, which is one very important part of the overall financial system. As you develop an understanding of the problems faced by corporations, it is important to realize that business finance is inextricably linked to government finance, personal finance, and international finance—the three other major agents in the financial system—because collectively they determine what happens in the financial system. The financial system is one huge market for borrowing and lending money—what happens in one part of the system affects all other parts.

## Summary of Learning Objectives

### 1.1 Define finance and explain what is involved in the study of finance.

Finance is the study of how and under what terms savings (money) are allocated between lenders and borrowers.

Finance is not just about how resources are allocated but also under *what terms* and through *what channels* the allocations are made. Whenever funds are transferred, a financial contract comes into existence, and these contracts are called financial securities. As a result, the study of finance requires a basic understanding of securities and corporate law and the institutions that facilitate and monitor this exchange of funds.

### 1.2 List the major financial and real assets held by Canadians.

The four major sectors of the economy are government, business, households, and non-residents. On an aggregate level, the first three sectors own real assets. Households own positive net financial assets, while governments and businesses own negative net financial assets, which means they are net debtors. Non-residents own a small portion of positive net financial assets.

### 1.3 Explain how money is transferred from lenders to borrowers and the role played by market and financial intermediaries.

Money is transferred from lenders to borrowers through the following three channels: (1) financial intermediaries that transform the nature of the securities they issue and invest in, (2) market intermediaries that simply make the markets work better, and (3) non-market transactions in which the market is not involved.

### 1.4 Identify the basic types of financial instruments that are available and explain how they are traded.

The major types of financial instruments are debt and equity. Debt instruments are loans. Equity instruments involve ownership. Financial markets are divided into two divisions: primary and secondary (secondary markets come in two types: auction and dealer markets).

### 1.5 Explain the importance of the global financial system and how Canada is impacted by global events.

In addition to the domestic financial markets discussed above, global financial markets represent important sources of funds for borrowers and provide investors with important alternatives. Indeed, Canadian debt and equity markets represent only a small proportion of the total global marketplace. Therefore, it makes sense for Canadians to borrow and invest abroad, which has become easier to do in today's global business environment as investment barriers are relaxed.

## Key Terms

auction markets, p. 1-16
brokers, p. 1-16
Canadian Securities Exchange (CSE), p. 1-17
capital market securities, p. 1-15
common share, p. 1-14
credit crunch, p. 1-8
Crown corporations, p. 1-11
dealer markets, p. 1-16
debt instruments, p. 1-14
equity instruments, p. 1-14
exchanges, p. 1-16

finance, p. 1-1
financial assets, p. 1-4
financial intermediaries, p. 1-7
fourth market, p. 1-17
intermediation, p. 1-7
market capitalization, p. 1-16
market intermediaries, p. 1-7
marketable financial assets, p. 1-15
money market securities, p. 1-15
Montreal Exchange (ME), p. 1-16
New York Stock Exchange (NYSE), p. 1-19

non-marketable financial assets, p. 1-14
over-the-counter (OTC)
    markets, p. 1-16
preferred shares, p. 1-14
primary markets, p. 1-15
real assets, p. 1-3
secondary markets, p. 1-15
third market, p. 1-17
TMX Group Limited, p. 1-16
Toronto Stock Exchange or TSX, p. 1-16
TSX Venture Exchange (TSVX), p. 1-16

# Questions and Practice Problems

## Multiple Choice Questions

1. **(LO 1.1)** Which of the following is *true* about finance?
   a. Finance is the study of how and under what terms savings (money) are allocated between lenders and borrowers.
   b. Finance is different from economics because economics does not study how resources are allocated.
   c. All parts of finance are not integrated.
   d. Business finance is the only important part of finance.

2. **(LO 1.2)** According to Canada's national balance sheet, which of the following items is *not* a real asset?
   a. Land
   b. Machinery and equipment
   c. Stocks
   d. Residential structures

3. **(LO 1.2)** According to Canada's national balance sheet, which of the following items is *not* a financial asset?
   a. Consumer credit
   b. Loans
   c. Mortgages
   d. Real property

4. **(LO 1.2)** Explain why real assets are not perceived to be as *liquid* as financial assets.

5. **(LO 1.3)** You have hired someone to purchase 100 shares of a technology firm for your portfolio. The person you have hired is acting as a
   a. financial intermediary.
   b. market intermediary.
   c. financial principal.
   d. market principal.

6. **(LO 1.3)** Which of the following is a *correct* combination of primary fund lenders and fund borrowers in the financial system?
   a. Households and government
   b. Households and non-residents
   c. Businesses and households
   d. Government and non-residents

7. **(LO 1.3)** Which of the following financial intermediaries does *not* transform the nature of the underlying financial securities?
   a. Banks
   b. Insurance firms
   c. Mutual funds
   d. Pension funds

8. **(LO 1.4)** A small investor from New Brunswick has just purchased 100 common shares of a telecommunications firm on the Toronto Stock Exchange. This is the first time the investor has purchased this stock. This transaction is an example of
   a. a primary market transaction because it is the first time the investor has bought the stock.
   b. a primary market transaction because the money the investor has invested will go directly to the firm.
   c. a secondary market transaction because the investor has bought the stock from other investors.
   d. none of the above; this is a large block trade and will be done using the OTC market (the "third market").

9. **(LO 1.4)** Compare and contrast marketable versus non-marketable assets.

10. **(LO 1.5)** Which of the following statements is *true* about the global financial system?
    a. Canadian debt and equity markets represent the majority of the global financial market.
    b. Canada's net international investment position is always negative in any year.
    c. The globalization of the equity markets means that the linkages between the global markets are getting tighter.
    d. Canada's financial system is completely separated from the global financial market.

## Practice Problems

### Intermediate

**11. (LO 1.2)** You are examining the economy of a very small, completely isolated island nation. There are only three people on this island: Fred, Robinson, and Friday. Fred owns a house valued at $1,000 and owes Friday $500. Robinson owns a house valued at $3,000 and owes Friday $2,000. Friday's house is valued at $1,500. Derive the balance sheet of this island economy.

**12. (LO 1.3)** List the four major financial sectors in the financial system and discuss how they relate to one another.

**13. (LO 1.3)** Explain how banks, pension funds, insurance firms, and mutual funds work in the financial system.

**14. (LO 1.3)** Describe why financial and market intermediaries exist in our financial system.

**15. (LO 1.4)** Describe the two major types of secondary markets.

### Challenging

**16. (LO 1.4)** What are secondary market transactions? How do secondary markets facilitate the primary markets?

# Business (Corporate) Finance

In Chapter 1, we discussed the financial system and provided the context for the discussion of business finance. In this chapter, we discuss the role of the corporation and provide the background that is necessary to analyze how its investment and financing decisions are made. In the process, we discuss the goals of the corporation and how its internal affairs are organized. These days, corporations are being called upon more than ever to act in a manner that is socially, economically, and environmentally responsible. However, sometimes being a good corporate citizen can put a firm at odds with its fundamental obligation, which is to maximize shareholder value. We conclude with a description of some available jobs in the field.

## 2.1 | Types of Business Organizations

**LEARNING OBJECTIVE 2.1**

List the four forms of business organizations and describe the advantages and disadvantages of each.

In Chapter 1, we distinguished between real assets and financial assets, with real assets for the household being tangible things, such as houses, dishwashers, computers, and cars, while financial assets are loans, in the broadest sense, to other people and institutions. However, this discussion of Canadian households was limited by Statistics Canada's (StatsCan's) division of the economy into four main segments: households, business, government, and foreign (non-resident). The reason for this division is that the business sector makes the real investment decisions that increase our wealth over time. In contrast, the real investment decisions of households are to buy consumer durables—that is, consumption items that generate value over future periods. Ultimately, we can say that households consume—it's just that some of this consumption is of non-durables, like food, and some of it is of durables, like cars. The business sector, conversely, makes very different real investment decisions, which are intended to increase its ability to produce goods and services in the future—that is, to generate future growth in consumption and wealth.

As we noted in Chapter 1, StatsCan considers Canadian households to comprise "persons and unincorporated businesses," so some business is conducted within the household, rather than in the business sector. Businesses can be organized in different ways. The four major forms of business organizations are:

- sole proprietorships
- partnerships
- trusts
- corporations

We discuss each of these in this section.

## Sole Proprietorships

**sole proprietorship** a business owned and operated by one person

A **sole proprietorship** is a business owned and operated by one person. Starting one is as simple as drumming up business. Many important businesses have been started by someone trying to meet a market need, whether it's the neighbour's son who set up a lemonade stand one hot summer day or the daughter who cleans up yards in her spare time. These people have both started sole proprietorships, in which one person starts working on their own rather than for someone else.

The big advantage of a sole proprietorship is that setting one up is easy—no paperwork is involved, and the owner needs only to start doing business. Of course, if the business begins to grow, the owner might want to register a business name, or even patent a particular business process to keep imitators away or at least make them pay a royalty.[1] Purchasing some business cards is helpful too. However, the critical thing is that the business is almost inseparable from the owner; if that lemonade turns out to be bad, or if part of that yard isn't cleaned up, then the business owner is personally liable. This isn't a big factor for most very small businesses, but if that person's web page inadvertently damages a client by directing traffic elsewhere, then the owner is personally liable. More to the point, an owner can be sued for damages. If that person has other assets, they could lose them or, in extreme cases, be forced into bankruptcy and lose everything because of a bad decision made in that sole proprietorship. This accountability is referred to as **unlimited liability**, because an owner is liable not only to the extent of what is invested in the business but also for any other assets owned. Lawyers generally advise wealthy people not to operate a sole proprietorship.

**unlimited liability** the liability not only for what is invested in the business but also for any other assets owned

Sole proprietorships do have financial implications. The sources of finance available for sole proprietorships are the same ones that are available to individuals. No complicated finance options are available—owners borrow from relatives and friends, or from the bank, through either a loan or a credit card. If a business creates some revenue, its owner can use one of the many government programs designed to stimulate small businesses. If a business grows and the owner wants to sell it, this can be problematic, because all the contacts and relationships are personal and belong to the owner, since legally the owner and the business are identical. Selling a profitable window-cleaning business may mean visiting every contact and explaining that someone new is taking over the business and will be serving them in the future. The fact is, there is no continuity in a sole proprietorship, which makes it difficult to sell. And, of course, it dies with the owner.

Because legally a sole proprietorship is inseparable from the individual, the owner has to report the income to the Canada Revenue Agency (CRA) on an annual income tax return. Sole proprietors have to keep the same accounting records as big businesses do and report the income after deducting all reasonable expenses. However, the net income is simply added to any regular salary income and taxed at ordinary tax rates. For this reason, StatsCan cannot separate persons and unincorporated businesses from households, because most of the data come from individual income tax returns.

---

[1]Most provinces have agencies that, for a fee, will register business names and search to make sure someone isn't already conducting similar business with a similar name. In Ontario, for example, ServiceOntario offers these services; in British Columbia it is BC Registry Services.

# Partnerships

Suppose you are working on a new web page and need some help from a friend. The two of you start working together. After a while, it becomes a solid relationship and you always work together on jobs for clients. This relationship is a **partnership**, rather than a sole proprietorship. Some of the most prominent and successful businesses started out as partnerships—consider Bill Gates and Paul Allen (Microsoft Corporation), who started a partnership working on personal computers in their parents' garages. A partnership can be formalized by having a lawyer create a partnership agreement. The agreement sets out how decisions are made, such as how each partner can buy out the other in the event that one wants to dissolve the partnership. If the partnership grows, the owners also need to document how new partners enter and their attendant obligations, as well as how others can cash out. The partnership agreement further stipulates how the partnership's income is allocated among the partners. Individuals have to be careful with partnerships, since a legal agreement is not required to be considered a partner. Sometimes a partnership can be implied by the actions of a group of people working together. This becomes a problem when a disaffected party sues everyone associated with a business, even people who are not formal partners.

**partnership**   a business owned and operated by two or more people

Some very big firms traditionally operated as partnerships, most of which were in the professional services area, such as accounting firms, investment banking firms, doctors' offices, and dentists' offices. Such firms needed more than one person to deliver a full range of services, yet "society" judged it important to hold each member individually responsible both for their own actions and for the actions of their colleagues. However, over time, the increasing complexity of partnership operations—for example, in the accounting and investment banking areas—weakened this argument. With hundreds of partners, it is difficult to justify making all the partners responsible for the actions of one rogue partner. As a result, the importance of traditional partnerships has diminished.

Partnerships are still important for smaller firms because they maintain the integration of partnership income with other income for each partner. However, newer partnership models have emerged that maintain this tax treatment while removing the unlimited personal liability. The two main partnership forms are limited liability partnerships (LLPs) and limited and general partnerships.

LLPs are the latest form of organization for professional firms. Each partner has limited liability in the event of a lawsuit against the firm; however, each partner's income is still included as ordinary income and filed by using an individual tax return. Two industries that are dominated by LLPs are legal firms and accounting firms. Borden Ladner Gervais LLP and Gowling Lafleur Henderson LLP are two of the largest law firms in Canada, with 713 and 668 lawyers, respectively, as of December 2018. In 2017, Deloitte LLP was the largest accounting firm in Canada, generating revenue of $2.3 billion. At that time, Deloitte had 6,636 professional staff and 957 partners. Notice the LLP designation is included after each firm's name, indicating a limited liability partnership. Clearly, with the larger firms having hundreds of partners, it is unreasonable to impose unlimited liability on them all.

Limited and general partnerships are generally used for tax reasons. In this case, a general partner operates the business, and limited partners are passive investors. As long as the limited partners are not active in the business, they have the advantage of **limited liability**, in that all they can lose is their initial investment. The general partner, conversely, has unlimited liability as the operator of the business. In practice, most general partners are corporations (discussed later in this section) and indirectly benefit from limited liability. Limited partnerships are often used in tax shelters; for this reason, Canada Revenue Agency looks at them very carefully to make sure they are not a vehicle for tax avoidance; however, there are also legitimate reasons to set up a limited partnership.

**limited liability**   the liability for only the initial investment

Until 2010, Canada had some very large firms organized as partnerships. For example, the largest natural gas distribution company in Quebec is Gaz Métro, which had 2009 sales of $2.25 billion and profit of $158 million. Part of Gaz Métro was then publicly owned through Gaz Métro Limited Partnership (GMLP). However, the federal government changed the tax treatment of limited partnerships, along with that of income trusts (discussed next), and GMLP converted to a regular corporation, Valener, in October 2010.

# Trusts

**trust** a legal organization in which assets are owned by one party and managed or controlled by a different party

The trust structure is not new by any means and is, in fact, a standard part of the lawyer's tool kit. **Trusts** are used to separate ownership from control. For example, a standard part of estate planning is transferring assets in trust to children to minimize any tax burden and yet control the use of those assets until death. In this way, ownership has been transferred to one party, but control stays with the transferring party. Traditionally, open-end mutual funds have been organized as trusts. The mutual fund is owned by the unitholders, yet day-to-day control is exercised by the fund manager under the supervision of a board of directors, which appoints the manager. More important, because it is a trust, the income earned by the mutual fund passes through without any tax to the unitholders, who are then subject to taxes on the income received. The use of trusts expanded dramatically during the 2000s, from personal finance and mutual funds to **income trusts** and **royalty trusts**, which became very important in the Canadian financial system to the extent that they jeopardized the federal government's corporate income tax revenues. Income and royalty trusts are set up to invest in the shares and debt obligations of a company. Because they are trusts, all the income passes through without any tax. **Figure 2.1** is a simplified example of an income trust structure.

**income trust** and **royalty trust** a trust set up to invest in the shares and debt obligations of a company

Figure 2.1 shows that, because the trust owns both the debt and the equity of the company, the use of debt by the company can be maximized to reduce (or eliminate) any corporate income tax. The interest, dividends, and other payments then flow through to the trust, and provided the trust pays out most (or all) of its income to its unitholders, there is no tax paid. This is because interest payments on debt are a tax-deductible expense to the corporation, as we will discuss later, but it is unlikely that non-payment of interest will cause default since the trust is both the debt holder and the equity holder. In the jargon of finance professionals, trusts are "tax efficient." From 1998, and for almost 10 years, the use of trusts to structure business activity exploded. By March 31, 2006, there were 238 income trusts listed on the Toronto Stock Exchange (TSX), up from 73 in 2001 and only a handful in the mid-1990s. In fact, the total market capitalization of income trusts grew from $1.4 billion in 1994 to $192 billion by March 2006, representing approximately 10 percent of the quoted market value of the TSX.[2]

**FIGURE 2.1** Simplified Example of an Income Trust Structure

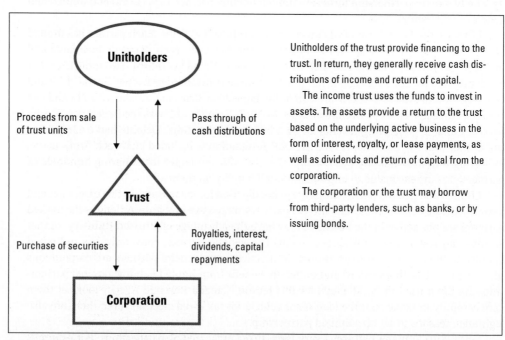

Unitholders of the trust provide financing to the trust. In return, they generally receive cash distributions of income and return of capital.

The income trust uses the funds to invest in assets. The assets provide a return to the trust based on the underlying active business in the form of interest, royalty, or lease payments, as well as dividends and return of capital from the corporation.

The corporation or the trust may borrow from third-party lenders, such as banks, or by issuing bonds.

**Source:** Figure 1 from *Tax and Other Issues Related to Publicly Listed Flow-Through Entities*, a consultation paper from Department of Finance Canada, September 2005, www.fin.gc.ca/activty/pubs/toirplf_1-eng.asp. Reproduced with the permission of the Department of Finance, 2015.

[2]Statistics from the TSX website at www.tsx.com.

As a result of this growth, the TSX fully incorporated income trusts into the Standard & Poor's/ Toronto Stock Exchange (S&P/TSX) Composite Index as of March 2006, completing a gradual process that was initiated in November 2005.

The tax-efficient structure of trusts, along with their popularity among investors, led many corporations to convert to the trust structure between 2000 and 2006. This fuelled concerns regarding the government's loss of corporate tax revenue, because the trust structure eliminates most of the income taxes paid by businesses. In addition, it generated a great deal of worry and speculation regarding the effect that this trend would have on the future growth of businesses in the Canadian economy, since trusts are inclined to pay out their earnings rather than reinvest in the business. All these worries came to a head in the fall of 2006 in response to announcements by Canadian telecommunications giants TELUS Corporation and BCE Inc. that they would be converting to the trust structure. Not only would these conversions add another $50 billion or so in market capitalization to the income trust market, but their conversion was also taken as a warning sign that many other large corporations could follow suit. As a result of these concerns, on October 31, 2006, the federal government announced that the distributions made by newly created trusts would be taxed at prevailing corporate tax rates, and that this new tax would apply to existing trusts beginning in 2011. Following this announcement, income trust prices dropped about 12.4 percent on average, wiping out nearly $20 billion in shareholder wealth. The market prices of the shares of BCE and TELUS were also hit hard, as the market anticipated, correctly, that they would cancel their plans to convert to the trust structure.

Since the change in tax policy by the federal government, large numbers of income trusts have converted back to regular corporate status, discussed next. However, the income trust sector remains an important investment vehicle for Canadians. Moreover, in many ways it has reverted to its original status, since most of the income trusts are now real estate investment trusts and royalty trusts, rather than regular corporate activity.

# Corporations

**Corporations** are easy to recognize because they have "Inc." for incorporated, "Ltd." for limited, or, in Europe, "PLC" for private limited corporation after their names. In each case, the abbreviations or initials indicate that the owners have the benefit of limited liability, so the maximum they can lose is their investment—that is, they cannot be forced to invest more in the firm to make up for any losses the firm incurs. Unlike a partnership or sole proprietorship, a business that operates as a corporation separates personal assets from any malfeasance or failure at the corporate level. Although the courts have occasionally "pierced the corporate veil" and extended that liability, it is very rare and happens only when significant public policy concerns are involved.

How a corporation is formed depends on provincial corporate law; however, it is generally by either a certificate of incorporation or letters patent. The articles of incorporation then indicate the most basic information about the firm, such as its mailing address, name, line of business, number of shares issued, names and addresses of the officers of the firm (that is, the people who can legally bind the firm by signing cheques), and so on. The critical feature is that the corporation is a distinct legal entity. For this reason, the corporation is entitled to sign contracts, file tax returns, borrow money, make investments, sue, and be sued—all in its own name.

As a distinct legal entity, the corporation has significant advantages over a partnership or a sole proprietorship. One advantage is that a corporation is "immortal." Early limited companies had to renew their charter or incorporation periodically, since politicians worried about the public policy implications of having a legal entity with an indefinite life; however, as the operations of corporations have become better understood, these concerns have waned. This indefinite life means that, unlike people, corporations can borrow by using debt that will be paid off in 40, and sometimes 50, years' time. Individuals, with finite lives, would have difficulty getting these terms from a bank. It also means that transferring and selling assets is relatively easy because all the contracts go with the company, and the share ownership is simply transferred.

The most difficult aspects of corporations are their control and taxation (we will deal with taxes in Chapter 3). In partnerships and sole proprietorships, the owners run the business; in corporations, the owners are the shareholders. For smaller companies this isn't a problem, but for larger companies it becomes a serious concern: they usually have a very clear separation of ownership by the shareholders and control by management. This division is the fundamental

**corporation** a business organized as a separate legal entity under corporate law, with ownership divided into transferable shares problem of the governance structure of large companies. We will discuss governance later in the chapter and in Chapter 15 because it is integral to the role of mergers and acquisitions and to understanding valuation. Corporations also face the issue of double taxation, since the corporation is taxed on its income, and then shareholders are taxed when they receive dividends that the corporation pays to them from this same income.

Every company has a set of bylaws that indicates how it is run. Some of the content of the bylaws is determined by corporate law, but most is discretionary and up to the company. What is not discretionary is the requirement that the company have a board of directors (BOD) whose responsibility is to "manage or supervise the management of the business and affairs of the corporation."[3] These directors are appointed at the annual general meeting of the company and serve at the discretion of the shareholders, which means that they can be removed without cause.[4]

In theory, the BOD is elected by the shareholders and acts in their best interests. The directors' statutory responsibilities are enshrined in the *Canada Business Corporations Act* (*CBCA*), in Section 122 (1):

> Every director and officer of a corporation in exercising their powers and discharging their duties shall
>
> *(a)* act honestly and in good faith with a view to the best interests of the corporation; and
>
> *(b)* exercise the care, diligence, and skill that a reasonably prudent person would exercise in comparable circumstances.

Essentially, this legal requirement means that members of the BOD have to exercise the normal standards of professionalism expected of people in their position. This standard is known as the "due diligence" standard, and as long as it is met, members of the BOD cannot be sued for negligence. What should their goals be? The *CBCA* says only that they must act in the best interests (honestly and in good faith) of the corporation, but what are the best interests of the corporation? To answer this, we have to discuss corporate goals.

---

**Concept Review Questions**

1. Describe the main advantages and disadvantages of sole proprietorships and partnerships.
2. How are trusts distinct from corporations?
3. What are the main advantages and disadvantages of the corporation structure?

---

## 2.2 | The Goals of the Corporation

**LEARNING OBJECTIVE 2.2**

Describe the goals of the firm and the pressures exerted on corporations by various stakeholders.

You might remember from your economics course that the goal of the firm is to maximize its profits. However, many have challenged this objective, and the major reasons are illustrated in **Figure 2.2**.

---

[3]Section 121 of the *Canada Business Corporations Act* allows the BOD to delegate this responsibility to officers of the corporation.

[4]In the United States, this is not the case; directors can only be removed for cause before the end of their term of appointment. This means that it is technically possible for a person to own 51 percent of a company and yet not be able to immediately remove the board of directors and control that company.

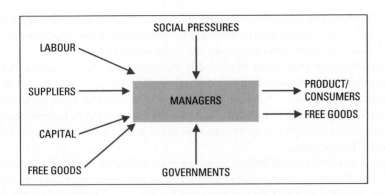

**FIGURE 2.2** **The Firm as an Input-Output Function**

What Figure 2.2 illustrates is that the firm is essentially an input-output mechanism. It takes inputs, such as raw materials, labour, and supplies, and transforms those inputs into something more useful to society when it produces goods or services. For all firms, this activity is regulated both by implicit societal pressures to be good and by laws passed by government to prevent firms from doing things it regards as bad. For example, minimum wage and employment laws prevent firms from paying wages that are too low or using underage labour. Similarly, laws on environmental protection, packaging of goods, and so on ensure that the firm operates according to what is in consumers' interests. Apart from obeying the law, for sole proprietorships and partnerships, this is the end of the story; those firms are then run in the interests of their owners. Normally, this means that the firms enhance the owners' welfare and make profits.

In finance, we extend the idea of the firm's goal being to maximize its profits, because what the firm should really do is enhance the owner's wealth. Wealth is different from profits because it reflects the value of all profits—not just today's but also those expected in the future—where profits refer to genuine economic profits and not what the accountant creates (i.e., accounting profits). When this definition of the firm's goal is applied to publicly traded firms, the goal of the firm is to maximize its market value or, alternatively, maximize shareholder value: the firm should take resources and create products that society values more highly than it values the inputs. Note that there are two very important things in Figure 2.2 that we have not discussed: the existence of externalities and the role of managers.

Externalities are things that the firm doesn't pay for or charge for, but which affect others. As a result, if the firm creates value without taking into account its impact, it may make decisions that are not in the public's best interests. A classic example on the input side is the use of water. Should firms be allowed to use water without paying a true market price for it? Water is something that Canada has in abundance, and it would be relatively easy to set up a plant to export water to, say, the U.S. southwest, which is largely desert. In fact, it is possible to reverse the flow of water down the Mackenzie Valley, moving it down the Colorado River to Arizona and California, instead of having it go to the Arctic. This was an issue in the Free Trade Agreement (FTA) between the United States and Canada: would the United States have the right to Canadian water, and would refusing a U.S. request for water be a violation of trade under the FTA? Clearly, large-scale diversion of water entails a cost that is not captured in the rates the public pays for water, and to charge this lower rate for large-scale water diversion is almost certainly not in the best interests of Canada, even though it may be in the best interests of people sponsoring the idea.

Another important example of externalities is greenhouse gas (GHG) emissions. At the time of writing, the Canadian federal government was in the process of imposing taxes on such emissions in the form of a so-called carbon tax. The decision to implement this tax in provinces without acceptable GHG emissions policies has been legally challenged by Saskatchewan, with Ontario and New Brunswick also opposing the imposition of the tax.

Finally, the "too big to fail" issue creates externalities, and has become extremely political in the aftermath of the 2008–9 financial crisis. During the financial crisis, the U.S. banking system was on the verge of collapse, and two of the Big Three U.S. car manufacturers became insolvent. True to form, the U.S. government bailed out GM and Chrysler, since the financial markets were so fragile at that time that the bankruptcy of the largest car company in the world was considered unthinkable. By April 2009, GM had received $19.2 billion in emergency bailout money from the U.S. government. On June 1, 2009, it was reorganized, and a new GM emerged with the company's good assets, while all the bad assets were left for Motors

Liquidation Corporation, the successor to the old GM. GM may indeed have been "too big to fail" as far as the company was concerned, but the shareholders lost almost every cent, and Fritz Henderson, temporary chief executive, was soon out of a job.

The main message from these examples is that very large firms are very visible, their actions often have a significant impact on other firms, and those actions are not necessarily in the best interests of Canada. After all, firms hold privileged status as corporations because they act in the owners' interests, so the government has the right to oversee their actions. Consequently, many argue that corporations should act in the "social interest," rather than in the interests of their owners.

The social welfare or social interest argument has validity for the largest firms in Canada because they are the ones that have these spinoff effects on others. Indeed, for the first time in a generation, policy-makers are considering reducing the size of major U.S. firms due to the significant problems their failure imposed on the U.S. economy in 2008. However, for most firms, what is good for the firm is also what is good for Canada; there are few spinoffs elsewhere. For this reason, the creation of shareholder value has been widely accepted as the proper goal for a corporation, not just by academic theorists but also by regulators. In 1994, the TSX issued a report entitled *Where Were the Directors?*—commonly called the Dey Report,[5] after its chairman, Peter Dey. The report's mandate was to look at the governance of Canadian companies after the serious recession of the early 1990s. The Dey Report concluded, in Section 1.11:

> We recognize the principal objective of the direction and management of a business is to **enhance shareholder value,** which includes balancing gain with risk in order to enhance the financial viability of the business.

As you will see, this is exactly what finance takes as the objective of the firm. Further, the idea of balancing gain with risk is what we refer to as the *risk-return trade-off*, and you will become very familiar with it as it comes up in connection with virtually every topic we discuss in this textbook.

---

## Concept Review Questions

1. What is the primary goal of the corporation?
2. What role does the board of directors serve?
3. Explain the costs imposed on society if firms become too big to fail, and discuss whether the government should break up large firms when they pose such risks.
4. Should the government allow one of the Big Six Canadian banks to fail if it loses money on its loan portfolio?

---

## 2.3 | The Role of Management and Agency Issues

**LEARNING OBJECTIVE 2.3**

Explain what agency costs are and how they affect the interests of management and shareholders.

Most finance academics, as well as the governance guidelines of the TSX, assess the goal of the firm to be that of the creation or maximization of shareholder value. The problem is that neither group actually runs a firm; that is what managers do.

---

[5]Toronto Stock Exchange, Committee on Corporate Governance in Canada, *Where Were the Directors? Guidelines for Improved Corporate Governance in Canada* (the Dey Report) (Toronto: TSE, December 1994).

In smaller firms, managers and owners are often the same people, which solves the problem. Even some quite large Canadian companies have a controlling shareholder who ensures that managers act in the shareholders' best interests. However, for many companies the shareholders are widely dispersed, and the firm's chief executive officer (CEO) is able to pack the BOD with cronies who will not challenge the CEO's authority. In other words, the firm has poor governance and few checks on management, and it may be run in management's interest rather than in the interests of the shareholders. Further, the interests of managers and shareholders do not necessarily coincide.

As management theorist Gordon Donaldson has stated:

> To say that management and shareholders have much in common is only to state the obvious. So do management and the labour force, consumers, or any other group having a vested interest in the corporate entity. But to extend this by saying that management, in pursuing the corporate objectives as it sees them, necessarily serves the best interest of the stockholders, in either the short or long run, misstates the facts in certain important respects. It also leads to confusion in and misinterpretation of financial policy.[6]

## The Agency Relationship and Agency Costs

Managers are employees, and we now think of them as agents working on behalf of the shareholders—this is referred to as an **agency relationship** in exactly the same way that we referred to agency transactions in Chapter 1 in the context of hiring a broker to act for and advise us. However, how hard managers work to serve the best interests of the shareholders depends on their personal interests and how they are compensated. This is one of the classic **agency problems** associated with the separation of ownership from management.

**agency relationship**  the relationship between the shareholders who own the company and the managers hired to work on their behalf

The costs associated with agency problems are referred to as **agency costs**. There are two major types of agency costs: (1) direct costs, which arise because suboptimal decisions are made by managers when they act in a manner that is not in the best interests of their company's shareholders, and (2) indirect costs, which are incurred in an attempt to avoid direct agency costs. Indirect costs include those that arise from any restrictions placed on the actions of management, those associated with monitoring the actions of managers (which includes any compensation paid to the BOD), and those associated with management compensation schemes that will provide managers with incentives to act in the shareholders' best interests. We elaborate on this last topic next.

**agency problems**  a problem that arises due to potential divergence of interests among managers, shareholders, and creditors

**agency costs**  the costs associated with agency problems

Suppose you hire the daughter of a friend to clean up your yard. You could sit on the back porch and watch her to make sure she does a good job. However, this monitoring of her work is expensive for you; after all, you probably hired her because your time is valuable and you have other things to do. Monitoring her continuously defeats the purpose. Instead, you can compensate her to try to meet your objectives. Suppose you pay her $10 an hour and think the job will take four hours. What might happen when you come back after four hours? Unless she expects repeat business, which means her reputation is at stake, she'll probably be only partly done, because with a cost-plus contract, her incentive is to stretch out the job. Conversely, if you agree on a fixed fee, say $40, you'll probably come back after four hours and discover that she left two hours earlier. Then you'll have to check everything, because she's probably taken short cuts. In this case, her personal incentive is to finish early. What you want to do is align her interests with yours so you don't have to monitor and check her behaviour.

Like your interests and those of your friend's daughter, the interests of managers and shareholders are usually fundamentally different. For example, shareholders tend to have a short-term interest in the firm and hold the shares and other securities of many entities in a large investment portfolio. If they see the managers acting contrary to what they would like, they are likely to sell their shares and go elsewhere rather than try to remove management through a costly proxy fight at the annual general meeting. It is simply too costly for most shareholders to fight to remove management in a large corporation; however, this is not to say it does not happen. For example, in 2012, U.S. hedge fund Pershing Square Capital Management waged an expensive, months-long war to successfully change the CEO of Canadian Pacific

---

[6]Donaldson, Gordon, "Financial Goals: Management vs. Stockholders." *Harvard Business Review* (May/June 1963).

Railway. All too often, such proxy fights to change management fail because it is so expensive and time-consuming for one party to bear the costs.

**moral hazard** the fact that individuals' behaviours may change if they are not exposed to the full consequences of their actions

Finally, in terms of agency costs, there is a special cost that has become a veritable "hot potato": **moral hazard**. Suppose that instead of hiring someone to clean up your yard, you accept your son's offer to volunteer to do the job. In this case, your son might think that he can do a quick job, knowing that you will finish it off—his behaviour changes because he knows that you will bail him out. So although your son might do a great job in someone else's yard, he does a poor job for you. If you think of your son as Lehman Brothers Holdings Inc. or Bear Stearns Companies, Inc., and the U.S. government as you, the parent, you can see how the concept of moral hazard became important in 2008.

In 1998, the U.S. government bailed out a hedge fund called Long-Term Capital Management (LTCM) because it was deemed to pose a systemic risk to the U.S. financial system—that is, it imposed an externality on others. This resulted in a common understanding that a financial institution could take risks because, in the event of failure, the U.S. government would bail out the institution. This is the moral hazard problem: knowing that the U.S. government had bailed out LTCM, the behaviour of other institutions changed. This problem is also why, on September 15, 2008, the U.S. government forced Lehman Brothers into bankruptcy, even though it was much larger than LTCM and its failure posed a much greater risk to the financial system. In retrospect, it is now acknowledged that forcing Lehman Brothers into bankruptcy was a huge mistake, since it triggered the credit crunch, financial market meltdown, and the worst recession since the Great Depression of the 1930s. The U.S. government's bailout of its banks after the Lehman crisis illustrates that moral hazard is still with us and, if left unchecked, could distort markets.

Despite the moral hazard problem, the fact remains that institutions that are too big to fail cannot be allowed to fail. As a result, a new acronym has entered the financial lexicon: SIFI, a systemically important financial institution, which is just another way of saying a bank that is too important to be allowed to fail. Allowing a SIFI to fail, it is argued, would trigger a global financial meltdown similar to what happened in 2008–9. Assuming we cannot break up SIFIs, we have to regulate them more carefully. In 2011, the Basel Committee on Banking Supervision opted for this approach in its new regulations (Basel 3). In 2018, 29 large international financial institutions were identified for this extra-careful supervision and more extensive regulation by the Financial Stability Board (FSB).[7] The list included only one Canadian bank (the Royal Bank of Canada); however, its presence is indicative of the critical importance of the other big Canadian banks, since they are similar in size.

---

### Concept Review Questions

1. Describe the nature of the basic owner–manager agency relationship.
2. Define agency costs and describe both types.

---

## 2.4 | Aligning Managers' and Owners' Interest

**LEARNING OBJECTIVE 2.4**
Explain the importance of aligning the interests of management with the interests of shareholders in a corporation.

We have discussed a variety of agency problems that explain why managers don't necessarily pursue the best interests of the shareholders—mainly because their investment in the

---

[7]Financial Stability Board, "2018 List of Global Systematically Important Banks (G-SIBs)," https://www.fsb.org/2018/11/2018-list-of-global-systematically-important-banks-g-sibs/.

**TABLE 2.1**   **Areas of Disagreement**

|  | Managers | Shareholders |
|---|---|---|
| Performance appraisal | Accounting ROI/cash | Market prices |
| Investment analysis | IRR of best division | WACC external |
| Financing | Retentions, debt, new equity | Debt, retentions, new equity |
| Risk | Preservation of firm | Portfolio |

corporation goes much deeper than that of a typical shareholder. Donaldson argued that the main implication was that managers of regular corporations tend to be more conservative than would seem justified by the shareholder approach, since they don't face the moral hazard problem of being too big to fail. Donaldson further analyzed four key areas and found that in each area, managers make different decisions than the ones shareholders would make. These are illustrated in **Table 2.1**.

For example, when being appraised, managers want to be judged relative to accounting numbers, such as profits and return on investment (ROI), because they can control these numbers. In contrast, shareholders are interested in the stock market performance, because they want managers to create shareholder value. Similarly, in investment analysis (choosing projects), managers want to choose the internal rate of return (IRR) of their best project, relative to other divisions of the firm or past performance, because, again, this is what they control.[8] In contrast, shareholders are interested in what they can do with the money, which can be measured by comparing the return on a project with the firm's weighted average cost of capital (WACC). If the firm can't meet the shareholders' criterion, shareholders believe it should give the money to them so they can invest elsewhere. Obviously, managers don't like this idea.

Managers and shareholders also differ in their approach to risk and financing. Donaldson argued that shareholders take a portfolio approach because they hold many securities. This allows them to diversify risk and have the firm be more aggressive, whereas managers see their careers totally tied up with the firm and act conservatively. This approach is carried over to financing, where managers follow a "pecking order": they want to retain earnings first, rather than pay them out in dividends; then use bank debt; and finally issue new equity only as a last resort. In contrast, shareholders want the firm to use debt, which makes the firm riskier at first; then use only shareholders' money by retaining earnings; and lastly issue new equity.

There is no question that Donaldson correctly identified the key differences in the goals of managers and shareholders. But this situation is like hiring your friend's daughter to work in your yard: it is a question of providing the correct incentive to get managers to do what you want. At the time Donaldson was writing, most managers were compensated through salaries and bonuses, which has changed as BODs have become more aware of the need to make managers act like shareholders.

**Table 2.2** lists the 10 highest-paid executives in Canada in 2017, with a breakdown of their compensation. The major components of income are base salary and bonus, other compensation, share-based awards, option-based awards, and pension value. Notice that, in all but one case, salary and bonus compensation is relatively low compared with the total package—most of which comes in the form of pension contributions and two types of share compensation: grants of restricted stock awarded under incentive plans, and stock options. With stock options, if the company's stock price goes above a certain level, the executive gets the right to buy the stock at a fixed lower price.

The idea behind share incentive plans is to have the interests of CEOs and senior managers coincide with those of shareholders. Often, shares are granted when the company reaches certain objectives, such as revenue targets or investment returns. In such cases, the manager has an incentive to get the share price up as high as possible. In the same way, if executives are given the right to buy shares at a price of $50 when they are selling for $40, then they

---

[8]We will discuss ROI, IRR, and WACC in later chapters.

**TABLE 2.2** **Canadian Executive Compensation, 2017**

| Executive | Organization Name | Salary and Bonus | All Other Compensation | Share-Based Awards | Option-Based Awards | Pension Value | Total Reported Compensation |
|---|---|---|---|---|---|---|---|
| Donald J. Walker | Magna International | $10,778,539 | $ 201,213 | $9,268,791 | $ 6,179,194 | $ 0 | $26,427,738 |
| Keith Creel | Canadian Pacific Railway | $ 3,855,886 | $ 926,402 | $4,407,788 | $10,516,630 | $ 398,894 | $20,105,600 |
| James Smith | Thomson Reuters | $ 5,967,336 | $1,421,705 | $5,711,865 | $ 5,711,861 | –$ 73,995 | $18,738,773 |
| Linda Hasenfratz | Linamar | $11,333,227 | $1,329,640 | $3,804,286 | $ 0 | $ 3,500 | $16,470,653 |
| Al Monaco | Enbridge | $ 4,385,051 | $ 124,742 | $2,660,109 | $ 3,485,190 | $5,606,710 | $16,261,802 |
| Doug Suttles | Encana | $ 4,264,999 | $ 385,569 | $8,379,632 | $ 2,793,203 | $ 0 | $15,823,403 |
| Mark Barrenechea | OpenText | $ 3,802,978 | $ 18,449 | $4,283,526 | $ 7,711,639 | $ 0 | $15,816,593 |
| Steven Williams | Suncor Energy | $ 4,604,769 | $ 173,309 | $5,077,224 | $ 4,847,100 | $ 117,600 | $14,820,002 |
| Alain Bellemare | Bombardier | $ 5,541,023 | $2,848,011 | $2,692,623 | $ 2,692,623 | $ 26,223 | $13,800,503 |
| David McKay | Royal Bank of Canada | $ 4,555,000 | $ 44,877 | $6,300,000 | $ 1,575,000 | $ 886,000 | $13,360,877 |

**Source:** Data retrieved from "CEO Compensation," *The Globe and Mail Report on Business*, June 21, 2018, p. B6. ©The Globe and Mail, Inc. All rights reserved. Reprinted by permission.

have an incentive to get the share price over $50 to trigger the option. If the share price never reaches $50, the options are worthless. Both types of share programs have the basic objective of aligning the interests of shareholders and managers, and traditionally have been used to trump the comments made by management theorists like Gordon Donaldson.

It's doubtful that share compensation schemes have successfully met their objectives, however. The stock market peaked in October 2000, and prices subsequently dropped almost 50 percent by the spring of 2002. Technology shares dropped even more: some investors purchased Nortel at $122 and saw it go bankrupt in the 2000s. Many may have purchased Research In Motion (RIM), now BlackBerry, shares and watched an eerily similar performance.[9] It would be nice to think that the senior management groups at Nortel, RIM, and other tech companies suffered those losses along with their shareholders. However, what happened was that the option grants and share incentive schemes were retooled to continue to provide incentives to management. So if the stock fell 50 percent and made existing options worthless, new ones were granted to continue to provide incentives for managers; the argument was that otherwise management would leave and go elsewhere.

Was such compensation necessary to keep these managers? Who would want to hire away the manager of a company whose stock price had fallen 50 percent? But then, the compensation committees of the BODs granting these options and share grants were not always completely independent of the CEO who received them.[10] The important point is that the interests of managers and shareholders are not aligned if, on the downside, managers do not suffer along with the shareholders. This is the issue discussed in Finance in the News 2.1,

---

[9]BlackBerry, formerly RIM, shares dropped from over $130 to under $7. James Balsillie and Mike Lazaridis, co-CEOs, both took in over $5 million in 2011 and were tied for 51st place on the Canadian executive compensation scale just as successive new RIM products bombed and the company's shares swooned. To their credit, Balsillie and Lazaridis moved aside to let new management take over.

[10]The compensation committees of the BOD are supposed to be made up of outside directors to avoid this conflict of interest. However, "independent" is an elastic term.

## 2.1 Finance in the News   HBC's Remuneration Practices Include a $54.8 Million Pay Package for the Executive Chairman

Hudson's Bay Company faced a fight from some of its most prominent investors Tuesday over its decision to award executives with multi-million-dollar pay packages despite two years of weak sales and sizable losses for the retailer.

The Ontario Teachers' Pension Plan, British Columbia Investment Management Corp. and the California Public Employees' Retirement System (CalPERS) said they voted against the company's remuneration practices that include a $54.8 million pay package for the retailer's executive chairman Richard Baker.

The "say on pay" vote—a non-binding motion that is growing in popularity at Canadian companies and aimed at collecting shareholder feedback—took place at the company's annual general meeting in Toronto and ended in the executives' favour.

However, CalPERS spokesperson Mike Osborn said in an email "we don't feel the company sufficiently linked pay with performance" and Teachers' said in its proxy vote statement that "in this case, we do not feel that the awards have been sufficiently justified."

Baker's compensation includes more than $37 million in share-based awards and more than $16.6 million in option-based awards. The company's other executives are due to earn totals between $1.4 million and $9.4 million, according to HBC's information circular.

After the vote passed, one shareholder in the audience criticized Baker's remuneration saying, "It is one thing to award a package. It is another to accept it and so I think accepting it reflects on (Baker)'s character, who not so long ago said the fair value was twice where these payouts are."

The shareholder called on Baker to address the issue, to which Baker replied "we appreciate your question. Thank you."

The majority of other stakeholders at the meeting focused on the value of the company's real estate, which at least one activist investor has previously pushed the company to think strategically about, given the retailer's rocky recent performance that included a $400-million loss in its first quarter compared with a loss of $221 million a year ago.

In October, Jonathan Litt, who is chief investment officer and founder of activist investor Land & Buildings Investment Management, said the company is really a real estate company, not a retailer, that has failed to outline a plan to unlock the "substantial real estate value trapped in the company."

**Source:** From "HBC Shareholders Challenge Executive Remuneration, Real Estate Plans." The Canadian Press, June 12, 2018. Available at https://www.cbc.ca/news/business/hbc-hudson-s-bay-shareholders-1.4703233.

which describes major institutional shareholders voting against HBC's pay practices in 2017—practices they viewed as excessive and not well aligned with performance given HBC's recent poor results. In fact, managers have an incentive to use short-sighted measures to pump up the share price so they can exercise their options or share grants. For the managers, this is a "heads they win, tails they don't lose" strategy.

One final wrinkle in the use of executive stock options is that this practice has been linked to outright fraud by senior managers in the United States. The U.S. Securities and Exchange Commission investigated 74 firms for "backdating" executive stock options grants.[11] The fraud was that senior managers would get the compensation committee to award them stock options and then date them to an earlier period, when the company's stock price was low. Effectively, this meant that on the approval date, the stock was already worth a large amount of money, so there was little incentive value to the grant. Committing this type of fraud was slightly more difficult in Canada, because the rules on reporting executive stock options were tighter than those in the United States. However, in March 2007, RIM admitted to having backdated options, and Jim Balsillie resigned as chairman of the BOD. In February 2009, RIM's co-CEOs, Jim Balsillie and Mike Lazaridis, agreed, along with Chief Operating Officer Dennis Kavelman, to pay $77 million in penalties, costs, and compensation to end the Canadian investigation into their option backdating.[12]

If compensation schemes have largely been used to reward management,[13] rather than to provide them with an incentive to act like shareholders, where does this leave the goal of the firm? Luckily, there is a more powerful argument: the threat of acquisition. Poor management translates into poor stock market performance and a share price that is less than its intrinsic value. If a firm owns assets with an intrinsic value of $50 a share, but is selling for $25 because management is incompetent and $25 reflects the value of the profits they are generating, then

---

[11]Henry, David, "How the Options Mess Got So Ugly and Expensive." *Business Week* (September 11, 2006).

[12]Middlemiss, Jim, "OSC and SEC: Different Views on Option Backdating." *Financial Post,* February 11, 2009. Accessed at *Financial Post* website, www.financialpost.com/.

[13]Does $75 million really provide managers with that much more incentive than, say, $10 million? Or, alternatively, how many millions does it take to motivate management?

more efficient managers can afford to bid for the firm to turn it around for a profit. This is termed the "market for corporate control," because it is based on teams of managers competing for the right to manage corporate assets.

The most important thing Canada can do is make sure that the assets in the country are managed as efficiently as possible so that the country is as wealthy as possible. This requires that the best managers are given the chance to manage assets. In turn, this means that hostile takeovers should be encouraged and managers should be prevented from mounting defensive measures that simply entrench their ability to mismanage our corporate assets. Finance people believe the best defence against mergers and acquisitions (which we will discuss extensively in Chapter 15) is a high stock price. Ultimately, it is this market for corporate control, not managerial incentives, that will ensure shareholder value creation is the objective of every well-run firm in Canada.

## Corporate Governance

The previous discussion regarding CEO compensation is a corporate governance issue. **Corporate governance** can be defined as a system of principles, policies, procedures, and clearly defined responsibilities and accountabilities used by stakeholders to overcome the conflicts of interest inherent in corporations. The major objectives are to:

**corporate governance** a system of principles, policies, procedures, and clearly defined responsibilities and accountabilities used by stakeholders to overcome the conflicts of interest inherent in corporations

1. Eliminate or mitigate conflicts of interest, particularly those between managers and shareholders.

2. Ensure the assets of the company are used efficiently and productively and in the best interest of its investors and other stakeholders.

An effective corporate governance system will define shareholder and stakeholder rights, as well as manager and director governance responsibilities. It will also establish accountabilities for responsibilities that are both identifiable and measurable. Key attributes include fairness and equitable treatment in dealings between managers, directors, and shareholders, as well as transparency and accuracy in disclosures regarding operations, performance, risk, and financial position.

One of the most important aspects of good corporate governance is the establishment of an effective board of directors. Aside from ensuring that all legal and regulatory requirements are met, the board's most important functions are to establish long-term strategic objectives, hire the CEO, establish CEO compensation packages, and review performance regularly. Some of the key attributes of an effective board are:

- A high level of independence (from management) of board members as a whole
- An independent chair of the board
- A well-qualified and diversified group of members
- Rigorous board self-assessment practices
- An independent audit committee and compensation committee

Corporate governance is critical to the ongoing success of companies—so much so that many sophisticated investors scrutinize corporate governance systems of companies they invest in. For example, the Canada Pension Plan Investment Board (CPPIB) proposes several guidelines regarding what it considers to be good corporate governance practices with respect to the following factors:[14]

1. Proxy voting and corporate governance, board and management responsibilities, long term perspective, sustainable investing, and how shares are voted

2. Shareholder voting

---

[14]CPP Investment Board, "Proxy Voting Principles and Guidelines," February 23, 2018, http://www.cppib.com/documents/1769/CPPIB_Proxy_Voting_Principles_and_Guidelines_EN_Wz3xvj0.pdf.

   3. Director elections

   4. Board of directors

   5. Director compensation

   6. Executive compensation

   7. The audit function

   8. Capital structure

   9. Corporate transactions

   10. Takeover protection

   11. Related party transactions

   12. Environmental and social factors

   13. Standards and guidelines of business conduct

The CPPIB is a member of the **Canadian Coalition for Good Governance (CCGG)**, which comprises large institutional investors (e.g., pension plans, mutual funds, and third-party money managers) that seek to promote good governance practices in the companies they own (mostly companies that are members of the S&P/TSX Composite Index). The coalition is rooted in the belief that good governance practices enhance shareholder value. At the time of writing, CCGG members managed almost $4 trillion in assets.[15] One of their initiatives is the "say-on-pay" vote, referred to in Finance in the News 2.1, which has now been adopted by a large number of firms. This vote is non-binding, in the sense that companies can still go ahead with their compensation plan even if shareholders vote against it. However, most firms, pay close attention to shareholders' opinion on the matter.

**Canadian Coalition for Good Governance (CCGG)** a Canadian coalition of large institutional investors who seek to promote good governance practices in the companies they own

---

### Concept Review Questions

   1. How have management compensation schemes been designed to better align owner–manager interests? How well have these schemes performed in this regard?

   2. What is moral hazard and why did it become the buzz word of the 2008 financial crisis?

---

## 2.5 | Corporate Finance

**LEARNING OBJECTIVE 2.5**

Identify the main corporate finance decisions involving the financial management of a firm's assets and its liabilities (corporate financing).

So what do senior managers do? To answer this question and provide the focus for this textbook, let's refer back to Chapter 1 and the discussion of how the wealth of a country and its people depends on its stock of assets. The government has primary responsibility for developing the country's human capital through its education policy, and is also responsible for realizing the value of its resources through royalties charged for the use of property. This leaves the management of physical assets, such as buildings, machinery and equipment, inventory, and other private assets, which raises some basic management problems and questions to answer:

---

[15]A list of its members, as well as its policies, can be found on the CCGG website at www.ccgg.ca.

1. How does a firm decide to expand its existing buildings or construct or buy another building?

2. How does a firm decide when to replace machinery and equipment? Just because a piece of equipment still works, does this mean that the firm should still use it?

3. How does a firm decide whether to buy or lease machinery and equipment?

4. How much stock or inventory should a firm carry? Should it keep stocks to meet every contingency or should it use just-in-time methods to reduce the investment?

**capital budgeting** or **capital expenditure analysis** the framework for analyzing investment or asset decisions

These decisions are some of the most important that a firm can make, and the framework for analyzing these investment or asset decisions is called **capital budgeting** or **capital expenditure analysis**. Unlike most decisions, a decision to open a mine or build a nuclear reactor commits a firm to a particular course of action and to spend money that is almost irreversibly sunk in a particular application, since often the investment has no or very little alternative use.

In addition to decisions about physical or real assets, firms have to consider the management of their financial assets, which raises some more basic questions.

1. How do firms decide to extend credit to customers to purchase their product—that is, why do firms finance other firms?

2. How do firms manage their cash? Cash is a non-interest-bearing asset, so it seems that corporate holdings of cash should be minimized. However, in 2012, Canadian firms had very significant cash hoards, and U.S. cash holdings are at record levels.

3. How do firms manage any temporary surplus cash?

4. Why do firms take minority stakes in other firms, or, more generally, how do they decide to buy 100 percent or less of another firm? This question leads us into corporate acquisitions and valuation.

**financial management** the process of managing the firm's investment decisions

The combination of the real asset decisions and these financial asset acquisition decisions represent acquisition or investment decisions. Generally, we talk about investment decisions in terms of **financial management**. However, this is only one side of the balance sheet. In addition, we have to consider how these assets are financed and answer some more basic questions.

1. How does a firm decide between raising money through debt or equity?

2. In terms of equity, how does a firm raise the equity: by retaining earnings or by issuing new equity?

**corporate financing** the sources of money for a company, which include using debt or equity, retaining earnings or issuing equity, going public, using bank debt or bonds, using the short-term money market, or borrowing from a bank

3. Why does a firm decide to go public and issue shares to the general public rather than remaining a non-traded private company?

4. If a firm decides to issue debt, what determines whether this is bank debt or bonds issued to the public debt market?

5. What determines whether firms access the short-term money market as opposed to borrowing from a bank?

**corporate finance** the financial management of assets and corporate financing decisions

These basic questions represent the core of liability management for corporations, which we refer to as their **corporate financing** decisions. Taken together, the financial management of assets and corporate financing decisions represent the area of **corporate finance**.

---

### Concept Review Questions

1. Describe the two key decision areas with respect to the financial management of assets.
2. What are some of the key corporate financing decisions made by firms?
3. What are the two key topics covered in the study of corporate finance?

## 2.6 | Finance Careers and the Organization of the Finance Function

**LEARNING OBJECTIVE 2.6**

List some finance jobs available with financial and non-financial companies.

Every manager should be a financial manager, in the sense that the ideas discussed in this textbook are important for all managers within a firm. However, when we think of finance jobs, we generally distinguish between jobs in corporate finance (i.e., within the finance function of a non-financial company, such as BCE) and "pure" finance jobs within a financial intermediary, such as the Royal Bank of Canada or Manulife Financial Corporation.

### Positions in Non-Financial Companies

Figure 2.3 shows the basic breakdown of the finance function within a non-financial corporation. The top person is the **chief financial officer (CFO)** or, in more traditional companies, the **senior vice-president of finance**. Under the CFO are the two main finance jobs: the **treasurer** and the **controller**. Although the breakdown of responsibilities will vary from firm to firm, generally the treasurer does the things that we discuss in this textbook and in the other finance courses normally taught at a university. The controller usually does the things normally discussed in accounting courses. As a result, anyone interested in working for a non-financial company, like Ford Motor Company of Canada, Ltd., or BCE, should study a lot of accounting, because what these firms regard as finance is heavily influenced by accounting.

The controller, for example, is responsible for compliance. This entails making sure that the firm meets its statutory legal responsibilities with securities commissions and other regulatory bodies, makes its tax payments to the government, fulfills its responsibility to prepare and file financial statements, and ensures that its internal control systems eliminate fraud so that the financial statements fairly represent the company's financial position. As part of this financial system, the controller is normally responsible for the management information system (MIS), because its main purpose is to collect the data required for internal audits and the preparation of the firm's financial statements. Finally, the system that produces the financial statements is the same system that generates budgets and targets for the upcoming year.

From this brief description of the controller's functions, it follows that finance jobs in the controller's department require training in financial accounting, management accounting, taxes, MIS, and control systems. These are all regarded as "finance" in non-financial companies.

In contrast, the treasurer has the pure finance job in a company. The treasurer's basic function is to manage the treasury, which is the company's chequebook. To do this, the treasurer has

**chief financial officer (CFO)**   the top financial manager in a company

**senior vice-president of finance**   in some companies, functions as the CFO

**treasurer**   one of the two main finance jobs in a non-financial firm; focuses on the finance side: forecasting, pension management, capital budgeting, cash management, credit management, financing, risk management

**controller**   one of the two main finance jobs in a non-financial firm; focuses on the accounting side: compliance, tax management, systems/MIS, internal audit, accounting, and budgeting

**FIGURE 2.3**   **Finance in a Non-Financial Company**

to manage the company's cash and decide to whom the company will extend credit—in other words, cash and credit management. The treasurer must then pay the bills and make sure that cash is available when needed. This means forecasting the firm's future cash position, determining its capital expenditure plans, and arranging both debt and equity financing. If the firm has a pension plan, the treasurer is also responsible for managing these financial assets the same way a portfolio manager in a mutual fund would manage them. As we noted in Chapter 1, the largest private pension plans manage billions of dollars. Finally, the treasurer is responsible for risk management. Traditionally, this has meant arranging adequate insurance and making sure the firm was covered if a fire burned down the building. However, over the past 30 years, many new techniques have emerged to manage financial risks, such as the risk of serious exchange rate or interest rate movements. These new techniques of financial risk management are the responsibility of the treasurer.

The important thing about finance jobs within a non-financial firm is that the jobs are very broad and need a strong dose of accounting and knowledge developed in other courses in a business school as well as in finance. This is also true, though to a lesser extent, for the finance jobs within a financial intermediary.

## Positions in Financial Companies

**analysts** first-level jobs in a financial institution, requiring an undergraduate degree; analysts are usually responsible for gathering and analyzing data, and providing general assistance to associates

**associates** second-level jobs in a financial institution, requiring an MBA or a professional designation, such as a CFA

**managers** third-level jobs in a financial institution

**account managers** people who manage a bank's relationships with companies, extending credit, helping to manage receivables and cash, and directing them to the bank's more specialized services

**banking associates** people who generate reports on companies, prepare industry reports, and perform background checks on credit applicants

Generally, in the major financial institutions, people start out as **analysts**, a position that requires an undergraduate degree, and then progress to **associates**. Analysts are usually responsible for gathering and analyzing data, and providing general assistance to associates. Normally, associates must have a master of business administration (MBA) or a professional designation, such as chartered professional accountant (CPA) or chartered financial analyst (CFA), before being promoted to **manager**. As we indicated earlier, the banks dominate the Canadian financial system, and Canadian banks offer different career paths, simply because they are such huge organizations. In traditional commercial banking, on the business lending side, the standard job is that of an **account manager** for small and medium-sized businesses. The job entails managing the bank's relationships with companies by extending credit, helping to manage their receivables and cash, and directing them to the bank's more specialized services, such as foreign exchange services, mergers and acquisitions, and specialized credit. **Banking associates** generate reports on companies, prepare industry reports, and perform the background checks (due diligence) needed before extending credit.

In the major chartered banks, investment banking is structured as a separate division, referred to as "investment dealers" or, increasingly, "capital markets" in Canada (such businesses are referred to as investment banks in the United States and in most other countries). People who work for investment dealers are either in sales/trading, or in "pure" investment banking. Pure investment banking, in turn, is divided into corporate financing and mergers and acquisitions (M&A), with jobs in both areas that mirror the corporate finance jobs in a non-financial company (i.e., analysts, associates, and managers).

Corporate financing workers, whether analysts, associates, or managers, advise their clients and help them access the capital markets to raise financing. Although a company may raise capital relatively infrequently, investment dealers constantly advise their clients on what is available in the capital market. On the M&A side, investment dealers, whether analysts, associates, or managers, advise their clients on suitable candidates for acquisition, or suggest how they can defend themselves against a hostile acquisition. This often involves restructuring operations, selling off divisions (divestitures), or changing the firm's financial structure.

**security analysts** people who monitor the valuations of companies and make recommendations to buy and sell a company's shares

Investment dealers, whether in corporate financing or M&A, derive part of their expertise from their knowledge of what is happening in the financial markets. Investment dealer **security analysts** monitor the valuations of the companies they follow and make recommendations to buy and sell a company's shares. They are generically referred to as sell-side analysts, because they generally recommend that their clients buy or sell securities. Their expertise in understanding a particular industry and their ability to value a company is vital to the dealer when it is considering how much a company would be worth if it were taken public and its shares sold in an initial public offering (IPO). **Sales** and **trading people** then execute trades on behalf of their clients and conduct proprietary trading for the dealer itself, using the bank's own capital. **Private bankers** and **retail brokers** help their clients manage their personal wealth. Retail brokers usually work with the general public and deal with small to medium-sized accounts, advising them on investment strategies to build their wealth. Private bankers deal with larger accounts and generally charge a flat fee of 1 percent of the value of the portfolio for their services; retail brokers generally charge per trade.

The larger insurance companies and pension funds, as we saw earlier, have significant long-term investments. As a result, they employ buy-side analysts to do research on which particular investments to buy or sell. In supporting these decisions, they have **financial** and **investment analysts** who do their own in-house research, performing detailed analyses of individual investments and making recommendations on overall financial strategy. **Portfolio managers** are the professionals in charge of the overall management of a portfolio. The analysts report to the portfolio managers, who make the ultimate decisions for their particular portfolio. Because these portfolios are very large, most of the larger companies employ **fixed income traders** or **equity traders** to implement their investment strategies and either buy or sell what are sometimes very large stakes in companies.

The final major sector with a significant number of finance jobs is management consulting and accounting firms. In their consulting practices, these firms need to analyze the financial health of a company, and often their advice contains a corporate finance element. Many of the smaller deals that do not involve significant capital market access are structured by accounting and consulting firms. The finance professionals are normally known as **corporate finance associates and consultants**, and they advise on restructuring, small-scale M&A, and corporate financing.

> **sales** and **trading people**   those who execute trades on behalf of their clients and conduct proprietary trading for the dealer itself by using the bank's own capital
>
> **private bankers**   people who help clients, usually people who have large accounts, manage their personal wealth
>
> **retail brokers**   people who help clients, usually people who have small to medium-sized accounts, manage their personal wealth
>
> **financial** and **investment analysts**   people who do research, perform detailed analyses of individual investments, and make recommendations on overall financial strategy
>
> **portfolio managers**   professionals in charge of the overall management of a portfolio
>
> **fixed income traders** or **equity traders**   people who implement a company's investment strategies and either buy or sell the stakes in companies
>
> **corporate finance associates and consultants**   finance professionals who advise on restructuring, small scale M&A, and corporate financing

---

### Concept Review Questions

1. List three finance positions within non-financial firms and briefly describe those positions.
2. Define the roles of analysts, associates and account managers for financial firms.
3. Distinguish between private bankers and retail brokers.

---

# Review

## Summary

In this chapter, we discuss the many different ways of organizing businesses, from sole proprietorships to trusts to corporations. We also discuss some of the pressures exerted on corporations, and point out that although finance people take it for granted that firms should create shareholder value, this is not always the case. One important consideration that can detract from this goal is the agency relationship that exists between owners and managers, who act as agents on behalf of the company's shareholders (owners). Agency costs arise because managers may not act in the best interests of shareholders or because they must be induced to act optimally.

We then discuss the main types of decisions made by corporations involving the financial management of their real and financial assets, as well as the associated corporate financing decisions. We conclude by discussing some of the major types of finance jobs that are available with both financial and non-financial companies. Many of these jobs require a solid background in accounting. This will lead us logically to the next section of this text, which reviews some of the most important concepts in financial accounting, at least from a finance point of view.

## Summary of Learning Objectives

### 2.1 List the four forms of business organizations and describe the advantages and disadvantages of each.

- Sole proprietorship: a business owned and operated by one person

  *Advantages*: it is easy to set up

  *Disadvantages*: the business is inseparable from the owner; there is unlimited legal liability; net income is taxed at personal marginal tax rate; financing is limited to the resources of the single owner
- Partnership: a business owned and operated by two or more people

  *Advantages*: it combines the financial resources and talents of its partners; liability is spread across the partners

  *Disadvantages*: income is taxed at the individual's marginal tax rate; there is unlimited legal liability
- Trust: a legal organization in which assets are owned by one party and managed or controlled by a different party

  *Advantages*: there is no taxation of funds flowing through the trust; ownership and control are separated

  *Disadvantage*: there are no funds left for investment because all cash is passed to unitholders
- Corporation: a business organized as a separate legal entity under corporate law, with ownership divided into transferable shares

  *Advantages*: ownership and control are separated; it has the potential to attract great amounts of financing by expanding the base of shareholders; it has the potential to attract and use the expertise of its board of directors; it has the potential to hire professional managers to build value

  *Disadvantages*: formality and structure may slow the speed of response of the organization; there is double taxation of corporate income tax and personal dividend tax

### 2.2 Describe the goals of the firm and the pressures exerted on corporations by various stakeholders.

Corporations are owned by the shareholders but managed by the executives. The link between the groups is the board of directors (BOD). The BOD has a fiduciary responsibility to represent the best interests of shareholders when dealing with the executives. The BOD hires and fires the senior executives. Other stakeholder groups, such as employees and the general public, may have an interest in the company's activities but do not have any legal sway over corporate decisions.

### 2.3 Explain what agency costs are and how they affect the interests of management and shareholders.

Agency costs are the costs associated with the agency problem. There are two major types of agency costs: (1) direct costs, which arise because suboptimal decisions are made by management when it acts in a manner that is not in the best interests of shareholders, and (2) indirect costs, which are incurred in an attempt to avoid direct agency costs. Indirect costs include those that arise from any restrictions placed on the actions of management, those associated with monitoring the actions of management, and those associated with management compensation schemes that provide managers with incentives to act in the shareholders' best interests.

### 2.4 Explain the importance of aligning the interests of management with the interests of shareholders in a corporation.

Management's personal interest and compensation may determine how hard it works to serve the best interests of the shareholders. This is the classic agency problem associated with the separation of ownership and management. Shareholders and management may disagree about performance appraisal, investment analysis, financing priorities, and risk consideration, which may result in management behaviour that reduces shareholders' value. Thus, it is important to align the interests of management with the interests of shareholders in order to maximize shareholders' value.

### 2.5 Identify the main corporate finance decisions involving the financial management of a firm's assets and its liabilities (corporate financing).

Financial managers in corporations make both short-term working capital decisions and long-term capital budgeting decisions. Both short- and long-term decisions have implications for the capital needs of the company.

### 2.6 List some finance jobs available with financial and non-financial companies.

- Finance jobs in corporations include chief financial officer, treasurer, and controller.
- Jobs in the investment industry include portfolio managers, brokers, traders, and analysts.
- Jobs on the buy side of the investment industry include buyers of securities.
- Jobs on the sell side of the investment industry include sellers of securities, such as investment dealers.
- Investment banking (corporate finance) jobs involve advising firms on their interactions with the capital markets. Investment bankers are involved with such events as new issues of securities and mergers.

## Key Terms

# Questions and Practice Problems

## Multiple Choice Questions

**1. (LO 2.1)** Which of the following businesses is the least likely to be operated as a partnership?

    **a.** Accounting firm

    **b.** Doctors' office

    **c.** Lawyers' office

    **d.** Steel foundry

**2. (LO 2.1)** Which of the following statements is *false*?

    **a.** The limited liability partnership (LLP) is one of the two main partnership forms.

    **b.** Limited liability partnerships (LLP) have more tax advantages than income trusts.

    **c.** In the limited and general partnerships form, the limited partners are passive investors.

    **d.** In the limited and general partnerships form, the general partner has unlimited liability.

**3. (LO 2.1)** Which statement about sole proprietorships is *false*?

    **a.** The business has unlimited liability.

    **b.** The business is easy to set up.

    **c.** The business is hard to sell.

    **d.** The income is taxed at a corporate rate.

**4. (LO 2.1)** Which of the following type of business organization does *not* have limited liability?

    **a.** Corporations

    **b.** Sole proprietorships

    **c.** Limited partnerships

    **d.** None of the above

**5. (LO 2.1)** Which of the following statements about corporations are *true*?

    **a.** A corporation is treated as a separate legal entity (person) for tax and legal purposes.

    **b.** A corporation has the potential to attract large amounts of capital/financing in contrast to other forms of businesses.

    **c.** The organizational response time of a corporation may be slowed due to the formality and structure involved.

    **d.** All of the above.

**6. (LO 2.1)** Which statement about trusts is *correct*?

    **a.** Compared with corporations, trusts provide greater tax advantages.

    **b.** Compared with corporations, trusts provide fewer tax advantages.

    **c.** Income usually passes through trusts, with corporate tax paid by the unitholders.

    **d.** Unitholders do not pay tax on the income received.

**7. (LO 2.1)** Which statement about corporations is *correct*?

    **a.** There is double taxation: corporations pay corporate tax and shareholders pay tax on dividends received.

    **b.** There is no separation of ownership and control.

    **c.** Corporations are taxed at the personal tax rate.

    **d.** Corporations are not as popular as sole proprietorships as a form of business organization.

**8. (LO 2.2)** Which of the following is the goal of a corporation?

    **a.** Operate in the legal sense

    **b.** Act in the "social interest"

    **c.** Maximize the wealth of its shareholders

    **d.** All of the above

**9. (LO 2.4)** Which of the following is the main concern from the point of view of a company's shareholders?

    **a.** IRR of all divisions when investment is analyzed

    **b.** Preservation of the firm where risk is concerned

    **c.** Accounting return on investment when performance is appraised

    **d.** Market prices when performance is appraised

10. **(LO 2.4)** What is the most important purpose of share incentive plans?

   a. Compensate straight salary

   b. Align the interests of managers and shareholders

   c. Reward management

   d. Boost the share price

11. **(LO 2.4)** Which statement about the areas of disagreement between managers and shareholders is *incorrect*?

   a. Performance appraisal: Managers use market prices while shareholders use accounting numbers like return on investment or cash.

   b. Investment analysis: Managers use the internal rate of return of the best division while shareholders use weighted average cost of capital.

   c. The order of financing: Managers prefer retentions to debt and prefer debt to new equity while shareholders prefer debt first.

   d. Risk concern: Managers' main concern is the preservation of the firm while shareholders' main concern is their portfolios.

12. **(LO 2.5)** Which of the following is *not* a concern related to capital budgeting?

   a. The percentage of debt financing in the capital structure

   b. Whether or not to replace old equipment to boost output

   c. Whether to purchase or lease machinery

   d. Inventory level

13. **(LO 2.6)** Who is the person in charge of the pure finance job (cash and credit management, risk management, etc.) in a company?

   a. Controller

   b. Treasurer

   c. Chief operating officer

   d. Accountant

14. **(LO 2.6)** Which of the following responsibilities does *not* usually belong to the controller?

   a. Compliance

   b. Credit management

   c. Tax management

   d. Budgeting

## Practice Problems

### Basic

15. **(LO 2.1)** List and define the four major forms of business organization.

### Intermediate

16. **(LO 2.1)** State the main differences and similarities between sole proprietorships and partnerships.

17. **(LO 2.1)** Summarize the main characteristics of corporations.

18. **(LO 2.1)** State the statutory responsibilities of directors that are described in the *Canada Business Corporations Act*.

19. **(LO 2.1)** Janice borrowed $100,000 from friends and family to start her company (a sole proprietorship). Business has been poor recently, and Janice has decided to cease operations and liquidate the firm. She expects to obtain $108,000 from selling the assets of the company. How much money will the debt holders receive, and how much will be left for Janice? Would these figures be different if the company had been a corporation?

20. **(LO 2.1)** Suppose Janice obtains only $93,000 when she sells all the assets of the firm described in practice problem 19. How much money would the debt holders receive if the business were a corporation? If it were a sole proprietorship? How much would Janice receive in each case?

21. **(LO 2.3)** Briefly describe the classic agency problem.

22. **(LO 2.4)** List the four areas of conflict of interest between shareholders and managers.

23. **(LO 2.4)** When you hired Dan to manage your business, you agreed to pay him a bonus of 10 percent of profits at the end of each year. The company now has a choice between two projects (it can take on only one of them). Project A will generate profits of $50,000 per year, and detailed financial calculations show that it will increase the value of the firm by $123,100. Project B will generate profits of $40,000 per year but will increase the firm's value by $125,600. Which project is Dan likely to choose and why? Which project would you, the owner of the firm, prefer?

24. **(LO 2.4)** What is the objective behind the stock option plan of executives? In reality, does it achieve this objective?

25. **(LO 2.5)** List the basic areas of capital budgeting.

26. **(LO 2.5)** List the basic areas of financial management.

27. **(LO 2.5)** List the basic questions related to corporate financing.

28. **(LO 2.6)** List the major jobs available in the financial industry.

29. **(LO 2.6)** Summarize the main responsibilities of the finance function (including CFO, treasurer, and controller) in a non-financial company.

30. **(LO 2.6)** As the CFO of your company, it falls to you to make the final decision on large expenditures. Recently, your controller has proposed purchasing a new computer system at a cost of $50,000. He believes the system will deliver savings of $60,000 in the accounting department and could be useful to other departments as well. Your treasurer takes a decidedly different view of the proposal. She claims that the company will have to borrow money to buy the computer system, and this will cost $11,000 in interest. As well, she is concerned that the amount of savings promised by the controller won't materialize. Should you purchase the computer system?

### Challenging

31. **(LO 2.4)** Describe the compensation structure of top Canadian executives.

# Financial Statements

---

**LEARNING OBJECTIVES**

After studying this chapter, you should be able to:

**3.1** Define what International Financial Reporting Standards (IFRS) are and state their significance for Canadian firms.

**3.2** Organize a firm's transactions and explain what are the most important accounting principles related to this task.

**3.3** Prepare a firm's financial statements.

**3.4** Analyze a firm's financial statements.

**3.5** Describe the Canadian tax system and explain the differences between how a corporation and an individual are taxed.

---

Accounting decisions can influence a company's stated performance, as well as perceptions regarding its future. Accounting is the language of business and one of the most important sources of corporate information. Gaining a good understanding of accounting is essential for any serious student of finance. As we discussed in Chapter 2, many "finance jobs" in non-financial companies require a significant knowledge of accounting. Even finance jobs with financial intermediaries require a good understanding of financial accounting. In Chapter 3, we review the salient features of financial accounting. This chapter is no substitute for a course in financial accounting, but it does deal with the issues that are vital to understanding finance. It will also help to explain how some accounting scandals occurred.

---

## 3.1 | Accounting Principles

**LEARNING OBJECTIVE 3.1**
Define what International Financial Reporting Standards (IFRS) are and state their significance for Canadian firms.

---

At its most basic level, accounting is simply an organized way of summarizing all of a firm's transactions and presenting them in such a way that external users can understand the firm's affairs. Clearly, problems arise when the firm tries to present its accounting statements in a way that does *not* fairly represent its affairs, either to creditors, like the bank, or to the common shareholders. Consequently, external users of the firm's financial statements have to become skilled in analyzing these statements and spotting signs that things may not be quite as management presents them. It is important to realize that management prepares the firm's financial statements, not the firm's auditors. Auditors, like Deloitte & Touche LLP, simply attest to whether or not the financial statements fairly represent the firm's financial position according to the appropriate accounting standards.[1]

# Canadian and International Standards

**International Financial Reporting Standards (IFRS)** an internationally recognized set of accounting guidelines adopted by many countries around the world (including Canada as of 2011)

Over the past decade, a new set of accounting guidelines, **International Financial Reporting Standards (IFRS)**, has gained prominence throughout the financial world. Up until approximately 2005, each country had its own accounting guidelines. However, with the increased globalization and prominence of international business, it became less suitable for each country to report financial results according to its own standards. For example, consider the situation of a Canadian investor wanting to invest in a Swiss company and desiring a full understanding of this company's financial health prior to investing. The investor would have had to obtain an understanding of the Swiss accounting rules before reviewing the company's statements. Thus, it is only natural that the accounting practices in various countries came to be standardized. Since 2005, approximately 120 countries around the world, including Canada, permit or require IFRS and/or have converged their local accounting standards with IFRS.

**generally accepted accounting principles (GAAP)** the set of basic principles and conventions applied in the preparation of financial statements

IFRS have been the primary accounting standards for publicly accountable enterprises in Canada since January 2011, replacing our previous standard, which we refer to as our "former" Canadian **generally accepted accounting principles (GAAP)** or as the "pre-changeover Canadian GAAP." Publicly accountable enterprises include any company that has issued debt or equity that is or will be traded in a public market, or any organization, such as a bank or a mutual fund, that holds assets in a fiduciary capacity for a broad group of outsiders as one of its primary businesses. Private companies or not-for-profit organizations have the option to report their financial results under IFRS but are not required to do so. These organizations have special accounting standards, which were also introduced in Canada in January 2011, and which are designed to meet their unique needs as well as the needs of the users of their financial statements. Private companies may report under IFRS or they may choose to report under Accounting Standards for Private Enterprises (ASPE), which is simpler than IFRS and therefore is often less costly for private companies. Not-for-profit organizations have special accounting standards designed to meet the unique needs of the users of their financial statements—for example, users often wish to review the effectiveness of the entity's stewardship of resources. Most small and mid-sized private Canadian companies have chosen to report under ASPE as it is fairly similar to the former Canadian GAAP. Larger private companies, such as Irving Oil, have opted to adopt IFRS. In some cases, larger organizations choose IFRS to prepare for an eventual public offering of their stock, because of their more complex accounting needs, or because it makes it easier for them to benchmark their financial statements against those of their industry peers.

Given the multiple accounting platforms that exist in Canada, the terminology of Canadian GAAP is used to encompass the different reporting possibilities—IFRS, ASPE, or not-for-profit or pension accounting.[2] There is also a separate set of standards applicable to public entities or government. The various reporting options acceptable under current Canadian GAAP are depicted in **Figure 3.1**.

There is one final accounting option for Canadian companies. Since March 2005, Canadian securities laws permit a public company whose stock is listed on both Canadian and American stock exchanges to prepare its financial statements under U.S. GAAP.[3] There were 187 companies listed on both Canadian and U.S. exchanges by the end of 2018, with about half of these being Canadian companies that are "inter-listed" in the United States.[4] Rather

---

[1]Much of this section was originally developed by Karine Benzancar, CMA, CPA, managing director of Knowledge Plus Corporation. We thank her very much for her assistance and her invaluable insights.

[2]Regulators resisted eliminating use of the term "GAAP" because many legal documents, such as loan agreements, would have to be revised if the terminology changed.

[3]This option is included in Canada Business Corporations Regulations, section 71.

[4]Toronto Stock Exchange, "Quarterly List of Interlisted Securities for NI 23-101—History," https://www.tsx.com/trading/toronto-stock-exchange/fee-schedule/ni-23-101, accessed March 13, 2019.

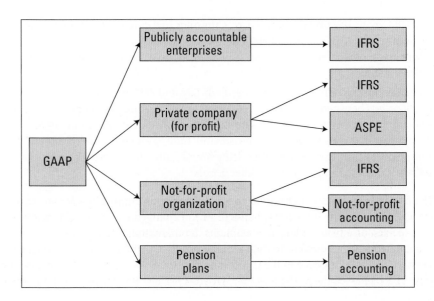

**FIGURE 3.1** Accounting
Options Available to Various
Forms of Organizations

than convert their financial statements to IFRS in 2011, some of these companies, such as
Magna International and Canadian Pacific Railway, chose to adopt U.S. GAAP instead. The
differences between U.S. GAAP and the former Canadian GAAP were much smaller than
those between Canadian GAAP and IFRS, so it was much easier and less expensive for these
companies to convert to U.S. GAAP.

The United States is one of the few developed countries that had not adopted IFRS at
the time this textbook was written. Instead, the Financial Accounting Standards Board
(FASB) in the United States has been working with the regulators of IFRS, the International Accounting Standards Board (IASB), located in London, England, to converge
U.S. GAAP with IFRS. Essentially, since 2002, the two regulators have been meeting
regularly to revise the U.S. accounting rules and modify IFRS to achieve consistency
between the two sets of accounting guidelines. The ultimate goal of the regulators is
to have one set of high-quality accounting standards that can be used throughout the
world. Although many of the standards have been converged, at the time of writing,
given the different viewpoints of the regulatory bodies, it is not expected there will be
perfect convergence.

## The Impact of Accounting Scandals

The question of whether a firm's financial statements fairly represent its financial position has been a major concern throughout time. Unfortunately, we have two prominent
Canadian examples—Nortel Networks Corp. and more recently Sino-Forest Corp., in which
the statements did not accurately reflect the company's position. Sino-Forest is a formerly
Canadian-listed, Hong Kong–based forestry company that had a market capitalization of
more than $6 billion before fraud allegations were levelled at it in 2011. It filed for bank-
ruptcy protection on March 30, 2012, and its shares were delisted from the Toronto Stock
Exchange in May 2012.

Concerns over accounting fraud hit all-time highs in the United States after the failure
of Enron Corporation in 2001. At the time, Enron was a respected and widely admired U.S.
company that had been ranked as high as seventh on the Fortune 500 list of U.S. companies.
Enron's collapse triggered dozens of lawsuits and criminal charges:

- Sixteen former Enron executives pleaded guilty to securities fraud, insider trading, and
conspiracy.
- Four former Merrill Lynch & Co., Inc., executives and one mid-level Enron finance executive were put in jail for misreporting loans.

- Merrill Lynch, JPMorgan Chase & Co., Citigroup Inc., and the Canadian Imperial Bank of Commerce (CIBC) paid US$400 million to settle allegations that they helped Enron "cook its books" and paid US$6.6 billion to settle a variety of shareholder lawsuits against them.

- The previous two CEOs of Enron, Kenneth Lay and Jeffrey Skilling, were found guilty on 29 counts between them. They stood trial for "misleading investors, analysts, auditors and employees through false and sanitized financial statements, empty hype and shady accounting manoeuvres in finance broadband, trading and retail energy units."[5] Kenneth Lay died less than two months after being found guilty. Jeffrey Skilling was sentenced to 24 years and 4 months in a U.S. federal prison.

The fallout from Enron's bankruptcy has had enormous implications for accounting and finance. Quite simply, the financial collapse of Enron changed the accounting landscape and what is expected of a firm's financial statements. So many individuals were hurt by the collapse, and it happened so quickly, to such a widely admired firm, that the U.S. Congress had to act to restore public confidence in the U.S. financial system. As a direct consequence, the U.S. Congress in 2002 passed the *Sarbanes-Oxley Act (SOX)*. The following are the main provisions of this act:

- the establishment of a Public Company Accounting Oversight Board to register and inspect public accounting firms and establish audit standards
- the separation of audit functions from other services, such as consulting, provided by the big accounting firms, with the auditors rotating every five years so that they do not get too close to the companies they are auditing
- the implementation of much stricter governance standards, including internal controls, with auditors reporting to the company's audit committee, which is to be composed of independent members of the board of directors (BOD) with the power to engage independent consultants
- the requirement that the company's annual report contain an internal control report that indicates the state of the firm's internal controls and assesses their effectiveness
- the requirement that both the chief executive officer (CEO) and the chief financial officer (CFO) "certify" that the firm's financial statements "fairly present, in all material respects, the operations and financial condition of the issuer"

As the key provisions of *SOX* indicate, the main targets are the company and its auditors. There was widespread belief that Enron's auditor, Arthur Andersen LLP, was too tight with Enron, as many former Andersen people worked with Enron, and the local auditors overruled head office in several key areas. Rotating the company's auditors every five years promotes their objectivity. Further, separating the non-audit functions of the major accounting firms from their audit functions helps prevent accounting firms from being in a conflict of interest. Previously, many felt the accounting firms were treating auditing as a "loss leader" to get consulting contracts. Consequently, they were not sufficiently objective in their audit responsibilities. This judgement is confirmed by the fact that the U.S. government set up an oversight body to regulate audit firms and take direct control of many accounting areas.

For U.S. companies, the major change is the requirement of stronger internal controls. One of the failures at Enron was apparently a weak audit committee that did not exercise proper oversight of the company's financial statements. Now the audit committee has to be composed of independent and unrelated members of the BOD who have the power to engage external consultants and have the external auditors report to them. Further, management has to report on, and the auditor has to comment on, the firm's internal controls, with the CEO and CFO certifying the statements are fair.

---

[5]This section is adapted from Hays, Kristen, "Trial of Enron Founder Ken Lay and Ex CEO Jeffrey Skilling Starts January 30." Associated Press, January 22, 2006.

## **3.1** Finance in the News   The Top 10 Canadian Accounting Stories of 2018

The past year was a turbulent one in the Canadian accounting profession. A year when politicians and regulators got serious about tax collection and financial reporting, following through on promises of reform and disclosure, setting the stage for the federal election in 2019. Here are the top 10 Canadian accounting stories of 2018 in reverse order of importance and impact:

**10.** Calls for tax reform go nowhere.

 **9.** G&M attacks the audit profession.

The feature article no one wants to talk about. "Why it's getting hard to trust the auditors," runs in The Globe and Mail's Report on Business Magazine (ROB Magazine), drawing a tenuous connection between accounting scandals at home and abroad to argue its canary in the coalmine warning. Like a bad smell in an elevator, everyone leaves quickly and gets on with their day.

 **8.** Big Four dominate Canadian consulting.

 **7.** Livent sends ripples through class-action waters.

 **6.** Stock market regulators say mind the non-GAAP.

 **5.** The CRA finally releases tax gap figures.

 **4.** Tax evaders rush to beat the CRA voluntary disclosure deadline.

 **3.** Auditor General says CRA fails audit.

In November, Canada's government auditor says the CRA is failing Audit 101, with "notable gaps" in how it treats taxpayers and how it measures its own compliance. To the amusement of Canadian Accountant, the CRA goes on a PR blitz prior to Michael Ferguson's report, leading us to reckon the Agency knew what was coming and wasn't entirely displeased with the AG's recommendations.

 **2.** Ontario's deficit. Worse than Watergate?

Soon after taking power in Ontario, Premier Doug Ford claims the provincial deficit is $8 billion higher than expected, based in part on the investigation of a select group of forensic accountants that includes Canadian Accountant's own Al Rosen. Ford trumpets "it's quite possibly the worst political cover-up in Ontario's history."

The province's chief accountant, Comptroller Cindy Veinot, requests on multiple occasions to meet with the Select Committee on Fiscal Transparency. The NDP members of the committee put forward a motion to call her as a witness and the PC members vote against the motion. Veinot resigns from the Ontario Public Service, saying she does not agree with the accounting decisions of the new government.

 **1.** Hydro accounting zaps two provincial elections.

B.C. and Ontario see governments change hands due in large part to the financial mess of deferral accounting at public utilities. In Ontario, Auditor General Bonnie Lysyk zaps Premier Kathleen Wynne twice over accounting issues that Lysyk claims hide the real nature of the provincial deficit. It's a shocking charge to voters who pull the plug on the provincial Liberals. No word yet on how the Tories will handle Hydro accounting in the future.

**Source:** Excerpted from Ellis, Colin, "The Top 10 Accounting Stories of 2018," *Canadian Accountant* (January 4, 2019). Available at http://www.canadian-accountant.com/content/business/the-top-10-canadianaccounting-stories-of-2018. Reproduced with the permission of CHT Business Media Inc.

*SOX* had a major impact in the United States, improving public confidence in the objectivity of the financial statements of U.S. companies. It also affected a significant number of Canadian companies (especially the large ones) that issue securities in the United States and have to comply with U.S. securities laws. Indeed, although Canada has had fewer accounting scandals, and those that have occurred are of a smaller scale than those in the United States, concerns over such misrepresentations and their impact on the business environment have dictated that Canadian regulatory authorities maintain strict controls over the auditing process, similar to those employed in the United States. On the other hand, increasing disclosure requirements does not solve many problems. It is still up to the users of these statements to identify the risks inherent in the disclosures.

Finance in the News 3.1 lists the "Top 10 Canadian Accounting Stories of 2018." It highlights the fact that concerns still exist regarding the audit function and the resulting fallout in terms of misrepresentations—and scandals—in extreme cases. In particular, stories 1, 2, 3, and 9 refer to issues and/or concerns regarding the audit function, accounting procedures, and the reliability of resulting information disclosures.

## **Concept Review Questions**

 **1.** What does IFRS stand for? What types of Canadian companies must prepare their financial statements in accordance with IFRS (or U.S. GAAP)?

 **2.** Who prescribes GAAP for U.S. companies?

 **3.** What are the major provisions of *SOX*?

## 3.2 | Organizing a Firm's Transactions

> **LEARNING OBJECTIVE 3.2**
>
> Organize a firm's transactions and explain what are the most important accounting principles related to this task.

## Bookkeeping

Table 3.1 presents a series of transactions that someone, let's call him Jim, has made in setting up a company to make widgets.

**TABLE 3.1  Jim's Widget Business**

1. December 1: Jim opens a business account with a $50,000 deposit.
2. December 5: Jim purchases a lathe for $30,000 using $20,000 cash and a $10,000 loan.
3. December 10: Jim buys $10,000 worth of inventory on credit.
4. December 11: Jim pays $5,000 to suppliers (creditors).
5. December 31: Jim sells $20,000 worth of widgets, $15,000 in cash and $5,000 on credit.
6. December 31: Jim recognizes cost of sales (inventory decline) of $8,000.
7. December 31: Jim pays hydro of $2,600 and rent of $2,400.
8. December 31: Jim withdraws $10,000 for himself.
9. January 5: Jim pays a further $5,000 to creditors.

The accountant must make sense of these transactions. Before we get into the accounting issues, we will first discuss bookkeeping, which is different from accounting. On December 1, Jim opened his business by putting in $50,000 of capital (i.e., he "capitalized" his business). The secret in bookkeeping and accounting is to recognize that every transaction is an exchange, so there must be two parallel transactions. This parallelism is called double-entry bookkeeping. For this transaction, the business received $50,000 in cash and gave Jim ownership rights, or capital, worth $50,000. Jim might decide that as far as his statements are concerned, this $50,000 represents 50,000 shares, each with a book value of $1.

By convention, increases in assets, like cash, are recorded as debits on the left side of a balance sheet. In contrast, increases in liabilities, like the capital owed to Jim, are recorded as credits on the right side of the balance sheet. So, after this transaction, the balance sheet for Jim's Widgets would look like this:

| Balance Sheet for Jim's Widgets (December 1) | | | |
|---|---|---|---|
| **Assets ($)** | | **Liabilities and Equity ($)** | |
| Cash | 50,000 | Owner's equity | 50,000 |
| Total assets | 50,000 | Total liabilities and equity | 50,000 |

**balance sheet** a snapshot of the financial position of a firm, listing assets on the left and liabilities and owner's equity on the right

The **balance sheet** is a snapshot of the firm's financial position, listing assets on the left side, and liabilities and owner's equity on the right side. In practice, the firm's bookkeeper wouldn't make up a balance sheet after every transaction; they would record the transaction in a journal or ledger and then post all the transactions to the firm's total balance sheet after a certain period. So balance sheets show the business's financial position at a particular time, such as the end of a year or a quarter. Because he is just starting out, Jim will be doing his own bookkeeping. What would the balance sheet look like after Jim purchases a lathe to make his widgets? Well, he has a lathe with a cost of $30,000, so he debits (increases) equipment on the assets side for $30,000, credits (reduces) cash by $20,000, and credits (increases) loans for $10,000, because he paid $20,000 in cash and now owes $10,000.

### Balance Sheet for Jim's Widgets (December 5)

| Assets ($) | | Liabilities and Equity ($) | |
| --- | --- | --- | --- |
| Cash | 30,000 | Loan | 10,000 |
| Equipment | 30,000 | Owner's equity | 50,000 |
| Total assets | 60,000 | Total liabilities and equity | 60,000 |

The second transaction illustrates a couple of things. First, in accounting parlance, "debit" means to increase an asset or decrease a liability, while "credit" means to increase a liability or decrease an asset. Because Jim paid $20,000 in cash, he credited cash for this amount. Second, the balance sheet still balances, but it has now increased by the amount of the equipment ($10,000) that was not paid for in cash.

For the third transaction, Jim buys $10,000 worth of inventory (i.e., stock, wood, and other supplies) that he needs to produce his widgets. Because he has good credit, the suppliers simply ship him the goods with invoices for him to pay. So he debits (increases) inventory for $10,000 and credits (increases) accounts payable to indicate that he has to pay $10,000 to his suppliers. For the fourth transaction, Jim pays $5,000 to his suppliers (creditors), so he credits (reduces) cash for $5,000 and debits (reduces) payables for $5,000. After these transactions on December 11, the balance sheet will look like this:

### Balance Sheet for Jim's Widgets (December 11)

| Assets ($) | | Liabilities and Equity ($) | |
| --- | --- | --- | --- |
| Cash | 25,000 | Payables | 5,000 |
| Inventory | 10,000 | Loan | 10,000 |
| Machinery | 30,000 | Owner's equity | 50,000 |
| Total assets | 65,000 | Total liabilities and equity | 65,000 |

By convention, items on balance sheets are listed in terms of their **liquidity**, which is how easily they are converted to cash. On the asset side, cash is the most liquid, then inventory, and finally machinery. On the liability side, payables are the most liquid, since they have to be paid in the normal course of business, then loans, and finally owner's equity.

**liquidity**   the ease with which assets and liabilities are converted to cash

Up to now, Jim has been buying things and getting ready to produce his widgets, so not much happens for the next few weeks. Then, at year end, he sells $20,000 worth of widgets, $15,000 for cash and $5,000 to someone who will pay in 30 days (Jim hopes). He debits (increases) cash for $15,000 and debits (increases) accounts receivable for $5,000, but what about sales (or revenues) of $20,000? For now, he will set up an account on the liability side for income from sales and call it the IS account. The balance sheet now looks as follows:

### Balance Sheet for Jim's Widgets (December 31)

| Assets ($) | | Liabilities and Equity ($) | |
| --- | --- | --- | --- |
| Cash | 40,000 | Payables | 5,000 |
| Receivables | 5,000 | Loan | 10,000 |
| Inventory | 10,000 | Owner's equity | 50,000 |
| Machinery | 30,000 | IS | 20,000 |
| Total assets | 85,000 | Total liabilities and equity | 85,000 |

It is now year end. Jim has to prepare his balance sheet, but he faces some special problems. So far, all the transactions have been mechanical and verifiable in that he had the invoices and the receipts to document the transactions. Therefore, the process has been simple bookkeeping, with very little judgement needed. However, Jim recognizes in transaction 6 from Table 3.1 that he has used $8,000 of his inventory, because he does a quick check of what he has on hand and finds that he is short this amount. Jim also recognizes in transaction 7 that some of the $5,000 he has paid in hydro and rent is for the future, because he had to pay two months' rent on moving in and he also had to make a $2,300 deposit for hydro. Finally, he knows that the $10,000 he took out of his business (transaction 8) can't all be salary, because it is excessive compared with his sales of $20,000. Jim also notices that his lathe is a bit worn, and he realizes that he will have to pay some interest on his loan soon. In short, Jim recognizes that although he could do his own bookkeeping, he can't do the accounting, so he has to set up a meeting to talk to an accountant.

# Accounting Conventions: The Basic Principles

What is the difference between an accountant and a bookkeeper? In a crude sense, the book-keeper manages all the transactions in a firm, while the accountant uses them to create the firm's financial statements. Accountants do this by applying the accounting standards we described previously so that other accountants can understand and accept what was done. As noted earlier, IFRS are a set of basic principles and conventions applied in preparing financial statements. These principles are accepted by securities regulators, like the Ontario Securities Commission (OSC), for use in preparing statements for securities offered to the general public.

The following are the most basic accounting principles:

1. The entity concept: the accounting is for an economic entity, such as a corporation.

2. The going concern principle: the statements must reflect the accounts on the basis that the firm is not in imminent threat of bankruptcy; otherwise, they have to be qualified.

3. A period of analysis: the statements are for a particular period of time, such as a year-end balance sheet or quarterly statement.

4. A monetary value: in Canada, accountants use historical cost accounting, in which trans-actions are for the dollars actually involved, with no restatement for inflationary effects.

5. The matching principle: the revenues must be matched against the costs that generated those revenues.

6. Revenue recognition: revenues are recognized only when there is a verifiable sale.

A particular entity's statements are prepared for a specific period, and the entity has to be a going concern (currently in business). The most powerful principle is the matching princi-ple, which leads to accrual accounting: costs and revenues have to match the period, even if the cash components of the transactions occur in other periods. This is the point at which the accountant's judgement is needed to match up these revenues and costs.

## General Themes of IFRS

According to IFRS, the primary objective of financial reporting standards is

> to provide financial information about the reporting entity that is useful to existing and potential investors, lenders, and other creditors in making decisions about providing resources to the entity.[6]

IFRS suggest that reported financial information should possess two fundamental quali-tative characteristics:

---

[6]IFRS Foundation/International Accounting Standards Board (IASB), "Conceptual Framework for Financial Reporting 2010" (London: IASB), paragraph OB2, p. 9.

1. Relevance: information is relevant if it could potentially affect users' decisions and has predictive and/or confirmatory power. This implies the information should be "material."

2. Faithful representation: the information provided should be complete, neutral (that is, bias-free), and free from error.[7]

IFRS suggest the following characteristics enhance the usefulness of relevant and faithfully represented information:

- Comparability: consistent comparisons can be made across entities and across time.
- Verifiability: information can be verified by an independent knowledgeable party.
- Timeliness: information is presented in a timely manner.
- Understandability: information is presented in as clear and concise a manner as is possible (given the nature of material information provided).[8]

The preceding paragraphs demonstrate that IFRS have a very strong focus on the users of financial statements and consist of a number of guidelines to encourage companies to provide enough detail and transparency on a company's financial health that readers of financial statements can make informed decisions. Although there are substantial guidelines in IFRS, there is also room for managerial discretion in deciding how to present the results. In fact, many industry professionals find that IFRS are more subjective than the former Canadian GAAP or U.S. GAAP; as a result, they find it challenging to compare financial results of different companies.

On the surface, in terms of format, a set of statements prepared using IFRS look very similar to the Canadian Pacific Railway Limited (Canadian Pacific (CP)) statements you will review in section 3.4, which were prepared using U.S. GAAP. There will still be an income statement, a balance sheet, and a statement of cash flows. However, the most significant difference between IFRS statements and U.S. GAAP lies in how the numbers are determined.

Since companies have a substantial amount of management judgement when it comes to reporting financial results, they present their financial statements with accompanying notes, which provide further detail on how the numbers in the statements are calculated. When reviewing financial statements, it is important to review not only the statements themselves, but also all the information presented in the notes.

For example, under IFRS, each company will make an accounting policy choice to report on the value of a company's fixed assets, based either on its historical value less any accumulated amortization or on its fair market value. Reporting on fair value provides the user of the financial statements with an understanding of what the asset is worth as of the balance sheet date; however, the process of determining fair value can be onerous and expensive for the company, especially for assets where fair values are constantly changing, such as real estate. Fair value reporting requires independent valuations by external appraisers and will require a number of accounting adjustments to accurately reflect the market value, making it more complex and expensive for companies to report in this fashion. Many companies in the real estate sector have chosen this valuation method, however, as it permits them to show higher asset values and equity on their balance sheet. The method of reporting (i.e., historical cost or fair value) will be described in the notes to the financial statements.

Differences between IFRS and other acceptable forms of financial reporting can be fairly significant. For example, U.S. GAAP does not permit companies to value fixed assets using market values; only historical costs, adjusted for amortization, are allowed. The same holds true for the Canadian GAAP that existed prior to 2011. When Brookfield Asset Management switched its reporting from the former Canadian GAAP, where it reported its fixed assets at historical cost, and began reporting real estate values on the basis of fair value, its equity almost tripled on its balance sheet, increasing from $7.5 million under the former Canadian GAAP to $23 million under IFRS.[9]

---

[7]Paraphrased from ibid., paragraphs QC5–18, pp. 17–19.
[8]Paraphrased from ibid., paragraphs QC19–34, pp. 19–22.
[9]Brookfield Asset Management financial statements, Q1 2009.

The impairment, or loss in value, of assets is also treated differently under IFRS and other forms of reporting, such as U.S. GAAP. For example, when an asset loses value, this loss in value is reflected in the company's financial statements. If subsequent events cause the asset's value to increase, IFRS require that higher asset value be reflected on the company's financial statements. In contrast, U.S. GAAP does not allow a company to increase the value of its assets once they have been reduced. An example of the impact of this policy can be seen in the 2003 financial statements of Lihir Gold, a company that reported $35 million of income under IFRS, $31 million of which resulted from reversing past impairments.[10]

In general, IFRS seek to present as much information as possible on the financial statements and to limit off-balance-sheet financing, a concept that can result in some of a company's financing costs not being reflected in the liabilities listed on their balance sheet. For example, if a company enters into an agreement to lease office space, typically the company's commitment is not seen on the balance sheet, even if it is a non-cancellable lease. This is an example of off-balance-sheet financing. Investors who are unaware of the extent of a company's off-balance-sheet financing can be unpleasantly surprised should the company end up in a position where it fails to meet its obligations. As of January 2019, IFRS standards require lessees to recognize virtually all leases on the balance sheet.

Another difference between IFRS and other forms of reporting is the volatility of income. If a company incurs large losses in one period that are offset by corresponding gains in another period, the company will present large fluctuations in income under IFRS; other forms of financial reporting tend to have more options to smooth out financial results over the periods in question. Although this characteristic of IFRS reporting causes income to be more volatile, it is a more accurate depiction of the company's true economic situation.

---

## Concept Review Questions

1. Differentiate between debits and credits with respect to assets and liabilities.
2. What is the primary objective of financial reporting under IFRS?
3. Explain what is meant by the matching principle. How is this principle related to the use of accrual accounting?

---

## 3.3 | Preparing Accounting Statements

**LEARNING OBJECTIVE 3.3**

Prepare a firm's financial statements.

---

## The Balance Sheet and the Income Statement

An accountant, armed with accrual accounting, looks at Jim's business and focuses on the matching and revenue recognition principles.

1. Inventory should be reduced by $8,000, and cost of sales of $8,000 should be expensed against revenues.
2. Of the $5,000 in payments, the accountant expenses $300 for hydro for the month and $1,200 for rent, and records the balance of $3,500 as a prepaid expense.

---

[10]Lihir Gold, 2003 F-20 SEC filing, reconciliation between U.S. GAAP and IFRS.

3. Of the $10,000 that Jim withdrew, the accountant indicates that $4,000 is a reasonable salary for the month and the balance of $6,000 reflects a reduction or return of capital.

4. The lathe has suffered wear and tear, and its value should be reduced. After looking at similar pieces of equipment, the accountant reduces the lathe's value by $2,000. This cost is offset against revenues.

5. The accountant advises Jim to record an expense of $100 for the interest that he owes but hasn't paid for the period.

6. Finally, the accountant will prepare Jim's tax return and recognize that, for tax purposes, Jim is able to write off $5,000 for wear and tear on the lathe, rather than the actual $2,000, because the government is giving special incentives for firms to buy more modern equipment.

After making these judgement calls, the accountant records these transactions to the special IS account that Jim inserted on the balance sheet:

- Inventory is credited (reduced) by $8,000, and the IS account debited (reduced) with cost of sales of $8,000.
- Cash is credited (reduced) by $5,000, of which $1,500 is debited to rent and hydro in the IS account, and $3,500 is debited to a new asset account called "prepaid expenses."
- Cash is credited (reduced) by $10,000 for Jim's withdrawal. Capital is debited (reduced) by $6,000, and the IS account is debited (reduced) by $4,000 for Jim's salary.
- The equipment account is credited (reduced) by $2,000 for the wear and tear on the lathe, and the IS account debited (reduced) by $2,000 for equipment wear and tear.
- The IS account is debited (reduced) by $100 for interest expense, and a new account is credited (increased) by $100 for accrued interest payable.
- Finally, the IS account is debited with $2,200 for total tax expense at a 50-percent tax rate, and two new accounts are created and credited $700 for accrued taxes payable and $1,500 for deferred income taxes.

The accountant has made a lot of judgement calls and has used the matching concept to match up Jim's Widgets' revenues and costs over the period, which in this case is from the start of the business until year end. After all this debiting and crediting, the balance sheet looks like this:

### Balance Sheet for Jim's Widgets (December 31)

| Assets ($) | | Liabilities and Equity ($) | |
|---|---|---|---|
| Cash | 25,000 | Payables | 5,000 |
| Receivables | 5,000 | Accruals | 800 |
| Inventory | 2,000 | Loan | 10,000 |
| Prepaids | 3,500 | Deferred taxes | 1,500 |
| Machinery | 28,000 | Owner's equity | 44,000 |
| | | IS | 2,200 |
| Total assets | 63,500 | Total liabilities and equity | 63,500 |

Those of you familiar with accounting will recognize the IS account listed below the owner's equity as the **income statement**. While Jim was adding these transactions to the balance sheet account, he was actually making up the income statement. For convenience, let's write out the transactions and record the income statement for Jim's Widgets.

The balance of $2,200 is Jim's net income. Now that the accountant knows that Jim's Widgets made $2,200 in profit or net income, they could ask Jim if he wants some of the $10,000 withdrawal as a dividend payment, rather than as salary or a withdrawal of capital. To make these decisions, Jim has to understand the tax consequences, which we will defer explaining for the moment.

**income statement**  a firm's financial statement showing the sales, expenses, and net profit for a given period

| Income Statement for Jim's Widgets ($) | |
|---|---|
| Revenues | 20,000 |
| Cost of sales | 8,000 |
| Hydro | 300 |
| Rent | 1,200 |
| Salaries | 4,000 |
| Depreciation (lathe) | 2,000 |
| Interest | 100 |
| Before-tax income | 4,400 |
| Tax expense | 700 |
| Deferred income tax | 1,500 |
| Net income | 2,200 |
| Dividends | 0 |
| Retained earnings | 2,200 |

The accountant reports one final number to Jim: because Jim capitalized his company with 50,000 shares, each with a $1 book value, his company earned $0.044 per share (i.e., $2,200/$50,000). This is the earnings per share (EPS) for Jim's Widgets and is a very important number, as you will see later. However, note that Jim could just as easily have capitalized his company using 10,000 shares with a book value of $5, in which case the $2,200 net income divided by the 10,000 shares would have given an EPS of $0.22. In isolation, the EPS is meaningless; it is only useful when we look at trends over time or compare it with other per-share figures, such as the stock price.

What is income? In economics, income is defined as the amount that can be withdrawn from a business while keeping it whole, in the sense of not encroaching on the capital value. However, although this is the guiding principle behind the matching and revenue recognition principles, in practice the correlation between the two is loose. In accounting, income is defined as the excess of revenues over expenses, which are estimated based on GAAP; accounting income typically differs substantially from economic income. For this reason, the external analyst must understand how the accountant creates the income statement and balance sheet.

## Changing Accounting Assumptions

Suppose that Jim's accountant interpreted three things differently:

1. On reflection, the accountant feels that the lathe has not deteriorated that much and expenses only $1,000 for wear and tear.
2. The accountant talks to Jim and decides to recognize another $5,000 in sales to a customer who has promised to buy some of Jim's widgets. Another $5,000 is added to receivables, because no cash has been received.
3. On reflection, the accountant feels that $2,000 of Jim's salary reflects the development of a unique style and also suggests that Jim patent this style.

Obviously, these new interpretations will influence Jim's balance sheet, as well as his profits. For now, we will focus our discussion on the impact that these three decisions have on Jim's profits, which jump to $6,200, as follows:

| Revised Income Statement for Jim's Widgets ($) | |
|---|---|
| Revenues | 25,000 |
| Cost of sales | 8,000 |
| Hydro | 300 |
| Rent | 1,200 |
| Salaries | 2,000 |
| Depreciation (lathe) | 1,000 |
| Interest | 100 |
| Before-tax income | 12,400 |
| Tax expense | 4,200 |
| Deferred income tax | 2,000 |
| Net income | 6,200 |
| Dividends | 0 |
| Retained earnings | 6,200 |

The extra $4,000 in retained earnings comes from the recognition of the extra $5,000 in sales ($2,500 after tax),[11] the reduction (or understatement) of Jim's wear and tear on the lathe by $1,000 ($500 after tax), and the reduction (or understatement) of Jim's salary by $2,000 ($1,000 after tax). These changes certainly make Jim's business look more profitable, and the balance sheet will be stronger as well. There is now an extra $5,000 receivable, the equipment is worth $1,000 more, and there is a new $2,000 account for patents and brand names. All in all, Jim's business looks much better, all because of different judgement calls made by Jim's accountant.

The three areas in which the accountant changed the financial statements are all classic areas of financial statement manipulation. WorldCom Corporation's accounting fraud was a simple case of deciding that the rental payments for telephone lines were an asset, rather than an expense. So instead of deducting them as expenses and reducing income, they were added to the balance sheet as assets, exactly like the $2,000 of Jim's salary. Bristol-Myers Squibb had to restate its financial statements after it was revealed that a significant component of its sales were actually to controlled distributors, where there was an agreement to buy them back under certain circumstances, exactly like the $5,000 in additional sales to someone who had "promised" to buy some of Jim's widgets. The understatement of wear and tear on Jim's lathe is another classic case where conservatism in writing down the value of an asset makes the company's income statement and balance sheet look better.

What these three examples, along with the other adjustments, indicate is the significant scope for judgement in the preparation of a firm's annual statements and the ongoing need to seriously examine the assumptions underlying these judgements. The examples emphasize the old phrase "figures can lie and liars can figure."

## Tax Statements

Let's assume that Jim decides against the aggressive adjustments discussed in the previous section and keeps to his original statements. We now consider the two tax accounts: taxes payable and deferred taxes. To understand the tax accounts, you have to understand that corporations are allowed to say different things to different people. In particular, they are allowed to present one set of accounts to Canada Revenue Agency (the tax authorities) and another to the investing public. There are limits on how different they can be, but Canada is not like northern European countries, where only one set of statements is used and the accounts given to the tax authorities are the same as those presented to the general public. One of the biggest differences in the statements in Canada is wear and tear.

What we have been calling "wear and tear" has traditionally been referred to by accountants as **depreciation** or **amortization**, because the asset is depreciating or reducing in value through time. For the financial statements, the accountant is allowed to use any reasonable (and GAAP-compliant) method for calculating depreciation (amortization). The most common method is to divide a depreciable asset's cost, less an estimated salvage value, by its estimated useful life and expense that amount per year. This is referred to as the "straight-line method." There are other, more sophisticated methods, such as by machine usage. However, for tax purposes, the government allows a special form of depreciation, which in Canada is called "capital cost allowance" (CCA). Essentially, every asset is allocated to a CCA asset class, and a fixed percentage of the undepreciated balance is allowed as an expense each year. So for tax purposes, Jim's income statement may look like this:

**depreciation** or **amortization**
the reduction in value of an asset over time

| Tax Return for Jim's Widgets ($) | |
| --- | --- |
| Revenues | 20,000 |
| Cost of sales | 8,000 |
| Hydro | 300 |
| Rent | 1,200 |
| Salaries | 4,000 |
| CCA | 5,000 |
| Interest | 100 |
| Taxable income | 1,400 |
| Tax expense | 700 |

---

[11]With an assumed 50-percent tax rate, all the changes on an after-tax basis are half the amounts.

The only difference from Jim's original income statement is that the CCA expense of $5,000 replaces the depreciation expense of $2,000. As a result, the tax bill for Jim's Widgets is only $700, despite the fact that the financial statements report $4,400 in before-tax income. So what is the deferred tax bill of $1,500? It's actually a figment of the accountant's imagination; it is the amount Jim's Widgets would pay if the government didn't allow accelerated depreciation for tax purposes (i.e., CCA). One thing should be made very clear: this is not money that is presently owed to the government. Canada Revenue Agency, like tax authorities all around the world, tries to collect all the money owed it. The deferred income taxes are entirely a result of the accountant's judgement in using depreciation for the financial statements that differs from the CCA allowed for tax purposes.

## Cash Flow Statements

By now, the element of judgement that permeates a firm's financial statements should be obvious. To outsiders, this is extremely annoying because external (non-accounting) observers tend to believe that there is one number that is waiting to be counted by the accountant, but this is not the case. A very good example to the contrary is provided by Nortel Networks Corporation. On March 11, 2006, Nortel announced that it was restating its financial results for at least the prior four years. This was Nortel's third attempt at preparing its financial statements for those years. Nortel's CFO, Peter Currie, blamed the misstatements on "misapplication of accounting theory."[12] However, an external telecommunications analyst expressed many people's frustration with Nortel by stating, "Really, how many accountants does it take to screw in a light bulb?"

How then can we assess the element of judgement in a firm's financial statements and determine how much money Jim has really made? One answer is to look at the third major

**cash flow statement** a summary of a firm's cash receipts and disbursements over a specified period

financial statement, the **cash flow statement**, which essentially undoes the effects of judgement as much as possible and tracks the actual flow of hard cash through a firm. There are two ways to calculate the cash flow statement: (1) examine the changes in the balance sheet accounts, or (2) add back non-cash items to net income.

An increase of cash occurs when you decrease an asset. For example, when Jim sells some of his inventory, if all else remains constant, this sale generates cash. Alternatively, cash is generated when liabilities increase—for example, if loans go up. So for Jim's Widgets, he can estimate the sources of cash from increases in liabilities and decreases in assets, and he can estimate the uses of cash as the opposite. For this example, because Jim started out with nothing and he knows what his year-end balance sheet looks like, the changes are easy to determine because it is just a rearrangement of the balance sheet. This is demonstrated below, where the net change in cash (or net cash flow) is $25,000, which corresponds to the $25,000 in the cash account on the balance sheet for Jim's Widgets. This makes sense because the beginning cash balance was zero.

| Sources and Uses of Funds for Jim's Widgets ($) | |
|---|---:|
| Increase in payables | 5,000 |
| Increase in accruals | 800 |
| Increase in loans | 10,000 |
| Increase in deferred taxes | 1,500 |
| Increase in owner's equity | 44,000 |
| Increase in retained earnings | 2,200 |
| Total sources of cash | 63,500 |
| Increase in receivables | 5,000 |
| Increase in inventory | 2,000 |
| Increase in prepaid expenses | 3,500 |
| Increase in machinery | 28,000 |
| Total uses of cash | 38,500 |
| Increase in cash | 25,000 |

---

[12]Hamilton, Tyler, "Nortel Accounting Woes Continue." *Toronto Star*, March 11, 2006.

Another way to arrive at the same result is to start with the net income figure of $2,200 and then add back the non-cash items in the income statement. This version of the cash flow statement is presented here:

| Cash Flow Statement for Jim's Widgets ($) | |
|---|---|
| Net income | 2,200 |
| Depreciation | +2,000 |
| Deferred income taxes | +1,500 |
| Traditional cash flow | 5,700 |
| Increase in receivables | −5,000 |
| Increase in prepaids | −3,500 |
| Increase in inventory | −2,000 |
| Increase in accruals | +800 |
| Increase in payables | +5,000 |
| Increase in net working capital | −4,700 |
| Cash flow from operations | 1,000 |
| Capital expenditures | −30,000 |
| Free cash flow | −29,000 |

In Jim's case, the major non-cash items in the income statement are depreciation and deferred income taxes. Remember that depreciation is a non-cash item because the accountant just "charged off" $2,000 to represent the wear and tear on the lathe, but no cash was involved in this. Similarly, the only taxes Jim owed were those that were calculated using CCA, resulting in the $700 tax liability. The deferred or future income taxes were created from the accountant's judgement and do not reflect what is owed to the government. Adding these judgement calls back to net income indicates that Jim's Widgets had cash flow of $5,700. This figure is often referred to as the **traditional cash flow** figure.

> **traditional cash flow**   net income plus non-cash expenses, such as depreciation and deferred taxes

Historically, analysts have focused on traditional cash flow, since for many manufacturing firms depreciation is a major non-cash expense. Further, it adjusts for any aggressive choice of depreciation by adding back whatever was subtracted in the income statement. For example, if Jim had followed aggressive accounting practices and used depreciation of $1,000 instead of $2,000, this would have been added back in calculating traditional cash flow. Therefore, focusing on cash flow negates the effect of aggressive accounting for depreciation.

However, other subtle non-cash items are often even more important. For example, Jim's accounts receivable increased by $5,000 because $5,000 of his sales were credit sales and not cash sales. Instead of cash, all Jim got was someone's promise to pay him later. As a result, net income overstates cash flow by assuming that all sales are cash sales. Jim also paid $5,000 for rent and hydro, only $1,500 of which passed through the income statement; another $3,500 was classified as prepaid expenses but still involved cash payments. Similarly, Jim paid $10,000 for inventory but used only $8,000 of it, as $2,000 was still in inventory at the end of the year. Jim has to recognize that he paid $2,000 for this inventory. The sum of these three items is an increase in working capital and a decrease in cash of $10,500. We call this "working capital" simply because it represents short-term investments that turn over or are constantly "working."

Offsetting this increase in working capital is the fact that some of the expenses in the income statement similarly do not involve cash. For example, Jim recorded $100 in interest and $700 in taxes on the income statement as expenses, because the accountant wanted to match these expenses with Jim's revenues. However, neither the bank nor the government was actually paid, although the expenses have been accrued, and these obligations can be referred to as "accruals." Similarly, there are still accounts payable of $5,000 outstanding, which means that some of the inventory expenses on the income statement are not yet paid. When these two accounts of $5,800 are subtracted from the working capital of $10,500, net working capital increased by $4,700. The net working capital figure indicates that Jim made a cash investment of $4,700 in his widget business, reflecting the difference between what is recorded on the income statement and what went through his chequebook.

When we subtract the increase in net working capital of $4,700 from the traditional cash flow of $5,700, we get **cash flow from operations (CFO)** of $1,000. The value of looking at CFO is that it takes into account changes in net working capital. It brings to light any increases in receivables and inventory, so the analyst can ask why people aren't paying for their sales and why inventory is increasing. If sales are constant and yet the increase in net working

> **cash flow from operations (CFO)**   the result of subtracting the increase in net working capital from traditional cash flow

capital is significant, it is one sign that the firm's net income numbers might be aggressive. For example, remember Jim's possible use of aggressive accounting in recording $5,000 of sales prematurely. If Jim had done this, then net working capital would have increased by this $5,000, since the sales would have shown up as credit sales and increased receivables. As a result, subtracting this larger increase in net working capital when calculating CFO would have corrected for this aggressive accounting assumption.[13]

**free cash flow** the result of subtracting capital expenditures from cash flow from operations

The next step in the cash flow statement is to subtract capital expenditures (capex) of $30,000 from CFO. This gives a figure that is commonly called **free cash flow**, which is −$29,000 in Jim's case. Financial analysts focus on free cash flow to see whether a company is generating or using cash. In Jim's case, he is investing in his company and it is using cash. Free cash flow is important because it picks up the effect of all three of the aggressive accounting practices that Jim could have used. In the final case, where Jim could have claimed that $2,000 of his salary was to develop a brand or patent for his business, this would have been a capital expenditure. In that case, although Jim's income would have been higher, the increased capital expenditures would have been subtracted from CFO and reduced the free cash flow figure.

Financial analysts like to calculate free cash flow because it focuses on the financing of the firm: if the firm is using cash, it has to raise the money from somewhere. As a result, free cash flow indicates the firm's financing problems, or lack thereof. In practice, accountants prepare a variation of the free cash flow statement shown earlier that accounts for cash flow from financing (CFF) and is referred to as the cash flow statement. For Jim's Widgets, an abbreviated version of the cash flow statement would look like this:[14]

| Cash Flow Statement for Jim's Widgets ($) | |
|---|---:|
| Cash flow from operations | 1,000 |
| Cash flow from investing | −30,000 |
| Bank loan | 10,000 |
| Capital stock | 44,000 |
| Cash flow from financing | 54,000 |
| Change in cash | 25,000 |

This presentation of the cash flow statement simply takes free cash flow of −$29,000 and adds CFF of $54,000 to it. Because Jim still owes the bank $10,000 and has invested $44,000 in owner's equity, CFF is $54,000. When this amount is added to the free cash flow deficit of $29,000, we arrive at the net cash flow (or change in cash) figure of $25,000, as calculated in the sources and uses of funds statement.

Most financial analysts focus on the cash flow statement. However, one problem with this statement is that the same information can be presented in many different ways. In fact, both the name and the presentation of the cash flow statement has changed several times over the past 20 years in response to user concerns.

We now leave our simple example, which was designed to show the basic accounting principles involved in determining financial statements, to look at the actual financial statements of Canadian Pacific.

## Concept Review Questions

1. How is the balance sheet related to the income statement?
2. What happens to the net income figure when a firm's accountants make more aggressive accounting assumptions? Briefly explain.
3. How do cash flow statements alleviate the impact of most major accounting assumptions?
4. Why do income statements differ from tax statements? What is the major difference?

---

[13]However, in this case, Jim's figures would be down because he would accrue more income tax.
[14]This statement is abbreviated because it leaves out the calculation of CFO and cash flow from investing (or capex), which were calculated previously.

## 3.4 | Canadian Pacific Accounting Statements

---

**LEARNING OBJECTIVE 3.4**

Analyze a firm's financial statements.

---

Canadian Pacific (CP) is one of Canada's best known companies and one of Canada's two large railway companies (the other being Canadian National Railways Company or CN). We present and discuss CP's financial statements in this chapter, and in the next chapter we provide some tools that can be used to analyze these statements.

## Accompanying Statements

We begin by looking at the information the company files with its financial statements. **Figure 3.2** provides the "Certification by the Chief Executive Officer of the Registrants filed pursuant to Rule 13a-14(a) of the Exchange Act. Canadian Pacific Railway Limited" (Exhibit 31.1) from CP's 2018 annual report on its 10-K. CP's CFO must also sign an identical report that is included in the annual report. This report discusses the responsibility of management to ensure the integrity of the process by which the company's financial statements were prepared. Although CP is based in Calgary, it files its statements according to Securities and Exchange Commission (SEC) regulations (and according to the rules of *SOX*) in the form of a 10-K statement, since its common shares are listed on the New York Stock Exchange (NYSE), as well as on the Toronto Stock Exchange (TSX).[15]

Notice in Figure 3.2 that the CEO states: "Based on my knowledge, the financial statements, and other financial information included in this report, fairly present in all material respects the financial condition, results of operations and cash flows of the registrant as of, and for, the periods presented in this report." In essence, the CEO and CFO assume responsibility for the integrity of the financial statements, as well as for the process under which they were prepared. This is important to note, as it means the CEO and CFO are personally "liable" for the integrity of the financial statements.

**Figure 3.3** provides a sample of an independent auditor's report. Notice that the report is addressed to the shareholders and board of directors of the company. The section titled "Basis for Opinion" describes the scope of the auditor's examination, which includes various audits and tests to verify things were as management said they were, as well as "evaluating the accounting principles used and significant estimates made by management." Previously, auditors checked everything, but that isn't feasible now, so they do spot checks. Remember, a considerable amount of judgement is involved in the preparation of financial statements. The auditor also assessed the overall financial statement presentation.

The audit "Opinion" states that "in our opinion" the statements "present fairly, in all material respects, the financial position of" the company. The auditor does not say that the statements fairly present in an absolute sense, but simply that the company has chosen a set of allowable accounting principles and has prepared the statements fairly in accordance with those principles. This difference may seem picky, but sometimes financial statements that fairly present according to GAAP do not fairly present in an absolute sense.

## Canadian Pacific's Balance Sheet

CP's financial statements are relatively straightforward for 2017 and 2018, which is one reason we chose them. **Figure 3.4** shows CP's balance sheets for 2017 and for 2018 as presented in its 2018 annual report.

---

[15]Not all Canadian companies that list on U.S. exchanges prepare their annual reports using U.S. GAAP as CP has chosen to do. Many Canadian companies, such as BCE Inc., prepare their annual reports using IFRS.

**FIGURE 3.2** Canadian Pacific's "Certification by the Chief Executive Officer"

---

**Exhibit 31.1**

**Certification by the Chief Executive Officer of the Registrants filed pursuant to Rule 13a-14(a) of the Exchange Act.**

**Canadian Pacific Railway Limited**

I, Keith Creel, certify that:

1. I have reviewed this Annual Report on Form 10-K of Canadian Pacific Railway Limited;

2. Based on my knowledge, this report does not contain any untrue statement of a material fact or omit to state a material fact necessary to make the statements made, in light of the circumstances under which such statements were made, not misleading with respect to the period covered by this report;

3. Based on my knowledge, the financial statements, and other financial information included in this report, fairly present in all material respects the financial condition, results of operations and cash flows of the registrant as of, and for, the periods presented in this report;

4. The registrant's other certifying officer and I are responsible for establishing and maintaining disclosure controls and procedures (as defined in Exchange Act Rules 13a-15(e) and 15d-15(e)) and internal control over financial reporting (as defined in Exchange Act Rules 13a-15(f) and 15d-15(f)) for the registrant and have:

    a) Designed such disclosure controls and procedures, or caused such disclosure controls and procedures to be designed under our supervision, to ensure that material information relating to the registrant, including its consolidated subsidiaries, is made known to us by others within those entities, particularly during the period in which this report is being prepared;

    b) Designed such internal control over financial reporting, or caused such internal control over financial reporting to be designed under our supervision, to provide reasonable assurance regarding the reliability of financial reporting and the preparation of financial statements for external purposes in accordance with generally accepted accounting principles;

    c) Evaluated the effectiveness of the registrant's disclosure controls and procedures and presented in this report our conclusions about the effectiveness of the disclosure controls and procedures, as of the end of the period covered by this report based on such evaluation; and

    d) Disclosed in this report any change in the registrant's internal control over financial reporting that occurred during the registrant's most recent fiscal quarter (the registrant's fourth fiscal quarter in the case of an annual report) that has materially affected, or is reasonably likely to materially affect, the registrant's internal control over financial reporting; and

5. The registrant's other certifying officer and I have disclosed, based on our most recent evaluation of internal control over financial reporting, to the registrant's auditors and the audit committee of the registrant's board of directors (or persons performing the equivalent functions):

    a) All significant deficiencies and material weaknesses in the design or operation of internal control over financial reporting which are reasonably likely to adversely affect the registrant's ability to record, process, summarize and report financial information; and

    b) Any fraud, whether or not material, that involves management or other employees who have a significant role in the registrant's internal control over financial reporting.

Date: February 15, 2019

/s/ Keith Creel
_____

Keith Creel

President and Chief Executive Officer

**Source:** *Canadian Pacific Annual Report on 10-K 2018*, p. 138

---

**current assets** assets (cash and cash equivalents, short-term investments, accounts receivable, inventories, prepaid expenses, and other items) that are expected to be converted into cash within a year or operating cycle

**current liabilities** liabilities (e.g., accounts payable, notes payable, bank loans, and so on) that are due within a year or operating cycle

Figure 3.4 shows that in fiscal 2018, CP had total assets of $21.254 billion. This figure included $1.117 billion in current assets, including, among other items, $61 million in cash and cash equivalents, $815 million in accounts receivable, and $173 million in materials and supplies. These items are all called **current assets** because they are expected to be converted into cash within a year as receivables are collected, materials and supplies used, and so on. For longer-term assets, by far the largest item is properties (net) at $18.418 billion. Deferred income tax items arise due to timing differences between the tax and reporting values of certain assets and liabilities. CP reports a deferred income tax figure on its balance sheet of $3.518 billion under long-term liabilities (due from the company in the long term).

The $1.243 billion recorded as "Pension asset" reflects the difference between the estimated fair market value of CP's pension assets minus the estimated present value of the plan liabilities (referred to as the projected benefit obligation).

For **current liabilities**, CP reported accounts payable and accrued liabilities of $1.449 billion, $474 million of which was trade payables, and the rest of which represented

**FIGURE 3.3**   Canadian Pacific's Independent Auditor's Report

## Report of Independent Registered Public Accounting Firm
**To the Shareholders and the Board of Directors of Canadian Pacific Railway Limited**

### Opinion on the Financial Statements

We have audited the accompanying consolidated balance sheets of Canadian Pacific Railway Limited and subsidiaries (the "Company") as of December 31, 2018 and 2017, the related consolidated statements of income, comprehensive income, cash flows, and changes in shareholders' equity, for each of the three years in the period ended December 31, 2018, and the related notes and the financial statement schedule listed in the Index at Item 15 (collectively referred to as the "financial statements"). In our opinion, the financial statements present fairly, in all material respects, the financial position of the Company as of December 31, 2018 and 2017, and the results of its operations and its cash flows for each of the three years in the period ended December 31, 2018, in conformity with accounting principles generally accepted in the United States of America.

We have also audited, in accordance with the standards of the Public Company Accounting Oversight Board (United States) (PCAOB), the Company's internal control over financial reporting as of December 31, 2018, based on criteria established in *Internal Control—Integrated Framework (2013)* issued by the Committee of Sponsoring Organizations of the Treadway Commission and our report dated February 15, 2019, expressed an unqualified opinion on the Company's internal control over financial reporting.

### Change in Accounting Principle

As discussed in Note 2 to the financial statements, effective January 1, 2018, the Company has retrospectively changed its method of accounting for the presentation of current period service costs due to the adoption of the Accounting Standards Update No. 2017-07 Improving the Presentation of Net Periodic Pension Cost and Net Periodic Postretirement Benefit Cost.

### Basis for Opinion

These financial statements are the responsibility of the Company's management. Our responsibility is to express an opinion on the Company's financial statements based on our audits. We are a public accounting firm registered with the PCAOB and are required to be independent with respect to the Company in accordance with the U.S. federal securities laws and the applicable rules and regulations of the Securities and Exchange Commission and the PCAOB.

We conducted our audits in accordance with the standards of the PCAOB. Those standards require that we plan and perform the audit to obtain reasonable assurance about whether the financial statements are free of material misstatement, whether due to error or fraud. Our audits included performing procedures to assess the risks of material misstatement of the financial statements, whether due to error or fraud, and performing procedures that respond to those risks. Such procedures included examining, on a test basis, evidence regarding the amounts and disclosures in the financial statements. Our audits also included evaluating the accounting principles used and significant estimates made by management, as well as evaluating the overall presentation of the financial statements. We believe that our audits provide a reasonable basis for our opinion.

/s/ Deloitte LLP

Chartered Professional Accountants
Calgary, Canada
February 15, 2019

We have served as the Company's auditor since 2011.

Source: *Canadian Pacific Annual Report on 10-K 2018*, p. 118

a variety of accrued expenses.[16] The company also had $506 million representing the current portion of long-term obligations (i.e., the portion due to be repaid in the coming year). In total, CP had current liabilities of $1.955 billion. The main components of its long-term liabilities consisted of long-term debt of $8.190 billion, pension and other benefit liabilities of $718 million, and other long-term liabilities of $237 million, in addition to the $3.518 billion in deferred income taxes mentioned previously. CP's equity holders have contributed $6.636 billion in shareholders' equity, either through original contributions or by having net income retained and reinvested within the business.

In looking at CP's assets and liabilities, you should recognize the similarity to the simple statements prepared for Jim's Widgets. Of course, the preparation of the statements for a firm with $21.254 billion in assets is more complex than it is for Jim's Widgets, but, in principle, the same GAAP have been followed. Just as Jim's Widgets does, CP has cash, accruals, receivables, and properties.

---

[16]Note 16 of the consolidated financial statements provides a complete list of accounts payable and accrued liabilities.

**FIGURE 3.4** Canadian Pacific's Consolidated Balance Sheet

## CONSOLIDATED BALANCE SHEETS

| As at December 31 (in millions of Canadian dollars, except Common Shares) | 2018 | 2017 |
|---|---|---|
| **Assets** | | |
| **Current assets** | | |
| Cash and cash equivalents | $ 61 | $ 338 |
| Accounts receivable, net (Note 10) | 815 | 687 |
| Materials and supplies | 173 | 152 |
| Other current assets | 68 | 97 |
| | 1,117 | 1,274 |
| Investments (Note 12) | 203 | 182 |
| Properties (Note 13) | 18,418 | 17,016 |
| Goodwill and intangible assets (Note 14) | 202 | 187 |
| Pension asset (Note 21) | 1,243 | 1,407 |
| Other assets (Note 15) | 71 | 69 |
| **Total assets** | **$21,254** | **$20,135** |
| **Liabilities and shareholders' equity** | | |
| **Current liabilities** | | |
| Accounts payable and accrued liabilities (Note 16) | $ 1,449 | $ 1,238 |
| Long-term debt maturing within one year (Note 17, 18) | 506 | 746 |
| | 1,955 | 1,984 |
| Pension and other benefit liabilities (Note 21) | 718 | 749 |
| Other long-term liabilities (Note 19) | 237 | 231 |
| Long-term debt (Note 17, 18) | 8,190 | 7,413 |
| Deferred income taxes (Note 6) | 3,518 | 3,321 |
| **Total liabilities** | **$14,618** | **$13,698** |
| **Shareholders' equity** | | |
| Share capital (Note 20) | | |
| Authorized unlimited Common Shares without par value. Issued and outstanding are 140.5 million and 144.9 million at December 31, 2018 and 2017, respectively. | 2,002 | 2,032 |
| Authorized unlimited number of first and second preferred shares; none outstanding. | | |
| Additional paid-in capital | 42 | 43 |
| Accumulated other comprehensive loss (Note 8) | (2,043) | (1,741) |
| Retained earnings | 6,635 | 6,103 |
| | 6,636 | 6,437 |
| **Total liabilities and shareholders' equity** | **$21,254** | **$20,135** |

Commitments and contingencies (Note 24).

See Notes to Consolidated Financial Statements.

**Approved on behalf of the Board:**

| /s/ ANDREW F. REARDON | /s/ JANE L. PEVERETT |
|---|---|
| **Andrew F. Reardon, Director,** | **Jane L. Peverett, Director,** |
| **Chair of the Board** | **Chair of the Audit Committee** |

# Canadian Pacific's Income Statement

How much money did CP make in fiscal 2018? To see this, we look at the consolidated statements of income (also known as statement of earnings) as reported in **Figure 3.5**.

We can see from Figure 3.5 that in 2018, CP had revenues of $7.316 billion. Subtracting operating expenses of $4.485 billion from revenues gave it operating income of $2.831 billion, from which it deducted some other expenses and recoveries, including $453 million in net interest expense (i.e., interest expense less interest income), and $637 million in income tax expense. Overall, in 2018, CP produced $1.951 billion in net income. So when CP's net income is divided by the average (adjusted) number of shares outstanding, it produces a basic EPS figure of $13.65. Companies are also required to report "diluted" EPS, which is simply the adjusted net income divided by the total possible number of shares that could be outstanding if all potentially "dilutive" securities outstanding were converted into common shares. For example, a company might have some "convertible" bonds outstanding, which, under certain circumstances, could be converted into common shares. The diluted EPS takes into account all the potential shares that could "dilute" the EPS by spreading the net income over a greater number of shares. CP had minimal potential for equity dilution, so its diluted EPS figure is only $0.04 below its basic EPS figure at $13.61.

**FIGURE 3.5** **Canadian Pacific's Income Statement**

**CONSOLIDATED STATEMENTS OF INCOME**

| Year ended December 31 (in millions of Canadian dollars, except per share data) | **2018** | 2017 | 2016 |
|---|---|---|---|
| **Revenues (Note 3)** | | | |
| Freight | **$7,152** | $6,375 | $6,060 |
| Non-freight | **164** | 179 | 172 |
| **Total revenues** | **7,316** | 6,554 | 6,232 |
| **Operating expenses** | | | |
| Compensation and benefits (Note 2, 21, 22) | **1,468** | 1,309 | 1,356 |
| Fuel | **918** | 677 | 567 |
| Materials | **201** | 190 | 180 |
| Equipment rents | **130** | 142 | 173 |
| Depreciation and amortization | **696** | 661 | 640 |
| Purchased services and other (Note 11) | **1,072** | 1,056 | 905 |
| **Total operating expenses** | **4,485** | 4,035 | 3,821 |
| **Operating income** | **2,831** | 2,519 | 2,411 |
| Less: | | | |
| Other expense (income) (Note 4) | **174** | (178) | (45) |
| Other components of net periodic benefit recovery (Note 2, 21) | **(384)** | (274) | (167) |
| Net interest expense (Note 5) | **453** | 473 | 471 |
| **Income before income tax expense** | **2,588** | 2,498 | 2,152 |
| Income tax expense (Note 6) | **637** | 93 | 553 |
| **Net income** | **$1,951** | $2,405 | $1,599 |
| **Earnings per share (Note 7)** | | | |
| Basic earnings per share | **$13.65** | $16.49 | $10.69 |
| Diluted earnings per share | **$13.61** | $16.44 | $10.63 |
| **Weighted average number of shares (millions) (Note 7)** | | | |
| Basic | **142.9** | 145.9 | 149.6 |
| Diluted | **143.3** | 146.3 | 150.5 |

Certain of the comparative figures have been restated in order to be consistent with the 2018 presentation (Note 2).

See Notes to Consolidated Financial Statements.

**Source:** *Canadian Pacific Annual Report 2018*, p. 88

# Canadian Pacific's Cash Flow Statement

We examine CP's statement of cash flows in **Figure** 3.6. In terms of non-cash items, the biggest item is depreciation and amortization of $696 million, which represents an "expense," as fixed assets are depreciated; however, no cash is actually paid out. The net working capital adjustments are relatively minor, so cash flow from operations (CFO) of $2.712 billion is very close to

**FIGURE 3.6** Canadian Pacific's Consolidated Statement of Cash Flows

## CONSOLIDATED STATEMENTS OF CASH FLOWS

| Year ended December 31 (in millions of Canadian dollars) | 2018 | 2017 | 2016 |
|---|---|---|---|
| **Operating activities** | | | |
| Net income | $1,951 | $2,405 | $1,599 |
| Reconciliation of net income to cash provided by operating activities: | | | |
|     Depreciation and amortization | 696 | 661 | 640 |
|     Deferred income taxes (Note 6) | 256 | (210) | 320 |
|     Pension recovery and funding (Note 21) | (321) | (237) | (138) |
| Foreign exchange loss (gain) on long-term debt (Note 4) | 168 | (186) | (79) |
| Settlement of forward starting swaps on debt issuance (Note 17, 18) | (24) | — | — |
| Other operating activities, net | (79) | (113) | (198) |
| Change in non-cash working capital balances related to operations (Note 9) | 65 | (138) | (55) |
| **Cash provided by operating activities** | 2,712 | 2,182 | 2,089 |
| **Investing activities** | | | |
| Additions to properties | (1,551) | (1,340) | (1,182) |
| Proceeds from sale of properties and other assets (Note 11) | 78 | 42 | 116 |
| Other | 15 | 3 | (3) |
| **Cash used in investing activities** | (1,458) | (1,295) | (1,069) |
| **Financing activities** | | | |
| Dividends paid | (348) | (310) | (255) |
| Issuance of CP Common Shares (Note 20) | 24 | 45 | 21 |
| Purchase of CP Common Shares (Note 20) | (1,103) | (381) | (1,210) |
| Issuance of long-term debt, excluding commercial paper (Note 17) | 638 | — | — |
| Repayment of long-term debt, excluding commercial paper (Note 17) | (753) | (32) | (38) |
| Net repayment of commercial paper (Note 17) | — | — | (8) |
| Settlement of forward starting swaps on de-designation (Note 18) | — | (22) | — |
| Other | — | — | (3) |
| **Cash used in financing activities** | (1,542) | (700) | (1,493) |
| Effect of foreign currency fluctuations on U.S. dollar-denominated cash and cash equivalents | 11 | (13) | (13) |
| **Cash position** | | | |
| (Decrease) increase in cash and cash equivalents | (277) | 174 | (486) |
| Cash and cash equivalents at beginning of year | 338 | 164 | 650 |
| **Cash and cash equivalents at end of year** | $ 61 | $ 338 | $ 164 |
| | | | |
| **Supplemental disclosures of cash flow information:** | | | |
| Income taxes paid | $ 318 | $ 425 | $ 322 |
| Interest paid | $ 463 | $ 475 | $ 488 |

See Notes to Consolidated Financial Statements.

**Source:** *Canadian Pacific Annual Report 2018*, p. 91

the net income plus depreciation and amortization total of $2.647 billion, which is commonly referred to as "traditional cash flow." This similarity in numbers essentially indicates that CP is not prematurely recording sales, building up inventory, or avoiding paying its bills. Its net income figure is reliable.

In 2018, CP's cash flow from investing activities (CFI) was −$1.458 billion, mainly due to $1.551 billion in additions to properties, which is offset by sales of properties and other assets totalling $78 million, and other effects of $15 million. The 2018 net CFI figure is similar to the 2017 figure of −$1.295 billion. Firms that are growing and constantly investing in (that is, acquiring) new assets typically have negative CFI figures, such as is the case for CP.

The cash flow for financing (CFF) figure for 2018 of −$1.542 billion is due primarily to the purchase of $1.103 billion of CP stock, the payment of dividends ($348 million), and the repayment of $753 million in debt, all of which were offset to some extent by the issue of $638 million in long-term debt. This figure was much more negative than the 2017 figure of −$700 million, but close to the 2016 figure, largely due to the large share repurchases in 2016 and 2018 but not in 2017. Finally, adding the CFO, the CFI, and the CFF shows that CP had a net decrease in cash of $277 million in 2018, relative to a net increase in cash of $174 million in 2017.

The strength of CP can be seen when we use the information from the cash flow statement to estimate the company's free cash flow, as shown in **Table 3.2**.[17]

The company had 2018 total income of $1,951 million and cash flow from operations of $2,712 million. After deducting additions to properties (or capital expenditures) of $1,551 million, the 2018 free cash flow was $1,161 million, well above the 2017 figure of $842 million. The free cash flow can be viewed as the funds available to the company and its subsidiaries to pay dividends after taking care of investment requirements. CP's dividend payments were actually well below their free cash flow numbers in both 2017 and 2018, at $310 million and $348 million, respectively. This explains why the company was able to repurchase such a large number of CP shares in 2018. Overall, CP's financial statements are "clean," in the sense that there are very few adjustments that make the statements difficult to understand.

**TABLE 3.2**  Canadian Pacific's Free Cash Flow Estimated (*for the Years Ended December 31*)

| Free Cash Flow | 2018 ($Million) | 2017 ($Million) |
|---|---|---|
| Net income | 1,951 | 2,405 |
| Total cash flow from operations (CFO) | 2,712 | 2,182 |
| Additions to properties, or capital expenditures (capex) | (1,551) | (1,340) |
| Free cash flow | 1,161 | 842 |

**Source:** Data from *Canadian Pacific Annual Report 2018*

## Concept Review Questions

1. Who is responsible for the preparation of a company's financial statements?
2. What are the scope and purpose of the auditor's opinion?
3. Identify the main components of a firm's balance sheet and income statement.

[17]This is a typical definition for free cash flow; however, several variations exist.

## 3.5 | The Canadian Tax System

> **LEARNING OBJECTIVE 3.5**
>
> Describe the Canadian tax system and explain the differences between how a corporation and an individual are taxed.

Canadian taxes are levied on both personal and corporate income, but the government recognizes the potential for double taxation of income earned through a corporation and has designed a partially integrated system. We will explain what we mean by partially integrated as we develop our understanding of taxes. We begin by noting that the United States operates a classical system of double taxation, while Europe, by and large, operates a fully integrated system, which leaves Canada somewhere in the middle. How taxes are levied has important implications for corporate finance, so it is important to realize from the outset that the Canadian tax system differs in some fundamental ways from the U.S. system. As a result, corporate finance strategies that are based on the U.S. tax code are not always directly applicable in Canada or Europe.

## Corporate Taxes

As we saw in Chapter 2, corporations are distinct legal entities and are taxed as such. We saw in this chapter that corporations file income tax returns with Canada Revenue Agency that are determined in much the same way as they prepare their income statement for investors. However, we also noted that there are some differences. One main difference that we have discussed previously is that different methods are used to calculate amortization expense. Another major difference is in the treatment of investment income and expenses. We will now elaborate on these two issues.

CCA is amortization for tax purposes, and the government has designed it to be as simple as possible. First, all assets are allocated to one of a number of CCA asset classes. Five of the major ones are listed in **Table 3.3**.[18]

**undepreciated capital cost (UCC)** the undepreciated cost of assets, calculated by asset class and written off on a declining balance basis

Class 8 is, in fact, a general catch-all category, so when in doubt use a 20-percent CCA rate! The CCA rate is the rate that is applied to the **undepreciated capital cost (UCC)** of an asset class; the higher the rate, the faster the assets are depreciated. Notice that the general rates make sense in terms of the assets' economic lives. Computers may last a long time, but the rapid pace of technological progress means that you will generally replace them before they wear out. Their economic life is relatively short, and their CCA rate is high. In contrast,

**TABLE 3.3    Major CCA Asset Classes**

| Asset Class | Type of Assets | CCA Rate |
|---|---|---|
| Class 1 | Buildings | 4% |
| Class 8 | Office equipment | 20% |
| Class 10 | Computer hardware, system software | 30% |
| Class 43 | Manufacturing equipment | 30% |
| Class 50 | Computer/hardware | 55% |

---

[18]There is no category for land, since it is a non-depreciable asset.

buildings last much longer, so their CCA rate of 4 percent is much lower. The asset classes or pools have been designed so that CCA is applied to the balance of the pool at the end of the fiscal year. Rather than calculating CCA for each item separately, it is calculated for the pool as a whole. For most firms, unless they make a special election, their fiscal year is the same as the calendar year.

Prior to November 2018, there was an adjustment associated with CCA due to the fact that it is taken on the year-end balance. Therefore, Canada Revenue Agency allowed firms to apply only one-half of the CCA rate to net acquisitions of an asset class in the first year the assets are acquired. This is known as the **half-year rule**, which was implemented to reduce the incentive to purchase assets right at the end of the year and then claim a full year's CCA on them. Remember, CCA is a non-cash expense, but it reduces taxable income and therefore reduces current taxes payable. As a result, firms generally want to charge as much CCA as possible.

In November 2018, Canada Revenue Agency introduced the Accelerated Investment Incentive (AII) program to encourage additional investment by Canadian firms. This program changed the CCA rules over the period of November 2018–23, as well as over the "phase-out" period of 2024–27, as discussed in Finance in the News 3.2. For asset class 53 (machinery and equipment for manufacturing or processing) and classes 43.1 and 43.2 (specified clean energy equipment), the assets may be written off entirely upon acquisition. For other asset classes, over the entire November 2018–27 period, no half-year rule will be applied to net acquisitions. During the initial November 2018–23 period, an additional incentive allows CCA to be charged on an amount equal to the net acquisition cost plus 50 percent of this cost. This essentially means that in the year of acquisition, firms can charge three times the CCA amount that would have been charged under the old system, which applied the half-year rule (as illustrated in footnote 19). During the 2024–27 phase-out period, this additional incentive is eliminated, but the half-year rule will not be applied. This means that in the year of acquisition, firms can charge two times the CCA amount that would have been charged under the old system.

**half-year rule**   the rule by which Canada Revenue Agency allows firms to apply only one-half of the CCA rate to net acquisitions of an asset class in the first year the assets are acquired

---

## 3.2  Finance in the News   Accelerated Investment Incentive

The Government of Canada's 2018 Fall Economic Statement was tabled on November 21, 2018.

It proposes the following measures for eligible property:

Accelerated Investment Incentive—Providing an enhanced first-year allowance for certain eligible property that is subject to the Capital Cost Allowance (CCA) rules. In general, the incentive will be made up of two elements:

- applying the prescribed CCA rate for a class to up to one-and-a-half times the net addition to the class for the year

- suspending the existing CCA half-year rule (and equivalent rules for Canadian vessels and class 13 property)

Full Expensing for Manufacturers and Processors—Allowing businesses to immediately write off the full cost of machinery and equipment used for the manufacturing or processing of goods (class 53).

Full Expensing for Clean Energy Investments—Allowing businesses to immediately write off the full cost of specified clean energy equipment (classes 43.1 and 43.2).

You must acquire the eligible property after November 20, 2018, and it must be available for use before 2028 in order to qualify for the incentive or the full expensing measure. A phase-out will begin for property that becomes available for use after 2023.

. . .

As a result, eligible property currently subject to the half-year rule will, in essence, qualify for an enhanced CCA equal to three times the normal first-year deduction. Eligible property not subject to the half-year rule (e.g., patent, franchise or limited-period licence) will qualify for one-and-a-half times the normal first-year deduction. For more information, see Example 3.

. . .

Application and phase-out

. . .

For eligible property that would normally be subject to the half-year rule (or an equivalent rule) and that becomes available for use during the 2024–2027 phase-out period, the incentive will effectively suspend the half-year rule (and equivalent rules). In essence, you'll be able to calculate CCA at the rate relevant to that class without applying the half-year rule.

. . .

The enhanced first-year allowance is reduced to two times the normal first-year CCA deduction in the 2024–2027 period. . .

**Source:** Excerpted from Government of Canada, "Accelerated Investment Initiative," last modified February 8, 2019. Available at https://www.canada.ca/en/revenue-agency/services/tax/businesses/topics/sole-proprietorships-partnerships/report-business-income-expenses/claiming-capital-cost-allowance/accelerated-investment-incentive.html#Effects.

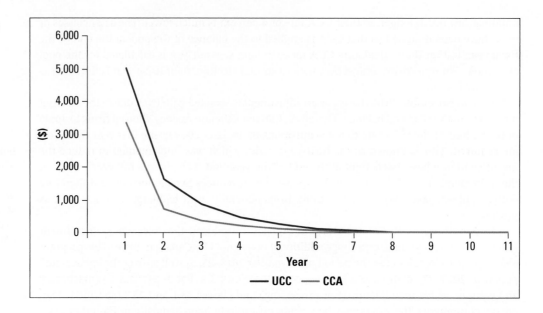

For example, suppose a company buys new assets for $5,000. Assume the CCA rate would be 45 percent of $5,000, or $2,250. After grossing up the $5,000 by 50 percent to $7,500 and applying the 45-percent CCA rate, the CCA charged would equal $3,375.[19] After deducting CCA of $3,375, the balance that remains to be depreciated (i.e., the associated UCC) is $1,625, which equals the asset class's UCC if it were the only asset in that class. For the following year, if no further assets in that asset class were acquired, the CCA would be 45 percent of the UCC of $1,625, or $731.25. Notice that although 45 percent seems to be a high depreciation rate, it is applied to the UCC, which declines each year, so the firm will actually be taking CCA on these assets forever, even though its economic life may be only three years. Therefore, approximately two-thirds of the asset's value will be depreciated after one year, and over 90 percent within three years, and virtually all of it will be depreciated after six years, as illustrated in **Figure** 3.7. Notice that although CCA expenses technically go on forever, for practical purposes they end after six years or so for this asset class. By year 10, the UCC is only $7.48 and CCA deductions are only $3.37, which is trivial when compared to the original investment of $5,000.

One advantage of using CCA asset classes or pools is that individual assets are not amortized separately, unless they are the only asset in the pool. This makes it easy to account for sales of assets: the proceeds are subtracted from, instead of added to, the pool, and the new AII rules (or previously the "old" half-year rules) only come into play only when the net acquisitions figure for an asset class is positive (i.e., when purchases exceed sales for that asset class). Example 3.1 illustrates how to apply the CCA system.

---

**EXAMPLE 3.1** | Calculating CCA

A company purchases an asset for $650,000. The asset is in asset class 10, which has a CCA rate of 30 percent (declining balance method). Assume this is the only asset in this class. Calculate the CCA associated with this asset class for the year of acquisition and for the subsequent two years.

**Solution**   For year 1, add 50 percent to the acquisition price of $650,000 to obtain $975,000, to which the CCA rate will be applied. Therefore, we can calculate CCA in year 1 as

$$CCA \text{ (year 1)} = (\$975,000)(0.30) = \$292,500$$

---

[19]Under the old system, using the half-year rule, only $1,125 (i.e., one-third of $3,375) would have been charged as CCA in the first year (i.e., ($5,000)(1/2)(0.45)).

Because the full CCA rate is applied to the UCC of the asset class in all years subsequent to the first year, we can calculate the CCA in years 2 and 3 as follows:

$$UCC \text{ (beginning of year 2)} = UCC \text{ (beginning of year 1)} - CCA \text{ (year 1)} = \$650{,}000 - \$292{,}500$$
$$= \$357{,}500$$
$$CCA \text{ (year 2)} = (UCC)(CCA \text{ Rate}) = (\$357{,}500)(0.30) = \$107{,}250$$
$$UCC \text{ (beginning of year 3)} = UCC \text{ (beginning of year 2)} - CCA \text{ (year 2)} = \$357{,}500 - \$107{,}250$$
$$= \$250{,}250$$
$$CCA \text{ (year 3)} = (UCC)(CCA \text{ Rate}) = (\$250{,}250)(0.30) = \$75{,}075$$

Other issues arise with respect to depreciable assets when they are sold. First, if the selling price is greater than the original capital cost, a **capital gain** arises, which is taxable. However, the converse is not true; when a depreciable capital asset is sold below its original purchase price, this does not generate a tax deductible **capital loss**, because this is expected (i.e., it is a depreciable asset and, as such, is expected to depreciate in value below its original cost). In fact, capital losses are generated only when a non-depreciable asset (such as land or financial assets) is sold at a price less than its original cost.

Aside from capital gains, additional tax consequences may arise in the form of **CCA recapture** or **terminal losses**. These may arise if the CCA asset class is terminated by selling the asset, which would occur only if there were no other assets included in that asset class for the firm. Under this scenario, the firm would have to pay additional taxes on "excess" CCA charged against the asset (or assets) if the salvage value is greater than the ending UCC for the asset (or asset class). The amount by which the salvage value exceeds the UCC is referred to as CCA recapture and is fully taxable.[20] However, if the salvage value is less than the ending UCC, the amount by which the UCC exceeds the salvage value is referred to as a terminal loss, which is fully tax deductible.[21] Finally, CCA recapture may occur even if an asset class is not terminated, if an asset (or assets) is (are) sold for a price that exceeds the remaining UCC for that asset class. Example 3.2 illustrates capital gains and CCA recapture, and Example 3.3 illustrates terminal losses.

**capital gain**   a taxable gain realized when an asset is sold at a price greater than its original cost

**capital loss**   a tax-deductible loss generated when a non-depreciable asset is sold at a price lower than its original cost

**CCA recapture**   a tax on the amount by which the salvage value (sale price) of an asset exceeds the undepreciated capital cost; occurs only if the asset class is terminated or if an asset is sold for a price that exceeds the remaining UCC for that asset class

**terminal loss**   a tax deduction equal to the amount by which the undepreciated capital cost exceeds the salvage value (sale price); occurs only if the asset class is terminated

---

**EXAMPLE 3.2** │ Capital Gains and CCA Recapture

Assume that, during year 3, the company from Example 3.1 sells for $700,000 the asset it purchased for $650,000. Estimate the tax consequences of this transaction, again assuming that this is the only asset in this class.

**Solution**   First, check for capital gains, which do occur in this example:

$$\text{Capital gains} = \text{Selling price} - \text{Original cost} = \$700{,}000 - \$650{,}000 = \$50{,}000$$

Next, determine whether a CCA recapture or terminal loss results. The CCA recapture (terminal loss) will equal the excess (deficit) amount of CCA that the firm charged, which can be determined as the difference between the lower of the selling price and the original cost, and the beginning UCC in year 3 (which was determined in Example 3.1):

$$\text{CCA recapture (terminal loss)} = \text{Lower of selling price and the original cost}$$
$$- UCC \text{ (beginning of year 3)}$$
$$= \$650{,}000 - \$250{,}250 = \$399{,}750$$

This number is positive, so it represents a CCA recapture of $399,750. The firm must claim this taxable amount on its income tax return.

---

[20]In other words, it is viewed as if the firm charged too much CCA (amortization), because the asset is sold for more than its depreciated book value for tax purposes (UCC). Therefore, the firm must pay back the amount of taxes it saved by charging too much CCA.

[21]In other words, the firm did not charge enough CCA, because the asset was sold below its book value for tax purposes (UCC). Therefore, the firm is permitted to amortize the asset to its selling price and deduct this charge for tax purposes.

---

**EXAMPLE 3.3** | Terminal Loss

Ignore Example 3.2 and now assume that, during year 3, the company from Example 3.1 sells for $200,000 the asset it purchased for $650,000. Estimate the tax consequences of this transaction, again assuming that this is the only asset in this class.

**Solution**   First, check for capital gains, which do not occur in this example, because the selling price of $200,000 is less than the original cost of $650,000.

Next, determine whether a CCA recapture or terminal loss results:

$$\text{CCA recapture (terminal loss)} = \text{Lower of selling price and the original cost} - \text{UCC}$$
$$= \$200,000 - \$250,250 = -\$50,250$$

The number is negative, so it represents a terminal loss of $50,250. The firm will deduct this amount on its income tax return.

---

Firms often make temporary investments while waiting to pay bills. These assets generate investment income. Similarly, CP has both debt and common shares outstanding, so it paid interest on its debt and dividends on its common shares. How investment income and expenses are treated for tax purposes is very important in finance. The basic rule is that interest is fully taxable when earned and fully deductible when paid. Usually, firms combine these two items into one "net interest" amount that is taxable.

Unlike interest, dividends are not tax deductible when paid since they are paid out of after-tax income. In return, when a Canadian corporation receives dividends from another Canadian corporation, they are not taxable, because they are paid out of the after-tax income of the issuing corporation. Otherwise, dividends flowing through multiple companies would attract tax at every stage, thereby increasing the effective tax rate. This represents another difference between accounting income and income for tax purposes. In particular, for accounting purposes, any dividends received are added to income. All else being constant, the different tax treatment of interest and dividends means that companies prefer to pay interest (issue debt) and receive dividend income. We will return to this preference when we discuss corporate financing issues in Chapter 21. In terms of taxable income, it means that firms with significant dividend income and high CCA deductions will appear to pay lower rates of tax on their financial statements.

The basic tax rates for Canadian corporate income for 2018 consisted of a federal and a provincial rate, and are provided in Table 3.4. The basic rate of federal corporate income tax was 15 percent for active businesses in 2018—that is, for non-investment income—with a 5-percent reduction to 10 percent for small businesses earning less than $500,000.[22] Provincial taxes run from 0 percent for small businesses in Manitoba, for an overall rate of 10 percent, to 16 percent for larger businesses in Nova Scotia, for an overall rate of 31 percent. **Operating losses** can also be important for corporations, since they can be used to reduce taxable income. If a company has a loss, it can carry it back three years to restate prior tax returns and get a refund on taxes that have been "overpaid." Alternatively, the operating loss can be stored and carried forward for 20 years to reduce future taxes payable.

**operating loss**   loss generated when a firm's tax deductions are greater than its taxable income; losses can be carried back three years to get a refund on taxes paid or carried forward for 20 years to reduce future taxes payable

## Personal Tax

Canada operates a progressive personal tax system in which the rates increase with income. For 2019, the basic federal income tax rates were the following:

---

[22]Note that this is the federal limit. At the time of writing, provincial limits were $500,000 in every province or territory except Manitoba, where it was set at $450,000 for 2018, but increased to $500,000 for 2019.

**TABLE 3.4**   **Corporate Income Tax Rates 2018 (%)**

|  |  | Rate (%) |
|---|---|---|
| Federal | General | 15 |
|  | Small business CCPC | 10 |
| Alberta | General | 12 |
|  | Small business CCPC | 2 |
| British Columbia | General | 12 |
|  | Small business CCPC | 2 |
| Manitoba | General | 12 |
|  | Small business CCPC | 0 |
| New Brunswick | General | 14 |
|  | Small business CCPC | 3 |
| Newfoundland and Labrador | General | 15 |
|  | Small business CCPC | 3 |
| Northwest Territories | General | 11.5 |
|  | Small business CCPC | 4 |
| Nova Scotia | General | 16 |
|  | Small business CCPC | 3 |
| Nunavut | General | 12 |
|  | Small business CCPC | 4 |
| Ontario | General | 11.5 |
|  | Small business CCPC | 3.5 |
| Prince Edward Island | General | 16 |
|  | Small business CCPC | 4.0 |
| Quebec | General | 11.7 |
|  | Small business CCPC | 8 |
| Saskatchewan | General | 12 |
|  | Small business CCPC | 2 |
| Yukon | General | 12 |
|  | Small business CCPC | 2 |

**CCPC:** Canadian-controlled private corporation

**Source:** Data from KPMG website, https://home.kpmg/ca/en/home/services/tax/canadiancorporate-tax-tables.html, accessed March 13, 2019

- 15 percent on the first $47,630 of taxable income
- 20.5 percent on the next $47,629 of taxable income
- 26 percent on the next $52,408 of taxable income
- 29 percent on the next $62,704 of taxable income
- 33 percent on taxable income above $210,371

In addition, each province operates a separate provincial tax system. It used to be that provincial taxes were a simple multiple of federal taxes, so that Ontario, for example, would add 52 percent (at its peak) of federal taxes. However, things have changed over the past 15 years, and most provinces have developed a parallel progressive tax system.

Table 3.5 provides the 2019 federal and provincial marginal tax rates. In looking at the tax rates, remember that these rates are marginal rates, which means they are the rates on the next dollar of income. For example, the top federal rate of 33 percent is applied to every dollar of income above $210,371. Someone earning over $220,000 in Nova Scotia would pay this federal rate of 33 percent, plus a provincial rate of 21 percent—effectively, the governments are more than equal partners for these individuals. Remember too that interest income is taxed as ordinary income: the marginal tax rate for investment income differs depending on whether

**TABLE 3.5** Provincial/Territorial Personal Income Tax Rates, 2019

| Provinces/Territories | Rate(s) |
|---|---|
| Federal | 15% on the first $47,630 of taxable income, +<br>20.5% on the next $47,629, +<br>26% on the next $52,408, +<br>29% on the next $62,704, +<br>33% on the amount over $210,371. |
| Alberta | 10% on the first $131,220 of taxable income, +<br>12% on the next $26,244, +<br>13% on the next $52,488, +<br>14% on the next $104,976, +<br>15% on the amount over $314,928. |
| British Columbia | 5.06% on the first $40,707 of taxable income, +<br>7.7% on the next $40,709, +<br>10.5% on the next $12,060, +<br>12.29% on the next $20,030, +<br>14.7% on the next $40,394, +<br>16.8% on the amount over $153,900. |
| Manitoba | 10.8% on the first $32,670 of taxable income, +<br>12.75% on the next $37,940, +<br>17.4% on the amount over $70,610. |
| Newfoundland and Labrador | 8.7% on the first $37,591 of taxable income, +<br>14.5% on the next $37,590, +<br>15.8% on the next $59,043, +<br>17.3% on the next $53,689, +<br>18.3% on the amount over $187,913. |
| New Brunswick | 9.68% on the first $42,592 of taxable income, +<br>14.82% on the next $42,592, +<br>16.52% on the next $53,307, +<br>17.84% on the next $19,287, +<br>20.3% on the amount over $157,778. |
| Northwest Territories | 5.9% on the first $43,137 of taxable income, +<br>8.6% on the next $43,140, +<br>12.2% on the next $53,990, +<br>14.05% on the amount over $140,267. |
| Nova Scotia | 8.79% on the first $29,590 of taxable income, +<br>14.95% on the next $29,590, +<br>16.67% on the next $33,820 +<br>17.5% on the next $57,000, +<br>21% on the amount over $150,000. |
| Nunavut | 4% on the first $45,414 of taxable income, +<br>7% on the next $45,415, +<br>9% on the next $56,838, +<br>11.5% on the amount over $147,667. |
| Ontario | 5.05% on the first $43,906 of taxable income, +<br>9.15% on the next $43,907, +<br>11.16% on the next $62,187, +<br>12.16% on the next $70,000, +<br>13.16% on the amount over $220,000. |
| Prince Edward Island | 9.8% on the first $31,984 of taxable income, +<br>13.8% on the next $31,985, +<br>16.7% on the amount over $63,969. |

*(continued)*

**TABLE 3.5**   **Provincial/Territorial Personal Income Tax Rates, 2019** (*continued*)

| Provinces/Territories | Rate(s) |
|---|---|
| Quebec | 15% on the first $43,790 of taxable income, +<br>20% on the next $43,785, +<br>24% on the next $18,980, +<br>25.75% on the amount over $106,555. |
| Saskatchewan | 10.5% on the first $45,225 of taxable income, +<br>12.5% on the next $83,989, +<br>14.5% on the amount over $129,214. |
| Yukon | 6.4% on the first $47,630 of taxable income, +<br>9% on the next $47,629, +<br>10.9% on the next $52,408, +<br>12.8% on the next $352,333, +<br>15% on the amount over $500,000. |

**Source:** Data from Canada Revenue Agency website, https://www.canada.ca/en/revenue-agency/services/tax/individuals/frequently-asked-questions-individuals/canadian-income-tax-rates-individuals-current-previous-years.html#federal, accessed March 13, 2019

the individual earns interest from debt, dividends from common shares, or capital gains from increases in security prices.

Both cash and stock dividends received by individuals from Canadian corporations are taxable using the dividend tax credit system, which provides for tax savings associated with dividend income. For "eligible" dividends (which essentially applies to those received from Canadian companies), the system works in the following manner. First, the amount of the dividend is "grossed up" (currently by 38 percent) to obtain the full taxable amount of dividend income included in taxable income. Then a federal dividend tax credit (currently 15.0198 percent) is applied to reduce the taxes owing. The appropriate provincial tax credit (which varies by province) is also applied. We will discuss how this interacts with corporate taxation later in the textbook (in chapters 21 and 22), when we consider how a firm should be financed. However, note for now that the tax rate on dividend income is always lower than that on interest income. Under recent rules, the dividend tax rates will be 20 to 25 percent lower than the marginal rates, depending on an investor's tax category and on the provincial rules.

The final source of investment income is capital gains. These are currently taxed on the basis that 50 percent of the capital gain (i.e., the taxable capital gain) is included as ordinary income. As a result, the effective rate is simply half that of ordinary income. If an individual incurs a capital loss, it can only be used to offset capital gains income, but not ordinary income. That being said, if there is an excess of capital losses, it can be carried back three years, to reduce any taxes paid on previous capital gains, or carried forward indefinitely. Of course, tax rates and tax rules are constantly changing, and we suggest that you check the newest tax rules.

## Concept Review Questions

1. Explain how to calculate the CCA expense for an asset class in a given year.
2. Explain why a firm cannot claim CCA recapture and a terminal loss for the same asset class in the same year.
3. Why would firms prefer to receive dividend income and make interest payments rather than make dividend payments and receive interest payments?
4. What form of investment income has the highest tax rate in Canada?

# Review

## Summary

This chapter provides a basic overview of accounting statements, beginning with a discussion of the principles on which they are constructed. We discuss the importance of using generally accepted accounting principles (GAAP) and the role of International Financial Reporting Standards (IFRS) in creating financial statements that adhere to somewhat uniform standards. We then illustrate how to apply these principles by developing a simple set of financial statements from a series of transactions that an entrepreneur makes in setting up a business. We look at the financial statements of a large company (CP) to show that these simple principles are the same basic ones needed to understand the financial statements of large corporations. Finally, because much accounting revolves around tax issues, we conclude the chapter with a brief discussion of the Canadian tax system.

## Summary of Learning Objectives

### 3.1 Define what International Financial Reporting Standards (IFRS) are and state their significance for Canadian firms.

International Financial Reporting Standards (IFRS) set out the basic conventions for preparing financial statements in Canada and in many countries around the world. They are intended to ensure that a firm's financial position is fairly represented to those who use the firm's financial statements (e.g., shareholders and creditors), and that these users are able to understand the firm's transactions. The emergence of a common set of international standards is becoming more important in today's global environment as it makes it easier to compare financial statements from companies based in different countries.

### 3.2 Organize a firm's transactions and explain what are the most important accounting principles related to this task.

The organization of a firm's transactions is presented in section 3.2. When organizing a firm's transactions, the most important accounting principles are:

**The entity concept:** The accounting is for an economic entity, such as a corporation.

**The going concern principle:** The statements must reflect the accounts on the basis that the firm is not in imminent threat of bankruptcy; otherwise, they have to be qualified.

**A period of analysis:** The statements are for a particular period of time, such as a year-end balance sheet or quarterly statement.

**A monetary value:** In Canada, accountants use historical cost accounting, in which transactions are for the dollars actually involved, with no restatement for inflationary effects.

*The matching principle:* The revenues must be matched against the costs that generated those revenues.

*Revenue recognition:* Revenues are only recognized when there is a verifiable sale.

### 3.3 Prepare a firm's financial statements.

The preparation of a firm's financial statements is presented in section 3.3.

### 3.4 Analyze a firm's financial statements.

A firm can be analyzed by comparing its historical statements with its current statements and by comparing its financial statements with those of other firms in the same industry. An analysis of the financial statements of CP is presented in section 3.4.

### 3.5 Describe the Canadian tax system and explain the differences between how a corporation and an individual are taxed.

Canadian taxes are levied on both personal and corporate income, but the government recognizes the potential for double taxation of income earned through a corporation and has designed a partially integrated system. For a corporation, amortization and interest payments are deducted before tax is paid, but dividends are paid after tax; for an individual, there are different deductibles—interest income is taxed as regular income, half of capital gains are taxed, and dividends are taxed but with a dividend tax credit.

## Key Terms

amortization, p. 3-13
balance sheet, p. 3-6
capital gain, p. 3-27
capital loss, p. 3-27
cash flow from operations (CFO), p. 3-15
cash flow statement, p. 3-14
CCA recapture, p. 3-27
current assets, p. 3-18

current liabilities, p. 3-18
depreciation, p. 3-13
free cash flow, p. 3-16
generally accepted accounting principles
  (GAAP), p. 3-2
half-year rule, p. 3-25
income statement, p. 3-11

International Financial Reporting Standards
  (IFRS), p. 3-2
liquidity, p. 3-7
operating loss, p. 3-28
terminal loss, p. 3-27
traditional cash flow, p. 3-15
undepreciated capital cost (UCC), p. 3-24

# Questions and Practice Problems

## Multiple Choice Questions

1. **(LO 3.2)** Which of the following is *correct*?

   a. IFRS are the primary accounting standards for publicly accountable enterprises in Canada.

   b. Canadian private companies are required to use IFRS.

   c. Canadian GAAP is issued by the International Accounting Standards Board (IASB).

   d. Canada has adopted U.S. GAAP.

2. **(LO 3.2)** What is the correct book entry when a firm increases its inventories by using its credit with a supplier?

   a. Credit inventories and debit cash.

   b. Credit inventories and debit accounts payable.

   c. Debit inventories and credit cash.

   d. Debit inventories and credit accounts payable.

3. **(LO 3.2)** Which of the following is *true*?

   a. Income reported may be more volatile under IFRS than U.S. GAAP.

   b. Reported losses in one period may be offset by reported gains in another period under IFRS.

   c. Under IFRS, firms are required to report fixed assets using historical cost.

   d. U.S. GAAP permits firms to value fixed assets using market value.

4. **(LO 3.2)** Which of the following is *not* an IFRS principle?

   a. The entity concept

   b. A period of analysis

   c. The idea that revenues must be matched against the costs that generated those revenues

   d. The idea that revenues are only recognized when cash is collected

5. **(LO 3.3)** Which of the following assets does *not* qualify for capital cost allowance (CCA)?

   a. Land

   b. Manufacturing equipment

   c. Building

   d. Computer

6. **(LO 3.3)** Which of the following is a source of cash inflows?

   a. Decrease of property, plant, and equipment

   b. Increase of accounts receivable

   c. Payment of dividends

   d. Decrease of accounts payable

7. **(LO 3.3)** Which of the following is a non-cash item?

   a. Receipt of dividends

   b. Payment of interest

   c. Amortization

   d. Purchase of inventory

8. **(LO 3.3)** Which of the following equations represents free cash flow?

   a. Net income + Depreciation + Deferred income taxes

   b. Net income + Depreciation + Deferred income taxes +/− Change in working capital

   c. Net income + Depreciation + Deferred income taxes +/− Change in working capital − Capital expenditures

   d. Net income + Depreciation + Deferred income taxes +/− Change in working capital − Capital expenditures +/− Financing cash flows

9. **(LO 3.3)** Which of the following is *not* classified as cash flow from financing?

   a. Issuance of long-term debt

   b. Repurchase of capital stock

   c. Payment of dividends

   d. Purchase of inventory

10. **(LO 3.3)** Which of the following is a cash outflow?

    a. Decrease in inventories

    b. Decrease in accounts receivable

    c. Issue of common shares

    d. Decrease in accounts payable

11. **(LO 3.3)** Which of the following is *not* classified as cash flow from operations?

    a. Issuance of long-term bonds

    b. Sale of goods

    c. Purchase of inventories

    d. Payment of employee salaries

**12. (LO 3.4)** Which of the following is *not* a current asset?

    **a.** Cash

    **b.** Marketable securities

    **c.** Inventories

    **d.** Land

**13. (LO 3.5)** Capital gains occur in which of the following cases?

    **a.** Selling price of the asset < Initial cost of the asset

    **b.** Selling price of the asset > Initial cost of the asset

    **c.** Selling price of the asset < Ending UCC

    **d.** Selling price of the asset > Ending UCC

**14. (LO 3.5)** Which of the following statements is *false*?

    **a.** Canada operates a progressive personal tax system.

    **b.** When dividends are received, they are preferentially taxed.

    **c.** When interest is earned, it is fully taxable.

    **d.** Ontario residents and Quebec residents pay the same federal and provincial tax.

## Practice Problems

### Basic

**15. (LO 3.2)** State three of the most basic principles of IFRS.

**16. (LO 3.2)** The balance sheet for a small firm shows total assets of $529,500 and total liabilities of $379,000. What is the shareholders' equity?

**17. (LO 3.3)** The firm in practice problem 16 had retained earnings of $15,000 at the beginning of the year. Its net income for the year was $7,500, and it paid out $4,000 in dividends. What are its retained earnings at the end of the year?

**18. (LO 3.3)** The balance sheet for a small corporation shows total assets of $525,600, common equity of $136,000, and retained earnings of $75,000. Calculate the total liabilities.

**19. (LO 3.3)** A firm had retained earnings of $18,000 at the beginning of the year. Its net income for the year was $14,300, and its dividend payout ratio is 30 percent. What are its retained earnings at the end of the year?

**20. (LO 3.3)** A firm's net earnings are $85 million and it has 60 million shares outstanding. Determine its earnings per share.

**21. (LO 3.3)** A firm borrowed $3 million and paid 10-percent interest this year. It also paid a dividend of $1 per share on 500,000 shares outstanding. What is the firm's cash flow from financing if it treats interest paid as a financing use of cash?

**22. (LO 3.5)** Mrs. Kwan lives in Ontario. Her annual salary is $225,000. What is the marginal tax on her salary?

**23. (LO 3.5)** GG Inc. just bought a computer for $4,000. It belongs to asset class 45 and has a CCA rate of 45 percent. Calculate the first-year and second-year CCA expenses. (Include the half-year rule.) (Assume this computer is the only asset in this asset class.)

**24. (LO 3.3)** Randy's Rowboats Ltd. purchased and began to use its first six rowboats for a total cost of $2,400. Randy believes the boats can be used for four years, providing the company with equal value each year. After four years, the boats will be worthless.

    **a.** Use your best judgement to determine a reasonable amount to charge to depreciation expense each year.

    **b.** Find the book value (cost less depreciation) of the boats for each of the four years they will be used.

    **c.** If the company expects to sell the rowboats for $400 after four years, determine the reasonable amount to charge to depreciation expense each year.

### Intermediate

**25. (LO 3.5)** The rowboats Randy purchased (see Practice Problem 24) have a CCA rate of 15 percent. Determine the amount of the capital cost allowance for each of the four years the boats will be used (include the "half-year rule").

**26. (LO 3.2)** List the correct bookkeeping entries when a firm sells $50,000 worth of inventories for $80,000 using credit sales. (Ignore the tax effect.)

**27. (LO 3.3)** Based on the figures in practice problems 16 and 17, how much money did the shareholders actually invest in the firm (i.e., what is the value of the share capital)?

*Use the following information to answer practice problems 28 to 31 about Finns' Fridges.*

Twin brothers David and Douglas Finn started a small business from their college dormitory room. Finns' Fridges purchased several small refrigerators to rent to other students for use in their rooms. At the end of their first year of operations, the brothers' records showed the following information.

| | |
|---|---:|
| Current assets (cash and accounts receivable) | $2,000 |
| Interest payable | 200 |
| Other current liabilities | 800 |
| Property and equipment (net) | 4,000 |
| Long-term liabilities | 3,200 |
| Owners' equity | 1,800 |
| Revenues | 2,000 |
| Interest expense | 200 |
| Depreciation expense | 1,000 |

**28. (LO 3.3)** Construct a balance sheet and income statement for the business, assuming no income tax.

**29. (LO 3.3)** Based on the balance sheet you created, how much working capital does Finns' Fridges have?

**30. (LO 3.3)** Suppose Finns' Fridges is subject to corporate income tax at a rate of 40 percent. What will the company's net income be after tax?

**31. (LO 3.3)** David and Douglas invested $500 each to capitalize Finns' Fridges. To allow for future flexibility (such as selling shares to other investors), they placed a "par value" of $10 on each share; thus each brother owns 50 shares. Based on the net income figure from Practice Problem 28, assuming no tax, what were the earnings per share (EPS) of Finns' Fridges for its first year of operations?

**32. (LO 3.3)** Corine's Candies Inc. paid dividends of $1 million during 2022. However, the company needed extra cash to open new stores, so it issued $1.4 million in new shares. What was Corine's cash flow from financing in 2022?

**33. (LO 3.3)** In 2022, a firm's revenue is $100,000, cost of sales is $40,000, rent is $15,000, depreciation is $3,000, and interest paid is $2,000. Its tax rate is 35 percent.

    **a.** Construct an income statement based on this information.

    **b.** If the company pays 20 percent of its net income as dividends, what is the increase in retained earnings for 2022?

**34. (LO 3.3)** In year 1, a firm had cash and cash equivalents of $150,000, accounts receivable of $35,000, and inventories of $23,000. In year 2, it had cash and cash equivalents of $80,000, accounts receivable of $20,000, and inventories of $15,000. Calculate the change in total current assets in dollars and as a percentage.

*Use the following information to answer practice problems 35 to 38.*

**Year 1 and Year 2 Balance Sheet ($million)**

|  | Y1 | Y2 |  | Y1 | Y2 |
|---|---|---|---|---|---|
| Cash | 100 | 112 | Accounts payable | 400 | 350 |
| Accounts receivable | 330 | 234 | Notes payable | 390 | 370 |
| Inventory | 410 | 435 | Current liabilities | 790 | 720 |
| Total | 840 | 781 | Long-term debt | 500 | 550 |
| Net fixed assets | 1,556 | 1,888 | Owners' equity |  |  |
|  |  |  | Common shares | 550 | 599 |
|  |  |  | Retained earnings | 556 | 800 |
|  |  |  | Total | 1,106 | 1,399 |
| Total assets | 2,396 | 2,669 | Total liabilities and owners' equity | 2,396 | 2,669 |

**35. (LO 3.3)** What is the firm's net working capital in year 2?

**36. (LO 3.3)** What is the firm's change in net working capital in year 2?

**37. (LO 3.3)** The firm's dividend payout ratio is 30 percent. What was the firm's year 2 net income?

**38. (LO 3.3)** The firm has 200 million shares outstanding. What is the firm's year 2 earnings per share?

*Use the following information to answer practice problems 39 to 41.*

**Balance Sheet ($million)**

|  |  |  |  |
|---|---|---|---|
| Cash | 100 | Accounts payable | 275 |
| Marketable securities | 15 | Notes payable (current) | 125 |
| Accounts receivable | 225 | Total | 400 |
| Inventory | 175 | Long-term debt | 250 |
| Total | 515 | Owner's equity |  |
| Net fixed assets | 385 | Common shares | 10 |
|  |  | Retained earnings | 240 |
|  |  | Total | 250 |
| Total assets | 900 | Total liabilities and owner's equity | 900 |

**39. (LO 3.3)** What is the firm's net working capital?

**40. (LO 3.3)** Suppose the firm uses all available cash to pay down accounts payable today, what will its net working capital be after?

**41. (LO 3.3)** Suppose the firm uses its entire cash and marketable securities balance to buy new property, plant and equipment today, what will its net working capital be after?

**42. (LO 3.4)** Using the net income and basic earnings per common share (EPS) figures from Canadian Pacific's (CP's) income statement (Figure 3.5), determine how many shares (approximately) the company had outstanding at the end of 2018.

**43. (LO 3.4)** Based on CP's balance sheet (Figure 3.4), the firm's total current assets changed between the two years. Which component of the current assets changed the most? By what dollar amount and percentage did it increase or decrease?

**44. (LO 3.4)** Use the total "Dividends paid" figure from the firm's cash flow statement (Figure 3.6) and your answer to practice problem 42 to estimate the dividends per common share outstanding for 2018.

**45. (LO 3.4)** Use the income statement for CP (Figure 3.5) to calculate the average tax rate (tax paid as a percentage of net income) in 2018.

**46. (LO 3.4)** What was the growth rate of sales at CP in 2017 and 2018? Did the sales growth rate increase or decrease?

**47. (LO 3.5)** Suppose firms A and B have identical revenues and operating expenses, so that each has earnings before depreciation and taxes of exactly $1 million. Both firms will report depreciation of $250,000 on their public financial statements. On its tax return, firm A claims $250,000 for CCA, whereas firm B is able to claim $400,000. Based on a tax rate of 30 percent of taxable income, how much tax will each firm pay?

**48. (LO 3.5)** What is the apparent tax rate (tax paid as a percentage of income before taxes) for firms A and B in practice problem 47?

**49. (LO 3.5)** Prince Rupert Fly 'n' Fish Inc. purchases one small plane in its first year of business for $90,000. In year 2, it purchases another plane for $100,000. Find the UCC at the end of year 3 if the CCA rate for aircraft is 25 percent. (Include the half-year rule.)

**50. (LO 3.5)** Suppose Prince Rupert Fly 'n' Fish Inc. (see Practice Problem 49) decides to sell its first aircraft for $50,000 in year 2 (purchased for $90,000 in year 1). As before, the second plane costs $100,000 and is bought and put in service in year 2. Find the UCC at the end of year 3. (Include the half-year rule.)

**51. (LO 3.5)** Tina's Business Inc. bought machines some time ago for $25,000. She decided to sell all the assets from this pool at the end of this year. The pool of assets had a UCC of $5,000 before the sale, and the whole asset class was sold for $45,000. Calculate the amount of any capital gain, and calculate the amount (if any) of CCA recapture and/or terminal loss.

## Challenging

Refer to practice problem 28.

**52. (LO 3.2)** David Finn notices that the local appliance store is now charging $210 for the same model of refrigerator his company bought for $200. Given that Finns' Fridges purchased 25 of these refrigerators, what should the company's balance sheet show as the value of property and equipment?

Refer to practice problem 28.

**53. (LO 3.3)** The Finn brothers are concerned that the financial statements for Finns' Fridges don't reflect the true state of affairs. The company's 25 customers were charged $10 for rent at the end of each month. Now that the academic year is over, five of these customers (students) have vacated their dormitory rooms without paying the last month's rent on the refrigerators. Moreover, one student seems to have taken the refrigerator with him when he left! Douglas doubts the company will ever receive the late rental fees or retrieve the stolen fridge. Based on this, construct a new balance sheet and income statement for the company.

**54. (LO 3.3)** Calculate cash flow from operations for Tina's Business Inc. using the following information.

| | |
|---|---|
| Net income | $80,000 |
| Depreciation | 6,000 |
| Deferred income taxes | 2,000 |
| Decrease in inventories | 10,000 |
| Decrease in accounts receivable | 2,000 |
| Decrease in accounts payable | 1,500 |
| Decrease in accruals | 2,200 |
| Decrease in prepaids | 3,600 |

**55. (LO 3.3)** Estimate cash flow from operations for KER Inc. using the following information.

| | |
|---|---|
| Net income | $90,000 |
| Depreciation | 10,000 |
| Deferred income taxes | 5,000 |
| Increase in inventories | 20,000 |
| Decrease in accounts receivable | 1,000 |
| Increase in accounts payable | 2,000 |
| Decrease in accruals | 2,500 |
| Decrease in prepaids | 5,000 |

**56. (LO 3.5)** Given the following income statement for GG Inc. and the adjustments to be made, rebuild its income statement.

**a.** GG Inc. should use the straight-line depreciation method, which incurred only $1,500 in depreciation.

**b.** GG Inc. forgot to record $6,000 in salary paid during the year.

**c.** GG Inc. should use the new corporate tax rate, which is 26.5 percent.

| GG Inc. Income Statement for Y2022 (unadjusted) | |
|---|---|
| Revenue | $100,000 |
| Cost of sales | 30,000 |
| Rent | 10,000 |
| Depreciation | 2,500 |
| Interest | 2,800 |
| Income before taxes | 54,700 |
| Taxes paid | 21,880 |
| Net income | $32,820 |

**57. (LO 3.5)** Suppose firms A and B have identical revenues and operating expenses, so that each has earnings before depreciation and taxes of $10 million. Both firms will report depreciation of $1 million on their public financial statements. On its tax return, firm A claims $1 million for CCA, whereas firm B claims $2 million. The tax rate is 30 percent of taxable income.

**a.** Is it legal to report different depreciation for financial statement and for tax purposes?

**b.** Which firm pays higher taxes?

**c.** How much tax will each firm pay?

**d.** What is the net income for each firm?

**58. (LO 3.3)** Tina's Business Inc. purchases one machine in its first year of business for $1,000,000. In year 2, it purchases another machine for $500,000. The CCA rate for these assets is 20 percent. (Include the half-year rule.)

**a.** Find the beginning UCC, CCA, and ending UCC in years 1 to 3 for the first machine.

**b.** Find the beginning UCC, CCA, and ending UCC in years 2 and 3 for the second machine.

**c.** Find the UCC at the end of year 3 for both machines in total.

**59. (LO 3.5)** Kash Kow Inc. pays out all its after-tax earnings to shareholders in the form of dividends. Suppose that in 2022 the company earned $1 per share before tax. Corporate income tax was paid at a rate of 25 percent. Suppose a high-income shareholder receiving this dividend has a combined federal and provincial personal tax rate of 42 percent. Assume this is an eligible dividend subject to a combined federal and provincial dividend tax credit of 21.42 percent.

**a.** How much of the original $1 per share would such a shareholder have left after all the taxes were paid?

**b.** Suppose instead of the eligible dividend, the taxpayer received interest income of $0.75. Assuming all else the same, how much would they have left after all taxes are paid?

**c.** Suppose instead, the taxpayer received interest income of $1. Assuming all else the same, how much would they have left after all taxes are paid?

**d.** Calculate and compare the average tax rates in the three scenarios.

# Financial Statement Analysis and Forecasting

---

**LEARNING OBJECTIVES**

After studying this chapter, you should be able to:

**4.1** Identify the issues to consider in applying consistent financial analysis.

**4.2** Explain why return on equity is a key financial ratio used to assess a firm's performance.

**4.3** Calculate, interpret, and evaluate the key ratios relating to financial leverage.

**4.4** Calculate, interpret, and evaluate the key ratios relating to financial efficiency.

**4.5** Calculate, interpret, and evaluate the key ratios relating to financial productivity.

**4.6** Calculate, interpret, and evaluate the key ratios relating to financial liquidity.

**4.7** Calculate, interpret, and evaluate the key ratios relating to the valuation of a company.

**4.8** Explain how to prepare financial forecasts using the percentage of sales method.

**4.9** Explain how external financing requirements are related to sales growth, profitability, dividend payouts, and sustainable growth rates.

**4.10** Apply financial forecasting to a real company.

---

If accounting is the language of business, what is it saying to us? Chapter 4 answers this question and shows how external interested parties can use financial statements to evaluate a firm. Ratio analysis is part of this process, as ratios provide insight into the aggregate numbers. Of course, no one uses financial statements in isolation; they look at additional information on the firm and the macroeconomic environment, and compare the firm's statements across time and with members of its peer group, such as other firms in the same industry or industry averages. However, in all cases, a major source of information is the firm's financial statements, and financial analysis provides a standard framework of evaluation.

Financial analysis is clearly important for the firm. Of course, financial analysis is also critical for a firm's creditors, like the bank, and for investment dealers, who need to advise the firm on its financing issues. In this chapter, we will introduce the basics of financial analysis and forecasting.

---

## 4.1 | Consistent Financial Analysis

---

**LEARNING OBJECTIVE 4.1**

Identify the issues to consider in applying consistent financial analysis.

---

In Chapter 3, you learned about the significant role that judgement plays in the preparation of a firm's financial statements. With so much judgement involved, it is reasonable to ask whether financial analysis based on these statements is a bit like building a sand castle.

To some extent it is, and this has led to significant efforts by third parties to reconcile and standardize the financial statements of firms. As discussed in Chapter 3, most countries have adopted International Financial Reporting Standards (IFRS), which allow users of financial statements to compare the financial statements of companies in the same industry that are based in different countries. However, despite efforts to harmonize accounting standards, important differences still persist. For example, two of the world's largest oil and gas companies are Exxon Mobil Corporation (United States) and BP PLC (United Kingdom). Exxon uses U.S. generally accepted accounting principles (U.S. GAAP) and BP PLC follows IFRS, which complicates a comparison of their financial statements.

Aside from the use of different accounting standards in preparing financial statements, an additional complication arises because there are no generally accepted financial ratios. Thus, it is important, when looking at ratios generated by another party, to determine how they are calculated. Some of the most basic ratios, such as return on equity, can vary when calculated by different institutions, even if the input data are the same.[1] Other ratios, such as the debt ratio, have multiple definitions and can vary quite widely in their calculation and, hence, their interpretation. Acting on the assumption that all ratios are prepared on the same basis can lead to misleading conclusions, and it is essential to always compare "apples with apples" and not "oranges."

---

### Concept Review Questions

1. What difficulties do analysts face when trying to compare the financial statements of firms that are based in different countries?
2. Why should people be aware of the precise definition of a financial ratio employed by those who calculate the ratio?

---

## 4.2 | A Framework for Financial Analysis

> **LEARNING OBJECTIVE 4.2**
> Explain why return on equity is a key financial ratio used to assess a firm's performance.

### Return on Equity (ROE) and the DuPont System

**return on equity (ROE)**   the return earned by equity holders on their investment in the company; net income divided by shareholders' equity

**Return on equity (ROE)** is one of the most commonly referenced ratios, and for good reason: it measures the return earned by the equity holders on their investment in the company. It is calculated as the net income (NI) divided by shareholders' equity (SE), as shown in Equation 4.1.[2]

$$ROE = \frac{NI}{SE}$$

[4.1]

We will calculate the 2018 ROE for Canadian Pacific Railway Limited (CP), using the figures reported in the company's financial statements, which were included in Chapter 3. (We will

---

[1]This is not because they make mistakes but because they employ different definitions of the same ratio.
[2]ROE can also be defined as NI available to the common shareholders (i.e., NI − preferred dividends) divided by common equity (CE). For CP, there is no difference, because the company does not have any preferred equity. For some firms, it can make a difference.

also use CP's figures to calculate the other ratios introduced in this chapter.) In 2018, NI was $1,951 million, while SE was $6,636 million, so CP's ROE was as follows:

$$ROE = \frac{NI}{SE} = \frac{\$1,951}{\$6,636} = 29.40\%$$

This is a healthy ROE figure that would be rated above average, which suggests that CP lies at the upper end of corporate profitability in Canada (or anywhere else for that matter).

ROE is not a "pure" financial ratio because it involves dividing an income statement (flow) item by a balance sheet (stock) item.[3] As a result, some people calculate the ROE as NI over the "average" SE—that is, the average of the starting and ending SE. This adjustment acknowledges that NI is earned throughout the year, so it makes sense to divide by an average of SE to recognize that not all of those funds were invested throughout the year. For example, the ending SE is partly the result of the retained earnings for the year, which, in turn, is dependent on the net income for the year; however, with three years of data, the use of the average SE causes the loss of an observation. This is why most analysts use the ending SE as the denominator simply to get more estimates of the ROE; that way, they can assess a trend over time. However, this tends to understate a firm's profitability on average, because the ending SE will usually exceed the average for the year if the firm is profitable.

The next step in financial analysis is to understand where CP's ROE came from. The most popular approach to "decomposing" ROE is attributable to the DuPont Corporation, which pioneered a variation of the expansion of the ROE shown in **Figure 4.1**.

The DuPont system provides a good starting point for any financial analysis and is commonly included in research reports as a way to summarize a firm's key financial ratios. Many analyst reports, such as those provided by Morningstar Inc., provide a DuPont analysis as a way of summarizing a company's financial performance. We will provide such an analysis next for CP, and you will see how all the reported figures and ratios are related as you proceed through this section, with particular emphasis on the 2018 numbers for CP.

The DuPont approach defines the firm's **return on assets (ROA)** as NI divided by total assets (TA), as shown in Equation 4.2.

**return on assets (ROA)** net income divided by total assets

$$ROA = \frac{NI}{TA} \qquad [4.2]$$

For CP in 2018,

$$ROA = \frac{NI}{TA} = \frac{\$1,951}{\$21,254} = 9.18\%$$

If the ROA is multiplied by TA and divided by SE, the TAs cancel out and produce the ROE. So what is TA divided by SE? This is called the **leverage ratio**, and it measures how many dollars of total assets are supported by each dollar of SE, or how many times the firm has "leveraged" the capital provided by the shareholders into total financing. It is shown in Equation 4.3.

**leverage ratio** total assets divided by shareholders' equity; it measures how many dollars of total assets are supported by each dollar of shareholders' equity, or how many times the firm has leveraged the capital provided by the shareholders into total financing

$$Leverage = \frac{TA}{SE} \qquad [4.3]$$

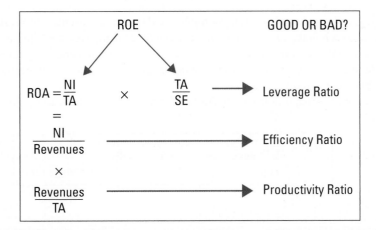

**FIGURE 4.1** **DuPont System**

---

[3]"Pure" ratios involve dividing an income statement item by another income statement item, or dividing a balance sheet item by another balance sheet item.

The 2018 leverage ratio for CP is as follows:

$$\text{Leverage} = \frac{\text{TA}}{\text{SE}} = \frac{\$21,254}{\$6,636} = 3.2028 = 320.28\%$$

Thus, CP has leveraged every dollar of shareholders' equity into $3.20 of total financing by using debt and other forms of liabilities to help finance its operations.

We interpret the ROA as saying that every dollar of total assets earned a return of 9.18 percent, but the shareholders didn't provide all this financing. They provided about 31.2 percent of the money to buy the firm's total assets (i.e., 1/3.2028)—that is, the firm leveraged each dollar of shareholders' equity by 3.2028. As a result, the ROE is the ROA of 9.18 percent multiplied by the leverage ratio of 3.2028, which gives an ROE of 29.40 percent. What this figure means is that part of the reason for CP's high ROE is that it is extremely profitable and has a high ROA of 9.18 percent. The rest of the story is that CP magnified this ROA using financial leverage. This is why, when we analyze corporate performance, we look at ROE, ROA, and a series of ratios that measure **financial leverage**, since how the firm finances its operations is very important.

**financial leverage**   the use of capital provided by shareholders to increase total financing

**net profit margin**   part of return on assets; net income divided by revenues

**turnover ratio**   part of return on assets; revenues divided by total assets

We can now decompose ROA into two of its major components: the firm's **net profit margin** and its (asset) **turnover ratio**, which we show in Equation 4.4 and Equation 4.5.

$$\text{Net profit margin} = \frac{\text{NI}}{\text{Revenues}} \qquad [4.4]$$

$$\text{Turnover ratio} = \frac{\text{Revenues}}{\text{TA}} \qquad [4.5]$$

Multiplying the two ratios together cancels the revenues figure on the bottom of net profit margin with the revenues figure on the top of the turnover ratio, leaving NI/TA, or, simply, the ROA, as shown in Equation 4.6.

$$\text{ROA} = \frac{\text{NI}}{\text{TA}} = \frac{\text{NI}}{\text{Revenues}} \times \frac{\text{Revenues}}{\text{TA}} \qquad [4.6]$$

For CP, the 2018 net profit margin or (return on revenues) was as follows:

$$\text{Net profit margin} = \frac{\text{NI}}{\text{Revenues}} = \frac{\$1,951}{\$7,316} = 26.67\%$$

So CP made profits of over 26 percent of revenues earned. We look at the net profit margin to determine how *efficiently* the firm converts revenues into profits. Later in the chapter, we will expand our analysis to include additional efficiency ratios.

So if every dollar of revenue earned CP 26.7 percent in profits, how many dollars of revenue did it generate from each dollar invested in assets, or, alternatively, what was its turnover ratio?

$$\text{Turnover ratio} = \frac{\text{Revenues}}{\text{TA}} = \frac{\$7,316}{\$21,254} = 0.3442$$

For 2018, with total assets of $21,254 million, CP generated revenues of $7,316 million. In other words, each dollar of assets generated about $0.3442 in revenues. The turnover ratio is a productivity ratio, as it measures how productive the firm is in generating revenues from its assets. As you will see, several productivity ratios can be calculated to determine the main drivers of this overall productivity.

Now we have the major ratios of the DuPont formula. Putting them all together produces Equation 4.7.[4]

$$\text{ROE} = \frac{\text{NI}}{\text{SE}} = \frac{\text{NI}}{\text{Revenues}} \times \frac{\text{Revenues}}{\text{TA}} \times \frac{\text{TA}}{\text{SE}} \qquad [4.7]$$
$$= \text{Net profit margin} \times \text{Turnover ratio} \times \text{Leverage ratio}$$

---

[4]This is the simplest and most commonly used version of the DuPont system. There are other versions, which we do not discuss here, many of which break ROE into five or more components.

For CP in 2018,

$$\text{ROE} = \frac{\text{NI}}{\text{SE}} = \frac{\text{NI}}{\text{Revenues}} \times \frac{\text{Revenues}}{\text{TA}} \times \frac{\text{TA}}{\text{SE}}$$

$$= 0.2667 \times 0.3442 \times 3.2028 = 29.40\% \text{ (as calculated at the start of this section)}$$

Each dollar of equity supported $3.2028 of assets, which, in turn, generated $0.3442 in revenues, which, in turn, generated a net profit margin of 26.67 percent. In other words, overall, the ROE is determined by leverage, turnover, and profit margin. So what does this mean?

## Interpreting Ratios

A single ratio on its own provides little information. To judge whether a given ratio is "good" or "bad" requires some basis for comparison. Two bases are commonly used for comparison:

1. The company's historical ratios, or the *trend* in its ratios

2. Comparable companies—for this purpose, we can use a similar company or use industry average ratios

Table 4.1 includes CP's DuPont analysis ratios for 2016–18.

Often, unique factors drive a particular firm's ratios and make them difficult to compare with the ratios of other firms. For example, if a firm has made a recent large acquisition of another firm, key profitability and turnover ratios often drop. For this reason, it is important to look at a firm's ratios over time. What we can observe from Table 4.1 is that CP was profitable in all three years, with ROEs ranging from 29.4 percent to 37.4 percent. We also observe a significant increase in profitability in 2017, as the net profit margin increased to 36.7 percent from 25.7 percent, which was the driving force behind this increase in ROE. Both the turnover ratio and the leverage ratio improved slightly over the three-year period, with the turnover ratio increasing slightly and the leverage ratio decreasing from 4.155 to 3.203.

So how does CP compare with its competition? In order to make such a comparison we look for a similar company, and Canadian National Railway Company (CN) is a logical candidate. CN is Canada's only other major railway company. It is larger than CP, with 2018 year-end total assets of $41.2 billion (versus $21.3 billion for CP), 2018 revenues of $14.3 billion (versus $7.3 billion for CP), and a 2018 year-end market capitalization of $73.3 billion (versus $34.0 billion for CP). Aside from CN, it also makes sense to look for similar U.S. railways, and there are four logical candidates—Union Pacific Corporation (UNP), CSX Corporation (CSX), Norfolk Southern Corporation (NSC), and Burlington Northern Santa Fe (BNSF). These four firms account for approximately 90 percent of the U.S. industry market share. Since BNSF was acquired by Berkshire Hathaway and is no longer publicly traded, we will use only the other three companies for comparison purposes. All three are larger than CP, but are reasonable comparators. For example, the total assets for UNP, CSX, and NSC respectively are $59.1, $36.7, and $36.2 billion (all in U.S. dollars). They also compare well to CP along several dimensions, such as product offerings and market presence.[5]

**TABLE 4.1    Canadian Pacific's DuPont Ratios**

|                   | 2018   | 2017   | 2016   |
|-------------------|--------|--------|--------|
| ROE               | 0.2940 | 0.3736 | 0.3457 |
| ROA               | 0.0918 | 0.1194 | 0.0832 |
| Net profit margin | 0.2667 | 0.3670 | 0.2566 |
| Turnover          | 0.3442 | 0.3255 | 0.3242 |
| Leverage          | 3.2028 | 3.1280 | 4.1550 |

[5]Also, recall that CP's financial statements have been prepared in accordance with U.S. GAAP, and we want to compare "apples with apples" to the greatest extent possible.

**TABLE 4.2** Canadian National and U.S. Industry Average DuPont Ratios

|  | Canadian National | | | U.S. Industry Average | | |
| --- | --- | --- | --- | --- | --- | --- |
|  | 2018 | 2017 | 2016 | 2018 | 2017 | 2016 |
| ROE | 0.2453 | 0.3293 | 0.2453 | 0.2430 | 0.3778 | 0.1645 |
| ROA | 0.1050 | 0.1457 | 0.0982 | 0.0882 | 0.1663 | 0.0574 |
| Net profit margin | 0.3022 | 0.4205 | 0.3024 | 0.2547 | 0.4987 | 0.1786 |
| Turnover | 0.3475 | 0.3466 | 0.3248 | 0.3453 | 0.3274 | 0.3180 |
| Leverage | 2.3363 | 2.2592 | 2.4969 | 2.7258 | 2.3126 | 2.8794 |

Table 4.2 provides the DuPont ROE data for CN and the averages for the three U.S. firms, which we label "U.S. Industry," for 2016–18. These ratios are comparable to CP's ratios, and it should be noted that all five firms have a December 31 fiscal year end.[6]

The ROE, ROA, net profit margin, and turnover ratio for CP are all similar to the 2016–18 figures for CN and the U.S. averages, while the CP leverage ratio has been higher. In 2018, CP's ROE of 29.4 percent was higher than those of CN and the U.S. industry average, while CP's ROA of 9.2 percent was slightly below CN's figure of 10.5 percent, and slightly above the U.S. industry average of 8.8 percent. The higher ROE is reflective of CP's higher leverage ratio.

Overall, we could say that CP's profitability has improved significantly and is currently similar to that of CN and superior to that of the U.S. railroads. CP also displays average asset turnover and is slightly more highly levered. However, we should consider any possible contributing factors before reaching final conclusions. To get a better understanding of these results, we will extend the analysis of the leverage, efficiency, and productivity ratios.

---

### Concept Review Questions

1. What three areas of a firm's operations does the DuPont system provide information about?
2. All else being equal, list three factors that will lead to higher ROE ratios.
3. What can we use as a basis for comparison when looking at financial ratios? What kind of information can we gain from this comparison?

---

## 4.3 Leverage Ratios

---

**LEARNING OBJECTIVE 4.3**

Calculate, interpret, and evaluate the key ratios relating to financial leverage.

---

Leverage is synonymous with magnification. It is good when a firm is low risk and earns a healthy ROA, since it magnifies these high ROAs into even higher ROEs. However, when the firm loses money, the use of leverage magnifies ROEs on the downside as well. This can get the firm into serious trouble.

We will discuss the leverage decision in more detail when we discuss the firm's capital structure in chapters 20 and 21. But for now, we will introduce the major ratios to consider

---

[6]The choice of fiscal year end can have a significant impact on reported financial ratios, based on annual financial statements, especially for firms that face a seasonal sales cycle. As a result, several balance sheet items, such as loans outstanding, accounts receivable, inventory, and accounts payable, will vary considerably during the year. The analyst must be aware of these factors when evaluating the ratios and also when comparing to other "similar" firms that choose different fiscal year ends.

when discussing financial leverage. There are basically three types: stock ratios, flow ratios, and other ratios.

**Stock ratios** indicate the amounts of debt outstanding at a particular time. For leverage, there are three basic stock ratios: the leverage ratio (discussed previously), the debt ratio, and the debt-equity ratio. The **debt ratio** is defined as total liabilities (TL) divided by total assets (TA), as shown in Equation 4.8.[7]

$$\boxed{\text{Debt ratio} = \frac{\text{TL}}{\text{TA}}} \qquad [4.8]$$

For CP in 2018,

$$\text{Debt ratio} = \frac{\text{TL}}{\text{TA}} = \frac{\$14{,}618}{\$21{,}254} = 0.6878$$

The debt ratio is just a rearrangement of the leverage ratio, which for CP was 3.2028.[8] The debt ratio as defined includes all liabilities, including money that a company owes suppliers. But in a broad sense, these liabilities are not debt in the way that bank debt is debt. These liabilities arise as a result of normal operations, not from someone deciding to invest in, or lend money to, CP.

To capture the use of "genuine" debt, we estimate the amount of interest-bearing debt the firm has outstanding relative to shareholders' equity. The sum of interest-bearing debt and shareholders' equity is referred to as **invested capital** to distinguish it from total assets, some of which are financed as a result of normal business operations. CP's interest-bearing debt total of $8,696 million is calculated as follows:

$506 million (Current portion of long-term debt) + $8,190 million (Long-term debt)

So the company's **debt-equity (D/E) ratio** is simply debt (D) divided by shareholders' equity (SE), as shown in Equation 4.9.

$$\boxed{\text{D/E ratio} = \frac{\text{D}}{\text{SE}}} \qquad [4.9]$$

For CP in 2018,

$$\text{D/E ratio} = \frac{\text{D}}{\text{SE}} = \frac{\$8{,}696}{\$6{,}636} = 1.3104$$

This means that for every dollar of equity contributed by shareholders, CP borrowed $1.31 in interest-bearing debt.

The D/E ratio's advantage over the debt ratio is that it measures the use of interest-bearing debt. This is important because it is the promise to pay interest that makes debt risky. For example, CP does not face risk as a result of its tax-collecting activities on behalf of the government, because its creditors think well enough of it to ship supplies on credit, or because an accountant has decided to generate accruals in terms of future employee benefits. CP does face risk through its interest-bearing debt. In this respect, analysts often "net out" interest-bearing debt by subtracting cash and cash equivalents. In CP's case, these two items total $8,635 million, (i.e., $8,696–$61).

This discussion of the role of interest-bearing debt should remind you that not only is it important to determine the amount of debt, but it is also equally, if not more, important to evaluate how much the debt costs. More generally, we look at measures that indicate the flow of fixed commitments to income, which provides an estimate of a firm's ability to service its debt obligations. Of course, this concept also relates to individuals, as demonstrated in Finance in the News 4.1. This article discusses the debt-to-income ratio for individuals, which sat at $1.79 per dollar of disposable income (or 179 percent) during the last quarter of 2018. The article also discusses the importance of servicing debt, noting that a record 15 percent of disposable income was being used to service debt at that time.

The most important debt coverage measure, or at least the one most commonly referred to, is the **times interest earned (TIE)**, or coverage, ratio. This is defined as earnings before interest and taxes (EBIT) divided by interest expense (I), as shown in Equation 4.10:

$$\boxed{\text{TIE} = \frac{\text{EBIT}}{\text{I}}} \qquad [4.10]$$

**stock ratios**   the amounts of debt outstanding at a particular time

**debt ratio**   total liabilities divided by total assets

**invested capital**   the sum of interest-bearing debt and shareholders' equity

**debt-equity (D/E) ratio**   debt divided by shareholders' equity

**times interest earned (TIE)** earnings before interest and taxes divided by interest expense; also called the "coverage ratio"

---

[7]There are many variations of this ratio that include the use of total debt or total long-term debt in the numerator and/or divide by total capital instead of total assets.

[8]In fact, the leverage ratio is simply one divided by one minus the debt ratio (i.e., 1/(1 − 0.6878) = 3.203).

---

### 4.1 Finance in the News  Canadian Households Now Using 14.9% of Income for Debt Payments

The average Canadian household was using a record 14.9 per cent of its disposable income to meet debt obligations, Statistics Canada said on Wednesday.

The measure was "just a whisker" below the record high reached at the end of 2017, noted BMO economist Priscilla Thiagamoorthy. And a growing share of Canadians' income—7.3 per cent, the most in nine years—is going toward interest charges, she added.

Total debt repayments outpaced the growth of disposable income in the last three months of the year, StatsCan said. Between October and December, Canadians' household debt reached a seasonally-adjusted average of $1.79 for every dollar of disposable income, up slightly from $1.78 in the June to September period.

Debt is eating up an increasing share of household disposable incomes even as Canadians pull back on borrowing. Although the end of 2018 saw a pick-up in mortgage loans, on an annual basis household borrowing declined 19.5 per cent in 2018 to the lowest level since 2014.

Rising debt-servicing costs will likely continue to squeeze Canadians' wallets for the foreseeable future, RBC economist Josh Nye wrote in a note to clients.

Even if the Bank of Canada keeps rates on hold for the rest of the year, the share of income Canadians will have to devote to mandatory debt repayments will probably keep edging up as homeowners renew fixed-rate mortgages at higher interest rates, he added.

Most Canadians will likely be able to manage higher borrowing costs by trimming consumption, according to Nye.

"We think the increase in debt servicing costs is more of a headwind to consumer spending than a financial stability risk," he wrote.

But while most households will be able to keep up with higher interest payments, they'll have a harder time making an actual dent in their debt. As a result, the debt-to-income ratio is likely to remain roughly stable, as it has been since the central bank began its rate-hiking, according to Nye.

"It will take a long period of household incomes outpacing credit growth to deliver meaningful improvement in the debt-to-income ratio," he wrote. "We're not seeing that yet."

**Source:** Excerpted from Alini, Erica, "Canadian Households Now Using 14.9% of Income for Debt Payments," Global News, March 14, 2019. ©2019, Available at https://globalnews.ca/news/5055092/canada-household-debt-service-ratio/. Reproduced with the permissions of Global News, a division of Corus Entertainment Inc. Corus News. All rights reserved.

---

We estimate the TIE for CP in 2018 by first estimating the earnings before interest and taxes (EBIT) figure of $3,041 million, which equals the operating income figure of $2,831 million minus $174 million in other expenses plus $384 million in net periodic benefit recoveries. We then divide this EBIT figure by the net interest expense figure of $453 million, as shown here. (All figures are found in CP's income statement, which we presented in Chapter 3.)

$$\text{TIE} = \frac{\text{EBIT}}{\text{I}} = \frac{\$3,041}{\$453} = 6.7130$$

So how do we evaluate the TIE? It means that for every dollar of interest expense, CP had approximately $6.71 of income available to pay interest and taxes. This demonstrates that CP is in a stable position in the sense that the company is very able to cover its interest payments from the profits it generates.[9]

**cash flow to debt ratio** a measure of how long it would take to pay off a firm's debt using its cash flow from operations; cash flow from operations divided by debt

A final ratio that is normally calculated is a mixture of the previous ratios. The **cash flow to debt ratio** measures how long it would take to pay off a firm's debt (D) using its cash flow from operations (CFO). It is calculated as shown in Equation 4.11:

$$\text{Cash flow to debt ratio} = \frac{\text{CFO}}{\text{D}} \qquad [4.11]$$

For CP in 2018,

$$\text{Cash flow to debt ratio} = \frac{\text{CFO}}{\text{D}} = \frac{\$2,712}{\$8,696} = 0.3119$$

Given its CFO of $2,712 million and its total interest-bearing debt outstanding of $8,696 million, CP could pay off 31.2 percent of its debt within a year if it devoted its operating cash flow to debt repayment. This indicates, once again, CP's strong credit position.

So what is the overall assessment of CP's leverage position in 2018? The stock ratios (i.e., debt ratio, leverage ratio, and D/E ratio) indicate moderate levels of debt, while the interest coverage ratio and cash flow to debt ratios indicate that CP's earnings or the related operating cash flows can very easily support the required debt payments.

---

[9]There are other coverage ratios, variations of the TIE, that are adjusted to include the impact of other fixed charges, such as preferred share dividends, lease obligations, and sinking fund payments. These will be discussed later when we talk about other contractual commitments attached to different types of securities.

**TABLE 4.3**   Canadian Pacific, Canadian National, and U.S. Industry Average Leverage Ratios

| | Canadian Pacific | | | Canadian National | | | U.S. Industry Average | | |
|---|---|---|---|---|---|---|---|---|---|
| | 2018 | 2017 | 2016 | 2018 | 2017 | 2016 | 2018 | 2017 | 2016 |
| Leverage | 3.2028 | 3.1280 | 4.1550 | 2.3363 | 2.2592 | 2.4969 | 2.7258 | 2.3126 | 2.8794 |
| Debt ratio | 0.6878 | 0.6803 | 0.7593 | 0.5720 | 0.5574 | 0.5995 | 0.6295 | 0.5668 | 0.6522 |
| D/E ratio | 1.3104 | 1.2675 | 1.8772 | 0.7125 | 0.6501 | 0.7369 | 0.9988 | 0.6953 | 0.8476 |
| TIE | 6.7130 | 6.2812 | 5.5690 | 12.6196 | 11.5800 | 11.2646 | 8.2871 | 8.2954 | 7.3217 |

To gain additional insight, look at the trend in CP's leverage ratios, and compare them with those of CN and the U.S. industry average, shown in Table 4.3.

CP's leverage ratios show that the amount of debt as a percentage of total financing has decreased since 2016; however, the company's coverage ratio has increased. Comparing CP with CN and the U.S. industry average, we can see that CP had more debt and lower coverage ratios than both. Based on the foregoing, we could conclude that CP's debt levels and coverage have improved since 2016, but they still possess more than average debt with less than average coverage. However, overall they seem to be in a relatively good position with respect to leverage.

---

### Concept Review Questions

1. Why is it important to look at stock and flow leverage ratios to assess a firm's debt situation?
2. Briefly explain what type of information is provided about a firm's leverage position by the debt ratio, the D/E ratio, the TIE ratio, and the cash flow to debt ratio.

---

## 4.4  Efficiency Ratios

### LEARNING OBJECTIVE 4.4
Calculate, interpret, and evaluate the key ratios relating to financial efficiency.

**Efficiency ratios** measure how efficiently a dollar of revenue is turned into profits, so we start with CP's 2018 net profit margin of 26.7 percent, which is a very healthy figure. However, it is a measure of overall profitability and is frequently broken out into its major components. How this is done depends on the type of firm and the amount of data presented in its financial statements. Unfortunately, not all firms present a good breakdown of their cost structure on their income statements.

When looking at a firm's cost structure, economists like to think in terms of variable and fixed costs, where variable costs vary with the amount of production, and sales and fixed costs do not. Suppose a firm has revenues of $120 and variable costs of $72, or 60 percent of revenues. This means that the firm has a contribution margin of 40 percent, or $48 is available to contribute to the firm's fixed costs and profits. With fixed operating costs of $31 and fixed interest costs of $5, the firm has taxable income of $12. With a 50-percent income tax rate, its net income and taxes are both $6, and the firm has a net profit margin of 5 percent. This example is illustrated in Table 4.4, which also shows what happens with a 10-percent increase and decrease in revenues.

**efficiency ratios** ratios that measure how efficiently a dollar of revenue is turned into profits

**TABLE 4.4** Profit Margin and Revenue Variability

| Revenues | $120 | $132 | $108 |
|---|---|---|---|
| Contribution margin (40%) | 48 | 53 | 43 |
| Fixed operating cost | 31 | 31 | 31 |
| Fixed interest cost | 5 | 5 | 5 |
| Tax | 6 | 8.5 | 3.5 |
| Net income | 6 | 8.5 | 3.5 |
| Net profit margin | 5% | 6.4% | 3.2% |

If the firm sells more and revenues increase to $132, then only the variable costs increase. The gross profit, which is revenues minus variable costs, also increases by 10 percent to $53. However, because the fixed production and interest costs stay the same, the taxable income increases from $12 to $17 or 40 percent, and the net profit margin increases to 6.4 percent. Conversely, if revenues decrease by 10 percent to $108, the process works in reverse and the existence of the fixed costs causes net income to drop by 40 percent.[10]

This example indicates that the more fixed costs the firm has, the greater its income variability. Note that although revenues varied by +/−10 percent, net income varied by +/−40 percent. We will discuss this more in chapters 20 and 21, when we discuss the financial and business risk of the firm. However, as shown in Equation 4.12, we can estimate the **degree of total leverage (DTL)** as the contribution margin (CM) divided by the earnings before taxes (EBT).[11]

**degree of total leverage (DTL)** contribution margin divided by earnings before taxes

$$DTL = \frac{CM}{EBT}$$ [4.12]

For the previous example,

$$DTL = \frac{CM}{EBT} = \frac{\$48}{\$12} = 4.0$$

The DTL for our example firm shows a very significant exposure of profits to variability in revenues, because every 1-percent change in revenues causes a 4-percent change in earnings before taxes. This exposure depends on the firm's cost structure, which is crucial to the risk of the firm. It also allows the firm to estimate its **break-even point (BEP)**, which is the level of revenues at which the firm covers all its operating and fixed costs. In the previous example, the firm needs revenues of $90 to cover these costs; if revenues fall below this level, it loses money.

This $90 break-even point is calculated as the total fixed costs (FC) divided by the contribution margin ratio, as shown in Equation 4.13:

**break-even point (BEP)** the level of revenues at which the firm covers all its operating costs and fixed costs; total fixed costs divided by the contribution margin ratio

$$BEP = \frac{FC}{CM}$$ [4.13]

For our example firm,

$$BEP = \frac{FC}{CM} = \frac{\$31 + \$5}{0.4} = \$90$$

The contribution margin ratio is just the complement of the variable costs as a percentage of revenues, so with variable costs at 60 percent of revenues, the contribution margin is 40 percent or 0.4. Dividing the fixed operating and interest costs of $36 by 40 percent produces the break-even point of $90.

Clearly, it is important for the firm to know its break-even point and how its profits vary with revenues. As a result, internally it will have the information to estimate these important values. However, externally, the firm is not required to present this information in its financial statements. Further, the proxies that are available are often poor. From your managerial cost accounting course, you know that the cost of sales includes variable production costs, as well

---

[10]The actual numbers are rounded.

[11]We don't use net income to estimate the DTL. With a 50-percent tax rate, half the gain accrues to the government in income taxes because income taxes are not a fixed payment.

as the allocation of factory overhead—that is, it includes fixed costs. If the firm does only one thing, this factory overhead can include almost all of its operating fixed costs. Unfortunately, what is presented for most companies, including CP, does not allow a breakout of variable and fixed costs, so we cannot estimate its break-even point or contribution margin, or the sensitivity of its profits to revenue increases or decreases.

However, consistent with the basic idea of calculating the contribution margin—that is, revenues minus variable costs—we can calculate a variation of the break-even point: the **gross profit margin**. Equation 4.14 shows that this ratio is defined as revenues (Rev) minus the cost of sales (COS) divided by revenues.

**gross profit margin**  revenues minus the cost of sales divided by revenues

$$\text{Gross profit margin} = \frac{\text{Rev} - \text{COS}}{\text{Rev}} \qquad [4.14]$$

For CP in 2018,

$$\text{Gross profit margin} = \frac{\text{Rev} - \text{COS}}{\text{Rev}} = \frac{(\$7{,}316 - \$2{,}717)}{\$7{,}316} = 62.86\%$$

A gross margin of 62.9 percent indicates that 62.9 percent of CP's revenues is available to cover its cost of sales. However, this margin is more useful for manufacturing firms as a measure of production efficiency, and is not very meaningful for a railway like CP. Railway analysts and railway management tend to focus on operating profitability, which is discussed next.

The other expenses, apart from the cost of sales, that firms normally incur are period costs, which are often loosely called fixed costs, because, in the short run, they are unrelated to revenues. These costs consist of advertising, research and development, general sales and administrative expenses, and amortization expenses.

The final ratio is the **operating margin**, which is defined as **operating income (OI)** divided by revenues, as in Equation 4.15.

**operating margin**  operating income (OI) divided by revenues

**operating income (OI)**  revenue minus operating expenses

$$\text{Operating margin} = \frac{\text{OI}}{\text{Rev}} \qquad [4.15]$$

For CP, this ratio is relatively easy to calculate, since operating income (or earnings before interest and taxes—EBIT) is reported in the income statement, but this is not always the case.[12]

The operating income figure for CP in 2018 was $2,831 million. For CP, the 2018 operating margin was as follows:

$$\text{Operating margin} = \frac{\text{OI}}{\text{Rev}} = \frac{\$2{,}831}{\$7{,}316} = 38.70\%$$

For reference, 38.70 percent is a solid operating margin and is in line with CP's 2017 and 2016 figures of 38.43 percent and 38.69 percent. This indicates the company presently has good control over its operating costs and has improved a lot in this regard. In fact, this was the main issue raised in the 2012 proxy fight launched by Pershing Square, who noted that CP had a much lower operating margin than CN and comparable U.S. railways.[13] **Table 4.5** provides the efficiency ratios for CP and CN, as well as the U.S. industry average for 2016–18,

**TABLE 4.5  Canadian Pacific, Canadian National, and U.S. Industry Average Efficiency Ratios**

|  | Canadian Pacific | | | Canadian National | | | U.S. Industry Average | | |
|---|---|---|---|---|---|---|---|---|---|
|  | 2018 | 2017 | 2016 | 2018 | 2017 | 2016 | 2018 | 2017 | 2016 |
| Net profit margin | 0.2667 | 0.3670 | 0.2566 | 0.3022 | 0.4205 | 0.3024 | 0.2547 | 0.4987 | 0.1786 |
| Operating profit margin | 0.3870 | 0.3843 | 0.3869 | 0.3836 | 0.4020 | 0.4180 | 0.3694 | 0.3506 | 0.3267 |
| Gross profit margin | 0.6286 | 0.6463 | 0.6348 | N/A | N/A | N/A | 0.3944 | 0.4006 | 0.3848 |

[12]Some analysts use EBITDA, or earnings before interest, tax, depreciation, and amortization, in their calculations since it is less susceptible to the effects of accounting judgement with respect to amortization.

[13]Technically, Pershing Square referred to CP's higher than average "operating ratio," which is a key indicator used by railway analysts and management, and is defined as "operating expenses divided by revenue." It is easy to see that this is simply "1 − operating margin."

which allows us to further evaluate CP's efficiency results. We can see that CP's profitability, like CN's and the U.S. railways', improved during 2017, then declined but remained healthy. CP was slightly less profitable than CN in 2018, and slightly more profitable than the U.S. railways that year.

---

### Concept Review Questions

1. What useful information is provided by the contribution margin, the degree of total leverage, and the break-even point?

2. Why is it uncommon to see those three ratios reported by companies for external users of their financial statements?

3. What useful information is provided by the net profit margin, the gross profit margin, and the operating margin?

---

## 4.5 | Productivity Ratios

---

**LEARNING OBJECTIVE 4.5**

Calculate, interpret, and evaluate the key ratios relating to financial productivity.

---

If the efficiency ratios measure how efficiently the firm turns revenues into profits, the next question is how productive the firm is in generating revenues from its assets. You saw that the turnover ratio is determined by dividing revenues by total assets, so the key to looking at different **productivity ratios** is to look at variations of the turnover ratio for each major asset class. For example, we can see how productive the firm is in using receivables, inventory, and plant and equipment, because these are the major categories of assets that all firms have.

We begin by defining the **receivables turnover ratio** as revenues (Rev) divided by accounts receivable (AR), as shown in Equation 4.16.

**productivity ratios** measurements of how productive the firm is in generating revenues from its assets

**receivables turnover ratio** revenues divided by accounts receivable (AR)

$$\text{Receivables turnover} = \frac{\text{Rev}}{\text{AR}}$$ [4.16]

For CP in 2018,

$$\text{Receivables turnover} = \frac{\text{Rev}}{\text{AR}} = \frac{\$7{,}316}{\$815} = 8.9767$$

For every dollar invested in receivables (i.e., credit extended to purchasers), CP generated $8.9767 in revenues. Alternatively, we can say that CP turned its AR account over 8.98 times during the year, on average.

The turnover ratio is useful, but it is common to calculate a variation of it called the **average collection period (ACP)**. To do this, divide the average daily credit sales into the accounts receivable, because only credit sales generate receivables; cash sales, obviously, generate cash! However, CP, like most companies, does not break out sales into cash and credit sales—at least, not in its external financial statements. Therefore, it is common to use average daily sales (ADS) or average daily revenue (ADR) in the denominator, which equals annual sales (or revenues) divided by 365 days. When we define ACP in this manner, ACP is 365 divided by the receivables turnover ratio, because if AR are "turned over" 10 times a year, it implies that the firm takes an average of 36.5 days to collect on its AR. Therefore, we can define the ACP as shown in Equation 4.17.

**average collection period (ACP)** accounts receivable divided by the average daily revenue

$$\text{ACP} = \frac{\text{AR}}{\text{ADR}} = \frac{365}{\text{Receivables turnover}}$$ [4.17]

For CP in 2018,

$$ACP = \frac{AR}{ADR} = \frac{365}{\text{Receivables turnover}} = \frac{365}{8.9767} = 40.6608$$

This implies its receivables were paid on average within 40.7 days. For CP, this is not a critical ratio, since it does not carry much in the way of receivables.

The second major current asset category for many companies is inventory, which is to be sold or transformed into a final product. However, CP does not provide a figure labelled as inventory since it provides a service for its customers. The company does have to maintain materials and supplies to provide this service, and it reports this number on its balance sheet, so we will use this number to calculate inventory ratios, since it is similar to inventory in the traditional sense. As one might expect, this is not a significant investment amount for CP ($173 million in 2018). Conceptually, the **inventory turnover ratio** is calculated as the cost of sales divided by inventory, because when a widget is sold, its financial cost moves from inventory (INV) and is expensed through cost of sales. This ratio is shown in Equation 4.18.

**inventory turnover ratio**  the cost of sales (or sales) divided by inventory

$$\boxed{\text{Inventory turnover} = \frac{COS}{INV}} \qquad [4.18]$$

For CP in 2018,

$$\text{Inventory turnover} = \frac{COS}{INV} = \frac{\$2,717}{\$173} = 15.7052$$

For some firms, the data on cost of sales (or cost of goods sold) is not reliable. This is because of accounting differences in how such items as factory overhead are treated.[14] In addition, publicly available ratios and industry ratios are frequently calculated using revenue due to the difficulty of determining cost of goods sold, which is often not separated out on corporate income statements. As a result, the cost of sales is regularly replaced by revenues in the inventory turnover ratio, as shown in Equation 4.19.

$$\boxed{\text{Inventory turnover} = \frac{Rev}{INV}} \qquad [4.19]$$

When we calculate CP's 2018 inventory turnover ratio using this equation, we get

$$\text{Inventory turnover} = \frac{Rev}{INV} = \frac{\$7,316}{\$173} = 42.2890$$

Notice the large difference in the inventory turnover ratio figures, depending on which version of the two equations is used. This difference makes it clear why we have stressed the importance of determining precisely how a ratio is calculated (i.e., so we can compare "apples with apples"). Just as we did with the receivables turnover ratio, it is common to invert the inventory turnover ratio and call it the **average days revenues in inventory (ADRI)**, as shown in Equation 4.20.

**average days revenues in inventory (ADRI)**  inventory divided by average daily revenues

$$\boxed{ADRI = \frac{INV}{ADR} = \text{Inventory turnover}} \qquad [4.20]$$

For CP in 2018,

$$ADRI = \frac{INV}{ADR} = \frac{\$173}{(\$7,316/365)} = 8.6311$$

Notice that this equals 365 divided by the inventory turnover ratio of 42.2890. So in 2018, CP had 8.6 days of revenues tied up in materials and supplies (inventory) and 40.7 days in receivables.

The final productivity ratio is the **fixed asset turnover ratio**, calculated as revenues divided by net fixed assets (NFA), which is simply the depreciated value of the fixed assets, as shown in Equation 4.21.

**fixed asset turnover ratio**  revenues divided by net fixed assets

$$\boxed{\text{Fixed asset turnover} = \frac{Rev}{NFA}} \qquad [4.21]$$

---

[14]Also, in the case of CP, the COS is not very meaningful, as discussed in the previous section.

**TABLE 4.6** Canadian Pacific, Canadian National, and U.S. Industry Average Productivity Ratios

| | Canadian Pacific | | | Canadian National | | | U.S. Industry Average | | |
|---|---|---|---|---|---|---|---|---|---|
| | 2018 | 2017 | 2016 | 2018 | 2017 | 2016 | 2018 | 2017 | 2016 |
| TA turnover | 0.3442 | 0.3255 | 0.3242 | 0.3475 | 0.3466 | 0.3024 | 0.3453 | 0.3274 | 0.3180 |
| Receivables turnover | 8.9767 | 9.5400 | 10.5448 | 12.2506 | 13.2530 | 13.7566 | 12.1647 | 12.3451 | 12.7052 |
| ACP | 40.6609 | 38.2600 | 34.6142 | 29.7945 | 27.5409 | 26.5329 | 30.0974 | 29.9096 | 29.6134 |
| Inventory (materials and supplies) turnover (using sales) | 42.2890 | 43.1184 | 33.8696 | 25.7110 | 30.7571 | 33.1600 | 44.2338 | 35.5172 | 31.1610 |
| ADRI | 8.6311 | 8.4651 | 10.7766 | 14.1963 | 11.8672 | 11.0072 | 8.7641 | 10.8177 | 12.0105 |
| FA turnover | 0.3972 | 0.3852 | 0.3734 | 0.3791 | 0.3814 | 0.3566 | 0.3949 | 0.3729 | 0.3611 |

For CP in 2018,

$$\text{Fixed asset turnover} = \frac{\text{Rev}}{\text{NFA}} = \frac{\$7,316}{\$18,418} = 0.3972$$

As firms depreciate their assets, the fixed asset turnover ratio automatically increases, so many analysts also look at the fixed asset turnover ratio by using gross assets, which is the undepreciated cost of the fixed assets (i.e., without any depreciation deducted). CP had fixed assets with an initial cost in 2018 of $26,382 million, but had accumulated depreciation of $7,964 million. So its fixed assets are approximately 30 percent depreciated (i.e., $7,964/$26,382 = 0.3019).

In **Table 4.6**, we provide some context for CP's 2018 ratios as calculated earlier by reporting its historical ratios, as well as those for CN and the U.S. industry average.

There are several things to note from Table 4.6. First, all four of CP's turnover ratios were fairly steady throughout the three-year period. The receivables and inventory turnover ratios are not particularly important for any of these companies, since they all maintain relatively low levels of receivables and materials and supplies (inventories), consistent with the capital-intensive nature of their businesses. CP had similar fixed asset and total turnover ratios to those of both CN and the U.S. industry averages.

---

### Concept Review Questions

1. What information can be gained by examining a firm's receivables turnover, inventory turnover, and fixed asset turnover ratios?
2. Why is it common to estimate the ACP by using total revenues rather than credit sales, and to estimate inventory turnover by using revenues rather than cost of sales?

---

## 4.6 | Liquidity Ratios

### LEARNING OBJECTIVE 4.6
Calculate, interpret, and evaluate the key ratios relating to financial liquidity.

As we discussed previously, DuPont analysis shows that, together, the leverage, efficiency, and productivity ratios help explain a firm's good or poor performance in terms of ROE. However, some financial statement users have a different interest when examining financial statements. Banks, for example, and suppliers shipping to CP on credit, want to know whether a firm has the means to pay off its debts. This leads to a focus on the liquidity of the company. As mentioned in Chapter 3, **liquidity** refers to how easily something can be converted into cash.

The focus in analyzing the liquidity of the company is on the overall liquidity of a firm's assets and on the available assets to meet current liabilities. In terms of overall liquidity, we look at the ratio of current assets (CA) to total assets (TA). This is referred to as the **working capital ratio** because current assets are often called **working capital**.[15] This is defined in Equation 4.22.

**liquidity**   the ease with which something can be converted into cash

**working capital ratio**   current assets divided by total assets

**working capital**   current assets

$$\text{Working capital ratio} = \frac{\text{CA}}{\text{TA}} \qquad [4.22]$$

For CP in 2018,

$$\text{Working capital ratio} = \frac{\text{CA}}{\text{TA}} = \frac{\$1,117}{\$21,254} = 0.0526$$

For CP, this ratio indicates that its assets are not extremely liquid, with only 5.3 percent supposedly converting to cash within a year. Overall, CP consists of larger amounts of net fixed assets and smaller amounts of current assets. So how liquid are these current assets?

One of the most important liquidity ratios is the **current ratio**, also called the bankers' ratio, which is estimated as current assets divided by current liabilities (CL), as shown in Equation 4.23.

**current ratio**   also called the "bankers' ratio"; current assets divided by current liabilities

$$\text{Current ratio} = \frac{\text{CA}}{\text{CL}} \qquad [4.23]$$

For CP in 2018,

$$\text{Current ratio} = \frac{\text{CA}}{\text{CL}} = \frac{\$1,117}{\$1,955} = 0.5714$$

CP has \$0.57 in current assets for every dollar in current liabilities. This ratio is important for bankers because bank loans are normally short term and included in current liabilities. So a current ratio of 0.57 means that CP does not have enough assets that will be soon converted to cash and may be available to help pay off a bank loan. This is probably not a critical ratio, given the low percentage of current assets and current liabilities associated with CP's operations. However, if a bank has to seize assets or force a firm to liquidate assets, this is a sign that some of the firm's assets are probably not worth much. In particular, the inventory of a bankrupt or failing firm is normally not worth its book value, while it is unlikely a creditor could ever recover any funds from prepaid expenses. For this reason, banks also look at the **quick ratio** or **acid test ratio**, which is cash (C) plus marketable securities (MS) plus accounts receivable (AR) divided by current liabilities, as shown in Equation 4.24.[16]

**quick ratio** or **acid test ratio**   cash plus marketable securities plus accounts receivable divided by current liabilities

$$\text{Quick ratio} = \frac{\text{C} + \text{MS} + \text{AR}}{\text{CL}} \qquad [4.24]$$

For CP in 2018,

$$\text{Quick ratio} = \frac{(\text{C} + \text{MS} + \text{AR})}{\text{CL}} = \frac{(\$61 + \$815)}{\$1,955} = 0.4481$$

For CP in 2018, the quick ratio is less than 1, which indicates the company could not pay off all its current liabilities from its "quick" (i.e., most liquid) assets. **Table 4.7** contains

**TABLE 4.7**   **Canadian Pacific, Canadian National, and U.S. Industry Average Liquidity Ratios**

|  | Canadian Pacific | | | Canadian National | | | U.S. Industry Average | | |
|---|---|---|---|---|---|---|---|---|---|
|  | 2018 | 2017 | 2016 | 2018 | 2017 | 2016 | 2018 | 2017 | 2016 |
| Current ratio | 0.5714 | 0.6421 | 0.7491 | 0.7794 | 0.5498 | 0.7003 | 0.9860 | 0.9575 | 1.0622 |
| Quick ratio | 0.4481 | 0.5166 | 0.5605 | 0.5509 | 0.3859 | 0.5143 | 0.7676 | 0.7018 | 0.8285 |

---

[15]Some people refer to working capital as current assets minus current liabilities, which we would refer to as "net working capital."

[16]Sometimes the quick ratio is calculated as current assets minus inventory divided by current liabilities, which would include prepaid expenses.

the current and quick ratios for CP and CN, as well as the U.S. industry average for 2016–18. CP's current ratios declined over the period and were lower than those for CN in 2018 and well below the U.S. industry average in 2018 of 0.9860. CP's 2018 quick ratio was below CN's, while its quick ratios were well below those of the U.S. industry average for all three years. Overall, CP seems to display lower than average liquidity, although it is likely not a huge area of concern, as discussed previously.

Before we proceed to the next section, we will elaborate on the concept of adjusting book values to realizable values in the event of bankruptcy. We introduced this concept when we treated inventory as worthless when calculating the quick ratio, which is an extreme example of asset adjustment. The objective is really to estimate a realizable value in the event of liquidation.

Finance in the News 4.2 discusses the importance of estimating the liquidation value of a company from an investing perspective, as advocated by legendary investing guru Benjamin Graham (Warren Buffett's mentor). The article discusses the rationale underlying the purchase of stocks in companies that are trading for less than their liquidation value.

While Graham suggests that the liquidation value of assets "will vary according to their character," he does provide some general guidelines, which can be adjusted according to the specific situation. He suggests valuing cash at 100 percent of its book value, because it is cash. Accounts receivable are valued at 75 to 90 percent, with an average of 80 percent; inventory between 50 and 75 percent, with an average of 66.6 percent; and fixed assets between 1 and 50 percent, with an approximate average of 15 percent. Liabilities should be valued at 100 percent, since this is the amount due.

---

## 4.2 Finance in the News    About Liquidation Value Investing

Liquidation value investing is the purchase of securities at a discount to the value of the securities in a liquidation.

The rationale for such an investment is straightforward. In the 1934 edition of *Security Analysis*, Benjamin Graham argued that the phenomenon of a stock selling persistently below its liquidation value was "fundamentally illogical." In Graham's opinion, it meant:

1. The stock was too cheap, and therefore offered an attractive opportunity for purchase and an attractive area for security analysis; and

2. Management was pursuing a mistaken policy and should take corrective action, "if not voluntarily, then under pressure from the stockholders."

Graham understood why these sort of stocks—also known as "net-net", "net-quick" or "net current asset value" stocks—traded at a discount to liquidation value:

"Common stocks in this category almost always have an unsatisfactory trend of earnings."

. . .

Graham then considered why investors should even contemplate liquidating values when companies were not going to liquidate, responding:

"The stockholders do not have it in their power to make a business profitable, but they do have it in their power to liquidate it. At bottom it is not a theoretical question at all; the issue is both very practical and very pressing.

. . .

"In its simplest terms the question comes down to this: Are these managements wrong or is the market wrong? Are these low prices merely the product of unreasoning fear, or do they convey a stern warning to liquidate while there is yet time?"

### How to determine a company's liquidation value

In *Security Analysis*, Graham wrote that, in determining the liquidation value, the current-asset value generally provides a rough indication:

"A company's balance sheet does not convey exact information as to its value in liquidation, but it does supply clues or hints which may prove useful. The first rule in calculating liquidating value is that the liabilities are real but the assets are of questionable value. This means that all true liabilities shown on the books must be deducted at their face amount. The value to be ascribed to the assets however, will vary according to their character."

Graham then provided the following guide for determining the value of various types of assets in a liquidation:

- Cash assets (including securities at market) – 100%

- Receivables (less usual reserves) – between 75% to 90% with an average of 80%. Graham noted that retail installment accounts should be valued for liquidation at a lower rate, between 30% to 60% with an average of about 50%

- Inventories (at lower of cost or market) – between 50% to 75% with an average of 66.6%

- Fixed and miscellaneous assets (real estate, buildings, machinery, equipment, nonmarketable investments, intangibles etc.) – between 1% to 50% with an approximate average of 15%.

**Source:** Excerpted from Carlisle, Tobias, "About Liquidation Value Investing." Greenbackd.com, December 1, 2008. Available at http://greenbackd.com/2008/12/01/about-liquidation-value-investing. Reprinted by permission.

Several things are important in this simple approach. First, the discounts from book value increase as the liquidity of the asset deteriorates; for example, receivables are worth 80 percent; inventories, 66.6 percent; and fixed assets, 15 percent. This occurs because a bank seizing the receivables has to wait only 30 or 60 days for customers to pay their bills. In contrast, the inventory of a failed firm is often not worth much, while plant and equipment often entail significant costs in physically removing them from one location and transporting them to another. The true liquidation value could deviate significantly from the figure calculated, and in order to value a company that is on the brink of liquidation, one would have to go through the assets in more detail. For example, 80 percent is slightly higher than the more commonly used percentages of 70 to 75 percent for collecting on receivables; however, any of these figures could be high depending on the quality and age of the receivables. Similarly, valuing inventory even at 50 percent (which is the commonly used percentage) might be too high, especially if a lot of it is in the form of work in progress and/or obsolete inventory. On the other hand, it is possible that fixed assets might sell for their book value or more and not 15 percent, depending on the market value of real estate in the company's market—remember that fixed assets are carried at historical cost less depreciation.

While the liquidation value is a useful figure, as is the book value, the "market" value could be, and often is, much higher. This is because company market value is based on the company's value as a going concern; for profitable companies, the value of the assets in use is significantly more than their value to someone else. This leads to the final set of ratios that analysts often consider, which includes valuation ratios. These summarize how the market values the firm's operations.

---

### Concept Review Questions

1. What type of financial statement user will be most interested in a firm's liquidity ratios?
2. What useful information do we obtain from a firm's working capital, current, and quick ratios?
3. Why might bankers focus more on the quick ratio than on the current ratio?

---

## 4.7 | Valuation Ratios

---

**LEARNING OBJECTIVE 4.7**

Calculate, interpret, and evaluate the key ratios relating to the valuation of a company.

---

We will discuss common share valuation in Chapter 7, but at this stage we introduce some of the standard ratios that people look at to understand the relative valuation of a company.

Some ratios that are useful in assessing a firm's relative value include earnings per share (EPS), which we discussed in Chapter 3, and the **equity book value per share (BVPS)**, which is the ending shareholders' equity (SE) divided by the ending number of shares outstanding, as shown in Equation 4.25.

**equity book value per share (BVPS)**  shareholders' equity divided by the number of shares outstanding

$$BVPS = \frac{SE}{\text{Number of shares}} \qquad [4.25]$$

For CP in 2018,

$$BVPS = \frac{SE}{\text{Number of shares}} = \frac{\$6,636}{140.5} = \$47.23$$

Usually, reporters of financial information will adjust the previous per-share values to reflect any changes in the number of shares outstanding.

**dividend yield** the dividend per share divided by the share price

In terms of valuation, one of the most basic ratios an analyst can look at is a company's **dividend yield**, which is the current dividend per share (DPS) divided by the current share price (P), as shown in Equation 4.26.

$$\text{Dividend yield} = \frac{\text{DPS}}{\text{P}}$$ [4.26]

For CP, the 2018 DPS was $2.5125, so at its year-end share price of $242.24, we obtain the following:

$$\text{Dividend yield} = \frac{\text{DPS}}{\text{P}} = \frac{\$2.5125}{\$242.24} = 0.0104 \text{ or } 1.04\%$$

A dividend yield of 1.04 percent is quite low. Equation 4.26 tells us that a low dividend yield can be caused by low dividend payouts or high share prices or both. Because investors are concerned about the firm's ability to sustain its dividend payments, one ratio that is useful to assess this ability is the **dividend payout ratio**, which is the DPS divided by the EPS, as shown in Equation 4.27.

**dividend payout ratio** the dividend per share divided by the earnings per share

$$\text{Dividend payout} = \frac{\text{DPS}}{\text{EPS}}$$ [4.27]

We will use the basic EPS in this equation. For CP in 2018 that was $13.65, so we obtain the following:

$$\text{Dividend payout} = \frac{\text{DPS}}{\text{EPS}} = \frac{\$2.5125}{\$13.65} = 0.1841$$

This ratio implies that, during 2018, CP paid out 18.41 percent of its earnings as dividends.

We would expect this from a capital-intensive business, such as CP, which invests regularly in long-term assets. This dividend payout ratio allows the company to reinvest about 82 percent of each dollar earned back into the company.

**price-earnings (P/E) ratio** the share price divided by the earnings per share

One of the most important and widely followed value ratios is the **price-earnings (P/E) ratio**, which is estimated as the share price (P) divided by the EPS, as shown in Equation 4.28.

$$\text{P/E} = \frac{\text{P}}{\text{EPS}}$$ [4.28]

For CP in 2018,

$$\text{P/E} = \frac{\text{P}}{\text{EPS}} = \frac{\$242.24}{\$13.65} = 17.75$$

This means that investors were willing to pay $17.75 for $1 of CP's 2018 earnings. The higher the ratio, the more investors will pay and vice versa. We will discuss the determinants of P/E ratios at some length in Chapter 7 but will note here that P/E ratios increase when share prices increase or when EPS declines. Usually, analysts focus on prices, which are reflected in the numerator of the P/E, and some would argue that a company's shares become too expensive when its P/E ratio gets too high. Conversely, others might argue that a high P/E ratio is warranted because they expect substantial growth in the company's future earnings or because they feel that the company's shares represent a relatively low-risk investment. In either event, from the firm's point of view, higher P/E ratios are a good thing, because they suggest that the markets have confidence in the firm, all else being equal. Remember that, in Chapter 2, we suggested the goal of the firm is to maximize shareholder wealth, which is reflected in share price.

The P/E ratio estimated earlier is based on the "trailing," or previous year's, EPS and is sometimes called the trailing P/E ratio. However, CP's fiscal year runs until the end of December, so at the time of writing this EPS was about three months old. The analysts following CP and making recommendations to investors estimated its 2019 fiscal EPS figure at $16.50. When we estimate the P/E ratio based on the current price and a forecast or expected EPS (EEPS) figure, we refer to it as the **forward P/E ratio**, as shown in Equation 4.29.

**forward P/E ratio** share price divided by the expected earnings per share

$$\text{Forward P/E} = \frac{\text{P}}{\text{EEPS}}$$ [4.29]

The analyst "consensus" EPS estimate for CP in 2019 was $16.50, while its 2018 year-end share price was $242.24, which gives us the following forward P/E ratio:

$$\text{Forward P/E} = \frac{P}{EEPS} = \frac{\$242.24}{\$16.50} = 14.68$$

Security analysts who recommend companies tend to use forward P/E ratios because they normally make shares look cheaper (i.e., as long as EPS continues to increase).

A forward P/E ratio of 14.68 means that if an investor held the stock for 14.7 years and the EPS stayed at the estimated 2019 value, the investor would get back in profits the $242.24 paid for the stock. In this sense, the P/E ratio is a simple example of a payback period, which will be discussed in Chapter 13. The higher the P/E ratio, the longer shareholders have to wait to recover the cost of their investment in future profits. Generally, low P/E shares are regarded as value stocks, since the payback period is shorter and there is less emphasis on any growth in the forecast EPS. In contrast, high P/E shares are generally regarded as *growth* stocks, because investors are relying more heavily on future growth in the EPS.

The P/E ratio and dividend yield are useful value indicators for many firms. However, P/E ratios are meaningless when EPS is negative or very low, while dividend yields will equal zero for firms that do not pay dividends. In such cases, analysts look for other ratios that provide an indication of a firm's relative value, and many relative value ratios exist. One commonly used ratio is the **market-to-book (M/B) ratio**, which is defined as the market price per share (P) divided by the book value per share (BVPS), as shown in Equation 4.30.

**market-to-book (M/B) ratio**
the market price per share divided by the book value per share

$$M/B = \frac{P}{BVPS} \qquad [4.30]$$

Using the 2018 book value and year-end price for CP,

$$M/B = \frac{P}{BVPS} = \frac{\$242.24}{\$47.23} = 5.1289$$

This ratio indicates that every dollar invested by the shareholders in CP was worth $5.13 as of the end of December 2018. A dollar invested in CP's operations is worth $5.13 in part because of the company's ROE of 29.40 percent. This ROE is attractive, and much better than what investors can get elsewhere, so they have bid up the share price to well above its book value.

Finally, another valuation ratio that is often considered is the **EBITDA multiple**, which is calculated as the **total enterprise value (TEV)** divided by earnings before interest, taxes, depreciation, and amortization (EBITDA), which is shown in Equation 4.31.

**EBITDA multiple**  the total enterprise value divided by earnings before interest, taxes, depreciation, and amortization

**total enterprise value (TEV)** equity market value plus the market value of the firm's debt

$$\text{EBITDA multiple} = \frac{TEV}{EBITDA} \qquad [4.31]$$

The total enterprise value is an estimate of the total market value of the firm, which equals the equity market value plus the market value of the firm's debt. This is the market value of what we called "invested capital" when we looked at the firm's financial statements. For CP, its December 2018 equity market value, at a $242.24 share price with 140.5 million shares outstanding, was $34,035 million. Usually, it is reasonable to assume that the book value of debt provides a sufficient approximation of its market value, although this will not always be the case.[17] We will make this assumption for CP's debt in 2018. Therefore, we add the amount of its total debt outstanding of $8,696 million (as calculated earlier) to the market value of its equity and estimate its total enterprise value at $42,731 million. Dividing this by the company's 2018 EBITDA of $3,737 million (calculated as CP's 2018 EBIT of $3,041 million + its depreciation and amortization of $696 million), we obtain the following:

$$\text{EBITDA multiple} = \frac{TEV}{EBITDA} = \frac{\$42,731}{\$3,737} = 11.43$$

This ratio is of particular interest when a firm is considering the takeover or purchase of another firm, since it values the whole firm and not just the common equity. It also recognizes that the firm can always issue or buy back common equity and debt.

---

[17]We will elaborate in Chapter 6 on why this assumption may not be reasonable.

**TABLE 4.8** Canadian Pacific, Canadian National, and U.S. Industry Average Valuation Ratios

| | Canadian Pacific | | | Canadian National | | | U.S. Industry Average | | |
|---|---|---|---|---|---|---|---|---|---|
| | 2018 | 2017 | 2016 | 2018 | 2017 | 2016 | 2018 | 2017 | 2016 |
| Dividend yield | 0.0104 | 0.0088 | 0.0093 | 0.0175 | 0.0156 | 0.0156 | 0.0180 | 0.0162 | 0.0210 |
| Dividend payout | 0.1841 | 0.1730 | 0.1680 | 0.2280 | 0.3160 | 0.3170 | 0.1500 | 0.4003 | 0.4257 |
| P/E | 17.75 | 18.70 | 19.00 | 13.00 | 20.30 | 20.00 | 8.30 | 24.97 | 20.27 |
| M/B | 5.13 | 6.00 | 6.00 | 4.20 | 5.10 | 4.60 | 3.57 | 4.40 | 3.20 |

In Table 4.8, we can see that CP's 2018 dividend yield of 1.04 percent is slightly above its 2017 value of 0.88 percent and is very low. CP's dividend yield is about 60 percent of CN's 2018 yield of 1.75 percent, and is even further below the 2018 U.S. industry average of 1.80 percent. The lower ratio for CP relative to both CN and the U.S. industry average is consistent with CP's dividend payout ratio of 18.4 percent in 2018, which is lower than CN's payout of 22.8 percent, but above the 2018 U.S. industry average of 15.0 (though the U.S. average was above 40 percent in both 2016 and 2017). This makes the numerator portion of this ratio lower for CP. In addition, CP's 2018 P/E ratio of 17.75 is well above the 13.0 figure for CN and the 8.3 U.S. average—this implies the figure for the CP denominator of the dividend yield ratio will be relatively higher. CP's M/B ratio decreased from 6.0 in 2016 and 2017 to 5.13 during 2018, but remained well above the figures for both CN (4.20) and the U.S. industry average (3.57).

Overall, our analysis of the valuation ratios provided in Table 4.8 suggests that, based on the P/E ratio, dividend yield, and M/B ratios, CP is valued higher than both CN and comparable U.S. railways.

## Summing up Valuation Ratios

Overall, what do we make of CP as a potential investment? Our financial analysis indicates that it has improved its operations dramatically and currently possesses high operating margins and good turnover, so it is very profitable. These strengths are reflected in CP's stock price, which is over five times its book value per share and is consistent with its high P/E ratio and EBITDA multiple.

### Concept Review Questions

1. What useful information do we obtain from the dividend yield, P/E ratio, M/B ratio, and EBITDA multiple?
2. Why are P/E ratios and dividend yields often not useful indicators of value?
3. Why is it so difficult to assess whether a firm is properly valued?

## 4.8 | Financial Forecasting

### LEARNING OBJECTIVE 4.8

Explain how to prepare financial forecasts using the percentage of sales method.

To do a reasonable job of financial forecasting, we first must complete a comprehensive financial analysis in order to develop a good understanding of the relationships in the firm's financial statements. Financial forecasting is a critical job for the firm, its financial advisors, and its external analysts. The firm cannot decide how to finance itself until it first assesses the nature of the financing need to determine whether funds are required in the short or long run, whether the financing needs will grow through time, whether the financing need arises from a problem that is self-correcting, and so on. The firm's financial advisors also must consider the firm's needs when recommending a financial strategy, just as the bank must consider these when structuring a loan or credit facility. Finally, equity investors must consider the firm's financing needs when buying the company's shares, because the last thing they want is to invest in a company only to find that it has to raise more money.

# The Percentage of Sales Method

The most important input in financial forecasting is an accurate sales forecast, because sales growth drives a firm's financing requirements. As a result, financial forecasting requires input from most of the divisional managers of the firm but particularly the marketing managers. This will become evident when we consider the most basic forecasting technique: the **percentage of sales method**. We will first consider a stylized example and then return to our study of CP.

The percentage of sales method involves the following steps:

**percentage of sales method** a method of financial forecasting that uses a fixed percentage of sales from the previous period to determine amounts in a future period

1. Determine which financial policy variables you are interested in.

2. Set all the non-financial policy variables as a percentage of sales.

3. Extrapolate the balance sheet based on a percentage of sales.

4. Estimate future retained earnings.

5. Modify and iterate until the forecast makes sense.

## A Naïve Forecast

Financial policy variables are the variables that the treasurer is concerned with. For example, the treasurer could be concerned with common equity (whether the firm has to issue equity or not), long-term funds (equity plus long-term debt), or the firm's total external financing requirement. To illustrate, we will assume that the treasurer is interested in total **external financing requirements (EFR)**. Let's look at a simple balance sheet for a hypothetical firm (Table 4.9) to see what this means.

**external financing requirements (EFR)** the money a firm has to raise by using equity or debt or both

This firm has total assets of $150 that have been financed with $80 of common equity, $40 of long-term debt, and $20 of short-term debt. Taken together, these are referred to as invested capital, because both the common shareholders and the bank and long-term debt investors have made a decision to invest in the firm. In contrast, the accruals and payables are referred to as **spontaneous liabilities** because as long as the firm is in business (i.e., a going concern), it will naturally generate payables and accruals: suppliers will ship goods on credit, and workers will work and collect their wages at the end of the month. In this sense, when we generate a five-year financial forecast, we assume these accounts will automatically increase with sales, and only the financial policy variables will initially be kept constant.[18]

**spontaneous liabilities** accruals and payables that arise during the normal course of business

**TABLE 4.9   Balance Sheet ($)**

| | | | |
|---|---|---|---|
| Cash | 5 | Accruals | 5 |
| Securities | 10 | Payables | 5 |
| Receivables | 10 | Bank debt | 20 |
| Inventory | 25 | Current liabilities | 30 |
| Current assets | 50 | Long-term debt | 40 |
| Net fixed assets | 100 | Common equity | 80 |
| **Total assets** | **150** | **Total liabilities and equity** | **150** |

[18]This is not to say that these amounts are ignored: some financially constrained firms will decide to delay paying bills in order to meet their financial targets. This means that payables will increase more than proportionally with sales. We will discuss this in Chapter 24.

**TABLE 4.10   Initial Forecast**

| | Base Case | % of Total Sales | 10% Sales Increase in Year 1 | 10% Sales Increase in Year 2 | 10% Sales Increase in Year 3 |
|---|---|---|---|---|---|
| Sales | $120 | | $132 | $145 | $160 |
| Cash | 5 | 4.2 | 5.5 | 6.1 | 6.7 |
| Marketable securities | 10 | 8.3 | 11 | 12.1 | 13.3 |
| Accounts receivable | 10 | 8.3 | 11 | 12.1 | 13.3 |
| Inventory | 25 | 20.8 | 27.5 | 30.3 | 33.3 |
| Net fixed assets | 100 | 83.3 | 110 | 121 | 133 |
| **Total assets** | **150** | **125** | **165** | **181.6** | **199.6** |
| Accruals | 5 | 4.2 | 5.5 | 6.1 | 6.7 |
| Accounts payable | 5 | 4.2 | 5.5 | 6.1 | 6.7 |
| Short-term debt | 20 | 16.7 | 20 | 20 | 20 |
| Long-term debt | 40 | 33.3 | 40 | 40 | 40 |
| Equity | 80 | 66.7 | 80 | 80 | 80 |
| **Total liabilities and equity** | **150** | **125** | **151** | **152.2** | **153.4** |
| Cumulative EFR | | | 14 | 29.4 | 46.2 |

*PERCENTAGES OF SALES (bracket spanning Cash through Accounts payable rows)*

The next step is to convert the non-policy variables to a percentage of sales. For the sake of our example, we will assume that sales are $120 and that the percentages that result from this sales level are reasonable for the future. In practice, we would look at the ratios over the previous five years or so, factor in current business conditions for the firm (e.g., new orders), and assess what values would be reasonable going forward.

The third step is to extrapolate the balance sheet based on the sales forecast by using these percentages of sales. For our purposes, we will assume that sales are forecast to increase by 10 percent a year. The result is the naïve initial forecast shown in **Table 4.10**.

The top line is the sales forecast, with sales going from the current level of $120 to $132 one year out, and then to $145, and finally to $160. Then we express all the asset accounts and the spontaneous liabilities as a percentage of sales, because these are the non-policy variables and are extrapolated based on the sales forecast. Take cash, for example: it is $5 or 4.2 percent of the $120 sales level, so based on a 10-percent sales growth forecast, it increases by 10 percent to $5.5, $6.1, and $6.7. The values of the other assets are also increased by 10 percent per year, resulting in a forecast value of $199.60 for total assets.

On the liability side, as discussed, we assume that spontaneous liabilities increase at the rate of sales, so we get a forecasted value of $13.40. Subtracting this figure from the total assets forecast of $199.60, we get the required invested capital figure of $186.20. However, recall that we assumed no change in the amount of invested capital, leaving only $140 in invested capital, which suggests a shortfall of $46.20. This shortfall is the balance sheet plug, which we have labelled as the EFR.[19] Notice that this is a cumulative not an annual requirement—that is, the firm needs to raise $46.20 in total financing over the next three years.

## Some Common Adjustments

The forecast derived in Table 4.10 is extremely naïve or simple. For one thing, it ignores any new equity that the firm will generate simply by retaining some of its future earnings. For another, it assumes that the existing debt will still be there in three years. In practice, some of it may need to be refinanced, or the bank may refuse to renew the short-term loans. However,

---

[19]Remember, the balance sheet has to balance.

| **TABLE 4.11** | Income Statement ($) |
| --- | --- |
| Sales | 120 |
| Gross operating profit | 48 |
| Fixed costs | 31 |
| EBIT | 17 |
| Interest | 5 |
| Taxes (50%) | 6 |
| Net income | 6 |
| Dividends | 3 |

we'll assume that all the debt can be renewed and focus on the retained earnings. To do this, we need to look at the firm's income statement (**Table 4.11**).

**Retained Earnings**   If Table 4.11 looks familiar, it's because it is the example we used before when looking at efficiency ratios, where the firm has a cost structure of 60-percent variable costs and fixed costs of $31. So at the current sales level of $120, the firm has EBIT of $17, from which it subtracts $5 in interest on the $60 of debt and pays 50-percent income taxes or $6. As a result, it has net income of $6 and a net profit margin of 5 percent. However, it pays out 50 percent of its earnings as dividends, so only $3 is retained within the firm. What is important is that the firm's retained earnings as a percentage of sales are its net profit margin, multiplied by one minus the dividend payout, which equals 2.5 percent (i.e., 5% × 0.5) in this example.

If we use this information to revise our simple initial forecast, we add 2.5 percent of sales each year to retained earnings, which leaves us with our first revision to our naïve forecast, depicted in **Table 4.12**.

The only difference between this revision and the initial forecast is that we have taken into account the future retained earnings of 2.5 percent per dollar of sales, which has reduced the EFR by $10.90. However, this forecast is still relatively naïve and does not make use of skills in financial analysis. We can improve on this naïve forecast. To do this, we will go through all the non-financial policy assumptions to see whether we can improve on them.

| **TABLE 4.12** | **First Revision of Forecast** | | | | |
| --- | --- | --- | --- | --- | --- |
| | Base Case | % of Total Sales | 10% Sales Increase in Year 1 | 10% Sales Increase in Year 2 | 10% Sales Increase in Year 3 |
| Sales | $120 | | $132 | $145 | $160 |
| Cash | 5 | 4.2 | 5.5 | 6.1 | 6.7 |
| Marketable securities | 10 | 8.3 | 11 | 12.1 | 13.3 |
| Accounts receivable | 10 | 8.3 | 11 | 12.1 | 13.3 |
| Inventory | 25 | 20.8 | 27.5 | 30.3 | 33.3 |
| Net fixed assets | 100 | 83.3 | 110 | 121 | 133 |
| **Total assets** | **150** | **125** | **165** | **181.6** | **199.6** |
| Accruals | 5 | 4.2 | 5.5 | 6.1 | 6.7 |
| Accounts payable | 5 | 4.2 | 5.5 | 6.1 | 6.7 |
| Short-term debt | 20 | 16.7 | 20 | 20 | 20 |
| Long-term debt | 40 | 33.3 | 40 | 40 | 40 |
| Equity | 80 | 66.7 | 83.3 | 86.9 | 90.9 |
| **Total liabilities and equity** | **150** | **125** | **154.3** | **159.1** | **164.3** |
| Cumulative EFR | | | 10.7 | 22.5 | 35.3 |

**Cash**   We have to recognize that the percentage of sales method automatically imposes a very strict relationship between the assets and sales. For example, when we assume that cash is 4.2 percent of sales, we assume that it will remain so whether sales are $10 or $1,000. Graphically, we are forcing the relationship between cash and sales to be a straight line going through the origin. A more reasonable assumption would be that there are economies of scale to managing cash and that the marginal impact of sales growth is less than the 4.2 percent of the average percentage of sales. For example, the true relationship at a sales level of $120 might be $2 plus 2.5 percent of sales so that the marginal impact of sales growth is only 2.5 percent of sales. **Figure 4.2** depicts the differences in the cash forecasts that arise by changing this assumption.

How cash varies with sales can be determined by statistically analyzing previous sales levels and cash balances. A linear relationship, as graphed in Figure 4.2, can be estimated with or without a constant by using an ordinary least squares (OLS) linear regression. This regression can be done in Excel or by using various other statistical packages. For our forecast, we assume that the treasurer has done this analysis and is satisfied that, over the three-year horizon, operations can be managed from existing cash balances and no further investment is required. Cash will be held constant at $5.

**Accounts Receivable and Inventory**   We will temporarily skip marketable securities and consider accounts receivable. Is it reasonable to assume they are a strict percentage of sales? In this case, it may be. Previously, when considering the investment in accounts receivable, we showed that the number of days of sales in receivables, or the ACP, gave essentially the same information as the receivables turnover ratio. As long as the firm maintains the same credit policy and the same mix between credit and cash sales, and the economy doesn't crash, then assuming a constant percentage of sales is reasonable. However, if the firm anticipates changing its credit policy and granting more lenient credit terms, then the percentage of sales tied up in receivables will increase, as it will if the proportion of credit to cash sales increases. Both of these events might happen in an economic downturn, where the firm might use more lenient credit to maintain its level of sales. Understanding the macroeconomic environment that generates the sales forecast will help the treasurer refine the percentage of sales tied up in receivables. For our purposes, we will assume that no slowdown is expected during the forecast period and that estimating receivables at 8.3 percent of sales is reasonable.

We treat inventory in a similar manner to receivables. As long as the inventory turnover ratio is expected to be constant, inventory will increase in line with sales. However, the same qualifications apply in terms of the macroeconomic environment. If a downturn is anticipated, then the firm might plan to increase the level of inventory in order to bolster sales by offering immediate delivery. In contrast, the firm might believe that it can reduce inventory, either because some of it is obsolete or because it plans to adopt new inventory management systems, such as "just-in-time" inventory planning. However, consistent with our treatment of receivables, we assume that using a constant percentage of sales is reasonable.

**FIGURE 4.2**   **Cash Forecast**

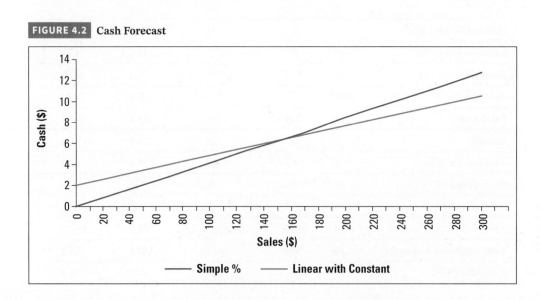

**Fixed Assets**  The next asset item is net fixed assets. Here, the reasonableness of assuming a constant percentage of sales largely depends on whether the firm is a single-plant or multi-plant firm. In a single-plant firm, assuming that a constant percentage of sales will be tied up in net fixed plant and equipment tends to be unreasonable; investment in plant and equipment usually lasts many years, and the firm does not replace a part of it each year. Instead, investment in plant and equipment is "lumpy." The firm will build its plant and equipment, and then each year the plant and equipment will reduce in value as the firm records depreciation. After a certain number of years, major refurbishment and replacement is needed, and the cycle begins again. For multi-plant firms, this effect gets smoothed out because the process is occurring over large numbers of plants.

**Marketable Securities**  This brings us back to the question of why firms hold marketable securities. Generally, firms do not create value by investing in marketable securities; they hold marketable securities as a temporary resting place for cash until it can be used. Suppose that the treasurer talks to the controller and realizes that the $10 in marketable securities is needed to fund a plant expansion next year, after which there will be no further capital expenditures over the forecast horizon. In this case, it makes no sense to extrapolate marketable securities into the future. Further, after the plant and equipment are expanded, the value of plant and equipment will decline in the future as they are depreciated. So we'll assume that the firm depreciates the plant and equipment by $10 per year, but in the first year it spends the $10 in marketable securities to maintain the plant and equipment at $100.

**Spontaneous Liabilities**  The final items to consider are the spontaneous liabilities. These act very much like accounts receivable, because the major item is accounts payable. As long as the firm does not anticipate changing its payment policy, its payables will increase in line with sales, so assuming that payables will remain a constant percentage of sales is reasonable.

## Second Revision of the Forecast

Making the adjustments discussed previously, we get the second revision to the forecast, which is shown in **Table 4.13**.

**TABLE 4.13**  **Second Revision of Forecast**

| | Base Case | % of Total Sales | 10% Sales Increase in Year 1 | 10% Sales Increase in Year 2 | 10% Sales Increase in Year 3 |
|---|---|---|---|---|---|
| Sales | $120 | | $132 | $145 | $160 |
| Cash | 5 | 4.2 | 5 | 5 | 5 |
| Marketable securities | 10 | 8.3 | 0 | 0 | 0 |
| Accounts receivable | 10 | 8.3 | 11 | 12.1 | 13.3 |
| Inventory | 25 | 20.8 | 27.5 | 30.3 | 33.3 |
| Net fixed assets | 100 | 83.3 | 100 | 90 | 80 |
| **Total assets** | **150** | **125** | **143.5** | **137.4** | **131.6** |
| Accruals | 5 | 4.2 | 5.5 | 6.1 | 6.7 |
| Accounts payable | 5 | 4.2 | 5.5 | 6.1 | 6.7 |
| Short-term debt | 20 | 16.7 | 20 | 20 | 20 |
| Long-term debt | 40 | 33.3 | 40 | 40 | 40 |
| Equity | 80 | 66.7 | 83.3 | 86.9 | 90.9 |
| **Total liabilities and equity** | **150** | **125** | **154.3** | **159.1** | **164.3** |
| Cumulative EFR | | | −10.8 | −21.7 | −32.7 |

**TABLE 4.14** Profit Margin and Sales

| Sales | $120 | $132 | $145 | $160 |
|---|---|---|---|---|
| Gross margin (40%) | 48 | 53 | 58 | 64 |
| Fixed costs | 31 | 31 | 31 | 31 |
| Interest | 5 | 5 | 5 | 5 |
| Tax | 6 | 8.5 | 11 | 14 |
| Net income | 6 | 8.5 | 11 | 14 |
| Net profit margin | 5% | 6.4% | 7.6% | 8.8% |

This revision has profoundly different implications for the treasurer. Before, the firm had an external financing requirement; now it will be able to repay some financing obligations because the EFR is negative. The reasons for this are that the firm no longer needs the increase in cash or the marketable securities and, more important, the plant and equipment don't need new money spent on them during the forecast period.

## Net Profit Margins

The next step is to consider changes in the net profit margin. Previously, we assumed that the net profit margin remained the same even when sales changed. However, if the 10-percent sales growth forecast is due to a recovery from a recession, then the firm may be able to achieve this growth without adding to its fixed costs. In this case, the net profit margin may also increase, if the firm's fixed costs are indeed fixed. Table 4.14 reports the income statements that arise if we maintain gross profits at 40 percent of sales but maintain fixed costs at $31.

Notice that the profit margin increases dramatically from 5 percent to 8.8 percent over the four-year period. This is the typical "recovery from recession" pattern, in which the firm lowers fixed costs during a recession, through restructuring and cost-cutting, so that the immediate impact of a recovery causes greatly improved profit margins.

## Dividend Payments

Finally, as we will discuss in Chapter 22, firms usually do not follow a constant dividend payout policy; they tend to cautiously increase dividends in line with sustainable earnings. We'll assume that the treasurer expects the dividend to stay at $3 for the next three years. This means that retained earnings will increase much more quickly than net income will. If this higher level of retained earnings is added to our forecast, we get the final forecast, as shown in Table 4.15.

The upshot of this final revision is that the surplus is even greater, and the treasurer has to develop a plan for managing these funds, rather than arranging for the firm to raise money. This is quite a different scenario indeed![20]

In considering how we changed the simple percentage of sales forecast, we have obviously exaggerated certain effects. For example, fixed costs are only fixed in the sense that they do not vary with sales. However, they still tend to increase over time as a result of wage increases and the general tendency to hire more staff as the firm's profits increase. Likewise, it would be difficult for the firm to maintain the dividend at $3 as profits and cash start to pile up. Alternative assumptions about the macroeconomic environment could soon cause the surplus to become a deficit. For example, if a slowdown is forecast, then a stable or declining sales forecast could cause the profit margin to contract while requiring more receivables and inventory as a percentage of sales. However, this is not the point of the exercise, because many different scenarios can be envisioned. What we wanted to demonstrate is how the simple percentage of sales forecasting method, when allied with basic skills in financial analysis, can produce an effective forecast. However, if it is employed "blindly," it may provide misleading results.

---

[20]Note that some "sophisticated" financial planning models build in a further refinement so that, as debt changes, so too do the firm's interest charges and net profit margin. This can be done quite easily in Excel by simultaneously solving for all values. However, we find that this extension generally adds little to the usefulness of financial planning, particularly now that interest rates are so low.

**TABLE 4.15** **Final Revision of Forecast**

| | Base Case | % of Total Sales | 10% Sales Increase in Year 1 | 10% Sales Increase in Year 2 | 10% Sales Increase in Year 3 |
|---|---|---|---|---|---|
| Sales | $120 | | $132 | $145 | $160 |
| Cash | 5 | 4.2 | 5 | 5 | 5 |
| Marketable securities | 10 | 8.3 | 0 | 0 | 0 |
| Accounts receivable | 10 | 8.3 | 11 | 12.1 | 13.3 |
| Inventory | 25 | 20.8 | 27.5 | 30.3 | 33.3 |
| Net fixed assets | 100 | 83.3 | 100 | 90 | 80 |
| **Total assets** | **150** | **125** | **143.5** | **137.4** | **131.6** |
| Accruals | 5 | 4.2 | 5.5 | 6.1 | 6.7 |
| Accounts payable | 5 | 4.2 | 5.5 | 6.1 | 6.7 |
| Short-term debt | 20 | 16.7 | 20 | 20 | 20 |
| Long-term debt | 40 | 33.3 | 40 | 40 | 40 |
| Equity | 80 | 66.7 | 85.5 | 93.5 | 104.5 |
| **Total liabilities and equity** | **150** | **125** | **156.5** | **165.7** | **177.9** |
| Cumulative EFR | | | −13 | −28.3 | −46.3 |

Moreover, even though the percentage of sales forecasting method can be improved for short-term forecasts, it is very accurate for multi-plant firms over longer periods of time, which brings us to simple formula forecasting techniques.[21]

---

### Concept Review Questions

1. Why is the sales forecast the most critical component of financial forecasting?
2. Describe the basic percentage of sales approach to financial forecasting. What is the main underlying premise of this forecasting approach?
3. What are some of the major limitations of the percentage of sales approach, and how may they be overcome?

---

## 4.9 Formula Forecasting

### LEARNING OBJECTIVE 4.9

Explain how external financing requirements are related to sales growth, profitability, dividend payouts, and sustainable growth rates.

Let's return to the simple percentage of sales forecasting method, as this works very well for longer periods and for multi-plant firms. From the initial forecast, total assets in our example

---

[21]In fact, to get a detailed picture of cash flow needs throughout the year for a firm with seasonal sales, a cash flow forecast is needed, using a detailed cash budget. This is discussed in Chapter 23. The percentage of sales method allows you to forecast more permanent financing required to support projected sales growth, but throughout the year, actual financing requirements may be considerably greater. This effect may be further complicated by the firm's choice of fiscal year end.

were 125 percent of sales, and spontaneous liabilities were 8.4 percent, so invested capital was the balance of 116.6 percent. As we discussed previously, when we subtract spontaneous liabilities from total assets, we get the firm's invested capital, or net assets, as a percentage of sales. We will denote this as $a$, which represents the treasurer's financial policy variable, because it is the total invested capital requirement of the firm as a percentage of sales.

According to the assumptions of the percentage of sales method, if the firm doesn't grow, there is no need for additional net assets. This is because the firm will not need to provide additional credit to customers (accounts receivable) or inventory to meet demand, and the firm's fixed assets should be able to continue to produce enough to meet demand. Consequently, the current level of invested capital is sufficient for the firm. The corollary is that positive EFR mainly arises as a result of sales growth. We represent this sales growth as $g$, so if current sales are $S$, next period's sales growth is $S \times g$, and the incremental capital required is $a \times S \times g$. In our previous example, current sales were $120, and the forecast sales growth rate was 10 percent, so incremental sales were expected to be $12. With the net asset requirement of 116.6 percent of sales, the firm will acquire additional invested capital of $14.

From this additional invested capital, we need to subtract the forecast retained earnings. As we noted before, this is the net profit margin multiplied by one minus the dividend payout. We represent the net profit margin as $PM$, and we denote one minus the payout ratio as $b$, which is commonly referred to as the **retention (or plowback) ratio**. Therefore, we can express the forecast retained earnings as $b \times PM \times (1 + g) \times S$. In our example, with current sales of $120, the forecast sales $[(1 + g) \times S]$ are $132, using a sales growth rate of 10 percent. In this case, the forecast retained earnings are 2.5 percent of $132 or $3.30, since we are assuming a 5-percent net profit margin ($PM$) and a retention ratio ($b$) of 50 percent. The EFR of $10.70 is then exactly what we calculated in the first revision of our percentage of sales forecast in Table 4.12.

Algebraically, we can represent this EFR as shown in Equation 4.32.

**retention (or plowback) ratio**   one minus the payout ratio

$$EFR = a \times S \times g - b \times PM \times (1 + g) \times S \qquad [4.32]$$

This is the invested capital requirement minus the forecast retained earnings. The advantage of the algebraic formulation is that it focuses on the key drivers of the EFR, which are the sales growth rate, the invested capital requirement, and the amount of earnings retained by the firm.

The EFR in our example can also be expressed as a linear function of the sales growth rate ($g$). We can see this more easily by dividing both sides of Equation 4.32 by the current sales level and rearranging, as shown in Equation 4.33.

$$\frac{EFR}{S} = -b \times PM + (a - b \times PM)g \qquad [4.33]$$

This line can be graphed with $EFR/S$ along the vertical ($y$) axis, and with $g$ along the horizontal ($x$) axis, as shown in **Figure 4.3**.

**FIGURE 4.3**   **External Financing Requirements**

This is an important graph. It tells us that for negative and low forecast sales growth rates, EFR is zero or even negative (i.e., cash is freed up). The reason for this is twofold: first, the firm generates profits from its sales, some of which ($b \times PM$) are retained within the firm; second, it also liberates some of its investment in accounts receivable and inventory, which both decline as sales fall. At this point, it is important to remember that this is the forecast growth rate. If the firm plans for positive sales growth, and then sales decline, this often results in more receivables and inventory than planned and generates a positive EFR. In fact, many firms run into severe financing problems when sales decline dramatically and they are not able to cut production quickly enough, so they just produce for inventory.

The graph indicates a basic principle in finance, which is that declining and low-growth firms tend to be cash cows, in that they generate cash. Notice from Equation 4.33 that at a zero growth rate, the firm does not need any new invested capital, so the EFR equals the forecast earnings retained within the business. Further, notice that the coefficient of growth is positive as long as $a > (b \times PM)$, which will almost always be the case. This means that the EFR increases as sales growth increases, all else being equal. In our example, $a > (b \times PM)$ because the sales growth causes the firm to increase its net assets by $a$, which in our example is 116.6 percent, and this is only partially offset by the retained earnings percentage of sales, which in our example is 2.5 percent. The result is that the sales growth generates an external financing need and problems for the treasurer. This is the norm—as sales grow, firms require external financing to support these sales, no matter how profitable they are.

Finance professors like linear relationships, such as those discussed here, because they generate a line that crosses the horizontal axis. This is very important, because it measures a break-even point. We have already discussed the break-even point, which is the sales level at which the firm covers its fixed costs. However, there is also a sales growth rate at which the firm neither generates nor needs financing—that is, it breaks even in the financing sense. This is the point in Figure 4.3 at which the line crosses the horizontal axis, which we call the **sustainable growth rate (g\*).**[22] We can find this point by setting *EFR/S* to zero in Equation 4.33 and solving for *g*, which leaves us with Equation 4.34.

**sustainable growth rate (g\*)** the sales growth rate at which the firm neither generates nor needs financing—that is, it breaks even in terms of financing

$$g^* = \frac{b \times PM}{(a - b \times PM)} \qquad [4.34]$$

For our example, we have the following:

$$g^* = \frac{b \times PM}{(a - b \times PM)} = \frac{0.5 \times 0.05}{(1.166 - 0.5 \times 0.05)} = 0.0219$$

Sales for the firm in our example can grow at 2.19 percent per year before the firm needs external financing. The fact that sales are forecast to grow at 10 percent generates the EFR in the first revision of our percentage of sales forecast.

If sales for the firm in our example do in fact grow at 10 percent per year and exceed the sustainable growth rate, then one of two things has to happen. Either the firm has to raise external funds or the parameters in our equation have to change. The parameters can be changed by increasing the net profit margin, decreasing the dividend payout rate, or decreasing the net investment in assets. In fact, these are the factors that we altered in our forecast revisions in section 4.8. By knowing the sustainable growth rate, as well as the target growth rate given by the marketing people, the treasurer gains valuable information about the nature of the financing problem facing the firm in the future—the rest of the effort is working out the details.

## Concept Review Questions

1. What four variables have a direct impact on a firm's need for external financing?
2. What is the nature of the relationship between EFR and the four variables described in this section?
3. Explain what the sustainable growth rate is and why it is important.

---

[22]See Higgins, Robert, "Sustainable Growth under Inflation." *Financial Management* 10 (Autumn 1981), pp. 36–40.

<table>
<tr><td>4.10</td><td></td></tr>
</table>

# 4.10 CP's External Financing Requirements

> **LEARNING OBJECTIVE 4.10**
> Apply financial forecasting to a real company.

There are some useful lessons to be learned by repeating the forecasting exercise using CP. We will keep the forecast as simple as possible, and make assumptions that are as realistic as possible. For this purpose, we begin by expressing CP's 2016–18 balance sheet accounts as a percentage of sales, which is shown in Table 4.16.

**TABLE 4.16** Canadian Pacific's Balance Sheet Accounts as a Percentage of Sales

| Assets | % of Sales (2016) | % of Sales (2017) | % of Sales (2018) | Average (2016–2018) | Use |
|---|---|---|---|---|---|
| **Current assets** | | | | | |
| Cash and cash equivalents | 0.0263 | 0.0516 | 0.0083 | 0.0287 | average |
| Accounts receivable, net | 0.0948 | 0.1048 | 0.1114 | 0.1037 | average |
| Materials and supplies | 0.0295 | 0.0232 | 0.0236 | 0.0255 | average |
| Deferred income taxes | 0.0000 | 0.0000 | 0.0000 | 0.0000 | average |
| Other current assets | 0.0112 | 0.0148 | 0.0093 | 0.0118 | average |
| **Total current assets** | **0.1619** | **0.1944** | **0.1527** | **0.1697** | sum |
| Investments | 0.0311 | 0.0278 | 0.0277 | 0.0289 | average |
| Properties | 2.6780 | 2.5963 | 2.5175 | 2.5972 | average |
| Goodwill and intangible assets | 0.0324 | 0.0285 | 0.0276 | 0.0295 | 2018 figure |
| Pension assets | 0.1717 | 0.2147 | 0.1699 | 0.1854 | 2018 figure |
| Other assets | 0.0091 | 0.0105 | 0.0097 | 0.0098 | 2018 figure |
| **Total assets** | **3.0842** | **3.0722** | **2.9051** | **3.0205** | sum |
| **Liabilities** | | | | | |
| Accounts payable and accrued liabilities | 0.2121 | 0.1889 | 0.1981 | 0.1997 | average |
| Long-term debt maturing within one year | 0.0040 | 0.1138 | 0.0692 | 0.0623 | 2018 figure |
| **Total current liabilities** | **0.2161** | **0.3027** | **0.2672** | **0.2620** | sum |
| Pension and other benefit liabilities | 0.1178 | 0.1143 | 0.0981 | 0.1101 | 2018 figure |
| Other long-term liabilities | 0.0456 | 0.0352 | 0.0324 | 0.0377 | 2018 figure |
| Long-term debt | 1.3894 | 1.1311 | 1.1195 | 1.2133 | 2018 figure |
| Deferred income taxes | 0.5730 | 0.5067 | 0.4809 | 0.5202 | 2018 figure |
| **Total liabilities** | **2.3419** | **2.0900** | **1.9981** | **2.1434** | sum |
| **Shareholders' equity** | | | | | |
| Share capital | 0.3212 | 0.3100 | 0.2736 | 0.3016 | 2018 figure |
| Additional paid-in capital | 0.0083 | 0.0066 | 0.0057 | 0.0069 | 2018 figure |
| Accumulated other comprehensive loss | −0.2887 | −0.2656 | −0.2793 | −0.2779 | 2018 figure |
| Retained earnings | 0.7014 | 0.9312 | 0.9069 | 0.8465 | 2018 figure + (NI − Div) |
| **Total shareholders' equity** | **0.7423** | **0.9821** | **0.9071** | **0.8772** | sum |
| **Total liabilities and shareholders' equity** | **3.0842** | **3.0722** | **2.9051** | **3.0205** | sum |

For most of the items, the percentages are similar for 2016, 2017, and 2018. This implies that using the percentage of sales forecasting approach is reasonable. The only notable exception is that long-term debt maturing within one year changed substantially through the years.

Table 4.16 also includes an additional column entitled "Use," which shows the assumption we will use to construct our forecast. You will note that we have simply used the 2016–18 average percentage of sales figures to forecast several balance sheet items, which simplifies our forecasting process considerably. We also used 2018 figures for several items that have no necessary close relationship with sales on an annual basis. For example, we use the 2018 figures for goodwill and intangible assets, pension assets, other assets, long-term debt maturing within a year, all long-term liabilities, and all shareholders' equity accounts except for retained earnings. These seem to be reasonable assumptions, since we see there has been little change in, for example, the long-term liabilities items. In addition, this is a useful assumption for forecasting purposes because long-term debt represents one of two major sources for external financing that CP might use to meet external financing requirements (EFR), with equity issues being another possibility.

The only other account that is not estimated as a direct percentage of sales is the retained earnings account, which we estimate using the procedures described in the preceding two sections. In particular, we have derived an equation that helps us to determine how retained earnings will increase in the future, based on forecasted sales growth, profit margins, and retention rates. We will use the 2016–18 average sales growth rate of 3.21 percent for CP to estimate future sales figures. This is conservative as sales decreased by 7.15 percent in 2016, grew by 5.17 percent in 2017, and grew by 11.63 percent in 2018. We use the 2018 operating profit margin for CP to estimate operating profits. We use the 2018 figure rather than a period average because it seems more representative, and it is very close to the 2016 and 2017 margins in any case.[23] We also use the 2018 dividend payout ratio of 18.41 percent to estimate future dividend payments and contributions to retained earnings. All of these estimates seem reasonable, for our purposes.

Based on these assumptions, we use a sales growth rate of 3.21 percent to construct our financial forecast for 2019–21, which is shown in **Table 4.17**.

Notice from Table 4.17 that the bottom line is the cumulative EFR. This is –$579 million for 2019, which means CP could actually pay down some debt that year. The projected cumulative EFR declines further to –$1,913 million and then to –$3,301 million in 2020 and 2021 respectively. This means the company could pay down a significant amount of debt during those years, or increase its capital spending, increase its dividend payout, and/or repurchase some more shares, as long as its sales continue to grow and its profit margins remain high.

The fact that CP produced negative EFR positions is hardly surprising if we look at its sustainable growth rate, which we can estimate by using the approach described in section 4.9. In 2018, total assets were 290.51 percent of sales, and spontaneous liabilities (accounts payable and accrued liabilities) were 19.81 percent, so net assets ($a$) were 270.70 percent. To estimate the sustainable growth rate, we also need to estimate the retained earnings percentage of sales, which is the profit margin times the retention rate. We use the 2018 figures for CP, which indicate a retention ratio ($b$) of 0.8216 and a net profit margin ($PM$) of 26.67 percent. By using Equation 4.34, we can estimate CP's sustainable growth rate as the following:

$$g^* = \frac{b \times PM}{(a - b \times PM)} = \frac{0.219121}{2.7070 - 0.219121} = 0.0881 = 8.81\%$$

This is a relatively high sustainable growth rate, reflecting CP's high profitability and relatively high retention rates. In fact, very few firms could grow at this rate without needing significant amounts of external financing. Notice that CP's revenues increased 3.21 percent on average over 2016–18, well below the estimated sustainable growth rate. Thus, it is not surprising that, based on the 3.21-percent sales growth estimate we forecast, CP would require only minimal financing for the next three years.

---

[23]While, for the sake of brevity, we have not reported our pro forma income statements here, we would note that our forecasted net income figures for 2019–21 were $2,241, $2,313, and $2,387 million, respectively. Combining these figures with the assumption that the number of common shares outstanding would remain at 140.5 million shares (the amount outstanding at the end of 2018) resulted in forecasted 2019–21 basic EPS figures of $15.95, $16.46, and $16.99.

**TABLE 4.17** Canadian Pacific Inc. Forecast ($Million)

| | 2019 ProForma | 2020 ProForma | 2021 ProForma |
|---|---|---|---|
| **Assets** | | | |
| **Current assets** | | | |
| Cash and cash equivalents | 217 | 224 | 231 |
| Accounts receivable, net | 783 | 808 | 834 |
| Materials and supplies | 192 | 198 | 205 |
| Deferred income taxes | 0 | 0 | 0 |
| Other current assets | 89 | 92 | 95 |
| **Total current assets** | **1,281** | **1,322** | **1,365** |
| Investments | 218 | 225 | 232 |
| Properties | 19,612 | 20,242 | 20,893 |
| Goodwill and intangible assets | 202 | 202 | 202 |
| Pension asset | 1,243 | 1,243 | 1,243 |
| Other assets | 71 | 71 | 71 |
| **Total assets** | **22,627** | **23,305** | **24,006** |
| **Liabilities** | | | |
| Accounts payable and accrued liabilities | 1,508 | 1,556 | 1,606 |
| Long-term debt maturing within one year | 506 | 506 | 506 |
| **Total current liabilities** | **2,014** | **2,062** | **2,112** |
| Pension and other benefit liabilities | 718 | 718 | 718 |
| Other long-term liabilities | 237 | 237 | 237 |
| Long-term debt | 8,190 | 8,190 | 8,190 |
| Deferred income taxes | 3,518 | 3,518 | 3,518 |
| **Total liabilities** | **14,677** | **14,725** | **14,775** |
| **Shareholders' equity** | | | |
| Share capital | 2,002 | 2,002 | 2,002 |
| Additional paid-in capital | 42 | 42 | 42 |
| Accumulated other comprehensive loss | −2,043 | −2,043 | −2,043 |
| Retained earnings | 8,528 | 10,492 | 12,531 |
| **Total shareholders' equity** | **8,529** | **10,493** | **12,532** |
| **Total liabilities and shareholders' equity** | **23,206** | **25,218** | **27,307** |
| **Cumulative EFR** | **−579** | **−1,913** | **−3,301** |
| Common shares outstanding (assumed) | 140.5 | 140.5 | 140.5 |

## Concept Review Question

1. What is the relationship between the sustainable growth rate, the actual sales growth rate, external financing requirements, and dividend payments?

# Review

## Summary

Almost all corporate finance questions involve an analysis of macroeconomic conditions, followed by a financial analysis of the firm. It is critical to understand the sources of a firm's profitability or lack thereof. The basic analysis is to look at the ROE and then break this out into operating profitability, leverage, efficiency, and productivity ratios, with a look at liquidity ratios to see what the firm's financial reserves are. These same skills in financial analysis are then needed for financial forecasting, for which the external financing requirement is essentially the plug in a forecast balance sheet. All forecasts hinge on a sales forecast. For longer-term forecasts, the sustainable growth rate represents an easy shortcut to estimating the types of financing problems a firm is likely to have.

## Summary of Learning Objectives

### 4.1 Identify the issues to consider in applying consistent financial analysis.

Despite efforts to harmonize accounting standards, important differences in generally accepted accounting principles (GAAP) still persist. An additional complication arises because there are no generally accepted financial ratios. Thus, it is always important, when looking at ratios generated by another party, to examine how they are calculated. Even some of the most basic ratios, such as return on equity (ROE), can vary when calculated by different institutions, even if the input data are the same.

### 4.2 Explain why return on equity is a key financial ratio used to assess a firm's performance.

The return on equity (ROE) ratio is an accounting measure of the return on the owners' investment. It is a very important ratio for financial analysts as it measures overall profitability from the owners' (shareholders') perspective. The DuPont system is a method for analyzing ratios, and it explains changes in ROE. In the DuPont system, ROE is shown to be a function of leverage, margin, and turnover.

### 4.3 Calculate, interpret, and evaluate the key ratios relating to financial leverage.

Leverage ratios measure the amount of borrowing that a company has done (debt) and the ability of the company to pay interest and repay principal on its debts. The calculation and evaluation of leverage ratios are presented in section 4.3.

### 4.4 Calculate, interpret, and evaluate the key ratios relating to financial efficiency.

Efficiency ratios measure margins and profitability. The calculation and evaluation of efficiency ratios are presented in section 4.4.

### 4.5 Calculate, interpret, and evaluate the key ratios relating to financial productivity.

Productivity ratios measure how efficiently a company uses its assets—that is, how much revenue it gets out of its assets. The calculation and evaluation of productivity ratios are presented in section 4.5.

### 4.6 Calculate, interpret, and evaluate the key ratios relating to financial liquidity.

Liquidity ratios reflect net working capital—the amount of short-term assets relative to the amount of short-term liabilities. Liquidity ratios are of particular interest to short-term lenders, who use the short-term assets as collateral. The calculation and evaluation of liquidity ratios are presented in section 4.6.

### 4.7 Calculate, interpret, and evaluate the key ratios relating to the valuation of a company.

Valuation ratios provide insight into whether stock prices are overvalued or undervalued. The calculation and evaluation of valuation ratios are presented in section 4.7.

### 4.8 Explain how to prepare financial forecasts using the percentage of sales method.

Financial forecasts help managers identify cash and capital shortages before they occur. Forecasting is also a critical part of discounted cash flow valuation—a primary tool of investment managers. Financial forecasting is usually performed using the percentage of sales method. Under this method, sales are forecast, and then most financial items are forecast using their historic ratio to sales, making adjustments to items when this assumption is not appropriate.

**4.9 Explain how external financing requirements are related to sales growth, profitability, dividend payouts, and sustainable growth rates.**

Financial forecasting yields a value for external financing requirements (EFR). EFR is the amount of capital (from outside sources) necessary to fund the forecasted increase in sales and the associated increased need for assets like inventory and fixed assets.

**4.10 Apply financial forecasting to a real company.**

See the example using CP in section 4.10.

## Key Terms

## Equations

| Equation | Description | Formula | Page |
|---|---|---|---|
| **[4.1]** | Return on Equity | $\text{ROE} = \dfrac{\text{NI}}{\text{SE}}$ | p. 4-2 |
| **[4.2]** | Return on Assets | $\text{ROA} = \dfrac{\text{NI}}{\text{TA}}$ | p. 4-3 |
| **[4.3]** | Leverage Ratio (Equity Multiplier) | $\text{Leverage} = \dfrac{\text{TA}}{\text{SE}}$ | p. 4-3 |
| **[4.4]** | Net Profit Margin | $\text{Net profit margin} = \dfrac{\text{NI}}{\text{Revenues}}$ | p. 4-4 |
| **[4.5]** | Turnover Ratio | $\text{Turnover ratio} = \dfrac{\text{Revenues}}{\text{TA}}$ | p. 4-4 |
| **[4.6]** | Return on Assets (DuPont) | $\text{ROA} = \dfrac{\text{NI}}{\text{TA}} = \dfrac{\text{NI}}{\text{Revenues}} \times \dfrac{\text{Revenues}}{\text{TA}}$ | p. 4-4 |
| **[4.7]** | Return on Equity (DuPont) | $\text{ROE} = \dfrac{\text{NI}}{\text{SE}} = \dfrac{\text{NI}}{\text{Revenues}} \times \dfrac{\text{Revenues}}{\text{TA}} \times \dfrac{\text{TA}}{\text{SE}}$ <br> $= \text{Net profit margin} \times \text{Turnover ratio} \times \text{Leverage ratio}$ | p. 4-4 |
| **[4.8]** | Debt Ratio | $\text{Debt ratio} = \dfrac{\text{TL}}{\text{TA}}$ | p. 4-7 |
| **[4.9]** | Debt-to-Equity Ratio | $\text{D/E ratio} = \dfrac{\text{D}}{\text{SE}}$ | p. 4-7 |
| **[4.10]** | Times Interest Earned (Coverage Ratio) | $\text{TIE} = \dfrac{\text{EBIT}}{\text{I}}$ | p. 4-7 |
| **[4.11]** | Cash Flow to Debt Ratio | $\text{Cash flow to debt ratio} = \dfrac{\text{CFO}}{\text{D}}$ | p. 4-8 |
| **[4.12]** | Degree of Total Leverage | $\text{DTL} = \dfrac{\text{CM}}{\text{EBT}}$ | p. 4-10 |

*(continued)*

| Equation | Description | Formula | Page |
|---|---|---|---|
| [4.13] | Break-Even Point | $BEP = \dfrac{FC}{CM}$ | p. 4-10 |
| [4.14] | Gross Profit Margin | $\text{Gross profit margin} = \dfrac{Rev - COS}{Rev}$ | p. 4-11 |
| [4.15] | Operating Profit Margin | $\text{Operating margin} = \dfrac{OI}{Rev}$ | p. 4-11 |
| [4.16] | Receivables Turnover | $\text{Receivables turnover} = \dfrac{Rev}{AR}$ | p. 4-12 |
| [4.17] | Average Collection Period | $ACP = \dfrac{AR}{ADR} = \dfrac{365}{\text{Receivables turnover}}$ | p. 4-12 |
| [4.18] | Inventory Turnover Ratio (Using COS) | $\text{Inventory turnover} = \dfrac{COS}{INV}$ | p. 4-13 |
| [4.19] | Inventory Turnover Ratio (Using Revenues) | $\text{Inventory turnover} = \dfrac{Rev}{INV}$ | p. 4-13 |
| [4.20] | Average Days Revenues in Inventory | $ADRI = \dfrac{INV}{ADR} = \text{Inventory turnover}$ | p. 4-13 |
| [4.21] | Fixed Asset Turnover | $\text{Fixed asset turnover} = \dfrac{Rev}{NFA}$ | p. 4-13 |
| [4.22] | Working Capital Ratio | $\text{Working capital ratio} = \dfrac{CA}{TA}$ | p. 4-15 |
| [4.23] | Current Ratio | $\text{Current ratio} = \dfrac{CA}{CL}$ | p. 4-15 |
| [4.24] | Quick (Acid Test) Ratio | $\text{Quick ratio} = \dfrac{C + MS + AR}{CL}$ | p. 4-15 |
| [4.25] | Equity Book Value per Share | $BVPS = \dfrac{SE}{\text{Number of shares}}$ | p. 4-17 |
| [4.26] | Dividend Yield | $\text{Dividend yield} = \dfrac{DPS}{P}$ | p. 4-18 |
| [4.27] | Dividend Payout Ratio | $\text{Dividend payout} = \dfrac{DPS}{EPS}$ | p. 4-18 |
| [4.28] | Price-to-Earnings Ratio (Trailing) | $P/E = \dfrac{P}{EPS}$ | p. 4-18 |
| [4.29] | Price-to-Earnings Ratio (Forward) | $\text{Forward } P/E = \dfrac{P}{EEPS}$ | p. 4-18 |
| [4.30] | Market-to-Book Ratio | $M/B = \dfrac{P}{BVPS}$ | p. 4-19 |
| [4.31] | Earnings before Interest, Taxes, Depreciation, and Amortization (EBITDA) Multiple | $\text{EBITDA multiple} = \dfrac{TEV}{EBITDA}$ | p. 4-19 |
| [4.32] | External Financing Required (EFR) | $EFR = a \times S \times g - b \times PM \times (1 + g) \times S$ | p. 4-28 |
| [4.33] | EFR/Sales | $\dfrac{EFR}{S} = -b \times PM + (a - b \times PM)g$ | p. 4-28 |
| [4.34] | Sustainable Growth Rate | $g^* = \dfrac{b \times PM}{(a - b \times PM)}$ | p. 4-29 |

# Questions and Practice Problems

## Multiple Choice Questions

**1. (LO 4.1)** Which of the following statements about consistent financial analysis is *correct*?

   **a.** Accounting standards are different across countries.

   **b.** If the input data are the same, the ratios for companies across countries are the same.

   **c.** We can directly compare ratios from annual reports of companies across countries.

   **d.** Debt ratio is calculated in the same way by companies across countries.

**2. (LO 4.2)** Which of the following ratios is *not* in the DuPont system?

   **a.** Net profit margin    **c.** Asset turnover

   **b.** Leverage    **d.** Current ratio

**3. (LO 4.2)** Which of the following components of the DuPont system for Hill Inc. is *correct* if sales are $6,500; earnings before tax (EBT) are $3,090; the tax rate is 40 percent; total liabilities are $30,900; and equity is $18,500?

   **a.** Net profit margin = 47.54 percent

   **b.** Asset turnover = 11.81 percent

   **c.** Leverage = 2.67

   **d.** Leverage = 0.53

**4. (LO 4.2)** To increase return on equity (ROE),

  **a.** increase equity, all else being unchanged.

  **b.** decrease debt outstanding, all else being unchanged.

  **c.** decrease corporate tax rate, all else being unchanged.

  **d.** decrease earnings after tax, all else being unchanged.

*Use the following information to answer practice problems 5 to 10.*

### Statement of Financial Position as at December 31, 2022 ($)

| | | | |
|---|---|---|---|
| Cash | 500,000 | Accounts payable | 600,000 |
| Marketable securities | 600,000 | Accrued liabilities | 190,000 |
| | | Wages payable | 250,000 |
| Inventory | 350,000 | Long-term debt | 2,000,000 |
| Equipment | 1,000,000 | Common shares | 2,800,000 |
| Land | 2,500,000 | Retained earnings | 90,000 |
| Patent | 980,000 | Total liabilities and equity | 5,930,000 |
| Total assets | 5,930,000 | | |

### Statement of Comprehensive Income 2022 ($)

| | |
|---|---|
| Sales | 1,290,000 |
| COGS | 380,000 |
| Wages | 200,000 |
| Interest | 150,000 |
| EBT | 560,000 |
| Tax | 224,000 |
| NI | 336,000 |

**5. (LO 4.3)** What is the company's debt ratio?

  **a.** 0.36

  **b.** 0.94

  **c.** 0.55

  **d.** 0.51

**6. (LO 4.3)** Calculate the debt-equity ratio and times interest earned ratio.

  **a.** 3.56; 0.32

  **b.** 0.95; 2.4

  **c.** 0.69; 3.4

  **d.** 0.69; 4.73

**7. (LO 4.4)** What is the company's gross profit and its operating margin? (Use EBIT as operating income.)

  **a.** 71 percent; 55 percent

  **b.** 65 percent; 47 percent

  **c.** 55 percent; 30 percent

  **d.** 70 percent; 49 percent

**8. (LO 4.5)** Which of the following is average days revenues in inventory?

  **a.** 84 days

  **b.** 70 days

  **c.** 66 days

  **d.** 99 days

**9. (LO 4.6)** Which of the following is the working capital ratio?

  **a.** 24.5 percent

  **b.** 18.5 percent

  **c.** 20.4 percent

  **d.** 15.5 percent

**10. (LO 4.3)** Which of the following is invested capital?

  **a.** $5,600,000

  **b.** $2,890,000

  **c.** $4,800,000

  **d.** $4,890,000

**11. (LO 4.3)** A financial ratio that measures the firm's ability to pay its interest obligations is

  **a.** debt ratio.

  **b.** debt-equity ratio.

  **c.** cash flow to debt ratio.

  **d.** times interest earned.

**12. (LO 4.6)** The current ratio is measured as

  **a.** current assets minus current liabilities.

  **b.** current assets divided by current liabilities.

  **c.** cash and cash equivalents divided by current liabilities.

  **d.** current liabilities divided by current assets.

**13. (LO 4.4)** The financial ratio measured as sales minus cost of goods sold, divided by sales, is the

  **a.** gross profit margin.

  **c.** degree of total leverage.

  **b.** break-even point.

  **d.** current ratio.

**14. (LO 4.5)** The average collection period is measured as

  **a.** accounts receivable divided by average daily sales.

  **b.** sales divided by accounts receivable.

  **c.** sales divided by inventory.

  **d.** 365 divided by inventory turnover.

**15. (LO 4.7)** The financial ratio measured as dividend per share divided by the current stock price is the

  **a.** dividend yield.

  **b.** book value per share.

  **c.** dividend payout.

  **d.** price-earnings ratio.

## Practice Problems

*Use the following information to answer the practice problems about Finns' Fridges.*

Finns' Fridges is a company created by twin brothers David and Douglas Finn, who rented small refrigerators to other students in their college dormitory. Use the following statements to answer the questions about Finns' Fridges.

### Statement of Financial Position for Finns' Fridges
### (End of the Year Indicated)

| | Year 1 ($) | Year 2 ($) |
|---|---|---|
| **Assets** | | |
| Cash | 1,150 | 493 |
| Property and equipment (net) | 3,840 | 3,888 |
| Total assets | 4,990 | 4,381 |
| **Liabilities and owners' equity** | | |
| Interest payable | 200 | 160 |
| Tax payable | 177 | 182 |
| Dividends payable | 200 | 210 |
| Long-term debt | 3,200 | 2,400 |
| Total liabilities | 3,777 | 2,952 |
| Common shares | 1,000 | 1,000 |
| Retained earnings | 213 | 429 |
| Total owners' equity | 1,213 | 1,429 |
| Total liabilities and owners' equity | 4,990 | 4,381 |

### Statement of Comprehensive Income for Finns' Fridges
### (For the Full Year Indicated)

| | Year 1 ($) | Year 2 ($) |
|---|---|---|
| Revenues (net of bad debts) | 1,950 | 2,200 |
| Selling and administrative expenses | 0 | 220 |
| Loss (stolen equipment) | 160 | 0 |
| EBITDA | 1,790 | 1,980 |
| Depreciation expense | 1,000 | 1,212 |
| EBIT | 790 | 768 |
| Interest expense | 200 | 160 |
| Earnings before tax | 590 | 608 |
| Tax (30%) | 177 | 182 |
| Net income | 413 | 426 |
| Earnings per share (100 shares) | 4.13 | 4.26 |
| Dividends per share | 2.00 | 2.10 |

## Basic

**16. (LO 4.2)** Find Finns' Fridges' return on equity (ROE) for years 1 and 2, using the owners' equity figure at the end of each year. Did this ratio improve or get worse between year 1 and year 2?

**17. (LO 4.2)** Use the definition of the leverage ratio in the DuPont system to determine if Finns' Fridges has become more or less leveraged between year 1 and year 2.

**18. (LO 4.2)** One key part of ROE in the DuPont system is the return on assets (ROA). Find the ROA for Finns' Fridges for both years and determine if it is increasing or decreasing.

**19. (LO 4.3)** The most recent financial statements for a large Canadian furniture and appliance rental chain show that its debt ratio was 0.256 and its debt-to-equity ratio (D/E) was 0.073. At the end of year 2, was Finns' Fridges more or less leveraged than this major competitor? (Remember to use only the interest-bearing liabilities—that is, long-term debt, when calculating the D/E ratio.)

**20. (LO 4.2)** At the end of 2021, Corine's Candies Inc. had total shareholders' equity of $13.8 million. In 2022, the company had net income of $5.2 million and paid out half this amount in dividends, resulting in shareholders' equity at the end of 2022 of $16.4 million. Use the average amount of shareholders' equity to determine Corine's ROE for 2022.

## Intermediate

**21. (LO 4.4)** The large competitor firm mentioned in practice problem 19 had net operating income of $4.426 million and sales of $30.16 million in its most recent accounting period. Find the operating margin for this competitor. Comment on Finns' Fridges' level of operating efficiency compared to this real-world business.

**22. (LO 4.2)** In the DuPont system, there are two components of ROA. Determine whether efficiency or productivity (or both) is responsible for the increase in ROA for Finns' Fridges from year 1 to year 2.

**23. (LO 4.3)** We can calculate cash flow from operations (CFO) as net income + non-cash expenses + change in working capital ignoring cash. In year 2, the change in working capital for Finns' Fridges was –$25. Find the CFO and use this figure to calculate the cash flow to debt ratio. How many years would it take the company to pay off its entire debt load if it devoted its cash flow to debt repayment?

**24. (LO 4.4)** Find the operating margin for Finns' Fridges for both years (you may assume that the net operating income is equal to the firm's EBIT). Was there an increase or a decrease in the operating margin, and is this a good trend or a bad one?

**25. (LO 4.5)** Calculate the fixed asset turnover for Finns' Fridges for years 1 and 2 (note that net fixed assets correspond to "property and equipment (net)" on the company's statement of financial position). Has the company become more or less productive in terms of generating sales from assets?

**26. (LO 4.6)** At the end of its most recent fiscal period, the large appliance rental company mentioned in practice problem 19 had a working capital ratio of 4.3 percent and a current ratio of 18.2 percent. Calculate these ratios for Finns' Fridges at the end of year 1 and year 2. Is the company more or less liquid than its competitor?

**27. (LO 4.8)** The Finn brothers are planning their third year of operations. As a first step in the process, create a "percentage of sales" statement of financial position for Finns' Fridges as at the end of year 2.

**28. (LO 4.8)**

   **a.** Suppose the Finns believe they can increase revenues to $2,600 in year 3. Use this figure and the percentage of sales

balance sheet (practice problem 27) to forecast the company's balance sheet at the end of year 3. Remember that the "financing" components (long-term debt and total owners' equity) should be left unchanged from the year 2 figures.

   **b.** The forecast balance sheet does not balance! Determine the amount of external financing required by Finns' Fridges based on the initial forecast.

**29. (LO 4.8)** To achieve the target level of revenues in year 3 ($2,600), Finns' Fridges will have to buy some more equipment. This will increase the depreciation expense to $1,422. Selling costs will be the same percentage of sales as in year 2, and the interest expense for the year will be $120. Use this information to determine the amount of net income the company should expect to earn in year 3.

**30. (LO 4.8)** Use the average dividend payout ratio from years 1 and 2, and the forecast net income figure from practice problem 29, to estimate the total amount of dividends that will be paid by the company in year 3.

**31. (LO 4.8)** Suppose that Finns' Fridges actually pays $270 in dividends in year 3. Determine the value of the retained earnings account at the end of year 3 based on the forecast net income calculated in practice problem 29.

**32. (LO 4.8)** The forecast for retained earnings (practice problem 31) changes the year 3 forecast for total liabilities and owners' equity to $4,771. With total assets forecast to be $5,177, determine how much external financing will be required in year 3.

**33. (LO 4.4)** Corine's Candies Inc. registered a gross profit margin of 75 percent on sales of $16 million in 2022. What would the company's income statement show for the cost of goods sold?

**34. (LO 4.7)** The shares of Corine's Candies Inc. are currently trading at $18.20. There are 4 million shares outstanding. The company's 2022 net income was $5.2 million. Find the market value of equity for the company and the P/E ratio of the shares.

**35. (LO 4.7)** Other candy-making firms have an average forward P/E ratio of 12 at this time. With a share price of $18.20, what are the expected 2023 EPS for Corine's Candies if its forward P/E ratio is the same as the industry average?

**36. (LO 4.7)** The managers of Corine's Candies like to use the EBITDA multiple to value the firm. EBITDA was approximately $10 million in 2022. Use the market value of equity from practice problem 34 and a debt value of $20 million to find the total enterprise value (TEV). Next, calculate the EBITDA multiple. Suppose the industry-average EBITDA multiple for candy producers is 8.65. Is the market valuing Corine's Candies Inc. higher or lower than its competitors?

**37. (LO 4.4)** For GG. Co., calculate the degree of total leverage (DTL) and break-even point of sales at which the firm covers all its operating and fixed costs, given the following information: sales are $5,050,000; variable cost is $1,850,000; net income is $685,750; tax rate (T) is 35 percent; and fixed cost is $2,100,000.

**38. (LO 4.4)** Calculate the degree of total leverage (DTL) and break-even point for a company, given the following information: sales are $400,000; variable cost is $130,000; net income is $180,000; tax rate ($T$) is 40 percent; fixed cost is $80,000.

**39. (LO 4.7)** Calculate book value per share, dividend yield, dividend payout, market-to-book ratio, earnings per share, and price-to-earnings ratio given the following information: shareholders' equity is $945,000; number of shares outstanding is 500,000; total dividends are $150,000; market price of each share is $9.50; net income is $433,000.

*Use the following information to answer the practice problems 40 to 53 about Excelsior Inc.*

### Year 2 Statement of Comprehensive Income ($Million)

| | | | |
|---|---|---|---|
| Net sales | 1,850 | Taxable income | 985 |
| Less: Cost of goods sold | 605 | Less: Taxes | 156 |
| Less: Depreciation | 180 | Net income | 829 |
| Earnings before interest and taxes | 1,065 | Addition to retained earnings | 244 |
| Less: Interest paid | 80 | Dividends paid | 585 |

### Year 1 and Year 2 December 31 Statement of Financial Position ($Million)

| | Year 1 | Year 2 | | Year 1 | Year 2 |
|---|---|---|---|---|---|
| Cash | 100 | 112 | Accounts payable | 400 | 350 |
| Accounts receivable | 330 | 234 | Notes payable | 390 | 370 |
| Inventory | 410 | 435 | Subtotal | 790 | 720 |
| Subtotal | 840 | 781 | Long-term debt | 500 | 550 |
| Net fixed assets | 1,556 | 1,888 | Owner's equity | | |
| | | | Common shares | 550 | 599 |
| | | | Retained earnings | 556 | 800 |
| | | | Subtotal | 1,106 | 1,399 |
| Total assets | 2,396 | 2,669 | Total liabilities and equity | 2,396 | 2,669 |

Number of shares = 100 million; share price = $15

**40. (LO 4.2)** Using the DuPont system, what are Excelsior Inc.'s net profit margin, asset turnover, and leverage ratio in year 2?

**41. (LO 4.2)** Use two approaches to determine ROE in year 2. (Hint: one approach is from the definition and the other is to use the DuPont system.)

**42. (LO 4.3)** Determine leverage ratios, including debt ratio and debt-equity ratio, in both years. Has Excelsior Inc. improved on its leverage ratios in year 2?

**43. (LO 4.3)** Determine Excelsior Inc.'s efficiency ratio of times interest earned in year 2.

**44. (LO 4.4)** Determine the company's efficiency ratios including gross profit margin and operating margin in year 2. Explain the differences.

**45. (LO 4.5)** Determine productivity ratios including receivables turnover and average collection period in year 2.

**46. (LO 4.5)** Determine productivity ratios including inventory turnover and average days revenue in inventory in year 2.

**47. (LO 4.5)** Determine net fixed asset turnover in year 2.

**48. (LO 4.6)** Determine liquidity ratios including working capital ratio, current ratio, and quick ratio for year 2. Explain the differences among the ratios.

**49. (LO 4.7)** Determine valuation ratios including book value per share, dividend yield, and dividend payout for year 2.

**50. (LO 4.9)** If Excelsior Inc. keeps the same dividend payout ratio, what are the expected total dividends in year 3 if profits and dividends are expected to grow at 5 percent per year?

**51. (LO 4.7)** Determine the price-earnings ratio, market-to-book ratio, and EBITDA ratio for year 2.

**52. (LO 4.9)** What sales growth rate must Excelsior Inc. achieve if it is to have a cash surplus?

**53. (LO 4.9)** If Excelsior Inc.'s expected sales growth rate is 5 percent, determine the external financing required. Will the corporation have a cash surplus or deficit?

## Challenging

**54. (LO 4.9)** Use the following information to create a revised forecast of the year 3 balance sheet for Finns' Fridges. Cash will increase by the forecast EBITDA amount (see practice problem 29); it will be reduced by $1,050 to purchase new equipment, $552 for year 2 payables, and $800 for debt repayment. The property and equipment (net) account will increase by $1,050 (new fridges purchased) but must be reduced by the $1,422 depreciation expense. Interest and tax payable will reflect the respective expenses on the forecast income statement (again, see practice problem 29). Dividends payable will be $270. Long-term debt will be reduced by $800, and the retained earnings figure is $718. With this revised forecast, determine if any additional external financing is required.

*Use the following information to answer practice problems 55 to 58 about Food Inc. All figures are in ($Million) unless indicated otherwise.*

| | Year 1 | Year 2 |
|---|---|---|
| Total sales | $46,693 | $46,702 |
| Less: Cost of goods sold | 32,537 | 32,913 |
| Gross profit | 14,156 | 13,789 |
| Less: Selling, general, and administrative expenses | 12,233 | 11,295 |
| Earnings before interest and taxes (EBIT) | 1,923 | 2,494 |
| Interest expense | 400 | 524 |
| Income tax expense | 606 | 443 |
| Net income | $ 917 | $ 1,527 |
| Price per share | $ 62.78 | $ 51.48 |
| Shares outstanding (millions) | 379.3 | 397.3 |
| Shareholder's equity | $12,119 | $13,012 |
| Total liabilities and shareholder's equity | $30,153 | $35,106 |

**55. (LO 4.2)** Using the DuPont system, what are Food Inc.'s net profit margin, asset turnover, and leverage ratio in Year 1? Has Food Inc. improved on its net profit margin in Year 2?

**56. (LO 4.2)** Use two approaches to determine ROE in Year 1. (Hint: one approach is from the definition and the other is to use the DuPont system.)

**57. (LO 4.3)** Has Food Inc.'s efficiency ratio of times interest earned improved in Year 2?

**58. (LO 4.7)** Determine the book value per share, market-to-book ratio, and price-earnings ratio for Year 1.

**59. (LO 4.9)** Use the year 2 financial statements for Finns' Fridges to determine the company's sustainable growth rate.

**60. (LO 4.9)** GG Co. shows the following information on its financial statements: interest-bearing debt is $900,000; shareholders' equity (SE) is $2,500,000; sales are $5,050,000; net income is $685,750; dividends are $200,000; and sales growth (g) is 5 percent. Calculate EFR/S and discuss the relationship between dividend payout and EFR. Calculate the sustainable growth rate for GG Co. Discuss the relationship between profit margin and EFR.

**61. (LO 4.9)** Suppose that GG Co. would like to grow its sales by 25 percent, which is greater than its sustainable growth rate (see practice problem 60). If all the other financial information remains unchanged, how much external financing will the company require?

**62. (LO 4.5)** Calculate the receivables turnover, inventory turnover, and average collection period for a firm, given the following accounting data: accounts receivable are $600,000; accounts payable are $305,000; inventory is $550,000; gross profit is $550,000; sales are $950,000. Interpret the receivables turnover, inventory turnover, and the average collection period.

# Time Value of Money

---

**LEARNING OBJECTIVES**

After studying this chapter, you should be able to:

**5.1** Explain the importance of the time value of money and how it is related to an investor's opportunity costs.

**5.2** Define simple interest and explain how it works.

**5.3** Define compound interest and explain how it works.

**5.4** Differentiate between an ordinary annuity and an annuity due, and explain how special constant payment problems can be valued as annuities and, in special cases, as perpetuities.

**5.5** Estimate the present value of growing perpetuities and annuities.

**5.6** Differentiate between quoted rates and effective rates, and explain how quoted rates can be converted to effective rates.

**5.7** Apply annuity formulas to value loans and mortgages, and set up an amortization schedule.

**5.8** Solve a basic retirement problem.

---

This chapter will introduce you to everyday problems, such as taking out a loan, setting up a series of payments, and valuing them. The ideas in this chapter are important for all types of financial problems: determining the payments on a weekly versus a monthly mortgage, buying versus leasing a new car, appropriately valuing a bond or stock, determining whether a company should expand production or abandon a product line, and deciding how much a company should be willing to pay for another company. Although each situation involves unique circumstances that will be covered in subsequent chapters, the basic framework used to evaluate them is the same and relies on material covered in this chapter. It cannot be stated too strongly that grasping the concepts presented in this chapter will be critical to the understanding of security valuation and to making better corporate investment decisions.

## 5.1 | Opportunity Cost

---

**LEARNING OBJECTIVE 5.1**

Explain the importance of the time value of money and how it is related to an investor's opportunity costs.

---

In this chapter, we are concerned with the **time value of money**. As we saw in chapters 1 and 2, the financial system is designed to transfer savings from lenders to borrowers, so that savers have money to spend in the future. To illustrate this concept, we used the example of

**time value of money** the idea that a dollar today is worth more than a dollar in the future

**medium of exchange**
something that can be used to
facilitate transactions

saving while working in order to have money when retired. Money, in this sense, represents our ability to buy goods and services—that is, it operates as a **medium of exchange** and has no value in and of itself. Of course, an investor could simply store the paper currency (tuck it under the mattress, perhaps) and spend it later; a dollar is always worth at least a dollar in the future.[1] However, this option ignores the fact that the saver has other uses for that dollar, which in economics are called the "opportunity costs" or "alternative uses." Opportunity costs, such as investing the dollar to earn a return, are what produce the time value of money.

The opportunity cost of money is the interest rate that would be earned by investing it. For this reason, we also call the interest rate the "price of money." Knowing this rate helps us determine the value of money received at different times. Suppose, for example, a person has three choices: they could receive $20,000 today, $32,000 in five years, or $2,500 per year indefinitely. This choice could, for example, be the payoff from a lottery (though we are certainly not advocating gambling!). Making a choice from these different options requires that we know how to value the dollars received at different times—that is, the winner needs to adjust for the time value of money.

**required rate of return** or
**discount rate**   the market
interest rate ($k$) or the investor's
opportunity cost

To make a decision, the person needs to know what the interest rate is. We will use $k$ as a standard notation throughout the textbook for the market interest rate. We will refer to this market interest rate by several other names later in the textbook, such as the **required rate of return** or **discount rate**. The reason for these different names will become clear later, but in all cases we are looking at the investor's opportunity cost—that is, what they can do with the money being invested. However, first we have to make some basic distinctions in terms of how this interest rate is earned, and we must distinguish between simple interest and compound interest.

---

### Concept Review Questions

1. Why does money have a "time value"?
2. What is an "opportunity cost"?

---

# Simple Interest

---

**LEARNING OBJECTIVE 5.2**
Define simple interest and explain how it works.

---

**simple interest**   interest paid
or received on only the initial
investment (the principal)

**Simple interest** is interest paid or received on only the initial investment (the principal). Although, in practice, simple interest is used for a limited number of applications, we introduce it first to contrast it with compound interest, which is used extensively.

In Example 5.1, the interest earned is $100 every year, regardless of the beginning amount each year, because interest is earned on only the original investment (principal). Interest is *not* earned on the accrued (or earned) interest.

---

[1]This ignores the fact that what we are really concerned about is what that dollar will buy in terms of goods and services—that is, its purchasing power. We discuss this later in the chapter.

---

**EXAMPLE 5.1** | Simple Interest I

Suppose someone invests $1,000 today for a five-year term and receives 10-percent annual simple interest on the investment. How much money would the investor have after five years?

**Solution**

Annual interest = $1,000 × 0.1 = $100 per year

| Year | Beginning Amount | Ending Amount |
|------|------------------|---------------|
| 1 | $1,000 | $1,100 |
| 2 | 1,100 | 1,200 |
| 3 | 1,200 | 1,300 |
| 4 | 1,300 | 1,400 |
| 5 | 1,400 | 1,500 |

---

Because the same amount of interest is earned each year—$100 in the example—we can use Equation 5.1 to find the value of the investment at any point in time.

$$\text{Value (time n)} = P + (n \times P \times k) \qquad [5.1]$$

where $P$ = principal and $n$ = number of periods.

Notice that $P \times k$ = interest. If we apply this equation to Example 5.1, $P = 1,000$, $n = 5$, and $k = 0.1$. The value at the end of year 5 = $1,000 + (5 \times \$1,000 \times 0.1) = \$1,500$. This is the amount shown in the table for Example 5.1 at the end of year 5.

The basic point of simple interest is that in order to determine the future value of an investment, we calculate the annual interest—in this case, $100—multiply this by the number of years of the investment, and add it to the starting principal.

Understanding simple interest helps solve our earlier problem involving the choice between receiving $20,000 today, $32,000 in five years, or $2,500 per year indefinitely. A person offered the choice between $20,000 today and $32,000 in five years can calculate the two annual interest payments. With the same 10-percent interest rate, the annual interest is $20,000 × 0.1 = $2,000 per year. In five years, it would generate $10,000 in interest, meaning that $20,000 today is worth $30,000 in five years. In this case, given the choice between $20,000 today and $32,000 in five years, with 10-percent simple interest, the correct choice is $32,000 in five years, because it is worth more. However, how do we solve the choice between these two options and $2,500 per year forever (indefinitely)?

---

**EXAMPLE 5.2** | Simple Interest II

We'll repeat Example 5.1 but assume that the investment is for 50 years.

**Solution**   Annual interest is still $100 per year ($1,000 × 0.1), so using Equation 5.1 we get

Value in year 50 = $1,000 + (50 × $1,000 × 0.1) = $1,000 + $5,000 = $6,000

---

One way to solve this problem (dealing with forever) is to assume a very long period of time, say 100 years. Receiving $2,500 each year for 100 years produces a future value of $2,500 × 100 = $250,000. We then compare this with investing $20,000 with 10-percent simple interest for 100 years, which has a future value of $20,000 + ($20,000 × 100 × 0.1) = $220,000. In this case, by assuming that "indefinitely" is 100 years, the solution would be to choose the $2,500 investment. However, apart from the fact that since simple interest is rarely offered, it turns out that we are missing something important, particularly when we invest for long periods. If we earn interest on the principal, then what about the interest earned on the subsequent interest payments, since these can be regarded as (smaller) subsequent principal investments?

---

**Concept Review Questions**

1. Explain how simple interest payments are determined.
2. Does simple interest take into account the time value of money? Explain.

---

## 5.3 Compound Interest

---

**LEARNING OBJECTIVE 5.3**

Define compound interest and explain how it works.

---

## Compounding (Computing Future Values)

**compound interest** interest that is earned on the principal amount invested *and* on any accrued interest

**Compound interest** is interest that is earned on the principal amount invested *and* on the future interest payments. Compound interest can result in dramatic growth in the value of an investment over time. This growth is directly related to the length of the period, as well as to the level of return earned, which we will demonstrate shortly. Before we get to that, an example will show how compound interest arrangements work.

---

**EXAMPLE 5.3** | Compound Interest I

Suppose someone invests $1,000 today for a five-year term and receives 10-percent annual *compound* interest. How much would the investor have after five years?

**Solution**   Annual interest is earned on the original $1,000 (principal) *and* on accrued interest.

| Year | Beginning Amount | Interest | Ending Amount |
|------|------------------|----------|---------------|
| 1 | $1,000 | $1,000 × 0.1 = $100 | $1,100 |
| 2 | 1,100 | 1,100 × 0.1 = $110 | 1,210 |
| 3 | 1,210 | 1,210 × 0.1 = $121 | 1,331 |
| 4 | 1,331 | 1,331 × 0.1 = $133.10 | 1,464.10 |
| 5 | 1,464.10 | 1,464.10 × 0.1 = $146.41 | 1,610.51 |

---

Unlike the annual interest for an investment earning simple interest, the amount of compound interest earned increases every year; the interest rate is applied to the *principal plus interest earned*, so the value of the investment increases. As a result, the interest received increases from $100 in year 1, to $146.41 in year 5; the ending amount of $1,610.51 is much higher than the $1,500 earned with simple interest.

To make the process clear, let's look at the first two years of interest using a little algebra. For the first year, everything is the same as the example with simple interest—that is, the ending amount is the starting principal plus the interest, or

$$\$1,000 + (\$1,000 \times 0.1) = \$1,100 = \$1,000 \times (1 + 0.1) \text{ or } PV_0 (1 + k)$$

where $PV_0$ = the present value today (i.e., at time 0). We have factored the $1,000 principal value, so to get the future value, we multiply the principal by 1 plus the market interest rate.

For year 2, the full $1,100 is **reinvested**—that is, we explicitly do not take the $100 of interest and spend it. As a result, we have the following equation:

**reinvest** continue to invest principal *as well as interest* each year

$$\$1,100 + (\$1,100 \times 0.1) = \$1,210 = \$1,100 \times (1 + 0.1) \text{ or } PV_0 (1 + k)^2$$

In this case, $1,100 is invested at the beginning of year 2 and earns the 10-percent interest. The interest earned increases to $110: the $100 interest on the starting principal plus $10 interest earned on the $100 of interest reinvested at the end of the first year. We can again factor the starting value of $1,100 and then factor the $1,000 principal value to get the formula for the future value at the end of year 2. This is the starting principal times 1 plus the interest rate squared. As we increase the period, we get the general formula

$$FV_n = PV_0 (1 + k)^n \qquad [5.2]$$

where $FV_n$ = the future value at time $n$.

Equation 5.2 is the basic compounding equation, and the last term, $(1 + k)^n$, is the **future value interest factor (FVIF)**.

Applying this equation to Example 5.3, we get $FV_5 = \$1,000(1 + 0.1)^5 = \$1,000(1.61051) = \$1,610.51$. This is $110.51 more than for the investment earning simple interest. **Figure 5.1** illustrates what happens with the two types of interest over time. Note that for the first few years the difference is minimal, but over time it gets bigger and bigger.

**future value interest factor (FVIF)** a term that represents the future value of an investment at a given rate of interest and for a stated number of periods: $(1 + k)^n$

Example 5.3 can also be solved using a financial calculator. Although the keystrokes (and variable names) used will vary from one calculator to the next, the basic procedures do not. We will illustrate with one commonly used calculator: the Texas Instruments (TI) BA II Plus.[2]

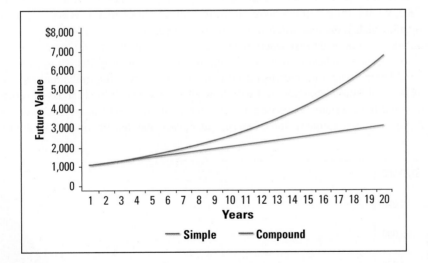

**FIGURE 5.1** **Simple versus Compound Interest at 10 Percent**

---

[2]CFA Institute's calculator policy states that only two types of calculators may be used on chartered financial analyst (CFA) exams. These include the Texas Instruments BA II Plus (including BA II Plus Professional) and the Hewlett Packard 12C (including the HP 12C Platinum, 12C Platinum 25th anniversary edition, 12C 30th anniversary edition, and HP 12C Prestige). See cfainstitute.org.

**EXAMPLE 5.3** | Solution Using a Financial Calculator

Input the following variables:

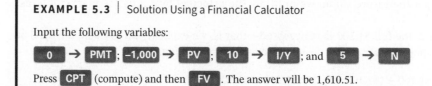

Press CPT (compute) and then FV. The answer will be 1,610.51.

PMT here refers to regular payments and will be discussed in a later section; FV is the future value; I/Y is the period interest rate; and N is the number of periods. The PV is entered with a negative sign on this calculator (this is not the case with all calculators) to reflect the fact that investors must pay money now to get money in the future. Alternatively, we could have left it positive. This would produce a negative sign in front of the FV, which we could simply ignore. We will do this in some of the ensuing applications.

Let us now extend the time horizon for Example 5.3, as we did for the example relating to simple interest.

**EXAMPLE 5.4** | Compound Interest II

Repeat Example 5.3, but assume the investment is for 50 years.

**Solution** Applying Equation 5.2 to this example, we get

$$FV_{50} = \$1,000 \, (1 + 0.1)^{50} = \$1,000 \, (117.39085) = \$117,390.85$$

Investing $1,000 for 50 years at an annual compound interest rate of 10-percent produces $117,390.85. Notice the huge difference between this amount and the future value of the same $1,000 invested for 50 years, but earning simple interest, which was a mere $6,000 ($1,000 + [50 × $100]). You can see the difference that compounding makes over this 50-year span in **Figure 5.2**. What is the difference between the two future values after 50 years? The answer is $111,390.85, which is the total interest-on-interest earned.

You might be tempted to ask whether a 50-year term is realistic. It is for many investments. Consider someone who begins investing for retirement in their early 20s. Those early investments could earn compound returns for 40 years or more before the individual retires. Further, assuming the individual does not withdraw all the savings on the first day of retirement (which would have serious tax consequences), and assuming that this person lives another 20 to 25 years after retirement, some investment dollars may not be touched for more than

**FIGURE 5.2** **Simple versus Compound Interest over 50 Years**

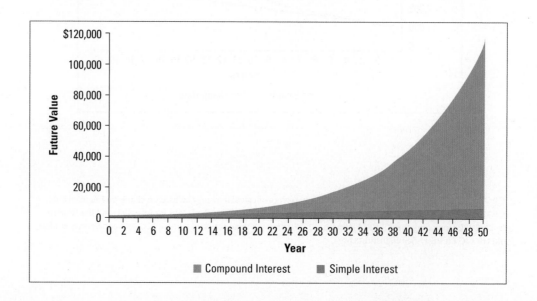

With sky-high prices in Toronto and Vancouver, saving up to buy a house is already tough enough for many Canadians. But stashing those savings into an RRSP can make your first home purchase even harder.

Canadians are justified in thinking of RRSPs as a way to save up for a down payment. There is, after all, something called the RRSP Home Buyer's Plan (HBP), which allows first-time homebuyers to withdraw $25,000 from their RRSP, tax free.

The thing is, there are a few drawbacks to the HBP.

### First, $25,000 isn't a lot of money when you're buying a house

The HPB cap is outdated, argues Ted Rechtshaffen, president of wealth advisory firm TriDelta Financial.

"$25,000 is kind of like a memory of when a can of Coke was 10 cents." Rechtshaffen told Global News.

When you're facing average home prices closing in on $1 million, as many B.C. and Ontario residents do, the maximum HBP withdrawal can feel like a drop in the bucket, even if you join forces with a spouse, partner or friend for a combined $50,000 contribution.

And if you decide to take out money in excess of the HBP cap, you'll have to pay tax on it, warned Rechtshaffen.

### Second, you will need to repay that money

The HBP is a loan: You can take money out today to buy a house, but you will have to eventually pay back all of it to avoid penalties.

Admittedly, the government is pretty generous with its repayment schedule: You have 15 years.

And yet, a growing number of Canadians are defaulting on their HBP loans.

Failure to make RRSP repayments under the HBP program were the driver behind Statistics Canada recording a 30 per cent increase in early RRSP withdrawals between 2000 and 2013.

Taking money out of your RRSP for an HBP loan doesn't count as an early withdrawal if you repay the funds. If you default,

however, you will have to pay tax on whatever portion of the loan you didn't pay back, just like a regular pre-retirement RRSP withdrawal.

### Third, paying back your HBP loan isn't straightforward

In order for money put into your RRSP to count as a repayment of an HBP loan, you have to designate it as such. Otherwise, the Canada Revenue Agency will consider it a regular contribution.

Many Canadians appear to be unaware of the rule, Statistics Canada noted in a recent research paper, as some individuals made RRSP contributions the same year they defaulted on their HBP loans.

If your RRSP contribution happens to be equal or greater than the HBP repayment, there are no tax consequences, as the tax refund you receive offsets the tax applied to your missed repayment. But defaulting on your HBP has always the effect of lowering your RRSP contribution room.

### What to do then?

For many first-time homebuyers, a TFSA can be a better savings vehicle, said Rechtshaffen.

Sure, there isn't a lot of room to save in a TFSA, especially after the Liberal government lowered the maximum contribution room from $10,000 to $5,500 in 2016. It will take some time to build up your savings.

Still, just like in an RRSP, if you invest your TFSA funds, your investments will grow tax free.

And once you do reach your down payment target, you'll be able to take the money out all at once with no tax consequences and no string attached.

50 years. Finance in the News 5.1 discusses the tradeoff that young would-be homeowners may be making by taking part in the Home Buyers' Plan and obtaining no-interest loans today at the expense of lower retirement income down the road.

Table 5.1 provides some evidence regarding the power of compound returns. It shows the future values that would have resulted from investing $1,000 at the beginning of 1938 and leaving that money invested for 81 years (until the end of 2018) in various investment assets.

Compound return represents the average annual growth rate in the value of $1 invested at the start of the period. Compound return thus involves the same reinvestment rate assumption as compound interest rate—that is, all future returns are reinvested. Compound return is also often referred to as the geometric return and differs from the simple average or arithmetic average. We will discuss the difference between the two in detail in Chapter 8. Notice the impressive power of compounding over such a long period: $1,000 invested in Canadian equities would have made you a millionaire in 2012, and invested in U.S. equities, a millionaire times four (easily). However, remember that the cost of this investment is that the $1,000 invested in 1938 would have been locked away and not touched for 81 years, so in all likelihood, whoever invested this money would have left it for their great-grandchildren!

| TABLE 5.1 | Ending Wealth of $1,000 Invested from 1938 to 2018 in Various Asset Classes | |
| --- | --- | --- |
| | **Annual Compound Return (%)** | **Year-End Value, 2018 ($)** |
| Government of Canada treasury bills | 4.53 | 36,184 |
| Government of Canada bonds | 5.76 | 93,333 |
| Canadian stocks | 9.77 | 1,901,852 |
| U.S. stocks | 10.99 | 4,655,775 |

**Source:** Data to 2008 are from the Canadian Institute of Actuaries; data from 2009 to 2018 are from the Statistics Canada CANSIM database and the Canadian Financial Markets Research Centre.

The dramatic difference in ending values results from differences in the rate of return. At a rate of return of 4.53 percent (i.e., the T-bill return), $1,000 would have grown to $36,184, while at 10.99 percent (i.e., the U.S. stock return), it would have grown to $4,655,775—more than 128 times as much. The difference in ending values is significant, even when the differences in returns are small. For example, consider the difference in ending values of nearly $3,000,000 when $1,000 is invested in Canadian stocks at 9.77 percent versus U.S. stocks at 10.99 percent. These data show why finance professionals struggle to increase the returns on their investments even by very small amounts. In fact, it is normal to look at returns down to 1/100 of 1 percent, which is called a **basis point**. Earning just a few basis points more on one investment causes the future value of the portfolio to compound that much faster. Unfortunately, this search for additional returns often leads investors to underestimate the associated risks, which can backfire. For example, during the period leading up to the 2007–8 financial crisis, many investors in search of slightly higher returns purchased securitized structured debt products offered by investment banks over, for example, government bonds. However, instead of earning higher returns, they ended up generating huge losses.

**basis point**   1/100 of 1 percent

Let's return to our two choices of $20,000 today or $32,000 in five years' time, assuming the investor now earns *compound* interest of 10 percent. Using the FVIF formula, we get $FVIF = (1 + k)^5 = (1.1)^5 = 1.61051$. The $20,000 compounds to $32,210. So the better choice is now $20,000 today, because it will grow to more than $32,000 in five years if invested at 10 percent with compound interest. However, we still have a problem comparing either of these single sums with the option of getting $2,500 a year forever. We could compound each of the $2,500 annual payments forward to, say, 100 years in the future, but there are easier ways of doing this, as we will discuss in section 5.4.

## Discounting (Computing Present Values)

So far we have been concerned with finding future values, but there is a problem with comparing future values: there are many of them! We could choose an arbitrary common period to make the comparisons, which solves this problem. The obvious choice is to compare values at the *current* time, so instead of calculating future values, we determine *present values*. This process is also called **discounting**. We will explain it with a simple example, Example 5.5.

**discounting**   finding the present value of a future value by accounting for the time value of money

---

**EXAMPLE 5.5** | Discounting

An investor estimates that she needs $1 million to live comfortably when she retires in 40 years. How much does she have to invest today, assuming a 10-percent interest rate on the investment?

**Solution**   To solve this example, first start with what is already known: the future value formula of Equation 5.2.

$$FV_n = PV_0 (1 + k)^n$$

where FVIF $= (1 + k)^n$. With a starting present value, we multiply by the FVIF to get the future value. This means we can divide the future value by the FVIF to get the present value. Rearranging Equation 5.2 to solve for $PV$ we get

$$PV_0 = \frac{FV_n}{(1+k)^n} = FV_n \times \frac{1}{(1+k)^n} \qquad [5.3]$$

Equation 5.3 is the basic discounting equation, and the last term, $1/(1 + k)^n$, is called the discount factor or **present value interest factor (PVIF)**. Some older textbooks have tables of PVIF and FVIF for various periods and interest rates, although they are simply reciprocals of each other. The use of computers and calculators makes these tables obsolete.

> **present value interest factor (PVIF)** a formula that determines the present value of $1 to be received at some time in the future, $n$, based on a given interest rate, $k$

Let's return to our example. If FV = \$1,000,000; $k = 0.1$; and $n = 40$, we get

$$PV = \$1,000,000 \times 1/(1.1)^{40} = \$1,000,000 \times (1/45.259256)$$
$$= \$1,000,000 \times 0.02209493 = \$22,094.93$$

We illustrate this in a timeline.

An investment of \$22,094.93 today, earning a 10-percent return per year, has a future value of \$1 million in 40 years. With a 10-percent market interest rate, \$22,094.93 today and \$1 million in 40 years' time are worth the same amount, so the two figures are financially equivalent.

We can also solve Example 5.5 using a financial calculator, as shown below.

**EXAMPLE 5.5** | Solution Using a Financial Calculator

Input the following variables:

Press **CPT** and then **PV**. This will give an answer of 22,094.93.

Now you know why we call this process "discounting." If people don't want to pay the full price for something, they ask for a discount or, in other words, they ask for something off the price. In the same way, \$1 million in 40 years is not worth \$1 million today, so you discount, or take something off, to get it to its true value. Discounting future values to find their present value is the same process, except that when we know the market interest rate, we can use Equation 5.3 to calculate the exact true value today.

There are two important points to note from Example 5.5 and Equation 5.3: first, discount factors (the PVIF) are always less than one as long as discount rates are positive (i.e., $k > 0$). This means that future dollars are usually worth less than the same dollars today. However, this is not always the case. In Germany in 2012, six-month treasury bills had an average yield that was slightly negative. Why, you might ask, wouldn't investors simply keep the money in cash? The answer is that the investors in question were major institutions, so going to the local bank to ask for €3.9 billion in ones and twos was not an option![3] Like the German government,

---

[3] In an attempt to reduce money laundering from illicit activity, most countries severely restrict the amount of money that can be withdrawn in cash. As a result, taking money out and "putting it under the bed" is only viable for very small investors.

major financial institutions are now considering imposing fees on deposits rather than paying interest, since the deposited money cannot be lent out to borrowers to earn positive rates of return for the bank.

The second important point is that discount factors are the reciprocals of their corresponding compound factors and vice versa ($PVIF = 1/FVIF$). This means that **the greater the discount rate, the greater the FVIF (and future value) and the smaller the PVIF (and present value), and vice versa.**

This last point has been important in recent years when interest rates have been abnormally low. Consider, for example, the impact of these low interest rates on pension funds, which were discussed briefly in Chapter 1. Pension funds estimate the present value of their future pension payouts to plan members (i.e., their liabilities) based on discounting these future pension payments using current interest rates. As a result of these very low interest rates, the present value of these pension liabilities has increased dramatically. This discount rate effect on the liability side of their funding equation was made worse by negative market returns in the order of 12 percent in the last half of 2018. Fortunately, the first quarter of 2019 saw a complete reversal back to positive returns of 12 percent, but multiple years of low interest rates combined with stagnant investment returns put many defined-benefit pension plans in a significant deficit position, as their assets did not increase as fast as the present value of their liabilities.

## Determining Rates of Return or Holding Periods

When we looked at the discounting problem, we noted that we simply divided through by the FVIF but essentially used the same future value equation. Let's look at this again.

$$FV_n = PV_0 (1 + k)^n$$

We have used this equation to solve for future values (*FV*) and present values (*PV*), but notice that we can solve for two other values: the interest rate (*k*) and the period (*n*). If both the present and future values are known, and we know either the interest rate or the period, we can solve for the last unknown. We illustrate this in Examples 5.6 and 5.7.

---

**EXAMPLE 5.6** | Finding the Rate of Return

Suppose we modify the lottery example used earlier. The "prize" is now a $20,000 investment that has a payoff of $32,000 in five years. We have the present and future values and the period, so we can solve for the interest rate. This is an important interest rate, called the internal rate of return (IRR), because it is the rate of return that is *internal* to the values in the problem. Many problems in finance are IRR problems for which we need to compare the rates of return earned on different investments.

**Solution**

$$FV = \$32,000; \ PV = \$20,000; \ n = 5$$

Using Equation 5.2, we get $\$20,000 = \$32,000/(1 + k)^5$.
We could solve for *k* in the following manner:

$$\$32,000/\$20,000 = 1.6 = (1 + k)^5$$

This is a simple problem, but it is still awkward to solve. One way to solve it is through trial and error, using a simple calculator. Put, say, 1.08 into memory and then enter 1 and press "multiply, memory recall, equals" five times. The result is 1.469. Doing the same thing with 10 percent (1.1) produces 1.6105, so we know that the internal rate of return is in between these two numbers and closer to 10 percent than to 8 percent. All we can then do is iterate to get closer and closer to 1.6. Eventually, we would end up with 9.856 percent. However, this is a laborious and inefficient process. Using a financial calculator makes these types of calculations much simpler, as we illustrate below.

---

**EXAMPLE 5.6** | Solution Using a Financial Calculator

Input the following variables:

| 0 | → | PMT | ; | 32,000 | → | FV | ; | −20,000 | → | PV | ; and | 5 | → | N |

Press **CPT** and then **I/Y** . This will give an answer of 9.856 percent. Notice that either FV or PV needs to be input as a negative number, because to "receive" one cash flow (either today or in the future) you need to "pay" (or invest) either today or in the future.

**EXAMPLE 5.7** | Solving for Time or "Holding" Periods

In this example, we use the same data as before but change the problem to ask how long we have to invest $20,000 at 10 percent to get $32,000.

**Solution**   With our data, we now have to solve the following for $n$:

$$\$32{,}000/\$20{,}000 = 1.6 = (1.1)^n$$

Unfortunately, solving this equation with a simple calculator is even more complicated than the IRR problem was. We could put 1.1 into memory, enter 1, and again press "multiply, memory recall, equals" five times to find that the period is between four and five years but closer to five. However, we can't be more accurate than this. If you are familiar with logarithms, you can take logs of both sides and solve for $n$ as follows:

$$n = \frac{\text{Ln (FV/PV)}}{\text{Ln } (1 + k)} = \frac{\text{Ln } 1.6}{\text{Ln } 1.1}$$

The natural log of 1.6 is 0.47 and the natural log of 1.1 is 0.09531, so the answer is 4.93 years. However, logarithm tables are rarely used. Using a financial calculator makes calculations of this type much easier.

**EXAMPLE 5.7** | Solution Using a Financial Calculator

Input the following variables:

| 0 | → | PMT | ; | 32,000 | → | FV | ; | −20,000 | → | PV | ; and | 10 | → | I/Y |

Press **CPT** and then **N** . This will give an answer of 4.9313 or 4.93 years.

We'll summarize what we have learned so far. We have Equation 5.2:

$$FV_n = PV_0 (1 + k)^n$$

This equation has four values. If we know any three of them, we can solve for the last one. Therefore, four different types of finance problems can be solved:

- **Future value problems:** How much will I have in $n$ years at $x$ percent if I invest $\$y$ today?
- **Present value problems:** What is the value today of receiving $\$z$ in $n$ years if the interest rate is $x$ percent?
- **IRR problems:** What rate of return will I earn if I invest $\$y$ today for $n$ years and get $\$z$?
- **Period problems:** How long do I have to wait to get $\$z$ if I invest $\$y$ today at $x$ percent?

All the problems that we have looked at are single-sum problems, looking at a single investment today and a single payoff in the future. In principle, we can solve almost any problem using the techniques we have discussed because, for example, valuing a series of receipts in the future can be done by valuing each one individually. However, special formulas exist for standard problems in finance for which the receipts or payments are the same each period. Think back to our first example about choosing between $20,000 today, $32,000 in five years, or $2,500 each year forever. The last choice involves valuing a constant $2,500 each year forever and is an example of an "annuity." In this case, it is a special class of annuity: a perpetual annuity, commonly referred to as a "perpetuity."

---

### Concept Review Questions

1. Explain how to compute future values and present values when using compound interest.
2. What is the relationship between FVIFs and PVIFs? Why does this make sense?
3. Why does compound interest result in higher future values than simple interest?

---

## 5.4 | Annuities and Perpetuities

**LEARNING OBJECTIVE 5.4**
Differentiate between an ordinary annuity and an annuity due, and explain how special constant payment problems can be valued as annuities and, in special cases, as perpetuities.

### The Importance of Investing Early

The example below illustrates the power of compound interest as time passes. Consider twins who follow two different investing approaches. Assume each earns a 12-percent annual return.

- Twin 1: At age 21, she decides to invest $2,000 per year (at year end) for six years, and then she makes no further contributions (total amount invested is $12,000). Note that she invests the same amount each year, so this is an example of an annuity. At age 65, she will have accumulated approximately $1.2 million for retirement.
- Twin 2: She postpones investing for six years, until she reaches age 27, and then invests $2,000 per year (at year end) for 38 years (total amount invested is $76,000). At age 65, she will also have accumulated approximately $1.2 million for retirement.

Notice that both twins have almost exactly the same ending amounts, but Twin 1 invested only $12,000 in total, while Twin 2 invested $76,000. This shows how the compounding effect is magnified as the time horizon increases.

We could solve these problems to find the ending value using "brute force," finding the future value of each payment the twins make individually. However, we will solve them after we develop more formally the concept of an annuity.

### Ordinary Annuities

**annuity** regular payments on an investment that are for the same amount and are paid at the same interval of time

**cash flows** the actual cash generated from an investment

So far, we have dealt with PV and FV concepts as they apply to only two cash flows—one today (i.e., the PV) and one in the future (i.e., the FV). In practice, we will often need to compare different series of receipts or payments that occur through time. An **annuity** is a series of payments or receipts, which we will simply call **cash flows**, that are for the same amount and paid at the same interval—that is, for example, they are paid annually, monthly, or weekly—over a given period. Annuities are common in finance; the ones you may be familiar with are car loans or mortgage payments. These involve an identical payment made at regular intervals for a loan based on a single interest rate.

**Ordinary annuities** involve end-of-period payments. Example 5.8 demonstrates how to determine the FV and PV of an ordinary annuity. We have the same values as in our earlier discussion: FV, PV, $n$, and $k$. However, now we have another term, PMT, for the regular annuity payment or receipt.

**ordinary annuities**   equal payments that are made at the end of each period of time

---

**EXAMPLE 5.8** │ FV and PV of an Ordinary Annuity

In 2018–19, the average NHL player earned $2.78 million per year, while the average career was approximately six years. Assuming a 41-percent tax rate, this would generate $1,640,200 in annual "disposable" (i.e., after-tax) income. Assume a player earning this average decides to invest 10 percent of his disposable income (i.e., $164,020) at the end of each year for the next six years (i.e., the average career span) and expects to earn 8 percent per year.

  **a.** How much will he have accumulated after six years?

  **b.** How much would he need to deposit today to have the same results?

**Solution**

  **a.** We can first display the series of payments on a timeline diagram, which shows when the cash flows occur.

Timelines are very useful in finance. You should get into the habit of presenting the data in a problem on a timeline. For example, from this diagram we can see that by the end of year 6, the first deposit of $164,020 will have earned a return for five years, because there are five years from the end of year 1 to the end of the period in year 6. Similarly, the second payment will earn a return for four years, the third for three years, the fourth for two years, the fifth for one year, and the final payment will not earn a return at all. Using this information, we could view this as a six-part problem in which we have to find the future value of each of the six payments.

$$FV_6 = \$164{,}020\,(1.08)^5 + \$164{,}020\,(1.08)^4 + \$164{,}020\,(1.08)^3 + \$164{,}020\,(1.08)^2 +$$
$$\$164{,}020\,(1.08)^1 + \$164{,}020\,(1)$$

$$= \$164{,}020\,(1.469328) + \$164{,}020\,(1.360489) + \$164{,}020\,(1.259712) +$$
$$\$164{,}020\,(1.1664) + \$164{,}020\,(1.08) + \$164{,}020\,(1)$$

$$= \$164{,}020\,(7.335929) = \$1{,}203{,}239 \text{ (rounded)}$$

We illustrate this in a timeline.

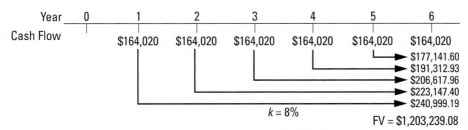

The player would have $1,203,239 after six years.

This would be our brute-force calculation, in which we solve the problem with six separate calculations. This approach is fine for a six-period annuity problem, but it would be tedious for a 25-year monthly mortgage problem that has 300 payments. Fortunately, there is a much quicker way (even without the use of a financial calculator or a spreadsheet). If we look closely at our solution, we can see that we are multiplying $164,020 by the sum of six future value interest factors (FVIF), based on an 8-percent return (i.e., the FVIF for $k = 8$ percent, with $n = 5, 4, 3, 2, 1,$ and 0, respectively).

The ordinary annuity equation, Equation 5.4, adds these FVIFs.

$$FV_n = PMT\left[\frac{(1+k)^n - 1}{k}\right]$$ [5.4]

*PMT* is the end-of-period annuity payment. This formula is usually called the future value annuity formula or FVAF to distinguish it from the single-sum FVIF. The advantage of Equation 5.4 is that it involves only one formula and can be solved easily, even on a simple calculator. Using this equation, we can solve Example 5.8a. as follows:

$$FV_6 = PMT\left[\frac{(1+0.08)^6 - 1}{0.08}\right] = \$164{,}020\,(7.335929) = \$1{,}203{,}239$$

We can get the FVAF for six years at 8 percent by using simple calculator keystrokes, putting 1.08 into memory, entering 1, and then pressing "times, memory recall, equals" six times, or by using Excel and entering = 1.08^6. Then we can take this number, subtract 1 from it, and divide by 0.08 to get 7.335929.

**b.** To find the present value, we can again view this as a six-part problem for which we have to find the present value of each of the six annual payments:

$$PV_0 = \$164{,}020\,(1/1.08)^6 + \$164{,}020\,(1/1.08)^5 + \$164{,}020\,(1/1.08)^4 + \$164{,}020\,(1/1.08)^3 +$$
$$\$164{,}020\,(1/1.08)^2 + \$164{,}020\,(1/1.08)^1$$

$$= \$164{,}020\,(0.630170) + \$164{,}020\,(0.680583) + \$164{,}020\,(0.735030) +$$
$$\$164{,}020\,(0.793832) + \$164{,}020\,(0.857339) + \$164{,}020\,(0.925926)$$

$$= \$164{,}020\,(4.622880) = \$758{,}245 \text{ (rounded)}$$

We illustrate this in a timeline.

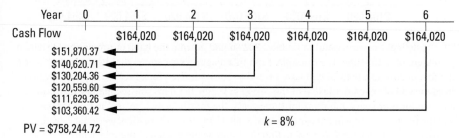

As before, notice that we are using brute force by multiplying $164,020 by the sum of the relevant six PVIF or discount factors, which add to 4.622880. Fortunately, the formula for determining the PV of ordinary annuities, Equation 5.5, will do this for us.

$$PV_0 = PMT\left[\frac{1 - \dfrac{1}{(1+k)^n}}{k}\right]$$ [5.5]

This formula is usually called the present value annuity factor or PVAF to distinguish it from the PVIF used for valuing single-sum problems. By using this equation to solve Example 5.8b, we get

$$PV_0 = \$164{,}020\left[\frac{1 - \dfrac{1}{(1.08)^6}}{0.08}\right] = \$164{,}020(4.622880) = \$758{,}245$$

Again, we can get the PVAF for six years at 8 percent by using a simple calculator with memory. For longer-period problems, we can use a financial calculator.

**EXAMPLE 5.8** | Solution Using a Financial Calculator

Input the following variables:

164,020 → PMT ; 6 → N ; 0 → PV ; and 8 → I/Y

Press CPT and then FV . This will give you an answer of −1,203,239. Remember that you get a negative value because the calculator is programmed to consider cash outflows and cash inflows.

Input the following variables:

164,020 → PMT ; 6 → N ; 0 → FV ; and 8 → I/Y

Press CPT and then PV . This will give an answer of −758,245.

In summary, the examples above illustrate the following relationships:

$758,245 today = $164,020 at the end of each of the next six years = $1,203,239 six years from today, assuming an annual interest rate of 8 percent.

## Annuities Due

Sometimes annuities are structured so that the cash flows are paid at the *beginning* of a period, rather than at the end. For example, leasing arrangements are usually set up like this, with the **lessee** making an immediate payment on taking possession of the equipment, such as a car. Such an annuity is called an **annuity due**. Example 5.9 demonstrates how to evaluate these cash flows.[4]

**lessee** a person who leases an item

**annuity due** an annuity (such as a lease) for which the payments are made at the beginning of each period

**EXAMPLE 5.9** | FV and PV of an Annuity Due

We will repeat Example 5.8, except we assume that the payments are made at the *beginning* rather than the end of each year.

  **a.** How much will the player have after six years?

  **b.** How much would the player have to deposit today to have the same result?

**Solution**

  **a.** We begin as before by depicting the data on a timeline.

| 0 | 1 | 2 | 3 | 4 | 5 | 6 |
|---|---|---|---|---|---|---|
| $164,020 | $164,020 | $164,020 | $164,020 | $164,020 | $164,020 | |

Notice that, as in Example 5.8, we have six cash flows of $164,020 each. However, each cash flow appears one period earlier, and thus each receives an extra period of interest at the rate of 8 percent. Using the brute-force approach applied in Example 5.8a, we can find the future value of each of the six payments.

$$FV_6 = \$164,020\,(1.08)^6 + \$164,020\,(1.08)^5 + \$164,020\,(1.08)^4 + \$164,020\,(1.08)^3 + \$164,020\,(1.08)^2 + \$164,020\,(1.08)^1$$

$$= \$164,020\,(1.586874) + \$164,020\,(1.469328) + \$164,020\,(1.360489) + \$164,020\,(1.259712) + \$164,020\,(1.1664) + \$164,020\,(1.08)$$

$$= \$164,020\,(7.922803) = \$1,299,498$$

---

[4]A strong note of caution is called for here. Changing a calculator's default setting may lead to undesired results. Most calculations do not depend on beginning-of-period cash flows, so telling the calculator to assume this is fine for one example but if left as the default will produce incorrect results when more common end-of-period cash flows are required. In particular, exam performance may be negatively affected!

We illustrate this on a timeline.

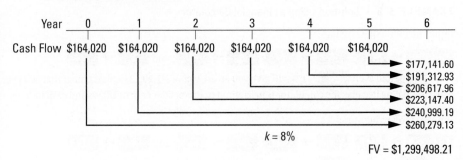

Notice that because each flow gets one extra period of compounding at 8 percent, the net result is that we multiply our answer to Example 5.8a by 1.08. In other words, the *FV* (annuity due) = [*FV* (ordinary annuity)](1 + *k*).

Therefore, we can alter Equation 5.4 to find the FV of an annuity due as follows:

$$FV_n = PMT\left[\frac{(1+k)^n - 1}{k}\right](1+k) \qquad [5.6]$$

This is *FVAF* (1 + *k*), so in practice we don't use a separate formula. However, we can now solve Example 5.9a as follows:

$$FV_6 = PMT\left[\frac{(1+0.08)^6 - 1}{0.08}\right](1.08) = [\$164,020(7.335929)](1.08) = \$1,203,239(1.08) = \$1,299,498$$

Note that the value of the annuity due, $1,299,498, is 1.08 times the value of the ordinary annuity that we calculated earlier, which was $1,203,239.

**b.** As before, to solve for the present value, we could view this as a six-part problem for which we have to find the present value of each of the six payments.

$$\begin{aligned}PV_0 &= [\$164,020\,(1/1.08)^6 + \$164,020\,(1/1.08)^5 + \$164,020\,(1/1.08)^4 + \\ &\quad \$164,020\,(1/1.08)^3 + \$164,020\,(1/1.08)^2 + \$164,020\,(1/1.08)^1]\times(1.08) \\ &= [\$164,020\,(4.622880)](1.08) = \$758,245(1.08) = \$818,904\end{aligned}$$

We illustrate this on a timeline.

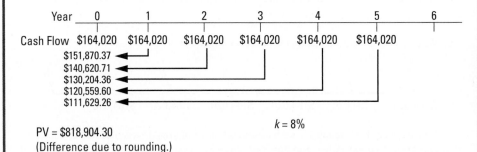

PV = $818,904.30
(Difference due to rounding.)

Note that, as in Example 5.9a, we are multiplying our answer to Example 5.8b by 1.08—that is, (1 + *k*). Accordingly, we can modify Equation 5.5 to arrive at the formula for determining the PV of an annuity due, which is given below:

$$PV_0 = PMT\left[\frac{1 - \dfrac{1}{(1+k)^n}}{k}\right](1+k) \qquad [5.7]$$

Equation 5.7 is PVAF (1 + *k* ). Using this to solve Example 5.9b, we get

$$PV_0 = \$164,020\left[\frac{1 - \dfrac{1}{(1.08)^6}}{0.08}\right](1.08) = [\$164,020(4.622880)](1.08) = \$758,245(1.08) = \$818,904$$

**EXAMPLE 5.9** | Solution Using a Financial Calculator

There is a "Begin" mode on the TI BA II Plus, as there is on most financial calculators. We need to activate "Begin" mode before solving this problem, which can be done as follows for the TI BA II Plus:

Press [2ND] [BGN] [2ND] [SET]. Then input the variables:

[0] → [PV]; [164,020] → [PMT]; [6] → [N]; and [8] → [I/Y]

Press [CPT] and then [FV]. This gives an answer of −1,299,498. As before, recognize that the negative sign is due to the need for a series of cash inflows matched by a cash outflow.

First, activate the "Begin" function [BGN]. Then input the following variables:

[0] → [FV]; [164,020] → [PMT]; [6] → [N]; and [8] → [I/Y]

Press [CPT] and then [PV]. This gives an answer of −818,904.

## Perpetuities

**Perpetuities** are special annuities in that they go on forever, so $n$ goes to infinity in the annuity equation. In this case, Equation 5.5 reduces to

$$PV_0 = \frac{PMT}{k} \qquad [5.8]$$

**perpetuity**  a special annuity that provides payments forever

Perpetuities are easy to value because all we do is divide the cash payment or receipt by the interest rate. This calculation is shown in Example 5.10.

**EXAMPLE 5.10** | Annuities and Perpetuities

a. An annuity pays $3,000 per year at year end and earns an annual return of 12 percent per year for 30 years. What is the present value?

b. What is the PV of a $3,000 per year annuity that goes on forever—that is, in perpetuity—if $k = 12$ percent?

**Solution**

a. $PV_0 = \$3,000 \left[ \dfrac{1 - \dfrac{1}{(1.12)^{30}}}{0.12} \right] = \$3,000\,(8.05518) = \$24,165.55$

b. $PV_0 = \dfrac{\$3,000}{0.12} = \$25,000$

Notice the small difference in the present value of these cash streams. This tells you that the PV of the cash flows of $3,000 per year from years 31 to infinity ($\infty$) is only $834.45—that is, $25,000 − $24,165.55. This is a very important result and is behind many financial innovations. It means that cash flows far in the future are of little value because of the discounting involved in the time value of money.[5]

[5]This has also been behind many misleading advertisements for which something is 100 percent backed by a government bond. The small print indicates that the bond pays off in 25 years so is not worth much today!

---

**EXAMPLE 5.10** | Solution Using a Financial Calculator

Input the following variables:

`0` → `FV` ; `3,000` → `PMT` ; `30` → `N` ; and `12` → `I/Y`

Press `CPT` and then `PV`. This will give an answer of −24,165.55.

---

We conclude by deriving the solution to the investing-early scenario described at the beginning of this section.

---

**EXAMPLE 5.11** | Investing Early

Solve for both twins from the scenario at the beginning of section 5.4.

**Solution** This must be solved as a two-part problem, which can then be solved in several ways. We first estimate the future value of the six $2,000 payments at the end of six years.

$$FV_0 = PMT\left[\frac{(1+k)^n - 1}{k}\right] = \$2,000\left[\frac{(1.12)^6 - 1}{0.12}\right] = \$2,000(8.11519) = \$16,230.38$$

Then we estimate the future value of the accumulated savings after 38 years (i.e., from age 27 to age 65).

$$FV_{38} = PV_0(1+k)^n = \$16,230.38(1.12)^{38} = \$16,230.38(74.17966) = \$1,203,964.13$$

Solve for Twin 2 from the scenario above.

$$FV_{38} = PMT\left[\frac{(1+k)^n - 1}{k}\right] = \$2,000\left[\frac{(1.12)^{38} - 1}{0.12}\right] = \$2,000(609.83053) = \$1,219,661.07$$

So they both end up with approximately $1.2 million.

---

# Annuities and Perpetuities Summarized

So far, we have discussed constant annuities and perpetuities—that is, where the cash flows remain the same for every period. However, sometimes we want to evaluate growing (or shrinking) perpetuities or annuities—that is, where the cash flows grow (or shrink) at a certain rate every period. We will consider situations in which these assumptions may be appropriate in Chapter 7 (for valuing stocks) and in chapters 13 to 15 (for evaluating long-term investments, and merger and acquisition decisions). Section 5.5 describes how to evaluate growing perpetuities and annuities.

---

## Concept Review Questions

1. Explain how to calculate the present value and future value of an ordinary annuity and an annuity due.
2. Define "perpetuity."
3. Why is the present value of $1 million in 50 years' time worth very little today?

**LEARNING OBJECTIVE 5.5**

Estimate the present value of growing perpetuities and annuities.

## Growing Perpetuities

Sometimes we may want to evaluate a stream of cash flows that will grow (or shrink) at a constant rate per period ($g$) indefinitely.[6] In this case, our payments ($PMT$) will change from one period to the next, as shown below:

$$PMT_1 = PMT_0(1 + g)$$
$$PMT_2 = PMT_1(1 + g) = PMT_0(1 + g)^2$$
$$PMT_3 = PMT_2(1 + g) = PMT_0(1 + g)^3$$

and so on.[7]

The present value of this stream of payments can be calculated as follows:

$$PV_0 = \frac{PMT_0(1 + g)^1}{(1 + k)^1} + \frac{PMT_0(1 + g)^2}{(1 + k)^2} + \frac{PMT_0(1 + g)^3}{(1 + k)^3} + \cdots + \frac{PMT_0(1 + g)^\infty}{(1 + k)^\infty} \quad [5.9]$$

Notice that what we are doing here is multiplying $PMT_0$ by a factor of $(1 + g)/(1 + k)$ every period. This is easily solved because it represents the sum of a geometric series, so we can reduce this to the following expression:

$$PV_0 = \frac{PMT_0(1 + g)}{k - g} = \frac{PMT_1}{k - g} \quad [5.10]$$

Equation 5.10 has several important points:

1. This relationship holds only when $k > g$. Otherwise, the answer is negative, which is uninformative.

2. Only *future* estimated cash flows and estimated growth in these cash flows are relevant.

3. The relationship holds only when growth in payments is expected to occur at the same rate indefinitely.

---

**EXAMPLE 5.12** | Valuing a Growing Perpetuity

You are attempting to determine the present value of cash flows to be generated by a rental property you are considering purchasing. You have estimated that the after-tax cash flows from this property will grow at 4 percent per year indefinitely due to rental increases. The cash flow this past year was $100,000, and the appropriate discount rate is 15 percent. Find the present value of these cash flows.

**Solution**

$$PMT_0 = \$100,000; g = 4\%; k = 15\%$$

Using Equation 5.10, we get

$$PV_0 = \frac{PMT_0(1 + g)}{k - g} = \frac{\$100,000(1 + 0.04)}{0.15 - 0.04} = \frac{\$104,000}{0.11} = \$945,454.55$$

---

[6]For example, in Chapter 7 we will make this assumption about dividends paid on common shares.
[7]Notice that if the cash flows are shrinking, it merely means that $g$ is a negative rate.

## Growing Annuities

Sometimes we may want to evaluate a stream of cash flows that will grow (or shrink) at a constant rate per period (*g*) over a given period of time, ending at some terminal point (*n*). Such a stream represents a growing annuity.

The present value of this stream of payments can be calculated as follows:

$$PV_0 = \frac{PMT_0(1+g)^1}{(1+k)^1} + \frac{PMT_0(1+g)^2}{(1+k)^2} + \frac{PMT_0(1+g)^3}{(1+k)^3} + \cdots + \frac{PMT_0(1+g)^n}{(1+k)^n} \qquad [5.11]$$

Notice that this equation is identical to Equation 5.9, except that the last payment occurs at time *n*—that is, the payments do not go on to infinity. With some work, Equation 5.11 reduces to the following expression:

$$PV_0 = \frac{PMT_1}{k-g} \times \left[ 1 - \left( \frac{1+g}{1+k} \right)^n \right] \qquad [5.12]$$

---

**EXAMPLE 5.13** | Valuing a Growing (Shrinking) Annuity

A mining company is attempting to determine the present value of cash flows to be generated from a new mining operation. They have estimated that the after-tax cash flows from this mine will shrink at a rate of 10 percent per year as the reserves are depleted, and that after 10 years the mine will be abandoned. Next year's cash flow is estimated to be $200,000, and the appropriate discount rate is 20 percent. Find the present value of these cash flows.

**Solution**

$$PMT_1 = \$200{,}000; g = -10\%; k = 20\%; n = 10$$

Using Equation 5.12, we get

$$PV_0 = \frac{PMT_1}{k-g} \times \left[ 1 - \left( \frac{1+g}{1+k} \right)^n \right] = \frac{200{,}000}{0.20-(-0.10)} \times \left[ 1 - \left( \frac{1+(-0.10)}{1+0.20} \right)^{10} \right] = \$629{,}124.32$$

---

### Concept Review Questions

1. Explain how to evaluate a growing perpetuity.
2. Explain how to calculate the present value of a growing annuity.

---

## 5.6 | Quoted versus Effective Rates

**LEARNING OBJECTIVE 5.6**

Differentiate between quoted rates and effective rates, and explain how quoted rates can be converted to effective rates.

# Determining Effective Annual Rates

So far, we have assumed that payments are made annually and that interest is compounded annually, so we have been able to use quoted rates to solve each problem. In practice, in many situations, payments are made (or received) at intervals other than annually (e.g., quarterly or monthly), and compounding often occurs more frequently than annually, so we need to be sure that we use the appropriate effective interest rate.

The **effective rate** for a period is the rate at which a dollar invested grows over that period. It is usually stated in percentage terms based on an annual period. To determine effective rates, we first recognize that the annual rates quoted by financial institutions will equal the annual effective rate only when compounding is done annually. We will use some examples to illustrate the process for determining effective rates.

**effective rate** the rate at which a dollar invested grows over a given period; usually stated in percentage terms based on an annual period

---

**EXAMPLE 5.14** | Effective versus Quoted Rates

**a.** Suppose someone invests $1,000 today for one year at a quoted annual rate of 16 percent compounded annually. What is the FV at the end of the year?

**b.** What if someone invests $1,000 at a quoted rate of 16 percent compounded quarterly?

**Solution**

**a.** FV = $1,000(1.16)$^1$ = $1,160

This means that each dollar grows to $1.16 by the end of the period, so we can say that the "effective" annual interest rate is 16 percent.

**b.** When the rate is "quoted" at 16 percent, and compounding is done quarterly, the appropriate adjustment (by convention) is to charge 16 percent/4 = 4 percent per quarter, so we have FV = $1,000(1.04)$^4$ = $1,170 (rounded).

Notice that even though the quoted rate is 16 percent, each dollar invested grows to $1.17—that is, by 17 percent—by the end of the period. In this case, we say that the "effective" annual interest rate is 17 percent.

---

We can use the following equation to determine the effective *annual* rate for any quoted annual rate, if given the compounding interval:

$$k = \left(1 + \frac{QR}{m}\right)^m - 1$$  [5.13]

where $k$ = effective annual rate, $QR$ = quoted rate, and $m$ = the number of compounding intervals per year.

Applying this equation to Example 5.14, we see the following:
For 5.14a, $m = 1$, $QR = 0.16$, and we get

$$k = \left(1 + \frac{0.16}{1}\right)^1 - 1 = 0.16 = 16\%$$

so the quoted and effective rates are the same.
For 5.14b, $m = 4$, $QR = 0.16$, so we get

$$k = \left(1 + \frac{0.16}{4}\right)^4 - 1 = 0.1699 = 17\%$$

The effective rate is higher than the quoted rate. This is why it is important to examine the compounding frequency of investments and loans; looking at the rate alone is often not enough.

When compounding is conducted on a continuous basis, we use Equation 5.14 to determine the effective annual rate for a given quoted rate.

$$k = e^{QR} - 1$$ [5.14]

where $e$ is the unique Euler number (approximately 2.718), which is found on your calculator and in Excel. It is used frequently in finance. If we use the Excel function "enter = exp (.16)," and subtract 1, we get 17.351 percent.

Example 5.15 shows that as the frequency of compounding increases, the effective annual rate also increases.

---

**EXAMPLE 5.15** | Effective Annual Rates for Various Compounding Intervals

What are the effective annual rates for the following quoted rates?

a. 12 percent, compounded annually

b. 12 percent, compounded semi-annually

c. 12 percent, compounded quarterly

d. 12 percent, compounded monthly

e. 12 percent, compounded daily

f. 12 percent, compounded continuously

**Solution**

a. Annual compounding, $m = 1$: $k = \left(1 + \frac{0.12}{1}\right)^1 - 1 = 12\%$

b. Semi-annual compounding, $m = 2$: $k = \left(1 + \frac{0.12}{2}\right)^2 - 1 = 12.36\%$

c. Quarterly compounding, $m = 4$: $k = \left(1 + \frac{0.12}{4}\right)^4 - 1 = 12.55\%$

d. Monthly compounding, $m = 12$: $k = \left(1 + \frac{0.12}{12}\right)^{12} - 1 = 12.68\%$

e. Daily compounding, $m = 365$: $k = \left(1 + \frac{0.12}{365}\right)^{365} - 1 = 12.747\%$

f. Continuous compounding: $k = e^{0.12} - 1 = 12.75\%$

---

Example 5.15 shows that as the compounding frequency increases, the quoted rate of 12 percent increases to a maximum effective rate of 12.75 percent, achieved with instantaneous or continuous compounding. However, the daily rate is almost the same, at 12.747 percent.

You can, of course, solve effective interest rate problems by using a calculator or Excel.

---

**EXAMPLE 5.15** | Solution Using a Financial Calculator

To solve for daily compounding, perform the following keystrokes:

`2ND` `ICONV`
`2ND` `CLR WORK`

The screen will show NOM = some value.
Make NOM = 12 (this is the nominal rate).

Then `ENTER` `↓` `↓`

This should show C/Y = some value.
For daily compounding, for example, input:
C/Y = 365 (this is the number of compounding periods per year)

Then `ENTER` `↓` `↓` , which should show EFF = some value.

Then `CPT` , which gives an answer of 12.747 percent.

---

# Effective Rates for "Any" Period

In Example 5.14b, the effective quarterly rate is 4 percent, because each dollar grows to $1.04 by the end of one quarter. Similarly, in Example 5.15 (which uses a quoted rate of 12 percent), the effective semi-annual rate for 5.15b is 6 percent (i.e., 12 percent/2), the effective quarterly rate for 5.15c is 3 percent (i.e., 12 percent/4), and the effective monthly rate for 5.15d is 1 percent (i.e., 12 percent/12).

However, suppose we need to know the effective monthly rate associated with the annual effective rate of 12.36 percent from Example 5.15b, perhaps to make monthly payments on a loan. It is not appropriate to divide 12.36 percent by 12, because it is an effective rate, not a quoted rate. Remember, we are looking for the effective monthly rate (i.e., how much $1 would grow over a given month), based on an annual effective rate of 12.36 percent. In this case, we know that after 12 compounding intervals at a monthly effective rate of $k_{monthly}$, each $1 would have grown to $1.1236. In other words, we have

$$(1 + k_{monthly})^{12} = 1.1236$$

We could solve this equation by taking the 12th root of each side:

$$(1 + k_{monthly}) = (1.1236)^{1/12}$$

So $k_{monthly} = (1.1236)^{1/12} - 1 = 0.0097588$ or 0.97588 percent.

We can verify this by compounding $1 at the rate of 0.97588 percent per month for 12 months as follows: $(1.0097588)^{12} = 1.1236$. In other words, investing $1 at 0.97588 percent per month produces the same amount at the end of one year (1.1236) as does investing $1 for one year with semi-annual compounding at 6 percent per six-month period.

The following equation, which is a variation of Equation 5.13, can be used to determine the effective rate for any period, given any quoted rate:

$$k = \left(1 + \frac{QR}{m}\right)^{\frac{m}{f}} - 1 \qquad [5.15]$$

where $f$ = frequency of payments per year (i.e., $f = 1$ when we are looking for an annual effective rate; $f = 12$ when looking for a monthly effective rate, etc.). Notice that when $f = 1$, we have Equation 5.13.

In Excel, we can use the rate function. For example, if the annual rate is 12.36 percent and we want to know the effective monthly rate, we can use the following function,

$$= \text{Rate (nper, pmt, pv, fv, type)},$$

entering the following in the appropriate cell,

$$= \text{Rate (12, 0, -1, 1.1236, 0)},$$

where there are 12 periods and no intervening payments, and we are interested in a $1 outflow growing to 1.1236. Because we are not interested in annuities, we put in 0 for type. This produces the same answer: 0.97588 percent.

---

## Concept Review Questions

1. Why can effective rates often be very different from quoted rates?
2. Explain how to calculate the effective rate for any period.

## 5.7 | Loan or Mortgage Arrangements

**LEARNING OBJECTIVE 5.7**

Apply annuity formulas to value loans and mortgages, and set up an amortization schedule.

**mortgage** a loan, usually secured by real property, that involves "blended" equal payments (both interest and a principal repayment) over a specified payment period

**amortize** to retire a loan over a given period by making regular payments

One common and important application of annuity concepts takes the form of loan or **mortgage** arrangements. Typically, these arrangements involve "blended" payments for equal amounts that include both an interest and a principal repayment component. The loan payments are designed to **amortize** the loan, which means that, at the end of the loan term, the balance due (or principal outstanding) will equal zero—in other words, the loan and all associated interest obligations will have been paid off in their entirety. Note that both "amortize" and "mortgage" contain the French word *mort,* which means "death." So a mortgage is "killed off" over the mortgage period, and no money is owed at the end. Similarly, amortize means to "kill off" financially.

Because these loans involve equal payments at regular intervals, based on one fixed interest rate specified when the loan is taken out, the payments can be viewed as annuities. Therefore, we can determine the amount of the payment, the effective period interest rate, and so on, by using Equation 5.5 and recognizing that the PV equals the amount of the loan.

An amortization schedule divides the blended payments into the interest portion and the principal repayment portion. This is of importance to businesses, where the interest portion is a deductible expense for tax purposes. The interest portion is determined by applying the effective period interest rate to the principal outstanding at the beginning of each period. The remaining portion of the payment is then used to reduce the amount of principal outstanding. The example below shows the development of an amortization schedule.

It is important to understand how this amortization table is created. The loan is a simple annual payment loan, so the cost of the loan is the annual interest rate times the outstanding balance; in this case, 10 percent times $5,000, or $500. This is the first charge on the loan payments; the residual, which is $1,510.57 in the first year, goes to reduce the amount of the loan.

**EXAMPLE 5.16** | Loan Payments and Amortization Schedule

Determine the required year-end payments for a three-year $5,000 loan with a 10-percent annual interest rate. Complete an amortization schedule.

**Solution** First, determine the required payments by solving Equation 5.5 for *PMT*.

$$PMT = \frac{PV_0}{\left[\frac{1 - \frac{1}{(1+k)^n}}{k}\right]} = \frac{\$5,000}{\left[\frac{1 - \frac{1}{(1.10)^3}}{0.10}\right]} = \frac{\$5,000}{2.48685} = \$2,010.57$$

Second, determine the loan amortization schedule.

| Period | (1) Beginning Principal Outstanding | (2) PMT | (3) Interest [(1)*k] | (4) Principal Repayment [(2)–(3)] | Ending Principal Outstanding [(1)–(4)] |
|---|---|---|---|---|---|
| 1 | $5,000.00 | $2,010.57 | $500.00 | $1,510.57 | $3,489.43 |
| 2 | 3,489.43 | 2,010.57 | 348.94 | 1,661.63 | 1,827.80 |
| 3 | 1,827.80 | 2,010.57 | 182.77 | 1,827.80 | 0.00 |

**EXAMPLE 5.16** | Solution Using a Financial Calculator

Input the following variables:

$0 \rightarrow$ FV ; $5{,}000 \rightarrow$ PV ; $3 \rightarrow$ N ; and $10 \rightarrow$ I/Y

Press CPT and then PMT $= -2{,}010.57$.

For the next year, the outstanding balance on the loan is $3,489.43 and the cost of the loan goes down to $348.94, even though the payment is the same at $2,010.57. As a result, the amount going toward the repayment of the loan increases to $1,661.63.

Note that Excel users can automate the whole process of generating an amortization table by typing *amortization* into the online help and downloading the amortization template.

However, even though you can use Excel, you should practise generating your own schedule by using the PMT function and writing out each line separately, since Excel sometimes presents the data in a way that your instructor might not accept.

**EXAMPLE 5.17** | Determining the Principal Outstanding

Determine the principal outstanding on the loan in Example 5.16 after one year, without referring to the amortization schedule found in the solution.

**Solution** This problem can be solved by recognizing that the principal outstanding at any time on a loan equals the PV of all future payments at that time. For this example, we find the PV for the given payments and interest rate when $n = 2$ (i.e., the number of payments remaining on the loan after one year).

$$PV_0 = PMT \left[ \frac{1 - \frac{1}{(1+k)^n}}{k} \right] = \$2{,}010.57 \left[ \frac{1 - \frac{1}{(1.10)^2}}{0.10} \right]$$

$$= \$2{,}010.57(1.735537) = \$3{,}489.42$$

**EXAMPLE 5.17** | Solution Using a Financial Calculator

$0 \rightarrow$ FV ; $2{,}010.57 \rightarrow$ PMT ; $10 \rightarrow$ I/Y ; and $2 \rightarrow$ N

Press CPT and then PV $= -3{,}489.42$.

# Mortgages

In practice, loan repayments are often not made annually. Many loans call for quarterly, monthly, or even weekly repayments. For these arrangements, we need to convert the quoted annual rates into effective period rates that correspond to the frequency of payments, which can be done using Equation 5.15. This conversion is needed to determine the interest that accrued during the period in question, based on the principal outstanding at the beginning of the payment period (i.e., at the beginning of the month, week, etc.), because that amount will be reduced after the payment is made.

Mortgages represent an example of a loan that requires that payments be made more frequently than annually. In fact, mortgage payments must be made at least monthly, and many offer the opportunity to make biweekly or weekly payments. In Canada, mortgages are further complicated by the fact that compounding is done on a semi-annual basis, similar to bonds, which we will discuss in Chapter 6. When we deal with mortgages in Canada, $m = 2$ in

Equation 5.15, while $f > 2$ (in fact, $f$ must be greater than or equal to 12, since payments must be made at least monthly).

Finally, one other thing to be familiar with is the distinction between the "term" and the "amortization period" associated with long-term loans, such as mortgages. In particular, the term of a loan refers to the period for which investors can "lock in" at a fixed rate. This is usually shorter than the period over which the loan is to be repaid, or amortized, which is called the amortization period. The payments are based on the amortization period. It is this fact that helps make mortgage payments more affordable. For example, a loan with a 25-year amortization period may be structured so that the investor locks in a fixed rate of 6 percent for five years (which is the term of the loan). The payments for this loan would be determined based on the 6-percent quoted rate, assuming equal payments for 25 years even though after five years the payments will change if the interest rate on the mortgage changes.

The choice of amortization period can have a large impact on the amount of each mortgage payment (and hence on the maximum amount mortgagees can borrow), and also on the total amount of interest paid during the duration of the loan. Finance in the News 5.2 demonstrates this point clearly by showing that a $400,000 mortgage loan that is amortized over 30 years instead of 25 years will lead to a monthly payment reduction of over $200. This reduced monthly payment comes with a cost in that the total interest paid over the life of the 30-year mortgage is more than $45,000 higher than for the 25-year mortgage. On the whole, the increase in the time it would take to pay off the longer mortgage is balanced by the fact that Canadians are living and working longer.

## 5.2  Finance in the News    A Housing Policy with Millennials in Mind

Politically, the federal government has to do something to make home buying more affordable.

The polling firm Abacus Data says millennials will make up the largest group of eligible voters in the election coming this fall, and housing affordability is their top priority.

The government is under pressure to respond in a way that helps young people realize their urgent desire to become owners while preventing them from financially maiming themselves and the economy by purchasing homes they can't properly afford.

The best thing the government could do for housing from a pure policy point of view is to maintain the status quo and see whether the cooling trend in sales continues. But that might not bring relief fast enough for all the people stressing about housing affordability.

The emotional health of this country seems to depend on people, particularly young adults, being able to buy houses. Renting compares well in a financial sense if you invest the savings over not owning, but there is no sign that society is ready to accept it as anything more than a stopgap. Also, renting is stupid expensive in cities such as Toronto and Vancouver.

Here's how the government should help millennials buy a home: Leave the stress tests for mortgage applicants in place, but increase the maximum amortization period for people with small down payments to 30 years from 25. Finance Minister Bill Morneau is reportedly considering the 30-year option.

This isn't an ideal approach because it will stimulate the market and probably cause prices to rise. But it will make housing more affordable on the whole and ease the financial pressure on new buyers.

Mortgages with a 30-year amortization are actually available now for buyers who have a down payment of 20 per cent or more and thus don't need to pay for mortgage default insurance. According to the Office of the Superintendent of Financial Institutions, about 47 per cent of uninsured mortgages had amortizations longer than 25 years in mid-2018.

Thirty-year mortgages were widely available until 2012, when the federal government made them off limits for people putting less than 20 per cent down. A press release issued at the time said this measure would "reduce the total interest payments Canadian families make on their mortgages, helping them build up equity in their homes more quickly and pay off their mortgages sooner."

It's true—longer amortization periods are bad personal finance because you pay more mortgage interest. But they also make houses more affordable by reducing the monthly costs of owning a home.

Here's an example I used in a column last fall about the benefits of 30-year mortgages: Let's start with a $500,000 house bought with the combination of $100,000 down and a five-year, fixed-rate mortgage at 3.5 per cent. Total interest paid is $199,123 for 25 years and $244,595 over 30 years—that's a 22.8-per-cent increase for using a 30-year amortization. The monthly payment is $1,997 for a 25-year amortization and $1,790 for 30 years—a significant saving for cash-hungry families.

The case for the 30-year mortgage amortization is backed by demographics. Canadians are living and working longer—why can't this be reflected in the payback period for mortgages?

Resurrecting the 35- and 40-year mortgages that used to be widely available is pushing it, but 30 years seems right for the times.

Mortgage stress tests require that home buyers are able to afford making their payments if interest rates surge. People who make a living from the sale of homes argue, with some justification, that the stress test requires buyers to weather more of a rate increase than we're likely to see in today's slow-growth economy.

The stress test might be overkill as a way of ensuring people can afford higher rates, but in a backhanded way, it's good for your personal finances. To pass a stress test, you might have to buy a less-expensive home than you planned. Your mortgage payments will be more manageable, as might other ownership costs.

Ideally, the government would act on housing only when the market blows too hot or cold. In the real world, that won't fly, so bring on the 30-year mortgage.

**Source:** Carrick, Rob, "A Housing Policy with Millennials in Mind." *The Globe and Mail*, February 8, 2019. Available at www.theglobeandmail.com.

**EXAMPLE 5.18** | Determining Mortgage Payments and Amortization Schedule

Determine the monthly payments and the amortization schedule for the first three months of a $200,000 mortgage loan with an amortization period of 25 years, based on a quoted rate of 6 percent and a 10-year term.

**Solution**   First, determine the effective period rate. Because it is a Canadian mortgage, we know that $m = 2$. Since payments are made monthly, we need to find the effective monthly rate, so $f = 12$. Using Equation 5.15,

$$k_{monthly} = \left(1 + \frac{0.06}{2}\right)^{\frac{2}{12}} - 1 = 0.4938622\%$$

Second, determine the required monthly payments by using Equation 5.5. There are 300 payments in total, since $n = 25$ years $\times$ 12 months $= 300$. PV $= 200,000$ (i.e., the loan amount).

$$PMT = \frac{PV_0}{\left[\dfrac{1 - \dfrac{1}{(1 + k)^n}}{k}\right]} = \frac{\$200,000}{\left[\dfrac{1 - \dfrac{1}{(1.004938622)^{300}}}{0.004938622}\right]} = \frac{\$200,000}{156.2972258} = \$1,279.61$$

Third, construct an amortization schedule similar to the one in Example 5.16 above.

| Period | (1) Beginning Principal Outstanding | (2) PMT | (3) Interest $[k \times (1)]$ | (4) Principal Repayment $[(2)-(3)]$ | Ending Principal Outstanding $[(1)-(4)]$ |
|---|---|---|---|---|---|
| 1 | $200,000.00 | $1,279.61 | $987.72 | $291.89 | $199,708.11 |
| 2 | 199,708.11 | 1,279.61 | 986.28 | 293.33 | 199,414.78 |
| 3 | 199,414.78 | 1,279.61 | 984.83 | 294.78 | 199,120.00 |

**EXAMPLE 5.18** | Solution Using a Financial Calculator

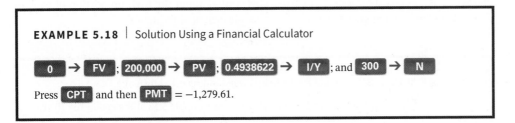

Press **CPT** and then **PMT** $= -1,279.61$.

Note that unlike the simple annual payment loan, for which the cost of the loan was the annual interest cost, now the cost is the monthly interest rate of 0.4938622 percent, because we have a monthly amortization schedule. It is this monthly rate applied to the outstanding balance that determines how much of the mortgage's monthly payments represent the cost of the loan. As is clear from the amortization schedule, little of the early payments go toward reducing the principal. The greater portion of the early payments is for interest. This is true for all long-term loans because, by definition, the repayment of the loan is being done over a longer period. As time passes, the interest cost of the fixed payments continues to decrease, and the payment of principal correspondingly increases. The reason for this is simply that the interest rate is the cost of borrowing money, and this cost has to be subtracted first from the monthly payment.

Excel simplifies the whole process. However, note that Excel reports mortgage costs according to U.S., not Canadian, practice. In Canada, mortgage rates are quoted equivalent to bonds, so a 6-percent quoted mortgage rate is actually 3 percent every six months, and the monthly rate is then determined as a monthly rate that compounds to 3 percent over six months or 0.4938622 percent. In the United States, the same 6-percent quote means 0.5 percent per month. In other words, the annual rate is simply divided by 12. As a result, the same quoted mortgage rate in the United States and Canada will produce different results. The first three months of the Excel amortization table for Example 5.18 are shown in **Figure 5.3**.

FIGURE 5.3 **Mortgage Loan Payments**

| Enter values | |
|---|---|
| Loan amount | $ 200,000.00 |
| Annual interest rate | 0.06 |
| Loan period in years | 25 |
| Number of payments per year | 12 |
| Start date of loan | 06/11/2021 |
| Optional extra payments | $ - |

| Loan summary | |
|---|---|
| Scheduled payment | $ 1,288.60 |
| Scheduled number of payments | 300 |
| Actual number of payments | 300 |
| Total early payments | $ - |
| Total interest | $ 186,580.84 |

**Lender Name:**

| Pmt No. | Payment date | Beginning balance | Scheduled payment | Extra payment | Total payment | Principal | Interest | Ending balance | Cumulative interest |
|---|---|---|---|---|---|---|---|---|---|
| 1 | 06/12/2021 | $ 200,000.00 | $ 1,288.60 | $ - | $ 1,288.60 | $ 288.60 | $ 1,000.00 | $ 199,711.40 | $ 1,000.00 |
| 2 | 06/01/2022 | 199,711.40 | 1,288.60 | - | 1,288.60 | 290.05 | 998.56 | 199,421.35 | 1,998.56 |
| 3 | 06/02/2022 | 199,421.35 | 1,288.60 | - | 1,288.60 | 291.50 | 997.11 | 199,129.86 | 2,995.66 |

Note that for the first month, the interest payment is simply 0.5 percent times the principal of $200,000, or $1,000, versus $987.72 for the true (Canadian) cost. Also note that the monthly payment is $9 higher, at $1,288.60.

Excel is a wonderful software program, but before using the sophisticated functions, always check the answers by using the basic functions to make sure that the macros written by the programmers are consistent with what you want to estimate. It is worth mentioning that for Canadian mortgages, you can check with a variety of mortgage calculators, available free on the Internet, that also produce amortization schedules.[8]

One item of interest to a mortgagee would be how much of the loan has been retired after a certain time. We can solve this problem in the same manner that we did in Example 5.17.

Notice in Example 5.19 that slightly less than 25 percent of the loan has been repaid after 10 years, even though 40 percent of the amortization period (i.e., 10 out of 25 years) has elapsed. This is consistent with our earlier observation about the high proportion of each of the early payments that goes toward interest versus principal reduction.

---

**EXAMPLE 5.19** | Determining the Principal Outstanding on a Mortgage

Determine the principal outstanding on the mortgage in Example 5.18 at the end of the 10-year term.

**Solution** Trying to solve this by constructing an amortization schedule to the end of 10 years would be cumbersome. However, it is easily solved by recognizing that the principal outstanding is the PV of all future payments after 10 years. We find the PV for the payments when $n = 15$ years $\times$ 12 months $= 180$ months—that is, for the balance of the payments after 10 years.

$$PV_0 = \$1,279.61 \left[ \frac{1 - \dfrac{1}{(1.004938622)^{180}}}{0.004938622} \right] = \$1,279.61(119.0642325) = \$152,355.78$$

---

**EXAMPLE 5.19** | Solution Using a Financial Calculator

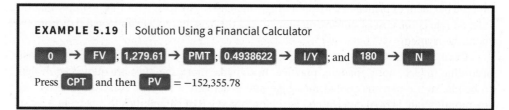

Press **CPT** and then **PV** $= -152,355.78$

---

[8]A well-presented calculator is available on the website of the Government of Canada: https://itools-ioutils.fcac-acfc .gc.ca/MC-CH/MCCalc-CHCalc-eng.aspx.

## Concept Review Questions

1. Explain how loan and mortgage payments can be determined using annuity concepts.
2. What complications arise when dealing with mortgage loans in Canada?

## 5.8 Comprehensive Examples

### LEARNING OBJECTIVE 5.8
Solve a basic retirement problem.

We conclude this chapter by providing a few comprehensive examples that involve applying the concepts you have learned to more challenging situations. The second of these examples is a common problem facing investors with respect to planning for retirement.

Notice that the two problems in this section appear complicated at first but are quite manageable if you break them down into their components. Timelines are useful for this purpose because they help you visualize what information you have and what is needed to solve the problem. If you are able to solve these problems, then you have a good understanding of the basic concepts involving the time value of money.

---

**EXAMPLE 5.20** | Multiple Annuities

a. What is the PV of $1,000 received at year end for the next four years, followed by $2,000 per year end for years 5 to 7, assuming a 10-percent rate of interest, compounded annually?

b. Suppose an investor needed $15,000 at the end of seven years and can only invest $1,000 per year for years 1 to 4 (as above). How much would the investor need to deposit in each of years 5 to 7 to achieve this objective, assuming a 10-percent interest rate as above?

**Solution**

a. This problem is best solved by first constructing a timeline:

Notice that we can view this problem in several ways. It can be viewed as a four-year annuity of $1,000 followed by a three-year annuity of $2,000, or as a seven-year annuity of $1,000, with a three-year annuity of an "extra" $1,000 beginning at the end of year 5, and so on. Also, we could solve it by finding the future value of both annuities at $t = 7$ and then discounting them, or by finding the PV of the second annuity at $t = 4$ and discounting it back to $t = 0$, which is the approach we have chosen.

Viewing this problem as a four-year ordinary annuity (A1) that pays $1,000 per year, followed by a three-year ordinary annuity (A2) that pays $2,000 per year, we can determine the PV as follows:

$$PV(A1) = \$1,000 \left[ \frac{1 - \frac{1}{(1.10)^4}}{0.10} \right] = \$1,000(3.16987) = \$3,169.87$$

$$PV(A2) = \$2,000 \left[ \frac{1 - \frac{1}{(1.10)^3}}{0.10} \right] \left[ \frac{1}{(1.10)^4} \right] = \$2,000(2.48685)(0.683013) = \$3,397.10$$

We illustrate this in a timeline.

Notice that for PV(A2), we first determine the PV of the three-year annuity starting at time $t = 4$ (i.e., \$4,973.70), and then we discount this amount back to today.

**EXAMPLE 5.20a** | Solution Using a Financial Calculator

Enter the following:

**0** → **FV** ; **1,000** → **PMT** ; **10** → **I/Y** ; and **4** → **N**

Press **CPT** and then **PV** = −3,169.87

Then enter the following:

**0** → **FV** ; **−2,000** → **PMT** ; **10** → **I/Y** ; and **3** → **N**

Press **CPT** and then **PV** = 4,973.70

This is the PV of the three-year annuity at time $t = 4$, which must be discounted back to time $t = 0$. Next, enter the following:

**0** → **PMT** ; **4,973.70** → **FV** ; **10** → **I/Y** ; and **4** → **N**

Press **CPT** and then **PV** = −3,397.10

So the PV(Total) = PV(A1) + PV(A2) = \$3,169.87 + \$3,397.10 = \$6,566.97.

In all these problems, the interest rate need not be the same over the two periods. For our example, the interest rate for the second three-year period could be 10 percent, while for the first four periods it could be 5 percent. In this case, the Excel solution would be

$$= PV(0.05, 4, 1000, 0, 0) + PV(0.05, 4, 0, PV(0.1, 3, -2000, 0, 0), 0)$$

and the value increases to \$7,637.83.

**b.** This problem can also be best represented by using a timeline:

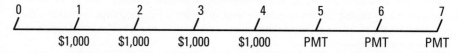

We can solve this problem in several ways. We have chosen to solve it by finding the future value of the first annuity (A1) at $t = 7$, and then determining the FV of the second annuity (A2) at $t = 7$, required to achieve the \$15,000 target. Then, knowing the required FV of the three-year annuity, we can determine the payments for years 5 to 7.

Determine the FV of A1 at time $t = 4$:

$$FV_4(A1) = \$1,000 \times \left[\frac{(1 + 0.10)^4 - 1}{0.10}\right] = \$1,000\,(4.641) = \$4,641$$

Second, determine the FV of A1 at time $t = 7$:

$$FV_7(A1) = \$4,641 \times (1.1)^3 = \$4,641(1.331) = \$6,177.17$$

Third, determine the required FV of A2 at time $t = 7$:

$$\text{Required } FV_7(A2) = \text{Required amount} - FV_7(A1) = 15,000 - 6,177.17 = \$8,822.83$$

We illustrate this on a timeline.

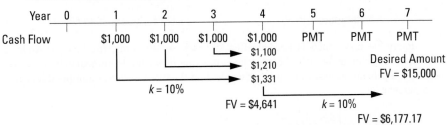

Fourth, determine the required payments for A2:

$$PMT = \frac{\$8,822.83}{\left[\frac{(1.10)^3 - 1}{0.10}\right]} = \frac{\$8,822.83}{3.31} = \$2,665.51$$

---

**EXAMPLE 5.20b** | Solution Using a Financial Calculator

Enter the following:

$\boxed{0} \rightarrow \boxed{PV}$ ; $\boxed{-1,000} \rightarrow \boxed{PMT}$ ; $\boxed{10} \rightarrow \boxed{I/Y}$ ; and $\boxed{4} \rightarrow \boxed{N}$

Press $\boxed{CPT}$ and then $\boxed{FV}$ = 4,641

Second, enter the following:

$\boxed{0} \rightarrow \boxed{PMT}$ ; $\boxed{4,641} \rightarrow \boxed{PV}$ ; $\boxed{10} \rightarrow \boxed{I/Y}$ ; and $\boxed{3} \rightarrow \boxed{N}$

Press $\boxed{CPT}$ and then $\boxed{FV}$ = −6,177.17

Third, enter the following:

$\boxed{0} \rightarrow \boxed{PV}$ ; $\boxed{8,822.83} \rightarrow \boxed{FV}$ ; $\boxed{10} \rightarrow \boxed{I/Y}$ ; and $\boxed{3} \rightarrow \boxed{N}$

Press $\boxed{CPT}$ and then $\boxed{PMT}$ = −2,665.51

---

**EXAMPLE 5.21** | Retirement Problem

An investor plans to retire 35 years from today and have sufficient savings to guarantee $48,000 each year for 20 years. Assume retirement withdrawals will be made at the beginning of each of the 20 years. The investor estimates that at the time of retirement, he can sell his business for $200,000. The expectation is that interest rates will be relatively stable at 8 percent a year for the next 35 years. Thereafter, the interest rate is expected to decline to 6 percent forever. The investor wants to make equal annual deposits at the end of each of the next 35 years. How much should be deposited each year in order to meet the stated objective?

**Solution**   A timeline helps visualize the problem:

| 0 | 1 | ... | 35 | 36 | ... | 54 | 55 |
|---|---|---|---|---|---|---|---|
| | PMT | PMT | PMT<br>$200<br>−$48 | −$48 | | −$48 | 0 |

$k = 8\%$ for years 1 to 35                    $k = 6\%$ for years 35 to 55

First, determine how much is needed after 35 years. At this time, the investor wants a 20-year annuity due of $48,000, because he is drawing down funds immediately on retirement, at a 6 percent interest rate. In other words, find the PV of a 20-year annuity due, when $k = 6$-percent:

$$PV_{35} = \$48,000\left[\frac{1 - \frac{1}{(1.06)^{20}}}{0.06}\right](1.06) = \$48,000(11.46992122)(1.06) = \$583,589.59$$

Second, subtract the $200,000 expected from the sale of the business, leaving the amount needed to be raised through investments:

$$\text{Need FV}_{35} = \$583,589.59 - \$200,000 = \$383,589.59$$

Third, determine the required year-end payments over the next 35 years:

$$\text{PMT} = \left[\frac{\$383,589.59}{\frac{(1.08)^{35} - 1}{0.08}}\right] = \frac{\$383,589.59}{172.3168037} = \$2,226.07$$

---

**EXAMPLE 5.21** | Solution Using a Financial Calculator

First, set your calculator to "Begin" mode and then enter

`0` → `FV` ; `48,000` → `PMT` ; `6` → `I/Y` ; and `20` → `N`

Press `CPT` and then `PV` = −583,589.59

Finally, take your calculator out of "Begin" mode.

Enter `0` → `PV` ; `383,589.59` → `FV` ; `8` → `I/Y` ; and `35` → `N`

Press `CPT` and then `PMT` = −2,226.07

---

## Lessons to Be Learned

Example 5.21 demonstrates a relatively simple version of the basic retirement "problem" that is central to finance, as it relates to all individual investors, as well as pension funds. Notice that this problem is based on "assumed" returns of 8 percent per year during the investor's "earnings" phase. So what options do investors have when the invested funds do *not* earn this rate of return and they find themselves in a shortfall position?

Basically, they have four options: (1) increase their contributions; (2) try to earn a higher rate of return (although they do not have control over capital market returns, so this might involve taking on more risk, which could backfire and result in even lower returns); (3) reduce the amount withdrawn upon retirement; and/ or (4) postpone retirement (i.e., work longer).

Unfortunately, many individuals, as well as many pension plans, have been forced to deal with this situation over the past few years, as their investment funds were hit by volatile and weak market returns. In addition, many pension plans have been dealing with severe underfunding problems and have been forced to consider (or implement) some combination of reducing benefits paid to retirees and/or increasing required contributions. All of this comes at a time when the returns offered by "safe" investments (i.e., government debt securities) are very low, and stock returns have been volatile, thus requiring some tough decisions by investors at all levels.

## Concept Review Questions

1. Explain how timelines can be used to break a complicated time value of money problem into manageable components.
2. Demonstrate how to solve a typical retirement problem.

# Review

## Summary

In this chapter, we demonstrate how to compare cash flows that occur at different points in time, after accounting for the time value of money. This process is applied to virtually every topic that is studied in finance, so it is extremely important. We show how to determine economically equivalent future values from values that occur in previous periods by applying the process of compounding at an appropriate rate of return. Similarly, we show how to determine economically equivalent present values (in today's dollars) for cash flows that occur in the future by discounting them, which is the reciprocal of compounding. These processes can be applied to several cash flows simultaneously.

Annuities represent a special type of cash flow stream involving equal payments at the same interval, with the same interest rate being applied throughout the period. We see that these kinds of cash flow streams are commonplace in finance applications (e.g., loan payments), and that there are relatively simple formulas that enable us to determine the present or future value of these cash flows. Infinite cash flow streams, namely perpetuities, are also considered, and a formula is applied to permit the determination of the present value of these infinite streams. Similarly, a formula is derived to find the present value of a growing perpetuity, which will be more important in Chapter 7 when equity securities are valued. Analogous to the growing perpetuity problem, the growing annuity is also introduced. In addition, we illustrate how to adjust quoted interest rates to find effective rates, which is important because compounding often takes place at other than annual intervals. Finally, we conclude with some more involved applications of the concepts discussed in the chapter.

## Summary of Learning Objectives

### 5.1 Explain the importance of the time value of money and how it is related to an investor's opportunity costs.

Time value of money is the idea that money invested today has more value than the same amount invested later. This concept helps us to understand how interest is earned and why investors are indifferent to investment today and future value later.

The opportunity cost of money is the interest rate that would be earned by investing it. For this reason, we also call the interest rate the "price of money."

### 5.2 Define simple interest and explain how it works.

Simple interest is interest earned on the original principal. The growth in the value of an investment is simply the sum of annual interest earned.

### 5.3 Define compound interest and explain how it works.

Compound interest is interest earned on the principal amount invested and on any accrued interest. Compound interest can result in dramatic growth in the value of an investment over time.

### 5.4 Differentiate between an ordinary annuity and an annuity due, and explain how special constant payment problems can be valued as annuities and, in special cases, as perpetuities.

Annuities are streams of identical payments made at regular time intervals. An ordinary annuity has payments at the end of each period. An annuity due has the same number of payments as an ordinary annuity, but the payments occur at the beginning of each period. The present value of an ordinary annuity can be found with a formula that is equal to the sum of the present value factors. The future value of an ordinary annuity can be found with a formula that is equal to the sum of the future value factors. To get the present and future value factors for an annuity due, multiply the ordinary annuity factors by $(1 + k)$. Perpetuities are streams of identical payments made at regular time intervals, forever. The present value of a perpetuity is easy to calculate because all that is needed is to divide the identical payments by the discount rate.

### 5.5 Estimate the present value of growing perpetuities and annuities.

Growing perpetuities can be solved using Equation 5.10, while growing annuities can be solved using Equation 5.12.

## 5.6  Differentiate between quoted rates and effective rates, and explain how quoted rates can be converted to effective rates.

Quoted rates are also called stated rates or annual percentage rates, which are measured annually and used for quoting purposes. The effective rate for a period is the rate at which a dollar invested grows over that period. It is usually stated in percentage terms based on an annual period. The relation can be found in the formula $k = \left(1 + \dfrac{QR}{m}\right)^m - 1$, where $QR$ is the quoted rate, $m$ is the compounding frequency, and $k$ is the annual effective rate.

## 5.7  Apply annuity formulas to value loans and mortgages, and set up an amortization schedule.

Loans can be valued as annuities since they meet the three characteristics of an annuity: they have equal payments, are for a fixed period of time, and are based on the same discount rate.

To set up an amortization schedule, five variables are calculated for each period: beginning principal outstanding, payment, interest, principal repayment, and ending principal outstanding.

## 5.8  Solve a basic retirement problem.

A simple retirement problem can be solved by equating the present value of the retirement annuity and the future value of the savings annuity. Comprehensive examples are presented in section 5.8.

## Key Terms

amortize, p. 5-24
annuity, p. 5-12
annuity due, p. 5-15
basis point, p. 5-8
cash flows, p. 5-12
compound interest, p. 5-4
discounting, p. 5-8

effective rate, p. 5-21
future value interest factor (FVIF), p. 5-5
lessee, p. 5-15
medium of exchange, p. 5-2
mortgage, p. 5-24
ordinary annuities, p. 5-13
perpetuity, p. 5-17

present value interest factor (PVIF), p. 5-9
reinvest, p. 5-5
required rate of return or discount rate, p. 5-2
simple interest, p. 5-2
time value of money, p. 5-1

## Equations

| Equation | Description | Formula | Page |
|---|---|---|---|
| [5.1] | Future Value (Simple Interest) | $\text{Value (time n)} = P + (n \times P \times k)$ | p. 5-3 |
| [5.2] | Future Value (Compound Interest) | $FV_n = PV_0 (1 + k)^n$ | p. 5-5 |
| [5.3] | Present Value | $PV_0 = \dfrac{FV_n}{(1+k)^n} = FV_n \times \dfrac{1}{(1+k)^n}$ | p. 5-9 |
| [5.4] | Future Value (Ordinary Annuity) | $FV_n = PMT\left[\dfrac{(1+k)^n - 1}{k}\right]$ | p. 5-14 |
| [5.5] | Present Value (Ordinary Annuity) | $PV_0 = PMT\left[\dfrac{1 - \dfrac{1}{(1+k)^n}}{k}\right]$ | p. 5-14 |
| [5.6] | Future Value (Annuity Due) | $FV_n = PMT\left[\dfrac{(1+k)^n - 1}{k}\right](1+k)$ | p. 5-16 |
| [5.7] | Present Value (Annuity Due) | $PV_0 = PMT\left[\dfrac{1 - \dfrac{1}{(1+k)^n}}{k}\right](1+k)$ | p. 5-16 |
| [5.8] | Present Value (Perpetuity) | $PV_0 = \dfrac{PMT}{k}$ | p. 5-17 |
| [5.9] | Growing Perpetuity (long version) | $PV_0 = \dfrac{PMT_0(1+g)}{(1+k)^1} + \dfrac{PMT_0(1+g)^2}{(1+k)^2} + \dfrac{PMT_0(1+g)^3}{(1+k)^3} + \cdots + \dfrac{PMT_0(1+g)^\infty}{(1+k)^\infty}$ | p. 5-19 |

*(continued)*

| Equation | Description | Formula | Page |
|---|---|---|---|
| [5.10] | Growing Perpetuity (reduced version) | $PV_0 = \dfrac{PMT_0(1+g)}{k-g} = \dfrac{PMT_1}{k-g}$ | p. 5-19 |
| [5.11] | Growing Annuity (long version) | $PV_0 = \dfrac{PMT_0(1+g)}{(1+k)^1} + \dfrac{PMT_0(1+g)^2}{(1+k)^2} + \dfrac{PMT_0(1+g)^3}{(1+k)^3} + \cdots + \dfrac{PMT_0(1+g)^n}{(1+k)^n}$ | p. 5-20 |
| [5.12] | Growing Annuity (reduced version) | $PV_0 = \dfrac{PMT_1}{k-g} \times \left[1 - \left(\dfrac{1+g}{1+k}\right)^n\right]$ | p. 5-20 |
| [5.13] | Effective Annual Rate | $k = \left(1 + \dfrac{QR}{m}\right)^m - 1$ | p. 5-21 |
| [5.14] | Effective Annual Rate (with continuous compounding) | $k = e^{QR} - 1$ | p. 5-22 |
| [5.15] | Effective Period Rate (for any period $f$) | $k = \left(1 + \dfrac{QR}{m}\right)^{\frac{m}{f}} - 1$ | p. 5-23 |

# Questions and Practice Problems

## Multiple Choice Questions

1. **(LO 5.2, 5.3)** What is the total amount accumulated after six years if someone invests $1,000 today with a simple annual interest rate of 8 percent? How about with a compound annual interest rate of 8 percent?

   a. $1,400, $1,469

   b. $1,469, $1,400

   c. $1,480, $1,587

   d. $1,600, $1,816

2. **(LO 5.2, 5.3)** An investment of $5,000 invested for three years has an expected future value of $6,200. The simple annual interest rate is closest to _____ and the compound annual interest rate is closest to _____.

   a. 7.01 percent; 8.41 percent

   b. 7.43 percent; 8.00 percent

   c. 8.00 percent; 7.43 percent

   d. 8.41 percent; 7.01 percent

3. **(LO 5.2, 5.3)** At the end of 2022, Malcolm invested $10,000 in two bank accounts. The expected value of each bank account for the years 2022 to 2033 are represented in the following graph. In the graph, "Series 1" represents an account paying _____ interest, while "Series 2" represents an account paying _____ interest.

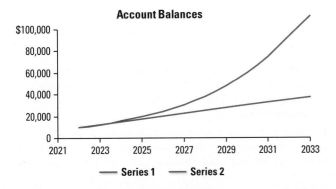

**Account Balances**

— Series 1    — Series 2

   a. simple; compound

   b. compound; simple

   c. simple; simple

   d. compound; compound

4. **(LO 5.2, 5.3)** Which of the following has the largest future value if $1,000 is invested today?

   a. Five years with a simple annual interest rate of 10 percent

   b. Ten years with a simple annual interest rate of 8 percent

   c. Eight years with a compound annual interest rate of 8 percent

   d. Ten years with a compound annual interest rate of 7 percent

*Interest rates in the following questions are compound rates unless otherwise stated.*

5. **(LO 5.3)** Suppose an investor wants to have $15 million to retire 25 years from now. How much would she have to invest today if her annual rate of return is equal to 5 percent?

   a. $6,666,667

   b. $4,429,542

   c. $600,000

   d. $21,345

6. **(LO 5.2, 5.3)** Which of the following is *false*?

   a. The longer the time period, the smaller the present value, given a $100 future value and holding the interest rate constant.

   b. The greater the interest rate, the greater the present value, given a $100 future value and holding the time period constant.

   c. A future dollar is always less valuable than a dollar today if interest rates are positive.

   d. The discount factor is the reciprocal of the compound factor.

7. **(LO 5.3)** Maggie deposits $10,000 today and is promised a return of $16,000 in eight years. What is the implied annual rate of return?

   a. 5.86 percent

   b. 7.16 percent

   c. 6.39 percent

   d. 6.05 percent

8. **(LO 5.3)** How long will it take Mike to triple his investment if he can earn an annual rate of return of 9 percent?

   **a.** 15.5 years

   **b.** 13.9 years

   **c.** 12.7 years

   **d.** 10 years

9. **(LO 5.4)** Which of the following statements is *incorrect*?

   **a.** An ordinary annuity has payments at the end of each year.

   **b.** An annuity due has payments at the beginning of each year.

   **c.** A perpetuity is considered a perpetual annuity.

   **d.** An ordinary annuity has a greater PV than an annuity due if they both have the same periodic payments, discount rate, and time period.

10. **(LO 5.4)** Jan plans to invest $2,000 in an equity fund every year end beginning this year. The expected annual return on the fund is 15 percent. How much would she expect to have at the end of 20 years?

   **a.** $237,620

   **b.** $176,424

   **c.** $204,887

   **d.** $178,424

11. **(LO 5.4)** Jan plans to invest $2,000 in an equity fund every year end beginning this year. The expected annual return on the fund is 15 percent. She plans to invest for 20 years. What is the present value of Jan's investments?

   **a.** $12,625

   **b.** $12,519

   **c.** $14,396

   **d.** $12,396

12. **(LO 5.4)** What is the present value of a perpetuity with an annual year-end payment of $1,500 and expected annual rate of return equal to 12 percent?

   **a.** $14,000

   **b.** $13,500

   **c.** $11,400

   **d.** $12,500

13. **(LO 5.4)** What is the present value of a perpetuity with an annual payment of $1,500 if the first payment is due immediately? The expected annual rate of return is equal to 12 percent.

   **a.** $14,000

   **b.** $13,500

   **c.** $11,400

   **d.** $12,500

14. **(LO 5.7)** Ten years ago you borrowed $300,000. The term of the loan was 20 years and required monthly payments of $3,303.26. The interest rate on the loan was 12 percent compounded monthly. You have just made the 120th payment. What is the principal outstanding?

   **a.** $212,583

   **b.** $230,239

   **c.** $191,866

   **d.** $150,000

15. **(LO 5.4)** Which of the following statements is *correct*?

   **a.** The future value of a perpetuity cannot be computed.

   **b.** The future value of a perpetuity can be computed.

   **c.** The present value of a perpetuity cannot be computed.

   **d.** The present value of an annuity cannot be computed.

## Practice Problems

### Basic

16. **(LO 5.2)** Dmitri Chekov has made an investment of $25,000 that promises to pay him 8 percent simple interest per year for 10 years. Determine how much interest he will earn in the:

   **a.** first year

   **b.** ninth year

17. **(LO 5.2)** After a summer of travelling (and not working), a student finds himself $1,500 short for this year's tuition fees. His parents have agreed to lend him the money for three years at a simple interest rate of 6 percent, with interest due at the end of each year.

   **a.** How much interest will he owe his parents after one year?

   **b.** How much money will he have paid, in total, at the end of three years?

18. **(LO 5.2)** Your sister has been forced to borrow money to pay her tuition this year. If she makes annual interest payments on the loan at year end for the next three years, and the loan is for $2,500 at a simple interest rate of 6 percent, how much will she pay each year?

19. **(LO 5.2)** Khalil's summer job has given him $1,200 more than he needs for his tuition this year. The local bank pays simple interest at a rate of 0.5 percent per month. How much interest will he earn in one year if the interest is not compounding?

20. **(LO 5.3)** A new Internet bank pays compound interest of 0.5 percent per month on deposits. How much interest will Khalil's summer savings of $1,200 earn in one year with this online bank account?

21. **(LO 5.2, 5.3)** History tells us that a group of Dutch colonists purchased the island of Manhattan from the Native American residents in 1626. Payment was made with wampum (likely glass beads and trinkets), which had an estimated value of $24. Suppose the Dutch had invested this money back home in Europe and earned an average return of 5 percent per year. Determine how much this investment would be worth 394 years later (rounding to the nearest dollar), using:

   **a.** simple interest

   **b.** compound interest

22. **(LO 5.3)** David has been awarded a scholarship that will pay $5,000 one year from now. However, he really needs the money today and has decided to take out a loan. If the interest rate is 6 percent, how much can he borrow so that the scholarship will just pay off the loan?

23. **(LO 5.3)** On the advice of a friend, Gilda invests $20,000 in a mutual fund that has earned 10 percent per year, on average, in recent years. If this rate of return continues, determine how much her investment will be worth in:

   **a.** one year

   **b.** five years

   **c.** 10 years

24. **(LO 5.3)** When Jon graduates in three years, he wants to throw a big party, which will cost $800. To have this amount available, how much does he have to invest today if he can earn a compound return of 5 percent per year?

25. **(LO 5.4)** A retired teacher, would like to donate some money to his alma mater to endow a $1,000 annual scholarship. The university will manage the funds and expects to earn 3 percent per year. How

much will the teacher have to donate so that the endowment fund never runs out?

**26. (LO 5.6)** Bank A pays 7.25-percent interest compounded semi-annually, Bank B pays 7.2 percent compounded quarterly, and Bank C pays 7.15 percent compounded monthly. Which bank pays the highest effective annual rate?

**27. (LO 5.6)** Jimmie is buying a new car. His bank quotes a rate of 9.5 percent per year for a car loan. Calculate the effective annual rate if the compounding occurs:

    **a.** annually

    **b.** quarterly

    **c.** monthly

**28. (LO 5.6)** If Alysha puts $50,000 in a savings account paying 6 percent per year, determine how much money she will have in total at the end of the first year if interest is compounded:

    **a.** annually

    **b.** monthly

    **c.** daily

**29. (LO 5.4)** Public corporations have no fixed lifespan; as such, they are often viewed as entities that will pay dividends to their shareholders in perpetuity. Suppose a firm pays a dividend of $2 per share every year. If the discount rate is 12 percent, what is the present value of all the future dividends?

**30. (LO 5.4)** Mary-Beth is planning to live in a university residence for three years while completing her degree. The annual cost for food and lodging is $9,500 and must be paid at the start of each school year. What is the total present value of Mary-Beth's residence fees if the discount rate (interest rate) is 6 percent per year?

**31. (LO 5.4)** At the age of 10, Felix decided that he wanted to attend a very prestigious (and expensive) university. How much will his parents have to save each year to accumulate $60,000 by the time Felix needs the funds in eight years? Assume Felix's parents can earn 7 percent (compounded annually) on their savings, and that each year's savings are deposited at the end of the year.

**32. (LO 5.5)** An investment promises to pay you $100 per year starting in one year. The cash flow from the investment is expected to increase by 3 percent per year forever. If alternative investments of similar risk earn a return of 9 percent per year, determine the maximum you would be willing to pay for the investment.

**33. (LO 5.8)** Jack is 28 years old now and plans to retire in 35 years. He works in a local bank and has an annual after-tax income of $45,000. His expected annual expenditure is $36,000, and the rest of his income will be invested at the beginning of each of the next 35 years at an expected annual rate of return of 12.6 percent. Calculate the amount Jack will have accumulated when he retires.

**34. (LO 5.8)** Tommy has a goal of amassing $1 million by the time he retires. However, there always seems to be a reason not to save money, so he put it off for many years. Finally, with just 15 years before his retirement, he begins to save. Fortunately, Tommy's executive-level job allows him to save $30,000 per year. If these savings earn 10 percent per year, will Tommy achieve his $1-million goal at the desired time?

## Intermediate

**35. (LO 5.1)** Franklin is trying to decide whether or not to take a philosophy course next semester. He finds the topic interesting, but being a business student, he wants to measure the cost of taking the course. After detailed thought and analysis, he has identified the following items that he feels may be relevant to his decision:

Tuition fees for the course: $800

Textbook for the course: $300

Rent for his apartment: $5,000

Food for next semester: $3,200

Currently Franklin earns $3,000 per semester as a teaching assistant. Franklin estimates that the philosophy course will require considerable study so he will have to reduce his teaching assistant hours by 30 percent. Determine the cost of taking the philosophy course.

**36. (LO 5.4)** Grace, a retired librarian, would like to donate some money to her alma mater to endow a $5,000 annual scholarship. The first scholarship will be awarded in five years. The university will manage the funds and expects to earn 3 percent per year. How much will Grace have to donate so that the endowment fund never runs out?

**37. (LO 5.4)** Muriel would like to support the education of her favourite grand-nephew, Stephen, who plans to begin university in three years. How much will Muriel have to invest today, at 5 percent, to be able to give Stephen $6,000 at the end of each year for four years?

**38. (LO 5.4)** You have just won $50 million in a lottery and are offered two options: receive $40 million today or receive $5 million per year for the next 10 years. At what interest rate are you indifferent to the choice between the two options? If the interest rate is greater than the indifference rate, which do you prefer and why? If the interest rate is less than the indifference rate, which do you prefer and why?

**39. (LO 5.6)** A bank is currently offering a savings account paying an interest rate of 9 percent compounded quarterly. It would like to offer another account, with the same effective annual rate, but compounded monthly. What is the equivalent rate compounded monthly?

**40. (LO 5.6)** Calculate the effective annual rates for the following:

    **a.** 24 percent, compounded daily

    **b.** 24 percent, compounded quarterly

    **c.** 24 percent, compounded every four months

    **d.** 24 percent, compounded semi-annually

    **e.** 24 percent, compounded continuously

    **f.** Calculate the effective monthly rate for parts a to d.

**41. (LO 5.4)** Jane's parents save $1,000 per year for 17 years to pay for her university tuition costs. They deposit the money into a Registered Education Savings Plan (RESP) account so that no tax is payable on the interest income. This RESP account provides a return of 6 percent per year.

    **a.** How much will Jane's account be worth when she begins her university studies?

    **b.** As an incentive to save for higher education, the government will add 20 percent to any money contributed to an RESP each year. Including these grants, how much will Jane have in her account?

**42. (LO 5.4)** Stephen has learned that his great-aunt intends to give him $6,000 each year he is studying at university. Tuition must be paid in advance, so Stephen would like to receive his payments at the beginning of each school year. How much will his great-aunt have to invest today at 5 percent to make the four annual (start-of-year) payments? Assume that Stephen will be starting school in five years.

**43. (LO 5.4)** Felix will need $15,000 per year for four years to pay for tuition. How much will Felix's parents have to invest at the end of each year for the eight years before he begins his studies if their savings earn compound interest at 7 percent per year? Assume the tuition payments occur at the end of each year.

**44. (LO 5.5)** Shirley has been offered two perpetuities: Grow and Shrink. Grow promises her $100 in one year and an annual cash flow that will increase by 4 percent per year forever. Shrink, in contrast, promises her $1,000 in one year but the annual cash flow will decline by 2 percent forever. If her opportunity cost is 5 percent per year and both annuities cost $1,000, which annuity offers her the greater value?

**45. (LO 5.5)** An investment promises to pay you $100 per year starting immediately. The cash flow from the investment is expected to increase by 3 percent per year forever. If alternative investments of similar risk earn a return of 9 percent per year, determine the maximum you would be willing to pay for the investment.

**46. (LO 5.5)** An investment promises to pay you $100 per year starting in five years. The cash flow from the investment is expected to increase by 3 percent per year forever. If alternative investments of similar risk earn a return of 9 percent per year, determine the maximum you would be willing to pay for the investment.

**47. (LO 5.4, 5.6)** To start a new business, Su Mei intends to borrow $25,000 from a local bank. If the bank asks her to repay the loan in five equal annual instalments of $6,935.24, determine the bank's effective annual interest rate on the loan transaction. With annual compounding, what nominal rate would the bank quote for this loan?

**48. (LO 5.4, 5.6)** The Business Development Bank is willing to loan Su Mei the $25,000 she needs to start her new business. The loan will require monthly payments of $556.11 over five years.

   **a.** What is the effective monthly rate on this loan?

   **b.** With monthly compounding, what is the nominal (annual) interest rate on this loan?

**49. (LO 5.6)** After losing money playing online poker, Scott visits a loan shark for a $750 loan. To avoid a visit from the "collection agency," he will have to repay $800 in just one week.

   **a.** What is the nominal interest rate per week? Per year?

   **b.** What is the effective annual interest rate?

**50. (LO 5.7)** Josephine needs to borrow $180,000 to purchase her new house in Yarmouth, Nova Scotia. She would like to pay off the mortgage in 20 years, making monthly payments. For the initial three-year term, Providence Bank has offered her a quoted annual rate of 6.4 percent.

   **a.** What is the effective annual interest rate?

   **b.** What is the effective monthly interest rate?

   **c.** How much will Josephine's monthly mortgage payments be?

   **d.** Yarmouth Credit Union will provide Josephine with a mortgage at a rate of 6.36 percent, but unlike most Canadian mortgages, the compounding will occur monthly. Should Josephine take the mortgage loan from Yarmouth Credit Union or from Providence Bank?

**51. (LO 5.7)** A lakefront house in Kingston, Ontario, is for sale with an asking price of $699,000. The real estate market has been quite active, so the house will almost certainly attract several offers, and may sell for more than the asking price. Charlie is very eager to purchase this house, but is concerned that he may not be able to afford it. He has $130,000 available for a down payment, and can pay up to $3,000 per month on a mortgage loan. As Charlie is a long-time customer, his bank has offered him a great mortgage rate of 3.9 percent on a one-year term. If the loan will be amortized over 25 years, what is the most that Charlie can afford to pay for the house?

**52. (LO 5.8)** Timmy sets himself a goal of amassing $1 million in his retirement fund by the time he turns 61. He begins saving $3,000 at the end of each year, starting on his 21st birthday (40 years of saving).

   **a.** If his savings earn 10 percent per year, will Timmy achieve his goal?

   **b.** At what age will the value of Timmy's savings plan be worth $1 million?

**53. (LO 5.8)** Paul and Maria want to have enough money to travel around the world when they retire. They both just turned 30 and will retire when they turn 60. They earn a total of $9,000 after taxes each month. Their monthly expenditures include $3,000 in mortgage payments, $850 in car payments, and $1,450 in other expenses. They approached a fund manager and decided to invest the rest of their income at the end of each year. They expect to earn a 10-percent annual rate of return for each of the next 30 years. When they retire, they will sell their cottage for an expected price of $150,000.

   **a.** Determine how much they will have when they retire.

   **b.** How much can Paul and Maria withdraw annually at the beginning of each year after they retire if they expect to live until they are 90?

## Challenging

**54. (LO 5.1, 5.3)** Veda has to choose between two investments that have the same cost today. Both investments will ultimately pay $1,300 but at different times, as shown in the table below. If Veda does not choose one of these investments, she could leave the funds in a bank account paying 5 percent per year. Which investment should Veda choose?

| Year | Investment A | Investment B |
|------|--------------|--------------|
| 1 | $ 0 | $200 |
| 2 | $500 | $400 |
| 3 | $800 | $700 |

**55. (LO 5.4)** A firm has just declared that its dividend next year will be $3 per share. That rate of payment will continue for an additional four years, after which the dividends will fall back to their usual $2 per share. The discount rate is 12 percent. What is the present value of all the future dividends?

**56. (LO 5.4)** After living in a university residence for one year, Mary-Beth decides to rent an apartment for the remaining three years of her degree. She has found a nice location that will cost $950 per month. Rent for the first and last month must be paid up front. How much money would Mary-Beth need to have in her bank account right now to be sure she will always have enough for rent? The bank account pays 4.5-percent interest, compounded monthly.

**57. (LO 5.4)** A 65-year-old man intends to use his retirement funds to purchase an annuity from a life insurance company. Given the amount of money the man has available to invest, the insurance company is able to offer two alternatives. The first option is to receive $2,785 at the end of each month for as long as he lives; the second option is to receive $3,500 at the end of each month, but for only 20 years (payments will be made to his estate if he should die before that time). The relevant interest rate is 6 percent per year compounding monthly. How long must the man live so that the first option is a better deal?

**58. (LO 5.4)** Two friends, Abe and Betty, are planning for their retirement. Both are 20 years old and plan on retiring in 40 years with $1 million each. Betty plans on making annual deposits beginning in one year (total of 40 deposits) while Abe plans on waiting and then depositing twice as much as Betty deposits. If both can earn 5 percent per year, how long can Abe wait before he has to start making his deposits?

**59. (LO 5.1, 5.2, 5.3, 5.4)** You are planning on buying your first home and need to borrow $250,000 from the bank. The manager offers you two mortgages: the long option will take 25 years to be paid off, and your annual payment will be $17,738. The short option will take only 10 years to be paid off, and your annual payment will be $35,200. The manager offers you the following advice: if you take the long option, you will pay $193,450 in interest ($17,738 × 25 − $250,000), while if you take the short option, you will pay only $102,000 in interest ($35,200 × 10 − $250,000)—a savings of over $91,000. Do you agree or disagree with the manager's advice? Briefly explain your reasoning. Hint: consider opportunity cost.

**60. (LO 5.4, 5.6)** Amanda would like to borrow $50,000 to pay one year's tuition at a private U.S. university. She would like to make quarterly payments and finish repaying the loan in five years. If the bank is quoting her a rate of 6 percent compounded monthly, determine her quarterly payment.

**61. (LO 5.4, 5.6)** Wilma would like to borrow $250,000 to start her own business. She would like to make monthly payments to repay the loan in 10 years. If the bank is quoting her a rate of 6 percent compounded quarterly, determine her monthly payment.

**62. (LO 5.3, 5.4)** Roger has his eye on a new car that will cost $20,000. He has $15,000 in his savings account, earning interest at a rate of 0.5 percent per month.

    **a.** How long (to the nearest month) will it be before he can buy the car?

    **b.** How long will it be before Roger can buy the car if, in addition to his existing savings, he can save $250 per month?

**63. (LO 5.3, 5.6)** How many years will it take for an investment to double in value if the rate of return is 9 percent and compounding occurs:

    **a.** annually?

    **b.** quarterly?

**64. (LO 5.4)** Céline has just won a lottery. She will receive a payment of $6,000 at the end of each year for nine years. As an alternative, she can choose an immediate payment of $50,000.

    **a.** Which alternative should she pick if the interest rate is 5 percent?

    **b.** What would the interest rate have to be for Céline to be indifferent between the two alternatives?

**65. (LO 5.5)** Xiang wishes to have $1 million in 25 years. He cannot afford to make large deposits at the moment; however, he believes that he will be able to increase his deposits by 4 percent per year for the next 25 years. He will make his first deposit in one year. If his opportunity cost is 6 percent, how large an initial deposit is needed? If instead of increasing his deposit each year, Xiang invested the same amount each year, how large a deposit would he need to make each year?

**66. (LO 5.7)** Alysha has decided to use $150,000 in savings to make a down payment on a house. She will live in the house for the next two years while still at university and then sell it when she graduates. The bank has offered her a mortgage rate of 5.1-percent compounded semi-annually on a two-year term, with an amortization period of 25 years. The house she is interested in purchasing costs $380,000.

    **a.** If two friends rent rooms from Alysha and pay her $475 each for rent at the end of each month, how much additional money does she need to meet her monthly mortgage payment?

    **b.** In two years, Alysha wants to sell the house for a high enough price to cover the remaining principal amount on the mortgage, as well as recoup her down payment. What is the minimum sale price she should accept?

**67. (LO 5.6, 5.7)** Jimmie wishes to buy a new car that will cost $29,000.

    **a.** How much will his monthly car payments be if he obtains a loan that is amortized over 60 months, and the nominal interest rate is 8.5 percent per year with monthly compounding?

    **b.** Create an amortization schedule for Jimmie's car loan. What portion of the first monthly payment goes toward repaying the principal amount of the loan? What portion of the last monthly payment goes toward the principal?

    **c.** Using the amortization schedule, determine how much Jimmie still owes on the car loan after three years of payments on the five-year loan. What is the present value of this amount?

**68. (LO 5.6, 5.7)** Michelle is offered a loan of $30,000 that requires 60 monthly payments of $622.75. What is the effective annual interest rate on this loan? What would the quoted rate be?

**69. (LO 5.7)** Five years ago, Franklin borrowed $250,000 to purchase a house in Sandy Lake. At the time, the quoted rate on the mortgage was 6 percent, the amortization period was 25 years, the term was five years, and the payments were made monthly. Now that the term of the mortgage is complete, Franklin must renegotiate his mortgage. If the current market rate for mortgages is 8 percent, what is Franklin's new monthly payment?

**70. (LO 5.7)**

    **a.** Determine the month-end payment for a $200,000, 10-year loan with an interest rate of 12 percent, compounded monthly, assuming there is no down payment.

    **b.** Calculate the outstanding loan amount after 18 months.

    **c.** Redo part a, assuming it is a mortgage loan with 12-percent annual interest rate and monthly payments.

**71. (LO 5.8)** Investor A just turned 20 years old and currently has no investments. She plans to invest $5,500 at the end of each year for eight years, beginning in five years. The rate of return on her investment is 15 percent, continuously compounded. Investor B is 40 years old and he has just started to invest an equal amount of money at the beginning of every year. He will invest for 10 years. The rate of return on his investment is 16 percent, compounded quarterly. Determine the yearly payment Investor B has to make in order to have the same present value as Investor A.

# Cases

### Case 5.1    Invest, Save, or Spend?

Shanna Mathieson, a recent business school graduate, is thinking about how to manage her finances over the next few years. In the short term, she would like to save for a down payment on a house and for a Caribbean vacation. Thinking about the long term, she would like to start investing for her retirement. Shanna's target date for buying a house is four years from now. If the Caribbean vacation goes ahead, it will happen one year from now—to mark her best friend's birthday. Currently 22 years old, Shanna believes that it would be great if she could retire at age 65.

    Shanna's business degree and student work experience have really paid off—two months ago she accepted an offer with a local agricultural lender as a financial analyst. Her starting salary was $48,000 per year, or $34,560 after taxes and other payroll deductions.

If Shanna buys a house, she expects to spend $325,000, of which 15 percent, or $48,750, would be required as a minimum down payment. Shanna's grandparents have told her that they will cover her down payment, and they've made it clear that this is as high as they can go. Shanna wonders if saving as much as she can now and forgoing some pleasures in life might have benefits later, through either a larger down payment or a larger retirement account. If she goes ahead with the Caribbean vacation, she plans to do it in a big way and spend $5,000. If she focuses only on her retirement savings she will contribute any net monthly cash flow to her Registered Retirement Savings Plan (RRSP) account. Any money deposited in this account will grow without tax, during the contribution phase.

1. Mortgage calculations:

   a. Shanna's estimate for her nominal mortgage interest rate is 4.5 percent. This rate would be compounded semi-annually while her payments would be made monthly. What is the effective monthly interest rate that she would pay?

   b. Calculate her monthly mortgage payment, assuming a $48,750 down payment and a mortgage maturity of 25 years.

2. After employment deductions and all of her living expenses, Shanna has $840 of net cash flow every month. The local economy has been weak and she's not expecting any change to her income or net cash flow in the four years leading up to her planned house purchase.

   a. If Shanna saves all of her monthly net cash flow at a short-term savings rate of 1.5 percent (compounded monthly) for the next four years, how much will she have?

   b. If in four years' time she adds all of her saved money to her grandparents' gift, how large will her down payment be?

   c. Calculate her monthly mortgage payment, considering the increased down payment calculated in part b above. The mortgage maturity remains at 25 years.

3. If Shanna puts all of her monthly net cash flow into her RRSP account and earns the long-term annual savings rate of 6.5 percent (compounded monthly) for the next four years,

   a. what will the value of the account be at age 26?

   b. what will the account value be at age 65, if she continues to make the same monthly contributions and earns the same long-term savings rate?

4. If in one year Shanna takes $5,000 out of her savings account to pay for her Caribbean trip, her account balance will decrease to $5,386. If she invests this remaining money at the long-term savings rate and then saves her net cash flow for another three years,

   a. what will the value of her account be at age 26?

   b. how much less will she have saved at age 26, because of the $5,000 Caribbean trip?

   c. How much less will she have saved at age 65 as a result of this $5,000 expenditure?

### What Should Shanna Do?

In making financial decisions, it is common to struggle with how much to spend, how much to save for short-term needs, and how much to put away for long-term needs. Whether an individual has a small or large income, making reasonable saving and spending goals can be challenging, just as Shanna's situation demonstrates. What should Shanna do? She wants to enjoy life, cover her immediate spending needs, and plan for her financial future. How can she use time value of money concepts to her advantage?

# Bond Valuation and Interest Rates

---

**LEARNING OBJECTIVES**

After studying this chapter, you should be able to:

**6.1** Describe the basic structure and the various features of different types of bonds.

**6.2** Explain how to value a bond given an appropriate discount rate.

**6.3** Determine the discount rate or yield for a given market value of a bond.

**6.4** List and describe the factors, both domestic and global, that affect interest rates.

**6.5** List and describe the characteristics and pricing of other debt instruments.

**6.6** Explain how interest rate parity works.

**6.7** Determine the discount rate or yield for a callable bond.

---

Chapter 5 introduced the basic concept of the time value of money. In this chapter, we discuss bonds, which provide investors with predetermined future payments. As such, the analysis of bonds provides an important application of compounding and discounting. Understanding the topics covered in this chapter will increase your ability to apply the tools of valuation and improve your knowledge of financial securities.

The importance of bond and money markets to the global financial system and the overall global economy has gained more attention than usual over the past few years. Bond markets represent a major source of financing for companies, financial institutions, and governments. Thus, the fallout from collapses in corporate bond and commercial paper markets contributed greatly to the financial crisis of 2007 and 2008 and forced central banks to take action to support these markets. The European debt crisis has been one of the most important stories since 2009, while other issues, such as the downgrading of the United States' credit rating, have also been prevalent.

Throughout this textbook, we will refer to bonds generically as long-term debt instruments that promise fixed payments to their owners. However, specific terms are used depending on the maturity of the bond. Short-term bonds, with a maturity of less than one year, are called bills or paper; those with maturities between one and 10 years are called notes; and those with terms of longer than 10 years are called bonds. In spite of their different names, all of these instruments are valued in the same manner.

In Canada, the main bond issuers include federal, provincial, and municipal governments; government agencies (e.g., Canada Mortgage and Housing Corporation, Hydro-Québec); corporations; and non-resident issuers (e.g., the Maple bond market). The main purchasers are institutional investors—in particular, insurance companies, pension funds, and bond mutual funds.

# The Basic Structure of Bonds

---

**LEARNING OBJECTIVE 6.1**

Describe the basic structure and the various features of different types of bonds.

---

**bonds** long-term debt instruments that promise fixed payments and have maturities of more than 10 years

The key feature of a **bond** is that the issuer agrees to pay the bondholder (investor) a regular series of cash payments and to repay the full principal amount by the maturity date. These promises are stipulated in the bond contract and are a fixed contractual commitment. (You will hear this phrase again, as it is important in corporate financing.) Although many payment structures are possible, the traditional "coupon-paying" bond provides for identical payments at regular intervals (usually semi-annually or annually), with the full principal to be repaid at the stated maturity date. We call the interest payment a "coupon" because at one time bonds literally had coupons, and the investor had to cut the coupon from the bond certificate and send it in for payment.[1] Today, almost all bonds in Canada are registered, and the payments are made directly into individual bank accounts, providing a record of who has paid and who has received the interest. When the principal payment is made in one lump sum at maturity, it is called a **bullet payment** or **balloon payment**.

**bullet payment** or **balloon payment** a principal payment made in one lump sum at maturity

Bonds are often referred to as fixed income securities because the interest payments and the principal repayment are specified, or fixed, at the time the bond is issued. In other words, the bond purchaser knows the amount and timing of the future cash payments to be received, barring default by the issuer. However, if the buyer decides to sell the bond before maturity, the price received will depend on the level of interest rates at that time, which we will illustrate shortly.

To understand how bonds are valued, we can use timelines, introduced in Chapter 5. A typical pattern of cash payments is depicted in **Figure 6.1**. Two things are obvious. First, the structure of the payments differs from that of the loan or mortgage discussed in Chapter 5, because those involved "blended" payments that included both interest and principal components. In contrast, a typical bond has interest payments throughout its life and a balloon payment of principal at maturity. Second, a bond can be viewed as two separate components: an annuity, consisting of the identical and regular interest payments; plus a lump-sum principal payment at maturity. In this way, valuing a traditional bond becomes a straightforward application of the time value of money concept developed in Chapter 5.

Note: $I$ = interest payments; $F$ = principal repayment (face value)

**FIGURE 6.1** **Cash Flow Pattern for a Traditional Coupon-Paying Bond**

## Basic Bond Terminology

**bond indenture** a legal document that specifies the payment requirements and all other salient matters relating to a particular bond issue, held and administered by a trust company

Before discussing how to value bonds, we will introduce some terminology and institutional features attached to different types of bonds. Most bonds are sold to a variety of investors, and someone must make sure that the payments are made on time. This problem is solved by including all relevant details for a particular bond issue in a **bond indenture** that is held and administered by a trust company. This is a legal document that specifies the payment requirements, all other salient matters relating to the issue (such as any assets that might serve as

---

[1] The coupons were attached to the bond and could be mailed in by whoever had the bond. Such bonds were called "bearer bonds" and are still widely used in parts of the world where personal tax rates are high.

security or **collateral** for the bond), any protective provisions, and other additional features. The trust company (or **fiduciary**) makes sure that these **covenant provisions** within the indenture are observed by the issuer. In this way, the bond is a legal contract between the issuer and the holder, and the trust company has the job of ensuring that the terms of the contract are upheld. Any change to the contract normally requires the approval of bondholders representing from one-half up to two-thirds of the value of the outstanding bonds.

All bond indentures include the basic features attached to the cash payments. The **par value**, also known as **face value** or **maturity value**, represents the amount that is paid at maturity for traditional bonds. The par value of most bonds is $1,000, although bond prices are typically quoted based on a par value of $100. In other words, if the price of a bond is quoted at $99.583, a $1,000 par value bond would be selling for $995.83. The **term to maturity** of the bond is the time remaining until the maturity date. The regular **interest payments**, or **coupons**, for any bond are determined by multiplying the coupon rate (which is stated on an annual basis) by the par value of the bond. For example, a bond with a coupon rate of 6 percent and a par value of $1,000 would pay coupons of $60 if they are paid annually, or $30 every six months if they are paid semi-annually.

## Security and Protective Provisions

Technically, bonds are debt instruments that are secured by real assets. They are often called **mortgage bonds**. However, not all bonds are secured by real property. For example, **debentures** are similar to bonds but are generally unsecured, or are secured by a general floating charge over the company's unencumbered assets (i.e., those assets that have not been pledged as security for other debt obligations). Government bonds are debentures because no specific security is pledged as collateral. However, they are referred to as bonds as a matter of convention.

**Collateral trust bonds** are secured by a pledge of other financial assets, such as common shares, bonds, or treasury bills. **Equipment trust certificates** are secured by equipment, such as the rolling stock of a railway. The assets pledged as security are owned by investors through a lease agreement with, in this case, a railway until the loan has been retired. The certificates have serial numbers that dictate their maturity date, with a certain amount maturing every year.

**Protective covenants** are clauses in the trust indenture that restrict the actions of the issuer. Negative covenants prohibit certain actions. For example, a company may be restricted from making a dividend payment larger than a certain amount or prevented from pledging its assets to another lender. Positive covenants specify actions that the firm agrees to undertake. For example, a company may promise to provide quarterly financial statements or maintain certain working capital levels.

## Additional Bond Features

So far, we have focused our discussion on traditional or regular coupon-paying bonds that provide for full principal repayment at the maturity date. However, some bonds have additional features (or options) that may provide for some, or all, of the principal to be repaid before maturity. We discuss a few of the more common provisions here.

**Callable bonds** give the issuer the option to "call," or repurchase, outstanding bonds at predetermined **call prices** (generally at a premium over par) at specified times. A necessary condition for a company to call back its bonds is that market interest rates have declined. The company may choose to redeem its bonds and issue new bonds to take advantage of lower interest rates. This is not a sufficient reason to call the bonds, however, because there are costs associated with a new bond issue, and the savings realized from lower interest rates may not be enough to overcome the additional costs. These types of bonds create an additional risk for the bondholder; hence, the call price usually exceeds the par value to provide an incentive for investors to buy the bonds initially. Conversely, **retractable** (or putable) **bonds** allow the bondholder to sell the bonds back to the issuer at predetermined prices at specified times earlier than the maturity date. In this way, the maturity of the bond is retracted, or shortened. As opposed to callable bonds, a necessary condition for holders of retractable bonds to exercise

---

**collateral**   assets that can serve as security for the bond in case of default

**fiduciary**   a third party who acts to ensure that the best interests of bondholders are upheld

**covenant provisions**   clauses within the indenture that lay out the legal rights of the bondholder and the obligations of the issuer

**par value, face value,** or **maturity value**   the amount paid at maturity for traditional bonds

**term to maturity**   time remaining to maturity date

**interest payments** or **coupons**   amounts paid on a bond at regular intervals

**mortgage bonds**   debt instruments that are secured by real assets

**debentures**   debt instruments that are similar to bonds but are generally unsecured or are secured by a general floating charge over the company's unencumbered assets

**collateral trust bonds**   bonds secured by a pledge of other financial assets, such as common shares, bonds, or treasury bills

**equipment trust certificates** a type of debt instrument secured by equipment, such as railway rolling stock

**protective covenants**   clauses in a trust indenture that restrict the actions of the issuer; covenants can be positive or negative

**callable bonds**   bonds that give the issuer the option to "call," or repurchase, outstanding bonds at predetermined prices at specified times

**call prices**   prices, generally at a premium over par, at which issuers can repurchase bonds

**retractable bonds**   bonds that the bondholder can sell back to the issuer at predetermined prices at specified times earlier than the maturity date

**extendible bonds** bonds that allow the bondholder to extend the maturity dates of the bonds

their option is that market interest rates have gone up. In contrast, **extendible bonds** allow the bondholder to extend the maturity date of the bond. "Extendibles" and "retractables" give bondholders the flexibility to change the maturity of the bonds to their advantage. We will discuss why they might want to do this after we show how bonds are valued.

**sinking fund provisions** the requirement that an issuer set aside funds each year to be used to pay off the debt at maturity

**Sinking fund provisions** require the issuer to set money aside each year so that funds are available at maturity to pay off the debt. Provisions are made in two ways. In the first, the firm repurchases a certain amount of debt each year so that the amount of debt goes down. In the second, the firm pays money into the sinking fund to buy other bonds, usually government bonds, so that money is available at maturity to pay off the debt, although the amount due at maturity is unchanged. Sinking fund provisions benefit the issuers, because they allow the issuers to avoid paying the entire face value of the issue at the maturity date. However, if the bonds are actually repurchased, sinking fund provisions are not always beneficial to investors, because the bonds may be randomly called and repaid. Furthermore, the bonds are normally repaid at par value, and the investors may suffer a loss if the bonds are worth more. Finally, as the amount of the issue declines, there may be a loss of liquidity as the bonds become less attractive. These disadvantages are offset by the operation of a sinking fund in which funds are used to buy government bonds.

**purchase fund provisions** the requirement that a certain amount of debt be repurchased only if it can be repurchased at or below a given price

**Purchase fund provisions** are similar to sinking fund provisions, but require the repurchase of a certain amount of debt only if it can be repurchased at or below a given price. These provisions are generally advantageous to the debt holder, since they provide some liquidity and downward price support for the market price of the debt instruments.

**convertible bonds** bonds that can be converted into common shares at predetermined conversion prices

**Convertible bonds** can be converted into common shares at predetermined conversion prices. Convertible bonds may be offered to make debt issues more attractive to investors. These are discussed in greater depth in Chapter 19.

From this brief review of the institutional features attached to bonds, two things should be very clear: a bond is a contract, and what is in that contract varies from one bond to another. Unlike common shares, which we discuss later, each bond contract has to be reviewed separately, because one differs from another. If investors don't recognize this, the differences can come back to haunt them years after the bond has been issued.[2]

---

### Concept Review Questions

1. In what ways are bonds different from mortgages?
2. How is a traditional bond structured?
3. What is a bond indenture?
4. What is the difference between a positive and a negative covenant provision?
5. How do callable bonds differ from retractable and extendible bonds?
6. How do sinking funds work?

---

## 6.2 | Bond Valuation

### LEARNING OBJECTIVE 6.2
Explain how to value a bond given an appropriate discount rate.

We are now ready to examine how bonds are valued. Once investors know the par value, the term to maturity, and the coupon rate, they know both the amount and the timing of all the future promised payments on a bond. The price of a bond is determined by discounting

---

[2]In particular, issuers have to do only what they have contracted to do in the indenture. A famous case involved bonds issued by CP Railway that were redeemable "after 1953." Investors expected the bonds to be redeemed in 1954 and sued the company when it refused. The company won the suit.

these future payments using an appropriate discount rate, often referred to as the "market rate of interest." We will discuss the factors that affect this discount rate in greater detail later in the chapter. For now, you should be aware that the discount rate is a function of market conditions (i.e., other market interest rates) as well as factors specific to the issue and issuer.

The price of a bond equals the present value of the future payments on the bond, which is the present value of the interest payments and the par value repaid at maturity. By using the concepts developed in Chapter 5, we can use Equation 6.1 to price the bond:

$$B = I \times \left[ \frac{1 - \frac{1}{(1 + k_b)^n}}{k_b} \right] + F \times \frac{1}{(1 + k_b)^n} \qquad [6.1]$$

where $B$ = the bond price
$I$ = interest (or coupon) payments
$k_b$ = the bond discount rate (or market rate)
$n$ = the term to maturity
$F$ = the face (par) value of the bond

In Equation 6.1, note that the interest or coupon payments are multiplied by the standard present value annuity factor (PVAF) developed in Chapter 5, while the par value is multiplied by the present value interest factor (PVIF). Valuing a traditional bond is an example of applying the time value of money concept. Using interest factors, Equation 6.1 can be written more compactly as:

$$B = I \times PVAF(k_b, n) + F \times PVIF(k_b, n) \qquad [6.2]$$

---

**EXAMPLE 6.1** | Bond Valuation with Annual Coupons I

Find the price of a $1,000 par value bond that matures in 10 years if it pays interest annually, if it is based on a 6-percent coupon rate, and if the market rate of interest is 7 percent.

**Solution**

$$F = \$1,000; I = \text{coupon rate} \times F = 0.06 \times \$1,000 = \$60; n = 10; k_b = 0.07$$

With this information, we can use Equation 6.1 to find the price, or we can solve it by using a financial calculator.

$$B = \$60 \times \left[ \frac{1 - \frac{1}{(1.07)^{10}}}{0.07} \right] + \$1,000 \times \frac{1}{(1 + 0.07)^{10}}$$

$$= (\$60 \times 7.02358) + (\$1,000 \times 0.50835) = \$421.41 + \$508.35 = \$929.76$$

or $B = \$60 \times PVAF(7\%, 10) + \$1,000 \times PVIF(7\%, 10) = \$929.76$

We illustrate this with a timeline.

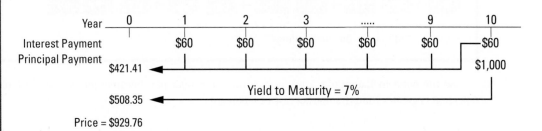

---

**EXAMPLE 6.1** | Solution Using a Financial Calculator

Input the following variables:

$$\boxed{-60} \to \boxed{\text{PMT}} ; \boxed{10} \to \boxed{\text{N}} ; \boxed{-1{,}000} \to \boxed{\text{FV}} ; \boxed{7\%} \to \boxed{\text{I/Y}} ; \boxed{\text{CPT}} \boxed{\text{PV}} = \$929.76$$

As in Chapter 5, with the calculator solution we have to be careful with the signs. The calculator program assumes that there is an outflow (negative value) for an investment and then a payoff (positive value). A negative PV result (−$929.76) would be obtained if both PMT and FV were set as positive.

---

**discount** the difference between a bond's par value and the price it trades at when it trades below the par value

In Example 6.1, the bond trades at a **discount** from its par value. This happens because the coupon rate is less than the market interest (discount) rate, which means that investors require a return greater than 6 percent on equivalent bonds under current market conditions. Because the future payments are fixed, the only way to get a return higher than the coupon rate on this bond is to pay less than the par value for it. If an investor bought the bond at its par value of $1,000 and held it to maturity, they would earn a return equal to the coupon rate of 6 percent. In other words, the person would invest $1,000, get a 6-percent return on that investment per year—that is, $60 in interest each year—and then receive $1,000 back at maturity. Thus, when market rates equal the coupon rate, bonds trade at par.[3] Similarly, if market interest rates are below the coupon rate of 6 percent, the bond will trade at a **premium** to par, which we illustrate in Example 6.2.

**premium** the difference between a bond's par value and the price it trades at when it trades above the par value

---

**EXAMPLE 6.2** | Bond Valuation with Annual Coupons II

Find the price of a $1,000 par value bond that matures in 10 years. It pays interest annually, is based on a 6-percent coupon rate, and the market rate of interest is 5 percent.

**Solution**

$$F = \$1{,}000; I = \text{coupon rate} \times F = 0.06 \times \$1{,}000 = \$60; n = 10; k_b = 0.05$$

We can use Equation 6.1 to find the price. We can also find the price by using a financial calculator.

$$B = \$60 \times \left[ \frac{1 - \dfrac{1}{(1.05)^{10}}}{0.05} \right] + \$1{,}000 \times \frac{1}{(1 + 0.05)^{10}}$$

$$= (\$60 \times 7.72173) + (\$1{,}000 \times 0.61391) = \$463.30 + \$613.91 = \$1{,}077.21$$

or alternatively $B = \$60 \times \text{PVAF}(5\%, 10) + \$1{,}000 \times \text{PVIF}(5\%, 10) = \$1{,}077.21$

---

**EXAMPLE 6.2** | Solution Using a Financial Calculator

Input the following variables:

$$\boxed{-60} \to \boxed{\text{PMT}} ; \boxed{10} \to \boxed{\text{N}} ; \boxed{-1{,}000} \to \boxed{\text{FV}} ; \boxed{5\%} \to \boxed{\text{I/Y}} ; \boxed{\text{CPT}} \boxed{\text{PV}}$$

$= \$1{,}077.22$ (difference due to rounding)

---

So the bond in Example 6.2 trades at a premium over par, because the coupon rate of 6 percent is greater than the market rate of 5 percent.

---

[3]Bonds are often issued at (or very close to) par by setting the coupon rate equal to the market rate at the time of issue.

The two examples assume that interest payments (or coupons) are made annually. However, in reality, most bonds pay coupons semi-annually. Fortunately, this does not change the valuation process, but we must make the appropriate adjustments to reflect the fact we are dealing with semi-annual periods rather than annual ones. Specifically, we must divide the annual coupon payments by two to determine the amount of semi-annual coupons and multiply the number of years to maturity by two to obtain the number of semi-annual periods to maturity. Finally, we need a semi-annual discount rate because that coincides with the frequency of payments. For bonds, as a matter of convention, the appropriate adjustment is to divide the market bond yield by two to obtain the six-month market yield (notice that this implies that the bond yields are not effective rates). Example 6.3 shows how to apply this process.

---

**EXAMPLE 6.3** | Bond Valuation with Semi-Annual Coupons

Determine the price of a 15-year bond that pays interest semi-annually and has a par value of $1,000 and a coupon rate of 5 percent, when the appropriate market rate is 6 percent.

**Solution**

Semi-annual market rate: $k = 6\%/2 = 3\%$

Term to maturity (in semi-annual periods): $n = 15 \text{ years} \times 2 = 30$

Semi-annual coupons: $I = \text{coupon rate}/2 \times F = 0.05/2 \times \$1,000 = \$25$

$$B = \$25 \times \left[ \frac{1 - \frac{1}{(1.03)^{30}}}{0.03} \right] + \$1,000 \times \frac{1}{(1 + 0.03)^{30}}$$

$$= (\$25 \times 19.60044) + (\$1,000 \times 0.041199) = \$490.01 + \$411.99 = \$902.00$$

or alternatively B = $25 × PVAF(3%, 30) + $1,000 × PVIF(3%, 30) = $902.00

We illustrate this with a timeline.

---

**EXAMPLE 6.3** | Solution Using a Financial Calculator

Input the following variables:

= $902.00

---

# Factors Affecting Bond Prices

The examples above illustrate the most important property of fixed income investments, such as bonds: *if interest rates decrease, the market prices of bonds increase and vice versa*. In addition, the difference in yields between Canadian government bonds and U.S. treasury bonds has an important impact on the value of the Canadian dollar.

Consider a bond that has a 4-percent coupon paid semi-annually and that matures in 10 years. If the yield is less than 4 percent, the bond trades at a premium. If the yield is greater than 4 percent, the bond trades at a discount, as you can see when we look at yields to maturity ranging from 0 percent to 10 percent (**Table 6.1**).

**Table 6.1**   **Bond Yields**

| Yield to Maturity | Discount Rate Per Period | Number of Periods | Coupon Payment | Face Value | Price |
|---|---|---|---|---|---|
| 0% | 0.0% | 20 | $20 | $1,000 | $1,400.00 |
| 1% | 0.5% | 20 | $20 | $1,000 | $1,284.81 |
| 2% | 1.0% | 20 | $20 | $1,000 | $1,180.46 |
| 3% | 1.5% | 20 | $20 | $1,000 | $1,085.84 |
| 4% | 2.0% | 20 | $20 | $1,000 | $1,000.00 |
| 5% | 2.5% | 20 | $20 | $1,000 | $922.05 |
| 6% | 3.0% | 20 | $20 | $1,000 | $851.23 |
| 7% | 3.5% | 20 | $20 | $1,000 | $786.81 |
| 8% | 4.0% | 20 | $20 | $1,000 | $728.19 |
| 9% | 4.5% | 20 | $20 | $1,000 | $674.80 |
| 10% | 5.0% | 20 | $20 | $1,000 | $626.13 |

You can also see this inverse relationship between yields and bond values in **Figure 6.2**, in which we depict the bond price-yield curve for this bond for yields from 0 percent to 10 percent.

**Figure 6.3** provides a general depiction of the bond price-yield curve for any regular coupon-paying bond. We can also see clearly from this graph that the relationship between market rates and bond price is *not* linear; the curve representing this relationship is convex. This fact is evident if we look at the bond pricing equation, in which the discount rate is raised to powers other than one.

The shape of this curve shows two additional factors in the relationship between bond prices and market rates. First, for a given change in interest rates, bond prices will increase

**FIGURE 6.2**  Value of $1,000 Face Value Bond, with a 4-Percent Semi-Annual Coupon Maturing in 10 Years For Different Yields to Maturity

**FIGURE 6.3** **Bond Price-Yield Curve**

more when rates decrease than they will decrease when rates increase. Note, for example, that the curve is steeper to the left of any point than it is to the right, which indicates that the impact of decreasing interest rates is different from the impact of increasing ones. Second, the curve is steeper for lower interest rates, which means that a given change in interest rates will have a much greater impact on bond prices when rates are lower than it will if they are higher.

The second-most-important property of bonds is that *the longer the time to maturity, the more sensitive the bond price is to changes in market rates.* Intuitively, this makes sense, because the longer the term to maturity, the longer the investor has "locked-in" fixed payments based on the bond's coupon rate. When market rates rise above this rate, the bond price will fall more because the coupon rate is unattractive relative to prevailing rates for a longer period. The longer an investor is locked in, the greater the disadvantage and the more the bond price will fall to adjust. Similarly, when rates fall below the coupon rate, the longer an investor is locked in, the greater the attractiveness of the higher coupon. Example 6.4 illustrates this property.

---

**EXAMPLE 6.4** | Estimating Prices for Bonds with Different Terms to Maturity

Consider the bond from Example 6.3 with a $1,000 par value and a coupon rate of 5 percent, paying interest semi-annually, with market rates at 6 percent. Recalculate the price on this bond, assuming that the term to maturity is not 15 years, but is either

**a.** 5 years, or

**b.** 30 years

**Solution**

$$k = 3\%; I = \$25; F = \$1,000$$

**a.** $n = 5 \text{ years} \times 2 = 10$

$B = \$25 \times \text{PVAF}(3\%, 10) + \$1,000 + \text{PVIF}(3\%, 10)$

$= (\$25 \times 8.53020) + (\$1,000 \times 0.74409) = \$213.26 + \$744.09 = \$957.35$

**b.** $n = 30 \text{ years} \times 2 = 60$

$B = \$25 \times \text{PVAF}(3\%, 60) + \$1,000 \times \text{PVIF}(3\%, 60)$

$= (\$25 \times 27.67556) + (\$1,000 \times 0.16973) = \$691.89 + \$169.73 = \$861.62$

**EXAMPLE 6.4a** | Solution Using a Financial Calculator

Input the following variables:

$-25 \rightarrow$ PMT ; $10 \rightarrow$ N ; $-1{,}000 \rightarrow$ FV ; $3\% \rightarrow$ I/Y ; CPT PV

$= \$957.35$

**EXAMPLE 6.4b** | Solution Using a Financial Calculator

Input the following variables:

$-25 \rightarrow$ PMT ; $60 \rightarrow$ N ; $-1{,}000 \rightarrow$ FV ; $3\% \rightarrow$ I/Y ; CPT PV

$= \$861.62$

Bond prices' sensitivity to interest rates is directly related to interest rate levels and to the term to maturity. It is also related to the level of the coupon rate associated with the bond, although this factor is much less important than either interest rate levels or the term to maturity. In particular, the price of bonds with lower coupon rates will be more sensitive to interest rates than the price of higher-coupon-paying bonds will be. This is intuitive, if we recall from Chapter 5 that the compounding (or discounting) effect is accentuated with time, which suggests that a change in the discount rate will have the greatest impact on the most distant cash flows, including the par value to be received at maturity in the case of bonds. For bonds that pay lower coupons, the principal repayment, which occurs at the maturity date, represents a higher proportion of the total payments to be received by the bondholder. As a result, the prices of such bonds will fluctuate more for a given change in interest rates than will otherwise identical higher-coupon-paying bonds. Example 6.5 illustrates this property.

**EXAMPLE 6.5** | Estimating Prices for Bonds with Different Coupon Rates

Consider the semi-annual, $1,000 par value, 5-percent bond examined in Example 6.3 (call it Bond 1) along with another 15-year bond that pays semi-annual coupons based on a 6-percent coupon rate (Bond 2). Calculate the price of each bond when market rates are

**a.** 5 percent
**b.** 6 percent

**Solution**

For both bonds: $F = \$1{,}000$; $n = 30$

For Bond 1: $I = \$25$

For Bond 2: $I = \$30$

**a.** $k = 5\%/2 = 2.5\%$

Bond 1: $B = \$1{,}000$ (i.e., it trades at par, since market yield = coupon rate)
Bond 2: $B = \$30 \times \text{PVAF}(2.5\%, 30) + \$1{,}000 \times \text{PVIF}(2.5\%, 30)$
$= (\$30 \times 20.93029) + (\$1{,}000 \times 0.47674) = \$627.91 + \$476.74 = \$1{,}104.65$

**b.** $k = 6\%/2 = 3\%$

Bond 1: $B = \$25 \times \text{PVAF}(3\%, 30) + \$1{,}000 \times \text{PVIF}(3\%, 30)$
$= (\$25 \times 19.60044) + (\$1{,}000 \times 0.41199) = \$490.01 + \$411.99 = \$902.00$
Bond 2: $B = \$1{,}000$ (i.e., it trades at par, since market yield = coupon rate)

---

**EXAMPLE 6.5** | Solution Using a Financial Calculator

**a.** Bond 2 :

$-30 \rightarrow$ PMT ; $30 \rightarrow$ N ; $-1{,}000 \rightarrow$ FV ; $2.5\% \rightarrow$ I/Y ; CPT PV

$= \$1{,}104.65$

**b.** Bond 1:

$-25 \rightarrow$ PMT ; $30 \rightarrow$ N ; $-1{,}000 \rightarrow$ FV ; $3\% \rightarrow$ I/Y ; CPT PV

$= \$902.00$

---

As we would expect, based on our discussion, if we look at the change in the price of each bond in Example 6.5 for a 1-percent change in interest rates, we can see that Bond 1 (with the lower coupon rate) experienced a higher percentage change (decline) in price than Bond 2 (the higher-coupon-rate bond) did, although the difference is not dramatic.

Percentage change in price of Bond 1
$= (\$902 - \$1{,}000)/\$1{,}000 = -0.0980 = -9.8\%$

Percentage change in price of Bond 2
$= (\$1{,}000 - \$1{,}104.65)/\$1{,}104.65 = -0.0947 = -9.5\%$

The sensitivity of bond prices to changes in interest rates is generally referred to as **interest rate risk**. All else remaining constant, longer-term bonds with lower coupon rates and lower market yields will possess greater interest rate risk than will shorter-term, higher-coupon bonds with higher market yields. An important measure of interest rate risk, **duration**, incorporates all these factors into a single measure. Technically, duration measures the approximate percentage change in the price of a bond for a given change in the appropriate market interest rate. For example, the price of a bond with a duration of 10 would be expected to increase approximately 10 percent if interest rates fell 1 percent. This approximation tends to work quite well for small changes in interest rates, but is less accurate for larger changes in rates due to the convexity of the price-yield curve.

While a detailed discussion of duration is beyond the scope of this textbook, we note the following important points:

**interest rate risk**   the sensitivity of bond prices to changes in interest rates

**duration**   an important measure of interest rate risk that incorporates several factors

1. The prices of bonds with higher durations are more sensitive to interest rate changes than are those with lower durations.

2. All else being equal, durations will be higher when (1) market yields are lower, (2) bonds have longer maturities, and (3) bonds have lower coupons.[4]

---

[4]Excel has a duration function—DURATION (settlement, maturity, coupon, yld, frequency, basis)—where all of the same factors needed to value a bond are the inputs. The duration function measures the sensitivity of the bond to interest rate changes.

# Bond Quotes

Table 6.2 shows some typical bond quotes that appear in the financial media.

**Table 6.2  Selected Bond Quotes on May 15, 2019**

**Canada T-Bills**

| Issuer | Coupon | Maturity | Price | Yield |
|---|---|---|---|---|
| Canada 1-Month | N/A | Jun 2019 | 99.87 | 1.68 |
| Canada 2-Month | N/A | Jul 2019 | 99.75 | 1.67 |
| Canada 3-Month | N/A | Aug 2019 | 99.61 | 1.71 |
| Canada 6-Month | N/A | Oct 2019 | 99.22 | 1.70 |
| Canada 1-Year | N/A | Apr 2020 | 98.40 | 1.69 |

**Canada Benchmarks**

| Issuer | Coupon | Maturity | Price | Yield |
|---|---|---|---|---|
| Canada 2-Year | N/A | 2021 | 100.34 | 1.57 |
| Canada 5-Year | N/A | 2024 | 103.29 | 1.53 |
| Canada 10-Year | N/A | 2029 | 105.46 | 1.66 |
| Canada 30-Year | N/A | 2049 | 119.38 | 1.89 |

**Provincials**

| Issuer | Coupon | Maturity | Price | Yield |
|---|---|---|---|---|
| Alberta | 1.25 | Jun 2020 | 99.47 | 1.77 |
| Manitoba | 1.55 | Sep 2021 | 99.51 | 1.77 |
| Ontario | 1.35 | Mar 2022 | 98.76 | 1.81 |
| Quebec | 3.50 | Dec 2022 | 105.60 | 1.86 |
| British Columbia | 2.70 | Dec 2022 | 103.08 | 1.81 |
| Manitoba | 2.55 | Jun 2023 | 102.38 | 1.94 |
| Newfoundland | 2.30 | Jun 2025 | 100.33 | 2.24 |
| Ontario | 2.60 | Jun 2026 | 101.21 | 2.21 |
| Nova Scotia | 2.10 | Jun 2027 | 98.55 | 2.30 |

**Corporates**

| Issuer | Coupon | Maturity | Price | Yield |
|---|---|---|---|---|
| Laurentian Bank | 2.750 | Apr 2021 | 100.63 | 2.42 |
| TELUS | 2.350 | Mar 2022 | 100.04 | 2.34 |
| Saputo | 1.939 | Jun 2022 | 98.28 | 2.53 |
| CIBC | 2.300 | Jul 2022 | 100.38 | 2.18 |
| Enbridge | 3.190 | Dec 2022 | 102.51 | 2.45 |
| Ford Canada | 3.742 | May 2023 | 99.79 | 3.80 |
| Emera | 2.900 | Jun 2023 | 102.79 | 3.62 |
| Bell Canada | 2.700 | Feb 2024 | 100.41 | 2.61 |
| Brookfield | 4.300 | Mar 2024 | 102.79 | 3.66 |

**Source:** Data from Perimeter Markets Inc., www.pfin.ca

Let's consider the following quote from the table:

| Issuer | Coupon | Effective Maturity | Price | Yield |
|--------|--------|--------------------|-------|-------|
| Alberta | 1.25 | Jun 2020 | 99.47 | 1.77 |

This quote shows the issuer (Alberta—that is, the Province of Alberta), the associated coupon rate (1.25 percent), the month and year the bond matures (June 2020), the May 15, 2019, trading day's price ($99.47), and the associated yield to maturity (1.77 percent). The price is based on $100 of face value. For example, if the face value of the bond was $1,000, you would have to pay $994.70 ($1,000 × 0.9947) plus accrued interest (discussed below) to purchase the bond. The yields refer to the market (discount) rates that we have been using to value bonds. These are discussed in the next section.

Notice that the Province of Alberta bond was trading at a discount, because the yield was above the coupon rate of 1.25 percent. This is true of many of the bonds listed in Table 6.2. However, several bonds were also trading above par at that time, including the Province of Quebec bond (at $105.60) shown in Table 6.2. This is because bonds are issued at various points in time, and the coupon rates are set approximately equal to prevailing market rates at that time. Therefore, with different levels of prevailing interest rates, at any given point we will observe some bonds trading at discounts and others trading at premiums.

## Cash Prices versus Quoted Prices

The prices discussed in this section, as well as those reported in the media, such as in Table 6.2, are typically referred to as "quoted" prices. These differ from the actual prices investors pay for bonds whenever bonds are sold at a date other than the date of a coupon payment. The reason is that interest will accrue to bondholders between such payment dates. For example, investors who held bonds for 45 days since the last coupon was paid have "earned" 45 days of interest, even though they will not receive those 45 days of interest if they sell the bonds now because coupons are paid semi-annually—in fact, the bond purchasers will receive those 45 days of interest when they receive the next scheduled coupon payment. As a result, a bond purchaser must pay the bond seller the quoted price plus the accrued interest on the bond. This amount is referred to as the "cash price" of the bond. Example 6.6 demonstrates how the cash price is calculated.

---

**EXAMPLE 6.6** | The Cash Price of a Bond

Consider the bond in Example 6.3, which pays interest semi-annually, has a $1,000 maturity value and a 5-percent coupon rate, and is sold on July 14 at a quoted price of $902. Assume this bond matures on June 30, which implies the semi-annual interest payments on this bond are made on June 30 and on December 31. Calculate the cash price of this bond.

**Solution** The cash price for this bond would equal $902 plus 14 days of accrued interest at the coupon rate of 5 percent. Each coupon is valued at 2.5 percent of $1,000 or $25. There are a total of 184 days from July 1 to December 31. In other words,

Cash price = Quoted price + Accrued interest

Cash price = $902 + ($1,000 × 0.025 × [14/184]) = $902 + $1.90 = $903.90

Note that we have to choose a convention in terms of how much interest has been earned. Because this is a Canadian bond, we use the Canadian day count, which uses the actual number of days that have elapsed and assumes there are 365 days in a year.

---

## Concept Review Questions

1. What time value of money formula do we need to value a bond?
2. When market interest rates are above the coupon rate on a bond, is it a premium or discount bond?
3. If market interest rates go up, what happens to bond prices?
4. Which types of bonds have more interest rate risk: short-term or long-term bonds?
5. What is the day count convention in Canada and in the United States?

# Bond Yields

---

### LEARNING OBJECTIVE 6.3
Determine the discount rate or yield for a given market value of a bond.

---

## Yield to Maturity

**yield to maturity (YTM)** the discount rate used to evaluate bonds

The discount rate used to evaluate bonds is referred to as the **yield to maturity (YTM)**. It is the yield that an investor would realize if they bought the bond at the current price, held it to maturity, received all the promised coupon payments on their scheduled dates, and reinvested all the coupons received at the YTM. Given the price of a bond and all the details regarding the amount and timing of interest and principal repayments, we can always estimate the bond's YTM using Equation 6.1, which is reproduced below.

$$B = I \times \left[ \frac{1 - \frac{1}{(1 - k_b)^n}}{k_b} \right] + F \times \frac{1}{(1 + k_b)^n}$$

The difference is that now we will solve for $k_b$, given $B$, instead of solving for $B$, given $k_b$. $k_b$ represents the discount rate that equates the known market price ($B$) with the present value of the future interest payments and face value repayment. This rate is simply a special form of internal rate of return (IRR), which will be discussed in detail in Chapter 13. For bonds that pay annually, $n$ is the number of years to maturity, and YTM is $k_b$. For semi-annual bonds, $n$ is the number of years to maturity multiplied by two, and YTM is $k_b$ multiplied by two.

Unfortunately, as we will learn in Chapter 13, solving for IRRs is difficult because of the various powers involved in Equation 6.1: solutions may require logarithms, a business calculator, Excel, or a lot of time-consuming trial and error. The same problems occur in calculating the YTM on a bond. In fact, an exact algebraic solution for the YTM is not generally available. Fortunately, financial calculators and Excel are good at repetitive calculations and can solve the problem easily. However, if you don't have access to a financial calculator or Excel, you have to use a trial-and-error approach to estimate the approximate yield that satisfies Equation 6.1.[5] In Example 6.7, we will use the formula with trial and error, and then find the solution using a financial calculator.

---

**EXAMPLE 6.7** | Estimating the YTM on an Annual-Pay Bond

Estimate the YTM on a 10-year, 5-percent bond that pays annual coupons and is selling for $980.

**Solution**

$$B = \$980; F = \$1,000; I = 0.05 \times \$1,000 = \$50; n = 10$$

$$\$980 = \$50 \times \left[ \frac{1 - \frac{1}{(1 + k_b)^{10}}}{k_b} \right] + \$1,000 \times \frac{1}{(1 + k_b)^{10}}$$

Essentially, we begin by estimating the discount rate, $k_b$. We try the coupon rate first, even though we know the yield must be greater than 5 percent, as the bond is selling at a discount. Substituting this rate into the equation for $k_b$ gives us a price of $1,000. Therefore, $k_b$ must be higher than this rate because $1,000 is more than the price we want ($980). Substituting 6 percent for $k_b$ gives us a price of $926.40, so 6 percent is too high a discount rate. Therefore, we know that the rate we are looking for is between 5 percent and 6 percent.

---

[5]An approximation formula does exist, but it can be off by a significant amount sometimes, especially for longer-term bonds that are trading at prices quite different from their par value.

We can obtain a close approximation by using linear interpolation, which involves setting up two equivalent ratios:

| Rate | Price |
|------|-------|
| 5% | $1,000 |
| $k_b$ | $980 |
| 6% | $926.40 |

We find $k_b$ by forming one ratio of the rates and putting the corresponding prices in the same position in a ratio of the prices:

$$\frac{k_b - 5}{6 - 5} = \frac{\$980 - \$1,000}{\$926.40 - \$1,000}$$

$$\frac{k_b - 5}{1} = \frac{-\$20}{-\$73.60} = 0.2717$$

So, $k_b = 5.27$ percent.

Since this is an annual-pay bond, the YTM $= k_b = 5.27$ percent. Notice that this is close to the more accurate solution of 5.26 percent obtained using a financial calculator.

We illustrate this with a timeline.

---

**EXAMPLE 6.7** | Solution Using a Financial Calculator

Input the following variables:

50 → PMT ; –980 → PV ; 1,000 → FV ; 10 → N

Then, CPT I/Y will give 5.26 percent, which is an annual rate, so YTM (annual) = 5.26 percent (correct to two decimal places).

---

We follow the same process to estimate the YTM on a bond that pays semi-annual coupons, except that we first solve Equation 6.1 for a semi-annual rate ($k_b$), which we then convert to an annual rate by multiplying it by two.[6] Example 6.8 demonstrates this process.

---

**EXAMPLE 6.8** | Estimating the YTM on a Semi-Annual Bond

Estimate the YTM on a 20-year, 6-percent bond that pays semi-annual coupons and is selling for $1,030.

**Solution**

$$B = \$1,030; F = \$1,000; I = 0.06/2 \times \$1,000 = \$30; n = 20 \times 2 = 40$$

$$\$1,030 = \$30 \times \left[\frac{1 - \dfrac{1}{(1 + k_b)^{40}}}{k_b}\right] + \$1,000 \times \frac{1}{(1 + k_b)^{40}}$$

---

[6]We multiply the semi-annual rate by two in order to reflect the manner in which bond yields are quoted. As discussed previously, bond yields are not effective annual rates when semi-annual coupons are paid.

**EXAMPLE 6.8** | Solution Using a Financial Calculator

Input the following variables:

`30` → `PMT` ; `−1,030` → `PV` ; `1,000` → `FV` ; `40` → `N`

Then, `CPT` `I/Y` will give 2.873 percent, which is a semi-annual rate ($k_b$), so we multiply by two to find the annual YTM: 2.873% × 2 = 5.75% (rounded to two decimal places).

# Current Yield

**current yield (CY)** the ratio of the annual coupon interest divided by the current market price

The **current yield (CY)** is defined as the ratio of the annual coupon interest divided by the current market price. As such, it is not a true measure of the return to a bondholder because it disregards the bond's purchase price relative to all the future cash flows and uses just the next year's interest payment. The current yield is also sometimes referred to as the flat or cash yield. It can be calculated using Equation 6.3.

$$CY = \frac{\text{Annual interest}}{B}$$ [6.3]

**EXAMPLE 6.9** | Current Yield

Determine the current yield for the bond used in Example 6.8, which was trading for $1,030.

**Solution**

$B = \$1,030$; annual interest = $30 × 2 = $60 (or simply $1,000 × 0.06)

$$CY = \frac{\$60}{\$1,030} = 0.0583 \ or \ 5.83\%$$

Notice that the current yield does not equal the coupon rate of 6 percent or the YTM of 5.75 percent. This will hold unless the bond is trading at its face value, in which case all three rates will be equal. It is clear that whenever bonds trade at a premium, the CY will be less than the coupon rate but greater than the YTM (as in Example 6.9); and whenever they trade at a discount, the CY will be greater than the coupon rate but less than the YTM, as shown here:

| Price-Yield Relationships | |
|---|---|
| **Bond Price** | **Relationship** |
| Par | Coupon rate = CY = YTM |
| Discount | Coupon rate < CY < YTM |
| Premium | Coupon rate > CY > YTM |

## Concept Review Questions

1. Why is there no simple analytical formula for the yield to maturity?
2. When bonds sell above their par value, is the yield to maturity greater or less than the coupon rate?

# Interest Rate Determinants

---

**LEARNING OBJECTIVE 6.4**
List and describe the factors, both domestic and global, that affect interest rates.

---

## Base Interest Rates

Interest rates are usually quoted on an annual percentage basis. However, it is common to refer to changes in interest rates in terms of "basis points," each of which represents 1/100th of 1 percent. For example, a decrease of 10 basis points indicates that interest rates declined by 0.1 percent.

As we discussed in Chapter 5, the interest rate is the price of money and, just like the price of any other commodity, it is determined by the laws of supply and demand. In the case of interest rates, it is the supply of and demand for "loanable funds." All else being constant, as the demand for loanable funds increases, so does their price and, as a result, interest rates increase. Conversely, interest rates decrease as the supply of loanable funds increases. The interest rates that we have been discussing so far are called **nominal interest rates**, because they are the rates charged for lending today's dollars in return for getting dollars back in the future, without taking into account the purchasing power of those future dollars. One of the most important factors in determining these nominal interest rates is the expected rate of inflation, because this determines the purchasing power of those future dollars.

In structuring our discussion of actual interest rates, we refer to the base rate as the **risk-free rate (RF)**. We will discuss risk at length shortly, but the term "risk free," although conventional, is a bit of a misnomer. What it actually refers to is **default free**, in that the investors know exactly how many dollars they will get back on their investment. It is common to use the yield on short-term government treasury bills (T-bills), which are discussed in greater detail later in this chapter, as a proxy for this risk-free rate. Federal government T-bill yields are considered risk free because they possess no risk of default: the government essentially controls the Bank of Canada and can always have it buy any bonds that are issued, using Bank of Canada banknotes. Furthermore, government T-bills have little interest rate risk because their term to maturity is short.

As a result, we have the approximate relationship as shown in Equation 6.4:

$$\boxed{RF = \text{Real rate} + \text{Expected inflation}} \qquad [6.4]$$

This relationship is an approximation of the direct relationship between inflation and interest rates that is often referred to as the "Fisher effect," after Irving Fisher, who described how investors attempt to protect themselves from the loss in purchasing power caused by inflation by increasing their required nominal yield.[7] As a result, interest rates will be low when expected inflation is low and high when expected inflation is high.

The "precise" Fisher relationship is shown in Equation 6.5:

$$\boxed{RF = [(1 + \text{Real rate})(1 + \text{Expected inflation})] - 1} \qquad [6.5]$$

Applying a bit of algebra, we see that the risk-free rate is not only the sum of the real rate and the expected inflation rate, but also the cross-product term, real rate × expected inflation:

$$RF = \text{Real rate} + \text{Expected inflation} + (\text{Real rate} \times \text{Expected inflation})$$

**nominal interest rates**  the rates charged for lending today's dollars in return for getting dollars back in the future, without taking into account the purchasing power of those future dollars

**risk-free rate (RF)**  the rate of return on risk-free investments, which is often used as the base interest rate

**default free**  having no risk of non-payment

---

[7]See Fisher, Irving, "Appreciation and Interest." *Publications of the American Economic Association* (August 1896), pp. 1–110.

**FIGURE 6.4** Interest Rates and Inflation

**Source:** Data from Bank of Canada

We often see the approximation (Equation 6.4), simply because the cross-product term (the rightmost term) is generally small when inflation rates are low, and can therefore be ignored.

The average return on Government of Canada T-bills over the 1938 to 2018 period was 4.53 percent. Over the same period, inflation averaged 3.61 percent, which indicates that the average real return over this period was 0.92 percent, or 92 basis points.[8]

The graph in **Figure 6.4** provides the history of the annual inflation rate as measured by the consumer price index (CPI) and the yield to maturity on long-term Government of Canada bonds over the 1958 to 2018 period. Notice that the level of nominal interest rates generally tracked the increase in inflation throughout the 1960s and early 1970s, until inflation unexpectedly peaked at more than 12 percent in 1974, at which point the actual inflation rate exceeded government bond yields. Since then, interest rates have generally declined with the rate of inflation.

As we just discussed, one measure of the real rate is the difference between the ongoing inflation rate and the long-term bond rates, which averaged 6.81 percent over the 1958 to 2018 period. This difference was larger throughout the 1980s and 1990s, before narrowing considerably after 2002. Since then, interest rates have remained abnormally low relative to inflation rates for several reasons (which are discussed in the remainder of this chapter).

---

**EXAMPLE 6.10** | Estimating the Real Rate of Return

If T-bill rates are currently 4.5 percent and the expected level of inflation is 2 percent, estimate the approximate real rate of return.

**Solution**

$$\text{Real rate} = 4.5 - 2 = 2.5\%$$

---

## Global Influences on Interest Rates

We have already discussed the effect that global factors have played in influencing domestic interest rates, which has been painfully obvious over the past few years. For example, the excellent returns experienced by Canadian and U.S. bond markets during 2011 were a direct result of the influence of the European debt crisis, which led bond investors to seek safer places

---

[8]Notice that we are looking at returns "after the fact" in this example. In practice, the return is based on expected inflation, which will usually not be the same as actual inflation.

for their funds. While global influences can dominate in times of such crises, these effects are present even under normal circumstances, as discussed below.

Although interest rate levels vary from one country to the next, global interest rates interact with one another. This occurs because most countries have now removed foreign exchange restrictions, allowing capital to flow from one country to another in search of higher rates of return. As a result, interest rates in Canada are heavily influenced by prevailing rates in other countries, especially those in the United States. This influence is inevitable in today's capital markets because money is the most generic of all commodities. If there are no restrictions, one price will prevail in the capital market.

Exactly how do foreign interest rates affect domestic interest rates? For example, why do investors not invest in the bonds of countries that are offering higher interest rates, and why do companies not issue bonds in countries with lower rates? The answer to these questions lies in the functioning of foreign exchange markets. For example, although it may be tempting to buy bonds in countries offering higher interest rates, the additional gains could easily be cancelled out (and large losses could even be incurred) as a result of adverse movements in the foreign exchange rates prevailing when funds are converted back into the domestic currency. In other words, investing or issuing debt abroad creates foreign exchange risk, which offsets the potential advantages that may arise from inter-country interest rate differentials.

The **interest rate parity (IRP) theory** demonstrates how differences in interest rates between countries are offset by expected changes in exchange rates. If this were not the case, capital would flow from countries with low interest rates to those with high interest rates, increasing the supply of capital in the country with higher rates, which would ultimately drive down borrowing costs. Similarly, the capital outflows from countries with low rates would cause their rates to rise in order to have the supply of funds equal the demand for these funds.

**interest rate parity (IRP) theory** a theory that demonstrates how differences in interest rates between countries are offset by expected changes in exchange rates

The IRP theory, which is discussed in greater detail in Appendix 6A, uses forward currency exchange rates to describe the precise relationship between interest rates and currency levels, because forward currency contracts can be used to eliminate foreign exchange risk. Essentially, the IRP theory states that forward exchange rates, which can be locked in today in order to eliminate foreign exchange risk, will be established at levels that ensure investors will end up with the same amount whether they invest at home or in another country (with no foreign exchange risk). Important factors that affect both interest rates and currency exchange rates are inflation and inflation differentials between countries. For example, if Canadian inflation exceeded that in the United States, we would expect that interest rates would be higher in Canada than in the United States. However, the inflation would cause the value of our currency to depreciate in relation to the U.S. dollar so that we could remain competitive in international trade. Thus, a U.S. investor who bought Canadian bonds in an attempt to benefit from our higher rates would lose these gains when they converted the Canadian-dollar payments back into U.S. dollars.

In short, although interest rates are heavily influenced by inflation and other domestic macroeconomic variables, global factors, such as foreign exchange rates and inflation differentials, also play an important role in the level of interest rates at any given time.

## The Term Structure of Interest Rates

So far, we have discussed the major factors affecting the base level of interest rates, or RF, which we use as a proxy for the yield on short-term government T-bills. The yields on other debt instruments will differ from RF for several reasons. One important factor affecting debt yields is the term to maturity. This is obvious if we look at the Canadian bond quotes from Table 6.2, where we can see various yield levels for bonds with different maturity dates, even though they were issued by the same entity. For example, the Government of Canada benchmarks are yields ranging from 1.53 percent for bonds maturing in 2024 to 1.89 percent for bonds maturing in 2049.

**term structure of interest rates** the relationship between interest rates and the term to maturity on underlying debt instruments

The relationship between interest rates and the term to maturity on underlying debt instruments is referred to as the **term structure of interest rates**. The graphic representation of this relationship (as displayed in **Figure 6.5**) is often referred to as the **yield curve**. Yield curves must be constructed based on interest rates on debt instruments that are from the same issuer. Otherwise, default risk (discussed below) and other risk factors, in addition to maturity differentials, will affect the difference in yields. Therefore, the yield curve is almost

**yield curve** the graphic representation of the term structure of interest rates, based on debt instruments from the same issuer

**FIGURE 6.5** Historical Yield Curves, 1990, 1994, 1998, 2004, 2012, 2015, and 2019

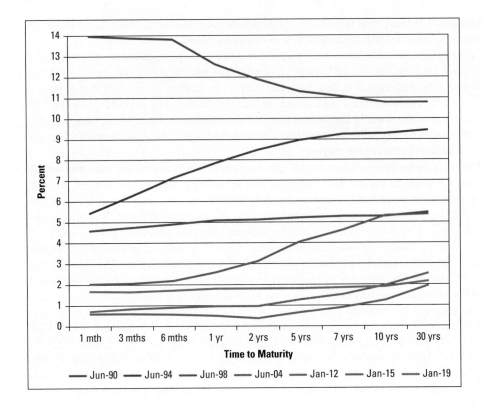

always constructed using federal government issues because they possess the same default risk, as well as similar issue characteristics. In addition, the government tends to have a large number of issues outstanding at any given time, so we can construct a yield curve with rate estimates for a wide variety of maturities.

Figure 6.5 shows seven historical Government of Canada yield curves at the end of June in 1990, 1994, 1998, and 2004, and as at January 2012, January 2015, and January 2019. Although yield curves are usually upward sloping, they can assume a wide variety of shapes, which is evident in this figure. The 2015 yield curve slopes upward, with one-month rates sitting at 0.6 percent and longer-term rates at just over 1.9 percent. This illustrates that although long-term government bonds are virtually free from default risk—just as short-term government T-bills are—long-term bonds typically yield more than medium-term bonds, which in turn typically yield more than T-bills.

Similar to the curves for 2015 and 2012, the curves for 1994 and 2004 are upward sloping. However, these four curves vary significantly in terms of their shapes and their starting points, with long-term rates exceeding the short-term rates by about 4 percent in 1994 and 2004, but by less than 2 percent in 2015 and 2012. In addition, the short-term rates vary from under 1 percent in 2015 and 2012 to just more than 2 percent in 2004 and almost 6 percent in 1994. The downward-sloping (or inverted) yield curve from 1990, when short-term rates exceeded long-term rates, is less common. Some market participants believe these inverted curves indicate that short-term rates will fall. In fact, short-term interest rates did decline in the subsequent 1991–1993 period. Another less common shape is the relatively flat yield curves in 1998 and in 2019, which indicate that long- and short-term rates are similar.

Several theories attempt to account for the various shapes and movements of the yield curve. We describe three of the most popular theories here.

**liquidity preference theory**
a theory that suggests that investors prefer short-term debt instruments because they exhibit less interest rate risk, while debt issuers prefer to lock in borrowing rates for longer periods to avoid the risk of having to refinance at higher rates

1. The **liquidity preference theory** suggests that investors prefer short-term debt instruments (i.e., more liquid instruments) because they exhibit less interest rate risk, while debt issuers prefer to lock in borrowing rates for longer periods to avoid the risk of having to refinance at higher rates. Therefore, issuers must provide investors with higher yields to induce them to invest in longer-term bonds. As a result, yield curves will generally be upward sloping because long-term rates will be higher than short-term rates. Although this theory is intuitive and does a good job of explaining why yield curves are usually upward sloping, it is somewhat less convincing when the yield curve is inverted (or flat), as it suggests that

investors expect long-term rates to decline, and the magnitude of the decline dominates (or equals) the premium that investors usually expect when lending for longer periods of time.

2. The **expectations theory** argues that the yield curve reflects investor expectations about future interest rates. Therefore, an upward-sloping yield curve reflects expectations of interest rate increases in the future, and a downward-sloping curve reflects expectations of interest rate decreases in the future. Unlike the liquidity preference theory, this theory provides a reasonable explanation for downward-sloping and flat term structures, as well as for upward-sloping curves. However, it does not account for the predominance of upward-sloping curves, because it is unreasonable to believe that people expect rates to increase most of the time.

3. The **market segmentations theory** suggests that distinct markets (or market segments) exist for interest rate securities of various maturities (for example, bank deposits constitute a market at the short end of maturities, and pension plans a market at the long end), and that rates are determined within these independent market segments by the forces of supply and demand within that market. The resulting term structure merely depicts the consequences of the forces of supply and demand within these markets.

Each of these theories provides useful insights into the factors that affect the shape of term structures. However, each theory has its limitations and therefore does not provide a comprehensive explanation. It is best to realize that liquidity preferences by investors, investor expectations about interest rates, and the demand and supply forces within various maturity segments all affect the shape of the yield curve at any given time, and that the relative importance of each of these factors will vary through time.

## Risk Premiums

In addition to differences in terms to maturity, the yield on bonds will differ from the risk-free rate because of additional risks or features associated with these instruments. In other words, investors expect extra compensation for assuming additional risks, and therefore they require higher returns. We can express this relationship using Equation 6.6.

$$k_b = RF +/- \text{Maturity yield differential} + \text{Spread} \qquad [6.6]$$

The maturity yield differential refers to the term structure impact, which we discussed in the section above, so we now turn our attention to the last term in Equation 6.6. The **spread** is a difference in yield that compensates the investor for the assumption of additional risks, which may include some or all of (1) default or credit risk, (2) liquidity, and (3) issue-specific features. We will discuss each of these in turn.

The most obvious difference in yield arises because of the different levels of **default risk** associated with the bond issuer. In other words, bondholders require higher yields to compensate them for the possibility that the borrower may default on the promised debt payments. This factor is an obvious influence on the yields shown in Table 6.2. For example, consider the Quebec bond with a 3.50-percent coupon, maturing in December 2022 and yielding 1.86 percent, and the Enbridge bond with a lower coupon of 3.19 percent, maturing the same month and yielding 2.45 percent. The higher rate of return for Enbridge is primarily accounted for by the risk of default.

**Debt ratings** are assigned by professional debt-rating services, which perform detailed analyses of bond issuers to determine their ability to sustain their required payments of interest and principal. The ratings may be modified by "high" or "low" to indicate the relative ranking within a category. **Figure 6.6** lists the debt-rating categories for Standard & Poor's (S&P), Dominion Bond Rating Service (DBRS), and Moody's.

**Investment-grade debt** is debt with a rating at or above BBB (DBRS, S&P, and Fitch Ratings) or Baa (Moody's). In other words, investment-grade debt includes the top four major classes. **Speculative debt** has a credit rating below investment grade. If a rated bond is not investment grade, then it is speculative. Some other names for speculative debt are "high-yield debt," "junk bond," or "low-grade debt."

**expectations theory**   a theory that argues that the yield curve reflects investor expectations about future interest rates

**market segmentations theory**   a theory that suggests that distinct markets (or market segments) exist for interest rate securities of various maturities, and that rates are determined within these independent market segments by the forces of supply and demand within that market

**spread**   a difference in yield that compensates the investor for the assumption of additional risks

**default risk**   the risk associated with the bond issuer and its ability to pay

**debt ratings**   ratings assigned by professional debt-rating services after detailed analyses of bond issuers to determine their ability to sustain the required interest and principal payments

**investment-grade debt**   debt obligation with a credit rating of AAA, AA, A, or BBB (or Aaa, Aa, A, or Baa)

**speculative debt**   debt that is not investment grade, being rated below BBB or Baa; also commonly referred to as "high-yield debt," "junk bonds," or "low-grade debt"

**FIGURE 6.6** **Debt-Rating Categories for Standard & Poor's, Dominion Bond Rating Service, and Moody's**

| S&P and DBRS | Moody's | Description | | |
|---|---|---|---|---|
| AAA | Aaa | highest credit quality | } High quality | } Investment grade |
| AA | Aa | very good quality | | |
| A | A | good quality | } Medium grade | |
| BBB | Baa | medium quality | | |
| BB | Ba | lower medium quality | | } Non-investment grade |
| B | B | poor quality | | |
| CCC | Caa | speculative quality | | |
| CC | Ca | very speculative quality | | |
| D | C | default | | } In default |
| Suspended | | rating suspended | | |

**Sources:** Standard & Poor's, www.standardandpoors.com; DBRS, www.dbrs.com; Moody's, www.moodys.com

Why have an issue evaluated by a credit-rating firm? The answer is that many investors want to have, or are required to have, a third-party assessment of the creditworthiness of the debt. For example, many pension funds and insurance companies (the two largest holders of bonds) are restricted to investing in investment-grade debt.

Is all debt rated? No, it isn't. Some issuers will place an issue directly with an investor and will not have the issue rated if the investor does not require it.

National governments issue debt obligations (referred to as sovereign debt). In theory, this debt is considered to be risk free because the government can print money or raise revenues through taxes to meet the cash flow obligations of this sovereign debt. We say "in theory" because there have been situations in which this debt has been viewed as not risk free. This has been the case in recent memory for many European countries facing possible debt default, including Greece, Ireland, Italy, Portugal, and Spain. Other nations have defaulted in the past, including Venezuela, Russia, Argentina, Ivory Coast, Ukraine, and Belize. In some cases, the debt has been restructured, allowing the nation to repay the debt under more favourable terms.[9]

Sovereign debt ratings are similar to those of corporate debt ratings in terms of a ratings scheme, but the factors are different. Sovereign debt ratings take into account:

- fiscal performance
- debt burden
- external liquidity and international investment position
- institutional effectiveness
- political risks
- monetary flexibility
- economic structure
- growth prospects

Consider the case of Greece, which is part of the European Union. As the country's economic conditions worsened, its debt credit rating deteriorated over time and has only recently started to improve (**Table 6.3**).

These credit ratings reflect the burgeoning debt relative to the country's gross domestic product (GDP). For example, the ratio of debt to GDP climbed from 94 percent in 1999 to 142.8 percent in 2010. Additionally, GDP growth went from positive 1 percent in 2008 to negative 2 percent and negative 4.5 percent in 2009 and 2010, respectively. Moody's, in a report issued in March 2015, estimated the probability of Greece defaulting on its debt as nearly 6 percent. This is in sharp contrast to a country like Jamaica, with debt classified as lower medium quality (BB), which has an estimated probability of default of only 1 percent. Greece is part of the

---

[9]An exception is the case of Ecuador in 2008. That country's government simply decided not to pay its debts on the basis of moral grounds, though the country likely could have paid its debts.

**TABLE 6.3**  Greek Debt Credit Rating

| Date | Debt Rating |
|------|-------------|
| March 26, 1997 | A− |
| March 13, 2001 | A |
| June 10, 2003 | A+ |
| November 17, 2004 | A |
| January 14, 2009 | A− |
| December 16, 2009 | BBB+ |
| April 27, 2010 | BB+ |
| March 29, 2011 | BB− |
| May 9, 2011 | B |
| June 13, 2011 | CCC |
| July 27, 2011 | CC |
| March 21, 2014 | C |
| March 20, 2015 | CCC− |
| January 7, 2019 | B+ |

**Source:** Data from Standard & Poor's Ratings Services, www.spratings.com

European Union and, as such, cannot print more money and must seek assistance from the European Central Bank. It therefore has limited flexibility in dealing with its economic woes.

As the example of Greece illustrates, the credit ratings of countries reflect varying economic conditions. The ratings for 16 major nations as of January 7, 2019, are listed in **Table 6.4**.

On August 5, 2011, Standard & Poor's lowered the rating on the debt of the United States from AAA to AA+. The United States had had an AAA rating since 1917. This downgrade followed a rancorous debate over the debt ceiling, the budget, and deficit spending.[10]

**TABLE 6.4**  Credit Ratings for Various Countries

| Country | Credit Rating as of January 7, 2019 |
|---------|-------------------------------------|
| Australia | AAA |
| Brazil | BB− |
| Canada | AAA |
| France | AA |
| Germany | AAA |
| Iceland | A |
| Israel | AA− |
| Italy | BBB |
| Japan | A+ |
| Mexico | BBB+ |
| People's Republic of China | A+ |
| Portugal | BBB− |
| Russian Federation | BBB− |
| Sweden | AAA |
| United Kingdom | AA |
| United States | AA+ |

**Source:** Data from Standard & Poor's Ratings Services, www.spratings.com

[10]Congress passed the *Budget Control Act of 2011* [Public Law 112–25, S. 365], and the bill was signed into law on August 2, 2011. The bill increased the country's debt limit, attempting to avert a credit downgrade or default on the debt. Standard & Poor's downgraded the U.S. debt within one week of the bill being signed into law. This debt crisis brought to the forefront the issue of how much debt the federal government should or could bear.

The United States managed to regain its AAA credit rating but has since been downgraded again, while Canada has succeeded in retaining its AAA credit rating and managed to exit the storm brought about by the worldwide financial crises relatively unscathed.

Table 6.5 presents a comparison of government-issued debt ratings by region. Europe is relatively strong with few low-rated countries (out of 50 rated) and eight AAA-rated countries (Denmark, Germany, the Netherlands, Luxembourg, Liechtenstein, Norway, Sweden, and Switzerland). In the Americas, only Canada is AAA-rated. The Asia-Pacific region includes Singapore and Australia in the AAA-rated category, while the Middle East and Africa have significantly lower-rated sovereign debt.

Most of the differences in yields for bonds of the same term to maturity that we observe as we move from Government of Canada bonds to provincial government bonds to corporate bonds are due to differences in the default risk associated with the issuers. However, a portion of the difference is also due to the fact that Government of Canada bonds trade more actively than provincial bonds, which trade more actively than most investment-grade corporate bonds, which trade more actively than junk bonds. In other words, some bonds are more liquid than others, meaning they are easier to buy and sell and the required price concessions are lower. Bonds that are less liquid generally have to offer investors a higher yield to compensate for this illiquidity. This additional yield is referred to as the **liquidity premium**. Researchers at the Bank of Canada have estimated that 63 percent of the difference in spreads for investment-grade issuers results from liquidity rather than risk differences.[11] This is reversed for non-investment-grade issuers, with changes in default risk dominating.

**liquidity premium** an additional yield offered on bonds that are less liquid

The importance of good fiscal management is highlighted in Finance in the News 6.1. We suggest that excessive fiscal spending may contribute to election successes, but that this type of strategy will have longer-term political consequences for governing parties.

**issue-specific premiums** premiums that arise when bonds have features that cause them to be more or less attractive to investors, relative to straight (option-free) bonds

**Issue-specific premiums** arise when bonds have features that cause them to be more or less attractive to investors, relative to straight (option-free) bonds. For example, as discussed earlier in the chapter, the call feature is detrimental to bondholders because these bonds are likely to be called by the issuer when interest rates are low (so that they can be refinanced at lower rates), which is exactly when the market prices of these bonds are increasing. As a result, investors will not pay as much for a callable bond as they would for an otherwise identical non-callable bond (i.e., they will demand a higher return). Conversely, retractable bonds permit investors to sell the bonds back to the issuer at predetermined prices when interest rates rise (and bond prices fall), which provides protection against rising rates. Similarly, extendible bonds will only be extended by investors if the coupon rates on such bonds are competitive. If rates increase, the investors will choose not to extend and could invest in other

**TABLE 6.5    Government-Issued Debt Ratings by Region**

| Region | Sovereign Ratings as of December 31, 2018 | | | | | | |
|---|---|---|---|---|---|---|---|
| | ≥CCC | ≥B | ≥BB | ≥BBB | ≥A | ≥AA | =AAA |
| Europe (50) | 50 | 48 | 39 | 29 | 24 | 13 | 8 |
| Americas (31) | 29 | 25 | 16 | 12 | 4 | 2 | 1 |
| Asia-Pacific (21) | 21 | 21 | 13 | 11 | 8 | 5 | 2 |
| Middle East (11) | 11 | 11 | 7 | 6 | 4 | 2 | 0 |
| Africa (20) | 19 | 14 | 3 | 1 | 0 | 0 | 0 |

**Source:** Data from Standard & Poor's Ratings Services, www.spratings.com

[11]Garcia, A., and Yang, J., "Understanding Corporate Bond Spreads Using Credit Default Swaps." *Bank of Canada Review* (Autumn 2009).

## 6.1 Finance in the News    Fiscal Restraint Still *de Rigueur*; Trump Drunk on Deficits, Canada Should Resist

Remember when you had to balance a budget to get elected in Canada? It was the highest form of economic stewardship in the late 1990s and for at least the first decade of the new millennium. The idea was so entrenched that even Thomas Mulcair's New Democratic Party thought it had to promise a surplus to beat Stephen Harper's Conservatives in the 2015 election.

The NDP won't be making that mistake again. "I think maybe it's no longer a big issue," New Democratic leader Jagmeet Singh told journalist Paul Wells in front of an audience in Ottawa earlier this month. Wells had asked Mulcair's replacement whether the closest thing Canada has to a socialist party still thought balanced budgets were crucial. "I'm opposed to austerity in all its forms," Singh said.

The aftermath of the Great Recession is now what scares voters in Canada and the United States, not stories about bond vigilantes.

At the end of January, New Brunswick Finance Minister Cathy Rogers postponed her (Liberal) government's plan to erase the province's deficit in 2019. Instead, she and Premier Brian Gallant chose to set the stage for the September election with a budget that cuts small-business taxes and spends a little extra on economic development, youth employment, and taking care of seniors.

I know what some of you conservatives are thinking: What do you expect from vote-buying Liberals and freespending socialists? But it's not like you guys have much credibility on the subject, given the recent performance of the political wing of your movement in Washington.

Rogers and the New Brunswick Liberals at least are talking about balancing the budget in the near future (2020, instead of 2019). President Donald Trump on Monday presented a budget proposal that would run up deficits of more than US$7 trillion over the next decade, twice what the White House forecast last spring, according to Politico.

House Speaker Paul Ryan, one of the more vigorous critics of former president Barack Obama's deficit spending, called the Trump plan "thoughtful" and "responsible."

Thoughtful? We can debate.

But there is nothing responsible about Trump's profligacy. Even Obama's economists think it's too much.

"I consider myself a deficit dove," tweeted Jason Furman, one of the previous president's top economic advisers, adding that he's fine with a budget shortfall of 3 per cent of gross domestic product. "But, deliberately sending an essentially full employment economy into deficits of 5 to 7 per cent is nuts."

Canadian governments have an opportunity here if they can resist getting drunk on last year's good economic fortune.

There's little anyone can do to stop Trump from wreaking havoc with the international trade, and his tax cuts will lure investment that might otherwise have occurred in Canada. But Trump needn't influence the spending decisions of Finance Minister Bill Morneau, who said Tuesday that the next budget will be on Feb. 27, or his provincial and territorial counterparts. There's an argument to be had about whether Canada needs lower taxes on investment to remain competitive.

But we should keep in mind there will also be an advantage to having sound finances, a goal that Trump's America has abandoned.

Some think the recent chaos in financial markets is the work of those vigilantes mentioned above. Bond yields jumped before stock prices plunged. That might have had something to do with investors deciding there are safer bets than lending the Trump administration money at 2.5 per cent, the yield on 10-year Treasury debt at the start of the year.

The yield on the U.S. benchmark now is around 2.9 per cent. A possible reason: Now that all of the world's major economies are growing again, investors have options. That means the United States will have to pay more to finance its spending than it has had to in years.

Interest rates will be rising most everywhere as central banks lift borrowing costs to stay ahead of inflation. Still, those places with reputations for sound fiscal management will have an advantage because creditors will accept lower risk premiums to finance their debt. Canada is one of those places. The federal government is one of a small number of sovereigns that survived the financial crisis with its credit rating intact, and five of 10 provinces have balanced budgets.

The prospect of relatively lower interest rates and stable bond markets is something finance ministers should protect, not exploit for short-term gains. That doesn't mean rushing to balance budgets for the sake of it. The economics profession is less convinced of the necessity of this than it was in the 1990s, and as Harper discovered, voters won't stand for it.

But it might mean signalling to those bond vigilantes that Canada is committed to reducing its debt.

For example, New Brunswick's deficit remains fairly small, but its debt is projected to stay fairly large at around 45 per cent of GDP. DBRS Ltd., the bond-rating agency, was unimpressed. It said it was "concerned" about Rogers's budget and that it "questions the credibility of the multi-year plan to return to balance."

Reputations are won and lost. The International Monetary Fund has been advising Prime Minister Justin Trudeau for a couple of years to legislate a commitment to reduce the debt relative to GDP in order to retain the confidence of markets. Dozens of countries do this, but Trudeau and Morneau refuse. They should reconsider. It could be their secret weapon in their fight against Trump's efforts to upend the Canadian economy.

bonds that offer higher coupon rates. Because extendible and retractable bonds, as well as convertible bonds, offer the investor an additional privilege, they will trade at higher prices than otherwise identical straight bonds (i.e., they will provide a lower return).

All three of these factors are embedded in what is commonly called the corporate spread over equivalent-maturity Canada bonds. In practice, it is difficult to separate these three components of the corporate spread. The *Lessons to Be Learned* feature here discusses the corporate yield spread, as measured by the difference between AAA-rated bonds and BBB-rated bonds. These spreads vary over time with the business cycle and often provide clues as to future economic activity. Notice that despite the variation, the AAA-rated bonds always provide lower yields than their riskier BBB-rated counterparts.

## Lessons to Be Learned

Corporate bond yields change along with the changing economy. Not only do credit spreads—the difference between corporate bond yields and government yields—increase in a recession, but the spread between yields on corporate bonds that have different credit risks increases, as indicated by the spread between yields on AAA-rated bonds and BBB-rated bonds. We can see these characteristics when examining the credit spreads leading up to and following the financial crisis of 2008 and 2009, illustrated in **Figure 6.7**.

In fact, the credit spreads began to widen several months before the recession and peaked in the fall of 2009. The spreads narrowed again during the recovery period in 2010, although they remained at high levels because of uncertainty over the economic recovery, the European debt crisis, and similar matters.

**FIGURE 6.7** Default Credit Spreads, December 1979 to December 2009

**Source:** Data from Datastream

## Concept Review Questions

1. How does the expected rate of inflation affect nominal interest rates?
2. Why do interest rates differ between Canada and the United States?
3. Why do interest rates on different-maturity Canada bonds differ?
4. What is a corporate spread?

## 6.5 | Other Types of Bonds/Debt Instruments

**LEARNING OBJECTIVE 6.5**
List and describe the characteristics and pricing of other debt instruments.

## Treasury Bills

Treasury bills (T-bills) are short-term government debt obligations that mature in one year or less. Partly because of this short term to maturity, they do not make regular interest payments but are sold at a discount from their par (or face) value, which is paid on the maturity date. The interest earned is the difference between the purchase price and the face value. In Canada,

T-bills are issued by the federal government and, in recent years, have also been issued by many provincial governments.

Similar to bonds, T-bills can be priced by estimating the present value of the expected future payment (i.e., the par value that is to be repaid at maturity). Equation 6.7 is used to value T-bills in Canada, with $k_{BEY}$ being the bond equivalent yield and $n$ the term to maturity expressed as number of days.

$$P = \frac{F}{\left(1 + k_{BEY} \times \frac{n}{365}\right)} \qquad [6.7]$$

---

**EXAMPLE 6.11** | Determining the Price of T-bills

Find the price of a 91-day T-bill with a face value of $10,000 that has a quoted yield of 4.2 percent.

**Solution**

$$F = \$10,000; k_{BEY} = 0.042; n = 91$$

$$P = \frac{F}{\left(1 + k_{BEY} \times \frac{n}{365}\right)} = \frac{\$10,000}{1.010471233} = \$9,896.37$$

---

Similar to bonds, T-bill prices are usually quoted on the basis of $100 of par value, so the price quote for the T-bill in Example 6.11 would be $98.9637.

Rearranging Equation 6.7, we can determine the yield on T-bills in percentage form using Equation 6.8:

$$k_{BEY} = \frac{F - P}{P} \times \frac{365}{n} \times 100 \qquad [6.8]$$

---

**EXAMPLE 6.12** | Estimating the Yield on a T-bill

Estimate the yield on a 182-day T-bill that is currently selling at a price of $98.20.

**Solution**

$$F = \$100; P = \$98.20; n = 182$$

$$k_{BEY} = \frac{\$100 - \$98.20}{\$98.20} \times \frac{365}{182} \times 100 = 0.018329939 \times 2.005494505 \times 100 = 0.03676 \times 100 = 3.676\%$$

---

In the United States, yields on T-bills are usually quoted based on the "bank discount yield," which is determined by using a different procedure from that used to calculate the bond equivalent yield in Canada. The differences arise because of the use of face value instead of price in the denominator of the first term, and because 360 days is used instead of 365 days to annualize the rate. The resulting equation, in which $k_{BDY}$ is the bank discount yield, is:

$$k_{BDY} = \frac{F - P}{P} \times \frac{360}{n} \times 100$$

## Zero Coupon Bonds

A **zero coupon bond** (or, simply, "zero") is structured similarly to a long-term T-bill, in the sense that it does not make regular interest payments but is issued at a discount and repays the par value at the maturity date. The return earned represents the difference between the purchase price and the redemption price. Obviously, the lower the price paid for the bond, the higher the return. "Zeroes" were initially created by financial intermediaries who purchased traditional bonds, stripped the cash flows (both the interest and the principal repayment components) from

**zero coupon bond** a bond that is issued at a discount, pays no coupons, and repays the par value at the maturity date; also commonly referred to simply as a "zero" them, and sold these cash flows separately. Today, most zeroes are created this way, but some are also initially issued as zero coupon bonds. These instruments are very popular with financial institutions, which often use them for hedging purposes to cover their outstanding liabilities. Zeroes are ideally suited for this purpose because, unlike traditional bonds, they do not prevent investors from reinvesting interest payments that are received before maturity.

Zero coupon bonds are easy to evaluate using a variation of Equation 6.1 in which we drop the first term (because there are no interest payments to discount). This leaves us with Equation 6.9.

$$B = F \times \frac{1}{(1 + k_b)^n} \qquad [6.9]$$

Remember that, by convention, we value these bonds by assuming semi-annual discounting periods and convert our quoted yield to a semi-annual yield. Therefore, the number of periods should also be expressed in terms of semi-annual periods.

**EXAMPLE 6.13** | Estimating the YTM on a Semi-Annual Bond

Determine the price of a 15-year zero coupon bond with a face value of $1,000 and a market yield of 5 percent.

**Solution**

$$F = \$1,000; n = 15 \text{ years} \times 2 = 30; k_b = 0.05/2 = 0.025$$

$$B = \$1,000 \times \frac{1}{(1 + 0.025)^{30}} = \$1,000 \times 0.47674 = \$476.74$$

**EXAMPLE 6.13** | Solution Using a Financial Calculator

Input the following variables:

0 → PMT ; 30 → N ; 1,000 → FV ; 2.5% → I/Y ; CPT PV

= −$476.74

From Equation 6.8, notice that if market rates fell, the price of the zero would increase and vice versa, just as is the case for a regular coupon-paying bond. In fact, the market prices of zeroes are even more sensitive to interest rate changes, because they make no coupon payments at all.

Finally, it is relatively straightforward to solve for the YTM on a zero if we are given the price. In particular, we can rearrange Equation 6.9 to determine an exact solution for the semi-annual rate ($k_b$), as shown in Equation 6.10. This value is then doubled to find the annual YTM. Notice that this differs from coupon-paying bonds, for which there was no finite solution for YTM.

$$k_b = \left[\frac{F}{B}\right]^{\frac{1}{n}} - 1 \qquad [6.10]$$

**EXAMPLE 6.14** | Estimating the YTM on a Zero Coupon Bond

Determine the YTM on a 10-year zero coupon bond with a face value of $1,000 that is selling for $560.

**Solution**

$$F = \$1,000; n = 10 \text{ years} \times 2 = 20; PV = \$560$$

$$k_b = \left[\frac{\$1,000}{\$560}\right]^{\frac{1}{20}} - 1 = (1.785714286)^{\frac{1}{20}} - 1 = 1.0294 - 1 = .0294 = 2.94\%$$

**EXAMPLE 6.14** | Solution Using a Financial Calculator

Input the following variables:

$= 2.94\%$

Doubling this gives a YTM of 5.88 percent.

# Floating Rate and Real Return Bonds

**Floating rate bonds (floaters)** have adjustable coupons that are usually tied to some variable short-term rate, such as the T-bill rate, although many variations exist. They differ significantly from traditional fixed-income bonds because the coupon rates increase as interest rates increase and vice versa. Therefore, floaters provide protection against rising interest rates and tend to trade near their par value.

Government of Canada **Real Return Bonds** provide investors with protection against inflation by providing a real yield in which a nominal yield is adjusted for inflation. This is achieved by pegging the face value to the rate of inflation (as measured by the CPI) and having the coupon rate apply to the inflation-adjusted face value.

**floating rate bonds (floaters)**   bonds that have adjustable coupons that are usually tied to some variable short-term rate

**Real Return Bonds**   bonds issued by the Government of Canada that provide investors with protection against inflation

# Canada Savings Bonds

**Canada Savings Bonds (CSBs)** differ significantly from the bonds discussed above. Because they cannot be traded, CSBs have no secondary market and therefore their prices do not change over time. They are registered in the name of the investor at the time of purchase and can be cashed out by the owner, at their full par value plus eligible accrued interest, at any bank in Canada at any time. Currently, CSBs may be purchased only by individuals, estates, and certain trusts. This restriction differs significantly from the restrictions on traditional bonds, which tend to be held mainly by institutional investors.

The rates of return on CSBs may vary through time. At present, CSBs are available in two forms: (1) regular interest bonds, which pay out the annual interest amounts; and (2) compound interest bonds, which reinvest the interest, meaning interest is also earned on accumulated interest (producing the power of compounding, as discussed in Chapter 5).

**Canada Savings Bonds (CSBs)**   bonds issued by the Government of Canada that cannot be traded and therefore have no secondary market, which means their prices do not change over time

## Concept Review Questions

1. How does the formula for determining the price of a T-bill resemble the formula for determining the price of a zero coupon bond? Why is this so?
2. How do U.S. bank discount yields differ from bond equivalent yields?
3. How do floaters and Real Return Bonds provide protection against inflation?

## APPENDIX 6A   Interest Rate Parity

**LEARNING OBJECTIVE 6.6**

Explain how interest rate parity works.

Interest rates vary from one country to the next, yet wise investors do not invest merely in the bonds of countries that are offering the highest interest rates. Any attempt to exploit such opportunities would expose investors to foreign exchange risk, which offsets the potential advantages that may arise from inter-country interest rate differentials. The interest rate parity (IRP) theory demonstrates why the differences in interest rates between countries should be offset by forward exchange rates. In particular, the IRP states that the relationship shown in Equation 6A.1 should hold or else "arbitrage opportunities" (i.e., the opportunity to earn riskless profits) will exist.

$$\frac{F}{S} = \frac{(1 + k_{domestic})}{(1 + k_{foreign})} \qquad [6A.1]$$

where

$F$ = the current forward exchange rate, expressed in number of units of domestic currency required to purchase one unit of the foreign currency

$S$ = the current spot exchange rate

$k_{domestic}$ = the domestic interest rate

$k_{foreign}$ = the foreign interest rate

Example 6A.1 uses this equation to determine the predicted forward exchange rate.

---

**EXAMPLE 6A.1** | Using Interest Rate Parity (IRP)

Assume British interest rates are currently 10 percent on one-year British T-bills. Assume that sterling is quoted at £1 = C$1.75 and the interest rate on one-year T-bills in Canada is 6 percent. Find the one-year forward exchange rate.

**Solution** Notice that the interest rate differential for the specified one-year term is 4 percent, which implies that the forward exchange rate should be approximately 4 percent lower (in Canadian dollar terms) than the spot rate to ensure that IRP holds.

To be more precise, we can rearrange the IRP equation to solve for the forward rate:

$$F = S \times \frac{(1 + k_{domestic})}{(1 + k_{foreign})} = \$1.75 \times \frac{1.06}{1.10} = \$1.6864$$

---

The IRP implies that an investor cannot benefit from higher foreign interest rates without assuming risk, which is demonstrated in Example 6A.2.

---

**EXAMPLE 6A.2** | No Arbitrage Opportunity When IRP Holds

Determine the ending wealth of two Canadian investors with C$1,000 to invest, assuming the conditions identified in Example 6A.1 exist. Investor 1 invests domestically, while Investor 2 invests in Britain and eliminates foreign exchange risk using the forward contract.

**Solution**

Investor 1: Ending wealth = C$1,000 × 1.06 = C$1,060

Investor 2: First, convert C$ into £: C$1,000/1.75 = £571.43
Second, £571.43 invested at 10% grows to £628.57
Third, convert £ into C$ through forward contract = £628.57 × 1.6864 = C$1,060.02

Notice that if this is the prevailing forward rate, neither investor is better off by investing in either country (the $0.02 difference is due to rounding error).

---

Why does this relationship hold? If it didn't, investors could earn arbitrage (riskless) profits without putting up any initial investment. Example 6A.3 demonstrates how.

---

**EXAMPLE 6A.3** | An Arbitrage Opportunity When IRP Does Not Hold

In Example 6A.2, if the forward exchange rate was set at C$1.70 instead of C$1.6864, demonstrate how an investor (arbitrageur) could earn arbitrage (riskless) profit. Assume that anyone can borrow and lend (invest) at the quoted rates.

**Solution**   When the arbitrageur observes the forward price of C$1.70, she would first note that it violates IRP, because $F \neq 1.75\,(1.06) / (1.1) = C\$1.6864$.

This means that the forward rate is pricing sterling too dearly and Canadian dollars too cheaply. The arbitrageur will therefore want to sell sterling for Canadian dollars through the forward contract. She borrows Canadian dollars to buy sterling now in the spot market, and invests it in Britain until the maturity date of the forward contract.

Assuming the arbitrageur borrows C$2 million, we obtain the following:

1. Borrow C$2 million (at 6 percent) to buy sterling today. Convert C$2 million at spot of $(1/C\$1.75) = £1,142,857$.

2. Invest in sterling for one year at 10 percent.

3. The total investment at maturity = £1,142,857(1.1) = £1,257,143.

   Convert back to Canadian dollars at the C$1.70 forward rate: £1,257,143 × C$1.70 = C$2,137,143.

   Pay back loan: (C$2 million)(1.06) = C$2.12 million.

   Arbitrage profit = C$2,137,143 − C$2,120,000 = C$17,143

The arbitrageur would make a riskless (arbitrage) profit (of C$17,143) without assuming any risk and without making any initial investment of her own funds

---

The condition in Example 6A.3 could not persist, however. As investors rushed to exploit such an opportunity, the forward price would quickly fall to C$1.6864.[12]

In similar fashion, if the forward exchange rate were $1.66, arbitrageurs would note that this violates IRP because the rate is £1 = C$1.6864. However, this time the forward rate prices sterling too cheaply and Canadian dollars too dearly. Investors will want to sell Canadian dollars for sterling through the forward contract, which means they will borrow sterling (at 10 percent), convert it to Canadian dollars in the spot market, and invest the amount in Canada (at 6 percent) until the maturity date of the forward contract.

---

| APPENDIX 6B | # The Yield for Callable Bonds |

## LEARNING OBJECTIVE 6.7
Determine the discount rate or yield for a callable bond.

# Yield to Call

We mentioned earlier that bonds often have flexible maturity dates because some bonds are callable by the issuer; for others, the maturity can be retracted or extended by the investor. This means that we can calculate the yield to maturity for these different dates. Suppose, for example, that the bond in Example 6.8 was callable after five years at par.[13] This means

---

[12]Although the example illustrates the existence of an arbitrage possibility, it disregards transaction costs and the fact that borrowing and lending rates are not usually equal. Both of these factors affect the potential for arbitrage and explain why IRP need not hold precisely, but rather should hold within reasonable boundaries.

[13]In practice, many callable bonds have more than one call date.

that it is possible the bond will not be outstanding for 20 years, because it may be called after five years. The yield that is associated with a bond's first call date is known as its yield to call (YTC). It can be estimated in the same way as we estimated the YTM, using Equation 6.1, except that we replace the time to maturity ($n$) with the time to first call ($c$); we replace the face value ($F$) with the call price ($CP$); and we denote the appropriate discount rate as $k_c$ instead of $k_b$. This gives us Equation 6B.1.

$$B = I \times \left[ \frac{1 - \frac{1}{(1 + k_c)^c}}{k_c} \right] + CP \times \frac{1}{(1 + k_c)^c} \qquad [6B.1]$$

**EXAMPLE 6B.1** | Estimating the Yield to Call (YTC)

Estimate the YTC on a 20-year, 6-percent bond that is callable in five years at a call price of $1,050, if the bond pays semi-annual coupons and is selling for $1,030.

**Solution**

$$B = \$1,030; CP = \$1,050; I = 0.06/2 \times 1,000 = \$30; n = 5 \times 2 = 10$$

$$\$1,030 = \$30 \times \left[ \frac{1 - \frac{1}{(1 + k_c)^{10}}}{k_c} \right] + \$1,050 \times \frac{1}{(1 + k_c)^{10}}$$

We illustrate this with a timeline.

**EXAMPLE 6B.1** | Solution Using a Financial Calculator

Input the following variables:

30 → PMT ; –1,030 → PV ; 1,050 → FV ; 10 → N

Then, CPT I/Y will give 3.081 percent. This is a semi-annual rate ($k_c$), so we multiply by two to find the annual YTC: $3.081\% \times 2 = 6.16\%$.

Notice that in Example 6B.1, the YTC is greater than the coupon rate, because the call price of $1,050 is greater than the bond's current price of $1,030. This is the same bond used in Example 6.8, where the YTM was calculated as 5.75 percent. So what can we say about the 5.75-percent YTM, compared with the 6.16-percent YTC? Because the call price is above its current market price, it is unlikely that the bond would be called back by the issuer, so it is selling based on its YTM rather than its YTC. It would trade on its YTC if it were likely the bond would be called, which would occur if the bond were trading above its call price and, correspondingly, if the YTC were lower than the YTM. Generally, the bond trades off whichever of the two is lower. We can confirm this by looking at five-year and 20-year yields on equivalent non-callable bonds.

## Concept Review Question

1. Is the yield to call always greater than the yield to maturity?

# Review

## Summary

In this chapter, we discuss the nature of bonds as an investment. We examine the standard format of a traditional coupon-paying bond and consider additional features or variations of this structure. We then examine how these instruments can be valued, using the discounting concepts developed in Chapter 5, after we determine an appropriate

discount rate. One of the most important factors affecting bond prices is the level of interest rates. The most important property of bond prices is that they increase when interest rates decrease and vice versa. Finally, we consider the various factors, both domestic and global, that affect the basic levels of market interest rates.

## Summary of Learning Objectives

### 6.1  Describe the basic structure and the various features of different types of bonds.

A bond is a security that represents a loan from the buyer (investor) to the issuer. The issuer of the bond promises a series of cash payments to the buyer—the cash payments represent interest and repayment of principal. Bonds are often referred to as "fixed income securities" because the interest payments and the principal repayment are specified, or fixed, at the time the bond is issued. A coupon bond pays the bondholder semi-annual or annual interest payments (coupons) and the face value at the maturity date.

### 6.2  Explain how to value a bond given an appropriate discount rate.

The cash price of a bond is equal to the present value of the promised cash payments. The cash price of a bond is the sum of the quoted price and accrued interest. The bond prices shown in newspapers or on websites are the quoted price and not the cash price. The quoted price is the sum of the discounted future cash flow. Thus, discount rate plays an important role in bond pricing: the higher the discount rate, the lower the bond prices.

### 6.3  Determine the discount rate or yield for a given market value of a bond.

The yield to maturity (YTM) is the discount rate that equates future payments with the current selling price. It represents the return investors would get if they purchased the bond at the given price, held it to maturity, and reinvested all interest payments at this rate of return.

### 6.4  List and describe the factors, both domestic and global, that affect interest rates.

Interest rates are affected by domestic factors, including inflation, default risk, and liquidity risk. They are also affected by global factors, including foreign interest rates and foreign exchange risk.

### 6.5  List and describe the characteristics and pricing of other debt instruments.

Other debt instruments include treasury bills, zero coupon bonds, floating rate bonds, and Real Return Bonds. The price equals the sum of the discounted future cash flow.

### 6.6  Explain how interest rate parity works.

Interest rates vary from one country to another, yet wise investors do not invest merely in the bonds of countries that are offering the highest interest rates. Any attempt to exploit such opportunities would expose investors to foreign exchange risk, which offsets the potential advantages that may arise from inter-country interest rate differentials. The interest rate parity (IRP) theory demonstrates why the differences in interest rates between countries should be offset by forward exchange rates. In particular, the IRP states that the relationship shown in Equation 6A.1 should hold or else "arbitrage opportunities" (i.e., the opportunity to earn riskless profits) will exist.

### 6.7  Determine the discount rate or yield for a callable bond.

The yield to call (YTC) of a callable bond is the discount rate that equates future payments with the current selling price. It represents the return investors would get if they purchased the bond at a given price, held it until it was called, and received the call price for the bond when called. It further assumes that all interest payments are reinvested at the YTC rate.

## Key Terms

balloon payment, p. 6-2
bond indenture, p. 6-2
bonds, p. 6-2

bullet payment, p. 6-2
call prices, p. 6-3
callable bonds, p. 6-3

Canada Savings Bonds (CSBs), p. 6-29
collateral, p. 6-3
collateral trust bonds, p. 6-3

## Equations

| Equation | Description | Formula | Page |
|---|---|---|---|
| **[6.1]** | Bond Valuation and Yield to Maturity | $B = I \times \left[ \dfrac{1 - \dfrac{1}{(1 + k_b)^n}}{k_b} \right] + F \times \dfrac{1}{(1 + k_b)^n}$ | p. 6-5 |
| **[6.2]** | Bond Valuation Using Interest Factors | $B = I \times \text{PVAF}(k_b, n) + F \times \text{PVIF}(k_b, n)$ | p. 6-5 |
| **[6.3]** | Current Yield | $CY = \dfrac{\text{Annual interest}}{B}$ | p. 6-16 |
| **[6.4]** | Fisher Relationship (approximation) | $RF = \text{Real rate} + \text{Expected inflation}$ | p. 6-17 |
| **[6.5]** | Fisher Relationship (precise) | $RF = [(1 + \text{Real rate})(1 + \text{Expected inflation})] - 1$ | p. 6-17 |
| **[6.6]** | Bond Yield Components | $k_b = RF +/- \text{Maturity yield differential} + \text{Spread}$ | p. 6-21 |
| **[6.7]** | T-Bill Price | $P = \dfrac{F}{\left(1 + k_{BEY} \times \dfrac{n}{365}\right)}$ | p. 6-27 |
| **[6.8]** | T-Bill Yield | $k_{BEY} = \dfrac{F - P}{P} \times \dfrac{365}{n} \times 100$ | p. 6-27 |
| **[6.9]** | Price—Zero Coupon Bond | $B = F \times \dfrac{1}{(1 + k_b)^n}$ | p. 6-28 |
| **[6.10]** | YTM—Zero Coupon Bond | $k_b = \left[\dfrac{F}{B}\right]^{\frac{1}{n}} - 1$ | p. 6-28 |
| **[6A.1]** | Interest Rate Parity | $\dfrac{F}{S} = \dfrac{(1 + k_{domestic})}{(1 + k_{foreign})}$ | p. 6-30 |
| **[6B.1]** | Yield to Call | $B = I \times \left[ \dfrac{1 - \dfrac{1}{(1 + k_c)^c}}{k_c} \right] + CP \times \dfrac{1}{(1 + k_c)^c}$ | p. 6-32 |

# Questions and Practice Problems

## Multiple Choice Questions

1. **(LO 6.1)** Which of the following statements concerning bonds is *incorrect*?

    **a.** They involve blended payments of principal and interest.

    **b.** They have a fixed maturity date, at which time the issuer repays the full principal amount.

    **c.** Bondholders are paid a series of fixed periodic amounts before the maturity date.

    **d.** The bond indenture is a legal document, specifying payment requirements and so on.

2. **(LO 6.1)** Which of the following statements is *incorrect*?

    **a.** Callable bonds give the bond issuer an option to call the bond at a predetermined price.

    **b.** All debentures are secured bonds.

    **c.** Extendible bonds allow bondholders to extend the maturity date.

    **d.** Convertible bonds give the bondholders an option to convert into common shares at a predetermined conversion ratio.

3. **(LO 6.2)** What is the price of a 10-year, 8-percent, annual coupon bond when the market rate is 6 percent? The face value is $100.

    **a.** $114.72

    **b.** $110.57

    **c.** $107.71

    **d.** $113.42

4. **(LO 6.2)** Which of the following bond prices is most sensitive to market rate changes? The par value is $100 for all.

    **a.** 5-year, 5-percent coupon rate, yield 5.5 percent

    **b.** 3-year, 8-percent coupon rate, yield 5.6 percent

    **c.** 7.5-year, 4.5-percent coupon rate, yield 5.5 percent

    **d.** 10-year, 4.5-percent coupon rate, yield 5.5 percent

5. **(LO 6.3)** What is the yield to maturity on an eight-year, 9-percent bond that pays interest semi-annually, which is now priced at $980? Use a financial calculator.

    **a.** 9.05 percent

    **b.** 9 percent

    **c.** 4.68 percent

    **d.** 9.36 percent

6. **(LO 6.3)** Which of the following statements is *correct*?

    **a.** Current yield is the ratio of annual coupon payment divided by the par value.

    **b.** When the coupon rate is higher than the market rate, the bond is priced at a discount.

    **c.** When the market rate is higher than the coupon rate, the bond is priced at a premium.

    **d.** If a bond is at a discount, the coupon rate is less than the current yield, which is less than YTM.

7. **(LO 6.4)** Which statement is incorrect?

    **a.** The liquidity preference theory states that investors prefer short-term debt.

    **b.** According to the expectations theory, a downward-sloping yield curve implies that interest rates are expected to decline in the future.

    **c.** The risk premium in the bond yield reflects default risk, liquidity risk, and issue-specific features.

    **d.** A debt rating of AAA is a worse rating than BB for S&P.

8. **(LO 6.5)** What is the quoted price of a 182-day Canadian T-bill that has a face value of $10,000 and a quoted yield of 3 percent?

    **a.** $9,778.67

    **b.** $9,852.62

    **c.** $97.7867

    **d.** $98.5262

9. **(LO 6.5)** Which of the following statements is *false*?

    **a.** Zero coupon bonds are deep-discount bonds.

    **b.** Zero coupon bonds are often created when cash flows are stripped from traditional bonds.

    **c.** Floating rate bonds provide protection against decreasing interest rates.

    **d.** There are two forms of return available for Canada Savings Bond buyers: regular interest and compound interest.

10. **(LO 6.6)** Which statement is *correct* according to interest rate parity (IRP) theory?

    **a.** IRP states that differences in interest rates between countries cannot be totally offset by expected changes in exchange rates.

    **b.** Forward exchange rates may be locked in today to eliminate foreign exchange risk and ensure investors can profit from moving capital to countries with higher interest rates.

    **c.** Inflation differentials between countries affect both interest rates and currency exchange rates.

    **d.** The country with a higher inflation rate will see its currency appreciate against another country with a lower inflation rate.

## Practice Problems

### Basic

11. **(LO 6.1)** Describe the difference between positive and negative bond covenants.

12. **(LO 6.1)** How are the cash flows of an amortizing loan different from those of a coupon bond?

13. **(LO 6.2)** State the relationship between market rates and bond prices.

14. **(LO 6.2)** Under what circumstances can a zero-coupon bond be selling at a premium?

15. **(LO 6.2)** Calculate the price of the following bond: FV = $1,000; coupon rate = 6 percent, paid semi-annually; market rate = 5 percent; term to maturity = 10 years.

16. **(LO 6.2)** Describe the relationship between bond interest rate risk and the coupon rate, the market yield, and the term to maturity.

17. **(LO 6.2)** Calculate the cash price of the following bond, sold on September 21: par = $1,000; coupon rate = 4 percent, paid on January 1 and July 1; quoted price = $956. Explain why the cash price is different from the quoted price.

**18. (LO 6.2)** A bond is currently trading at $841.70. It has 15 years to maturity. If you require a rate of return of 12 percent, what should be the bond's coupon rate if the bond pays semi-annual coupons?

**19. (LO 6.4)** Suppose that a 6-percent, annual-pay, Government of Canada bond that matures in two years has a yield to maturity of 6.75 percent. If inflation is expected to be 2.5 percent per year over the next two years, what coupon rate would you expect to find on a Real Return Bond that is otherwise identical?

**20. (LO 6.4)** Suppose the inflation rate in Canada, as measured by the CPI, has been averaging 3.5 percent in recent years. The most recent Bank of Canada announcement indicates that it expects 3.2-percent inflation over the next year. If the real rate of return on Canadian T-bills is 2.5 percent, what is the nominal risk-free rate?

**21. (LO 6.4)** The following values are the spread for corporate bond yields.

| Bond Rating | Spread over AAA |
|---|---|
| AA | 30 basis points |
| A | 45 basis points |
| BBB | 70 basis points |
| BB | 110 basis points |

**a.** One-year T-bills are trading with a YTM of 6 percent. What yield would you expect to find on A-rated corporate bonds maturing in one year?

**b.** Five-year government bonds have a maturity yield differential of 50 basis points. What yield would you expect to observe on non-investment-grade (BB-rated) corporate bonds with a five-year maturity?

**22. (LO 6.4)** Using the Fisher relationship, calculate the exact real interest rate and the approximate real rate, given a T-bill rate of 8 percent and an expected inflation rate of 3.6 percent.

**23. (LO 6.5)** If you have a retractable bond, under what conditions will you exercise your right to sell the bond back to the bond issuer?

**24. (LO 6.4)** If a bond-rating agency downgrades the rating of a bond, how will it affect the price of that bond?

## Intermediate

**25. (LO 6.2)** Calculate the price of a bond with FV of $1,000, a coupon rate of 8 percent (paid semi-annually), and five years to maturity when:

**a.** $k_b = 10$ percent.

**b.** $k_b = 8$ percent.

**c.** $k_b = 6$ percent.

**26. (LO 6.2)** Suppose that, several years ago, the Canadian government issued three very similar bonds; each has a $1,000 face value and a 10-percent coupon rate and will mature in five years. The only difference between the bonds is the frequency of the coupon payments. If the market yield is now 5.5 percent, determine the price of the bond that pays coupons:

**a.** annually.

**b.** semi-annually.

**c.** monthly.

**27. (LO 6.2)** The following is data for two bonds at a time when the market yield is 7 percent.

| Bond | Coupon Rate | Price |
|---|---|---|
| A | 6% | $958.42 |
| B | 8% | $1,041.58 |

These bonds are otherwise identical (FV = $1,000, five years to maturity, semi-annual coupon payments). Which bond's price will change more, and by how much, if the market yield increases by 100 basis points?

**28. (LO 6.2)** The following two bonds are identical (FV = $1,000, 8-percent coupon rate paid semi-annually), except that they mature at different times.

| Bond | Time to Maturity | Price |
|---|---|---|
| C | 3 years | $1,026.64 |
| D | 8 years | $1,060.47 |

If the market yield, currently 7 percent, increases by 100 basis points, which bond's price will change more and by how much?

**29. (LO 6.2)** It is now May 1, 2022, and Peter has just purchased a five-year U.S. government bond (FV = $1,000) with a quoted price of $93.863. This bond has a 6-percent coupon rate, and the last semi-annual coupon payment was made on January 1, 2022.

**a.** How much will Peter pay for this bond?

**b.** Had this been a Canadian government bond, what would be the cash price?

**30. (LO 6.2)** Calculate the price change for a 1-percent decrease in market yield for the following bond: par = $1,000; coupon rate = 6 percent, paid semi-annually; market yield = 6 percent; term to maturity = 10 years.

**31. (LO 6.2)** You bought a bond last year for $102.50 and just sold it for $98.50. What has happened to the interest rate over that period?

**32. (LO 6.3)** An 8-percent annual coupon bond with 12 years left to maturity is selling for $928. What is the YTM of the bond?

**33. (LO 6.3)** A nine-year, 6.5-percent coupon bond is selling for 106.2 percent of par. What is the bond's market yield if it makes semi-annual coupon payments?

**34. (LO 6.3)** For each of the following YTM figures, calculate the price and current yield for a two-year, 7-percent, annual-pay bond with a face value of $1,000.

**a.** YTM = 6 percent

**b.** YTM = 7 percent

**c.** YTM = 8 percent

**35. (LO 6.3)** For each of the following YTM figures, calculate the price and current yield for a 10-year, 5-percent, semi-annual-pay bond with a face value of $1,000.

**a.** YTM = 4 percent

**b.** YTM = 5 percent

**c.** YTM = 6 percent

**36. (LO 6.3)** A company is contemplating issuing new 15-year bonds at par. The company currently has 5.5-percent coupon bonds on the market selling for $936. The bonds pay semi-annual interest and have 15 years until maturity. What coupon rate should the company set on its new bonds?

**37. (LO 6.5)** At maturity, each of the following zero coupon bonds (pure discount bonds) will be worth $1,000. For each bond, fill in the missing quantity in the following table. Assume semi-annual compounding.

| | Price | Maturity (Years) | Yield to Maturity |
|---|---|---|---|
| A | $450 | 10 | |
| B | $400 | | 6% |
| C | | 15 | 12% |

**38. (LO 6.5)** Calculate the bank discount yield on a 92-day U.S. T-bill that is currently quoted at $97.75. Find the bond equivalent yield on a 92-day Canadian T-bill with the same quoted price.

**39. (LO 6.5)**

    **a.** What is the value of a 10-year, zero coupon bond with a face value of $1,000 when the market rate is 8 percent?

    **b.** Calculate the YTM of the above zero coupon bond if the current price is $760.

**40. (LO 6.5)** A 90-day U.S. T-bill has a bank discount yield ($k_{BDY}$) of 4.673 percent. Find the quoted price. Find the bond equivalent yield ($k_{BEY}$) on a 90-day Canadian T-bill with the same quoted price.

**41. (LO 6.5)** Altech Inc. has a convertible bond with a face value of $1,000 and coupon rate of 6 percent. The bond will mature in 10 years, and its current price is $950. The bond can be converted at any time into 25 shares of Altech Inc., whose current share price is $40. If the holder decides to convert the bond into shares, what is the percentage premium/discount of the conversion relative to the current share price?

**42. (LO 6.3)** A bond has a yield to maturity of 8 percent and a current yield of 6 percent. Is the bond trading at par, at a premium, or at a discount? What can you say about the coupon rate?

**43. (LO 6.3)** Explain yield to maturity in terms of the spot rate.

**44. (LO 6.3)** The present value of a dollar to be received one year from today is $0.927644. The present value of a dollar to be received two years from today is $0.854172. What is the price of a bond that pays an annual coupon of 7 percent and matures in two years? Find its yield to maturity.

**45. (LO 6.5)** You are a financial advisor and one of your clients comes to you with a convertible bond that has a coupon rate of 8 percent. The market interest rate is 6 percent. The share price of the company that issued the bond is going down, and you don't expect the company to recover in the near future. Your client is thinking of converting the bond into shares and wants your advice. What will you recommend to your client?

**46. (LO 6.6)** Adam has saved C$1,000 and plans to go surfing in Australia next summer. He won't need the money for a year, so he decides to invest it. Adam could invest the money in Canada, where a T-bill will earn 4.5 percent, and then convert it to Australian dollars (AU$) just before he leaves. Alternatively, Adam could convert the funds today and invest in an Australian T-bill earning 5.2 percent. Which approach should he take if the currency spot rate is C$0.90431/AU$ and the one-year forward rate is C$0.89829/AU$?

## Challenging

**47. (LO 6.2)** A 20-year semi-annual bond has just been issued with its coupon rate set at the current market yield of 6 percent. How much would the price of the bond change (in percentage terms) if the market yield suddenly fell by 50 basis points? How much would the price change if the yield rose by 50 basis points?

**48. (LO 6.2)** Consider a bond with five years to maturity, FV of $1,000, and a coupon rate of 6.5 percent (semi-annual payments).

    **a.** Calculate the price of this bond if the market yield is: i) 7.75 percent; ii) 5.25 percent.

    **b.** In each case, calculate the percentage change in the price of the bond if the market yield rises by 1 percent.

**49. (LO 6.2)** A zero coupon bond has a par value of $1,000 and will mature in eight years.

    **a.** Calculate the current price of this bond if the market yield is: i) 7.75 percent; ii) 5.25 percent.

    **b.** In each case, calculate the percentage change in the price of the bond if the market yield rises by 1 percent.

**50. (LO 6.3)** A bond with semi-annual coupons at a rate of 10 percent will mature in one year. If the bond's price is $1,010, use the trial-and-error method to find the YTM. Check your answer by using a financial calculator. What would the YTM be if the bond made annual coupon payments?

**51. (LO 6.4)** Sapna would like to receive a real return of 5 percent per year on a bond investment at a time when the expected inflation rate is 2.5 percent. How much would she be willing to pay for a bond maturing in two years if it pays annual coupons at a (nominal) rate of 7 percent? If a Real Return Bond were available with a 4.5-percent coupon (annual payments) and the same two-year maturity, how much would Sapna be willing to pay for it to achieve her desired rate of return?

**52. (LO 6.2, 6.3, 6.5)** The Slice & Dice Investment Co. needs some help understanding the intricacies of bond pricing. It has observed the following prices for zero coupon bonds that have no risk of default:

| Maturity | Price per $1 Face Value |
|---|---|
| 1 year | $0.97 |
| 2 years | 0.90 |
| 3 years | 0.81 |

    **a.** How much should Slice & Dice be willing to pay for a three-year bond that pays a 6-percent coupon, assuming annual coupon payments start one year from now?

    **b.** What is the yield to maturity of the three-year coupon bond?

    **c.** Suppose Slice & Dice purchases this coupon bond and then "un-bundles" it into its four component cash flows: three coupon payments and the par value amount. At what price(s) can Slice & Dice resell each of the first three cash flows (the coupon payments) today?

    **d.** The remaining cash flow (the face value amount) is a "synthetic" three-year, zero coupon bond. How much must this "strip bond" be sold for if Slice & Dice is to break even on the investment?

    **e.** What is the yield to maturity on the synthetic three-year, zero coupon bond?

    **f.** Why are the answers for parts b and e different?

**53. (LO 6.6)** Bower is a Canadian investor. He noticed that the euro spot rate is currently quoted at C$1.4768 per euro. The European interest rate is 6 percent on one-year T-bills, and the one-year interest rate in Canada is 3 percent. The one-year forward rate is C$1.409/euro. Determine whether there is an arbitrage opportunity. State the transactions Bower should apply to profit from the arbitrage opportunity if one exists. Explain what would happen if many other investors also seized such an arbitrage opportunity, if one existed.

**54. (LO 6.7)** A bond that matures in 10 years is callable in three years at a call price of $1,025. The bond has a semi-annual coupon rate of 8 percent. If the YTM is 7.3 percent and the YTC is 6.92 percent, what is the bond's current price? Is this bond likely to be called?

**55. (LO 6.7)** A 12-year, 7.5-percent bond is callable in four years at a call price of $1,045. If the bond pays semi-annual coupons and is selling for $1,038, what is the YTM and YTC of the bond? Is this bond likely to be called?

# Case

### Case 6.1 General Gas Ltd. Bond Valuation

General Gas Ltd., a natural gas pipeline company, has contacted your office for advice on an upcoming bond issue. You work for an investments services firm and your specialization is in fixed income, helping companies to finance and to refinance with bonds. The company's CFO provided some preliminary information, and the issue is going to be impressive. At $500 million, it will take some time and effort to raise the funds. Details of the issue are listed below.

> Number of bonds: 50,000
>
> Face value: $10,000
>
> Coupon rate: 4.5%
>
> Frequency: semi-annual
>
> Initial price: par value
>
> Settlement: January 1, 2022
>
> Maturity: December 31, 2040

News of the upcoming issue has gotten out quickly, and you've already received calls from interested investors. One firm in particular has expressed a desire to invest $50 million as soon as the bonds are available, and other firms have demonstrated that they too will make significant investments. In anticipation, your supervisor has asked you to calculate several values.

1. Although the costs associated with raising the money will be based on a small percentage, at 0.62 percent of the final issue value, General Gas expects to pay a significant amount to have your firm handle the offer. How much will General Gas pay for your company's services? Remember that General Gas must be left with exactly $500 million once all issue fees (also known as flotation costs) have been paid.

2. It is now July 1, 2022. While the bond issue went well and received an initial rating of BBB, the bond is now priced at a discount, at $97.50.

   **a.** Calculate the YTM used by the market to price the bond.

   **b.** What are some factors that may have led to this change in the YTM and subsequent price decline, six months after issue?

*Note: Experts have said that market rates have changed because of major bond defaults in another country and a flight to quality in Canada.*

3. It is now January 1, 2023 (18 years remaining). The Bank of Canada has taken steps to settle the Canadian interest rate environment and the market yield to maturity (YTM) has dropped to 4.0 percent.

   **a.** Calculate the price of the bond, using the new YTM.

   **b.** Recalculate the price of the bond using a YTM of 5.0 percent.

   **c.** How sensitive is the bond's price to changes in the YTM? Compare the price based on a yield of 4.0 percent to the price based on a yield of 5.0 percent.

### An "Interesting" Rate Discussion

Prior to the bond's issue you meet with Deb Enshire, a long-term client that would like to learn more about General Gas's upcoming borrowing. Deb is 70 years old and very wealthy, having inherited $20 million when she was only 30. Deb is risk averse in many ways, and this guided her investment decisions in 1975 when she inherited her wealth—she took almost all of the money and invested in long-term bonds. Since then her bond portfolio has performed well and she has had several years where her returns were greater than 10 percent. You tell her that General Gas, a triple-B rated firm, is about to offer 19-year semi-annual pay bonds with an annual coupon of 4.5 percent. Deb scoffs. She thinks that the current bond rate environment is ridiculously low and that her bond strategy is no longer appropriate.

4. By comparing current low rates (which are well below 10 percent) to her years of double-digit bond returns, what is Deb failing to consider?

5. Further to your answer in question 4 above, what are the potential implications for Deb's portfolio?

6. Deb does a lot of reading, and during your meetings with her she occasionally goes off on a tangent based on what she has been reading. Today's meeting is no exception and she has asked you to explain the significance of interest rate parity if she were to invest in a bond similar to General Gas's, but with a U.S. company.

# Equity Valuation

---

**LEARNING OBJECTIVES**

After studying this chapter, you should be able to:

**7.1** Identify the basic characteristics of equity securities (i.e., preferred shares and common shares).

**7.2** Explain how to value preferred shares.

**7.3** Explain how to value common shares using the dividend discount model.

**7.4** Explain how to value common shares using the price-earnings (P/E) ratio.

**7.5** Apply the principles of fundamental valuation and relative valuation.

**7.6** Explain how speculative price bubbles occur.

**7.7** Explain how to value common shares using additional relative value ratios.

---

There are a number of factors that have affected the value of common shares over time. These include (1) "intangibles" that can generate future cash flows, (2) dividends, and (3) earnings power. We discuss each of these factors in this chapter. Recall that in Chapter 6 we discussed how to estimate the value of bonds based on the present value of their expected future cash flows and how to estimate the implied yield based on given prices. In this chapter, we apply the same concepts to equity valuation. We begin by examining how to evaluate both preferred and common shares based on the present value of their expected future dividend stream. We proceed to show how this approach is related to the fundamentals that affect stock prices (i.e., future profitability and dividends, interest rates, and risk). We conclude with a discussion of relative valuation approaches and show how they too can be related to company fundamentals.

---

## 7.1 | Equity Securities

---

**LEARNING OBJECTIVE 7.1**

Identify the basic characteristics of equity securities (i.e., preferred shares and common shares).

---

**Equity securities** are ownership interests in an underlying entity, usually a corporation. Generally, equity securities have no fixed maturity date. Equities pay dividends from after-tax earnings, so, unlike interest payments, they do not provide the issuer with a tax-deductible expense. However, shareholders pay lower taxes on dividends received from Canadian corporations than they would on interest payments, as discussed in Chapter 3.

By far the most common type of equity security is the **common share**, which represents a certificate of ownership in a corporation. A purchaser of 200 common shares owns

**equity securities** ownership interests in an underlying entity, usually a corporation

**common share** a certificate of ownership in a corporation; the most common type of equity security

($200/n \times 100$) percent of the corporation (where $n$ is the total number of common shares outstanding). Common shareholders represent the true "owners" of the corporation. They are the residual claimants of the corporation, which means that they are entitled to income remaining only after all creditors and preferred shareholders (discussed below) have been paid. Similarly, in the case of liquidation of the corporation, common shareholders are entitled to the remaining assets only after all other claims have been satisfied. As owners, they can exert control over the corporation through their power to vote, which allows them to elect the board of directors and to vote on major issues, such as takeovers, corporate restructuring, and so on. In Chapter 19, we discuss the characteristics of common shares in more detail.

**preferred share** the other major type of equity security, which gives the owner a claim to a fixed amount of equity that is established when the shares are first issued

The other major category of equities is **preferred shares**. These provide the owner with a claim to a fixed amount of equity that is established when the shares are first issued. Most preferred shares have preference over common shares with respect to income and assets (in the event of liquidation), but they rarely have any voting rights. Traditionally, preferred shares have no maturity date, but over the past 30 years preferred shares have increasingly been issued with a fixed maturity date, similar to a bond. The main difference between preferred shares and bonds is that the board of directors declares any dividends. Unlike interest payments, dividends are not a legal obligation of the firm until that declaration is made. Usually no payments can be made to common shareholders until preferred shareholders have been paid the entire amount of the dividends they are due. We discuss the characteristics of preferred shares in more detail in Chapter 19.

## Valuation of Equity Securities

A commonly used method for valuing equity securities follows the discounted cash flow approach used to estimate the value of bonds. Specifically, we estimate the expected future cash flows associated with the security and then determine the discounted present value of those future cash flows, based on an appropriate discount rate ($k$). The discount rate for equities will equal the risk-free rate of return plus a risk premium (as was the case for bonds). This is shown in Equation 7.1 below.

$$k = RF + \text{Risk premium} \qquad [7.1]$$

where $k$ = the required return on an equity security and $RF$ = the risk-free rate of return.

Recall from Chapter 6 that the risk-free rate comprises the real rate of return plus expected inflation and is often proxied by the return on short-term government T-bills. However, for long-lived investments like common shares, the use of a short-term interest rate often introduces problems, since it is directly affected by the Bank of Canada's monetary policy. To offset this, many analysts use long-term Canada bond yields as the risk-free rate.[1] The risk premium will be based on an estimate of the risk associated with the security; the higher the risk, the higher the risk premium, because investors will require a higher return as compensation. We will discuss the factors affecting the risk premium and methods for estimating a discount rate for equities in chapters 8 and 9.

In addition to determining the discount rate, investors must estimate the size and timing of the expected cash flows associated with an equity security. Obtaining this estimate is straightforward for a bond, because the amount and timing of the coupons and principal repayments are specified in the bond indenture. For equities, this issue is more complex, especially for common shares, as will be discussed shortly. We will first deal with preferred shares because they are easier to value.

### Concept Review Questions

1. How do equity shareholders exert their influence over a company?
2. What are the two main components of the required rate of return on equity securities?

[1]For example, 91-day treasury bills are only risk free over a 91-day horizon.

## 7.2 | Preferred Share Valuation

> **LEARNING OBJECTIVE 7.2**
>
> Explain how to value preferred shares.

As mentioned above, traditional preferred shares have no maturity date and pay dividends of a fixed amount at regular intervals indefinitely, as depicted in **Figure 7.1**:

where $D_p$ = dividend payments

**FIGURE 7.1** The Cash Flow Pattern for a Straight Preferred Share

Because the payments are essentially fixed when the preferred shares are issued, such shares are often referred to as fixed income investments, just as bonds are. The payment of a fixed dividend amount at regular intervals indefinitely means we can view these investments as "perpetuities," which were discussed in Chapter 5. The value of preferred shares can be estimated using Equation 7.2, which determines the present value of a perpetuity. $P_{ps}$ is the market price (or present value), $D_p$ is the dividend amount (or payment), and $k_p$ is the required rate of return on the preferred shares (or discount rate).

$$P_{ps} = \frac{D_p}{k_p}$$

[7.2]

The amount of the dividend payments is usually based on a stated par (or face) value and a stated dividend rate, which is similar to the coupon rate on a bond. For example, a preferred share with a par value of $100 and a 4-percent dividend rate would pay an annual dividend of $4 per year. In practice, dividends are paid quarterly; however, for valuation purposes, we will assume they are paid annually.[2] This will not have a big influence on the valuation process because of the long time period involved (i.e., assuming the dividends are paid to infinity).

---

**EXAMPLE 7.1** | Determining the Market Price of Preferred Shares

Determine the market price of a $50 par value preferred share that pays annual dividends based on a 4-percent dividend rate when market rates are

**a.** 4 percent.

**b.** 5 percent.

**c.** 3 percent.

**Solution**

$$D_p = \$50 \times 0.04 = \$2.00$$

**a.** $P_{ps} = \dfrac{D_p}{k_p} = \dfrac{\$2.00}{0.04} = \$50.00$

**b.** $P_{ps} = \dfrac{\$2.00}{0.05} = \$40.00$

**c.** $P_{ps} = \dfrac{\$2.00}{0.03} = \$66.67$

---

[2]We will also assume annual dividends when valuing common shares, even though they also usually pay quarterly dividends.

Notice that, like bonds, preferred shares will trade at par when the dividend rate equals the market rate, at a discount from par when market rates exceed the dividend rate, and at a premium when market rates are less than the dividend rate. Also note that the market prices of preferred shares increase when market rates decline, and vice versa.

Equation 7.2 can be rearranged to determine the required rate of return on the preferred shares for a given market price, as follows:

$$k_p = \frac{D_p}{P_{ps}}$$ [7.3]

---

**EXAMPLE 7.2** | Estimating the Required Rate of Return on Preferred Shares

Determine the required rate of return on preferred shares that provide a $5 annual dividend if they are selling for $70.

**Solution**

$$k_p = \frac{D_p}{P_{ps}} = \frac{\$5}{\$70} = 7.14\%$$

---

Finance in the News 7.1 deals with income opportunities in the preferred share market. Normally, preferred share investments do poorly when interest rates rise, since the dividends that they pay are generally fixed. But preferred shares that offer a spread above a reference rate, such as Canadian government bonds, do well as interest rates rise, since they offer investors an increased income. This class of preferred shares has the dividend rate reset at regular, pre-specified points in time. When the outlook for increased market rates diminishes, this class of preferred shares will decline in price and represent a buying opportunity.

---

## 7.1 Finance in the News    Brookfield Blue Chips Can Be Found in the Preferred-Share Bargain Bin

Rate-reset preferred shares were built for the kind of world we were living in until this fall.

The sudden reversal of investor expectations for interest-rate increases has pushed rate-reset preferreds into a tailspin that is a bit reminiscent of the harrowing plunge of 2015. Rate-resets turned out to be a great buy back then. Can the same be true of the most recent setback?

Portfolio manager Dustin Van Der Hout of Richardson GMP believes there are some bargains to be had in the rate-reset preferred market. As examples, he highlights a pair of issues from Brookfield Asset Management Inc.—BAM.PR.R and BAM.PF.B.

Rate-resets thrive when there are expectations of rising rates ahead. Until fall 2018, that was exactly the outlook.

Now, investors are worrying that economic growth has peaked and rates may not rise much further.

Rate-resets offer a yield that is set every five years using a spread over the five-year Government of Canada bond.

Rising rates offer the opportunity to get a higher yield from a rate-reset, while falling rates mean you could get less.

As a proxy for the rate-reset preferred market, let's use the BMO Laddered Preferred Share Index ETF (ZPR-T). It's down 7.3 per cent for the year through Nov. 30 on a total-return basis, which means dividends are included.

Mr. Van Der Hout said he's buying certain rate-reset preferred-share issues at current prices. "I'm building a core position now at these prices," he said. "I'm saying to clients, 'Hey, get ready because if this sells off more, we're going to stock up again like we did in 2015.'" The rate-reset market is divided by Mr. Van Der Hout into two parts—the old generation of rate-resets, which tend to offer smaller spreads over the five-year Canada bond, and a newer generation that offered juicier spreads to spark investor interest in this type of preferred share.

The newer rate-resets have done well lately. Mr. Van Der Hout said some have basically sidestepped the recent decline and are trading near or even above their $25 issue price. The older rate-resets are the ones that are suffering and it's there that Mr. Van Der Hout sees some value.

He said BAM.PR.R resets in June, 2021, with a spread of 2.3 per cent over the five-year Canada bond yield, which has recently been around 2.06 per cent.

That works out to a yield of 4.36 per cent, which in turn suggests an annualized dividend of $1.09 based on the $25 issue price.

With BAM.PR.R closing at $16.35 on Monday, that $1.09 dividend would produce a yield of 6.67 per cent. The current yield is 4.6 per cent. BAM.PF.B has a current yield of 5.5 per cent and comes up for reset in March, 2019.

Based on the closing price Monday of $19, he calculates a yield of about 6.2 per cent after reset.

"For Brookfield, which I feel is one of the highest-quality companies in Canada, that is amazing," Mr. Van Der Hout said.

**Concept Review Questions**

1. In what ways are preferred shares different from bonds?
2. How is a traditional preferred share valued?
3. How can we estimate the investor's required rate of return for a traditional preferred share?

# 7.3 Common Share Valuation: The Dividend Discount Model (DDM)

**LEARNING OBJECTIVE 7.3**

Explain how to value common shares using the dividend discount model.

## The Basic Dividend Discount Model

Valuing common shares involves several complications that arise with respect to the appropriate future cash flows that should be discounted. Which cash flows should be discounted? The most popular model for valuing discounted cash flows, which is discussed below, uses dividends. However, unlike bonds or even preferred shares, there is no requirement that common shares pay dividends at all. In addition, the level of dividend payments is also discretionary, which means we must make estimates regarding the amount and timing of any dividend payments.

The **dividend discount model (DDM)** assumes that common shares are valued according to the present value of their expected future cash flows. Based on this premise, today's price can be estimated using Equation 7.4, if we have an *n*-year holding period.

**dividend discount model (DDM)** a model for valuing common shares that assumes they are valued according to the present value of their expected future dividends

$$P_0 = \frac{D_1}{(1 + k_c)^1} + \frac{D_2}{(1 + k_c)^2} + \cdots + \frac{D_n + P_n}{(1 + k_c)^n}$$ [7.4]

where

$P_0$ = the estimated share price today

$D_1$ = the expected dividend at the end of year 1

$P_n$ = the expected share price after *n* years

$k_c$ = the required return on the common shares

Consider Example 7.3, in which the investor plans to hold the stock for one year.

---

**EXAMPLE 7.3** | Estimating the Price of a Common Share for a One-Year Holding Period

An investor buys a common share and estimates she will receive an annual dividend of $0.50 per share in one year. She estimates she will be able to sell the share for $10.50. Estimate its value, assuming the investor requires a 10-percent return on this investment.

**Solution**

$$P_0 = \frac{\$0.50 + \$10.50}{(1 + 0.10)^1} = \$10.00$$

According to the DDM, the selling price at any point (say, time $n$) will equal the present value of all the expected future dividends from period $n + 1$ to infinity. So the price next year, for example, is the present value of the expected dividend and share price for year 2. By repeatedly substituting for the future share price, we replace it with the present value of the dividend and share price expected the following year. As a result, we remove $P_n$ in Equation 7.4 and eventually get the following:

$$P_0 = \frac{D_1}{(1 + k_c)^1} + \frac{D_2}{(1 + k_c)^2} + \ldots + \frac{D_\infty}{(1 + k_c)^\infty} = \sum_{t=1}^{\infty} \frac{D_t}{(1 + k_c)^t} \qquad [7.5]$$

In other words, the price today is the present value of all future dividends to be received (i.e., from now to infinity).

Why use dividends? Well, if investors buy a particular stock, the only cash flows they will receive until they sell the stock will be the dividends. Although a firm's residual earnings technically belong to the common shareholders, corporations generally do not pay out all their earnings as dividends. Another reason is that dividends can only be paid out of earnings (otherwise they are a return of capital), so dividends are a good signal of the long-run earnings of the firm. Of course, it is really the earnings that are important, since without them the corporation could not sustain dividend payments for long. In fact, earnings receive more attention from investors than any other single variable. However, corporations typically reinvest a portion of their earnings to enhance future earnings and, ultimately, future dividends.

Equation 7.5 is the workhorse of share valuation because it says that the value of a share is the present value of expected future dividends. However, by repeatedly substituting for the share price, we are implicitly making a very important assumption: that investors are rational. We assume that, at each point, investors react rationally and value the share based on what they rationally expect to receive the next year. This assumption specifically rules out "speculative bubbles," which illustrate what is colloquially known as the "bigger fool theorem."

Suppose, for example, a broker tells a client to buy XYZ at $30. The investor refuses because the stock is worth only $25. The broker replies, "I know, but there is momentum behind it and I am seeing a lot of interest. I think it will go to $40 by next year." The investor is a fool to pay $30 for something she thinks is worth $25, but it is not the fool theorem but the bigger fool theorem. If the investor does buy it, she is a fool, but she is also assuming that an even bigger fool will buy it in a year's time for $40.

This type of speculative bubble, in which prices keep increasing and become detached from reality, is specifically ruled out by the assumption of rational investors coolly calculating the present value of the expected cash flows each year, so that prices never get detached from these fundamentals. Of course, there have been speculative bubbles when it has been very difficult to estimate these fundamental values. In Appendix 7A, we review the famous bubble involving the South Sea Company in 1720, when Sir Isaac Newton almost bankrupted himself and then proclaimed, "I can calculate the motions of the heavenly bodies, but not the madness of people." The madness of people was what caused the share price of the South Sea Company to become completely detached from its fundamentals. The Internet bubble of the late 1990s, in which the price of shares in Nortel Networks Corporation rose from $20 to $122 and then fell back to less than $2, indicates that the madness of people may not have changed much in almost 300 years. However, it is difficult to build pricing models based on irrationality, so we will continue with the development of models based on fundamental cash flows.

## The Constant Growth DDM

Obviously, it is impractical to estimate and discount *all* future dividends one by one, as required by Equation 7.5. Fortunately, this equation can be simplified into a usable formula by assuming that dividends grow at a constant rate ($g$) indefinitely. We can then estimate all future dividends, assuming we know the most recent dividend paid ($D_0$).

$$D_1 = D_0(1 + g)$$

$$D_2 = D_1(1 + g) = D_0(1 + g)^2$$

$$D_3 = D_2(1 + g) = D_0(1 + g)^3$$

and so on.

Therefore, assuming constant growth in dividends to infinity, Equation 7.5 reduces to the following expression:

$$P_0 = \frac{D_0(1 + g)^1}{(1 + k_c)^1} + \frac{D_0(1 + g)^2}{(1 + k_c)^2} + \ldots + \frac{D_0(1 + g)^\infty}{(1 + k_c)^\infty}$$  [7.6]

In Equation 7.6 we are multiplying $D_0$ by a factor of $(1 + g)/(1 + k)$ every period. This represents a "growing perpetuity," which is easily solved because it represents the sum of a geometric series. In fact, Equation 7.6 reduces to the following expression, which is the constant growth version of the DDM, or simply the **constant growth DDM**:

$$P_0 = \frac{D_0(1 + g)}{k_c - g} = \frac{D_1}{k_c - g}$$  [7.7]

**constant growth DDM**   a version of the dividend discount model for valuing common shares, which assumes that dividends grow at a constant rate indefinitely

There are several important points to note about Equation 7.7.

1. This relationship holds only when $k_c$ is greater than $g$. Otherwise, the value is negative, which is uninformative.[3]

2. Only *future* estimated cash flows and estimated growth in these cash flows are relevant.

3. The relationship holds only when growth in dividends is expected to occur at the same rate indefinitely.

---

**EXAMPLE 7.4** | Using the Constant Growth DDM

Assume a company is currently paying $1.10 per share in dividends. Investors expect dividends to grow at an annual rate of 3 percent indefinitely, and they require a 10-percent return on the shares. Determine the price of these shares.

**Solution**

$$D_1 = (\$1.10)(1 + 0.03) = \$1.133$$

$$P_0 = \frac{D_1}{k_c - g} = \frac{\$1.133}{0.10 - 0.03} = \$16.19$$

---

## Estimating the Required Rate of Return

The constant growth DDM can be rearranged as Equation 7.8 to obtain an estimate of the rate of return required by investors on a particular share.

$$k_c = \frac{D_1}{P_0} + g$$  [7.8]

The first term $(D_1/P_0)$ in Equation 7.8 represents the expected dividend yield on the share, which we discussed in Chapter 4. Therefore, we may view the second term, $g$, as the expected capital gains yield, because the total return must equal the dividend yield plus the capital

---

[3]The negative answer occurs because if $g$ is greater than $k_c$ in Equation 7.7, each future dividend is worth more in today's terms than the previous one. The value never converges to a finite amount but instead increases to infinity. Note that this does not rule out the possibility that $g$ could be negative.

gains yield. It is important to recognize that this equation provides an appropriate estimate for required return *only* if the conditions of the constant growth DDM are met (i.e., in particular, the assumption regarding constant growth in dividends to infinity must be satisfied).

---

**EXAMPLE 7.5** | Estimating the Required Rate of Return Using the DDM

The market price of a company's shares is $15 each; the estimated dividend at the end of this year ($D_1$) is $0.60; and the estimated long-term growth rate in dividends ($g$) is 3 percent. Estimate the implied required rate of return on these shares.

**Solution**

$$k_c = \frac{D_1}{P_0} + g = \frac{\$0.60}{\$15} + 0.03 = 0.04 + 0.03 = 0.07 = 7\%$$

---

The result in Example 7.5 suggests that the expected return on these shares comprises an expected dividend yield of 4 percent and an expected capital gains yield of 3 percent.

## Estimating the Value of Growth Opportunities

The constant growth DDM can also provide a useful assessment of the market's perception of growth opportunities available to a company, as reflected in its market price. Let's begin by assuming that a firm with no profitable growth opportunities should not reinvest residual profits in the company, but rather should pay out all its earnings as dividends. Under these conditions, we have $g = 0$ and $D_1 = EPS_1$, where $EPS_1$ represents the expected earnings per common share in the upcoming year. Given these assumptions, the constant growth DDM reduces to the following expression:

$$P_0 = \frac{EPS_1}{k_c}$$
[7.9]

We are not likely to find a company that has exactly "zero" growth opportunities, but the point is that we can assume the share price of any common stock that satisfies the assumptions of the constant growth DDM will be made up of two components: its no-growth component and the remainder, which is attributable to the market's perception of the growth opportunities available to that company. We denote this as the present value of growth opportunities (PVGO). These growth opportunities will generally represent a company's ability to generate substantial growth in future profits and cash flows. This growth may be attributable to several factors, including the prospects for its industry, its competitive position within that industry, the value of its "brand" name, and its long-term investment and research and development programs. We will discuss these issues in greater detail throughout the text, and in chapters 13, 14, and 20 in particular.

Taking into account PVGO, we get Equation 7.10.

$$P_0 = \frac{EPS_1}{k_c} + PVGO$$
[7.10]

---

**EXAMPLE 7.6** | Estimating PVGO

A company's shares are selling for $20 each in the market. The company's EPS is expected to be $1.50 next year, and the required return on the shares is estimated to be 10 percent. Estimate the PVGO per share.

**Solution** This can be solved by rearranging Equation 7.10 to solve for PVGO.

$$PVGO = P_0 - \frac{EPS_1}{k_c} = \$20 - \frac{\$1.50}{0.10} = \$20 - \$15 = \$5$$

# Examining the Inputs of the Constant Growth DDM

From Equation 7.7, we can see that the constant growth DDM predicts that, all else remaining equal, the price of common shares ($P_0$) will *increase* as a result of

1. an increase in $D_1$

2. an increase in $g$

3. a decrease in $k_c$

This list illustrates the intuitive appeal of the DDM. It links common share prices to three important fundamentals: corporate profitability, the general level of interest rates, and risk. In particular, expected dividends are closely related to profitability, as is the growth rate of these dividends, while the required rate of return is affected by the base level of interest rates ($RF$) and by risk (as reflected in the risk premium required by investors). In particular, *all else being equal,* the DDM predicts that common share prices will be higher when profits are high (and expected to grow), when interest rates are lower, and when risk premiums are lower.

We can usually assume that current dividends ($D_0$) are given, so it is the movements in $k_c$ and $g$ that determine the price of a share (i.e., because $k_c - g$ is the denominator, and because $D_0 [1 + g]$ is the numerator). In fact, given the long period involved in the discount process (i.e., to infinity), price estimates are very sensitive to these inputs, as illustrated in Example 7.7 and Example 7.8.

---

**EXAMPLE 7.7** | More Pessimistic Inputs of the Constant Growth DDM

Revisit the company in Example 7.4 that is currently paying $1.10 per share in dividends. This time, revise the expectations for annual growth in dividends to 2 percent (from 3 percent) and revise the estimated required rate of return to 11 percent (from 10 percent). Re-estimate the price of these shares.

**Solution**

$$D_1 = (\$1.10)(1 + 0.02) = \$1.122$$

$$P_0 = \frac{D_1}{k_c - g} = \frac{\$1.122}{0.11 - 0.02} = \$12.47$$

---

Notice the substantial drop in price (i.e., 23 percent, from $16.19 to $12.47) that results when we increase the discount rate from 10 percent to 11 percent and lower the growth rate from 3 percent to 2 percent (which both have negative effects on stock prices). Similarly, Example 7.8 illustrates the large price increase that results from the use of improved estimates for these inputs.

---

**EXAMPLE 7.8** | More Optimistic Inputs of the Constant Growth DDM

Redo Example 7.7 by assuming annual growth in dividends is 4 percent and the required rate of return is 9 percent.

**Solution**

$$D_1 = (\$1.10)(1 + 0.04) = \$1.144$$

$$P_0 = \frac{D_1}{k_c - g} = \frac{\$1.144}{0.09 - 0.04} = \$22.88$$

---

In this case, the price estimate is 41.3 percent higher than the original estimate of $16.19, yet we changed each of our inputs by only 1 percentage point. Obviously, we need to be careful when determining these inputs, which are in fact merely estimates.

## Estimating DDM Inputs

Estimating the inputs into the constant growth DDM generally requires a great deal of analysis and judgement. Assuming we know the most recent year's dividend payment ($D_0$), we need to estimate g because $D_1 = D_0(1 + g)$. As discussed earlier, the discount rate for equities will equal the risk-free rate of return plus a risk premium, as depicted in Equation 7.1. We defer further discussion of estimating the discount rate for equities to chapters 8 and 9.

**sustainable growth rate**
the earnings retention ratio multiplied by return on equity

Several methods can be used to estimate the expected annual growth rate in dividends (g). One of the most common approaches is to determine the company's **sustainable growth rate**, which can be estimated by multiplying the earnings retention ratio by the return on equity, as shown in Equation 7.11:

$$g = b \times ROE \qquad [7.11]$$

where $b$ = the firm's earnings retention ratio = 1 − the firms's dividend payout ratio; and $ROE$ = the firm's return on common equity = net profit/common equity (as defined in Chapter 4).

Growth in earnings (and dividends) will be positively related to the proportion of each dollar of earnings reinvested in the company ($b$) multiplied by the return earned on those reinvested funds, which we measure using ROE. For example, a firm that retains all its earnings and earns 10 percent on its equity would see its equity base grow by 10 percent per year. If the same firm paid out all of its earnings, it would not grow. Similarly, a firm that retained a portion ($b$) of its earnings would earn 10 percent on that portion, resulting in $g = b \times ROE$.[4]

---

**EXAMPLE 7.9** | Estimating a Firm's Sustainable Growth Rate

A firm has an ROE of 12 percent, and its dividend payout ratio is 30 percent. Use this information to determine the firm's sustainable growth rate.

**Solution**

$$g = b \times ROE = (1 - 0.3) \times 0.12 = 0.7 \times 0.12 = 0.084 = 8.4\%$$

---

Recall from Chapter 4 that we can use the DuPont system to decompose ROE into three factors, as shown in Equation 7.12.

$$\begin{aligned} ROE &= (\text{Net income/Sales}) \times (\text{Sales/Total assets}) \times (\text{Total assets/equity}) \\ &= \text{Net profit margin} \times \text{Turnover ratio} \times \text{Leverage ratio} \end{aligned} \qquad [7.12]$$

The ROE, and hence g, increases with higher profit margins, higher asset turnover, and higher debt (although higher debt implies higher risk and, therefore, higher $k_c$).

---

**EXAMPLE 7.10** | Estimating a Firm's Sustainable Growth Rate Using the DuPont System

A company just paid an annual dividend of $1 per share and had an EPS of $4 per share. Its projected values for net profit margin, turnover ratio, and leverage ratio are 4 percent, 1.25, and 1.4, respectively. Determine the firm's sustainable growth rate.

---

[4]A major weakness of this approach is its reliance on accounting figures to determine ROE, because it is based on book values and the accrual method of accounting. As a result, it may not represent the "true" return earned on reinvested funds.

**Solution**

$$ROE = 0.04 \times 1.25 \times 1.4 = 0.07 = 7\%$$

$$\text{Payout ratio} = DPS/EPS = \$1/\$4 = 0.25, \text{ so } b = 1 - 0.25 = 0.75$$

$$g = b \times ROE = 0.75 \times 7\% = 5.25\%$$

Another method of estimating $g$ is to examine historical rates of growth in dividends and earnings levels, including long-term trends in these growth rates for the company, the industry, and the economy as a whole. Predictions regarding future growth rates can be determined based on these past trends by using arithmetic or geometric averages, or by using more involved statistical techniques, such as regression analysis. Finally, an important source of information regarding company growth, particularly for the near term, can be found in analyst estimates. Investors are often especially interested in "consensus" estimates, because market values are often based to a large extent on these estimates. However, a word of caution is in order: analysts have been shown to be biased—that is, they tend to be overly optimistic—in part because their major source of information is frequently the company itself. Research by Easton and Sommers has put the "optimism" bias in analysts' growth forecasts at an average of 2.84 percent.[5] As a result, analyst forecasts tend to be used with the two-stage growth model (discussed in the next section) to mitigate this optimism.

It is important to remember, when applying any of these approaches, that "future" growth is being estimated, and the inputs require judgement on the part of the analyst. If researchers believe past growth will be repeated in the future, or if they want to eliminate period-to-period fluctuations in $b$ and ROE, they may choose to use three- to five-year averages for these variables. Conversely, if the company has changed substantially, or if analysts have good reason to believe the ratios for the most recent year are the best indicators of future sustainable growth, they will use these figures. In addition, an analysis of macroeconomic, industry-specific, and company-specific factors may lead researchers to develop predicted values for these variables independent of their historical levels.

## The Multiple-Stage Growth Version of the DDM

The constant growth DDM relationship holds only when we are able to assume constant growth in dividends from now to infinity. In many situations, it may be more appropriate to estimate dividends for the most immediate periods up to some point ($t$), after which it is assumed there will be constant growth in dividends to infinity. Several situations lend themselves to this structure. For example, it is reasonable to assume that competitive pressures and business-cycle influences will prevent firms from maintaining extremely high growth in earnings for long periods. In addition, short-term earnings and dividend estimates should be much more reliable than those covering a longer period, which are often calculated using very general estimates of future economic, industry, and company conditions. To use the best information available at any point, it may make the most sense to estimate growth as precisely as possible in the short term before assuming some long-term rate of growth.

Equation 7.13 can be applied when steady growth in dividends to infinity does not begin until period $t$:

$$P_0 = \frac{D_1}{(1 + k_c)^1} + \frac{D_2}{(1 + k_c)^2} + \ldots + \frac{D_t + P_t}{(1 + k_c)^t} \qquad [7.13]$$

where $P_t = \dfrac{D_{t+1}}{k_c - g}$

Notice that this is Equation 7.4, with $n$ replaced by $t$ and with an estimate for $P_t$. **Figure 7.2** depicts the cash flows associated with this type of valuation framework.

---

[5]Easton, Peter D., and Sommers, Gregory A., "Effect of Analysts' Optimism on Estimates of the Expected Rate of Return Implied by Earnings Forecasts." *Journal of Accounting Research* 45, no. 5 (December 2007), pp. 983–1016.

**FIGURE 7.2** The Cash Flow Pattern for Multiple-Stage Growth in Dividends

Essentially, whenever we use multiple-period growth rates, we estimate dividends up to the beginning of the period in which it is reasonable to assume constant growth to infinity. Then we can use the constant growth DDM to estimate the market price of the share at that time ($P_t$). Finally, we discount all the estimated dividends up to the beginning of the constant growth period, as well as the estimated market price at that time.[6] This provides us with today's estimate of the share's market price.

---

**EXAMPLE 7.11** | Using the Multiple-Stage DDM

A company is expected to pay a dividend of $1.00 at the end of this year, a $1.50 dividend at the end of year 2, and a $2.00 dividend at the end of year 3. It is estimated dividends will grow at a constant rate of 4 percent per year thereafter. Determine the market price of this company's common shares if the required rate of return is 11 percent.

**Solution**  First, estimate dividends up to the start of constant growth to infinity. In this example, they are all given, so no calculations are required:

$$D_1 = \$1.00$$
$$D_2 = \$1.50$$
$$D_3 = \$2.00$$

Second, estimate the price at the beginning of the constant growth to infinity period:

$$D_4 = (\$2.00)(1 + 0.04) = \$2.08$$

$$P_3 = \frac{D_4}{k_c - g} = \frac{\$2.08}{0.11 - 0.04} = \$29.71$$

Third, discount back the relevant cash flows to time 0:

$$P_0 = \frac{\$1.00}{(1 + 0.11)} + \frac{\$1.50}{(1 + 0.11)^2} + \frac{\$2.00 + \$29.71}{(1 + 0.11)^3} = \$0.90 + \$1.22 + \$23.19 = \$25.31$$

---

**EXAMPLE 7.11** | Solution Using a Financial Calculator

Input the following variables:

($D_1$) [1] → [N] ; [11%] → [I/Y] ; [0] → [PMT] ; [−1.00] → [FV] ; [CPT] [PV]
= $0.90

($D_2$) [2] → [N] ; [11%] → [I/Y] ; [0] → [PMT] ; [−1.50] → [FV] ; [CPT] [PV]
= $1.22

($D_3 + P_3$) [3] → [N] ; [11%] → [I/Y] ; [0] → [PMT] ; [−31.71] → [FV] (i.e.,
$2.00 + $29.71); [CPT] [PV] = $23.19

Then we add these figures to get $25.31, as above.

---

[6]Recall that $P_t$ represents the present value of all the expected dividends from time $t + 1$ to infinity, so we are essentially discounting *all* the expected future dividends associated with the stock.

A well-known version of the multiple-stage growth DDM is the two-stage growth rate model, which assumes growth at one rate for a certain period, followed by a steady growth rate to infinity. This is illustrated in Example 7.12.

---

**EXAMPLE 7.12** | Two-Stage Dividend Growth

A company just paid a dividend of $2 per share. An investor estimates that dividends will grow at 8 percent per year for the next two years and then grow at an annual rate of 3 percent to infinity. Determine the market price of this company's common shares if the required rate of return is 12 percent.

**Solution**   First, estimate dividends up to the start of constant growth to infinity. In this example, we use the first-period growth rate of 8 percent:

$$D_1 = (\$2.00)(1.08) = \$2.16$$
$$D_2 = (\$2.16)(1.08) = \$2.3328$$

Second, estimate the price at the beginning of the constant growth to infinity period:

$$D_3 = (\$2.3328)(1 + 0.03) = \$2.402784$$

$$P_2 = \frac{D_3}{k_c - g} = \frac{\$2.402784}{0.12 - 0.03} = \$26.70$$

Third, discount the relevant cash flows back to time 0:

$$P_0 = \frac{\$2.16}{(1.12)^1} + \frac{\$2.3328 + \$26.70}{(1.12)^2} = \$1.93 + \$23.14 = \$25.07$$

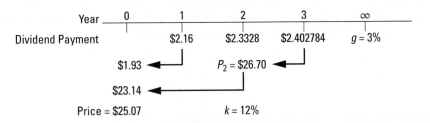

---

**EXAMPLE 7.12** | Solution Using a Financial Calculator

Input the following variables:

$(D_1)$ `1` → `N` ; `12%` → `I/Y` ; `0` → `PMT` ; `-2.16` → `FV` ; `CPT` `PV`
= $1.93

$(D_2 + P_2)$ `2` → `N` ; `12%` → `I/Y` ; `0` → `PMT` ; `-29.03` → `FV`

(i.e., $2.33 + $26.70); `CPT` `PV` = $23.14

Then we add these figures to get $25.07, as above.

---

# Limitations of the DDM

Although the DDM provides significant insight into the factors that affect the valuation of common shares, it is based on several assumptions that are not met by a large number of firms, especially in Canada. In particular, it is best suited for companies that (1) pay dividends based on a stable dividend-payout history that they want to maintain in the future, and (2) are growing at a steady and sustainable rate. As such, the DDM works reasonably well for large corporations in mature industries with stable profits and an established dividend policy.

In Canada, the banks and utility companies fit this profile, while in the United States, there are numerous NYSE-listed companies of this nature. Not surprisingly, the DDM does not work well for and/or is difficult to apply to many resource-based companies, which are cyclical in nature and often display erratic growth in earnings and dividends. Many of these companies (especially the smaller ones) do not distribute much in the way of profits to shareholders as dividends. The model will also not work well for firms in distress, firms that are in the process of restructuring, firms involved in acquisitions, and private firms. Finally, if a company enters into substantial share-repurchase arrangements, the model will require adjustments, because share repurchases also represent a method of distributing wealth to shareholders.

Due to the limitations of the DDM discussed above, and because common share valuation is a challenging process, involving, as it does, predictions for the future, analysts often use several approaches to value common shares. This is evident from the survey results reported in **Table 7.1**. The study surveyed the percentage of analysts who use a particular share valuation method, and the fact that the percentages far exceed 100 percent suggests that most analysts use several methods.

In addition to the DDM and the relative valuation approaches discussed in the next section, another discounted cash flow approach—the free cash flow approach—is used frequently, which is obvious from Table 7.1. The free cash flow approach is implemented in almost the same way as the DDM, except that instead of discounting estimated future dividends, you discount expected future free cash flows. The underlying rationale is that dividends are discretionary, and many firms may choose not to pay out the amount of dividends they could. Therefore, instead of using dividends, you use free cash flow, which is in some sense a measure of what a firm could pay out if it chose, after taking account of expenses, changes in net working capital, and capital expenditures. We will not discuss this model in detail but would note that there are two variations of this approach: (1) using free cash flows to equity holders and discounting them using the required return to equity holders (as in the DDM), and (2) using free cash flows to the firm and discounting them using the firm's weighted average cost of capital (which will be discussed in Chapter 20).[7] This approach is often more appropriate when firms do not pay out a significant portion of their earnings as dividends or pay out well below their capacity.

**TABLE 7.1** **Common Share Valuation Approaches**

| Method Used | Percentage |
| --- | --- |
| Price-earnings (P/E) approach | 88.1 |
| Discounted free cash flow approach | 86.8 |
| Enterprise value multiple approach | 76.7 |
| Price-to-book-value approach | 59.0 |
| Price-to-cash-flow approach | 57.2 |
| Price-to-sales approach | 40.3 |
| Dividend-to-price or price-to-dividend approaches | 35.5 |
| Dividend discount model approach | 35.1 |

**Source:** From "Valuation Methods" presentation, October 2007, produced by Tom Robinson, Ph.D., CFA, CPA, CFP®, Head, Educational Content, CFA Institute. Copyright 2007, CFA Institute. Reproduced and republished with permission from CFA Institute. All rights reserved.[8]

---

[7]Free cash flow available to equity holders can be estimated as Net income + Depreciation and Amortization + Deferred taxes − Capital spending +/− Change in net working capital − Principal repayments + New external debt financing. Free cash flow to the firm can be estimated as Net income + Depreciation and Amortization + Deferred taxes − Capital spending +/− Change in net working capital + Interest expense × (1 − Tax rate).

[8]The results are based on a survey of about 13,500 CFA Institute members, 2,369 of whom accepted the invitation. Of those surveyed, 2,063 evaluate individual securities in order to make an investment recommendation or portfolio decision. They are primarily buy-side investment analysts and portfolio managers. For those managing portfolios, the sample was split fairly equally between members managing institutional and individual (private wealth) portfolios.

Finance in the News 7.2 highlights the importance of a recent innovation in investment strategy. Ethical considerations are becoming increasingly important to investors who want to promote companies seen to be adopting policies that preserve limited global resources without leaving behind a negative footprint, while still earning an acceptable return. Ethical investing forms an integral part of an investment approach that recognizes the fact that decent returns can be earned while limiting increases in risk.

## 7.2 Finance in the News   A Dow-Sized Dilemma: Ethical Investors and Trump

Ethical investors take a principled approach to their portfolios, but they now face a dilemma: Is the entire U.S. stock market looking like a no-go zone?

The alarming shift in U.S. policy under President Donald Trump—defending the use of torture, trampling women's rights, closing the door on refugees and targeting immigrants as a threat to national security—has raised the question of whether investors should be doing something to voice their concerns.

Selling U.S. stocks sends a message, especially if it causes a market downturn that forces the White House to reconsider its actions.

Typically, ethical or responsible investing avoids specific stocks and sectors, rather than entire countries. Gun, tobacco and gambling companies are out. So are companies that harm the environment, employ unsound labour practices and pack their boards of directors with old, white men.

What's left are sound companies that investors can own with pride. Portfolio managers also believe these companies will perform well because they are positioned for the long term.

But surely something bigger must be gnawing at ethical investors today. If these investors can't stomach the idea of a company that makes cigarettes, how are they going to sleep at night knowing that their silence is reflected in the performance of their U.S. index funds?

U.S. boycott wouldn't be easy, of course.

U.S. stocks account for 60 per cent of the developed global stock market in terms of their weighting in the MSCI World Index.

The next largest country, Japan, is about 9 per cent and Canada is less than 4 per cent.

This means that large, institutional investors would have a tough time avoiding U.S. stocks.

Small investors are more nimble, but would be at risk of creating very lop-sided portfolios with an overwhelming tilt toward, say, Canada and Europe.

They could miss out on gains.

Since early November, U.S. stocks have rallied 9 per cent and the Dow Jones industrial average recently surged to a record high above 20,000, reflecting hope that Mr. Trump's economic policies will boost growth and employment As well, avoiding all

U.S. stocks means taking a pass on progressive companies such as Google Inc. and Apple Inc., which could be opposing Mr. Trump's social policies. Clearly, a broad boycott would cause some collateral damage.

Experts in ethical investing actually discourage a broad boycott, arguing that companies shouldn't be punished for the actions of one government.

"I would be reticent to say that we should all sell our U.S. equities. I think that would be rather irresponsible," said Milla Craig, a Montreal-based consultant at Millani Perspectives, which focuses on business sustainability and responsible investing.

"We have to look at this on a global basis," she added. "Some of the leading companies in the world are U.S.-based companies."

Dustyn Lanz, a spokesperson for the Responsible Investment Association, said in an e-mail: "The shift toward responsible investing is much bigger than one president."

It's a fair point, but it doesn't address the importance of sending a message to the Trump administration.

Consumers appear to be getting on board with this approach. The Economist noted that a sizable share of European travellers say they are less likely to visit the United States, which suggests that tourists are willing to vacation elsewhere.

Investors could send a similar message.

I've written numerous articles that touted the benefits of investing in tobacco stocks and many readers have vilified me for my unprincipled approach to investing. They tell me that their principles are more important than the big dividends and profits that flow from cigarette sales.

These principles are now being put to the test.

If the Trump administration is good for the U.S. stock market, ethical investors need to ask themselves if they're okay with that.

And if they are, well, take another look at tobacco stocks.

## Concept Review Questions

1. Why is share value based on the present value of expected future dividends?
2. What is the "bigger fool theorem" of valuation?
3. Why does an increase in the expected dividend growth rate increase share prices?
4. Why can't the expected growth rate exceed the investor's required return in the constant growth model?
5. How can we estimate future growth rates?

## 7.4 | Using Multiples to Value Shares

> **LEARNING OBJECTIVE 7.4**
> Explain how to value common shares using the price-earnings (P/E) ratio.

### The Basic Approach

**price-earnings (P/E) ratio**
the share price divided by the earnings per share; the most commonly used relative valuation multiple

Relative valuation approaches determine the value of common shares by comparing the market prices of similar companies relative to some common variable, such as earnings, cash flow, book value, or sales. Conceptually, these approaches are relatively simple to apply: all we need to do is find a group of comparable firms and then use their financial data and market values to infer the value of the firm in question. However, finding comparable firms is difficult: what firm is similar to Microsoft, for example? Even after we find a group of comparable firms, we have to estimate the appropriate multiple because values will differ even for comparable firms, so the exercise involves substantial analysis and judgement. We will illustrate the approach by using the most commonly used relative valuation multiple: the **price-earnings (P/E) ratio**. In the first edition of *Security Analysis* (1934), Benjamin Graham and David L. Dodd described common stock valuation based on price-earnings ratios as the standard method of that era. Table 7.1 suggests that, over 85 years later, the P/E ratio is still the most familiar valuation measure. Recall that the P/E ratio, which was introduced in Chapter 4, represents the number of times investors are willing to pay for a company's earnings, as expressed in the share price, or the share price divided by the earnings per share. The P/E approach is implemented by estimating the firm's earnings per share (EPS) and multiplying that figure by an appropriate (or justifiable) P/E multiple. The typical P/E formulation uses estimated earnings per share ($EPS_1$) for the next 12 months. The basic valuation equation can then be expressed as shown in Equation 7.14.

$$P_0 = \text{Estimated } EPS_1 \times \text{Justified P/E ratio} = EPS_1 \times P_0/E_1 \qquad [7.14]$$

Notice that the P/E ratio used in Equation 7.14 differs from the one we discussed in Chapter 4. This one is based on expected future earnings ($EPS_1$) and is called the "leading P/E ratio." By comparison, when we analyze financial ratios, the reported P/E ratios are based on earnings over the previous 12 months ($EPS_0$), which are called "lagging P/E ratios." For valuation purposes, we typically focus on the leading P/E ratio, because market values are based on expectations about the future.

Using the P/E ratio is easy: if the firm's forecast earnings per share are $2 and the P/E ratio for comparable firms is 20X, then the P/E approach would say that a fair share price is $40. We can see from this example why this approach is also called "using multiples." In this case, the multiple of earnings is 20X. What this means is that if this level of earnings stays constant, it will take 20 years to earn back the price of the shares. In this sense, the multiple is an example of a payback period. The higher the multiple, the longer the payback period and the more the investor is expecting earnings to increase. Alternatively, it could be that the shares are simply more expensive shares.

**relative valuation** valuing a firm relative to other comparable firms

We can also see why the approach is commonly called **relative valuation**: we are valuing the firm relative to other comparable firms. This means that if the comparable firms are all overvalued, then using the P/E approach will overvalue the firm in question. If the market is in a speculative bubble, the P/E approach will not detect it directly. In that case, what we need is some yardstick or benchmark P/E. We can approximate this by looking at the P/E ratio for the S&P/TSX Composite Index, which is shown in **Figure 7.3**.

The P/E in Figure 7.3 is based on trailing or lagging earnings for the firms in the S&P/TSX Composite Index. It vividly demonstrates the problems with the P/E ratio: very low earnings cause the value of the P/E to skyrocket. Despite the fact that the P/E is based on approximately 250 companies, these problems are not minimal.[9] In the early 1990s, Canada experienced a severe recession as a result of high interest rates as well as the costs of adjusting to free trade

---

[9]There were 241 companies in the S&P/TSX Composite Index in December 2018.

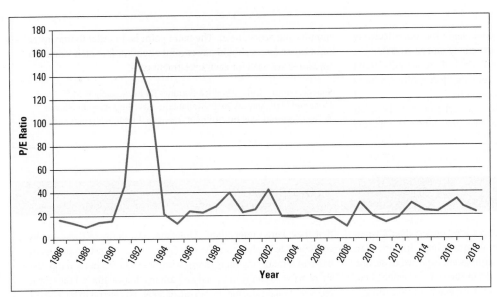

**FIGURE 7.3**  **S&P/TSX Composite P/E Ratios**

**Sources:** Data from Datastream and Capital IQ

with the United States, and many Canadian companies incurred large losses. Earnings for corporate Canada almost disappeared, causing the P/E to increase dramatically. For this reason, the P/E is often set at a maximum of 100.

As we can see from Figure 7.3, P/E ratios for the index typically hover around 20X. In fact, the median value over the 1986 to 2018 period was 22.68.[10] When P/E ratios fall below 15X, we tend to think the stock market is undervalued; when the P/E creeps above 20X, we take it as a warning signal that equities are overvalued. In the early part of 2019, the P/E ratio for the S&P/TSX Composite Index was significantly above its typical level and regularly exceeded 22X.

The P/E ratio is an attractive (and commonly reported) statistic for investors and analysts for several reasons. First, it relates the price to the earnings owned by the shareholders. Second, it is easy to calculate and, as a result, is commonly available. This makes comparisons relatively straightforward. Third, it is intuitive, as it indicates the payback period and can be related to a number of other firm characteristics, such as growth opportunities and risk. The question of whether the P/E ratio works well in practice is discussed in Finance in the News 7.3.

## 7.3  Finance in the News    Do Price-Earnings Ratios Actually Work?

Most investors assume that stocks, despite the occasional value trap, with low valuations always outperform more expensive issues as a matter of faith. Over the extreme long term, this faith is justified, particularly in terms of risk-adjusted returns.

In the past 13 years, however, the actual performance data are far more mixed—in most sectors, valuation levels had no relationship to future performance at all. In some cases, the results contradict the conventional wisdom that cheaper stocks are better investments.

Breaking the TSX into industry subsectors, this column will detail where a focus on valuations has worked for investors and where they haven't. There are numerous surprises.

The analysis uses the two most popular valuation measures—trailing 12-month price-to-earnings and price-to-book ratios—for each major subindex and compares them with index performance in the subsequent two years.

In each case, I was looking for the high negative correlation levels that would indicate that future performance rose as valuations declined or, conversely, that as valuations climbed and stocks became more expensive, performance weakened. In short, high

negative correlations would indicate that buying cheap stocks added to positive market returns.

(Correlation analysis provides a mathematical value between the minimum minus-1.0, which would indicate all monthly data points saw future performance go in one direction and valuation levels in another, and positive-1.0.)

Only one of the readings was positive: the relationship between price earnings ratio and future performance for materials stocks. This means that *P/E* ratios were no help to investors in the sector—materials stocks performed better the more expensive they got (in terms of *P/E*).

Similarly, the very small negative correlation indicates that price-to-book-values ratios were very little help for investors in industrial stocks.

The most helpful results were, in order, price to book value for utilities stocks, *P/B* for banks, *P/E* for consumer staples stocks, *P/E* for energy stocks and *P/B* for consumer discretionary.

Average price to book levels have worked remarkably well for investors in Canadian utilities stocks.

[10]The average, which is 30.04, is less meaningful, since it is impacted by the outliers exceeding 100.

Time periods where price to book value has not effectively predicted future returns have been extremely rare since 2002.

Outside of March 2003 to April 2004, there actually aren't any. In addition, current valuation levels project positive returns for the utility sector for the next few months.

The usual caveats apply—historical relationships between valuations and investment returns may not continue into the months and years ahead. The main point is: In order to maximize returns, investors should pay careful attention to which valuation measures are used for each investment type.

**Source:** Barlow, Scott, "Do Price-Earnings Ratios Actually Work?" *The Globe and Mail*, May 29, 2015. Available at www.theglobeandmail.com. © The Globe and Mail Inc. All rights reserved. Reprinted by permission.

## Lessons to Be Learned

It is common to hear that stock prices are "undervalued" when their P/E ratio is low, or overvalued when it is high. In particular, P/E ratios will be low when future earnings are expected to decline or to grow more slowly than they did in the past, or when there is a great deal of risk associated with the expected future earnings. Many investors learned this lesson the hard way as they poured money into the shares of banks and other companies in the financial sector during the summer and fall of 2008, based on the belief that they were undervalued. Unfortunately, many of these stocks continued to decline, and some of the financial institutions went bankrupt, rendering their shares worthless. On the other hand, the share prices of many financial institutions that weathered the storm recovered nicely during the spring of 2009. The lesson to be learned is that sometimes low P/E ratios represent a buying opportunity, but in other cases they may be a sign of bad things to come. Only detailed analysis (and a little luck) can tell the difference.

# Applying the P/E Ratio Approach

Equation 7.14 suggests that we need two estimates in order to implement the P/E ratio approach. Unfortunately, obtaining reasonable estimates requires a substantial amount of analysis and also an element of judgement. $EPS_1$ can be determined using several approaches, which are similar to those described above for estimating future dividends. In particular, we can analyze historical earnings data, project trends, analyze the company's present situation, and forecast future earnings (see our discussion of forecasting financial statements in Chapter 4). In addition, the use of analyst estimates (and consensus estimates) may provide reasonable forecasts of $EPS_1$.

Estimating justifiable P/E ratios is even more involved, and several approaches are typically used. One commonly used approach is to find *comparable* companies and estimate an appropriate P/E ratio for the company being analyzed based on a comparison of this company with the others in terms of risk and growth opportunities. This method often involves using an industry-average P/E ratio, which is then scaled up or down, based on an assessment of whether the company is above or below average. Unfortunately, this approach involves a great deal of subjectivity regarding several company-specific characteristics, including risk, potential for growth, and the overall financial health of the company. In addition, it may build market errors into the value estimation process. For example, even though a firm may be average within its industry, the industry-average P/E ratio may be too high if the market has overvalued this particular industry at a particular time.

Another commonly used approach is to examine historical averages for the company or the company's industry. However, using historical averages may be inappropriate if the company has changed substantially or if market and industry conditions have changed or are changing.

Given these potential problems associated with the use of industry or historical averages to estimate the appropriate P/E ratio, it is beneficial to obtain corroborating estimates based on economic, industry, and company fundamentals, if possible. Fortunately, the P/E ratio can be estimated by relating it to the fundamentals in the DDM.[11] We will illustrate this by using the simplest DDM model, the constant growth model:

$$P_0 = \frac{D_1}{k_c - g}$$

---

[11]Like the DDM, this method for estimating P/E ratios will work best for companies with relatively stable dividend and growth patterns.

Dividing both sides of this equation by expected earnings ($EPS_1$), we get Equation 7.15.

$$\boxed{\frac{P_0}{EPS_1} = \frac{P}{E} = \frac{D_1/EPS_1}{k_c - g}}$$ [7.15]

We are left with the P/E ratio on the left side of the equation. Notice that $D_1/EPS_1$ is the expected dividend payout ratio at time 1.

Equation 7.15 indicates that the following fundamental factors affect the justified P/E ratio, and hence share prices:

1. the expected dividend payout ratio ($D_1/EPS_1$)
2. the required rate of return ($k_c$)
3. the expected growth rate of dividends ($g$)

Notice that *expected earnings*, not historical earnings, is the relevant input. Also note that $k$ and $g$ are typically the most important factors in the determination of the P/E ratio because a small change in either can have a large effect on its value.

The following relationships should hold, *all else being equal*:

1. The higher the expected payout ratio, the higher the P/E.
2. The higher the expected growth rate, $g$, the higher the P/E.
3. The higher the required rate of return, $k_c$, the lower the P/E.

However, "all else being equal" is a brave assumption, because many of these variables are interrelated. For example, raising the payout ratio and thus increasing the dividend seems to increase the P/E, but raising the payout may also reduce growth, because one estimate of the growth rate is the sustainable growth rate, where $g = (1 - \text{Payout}) \times \text{ROE}$. We might also try to increase the growth rate by taking on risky investment projects that could increase future earnings and dividends, but this could also cause the discount rate, $k$, to increase (i.e., recall $k = RF + \text{Risk premium}$). However, we can say that P/E ratios tend to be higher when future growth in earnings and dividends is also expected to be high, and when interest rates or risk premiums are low (because they both affect $k_c$).

---

**EXAMPLE 7.13** | Using the P/E Ratio Approach

Assume that a firm has just reported an EPS of $2 and expects to maintain a 40-percent payout ratio. Estimate the firm's P/E ratio and its market price, assuming its ROE is 10 percent and investors require a 9-percent return on their shares.

**Solution**   First, estimate growth:

$$g = (1 - \text{Payout})(\text{ROE}) = (1 - 0.4)(10\%) = 6\%$$

Second, estimate earnings per share for the next 12 months:

$$EPS_1 = (EPS_0)(1 + g) = (\$2.00)(1.06) = \$2.12$$

Third, estimate the price-earnings ratio:

$$\frac{P}{E} = \frac{D_1/EPS_1}{k_c - g} = \frac{0.40}{0.09 - 0.06} = 13.33$$

Fourth, estimate the current share price:

$$P_0 = EPS_1 \times P_0/E_1 = (\$2.12)(13.33) = \$28.26$$

---

In Example 7.14, we assume the payout ratio remains constant at 40 percent, but we vary the main subjective inputs, $k_c$ and $g$, to assess the effect on the P/E ratio and on price.

Notice the wide range of P/E and price estimates that arise for relatively small changes in our estimates of $k_c$ and $g$.

**EXAMPLE 7.14** | Varying the Inputs for the P/E Ratio Approach

Revisit the firm in Example 7.13, assuming the same reported EPS of $2 and the same payout ratio of 40 percent. However, now assume that the growth rate and required return on the shares are, respectively,

**a.** 5 percent and 10 percent

**b.** 7 percent and 8 percent

**Solution**

**a.** $EPS_1 = (\$2.00)(1.05) = \$2.10$

$$\frac{P}{E} = \frac{0.40}{0.10 - 0.05} = 8$$

So $P_0 = (\$2.10)(8) = \$16.80$

**b.** $EPS_1 = (\$2.00)(1.07) = \$2.14$

$$\frac{P}{E} = \frac{0.40}{0.08 - 0.07} = 40$$

So $P_0 = (\$2.14)(40) = \$85.60$

## Limitations of P/E Ratios

Aside from the difficulties in estimating an appropriate P/E ratio and in estimating future EPS, there are several other practical concerns regarding the use of P/E ratios. First, P/E ratios are uninformative when companies have negative, or very small, earnings. As we saw for the S&P/TSX Composite in Figure 7.3, we sometimes get large or meaningless numbers for the P/E ratio, even when we aggregate across all companies. For a particular firm, the potential for these problems is much higher. Second, the volatile nature of earnings implies a great deal of volatility in P/E multiples. For example, the earnings of cyclical companies fluctuate dramatically throughout a typical business cycle. For these reasons, P/E ratios are normally based on smoothed or normalized estimates of earnings for the forecast year.

### Concept Review Questions

1. Why can the P/E ratio be viewed as a type of payback period?
2. What drives P/E ratios?
3. Why do P/E ratios differ even between comparable firms?
4. How are multiples linked to a discounted cash flow valuation?

## 7.5 A Simple Valuation Example

**LEARNING OBJECTIVE 7.5**

Apply the principles of fundamental valuation and relative valuation.

Let us now apply our understanding of the two primary valuation techniques, namely the multiple-stage DDM and P/E multiple valuation. For the DDM valuation, we will assume that even though a company may experience a period of high growth in earnings and dividends, eventually, as the company matures, it reaches a stage of fairly stable growth that

**TABLE 7.2** Forecast of Annual Dividend Growth

| Year | Annual Dividend Growth[12] |
|---|---|
| 1 | $2.00 forecast |
| 2 | 10% |
| 3 | 9.09% |
| 4 | 12.5% |
| 5 | 11.11% |
| 6 | 3.33% |
| 7 | 3.23% |
| 8 | 3.12% |

can be expected to continue for the foreseeable future. A forecast of dividends for imaginary company XYZ Inc. over the next eight years produces the growth estimates shown in **Table 7.2**.

The geometric mean[13] growth rate in dividends for years 2 to 5 is

$$((1 + 0.1000)(1 + 0.0909)(1 + 0.1250)(1 + 0.1111))^{1/4} - 1 = 0.106677$$

The geometric mean growth rate in dividends for years 6 to 8 is

$$((1 + 0.0333)(1 + 0.0323)(1 + 0.0312))^{1/3} - 1 = 0.03227$$

We will therefore assume that the annual dividend growth rate for years 2 to 5 is 10.7 percent; thereafter, dividend growth will stabilize and remain at approximately 3.2 percent per year. For many companies like this one, the initial annual dividend ($2 in this case) will be relatively easy to forecast. After that, we will apply our dividend growth forecasts to value the company at the beginning of year 1. Assume further that the appropriate discount rate for the company is 8 percent. If we were to first value company shares according to the constant growth DDM, we would use Equation 7.7 and the long-term growth rate of 3.2 percent to obtain the following result:

$$P_0 = \frac{D_1}{k_c - g} = \frac{\$2.00}{0.08 - 0.032} = \$41.67$$

We should recognize, however, that the prospect of higher dividend growth in the next few years should translate into a higher estimate for the share price. To ignore this fact would likely lead us to underestimate the company's true value. When we factor in a period of higher growth and rely on the multiple-stage DDM, we will arguably obtain a better estimate of share value. Applying Equation 7.13 we get:

$$P_0 = \frac{\$2.00}{(1 + 0.08)} + \frac{\$2.00\,(1.107)}{(1 + 0.08)^2} + \frac{\$2.00\,(1.107)^2}{(1 + 0.08)^3} + \frac{\$2.00\,(1.107)^3}{(1 + 0.08)^4} + \frac{\$2.00\,(1.107)^4}{(1 + 0.08)^5}$$

$$+ \frac{\$2.00\,(1.107)^4(1.032)}{(0.08 - 0.032)} \times \frac{1}{(1.08)^5}$$

$$= \$1.85 + \$1.90 + \$1.95 + \$1.99 + \$2.04 + \$43.95 = \$53.68$$

It comes as no surprise that we have obtained a higher (by nearly 29 percent) estimate of the value of company shares. The multiple-stage DDM is a particularly useful valuation approach when a company is not yet in its mature phase and is likely to experience a period of higher growth before eventually settling down to a long-term period of stable growth. Using the calculator's CF function will make life a lot easier once we get some practice. We will see more examples of this type in Chapter 13.

[12]For simplicity, assume that each dividend is paid at the end of the year.
[13]We introduce the geometric mean here but discuss it in more detail in Chapter 8.

CF 2ND CLR WORK

ENTER ↓

2.00 ENTER ↓

↓ (Note: these arrows are necessary to accept each frequency, which by default is equal to 1. In this example, each cash flow is different and needs to be entered only once.)

2.00 × 1.107 = ENTER ↓

↓

1.107 $y^X$ 2 = × 2.00 = ENTER ↓ (Note: The order of calculation has been reversed, as it is generally easier to calculate the exponent first.)

↓

1.107 $y^X$ 3 = × 2.00 = ENTER ↓

↓

1.107 $y^X$ 4 = × 2.00 = STO 1 × 1.032 = ÷ 0.048 = + RCL 1 = ENTER ↓

↓

NPV 8 ENTER ↓

CPT → 53.6820475

In the long set of keystrokes before the NPV input, you are first calculating $D_t$ in year 5 $(1.107^4 \times 2.00)$, then storing this value (STO 1). Then, with the stored value still displayed, proceed to calculate $P_t$ by multiplying by the long-run dividend growth rate, then dividing by 0.048, which is the required rate of return less the long-run dividend growth rate $(k_c - g)$. Finally, obtain the year 5 cash flow by adding back the value for $D_t$ by recalling it from memory (RCL 1). Inputting NPV 8 tells the calculator to discount all cash flows by 8 percent. CPT displays the sum of the series of present value calculations.

Continuing with this example, we will carry out a P/E multiple valuation of our imaginary company, relying on the P/E estimates of companies in the same industry.[14] We therefore obtain several forward P/E $(P_0/E_1)$ estimates from comparable firms in the same industry as XYZ Inc, shown in **Table 7.3**.[15]

The arithmetic mean of these estimates is $\dfrac{15.07 + 14.05 + 13.72}{3} = 14.28$.

Using this information, we can obtain a share price estimate using relative valuation based on a P/E multiple.

**TABLE 7.3**   **Industry P/E Estimates**

| | |
|---|---|
| Forward P/E Estimate for Company 123 | 15.07 |
| Forward P/E Estimate for Company ABC | 14.05 |
| Forward P/E Estimate for Company D3E | 13.72 |

[14]This approach is generally referred to as the *method of comparables*; its economic rationale is the *law of one price*, which, simply stated, maintains that two identical assets should sell at the same price.

[15]I/B/E/S (the Institutional Brokers' Estimate System), Datastream, and Morningstar are well-known companies that provide earnings and P/E ratio estimates.

We first estimate growth by noting that the firm has recently stated that it plans to pay out 55 percent of its earnings in the form of dividends. Moreover, an examination of the company's financial statements provides a current estimate of ROE = 9 and current EPS = $3.60. Therefore:

$$g = (1 - \text{Payout})(\text{ROE}) = (1 - 0.55)(9\%) = 4.05\%$$

Next, estimate EPS for the following year:

$$\text{EPS}_1 = (\text{EPS}_0)(1 + g) = (\$3.60)(1.0405) = \$3.75$$

Finally, we obtain an estimate of the share price:

$$P_0 = \text{EPS}_1 \times P_0/E_1 = (\$3.75)(14.28) = \$53.55$$

This estimate is very much in line with the one obtained using the multiple-stage DDM, which would tend to give the analyst some degree of assurance that the valuation estimate is reasonable. Additional estimates, possibly using other multiples (as in Appendix 7B), would serve to reinforce this belief.

### Concept Review Question

1. What are some of the key assumptions that must be made when applying the valuation concepts discussed in this chapter to an actual valuation situation?

## APPENDIX 7A | A Short Primer on Bubbles[16]

### LEARNING OBJECTIVE 7.6

Explain how speculative price bubbles occur.

In 1711, the South Sea Company (SSC) was given a monopoly on all English trade to the South Seas—that is, South America.[17] Unfortunately, South America was largely under the control of Spain, and England was at war with Spain. Nevertheless, the hope was that in the ensuing peace, England would be able to dictate a freeing-up of trade to the company's benefit. As it turned out, the peace was to England's benefit but not very much to the company's. Meanwhile, John Law, a Scottish promoter in France, set up the Mississippi Company, which was draining investment from England to France. In response, the South Sea Company offered to have investors convert England's national debt into shares of the company. The company would pay a one-time fee to the government for this conversion and receive the fixed annual payments on the national debt. The certainty of receiving the interest payments would allow the company to borrow to fund its South Seas trade.

It was an audacious plan in an age of optimism and jubilation at England's defeat of both Spain and France. In April 1720, the government accepted the offer, and the stock price took off. It was clear that the plan could be accepted only if the stock price went up enough to encourage investors to convert their national debt into SSC equity. Consequently, the company issued shares on an instalment basis. As the cash came in, the company lent it back so that

---

[16]This appendix is based on Booth, Laurence, "Investments, 'Alternative' Investments, and Bubbles." In *Advisor's Guide to New Investment Opportunities* (2001), pp. 12–19.

[17]See Harrison, Jim, "The Damn'd South Sea." *Harvard Magazine* (May–June 1999).

investors could buy more shares. The stock obviously took off, and in doing so sucked in a whole group of neophyte investors.

It also spawned imitators. One of the most interesting of these declared that it was "a company for carrying on an undertaking of great advantage, but nobody was to know what it is." Prices soared, and small investors got in for fear of missing out. Sir Isaac Newton sold his stock in the SSC in April 1720 for a 100-percent gain. However, the company's stock price rocketed up from £300 to its peak of more than £1,000 and Newton bought back in. In August, the bubble burst, and by September prices were back to £300. The *London Gazette* was full of bankruptcy announcements, and Newton lost £20,000. Philosophically, he made his famous statement, "I can calculate the motions of the heavenly bodies, but not the madness of people."

We have learned from this, haven't we? Leaving aside the Great Crash of 1929, there is the little matter of the Crash of 2000, and our recent experience with technology and Internet stocks. The most recent crashes stemmed from the high valuation of the equity market as a result of the long bull markets of the late 1990s.

Long bull markets pull in inexperienced investors who have unrealistic expectations. As we saw in Chapter 5, over long periods, average returns of the equity market have exceeded 10 percent a year, which is not enough to get investors really excited. However, a couple of 25-percent-plus years bring in the people who then come to expect 25-percent-plus returns. Moreover, plenty of people are willing to tell them that they can get 25-percent returns and that this time it is different: it is a new world of investing with new metrics.

In the September 1999 issue of *Atlantic Monthly,* James Glassman and Kevin Hassett discussed their prediction that the Dow would go to 30,000. They stated, "Stocks were undervalued in the 1980s and 1990s and they are undervalued now. Stock prices could double, triple or even quadruple tomorrow and still not be too high." They went on to suggest that "a profound change has occurred in the attractiveness of stocks since the early 1980s, as investors have become more rational. The old limits of yields and P/Es do not apply anymore, if they ever did." And finally they insisted: "In truth there is no extra risk in stocks."[18]

A familiar refrain during times of speculative bubbles is "This time it is different." After all, the little investors get in only after a run-up in prices, so it has to be different this time; otherwise, they have missed the boat. On May 15, 1929, the publications *Outlook* and *Independent* remarked, "But apparently there has been a fundamental change in the criteria for judging security values. Widespread education of the public in the worth of equity securities has created a new demand." Similarly, before the correction in 1969, *Barron's* stated, "The failure of the general market to decline during the last three years despite its obvious vulnerability, as well as the emergence of new investment characteristics, has caused investors to believe that the U.S. has entered a new investment era to which old guidelines no longer apply."[19]

The fact is that "old guidelines" are perennial; the only thing that changes is that the old investors die off and a new generation has to learn the same old lessons. Does that 1720 English company that promised "carrying on of an undertaking of great advantage, but nobody was to know what it is," sound familiar? It should. On January 25, 2000, Michael Lewis, the author of *Liar's Poker,* pointed out that there was an Internet company, NetJ.com, that had filed statements with the U.S. Securities and Exchange Commission with the confession that "the company is not currently engaged in any substantial activity and has no plans to engage in any such activity in the foreseeable future." The company had $127,631 in accumulated losses and so little money on hand that the directors would have had to chip in to pay any filing costs to raise capital. The only snag was that NetJ.com had a market capitalization of $22.9 million.

[18]They also went through an interesting valuation of Cisco, in which they stated, "Using the standard formula for calculating a stock's present value according to the flow of cash it generates over time, we find that Cisco's PRP should be $399 a share. In other words, Cisco's price last June would need to sextuple. Its P/E would rise to 539 (no that's not a misprint)." See Glassman, James, and Hassett, Kevin, "Dow 36,000." *Atlantic Monthly* 284, no. 3 (September 1999).

[19]Quoted in Stack, Jim, *The New Paradigm Era or Bubble* (Whitefish, MT: InvesTech Research, 1997).

| APPENDIX 7B | # Additional Multiples or Relative Value Ratios |
|---|---|

**LEARNING OBJECTIVE 7.7**
Explain how to value common shares using additional relative value ratios.

The **market-to-book (M/B) ratio**, which was defined in Chapter 4 as the market price per share divided by the book value per share, can also be used to value stocks. This is achieved by multiplying a justifiable M/B ratio by a company's book value per share (which was also defined in Chapter 4). Recall that the book value per share equals the book value of equity (i.e., assets minus liabilities) divided by the number of common shares outstanding. As such, valuing stocks relative to their M/B is an attractive approach for several reasons. Book value provides a relatively stable, intuitive measure of value relative to market values, which can be easily compared to those of other companies, provided accounting standards do not vary greatly across the comparison group. Using book value eliminates the problems arising from the use of P/E multiples, because book values are rarely negative and do not exhibit the volatility associated with earnings levels. However, book values may be sensitive to accounting standards and may be uninformative for companies that do not have a large proportion of fixed assets, such as service firms.

> **market-to-book (M/B) ratio** market price per share divided by the book value per share

The use of the M/B ratio fell out of favour in the 1980s and 1990s when high rates of inflation distorted the book value of equity for many firms because of their use of historical cost accounting in an inflationary period. However, the low rate of inflation of the past 10 to 15 years has removed most of these problems, while changes in accounting standards have made the book value of equity more useful.[20]

The **price-to-sales (P/S) ratio** possesses several properties that make it attractive for valuation purposes. It is similar to the P/E and M/B approaches in that it is implemented by multiplying a justifiable P/S ratio by the sales per share figure. Unlike earnings and book value, sales are relatively insensitive to accounting decisions and are never negative. Sales are not as volatile as earnings levels, hence P/S ratios are generally less volatile than P/E multiples. In addition, sales figures provide useful information about corporate decisions, such as pricing. However, sales do not provide information about expenses and profit margins, which are important determinants of company performance.

> **price-to-sales (P/S) ratio** market price per share divided by sales per share

Another commonly used relative valuation ratio is the **price-to-cash-flow (P/CF) ratio**, for which cash flow (CF) is often estimated as Net income + Depreciation and amortization + Deferred taxes. (Some analysts focus on "free" cash flow available to equity holders, as defined previously.) By focusing on cash flow rather than accounting income, this ratio alleviates some of the accounting concerns regarding measures of earnings. The **market (enterprise) value to EBIT ratio** or the **market (enterprise) value to EBITDA ratio** can also be used. Using earnings before interest and taxes (EBIT) or earnings before interest, taxes, depreciation, and amortization (EBITDA) instead of net income eliminates a significant proportion of the volatility in EPS figures caused by the use of debt and amortization (which is a non-cash expense). We use the market value of the firm's capital (both debt and equity) to reflect the fact that EBIT and EBITDA represent income available to both debt and equity holders. However, although there are many different valuation ratios or "multiples," they are all related to the fundamental valuation drivers, as we now show.

> **price-to-cash-flow (P/CF) ratio** market price per share divided by per share cash flow

> **market (enterprise) value to EBIT ratio** total firm market value divided by earnings before interest and taxes

> **market (enterprise) value to EBITDA ratio** total firm market value divided by earnings before interest, taxes, depreciation, and amortization

Analysts may choose to display the range of possible value estimates in convenient chart form in order to assess the merits of each approach prior to making a specific recommendation of buy, hold, or sell. One such chart is shown in **Figure 7B.1**.

---

[20]At one point, firms were required to write off goodwill, which seriously affected both earnings and the book value of equity. Now the goodwill arising from an acquisition is written off only when it is impaired by a drop in value. This is what caused the huge losses to Nortel and JDS Uniphase in 2002.

**FIGURE 7B.1** **Summary of Different Valuation Ratios**

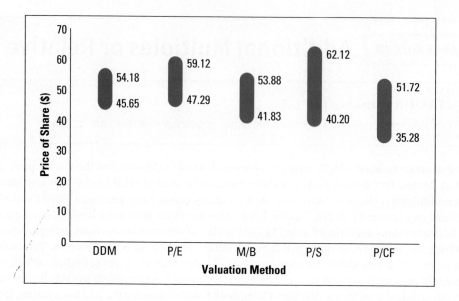

Suppose an investor requires a 15-percent return on their shares, expects the firm to pay a $1 dividend, and expects dividends and earnings to grow at 10 percent. In this case, we can use the constant growth model to value the shares at $20.

$$P = \frac{\$1}{0.15 - 0.10} = \$20$$

If 0.5 million shares are outstanding, this firm would have a total market value for the equity or equity market capitalization (cap) of $10 million.

If the firm has the income statement forecast and financial data shown in **Table 7B.1**, we can link all these valuation multiples.

For example, the share price is $20 and the dividend is $1, so the dividend yield is 5 percent (i.e., 1/20). In valuing this company, one valuation metric is to simply compare its dividend yields to those of other comparable companies. A high dividend yield relative to other

**TABLE 7B.1** **Income Statement Forecast**

| | |
|---|---|
| Sales volume | 1 million units |
| Unit price $10 | $10 million |
| Variable costs | 5.0 |
| Fixed cash costs | 1.7 |
| EBITDA | 3.3 |
| Depreciation | 0.8 |
| EBIT | 2.5 |
| Interest | 0.5 |
| EBT | 2.0 |
| Income tax (@50 percent) | 1.0 |
| Net income | 1.0 |
| Dividends | 0.5 |
| Book value of equity | 5.0 |
| Book value of debt | 5.0 |

companies might indicate an undervalued stock. Another way to use the dividend yield is to take its reciprocal and look at the dividend multiple—that is, the market price divided by the dividend. In this case, it is selling at 20X its dividend.

In practice, we don't often talk about the dividend multiple because the dividend yield provides the same information, and yields on stocks are often compared directly with yields on income trusts, bonds, and other interest-earning securities. However, there is a fundamental problem with using dividend multiples: many firms do not pay dividends. To get around this problem, we can work up the income statement and use the next item, which is earnings. In this case, with an equity market value of $10 million and $1 million in net income, the P/E ratio is 10X. Immediately we can see that although many firms don't have dividends, they should all expect to have some earnings. The problem here is that earnings are cyclical and industry specific, so let's move up the income statement a bit farther.

The next item is earnings before interest and tax (EBIT), which in our example is $2.5 million. The difference between EBIT and net income is that EBIT does not belong to the shareholders; some of it flows through to the firm's creditors and some to the government. This is why we usually calculate the total firm (enterprise) value (EV)—that is, the value of the debt plus the value of the equity—for all the ratios "above" net income. For our example, this comes to $15 million (the debt market value is assumed to be the book value of $5 million). The EV/EBIT multiple is then 6X (EBIT of $2.5 million divided into the total market value of $15 million).

However, as we know from our accounting discussion, depreciation is a non-cash charge, so we go farther up the income statement and add depreciation to get EBITDA. This adds back all the accounting items that do not involve cash. Depreciation of fixed assets is by far the largest component, but there are also some other amortizations, such as issue costs attached to debt, and so on. Again, with a total value of $15 million, the EV/EBITDA multiple is 4.5X. The EV/EBITDA multiple is the most commonly used multiple when firms look at acquiring other firms; it is a good proxy for the cash flow the firm generates, which can be used by the acquiring firm. Another good valuation is to look at the contribution generated by the firm, which is EBITDA with all the fixed costs added back. In our example, this is $5 million, giving a 3X multiple. This is useful for firms valuing other firms when they can consolidate operations and remove the fixed costs.

The final valuation multiple comes from going right to the top line, instead of the bottom line, and looking at sales. In our case, the sales multiple is a $10-million common equity value for buying $10 million in revenues or 1.0X. This would be useful if the entire sales of the firm could be switched to another firm and the existing plant and facilities closed down. Another variant is to look at the equity value per unit of sales. In our case, $10 million for 1 million unit sales means that the firm's shares are selling for $10 per unit of sales.

If we add to these valuation multiples the market-to-book ratio, which in our case is 2X (i.e., $10 million/$5 million), and the firm's return on equity (ROE) of 20 percent, we have a comprehensive list of key valuation ratios for the firm, all flowing from the fundamental valuation model.

Not all of these ratios are equally useful for every firm. Cable companies, for example, usually sell on a value per unit of output—in their case, a price per subscriber, because the more subscribers a cable company has, the more revenue it can generate. "Old-line" manufacturing firms generally sell on a market-to-book or P/E ratio basis because they tend to have stable earnings. Growth companies with large amounts of amortization because of their increasing asset base tend to sell on EBITDA or sales multiples. However, in all cases, these valuation multiples are simply shortcuts for the fundamental discounted cash flow valuation.

## Concept Review Question

1. What other relative valuation multiples are useful in valuation?

# Review

## Summary

This chapter reviews the basic approaches to valuing preferred and common shares. It begins by introducing the preferred share valuation process, which is based on estimating the present value of expected future dividends. This approach is then extended to common stock valuation in the form of the dividend discount model (DDM). We show how the constant growth version of the DDM is related to the fundamentals that affect stock prices (i.e., future profitability and dividends, interest rates, and risk). We then show how the multiple-growth version of the DDM could be used to estimate common share prices. We conclude by examining relative valuation models, the P/E ratio approach in particular, and how they interact with the discounted cash flow model. Throughout our discussion, we highlight the importance of recognizing the sensitivity of the valuation process to assumptions regarding input variables, such as growth rates, discount rates, and general market conditions, and the fact that valuation is as much an art as it is a science.

## Summary of Learning Objectives

### 7.1 Identify the basic characteristics of equity securities (i.e., preferred shares and common shares).

Equity securities are ownership interests in a company. Common shares have voting rights and pay a dividend (at the discretion of the board of directors). Preferred shares have no voting rights and pay a fixed, regular dividend. Preferred shares have a par value. In the event of bankruptcy or liquidation, preferred shareholders are entitled to their par value before common shareholders are paid (if there is enough money to pay the par value after creditors are paid).

### 7.2 Explain how to value preferred shares.

Preferred shares are valued as perpetuities, with annual dividends divided by the discount rate.

### 7.3 Explain how to value common shares using the dividend discount model.

The general framework is that price equals the sum of the discounted future cash flow. So we need to estimate the amount and timing of future cash flow and the appropriate discount rate. In the dividend discount model, we make simplifying assumptions that the dividend grows at a constant rate.

### 7.4 Explain how to value common shares using the price-earnings (P/E) ratio.

The common share price is the benchmark P/E ratio multiplied by the firm's earnings.

### 7.5 Apply the principles of fundamental valuation and relative valuation.

The application of the principles of fundamental valuation and relative valuation are presented as an example in section 7.5.

### 7.6 Explain how speculative price bubbles occur.

Speculative bubbles illustrate what is colloquially known as the "bigger fool theorem." Suppose, for example, a broker tells a client to buy XYZ at $30. The investor refuses because the stock is worth only $25. The broker replies, "I know, but there is momentum behind it and I am seeing a lot of interest. I think it will go to $40 by next year." The investor is a fool to pay $30 for something she thinks is worth $25, but this is not the fool theorem but the bigger fool theorem. If the investor does buy it, she is a fool, but she is also assuming that an even bigger fool will buy it in a year's time for $40.

### 7.7 Explain how to value common shares using additional relative value ratios.

The common share price is the benchmark relative value ratio multiplied by some measure of the firm's performance, such as earnings, book assets, and so on, which is the other side of the ratio.

# Key Terms

common share, p. 7-1
constant growth DDM, p. 7-7
dividend discount model (DDM), p. 7-5
equity securities, p. 7-1
market (enterprise) value to EBIT ratio, p. 7-25

market (enterprise) value to EBITDA ratio, p. 7-25
market-to-book (M/B) ratio, p. 7-25
preferred share, p. 7-2
price-earnings (P/E) ratio, p. 7-16

price-to-cash-flow (P/CF) ratio, p. 7-25
price-to-sales (P/S) ratio, p. 7-25
relative valuation, p. 7-16
sustainable growth rate, p. 7-10

# Equations

| Equation | Description | Formula | Page |
|---|---|---|---|
| **[7.1]** | Required Rate of Return on a Risky Security | $k = RF + \text{Risk premium}$ | p. 7-2 |
| **[7.2]** | Market Price of Preferred Shares | $P_{ps} = \dfrac{D_p}{k_p}$ | p. 7-3 |
| **[7.3]** | Required Return on Preferred Shares | $k_p = \dfrac{D_p}{P_{ps}}$ | p. 7-4 |
| **[7.4]** | Dividend Discount Model (DDM) (over $n$ Periods) | $P_0 = \dfrac{D_1}{(1+k_c)^1} + \dfrac{D_2}{(1+k_c)^2} + \ldots + \dfrac{D_n + P_n}{(1+k_c)^n}$ | p. 7-5 |
| **[7.5]** | Dividend Discount Model (DDM) | $P_0 = \dfrac{D_1}{(1+k_c)^1} + \dfrac{D_2}{(1+k_c)^2} + \ldots + \dfrac{D_\infty}{(1+k_c)^\infty} = \sum\limits_{t=1}^{\infty} \dfrac{D_t}{(1+k_c)^t}$ | p. 7-6 |
| **[7.6]** | Dividend Discount Model (DDM) with Constant Growth | $P_0 = \dfrac{D_0(1+g)^1}{(1+k_c)^1} + \dfrac{D_0(1+g)^2}{(1+k_c)^2} + \ldots + \dfrac{D_0(1+g)^\infty}{(1+k_c)^\infty}$ | p. 7-7 |
| **[7.7]** | Constant Growth Dividend Discount Model (DDM) | $P_0 = \dfrac{D_0(1+g)}{k_c - g} = \dfrac{D_1}{k_c - g}$ | p. 7-7 |
| **[7.8]** | Implied Rate of Return (Using Constant Growth DDM) | $k_c = \dfrac{D_1}{P_0} + g$ | p. 7-7 |
| **[7.9]** | No-Growth Value | $P_0 = \dfrac{EPS_1}{k_c}$ | p. 7-8 |
| **[7.10]** | Price in Terms of Assets in Place and Present Value of Growth Opportunities | $P_0 = \dfrac{EPS_1}{k_c} + PVGO$ | p. 7-8 |
| **[7.11]** | Sustainable Growth Rate | $g = b \times ROE$ | p. 7-10 |
| **[7.12]** | DuPont Equation (Three-Point) | $ROE = (\text{Net income/Sales}) \times (\text{Sales/Total assets}) \times (\text{Total assets/equity})$ $= \text{Net profit margin} \times \text{Turnover ratio} \times \text{Leverage ratio}$ | p. 7-10 |
| **[7.13]** | Dividend Discount Model (DDM) with Delayed Growth until Time $t$ | $P_0 = \dfrac{D_1}{(1+k_c)^1} + \dfrac{D_2}{(1+k_c)^2} + \ldots + \dfrac{D_t + P_t}{(1+k_c)^t}$ | p. 7-11 |
| **[7.14]** | P/E Ratio Approach | $P_0 = \text{Estimated } EPS_1 \times \text{Justified P/E ratio} = EPS_1 \times P_0/E_1$ | p. 7-16 |
| **[7.15]** | P/E Ratio (Using Constant Growth DDM) | $\dfrac{P_0}{EPS_1} = \dfrac{P}{E} = \dfrac{D_1/EPS_1}{k_c - g}$ | p. 7-19 |

# Questions and Practice Problems

## Multiple Choice Questions

**1. (LO 7.1)** Jason bought 46,000 shares of CTB Inc. on January 12, 2022. At that time, CTB Inc. had 2 million common shares outstanding. Calculate the portion of CTB Inc. that Jason owns.

- **a.** 2.3 percent
- **b.** 1.4 percent
- **c.** 6.0 percent
- **d.** 1.5 percent

**2. (LO 7.1)** You bought 100 shares at $20 each. At the end of the year, you received a total of $250 in dividends, and your stock was worth $2,250 total. What was your total return?

- **a.** 45 percent
- **b.** 50 percent
- **c.** 90 percent
- **d.** 25 percent

**3. (LO 7.1)** Which of the following is *not* a difference between equity securities and debt securities?

- **a.** Incur a tax-deductible expense
- **b.** Have a fixed maturity date
- **c.** Always involve fixed periodic payments
- **d.** Represent ownership of the security

**4. (LO 7.1)** Given that the government short-term T-bill yield is 3 percent, and the risk premium of Takashi Group is 5.5 percent, calculate Takashi Group's required rate of return.

- **a.** 8.5 percent
- **b.** 10.5 percent
- **c.** 7.25 percent
- **d.** 11.5 percent

**5. (LO 7.3)** Which of the following statements about equities is *correct*?

- **a.** Every firm pays dividends to common shareholders each year.
- **b.** Preferred dividends are usually paid annually in practice.
- **c.** Common shareholders are entitled to a firm's earnings before preferred shareholders.
- **d.** Common shareholders can vote on issues, such as mergers, election of board members, and so on.

**6. (LO 7.3)** Westlake Ltd. just paid a dividend of $2 per share, which is expected to grow at a constant rate of 6.5 percent indefinitely. The T-bill rate is 4 percent and the risk premium of Westlake Ltd. is 7.5 percent. Calculate Westlake's current share price.

- **a.** $42.60
- **b.** $41.80
- **c.** $46.05
- **d.** $40.00

**7. (LO 7.3)** Grace Holdings recently paid an annual dividend of $1.50 per share, and its estimated long-term growth rate in dividends is 4 percent. The current market price of each share is $26. The implied rate of return on the share is

- **a.** 9.77 percent.
- **b.** 10 percent.

- **c.** 12.5 percent.
- **d.** 13.33 percent.

**8. (LO 7.2)** Park Recreational Vehicles Ltd. shares are currently selling for $37.50 each. You bought 200 shares one year ago at $34 and received dividend payments of $1.50 per share. What was your total dollar capital gain this year?

- **a.** $400
- **b.** $300
- **c.** $700
- **d.** None of the above

**9. (LO 7.1)** Park Recreational Vehicles Ltd. shares are currently selling for $37.50 each. You bought 200 shares one year ago at $34 and received dividend payments of $1.50 per share. What was your total dollar return?

- **a.** $700
- **b.** $1,000
- **c.** $300
- **d.** None of the above

**10. (LO 7.3)** Limestone Co. just paid a dividend of $1.50 per share and its EPS is $3.00. Its book value per share (BVPS) is $36. Calculate Limestone's sustainable growth rate.

- **a.** 20.83 percent
- **b.** 25 percent
- **c.** 4.17 percent
- **d.** 5.25 percent

**11. (LO 7.3)** A firm can increase its dividend payout by doing any one of the following, except:

- **a.** by increasing its after-tax profit (net income)
- **b.** by decreasing the number of shares it has outstanding
- **c.** by increasing its retention rate
- **d.** by increasing its dividend payout rate

**12. (LO 7.3)** The sustainable growth rate is negatively related to

- **a.** net profit margin.
- **b.** leverage ratio or equity multiplier.
- **c.** payout ratio.
- **d.** retention ratio.

**13. (LO 7.3)** Which of the following is *not* a limitation of the DDM?

- **a.** It cannot be applied to firms without dividend payments.
- **b.** It can be applied only to constantly growing firms.
- **c.** It cannot be used to value private firms.
- **d.** It cannot be applied to firms with negative earnings.

**14. (LO 7.3)** Which of the following statements is *false*?

- **a.** The dividend discount model values a stock based on forecasted future dividends
- **b.** It is not unusual for firms to pay out 100% of their earnings to shareholders in the form of dividends during periods of high growth

c. Mature firms tend to have earnings that exceed their investment needs, thus facilitating dividend payments

d. Estimating dividends, especially those far in the future, is difficult.

**15. (LO 7.4)** Which of the following is *false* regarding the relative valuation approach?

   **a.** The most commonly used one is the P/E ratio approach.

   **b.** The M/B ratio may be used instead of the P/E ratio if the firm has negative earnings.

   **c.** We can use the average P/E ratio of the firm's industry when appropriate.

   **d.** The leading P/E ratio can be estimated as (Payout ratio)$(1+g)/(k-g)$.

**16. (LO 7.4)** High P/E ratios tend to indicate that a firm will _____, all things being equal.

   **a.** grow quickly

   **b.** grow at the same speed as the average firm

   **c.** grow slowly

   **d.** not grow

## Practice Problems

### Basic

**17. (LO 7.2)** Describe the characteristics of preferred shares.

**18. (LO 7.3)** List the elements needed for the calculation of a share price using the constant growth DDM.

**19. (LO 7.3)** Describe the constant growth DDM valuation method.

**20. (LO 7.3)** Describe how to estimate the present value of growth opportunities (PVGO) and what it represents.

**21. (LO 7.2)** Fill in the missing information in the following table:

**Preferred Shares in Canada**

| Company | Price | Par Value | Required Return | Dividend Rate | Dividends Paid per Share |
|---|---|---|---|---|---|
| A | | $100 | 8% | 5% | $5.00 |
| B | $60 | $50 | 3% | | |
| C | $70 | $75 | | | $8.00 |
| D | $50 | $50 | | 14% | |
| E | $150 | $30 | 7% | | |
| F | | $100 | 4% | | $9.50 |
| G | | | 7% | 9% | $18.00 |
| H | $18 | | 5% | 6% | |

**22. (LO 7.1)** The preferred shares of Chinook Electrical Co. have a par value of $100 and a dividend rate of 8 percent. The current price is $105. If the risk-free rate is 2.5 percent, what is the risk premium associated with these preferred shares?

**23. (LO 7.3)** FinCorp Inc. purchased a stock for $48. It expects to receive a dividend of $4 in one year and to sell the stock immediately afterwards.

   **a.** If the sale price is $65, what is the expected one-year holding period return?

   **b.** If the sale price is $38, what is the expected one-year holding period return?

   **c.** If the actual return was −5 percent, what was the sale price?

   **d.** If the actual return was 18 percent, what was the sale price?

**24. (LO 7.3)** Fill in the missing information in the following table:

**Common Shares in Canada**

| Company | Price | Required Return | Dividend Growth | Current Dividend | Dividend Expected in 1 Year |
|---|---|---|---|---|---|
| A | | 15% | | $4.50 | $5.00 |
| B | $600 | 3% | 1% | | |
| C | $70 | | 5% | | $8.00 |
| D | $55 | | | $10.00 | $11.00 |
| E | | 14% | 6% | $9.50 | |
| F | | 15% | 0% | | $18.00 |
| G | $40 | 5% | −2% | | |

**25. (LO 7.3)** ToolWerks Company is expected to earn $12 million next year. There are 4 million shares outstanding and the company uses a dividend payout ratio of 30 percent. The required rate of return for companies like ToolWerks is 10 percent. The current share price of ToolWerks is $45.

   **a.** What are the expected earnings per share for ToolWerks?

   **b.** What are the expected dividends per share for ToolWerks?

   **c.** What is the dividend growth rate expected for ToolWerks?

   **d.** What is the present value of growth opportunities for this firm?

**26. (LO 7.3)** Determine the present value of growth opportunities for a company with a leading EPS of $1.85, a required rate of return of 8 percent, and a current stock price of $50.

**27. (LO 7.3)** Oak Furniture Company's most recent earnings were $300,000. From these earnings, it paid dividends on common equity totalling $175,000. There are 50,000 common shares outstanding. The ROE for Oak Furniture is 12 percent. Determine the following:

   **a.** i) Earnings per share

     ii) Which can you calculate: leading or lagging EPS?

   **b.** Dividends per share

   **c.** Earnings retention ratio

   **d.** Sustainable growth rate

**28. (LO 7.4)** List three reasons why one firm may have a higher leading P/E ratio than a comparable firm.

### Intermediate

**29. (LO 7.3)** FinCorp Inc. purchased a stock for $50. It expects to hold the stock for two years, receive a dividend of $1.50 at the end of each year, and sell the stock immediately after receiving the second dividend. Assume dividends are held in a zero-interest savings account.

   **a.** If the sale price is $75, what is the expected annual return?

   **b.** If the sale price is $35, what is the expected annual return?

   **c.** If the actual return was −4 percent, what was the sale price?

   **d.** If the actual return was 15 percent, what was the sale price?

**30. (LO 7.3)** State the relationship that the required rate of return, the expected growth rate, and expected dividends have with the market share price, according to the constant growth DDM.

**31. (LO 7.3)** At a press conference that just concluded, the president of Danu Inc. announced that although the company had just paid a dividend of $0.95/share, they have decided to stop paying any dividends for the next three years. The company will use the time (and funds) to completely update their technology platforms and operations. In four years, Danu Inc. will once again begin to pay out 65% of its annual earnings as dividends. The first reinstated dividend is expected to be $1.40/share. Danu Inc. has a return on equity (ROE) of 12.5% and investors have a required rate of return on the stock of 13.5%. After year 4, dividends are expected to grow at the company's sustainable growth rate.

    **a.** Use the dividend discount model to estimate the stock price of Danu Inc. today.

    **b.** Jim Novak, who purchased shares in Danu Inc. a year ago for $10/share and who has already received the recent $0.95/share dividend, wants to sell his shares today at the price found in part (a). Calculate Jim's 1-year holding period return (HPR) for the period that he held the shares.

**32. (LO 7.2)** Star Corporation has issued $1 million in preferred shares to investors with a 6.75-percent annual dividend rate on a par value of $100. Assuming the firm pays dividends indefinitely and the required rate is 11.5 percent, calculate the price of the preferred shares.

**33. (LO 7.4)** Calculate the leading P/E ratio, given the following information: retention ratio = 0.4, required rate of return = 10 percent, expected growth rate = 6 percent.

**34. (LO 7.3)** You have just been to see your broker at Acclaim Capital Inc. for advice about investing in Empire Bank. The broker indicates that Empire Bank has three different types of securities: debt, preferred shares, and common shares. She states: "Debt is safe because it is a bank and Canadian banks are safe. Empire Bank preferred shares entitle you to vote at the annual general meeting. Empire Bank has paid a common share dividend of $2.50 per year for the past 18 years so you are guaranteed to receive $2.50 next year; if you don't, the bank will go bankrupt." Comment on your broker's statement. Is she correct?

**35. (LO 7.3)** Ibis Company is expected to pay a $1.50 dividend next year. Dividends are expected to grow at 3 percent forever and the required rate of return is 7 percent.

    **a.** What is the price of Ibis today?

    **b.** What is the expected dividend yield?

    **c.** What is the expected capital gains yield?

    **d.** In one year, immediately after the dividend is paid,

        **i.** what is the price of the stock?

        **ii.** what was the one-year holding period return?

    **e.** Looking forward one year, what are the expected dividend and capital gains yields?

    **f.** In year 10, immediately after the dividend is paid,

        **i.** what is the price of the stock?

        **ii.** what was the one-year holding period return (year 9 to 10)?

        **iii.** Looking forward one year, what are the expected dividend and capital gains yields?

**36. (LO 7.4)** Parker Imports Ltd. is expected to pay a $2 dividend in one year. The required rate of return is 9 percent. The firm uses a dividend payout ratio of 25 percent. Calculate the leading P/E ratio in the following cases:

    **a.** Expected growth rate = 4 percent

        **i.** Today

        **ii.** In one year (immediately after dividend paid)

    **b.** Expected growth rate = 8 percent

        **i.** Today

        **ii.** In one year (immediately after dividend paid)

    **c.** If a firm is expected to have a constant dividend growth rate, do you expect the P/E ratio to change over time? Explain.

**37. (LO 7.3)** Spinnaker Supplies Ltd. currently doesn't pay any dividends but is expected to start paying dividends in five years. The first dividend is expected to be $1.80 and is expected to grow at 4.5 percent thereafter. The required rate of return for the firm is 10.5 percent. What is Spinnaker's current stock price?

**38. (LO 7.3)** Latta Incorporated has announced an annual dividend of $5. The firm has zero growth and the required rate of return for this type of firm is 10 percent. Assuming that the ex-dividend date is January 20, calculate the expected stock price for Latta on January 19 and January 21.

**39. (LO 7.3)** OK Natural Foods' current dividend is $5. You expect the growth rate to be 0 percent for years 1 to 5, and 2 percent for years 6 to infinity. The required rate of return on this firm's equity is 10 percent. Determine the following:

    **a.** The expected dividend at the end of year 5

    **b.** The expected dividend at the end of year 6

    **c.** The expected price of the stock at the end of year 5 (immediately after the year 5 dividend)

    **d.** The price of the stock today

**40. (LO 7.3)** Peak's Organic Foods' current dividend is $4. You expect the growth rate to be 10 percent for years 1 to 5, and 3 percent from years 6 to infinity. The required rate of return on this firm's equity is 12.5 percent. Determine the following:

    **a.** The expected dividend at the end of year 5

    **b.** The expected dividend at the end of year 6

    **c.** The expected price of the stock at the end of year 5 (immediately after the year 5 dividend)

    **d.** The price of the stock today

**41. (LO 7.3)** Peele Clothiers Ltd.'s current dividend is $3.60. Dividends are expected to grow by 9 percent for years 1 to 3, 6 percent for years 4 to 7, and 2 percent thereafter. The required rate of return on the stock is 12 percent. What is the current stock price for Peele?

**42. (LO 7.3)** Prime Tire's current dividend is $4. Dividends are expected to grow by 25 percent for years 1 to 3 and 10 percent thereafter. The required rate of return on the stock is 15 percent. What is Prime's current stock price?

**43. (LO 7.3)** Investors demand a rate of return of 15 percent on Sweet Life Food Inc.'s common shares. These shares are currently trading at $20 per share. Dividend payout for the current year is expected to be $1 per share.

    **a.** What is the implied long-term growth rate that shareholders expect?

    **b.** If, because of a recession, the dividend growth rate is projected to be 0, what will be the new share value?

    **c.** Conversely, if, because of a booming economy, investors reassess their growth expectations to 15 percent per year, what will happen to the market price of Sweet Life Food's common shares?

**44. (LO 7.3)** Karlyle Inc. has just paid a dividend of $4. An analyst forecasts annual dividend growth of 9 percent for the next five years; then dividends will decrease by 1 percent per year in perpetuity. The required return is 12 percent (effective annual return, EAR). What is the current value per share according to the analyst?

**45. (LO 7.3)** Next year Dillon Mechanical Inc.'s EPS is expected to be $4. The firm is not expected to pay any dividends for the next four years. In year 5, a dividend of $1.50 is expected and subsequent dividends are expected to grow at 5 percent per year. The next year's EPS of another firm, Sterling Inc., is expected to be $6. Sterling has just paid a dividend of $6 (cheques were mailed out today). Its dividends are expected to grow at 2 percent per year. Assume that the cost of capital for both firms is 15 percent.

**a.** What should be the current share price of Dillon Mechanical Inc.?

**b.** What should be the current share price of Sterling Inc.?

**c.** What is the PVGO of Dillon Mechanical?

**d.** What is the PVGO of Sterling?

**46. (LO 7.3)** Apex Financial Ltd. is concerned about the impact of errors in its estimates of the future dividend payout ratio for Barnett Steel Corporation. Assume that the current dividend is $1, ROE is fixed at 10 percent, and the required rate of return is 15 percent. Using Excel, calculate the current stock price for dividend payout ratios ranging between 5 percent and 75 percent in 5-percentage-point increments. Is the percentage change in the stock price for a 5-percentage-point change in dividend payout ratio constant?

## Challenging

**47. (LO 7.1, 7.2, 7.3)** Global Systems Inc. has just paid $2.40 in dividends ($D_0 = \$2.40$). The firm is expected to continue paying dividends in perpetuity.

**a.** Suppose that the dividends are constant ($D_i = \$2.40$ for all $i$). What will be the stock price of a share of Global Systems Inc. in 22 years if the required rate of return is 10.5 percent?

**b.** Suppose that the dividends are expected to grow by 4 percent each year in perpetuity. What will be the price of a share of Global Systems Inc. in 22 years if the required rate of return is 10.5 percent? What will be the price in 18 years and in 28 years?

**48. (LO 7.3)** Dillon Mechanical Inc.'s first dividend of $2 per share is expected to be paid six years from today. From then on, dividends will grow by 10 percent per year for five years. After five years, the growth rate will slow to 5 percent per year in perpetuity. Assume that Dillon's required rate of return is 15 percent. What is the price of a share of Dillon Mechanical today?

**49. (LO 7.3)** TelTec Inc. stock is expected to sell for $10 per share four years from now. TelTec has just paid a dividend of 50 cents per share. Dividends are expected to grow at a rate of 5 percent per year for the next four years. Assume that the required rate of return for TelTec stock is 15 percent.

**a.** What is the expected constant growth rate beginning in year 5?

**b.** What will the price of TelTec stock be five years from now?

**c.** What is TelTec's current stock price?

**50. (LO 7.3)** JINX Ltd. had earnings per share of $5 as of December 31, 2022, but paid no dividends. Earnings were expected to grow at 15 percent per year for the following five years. JINX Ltd. will start paying dividends for the first time on December 31, 2027, distributing 50 percent of its earnings to shareholders. Earnings growth will be 6 percent per year for the next six years (that is, from January 1, 2028, through to December 31, 2033). Starting on December 31, 2033, JINX Ltd. will begin to pay out 80 percent of its earnings in dividends and earnings growth will stabilize at 2 percent per year in perpetuity. The required rate of return on JINX stock is 10 percent. What should be the current share price of JINX?

**51. (LO 7.3)** TelTec Inc. has a patent that will expire in two years. The firm is expected to grow at 10 percent for the next two years and dividends will be paid at year end. It just paid a dividend of $1. After

two years, the growth rate will decline to 4 percent immediately, and the firm will grow at this rate forever. If the required rate of return is 11 percent, value the firm's current share price.

**52. (LO 7.7)** INV Design Ltd. just paid a dividend of $4 and its current earnings per share is $6. The current T-bill rate is 3.5 percent and INV's risk premium is 10 percent. The net profit margin, asset turnover, and debt-to-equity (D/E) ratios are 15 percent, 1.25, and 0.6, respectively. Calculate the current share price by using the P/E ratio approach.

**53. (LO 7.2)** Dillon Mechanical Ltd.'s preferred shares have a par value of $50, a dividend rate of 7 percent, and trade at a price of $70. Sherwood Inc.'s preferred shares have a par value of $60, have a dividend rate of 4 percent, and trade at a price of $45. Which company's preferred stock is riskier?

**54. (LO 7.3)** Barchuk Mining Inc.'s shares are currently selling for $120. The current dividend is $5 and the required rate of return is 10 percent. What is the expected dividend growth rate?

**55. (LO 7.3)** Apex Financial Ltd. is interested in investing in Scion Systems Inc. Scion's current dividend is $5.50 and its shares are selling for $40. The required rate of return for firms like Scion is 8 percent. Apex has conducted an extensive analysis of the company and believes that the dividend growth rate should be 5 percent.

**a.** Should Apex buy the stock at $40? Why or why not?

**b.** Do you expect the stock price to stay at $40? Explain.

**56. (LO 7.4)** As part of your duties at Apex Financial Ltd. you have been asked to review the analysis carried out by a rival company— Prime Group—of the WX Media Company. WX has had a constant P/E ratio for the past five years. Prime's analyst has made the following statement: "WX's constant P/E ratio is due to zero growth in its earnings, and therefore, WX is not a good investment." Comment on Prime's statement.

**57. (LO 7.3)** Selkirk Inc. has an expected profit margin of 10 percent, a turnover ratio of 1.8, and a leverage ratio of 0.3. The leading EPS is $2.50 and the firm uses a dividend payout ratio of 35 percent. The required return on firms with Selkirk's risk characteristics is 5 percent. Calculate the expected current stock price of Selkirk.

**58. (LO 7.3)** Larch Foods Inc.'s current dividend is $5. Dividends are expected to decline by 4 percent per year for the next three years, and then remain constant thereafter. The required rate of return for this type of company is 12 percent. What is the current stock price for Larch Foods?

**59. (LO 7.3)** Apex Financial Ltd. has completed a fundamental analysis of Spark Energy Inc. Spark Energy is a young company and expects to invest heavily in facilities and research and development during the next five years. It expects to reap the benefits of its research and development during years 6 to 10. However, it expects rivals to enter the market and margins and profitability to stabilize at a lower level after year 10. The details of the analysis are presented below:

| Period | Net Profit Margin | Turnover | Leverage | Dividend Payout Ratio |
|---|---|---|---|---|
| Years 1-5 | 1% | 0.75 | 3.0 | 0.05 |
| Years 6-10 | 15% | 3.00 | 2.0 | 0.10 |
| Years 11-? | 5% | 1.40 | 1.0 | 0.50 |

The current dividend for Spark Energy is $3 and the required rate of return for this type of firm is 15 percent. Determine the current stock price for Spark Energy.

# Cases

Case 7.1 Southside Solar Solutions

Southside Solar Solutions (known as "S3") is a Vancouver-based solar power equipment builder and installer. Joey Hahn founded the company six years ago intending primarily to serve the market in Vancouver. Demand has increased quickly and the company has struggled to keep up, particularly with a broadened client base and increased geographical coverage. Rural communities have kept the company hopping, and this may be just the beginning.

Three years ago in 2019, S3 went public, raising C$85 million, and the company has continued to grow quickly since that time. S3 has been applauded for its sustainable manufacturing and its focus on environmental sensitivity. Despite strong demand and high resource utilization, the company reported negative net income in each of 2018–20; however, it became profitable in 2021 (last year) and Hahn expects it to remain so going forward. Hahn believes S3 has been investing for future growth and the previous years of losses were just the outcome of a highly aggressive and perfectly appropriate growth strategy. In his words, S3 will be the leader in its segment and the innovator that other companies are unable to catch; it will just take some short-term sacrifice to achieve excellent long-term results.

You work for a finance firm that provides private client financial services. Your role is unusual because although you are a stock analyst, you also work directly with clients. Many financial advisory firms would divide these roles between two employees; however, you are performing double-duty.

1. **Stock valuation using constant growth**

   Your supervisor has asked you to calculate the value of S3 common shares. He would like you to use the constant growth dividend discount model and the dividends (2018–21) and expected dividends (2022–25) listed below, which were supplied by the CEO. The required return for S3 stock is 13 percent.

   **S3 Dividends per share (in C$): Past, Present, and Projected**

   | 2018 | 2019 | 2020 | 2021 | 2022 | 2023 | 2024 | 2025 |
   |---|---|---|---|---|---|---|---|
   | 0 | 2.16 | 0 | 0.25 | 1.06 | 1.33 | 1.66 | 2.07 |

   *Note*: Hahn expects the company's dividend to grow at 4 percent after 2025. Also, the most recent dividend payment was at the end of 2021. This is the dividend "just paid."

2. **Choosing an appropriate discount rate**

   Selecting a discount rate is an important part of a stock valuation exercise. This is evident in Southside's case because increasing the discount rate from 13 percent to 15 percent causes a decrease in the calculated share price of $3.67, or 19.3 percent. List and briefly describe three reasons that might lead an analyst to increase or decrease the discount rate in a stock valuation exercise.

3. **Valuation by P/E ratio**

   S3's management has provided a forward EPS estimate of $3.00 for 2022, which you believe is reasonable. Based on this and your price forecasts, the company has a forward P/E ratio of 16.0. Your boss told you that analysts have suggested that S3's forward P/E ratio is 14.5, which means that if your calculations are correct, S3's share price could rise substantially once the market learns what you already know. This is a big deal—if you're correct it means that the market consensus has missed S3's value by about $4.06 per share. Your firm could simply buy as many shares as possible based on the current market valuation and sell once the market adjusts. List and discuss three reasons why you should be very careful in assuming that your estimates are better than the analysts that your boss has been following.

4. **Required return for Westside Winds**

   As a quick side project you've been asked to take a look at another company in a similar sector, the Westside Winds Company, which is a wind power equipment builder. Common shares in Westside Winds sell for $38.63 per share and it is expected that the company will pay a $1.97 dividend at the end of this year. In the past, Westside Winds has paid dividends every period, with a steady long-term growth rate of 2.9 percent. What required return has the market used in calculating a price for this stock?

5. **Can a nondividend payer have value?**

   Some public companies that have never paid a dividend are still popular with investors, even when there is no forecast that the company will ever pay a dividend. This could be true for S3. Hahn has forecasted strong dividend growth, but he could be wrong. Is it possible that S3 stock could still be an attractive purchase even if the company had no immediate plans for a dividend? Why would investors buy such a stock?

**Fifty-Five Years Old and Planning For Retirement**

Jane is a 55-year-old investor with a secure job that pays well. She has saved and invested steadily through her working years and is thinking about early retirement at age 60. She has maintained a thoughtful, well-diversified portfolio throughout her investing years; however, over the past six months she's become very intrigued by S3. Jane uses a solar energy system in her own home and other alternative power systems, and she believes that she is very knowledgeable about companies like S3. Because of her confidence she believes that she can devote a large portion of her portfolio to S3 stock and two or three other alternative energy companies. A friend suggested that it would be unwise to depart from her historical diversified investment strategy and Jane replied that there was no better time for her to do this, for two reasons. Reason one was that never before had she known so much about the company and sector that she was considering. Reason two was that she was getting close to retirement and it was more important now than ever to boost her returns as much as possible. What would you say to Jane?

# Risk, Return, and Portfolio Theory

**LEARNING OBJECTIVES**

After studying this chapter, you should be able to:

**8.1** Distinguish between ex post and ex ante returns and explain how they are estimated.

**8.2** Distinguish between arithmetic and geometric means.

**8.3** Explain how common risk measures are calculated and what they mean.

**8.4** Describe what happens to risk and return when securities are combined in a portfolio.

**8.5** Explain what is meant by the "efficient frontier."

**8.6** Explain what diversification is and why it is important to investors.

**8.7** Construct two-security portfolio risk-return frontiers.

**8.8** Explain the risk-management technique called Value at Risk (VaR).

Chapter 8 defines risk and return, which is the basic relationship in finance. Unfortunately, at any point in time, people tend to focus on only one of the "Rs." When times are good, nobody thinks about risk; when times are bad, people see only risks—the truth lies somewhere between. This chapter establishes the relationship between risk and return, with particular emphasis on equity securities. As such, it lays the foundation for Chapter 9, which discusses some of the most important concepts in finance.

## 8.1 | Measuring Returns

**LEARNING OBJECTIVE 8.1**

Distinguish between ex post and ex ante returns and explain how they are estimated.

In Chapter 7, we discussed the basics of the discounted cash flow (DCF) valuation and relative valuation of equities and finished with a valuation example of common shares that placed the company's stock price in the $53.55 to $53.68 range.

Risk is typically defined as "the possibility of incurring harm." Purchasing a company's shares at a price that is above their estimated value and then holding them may seem to be a bit of a gamble, but no one can say for sure—there is an element of uncertainty, or risk, involved. This chapter is concerned with ways to analyze and manage this risk. First, we develop some basic definitions.

# Ex Post versus Ex Ante Returns

**ex post returns** past or
historical returns

**ex ante returns** future or
expected returns

We must distinguish between **ex post returns** and **ex ante returns**. "Ex post" means "after the fact," so ex post returns are past or historical returns. "Ex ante" means "before the fact," so ex ante returns are expected returns. Advertisements for mutual funds and other investments show historical, or ex post, returns. Then, in smaller print, they have a disclaimer that says past returns do not necessarily reflect future, or ex ante, returns. Of course, what investors are interested in are these future or expected returns, but their judgement in terms of what they can reasonably expect is informed by what has happened in the past. The 33-percent negative return on Toronto Stock Exchange (TSX) stocks during 2008 shows that sometimes what happens is outside of what anyone expects. Even the experts never anticipated such a collapse in stock markets. Similarly, at the end of 2008, few would have predicted a banner year in 2009, when stocks returned 35 percent.

So how can investors measure these ex post or historical returns? As we saw in chapters 6 and 7, the return on an investment consists of two components: the income yield and the capital gain (or loss) yield. The **income yield** is the return earned in the form of a periodic cash flow received by the investors. These cash flows are interest payments (typically in the form of coupons) from bonds and dividends from equities. The income yield measures these cash receipts by dividing them by the purchase price or the beginning-of-period market price. This is shown in Equation 8.1.

**income yield** the return earned
by investors as a periodic cash
flow

$$\text{Income yield} = \frac{CF_1}{P_0} \qquad [8.1]$$

where

$CF_1$ = the expected cash flows to be received

$P_0$ = the purchase price (or beginning market price)

The graph in **Figure 8.1** shows the earnings yield (E/P) on the S&P/TSX Composite Index and the yield to maturity on the long Canada bond since 1986.[1] Notice that since 2005, earnings yields have been higher than bond yields (especially in 2008 and 2011) due to declines in stock prices, and also because bond yields remained extremely low over this period.

Remember that the yield to maturity on the long Canada bond is the return earned by buying the bond and holding it to maturity. In this sense, it is also an expected return over that very long investment horizon. Investors often compare bond yields to the aggregate market dividend yield, such as that on the S&P/TSX Composite Index in Canada. The dividend yield, on the other hand, is the cash that investors can expect to earn if the dividend payments over the next year are the same as they were over the previous period. The dividend yield is a measure of the current dividend payments divided by the current value of the index; it is not a forecast of future dividends. The dividend yield on the TSX was very similar to that on long Canada bonds during the 1950s. During that decade,

**FIGURE 8.1** **Market Yields,
1986 to 2018**

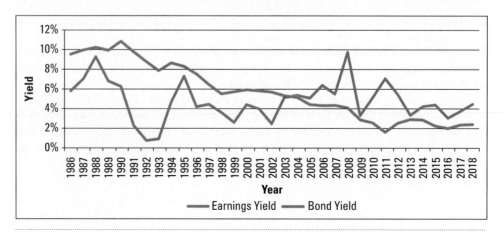

[1]The earnings yield depicted here is measured as $EPS_0/P_0$—that is, it is based on earnings per share over the previous 12 months, not the expected EPS.

| TABLE 8.1 | Average Yield Gap between Common Shares and the Long Canada Bond (%) |
|---|---|
| 1950s | 0.82 |
| 1960s | 2.35 |
| 1970s | 4.54 |
| 1980s | 8.14 |
| 1990s | 5.51 |
| 2000s (to 2018) | 1.16 |
| Overall | 3.08 |

Canada bonds yielded, on average, only 0.82 percent more than the S&P/TSX dividend yield. In fact, during December 1957, the dividend yield on the TSX was 4.41 percent, exceeding the 3.83-percent yield on the long Canada bond. Obviously, 4.41 percent dominates 3.83 percent, so a piece of the puzzle is missing; otherwise, everyone would buy common shares and no one would buy long Canada bonds. The missing piece is the risk attached to investing in common shares.

After the late 1950s, the yield gap between common shares and the long Canada bond became significant, as **Table 8.1** indicates. The spread increased to 2.35 percent in the 1960s, 4.54 percent in the 1970s, and 8.14 percent in the 1980s. The average yield gap decreased to 5.51 percent in the 1990s and to 1.16 percent so far in the 2000s. In fact, the spread was slightly negative in 2008, and hit −1.33 percent by the end of 2011 (and continued to be negative up to 2018), as bond yields fell to 1.52 percent and dividend yields were 2.85 percent due to the relatively low level of stock prices.

The main reason this yield gap has varied so much over time is that the return to investors is not just the income yield but also the capital gain (or loss) yield.

The **capital gain** (or **capital loss**) component measures the appreciation (or depreciation) in the price of the asset from some starting price, usually the purchase price or the price at the start of the year. Dividing this gain or loss by the price produces the capital gain (or loss) yield or return, as expressed in Equation 8.2.

$$\text{Capital gain (or loss) yield} = \frac{P_1 - P_0}{P_0} \qquad [8.2]$$

**capital gain** the appreciation in the price of an asset from some starting price, usually the purchase price or the price at the start of the year

**capital loss** the depreciation in the price of an asset from some starting price, usually the purchase price or the price at the start of the year

where $P_1$ = the selling price or current market price.

When we take the capital gain (or loss) yield into account, it is clear why the yield gap between equities and bonds has varied so much over time. The yield on the long Canada bond is a fixed return earned by buying and holding the bond to maturity. In contrast, as a firm retains money for reinvestment, that firm should become more valuable over time; investing in such a firm's common shares should give rise to significant long-term capital gains. In addition, common shares should gain from inflation over the long run as their prices and cash flows are not fixed; in aggregate, they should increase with inflation. As a result, we would expect the yield gap to increase with the rate of inflation, which it generally does. Remember, for example, from Figure 6-4, that the high level of long Canada bond yields coincided with the very high rates of inflation in the 1970s into the 1980s, when the yield gap was the highest.

To get the complete picture of the return from investing in bonds versus common shares, we have to add the income yield and the capital gain (or loss) yield together. The **total return** is then calculated using Equation 8.3.

**total return** income yield plus the capital gain (or loss) yield

$$\text{Total return} = \text{Income yield} + \text{Capital gain (or loss) yield}$$
$$= \frac{CF_1 + P_1 - P_0}{P_0} \qquad [8.3]$$

---

**EXAMPLE 8.1** | Calculating Returns

Estimate the income yield, capital gain (or loss) yield, and total return for the following securities over the past year:

**a.** A $1,000 par value, 4-percent bond that was purchased one year ago for $990 and is currently selling for $995.

**b.** A stock that was purchased for $20, provided four quarterly dividends of $0.25 each, and is currently worth $19.50.

**Solution**

**a.** $CF_1 = 0.04 \times \$1,000 = \$40; P_0 = \$990; P_1 = \$995$

Income yield $= \$40/\$990 = 0.0404 = 4.04\%$

Capital gain (or loss) return $= (\$995 - \$990)/\$990 = 0.0051 = 0.51\%$

Total return $= 4.04\% + 0.51\% = 4.55\%$

Or total return $= (\$40 + \$995 - \$990)/\$990 = 0.0455 = 4.55\%$

**b.** $CF_1 = \$0.25 \times 4 = \$1.00; P_0 = \$20; P_1 = \$19.50$

Income yield $= \$1/\$20 = 0.05 = 5\%$

Capital gain (or loss) return $= (\$19.50 - \$20)/\$20 = -0.025 = -2.5\%$

Total return $= 5\% - 2.5\% = 2.5\%$

Or total return $= (\$1 + \$19.50 - \$20)/\$20 = 0.025 = 2.5\%$

---

In Example 8.1, notice that the bond has not been held to maturity, so the return over one year may be different from the yield to maturity. In this case, the bond has increased in value from $990 to $995, so there is a capital gain of 0.51 percent from holding the bond, in addition to the income yield of 4.04 percent, so the total return is 4.55 percent. This raises an important question: in calculating the rate of return, does it matter whether or not the bond is sold? Take part b in Example 8.1, where there is a capital loss of 2.5 percent. This reduces the return from holding the common share from 5 percent to 2.5 percent, so it is less than the return from the bond. Should we add this capital loss to the overall return if we do not actually sell the shares?

The answer may seem obvious to most people, but psychologists have observed that people make different decisions if they own something than if they do not own it. For example, people will keep something for years because it cost $100 and is "valuable," even after they see the identical object selling for $1 in a flea market, and yet wouldn't buy it for $1. Owning assets includes an attachment effect, and, with such an attitude, many people refuse to accept capital losses in the total return calculation until they actually sell the asset and realize them. Until then, people refer to them as **paper losses**, with the implication that they are not real. This attitude is reinforced by the tax rules: capital gains and losses are only taxable on realization.

A second important point is that our decision to acknowledge paper gains and losses depends, in part, on our "investment horizon." For example, we can look at rates of return over daily, weekly, monthly, annual, or even longer periods. A **day trader** is someone who buys and sells based on intraday price movements. In that case, the total return for a day's trading will include the effect of capital gains and losses daily and sometimes over even shorter periods. In contrast, most people review their investments less frequently, perhaps quarterly or sometimes annually. For them, the intraday price variability and total return are not a concern. What is of concern is the total return over, say, a quarter or a year. They are not concerned about rates of return over shorter periods or the paper losses that are involved.[2]

**paper losses** capital losses that people do not accept as losses until they actually sell and realize them

**day trader** someone who buys and sells based on intraday price movements

---

[2]This brings to mind the philosophical question "Does a tree falling in a forest make a noise if there is no one there to hear it?" Similarly, does a daily total return matter to an investor who reviews their investments only once a month? Perhaps it depends on the month—during September 2008, when global stock markets plummeted, it could have mattered a lot!

The contrary view is that investors have to **mark to market** the prices of all financial securities over the relevant investment horizon. This means that investors always carry securities at the current market value regardless of whether they sell them. As a result, the total return includes the effect of paper gains and losses on securities not yet sold. This view is based on the basic opportunity cost argument, which asks what the alternative use is for the funds tied up in the investment. Clearly, an investor cannot sell the security at its historical cost; they can sell at the current market value, and this is the value that can be reinvested elsewhere. In this textbook, we will always mark to market and consider the total return as including paper gains and paper losses over the relevant investment horizon, because this reflects the economic value of past investment decisions.

**mark to market** carrying securities at the current market value regardless of whether they are sold

---

### Concept Review Questions

1. What is the difference between ex ante and ex post returns?
2. Why do the income and capital gains components of the total return differ between common shares and bonds?

---

## 8.2 | Types of Average Returns

### LEARNING OBJECTIVE 8.2
Distinguish between arithmetic and geometric means.

How can we measure these ex post or historical returns? Recall Table 5-1 from Chapter 5, which reported the geometric average annual rates of return for various types of investments from 1938 to 2018. These returns assume that the investor buys and holds the security for each year. Part of that table is reproduced in **Table 8.2**. It is important that you understand how these returns are calculated.

The **arithmetic mean** or **arithmetic average** is the most commonly used value in statistics. It is calculated as the sum of all of the returns divided by the total number of observations, as expressed in Equation 8.4.

**arithmetic mean** or **arithmetic average**  the most commonly used value in statistics; the sum of all returns divided by the total number of observations

$$\text{Arithmetic mean (AM)} = \frac{\sum\limits_{i=1}^{n} r_i}{n} \qquad [8.4]$$

where

$r_i$ = the individual returns

$n$ = the total number of observations

The **geometric mean**, in contrast, measures the compound growth rate over multiple periods, which was discussed in Chapter 5. For investments, this is the growth rate in the value invested or, equivalently, the compound rate of return. Recall that in Chapter 5, Table 5.1 showed that the future value of $1,000 invested in Canadian stocks at the start of 1938 would have grown to $1,901,852 by the end of 2018 (i.e., after 81 years) if all the income was reinvested each period. In fact, the precise geometric mean return was 9.769999741 percent, which means that $1,000 invested in 1938 and compounded at 9.77 percent grew to $1,901,852 after 81 years, or $FV = (\$1,000)(1.09769999741)^{81} = \$1,901,852$. In fact, the geometric mean is the rate of return used to find the future value, as discussed in Chapter 5. It is calculated using Equation 8.5.

**geometric mean**  the average or compound growth rate over multiple time periods

$$\text{Geometric mean (GM)} = [(1 + r_1)(1 + r_2)(1 + r_3)\ldots(1 + r_n)]^{1/n} - 1 \qquad [8.5]$$

**TABLE 8.2** Average Investment Returns and Standard Deviations, 1938 to 2018

| | Annual Arithmetic Mean (%) | Annual Geometric Mean (%)[3] | Standard Deviation of Annual Returns (%) |
|---|---|---|---|
| Government of Canada treasury bills | 4.68 | 4.53 | 3.91 |
| Government of Canada bonds | 6.09 | 5.76 | 8.26 |
| Canadian stocks | 10.99 | 9.77 | 16.37 |
| U.S. stocks[4] | 12.32 | 10.99 | 17.05 |

**Sources:** Annual geometric mean data are from the Canadian Institute of Actuaries (data to 2008) and from Statistics Canada CANSIM database (data from 2011 to 2018). Other data are from the Canadian Institute of Actuaries and from Datastream.

---

**EXAMPLE 8.2** | Calculating Arithmetic Mean and Geometric Mean

Estimate the arithmetic mean (AM) and geometric mean (GM) for the following returns: 4.3 percent, 3.2 percent, 5.6 percent, 10.5 percent, and −7.6 percent.

**Solution**

$$AM = (4.3 + 3.2 + 5.6 + 10.5 - 7.6)/5 = 16/5 = 3.2\%$$

$$GM = [(1.043)(1.032)(1.056)(1.105)(0.924)]^{1/5} - 1 = (1.1605455)^{1/5} - 1 = 1.0302 - 1$$
$$= 0.0302 \text{ or } 3.02\%$$

---

In Example 8.2, notice that the geometric mean is less than the arithmetic mean. This will always be the case unless the values are all identical. The more the returns vary, the bigger the difference between the AM and GM will be.

We will formally discuss statistical measurement of how much returns vary in section 8.3, but note that the last column in Table 8.2 gives the **standard deviation** of the annual returns. The standard deviation measures the "typical" variation of the return: the larger the standard deviation, the more variable the return. When the standard deviation is squared, we get a measure called the variance. The difference between the AM and GM returns is approximately half this variance.

**standard deviation** a measure of risk over all the observations; the square root of the variance, denoted as $\sigma$

For example, the standard deviation of the annual treasury bill (T-bill) returns was 3.91 percent or 0.0391. Squaring this to get the variance gives us 0.00152881, and half this is 0.000764405 or 0.0764405 percent. Note that the difference between the AM and GM T-bill returns is 4.68 percent minus 4.53 percent, or 0.15 percent. So the approximation is reasonably close. For Canadian equities, the standard deviation and variance were 16.37 percent (or 0.1637) and 0.02679769 respectively, so half the variance is 1.3399 percent. In this case, the difference between the AM and GM equity returns is 10.99 percent minus 9.77 percent or 1.22 percent, so the approximation is fairly precise.

As we indicated before, the more variable the annual returns, the bigger the difference between the AM and GM measures of return. Looking again at Table 8.2, the biggest difference is for the common stock returns and then the long bond returns. The smallest is for the T-bill returns. So when should we use the AM and when the GM to describe the average return from an investment? The answer depends on what we are trying to do.

The AM is appropriate when we are trying to estimate the typical return for a given period, such as a year. If we wanted to know the best estimate for the rate of return over the next year, we would use the AM of the annual rates of return because, by definition, this measures the average annual rate of return. We use the GM when we are interested in determining the "true" average rate of return over multiple periods—for instance, if we wanted to know how our investment (and wealth) will grow over time. We use the GM because it measures the compound rate of growth in our investment value over multiple periods. In this sense, the difference between the AM and GM is dependent on the relevant investment horizon.

[3]This was referred to as the annual compound return in Table 5.1. This is because the geometric mean is the mean used in compounding.
[4]The return on U.S. stocks is the return when converted to Canadian dollars.

If the investment horizon is one year, the AM is the best estimate. If the investment horizon is multiple years, the GM is better. Example 8.3 demonstrates why the geometric mean is superior for estimating returns over multiple periods.

---

**EXAMPLE 8.3** | Geometric Mean versus Arithmetic Mean

Estimate the annual arithmetic mean return and the geometric mean return on an investment that is purchased for $100, rises to $110 after one year, and falls to $100 by the end of the second year. Assume the investment provided no income during the two-year period.

**Solution**

$$\text{Total return (Year 1)} = (\$110 - \$100)/\$100 = 0.1 = 10\%$$
$$\text{Total return (Year 2)} = (\$100 - \$110)/\$110 = -9.09\%$$
$$\text{AM} = (10 - 9.09)/2 = 0.455\%$$
$$\text{GM} = [(1.1)(0.9091)]^{1/2} - 1 = 0.0000 = 0.00\%$$

---

The annual arithmetic mean return is 0.455 percent because this is simply the average of the two annual rates of return. However, to tell an investor that they have made on average 0.455 percent, when the investment is worth exactly what it started with, is misleading. In contrast, the geometric mean or compound rate of return provides the correct annual return of 0 percent.[5]

Why the AM and GM differ in Example 8.3 can be seen by looking at the two rates of return. As we mentioned before, the annual rates of return have to vary to make a difference between the AM and GM, which they did in Example 8.3. Now notice that the gain of 10 percent is made when the investment is worth $100, whereas the loss of 9.09 percent is made when the investment is worth $110. Clearly, a gain of 10 percent on $100 is $10 and a loss of 9.09 percent on $110 is also $10, which is why the investor ends up with the same $100 that they started with. However, the AM simply averages the annual rates of return without taking into account that the amount invested varies across time. For this reason, the GM is a better way to estimate the average return when we are interested in the performance of an investment over time.

## Estimating Expected Returns

Although it is important to be able to estimate the ex post returns realized from past investments, investors are generally interested in the returns they *expect* to realize from an investment made today. In practice, **expected returns** are often estimated based on historical averages, but the problem is that there is no guarantee the past will repeat itself. For example, the years 1938 to 2018 included World War II (1939–45), a period of significant inflation (the 1970s and into the 1980s), a recession caused, in part, by the passing of the North American Free Trade Agreement between Canada, the United States, and Mexico (early 1990s), a bubble in technology stock prices, and a catastrophic 2008 for investors at the height of the recent financial crisis. For investors interested in expected returns, such events as these can have unexpected effects.

**expected returns**   estimated future returns

An alternative approach is to use all available information to assess the most likely returns under various future scenarios and then attach probabilities to the likelihood of each occurring. Using this approach, the expected return is estimated as the weighted average of the expected returns under each scenario; the weights correspond to the probability of each scenario actually occurring. This is expressed by Equation 8.6.

$$\text{ER} = \sum_{i=1}^{n}(r_i \times \text{Prob}_i)$$   [8.6]

where

$ER$ = the expected return on an investment

$r_i$ = the estimated return in scenario $i$

$Prob_i$ = the probability of state $i$ occurring

---

[5]In fact, the return would be negative in this case if we also considered opportunity cost.

**EXAMPLE 8.4** | Estimating Expected Returns

Suppose you are given the following information for two stocks, A and B, where the return on each varies with the state of the economy.

| State of the Economy | Probability of Occurrence | Expected Return on Stock A in This State | Expected Return on Stock B in This State |
|---|---|---|---|
| High growth | 0.1 | 60% | 5% |
| Moderate growth | 0.2 | 20% | 25% |
| No growth | 0.5 | 10% | 5% |
| Recession | 0.2 | −25% | 0% |

Estimate the expected return for each stock.

**Solution**

$$ER_A = 0.1(60) + 0.2(20) + 0.5(10) + 0.2(-25) = 10\%$$
$$ER_B = 0.1(5) + 0.2(25) + 0.5(5) + 0.2(0) = 8\%$$

Conceptually, the expected return in Example 8.4 is calculated the same way we calculate AM from historical data; the only difference is how we calculate the probabilities. In Example 8.4, we estimate the probabilities of each event directly. For example, economists might estimate the likelihood of different economic growth scenarios for the upcoming year, and security analysts will estimate the prospects for each firm. This sort of scenario data can then be packaged into data similar to what we have in the table in Example 8.4. In contrast, the AM simply assumes that each observation is equally likely, so the probability of each event is reflected in the number of times we observe it in the data. For example, the data from 1938 to 2018 will reflect the historical probabilities of the four different economic scenarios in the table without paying any attention to where we are today.

There are pros and cons to each method of determining expected rates of return. For short-term forecasts, the scenario-based approach makes more sense, because where we are today has a huge bearing on what is likely to happen over a short period. However, for longer-run forecasts, the historical approach tends to be better because it reflects what actually happens, even if it was not expected. In the next sections, we will use the scenario-based approach.

## Concept Review Questions

1. Why is the GM return a better estimate of long-run investment performance than the AM return?
2. Why might a scenario-based estimate be more accurate for a short-run expected return than a historical AM estimate?

## 8.3 | Measuring Risk

**LEARNING OBJECTIVE 8.3**
Explain how common risk measures are calculated and what they mean.

We have already touched on the idea of risk several times. Risk is the probability of incurring harm, and, for investors, harm generally means losing money or earning an inadequate rate of return. In the rest of this chapter, we will use the term "risk" to mean the probability that the

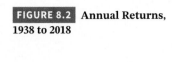
**FIGURE 8.2** **Annual Returns, 1938 to 2018**

actual return from an investment is less than the expected return.[6] This means that the more variable the possible returns, the greater the risk. We can see this in **Figure 8.2**, which graphs the actual returns for Canadian T-bills versus Canadian stocks from 1938 to 2018. These two investments represent two ends of the investment spectrum. Averages were reported for these and for Canadian long-term bonds and U.S. stocks in Table 8.2. One thing that is obvious from the graph is the wide variation in returns for Canadian stocks relative to the returns for Canadian T-bills. (The variability of returns for U.S. stocks is similar to that of Canadian stocks, while long-term bond variability falls somewhere between the two extremes.) For example, Canadian stock returns varied from a maximum of 48.43 percent to a minimum of −33.00 percent, while T-bill returns varied much less, with a maximum of 20.37 percent and a minimum of 0.37 percent.

The difference between the maximum and minimum values is called the **range**, so Canadian common stocks had a range of annual returns of 81.43 percent, which is greater than that for Canadian T-bills at 20 percent. The range summarizes the visual evidence that the returns on common stocks are more variable than those for bonds or T-bills.

**range** the difference between the maximum and minimum values

## Standard Deviation

A more accurate measure of risk is the standard deviation, because the range uses only two observations, the maximum and minimum, whereas the standard deviation uses all the observations.

We reported the standard deviation of the 1938 to 2018 annual returns in Table 8.2 and discussed it when we pointed out the difference between the AM and GM returns. The standard deviation, like the range, clearly shows that common stock returns had a higher standard deviation in their annual returns than did bonds and T-bills over this period. This ranking of investments according to risk mirrors the ranking in terms of AM and GM returns, and it hints at a basic result in finance: risk and return go hand in hand. In other words, we normally see a trade-off between risk and return: securities offering higher expected rates of return tend to be riskier. So let's measure this risk using the standard deviation.

[6]Often, risk is defined as the probability that the actual return is less than the risk-free rate, because this reflects the alternative investment. However, for our purposes this distinction is not material.

The definition of the standard deviation for a series of historical or ex post returns is shown in Equation 8.7.

$$\text{Ex post } \sigma = \sqrt{\frac{\sum\limits_{i=1}^{n}(r_i - \bar{r})^2}{n-1}} \qquad [8.7]$$

where

$\sigma$ = the standard deviation

$\bar{r}$ = the average return

$r_i$ = the return in year $i$

$n$ = the number of observations

**variance**  the standard deviation squared; denoted as $\sigma^2$ and expressed in units of $\%^2$

The term inside the square root sign in Equation 8.7 is called the **variance**, which is denoted as $\sigma^2$. Therefore, the standard deviation is the square root of the variance, and, conversely, the variance is the square of the standard deviation. We focus on the standard deviation because it is easier to interpret: the standard deviation for a series of returns is expressed in the same unit as the returns—that is, as a percentage. In contrast, the variance is expressed as $\%^2$, which makes its interpretation less obvious. Also note that by definition, the calculation of the standard deviation uses the arithmetic mean as opposed to the geometric mean.

---

**EXAMPLE 8.5** | Calculating the Ex Post Standard Deviation

Estimate the standard deviation of the returns provided in Example 8.2 (i.e., 4.3 percent, 3.2 percent, 5.6 percent, 10.5 percent, and −7.6 percent).

**Solution**  Recall from Example 8.2 that the arithmetic mean for this series of returns was 3.2 percent. Therefore, we can estimate the standard deviation as follows:

$$\sigma = \sqrt{\frac{(4.3 - 3.2)^2 + (3.2 - 3.2)^2 + (5.6 - 3.2)^2 + (10.5 - 3.2)^2 + (-7.6 - 3.2)^2}{5 - 1}}$$

$$= \sqrt{\frac{1.21 + 0 + 5.76 + 53.29 + 116.64}{4}} = \sqrt{\frac{176.9}{4}} = \sqrt{44.225} = 6.65\%$$

Notice that the variance of this return series is $44.225\,\%^2$.

---

The standard deviation, as we have measured it, estimates the variability of the returns over the sample period. In the case of Example 8.5, this is 6.65 percent. For the investment returns from 1938 to 2018, the standard deviation of the annual returns for Canadian common shares was 16.37 (17.05 percent for U.S. stocks); that for bonds was 8.26 percent. This raises the question of whether this relative risk was constant over the entire period. The graph in **Figure 8.3** shows the ratio of the standard deviation of the returns on common shares to that on long Canada bonds over the 1947 to 2018 period. To see how this has changed over time, the estimates are based on rolling 10-year periods going back to 1938, so the first estimate is the ratio for 1938 to 1947, the second for 1939 to 1948, and so on.

What is clear is that the relative risk of equities versus bonds has not been constant over this long period. Until the 1960s, the annual rates of return on common shares were about four to six times more variable than those on bonds. During the 1960s, they were approximately three times as volatile. Since then, they have been approximately twice as variable, until the 2009 to 2018 period, when the ratio increased markedly into the 4 to 6 range. Just as the AM estimate of the annual return reflects the economic circumstances of the period over which it is estimated, so too does the standard deviation. For this reason, we also calculate the scenario-based standard deviation as a measure of risk.

**FIGURE 8.3** **Relative Uncertainty: Equities versus Bonds**

The scenario-based standard deviation can be estimated using Equation 8.8 (where all variables are as defined in Equation 8.6). We will refer to this as the "ex ante measure" because we are explicitly taking into account updated probabilities of future events happening.

$$\text{Ex ante } \sigma = \sqrt{\sum_{i=1}^{n}(\text{Prob}_i)(r_i - ER)^2} \qquad [8.8]$$

---

**EXAMPLE 8.6** | Estimating Ex Ante Standard Deviations

Estimate the standard deviations for stocks A and B from Example 8.4, using the information provided in that example.

**Solution**

$$\sigma_A = \sqrt{0.10(60-10)^2 + 0.20(20-10)^2 + 0.50(10-10)^2 + 0.20(-25-10)^2}$$
$$= \sqrt{250 + 20 + 0 + 245} = \sqrt{515} = 22.69\%$$

$$\sigma_B = \sqrt{0.10(5-8)^2 + 0.20(25-8)^2 + 0.50(5-8)^2 + 0.20(0-8)^2}$$
$$= \sqrt{0.9 + 57.8 + 4.5 + 12.8} = \sqrt{76.00} = 8.72\%$$

Notice that A has the higher standard deviation; therefore, it appears to have the most risk, based on the variability of the forecast for its expected return.

---

## Coefficient of Variation

The **coefficient of variation (CV)** is an alternative measure of risk compared to the variance or standard deviation. Equation 8.9 provides the calculation of this statistic.

$$\text{Coefficient of variation (CV)} = \frac{\text{Standard deviation of returns}}{\text{Arithmetic mean return}} \qquad [8.9]$$

**coefficient of variation (CV)** a standardized measure of dispersion that can be used to compare the risks of two investments with different arithmetic means

Since both the standard deviation and arithmetic mean returns are typically expressed as percentages, the measurement of the coefficient of variation is unit-free. As demonstrated in Example 8.7, this provides an advantage in that comparisons regarding risk can be made for different investment opportunities without regard for scale. Higher risk is consistent with a higher coefficient of variation.[7]

---

**EXAMPLE 8.7** | Using the Coefficient of Variation to Make Investment Decisions

A portfolio manager is considering investing in either the Canadian stock market or the U.S. stock market, and gathers data on the annual returns of two indexes over the 1999 to 2018 period:

|  | Canadian Stock Market Index | U.S. Stock Market Index |
|---|---|---|
| Standard deviation of returns | 16.74% | 14.97% |
| Arithmetic mean return | 6.78% | 4.46% |

Based on these data and relying on the coefficient of variation, which one of the investments should the manager select?

**Solution**

|  | Canadian Stock Market Index | U.S. Stock Market Index |
|---|---|---|
| Coefficient of variation | 16.74%/6.78% = 2.47 | 14.97%/4.46% = 3.36 |

Relying solely on the coefficient of variation, the manager should select the Canadian stock market index for investment. Although it has a higher dispersion (or spread) as measured by the standard deviation, the Canadian index has a higher arithmetic mean return, resulting in a lower coefficient of variation. Put another way, the U.S. index has 3.36 units of risk per unit of mean return while the Canadian index has only 2.47 units of risk per unit of mean return.

---

**Concept Review Questions**

1. Why is the range sometimes a poor measure of risk?
2. What is the difference between a scenario-based (probability) estimate of risk versus a historical data-based estimate of risk?
3. Why would we sometimes want to use scenario-based risk measures rather than the standard deviation of actual returns over a long period?
4. When would the coefficient of variation be a useful measure of risk and what are its limitations?

---

## 8.4 | Expected Return and Risk for Portfolios

**LEARNING OBJECTIVE 8.4**

Describe what happens to risk and return when securities are combined in a portfolio.

---

[7]Having a mean value in the denominator could present problems. Clearly, a mean of zero will produce an undefined coefficient of variation, and a very small mean will inflate the coefficient of variation and limit its usefulness. A negative coefficient of variation is not meaningful.

A **portfolio** is a collection of securities, such as stocks and bonds, that are combined and considered a single asset. A portfolio may refer to the holdings of a single investor or to holdings that are managed as a unit by one or more portfolio managers on behalf of their clients. It is a basic proposition in finance that securities should be managed within a portfolio, rather than individually, because it is possible to realize risk-reduction gains by combining securities into a portfolio. The study of portfolios and the potential gains related to them is called **modern portfolio theory (MPT)**, and we will be using the statistical ideas that we have just discussed to explore it. The basic idea is as simple as the old adage "don't put all your eggs in one basket": investors should diversify their investments so that they are not unnecessarily exposed to a single negative event. MPT takes this basic idea and operationalizes it to show how to form portfolios with the highest possible expected rate of return for any given level of risk. First, we will examine how to calculate the expected return and risk of a portfolio.

The expected return on a portfolio is simply the weighted average of the expected returns on the individual securities in the portfolio, as expressed in Equation 8.10. The "portfolio weight" of a particular security is the percentage of the portfolio's total value that is invested in that security. These weights sum to one, because 100 percent of the portfolio must be invested in something, even if it is simply cash.

$$ER_p = \sum_{i=1}^{n}(w_i \times ER_i) \qquad [8.10]$$

where

$ER_p$ = the expected return on the portfolio

$ER_i$ = the expected return on security $i$

$w_i$ = the portfolio weight of security $i$

The result of Example 8.8 means that if an investor puts 70 percent of their investment in security B, the remaining 30 percent has to be in A. We can simplify the expected return formula in the two-security case to make it more informative. Let us define $w$ as simply the weight placed on security A, so that $(1 - w)$ is the weight placed on security B. In this case, we can rearrange the expected return for a two-security portfolio formula to get Equation 8.11.

$$ER_p = ER_B + w(ER_A - ER_B) \qquad [8.11]$$

> **EXAMPLE 8.8** | Estimating Expected Portfolio Return
>
> Using the data from Example 8.4, estimate the expected return for a portfolio that has $600 invested in stock A and $1,400 invested in stock B.
>
> **Solution**
>
> $$\text{Portfolio value} = \$600 + \$1,400 = \$2,000$$
> $$w_A = \$600/\$2,000 = 0.3$$
> $$w_B = \$1,400/\$2,000 = 0.7$$
> $$ER_p = w_A ER_A + w_B ER_B = (0.3)(10\%) + (0.7)(8\%) = 8.6\%$$

For example, if we place a weight of 0 on A, then, by definition, 100 percent is invested in B, and we expect to earn 8 percent, the expected return on B. Conversely, if we invest 100 percent in A and nothing in B, then we expect to earn 10 percent. Incrementally, as we increase $w$ and put more money (weight) in A, we pick up the difference in the expected returns between A and B, which, with the numbers from Example 8.8, is 2 percent. In financial terms, the cost of investing in A is the lost 8-percent expected return from not investing in B, whereas the benefit is its expected return of 10 percent. There is a net advantage in terms of expected return of 2 percent.

**portfolio** a collection of securities, such as stocks and bonds, that are combined and considered a single asset

**modern portfolio theory (MPT)** the theory that securities should be managed within a portfolio, rather than individually, to create risk-reduction gains; also stipulates that investors should diversify their investments so as not to be unnecessarily exposed to a single negative event

**FIGURE 8.4** Expected Portfolio Return

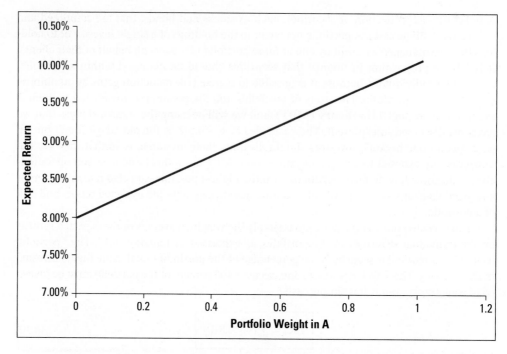

We graph this relationship in **Figure 8.4**. Note that the graph sets the base return at 8 percent, where everything is invested in B, and then increases to 10 percent as we invest more and more in A.[8]

Regardless of the number of assets held in a portfolio or the portfolio weights, the expected return on the portfolio is *always* a weighted average of the expected return on each individual asset. However, this is *not* the case for the portfolio standard deviation, because we must account for correlations, or co-movements, among the individual security returns included in the portfolio, which in turn affect the variability in total portfolio returns. Therefore, the standard deviation for a portfolio will reflect the weighted impact of the individual securities' standard deviations and the relationship among the co-movements of the returns on those individual securities.

The standard deviation of a two-security portfolio can be estimated using Equation 8.12. Notice that the first two terms inside the square root sign account for the weighted standard deviations (or variances) of individual securities, while the third term accounts for the weighted co-movement of the returns on the two securities. This is denoted by the **covariance** of the returns on A and B ($COV_{AB}$), which we define below.

**covariance** a statistical measure of the correlation of the fluctuations of the annual rates of return of different investments

$$\sigma_p = \sqrt{(w_A)^2(\sigma_A)^2 + (w_B)^2(\sigma_B)^2 + 2(w_A)(w_B)(COV_{AB})} \qquad [8.12]$$

where

$\sigma_p$ = the portfolio standard deviation

$COV_{AB}$ = the covariance of the returns on security A and security B

The covariance is calculated using Equation 8.13.[9]

$$COV_{AB} = \sum_{i=1}^{n} Prob_i (r_{A,i} - \bar{r}_A)(r_{B,i} - \bar{r}_B) \qquad [8.13]$$

where $r_{A,i}$ = the *i*th return on security A.

---

[8]For the purposes of this discussion, we have limited the investment weights to a range from 0 percent to 100 percent. However, if we are allowed to "short sell" either security, then the weights can be less than 0 (i.e., negative) and more than 100 percent. Short selling means investors sell shares in a stock that they do not own. This can be done through a broker, who "lends" investors shares that they can sell on the condition that the investors agree to "replace" these borrowed shares in the future (i.e., by buying them in the market). Thus, it provides investors with a way to profit from the belief that share prices will decrease. There are several technicalities associated with short selling that we will not discuss here. The main implication of short selling for our present discussion is that investors can maintain a negative position in one of the two stocks, so they can short sell A and use the proceeds to invest in B and vice versa.

[9]The ex post covariance can be calculated as $COV_{AB} = \dfrac{\sum_{i=1}^{n}(r_{A,i} - \bar{r}_A)(r_{B,i} - \bar{r}_B)}{n - 1}$

---

**EXAMPLE 8.9** | Estimating Covariance

Using the data from Example 8.4, estimate the covariance of the returns on securities A and B.

**Solution**

$$COV_{AB} = 0.1(60 - 10)(5 - 8) + 0.2(20 - 10)(25 - 8) + 0.5(10 - 10)(5 - 8)$$
$$+ 0.2(-25 - 10)(0 - 8) = -15 + 34 + 0 + 56 = 75\%^2$$

---

**EXAMPLE 8.10** | Estimating Portfolio Standard Deviation Using Covariance

Use the covariance estimate in Example 8.9 to estimate the standard deviation of the portfolio described in Example 8.8, which has 30 percent invested in stock A and 70 percent invested in stock B.

**Solution**    Using Equation 8.12, we get:

$$\sigma_p = \sqrt{(0.30)^2(22.69)^2 + (0.70)^2(8.72)^2 + 2(0.30)(0.70)(75)}$$
$$= \sqrt{46.335 + 37.259 + 31.500} = \sqrt{115.094} = 10.73\%$$

---

Notice that the portfolio standard deviation of 10.73 percent is less than the weighted average of the standard deviations of each individual security, which is 12.91 percent—that is, $(0.30)(22.69) + (0.70)(8.72)$. This is always the case, except for one special situation, which we will discuss momentarily. However, before this discussion, we will demonstrate, in **Figure 8.5**, the implication of the difference between the portfolio standard deviation and the weighted average of the standard deviations of each security by graphing the standard deviation of the return on the portfolio as we put a greater share of our investment in the riskier security.

We start out with the standard deviation of the portfolio at 8.72 percent because all funds are in B, and we finish up at 22.69 percent because all funds are in A, but the line between these points is not a straight one. In fact, the standard deviation of the portfolio's return barely moves as we increase investment in the riskier security to 20 percent, even though we expect to earn a higher rate of return. This is a clear win for the investor: more expected return and virtually the same amount of risk.

The curve that shows the standard deviation of the portfolio's return as we increase the investment in the risky security is distinctly "bowed." To see this, think of rotating the graph 180 degrees and then pulling on the bottom of the bow: you get the shape of the standard deviation of the portfolio return. We will return to this bow shape again as it is one of the most important ideas in MPT. For now, we turn to a discussion of another measure of return co-movements.

Although covariance provides a useful measure of the relationship of the co-movements of returns on individual securities, it is difficult to interpret intuitively because, as was the case with the variance, the unit is percent squared ($\%^2$). Fortunately, covariance is related to another statistical measure, the **correlation coefficient** ($\rho_{AB}$), which can be interpreted

**correlation coefficient**    a statistical measure that identifies how security returns move in relation to one another; denoted by $\rho_{AB}$

**FIGURE 8.5**    **Portfolio Risk**

more intuitively. The correlation coefficient is related to covariance and individual standard deviations according to the relationship shown in Equation 8.14.

$$\rho_{AB} = \frac{COV_{AB}}{\sigma_A \sigma_B}$$

[8.14]

This equation can be solved for covariance to provide Equation 8.15.

$$COV_{AB} = \rho_{AB} \sigma_A \sigma_B$$

[8.15]

Finally, we can replace the covariance term in Equation 8.12 to produce Equation 8.16, which is commonly used to estimate portfolio standard deviation.

$$\sigma_p = \sqrt{(w_A)^2 (\sigma_A)^2 + (w_B)^2 (\sigma_B)^2 + 2(w_A)(w_B)(\rho_{AB})(\sigma_A)(\sigma_B)}$$

[8.16]

---

**EXAMPLE 8.11** | Estimating Portfolio Standard Deviation Using the Correlation Coefficient

Redo Example 8.10 using Equation 8.16 instead of Equation 8.12.

**Solution**    First, we need to estimate the correlation coefficient between the returns on stocks A and B.

$$\rho_{AB} = \frac{COV_{AB}}{\sigma_A \sigma_B} = \frac{75}{(22.69)(8.72)} = 0.379$$

By using Equation 8.16, we get:

$$\sigma_p = \sqrt{(0.30)^2 (22.69)^2 + (0.70)^2 (8.72)^2 + 2(0.30)(0.70)(0.379)(22.69)(8.72)}$$

$$= \sqrt{46.335 + 37.259 + 31.495} = \sqrt{115.089} = 10.73\%$$

---

Example 8.11 yields the same answer as Example 8.10. We can now separate the standard deviation component from the correlation component. This is useful because we already have the standard deviation of both securities in the first two terms, so the correlation coefficient is the only new information.

## Correlation Coefficient

The correlation coefficient measures how security returns move in relation to one another. It is a relative measure that has a maximum value of +1.0, which denotes perfect positive correlation, and a minimum value of −1.0, which denotes perfect negative correlation. Positive correlation coefficients imply that the returns on security A tend to move in the same direction as those on security B. In other words, when the return on security B increases, the return on security A also tends to increase, and vice versa. It doesn't mean that they always increase together; if they did, they would be perfectly positively correlated. Negative correlation coefficients imply the opposite: the returns on security A tend to move in the opposite direction to those on security B. In other words, on average, when the return on security B increases, the return on security A tends to decrease, and vice versa.

The closer the absolute value of the correlation coefficient is to one, the stronger the relationship between the returns on the two securities. In fact, when $\rho_{AB} = +1$—that is, perfect positive correlation—and we know the return on one security, we can predict the return on the other security with certainty.[10] The same applies when we have $\rho_{AB} = -1$, perfect negative

---

[10]Technically, when $\rho = +1$ or −1 and we plot the returns of one asset on the *x*-axis and the returns of the other security on the *y*-axis, a line drawn through all the points would be straight. Such a line would be upward sloping when $\rho = +1$, and it would be downward sloping when $\rho = -1$.

correlation, which implies the returns have a perfect negative relationship with each other. When $\rho_{AB} = 0$ (i.e., zero correlation), there is no relationship between the returns on the two securities. In that case, knowing the return on one security provides no useful information for predicting the return on the second security. We illustrate various correlations in **Figure 8.6**, including perfect positive and perfect negative correlation, positive correlation, negative correlation, and no correlation. You can recognize perfect positive and perfect negative correlation right away, because the pairwise observations of returns lie on a perfectly straight line.

**FIGURE 8.6**   **Correlation between the Returns on Stocks**

The extreme correlation coefficient values described above do not occur for traditional common shares in practice, because so many different factors influence security returns. Generally, returns display positive correlations with one another, but they are less than one. This is logical because all securities tend to follow the movements of the overall market. As expected, the correlations tend to be higher among securities whose companies are similar in nature—for example, if they are in the same industry, are about the same size, and so on. The correlation coefficient on the common share returns for the Big Six Canadian banks tends to be high, in the 0.7 to 0.8 range, while the correlation coefficient between bank stocks and mining stocks tends to be much lower, in the 0.2 to 0.4 range. The correlation coefficient of 0.379 in Example 8.11 indicates the two securities are not in the same industry or are not affected similarly by common economic forces.

**Figure 8.7A** provides a scatter plot diagram of the returns on Canadian common shares relative to those on U.S. common shares. As expected, these returns possess a high and positive correlation coefficient of 0.6552. Indeed, the graph shows that the returns tend to move in the same direction—that is, they both tend to be high or low at similar times. The fitted trendline is clearly upward sloping, and the points are relatively close to this line. **Figure 8.7B** depicts the returns on Canadian common shares relative to those on 91-day T-bills, which

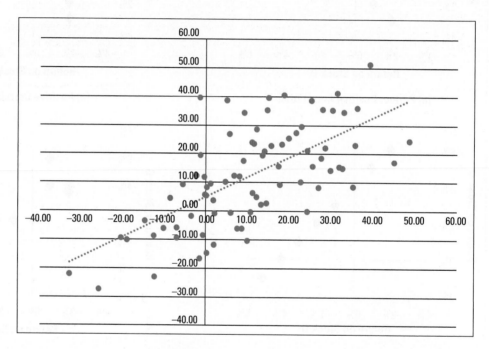

**FIGURE 8.7A** Canadian versus U.S. Stock Returns, 1938 to 2018 (Correlation Coefficient = 0.6552)

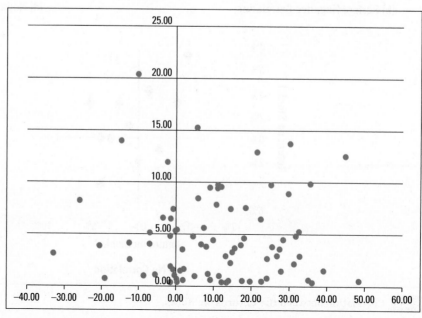

**FIGURE 8.7B** T-Bill Returns versus Canadian Stock Returns, 1938 to 2018 (Correlation Coefficient = −0.0372)

display a correlation coefficient that is close to zero, but is slightly negative ($-0.0372$). The graph shows that knowing the return on one security provides little information about the return on the other. In other words, it would be hard to draw a line through these returns that depicts any kind of relationship.[11]

Finally, we can compare the correlation coefficient with the covariance. As noted in Equation 8.15, the covariance is the correlation coefficient multiplied by the two standard deviations. As a result, the covariance measures the strength, or magnitude, of the relationship between two variables. For example, two variables might be perfectly correlated, so that they always move together, but one of them might barely move at all: it might always go up when the other goes up, and vice versa, but not by very much. As a result, the covariance between these two variables might be lower than that between two other variables that are not so highly correlated.

## Correlation Coefficients and Portfolio Standard Deviation

Recall that Equation 8.16 showed that the correlation between the returns on the two securities included in a portfolio affected the portfolio standard deviation. Holding the weights and the individual standard deviations constant, it is clear that the lower the correlation coefficient, the lower the standard deviation, a conclusion illustrated by Example 8.12.

---

**EXAMPLE 8.12** | Estimating Portfolio Standard Deviation as the Correlation Coefficient Changes

Redo Example 8.11 using Equation 8.16, but now assume that the correlation coefficient between the returns on A and B is

  **a.** $-1$

  **b.** 0

  **c.** 0.6

  **d.** 1

**Solution**

  **a.** $\sigma_p = \sqrt{(0.30)^2(22.69)^2 + (0.70)^2(8.72)^2 + 2(0.30)(0.70)(-1)(22.69)(8.72)}$

    $= \sqrt{46.335 + 37.259 - 83.100} = 0.703\%$

  **b.** $\sigma_p = \sqrt{(0.30)^2(22.69)^2 + (0.70)^2(8.72)^2 + 2(0.30)(0.70)(0.0)(22.69)(8.72)}$

    $= \sqrt{46.335 + 37.259 + 0} = 9.143\%$

  **c.** $\sigma_p = \sqrt{(0.30)^2(22.69)^2 + (0.70)^2(8.72)^2 + 2(0.30)(0.70)(0.6)(22.69)(8.72)}$

    $= \sqrt{46.335 + 37.259 + 49.860} = 11.552\%$

  **d.** $\sigma_p = \sqrt{(0.30)^2(22.69)^2 + (0.70)^2(8.72)^2 + 2(0.30)(0.70)(1.0)(22.69)(8.72)}$

    $= \sqrt{46.335 + 37.259 + 83.100} = 12.911\%$

---

There are several things to note from Example 8.12. First, the lower the correlation coefficient, the lower the portfolio standard deviation. In fact, the portfolio standard deviation for Example 8.12a is much lower than either individual standard deviation and is actually very close

---

[11]If we did draw a line, it would be downward sloping, as indicated by the slight negative correlation coefficient. However, the small absolute value of the coefficient indicates that it would not fit the data very well.

to zero. Obviously, the benefits will be greater as the correlation coefficient approaches −1. This highlights the importance of security return correlations in determining portfolio risk.

Second, the portfolio standard deviation is less than the weighted average of the individual security standard deviations (of 12.911 percent) in parts a to c, as it was in Example 8.11, for which the correlation coefficient was +0.379. Only in Example 8.12d, for which the correlation coefficient equals +1, which is its highest possible value, was it a weighted average. Because +1 is the maximum value for the correlation coefficient, it must be the case that for all other possible correlation coefficients, we have $\sigma_p < w_A\sigma_A + w_B\sigma_B$. This implies there will be benefits from diversification as long as $\rho_{AB}$ is less than +1, which is virtually always the case.

This result is very important because we have just shown the secret of MPT: by combining securities in a portfolio, we can reduce risk. This risk reduction increases as we combine securities that are less than perfectly correlated. It supports the basic finance argument that investors should hold diversified portfolios; otherwise, they are throwing away the magic of diversification, which is that they can lower risk without cost. We will return to this concept shortly, but first we graph the standard deviation of the portfolio return as the correlation coefficient changes in **Figure 8.8**.

This graph shows several interesting things. First, the slope is not linear, as discussed before. This means that to demonstrate the effect of the correlation coefficient, we can use a zero correlation as an example, because this simplifies the arithmetic. Second, with perfectly negative correlation, the variability of the portfolio is reduced to almost zero, which means there is almost no risk. In fact, whenever the correlation coefficient equals −1, there exists one set of portfolio weights for the two securities such that we can eliminate risk completely. This suggests that to discuss how the standard deviation and expected return of a portfolio vary as we change its composition, we can look at three special cases: when the correlation coefficient between the two securities is zero, +1, or −1.

Let's go back to Equation 8.16, which, for ease of reference, we repeat below.

$$\sigma_p = \sqrt{(w_A)^2(\sigma_A)^2 + (w_B)^2(\sigma_B)^2 + 2(w_A)(w_B)(\rho_{AB})(\sigma_A)(\sigma_B)}$$

The three special cases produce simplified versions of the standard deviation of the portfolio's return, shown below.[12]

$$\text{If } \rho = 0 \quad \sigma_p = \sqrt{(w_A)^2(\sigma_A)^2 + (w_B)^2(\sigma_B)^2}$$

$$\text{If } \rho = +1 \quad \sigma_p = \sqrt{(w_A)^2(\sigma_A)^2 + (w_B)^2(\sigma_B)^2 + 2(w_A)(w_B)(\sigma_A)(\sigma_B)}$$

$$\text{If } \rho = -1 \quad \sigma_p = \sqrt{(w_A)^2(\sigma_A)^2 + (w_B)^2(\sigma_B)^2 - 2(w_A)(w_B)(\sigma_A)(\sigma_B)}$$

The zero correlation coefficient case is obvious, as the covariance term disappears. However, in the other two cases, the correlation coefficient also disappears because it is either +1 or −1. We now get a perfect square: for a perfect positive correlation, think $(a + b)^2$,

**FIGURE 8.8** **The Impact of the Correlation Coefficient**

---

[12]Remember these, as they often appear on tests and exams.

and for a perfect negative correlation, $(a - b)^2$, where $a$ is the standard deviation of security A times its portfolio weight (i.e., $w_A \sigma_A$) and $b$ is the same for security B (i.e., $w_B \sigma_B$). This allows us to simplify the equation for the standard deviation of the portfolio return.

Figure 8.5 showed how the portfolio risk (standard deviation) varied with the composition of the portfolio (i.e., based on the weights invested in A and B) for our example case, in which the correlation coefficient was 0.379. Now we can consider how the variability changes with the portfolio composition for these three special cases, because they contain everything of interest. The results are shown in **Figure 8.9**.

Note that with perfect positive correlation, the variability changes in a linear (straight line) fashion with the portfolio weights. As we discussed before, in this case, the standard deviation of the portfolio is a weighted average of each security's standard deviation, which is similar to the expected return. However, when the correlation is less than perfectly positive, the relationship is "bowed." It becomes more bowed as the correlation decreases until, with a perfect negative correlation, we can remove all risk. In this case, the bow becomes two straight lines that touch the horizontal axis. At this point in the $\rho = -1$ case, we can create a portfolio with a standard deviation of zero and no variability at all.

To calculate the portfolio that removes all risk (i.e., creates a portfolio with no variability), consider the special case of Equation 8.16, which reduces to Equation 8.17 when $\rho = -1$.

$$\sigma_p = w\sigma_A - (1 - w)\sigma_B \qquad [8.17]$$

Here we have set the portfolio weights as $w$ and $(1 - w)$ rather than $w_A$ and $w_B$ because they have to add to 100 percent. If we set the standard deviation of the portfolio equal to zero, we can solve for this weight using Equation 8.18.

$$w = \frac{\sigma_B}{\sigma_A + \sigma_B} \qquad [8.18]$$

In our case, the weight is 27.76 percent, so if we put 27.76 percent of our investment in security A and 72.24 percent in the lower-risk security B, we get a portfolio that is risk free—that is, it has no variability at all. We can see this point in Figure 8.9, in which the two lines for the perfect negative correlation case touch the horizontal axis at just below 0.3.

The perfect negative correlation case is of great importance in finance, because it is the basis of hedging (taking an offsetting position so as to minimize risk; we will discuss hedging in more detail in chapters 11 and 12, when we deal with futures and options). Note that

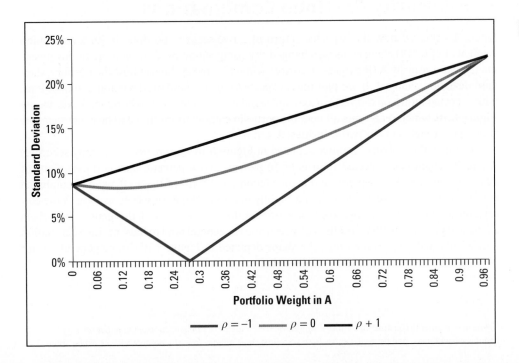

**FIGURE 8.9** **Portfolio Risk and Composition**

although the two securities in our example are perfectly negatively correlated, we do not create an equally weighted portfolio in which we invest the same amount in each security. Instead, we put 27.76 percent in the security with the greater standard deviation and 72.24 percent in the one with the smaller standard deviation. This is because when A goes up, B goes down, but they go up and down by different amounts, as indicated by their different standard deviations. As a result, we have to put more in the lower-variability security B to compensate for the fact that it does not move as much as security A. Only if the securities are equally risky, as well as being perfectly negatively correlated, would we form an equally balanced portfolio to remove risk.

---

### Concept Review Questions

1. Why is the expected return on a portfolio a weighted average of the expected returns of the underlying securities?

2. Why is portfolio standard deviation not a weighted average of the standard deviations of the underlying securities?

3. What is the difference between the covariance and the correlation coefficient?

4. Why is all risk removed in a two-security portfolio if the securities are perfectly negatively correlated?

5. Is the zero-risk portfolio described in Question 4 generally equally weighted in both securities? Explain.

---

## 8.5 | The Efficient Frontier

**LEARNING OBJECTIVE 8.5**

Explain what is meant by the "efficient frontier."

### Two-Security Portfolio Combinations

Figure 8.4 showed how the expected return of a two-security portfolio (with a correlation coefficient of 0.379) changed as we changed the composition by shifting more of our investment toward security A (the riskier security), while Figure 8.5 showed how the portfolio standard deviation changed. If we plot these expected return–standard deviation combinations, with expected return on the vertical axis and standard deviation on the horizontal axis, we get **Figure 8.10**, which represents all possible portfolio combinations that can be constructed by varying the weights in our two securities, A and B.[13]

The hyperbola-shaped frontier depicted in Figure 8.10 was created using only securities A and B, which had expected returns of 10 percent and 8 percent, standard deviations of 22.69 percent and 8.72 percent, and a correlation coefficient of 0.379. If we had combined two other securities, we would obtain a slightly different shape. However, as long as the correlation coefficient is not close to either extreme value (i.e., −1 or +1), this general hyperbola shape will prevail. Further, because risky securities in general tend to have positive correlation coefficients that are less than one, the shape depicted in Figure 8.10 can be generalized for portfolios formed by using most actual securities.

---

[13]Note that in order to construct this entire diagram, we have allowed the weights invested in either security to assume values above 1 and below 0 (i.e., we have permitted short selling—refer to footnote 8 for an explanation).

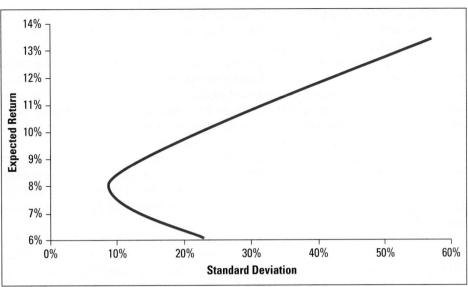

**FIGURE 8.10**  Two-Security Portfolios

## The Efficient Frontier

We can generalize from the two-security to the *n*-security case, for which the expected return will continue to be a weighted average of the expected returns on the individual securities, regardless of the number of securities in the portfolio. As a result, Equation 8.10 for estimating portfolio expected returns still applies, and the portfolio weights still have to sum to 100 percent. However, calculating the standard deviation on a portfolio of more than two securities becomes cumbersome quickly as the number of securities increases. For example, a three-security portfolio can be calculated using Equation 8.19, which has three weighted variance terms and three weighted co-movement terms.

$$\sigma_p = \sqrt{\begin{array}{l}(w_A)^2(\sigma_A)^2 + (w_B)^2(\sigma_B)^2 + (w_C)^2(\sigma_C)^2 + 2(w_A)(w_B)(\rho_{AB})(\sigma_A)(\sigma_B) \\ + 2(w_A)(w_C)(\rho_{AC})(\sigma_A)(\sigma_C) + 2(w_B)(w_C)(\rho_{BC})(\sigma_B)(\sigma_C)\end{array}}$$ [8.19]

The four-security portfolio would similarly have four variance terms and six co-movement terms: the five-security portfolio would have five variance terms and 10 co-movement terms; and so on. A 100-security portfolio would have 100 variance terms and 4,950 co-movement terms.[14] Obviously, the more securities in a portfolio, the greater the relative impact of the security co-movements on the overall portfolio risk, and the lower the relative impact of the individual risks. (We will elaborate on this last point in the next section.)

Harry Markowitz, who is considered the father of modern portfolio theory, was awarded the 1990 Nobel Prize in Economics as a result of his work in this field during the 1950s. One of his main contributions was to show investors how to optimally diversify their portfolios. His arguments, which are developed below, are based on several assumptions. Three of them, which follow, are the most important for our present discussion.

1. Investors are rational decision-makers.
2. Investors are **risk averse**, which means that they like expected returns and dislike risk, and therefore require compensation to assume additional risk.
3. Investor preferences are based on a portfolio's expected return and risk (as measured by variance or standard deviation).

Based on these assumptions, Markowitz introduced the notion of **efficient portfolios**, which dominate other portfolios that could be constructed from a given set of available securities. Efficient portfolios are those that offer the highest expected return for a given level of risk or offer the lowest risk for a given expected return. Investors can identify efficient portfolios

**risk averse**   to dislike risk and require compensation to assume additional risk

**efficient portfolios**   those portfolios that offer the highest expected return for a given level of risk or offer the lowest risk for a given expected return

---

[14]We can represent all these terms in a compact way using matrix algebra.

by specifying an expected portfolio return and minimizing the portfolio risk at this level of return, or by specifying a portfolio risk level they are willing to assume and maximizing the expected return given that level of risk.

The first step in the Markowitz analysis is to determine the expected return-risk combinations available to investors from a given set of securities by allowing the portfolio weights to vary, just as we did in Figure 8.10 when we considered only two securities. The entire curve, which is referred to as the **minimum variance frontier**, is illustrated in **Figure 8.11**.[15] Although our discussion has focused on plotting expected return against standard deviation, remember that the variance is just the standard deviation squared.

Notice that the shape is virtually identical to the frontier we constructed using only two securities in Figure 8.10. However, although the shape is similar, by using all available securities, we can generate a set of more efficient portfolios, in the sense that the portfolios will offer higher expected return for a given risk level or lower risk for a given expected return level.

The other difference between figures 8.10 and 8.11 is that we have included five portfolios marked A through E in Figure 8.11. All the portfolios that lie along the efficient frontier, including B, D, and E, can be attained by combining the underlying securities. They are referred to as the **attainable portfolios**. Portfolios A and C, conversely, which lie above and below the efficient frontier, are not attainable. Portfolio A is not attainable in the sense that there is no way the underlying securities can be combined in such a way as to achieve this combination of expected return and risk. It is simply impossible. Portfolio C is unattainable in a different sense: it can be attained only by deliberately wasting money—that is, by simply not investing some portion of wealth and leaving money to earn zero return. It means that the portfolio is not formed by efficient combinations of the underlying securities.

This leaves us with portfolios B, D, and E, which do lie on the minimum variance frontier. We can ignore portfolio D, because it is a dominated portfolio, even though it lies on the minimum variance frontier. Like portfolio C, which is inefficient (as well as dominated), portfolio D offers a lower expected rate of return for the same risk as another portfolio on the upper half of the minimum variance frontier. We can see this by drawing a vertical line through D. The point where that line intersects the top part of the minimum variance frontier indicates a portfolio with the same standard deviation of return but a higher expected rate of return. Portfolio E is a special portfolio: it lies on the efficient frontier and also has the minimum amount of portfolio risk available from any possible combination of available securities. It is referred to as the **minimum variance portfolio (MVP)**.

**minimum variance frontier** the curve produced when determining the expected return-risk combinations available to investors from a given set of securities by allowing the portfolio weights to vary

**attainable portfolios** portfolios that may be constructed by combining the underlying securities

**minimum variance portfolio (MVP)** a portfolio that lies on the efficient frontier and has the minimum amount of portfolio risk available from any possible combination of available securities

**FIGURE 8.11** The Minimum Variance Frontier

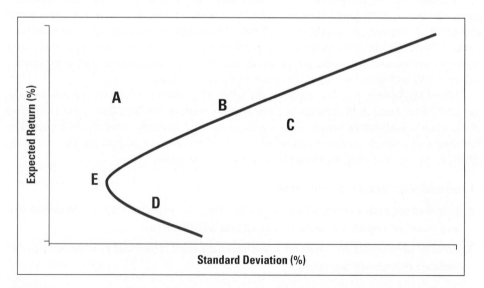

[15]Appendix 8A shows how to solve for all available portfolio weights in the two-security case, but this is impractical when a large number of securities are available. However, the problem can easily be solved using a quadratic programming model that chooses optimal "portfolio weights" in the available securities in order to minimize the risk of the portfolio for a given level of expected return. This optimization problem is subject to a wealth constraint (i.e., the sum of the weights in the individual securities must equal total wealth or 1) and is also constrained by the return-risk characteristics of the available set of securities.

The importance of the MVP is that portfolios lying below it, on the bottom segment of the minimum variance frontier, are dominated by portfolios on the upper segment. The segment of the minimum variance frontier above the global minimum variance portfolio, therefore, offers the best risk-expected return combinations available to investors from this particular set of securities. This segment includes the set of efficient portfolios that is commonly referred to as the **efficient frontier**. Rational, risk-averse investors will be interested in holding only those portfolios, like B, that offer the highest expected return for their given level of risk. (We will discuss risk aversion further in Chapter 9.) In this sense, these portfolios are not dominated by other attainable portfolios. In fact, the efficient frontier is the cornerstone of MPT.

**efficient frontier** the set of portfolios that offer the highest expected return for their given level of risk; the only portfolios that rational, risk-averse investors will want to hold

Finally, the particular portfolio chosen by an investor will depend on their risk preferences. A more aggressive (i.e., less risk averse) investor might choose portfolio B, while a more conservative (i.e., more risk averse) investor might prefer portfolio E (i.e., the MVP).

---

## Concept Review Questions

1. How do you form the minimum variance frontier in the two-security case?
2. What assumptions about investors underlie Markowitz's theories regarding efficient portfolios?
3. Why is the efficient frontier bowed?
4. What is an unattainable portfolio, and what is a dominated portfolio?

---

## 8.6 | Diversification

### LEARNING OBJECTIVE 8.6
Explain what diversification is and why it is important to investors.

## Domestic Diversification

We previously demonstrated that the expected portfolio return is always a weighted average of individual security returns, and as long as $\rho_{AB}$ is less than $+1$, portfolio risk is always less than a weighted average (i.e., $\sigma_p < w_A \sigma_A + w_B \sigma_B$) of the risk of the two (or more) securities. Therefore, there is a benefit to combining securities into portfolios. In other words, we can eliminate risk by investing our funds across several securities, or by "not putting all of our eggs in one basket." This principle is called **diversification**. We have already seen how Markowitz showed that efficient diversification leads investors to hold a portfolio along the efficient frontier, which is one of the cornerstones of MPT. However, we have also seen that calculating all those correlation coefficients and generating the efficient frontier is not easy. So an important question is how good is random or naïve diversification?

**diversification** the process of investing funds across several securities, which results in reduced risk

**Random diversification** or **naïve diversification** refers to the act of randomly diversifying without regard to relevant investment characteristics, such as company size, industry classification, and so on. An investor practising naïve diversification randomly selects a relatively large number of securities. **Figure 8.12** plots the actual monthly data for Canadian stocks over the 1985–97 period, based on the data reported in **Table 8.3**, to illustrate naïve diversification in practice. Portfolio risk for a randomly selected portfolio was reduced to approximately 4.5 percent per month over this period. As securities are added to the portfolio, the total risk associated with the portfolio declines rapidly. The first few stocks cause a large decrease in portfolio risk. Based on these data, 46 percent of portfolio standard deviation is eliminated as we go from one to 10 securities.

**random diversification** or **naïve diversification** the act of randomly buying securities without regard to relevant investment characteristics, such as company size, industry classification, and so on

**FIGURE 8.12** Diversification with Canadian Stocks (Average Portfolio Risk January 1985 to December 1997)

**Source:** From Cleary, S., and Copp, D., "Diversification with Canadian Stocks: How Much Is Enough?" Canadian Investment Review (Fall 1999), Figure 1. Copyright 1999. Reproduced with the permissions of Canadian Investment Review.

**TABLE 8.3**  Monthly Canadian Stock Portfolio Returns, January 1985 to December 1997

| Number of Stocks in Portfolio | Average Monthly Portfolio Return (%) | Standard Deviation of Average Monthly Portfolio Return (%) | Ratio of Portfolio Standard Deviation to Standard Deviation of a Single Stock | Percentage of Total Achievable Risk Reduction (%) |
|---|---|---|---|---|
| 1 | 1.51 | 13.47 | 1.00 | 0.00 |
| 2 | 1.51 | 10.99 | 0.82 | 27.50 |
| 3 | 1.52 | 9.91 | 0.74 | 39.56 |
| 4 | 1.53 | 9.30 | 0.69 | 46.37 |
| 5 | 1.52 | 8.67 | 0.64 | 53.31 |
| 6 | 1.52 | 8.30 | 0.62 | 57.50 |
| 7 | 1.51 | 7.95 | 0.59 | 61.35 |
| 8 | 1.52 | 7.71 | 0.57 | 64.02 |
| 9 | 1.52 | 7.52 | 0.56 | 66.17 |
| 10 | 1.51 | 7.33 | 0.54 | 68.30 |
| 12 | 1.51 | 7.03 | 0.52 | 71.58 |
| 14 | 1.51 | 6.80 | 0.50 | 74.19 |
| 16 | 1.52 | 6.63 | 0.49 | 76.04 |
| 18 | 1.52 | 6.51 | 0.48 | 77.41 |
| 20 | 1.52 | 6.39 | 0.47 | 78.65 |

*(continued)*

| TABLE 8.3 | Monthly Canadian Stock Portfolio Returns, January 1985 to December 1997 *(continued)* | | | |
|---|---|---|---|---|
| Number of Stocks in Portfolio | Average Monthly Portfolio Return (%) | Standard Deviation of Average Monthly Portfolio Return (%) | Ratio of Portfolio Standard Deviation to Standard Deviation of a Single Stock | Percentage of Total Achievable Risk Reduction (%) |
| 22 | 1.52 | 6.25 | 0.46 | 80.30 |
| 24 | 1.52 | 6.15 | 0.46 | 81.32 |
| 26 | 1.52 | 6.07 | 0.45 | 82.25 |
| 28 | 1.52 | 5.99 | 0.44 | 83.18 |
| 30 | 1.52 | 5.91 | 0.44 | 84.06 |
| 35 | 1.52 | 5.76 | 0.43 | 85.68 |
| 40 | 1.52 | 5.62 | 0.42 | 87.24 |
| 45 | 1.52 | 5.50 | 0.41 | 88.56 |
| 50 | 1.52 | 5.41 | 0.40 | 89.64 |
| 60 | 1.52 | 5.25 | 0.39 | 90.40 |
| 70 | 1.51 | 5.12 | 0.38 | 92.86 |
| 80 | 1.51 | 5.02 | 0.37 | 94.00 |
| 90 | 1.51 | 4.93 | 0.37 | 94.94 |
| 100 | 1.51 | 4.86 | 0.36 | 95.70 |
| 150 | 1.51 | 4.64 | 0.34 | 98.18 |
| 200 | 1.51 | 4.51 | 0.34 | 99.58 |
| 222 | 1.51 | 4.48 | 0.33 | 100.00 |

**Source:** From Cleary, S., and Copp, D., "Diversification with Canadian Stocks: How Much Is Enough?" *Canadian Investment Review* (Fall 1999), Table 1. Copyright 1999. Reproduced with the permission of Canadian Investment Review.

Figure 8.12 also demonstrates that the benefits of random diversification do not continue indefinitely. As more and more securities are added, the marginal risk reduction per security becomes extremely small, eventually producing an almost negligible effect on total portfolio risk. For example, going from 10 to 20 securities eliminates an additional 7 percent of the monthly portfolio standard deviation, but going from 20 to 30 securities eliminates only 3 percent of the monthly standard deviation. Thus, although a large number of securities are not required to achieve substantial diversification benefits, the monthly portfolio risk levels out as additional securities are added to the portfolio.

The part of the total risk that is eliminated by diversification is the company-specific **unique (non-systematic) risk** or **diversifiable risk**. The part that is *not* eliminated by diversification is the **market (systematic) risk** or **non-diversifiable risk**. This portion of the risk cannot be eliminated because all the securities in the portfolio will be directly influenced by overall movements in the general market or economy. Total risk is often divided into these two components, which are additive, as reflected in Equation 8.20.

**unique (non-systematic) risk** or **diversifiable risk** the company-specific part of total risk that is eliminated by diversification

**market (systematic) risk** or **non-diversifiable risk** the systematic part of total risk, directly influenced by overall movements in the general market or economy, that cannot be eliminated by diversification

$$\boxed{\text{Total risk} = \text{Market (systematic) risk} + \text{Unique (non-systematic) risk}} \qquad [8.20]$$

**FIGURE 8.13**  Total and
**Market Risk for Different-Size
Portfolios, Assuming Naïve
Diversification**

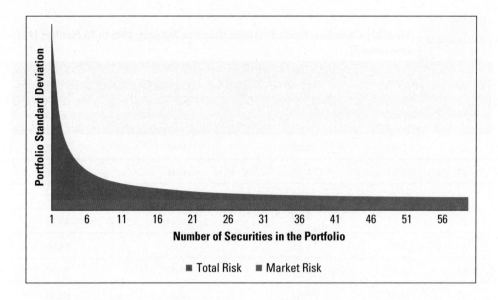

We show the total and market risk components in **Figure 8.13**.

The declining relationship between portfolio risk and the number of securities in a portfolio, illustrated in Figure 8.12 for Canadian stocks, is a well-known result that holds for diversification among stocks in all developed domestic stock markets around the world. Figure 8.12 highlights the benefits, in terms of risk reduction, of holding a well-diversified portfolio, when diversification is achieved by random security selection. Not surprisingly, diversification can be achieved more efficiently when we take a structured approach to forming portfolios, consciously selecting securities that can be expected to have lower correlations among their returns (i.e., choosing them from different industries).

A common and logical question to ask is "How many stocks should I hold to be well diversified?" While the number of stocks for adequate diversification is much debated, 20 to 30 stocks seems to be the most accepted range, representing a compromise between higher transaction and monitoring costs and additional benefits from more diversified holdings. As might be expected, there is no general agreement on the appropriate number of stocks to hold, with advocates existing on both sides of the fence.

## International Diversification

Our discussion above assumed random diversification in domestic securities only. However, it is reasonable to assume that if domestic diversification is good for reducing risk, international diversification must be better. This is logical, because we would expect the returns among stocks in different global markets to have lower correlation coefficients than those in the same market. **Figure 8.14** demonstrates the benefits of international diversification in reducing portfolio risk, based on evidence provided in a classic research article by Bruno Solnik. Throughout the entire range of portfolio sizes, the risk is reduced when international investing is compared with investing in only domestic stocks (U.S. stocks in this example), and the difference is dramatic—about one-third less. Several studies confirm similar risk-reduction benefits are available to Canadian investors who diversify internationally.

Although almost all experts agree that diversification in general, and international diversification in particular, is one of the most critical components of good portfolio management, evidence suggests the benefits of international diversification have been declining as global equity markets become more integrated, to the point where many have suggested it is not a worthwhile exercise. This has especially been the case in Canada, where our heavy exposure to resource stocks has served us well over the first decade of the millennium. Indeed, over the period from 2000 to 2010, the Canadian stock market yielded an average annual return of 6.6 percent, while global and U.S. stocks lost 1.6 and 2.3 percent respectively. However, there are still many valid reasons to diversify globally to some extent. Finance

**Source:** Solnik, Bruno, "Why Not Diversify Internationally Rather Than Domestically?" *Financial Analysts Journal* (July/August 1974). Copyright 1974, CFA Institute. Reproduced and republished from *Financial Analysts Journal* with permission from CFA Institute. All rights reserved.

in the News 8.1 discusses a few of these reasons amid the real concern that many average Canadians run the risk of outliving their assets. The first two reasons allude to the inadequate diversification provided by Canadian markets, which are dominated by resource stocks and financials, and are underweight in many other industries, such as health care and technology. The remaining reasons refer to the influence of currency value, and the fact that recent returns do not necessarily imply future returns. The weakening of the Canadian dollar relative to the U.S. dollar (US$1 = C$1.32, June 2019) further highlights the importance of international diversification.

## 8.1 Finance in the News   The Risk of Outliving Assets Is Real; and Defending against It Is No Small Task

"The real risk people need to manage when investing in their future is the risk of outliving their retirement savings"—Han Yik, Head of the Institutional Investors Industry, World Economic Forum. Our shift to goals-based benchmarking about two years ago has been a real eye-opener especially during our discussions with families regarding their specific savings objectives.

The most common concern that comes up during our interview process is whether there is going to be enough built-up savings to maintain a desired lifestyle into retirement. This could mean having the ability to buy a U.S. vacation property, finally getting to that renovation, or simply having the freedom to not have to worry about one's financial affairs, especially during unexpected events.

It is not surprising that making savings last is a top concern. According to a report released last week by the World Economic Forum, retirees in six major economies are expected to outlive their savings by eight to 20 years on average. Here in Canada, the report estimates that men will outlive their savings by 9.9 years and women by 12.7 years.

When it comes to addressing the problem, skipping that daily coffee purchase simply isn't going to cut it. Rather, people are going to have to take a much more proactive and serious approach to how their wealth is being accumulated and managed. This could mean adjusting savings rates and lifestyles, in addition to potentially onboarding risk sooner to account for increased longevity and future retirement needs. Unfortunately for those further along and about to enter retirement, what worked in the past is no longer an option. Baby boomers can't

deploy the same low-risk GIC-buying strategies as their parents did because, with interest rates setting record lows, they are insufficient to meet spending needs while preserving desired estate values. Making matters worse, few have defined benefit pension plans, so return shortfalls will have a direct impact on financial well-being.

As a result, in some cases adjustments will have to be made to spending rates in retirement and/or expected ultimate estate values.

The WEF report discusses undertaking what they call a decumulation review which means setting a realistic forward assumption of what one will spend in retirement.

While many have a rough idea of their financial picture most do not have it specifically mapped out in a formalized cash-flow forecast that factors in future incomes and expenses. This is a great first step that should be undertaken before making any changes to how one's portfolio is being managed. Once complete, a capital asset forecast can be done under different asset allocation scenarios between fixed income and equities using conservative return assumptions to show the impact on one's financial position over time.

Finally, once an allocation and a reasonable return target is set, the portfolio should be managed to mitigate risk as much as possible to achieve that goals-based return.

For example, the WEF report suggests the concurrent need to manage this risk through proper portfolio diversification, including moving beyond domestic bias and into international markets. We see this all the time with Canadian equities often dominating a portfolio, meaning that approximately 50 per cent of their equity position is exposed to financials and energy compared to only 25 per cent in global markets.

As I highlighted in a recent column, we would take this a step further by also recommending looking at the types of fixed income in a portfolio along with diversification by global market capitalization, REITs, low volatility and possibly some alternative strategies.

Overall, investing in one's financial future involves a bit of upfront work but having a formal plan and a systematic approach to managing risk will go a long way to securing the desired retirement.

## Lessons to Be Learned

During the fall of 2008, stock markets around the world fell dramatically, and they fell in tandem. In other words, the correlation among equity returns was extremely high, with most global stock market returns displaying correlations greater than 0.95 with the returns on the S&P 500 Composite Index. For example, the S&P/TSX Composite Index displayed a 0.97 coefficient with the S&P. This led many market observers to question the value of diversification. Consider the following quote from Louis Gagnon: "Diversification works on the way up when we don't need it and it fails miserably when we do."[16] What does this mean for investors? First of all, it suggests that diversification is no guarantee that you can never lose money, which is of course true—there are always risks associated with investing.

So what does diversification do for us? Consider the following two points. First, even though diversification within and across stock markets would not have prevented investors from experiencing large losses on their common equity holdings, they would have been much better off than if they had not been diversified. For example, investors would have suffered if their investments had been concentrated in financial companies. Many of those stock prices declined by as much as 90 percent, before some rebounded somewhat in the spring of 2009. Of course, if investors were holding only those stocks that didn't recover, they would have been hit really hard.

Second, being diversified across asset categories would have helped cushion the blow. Recall from Figure 8.7B, for example, the low correlation between stock returns and T-bill returns, which was $-0.0372$. Similarly, the correlation coefficient between stock returns and government bond returns over the 1938 to 2018 period was also close to zero (0.0106). So being invested in various asset categories would have softened the blow, due to the low correlations across the asset classes. For example, an investment in the S&P/TSX 60 ETF (exchange traded fund) would have lost 29.32 percent over the March 2008 to March 2009 period, while an equally weighted portfolio of the ETF and T-bills would have lost only 13.94 percent. On the other hand, the ending wealth for $1,000 invested in this equally weighted portfolio over the 1938 to 2018 period would have been $262,734, versus an ending wealth of $1,901,852 if invested entirely in stocks. That is obviously a big sacrifice in returns if investors were in it for the long term and could live with the additional risk (i.e., the standard deviation of the equally weighted portfolio was 10.14 percent versus 16.37 percent for the stock portfolio). On the other hand, if investors had a short-term investment horizon and/or a low risk tolerance for other reasons, the reduction in risk might have been well worth it— recall that, at the beginning of this chapter, we said there is a trade-off between risk and return!

## Concept Review Questions

1. What is naïve diversification?
2. What is the difference between diversifiable and non-diversifiable risk?
3. Why is it logical to believe that international diversification will provide benefits to investors?

---

[16]Ladurantaye, Steve, "World Markets Start Trading on Their Own Merits." *The Globe and Mail*, April 14, 2009.

# Two-Security Portfolio Frontiers

## LEARNING OBJECTIVE 8.7
Construct two-security portfolio risk-return frontiers.

Figures 8.4 and 8.9 show how the expected return and the standard deviation of a portfolio change as we change the portfolio's composition by shifting more of our investment toward security A, which is the riskier security. Rather than creating two graphs, we can combine them into one that implicitly shows all the portfolios. We do this by noting, from Equation 8.11, that rather than writing the expected return as the portfolio weight is varied, we instead write the portfolio weight as we change our expected return, as shown in Equation 8A.1.

$$w = \frac{ER_p - ER_B}{(ER_A - ER_B)} \qquad\qquad [8A.1]$$

Or, using the numbers in our example,

$$w = \frac{ER_p - 8\%}{2\%}$$

Think about this by supposing that an investor wants a portfolio with an expected rate of return of 8 percent. In this case, look at the equation above, substitute 8 percent for $ER_P$, and learn that a zero weight has to be placed in security A—that is, the 8-percent expected return can be met with 100 percent in B. If the expected return on the portfolio is set at 10 percent, then we get 2 percent in the numerator and denominator of Equation 8A.1, and the portfolio weight has to be 100 percent—that is, all the investment has to be placed in security A. Between these two expected returns, we get different portfolio weights as we vary how much is invested in each security.[17]

We can now use Equation 8A.1 to remove the portfolio weights in Equation 8.16 and express the standard deviation of the portfolio solely in terms of the expected returns, standard deviations, and the correlation coefficient, as is done in Equation 8A.2.

$$\sigma_p = \sqrt{\left(\frac{ER_p - ER_B}{ER_A - ER_B}\right)^2 (\sigma_A)^2 + \left(1 - \frac{ER_p - ER_B}{ER_A - ER_B}\right)^2 (\sigma_B)^2 + 2\left(\frac{ER_p - ER_B}{ER_A - ER_B}\right)\left(1 - \frac{ER_p - ER_B}{ER_A - ER_B}\right)(\rho_{AB})(\sigma_A)(\sigma_B)} \qquad [8A.2]$$

Although this is cumbersome, it indicates all the combinations of expected return and risk (standard deviation) created from these two securities.

With our example, we can substitute in and get the following:

$$\sigma_p = \sqrt{\left(\frac{ER_p - 8\%}{2\%}\right)^2 (22.69\%)^2 + \left(1 - \frac{10\% - ER_p}{2\%}\right)^2 (8.72\%)^2 + 2\left(\frac{ER_p - 8\%}{2\%}\right)\left(1 - \frac{10\% - ER_p}{2\%}\right)(\rho_{AB})(22.69\%)(8.72\%)}$$

This is a bit simpler, but you need to enter the numbers into Excel to work everything out. If you do this, you will get **Figure 8A.1** for our three special cases and anything in between.

As we saw before, if we start out with all investment in security B ($w = 0$), we get an 8-percent expected return and a standard deviation of 8.72 percent. If we move to a portfolio

---

[17]As we mentioned before, there is no conceptual reason why the weights can't be more than 100 percent, and we will relax this constraint later.

**FIGURE 8A.1** Two-Security Portfolios (Efficient Frontier)

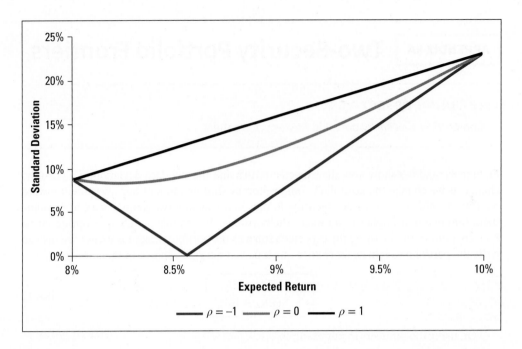

with 100 percent invested in A, we get a 10-percent expected return and a 22.69-percent standard deviation. In between, interesting things happen! Notice that the risk of the portfolio falls as we add the risky security A, unless the securities are perfectly correlated; this decline is much more dramatic if the securities are negatively correlated. Regardless, adding A to the portfolio increases the expected return and lowers the risk, which means the investor is better off. It also means that no one should hold security B in isolation. (Think about why an investor might want to hold A in isolation.) Eventually, the risk-reduction opportunity from holding A falls and the risk is minimized, after which the standard deviation of the portfolio's return starts to increase.

These diagrams show all the combinations of expected return and standard deviation that result from creating portfolios of the two securities. Now we can return to our example, in which the correlation coefficient was 0.379, and graph the efficient frontier with a non-special correlation coefficient. We can also flip the axes, because normally, in finance, we have the expected return on the vertical axis and the standard deviation or risk on the horizontal axis, as shown in **Figure 8A.2.**[18]

**FIGURE 8A.2** Two-Security Portfolios

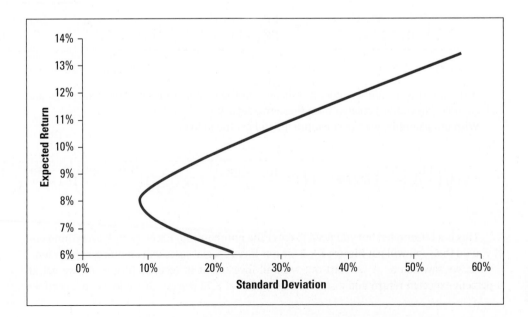

---

[18]Notice that we have also allowed the security weights to go below zero or above one in order to construct Figure 8A.2.

**APPENDIX 8B** # Value at Risk (VaR)

### LEARNING OBJECTIVE 8.8
Explain the risk-management technique called Value at Risk (VaR).

Value at risk (VaR) is arguably the financial industry's premier risk-management technique. It is a measure of potential loss (in money terms) that could be exceeded (minimum loss) at a given level of probability. Lower probability will equate to higher potential loss, all else being equal. For example a $1-million daily VaR at 5 percent means a 5-percent chance of losing at least $1 million in one day (or a 95-percent chance that one day's losses will be lower than $1 million).

There are three common ways to estimate VaR. The first is to use the analytical (variance-covariance) method. This approach assumes that portfolio returns are normally distributed. It requires an estimate of the expected return and standard deviation of returns on the portfolio. Using an expected return of zero is generally appropriate for estimating daily VaR, but not for longer-term measures of VaR.

For example, using this approach, we can use Equation 8B.1 to estimate the daily VaR as follows:

$$\boxed{\text{Daily VaR} = \text{Dollar value of position} \times \text{Portfolio return volatility}} \qquad [8B.1]$$

where portfolio return volatility is defined as the portfolio period standard deviation multiplied by the appropriate Z-score (from the normal distribution normalized Z-scores).

---

**EXAMPLE 8B.1** | Estimating Daily VaR

Estimate the 5-percent daily VaR of a $2-million position in the market, which has a 2-percent daily standard deviation in price changes.

**Solution**   Since we are looking for the 5-percent VaR, we use the Z-score of 1.65.

$$\text{Daily VaR} = \text{Dollar value of position} \times \text{Portfolio return volatility}$$
$$= \$2,000,000 \times (1.65 \times 0.02) = \$66,000$$

---

For a 5-percent VaR estimate, we would use a Z-score of 1.65 (rounded from 1.645), since 95 percent of the observations would lie above a Z-score of $-1.645$. This can be seen in **Figure 8B.1**. For a 99-percent VaR, we would use a Z-score of 2.33, since 99 percent of the observations would lie above a Z-score of $-2.33$.

The main advantage of the analytical method is its simplicity. The main disadvantage is its reliance on assumptions, particularly that of normal distribution of returns. In addition, it requires estimates of standard deviation of returns.

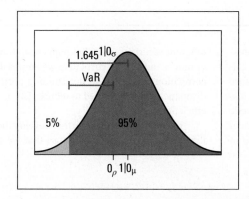

**FIGURE 8B.1** **Standardized Normal Distribution**

VaR can also be estimated using the historical method, which uses actual daily returns from some user-specified past period. If you have 1,000 observations, the 1-percent and 5-percent probabilities would be of a loss greater than the 10th- or 50th-worst out of the observations, respectively. As the name suggests, this approach reflects historical results, not the future, which is of course what concerns us. The main advantage is that it is nonparametric (i.e., we don't need to assume a certain probability distribution, such as the normal one). The main disadvantages are that the future could differ significantly from the past, and there is a somewhat limited number of past observations.

In order to overcome the problem of a limited number of observations associated with the historical method, the Monte Carlo simulation method synthesizes additional observations. For example, we might generate 10,000 real and synthetic observations. These observations are generated by using historical variance and covariance estimates and then employing a random number generator to synthesize observations. The objective is to replicate the distribution of observed outcomes with synthetic data.

The Monte Carlo method produces random outcomes to examine the effects of particular sets of risks, using a probability distribution for each variable of interest. We can use normal or non-normal distributions for modelling purposes. As a result, this method is often useful for determining important risk-management information about various sources of risk. For large portfolios, this approach may require extensive commitments of computer resources.

The advantages of VaR are that it quantifies potential loss in simple terms, is widely accepted by regulators, and is versatile. The limitations are that it can be difficult to estimate, and various estimation methods can lead to significant estimate differences. It can create a false sense of security for risk managers, and it may underestimate the severity of worst-case returns.

Based on the strengths and limitations of VaR, there is substantial debate about its usefulness. Consider the following comments from an article in the *GARP Risk Review*.[19] One of the co-authors, Aaron Brown, espouses the benefits of VaR, stating that "a risk manager has two jobs: make people take more risk the 99 percent of the time it is safe to do so, and survive the other 1 percent of the time. VaR is the border." The second co-author, David Einhorn, compares VaR to "an airbag that works all the time, except when you have a car accident." He further charges that VaR:

- led to excessive risk-taking and leverage at financial institutions
- focused on the manageable risks near the centre of the distribution and ignored the tails
- created an incentive to take "excessive but remote risks"
- was "potentially catastrophic when its use creates a false sense of security among senior executives and watchdogs"

---

[19] Einhorn, David, and Brown, Aaron, "Private Profits and Socialized Risk." *GARP Risk Review* (June/July 2008).

# Review

## Summary

In this chapter, we discuss the expected return and risk characteristics of risky securities. We show how the standard deviation is calculated, and how it is commonly used as a measure of risk because it represents the variability in a security's rate of return. We also discuss different definitions of rates of return, including the arithmetic and geometric rates of return, and explain why they differ. We then discuss how portfolios are formed by varying the weight invested in different securities and what happens to the portfolio's expected rate of return and risk. In particular, we emphasize the importance of the correlation coefficient in determining portfolio risk and show how diversification can be used to reduce risk, as well as how to create the efficient frontier.

In Chapter 9, we will further develop these ideas. At the moment they are mechanical, in the sense that we show how a given set of securities can be combined into efficient portfolios. This won Harry Markowitz the Nobel Prize, but it was left to one of his students, William Sharpe, to take these ideas and think through what it means for a capital market dominated by Markowitz-type investors, rationally forming efficient portfolios using the ideas in this chapter. This led to another seminal idea in finance and another Nobel Prize.

## Summary of Learning Objectives

### 8.1 Distinguish between ex post and ex ante returns and explain how they are estimated.

"Ex post" means "after the fact," so ex post returns are past or historical returns. "Ex ante" means "before the fact," so ex ante returns are expected returns. They are defined as the sum of dividends and capital gain (loss) divided by the beginning-of-period price.

### 8.2 Distinguish between arithmetic and geometric means.

The arithmetic mean is the most commonly used value in statistics. It is the sum of all returns divided by the total number of observations. The geometric mean is the average or compound growth rate over multiple time periods.

### 8.3 Explain how common risk measures are calculated and what they mean.

A common ex post risk measure is the ex post standard deviation, which is the standard deviation of the historical return. Ex ante standard deviation is scenario-based, which is given by Equation 8.8.

### 8.4 Describe what happens to risk and return when securities are combined in a portfolio.

Expected return will be the value weighted return of securities. Risk measure is the standard deviation, which decreases with the number of securities in the portfolio unless all securities are perfectly correlated.

### 8.5 Explain what is meant by the "efficient frontier."

Efficient frontier is the set of portfolios that offer the highest expected return for their given level of risk—the only portfolios that rational, risk-averse investors will want to hold.

### 8.6 Explain what diversification is and why it is important to investors.

Diversification is the process of investing funds across several securities, which results in reduced risk. It is important to investors because it reduces risk.

### 8.7 Construct two-security portfolio risk-return frontiers.

With two securities with known expected returns, standard deviation, and correlation coefficient, we can construct the risk-return frontier by changing the weight of the securities and calculating and plotting the expected return and standard deviation of the portfolio of these two securities.

### 8.8 Explain the risk-management technique called Value at Risk (VaR).

Value at risk (VaR) is a risk-management technique that estimates the potential minimum loss that could be exceeded at a given level of probability. There are several methods of estimating VaR. They include the analytical, historical, and Monte Carlo simulation methods.

## Key Terms

arithmetic average, p. 8-5
arithmetic mean, p. 8-5
attainable portfolios, p. 8-24
capital gain, p. 8-3
capital loss, p. 8-3
coefficient of variation (CV), p. 8-11
correlation coefficient, p. 8-15
covariance, p. 8-14
day trader, p. 8-4
diversifiable risk, p. 8-27
diversification, p. 8-25
efficient frontier, p. 8-25
efficient portfolios, p. 8-23

ex ante returns, p. 8-2
ex post returns, p. 8-2
expected returns, p. 8-7
geometric mean, p. 8-5
income yield, p. 8-2
mark to market, p. 8-5
market (systematic) risk, p. 8-27
minimum variance frontier, p. 8-24
minimum variance portfolio (MVP), p. 8-24
modern portfolio theory (MPT), p. 8-13
naïve diversification, p. 8-25
non-diversifiable risk, p. 8-27
paper losses, p. 8-4

portfolio, p. 8-13
random diversification, p. 8-25
range, p. 8-9
risk averse, p. 8-23
standard deviation, p. 8-6
total return, p. 8-3
unique (non-systematic) risk, p. 8-27
variance, p. 8-10

# Equations

| Equation | Description | Formula | Page |
|---|---|---|---|
| [8.1] | Income Yield | $\text{Income yield} = \dfrac{CF_1}{P_0}$ | p. 8-2 |
| [8.2] | Capital Gain (Loss) Yield | $\text{Capital gain (or loss) yield} = \dfrac{P_1 - P_0}{P_0}$ | p. 8-3 |
| [8.3] | Total Return | $\text{Total return} = \text{Income yield} + \text{Capital gain (or loss) yield}$ $= \dfrac{CF_1 + P_1 - P_0}{P_0}$ | p. 8-3 |
| [8.4] | Arithmetic Mean (AM) | $\text{Arithmetic mean (AM)} = \dfrac{\sum_{i=1}^{n} r_i}{n}$ | p. 8-5 |
| [8.5] | Geometric Mean (GM) | $\text{Geometric mean (GM)} = [(1 + r_1)(1 + r_2)(1 + r_3)\ldots(1 + r_n)]^{1/n} - 1$ | p. 8-5 |
| [8.6] | Expected Return (Individual) | $ER = \sum_{i=1}^{n}(r_i \times Prob_i)$ | p. 8-7 |
| [8.7] | Standard Deviation for Individual Returns Ex Post | $\text{Ex post } \sigma = \sqrt{\dfrac{\sum_{i=1}^{n}(r_i - \bar{r})^2}{n - 1}}$ | p. 8-10 |
| [8.8] | Standard Deviation for Individual Returns Ex Ante | $\text{Ex ante } \sigma = \sqrt{\sum_{i=1}^{n}(Prob_i)(r_i - ER)^2}$ | p. 8-11 |
| [8.9] | Coefficient of Variation (CV) | $\text{Coefficient of variation (CV)} = \dfrac{\text{Standard deviation of returns}}{\text{Arithmetic mean return}}$ | p. 8-11 |
| [8.10] | Expected Portfolio Return | $ER_p = \sum_{i=1}^{n}(w_i \times ER_i)$ | p. 8-13 |
| [8.11] | Expected Return on a Two-Security Portfolio | $ER_p = ER_B + w(ER_A - ER_B)$ | p. 8-13 |
| [8.12] | Standard Deviation of a Two-Security Portfolio (Using Covariance) | $\sigma_p = \sqrt{(w_A)^2(\sigma_A)^2 + (w_B)^2(\sigma_B)^2 + 2(w_A)(w_B)(COV_{AB})}$ | p. 8-14 |
| [8.13] | Covariance of Returns | $COV_{AB} = \sum_{i=1}^{n} Prob_i(r_{A,i} - \bar{r}_A)(r_{B,i} - \bar{r}_B)$ | p. 8-14 |
| [8.14] | Correlation Coefficient of Returns | $\rho_{AB} = \dfrac{COV_{AB}}{\sigma_A \sigma_B}$ | p. 8-16 |
| [8.15] | Covariance of Returns (Using Correlation Coefficient) | $COV_{AB} = \rho_{AB}\sigma_A\sigma_B$ | p. 8-16 |
| [8.16] | Standard Deviation of a Two-Security Portfolio (Using Correlation Coefficient) | $\sigma_p = \sqrt{(w_A)^2(\sigma_A)^2 + (w_B)^2(\sigma_B)^2 + 2(w_A)(w_B)(\rho_{AB})(\sigma_A)(\sigma_B)}$ | p. 8-16 |

*(continued)*

| Equation | Description | Formula | Page |
|---|---|---|---|
| **[8.17]** | Standard Deviation of a Two-Security Portfolio (where Correlation Coefficient $= -1$) | $\sigma_p = w\sigma_A - (1-w)\sigma_B$ | p. 8-21 |
| **[8.18]** | Portfolio Weights to Obtain Portfolio Standard Deviation $= 0$ (where Correlation Coefficient $= -1$) | $w = \dfrac{\sigma_B}{\sigma_A + \sigma_B}$ | p. 8-21 |
| **[8.19]** | Standard Deviation of a Three-Security Portfolio | $\sigma_p = \sqrt{\begin{array}{l}(w_A)^2(\sigma_A)^2 + (w_B)^2(\sigma_B)^2 + (w_C)^2(\sigma_C)^2 + 2(w_A)(w_B)(\rho_{AB})(\sigma_A)(\sigma_B) \\ + 2(w_A)(w_C)(\rho_{AC})(\sigma_A)(\sigma_C) + 2(w_B)(w_C)(\rho_{BC})(\sigma_B)(\sigma_C)\end{array}}$ | p. 8-23 |
| **[8.20]** | Total Risk Decomposition | Total risk = Market (systematic) risk + Unique (non-systematic) risk | p. 8-27 |
| **[8A.1]** | Portfolio Weight (in Terms of ERs) | $w = \dfrac{ER_p - ER_B}{(ER_A - ER_B)}$ | p. 8-31 |
| **[8A.2]** | Standard Deviation of a Two-Security Portfolio (in Terms of ERs) $\sigma_p = \sqrt{\left(\dfrac{ER_p - ER_B}{ER_A - ER_B}\right)^2(\sigma_A)^2 + \left(1 - \dfrac{ER_p - ER_B}{ER_A - ER_B}\right)^2(\sigma_B)^2 + 2\left(\dfrac{ER_p - ER_B}{ER_A - ER_B}\right)\left(1 - \dfrac{ER_p - ER_B}{ER_A - ER_B}\right)(\rho_{AB})(\sigma_A)(\sigma_B)}$ | | | p. 8-31 |
| **[8B.1]** | Value at Risk (Daily) | Daily VaR = Dollar value of position $\times$ Portfolio return volatility | p. 8-33 |

# Questions and Practice Problems

## Multiple Choice Questions

**1. (LO 8.1)** Calculate the capital gain return for a stock that was purchased at $32 one year ago and is now worth $34. It paid four quarterly dividends of $1.50 per share each throughout the year.

    **a.** 9.75 percent

    **b.** 6.25 percent

    **c.** 13.50 percent

    **d.** 11.00 percent

**2. (LO 8.1)** In Question 1, what is the total return of the security?

    **a.** 13 percent

    **b.** 20 percent

    **c.** 16 percent

    **d.** 25 percent

**3. (LO 8.2)** Which of the following is *false*?

    **a.** The income yield of a security that has a $3 cash flow during a period, with a beginning price of $15, is 20 percent.

    **b.** The arithmetic mean is always less than the geometric mean of a series of returns.

    **c.** The geometric mean of 50 percent and −50 percent is −13.4 percent.

    **d.** The greater the dispersion of a distribution, the greater the spread between the geometric mean and the arithmetic mean.

**4. (LO 8.2)** The geometric average annual return for a small market capitalization portfolio is 5 percent per year for the first 5 years and 12 percent per year for the next 10 years. The geometric average annual return for the entire 15-year period is:

    **a.** 9.11 percent

    **b.** 9.23 percent

    **c.** 9.95 percent

    **d.** 9.62 percent

**5. (LO 8.2)** Calculate the expected return on a stock that has a 25-percent probability of a 30-percent return, a 40-percent probability of a 40-percent return, and a 35-percent probability of a 15-percent return.

    **a.** 28.75 percent

    **b.** 33.50 percent

    **c.** 30.25 percent

    **d.** 24.00 percent

**6. (LO 8.3)** In Question 5, what is the standard deviation?

    **a.** 11.33 percent

    **b.** 9.87 percent

    **c.** 13.67 percent

    **d.** 10.83 percent

**7. (LO 8.3)** Which of the following is *false?*

  **a.** The expected return of a portfolio is always the weighted average of the expected return of each asset in the portfolio.

  **b.** Covariance measures the co-movement between the returns of individual securities.

  **c.** The standard deviation of a portfolio is always the weighted average of the standard deviations of individual assets in the portfolio.

  **d.** Standard deviation is easier to interpret than variance as a measure of risk.

**8. (LO 8.4)** The correlation coefficient

  **a.** equals covariance times the individual standard deviations.

  **b.** measures how security returns move in relation to one another.

  **c.** may be greater than +1.

  **d.** shows a stronger relationship between the returns of two securities when its absolute value is closer to 0.

**9. (LO 8.4)** Which of the following is *false?*

  **a.** The standard deviation of a portfolio that contains two individual securities is the weighted average of individual standard deviations only when the correlation coefficient is equal to +1.

  **b.** It is impossible to eliminate all the risk for a two-security portfolio.

  **c.** There are $n(n-1)/2$ co-movement terms and $n$ variance terms for an $n$-security portfolio.

  **d.** The more securities added, the lower the marginal risk reduction per security added.

**10. (LO 8.5)** According to the diagram below, which statement is *false?*

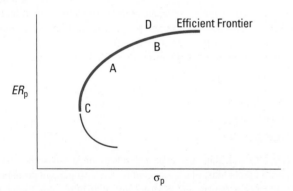

  **a.** Portfolio C is the minimum variance portfolio (MVP).

  **b.** Portfolios on the upper segment above C dominate those on the bottom segment below C.

  **c.** Portfolios A, B, and D are attainable, but C is not.

  **d.** A more risk-averse investor will prefer portfolios on the left side of the efficient frontier.

**11. (LO 8.6)** Which of the following correlation coefficients will provide the greatest diversification benefits for a given portfolio?

  **a.** 0

  **b.** 0.5

  **c.** 1

  **d.** −0.9

## Practice Problems

### Basic

**12. (LO 8.2)** Explain when to use the arithmetic mean and when to use the geometric mean to describe a return series.

**13. (LO 8.5)** State three of the most important assumptions underlying Markowitz's notion of efficient portfolios.

**14. (LO 8.2)** FinCorp Inc. conducted an extensive analysis of the economy and concluded that the probability of a recession next year is 30 percent, the probability of a boom is 45 percent, and the probability of a stable economy is 25 percent. Your boss has estimated that the price of PakCom Ltd. will be $60 if there is a recession, $110 if there is a boom, and $85 if the economy is stable. Currently, PakCom is trading for $83. Calculate the ex ante expected return on PakCom.

**15. (LO 8.1)** On Monday you invested $182 in Dettall Ltd. Dettall has earned daily returns of −8 percent, 18 percent, −30 percent, 6 percent, 7 percent, and −5 percent. If you determine that the appropriate measure is the geometric mean, what is the value of your investment at the end of the six days?

**16. (LO 8.4)** To achieve a zero standard deviation for a portfolio, calculate the weights of stock A and stock B, assuming the correlation coefficient is −1.

| State of the Economy | Probability of Occurrence | Expected Return on Stock A in This State | Expected Return on Stock B in This State |
|---|---|---|---|
| High growth | 25% | 40% | 55% |
| Moderate growth | 20% | 20% | 25% |
| Recession | 55% | −10% | −20% |

### Intermediate

**17. (LO 8.1)** At the beginning of the year you bought 300 shares of Lycel Ltd. at $84 each. During the year you received dividends of $780. At the end of the year the stock is trading for $87 and you decide to sell all your shares. Calculate your capital gain, total dollar return, and percentage return.

**18. (LO 8.1)** At the beginning of last year you invested $24,000 in 1,500 shares of Goran Products Inc. During the year you received $3,750 as a dividend. At the end of the year you sold the shares for $15 each. Calculate your total dollar return, capital gain, percentage return, and dividend yield.

**19. (LO 8.2, 8.3)** You have observed the following returns: 18 percent, −15 percent, 8 percent, 6 percent, and −12 percent.

  **a.** Calculate the geometric mean return.

  **b.** Calculate the arithmetic mean return.

  **c.** Calculate the variance and standard deviation of returns.

**20. (LO 8.2, 8.3, 8.4)** You observed the following daily returns for two companies, ABC and DEF.

| | Daily returns | |
|---|---|---|
| | **ABC** | **DEF** |
| Monday | 5% | −4% |
| Tuesday | −4% | 18% |
| Wednesday | 15% | −6% |
| Thursday | −3% | 12% |
| Friday | 6% | 5% |

**a.** Calculate the following for each stock:

   **i.** Five-day cumulative return

   **ii.** Geometric mean daily return

   **iii.** Arithmetic mean daily return

   **iv.** Standard deviation of daily returns

   **v.** Coefficient of variation

**b.** Calculate the covariance and correlation between the two stocks.

**21. (LO 8.4)** FinCorp Inc. is exploring different portfolio allocations between two stocks. Complete the following table.

| | Case 1 | Case 2 | Case 3 | Case 4 | Case 5 |
|---|---|---|---|---|---|
| $ invested in stock 1 | $500 | | | $200 | |
| $ invested in stock 2 | $500 | | $5,000 | | |
| Total $ invested | | $2,000 | $5,000 | | $1,000 |
| Weight in stock 1 | | 20% | | 40% | 15% |
| Weight in stock 2 | | | | | |
| Expected return of stock 1 | 8% | 3% | | 5% | 2% |
| Expected return of stock 2 | 3% | | | | 10% |
| Expected return of portfolio | | 8% | 6% | 7% | |

**22. (LO 8.4)** Your portfolio consists of two securities: Transcomm and MidCap. The expected return for Transcomm is 15 percent, while for MidCap it is 5 percent. The standard deviation is 6 percent for Transcomm and 20 percent for MidCap. If 55 percent of the portfolio is invested in Transcomm, calculate the portfolio standard deviation if

**a.** the correlation between the stocks is 0.8.

**b.** the correlation between the stocks is −0.8.

**23. (LO 8.4)** FinCorp Inc. is exploring the risk of different portfolio allocations between two stocks. Complete the following table.

| | Case 1 | Case 2 |
|---|---|---|
| Weight in stock 1 | | 15% |
| Weight in stock 2 | 25% | |
| Standard deviation of stock 1 | 15% | 2% |
| Standard deviation of stock 2 | 3% | 10% |
| Covariance between stocks 1 and 2 | | |
| Correlation between stocks 1 and 2 | −0.2 | 0.4 |
| Portfolio variance | | |
| Portfolio standard deviation | | |

**24. (LO 8.4)** You have the following return data on six stocks:

| Day | XYZ | ABC | DEF | GHI | JKL | MNO |
|---|---|---|---|---|---|---|
| Monday | 1% | −18% | 3% | 6% | 7% | 3% |
| Tuesday | 2% | −15% | 8% | 3% | 5% | −4% |
| Wednesday | 3% | −12% | 13% | 1% | 3% | 8% |
| Thursday | 4% | −9% | 18% | 3% | 2% | −2% |
| Friday | 5% | −6% | 22% | −5% | 0% | 0% |

**a.** Graph the returns of each stock (ABC, DEF, GHI, JKL, and MNO) against the returns of XYZ.

**b.** Based on the five graphs, which stocks are positively correlated with XYZ?

**c.** Based on the five graphs, which stocks are negatively correlated with XYZ?

**d.** Based on the five graphs, which stocks are uncorrelated with XYZ?

**e.** Calculate the correlation between the five stocks and XYZ to check your results from parts b to d.

**25. (LO 8.2)** Calculate the annual arithmetic mean and geometric mean return on the following security, and state which method is more appropriate for the situation: purchase price = $30; first-year dividend = $5; price after one year = $35; second-year dividend = $5; selling price after two years = $28.

**26. (LO 8.3)** Calculate the ex post standard deviation of returns for the following: 50 percent, 30 percent, 20 percent, 35 percent, 55 percent.

**27. (LO 8.4)** An investor owns a portfolio of $60,000 that contains $15,000 in stock A, with an expected return of 12 percent; $20,000 in bonds, with an expected return of 8 percent; and the rest in stock B, with an expected return of 20 percent. Calculate the expected return of the portfolio.

**28. (LO 8.2, 8.3)** On January 1, FinCorp Inc. published the following forecasts for the economy:

| State of the Economy | Probability | Forecasted Quarterly Returns |
|---|---|---|
| Poor | 20% | −3% |
| Average | 50% | 5% |
| Boom | 30% | 8% |

During the year you observed quarterly returns of 2 percent, −5 percent, 3 percent, and 8 percent.

**a.** Calculate the ex ante expected quarterly return.

**b.** Calculate the ex ante standard deviation of quarterly returns.

**c.** Calculate the ex post average quarterly return.

**d.** Calculate the ex post standard deviation of quarterly returns.

**e.** Explain the difference between the ex ante and ex post returns.

**29. (LO 8.2)** On January 1, FinCorp Inc. completed its analysis of the prospects for the Geriatric Toy Store and concluded that there was a 25-percent chance the stock price would be $150 in one year and a 75-percent chance the stock price would be $200. Six months later, FinCorp Inc. revised its estimated probabilities to a 40-percent chance of a stock price of $150 and a 60-percent chance of $200. If the market agrees with FinCorp Inc.'s revised probabilities, what is the expected change in stock price from January 1 to July 1? Assume the discount rate is zero.

**30. (LO 8.2)** As an analyst for FinCorp Inc., you are responsible for many firms, including ADFC. Currently you have a "hold" recommendation on ADFC.[20] The current price of ADFC is $140. You have conducted an extensive analysis of the industry and you feel that the probability the firm will capture a substantial share of the new market is 35 percent. If the firm is able to capture the new market, you are expecting earnings to grow at a rate of 45 percent per year for the next five years. In that case, the stock price would rise to $220 due to the unusually high growth rate of future earnings. However, you feel there is a 40-percent probability that the firm will face serious

---

[20] Basically, you are indicating that you believe the stock is fairly priced—it isn't a bargain, so people who don't currently own it shouldn't buy, and it isn't overpriced, so people who own it shouldn't sell.

difficulties in the near future, in which case the stock price will fall to $100, and the earnings growth rate will drop to 3 percent. There is a 25-percent chance that nothing will change for the firm and its earnings growth rate will remain at 12 percent. Should you change your recommendation?

**31. (LO 8.2)** FinCorp Inc. has been using the services of San Bernadino Brokerage Company (SBBC) for the past six months. SBBC has informed FinCorp Inc. that the geometric mean monthly return was 6 percent and that over the past six months FinCorp Inc. earned 16 percent, 19 percent, −23 percent, 14 percent, −8 percent, and an unknown amount in the last month. Determine the missing return.

**32. (LO 8.2)** Savita wants to find a new investment for her portfolio. She is looking for a safe investment that provides stable returns. She is considering the following investment options:

- Stock: XYZ Corp., a mature company with strong financial and operational performance, with an expected rate of return of 7.25 percent and a standard deviation of 16.8 percent.

- Bond: An investment-grade bond with an expected rate of return of 8.74 percent and a standard deviation of 6.29 percent.

- ETF: An ETF that tracks the performance of the S&P 500 index, with an expected rate of return of 10.11 percent and a standard deviation of 14.65 percent.

To find the most suitable investment, Savita decides to calculate the coefficient of variation for each option. Which one of the investments should Savita choose?

**33. (LO 8.4)** You wish to combine two stocks, Encor and Maestro, into a portfolio with an expected return of 16 percent. The expected return of Encor is 2 percent with a standard deviation of 1 percent. The expected return of Maestro is 25 percent with a standard deviation of 10 percent. The correlation between the two stocks is 0.4.

    **a.** What is the composition (weights) of the portfolio?

    **b.** What is the portfolio standard deviation?

**34. (LO 8.4)** You wish to combine two stocks, Peledon and Mexcor, into a portfolio with a standard deviation of 6 percent. The expected return of Peledon is 2 percent with a standard deviation of 1 percent. The expected return of Mexcor is 25 percent with a standard deviation of 10 percent. The correlation between the two stocks is 0.4.

    **a.** What is the composition (weights) of the portfolio?

    **b.** What is the expected return on the portfolio?

**35. (LO 8.4)** Calculate the covariance and correlation coefficient between the two securities of a portfolio that has 60 percent in stock X (with an expected return of 40 percent and a standard deviation of 12 percent) and 40 percent in stock Y (with an expected return of 30 percent and a standard deviation of 15 percent). The portfolio standard deviation is 6 percent.

**36. (LO 8.4)** Using the following information, calculate the expected return and the standard deviation of ABC.

| State of the Economy | Probability | ABC Stock Return (%) |
|---|---|---|
| Depression | 0.15 | −5 |
| Recession | 0.2 | 1 |
| Normal | 0.4 | 6 |
| Boom | 0.25 | 18 |

**37. (LO 8.4)** Five years ago, your dad bought 250 shares of ABC for $6 each and 300 shares of DEF for $7.50 each. He has now given you all

his shares, when both stocks are trading at $8. What are the weights of the two stocks in your portfolio?

**38. (LO 8.4)** The expected return of ABC is 16 percent, and the expected return of DEF is 27 percent. Their standard deviations are 10 percent and 23 percent, respectively. If a portfolio is composed of 40 percent ABC and the remainder DEF, calculate the expected return and the standard deviation of the portfolio, given a correlation coefficient between ABC and DEF of 0.45. Calculate the standard deviation if the correlation coefficient is −0.45.

## Challenging

**39. (LO 8.1)** Data on the daily performance of Carraway Corporation have been partially completed in the following table. Fill in the missing data.

**Carraway Corporation Performance**

| | Opening Price | Dividend | Closing[†] Price | Income Yield | Capital Gain | Total Daily Return |
|---|---|---|---|---|---|---|
| Monday | $100 | $7 | $115 | | | |
| Tuesday | $115 | $2 | | | 7% | |
| Wednesday | | $8 | | | | 10% |
| Thursday | | | | 4% | 3% | |
| Friday | | $0 | | | | 15% |

†The closing price on one day is assumed to be the opening price for the next day.

**40. (LO 8.4)** FinCorp Inc. is interested in the tradeoff between investing in two stocks, ABC and DEF. The expected return on ABC is 6 percent and on DEF is 18 percent.

    **a.** Graph the relationship between the expected return on the portfolio and the weight in DEF.

| Weight in DEF | Portfolio Return |
|---|---|
| 0% | 6% |
| 1% | 6.12% |
| 2% | 6.24% |
| 3% | 6.36% |
| — | — |
| — | — |
| — | — |
| 99% | 17.88% |
| 100% | 18% |

    **b.** What is the tradeoff between investing in ABC and DEF (i.e., if we increase the weight in DEF by 1 percent, what is the change in the expected return on the portfolio)?

    **c.** Your boss has just looked at your results and disagrees. He says the tradeoff between DEF and ABC is negative and, therefore, your results are wrong. Explain to your boss how you are both correct.

**41. (LO 8.4)** Calculate the correlation coefficient ($\rho_{AB}$) for the following situation:

| State of the Economy | Probability of Occurrence | Expected Return on Stock A in This State | Expected Return on Stock B in This State |
|---|---|---|---|
| High growth | 25% | 40% | 55% |
| Moderate growth | 20% | 20% | 25% |
| Recession | 55% | −10% | −20% |

**42. (LO 8.4)** An investor purchased 600 shares of stock A at $23 per share and 1,000 shares of stock B at $34 per share one year ago. Stock

A and stock B paid quarterly dividends of $1 per share and $1.50 per share, respectively, during the year. One year later, the investor sold both stocks at $32 per share. Calculate the total return of stock A and stock B and the total return of the portfolio.

**43. (LO 8.4)** In practice problem 42, the correlation coefficient $\rho_{AB}$ is 0.4 and the standard deviations of stock A and stock B are 28 percent and 15 percent, respectively. Calculate the standard deviation of the portfolio.

**44. (LO 8.4)** FinCorp Inc. is exploring the risk of different portfolio allocations between two stocks. Complete the following table.

|  | Case 1 | Case 2 |
|---|---|---|
| Weight in stock 1 | 35% | 40% |
| Weight in stock 2 |  |  |
| Standard deviation of stock 1 | 3% |  |
| Standard deviation of stock 2 | 25% | 20% |
| Covariance between stocks 1 and 2 |  | 0.022 |
| Correlation between stocks 1 and 2 |  |  |
| Portfolio variance | 0.027 |  |
| Portfolio standard deviation |  | 26% |

**45. (LO 8.4)** You are interested in using short selling to increase the possible returns from your portfolio.[21] You have short sold $200 of ABC and invested $1,200 in DEF. The following data are available on ABC and DEF:

|  | ABC | DEF |
|---|---|---|
| Expected return | 3% | 15% |
| Standard deviation | 7% | 35% |

The correlation between ABC and DEF is 0.4. Calculate the expected return and standard deviation of the portfolio. (Hint: The total invested is $1,000, and while individual weights can be greater than one or less than zero, the sum of the weights must still be one.)

**46. (LO 8.4)** The expected return of ABC is 15 percent, and the expected return of DEF is 23 percent. Their standard deviations are 10 percent and 23 percent, respectively, and the correlation coefficient between them is zero.

a. What is the expected return and standard deviation of a portfolio composed of 25 percent ABC and 75 percent DEF?

b. What is the expected return and standard deviation of a portfolio composed of 75 percent ABC and 25 percent DEF?

c. Would a risk-averse investor hold a portfolio made up of 100 percent of ABC?

**47. (LO 8.4)** Using the following information, calculate the expected return and standard deviation of a portfolio with 50 percent in ABC and 50 percent in DEF. Then calculate the expected return and standard deviation of a portfolio where you invest 40 percent in ABC, 40 percent in DEF, and the rest in T-bills with a return of 3.5 percent.

| State of the Economy | Probability | ABC Stock Return (%) | DEF Stock Return (%) |
|---|---|---|---|
| Depression | 0.1 | −5 | −7 |
| Recession | 0.2 | −2 | 2 |
| Normal | 0.4 | 5 | 6 |
| Boom | 0.3 | 10 | 15 |

**48. (LO 8.4)** You are assigned to manage the wealth of the firm's clients who insist on only holding stocks ABC and DEF in a portfolio together. Assuming you are prohibited from short selling (negative portfolio weights) and 100 percent of their wealth must always be invested, construct a portfolio for your clients with an expected rate of return of 14 percent. Stocks ABC and DEF have the following characteristics:

- Expected return on stock ABC = 15 percent
- Standard deviation on stock ABC = 18 percent
- Correlation (ABC, DEF) = −0.22
- Expected return on stock DEF = 11 percent
- Standard deviation on stock DEF = 15 percent

a. What percentage of the portfolio must be invested in stock ABC to achieve this goal by construction?

b. Calculate the standard deviation of the portfolio constructed in part a.

**49. (LO 8.5)** You are interested in two stocks: Alcon and Beldon. Both stocks have an expected return of 8 percent. The standard deviation of Alcon is 3 percent, and the standard deviation of Beldon is 5 percent. You want the weights to be greater than or equal to zero. You want to minimize the standard deviation of the portfolio. What should the portfolio composition be if

a. the correlation between the two stocks is −0.8?

b. the correlation between the two stocks is 0.8?

**50. (LO 8.5)** You are interested in two stocks: Alcon and Beldon. Both stocks have a standard deviation of 8 percent. The expected return of Alcon is 10 percent, and the expected return of Beldon is 20 percent. You want the weights to be greater than or equal to zero. You want to maximize the expected return of the portfolio. What should the portfolio composition be if

a. the correlation is 0.0?

b. the correlation is 1?

**51. (LO 8.5)** FinCorp Inc. wishes to examine the effect of correlation on the efficient frontier that can be created by investing in ABC and FGI. The expected return of ABC is 6 percent, with a standard deviation of 10 percent. The expected return of FGI is 10 percent, with a standard deviation of 25 percent. Graph the efficient frontier for

a. a correlation of 0.0.

b. a correlation of −0.5.

c. a correlation of 0.5.

**52. (LO 8.5)** You have observed the following monthly returns for ABC and DEF.

| Monthly Returns | | |
|---|---|---|
|  | ABC | DEF |
| January | 6% | 1% |
| February | −3% | 3% |
| March | −2% | 5% |
| April | −1% | 7% |
| May | 0% | 2% |
| June | 3% | 1% |
| July | 4% | −3% |
| August | 8% | −2% |
| September | 5% | −4% |
| October | 3% | −2% |
| November | 4% | 1% |
| December | 5% | 2% |

[21] When you short sell, you borrow stock from a broker and sell it. At a later date, you will have to buy the same number of shares back and return them to the broker.

a. Graph the relationship between the weight in ABC and the portfolio returns (restrict all weights to be greater than or equal to zero).

b. Graph the relationship between the weight in ABC and the portfolio standard deviation (use the same weights as in part a).

c. Using the data you have created in parts a and b, graph the relationship between the risk and return for the portfolio (put return on the y-axis).

d. Which portfolio weights do you prefer and why?

53. **(LO 8.5)** FinCorp Inc. wants to examine a "real" efficient frontier involving BlackBerry (BB.TO) and the Royal Bank (RY.TO).

a. Using monthly data for these two companies from January 2018 to December 2018, graph the relationship between risk and return.

b. Explain the difference between the frontier you developed in part a and the efficient frontier.

c. Where do you expect the S&P/TSX Composite Index to plot relative to the frontier? Explain.

d. Download the S&P/TSX Composite Index data for the same period (ticker: ^GSPTSE) and plot the S&P/TSX on your graph.

e. Based on your graph, is the S&P/TSX an efficient portfolio? Explain.

f. What do you expect will happen to the frontier if you increase the number of stocks? Explain your reasoning.

# The Capital Asset Pricing Model (CAPM)

This chapter continues the discussion of the relationship between risk and return initiated in Chapter 8. We expand upon this discussion and use it to develop asset pricing models, including the capital asset pricing model, which formalizes the risk-return relationship.

## 9.1 The New Efficient Frontier

### The Efficient Frontier with Risk-Free Borrowing and Lending

In Chapter 8, we introduced the efficient frontier, which is depicted in **Figure 9.1**. Recall that the portfolios of risky securities that lie along the efficient frontier—that is, on the curve above the minimum variance portfolio (MVP)—are efficient and dominate all other possible portfolios of risky securities. This means that for a given level of risk, as defined by the standard deviation of their return, these portfolios offer the highest expected rate of return (ER). As we showed in Chapter 8, the derivation of the efficient frontier is a mechanical exercise.

FIGURE 9.1 Efficient Portfolios

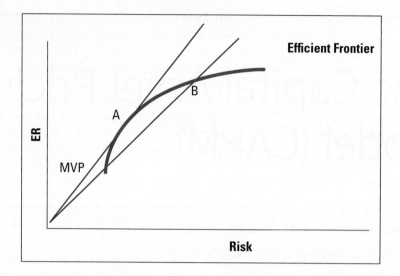

In the two-security case in Appendix 8A, we showed how to generate the efficient frontier from the expected return and standard deviation for each security and the correlation coefficient between their returns. The procedure is slightly cumbersome, but we can calculate the expected return on the portfolio, estimate its standard deviation, and graph the efficient frontier, which is what we did for Figure 8A.2. As the number of securities increases, the complexity of this mechanical exercise increases as well, but the general principle doesn't become more complex, because it is still mechanical. What we didn't fully explain in Chapter 8 are the reasons for graphing the efficient frontier.

In considering how investors make decisions between different securities, we assume that investors are "risk averse": that is, they will not willingly undertake fair gambles. Consider a game in which a coin is tossed. If it comes up heads, someone pays the player $100, but if it comes up tails, the player pays $100. The player will likely wait and see the coin tossed many times to make sure that the game is fair and that the odds really are 50-50. In this case, it is called a "fair gamble" because the expected payoff is 0—that is, the expected payoff $= 0 = 0.50 \times$ (+$100) + 0.50 × (−$100). If someone turns down a fair gamble, they are defined as risk averse. A risk-averse person prefers the risk-free situation to gambling on a risky situation where there is an equal probability of winning or losing the same amount of money.

**risk premium**  the expected payoff that induces a risk-averse person to enter into a risky situation

The corollary to turning down a fair gamble is that the risk-averse person needs a **risk premium** to be induced to enter into a risky situation. For example, someone might be willing to take part in the game if the heads payoff were $150 instead of $100. In this case, the expected payoff increases to $25, and it is no longer a fair gamble because there is a risk premium of $25. Another person might require that the heads payoff increase to $200 before undertaking the gamble, so the risk premium increases to $50. The second individual is more risk averse and requires a larger expected payoff or risk premium to get into the risky situation. Generally, investor behaviour is consistent with risk aversion and the existence of risk premiums to induce individuals to bear risk. We can represent this risk aversion in terms of the required risk premium per unit of risk, with higher risk premiums indicating greater risk aversion.

We can also reverse the situation by putting the individual in a risky situation and asking how much they are willing to pay to get out of the risky situation. Suppose, for example, someone is faced with a fair gamble; how much would they pay to get out of it? A very risk-averse individual would pay a large amount, say $25, to get out of a fair gamble with equally likely payoffs of +/−$100. In this case, the payment to get out of a risky situation is called an **insurance premium**.

**insurance premium**  the payment to get out of a risky situation

Recall that in Chapter 1 we discussed the basic institutions in the financial market and listed the major Canadian companies. One set of institutions was the insurance companies, including Manulife Financial Corporation, Sun Life Financial Inc., and Great-West Lifeco Inc., which all had more than $270 billion in assets and $26 billion in revenues. These companies buy risky situations from individuals and institutions that do not want to bear them themselves. The risk of a house burning down, a car being stolen, or a spouse dying prematurely are all risks that individuals are willing to pay an insurance company to bear so that the individuals reduce the probability they will suffer financial harm. In this case, the gross profit margin on most insurance products is about 50 percent, so only 50 cents of every insurance premium dollar actually goes to pay claims; the remainder ends up in administrative expenses, profits, and taxes. The fact that individuals are willing to pay insurance premiums that generate 50-percent gross margins indicates how risk averse they are.[1]

The existence of insurance markets indicates how risk aversion creates a demand to remove risk, whereas the existence of capital markets indicates how risk aversion generates the risk premiums required to induce people to bear risk. In the following discussion, we will assume that investors are risk averse—that is, they require a risk premium to bear risk—and that the more risk averse they are, the higher the risk premium they require. Further, we will continue to assume that we can represent risk in terms of the standard deviation of the return on the portfolio. These assumptions lead to the conclusion that investors will choose only portfolios on the efficient frontier above the MVP.

We can't say where on the efficient frontier a particular person will be, because individuals differ in terms of their risk aversion. However, a very risk-averse individual might choose portfolio A, shown in Figure 9.1, and a less risk-averse individual might choose portfolio B. Why do we know that the investor choosing A is more risk averse than the investor choosing B? The line going through A to the origin is steeper than the line through B and the origin. The slope of the line is the height, which is the expected return on the portfolio, divided by the length, which is the standard deviation of the portfolio. Because the line through A is steeper than the line through B, the individual who invests in A requires a higher expected rate of return per unit of risk—that is, they are more risk averse.

Many lines go through the origin and touch different points on the efficient frontier. Portfolios on the flatter lines are chosen by less risk-averse investors. These investors choose a portfolio with a lower expected rate of return per unit of risk and gradually move out along the efficient frontier. Apart from knowing that investors differ in terms of their risk aversion, we know only that their preferred portfolio will lie somewhere along the efficient frontier.[2]

The origin is the point with a zero expected rate of return and zero risk. Zero risk is another way of describing a risk-free asset, such as a treasury bill (T-bill), where the return on the asset is guaranteed with no possibility of earning more or less. We usually use T-bills as the example of a risk-free asset simply because they are obligations of the Government of Canada, which also has a monopoly on issuing Government of Canada bank notes. T-bills are default free because investors know that they will always be paid off in full.[3] While this is a reasonable assumption for Canada, the United States, and most countries, the concept of risk-free government debt has come under many challenges in recent years, with the European debt crisis and the restructuring of the Greek government's debt obligations, for example. This is nothing new, since other nations have defaulted on their debt obligations in the past, such as Venezuela, Russia, Argentina, the Ukraine, Ecuador, and Pakistan, among others.

## Risk-Free Investing

Consider any point on the efficient frontier in Figure 9.1, such as portfolio A. Now assume an investor places a portion of their wealth ($w$) in risky portfolio A, and the remainder ($1 - w$) in the risk-free asset, the T-bill. Remember that the expected return on a portfolio is always a weighted average of the expected returns on the individual assets, so we can estimate the

---

[1]It could also indicate that people do not understand the probabilities or the payoffs. People seem to be willing to pay very high premiums to remove low-probability risks that offer relatively low payoffs.

[2]The previous discussion may seem a bit loose for those with extensive economics training. We could represent each individual by their indifference curve, symbolizing their risk aversion and personal trade-off between risk and return. However, this adds little to our discussion.

[3]Treasury bills have not always been default free. John Ilkiw points out that sovereign debt used to be very risky because monarchs were above the law, as it was their law, and could repudiate debt without recourse. Only with the establishment of the Bank of England and parliamentary assumption of the British national debt in 1688 did the notion of a risk-free asset come into being. Interest rates on British debt dropped noticeably, by 4 percent, after this assumption as the default risk of lending to the government disappeared. In some parts of the world, government debt still remains risky. See Ilkiw, John, "The 100% Guarantee—The Reign of the Risk-Free Rate: Past Times, Present Value." *Canadian Investment Review* 19, no. 3 (Fall 2006), p. 7.

expected return on this portfolio according to Equation 8.11, reproduced here as Equation 9.1, with $RF$ in place of $ER_B$.

$$ER_p = RF + w\,(ER_A - RF)$$
[9.1]

$ER_P$ is the expected return on the portfolio that starts out with $w = 0$, because 100 percent is invested in the T-bill. As $w$ increases, more is placed in the risky portfolio, so the investor picks up $ER_P$ at the cost of taking money out of the T-bill. As a result, the expected return on the portfolio increases by the difference: $ER_A - RF$.

We can estimate the standard deviation on this portfolio using Equation 8.16 from Chapter 8, which is reproduced below.

$$\sigma_p = \sqrt{(w_A)^2(\sigma_A)^2 + (w_B)^2(\sigma_B)^2 + 2(w_A)(w_B)(\rho_{AB})(\sigma_A)(\sigma_B)}$$

If we replace $RF$ for risky portfolio B, $w$ for $w_A$, and $(1 - w)$ for $w_B$, we get the following:

$$\sigma_p = \sqrt{(w)^2(\sigma_A)^2 + (1 - w)^2(\sigma_{RF})^2 + 2(w)(1 - w)(\rho_{A,RF})(\sigma_A)(\sigma_{RF})}$$

With the risk-free asset, we know exactly what we are going to get, so the standard deviation of its return is zero. Because the return does not vary, the correlation between the return on the risk-free asset and that on risky portfolio A is also zero. So the standard deviation reduces to

$$\sigma_p = \sqrt{(w)^2(\sigma_A)^2 + (1 - w)^2(0)^2 + 2(w)(1 - w)(\rho_{A,RF} = 0)(\sigma_A)(0)} = \sqrt{w^2\sigma_A^2}$$

Taking the square root of the final term leaves us with Equation 9.2.[4]

$$\sigma_p = w\sigma_A$$
[9.2]

Equation 9.2 is very important as it shows that portfolio risk increases in direct proportion to the amount invested in the risky asset. Therefore, the higher the portfolio allocation (weight) directed to the risky asset, the higher the portfolio risk. Because both the expected return and the standard deviation of a portfolio comprising a risky asset and a risk-free asset ($RF$) *can* be represented by a line that is based on the weights invested in $RF$ and in the risky asset, all of the expected returns and risks for various portfolio combinations can be expressed as a straight line. We can show this by rearranging Equation 9.2 in terms of the portfolio weight:

$$w = \frac{\sigma_p}{\sigma_A}$$

Substituting for $w$ in Equation 9.1, we get Equation 9.3.

$$ER_p = RF + \left(\frac{ER_A - RF}{\sigma_A}\right)\sigma_p$$
[9.3]

Equation 9.3 is the equation of a straight line. It indicates that the line touches the vertical axis at the risk-free rate and then has a constant slope. The slope is the rise over the run, or the increased expected return divided by the increased risk. The increased expected return, as discussed, is the incremental return on the risky portfolio minus the lost return by taking money out of the risk-free asset. We represent this portfolio in **Figure 9.2**.

The interpretation of this figure is the same as before: if $w = 0$, all the investment is in the risk-free asset (T-bill), and the portfolio has no risk and earns $RF$. As $w$ increases, the expected return on the portfolio increases by ($ER_A - RF$), and its risk by $\sigma_p$ until $w = 100$ percent, the

---

[4]Technically, this equation holds when short selling is not permitted, so that $w$ is positive. If short selling were permitted, this would need to be replaced by the absolute value of $w$.

**FIGURE 9.2** Efficient Portfolios and a Risk-Free Asset

expected return is $ER_A$, and the risk is $\sigma_A$. Portfolios formed from A and the risk-free asset are formed using $RF$ and other portfolios on the efficient frontier. In each case, the equation will be the same as in Equation 9.3. In particular, think about portfolio T in **Figure 9.3**.

All portfolios composed of risky portfolio T and the risk-free rate lie along the line $RF$ to T and offer a higher expected rate of return for the same risk as portfolios composed of the risk-free rate and risky portfolio A. Portfolio T is called the **tangent portfolio**, because it is the risky portfolio on the efficient frontier whose tangent line cuts the vertical axis at the risk-free rate. Portfolios composed of the risk-free rate and portfolio T offer the highest expected rate of return for any given level of risk and represent the **new (or super) efficient frontier**, which is depicted in **Figure 9.4**.

**tangent portfolio**   the risky portfolio on the efficient frontier whose tangent line cuts the vertical axis at the risk-free rate

**new (or super) efficient frontier**   portfolios composed of the risk-free rate and the tangent portfolio that offer the highest expected rate of return for any given level of risk

**FIGURE 9.3** Tangent Portfolios

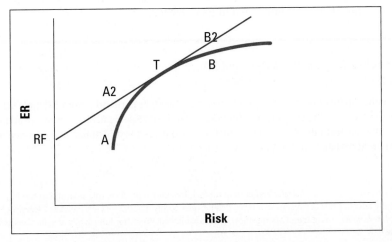

**FIGURE 9.4** The New Efficient Frontier

Consider, for example, portfolio A, which was optimal for a very risk-averse investor without the risk-free asset. Now this investor could hold a portfolio of the risk-free asset and risky portfolio T, which offers a higher expected rate of return for the same risk as A. This is the new portfolio A2. What this demonstrates is that a portfolio partially invested in the risk-free asset reduces the portfolio risk but can achieve a higher expected rate of return than any portfolio on the efficient frontier of risky assets.

---

**EXAMPLE 9.1** | Expected Return and Standard Deviation for a Two-Asset Portfolio That Includes Investment in a Risk-Free Asset

Assume that portfolio T has an expected return of 8 percent, with a standard deviation of 25 percent, and the risk-free rate is 3 percent. Estimate the expected return and standard deviation for a portfolio that has 30 percent invested in the risk-free asset and 70 percent in T.

**Solution**

$$w = 0.7; (1 - w) = 0.3$$

Therefore,

$$ER_P = (0.3)(3\%) + (0.7)(8\%) = 0.9\% + 5.6\% = 6.5\%$$

and

$$\sigma_p = (0.7)(25\%) = 17.5\%$$

---

# Risk-Free Borrowing

Now consider a less risk-averse investor who held portfolio B in Figure 9.4. They could now hold portfolio B2 and get a higher expected rate of return for the same level of risk as B. However, creating portfolio B2 involves having more than 100 percent invested in the risky portfolio T ($w > 100$ percent), and thus having a negative or **short position** in the risk-free asset. We create a short position in the risk-free asset by borrowing. One way to do this is to buy stocks on "margin," which means the investor borrows part of the purchase price from the stockbroker. For example, some stocks have margin requirements as low as 30 percent, indicating an investor could buy $1,000 worth of stocks by investing only $300 and borrowing the remaining $700 from the broker. In this case, the portfolio weights are $w = \$1,000/\$300$ or 333 percent in the risky asset and −233 percent in the risk-free asset. Of course, investors must pay interest on the borrowed money. In addition, short sellers face other risks, including experiencing unlimited losses (i.e., there is "theoretically" no maximum price the share prices could hit); being asked to "cover" their short position (by purchasing the amount of shares sold short); and having to cover dividends paid on the underlying stock while they are in the short position.

For simplicity, we assume that short sellers borrow at the same risk-free rate as investors can lend at.[5] This situation is illustrated in Example 9.2.

**short position** a negative position in an asset; the investor achieves a short position by borrowing part of the asset's purchase price from the stockbroker

---

**EXAMPLE 9.2** | Expected Return and Standard Deviation for a Two-Asset Portfolio That Includes Borrowing at the Risk-Free Rate

Assume that an investor invests all of her wealth ($1,000) in portfolio T from Example 9.1, with an expected return of 8 percent and a standard deviation of 25 percent. She borrows an additional $700 at the risk-free rate of 3 percent, which she also invests in T. Estimate the expected return and standard deviation for this portfolio.

---

[5]Although borrowing rates are generally higher than the risk-free rate in practice, this assumption can be relaxed without greatly affecting our key results. For more details, refer to any investments text, such as Cleary, W. S., and Jones, C.P., *Investments: Analysis and Management,* 3rd Canadian ed. (Toronto: John Wiley & Sons Canada Ltd., 2009), p. 236.

**Solution**

$$w = \$1{,}700/\$1{,}000 = 1.7; (1 - w) = 1 - 1.7 = -0.7$$

Therefore,

$$ER_P = (-0.7)(3\%) + (1.7)(8\%) = -2.1\% + 13.6\% = 11.5\%$$

and

$$\sigma_p = (1.7)(25\%) = 42.5\%$$

The portfolio described in Example 9.2 is similar to B2 and lies on the straight line depicted in Figure 9.4 beyond portfolio T, as would any portfolio formed by borrowing funds at *RF* and investing them in portfolio T.

## The New Efficient Set and the Separation Theorem

We showed above that any point along the tangent line from the risk-free rate is attainable by either investing in or borrowing at *RF*, and then investing all remaining proceeds in risky portfolio T. From Figure 9.4, we see that all the points along this line dominate all the points on the efficient frontier, except for point T. As we showed, A2 is better than A and B2 is better than B. Therefore, allowing for the possibility of risk-free investing and borrowing has expanded the efficient set and provided investors with a *more efficient* set of portfolios from which to choose. This line is often called the new (or super) efficient frontier, or the previous efficient frontier is specifically referred to as the "efficient frontier of risky portfolios" to distinguish it from the efficient frontier of the risk-free asset and the tangent portfolio.

Investors can achieve any point on this new efficient frontier by borrowing or investing desired amounts at *RF* and investing the remainder in one portfolio of risky assets, which is the tangent portfolio T. Therefore, each investor can choose the point on this line that suits their personal risk preferences: more risk-averse investors can choose portfolios like A2, which are heavily invested in the risk-free asset (T-bills); whereas more aggressive investors can choose portfolios like B2, which involve borrowing.

A very important concept arises from this discussion. Suppose investors all agree on the expected rates of return and the risk attached to each security. In that case, the efficient frontier of risky assets is the same for all investors. This would occur, for example, if the investors were clients of an investment company that estimated all these values and then discussed the best portfolio for a particular client. It would no longer be necessary to match each investor's risk preferences with a specific risky portfolio. Instead, the investment company would recommend the same tangent portfolio to all its clients. It might then refer to this portfolio as its model portfolio, and some investors would invest in this and the risk-free asset (T-bills), whereas others would borrow to invest in the model portfolio.

Suppose, further, that all investment companies agreed on the set of expected returns and the risk attached to the securities. In that case, the tangent or model portfolio would also be the same. This result provides the basis for the **separation theorem**, which states that the *investment decision*—that is, the decision on how to construct the portfolio of risky assets—is separate from the *financing decision*—that is, the decision about how much should be invested or borrowed at the risk-free rate. In other words, tangent portfolio T is optimal for every investor regardless of their degree of risk aversion. Further, if everyone holds the same portfolio, it must be the **market portfolio** of all risky securities, because every security has to be held by someone.

Theoretically, the market portfolio should contain all risky assets worldwide, including stocks, bonds, options, futures, gold, real estate, and so on, in their proper proportions. Such a portfolio, if it could be constructed, would be completely diversified. However, in practice, the market portfolio is unobservable, so we use proxies to measure its behaviour. Common stock

**separation theorem** the theory that the investment decision (how to construct the portfolio of risky assets) is separate from the financing decision (how much should be invested or borrowed at the risk-free rate)

**market portfolio** a portfolio that contains all risky securities in the market

market indexes, such as the S&P/TSX Composite Index in Canada and the S&P 500 Composite Index in the United States, are often used as proxies.

The fact that every investor would hold the same portfolio (the market portfolio) is referred to as an "equilibrium condition," because supply equals demand for all the risky securities, and we replace T with M, which is not just the tangent portfolio but also the market portfolio. This hypothesis is the basis for the most common model we use in finance to price securities, the capital asset pricing model, which is discussed in the next section.

---

### Concept Review Questions

1. What is risk aversion and how do we know investors are risk averse?
2. What is the risk of a portfolio consisting of a risk-free asset and a risky security?
3. Why is the tangent portfolio so important?
4. How do we generate a portfolio with a higher expected rate of return than that of the tangent portfolio?

---

## 9.2 | The Capital Asset Pricing Model (CAPM)

---

**LEARNING OBJECTIVE 9.2**

Explain how modern portfolio theory is extended to develop the capital market line (CML).

---

**capital asset pricing model (CAPM)** a pricing model that uses one factor, market risk, to relate expected returns to risk

Professor William Sharpe of Stanford University won the Nobel Prize for developing the best-known equilibrium asset pricing model, the **capital asset pricing model (CAPM)**, which relates expected returns to risk. The initial development of the CAPM was based on a number of assumptions that we have already briefly discussed:

1. All investors have identical expectations about expected returns, standard deviations, and correlation coefficients for all securities.
2. All investors have the same one-period time horizon.
3. All investors can borrow or lend money at the risk-free rate of return (*RF*).
4. There are no transaction costs.
5. There are no personal income taxes, so investors are indifferent whether they receive capital gains or dividends.
6. There are many investors, and no single investor can affect the price of a stock through their buying and selling decisions. Therefore, investors are price-takers.
7. Capital markets are in equilibrium.

These assumptions may appear unrealistic at first. For example, the assumption of identical expectations is needed so that the efficient frontier of risky portfolios is the same for all investors. However, not all investors matter; the most important are the big institutions that invest most of the money. They all have access to the same information, and they all have expert security analysts analyzing the data. Similarly, borrowing rates differ from lending rates for small investors, but for large institutional investors the difference is not material. The same applies to transaction costs. The result is that most of the assumptions can be relaxed without significantly affecting the CAPM or its main implications. However, before discussing the CAPM, we will discuss what happens to the overall capital market.

# The Market Portfolio and the Capital Market Line (CML)

The assumptions for the CAPM listed above give rise to the following important implications, which have been discussed previously:

1. The "optimal" risky portfolio is the one that is tangent to the efficient frontier on a line that is drawn from *RF*, as shown in Figure 9.4. This portfolio will be the same for all investors.

2. This optimal risky portfolio will be the "market portfolio" (M), which contains all risky securities. The value of this portfolio will equal the aggregate of the market values of all the individual assets composing it. Therefore, the weights of these assets in the market portfolio will be represented by their proportionate weight in its total value.

Figure 9.5 is similar to Figure 9.4, but it does not include the efficient frontier portion, and the only portfolio is M, the tangent portfolio, because the market portfolio (M) is the optimal portfolio of risky securities that is combined with *RF*. Recall that this line produces the highest attainable expected return for any given risk level; therefore, it includes only efficient portfolios. Further, all rational, risk-averse investors will seek to be on this line. In Figure 9.5, it is called the **capital market line (CML)**.

**capital market line (CML)** a line depicting the highest attainable expected return for any given risk level that includes only efficient portfolios; all rational, risk-averse investors want to be on this line

We can see from Figure 9.5 that the CML has an intercept of *RF*, just like any portfolio consisting of the risk-free asset and a risky portfolio. But the risky portfolio is not arbitrary: now it is the market portfolio. So we have a special version of Equation 9.3:

$$\text{Slope of the CML} = \frac{ER_M - RF}{\sigma_M}$$  [9.4]

As in Equation 9.3, the slope of the capital market line is the incremental expected return divided by the incremental risk. However, this is a special trade-off of risk and return called the **market price of risk** for efficient portfolios or the equilibrium price of risk in the capital market. It indicates the additional expected return that the market demands for an increase in a portfolio's risk. Adding the risk-free rate (*RF*) gives the CML as:

**market price of risk** the incremental expected return divided by the incremental risk; indicates the additional expected return that the market demands for an increase in risk

$$ER_p = RF + \left[\frac{ER_M - RF}{\sigma_M}\right]\sigma_p$$  [9.5]

where

$ER_M$ = the expected return on the market portfolio M

$\sigma_M$ = the standard deviation of returns on the market portfolio

$\sigma_p$ = the standard deviation of returns on the efficient portfolio being considered

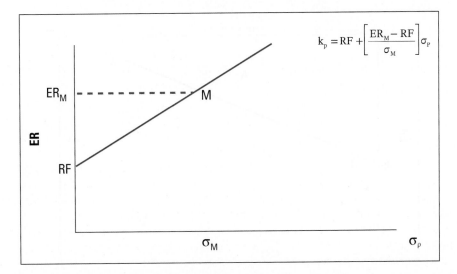

$$k_p = RF + \left[\frac{ER_M - RF}{\sigma_M}\right]\sigma_p$$

**FIGURE 9.5** The Capital Market Line (CML)

**required rate of return** the rate of return investors need to tempt them to invest in a security

The CML is a special version of Equation 9.3 in another important way. As always, the CML indicates an expected rate of return, just as Equation 9.3 gave the expected return on a portfolio of A and the risk-free rate. However, now we have made enough assumptions to identify the portfolio as the market portfolio and as an equilibrium condition in the capital market, where supply equals demand. As a result, the CML determines not just an expected rate of return but also a **required rate of return**, which we denote as $k_p$.

---

**EXAMPLE 9.3** | Using the CML to Determine the Required Rate of Return

Assume the risk-free rate is 3 percent. The expected return on the market is 7 percent, and it has a standard deviation of 15 percent. Determine the required rate of return necessary for investors to hold an efficient portfolio with a standard deviation of 20 percent.

**Solution**

$$k_p = RF + \left[ \frac{ER_M - RF}{\sigma_M} \right] \sigma_p = 3 + \left[ \frac{7 - 3}{15} \right](20) = 3 + (0.267)(20)$$

$$= 3 + 5.34 = 8.34\%$$

---

Notice that the required return on the portfolio in Example 9.3 is greater than that expected for the market portfolio, because it has a higher standard deviation.

Having defined the CML and worked through Example 9.3, we can talk in more detail about the difference between expected and required rates of return. Suppose the CML is as graphed in **Figure 9.6**, and we are looking at three portfolios: A, B, and C. The CML is drawn so that only portfolio B lies on the CML. For this portfolio, the expected rate of return is the same as the required rate of return, so the portfolio is "fairly priced." Portfolio C is drawn so that the expected portfolio return is higher than that of B. However, this portfolio is below the CML, which indicates that the required rate of return is higher than this expected rate of return. If we look at just the expected rate of return, C would seem to be a good buy, but this is wrong because it is a very risky portfolio. Given its risk, it is a bad buy and its price would drop, forcing up its expected rate of return until it was fairly priced and the expected and required rates of return were the same. Portfolio A presents the opposite situation: it has a high expected rate of return and relatively low risk. In this case, the expected rate of return exceeds the required rate of return, and investors would bid up its price and cause its expected rate of return to fall until it lies on the CML.

It is also important to recognize that the CML must always slope *upward*, because with risk-averse investors the risk premium must always be positive, and the CML predicts *required* returns. As a result, risk-averse investors will not invest unless they expect to be compensated for bearing risk. The greater the risk, the greater the required rate of return. However, as we

**FIGURE 9.6** **Expected and Required Rates of Return**

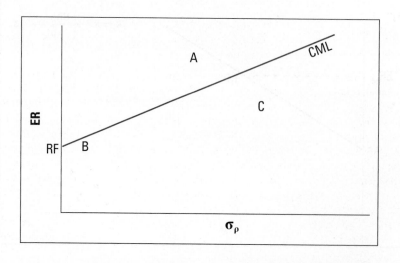

discussed in Chapter 8, there is a big difference between ex post and ex ante returns. After-the-fact (ex post) returns can be (and often have been) less than the T-bill yield. If this were never the case, investing in the equity market would have no risk and no one would hold T-bills. The observation of ex post poor returns on risky securities does not negate the validity of the CML; however, it merely indicates that returns actually realized differ from those that were expected. In other words, investors sometimes get it wrong and their expectations are not realized. If investors were never wrong, there would be no risk in the equity market!

The ideas that we have just described have become a critical part of the evaluation of investment performance in a financial system. Consider the slope of the CML in Equation 9.4 again. In equilibrium, all portfolios should lie along the CML, as those offering expected rates of return that are higher than required will have their prices bid up and vice versa. The CML is based on expected rates of return, so it is ex ante. However, if expectations are realized—if, on average, the actual return is what was expected—we can use the CML to judge the performance of different portfolios ex post—that is, the actual portfolio performance.

## Risk-Adjusted Performance and Sharpe Ratios

When the ideas underlying the CML are used in this way, it leads to a discussion of the **Sharpe ratio**, named after William Sharpe of Stanford University, who developed the ratio and first applied it to assessing portfolio performance. The Sharpe ratio generally uses realized (or ex post) returns, and is formally defined as

**Sharpe ratio**  a measure of portfolio performance that describes how well an asset's return compensates investors for the risk taken

$$\text{Sharpe ratio} = \frac{ER_p - RF}{\sigma_p} \qquad [9.6]$$

When the portfolio is the market portfolio, the Sharpe ratio is the ex post version of Equation 9.4, which is the ex post slope of the CML. So what would be typical values for the Sharpe ratio? Table 8.2 showed that from 1938 to 2018, the arithmetic mean return for Canadian equities was 10.99 percent and for T-bills was 4.68 percent, so the ex post excess return of equities over T-bills was 6.31 percent. If the T-bill return is taken to be the risk-free rate, and if the standard deviation for equities is 16.37 percent (also taken from Table 8.2), the ex post Sharpe ratio for Canadian equities in this period was 0.385 (i.e., 6.31/16.37). What this means is that for every 1-percent increase in risk (standard deviation of the portfolio's return), the Canadian equity market rewarded the investor with an extra 0.385 percent of return.

Sharpe ratios are commonly used to assess the performance of portfolios, including professionally managed funds, as discussed in Finance in the News 9.1. The reason is that it measures excess returns (i.e., returns in excess of a risk-free rate) and scales them by the volatility of the returns. In other words, its value is increasing in returns but is decreasing in risk, all else being equal. As Finance in the News 9.1 suggests, the "trick" to effective fund management is "to capture high returns without taking on too much risk."

### 9.1  Finance in the News    CAPM and the Sharpe Ratio

William Sharpe, an American academic and consultant, is one of the founders of what is known universally as the capital asset pricing model (CAPM) and also of a ratio that bears his name that is used to measure the riskiness of an investment relative to the returns it generates.

We can deal with the CAPM first by noting that Sharpe's main contribution to portfolio theory was the insight that an individual investment contained two types of risk: specific risk, unique to that investment; and market risk, sometimes called systemic risk. Specific risk can be removed through diversification.

Coping with systemic risk is what really plagues investors, according to Sharpe.

The CAPM evolved as a way of quantifying this risk. Sharpe found that the return on an individual investment or portfolio of investments should equate to the risk-free rate of return plus the excess return that the market provided over that risk-free rate multiplied by a factor, which Sharpe called beta. Beta is the measure of an individual investment's (or portfolio's) sensitivity to the movement in the market.

Each individual investment has a beta, which varies over time and for the time period chosen over which to measure it. A beta for a stock with measurements taken hourly over the course of a week, for example, might be different to one calculated daily over a period of three months. In both cases, though, beta means the same thing. A stock with a beta of 1.5 could, for example, be expected to rise 15 percent if the market rose 10 percent and fall 15 percent if the market fell 10 percent.

Beta is found by statistical analysis of share price returns compared with the market's returns over precisely the same period. Betas of individual stocks can be combined together to give a portfolio beta. The importance of Sharpe's model is that it allows one to predict the expected return from a portfolio given its beta, the market rate of return and the risk-free rate.

Say the portfolio beta was 2.0, the risk-free rate 3 percent, and the market rate of return 7 percent. Then the market's excess return is 4 percent $(7 - 3)$, the portfolio's excess return is 8 percent $(2 \times 4$, multiplying market excess return by beta), and the portfolio's total expected return is 11 percent $(8 + 3$, the portfolio's excess return plus the risk-free rate). What this means is that it is possible, by knowing these individual components of the CAPM, to establish whether the current price of an investment is consistent with it or not, in other words whether or not the investment is cheap or dear.

One other offshoot of Sharpe's work is a ratio for standardizing the measuring of the performance of funds, notably hedge funds. Known as the Sharpe ratio, this compares the excess return that a fund earns, over and above the risk-free rate, with the volatility of those returns. The argument underlying this is that any investment manager can earn higher returns by assuming more risk.

Risk is equated with volatility of returns. The trick is to capture high returns without taking on too much risk.

By comparing excess return with volatility, investments can be ranked on the basis of degree of return provided per unit of risk. The higher is the Sharpe ratio, the more favourable are the risk-return characteristics of the individual investment or fund. Just as funds can have Sharpe ratios, so too can markets.

This might all sound rather dry and academic, but the work of Sharpe and others led directly to the creation of index-tracking investments.

Sharpe, for example, by devising the concept of beta, demonstrated that it would not be necessary for an index-tracking portfolio to hold all of the constituents of an index in the exact proportions they represented for it to produce a performance that matched the index. All one needed to do was construct a portfolio that had, over time, a consistent beta of 1 and it would mimic the performance of the index.

It is perhaps significant that among the firms that used Sharpe's services as a consultant was Wells Fargo. Back in the mists of time, Wells Fargo Nikko Investment Advisors was a predecessor firm of Barclays Global Investors, creator of the iShares concept and now the biggest providers of exchange traded index funds for investors. If you hold an index-tracking investment, you have Sharpe to thank for the fact that the product is available for you to invest in.

**Source:** Temple, Peter, "CAPM and the Sharpe Ratio." *Interactive Investor,* March 24, 2011. First published on Interactive Investor www.iii.co.uk.

---

## Concept Review Questions

1. What is the slope of the CML, and why can it be viewed as the market price of risk for efficient portfolios according to the CML?
2. Assuming the CAPM holds, if the expected return on a diversified portfolio lies above the CML, should an investor buy or sell that portfolio?
3. When is the expected return equal to the required return?
4. Why is the Sharpe ratio frequently referred to as a "risk-adjusted" measure of performance?

---

## 9.3 | The CAPM and Market Risk

**LEARNING OBJECTIVE 9.3**

Explain how the capital asset pricing model's (CAPM) security market line (SML) is developed from the capital market line (CML), and how the SML can be used to estimate the required return on individual securities and portfolios.

The CML provides a method of estimating the required return on equity securities relative to their risk, but it applies only to efficient portfolios and not to individual securities. In addition, the risk premium is based on portfolio risk, as measured by the standard deviation of the return on the portfolio. In corporate finance, we are usually concerned with the risk attached to individual firms and the required return for investing in them. Recall from our discussion in Chapter 8 that as the number of securities included in a portfolio increases, unique

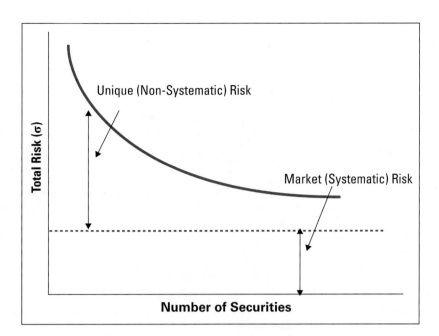

**FIGURE 9.7** Portfolio Risk and Diversification

(non-systematic or diversifiable) risk is eliminated, and only market (systematic or non-diversifiable) risk remains. This relationship is depicted in **Figure 9.7**.

Figure 9.7 shows that the average risk of an individual security—that is, a one-stock portfolio—is at the point where the curve gets very close to the vertical axis. Therefore, with randomly built diversified portfolios, the risk of a portfolio falls until it reaches a baseline and cannot be reduced below this market level. What this means is that part of a security's risk is diversifiable. Further, if it can be diversified away by holding a portfolio of more than, say, 20 securities, it is not important to rational investors. This is the key insight of the CAPM.

The CAPM points out that rational investors should not be compensated for unique or diversifiable risk, because it can be eliminated through diversification. This implies that market risk is the appropriate measure of risk to determine the risk premium required by investors for holding a risky security. We now introduce a new term, **beta ($\beta_i$),** which is a commonly used measure of market risk that relates the extent to which the return on a security moves with the return on the overall market. It is typically estimated by first plotting the returns on an individual security on the vertical axis relative to the returns for the market, which are plotted along the horizontal axis, and then fitting a line through the observations, as shown in **Figure 9.8**. The line is called the **characteristic line** and is determined by using a statistical technique called regression analysis. The slope of the line is the security's beta coefficient. For example, in Figure 9.8, the slope coefficient is 0.85, which indicates that if the market return goes up or down by 1 percent, the return on this security is expected to go up or down by 0.85 percent—that is, it changes by 0.85 of the return on the market.[6]

Estimating beta coefficients is tricky, because we are interested in the extent to which the security moves with the market over a future period. As always, we estimate beta coefficients by using historical data, which assumes that what has happened in the past is a good predictor for the future. Typically, betas are estimated using 60 months of monthly returns, but sometimes only 52 weeks of weekly returns are used. Betas change through time as the risk of the underlying security or portfolio changes. This is particularly important for individual securities, the betas for which can change dramatically over relatively short periods. Conversely, betas estimated for large portfolios or for industries are much more stable because they are averaged over many securities. Therefore, estimates of portfolio betas show less change from period to period and are much more reliable than the estimates for individual securities.

**beta ($\beta_i$)** a measure of market risk, or performance volatility, that relates the extent to which the return on a security moves with the return on the overall market; the covariance between an investment and the market divided by variance of the market

**characteristic line** a line of best fit through the returns on an individual security, plotted on the vertical axis, relative to the returns for the market, plotted along the horizontal axis

[6]The characteristic line is also often estimated by using excess returns. The excess return is calculated by subtracting the risk-free rate from both the return on the stock and the return on the market. In excess return form, the same analysis applies.

**FIGURE 9.8** The Characteristic Line for Security A

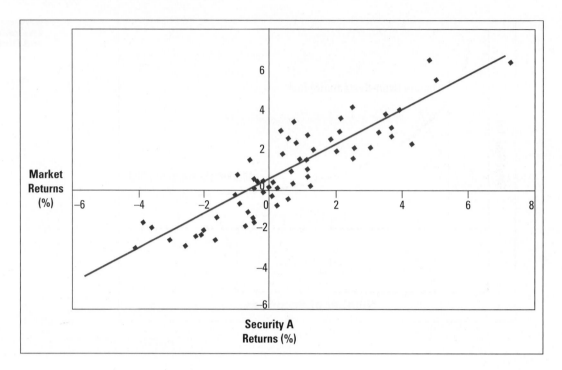

If we make some fairly common statistical assumptions, betas can be estimated using Equation 9.7.[7]

$$\beta_i = \frac{COV_{i,M}}{\sigma_M^2} = \frac{\rho_{i,M}\sigma_i}{\sigma_M}$$

[9.7]

Beta measures the risk of an individual stock or portfolio *relative* to the market portfolio. A beta of 1 implies that if the market increased (or decreased) by 1 percent, the return on the security (or portfolio) would increase (decrease) by 1 percent *on average*. Therefore, the market has a beta of 1. A security with a beta of 1.2 has returns that are 1.2 times as volatile as market returns, either up or down. In other words, if the market increased 10 percent, that security's returns would increase by 12 percent, and so on. Securities with betas greater than 1 are generally considered to be more volatile (or risky or more aggressive) than average. Similarly, securities with betas less than 1 are less volatile (less risky or more defensive). The risk-free asset has a beta of zero, because it has a covariance of zero with the market and has no risk. Finally, negative betas are possible, although they are rare. Equation 9.7 shows that negative betas can occur only if a security has a negative correlation coefficient with market returns, which is uncommon.[8]

---

**EXAMPLE 9.4** | Estimating Beta

The returns on stock X have a standard deviation of 20 percent and a correlation coefficient of 0.8 with market returns, which have a standard deviation of 15 percent. Estimate the beta for stock X.

**Solution**

$$\beta_x = \frac{\rho_{x,M}\sigma_x}{\sigma_M} = \frac{(0.80)(20)}{15} = 1.07$$

Notice that even though stock X has a higher standard deviation than the market, its beta is greater than one because of the correlation coefficient of 0.8.

---

[7]The technical assumptions required ensure that ordinary least squares (OLS) is the appropriate regression estimation approach to determine the equation of the characteristic line discussed above.

[8]This is the only way a negative beta is possible, because the standard deviation terms in Equation 9.7 are always positive. Gold stocks have sometimes had negative betas because, in the past, the price of gold tended to go in the opposite direction to the market; investors would invest in gold when they were nervous about future market movements. However, this relationship is not as strong as it used to be, and negative betas rarely occur, even for gold stocks.

**TABLE 9.1** Canadian Betas

| Company | Industry Classification | 2014 | 2019 |
|---|---|---|---|
| AGF Management Ltd. | Financials | 1.28 | 1.14 |
| Alamos Gold Inc. | Materials−Precious Metals & Minerals | 1.08 | 0.82 |
| Bank of Montreal | Financials−Banks | 0.62 | 0.99 |
| Bank of Nova Scotia | Financials−Banks | 0.67 | 0.98 |
| Barrick Gold Corp. | Materials−Precious Metals & Minerals | 1.00 | 0.77 |
| BCE Inc. | Communications−Telecommunications | 0.14 | 0.46 |
| Canadian Imperial Bank of Commerce | Financials−Banks | 0.77 | 0.94 |
| Cogeco Cable Inc. | Consumer Discretionary−Cable | 0.74 | 0.98 |
| Imperial Oil Ltd. | Energy−Oil & Gas: Integrated Oils | 1.23 | 0.96 |
| Magna International | Consumer Discretionary−Auto Parts | 1.28 | 1.36 |
| Royal Bank | Financials−Banks | 0.77 | 0.89 |
| Suncor Energy Inc. | Energy−Oil & Gas | 1.80 | 1.50 |
| Toronto-Dominion Bank | Financials−Banks | 0.68 | 0.83 |
| TMX Group Ltd. | Financials−Diversified Financials | 0.48 | 1.11 |
| WestJet Airlines Ltd. | Industrials−Transportation: Airlines | 0.57 | 0.61 |

Betas tend to vary a great deal between companies in different industries, because they possess different risk profiles. Although betas tend to be more similar for companies operating in the same industry, they can still vary substantially, because even companies within the same industry can differ across various dimensions, such as financial risk, size, and so on. These comments are validated by the betas reported in **Table 9.1** for several well-known Canadian companies that operate in a variety of industries. Betas for 2019 range from a low of 0.46 for BCE Inc. (a telecommunications company) to a high of 1.5 for Suncor Energy Inc. There are as many beta estimates as there are companies providing these estimates. This is due to variation in the time period selected, the length of time used for estimation and a variety of different adjustments that these different companies typically apply.

Table 9.1 also shows how betas change through time (as discussed previously). Notice that the betas for the banks increased markedly to a higher range from 0.83 to 0.99 in 2019 compared to the 0.62 to 0.77 range in 2014. Over this five-year period, the betas of BCE, Cogeco Cable, Magna, and TMX Group, also increased markedly, while those for AGF Management, Alamos Gold, Barrick Gold, Imperial Oil, and Suncor decreased significantly.

Unlike portfolio standard deviations, portfolio betas are weighted averages of the betas for the individual securities in the portfolio. Therefore, we can estimate the beta for an $n$-security portfolio by using Equation 9.8.

$$\beta_p = w_1\beta_1 + w_2\beta_2 + \cdots + w_n\beta_n \qquad [9.8]$$

Consider a security with a beta of zero. This means that its return is unrelated to the return on the market as a whole. As a result, all of the variability in this security's return is diversifiable by any investor holding a well-diversified portfolio. If this security is added to a diversified portfolio with a beta of 1, it will reduce the portfolio's beta. In contrast, if we add a security with a beta of 2 to the same portfolio, its beta will increase, thus increasing the risk of the portfolio and making it more sensitive to market movements.

---

**EXAMPLE 9.5** | Estimating a Portfolio Beta

An investor has a portfolio that consists of $10,000 invested in stock B, which has a beta of 1.2; $20,000 in stock C, which has a beta of 0.8; and $20,000 in stock D, which has a beta of 1.3. Estimate the beta of this portfolio.

**Solution**

$$w_B = \frac{\$10,000}{(\$10,000 + \$20,000 + \$20,000)} = 0.20; w_C = \frac{\$20,000}{\$50,000} = 0.40; w_D = \frac{\$20,000}{\$50,000} = 0.40$$

$$\beta_p = w_B\beta_B + w_C\beta_C + w_D\beta_D = (0.20)(1.2) + (0.40)(0.8) + (0.40)(1.3)$$

$$= 0.24 + 0.32 + 0.52 = 1.08$$

---

We can see from the result of Example 9.5 why diversified portfolios end up with only market risk. First, the beta on the market portfolio, by definition, is 1. We can see this from Equation 9.7 by substituting M for the standard deviation of the security and noting that a security is perfectly correlated with itself. So if the average beta is 1, as we randomly add securities to a portfolio, we eventually end up with an average risk portfolio with a beta of 1, composed of all market risk. This is also why most large portfolios made up of a large number of securities are essentially the same as the market portfolio and earn the same rate of return.[9]

## The Security Market Line (SML)

**security market line (SML)** the trade-off between market risk and the required rate of return for any risky investment, whether an individual security or a portfolio

Based on the argument made earlier that investors should be compensated for market risk, as measured by beta, it is easy to use the CML to derive the **security market line (SML)**, which is given in Equation 9.9.[10]

$$k_i = RF + (ER_M - RF)\beta_i$$

[9.9]

where

$k_i$ = the required return on security (or portfolio) $i$

$(ER_M - RF)\beta_i$ = the risk premium

The SML is the most important and widely used contribution of the CAPM, and it is depicted graphically in **Figure 9.9**. It represents the trade-off between market risk and the required rate of return for any risky investment, whether it is an individual security or a portfolio.

The SML slopes upward, which indicates that investors require a higher expected return on riskier—that is, higher-beta—securities. In essence, the SML formalizes the notion discussed previously at several junctures since Chapter 6: the required rate of return on an asset equals the risk-free rate plus a risk premium. According to the SML, the size of the risk premium varies directly with a security's market risk, as measured by beta.

**market risk premium** the risk premium as a function of market conditions; the expected return on the market minus the risk-free rate

The risk premium is also a function of market conditions, as reflected in the $ER_M - RF$ term, which is often referred to as the **market risk premium**. The historical averages provided in Table 8.2 of Chapter 8 suggest that the ex post risk premium from 1938 to 2018 in Canada was 6.31 percent (i.e., the average return on the market portfolio of Canadian common stocks was 10.99 percent, while the average T-bill return was 4.68 percent).

According to the SML, securities or portfolios with betas greater than the market beta of 1 will have larger risk premiums than the "average" stock and will therefore have larger required rates of return. Conversely, securities with betas less than that of the market are less risky and will have lower required rates of return.

---

[9]This is what is commonly referred to as "closet indexing," because although they charge large fees, most mutual funds have similar performance.

[10]For a formal derivation of the SML, refer to any investments textbook. For example, see Bodie, Z., et al., *Investments*, 8th Canadian ed. (Whitby, ON: McGraw-Hill Ryerson Ltd., 2015), pp. 237–38.

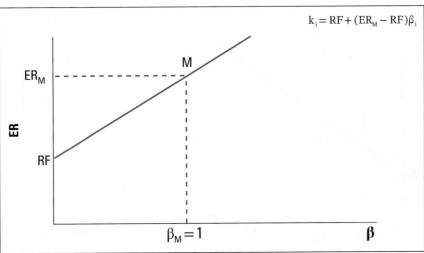

$$k_i = RF + (ER_M - RF)\beta_i$$

**FIGURE 9.9** **The Security Market Line (SML)**

---

**EXAMPLE 9.6** | Using the SML

Given that the expected return on the market is 8 percent and the risk-free rate is 3 percent, estimate

**a.** the market risk premium

**b.** the required return for security X in Example 9.4, which had a beta of 1.07

**c.** the required return for the portfolio in Example 9.5, which had a beta of 1.08

Solution

**a.** $ER_M - RF = 8 - 3 = 5\%$

**b.** $k_X = RF + (ER_M - RF)\beta_X = 3 + 5(1.07) = 3 + 5.35 = 8.35\%$

Notice that the required return for X is *greater* than the expected market return because its beta is greater than 1.

**c.** $k_p = RF + (ER_M - RF)\beta_p = 3 + 5(1.08) = 3 + 5.40 = 8.40\%$

Notice that the required return for this portfolio is *greater* than the expected market return because its beta is greater than 1.

---

## Lessons to Be Learned

Estimating required returns using the CAPM is fraught with difficulties. We need estimates of beta as well as the expected return on the market. Generally, betas are estimated using past data, with two years of weekly data or five years of monthly data being the most commonly employed approaches. Of course, what we really want is an estimate of beta for future periods, so beta estimates can and do vary through time as illustrated in Table 9.1. In many cases, they might not be good measures of a stock's future market sensitivity over a given period for a variety of reasons—we discuss one such instance in detail in Chapter 20.

Similarly, we often use historical averages to estimate the expected market return. Obviously, such estimates can often be way off the mark for any given period. Consider, for example, that the average Canadian stock market return over the 1938 to 2018 period was 10.99 percent, which is quite different from the −33-percent return experienced by the market in 2008, or the +35-percent return in 2009.

One has to keep in mind that beta represents the "average" market sensitivity and that this sensitivity may vary from one period to the next. The same applies to expected market returns. The realistic approach is to recognize that CAPM does a reasonable job of predicting returns on average, over the long run.

## The SML and Market Equilibrium

In equilibrium, the expected return on all properly priced securities will lie *on* the SML, just as the expected return on all portfolios will lie on the CML. As with the CML, when investors

**FIGURE 9.10** The SML and Security Valuation

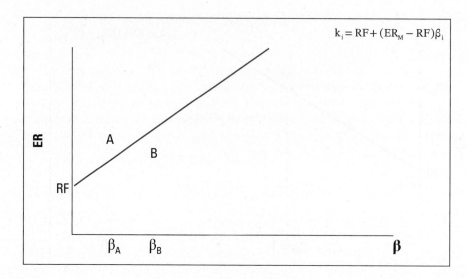

expect a return equal to the required return, the security is correctly priced. However, at any given time, some securities may be temporarily mispriced according to CAPM. Whenever analysis suggests that the expected return on a security differs from its required rate of return according to CAPM, then that security is either undervalued or overvalued. Securities or portfolios that have expected returns *greater* than their required rate of return are *undervalued,* because they provide investors with an expected return that is higher than the return required given their risk. As with the CML, undervalued securities will lie *above* the SML, reflecting the fact that the expected return exceeds the required return, which is the return along the SML that corresponds to the beta coefficient. Security A in **Figure 9.10** represents an example of an undervalued security. Similarly, securities or portfolios whose expected returns are *less* than their required rate of return, such as B in Figure 9.10, are *overvalued* and will lie below the SML.

If markets are efficient, we would expect prices to be correct (we will discuss the notion of market efficiency in Chapter 10). Therefore, whenever rational investors observe an undervalued security, such as A, they will rush to purchase it because it offers a higher expected return than its required return. As a result of this increase in demand for security A, its price will increase until it eventually equals the price level at which its expected return equals the required return according to the SML. In other words, security A's price will adjust until it lies along the SML. In similar fashion, selling pressure for security B (which is overvalued) would increase, causing B's price to decline until it too lies along the SML.

Of course, markets will not always be in equilibrium, and over a given period of time a security or portfolio might over- or under-perform the market and earn a return above or below that predicted by the SML. Let's consider the possibility that point A in Figure 9.10 depicts the actual returns and beta for portfolio A over some prior period in time, while $RF$ and $R_M$ represent the risk-free returns and market returns, respectively, over that same period. The risk-adjusted excess returns earned by portfolio A (i.e., the return above that predicted by this "ex post" SML) over this period would be referred to as the portfolio's "alpha." Alpha ($\alpha$) measures the risk-adjusted excess return (above or below that predicted by its beta) earned by a security or portfolio over a given period. It is a commonly used measure of portfolio manager performance. Of course, alpha need not always be positive; if point B in Figure 9.10 was also based on historical observations, it would indicate risk-adjusted "under-performance."

Alpha can be estimated by substituting ex post average returns (i.e., no more "expected" returns) into the SML and then rearranging as shown to create Equation 9.10.[11]

$$\alpha_i = (R_i - RF) - [\beta_i(R_M - RF)] \qquad [9.10]$$

Equation 9.10 indicates that $\alpha_i$ is the difference between the actual excess return on a security or portfolio during some period and the return that should have been earned according to its level of systematic risk (beta) and the use of the CAPM. This difference can

[11]Technically, alpha is the intercept coefficient estimate obtained when we regress past excess returns $(R_i - RF)$ on excess market returns $(R_M - RF)$, while the slope coefficient estimate is the beta.

be positive, negative, or zero. It is important to recognize the role of statistical significance in the interpretation of alpha. Although the estimated alpha may be positive or negative, it may not be significantly different (statistically) from zero. If it is not, we would conclude that the manager of the portfolio being evaluated performed as expected. That is, the manager earned an average risk-adjusted return, neither more nor less than would be expected given the risk assumed.

This discussion of the security market line is similar to the discussion of the capital market line. The two main differences are: (1) the measure of risk (CML uses standard deviation, while SML uses beta); and (2) the CML applies only to efficient portfolios, while the SML applies to individual stocks and portfolios.

## Using the SML to Estimate Long-Term Discount Rates

Technically, the CAPM is a one-period model, and the government T-bill rate should be used as the appropriate risk-free rate, since it is virtually guaranteed and does not fluctuate. However, analysts often use the CAPM to estimate the required return on common shares over many periods, such as when they are trying to estimate the share price using the dividend discount model or free cash flow models. As discussed in Chapter 7, these models require the discounting of expected cash flows that occur over many periods in the future. It is also normal to use the CAPM to estimate the cost of a firm's common equity financing component when estimating the firm's overall cost of capital. The cost of capital is then used to discount the expected future cash flows associated with capital expenditure decisions, which will be discussed in chapters 13, 14, and 20.

When using the CAPM to estimate a long-term required return on common equity, such as in the situations described above, analysts often use the yield on long-term government bonds instead of T-bills. Like T-bills, bond yields have virtually no default risk, but they do fluctuate widely in response to changes in interest rates (i.e., due to interest rate risk), as discussed in Chapter 6. So while T-bills represent a better one-period risk-free rate (because they don't fluctuate over one period), their rates often fluctuate from one period to the next. Long-term bond rates are more representative of the rate that could be obtained over longer investment horizons.

The market risk premium, as measured by the return on the market less the long-term government bond yield over the period from 1900 to 2016 averaged 5.1 percent in developed stock markets around the world.[12] **Figure 9.11** shows the required market risk premiums according to a 2016 survey of 6,932 analysts, companies, and finance professors in 71 countries around the world. Arithmetic means of medians in five different regions were obtained. Calculated means ranged from a low of 4.7 percent in Luxembourg to a high of 15.3 percent in Venezuela.

We will discuss the process of estimating the required rate of return on a firm's common equity in greater detail when we examine the cost of capital in Chapter 20. At this point, we will briefly review how to obtain the discount rate for CP.

If, in 2019, we were to run a regression of 60 months of returns for CP on returns for the S&P/TSX Index, we would obtain an estimate of the beta coefficient equal to 1.14. However, as

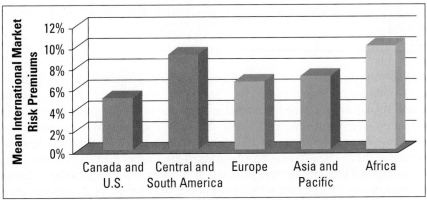

**FIGURE 9.11** Market Risk Premium Used in 71 Countries in 2016: A Survey with 6,932 Answers

**Source:** Fernandez, P., Ortiz Pizarro, A., and Fernández Acín, I., "Market Risk Premium Used in 71 Countries in 2016: A Survey with 6,932 Answers," SSRN (May 16, 2016), https://papers.ssrn.com/sol3/papers.cfm?abstract_id=2776636

[12]Dimson, E., Marsh, P., and Staunton, M., "Equity Premiums Around the World." In *Rethinking the Equity Risk Premium* (Research Foundation of the CFA Institute, December 2011); Fernandez, P., Ortiz Pizarro, A., and Fernández Acín, I., "Market Risk Premium Used in 71 countries in 2016"; and Fernandez, P., Aguirreamalloa, J., and Linares, P., "Market Risk Premium Used in 51 countries in 2013."

mentioned, beta estimates for individual stocks are always subject to some degree of estimation error. Therefore, it is common practice to also refer to industry beta estimates. Our estimate for CP is in line with the historical beta for this sector, which is typically in the range of 1 to 1.2. So to be conservative, and given that there is a case to be made that CP is an average stock and should have a beta close to that of the market as a whole, we have decided to use our low-end estimate of 1 as the beta estimate going forward; remember, we are interested in what the future beta is, and we use historical data for this purpose only (see Figure 20.7 for a series of CP estimates over time).

In 2019, the yield on long-term Government of Canada bonds over the previous five-year period was 2.9 percent, which we will use as our risk-free rate. The estimate of required market risk premiums in countries with developed markets, obtained from the survey that generated Figure 9.11, is close to 5 percent. Over time, the market risk premium has varied from 5 to 6 percent. If we first assume the low-end market risk premium, we get:

$$k_e = 2.9 + (5\%)(1) = 7.9\%$$

This is not totally unreasonable. However, if we were to use the high-end estimate of the market risk premium (6 percent), we would place the equity cost for CP at:

$$k_e = 2.9 + (6\%)(1) = 8.9\%$$

Taking a simple average of the two extremes leaves us with an estimate of:

$$k_e = (7.9\% + 8.9\%)/2 = 8.4\%$$

This is in line with the estimate obtained in Chapter 20.

## Concept Review Questions

1. Why is beta a measure of market risk for a security?
2. If a security's correlation with the market return increases, will its beta get larger or smaller?
3. What is a characteristic line, and why is it useful?
4. If the market risk premium increases, will securities become overvalued or undervalued?

## 9.4 | Alternative Asset Pricing Models

**LEARNING OBJECTIVE 9.4**

List alternative risk-based pricing models and describe how they differ from the CAPM.

The CAPM is a "single-factor" model because it suggests that the required return on equities is determined by only one risk factor: market risk. The CAPM is often criticized because it is based on several assumptions, many of which are called into question in the real world. In addition, a substantial amount of empirical evidence finds that the CAPM does not hold well in practice. In particular, although empirical estimates of the ex post SML suggest that it is indeed an upward-sloping straight line, the ex ante y-intercept has been found to be higher than *RF*, and the slope of the SML is less than that predicted by theory—that is, it is "flatter" than it should be. Although this research remains very controversial, a 1992 study of U.S. stock returns by Fama and French concluded that beta, the sole risk factor in the CAPM, possessed no explanatory power for predicting stock returns.[13] In addition, they found that two other factors (discussed in the next subsection) do a much better job of explaining common stock returns. Indeed, there is a great deal of controversy and debate about the validity of the CAPM, as discussed in Finance in the News 9.2.

[13]See Fama, E., and French, K., "The Cross Section of Expected Stock Returns." *Journal of Finance* 47 (1992), pp. 427–65.

## Benjamin Graham and Risk

Beta is a more or less useful measure of past price fluctuations of common stocks. What bothers me is that authorities now equate the beta idea with the concept of risk. Price variability yes; risk no. Real investment risk is measured not by the percent that a stock may decline in price in relation to the general market in a given period, but by the danger of a loss of quality and earnings power through economic changes or deterioration in management.

—Benjamin Graham

## Introduction

This paper draws on diverse sources, including

1. **MPT:** "Capital Ideas" by Peter Bernstein, recent articles by Harry Markowitz, William Sharpe, and Eugene Fama and Kenneth French,

2. **Benjamin Graham:** "The Intelligent Investor" by Ben Graham, and "Value Investing from Graham to Buffett and Beyond" by Bruce Greenwald et al.,

3. **Behavioural:** "Behavioural Investing" by James Montier.

This paper is not intended as another challenge to MPT—that significant body of theory consisting of mean-variance analysis (MVA) (Harry Markowitz—1952), the capital asset pricing model (CAPM) (William Sharpe—1964), and the efficient markets hypothesis (EMH) (Eugene Fama—1965).

There is already ample ongoing debate among very sophisticated commentators, including the above-noted original authors themselves, who acknowledge MPT's limitations and advocate broader perspectives. The paper is intended to discuss the MPT concept of risk, including the advice of the three original authors, discuss the value investors' concept of risk, and in conclusion, advocate the CFAI take a broader investor perspective with respect to its proposed risk management requirement. [. . .] Markowitz, Sharpe, Fama and French all suggest that alternatives to CAPM should be taught in finance courses.

## The Evidence

The above sets out the theory of beta as a measure of risk. As noted, a fairly large body of research challenges the theory. Value stocks (those with low price/earnings ratios (P/Es) and low price/book ratios (P/Bs)) have lower betas, but have higher returns than growth stocks. This is contrary to the notion that returns go hand in hand with risk—which is at the heart of MPT. Such research emerged not long after Sharpe's paper in 1964—with the first studies appearing in 1970 . . . and they are still coming. The . . . exhaustive study by Fama and French (2004) examined all NYSE, ASE, and NASDQ listed stocks between 1929 and 2003. It found there was almost no relationship between returns and beta.

As behaviouralist author James Montier says: "There is an overwhelming amount of evidence that CAPM simply does not work . . . CAPM woefully underpredicts the returns to low beta stocks and massively overestimates the returns to high beta stocks."

## Benjamin Graham and Value Investors' Concept of Risk

In addition to Benjamin Graham's quote at the very beginning, most value investors have different views on beta.

Warren Buffett says in Berkshire Hathaway's "1993 Annual Report":

We define risk, using the dictionary terms, as "the possibility of loss or injury." Academics . . . like to define investment "risk" differently, averring that it is the relative volatility of a stock or portfolio of stocks . . . compared to a large universe of stocks. Employing data bases and statistical skills, these academics compute with precision the "beta" of a stock . . . and then build . . . investment and capital allocation theories around this calculation . . . for a single statistic to measure risk . . . For the owners of a business—and that's the way we think of shareholders, the academics' definition of risk is far off the mark.

Charles Brandes says in "Value Investing Today":

Volatility is measurable, uncertainty is not . . . defining volatility as risk (as MPT does) obscures the true definition of investment risk as the possibility of losing money . . . Beta is used primarily by those who are looking at the whole market (or large numbers of stocks within it) and who don't look in detail at the fundamentals of specific companies. As I have shown for value investors, this concept is irrelevant and downright dangerous at worst.

An interesting thing about the value investor's definition of risk is that it is not a theory, nor an equation, but a common sense expression of how to avoid losing money. As Bernstein says in "Capital Ideas":

Ben Graham had devised a method for determining whether a stock is cheap or expensive. That method has stood many if not all the tests of time, but it is still not a theory. Graham told the investor what to do but said little about why his prescriptions would work.

Quite often Warren Buffett uses his investment in the Washington Post Company to explain risk. Buffett says:

Sometimes risk and reward are correlated in a positive fashion . . . the exact opposite is true in value investing. If you buy a dollar for 60 cents, it is riskier than if you buy a dollar for 40 cents, but the expectation for reward is greater in the latter case.

The Washington Post Company in 1973 was selling for $80 million in the market. At that time . . . the assets were worth $400 million, probably more. Now if the stock had declined even further to a price that made the valuation $40 million instead of $80 million, its beta would have been greater. And to people who think beta measures risk, the cheaper price would have made it look riskier. This is truly Alice in Wonderland.

## Conclusions and Recommendations

It is clear that MPT has some limitations. As noted, the theory on beta simply does not hold up well empirically. Fama and French's exhaustive study found that value stocks have lower risk but higher returns than growth stocks—a direct contradiction of MPT, and ironically, exactly what the value investors say. Helping to explain why this is so, Fama and French went on to show that the low betas of value stocks and high betas of growth stocks converge as value stocks surprise on the upside and growth stocks surprise on the downside.

On the other hand, as all three original authors say, MPT should still be taught. An example of the usefulness of the CAPM concept is: how would one explain the concept of "portable alpha" without using the CAPM concepts of alpha and beta.

The recent comments of Harry Markowitz, William Sharpe, and Eugene Fama and Kenneth French make eminent sense though. MPT is a useful, though not the only, theory that should be taught in finance courses.

I would suggest that Benjamin Graham's definition of risk is the correct one and that of MPT is not.

**Source:** Grantier, Bruce, *The CFA Institute Centre for Financial Market Integrity Proposed Risk Management Requirement, Asset Manager Code of Professional Conduct—Benjamin Graham and Risk*. Originally published by the Brandes Institute: www.brandes.com/institute. Bruce Grantier is an Advisory Board member of the Brandes Institute.

| TABLE 9.2 | Percentage of Analysts Using Various Methods to Estimate the Required Return on Common Shares | |
|---|---|---|
| CAPM | 68.2% | |
| APT | 4.8% | |
| Fama-French | 4% | |
| Bond yield plus risk premium | 42.7% | |
| Judgementally determined hurdle rate | 47.5% | |
| Other (Build up or market derived) | 6.3% | |

**Source:** Model Selection from "Valuation Methods" presentation, October 2007, produced by Tom Robinson, Ph.D., CFA, CPA, CFP®, Head, Educational Content, CFA Institute. Copyright 2007, CFA Institute. Reproduced and republished from "Valuation Methods" with permission from CFA Institute. All rights reserved. The results are based on a survey of about 13,500 CFA Institute members, 2,369 of whom accepted the invitation. Of those surveyed, 2,063 evaluate individual securities for the purpose of making an investment recommendation or portfolio decision. They were primarily buy-side investment analysts and portfolio managers. For those managing portfolios, the sample was fairly equally split between members managing institutional and individual (private wealth) portfolios.

An important theoretical problem associated with tests of the CAPM was identified by Richard Roll in 1976 and is commonly referred to as Roll's critique.[14] Roll argued that the CAPM cannot be tested empirically because the market portfolio, which consists of all risky assets, is unobservable. Therefore, researchers are forced to use market proxies, which may or may not be the optimal mean-variance efficient portfolio. In effect, Roll argued that tests of the CAPM are actually tests of the mean-variance efficiency of the chosen market portfolio. He showed that the basic CAPM results will hold whenever the chosen proxy is mean-variance efficient and will not hold if the converse is true. As a result, the empirical tests have no power.

Despite the criticisms of the CAPM, it remains, for both academics and practitioners, the most commonly used method of estimating the required rate of return on individual securities (see **Table 9.2**). Two of the other models listed (Fama-French and APT) are discussed below, while the remainder will be discussed in Chapter 20. One of the main reasons for the CAPM's staying power is its intuitive appeal for assessing the trade-off between risk and expected return, and the observation that individuals hold diversified portfolios. Further, the contenders have had at least as much difficulty as the CAPM in generating statistical support. However, in response to some of the problems associated with the CAPM, alternative asset pricing models have been developed, and two of the better-known alternatives are discussed in the next two sections. In contrast to the CAPM, both of these models are multi-factor models: they assume that more than one factor affects stock returns.

## The Fama-French Model

As mentioned in the previous section, Fama and French found that two additional factors, beyond market returns, affected stock returns. These factors are the market value of a firm's

---

[14]See Roll, R., "A Critique of the Asset Pricing Theory's Tests; Part I: On Past and Potential Testability of the Theory." *Journal of Financial Economics* 4 (1976), pp. 129–76.

common equity (MVE) and the ratio of a firm's book equity value to its market value of equity (BVE/MVE). Based on this discovery, they developed a three-factor pricing model. Like the CAPM, their model includes an overall market factor; however, it also includes MVE (which is related to firm size) and the BVE/MVE.[15]

The **Fama-French (FF) model** has become popular over the past decade because some believe it does a better job than the CAPM of explaining ex ante stock returns. For example, Ibbotson Associates, Inc., a major provider of financial information, now gives estimates of companies' required return on equity based on this model, in addition to estimates determined by the more widely recognized CAPM. However, the FF model has been criticized because it is not based on sound economic fundamentals, while the CAPM is. Further, many believe that the FF model is simply an example of "data mining," in which the data have been examined so many times that eventually some variables are bound to be discovered that explain returns better than the CAPM.

**Fama-French (FF) model** a pricing model that uses three factors (a market factor, the market value of a firm's common equity, and the ratio of a firm's book equity value to its market value of equity) to relate expected returns to risk

## The Arbitrage Pricing Theory (APT)

Another well-known multi-factor asset pricing model is the **arbitrage pricing theory (APT)**. The APT holds under very few assumptions, unlike the CAPM. In particular, the APT does not depend on the existence of an underlying market portfolio, and it allows for the possibility that several types of risk may affect security returns. In fact, APT is based on the **no-arbitrage principle**, which states that two otherwise identical assets cannot sell at different prices.

Development of the formal APT assumes that asset returns are linearly related to a set of indexes, which proxy risk factors that influence security returns. The underlying risk factors in the APT represent broad economic forces, which are unpredictable. The APT can be expressed as in Equation 9.11.

$$\boxed{ER_i = a_0 + b_{i1}F_1 + b_{i2}F_2 + \cdots + b_{in}F_n}$$ [9.11]

**arbitrage pricing theory (APT)** a pricing model that uses multiple factors to relate expected returns to risk by assuming that asset returns are linearly related to a set of indexes, which proxy risk factors that influence security returns

**no-arbitrage principle** a rule stating that two otherwise identical assets cannot sell at different prices

where

$ER_i$ = the expected return on security $i$

$a_0$ = the expected return on a security with zero systematic risk

$b_{ij}$ = the sensitivity of security $i$ to a given risk factor $j$

$F_i$ = the risk premium for a given risk factor $j$

Equation 9.11 demonstrates that a security's risk is based on its sensitivity to basic economic factors, while expected return increases proportionately to this risk. The sensitivity measures ($b_i$) play a role similar to beta in the CAPM, because they measure the relative sensitivity of a security's return to a particular risk premium. In fact, the APT would "collapse" into the CAPM if there were only one risk factor (market returns) influencing security returns.

The main problem with the APT is that the factors are not specified ahead of time. In fact, APT does not even specify the number of risk factors that exist, or state which factors will be the most important. As a result, these factors, as well as their relative importance, must be identified empirically. Most empirical evidence suggests that three to five factors influence security returns and are priced in the market. For example, Roll and Ross identify the following five systematic factors:[16]

1. changes in expected inflation

2. unanticipated changes in inflation

3. unanticipated changes in industrial production

4. unanticipated changes in the default-risk premium[17]

5. unanticipated changes in the term structure of interest rates

[15]See Fama, E., and French, K., "Size and Book-to-Market Factors in Earnings and Returns." *Journal of Finance* 50 (1995), pp. 131–55.

[16]Roll, R., and Ross, S., "An Empirical Investigation of the Arbitrage Pricing Theory." *Journal of Finance* 35, no. 5 (December 1980), pp. 1073–1103.

[17]This variable is commonly defined as the yield on long-term corporate bonds minus the yield on long-term government bonds.

---

## Concept Review Questions

1. Why is the CAPM called a single-factor model?
2. Describe some of the criticisms of the CAPM, including Roll's critique.
3. Briefly describe the strengths and weaknesses of the Fama-French model and the APT.

---

# Review

## Summary

In this chapter, we show how the efficient frontier can be expanded by introducing the possibility of risk-free borrowing and lending. Based on certain assumptions that underlie the capital asset pricing model (CAPM), we show that this new (or super) efficient frontier can be depicted as a straight line that begins at RF and is tangent to the old efficient frontier at point M, the market portfolio. This line is called the capital market line (CML) and depicts the required return for efficient portfolios based on their standard deviations.

The security market line (SML), which represents the most important contribution of the CAPM, can be derived from the CML. The SML provides a way to estimate the required return for any security or portfolio, based on its market risk, as measured by beta. Criticisms of the CAPM have led to the development of alternative asset pricing models. We conclude the chapter with a brief description of two of these models: the Fama-French model and the arbitrage pricing theory (APT).

## Summary of Learning Objectives

**9.1 Describe how the efficient frontier is affected once the possibility of risk-free borrowing and investing is introduced.**

Once the possibility of risk-free borrowing and investing is introduced, the efficient frontier becomes a straight line. The new (or super) efficient frontier portfolios are composed of the risk-free rate and the tangent portfolio that offer the highest expected rate of return for any given level of risk.

**9.2 Explain how modern portfolio theory is extended to develop the capital market line (CML).**

The "optimal" risky portfolio is the one that is tangent to the efficient frontier on a line that is drawn from RF, as shown in Figure 9.4. This portfolio will be the same for all investors. This optimal risky portfolio will be the market portfolio (M), which contains all risky securities. The value of this portfolio will equal the aggregate of the market values of all the individual assets composing it. Therefore, the weights of these assets in the market portfolio will be represented by their proportionate weight in its total value.

**9.3 Explain how the capital asset pricing model's (CAPM) security market line (SML) is developed from the capital market line (CML), and how the SML can be used to estimate the required return on individual securities and portfolios.**

Because of diversification, the individual risk can be diversified away, but the market risk remains. So the security price will finally depend on its co-movement with the market, which is measured by beta. Then CML is developed into SML. SML can be applied easily into asset pricing; see Equation 9.9.

**9.4 List alternative risk-based pricing models and describe how they differ from the CAPM.**

Alternative asset pricing models include the Fama-French model and the arbitrage pricing theory. The Fama-French model includes the market factor, value factor, and size factor, and is empirically successful. The arbitrage pricing theory introduces more factors, while CAPM has only one factor: the market portfolio.

## Key Terms

arbitrage pricing theory (APT), p. 9-23
beta ($\beta_i$), p. 9-13

capital asset pricing model (CAPM), p. 9-8
capital market line (CML), p. 9-9

characteristic line, p. 9-13
Fama-French (FF) model, p. 9-23

## Equations

| Equation | Description | Formula | Page |
|---|---|---|---|
| [9.1] | Expected Portfolio Return | $ER_p = RF + w(ER_A - RF)$ | p. 9-3 |
| [9.2] | Portfolio Standard Deviation (Risky Asset and Risk-Free Asset) | $\sigma_p = w\sigma_A$ | p. 9-3 |
| [9.3] | Expected Portfolio Return (Risky Asset and Risk-Free Asset) in Terms of Standard Deviations | $ER_p = RF + \left(\dfrac{ER_A - RF}{\sigma_A}\right)\sigma_p$ | p. 9-3 |
| [9.4] | Slope of CML | $\text{Slope of the CML} = \dfrac{ER_M - RF}{\sigma_M}$ | p. 9-9 |
| [9.5] | Capital Market Line (CML) | $ER_p = RF + \left[\dfrac{ER_M - RF}{\sigma_M}\right]\sigma_p$ | p. 9-9 |
| [9.6] | Sharpe Ratio | $\text{Sharpe ratio} = \dfrac{ER_p - RF}{\sigma_p}$ | p. 9-11 |
| [9.7] | Beta | $\beta_i = \dfrac{COV_{i,M}}{\sigma_M^2} = \dfrac{\rho_{i,M}\sigma_i}{\sigma_M}$ | p. 9-13 |
| [9.8] | Portfolio Beta | $\beta_p = w_1\beta_1 + w_2\beta_2 + \cdots + w_n\beta_n$ | p. 9-15 |
| [9.9] | Security Market Line (SML) | $k_i = RF + (ER_M - RF)\beta_i$ | p. 9-16 |
| [9.10] | Alpha | $\alpha_i = (R_i - RF) - [\beta_i(R_M - RF)]$ | p. 9.18 |
| [9.11] | Arbitrage Pricing Theory (APT) | $ER_i = a_0 + b_{i1}F_1 + b_{i2}F_2 + \cdots + b_{in}F_n$ | p. 9.23 |

# Questions and Practice Problems

## Multiple Choice Questions

**1. (LO 9.1)** What is the expected return and standard deviation of a portfolio consisting of $7,500 invested in a risk-free asset with an 8-percent rate of return, and $2,500 invested in a risky security with a 20-percent rate of return and a 25-percent standard deviation?

  **a.** 11 percent, 6.25 percent

  **b.** 17 percent, 18.75 percent

  **c.** 6.25 percent, 11 percent

  **d.** 18.75 percent, 17 percent

**2. (LO 9.1)** Which of the following statements is *correct*?

  **a.** The new efficient frontier is a curved line similar to the original efficient frontier.

  **b.** All the portfolios along the new efficient frontier dominate those along the original efficient frontier including the tangency portfolio.

  **c.** The weight of the risk-free asset is positive in calculating expected return when investors buy stocks on margin.

  **d.** Investors who are more risk averse invest to the left of the tangent portfolio.

**3. (LO 9.2)** What is the standard deviation of an efficient portfolio with a 16-percent expected rate of return, given that $RF$ is 4 percent, $ER_M$ is 10 percent, and $\sigma_M$ is 30 percent?

  **a.** 50 percent

  **b.** 20 percent

  **c.** 60 percent

  **d.** 120 percent

**4. (LO 9.3)** Which of the following statements is *false*?

   **a.** The standard deviation of a risk-free asset is zero.

   **b.** Portfolios on the efficient frontier dominate all other attainable portfolios for a given risk or return.

   **c.** The covariance of any combination of a risky security and a risk-free asset is zero.

   **d.** The risk measurement associated with the security market line (SML) is the standard deviation of the portfolio.

**5. (LO 9.3)** If portfolio A lies above the SML, portfolio A is

   **a.** overvalued.

   **b.** undervalued.

   **c.** properly valued.

   **d.** undetermined.

**6. (LO 9.3)** All of the following are differences between the CML and SML, except

   **a.** the slope.

   **b.** the risk measurement.

   **c.** the *y*-intercept.

   **d.** the application to the required return on individual securities.

**7. (LO 9.3)** A portfolio with a beta greater than one is

   **a.** more volatile than the market.

   **b.** less volatile than the market.

   **c.** as volatile as the market.

   **d.** not volatile.

**8. (LO 9.2, 9.3)** Which of the following statements are *true*:

   **i.** The excess return on an investment (over and above the risk free rate) is equal to its Beta ($\beta$) multiplied by the market risk premium according to the Capital Asset Pricing Model (CAPM).

   **ii.** The security market line (SML) is a graph of the expected return of a security as a function of systematic risk (Beta).

   **iii.** The equity (or market) risk premium can be estimated by calculating historical average excess returns of the market portfolio above the prevailing risk-free rate.

   **a.** i only

   **b.** i and ii

   **c.** ii and iii

   **d.** all of the statements

**9. (LO 9.3)** Which of the following statements is *false*?

   **a.** Systematic risk cannot be diversified away.

   **b.** The market portfolio includes all risky assets including stocks, bonds, real estate, derivatives, and so on.

   **c.** The market portfolio is observable.

   **d.** The *y*-intercept of both the SML and the CML is *RF*.

**10. (LO 9.3)** Systematic risk (beta)

   **a.** is also called unique risk.

   **b.** equals total risk divided by non-systematic risk.

   **c.** estimates do not change through time.

   **d.** measures of portfolios are more stable than those of individual assets.

## Practice Problems

### Basic

**11. (LO 9.1)** For the following decisions, indicate if they are consistent with risk aversion or risk loving.

   **a.** Buying a lottery ticket

   **b.** Buying fire insurance on your house

   **c.** Jaywalking on St. Catherine Street in Montreal

   **d.** Backing up your computer

**12. (LO 9.1)** Today, you observe the market portfolio has an expected return of 13 percent, with a standard deviation of 7 percent. The risk-free rate is 2 percent. If only the risk-free rate increases (i.e., there are no changes to the expected risk and returns of the risky securities), will the composition of the market portfolio change? Will the expected risk and return on the market portfolio change? Explain your reasoning.

**13. (LO 9.2)** State three of the assumptions underlying the capital asset pricing model (CAPM).

**14. (LO 9.2)** How do you determine if a portfolio or security is undervalued, correctly valued, or overvalued?

**15. (LO 9.3)** What is the beta of the following?

   **a.** Risk-free asset

   **b.** Market portfolio

**16. (LO 9.3)** If a security's total risk (variance) increases, does that mean the beta must have increased? Explain.

**17. (LO 9.3)** What would motivate an investor to invest in a stock whose beta is negative, implying its expected return is less than the risk-free rate?

**18. (LO 9.2)** Which security, A, B, or C, will provide the greatest return per unit of risk when combined with the risk-free asset with a 5-percent rate of return?

$$ER_A = 20 \text{ percent}, \sigma_A = 5 \text{ percent}$$
$$ER_B = 25 \text{ percent}, \sigma_B = 10 \text{ percent}$$
$$ER_C = 30 \text{ percent}, \sigma_C = 15 \text{ percent}$$

**19. (LO 9.3)** The current price of a stock is $20. It is expected to rise to $22 in one year and pay an annual dividend of $1 during the year. The *RF* is 4 percent, the $ER_M$ is 10 percent, and the stock's beta is 1.6. Determine whether the stock is overvalued, undervalued, or properly valued. Is the stock above, below, or on the SML?

**20. (LO 9.3)** The idea behind CAPM is that investors should not be compensated for diversifiable risk. Why not?

**21. (LO 9.3)** The risk-free rate is 5 percent, the risk premium is 6 percent, and stock A has an expected return of 15.5 percent. What is the beta of stock A?

**22. (LO 9.4)** State Roll's critique concerning the CAPM.

### Intermediate

**23. (LO 9.1)** Jackie borrowed $1,000 at the risk-free rate of 6 percent. She invested the borrowed money and her own money of $2,500 in a portfolio with a 15-percent rate of return and a 25-percent standard deviation. What is the expected return and standard deviation of her portfolio?

**24. (LO 9.2)** Calculate the missing values for the following five efficient portfolios. The expected return on the market is 8 percent, with a standard deviation of 5 percent, and the risk-free rate is 2 percent.

| Portfolio | Expected Return | Standard Deviation | Sharpe Ratio | Required Rate of Return |
|---|---|---|---|---|
| Portfolio 1 | 14% | 9% | | |
| Portfolio 2 | 10% | 7% | | |
| Portfolio 3 | 12% | 8% | | |
| Portfolio 4 | 9% | 5% | | |
| Portfolio 5 | 6% | 4% | | |

**25. (LO 9.3)** TrenStar Inc. obtained the following incomplete information from ABC Company and has given you the task of completing the table.

| | Security 1 Beta | Security 2 Beta | Weight in Security 1 | Portfolio Beta |
|---|---|---|---|---|
| Case 1 | 0.5 | 1.5 | 0.4 | |
| Case 2 | | 0.65 | 0.5 | 1.3 |
| Case 3 | 1.1 | 1.9 | | 2.1 |
| Case 4 | 1.25 | 0.8 | 0.75 | |
| Case 5 | 1.3 | | 0.2 | 3 |

**26. (LO 9.3)** Stock FM has a standard deviation of 28 percent and a correlation coefficient of 0.7 with market returns. The standard deviation of market return is 16 percent, and the expected return is 13.5 percent. The risk-free rate is 4.5 percent.

    **a.** What is the beta of stock FM?

    **b.** What is the required rate of return of stock FM by the CAPM model?

    **c.** Compare FM's required return to the expected market return. What causes the difference?

**27. (LO 9.3)** Estimate the beta of the following stock: market risk premium = 25 percent, $RF$ = 6 percent, $P_0$ = $10, expected dividend at the end of the year = $2.50, $P$ = $12.50. Assume the market is in equilibrium.

**28. (LO 9.3)** You are following five different stocks and need to issue a recommendation (buy, hold, or sell) to your customers. The market return is 10 percent, with a standard deviation of 15 percent. The risk-free rate is 3 percent. The CAPM is assumed to hold.

| Security | Expected Return | Standard Deviation | Beta | Recommendation |
|---|---|---|---|---|
| ABC | 15% | 19% | 1.6 | |
| RTS | 10% | 13% | 1.15 | |
| DKF | 8% | 10% | 0.65 | |
| OPL | 9% | 14% | 0.8 | |
| WEQ | 12% | 16% | 1.35 | |

To determine the recommendations, begin by calculating the required returns for each security using the CAPM. Comparing the expected and required returns will indicate which securities are underpriced, overpriced, or correctly priced.

**29. (LO 9.3)** You are valuing Vancouver Rain-Making Company (VRM) and need to calculate the following:

    **a.** Required rate of return (assume the market risk premium is 8 percent, the risk-free rate is 3 percent, and the beta is 1.28)

    **b.** Price of VRM based on the current dividend of $1.50 and a dividend growth rate of 5 percent

**30. (LO 9.3)** Which of the following are examples of systematic (market) risks? Which are examples of unsystematic (unique) risks?

    **a.** Inflation risk

    **b.** CFO's fraudulent activities

    **c.** Changes in interest rates

    **d.** Product tampering

    **e.** Political risk

    **f.** CEO's aversion to working on Fridays

**31. (LO 9.3)** Suppose you have a portfolio that has $100 in stock A with a beta of 0.9, $400 in stock B with a beta of 1.2, and $300 in the risk-free asset. You have another $200 to invest. You wish to achieve a beta for your whole portfolio to be the same as the market beta. What is the beta of the added security? Give an example of a firm that may have such a beta.

**32. (LO 9.3)** Portfolio A has a beta of 0.82. Portfolio B has a beta of 1.05. $RF$ is 3 percent and the market risk premium is 6 percent. Calculate the required rate of return of A and B. If the expected rate of return for both portfolio A and B is 8.5 percent, what investment strategy should apply?

**33. (LO 9.3)** Determine the beta of QTax based on the following information:

    • Market expected return is 9 percent; standard deviation is 12 percent

    • Risk-free rate is 3 percent

    • Current dividend is $4

    • Dividend growth rate is 4 percent

    • Current stock price is $32

**34. (LO 9.3)** Assuming CAPM is valid, can we have a situation where stock A has a required rate of return of 15 percent and a beta of 1.4, and stock B has a required rate of return of 20 percent and beta of 1.2?

**35. (LO 9.3)** Stock A has a beta of 1.8 and an expected return of 20 percent. Stock B has a beta of 1.2 and an expected return of 14 percent. If CAPM holds, what should the return on the market and the risk-free rate be?

**36. (LO 9.3)** The expected return on stock A is 15 percent. The expected return on stock B is 9 percent. Assuming CAPM holds, if the beta of stock A is higher than the beta of stock B by 0.4, what should the risk premium be?

**37. (LO 9.3)** The variance of the market returns is 0.0576, and the covariance of the returns on ABC stock and the market is 0.09504. If the risk-free rate is 5 percent and the market risk premium is 8 percent, what is the required rate of return of ABC?

**38. (LO 9.3)** You invested $100,000 in the following stocks:

| Stock | Amount | Beta |
|---|---|---|
| ABC | $20,000 | 0.8 |
| DEF | $30,000 | 1.2 |
| GHI | $15,000 | 1.35 |
| JKL | $35,000 | 1.15 |

If the risk-free rate is 5 percent and the market risk premium is 8 percent, what is the expected return on your portfolio?

**39. (LO 9.4)** Four risk factors, $F_1$, $F_2$, $F_3$, and $F_4$, have been identified to determine the required rate of return, as follows: $ER_i = a_0 + b_{i1}F_1 + b_{i2}F_2 + b_{i3}F_3 + b_{i4}F_4$, where $a_0$, is the expected return on a security with zero systematic risk. Calculate the required rate of return of a portfolio where $b_{i1}$, $b_{i2}$, $b_{i3}$, and $b_{i4}$ are 0.4, 0.7, 0.8, and 1.2, respectively; $RF$ = 4 percent; $F_1$ = 12 percent; $F_2$ = 6 percent; $F_3$ = 10 percent; and $F_4$ = 8 percent.

## Challenging

**40. (LO 9.1)** TrenStar Inc. is planning to offer several investments to investors and is in the process of designing its marketing materials. Each investment's value in the future will be related to the return on the S&P/TSX Composite Index over the year. The cost and value of the investments are outlined as follows:

| | | Value of Investment if: | |
|---|---|---|---|
| Investment | Cost Today | S&P/TSX Return < 0% | S&P/TSX Return > 0% |
| A | $7 | $ 0 | $15 |
| B | $12 | $15 | $15 |
| C | $9 | $20 | $ 0 |
| D | $0 | −$10 | $10 |
| E | $0 | $10 | −$10 |

Assume that the probability of the S&P/TSX falling (i.e., having a return less than 0 percent) is 40 percent and that the risk-free rate is zero. Risk-averse investors are willing to invest in a risky undertaking only if the expected value is sufficiently greater than the cost. Which investments will be preferred by a risk-averse investor? Explain your reasoning.

**41. (LO 9.1)** TrenStar Inc. has five clients with different risk and return preferences. The market portfolio has an expected return of 12 percent, with a standard deviation of 16 percent. The risk-free rate is 4 percent. Each client has $2,500 to invest. Fill in the missing information in the following table.

| Investor | Weight in Risk-Free Asset | $ Amount Invested in Risk-Free Asset | Expected Portfolio Return | Portfolio Standard Deviation |
|---|---|---|---|---|
| Charles | 25% | | | |
| Sonja | | Borrowed $1,000 | | |
| Fritz | | | 9% | |
| Eddy | | | 25% | |
| Nellie | | | | 6% |

**42. (LO 9.1)** A lawyer prosecuting a lawsuit against The Brokerage Company has hired you to conduct an investigation into the advice the company has been giving its clients. You observe that clients have invested in the following portfolios:

| Investor | Portfolio | Expected Return | Standard Deviation |
|---|---|---|---|
| Charles | A | 2% | 0.4% |
| Rina | B | 4% | 0.6% |
| Xiang | C | 5% | 0.3% |
| Amanda | D | 7% | 0.5% |
| Amir | E | 9% | 0.45% |
| Geeta | F | 10% | 0.7% |

Evaluate the advice The Brokerage Company has been giving its clients. (Assume that investors can invest only in one of the six portfolios.)

a. Evaluate the investors who are holding inefficient portfolios.

i. Which investors are holding inefficient portfolios? Examine it by a graph with standard deviation on the x-axis and expected return on the y-axis.

ii. The broker under investigation argues that these portfolios are appropriate because the investors are risk loving. Are inefficient portfolios appropriate for risk-loving investors?

b. Use return/risk to evaluate the investors who are holding efficient portfolios. Who is

i. the most risk averse?

ii. the least risk averse?

**43. (LO 9.1)** Three of your friends (Jean, Evan, and Lee) are having an argument about investments and, because you have taken this course, have come to you for advice. The possible investments are set out in the following table. (Assume you cannot mix risky investments.)

| Risky Portfolio | Expected Returns | Standard Deviation |
|---|---|---|
| A | 8% | 5% |
| B | 13% | 7% |
| C | 17% | 11% |

Jean says they should all invest in portfolio A because it has the lowest risk. Evan says they should all invest in portfolio C because it has the highest return. Lee is just confused.

a. If there is no risk-free asset, can you recommend the same portfolio for each of the friends? Why or why not?

b. If the expected risk-free rate is 2 percent, can you recommend the same set of risky assets for each of the friends? Why or why not?

c. Use Equation 9.3 to complete the table below and plot it.

| Standard Deviation | Portfolio of RF + A Expected Return | Portfolio of RF + B Expected Return | Portfolio of RF + C Expected Return |
|---|---|---|---|
| 0 | | | |
| 0.01 | | | |
| 0.02 | | | |
| 0.03 | | | |
| 0.04 | | | |
| 0.05 | | | |
| 0.06 | | | |
| 0.07 | | | |
| 0.08 | | | |
| 0.09 | | | |
| 0.10 | | | |
| 0.11 | | | |
| 0.12 | | | |

d. Does the existence of a risk-free asset make the friends better off? Explain your reasoning.

**44. (LO 9.3)** Obtain monthly returns for BlackBerry, the Royal Bank of Canada, and the S&P/TSX Composite Index for January to December 2018. (Note: Monthly historical prices, adjusted for dividends, are available from http://ca.finance.yahoo.com. To obtain the data, go to the website and search using the ticker symbol, BB.TO.)

a. Which firm do you expect to have a larger beta? Explain your reasoning.

b. Calculate the beta for each company.

c. Create a portfolio consisting of 50 percent in BlackBerry and 50 percent in Royal Bank.

i. Calculate the monthly returns for the portfolio and calculate the beta of the portfolio using those monthly returns.

ii. Using Equation 9.8, calculate the beta of the portfolio.

iii. Compare the two betas.

**45. (LO 9.2, 9.3)** Your client is confused. He owns shares in Whistler Snow-Making Company (WSMC) and wants you to explain your recommendation. Both of you agree on the following: WSMC has an expected return of 12 percent, a standard deviation of 9 percent, and a beta of 1.25; the expected return on the market is 8 percent, with standard deviation of 3 percent; and the risk-free rate is 4 percent.

Your client has a basic understanding of the CAPM and, based on the capital market line, feels he should sell the stock. However, you are recommending that he buy more of the stock (or at least hold what he has). Explain your recommendation to your client.

**46. (LO 9.2, 9.3)** Consider the following data for the stock returns of companies ABC and DEF:

| Stock | Beta | Standard Deviation | Covariance with Market Returns |
|-------|------|--------------------|--------------------------------|
| ABC   | ?    | 45%                | 0.0154                         |
| DEF   | 1.45 | 40%                | ?                              |

The expected return on the market index is 15% and the risk-free rate is 3.5%. Assume both stocks are priced correctly according to the CAPM.

**a.** Suppose the standard deviation of the market portfolio is 20%. What is the beta of stock ABC and the correlation coefficient of stock DEF with the market portfolio?

**b.** Suppose you wanted to form a portfolio using only stocks ABC and DEF that had the exact same expected return as the market. What fraction of your investment would need to be in ABC and what fraction in DEF?

**c.** Assuming the portfolio you constructed in part (b) has a standard deviation of 36.53%, comment on whether the portfolio or the market portfolio has a better risk-return trade-off?

**47. (LO 9.3)** You are forecasting the returns for PVC Company, a plumbing supply company, which pays a current dividend of $10. The dividend is expected to grow at a rate of 3 percent. You have identified two public companies, ABC and VJK, which appear to be comparable to PVC. ABC has the same total risk as PVC and a beta of 1.2. VJK, in contrast, has a very different total risk but the same market risk as PVC. VJK's beta is 0.75. The market risk premium is 5 percent and the risk-free rate is 1 percent.

**a.** Determine the required return for PVC using the appropriate beta.

**b.** Determine the price of PVC.

# Market Efficiency

**LEARNING OBJECTIVES**

After studying this chapter, you should be able to:

**10.1** Explain what market efficiency is and why it is important.

**10.2** Differentiate among the different levels of efficiency.

**10.3** Discuss the general consensus based on empirical evidence of market efficiency, as well as the existence of some well-known anomalies.

**10.4** Differentiate between behavioural finance and the traditional view of finance.

**10.5** Explain the implications of market efficiency.

In a statement made near the end of 2007, James Cayne, former CEO of Bear Stearns, blamed the company's fall on market irrationality, and there is no doubt investor panic contributed to the collapse. On the other hand, the head of the Financial Crisis Commission pointed to several valid risks and warning signs that led to the investment bank's decline, so one could argue that market participants had several good reasons to dump Bear Stearns stock. Indeed, never has the concept of market efficiency been more severely criticized by its detractors than it has been over the early part of this century, as stock markets, corporate bond markets, structured debt product markets, etc. have experienced unprecedented declines and associated levels of volatility. A number of high-profile finance professionals (legendary investors, Nobel laureates, etc.) have lined up on different sides of this issue, which attests to its importance. In addition, this debate has been fuelled by the rapid rise to prominence of the theory of behavioural finance, which challenges many of the key assumptions underlying market efficiency and many other theories of finance.

An understanding of these topics is critical for students of finance and financial professionals. In fact, market efficiency is central to most of the topics in finance. For example, the capital asset pricing model, which was discussed in Chapter 9, is based on the notion that markets are efficient, as are most of the theories and processes discussed throughout this textbook. In Chapter 10, we will examine some of the evidence on the issue and discuss the implications that arise for investors and businesses.

## 10.1 Defining Market Efficiency

**LEARNING OBJECTIVE 10.1**

Explain what market efficiency is and why it is important.

In chapters 5 to 9, we discussed valuing different types of securities and estimating discount rates or required rates of return. We did this because, in corporate finance, firms have to know what investors want when they invest in a firm's securities, which is why discount rates are also called required rates of return. Once a firm knows what investors want, it can then make decisions that increase the value of those securities and enhance shareholder value. Never forget that firms have owners, and it is a legal requirement, as well as managerial responsibility, that managers act in the owners' best interests. Correctly estimating discount rates is only part of the process. A second important element is whether or not market prices reflect the actions of managers. This introduces the question of market efficiency.

An **efficient market** is one in which the prices of all securities accurately reflect all relevant and available information about the securities. This definition implies that security prices, as determined in the capital markets, are "correct." In other words, the current price of a common share reflects all known information, both past and present, about the firm, including information about a company's earnings, financial strength, management strengths and weaknesses, and future plans as announced through press releases and the management discussion and analysis (MD&A) in its financial statements. As discussed in Chapter 7, prices will reflect rational expectations about what will happen in the future and will therefore mirror today's beliefs about future interest rate changes, future profits, potential mergers, and so on. Events that cause these beliefs about the future to change will have a corresponding impact on today's prices.

Several conditions must exist before markets can operate efficiently. One critical condition is integrity of the market, such that all market participants are treated fairly. This requirement is the reason that such a heavy emphasis is placed on **disclosure**: the revelation of all material facts so that everyone in the market is buying and selling based on the same disclosed material facts about the firm.

A lack of disclosure is one reason that "black markets," or smaller and more loosely regulated markets, tend to be less efficient and that the prices in these markets do not accurately reflect available information. In this case, information is either not disclosed, is disclosed late, or is disclosed in such a way that not all market participants are aware of what is going on. Information disclosure is an important part of **securities law**, and significant attention is devoted to maintaining and enforcing capital market regulations designed to ensure that all investors have equal access to, and an equal opportunity to react to, new and relevant information.[1] For example, insider trading laws prevent "insiders" from acting on private information before that information is made public.[2]

The technical definition of market efficiency suggests that market prices are *always* correct, which requires *instantaneous* and *perfect* price adjustments in response to the arrival of new information in the marketplace. This type of efficiency is not a practical reality; however, efficient markets do react quickly and relatively accurately to new information, and therefore prices are correct *on average*. This is a reasonable definition of an efficient market. We can expand on this logic and note that market efficiency is a matter of degree. In other words, more efficient markets process information faster and more accurately than do inefficient ones; therefore, the prices in these efficient markets are closer to the true values.

**efficient market** a market that reacts quickly and relatively accurately to new public information, which results in prices that are correct on average

**disclosure** the revelation of all material facts so that everyone in the market is buying and selling based on the same material facts about the firm

**securities law** the body of law that ensures, through capital market regulations, that all investors have equal access to, and an equal opportunity to react to, new and relevant information; the body of law that governs the buying and selling of securities

## Assumptions Underlying Market Efficiency

The following assumptions underlie the existence of efficient markets:

1. There are a large number of rational, profit-maximizing investors who actively participate in the market by analyzing, valuing, and trading securities. The markets are assumed to be competitive, which means that no one investor can significantly affect the price of a security.

---

[1] Securities law in Canada is a provincial responsibility. There has been considerable discussion about whether Canada needs a national regulator, but at the moment, critical provinces are unwilling to give up their responsibilities. As a result, information must be disclosed and securities registered in most provinces separately. However, there is a forum for coordination across the provinces, and increasingly *national* policies are being developed.

[2] Several definitions exist for "insiders." We suggest the use of a broad definition that includes any party that has access to private information about a security as a result of a special relationship with the underlying entity. For example, this would include anyone who sat on the board of directors for a corporation, as well as that company's officers, lawyers, bankers, and so on.

**2.** Information is costless and widely available to market participants at the same time.

**3.** Information arrives randomly; therefore, announcements are not related to one another.

**4.** Investors react quickly and fully to the new information, which is reflected in stock prices.

Although these conditions are stringent, and are not met in the strictest sense in the real world, they are not unreasonable today. A large number of market participants actively follow the prices of securities trading in the market and devour information that may affect these prices. For example, all the major investment banks have securities analysts whose job is to monitor companies and regularly report on their value through earnings forecasts and buy/sell/hold recommendations. These analysts are called **sell-side analysts**, because they work for the investment banks that underwrite and sell securities to the public. In chapters 1 and 2, we saw that there are many institutions in the Canadian capital market that invest in securities, such as insurance companies, mutual funds, and pension funds. These institutions also employ securities analysts to evaluate the research and recommendations produced by the sell-side analysts. Because these institutions buy securities, their analysts are commonly referred to as **buy-side analysts**.

With all these analysts following firms, we might expect prices to be rationally based on available information and economic fundamentals. In addition, there is an abundance of free or inexpensive information available about most actively traded securities; some would even argue that an overabundance of such information makes it difficult to separate the wheat from the chaff. This information generally arrives randomly and is not predictable. If it were predictable, the prices would already reflect the information. Therefore, it is reasonable to assume that markets could be efficient. However, whether they are efficient is another matter, as the assumptions above may hold to various degrees.

**sell-side analysts** securities analysts whose job is to monitor companies and regularly report on their value through earnings forecasts and buy/sell/hold recommendations; they work for the investment banks that underwrite and sell securities to the public

**buy-side analysts** securities analysts whose job is to evaluate the research and recommendations produced by the sell-side analysts; they work for institutions in the capital market that invest in securities

## The Historical Development of Market Efficiency

The assumption most commonly under attack is the belief that investors are rational. The argument, espoused by former Bear Stearns CEO James Cayne, is that analysts and market participants are human and may not process information rationally or efficiently. For example, "group think" may take over and, to paraphrase John Maynard Keynes, one of the greatest economists of the 20th century, it may be better to fail conventionally than succeed unconventionally.[3] It is indicative that Keynes's seminal work was published in 1936, after the great stock market crash and during the worst of the Great Depression, when financial economists were questioning the efficient functioning of markets, just as they do today. For example, Keynes noted:

> It might have been supposed that competition between expert professionals, possessing judgment and knowledge beyond that of the average private investor, would correct the vagaries of the ignorant individual left to himself. It happens, however, that the energies and skill of the professional investor and speculator are mainly occupied otherwise. For most of these persons are, in fact, largely concerned, not with making superior long-term forecasts of the probable yield of an investment over its whole life, but with foreseeing changes in the conventional basis of valuation a short time ahead of the general public. They are concerned, not with what an investment is really worth to a man who buys it "for keeps," but with what the market will value it at, under the influence of mass psychology, three months or a year hence.[4]

Apart from the fact that Keynes was a great investor and substantially increased the endowment of his college at Cambridge University in England, he raised the basic question of whether or not the actions of many specialist investors and analysts made the stock market more or less efficient. Keynes was under no illusions: he believed that their actions

---

[3]A common axiom used to be "No one ever got fired for buying IBM," either the computers or the stock. In fact, the argument that "everyone else is doing it," backed by extensive reports from respected security analysts, is very powerful.

[4]One of the best discussions of the role of information in the stock market remains Chapter 12, "The State of Long-Term Expectations," of Keynes's *The General Theory of Employment, Interest and Money* (London: Macmillan, 1936), pp. 147–64. Keynes invented what is now called macroeconomics.

destabilized markets. Further, he believed that the stock market should have high transaction costs—that is, it should be *operationally inefficient*—in order to keep out small investors who didn't know what they were doing and contributed to stock market instability.[5]

Keynes's view, in part, reflected the fact that he was writing in the 1930s, just after the stock market crash of 1929.[6] However, it was a common belief: Bernard Baruch, a prominent U.S. investor in the 1920s, reportedly exited the U.S. stock market just before the crash after hearing elevator boys talking about which stocks to invest in. However, as the memories of 1929 and its aftermath receded, the notion that speculation or the actions of specialist investors were stabilizing took hold again, essentially producing a return to the pre-Keynesian belief that markets were inherently stable.

In this view, if prices are pushed up too high, then other experts will sell the stocks, driving prices down to an equilibrium level. This is the basic idea we discussed in Chapter 9 in the context of the market portfolio, and it is the dominant view in finance. However, the Internet bubble of the 1990s, the stock market crash of 2000, and the global collapse of stock and credit markets during 2008 again had people questioning investor rationality, the stabilizing role of professional investors, and market efficiency in general. Academics who study finance and markets have rediscovered the idea that there are limits to arbitrage and that speculation can be destabilizing. The result is a field of financial thought known as *behavioural finance*, which suggests that investors make systematic mistakes in both their processing of information and their investing activities. We will discuss this topic in more detail later in the chapter.

Before we discuss the different levels of market efficiency, and the related empirical evidence, we should note a theoretical impediment to market efficiency known as the Grossman-Stiglitz paradox. Grossman and Stiglitz argued that markets can never be fully efficient. If they were, then all prices would be correct and would reflect all available information. Under this scenario, investors could realize no added value by conducting any type of information gathering or analysis, since prices would already reflect such information. Of course, the paradox is that if nobody has any incentive to gather and process information about security values, how can the prices reflect this information? However, not even the most ardent supporter of market efficiency would expect the market to be completely efficient. Hence, the key insight of the Grossman-Stiglitz argument lies in its message regarding the costs of information gathering and processing. It suggests that market participants will exert efforts to obtain and analyze information up to the point where the marginal benefits obtained from this process equal the associated marginal costs. Presumably, the more inefficient the market, the larger the potential benefits will be, since it is less likely that all information will be fully and properly reflected in market prices.

## The Components of Market Efficiency

**operational efficiency**
a market condition in which transaction costs are low

**allocational efficiency**
a market condition in which there are enough securities to efficiently allocate risk

**informational efficiency**
a market condition in which important information is reflected in share prices

There are three components to market efficiency. The first is **operational efficiency**. When a market is operationally efficient, it means that transaction costs are low. If it is too expensive to trade securities, it will be difficult for firms to raise capital, and investment will be lower than it should be. The second component is **allocational efficiency**. This means that there are enough securities to efficiently allocate risk. For example, a capital market in which firms can issue only short-term notes would not be very efficient, even if transaction costs were low. These two types of efficiency are important for Canadian capital markets but are not the main concern in this chapter. For now, take it as a given that the Canadian markets have a broad array of financial securities, from short-term treasury bills to common shares and what we will later call hybrids, and these are issued at relatively low cost. So on most criteria, the Canadian capital markets are both operationally and allocationally efficient. What is important in this chapter is whether the markets have **informational efficiency**.

---

[5]This idea was resurrected in the 1990s in the form of the "Tobin tax," which was a transaction tax suggested by James Tobin of Yale University to reduce short-term speculation.
[6]Some suggest that it took investors 30 years to get back to the price level of 1929, while others say that it took 25 years to fully recover losses, and still others believe that it was less than 5 years when dividends and deflation are considered. In any case, there is reason to conclude that many investors ignored the stock market throughout the 1930s and perhaps through the war years as well.

If managers make decisions that they think should increase market values—for example, if they decide to introduce a new product—they will call a press conference and announce the details. Investors will then analyze the information in the announcement, and market prices will likely increase. The managers will have the satisfaction of knowing that their owners (the shareholders) reacted positively to their decision. However, if share prices are chaotic (this is actually a technical term that means, loosely, that share prices reflect past actions in a predictable way that is magnified many times), they will not reflect the information in the press announcement; they will reflect these other past actions. If this occurs, managers will have no idea whether their owners agree or disagree with their decisions.

For shareholder value maximization to mean anything, there has to be a connection between the decisions made by managers and the level of share prices. In this way, share prices are like a score sheet used to evaluate management. The closer the link between the actions of managers and this score sheet, the more informationally efficient the capital market. It is therefore critical, in corporate finance, to understand how informationally efficient the capital market, and particularly the stock market, is. In this chapter, we will drop the adjective "informational" before references to "efficiency," because our focus is entirely on how to assess whether or not important information is reflected in share prices.

In Chapter 17, we will discuss the basics of securities regulation in Canada. However, the key element is that all **material facts** should be disclosed to the capital market. Material facts are anything that can be expected to affect the share price. In the previous example, we mentioned a press conference. In Ontario, it is a legal requirement for a firm to divulge material facts through a press release that is then filed with the securities commission.[7] If all material facts are disclosed to the stock market, managers should be able to see how good the score sheet is or, in other words, how efficient the capital markets are.

> **material facts**   anything that can be expected to affect the share price

We conclude this section by noting that it remains an open question as to how informationally efficient the capital markets are.[8] We will elaborate on this debate in the sections that follow and discuss some of the empirical evidence.

---

### Concept Review Questions

1. Define market efficiency in terms of information.
2. Discuss the reasonableness of the assumptions underlying market efficiency.
3. Distinguish from among operational efficiency, informational efficiency, and allocational efficiency.

---

## 10.2   The Efficient Market Hypothesis (EMH)

### LEARNING OBJECTIVE 10.2
Differentiate among the different levels of efficiency.

The **efficient market hypothesis (EMH)** states that markets are efficient. Therefore, in its strictest sense, it implies that prices accurately reflect *all* available information at any point in time. This statement goes well beyond our "weaker" definition of efficient markets, proposed in the previous section, where we said that prices in efficient markets are correct *on average*.

> **efficient market hypothesis (EMH)**   the theory that markets are efficient and, therefore, that prices accurately reflect all available information at any given time

---

[7]In other provinces, such as British Columbia, for example, the firm has to disclose material facts in a different way, such as by filing a material change form with the provincial securities commission.

[8]The equivalent of Bernard Baruch's elevator boys was the proliferation of day traders in the 1990s. These people gave up their full-time jobs to trade in and out of securities within the day.

Because the strictest form of the EMH represents such a high hurdle, it is common to break the EMH down into the following three different, and cumulative, levels, based on the extent to which prices reflect different types of available information:

**weak form EMH** the theory that security prices fully reflect all market data, which refers to all past price and volume trading information

1. The **weak form EMH** states that security prices fully reflect *all market data*, which refers to all past price and volume trading information. If markets are weak form efficient, historical trading data will already be reflected in current prices and should be of no value in predicting future price changes. In particular, weak form EMH implies that looking at graphs of previous stock prices is of no value. Consequently, technical trading rules based on "patterns" observed in previous prices should be of no value.

**semi-strong form EMH** the theory that all publicly known and available information, including market data, is reflected in security prices

2. The **semi-strong form EMH** states that *all publicly known and available information* is reflected in security prices. This includes information about earnings, dividends, corporate investments, management changes, and so on. It would also include market data, which are publicly available. Therefore, this version of the EMH encompasses the weak form. In other words, if a market is semi-strong form efficient, then it must also be weak form efficient. A market that quickly incorporates all publicly available information into its prices is semi-strong form efficient. Semi-strong form EMH implies that it is futile to analyze publicly available information, such as financial statements, in an attempt to identify underpriced or overpriced securities; similarly, buying "undervalued" stocks based on P/E ratios or dividend yields is of no value.

**strong form EMH** the theory that stock prices fully reflect all information, which includes both public and private information

3. The **strong form EMH** asserts that stock prices fully reflect *all information*, which includes both public and private information. It is obviously the most stringent form of market efficiency, and it encompasses both the weak and semi-strong versions, because market data and all other publicly available information must be reflected in prices, as well as any private information that is possessed by some market participants but not by all. Strong form EMH implies that no investor can take advantage even of "inside" information that has not yet been released to the stock market. In this case, the possession of superior information or the superior processing of information to identify mispriced securities is not possible, since the prices already properly reflect all information. Obviously, this is a very strong assertion. The role of inside information and market efficiency is discussed later in the chapter in Ethics and Corporate Governance 10.1.

---

**Concept Review Questions**

1. Explain the efficient market hypothesis (EMH).
2. Describe the various forms of the EMH.

---

## 10.3 | Empirical Evidence Regarding Market Efficiency

**LEARNING OBJECTIVE 10.3**
Discuss the general consensus based on empirical evidence of market efficiency, as well as the existence of some well-known anomalies.

A perfectly efficient market is one in which all information is reflected in stock prices quickly and fully. Therefore, all security prices equal their true economic (or intrinsic) value. In practice, not even the strongest supporters of the EMH would claim that markets are perfectly efficient, so it becomes a matter of degree—in other words, exactly how efficient are the markets?

Empirical tests of market efficiency tend to be organized around how market prices react to certain kinds of information, and it is common to organize the evidence with respect to the implications about the three different forms of the EMH discussed above.

Countless studies have been conducted to test market efficiency, and we can't discuss them all. However, we will present the general consensus reached on many of the issues involved. Before we begin this discussion, note that, in order to be valid, any evidence supporting the existence of market inefficiencies must be *consistent* over reasonably long periods, because random or short-lived inefficiencies may appear from time to time, even in efficient markets. Similarly, many researchers have produced evidence that is *statistically* significant, but it would be difficult to translate these findings into *economically* significant gains, after accounting for risk, trading costs, and so on. Therefore, it makes sense to talk about an economically efficient market, in which securities are priced correctly enough that investors cannot exploit any discrepancies and earn unusual returns after consideration of all risks and trading costs. In fact, it is common for people involved in finance to suggest "There is no such thing as a free lunch." In such a market, some securities could be priced slightly above their intrinsic values and some slightly below, and time lags could exist in the processing of information, but the discrepancies would be too small to be exploited economically.

## Weak Form Evidence

If markets are weak form efficient, current market prices will reflect all historical trading data. Therefore, past price changes (and total returns) should be unrelated to future price changes. This idea is related to the **random walk hypothesis**, which states that prices follow a random walk, with price changes over time occurring independently of one another. This hypothesis is logical if information arrives randomly, as it should, and if investors react to it immediately.

**random walk hypothesis**
the theory that prices follow a random walk, with price changes over time occurring independently of one another

### Statistical Tests

Several tests of weak form efficiency are possible. One approach is to test whether price changes are, in fact, independent of one another. This assertion can be statistically tested in many different ways, so we will mention only two of the more commonly cited tests here. Serial correlation tests measure the correlation between successive price changes for various lags, such as one day, two days, one month, and so on. There have been numerous variations of these tests performed on Canadian, U.S., and global stock price data throughout the years. The general consensus of these studies has been that the correlations between successive price changes are not related in an economically significant manner, even though some, but not all, studies found statistically significant relationships. In other words, the pattern is too weak to be exploited by investors.

Another statistical test of price-change independence is the runs (or signs) test, which involves classifying each price change by its sign (i.e., whether the price change was +, 0, or −), and then examining whether there are any "runs" in the series of signs. The evidence provided by numerous studies that used the signs test also supports return independence. In particular, although "runs" have been documented, they could be consistent with random price changes, because even a truly random series will display some runs. Consider the following quote from *Graham and Dodd's Security Analysis*: "Elaborate tests of the correlation of successive prices, runs, and filter rules find some weak relationships, but they are not sufficient to generate trading profits after taking account of transactions costs."[9]

Although the evidence reported above is far from exhaustive, we can say that, for the most part, it supports the notion that price changes in the capital markets are independent of one another.

### Technical Analysis

An alternative method of testing weak form efficiency is to examine specific trading rules that attempt to exploit historical trading data. If any such trading rule could be implemented in a manner that consistently generated abnormal risk-adjusted returns after trading costs, this evidence would contradict weak form efficiency.

---

[9]Cottle, Sidney, Murray, Roger F., and Block, Frank E., *Graham and Dodd's Security Analysis: Principles and Technique*, 5th ed. (New York: McGraw Hill, 1988).

**technical analysis** the analysis of historical trading information to identify patterns in trading data that can be used to invest successfully

**anomalies** exceptions to a rule or theory

**momentum** the tendency for stocks that have experienced high returns in the previous 3- to 12-month period to outperform in the subsequent 3- to 12-month period

**Technical analysis** involves the analysis of historical trading information in order to identify patterns in trading data that can be used to invest successfully. Technical analysts argue that simple statistical tests, such as the ones discussed above, are inconclusive because they are not applied to more sophisticated trading strategies. It is difficult to definitively refute this assertion because there are a virtually unlimited number of technical trading rules. However, most of the evidence suggests that technical trading rules, on average, have not been able to outperform a simple buy-and-hold strategy, after accounting for risk and trading costs.

## Violations of Weak Form Efficiency

Most evidence supports the notion that markets are weak form efficient. However, a few important exceptions, or **anomalies**, have been documented. (We will discuss some anomalies with respect to the other forms of market efficiency in the next subsections.) Anomalies are exceptions to a rule or theory—in this case, exceptions to market efficiency. We will discuss a few well-known anomalies; however, there is no guarantee that a trading strategy based on exploiting these anomalies would prove fruitful. Recall that any evidence supporting the existence of such market inefficiencies must be consistent over reasonably long periods of time to be valid; otherwise, sample selection could be a major contributing factor to the apparent validity of the evidence. In addition, given the widespread attention devoted to uncovering profitable anomalies, many findings are attributed to a process called *data mining*. This is the process of examining data in various manners and forms, and using various empirical approaches, until you find an interesting observation and/or the result you were looking for before you began the analysis. Consider the following quote from the late Fischer Black (co-developer of the Black-Scholes option pricing model and the CAPM): "Most so-called anomalies don't seem anomalous to me at all. They seem like nuggets from a gold mine, found by one of the thousands of miners all over the world." Documented anomalies are also often disputed based on the fact that while they may be statistically significant, it would be difficult to translate these findings into economically significant gains after accounting for risk, trading costs, and so on.

DeBondt and Thaler examined U.S. stock returns and found evidence that people overreact to information, and these overreactions lead to stock price "reversals."[10] They found that stocks that had performed poorly over the most recent three- to five-year periods ("losers") tended to outperform in the subsequent three- to five-year periods, while stocks that displayed superior performance in the past ("winners") tended to underperform in the future. Trading strategies designed to exploit this pattern are commonly referred to as "contrarian strategies," because the idea is based on the notion of investing *contrary* to the past performance record of stocks. Several subsequent studies have confirmed these results for U.S. stock returns; however, international evidence has been mixed. Interestingly, Kryzanowski and Zhang found no such pattern for Canadian stocks over a period (1950–88) similar to that studied by DeBondt and Thaler.[11] This tendency for stock prices to reverse contradicts weak form efficiency, because it implies that future stock returns can be predicted merely by examining past trading data.

An even more important contradiction of weak form efficiency is the existence of **momentum** in stock returns: stocks that have experienced high returns in previous 3- to 12-month periods tend to outperform in the subsequent 3- to 12-month periods. Notice that this pattern is in sharp contrast to the longer-term reversal pattern. There is strong empirical support for the existence of momentum in stock returns in most stock markets around the world. Probably the most famous of these studies dealing with U.S. stock returns was conducted by Jegadeesh and Titman in 1993.[12] They formed portfolios by ranking stocks based on their past 3- to 12-month returns and found that buying the top-performing stocks ("winners") and selling the worst-performing stocks ("losers") produced significant positive abnormal returns.

Several studies have confirmed the existence of this pattern in Canadian stock returns, as demonstrated in **Figure 10.1**. This figure shows that from 1980 to 1999, the returns for a "winner" portfolio (based on the most recent six-month performance) averaged 20.76 percent in the

[10]See DeBondt, W., and Thaler, R., "Does the Stock Market Overreact?" *Journal of Finance* 40, no. 3 (1985), pp. 793–805.
[11]See Kryzanowski, L., and Zhang, H., "The Contrarian Strategy Does Not Work in Canadian Markets." *Journal of Financial and Quantitative Analysis* 27 (1992), pp. 389–95.
[12]See Jegadeesh, N., and Titman, S., "Returns to Buying Winners and Selling Losers: Implications for Stock Market Efficiency." *Journal of Finance* 48 (1993), pp. 65–91.

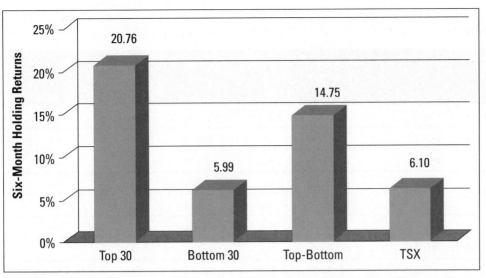

**FIGURE 10.1** Momentum in Canadian Stock Returns, 1980–99

**Source:** Adapted from Cleary,S., Schmitz,J., and Doucette,D., "Industry Affects Do Not Explain Momentum in Canadian Stock Returns." *Investment Management and Financial Innovations 2* (2005), pp. 49–60.

subsequent six-month period, well above the returns for the "loser" portfolio (5.99 percent) and the S&P/TSX Composite Index (6.10 percent).[13] Finance in the News 10.1 further suggests that such a strategy has generated higher returns than the market in 24 of the 26 years ending in 2011. Strong international evidence supports the existence of momentum.[14]

---

## 10.1 Finance in the News    The Momentum Approach to Stock Picking

### What Are We Looking For?

Momentum. Stocks that are going up have a tendency to keep going up—at least for the short term.

### More on Today's Screen

Craig McGee, senior consultant at CPMS, a division of Morning-star Canada, constructed the screen. He looked for rising stocks that are accompanied by improving expectations.

To make the list, a stock had to be:

- among the 350 largest stocks in the Canadian market, based upon market capitalization;

- among the 25 stocks in that group with the best combination of one-year total return, upward revisions in earnings estimates over the past 90 days, and positive earnings surprises, as calculated by CPMS.

### More about CPMS

CPMS provides quantitative North American equity research and portfolio analysis to primarily institutional clients. It covers more than 700 Canadian and 2,200 U.S. stocks, and spends a lot of time adjusting for unusual accounting items in each company's quarterly results to make sure screens can perform correctly.

### What We Learned

A momentum approach can work—if you can shoulder the hefty transaction costs involved in constantly shuffling your portfolio.

Mr. McGee tested how the particular momentum strategy outlined above would have performed over the past 25 years. He assumed an equally weighted 25-stock portfolio that was refreshed every three months.

He found that the approach would have generated an annualized return of 24.6 per cent since the end of 1985, nearly tripling the 8.3-per-cent return for the S&P/TSX Total Return Index over the same period. The portfolio outperformed the index in 24 of 26 years, and lagged behind only in 2008 and 2009.

Mr. McGee says the success of the strategy highlights the importance of focusing on stocks with improving expectations. He cautions, however, that the approach would have required a tremendous amount of discipline to follow in real life.

Someone taking this momentum approach would, on average, have turned over every stock in the portfolio more than twice a year. Transaction costs weren't factored into the return calculations, so the cost of buying and selling shares would have eaten into profits.

An investor would also have had to endure losing 46 per cent of his or her portfolio's value from the end of June 2008 to the end of February 2009. Momentum can work, it seems—but you have to be prepared for volatility along the way.

---

[13]See Cleary, S., Schmitz, J., and Doucette, D., "Industry Affects Do Not Explain Momentum in Canadian Stock Returns." *Investment Management and Financial Innovations* 2 (2005), pp. 49–60.

[14]For example, see Rouwenhorst, K.G., "International Momentum Strategies." *Journal of Finance* 53, no. 1 (February 1998), pp. 267–84.

**CPMS High Momentum Portfolio**

| Rank | Company | Symbol | Price $ (Feb. 3, 2012) | Market Cap ($ mil.) | 1-Year Total Return | 90-Day EPS Estimate | Latest Earnings Surprise |
|------|---------|--------|------------------------|---------------------|---------------------|---------------------|--------------------------|
| 1 | Poseidon Concepts Corp. | PSN-T | 15.26 | 1,237 | 573.50% | A+ | A− |
| 2 | EnerCare Inc. | ECI-T | 9.67 | 544 | 40.00% | A+ | A+ |
| 3 | Parkland Fuel Corp. | PKI-T | 13.11 | 844 | 17.70% | A+ | A+ |
| 4 | MEG Energy Corp. | MEG-T | 46.18 | 8,935 | 0.50% | A+ | A+ |
| 5 | Killam Properties Inc. | KMP-T | 11.86 | 585 | 20.10% | A+ | A+ |
| 6 | Argonaut Gold Inc. | AR-T | 8.69 | 796 | 83.30% | A+ | B+ |
| 7 | Black Diamond Group Ltd. | BDI-T | 18.99 | 708 | 65.10% | A− | A− |
| 8 | Northern REIT Stp Unit | NPR.UN-T | 31.5 | 927 | 19.00% | A+ | A− |
| 9 | Inter Pipeline Fund | IPL.UN-T | 18.31 | 4,832 | 28.20% | A− | A+ |
| 10 | Whitecap Resources Inc. | WCP-T | 9.63 | 695 | 41.80% | A+ | C− |
| 11 | lululemon athletica | LLL-T | 64.15 | 6,936 | 79.70% | A− | C− |
| 12 | Cdn. Utilities Ltd., A | CU-T | 61.56 | 7,856 | 18.80% | B− | A+ |
| 13 | Constellation Software | CSU-T | 84.98 | 1,487 | 72.20% | B− | B+ |
| 14 | Kirkland Lake Gold Inc. | KGI-T | 18.6 | 1,300 | 24.80% | A+ | C− |
| 15 | Major Drilling Grp Intl | MDI-T | 17.4 | 1,374 | 17.30% | B+ | A+ |
| 16 | Lumina Copper Corp. | LCC-X | 14.59 | 572 | 184.40% | B+ | B− |
| 17 | Endeavour Silver Corp. | EDR-T | 10.98 | 959 | 64.60% | A− | C− |
| 18 | Surge Energy Inc. | SGY-T | 9.77 | 693 | 15.60% | A+ | B− |
| 19 | TransForce Inc. | TFI-T | 17.03 | 1,627 | 32.00% | A− | B+ |
| 20 | Total Energy Serv. Inc. | TOT-T | 17.35 | 544 | 20.80% | B+ | A− |
| 21 | NGEx Resources Inc. | NGQ-T | 2.95 | 466 | 94.10% | C+ | C− |
| 22 | Algonquin Power Corp. | AQN-T | 6.02 | 820 | 27.10% | A− | B+ |
| 23 | Precision Drilling Corp | PD-T | 10.81 | 2,984 | 3.70% | B+ | A− |
| 24 | Open Text Corp. | OTC-T | 60.37 | 3,494 | 8.00% | B+ | A− |
| 25 | Wajax Corp. | WJX-T | 42.3 | 703 | 19.40% | C+ | A− |

Grades are relative to 738 securities in the CPMS Canadian database. **Source:** Morningstar Canada.

**Source:** From McGugan, Ian, "The Momentum Approach to Stock Picking." *The Globe and Mail*, February 8, 2012, p. B18. Available at www.theglobeandmail.com. ©The Globe and Mail, Inc. All rights reserved. Reprinted by permission.

There is also evidence of seasonal patterns in stock returns. The best-known pattern is the "January effect," sometimes called the Santa Claus Rally, since it occurs in the trading period following Christmas. Particularly for smaller firms, the returns are statistically higher in January than they are over the other 11 months of the year, with most of these returns arriving in the first five trading days. This pattern has been documented in the Canadian, U.S., and global markets. Evidence suggests the January effect is not as prevalent as it used to be, implying that market participants have "traded away" or exploited most of the pattern, as you would expect in a reasonably efficient market.

A wide array of reasons has been put forward to explain the January effect. One of the most commonly cited arguments is known as the "tax-loss selling hypothesis." This argument asserts that investors sell their "losers" of the previous year in late December to create capital losses, which can be used to offset their capital gains in order to reduce their taxes payable. By nature, many of these losers have lower prices and hence may be dominated by small cap stocks. This increased supply of stocks depresses the prices, so these stocks are bought in early January at relatively attractive prices. This demand then drives their prices up again. While this is a plausible argument, the evidence has only weakly supported the claim that this behaviour accounts for the January effect—i.e., while tax-loss selling may account for a portion of January returns, it does not explain all of it.

Another argument advanced is that professional portfolio managers engage in "window dressing" and attempt to get rid of their riskier holdings (i.e., small cap stocks, high-yield bonds, etc.) prior to December 31. According to the argument, this is a significant date because professional managers prepare their annual reports as of December 31, and these reports typically include portfolio holdings. As such, managers want their portfolios to look as attractive as possible for these widely distributed documents. After this critical date, managers may purchase riskier securities in an attempt to earn the associated higher expected returns. Similar to the tax-loss selling hypothesis, the evidence supporting this argument suggests it may explain some, but not all, of the January pattern.

Other seasonal patterns have been noted, such as the day-of-the-month effect, which reflects the fact that returns tend to be higher on the last trading day of the month and the first three trading days of the next month. The day-of-the-week effect refers to the fact that the average Monday return has historically tended to be negative and significantly different from the average returns for the other four weekdays, which are all positive. Although these patterns are interesting to note, it would be difficult and very risky to attempt to exploit them, because of the trading costs involved, and because the evidence refers to "averages," which means the effects do not occur all the time. Consider, for example, the following comment from Laszlo Birinya, Jr.: "Fact is that most seasonal tendencies are only 'statistically significant'—meaning you can write a dissertation on the subject, but don't try to make money on it."[15]

# Semi-Strong Form Evidence

Most tests of the EMH focus on the semi-strong version. This is logical, because most analysis of security prices, as well as most corporate finance decisions, involve the use of publicly available information. Most studies support the semi-strong EMH; however, some do not. We discuss two broad categories of testing the semi-strong form below.

### Stock Price Adjustments

One way of testing for semi-strong market efficiency is to examine the speed of adjustment of stock prices to announcements of significant new information. In a semi-strong form efficient market, prices would adjust quickly and accurately to this new information so that investors could not act on it and earn abnormally high risk-adjusted returns. In contrast, if the market overreacts or underreacts, or if there are time lags before stock prices adjust, and investors can exploit these flaws, then the market is not semi-strong form efficient.

**Figure 10.2** illustrates the price-adjustment process for an efficient market (A), for an inefficient market that overreacts to new information (B), and for an inefficient market that reacts too slowly to new information (C). In this example, the stock is trading at $20 on the announcement date of the significant event (*t*). Market A is efficient, and the price adjusts immediately and accurately to the new information, which is obviously good news, because the price increases to $23. Market B overreacts to the new information, which provides investors with a window of opportunity to earn abnormal profits as a result of the information if this overreaction occurs consistently and is of sufficient magnitude. In this case, investors could sell or short sell the stock shortly after the information becomes public and profit when the price subsequently declines. Market C, conversely, reacts too slowly to the new information, which again provides an opportunity for investors to exploit the information (i.e., by purchasing the stock after the information becomes public). Of course, many other possible patterns are displayed by inefficient markets.

---

[15]Birinya, Laszlo, Jr., "The Window Dressing Anomaly." *Forbes* (December 20, 1993).

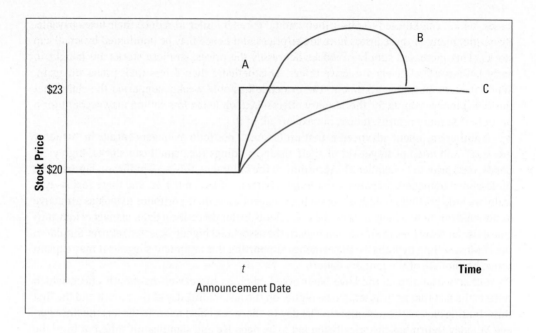

**FIGURE 10.2** Efficient and Inefficient Markets

There are numerous examples of these types of studies. Most of them take the form of an **event study**: stock returns are examined to determine the impact of a particular event on stock prices. Most of these studies support the notion that the market adjusts to new public information rapidly and accurately, and that investors could not earn **abnormal returns** based on inefficient market reactions to significant information announcements.

Many event studies have examined the impact of a variety of significant types of information events. For example, researchers have examined the price behaviour surrounding company-specific announcements regarding such events as stock splits, company takeovers, dividend changes, accounting changes, and so on. Researchers have also examined significant economy-wide announcements, such as unexpected interest rate changes, that could be expected to influence aggregate price levels. The results of most of these studies are similar: prices begin to react to the event before the announcement is made public, and the final price adjustment occurs rapidly when the actual announcement is made. This is depicted in **Figure 10.3**, which obviously alludes to the announcement of some positive news. Notice that this evidence supports the presence of the semi-strong form of market efficiency, because investors could not have earned abnormal returns after the information was made public. This evidence does not provide support for strong form efficiency, because the price increase that occurs

**event study** an examination of stock returns to determine the impact of a particular event on stock prices

**abnormal returns** returns that exceed the expected return on a stock according to a model of stock returns, such as the CAPM

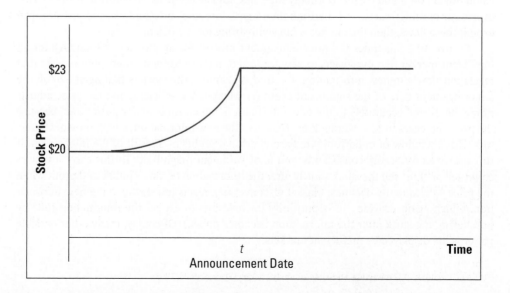

**FIGURE 10.3** The "Typical" Event Study Result for Good News Events

before the announcement suggests that some investors are profiting from private information about upcoming price changes by buying the securities before the information is made public.

One exception to the efficient processing of new information has been documented with respect to earnings "surprises." These refer to earnings announcements that either exceed or fall short of consensus earnings estimates. Several studies have confirmed that a lag exists in the adjustment of stock prices to earnings surprises. In particular, companies displaying the largest positive earnings surprises displayed superior *subsequent* performance, while *poor* subsequent performance was displayed by companies with low or negative earnings surprises. Although substantial price adjustments occurred before, and on the date of, the actual announcement, similar to those noted in the studies discussed above, the substantial adjustments occurring *after* the announcement date contradict semi-strong form efficiency. In addition, stocks that have experienced positive earnings forecast revisions have been found to produce positive abnormal returns subsequent to the revision, on average. The larger the revisions, the greater the excess returns. This also contradicts the semi-strong form of the EMH.

This anomaly may be related, to a certain extent, to the momentum anomaly discussed in the previous subsection. In particular, it has been argued that the slow reaction of markets to earnings announcements, as well as to other news items, contributes to the price momentum effect. In other words, prices react positively to good news (and negatively to bad news), but the full extent of the reaction is insufficient; therefore, prices will continue to appreciate (depreciate).

## Investor Returns

A second general method of testing for semi-strong market efficiency is to examine the performance of investors to see if they are able to use publicly available information to consistently generate abnormal risk-adjusted returns over sustained periods. A variety of active strategies have been tested, with most results suggesting that such strategies do not outperform a simple buy-and-hold strategy. Perhaps the strongest evidence of semi-strong market efficiency is the fact that professional fund managers, with all of their training, expertise, technological capability, and access to data, do not outperform the market on a risk-adjusted basis, on average. In fact, most studies indicate the performance of the average active portfolio manager, after expenses, is substantially worse than the performance of their passive benchmarks. Some studies suggest they may underperform their benchmarks by as much as 50 to 200 basis points. Empirical evidence also suggests that pension fund managers consistently underperform their benchmarks.

These results reflect how difficult it is to "beat the market" and are not meant as a commentary on the abilities of active managers. For example, consider the following comment from Charles Ellis, a well-known investment consultant and author, who has studied the results of professional managers over many years: "The problem is not that professional managers lack skill or diligence. Quite the opposite. The problem with trying to beat the market is that professional investors are so talented, so numerous, and so dedicated to their work that as a group they make it very difficult for any one of their number to do significantly better than the others, particularly in the long run."[16]

## Violations of Semi-Strong Form Efficiency

While an abundance of evidence supports semi-strong form efficiency, several exceptions have been noted. For example, some investment styles have been able to produce abnormal returns (an investment style is a method of forming portfolios that consist of stocks that have some common underlying characteristics). One of the most important of these exceptions is that "value" stocks have consistently outperformed "growth" stocks. Value stocks are generally those that have below-average price-to-earnings (P/E) and market-to-book (M/B) ratios and above-average dividend yields. They are thought to provide good value per dollar of market price. Growth stocks, conversely, have above-average P/E and M/B ratios, but below-average dividend yields. Their name refers to the fact that investors are willing to pay a premium for these companies because they expect them to display above-average future growth in earnings and share price.

Based on the value phenomena noted above, value investing has been a popular investment strategy for many years. In fact, this approach was advocated by Benjamin Graham and

---

[16]See Ellis, Charles, *Winning the Loser's Game* (New York: McGraw Hill, 2002).

David L. Dodd in their classic 1934 book *Security Analysis: Principles and Technique*, which remains a cornerstone of investment philosophy for many investment professionals to this day.[17] They argued that future growth was difficult to predict; therefore, investors should concern themselves with demonstrated performance. Graham and Dodd went on to show how analysts could identify bargain stocks by analyzing company financial statements.

Numerous studies of U.S., Canadian, and global market returns through the years have supported the superior returns generated by value stocks—in fact, there are too many studies supporting this assertion to even begin to list them. Of course, the higher returns could exist in perfectly efficient markets if value stocks are riskier than growth stocks. However, the evidence suggests this is not the case, at least not according to traditional risk measures, such as standard deviation and beta. In fact, most of the evidence suggests the opposite result with respect to risk—that is, value stocks appear to be less risky than growth stocks. This anomaly involving value stocks contradicts semi-strong market efficiency, because all the ratios used to categorize stocks in this manner are publicly available. The fact that this pattern has not disappeared in response to its widespread recognition by the investment community is troublesome to advocates of efficient markets. In efficient markets, when investors recognize this pattern, they should increase their demand for value stocks, driving up their prices and causing the excess returns to disappear. Similarly, the prices of growth stocks should decline in response to a decrease in demand for these types of stocks. However, these patterns have persisted. In any event, it is not a foolproof strategy because, in any given year, growth stocks could outperform value stocks, even though value stocks have continued to outperform over the long run.

Another commonly used investing style involves forming portfolios based on the "size" of the underlying common stocks. Size is commonly measured using the stock's market capitalization (or market cap), which equals the number of shares outstanding times the market price per share. This investing style has emerged in response to the **size effect** anomaly, which has been well documented in the finance literature since the early 1980s. The size effect refers to the fact that small cap stocks tend to outperform large cap stocks, even after adjusting for risk. Interestingly, a large portion (as much as 50 percent) of the size effect has occurred in January. In fact, the January effect noted in the previous section is driven to a large extent by the performance of small stocks and is sometimes referred to as the "small firm in January effect." However, small cap returns are generally more volatile, and while they have outperformed over a reasonably long period, in some years, such as 2008, they underperformed, so they are by no means a "free lunch." In addition, small caps generally have substantially higher trading costs than larger cap stocks because they tend to trade less actively.

Another long-standing semi-strong EMH anomaly is related to the information provided by Value Line Inc., one of the largest and best-known investment advisory services in the world, in its Value Line Investment Survey. Value Line ranks a large universe of stocks from 1 (best) to 5 (worst), based on its expectations regarding the stocks' performance over the next 12 months. Substantial evidence suggests that the performance of stocks in the first two categories has been clearly superior in the subsequent period, while the lower-ranked stocks have performed poorly. Of course, this evidence contradicts semi-strong form efficiency, because investors could profit by using these ratings after they have been made public. However, evidence also suggests that it would be hard to exploit this anomaly after trading costs, because the market adjusts relatively quickly to this information.

## Strong Form Evidence

The strong form version of the EMH asserts that prices reflect all public and private information, which is a very stringent requirement. For example, this suggests that insiders could not profit from inside information that is not known to the public, because prices would already reflect this information. However, it is impossible that prices could reflect all the information that is not publicly available. In fact, as discussed in *Finance in the News 10.2*, the senior director of corporate law at Apple made use of advance knowledge of Apple earnings—both good and bad—to earn superior returns and avoid losses on multiple share transactions over a seven-year period. It is not surprising that, on balance, the evidence does not support this version of the EMH.

**size effect** an anomaly in which small market cap stocks tend to outperform large cap stocks even after adjusting for risk

---

[17]Graham, Benjamin, and Dodd, David L., *Security Analysis: Principles and Technique* (New York: McGraw Hill, 1934).

---

### 10.2 Finance in the News    Apple Lawyer Charged with Insider Trading

#### Apple Lawyer Faces Insider Trading Allegations

Gene Daniel Levoff faces criminal and civil charges in New Jersey, where prosecutors allege that he illegally traded Apple securities ahead of quarterly earnings announcements with the benefit of material non-public information. Levoff was Apple's former global director of corporate law and corporate law secretary and was responsible for enforcing the firm's insider trading program. In that role, Levoff determined *"the criteria for those employees (including himself) restricted from trading around quarterly earnings announcements"*. He was also a member of Apple's Disclosure Committee, where he had access to material non-public information about Apple's financial results.

The SEC alleges that Levoff exploited his access to this financial information by trading in Apple securities in advance of quarterly earnings announcements. In one instance, it is alleged that Levoff sold almost all his Apple holdings upon discovering that the company was going to miss analysts' iPhone sales targets.

#### Similar Issues Have Arisen in Canada

The Levoff case bares resemblance to a recent Ontario Securities Commission ("OSC") case against the general counsel of a public company, who had a major role in enforcing the company's insider trading policy and advising when the company was in a 'blackout period' during which insiders were prohibited from trading.

In that case, the former GC and the OSC reached a settlement in June 2018 whereby the former GC acknowledged and admitted that *"he was in a position of high responsibility and trust and was subject to a high professional standard to avoid any appearance of conflicts of interest and any appearance of misuse of confidential information related to [his employer, a public company]"* and that *"the prudent course of action ... [as] general counsel would have been to err on the side of caution given his knowledge of [certain confiden-*

*tial matters] and refrain from purchasing [his employer's] securities at the time he did"*. The former GC undertook to make a voluntary payment of $30,000 to be designated for allocation or use by the OSC, obtain external legal advice in regard to any future trades in securities of issuers of which he is an insider, and successfully complete director education training. He was also reprimanded for his conduct and ordered to pay $10,000 in costs.

It is not just in-house counsel who must exercise caution. Outside counsel also walk a precarious line as a result of their access to their clients' confidential information. In one notable example, former Bay Street lawyer, Mitchell Finkelstein, was sanctioned by the OSC for misusing confidential information which he obtained while acting on deals and through his access to his firm's document management database. The OSC found that in passing on the material non-public information to a friend and investment advisors, who then traded on that information, Finkelstein had abused his position of trust.

#### Observations

Policies and procedures need to be in place in ensure ALL personnel who have access to confidential information act cautiously and transparently when making personal trading decisions. Officers and directors must ensure not only that these policies are widely and fully understood, but that they are consistently adhered to. Consideration needs to be given of the role of oversight to ensure that the gatekeepers charged with monitoring and enforcing the policies, are themselves satisfactorily complying with the high standards expected of them.

**Source:** From Ritchie, Lawrence E., Irving, Shawn & Whitmore, Seth, "Apple Lawyer Charged with Insider Trading." Copyright 2019. Reproduced with permission of Osler.

---

Strong form efficiency tests examine whether any group of investors has information, public or private, that allows it to earn abnormal profits consistently. Therefore, it is common to examine the performance of groups that are thought to have access to "private" information, such as insiders. Given insiders' access to privileged information, it is not surprising that several studies have found they have consistently earned abnormal returns on their stock transactions, which refutes strong form efficiency. However, some studies have found that their returns are only slightly better than average. It should be noted that the trading activity of insiders is restricted in order to protect the general investing public. Therefore, their potential to exploit this insider knowledge is limited.

## Summary of Empirical Evidence

Overall, based on the available empirical evidence, we can draw the following conclusions regarding the capital markets of Canada, the United States, and most developed countries:

1. Weak form efficiency is very well supported, and it is reasonable to conclude that markets are weak form efficient, although a few anomalies do exist.

2. Semi-strong form efficiency is well supported; however, more contradictory evidence exists for this version of the EMH than for the weak form.

3. Strong form efficiency is not very well supported by the evidence, and it is reasonable to conclude that markets are not strong form efficient in the strictest sense.

One final observation: in Chapter 9, we introduced the Fama-French three-factor model and noted that two of the factors are the size of the firm (measured by the market value of its common equity) and the ratio of the firm's book equity value to its market value of equity. As remarked in this chapter, small firms tend to outperform large ones, and value stocks outperform growth stocks. The market value of equity used by Fama-French identifies small and large firms, while the market-to-book ratio identifies value and growth stocks and is the reciprocal of the Fama-French risk factor. However, it is an ongoing debate as to whether the Fama-French "risk" factors identify riskier firms or simply identify these stock market anomalies or departures from efficiency. Eugene Fama, as the "temple guardian" of market efficiency, views these as risk factors and the market as efficient. Others are more sceptical; nevertheless, many investment professionals acknowledge the importance of many of these factors.

---

### Concept Review Questions

1. Is the weak form EMH well supported by empirical evidence? Discuss any exceptions.
2. Is the semi-strong form EMH well supported by empirical evidence? Discuss any exceptions.
3. Is the strong form EMH well supported by empirical evidence? Discuss any exceptions.

---

## 10.4 | Behavioural Finance

---

**LEARNING OBJECTIVE 10.4**

Differentiate between behavioural finance and the traditional view of finance.

---

**behavioural finance**  a field of financial thought that suggests that investor behaviour is not always rational but is influenced by psychological biases that cause investors to make systematic errors in judgement

According to a developing field of finance—**behavioural finance**—many of the anomalies described above have been attributed to human behaviour. Consider the following comment from David Dreman, a well-known financial commentator and huge supporter of value investing. Dreman argues that rather than basing their behaviour on logic, investor behaviour toward premium-priced stocks tends to favour these stocks because they are "fashionable" and "hot."

> Graham's observations that investors pay too much for trendy, fashionable stocks and too little for companies that are out-of-favour, was on the money . . . Why does this profitability discrepancy persist? There is an impressive and growing body of evidence demonstrating that investors and speculators don't necessarily learn from experience. Emotion overrides logic time after time.[18]

Dreman's comments about stocks being "fashionable" and investors letting "emotion" outweigh logic are references to some of the underlying tenets of behavioural finance.

Many of the theories and activities in finance are based on what is sometimes called "the traditional view of finance." This view suggests that investors:

1. consider all available information;
2. act rationally and do not make systematic errors, either in processing information or in implementing investment decisions; and
3. adhere to the basic tenets of modern portfolio theory (MPT), which implies they are risk averse, they diversify, and they consider risk in the context of a well-diversified portfolio.

---

[18]Dreman, David, "Ben Graham Was Right—Again." *Forbes* (May 6, 1996).

Conceptually, there seems to be little to dispute in the assertions above. However, in practice, human behaviour gets in the way. For example, a legendary investor, the late Peter Bernstein, suggested that, contrary to the traditional view of finance, the evidence "reveals repeated patterns of irrationality, inconsistency, and incompetence in the ways human beings arrive at decisions and choices when faced with uncertainty."[19] Behavioural finance examines human psychology in an attempt to explain how and why investor behaviour can deviate significantly from the predictions associated with the traditional view, which may lead to persistent market inefficiencies—that is, bubbles, crashes, etc.

Much of the rationale underlying behavioural finance is consistent with the thoughts expressed by Keynes, who was mentioned earlier in the chapter. Consider one of his famous quotations regarding the stock market: "Professional investment may be likened to those newspaper competitions in which the competitors have to pick out the 6 prettiest faces from 100 photographs, the prize being awarded to the competitor whose choice most nearly corresponds to the average preferences of the competitors as a whole."[20] That is, investors don't pick the stocks they like; they pick the ones they think other investors are going to like and which, as a result, will increase in price.

While Keynes's ideals no doubt influenced the development of behavioural finance, its roots as a formal field of finance can be attributed to the 1979 work of Tversky and Kahneman, who provided the first significant alternative to the expected utility theory underlying traditional rational financial decision-making. Contrary to what the standard theory predicts, they found evidence that people place different weights on gains and losses, being affected more adversely by a loss than they were affected positively by a gain of the same amount. Based on these results, Tversky and Kahneman developed "prospect theory" as a way to reconcile the observed behaviour that people exhibited when making decisions under uncertainty.

Indeed, the number of believers in the importance of behavioural finance continues to grow dramatically as people try to account for market bubbles and subsequent collapses. Robert Shiller, in the first edition of *Irrational Exuberance*, which examines the reasons underlying market bubbles and subsequent crashes, went so far as to say: "Much of the evidence is drawn from the emerging field of behavioural finance, which as the years go by, is looking less and less like a minor subfield of finance and more and more like a central pillar of finance theory."[21] Clear recognition of the impact of behavioural finance came in 2002, when the Nobel Prize in Economics was awarded to Daniel Kahneman, a Princeton psychologist, and Vernon Smith, of George Mason University, whose economic experiments were at odds with the efficient market hypothesis. Furthermore, two John Bates Clark medals in economics (awarded every two years) have gone to behaviourists.[22]

# Irrational Forces Motivating Investors

Behavioural finance suggests that investors are motivated by numerous "irrational" forces, such as overconfidence and extreme loss aversion. Recognizing these consistent errors in judgement provides us with the opportunity to avoid making such common errors ourselves, and/or to exploit market inefficiencies that present themselves due to the mistakes made by other market participants. Warren Buffett echoed these sentiments when he noted that in order to be a successful investor, "what you need is the temperament to control the urges that get other people into trouble in investing." This means that examining past trends and observed behaviours can be beneficial.

## Market Volatility and Loss Aversion

When the market is extremely volatile, it is often taken as an indicator that market prices may not reflect underlying fundamentals. One commonly used indicator of market volatility is the

---

[19]Bernstein, Peter L., *Against the Gods: The Remarkable Story of Risk* (Hoboken, NJ: Wiley, 1998); Bernstein, Peter L., *Capital Ideas: The Improbable Origins of Modern Wall Street* (Hoboken, NJ: Wiley, 2005).

[20]Keynes, John Maynard, "The State of Long-Term Expectations." Chapter 12 in *The General Theory of Employment, Interest and Money* (London: Macmillan, 1936), pp. 147–64.

[21]Shiller, Robert, *Irrational Exuberance* (Princeton, NJ: Princeton University Press, 2000).

[22]In 2013, Robert Shiller and Eugene Fama were awarded the Nobel Prize in Economics.

**FIGURE 10.4** Montreal Exchange (MX) Implied Volatility Index (VIXC) (December 2002–May 2019)

**Source:** https://m-x.ca/indicesmx_vixc_en.php

VIX Index, which measures investors' expectations of future volatility based on the implied volatilities derived from options-trading data on the Chicago Board Options Exchange. (Implied volatilities will be discussed in detail in chapter 12.) The Canadian version of the VIX Index is the Montreal Exchange Implied Volatility Index (VIXC). **Figure 10.4** depicts the value of the VIXC Index for the period from December 2002 to May 2019—a period during which stock prices plummeted in the fall of 2008, bounced up and down during the winter of 2009, and then showed signs of more permanent recovery in 2009 and 2010 as investors became more confident in the future of the economy and, hence, in future stock returns. Figure 10.4 shows that during the fall of 2008, the VIXC Index increased dramatically, mimicking the dramatic rise in investor uncertainty. It declined significantly during 2009 and 2010, returning to the upper end of previous values, before increasing again in 2011 above historical levels, reflecting concerns over the European debt crisis and its impact on stock markets.

**loss aversion** the tendency to place a heavier emphasis on losses than on comparable gains

One important behavioural bias is extreme **loss aversion**, as identified above by Tversky and Kahneman, which refers to investors' unwillingness to place "fair bets." This is not the same thing as **risk aversion**, which is an underlying assumption of traditional finance. Risk aversion implies that investors dislike risk but are willing to assume risk if they are adequately compensated in the form of higher expected returns. Loss aversion, on the other hand, implies that investors may engage in suboptimal investing decisions to avoid losses, which they dislike more than they like comparable gains.

**risk aversion** the tendency for investors to dislike risk while still being willing to assume it if they are adequately compensated

Loss aversion is related to several behavioural biases. For example, traditional finance suggests that investors will hold well-diversified portfolios that are consistent with their investing objectives in terms of return requirements and risk tolerance. Risk-averse investors will evaluate potential investments on this basis. In contrast, behavioural finance suggests that investors may invest too conservatively, especially if they have experienced losses recently. This could cause them to hold investments that are inappropriate for their investing objectives; as a result, their portfolios may not be adequately diversified. Loss aversion can also lead investors to hold on to "losers" too long (so they can avoid recognizing the loss) and sell "winners" too early (so they will realize the gains and avoid potentially losing these gains). This pattern of investing behaviour has been well documented.

Throughout history there have been numerous asset price "bubbles." For example, Sir Isaac Newton once said, "I can calculate the motions of heavenly bodies, but not the madness of people." He was referring to losses he experienced in 1720 while "following the herd" and investing in the South Sea Company, a London-based shipping company. Apparently Newton had sold all of his shares in the company in April 1720, after experiencing a gain of 100 percent on an original investment of £7,000. However, as the stock continued to soar, he was unable to stay on the sidelines and ended up buying an even larger number of shares near the peak of the market, eventually losing £20,000—a sizable amount at the time (see Chapter 7 for a fuller discussion of this bubble).

Certainly, there have been numerous examples of this herd-like mentality over the past decade and a half, as reluctant investors could no longer stand on the sidelines, but put their money into Internet stocks and U.S. real estate just as those bubbles were about to burst. It is indeed difficult to sit and watch as others make fantastic gains on their investments, without feeling you are missing out on a "sure thing." In contrast, traditional finance suggests that investors should make their decisions based on their perceived investing needs and their beliefs regarding the appropriateness of market prices.

Once these bubbles burst, loss-averse investors are reluctant to invest in anything but the safest investments and are slow to re-enter stock markets. This behaviour is sometimes referred to as the "snake bite" effect. It also reflects the fact that investors tend to give recent information more weight than more distant information. Of course, when recent news has been positive, this same trait fuels the bubbles. As Warren Buffett has said, "People tend to underestimate low probability events when they haven't happened recently, and overestimate them when they have." Traditional finance, on the other hand, suggests investors consider all available information and place the appropriate rational weight on each item, regardless of when it was received.

Consider, for example, one of the most prolific investors of all time, Peter Lynch. His Fidelity Magellan Fund beat the market in 11 of 13 years over the 1977–90 period, earning an average annual return of 29 percent, but Lynch regretted that many of his fund holders did not realize the full gains. How could this happen? Well, they did not stay fully invested in the fund, selling after periods of poor performance (i.e., selling low), then buying back after times of strong performance (i.e., buying high). Of course, this behaviour is the opposite of what you want to do as an investor, which is to buy low and sell high. Unfortunately, these tendencies to follow the herd and focus on the immediate past seem to be common behavioural flaws that doom many investors to experience subpar investment performance. Successful investing suggests, among other things, that you focus on your short-term and long-term investing objectives and risk tolerance, and design a portfolio that is consistent with these objectives.

## Investor Overconfidence and Anchoring

Another important behavioural flaw is investor overconfidence. This manifests itself in several ways. First, investors tend to focus on information that they consider important and downplay other pertinent information. They also tend to attribute their investing successes to their ability rather than to market factors. On the other hand, they tend to attribute investing failure to factors beyond their control. Overconfidence can lead investors to hold overly risky securities that might produce huge payoffs, which they take credit for, or huge losses, which they can blame on external factors they can't control. It might also lead them to hold poorly diversified portfolios, either because they hold too many risky securities or because they don't hold a sufficient number of securities. Clearly, this does not represent rational behaviour.

**Anchoring** refers to the tendency to become emotionally tied to some initial price or perception. For example, investors are often reluctant to sell investments below their original purchase price, or below some historically higher price (i.e., the price they could have sold it for a month ago). This may also cause them to not invest, because they could have done so at a lower price in the past. Investors can become anchored to some initial impression about the quality of an investment and either over- or undervalue it accordingly. This causes investors to adapt too slowly to new information as it is released. For example, they may assess the quality and value of a company's shares based on their embedded (historic) beliefs about the strength (or weakness) of the company, rather than in light of the actual health and future growth prospects of the company today. As a result, they may pay too much for companies whose fortunes have declined, or miss out on attractive "buy" opportunities for companies whose fortunes have improved.

Price anchoring tends to go hand in hand with **mental accounting**, which refers to the process of accounting for individual investments separately. This can cause investors to be

**anchoring**  the tendency to become emotionally tied to some initial price or perception

**mental accounting**  the process of accounting for individual investments separately poorly diversified, among other things. A good example of mental accounting is when investors employ different investing approaches to manage their investments, depending on the source of the money. In particular, investors often invest their "winnings" more aggressively than monies earned (this is known as the "house money effect"). This causes them to maintain separate mental accounts—i.e., "speculative" accounts, conservative accounts, and so on. Obviously, this can lead to poorly diversified portfolios that may not be consistent with investor objectives.

This discussion of behavioural investing flaws is far from exhaustive, but it does provide an overview of how psychological elements can affect the implementation of the investment decision. It is important to remember that these behaviours can be displayed by institutional investors as well as individual ones. After all, professional investors are also human and are subject to the same biases and emotional reactions as the rest of us. No matter what guidelines professional investors put in place in the form of clear, unambiguous investing restrictions and policies, the role of human behaviour usually comes into play at some point during the process.

## Market Efficiency and Speculative Bubbles

One of the most damaging observations related to the notion of market efficiency is the number of speculative bubbles in asset prices that have occurred so regularly throughout history, as discussed in Appendix 7A of Chapter 7. Bubbles refer to significant and generally unwarranted increases in asset prices that lead to unsustainably high price levels. Consider the following comment from *Manias, Panics, and Crashes* by Charles Kindleberger and Robert Aliber: "Bubbles always implode; by definition a bubble involves a non-sustainable pattern of price changes or cash flows."[23]

Some of the more notable bubbles through history include the Dutch Tulip Bulb bubble (1636), the South Sea bubble and the Mississippi bubble (1720), the late 1920s stock price bubble (1927–29), the Japanese bubble in real estate and stock prices (1985–89), the Internet bubble (1995–2000), and of course the U.S. real estate bubble (2008–9), which precipitated the sub-prime crisis and subsequent global financial crisis. An important behavioural trait contributing to these bubbles is the herd-like behaviour that investors have exhibited for centuries, which was discussed above. Of course, with almost all of these bubbles, there have been other important contributing factors, such as fraudulent representations, excessive availability of credit, and so on.

Consider, for example, the bubble in high-technology stock prices from 1995 to 2000, which translated into an average annual return of more than 40 percent for Nasdaq stocks over this period, prior to the market collapse in 2000. The Dow Jones Industrial Average (DJIA) also experienced dramatic increases over this period (tripling in value), as did high-tech stocks around the world. Indeed, as the DJIA surpassed 10,000 for the first time in 1999, it led many so-called experts to make bold predictions of the DJIA hitting 36,000, 40,000, and even 100,000 going forward. This kind of dramatic increase in prices inspired Robert Shiller to title his 2000 book *Irrational Exuberance*, reflecting an earlier comment made by Alan Greenspan, chairman of the U.S. Federal Reserve from 1987 to 2006, in reference to his concerns about market prices being overblown. At the time Shiller wrote the first edition, which was just before the "bursting of the tech bubble" during the summer of 2000, he suggested that this term was "a good description of the mood behind the market."

In the first edition, Shiller devoted considerable effort to describing some common behavioural biases that contributed to this bubble and to bubbles in general. In the preface to the second edition of his book, which was published in 2005, he elaborated on several of the behavioural traits he observed in investors while promoting his first text: herd behaviour, heavy emphasis on the importance of recent events, overconfidence, fear of regret, and so on. He then went on to note the existence of similar beliefs about the U.S. housing market, which subsequently collapsed in 2007, as illustrated in **Figure 10.5**.

---

[23]Kindleberger, Charles P., and Aliber, Robert, *Manias, Panics, and Crashes: A History of Financial Crises*, 5th ed. (Toronto: Wiley, 2005).

**FIGURE 10.5**  U.S. House Prices (1998–2007)

**Source:** Center for Responsible Lending/FHFA

## Lessons to Be Learned

One of the lessons of the 2008–9 financial crisis is that we don't always take these lessons to heart. Consider a few of the bubbles in our financial history. Alan Greenspan, former chairman of the Federal Reserve Bank of the United States, noted in a speech in 1996:

> Clearly, sustained low inflation implies less uncertainty about the future, and lower risk premiums imply higher prices of stocks and other earning assets. We can see that in the inverse relationship exhibited by price/earnings ratios and the rate of inflation in the past. But how do we know when irrational exuberance has unduly escalated asset values, which then become subject to unexpected and prolonged contractions as they have in Japan over the past decade?[24]

His comments were followed by declines in the stock markets around the world.

Robert Shiller used the phrase "irrational exuberance" to describe the dot.com frenzy in markets around the world, when stocks with few or no earnings prospects displayed values that made little sense using almost any valuation model. In his book *Irrational Exuberance*, published in 2000, Shiller discussed speculative bubbles in general, but also the speculative bubble that is often referred to as the "dot.com" or "Internet bubble."[25] The publication of this book preceded the bursting of the Internet bubble in 2000.

In the third edition of his book, published in 2016, Shiller added an analysis of the bond market.[26] He discussed the problems associated with personal bankruptcies leading to financial difficulties for financial institutions. The publication of this book preceded the sub-prime mortgage-fuelled boom that went bust in 2007.

The challenge, as you can see, is that participants in markets do not always learn, and there is a psychological dimension to how market participants value stocks.

One of the reasons the field of behavioural finance has grown so dramatically in importance is that it provides practical and useful insights for investors, corporate managers, and the ordinary person. This is because it is important to recognize why behavioural characteristics may lead others (whether professionals or not) toward certain decisions. However, it is probably even more important to recognize that we too are human, and many of our decisions can be influenced by these same emotions. Consider the following quote from Arnold S. Wood, partner, president, and CEO of Martingale Asset Management:

> Aristotle Onassis is famous for saying "The secret of business is to know something that nobody else knows." One must ask oneself, "What is it that I know that nobody else knows as well as I do?" The answer is yourself. This is not just a matter of casual introspection, nor is it a useless existential thought. It is a practical answer.[27]

[24]Greenspan, Alan, "The Challenge of Central Banking in a Democratic Society." Speech to the American Enterprise Institute, December 5, 1996.

[25]Shiller, Robert, *Irrational Exuberance* (Princeton, NJ: Princeton University Press, 2000).

[26]Shiller, Robert, *Irrational Exuberance*, 3rd ed. (Princeton, NJ: Princeton University Press, 2016).

[27]Wood, Arnold S., "Editor's Preface." In *Behavioral Finance and Investment Management*, pp. v–viii (Charlottesville, VA: Research Foundation of CFA Institute, December 2010).

> **Concept Review Questions**
>
> 1. Contrast behavioural finance with the traditional view.
> 2. Explain why behavioural flaws could result in investors holding portfolios that are not as predicted by modern portfolio theory.
> 3. Explain why behavioural traits can cause asset price bubbles.

## 10.5 | Implications of Market Efficiency

**LEARNING OBJECTIVE 10.5**

Explain the implications of market efficiency.

The EMH states that security prices will fully and accurately reflect all available information at any given time. The evidence suggests this strict interpretation of market efficiency does not hold; however, we can conclude that markets react quickly and relatively accurately to new public information. As a result, market prices are correct *on average*, and we can say that although markets may not be perfectly efficient, they are relatively efficient. This statement has several important implications for investors and for corporate officers.

Some of the implications for investors include the following:

1. Technical analysis, which involves examining trading data for patterns, is not likely to be rewarded by substantial abnormal returns, because markets appear to be weak form efficient.

2. Fundamental analysis based on various forms of publicly available information is also likely to be unsuccessful at generating abnormal profits, although some opportunities appear to be available. The implication is that to benefit from such data, the analysis must be of superior and consistent quality. Average, or below-average, analysis will likely be unfruitful. This notion is consistent with the subpar performance reported by the "average" professional portfolio manager.

3. In light of items 1 and 2 above, "active" trading strategies are unlikely to outperform "passive" portfolio management strategies on a consistent basis. Passive strategies involve buy-and-hold tactics and the purchase of such products as index mutual funds or exchange-traded funds (ETFs) that replicate the performance of a market index. The lack of success for active strategies is partially attributable to the extra costs associated with collecting and processing information, as well as to the additional trading costs associated with active strategies. Obviously, these extra costs can be justified only if the approach generates sufficient additional returns to compensate for them. Passive strategies minimize these costs and therefore provide "average" results.

A notable champion of efficient markets has been Burton Malkiel, renowned for his book *A Random Walk down Wall Street*, the first edition of which was published in the early 1970s. In it, he proclaimed that "the market prices stocks so efficiently that a blindfolded chimpanzee throwing darts at the Wall Street Journal can select a portfolio as [good as] those managed by the experts." Based on such beliefs, Malkiel was a staunch advocate of the benefits to investors of buying index funds, which hold the stocks comprising an underlying market index. Malkiel argued that these funds would outperform actively managed funds, especially on an after-tax basis, due to their reduced trading costs and greatly reduced management fees. In the eighth edition of his text, published in 2002, he stated: "Now, over thirty years later, I believe even more strongly in that original thesis, and there's more than a six figure gain to prove it." Malkiel was referencing the fact that

**FIGURE 10.6**  **Global ETFs (2000–April 2019)**

**Sources:** Data from www2.blackrock.com; www.etfgi.com.

a $10,000 investment in an S&P 500 Index Fund, made at the beginning of 1969, would have grown to $327,000 by June 2002 (after management expenses of 0.2 percent), versus $213,000 for the average actively managed equity fund. Malkiel was not alone in his beliefs, and index funds experienced dramatic growth during the 1970s, 1980s, and 1990s.

At the time Malkiel wrote his first edition, there were no such things as ETFs, which are similar to index funds in that they hold the securities comprising an underlying stock or bond index. However, ETFs are not mutual funds; their units trade on stock exchanges just like common shares, and the associated management expenses tend to be much lower. ETFs have experienced dramatic growth in the past 15 years. First launched in the early 1990s, ETFs grew steadily to reach about three dozen in number and $40 billion in assets before the end of the decade. As of the end of April 2019, propelled by their low cost, tax efficiency, and intraday liquidity advantages, ETFs exceeded 6,600 in number worldwide, with total assets under management (AUM) of over US$5.43 trillion, as can be seen in **Figure 10.6**. In Canada, as of the end of April 2019, there were nearly 700 funds, with over US$130 billion under management.

4. Whether investors decide to pursue a passive or active strategy, it is critical that they focus on the basics of good investing by defining their objectives in terms of expected return and acceptable risk levels, and by maintaining an adequately diversified portfolio. When markets are relatively efficient, as they appear to be, paying attention to these factors will do more to promote success than will the analysis of individual security prices.

Two of the most important implications of the preceding statement for corporate officers are the following:

1. The timing of security issues or repurchases is unimportant in an efficient market because prices will be correct, on average. In other words, prices will not become inflated, so there is no optimal time to sell new securities, and securities will not be undervalued, so there is no optimal time to repurchase outstanding securities.

2. If short-run momentum and overreaction continue, we would expect the opposite: that firms should sell equity after a price run-up and repurchase shares after a price decline. Therefore, management should monitor the price of the company's securities and determine whether price changes reflect new information or short-run momentum and/or overreaction.

## Concept Review Question

1. What are the main implications of the EMH for investors? For corporate officers?

## 10.1 Ethics and Corporate Governance   Capitol Gains

Earlier this year, Senate Majority Leader Bill Frist told the trustee in charge of managing his stock portfolio to sell all of his shares in Hospital Corporation of America, the giant company founded by the Senator's father and brother. Just two weeks after the shares were sold, H.C.A. announced that its earnings would not meet Wall Street expectations, and the company's stock price tumbled almost nine percent. Frist, it happened, had got out pretty much at the top, and his continued connections to H.C.A.—his brother, for instance, is on the company's board of directors—raised the possibility that he'd been tipped off.

Frist is now the target of a probe by the Securities and Exchange Commission, although he insists that he did nothing wrong, and that he sold the shares to defuse concerns about potential conflicts of interest. Frist's colleagues in the Senate, meanwhile, have remained noticeably quiet about the affair. Perhaps that's because he's far from the only senator to demonstrate uncanny investing smarts. Last year, Alan Ziobrowski, a professor at Georgia State, headed the first-ever systematic study of politicians as investors. Ziobrowski and his colleagues looked at six thousand stock transactions made by senators between 1993 and 1998. Over that time, senators beat the market, on average, by twelve percent annually. Since a mutual-fund manager who beats the market by two or three percent a year is considered a genius, the politicians' ability to foresee the future seems practically divine. They did an especially good job of picking up stocks at just the right time; their buys were typically flat before they bought them, but beat the market by thirty percent, on average, in the year after. By those standards, Frist actually looks like a bit of a piker.

Are senators really that smart? The authors of the study suggest a more likely explanation: at least some senators must have been trading "based on information that is unavailable to the public"—in other words, they were engaged in some form of insider trading. It's impossible to pin down exactly how it happened, but it's easy to imagine senators getting occasional stock tips from corporate supplicants, and their own work in Congress often deals with confidential matters that have a direct impact on particular companies.

That the senators have done this without a hint of censure shouldn't come as a surprise. Corporate insider trading is illegal, in theory, but prosecutions are rare. Economists have known for a long time that corporate insiders outperform the market by something like six or seven percent a year. The only way they could pull that off is by trading on privileged information. And some people think that's as it should be. Beginning in the nineteen-sixties, when Henry Manne published "Insider Trading and the Stock Market," many theorists have argued that insider trading is a victimless

offense, or even a positive good. After all, some investors always have better information than others, and if a well-informed trader didn't have the incentive of trading on what he knew, the stock market would dry up. Furthermore, since insider trading is, by definition, based on accurate information, it moves stock prices in the right direction. Isn't this just market efficiency in action?

Not really. Ultimately, insider trading is an inefficient way of achieving market efficiency, because insiders earn all their profits on the lag between when they start selling and when the market figures out what's going on. This gives them every reason to hoard information, with the result that stock prices are out of whack for longer than they otherwise would have been. Markets thrive on transparency, but insider trading thrives on opacity.

Insider trading therefore encourages executives to put their own interests before those of their shareholders. In fact, the real scandal of insider trading is not what's illegal but what's legal. For instance, although many companies have a rule that their employees can buy or sell company stock only during preordained periods, known as "trading windows," they don't need to announce in advance if they're going to buy or sell during a window. So executives who get bad news can still dump shares relatively freely (or, if they get wind of good news, buy freely).

**Discussion Questions**

1. **According to Henry Manne, insider trading is a victimless crime—even a positive good. Why do some argue that it is a good thing?**

2. **How do you think insider trading makes capital markets more efficient? If it were legal, what measures should be in place to make the markets even more efficient?**

3. **Why is insider trading illegal despite the claims of Manne? Would you participate in a market where insiders trade using information that is not available to you?**

4. **In this case, it is claimed that politicians have inside information as a result of their dealings with firms and lobbyists. What special policies would you recommend to manage the stock portfolios of politicians while they are in office?**

# Review

## Summary

In this chapter, we define an efficient market as one that reacts quickly and relatively accurately to new information; as a result, its prices are correct *on average*. The efficient market hypothesis (EMH) suggests that market prices fully and accurately reflect all available information.

The EMH is commonly broken down into three cumulative levels that are based on the extent to which prices reflect different types of available information. The weak form EMH states that security prices reflect all market data; the semi-strong form states that prices reflect all publicly known and available information; and the strong form states that prices reflect all public and private information.

Most of the assumptions required for markets to be efficient are reasonable; however, behavioural finance theory posits that some of the key assumptions related to human behaviour do not hold in the real world—namely investor rationality and risk aversion. Empirical evidence suggests that markets are reasonably efficient, but not perfectly so. In particular, the evidence suggests that markets are weak form efficient, are reasonably semi-strong form efficient, but are not strong form efficient. We discuss several important implications that arise from these conclusions, both for investors and for corporate decision-makers.

## Summary of Learning Objectives

### 10.1 Explain what market efficiency is and why it is important.

An efficient market is one in which the prices of all securities accurately reflect all relevant and available information about the securities. There are three components to market efficiency. The first is operational efficiency—whether transaction costs are low. The second is allocation efficiency—whether there are enough securities to efficiently allocate risk. The third is information efficiency, a market condition in which important information is reflected in share prices.

For shareholder value maximization to mean anything, there has to be a connection between the decisions made by managers and the level of share prices. In this way, share prices are like a score sheet used to evaluate management. The closer the link between the actions of managers and this score sheet, the more informationally efficient the capital market.

### 10.2 Differentiate among the different levels of efficiency.

(1) Weak form efficient market hypothesis (EMH) is the theory that security prices fully reflect all market data, which refers to all past price and volume trading information. (2) Semi-strong form EMH is the theory that all publicly known and available information, including market data, is reflected in security prices. (3) Strong form EMH is the theory that stock prices fully reflect all information, which includes both public and private information.

### 10.3 Discuss the general consensus based on empirical evidence of market efficiency, as well as the existence of some well-known anomalies.

Weak form efficiency is very well supported, and it is reasonable to conclude that markets are weak form efficient, although a few anomalies do exist. Semi-strong form efficiency is well supported; however, more contradictory evidence exists for this version of the EMH than for the weak form. Strong form efficiency is not very well supported by the evidence, and it is reasonable to conclude that markets are not strong form efficient in the strictest sense.

### 10.4 Differentiate between behavioural finance and the traditional view of finance.

Behavioural finance is a field of financial thought that suggests that investor behaviour is not always rational but is influenced by psychological biases that cause investors to make systematic errors in judgement. The traditional view of finance suggests that investors consider all available information; act rationally and do not make systematic errors, either in processing information or in implementing investment decisions; and adhere to the basic tenets of modern portfolio theory, which implies they are risk averse, they diversify, and they consider risk in the context of a well-diversified portfolio.

### 10.5 Explain the implications of market efficiency.

(1) Technical analysis, which involves examining trading data for patterns, is not likely to be rewarded by substantial abnormal returns, because markets appear to be weak form efficient. (2) Fundamental analysis based on various forms of publicly available information is also likely to be unsuccessful at generating abnormal profits, although some opportunities appear to be available. To benefit from such data, the analysis must be of superior and consistent quality. (3) "Active" trading strategies are unlikely to outperform "passive" portfolio management strategies on a consistent basis. Passive strategies involve buy-and-hold tactics and the purchase of products such as index mutual funds or exchange-traded funds (ETFs) that replicate the performance of a market index. (4) Whether investors adopt a passive or active strategy, it is critical that they focus on the basics of good investing by defining their objectives in terms of expected return and acceptable risk levels, and by maintaining an adequately diversified portfolio. When markets are relatively efficient, these factors may do more to promote success than the analysis of individual security prices.

## Key Terms

abnormal returns, p. 10-12
allocational efficiency, p. 10-4
anchoring, p. 10-19
anomalies, p. 10-8
behavioural finance, p. 10-16
buy-side analysts, p. 10-3
disclosure, p. 10-2
efficient market, p. 10-2
efficient market hypothesis (EMH), p. 10-5

event study, p. 10-12
informational efficiency, p. 10-4
loss aversion, p. 10-18
material facts, p. 10-5
mental accounting, p. 10-19
momentum, p. 10-8
operational efficiency, p. 10-4
random walk hypothesis, p. 10-7
risk aversion, p. 10-18

securities law, p. 10-2
sell-side analysts, p. 10-3
semi-strong form EMH, p. 10-6
size effect, p. 10-14
strong form EMH, p. 10-6
technical analysis, p. 10-8
weak form EMH, p. 10-6

# Questions and Practice Problems

## Multiple Choice Questions

**1. (LO 10.1)** Which of the following statements about an efficient market is *false*?

   **a.** Prices fully and accurately reflect all available information.

   **b.** Prices reflect information about a firm's future plans.

   **c.** Prices are always correct.

   **d.** Price changes are independent of one another.

**2. (LO 10.1)** Which of the following assumptions does *not* underlie the existence of efficient markets?

   **a.** There are a large number of irrational investors who actively participate in the market by analyzing, valuing, and trading securities.

   **b.** Information is costless and widely available to market participants at the same time.

   **c.** Information arrives randomly.

   **d.** Investors react quickly and fully to the information.

**3. (LO 10.1)** Which of the following is *not* a component of market efficiency?

   **a.** Allocational efficiency

   **b.** Informational efficiency

   **c.** Managerial efficiency

   **d.** Operational efficiency

**4. (LO 10.2)** Which of the following is *not* a form of the efficient market hypothesis (EMH)?

   **a.** Semi-strong

   **b.** Strong

   **c.** Semi-weak

   **d.** Weak

**5. (LO 10.2)** The main difference between the three forms of market efficiency is that

   **a.** the definition of excess returns differs.

   **b.** the definition of prices differs.

   **c.** the definition of information differs.

   **d.** There is no difference between the three forms.

**6. (LO 10.5)** Which of the following is useful in attempting to identify mispriced securities if the semi-strong form of EMH is assumed?

   **a.** Past stock price changes

   **b.** Earnings expectations

   **c.** Past and current published trading volumes

   **d.** Relevant insider information

**7. (LO 10.2)** Which of the following statements about the weak form EMH is *false*?

   **a.** Prices fully reflect all market data.

   **b.** Historical trading data should be of no value in predicting future price changes.

   **c.** Technical trading rules based on observed patterns should be of value.

   **d.** Prices reflect all past price and volume trading information.

**8. (LO 10.2)** Which of the following statements is *true*?

   **a.** The weak form of the EMH encompasses the semi-strong form.

   **b.** The strong form of the EMH encompasses the semi-strong form.

   **c.** The semi-strong form of the EMH encompasses the strong form.

   **d.** The strong form of the EMH does not encompass the weak form.

**9. (LO 10.3)** If a test is statistically significant,

   **a.** it must be economically significant as well.

   **b.** it cannot be economically significant at all.

   **c.** it could be economically significant if the test is still significant after accounting for risk, trading costs, and so on.

   **d.** None of the above.

**10. (LO 10.3)** Which of the following conclusions is *false*?

   **a.** Evidence strongly supports the weak form of EMH.

   **b.** Evidence strongly supports the semi-strong form of EMH, with more contradictory evidence than for the weak form.

   **c.** Evidence strongly supports the strong form of EMH.

   **d.** Evidence does not support the strong form of EMH.

**11. (LO 10.1)** In an efficient market,

   **a.** security prices react quickly to new information.

   **b.** security analysts will not enable investors to realize superior returns consistently.

   **c.** one cannot make money.

   **d.** a and b are both correct.

**12. (LO 10.2)** Which of the following statements about strong form EMH is *false*?

   **a.** It encompasses both the weak and semi-strong EMH.

   **b.** It is the most flexible form of market efficiency.

   **c.** It states that prices reflect both public and private information.

   **d.** It implies that no investor can take advantage of insider information.

**13. (LO 10.3)** Proponents of the efficient market hypothesis think technical analysts

   **a.** should focus on relative strength.

   **b.** should focus on resistance levels.

   **c.** should focus on support levels.

   **d.** are wasting their time.

**14. (LO 10.3)** According to proponents of the efficient market hypothesis, the best strategy for a small investor with a portfolio worth $25,000 is probably to

   **a.** perform fundamental analysis.

   **b.** invest in individual stocks.

   **c.** invest in derivative securities.

   **d.** invest in mutual funds.

**15. (LO 10.3)** Which of the following can be used to examine weak form efficiency?

    **a.** Runs test

    **b.** Serial correlation test

    **c.** Technical analysis

    **d.** All of the above

**16. (LO 10.5)** Although markets may not be perfectly efficient, they are relatively efficient. Which of the following is implied by this statement?

    **a.** Fundamental analysis based on publicly available information is likely to successfully generate abnormal profits.

    **b.** Technical analysis is not likely to be rewarded by substantial abnormal returns.

    **c.** As it relates to fundamental analysis, average or below-average analysis of publicly available information will likely be fruitful.

    **d.** As it relates to technical analysis and fundamental analysis, active trading strategies are likely to outperform passive portfolio management strategies.

**17. (LO 10.3)** Which of the following statements is *true*?

    **a.** Stock returns tend to produce statistically lower returns in January than in the other 11 months of the year.

    **b.** Average Monday returns tend to be negative, while average returns for the other four trading days tend to be positive.

    **c.** Growth stocks have consistently outperformed value stocks.

    **d.** Large cap stocks tend to outperform small cap stocks.

**18. (LO 10.3)** Which of the following characteristics is typical of a value stock?

    **a.** Below-average dividend yield

    **b.** Below-average P/E ratio

    **c.** Below-average M/B ratio

    **d.** b and c

**19. (LO 10.3)** If an investor observes a stock that experienced a price increase before an announcement of new information, as shown in the figure below, what can they conclude?

    **a.** The market is semi-strong form efficient.

    **b.** The market is strong form efficient.

    **c.** The market is not weak form efficient.

    **d.** The market is not efficient in any form.

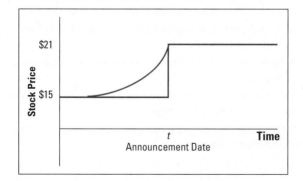

**20. (LO 10.4)** When investors dislike risk but are willing to undertake risk if they are compensated in the form of higher returns, this is an example of

    **a.** loss aversion.

    **b.** anchoring.

    **c.** mental accounting.

    **d.** risk aversion.

**21. (LO 10.4)** "The traditional view of finance" suggests that investors

    **a.** let emotion override logic.

    **b.** act irrationally and make systematic errors.

    **c.** consider all available information.

    **d.** are risk neutral.

**22. (LO 10.3)** Researchers have found that most of the size effect occurs

    **a.** during the spring months.

    **b.** during the summer months.

    **c.** in January.

    **d.** randomly.

## Practice Problems

### Basic

**23. (LO 10.1)** Identify the types of inefficiency (allocational, operational, or informational) described below:

    **a.** The Lower Red River stock market is characterized by very high transaction costs, and due to frequent flooding, transaction orders are often lost.

    **b.** In the markets of the country of Upper Lachine, firms can only issue very long-term debt (35-year maturity or more) and stock.

    **c.** The Middle Bow River Market is a small stock market where trading can only occur on Thursdays. Newspapers are published every day.

**24. (LO 10.1)** Explain whether each of the following is an example of informational efficiency.

    **a.** Every time my broker tells me to buy, the stock price subsequently goes down. Every time my broker tells me to sell, the stock price subsequently goes up.

    **b.** Three months after receiving the financial statements of the Canada Bank, I finally look at them and decide to trade. I rarely make money.

    **c.** I use a simple trading rule: if the stock has risen for the past three days—sell; if the stock has fallen for the past three days—buy. I usually make money.

    **d.** You have been studying the trading behaviour of the CEO of Parchyk Company and find that for the past 10 years, 90 percent of the time the stock rises after the CEO buys and 98 percent of the time the stock falls after the CEO sells stock.

    **e.** I carefully examine the financial statements of the firm, the industry prospects, and general economic conditions. Because of my skill, I am able to complete this analysis within five minutes of the financial statement disclosure. I usually make money.

**25. (LO 10.3)** Parker Investments Inc. has just completed an investigation of strong form efficiency in the Canadian stock market and has concluded that its evidence is statistically significant but not economically significant. Explain to your client how this is possible.

**26. (LO 10.1)** Which type of analyst, buy side or sell side, is more likely to "sell" their recommendation to the public?

**27. (LO 10.3)** Summarize the empirical conclusions regarding the three forms of the EMH.

**28. (LO 10.5)** State four important implications of the EMH for investors and two implications for corporate officers.

## Intermediate

**29. (LO 10.3)** Describe two common tests for the weak form and for the semi-strong form of the EMH.

**30. (LO 10.1)** State the main assumptions required for the existence of efficient markets.

**31. (LO 10.3)** What is the momentum effect? What form of the EMH does it contradict?

**32. (LO 10.2, 10.3)** According to recent studies, Berkshire Hathaway, a multinational conglomerate holding company led by Warren Buffet, had the highest Sharpe ratio out of all U.S. stocks and mutual funds from 1926 to 2011 that had been traded for more than 30 years. To place this performance further into context, Berkshire Hathaway's Sharpe ratio over the 35-year period between 1976 and 2011 was nearly double the overall stock market at 0.76. In order to achieve these returns, Warren Buffet buys stocks that are "safe" (with low beta and low volatility), "cheap" (value stocks with low price-to-book ratios), and high-quality (meaning stocks that are profitable, stable, growing, and with high payout ratios). Which form of the efficient market hypothesis does this violate, if any? Discuss.

**33. (LO 10.5)** Elvira, the CEO of AT Pharmaceutical Ltd., has hired Dome Financial Inc. to advise her on issuing new stock. Her company will need to issue more stock soon to finance the development of a new product—Hair Growth formula. Elvira has noticed that, on average, the stock price of pharmaceutical companies is higher in the spring than the rest of the year. She would like to issue the Hair Growth stock in the spring to obtain the highest price possible. Given your understanding of the efficiency of the Canadian market, what advice do you have for Elvira regarding the timing of the new stock issue?

**34. (LO 10.5)** You are on the board of directors of Marlin Company. The stock price of Marlin has suddenly increased by 20 percent, and the CEO has come to the board asking for a substantial pay increase. The CEO argues that the company's prospects have dramatically improved—after all, why else would the stock price increase? Do you feel that the CEO should receive a large pay increase? Explain.

**35. (LO 10.5)** On Monday, the stock of Wicker Company was trading at $25. The CEO was satisfied with this price as it reflected the prospects of the firm (future dividend growth and required rate of return). The firm's scientists worked all Monday night to complete a top secret project, which will dramatically improve the quality of Wicker's products and result in a huge increase in sales for the next 10 years. On Tuesday evening, you have dinner with the CEO (a client of yours), who is complaining that the "markets cannot be efficient" because the stock price of WC has not changed despite this dramatic change in the firm's prospects. Provide the CEO with two different explanations about why there was no reaction on Tuesday.

**36. (LO 10.5)** Assume that the information system is so advanced that the market, as confirmed by numerous unbiased studies, is

efficient. Investment firms therefore decide to retire all portfolio managers and financial analysts and let random choice govern the security selection process. What impact will this action have on market efficiency?

**37. (LO 10.4)** Distinguish between loss aversion and risk aversion.

## Challenging

**38. (LO 10.5)** The manager of Quest Adventures Ltd. is puzzled. Analysts are saying that the future prospects for his company are poor because the stock price has dropped 5 percent.

    **a.** Explain to the manager the relationship between stock prices and market expectations.

    **b.** Would you be as concerned about the company's future prospects if the company had a beta of 1.5 and the market had fallen 4 percent?

**39. (LO 10.5)** On the morning of March 15, Decker Marketing Inc. announced that it would pay its first dividend of $5 this year. The ex-dividend date will be July 3.

    **a.** If the announcement is a complete surprise to the market, what do you expect will happen to the stock price on March 15?

    **b.** If the announcement has been forecasted by the financial analysts, what do you expect to happen to the stock price on March 15?

    **c.** What do you expect to happen to the price of Decker Marketing Inc. on July 3?

**40. (LO 10.5)** On Monday evening, Codina Model Steam Engine Company announced that it would be restating its financial statements for the past five years, and its CFO was arrested for fraud. Interpret the following Tuesday's stock reactions:

    **a.** Stock price drops

    **b.** Stock price does not change

    **c.** Stock price increases

**41. (LO 10.4)** A news story about United Airline's decision to seek protection from creditors was originally published December 10, 2002, by the *Chicago Tribune*. The story was recirculated by a Florida news service in 2008. Following the recirculated story there was a steep sell-off in United's shares. When the story hit Bloomberg News, United's stock fell from about $12 per share to $3 per share. Once the truth was out, the stock got back to a slightly lower $10.

    **a.** Use your knowledge of behavioural biases among investors to explain the market reaction to the incorrect news.

    **b.** Why didn't the share price immediately return to $12 after the truth was known?

    **c.** Does this market behaviour contradict the efficient market hypothesis?

**42. (LO 10.4)** Would you expect investors to be more overconfident during a boom or a recession? Why?

**43. (LO 10.4)** How would you expect increasing access to the Internet to affect investor behaviour?

# Forwards, Futures, and Swaps

---

**LEARNING OBJECTIVES**

After studying this chapter, you should be able to:

**11.1** Describe forward contracts, including how they are used and priced.

**11.2** Explain what futures contracts are and why they can be viewed as the public market version of forward contracts.

**11.3** Describe the mechanics of simple swap structures, including interest rate swaps and currency swaps.

**11.4** Explain how the credit default swap market contributed to the financial crisis.

**11.5** Explain how the general principles of forward contracts can be applied to fixed income securities.

---

Suppose your teacher returned an English essay you had written, with the comment "This is derivative." You wouldn't be happy. Derivative means "not original," and the teacher's comment means your essay contained nothing new; it was derived from other things. So it is with derivative securities: they are not original because their behaviour is derived from other underlying assets—the securities on which derivative contracts are based. There are two basic types of derivative securities: (1) forwards, futures, and swaps, which are discussed in this chapter, and (2) options, which are discussed in Chapter 12.

---

## 11.1 Forward Contracts

---

**LEARNING OBJECTIVE 11.1**

Describe forward contracts, including how they are used and priced.

---

## Basic Characteristics of Forward Contracts

Appendix 6A introduced forward contracts in the discussion on interest rate parity (IRP). At that time, the forward rate was introduced as a forward foreign exchange rate. In fact, a **forward contract** is a price that is established today for future delivery, in contrast to a **spot contract**, which is a price that is established today for immediate delivery. The definition of immediate delivery depends on the nature of the underlying contract. For foreign exchange contracts, it is generally defined as the next day when exchanging the Canadian dollar for the U.S. dollar, and two days for many other less actively traded currencies. In contrast, forward delivery can be specified for almost any future date. **Table 11.1** shows the foreign exchange rates provided by Bloomberg for June 3, 2019.

**forward contract** a price that is established today for future delivery

**spot contract** a price that is established today for immediate delivery

| TABLE 11.1 | Foreign Exchange Rates (Foreign Currency per Canadian Dollar) | | | |
|---|---|---|---|---|
| | US($) | GB(£) | Jap(¥) | Euro(€) |
| Spot | 0.7419 | 0.5872 | 80.3900 | 0.6620 |
| 1 month | 0.7424 | 0.5867 | 80.2460 | 0.6609 |
| 3 month | 0.7433 | 0.5858 | 79.9700 | 0.6584 |
| 6 month | 0.7444 | 0.5846 | 79.5800 | 0.6549 |
| 9 month | 0.7454 | 0.5834 | 79.1620 | 0.6513 |
| 1 year | 0.7460 | 0.5825 | 78.7830 | 0.6480 |
| 2 year | 0.7480 | 0.5789 | 77.2880 | 0.6355 |

**Source:** Data from Bloomberg, intraday quotes on June 3, 2019

In each case, these prices reflect the amount of the foreign currency that one Canadian dollar would buy. The U.S. dollar rate of 0.7419, for example, means that if you exchanged one Canadian dollar on June 3, 2019, you could get 0.7419 U.S. dollars. The rates are mid-day rates for very large "wholesale" transactions between major banks, so these are not the rates that ordinary investors or retail clients of the bank would pay. At this point, the Canadian dollar (referred to as CDN by traders) was at a discount to the U.S. dollar. We can take the reciprocal of this rate, known as the "inverse" rate, to get the value of the Canadian dollar in terms of the U.S. dollar, which was 1.3479 (it would cost 1.3479 Canadian dollars to buy 1 U.S. dollar). Also note from the table that there is an extensive set of quotes for forward rates for the four major currencies out to two years in the table, with more distant dates also available from various suppliers. U.S.-dollar transactions out this long are routine since so much of Canada's trade is with U.S. customers or denominated in U.S. dollars. However, such long transactions are not as routine for the other currencies, so while it is possible to "do a forward" in two-year Japanese yen, you would need to make a call to one of the major banks to get an exact quote.

What do these quotes mean? In Chapter 5, we discussed the time value of money and emphasized that, because of the opportunity cost of money, a dollar in the future is not worth a dollar today; we can always invest a dollar today to get more than a dollar in the future. The time value of money is the reason we calculated present values. So it is with foreign currency; because forward rates are the price today for future delivery, they reflect the fact that foreign currency is not worth the same amount when it is received at different points in time.[1] For example, according to Table 11.1, if you bought US$1 million on June 3, 2019 (spot), the cost to a large wholesale investor would have been about C$1,347,891. However, if the investor wanted to fix a price on June 3 for US$1 million to be bought in two years' time, the investor would have had to pay about C$1.3369 million (using the reciprocal of 0.7480), indicating that U.S. dollars are worth less in the future than they are now relative to CDN.

This brings up an important feature associated with forward foreign exchange contracts: they are bank instruments. Buying or selling a forward contract requires that a customer have a banking relationship. It is not possible for ordinary individuals to access the forward foreign exchange market, as forward contracts are not traded in any open market. Instead, forwards are over-the-counter (OTC) markets. This means that they are traded OTC with a principal—in this case, the bank—in exactly the same way that we buy most things. We will return to this topic later, because it has important implications for the futures markets. Also note that although the quotes provided by Bloomberg are for discrete units of time—such as one month, two months, and so on—in practice, forwards can be tailored to any specific date in the future and for any amount of money. This makes them incredibly flexible.

---

[1]They are not present values because the Canadian dollars are received in the future.

# Using Forward Contracts

What can investors do with forwards? To make the arithmetic simple, suppose the Canadian dollar is trading at par with the U.S. dollar, as it was for much of 2012—that is, we assume the exchange rate is C$1.00 for US$1.00. To make it even simpler, suppose that both the spot and the one-year forward rates are quoted as 1.00. In this case, an investor decides to **speculate** on the value of the U.S. dollar in the future and is able to buy US$1 million forward. This obligates the investor to pay C$1 million and receive US$1 million in one year. Because the investor is speculating, they do not have any underlying U.S. dollars. This is called a **naked position**—that is, the investor is exposed to changes in the value of the **underlying asset**, which in this case is the U.S. dollar. Because the investor has agreed to buy U.S. dollars and sell Canadian dollars forward, they are **long** U.S. dollars and **short** Canadian dollars. In this case, "long" just means that an investor *owns* something and "short" means that an investor *owes* something, so by selling Canadian dollars forward for U.S. dollars, the investor is long U.S. dollars and short Canadian dollars. The payoff possibilities that arise from this position based on various exchange rates are depicted in **Figure 11.1**, where the horizontal axis is the value of the C$ in terms of the US$—that is, the inverse quote.

Continuing with our example, suppose that, in one year, the spot exchange rate for the U.S. dollar is either C$1.20 (i.e., the Canadian dollar depreciates or loses value) or C$0.80 (i.e., the Canadian dollar appreciates or increases in value). Of course, if the Canadian dollar appreciates in value, then the U.S. dollar depreciates (at least on a relative basis), and vice versa, because the exchange rate is just the ratio of Canadian dollars to U.S. dollars. If the Canadian dollar goes to 1.2, then each U.S. dollar is now worth C$1.20, so the U.S. dollar has appreciated in value and the Canadian dollar has depreciated. In this case, the investor fulfills the forward foreign exchange contract and exchanges C$1 million for US$1 million, and then immediately sells the U.S. dollars in the spot market to get C$1.2 million. In this case, the investor earns a profit of $200,000. If the opposite happens and the Canadian dollar appreciates to 0.8, the investor still has to fulfill the forward contract and sell C$1 million to get US$1 million. However, now when the investor sells the U.S. dollars in the spot market, they can be exchanged for only C$0.8 million, and the investor incurs a $200,000 loss.

If we denote the future spot price of Canadian for U.S. dollars as $S_T$, the forward price of Canadian for U.S. dollars as $F$, and the number of contracts entered into as $n$, the profit (loss) from a long position in a forward contract can be determined using Equation 11.1:

$$\text{Profit (loss) from long position} = (S_T - F) \times n \qquad [11.1]$$

The important point about a forward contract is that the investor *has* to fulfill the contract regardless of what happens to the value of the underlying asset. As a result, a forward contract has the possibility of either gains *or* losses, and the payoff is "linear" in the value of

**speculate**   make an educated guess about the future value of something in hopes of profiting from it

**naked position**   a position that leaves the investor exposed to changes in the value of the underlying asset

**underlying asset**   the securities on which derivative contracts are based

**long**   the investor owns something

**short**   the investor owes something

**FIGURE 11.1**  **Long Position in U.S. Dollars**

the underlying asset (that is, the payoff goes up "one for one" with increases in $S_T$ and goes down "one for one" with decreases in $S_T$).[2] Figure 11.1 shows the possible payoff from the forward contract as a 45-degree line going through the forward rate. If the spot exchange rate in the future exceeds the forward rate by $0.01, then the speculator earns $0.01 profit for every Canadian dollar sold forward for U.S. dollars, and vice versa. The reason for this payoff is that the forward contract is a legal contract between the speculator and the bank to exchange funds in the future at a price fixed today. However, think about the cost of the contract. The forward rate is the price for future delivery, but whereas the bank makes money by buying and selling forward contracts at slightly different prices,[3] there is no immediate cash outlay for the contract. It is a contract stipulating the terms for future delivery.

**credit (counterparty) risk**   the risk that a borrower will not fulfill a contract or make a required payment

This raises an interesting problem as far as the bank is concerned. If the Canadian dollar depreciates to 1.2, the investor will obviously execute the forward contract, buy the more valuable U.S. dollar, and make a profit of $200,000. However, if the Canadian dollar appreciates to 0.8, there is **credit risk** involved for the bank, as the investor suffers a loss of $200,000 and may decide to renege on the contract. This credit risk is also called **counterparty risk**, as it is the risk that the bank's counterparty to the transaction will not fulfill the contract. The bank can reduce this risk by dealing only with companies with which it already has a banking relationship and a line of credit. In this way, banks can control the risk that the counterparty imposes on them. This is an important issue that we will return to later in the chapter because it figured prominently in the financial crisis of 2008–9.

Finally, banks will sell forward contracts only for legitimate business purposes, and then only up to a company's approved credit limit. Banks do not want to be seen selling forward contracts for speculative purposes because this often runs counter to the objectives of the central bank, which may involve targeting a specific exchange rate. This is particularly true in countries where the bank regulator is that same central bank.

**hedging**   reducing the risk of adverse price movement by taking an offsetting position in a derivative to eliminate exposure to an underlying price

Most corporations and financial institutions become involved in forward markets for **hedging** purposes, rather than for speculation. In fact, most businesses and financial institutions are prohibited from engaging in speculation. Hedgers enter into derivative contracts to protect a short or long position in the underlying asset, as described below.

**exposure**   the extent to which value is affected by an external event, such as a change in exchange rate

Suppose, in the previous example, that a Canadian corporation is owed US$1 million by a U.S. company and expects to receive this in one year. In this case, the Canadian corporation has a naked position in U.S. dollars or, more formally, it has a U.S. dollar foreign exchange **exposure**, because it is long in the underlying asset (i.e., U.S. dollars). However, even though this position arises because of a commercial contract, the payoff is identical to the speculative purchase of the U.S. dollar forward that we just discussed. If the Canadian dollar depreciates to C$1.20, then the Canadian company will receive C$1.2 million when it exchanges the proceeds at the future spot rate. Alternatively, if the Canadian dollar appreciates to C$0.80, the Canadian company will receive only C$0.8 million. The only difference between the two payoffs is that one arises as the result of normal business operations and the other as the result of a speculative transaction.

This scenario of long U.S. dollar exposure is a standard problem facing Canadian companies that do business in the United States and invoice in U.S. dollars. In this case, if a Canadian company exports to the United States and waits for its U.S. customer to pay, it has long U.S. dollar exposure. Similarly, short U.S. dollar exposure arises when a Canadian company imports goods from the United States and then has to pay the U.S. dollar invoice at some future time, such as in 90 days. Because almost 90 percent of Canada's foreign trade is either with U.S. companies or denominated in U.S. dollars, these long and short U.S. dollar exposures are very common. A Canadian exporting company could avoid this problem by insisting that the U.S. company remit Canadian rather than U.S. dollars, but this normally isn't possible. Even if it were possible, it simply transfers the problem to the U.S. company. If a company cannot avoid this long U.S. dollar exposure, what can it do?

Most companies in this situation are not willing to speculate, because they are in business to manufacture and sell things, not to speculate on future exchange rates. In this regard,

---

[2]This is the distinction between the derivatives discussed in this chapter, which are linear, and those discussed in Chapter 12 (i.e., options), which are non-linear.

[3]The bank sells at the "ask" rate and buys at the "bid" rate. Its profit is the spread between these two rates, which differs according to the maturity of the contract and the size—that is, who the bank is dealing with.

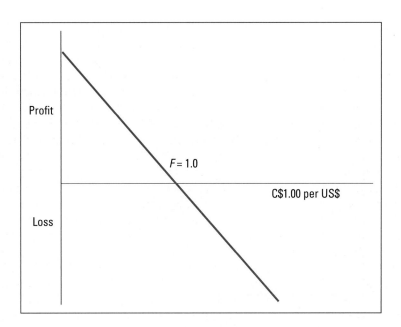

**FIGURE 11.2** **Short Position in U.S. Dollars**

however, note that doing nothing and exchanging the U.S. dollars when they are received is equivalent to engaging in currency speculation. Some large Canadian companies with extensive U.S. dollar business do find that it makes sense to hold U.S. dollar bank accounts and actively manage their U.S. dollar exposure, but most simply want to remove this exposure. Removing a naked position is called **covering** (or hedging). In fact, the dictionary definition of hedging describes it as betting on both sides in order to remove risk. From our previous discussion of forward markets, we know that the opposite of a firm's long position in U.S. dollars is a short position in U.S. dollar forward contracts, so the company needs to sell U.S. dollars forward for Canadian dollars. Before we discuss the "hedged" position, we should first consider the payoff diagram for a naked sale of U.S. dollars forward, which is depicted in **Figure 11.2**.

**covering**   removing a naked position

Notice that the payoff for the naked short position is the mirror image (or complete opposite) of the naked long position. If US$1 million is sold forward for C$1 million, and the Canadian dollar depreciates to C$1.20, then the forward contract loses money. In this case, the forward contract requires that US$1 million be exchanged for C$1 million. However, to get the US$1 million now requires C$1.2 million in the spot market, causing a C$200,000 loss. Alternatively, if the Canadian dollar appreciates to C$0.80, then buying US$1 million to fulfill the forward contract requires only C$800,000, meaning a C$200,000 profit. So the gains and losses from the naked short position are the exact opposite of a naked long position and can be determined by using Equation 11.2:

$$\boxed{\text{Profit (loss) from short position} = (F - S_T) \times n} \qquad [11.2]$$

Now consider the company with a long U.S. dollar exposure of US$1 million that buys a forward contract to sell U.S. dollars forward for Canadian dollars, thereby creating a US$1-million short position. That company's combined position is simply the sum of the two previous diagrams, shown in **Figure 11.3**.

If the Canadian dollar depreciates to C$1.20, the company earns a profit of $200,000 on its underlying U.S. dollar exposure but then loses $200,000 on the forward sale of U.S. dollars. Similarly, if the Canadian dollar appreciates to C$0.80, it loses $200,000 on its underlying U.S. dollar exposure but gains $200,000 on its forward sale of U.S. dollars. Regardless of what happens to the value of the exchange rate, it is locked in (or covered or hedged) against any future fluctuations in the exchange rate, so the company is no longer exposed to exchange rate changes.

We conclude this section with examples 11.1 to 11.4, which illustrate the profits that materialize from assuming various positions in forward contracts.

**FIGURE 11.3**  **Long and Short Forward Positions**

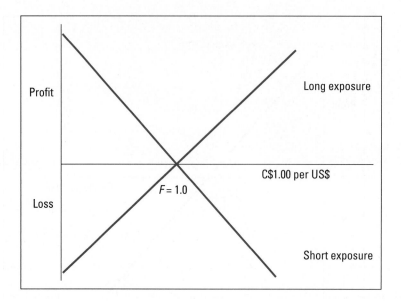

---

**EXAMPLE 11.1** | Profits from a Long Position

Suppose the spot exchange rate is C$1.50 per €1, while the six-month forward rate is C$1.52 per euro. What will be the profit for an investor who assumes a €100,000 long position in the forward contract if the spot rate in six months equals the following amounts?

    **a.** C$1.50 per euro

    **b.** C$1.55 per euro

**Solution**

    **a.** Profit (loss) long position $= (S_T - F) \times n = (\$1.50 - \$1.52) \times C\$100,000 = -\$2,000$ (loss)

    **b.** Profit (loss) long position $= (S_T - F) \times n = (\$1.55 - \$1.52) \times C\$100,000 = \$3,000$ profit

---

**EXAMPLE 11.2** | Profits from a Short Position

Assume another investor takes a €100,000 short position in the six-month euro forward contract discussed in Example 11.1. Determine the investor's profit (loss) if the spot rate in six months equals the following amounts:

    **a.** C$1.50 per euro

    **b.** C$1.55 per euro

**Solution**

    **a.** Profit (loss) short position $= (F - S_T) \times n = (\$1.52 - \$1.50) \times C\$100,000 = \$2,000$ profit

    **b.** Profit (loss) short position $= (F - S_T) \times n = (\$1.52 - \$1.55) \times C\$100,000 = -\$3,000$ (loss)

---

**EXAMPLE 11.3** | How to Hedge a Short Position in the Underlying Asset

Assume the spot rates and forward rates from Example 11.1. Suppose a firm has to pay a foreign supplier €100,000 in six months and decides to eliminate its foreign exchange exposure by entering into a six-month forward contract.

**a.** Should it enter into a short or a long forward position? For how much?

**b.** Assuming it enters into the appropriate forward position, determine the cost in Canadian dollars for the following future spot rates:

   **i.** C$1.50 per euro

   **ii.** C$1.55 per euro

**Solution**

**a.** Because the firm has a short position in the underlying asset (i.e., euros), it should take a long position in the forward contract. To hedge itself for the full amount of its obligation, it needs to enter into a €100,000 forward contract.

**b.** **i.** The cost in Canadian dollars = €100,000 × C$1.52 per euro = C$152,000

   **ii.** The cost in Canadian dollars = €100,000 × C$1.52 per euro = C$152,000

Notice that the cost is the same regardless of what the six-month spot rate is—thus, the position is hedged.

---

**EXAMPLE 11.4** | How to Hedge a Long Position in the Underlying Asset

Assume the spot rates and forward rates from Example 11.1. Suppose a firm expects to receive €100,000 in six months from a foreign customer and decides to eliminate its foreign exchange exposure by entering into a six-month forward contract.

**a.** Should it enter into a short or a long forward position? For how much?

**b.** Assuming it enters into the appropriate forward position, determine the proceeds in Canadian dollars for the following future spot rates:

   **i.** C$1.50 per euro

   **ii.** C$1.55 per euro

**Solution**

**a.** Because the firm has a long position in the underlying asset (i.e., euros), it should take a short position in the forward contract. To hedge itself for the full amount, it needs to enter into a €100,000 forward contract.

**b.** **i.** The proceeds in Canadian dollars = €100,000 × C$1.52 per euro = C$152,000

   **ii.** The proceeds in Canadian dollars = €100,000 × C$1.52 per euro = C$152,000

Notice that the proceeds are the same regardless of what the six-month spot rate is—thus, the position is hedged.

## Interest Rate Parity (IRP) Revisited

The simple examples above illustrate why the forward foreign exchange market is a bank market. The bank is selling forward contracts to its customers for commercial purposes to allow them to manage their foreign exchange exposure. The banks are not buying and selling foreign exchange for speculative purposes.[4] If a bank finds that it has sold too many U.S. dollar forward contracts to its customers, so that the bank itself is now exposed, it can either enter the inter-bank market to offset its exposure by trading with other banks or synthetically create forward foreign exchange contracts. A bank can synthetically create a forward contract through the interest rate parity (IRP) condition that was discussed in Appendix 6A.

$$\boxed{\dfrac{F}{S} = \dfrac{(1 + k_{domestic})}{(1 + k_{foreign})}} \qquad [11.3]$$

[4]Many banks have suffered huge losses when rogue traders incur losses on forward foreign exchange contracts and then hide these trades and take bigger positions in the hope of covering their losses, only to end up with even bigger losses. Allied Irish Bank lost US$691 million as a result of John Rusnak's rogue trading in the Japanese yen at its Baltimore (U.S.) office in 2003. Rusnak ended up with a 7½-year prison sentence for bank fraud.

Recall that in the IRP condition, the exchange rates are expressed as Canadian dollars per foreign currency. Equation 11.3 means that the ratio of the forward to the spot rate must equal the ratio of one plus the interest rate in both markets. If we rearrange this condition, it tells us what determines the forward rate:

$$F = S \times \frac{(1 + k_{domestic})}{(1 + k_{foreign})}$$

[11.4]

In other words, the forward rate is the ratio of one plus the interest rate in both markets times the spot rate. The important point is that all the Canadian banks deal in the spot market and can also borrow and lend in the major currencies. Thus, they can create a forward contract.

---

**EXAMPLE 11.5** | Estimating Forward Rates

Assume the one-year euro interest rate is presently 3.5 percent, and the one-year Canadian interest rate is 5 percent. Assume today's spot rate is C$1.50 for €1. Find the one-year forward exchange rate.

**Solution**  Notice that the interest rate differential for the specified one-year term is 1.5 percent, which implies that the forward exchange rate should be approximately 1.5 percent higher (in Canadian dollar terms) than the spot rate to ensure IRP holds.

To be more precise, we can use Equation 11.4 to solve for the forward rate:

$$F = S \times \frac{(1 + k_{domestic})}{(1 + k_{foreign})} = \$1.50 \times \frac{(1.05)}{(1.035)} = \$1.522$$

---

Suppose that a bank has sold too many U.S. dollar forward contracts and wants to create forward foreign exchange contracts to offset its own exposure. It can do so by first borrowing Canadian dollars for one year and then exchanging Canadian dollars for U.S. dollars at the spot rate. Finally, the bank would invest the U.S. dollar proceeds for one year at the U.S. interest rate. The result is that it knows exactly how many U.S. dollars it will own at the end of the year, because this is the amount invested times one plus the U.S. interest rate. It also knows exactly how many Canadian dollars it will owe, because this is the amount borrowed times one plus its borrowing cost. In effect, by borrowing Canadian dollars, converting them to U.S. dollars, and investing in the United States, the bank has synthetically sold Canadian dollars forward for U.S. dollars. This process generates a payoff identical to a straightforward sale of Canadian dollars for U.S. dollars, which is why interest rate parity tells us that the rates have to be the same. Otherwise, limitless profits could be made without assuming any risk—and the Canadian banks are not known for passing up the opportunity to make limitless profits!

For a bank with large-scale international operations, like all the major Canadian banks, these operations are routine. To synthetically create this forward contract, a Canadian bank would borrow in the Canadian money market by issuing what are termed "bankers' acceptances" (BAs). These are short-term notes that are fully guaranteed or "accepted" by the bank. The U.S. dollars would then be lent at what is referred to as the **London inter-bank offered rate (LIBOR)**. This is the key interest rate for Canadian banks when they are borrowing and lending U.S. dollars because it is a "free market" rate and not under direct government control. Further, it can be accessed by the banks to effect very large transactions.

**London inter-bank offered rate (LIBOR)**  the key interest rate for Canadian banks when borrowing and lending U.S. dollars; a "free market" rate that is not under direct government control

## Pricing Forward Contracts

The IRP condition is a special case for pricing forward contracts. The general condition is that investors can always create a forward position in a storable **commodity** by buying it spot and holding it for future delivery. It has to be storable because if its condition deteriorates, it will not be acceptable in fulfilling the contract. Similarly, a commodity is something like a precious metal, whose value is immediately recognizable and not subject to dispute. This is essentially what the bank did above to create a forward contract; it simply purchased U.S. dollars and then "stored" them in a one-year investment. The only difference was that it first borrowed the Canadian dollars and then exchanged them for U.S. dollars. However, suppose

**commodity**  something traded based solely on price, because it is undifferentiated and can be traded without requiring physical examination the storable commodity is a base metal that the investor has sold forward for $100. How is the forward synthetically created?

If the metal is currently selling for $80, it is regarded as having a forward **contango** of $20 or 25 percent. In this case, the investor borrows $80 and buys the metal spot. The investor then has to store it for a year, but because it is a storable commodity, at the end of the year the investor has the metal needed to meet the forward sale. The only question is the cost involved. First are the **storage costs**, which we assume are $5 for one year. Second are the financing costs, and we will assume the interest cost is 10 percent. With these assumptions, the investor can generate the metal for the forward sale at a future cost of $93. This is the principal and interest payment of $88 ($80 in principal and $8 interest) plus the storage cost of $5. If these were the actual prices and costs, an arbitrageur could generate gains of $7 simply by selling the metal forward for $100 and then buying it spot and storing it for a total cost of $93.

The above example is a simplified version of actual commodity arbitrage, because it assumes that there is no income or **convenience yield** associated with holding the asset.[5] However, this sort of commodity arbitrage is common with storable commodities.

The London Metal Exchange (LME) is the premier metal exchange in the world and traces its origins back to the Royal Exchange in 1751. The LME trades eight non-ferrous metals, including aluminum, copper, lead, nickel, zinc, and tin, as well as steel, molybdenum, and cobalt. To encourage the efficiency of the metal market, the LME lists major warehouses in 37 locations that accept and store metals. These warehouses are located around the world in the major markets, so that consumers can, if need be, take delivery. For example, the following is the first entry in its warehouse list:

> C. Steinweg NV
> Albert Dock, 131
> Vrieskaai,
> 2030 Antwerp
> AH, CA, PB, ZS

This indicates the company, C. Steinweg NV, in Antwerp, Belgium, accepts metals at this warehouse in the Albert Dock. The metals accepted at this location are primary aluminum (AH), copper (CA), lead (PB), and zinc (ZS). This particular warehouse does not accept some of the other metals, but C. Steinweg has other warehouses in the Albert Dock that do. The LME has strict guidelines that companies must follow to have their warehouses accepted for the list, so that people taking delivery know the quality of the metal they are buying. However, in actual practice, less than 1 percent of contracts are actually closed out with physical delivery.

The existence of these warehouses and an organized exchange means that it is very easy to buy spot, store, and then sell forward these commodities. A profit of $7 on a $100 forward sale is more than enough to increase the spot demand for the metal and generate a forward sale. In the process, the spot price rises and the forward price falls until there are no risk-free profits. If, for example, the forward price drops to $95 and the spot price rises to $81.82, then the arbitrage opportunity disappears. The difference between the spot and forward rate is $13.18 or 16.11 percent, made up of the interest cost of 10 percent plus the storage cost of 6.11 percent (i.e., $5/$81.82). Together, the storage and financing costs are referred to as the **cost of carry**, because they represent the total cost of buying the commodity spot and then carrying it or effecting physical delivery when the forward contract expires—in a year, for our example.

The cost of carry links spot and forward rates so that, unless it changes, spot and forward rates will move in unison. For example, if the price of the metal increases in the spot market from $81.82 to $90, then the forward rate will also increase. This also means that a future disruption in supply that changes the forward rate will also change spot rates, even if there is no change in spot market conditions. All that is required is that the items are storable commodities. If they are not storable, they can't be bought and held to meet future delivery, and the forward and spot markets would be disconnected. The items also have to be commodities, which essentially means that they are undifferentiated and can be traded without requiring physical examination. It would be difficult to buy spot and hold to meet future delivery if there was uncertainty about what was being delivered against the forward contract.

**contango**  when the forward price exceeds the spot price

**storage costs**  the price charged for holding a commodity for future delivery

**convenience yield**  the benefit or premium derived from holding the asset rather than holding a derivative

**cost of carry**  the total cost of buying a commodity spot and then carrying it or effecting physical delivery when the forward contract expires

---

[5] Note that when we were dealing with foreign currencies, the interest earned in the currency held could be viewed as the convenience yield.

Equation 11.5 expresses the relationship between cost of carry, and spot and forward prices:

$$\boxed{F = (1 + c) \times S}$$ [11.5]

where $c$ = the cost of carry, as a percentage of $S$, over the period in question.[6]

There was an enormous amount of arbitrage activity in the crude oil market toward the end of 2008. Huge tankers were being chartered simply so that arbitrageurs could buy oil spot and store it in the tankers to meet the delivery requirements on forward crude oil contracts. If that sounds strange, imagine it: tankers sitting idly offshore or moving aimlessly around for six months or even a year, simply to deliver crude oil against a forward contract.

---

**EXAMPLE 11.6** | Estimating Prices for Commodity Forward Contracts

Find the forward price for a one-year forward contract for a metal that is selling for $90 spot, if storage costs are $5 for the year and financing costs are 10 percent per year.

**Solution**

$$S = \$90; c = [(0.10 \times \$90) + \$5]/\$90 = 0.1556$$
$$F = (1 + 0.1556) \times \$90 = \$104$$

In comparison with our discussion above, notice that when the spot price increases by $8.18 (i.e., from $81.82 to $90), the forward price increases $9 (i.e., from $95 to $104).

---

**Concept Review Questions**

1. Why do forward contracts involve a credit risk for banks?

2. When would a speculator assume a long position in a forward contract on an underlying asset? When would a speculator assume a short position?

3. When would a hedger assume a long position in a forward contract on an underlying asset? When would a hedger assume a short position?

4. What is the relationship among spot rates, forward rates, and the cost of carry?

---

## 11.2 | Futures Contracts

**LEARNING OBJECTIVE 11.2**

Explain what futures contracts are and why they can be viewed as the public market version of forward contracts.

### The Mechanics of Futures Contracts

We started our discussion of derivatives with forward contracts for two reasons. First, they are primarily a bank instrument and represent one of the basic instruments used by

---

[6] Notice that interest rate parity is a special example of forward pricing in which the cost of carry is the ratio of one plus the interest rates in both countries. In other words, for IRP $(1 + c) = \dfrac{(1 + k_{domestic})}{(1 + k_{foreign})}$. Appendix 11A expands on this discussion, showing the relationship between forward interest rates and forward rate agreements (FRAs), which are interest-rate derivative products offered by banks.

corporations to manage their interest rate and foreign exchange rate exposures. The second reason is that they are centuries old. There are reports of forward-like contracts going back at least to the time of the Romans. Like the modern bank instruments of today, forwards have always been contracts between two parties and have largely been non-traded. However, over the past 35 years a new traded instrument that does much the same thing as a forward contract has rapidly developed. This is the **futures contract**. Remember that forward contracts involve credit risk, which is the reason investors need a line of credit with a bank before it will sell them. Once this requirement has been met, forwards are incredibly flexible in both the term and the amount of money involved. However, what makes them flexible for corporations also makes them difficult to trade. For something to be tradable, it has to be standardized so that people buying or selling it over the telephone or Internet know exactly what they are getting. The dramatic growth in the development of futures markets occurred because these problems have been solved. Let's look at how this happened.

First let's consider credit risk, which arises with the forward contract because the bank worries a borrower will renege on the forward contract if they suffer a loss. To solve this problem, all futures contracts are made with a futures exchange, not with an individual. Investor A might buy a futures contract and investor B might sell one, but instead of one contract between A and B, there are two contracts involving each individual and the exchange. The exchange then assigns responsibility for reducing the credit risk and making sure that delivery takes place to a **clearing corporation**. In Canada, the Canadian Derivatives Clearing Corporation (CDCC) of the Montreal Exchange handles these responsibilities for futures contracts, as well as option contracts, which we discuss in Chapter 12.

To ensure that people fulfill their contractual obligations, the CDCC enforces two types of **margins**: an **initial margin** and a **maintenance margin**. The margin is essentially a good faith deposit made by both the buyer and the seller to ensure they complete the transaction. In effect, it is a performance bond. The margin is set by each clearinghouse based on the risk involved in the underlying asset: the riskier the asset, the higher the margin. The initial margin is relatively small and varies between 2 percent and 10 percent of the value of the contract, but it is required of both the buyer and the seller. Usually, the brokerage house managing the transaction for the customer imposes a higher margin, particularly for new or smaller clients, but it is not permitted to impose smaller margins. (Members of CDCC are allowed to post margin by depositing securities; CDCC has an extensive list of securities issued by the U.S. and Canadian governments that it accepts, as well as Ontario and Quebec provincial bonds.)

All futures contracts are then marked to market each day, as the value of the contract changes. This means that all profits and losses on a futures contract are credited to investors' accounts every day to calculate their equity position in the underlying contract. If the equity position increases, these profits can be withdrawn; losses reduce investors' equity positions. Whenever an investor's equity position drops below the maintenance margin requirement (normally 75 percent of the initial margin), they will receive a **margin call** and will be forced to contribute more money, the **variation margin**, to bring the equity position back up to the initial level. If they fail to make this margin call, the position will automatically be closed out. This process of marking to market is called **daily resettlement** and is based on the contract's **settlement price**, which is normally, but not always, the daily closing price.

For example, suppose a futures contract is for 1,000 units of some underlying asset, and the starting unit price is $50; the contract value is $50,000. This is referred to as the **notional amount** of the contract, even though the investor does not have to come up with $50,000 to enter into it. The buyer and seller of this contract both need to deposit the initial margin requirement, which we assume is $2,000 (i.e., 4 percent of $50,000). Assume the maintenance margin is 75 percent of the initial margin (or $1,500). The buyer's commitment is to buy 1,000 units at $50, and the seller's commitment is to sell 1,000 units at $50. If the price closes up $0.25 on the first day, at $50.25, then the futures contract is now worth $250 to the buyer. This is because the buyer has contracted to buy the asset for $50,000, and it is now worth $50,250, so the equity increases from $2,000 to $2,250. Conversely, the seller's equity has declined from $2,000 to $1,750. Like all futures contracts, the gains and losses offset each other. In this case, the buyer has gained $250 at the expense of the seller, and the clearinghouse will transfer this $250 from the seller's account to the buyer's. The next day, the process

**futures contract**   a standardized exchange-traded contract in which the seller agrees to deliver a commodity to the buyer at some point in the future

**clearing corporation**   a company that is responsible for reducing the credit risk of futures contracts and option contracts and for making sure that delivery takes place

**margin**   a good faith deposit with a clearinghouse that is made by both the buyer and the seller to ensure they complete the transaction

**initial margin**   a relatively small deposit made with the clearinghouse, usually between 2 percent and 10 percent of the value of the contract

**maintenance margin**   a minimum amount that must be maintained in a margin account

**margin call**   a requirement to add money and increase an equity position to a minimum level

**variation margin**   the additional funds required to bring the margin account balance back up to its initial margin level when the maintenance margin level is breached

**daily resettlement**   the process of marking to market and adjusting investors' equity positions

**settlement price**   the price used to settle futures contracts; usually the daily closing price

**notional amount**   the dollar amount upon which a contract is valued

**offsetting** cancelling a futures position by making an equivalent but opposite transaction

starts all over again. If the buyer feels that, now that the price has gone up, they want to cancel the contract, the buyer makes an **offsetting** sale, and the purchase is cancelled. The buyer can then withdraw the $2,250.[7] In this case, the buyer has a $250 profit on the margin deposit of $2,000.

Suppose, instead, that both parties leave their contract outstanding, and the next day the price increases again, only this time it jumps to $51. Now the buyer's equity position has increased by $1,000 from its starting position, and the seller's equity position has correspondingly decreased by $1,000. The clearing corporation will transfer this amount from the seller's margin account, which means the seller's equity is now $1,000, below the maintenance margin. This drop in margin would result in the seller getting a call from the broker, telling them to post more money or the position will be closed. It is this daily resettling, combined with the enforcement of margin requirements, that ensures that both the buyer and the seller meet their commitments. This is the reason the margin is viewed as a performance bond: both the buyer and the seller have to post margin to make sure they deliver on their promise. The result is the elimination of credit risk, which means individuals can trade futures contracts without worrying about the identity of their counterparty—that is, the party they are trading with.

Examples 11.7 and 11.8 illustrate the concepts associated with marking to market.

---

**EXAMPLE 11.7** | Daily Marking to Market: Long Position

An investor enters into a long position in a futures contract that requires a $50,000 initial margin and has a maintenance margin that is 75 percent of this amount. The futures price associated with this contract is $20. Assume the spot price of the underlying asset closes at the following prices for the next five days: $20.50, $20.75, $21.00, $19.75, and $19.25. Estimate the daily profit (loss) for this investor, as well as the equity position, assuming no cash deposits or withdrawals are made to or from the account.

**Solution**

| Day | Spot Price | Daily Profit | Equity Position (Margin Balance) |
|---|---|---|---|
| 0 | $20 | – | $50,000 |
| 1 | $20.50 | $0.50 × 50,000 = $25,000 | $50,000 + $25,000 = $75,000 |
| 2 | $20.75 | $0.25 × 50,000 = $12,500 | $75,000 + $12,500 = $87,500 |
| 3 | $21.00 | $0.25 × 50,000 = $12,500 | $87,500 + $12,500 = $100,000 |
| 4 | $19.75 | −$1.25 × 50,000 = −$62,500 | $100,000 − $62,500 = $37,500 |
| 5 | $19.25 | −$0.50 × 50,000 = −$25,000 | $37,500 − $25,000 = $12,500 |

Notice that the investor would have received a margin call on day 5, when the equity position fell below the maintenance margin requirement of $37,500.

---

**EXAMPLE 11.8** | Daily Marking to Market: Short Position

An investor enters into a short position in a futures contract that requires a $50,000 initial margin and has a maintenance margin that is 75 percent of this amount. The futures price associated with this contract is $20. Assume the spot price of the underlying asset closes at the following prices for the next five days: $20.50, $20.75, $21.00, $19.75, and $19.25. Estimate the daily profit (loss) for this investor, as well as the equity position, assuming no cash deposits or withdrawals are made to or from the account.

---

[7]Similarly, investors with the short position in the futures contract could enter into an offsetting purchase to close their position. Entering into offsetting transactions is the most common way to close futures positions. Actual delivery of the underlying asset occurs very rarely, in less than 5 percent of all futures transactions.

**Solution**

| Day | Spot Price | Daily Profit | Equity Position (Margin Balance) |
|-----|-----------|--------------|----------------------------------|
| 0 | $20 | – | $50,000 |
| 1 | $20.50 | $-\$0.50 \times \$50,000 = -\$25,000$ | $\$50,000 - \$25,000 = \$25,000$ |
| 2 | $20.75 | $-\$0.25 \times \$50,000 = -\$12,500$ | $\$25,000 - \$12,500 = \$12,500$ |
| 3 | $21.00 | $-\$0.25 \times \$50,000 = -\$12,500$ | $\$12,500 - \$12,500 = \$0$ |
| 4 | $19.75 | $\$1.25 \times \$50,000 = \$62,500$ | $\$0 + \$62,500 = \$62,500$ |
| 5 | $19.25 | $\$0.50 \times \$50,000 = \$25,000$ | $\$62,500 + \$25,000 = \$87,500$ |

Notice that the investor would have received a margin call on day 1, when the equity position fell below the maintenance margin requirement of $37,500. Because the price continued to go up and additional losses were incurred, the investor might also have had to contribute on days 2 and 3 as well, depending on how much they contributed each day. Therefore, in practice, the margin account numbers after day 1 would reflect these contributions.

## Futures Contracts Markets

Producing a standardized contract requires that both the underlying asset and the term of the contract be standardized. The term of the contract is set by the individual exchange, but most exchanges follow the lead of the Chicago Mercantile Exchange (CME), which has been consolidating the derivatives exchange business by buying up exchanges around the world, including the Chicago Board of Trade (CBOT) and the New York Mercantile Exchange (NYMEX), which are all now part of the CME Group. The most common delivery months are March, June, September, and December. In practice, physical delivery rarely takes place, as most positions are closed out with an offsetting transaction before the final day of trading, which is generally a couple of days before delivery. In this way, futures contracts are designed to share the price risk and not actually transfer the underlying asset. Most futures generally have a rolling 18-month term. This means that, at any point, investors can normally buy and sell futures on the same commodity with six different maturity dates.

To standardize the underlying asset, the exchange specifies precisely what is being traded, so that even though delivery rarely takes place, people know exactly what they are buying or selling. For the rare occasions when delivery does take place, the exchange will specify both the location and how delivery will occur. This is why, for example, the London Metal Exchange keeps a list of recognized warehouses.

Finally, the exchange determines how much of the asset is traded in each contract. In the example above, we used $50,000 as a notional contract amount. In reality, the actual amount varies with the needs of the individuals who are trading. So what does all this mean in practice?

Understanding the futures market means understanding the basic distinction between futures on physical commodities and financial futures. Some of the major assets traded and the locations of the trading are shown in Table 11.2. However, these contracts are constantly changing as there have been enormous changes in futures markets over the past few years, with the CME Group consolidating several previously distinct exchanges. New market entrants have also appeared as the International Commodity Exchange (ICE) and the New York Stock Exchange (NYSE) have both bought smaller exchanges and expanded the range of contracts to compete with the CME Group.

Note the variety of commodities traded, ranging from traditional agricultural products to newer energy and base metal contracts. The CME even introduced both futures and options contracts on the regional Case/Shiller U.S. housing indexes. Essentially, we see that futures contracts exist on almost any asset that will generate sufficient interest from companies wanting to hedge risk against changes in its price or that will generate sufficient speculative trading activity. Also note the intense competition. Competition appears when new contracts are introduced, such as weather derivatives and futures contracts on real estate and the consumer price index; some of these survive, while others disappear due to lack of interest. Finance in the News 11.1 discusses the impact that increased volatility has had on bank stock investments.

**TABLE 11.2**     Major Futures Contracts and Markets

| Underlying Asset | Exchange |
| --- | --- |
| **Commodities** | |
| Wheat/oats/soybeans/rice | Chicago Board of Trade (CBOT) |
| Cattle/pigs/lumber/corn/milk | Chicago Mercantile Exchange (CME) |
| Crude oil/heating oil/natural gas/cocoa | New York Mercantile Exchange (NYMEX) |
| Cotton/orange juice/coffee/sugar | NY Cotton Exchange |
| Gold/silver/copper | The Commodity Exchange (Comex) |
| Lead/nickel/tin/aluminum/zinc | London Metal Exchange (LME) |
| Canola/western barley/wheat | International Commodity Exchange (ICE) |
| **Financial Futures** | |
| Treasury notes and bonds/DJIA | CBOT |
| S&P Index/Nikkei 225/C$/£/€ | CME |
| BAs/Canada bonds/TSX/S&P 60 Index | Montreal Exchange (MX) |
| German bonds/European equities | Euronext/NYSE Liffe |
| **Other** | |
| Weather derivatives | CME |

## 11.1  Finance in the News     Bank-Stock Volatility May Become the New Normal

The slowing economy is making it more difficult for equity analysts to accurately predict bank profits, suggesting that investors may want to get used to the kind of volatility that follows earnings misses.

Last quarter, four of the Big Six banks—Toronto Dominion, Nova Scotia, CIBC and National—fell short of earnings forecasts as higher credit losses stemming from slower growth took a toll on income statements.

A contributing factor was new accounting rules that forced banks to disclose expected losses.

"Last quarter was a bit of a wake-up call," said Rob Wessel, a former bank-equity analyst who runs Toronto-based Hamilton Capital Partners Inc. "Analysts are going to have more difficulty forecasting earnings, and therefore there's a greater chance of misses and beats."

And when analysts' forecasts are misaligned with actual results, stock volatility is sure to follow, particularly around earnings season. The banks' next round of quarterly financial statements is slated for late May.

Last year, Canadian banks adopted the accounting rules known as IFRS 9, which were formulated after the global financial crisis to improve reporting on financial assets.

Rather than simply booking loan losses when they are incurred, the banks have moved to a model that estimates losses before they happen. It's an imprecise process that requires banks to consider how macroeconomic and credit changes might affect their loan books.

In the banks' fiscal first quarter, covering the rocky November to January stretch for financial markets, cuts to Canadian growth forecasts, combined with a steep decline in the price of crude oil, as well as the housing market slowdown, all factored into a rise in loan loss provisions, the amount of money banks set aside to cover bad loans.

TD's loan losses rose to $850-million from $693-million in the same quarter last year, while CIBC's increased by 121 per cent year-over-year to $338-million.

That order of magnitude reflects a moderation of economic conditions, rather than a significant deterioration, CIBC Capital Markets analyst Robert Sedran said.

"We're at the point in the cycle where you should expect some noise on the loan-loss line," he said, adding that credit losses have nowhere to go but up.

"When you're at [a cyclical low in] loan losses, it creates potential risks."

Mr. Wessel said another potential source of friction is likely to contribute to a period of heightened volatility for bank stocks: big acquisitions south of the border.

There has been little in the way of consolidation in the U.S. banking industry in the years since the financial crisis. But the proposed US$28-billion merger of BB&T Corp. and SunTrust Banks Inc. has led to speculation about a coming wave of deal-making in the United States.

"Seeing a deal that large get approved signals to investors that the regulators are comfortable with M&A," Mr. Wessel said.

And for Canadian banks with big U.S. platforms, further expansion outside of Canada might make sense right now, said Norman Levine, the managing director at Toronto-based Portfolio Management Corp.

"The headwinds in Canada, between the consumer being so heavily in debt and economic growth looking to be substantially lower than in the U.S., are making U.S. acquisitions more attractive again," Mr. Levine said.

The concern for Canadian bank shareholders, however, is that a large acquisition is a fairly reliable trigger for that bank's stock to under-perform.

Last year, for example, the Bank of Nova Scotia's buying spree weighed on its share price.

Deals to acquire MD Financial Management and Jarislowsky Fraser Ltd. for a total of more than $3.5-billion coincided with Scotia's stock falling by 16 per cent in 2018, good for second last among the Big Six.

**Source:** Shufelt, Tim, "Bank-Stock Volatility May Become the New Normal." *The Globe and Mail,* April 27, 2019. ©2019 The Globe and Mail Inc. All rights reserved. Reprinted by permission.

It is interesting to note that relatively little trading takes place on Canadian exchanges. Commodity futures trading in Canada is concentrated in Winnipeg on ICE Canada, the former Winnipeg Commodity Exchange (WCE). ICE Canada trades western barley, durum wheat, and canola futures and has in the past also had contracts on rapeseed and other agricultural commodities. However, the wheat contract is in direct competition with the wheat contract on the CBOT, even though the CBOT contract is priced in U.S. dollars with a contract size of 5,000 bushels, while the Canadian contract is priced in Canadian dollars for 20 metric tonnes. The larger volume of trading in Chicago means that many Canadian farmers use the U.S. contract. As a result, the ICE contract has had an uneven history, with minimal contracts traded in Canada relative to the United States. In June 2006, just before trading in Canada was suspended, there was open interest of fewer than 5,000 contracts in Winnipeg versus open interest of more than 500,000 contracts on the CBOT. **Open interest** represents the number of contracts that are outstanding, so when someone buys and another person sells a futures contract, although two transactions are recorded with the exchange, the open interest is just one contract. Open interest, therefore, represents the true amount of futures market activity. Example 11.9 provides a scaled-down image of how open interest changes on a daily basis.

**open interest**  the number of contracts that are outstanding; the true amount of futures market activity

---

**EXAMPLE 11.9** | Calculating Open Interest

On a given day, a new futures contract starts to trade. There are four participants in the market, investors A, B, C, and D. Four sets of trades are recorded for the first day, as follows:

1. Investor A sells 3 contracts to investor B and 1 contract to investor C.
2. Investor B buys 2 contracts from investor D and 1 contract from investor A.
3. Investor C buys 2 contracts from investor D and 2 contracts from investor B.
4. Investor D sells 1 contract to investor A and 3 contracts to investor B.

What is the open interest at the end of the day?

**Solution**  We can follow each set of transactions by recording them in a table. A buy is recorded as a positive number and a sell is recorded as a negative number.

|  | Set 1 | Set 2 | Set 3 | Set 4 | Net |
|---|---|---|---|---|---|
| Investor A | −3, −1 | −1 |  | +1 | −4 |
| Investor B | +3 | +2, +1 | −2 | +3 | +7 |
| Investor C | +1 |  | +2, +2 |  | +5 |
| Investor D |  | −2 | −2 | −1, −3 | −8 |

We can see from the net result in the last column that there are a total of 12 contracts long (+7 + 5 = 12) and 12 contracts short (−4 − 8 = −12). Therefore, the open interest at the end of the day is 12 contracts.

---

Trading in financial futures was concentrated in Montreal when the Canadian exchanges were reorganized in 2000. In this reorganization, the Montreal Stock Exchange gave up trading in common stocks to the Toronto Stock Exchange, and the Toronto Futures Exchange closed down so that all derivatives trading would be concentrated in Montreal. Today, the major futures contracts traded on the Montreal Exchange (MX) are the bankers' acceptances futures contracts (BAX), those on two-year (CGZ) and 10-year (CGB) Government of Canada bonds, and one on the S&P/TSX 60 Index (SXF). In total, there is open interest of typically just under 1 million contracts, with the BAX accounting for slightly more than half the total.

## Trading/Hedging with Futures Contracts

To illustrate how financial futures work, let's look at the futures contract on the 10-year Government of Canada bond (CGB). The notional contract is for a $100,000 10-year Government of Canada bond at 6 percent. Prices for the CGB contract are quoted in the same way as for a regular bond—that is, they are quoted as a price per $100, such as $92.50, and then move in increments of $10 or 0.01 per $100.

In setting the initial margin requirement, the MX divides purchasers into speculators and hedgers, with the former posting a $2,350 margin and the latter $2,250. The MX classifies everyone as a speculator except for a small list of "institutions, counterparties, regulated entities, and bona fide hedgers as defined in its rules and procedures." As of June 10, 2019, the maximum position limit for the 10-year Canada bond future is set at 108,220 contracts, and individuals have to report to the MX when they have 250 or more contracts. This is to make sure that no single institution dominates trading.

With most futures contracts, the underlying asset is clearly specified, and the party responsible for delivering the asset has no choice. However, bond futures generally provide a choice. For example, if someone does choose to take delivery of the underlying asset in the CGB contract, the MX specifies a list of bonds with their "conversion factor" to make their values equivalent to the notional bond. The MX lists Government of Canada bonds that:

- have a remaining time to maturity of between 8 years and 10½ years as of the first day of the delivery month, calculated by rounding down to the nearest whole three-month period;
- have an outstanding amount of at least C$3.5-billion nominal value;
- are originally issued at 10-year auctions; and
- are issued and delivered on or before the 15th day preceding the first delivery notice day of the contract.

So what can an investor do with this bond future? Well, imagine that a portfolio manager on December 1, 2019, who owns $1 million in market value of long Canada bonds, plans to sell the bonds in four months, and wants to protect their value in case interest rates increase. Because the fund is long the Canada bond, the investor needs to sell (i.e., go short) long Canada bond futures to protect the value of the underlying bond portfolio. In this case, the manager sells 10 April 2020 10-year Government of Canada bond futures, because each contract has a notional value of $100,000.

If interest rates increase by April 1, 2020, then the market value of the fund's long Canada bonds will fall, causing a loss in their value. At the same time, the price of the futures contract falls, and because the futures have been sold, this generates a capital gain. This type of hedge, which we illustrated previously using forward contracts, is called a short hedge, because a futures sale or a short position in the futures contract is hedging a long position in the underlying asset.

Whether the gain on the futures contract exactly equals the loss on the long Canada bond portfolio depends on how sensitive both are to interest rate changes. If the bond portfolio's value changes exactly mimic those of the asset underlying the CGB contract, the portfolio will be completely hedged. However, when this is not the case, the investor will be exposed to **basis risk**. Basis risk is the risk associated with a hedged position that is attributable to the fact that the asset to be hedged is not identical to the asset used as the hedge. As a result, it may be impossible to create a perfectly hedged position because changes in the price of the underlying asset in the contract will not move in a totally predictable manner with respect to changes in the price of the asset position to be hedged. One of the advantages of forward contracts is that they can be structured to minimize (or even eliminate) basis risk. This is because,

**basis risk** the risk associated with a hedged position that is attributable to the fact that the asset to be hedged is not identical to the asset used as the hedge unlike futures contracts, forwards are not standardized and can therefore be tailor-made with respect to underlying assets and maturity dates.

In our example, if the bond portfolio is not exactly the same as the 6-percent notional 10-year Government of Canada bonds used in the futures contract, there is basis risk because their prices will not move identically. For bonds, this risk can be reduced by adjusting the number of bond futures sold to create a weighted hedge. In our example, perhaps selling 9.5 contracts would be more accurate than selling 10.[8] However, the principle remains the same—the portfolio manager can sell bond futures to hedge the portfolio's underlying exposure to long Canada bonds.

We conclude this section with an example of hedging foreign exchange risk. The CME trades a futures contract on the Canadian dollar to allow Americans to hedge their Canadian dollar exposure, but where is the U.S. dollar futures contract that Canadians can use to hedge their U.S. dollar exposure? The fact is, it doesn't exist, because the CME futures contract that involves a minimum 100 contracts, each with a notional value of C$100,000, works fine for Canadians as well. Foreign exchange rates are just reciprocals, so selling Canadian dollar futures on the CME is exactly the same as buying U.S. dollar futures—that is, the futures contract involves selling Canadian dollars and buying U.S. dollars. On June 25, 2019, the CME reported average daily volume on the US$/C$ futures contract in the month of May to be 78,867 contracts with open interest at the end of May 2019 of 148,109 contracts. Contracts list for a 20-month period on a March, June, September, December cycle. A significant amount of the trading volume involved Canadian parties hedging their U.S. dollar exposure, as well as Americans hedging their Canadian dollar exposure.

## Summary of Forward and Futures Contracts

Table 11.3 lists the major differences between forward and futures contracts. The bottom line is that forward contracts offer more flexibility because they are customized OTC contracts; however, they possess additional risks because the contracts are not actively traded and they possess credit risk. In other words, while forwards and futures serve the same basic purposes, one may be preferred over the other in some situations.

**TABLE 11.3**   **Forwards versus Futures**

|  | Forwards | Exchange Futures |
|---|---|---|
| Contracts | Customized | Standardized |
| Trading | Dealer or OTC markets | Exchanges |
| Default (credit) risk | Important | Unimportant—guaranteed by clearinghouse |
| Initial deposit | Not required | Initial margin and maintenance margin required |
| Settlement | On maturity date | Marked to market daily |

---

### Concept Review Questions

1. Define initial margin, maintenance margin, margin call, open interest, and notional amount.
2. Explain what is meant by "marked to market."
3. What is basis risk? Why is it important for hedgers?
4. Compare and contrast forwards and futures.

---

[8] In fact, the appropriate hedge ratio can be determined by calculating the bond's duration, but this is beyond the scope of our discussion.

<table>
</table>

| 11.3 | **Swaps** |

---

### LEARNING OBJECTIVE 11.3
Describe the mechanics of simple swap structures, including interest rate swaps and currency swaps.

---

**swap** an agreement between two parties to exchange cash flows in the future

**counterparties** two parties in a swap agreement

**interest rate swap** an exchange of interest payments on a principal amount in which borrowers switch loan rates

The final type of linear hedging contract we will discuss is the **swap**. A swap is an agreement between two parties, called **counterparties**, to exchange cash flows in the future. Note at the outset that this is a direct agreement between two parties; there is no formal exchange to guarantee performance, so the situation involves a dealer or OTC market, and there is credit risk. As a result, like forward contracts, swaps have evolved into a bank instrument, with the banks or swap dealers serving as intermediaries between the two counterparties to the swap. As with most things, the initial contracts were the simplest and the easiest to understand, so let's start with a simple **interest rate swap** example from the mid-1980s.[9]

## Interest Rate Swaps

We illustrate how an interest rate swap can be initiated by considering two hypothetical companies, A and B. Company A is a top-rated AAA company, whereas company B is a lower-rated BBB company. Credit (bond) ratings were discussed briefly in Chapter 6, and we'll look at them again in greater detail in Chapter 17, but for now, all you need to remember is that AAA is the highest rating a company can have, and although BBB is a good bond rating, it is the lowest "investment grade" rating. Assume that company A wants to raise debt and pay a floating interest rate, which is usually done to finance short-term receivables and credit that earn a short-term interest rate. Company B, conversely, wants long-term fixed rate financing, perhaps to finance the purchase of machinery and equipment. Both companies approach the capital market, and company A is quoted a rate of 10.8 percent for fixed rate financing or a floating rate of 0.25 percent over LIBOR. In contrast, company B is quoted fixed rate financing at 12 percent and floating rate financing at a 0.75-percent spread over LIBOR.

As mentioned earlier, corporate borrowing rates are not generally priced with reference to the Government of Canada treasury bill (T-bill) yield. Floating rate financing in Canadian dollars is generally priced relative to the bankers' acceptances (BA) rate, which is why the Montreal Exchange's most popular hedging contract is the BAX. In contrast, floating rate notes in U.S. dollars are normally priced off LIBOR. Why U.S. dollar financing would be based off a rate established in London, rather than New York, is partly a historical accident, but it is a rate that reflects true market activity. In contrast, rates in New York have historically reflected the intervention and credit controls established by U.S. monetary authorities and have not been true market rates.

Regardless of how the rates are determined and quoted, let's consider what these two companies would do. The quotes look reasonable; the BBB-rated borrower is quoted a higher yield in both the fixed rate and the floating rate markets and would have borrowed at 12 percent. The AAA company would have borrowed at LIBOR + 0.25 percent. However, 25 years ago, someone asked the basic question: why is the BBB company quoted a spread of 1.2 percent more than the AAA in the fixed rate market and only 0.5 percent more in the floating rate market? This person recognized that although firm A had an absolute financing advantage in both the fixed and the floating rate markets, it also had a **comparative advantage** in the fixed rate market, where its costs were 1.2 percent lower than those of firm B. In contrast, firm B had a comparative advantage in borrowing in the floating rate market, where it paid only 0.5 percent more than A.

**comparative advantage** a benefit that one firm has relative to another

---

[9]The example comes from the Bankers Trust sponsor's supplement to *Euromoney* (January 1986).

To take advantage of this difference in spreads, the companies should both borrow where they have a comparative advantage and then swap payments to get what they really want. From this, the swap market was born. So firm A should borrow what it does not need, which is fixed rate financing, say $50 million, at 10.8 percent, and B should borrow what it doesn't need through a floating rate note at LIBOR + 0.75 percent, say $50 million.

Company A then signs a five-year swap contract agreeing to make payments to B at LIBOR; in return, A will receive from B a fixed 10.9-percent rate. Thus, the overall cost to A is LIBOR − 0.1 percent, because it pays LIBOR to B and pays 10.8 percent on its direct financing, but it receives 10.9 percent from B through the swap. Therefore, A saves 0.35 percent over its direct quote, which was LIBOR + 0.25 percent. Firm B borrows at LIBOR + 0.75 percent and makes payments to A based on a 10.9-percent fixed rate, while receiving payments based on LIBOR from A. The net effect is that it ends up paying an 11.65-percent fixed rate (i.e., 10.9 percent + 0.75 percent) for financing and also saves 0.35 percent over its direct quote.[10] **Table 11.4** depicts the swap scenario, where borrowings are represented by minus signs.

A "fixed for floating" interest rate swap denominated in one currency, such as the one described in Table 11.4, is commonly referred to as a **plain vanilla interest rate swap**, reflecting the fact that it is the simplest and most commonly used type of swap. Although the example was developed to show that both parties gain 0.35 percent, in reality the amount they gain depends on negotiation between the two. However, in principle there is the spread in the spreads, which totals 0.7 percent and which can be shared in a variety of ways between the two parties.[11]

The comparative advantage argument is a basic one in finance: anyone offered a good deal in floating rate funds should borrow them, whether they are needed or not, and use a swap to exchange them for what is needed, locking in the financing advantage. In addition, although the swap market may have developed in response to such comparative advantages, today's swap markets have evolved beyond that. Today, many firms enter into swap arrangements to convert an existing fixed rate liability into a floating rate liability and vice versa. We discuss this in more detail later in this chapter.

The swap arrangement above is not without its problems. One main concern is that company A, which is a highly rated AAA company, is relying on the payments from B, a BBB-rated company, to make its fixed rate payments. In this example, firm A is assuming additional

**plain vanilla interest rate swap** the "fixed for floating" interest rate swap; the simplest and most commonly used type of swap

**TABLE 11.4 An Interest Rate Swap**

| | A | B |
|---|---|---|
| **Quotes** | **(AAA)** | **(BBB)** |
| Floating | LIBOR + 0.25 | LIBOR + 0.75 |
| Fixed | 10.8 | 12.0 |
| **Initial** | | |
| Floating | | −(LIBOR + 0.75) |
| Fixed | −10.8 | |
| **Swap** | B pays A fixed and A pays B floating | |
| | +10.9 | −10.9 |
| | −LIBOR | +LIBOR |
| **Net** | −(LIBOR − 0.1) | −11.65 |
| **Saving** | 0.35% | 0.35% |

[10]Note that this assumes the 0.75-percent credit spread over LIBOR is fixed; otherwise its "fixed" rate financing will vary with the credit spread.
[11]In practice, swap dealers will also "pocket" some of the spread as payment for their services.

credit risk. If B defaults, then A is stuck with its own 10.8-percent fixed rate financing and, depending on legal interpretation, may also have to continue to pay LIBOR to B even after B stops making the 10.9-percent fixed rate payment to A. For this reason, early swap contracts were directly negotiated between the two counterparties based on documentation used for parallel loan transactions and included "set-off" rights. These rights meant that if either party defaulted, the other party stopped making payments. This was soon changed, and the required payments for interest rate swaps became **net payments**. This meant that instead of exchanging the total amount of interest, parties involved in interest rate swaps exchanged payments representing the difference between the fixed and floating rates.

**net payments**   payments representing the difference between the fixed and floating rates

Table 11.5 shows how this would work for our interest rate swap example based on various values for LIBOR during the first five periods of the swap. The payments are assumed to be made every six months, which is the norm in practice, so the interest payments are half the quoted rates.

The implied cash flows depicted in Table 11.5 are from company A's point of view. A receives half the fixed rate of 10.9 percent from B each period, or 5.45 percent of the notional value of the swap; in return, A pays LIBOR. For the first six-month period, LIBOR is 8 percent, so A pays half this, or 4 percent, and receives 5.45 percent. The net cash payment is that B pays A 1.45 percent of the notional value of the swap, which is why the sign is positive. From B's perspective, all the signs would be reversed, as it pays the difference of 1.45 percent.

Notice from Table 11.5 that the net payments depend on how LIBOR changes, because the fixed rate does not vary. In the above example, LIBOR increases consistently, and by period 5 (two-and-a-half years away), when it has increased to 12 percent, A finds that it is making a net payment to B of 0.55 percent of the notional amount.

This example illustrates two important points. First, the net payment is expressed as a percentage of the notional amount. The actual cash flows would depend on the notional value of the swap—for a $10-million swap, the percentage would be multiplied by $10 million, so the period 1 payment would be $145,000 (i.e., $0.0145 \times \$10,000,000$); payment 2 would be $95,000; and so on. Equation 11.6 depicts the semi-annual payments from the fixed rate payee's perspective.[12]

$$\text{Payment (fixed rate payee)} = NP \times (\text{Fixed} - FR) \times \tfrac{1}{2} \qquad [11.6]$$

where $NP$ = notional principal, $Fixed$ = fixed rate, and $FR$ = floating rate (usually LIBOR).

Second, when only net payments are required, the credit risk from A's perspective decreases significantly because it no longer relies on B to make the entire fixed rate payment. All that A gets from B is the much smaller difference between the LIBOR and fixed rate, which may be positive or negative. If B does default, A is still at risk, but only for this future stream of differences, rather than for the full interest payments.

**TABLE 11.5**   **Interest Rate Swap Net Payments**

| Period | LIBOR (%) | Floating Pay (%) | Fixed Pay (%) | Net Pay (%) |
|--------|-----------|------------------|---------------|-------------|
| 1 | 8.0 | −4.0 | +5.45 | +1.45 |
| 2 | 9.0 | −4.5 | +5.45 | +0.95 |
| 3 | 9.8 | −4.9 | +5.45 | +0.55 |
| 4 | 11.0 | −5.5 | +5.45 | −0.05 |
| 5 | 12.0 | −6.0 | +5.45 | −0.55 |

---

[12] Notice that, to determine what the floating rate payee pays (receives), all we need to do is change the sign of the cash flow.

> **EXAMPLE 11.10** | Estimating Payments from an Interest Rate Swap
>
> Company C enters into a two-year, $1-million, plain vanilla interest rate swap and agrees to pay a fixed rate of 5 percent and receive LIBOR. Payments are exchanged every six months, based on LIBOR at the beginning of the six-month period. Determine the amount of the required semi-annual payments that C must make, assuming that LIBOR has the following values for each six-month period, beginning now: 5%, 5.5%, 5.25%, and 4.75%.
>
> **Solution**
> After 6 months: Payment = $1 million × (0.05 − 0.05) × ½ = $0
> After 12 months: Payment = $1 million × (0.05 − 0.055) × ½ = −$2,500 (i.e., they receive $2,500)
> After 18 months: Payment = $1 million × (0.05 − 0.0525) × ½ = −$1,250 (i.e., they receive $1,250)
> After 24 months: Payment = $1 million × (0.05 − 0.0475) × ½ = $1,250 (i.e., they pay $1,250)

# The Evolution of Swap Markets

As it turns out, the first swap was not an interest rate swap but a **currency swap** that involved IBM and the World Bank. At the time, the World Bank was required to borrow where it was cheapest in absolute dollars, which turned out to be either Swiss francs or German marks. In fact, it borrowed so much in those currencies that it made up the largest holding in most Swiss franc bond portfolios, and it ended up facing higher interest rates as a result. In contrast, it could issue U.S. dollar bonds quite easily because it was not a large U.S. dollar issuer. IBM, in contrast, was a well-known name but had never issued Swiss franc financing and was offered a good borrowing rate. Given our discussion of comparative advantage above, you might guess what happened next. IBM issued Swiss franc bonds, the World Bank issued U.S. dollar bonds, and each got its preferential rates. They then agreed to swap both the principal and the interest payments. In fact, the World Bank continued to make heavy use of currency swaps, and by the early 1980s it was routinely lowering its borrowing cost by a colossal 1.28 percent a year.[13]

*currency swap* the exchange of principal and interest in one currency for the same in another currency

The original swap transactions were extremely profitable for both counterparties, as indicated by the fact that the World Bank was able to lower its borrowing cost by 1.28 percent. This was because the credit spreads between risky borrowers and governments in different types of debt markets were largely unconnected. Theoretically, spreads in the floating rate and fixed rate markets should be the same, just as they should be between U.S. dollar and Canadian dollar financing. This is because most bonds have cross-default clauses in their debt contracts, so that default on any debt instrument anywhere in the world means a default on all debt obligations. As a result, the credit risk is the same. However, although the swap market has caused these spreads to narrow considerably, spread differences continue to exist. Swapping still makes sense, but it doesn't make as much sense as it used to.

Knowing what a swap is allows us to understand the reasons behind some strange actions. For example, we may see "tombstone" advertisements in the newspaper, in which a Canadian company announces that it has issued debt in New Zealand or Australian currencies. Taken on its own, this may not make much sense, especially if the company has no operations in New Zealand or Australia. However, when we realize that the company can swap those New Zealand or Australian dollars into Canadian dollars, we know that it has issued bonds in the foreign currencies because it got a "good" deal, and it then swapped the bonds for what it really needed—Canadian dollars. In fact, it has been estimated that as much as 75 percent of the bond issues in the international Eurobond market have ended up being swapped into something else.

The flip side to Canadian companies issuing foreign bonds in obscure locations is the recent development of the Maple bond market. Until January 2005, Canadian tax-preferred investors, such as pension funds, were restricted from holding more than 30 percent of the value of their portfolio in foreign-issued securities. To maximize the value of the 30-percent foreign content, investors tended to hold foreign equities rather than bonds. However, after the foreign content rule was removed, Canadian pension funds started buying Canadian

---

[13] Wallich, Christine, "The World Bank's Currency Swaps." *Finance and Development* (June 1984).

dollar-denominated bonds issued by foreign companies—a market that was quickly termed the Maple bond market. Similar to Canadian firms' issuing Kiwi or Aussie bonds in order to swap back into Canadian dollars, the proceeds of these Maple bonds were almost always swapped back into the currency needed by the issuer.

As swap markets have matured, another major change has taken place. Initially, the major investment banks would bring two parties together and arrange the swap for a fee. However, as the market's liquidity grew, the major banks increasingly acted as principals, directly signing a swap with one party, and then "warehousing" the swap until they could do an offsetting transaction with another party. This development was helped by the increasing standardization in the market. The International Swap Dealers Association (ISDA) has developed standard legal documentation so that everyone knows their rights and duties under a standard swap agreement. This standardization means that plain vanilla interest rate swaps and currency swaps have become commodities that can be bought and sold through a telephone call to a bank's swaps desk. As such, swaps have become traded commodities and major instruments for managing interest rate and currency exposures, with enormous ramifications that we will discuss shortly.

Consider, for example, the original IBM–World Bank currency swap. This was a primary market transaction, because both IBM and the World Bank used it to raise capital as cheaply as possible. In both cases, their intention was to raise the capital and then forget about it. However, once swaps became standardized, it was possible to constantly change the nature of an institution's liability stream.

Recall, for example, the foreign exchange exposure problem discussed earlier. At that time, we considered a firm that had a US$1-million receivable due in a year. Let's change this and say that a Canadian company has a five-year U.S. dollar bond outstanding, with fixed semi-annual interest payments of $1 million and a principal of US$30 million due in five years. In this case, the Canadian company has a U.S. dollar liability stream, so it is short the U.S. dollars. Now suppose the company looks at the current exchange rate and feels that it is at an all-time high and will depreciate in the future. As the Canadian dollar depreciates, it will cost the company more Canadian dollars to make those U.S. dollar interest and principal payments.

What can the company do? The most obvious thing is to repay the loan, but if this is a bond held by several U.S. institutions, that may not be possible. An alternative is to enter into a currency swap. The structure of currency swaps permits firms to adjust their foreign exchange exposure. In particular, one distinguishing feature of currency swaps is that, unlike interest rate swaps, they require the exchange of *all* cash flows. This is logical because exchange rates change as well as interest rates. Although this feature increases the credit risk associated with currency swaps, it also gives firms the opportunity to manipulate the underlying currency associated with a series of future cash flows that it expects to pay (or receive).

In this case, the company can talk to the swaps desk at its bank and swap the U.S. dollar liability stream for a Canadian dollar liability stream. Unlike the original IBM–World Bank currency swap, which was arranged by an investment bank between the two counterparties, the bank is now capable of executing a secondary market transaction with itself as a principal—that is, it doesn't need a counterparty. The reason is that a currency swap can be viewed as a series of forward transactions. Think of the firm's five-year bond not as one transaction but as 10 individual transactions. The first nine transactions involve a US$1-million outflow every six months for interest, while the last one is a US$31-million outflow for both the final interest payment and the principal payment. So rather than going through a search for a counterparty, the bank could always execute 10 forward sales of Canadian dollars for U.S. dollars and directly change the U.S. dollar liability stream into a Canadian dollar liability stream. Once it has been converted into a fixed Canadian dollar stream, an interest rate swap can convert it into any other Canadian dollar liability, such as a floating rate liability.

If currency swaps have become a bank market through their links to the forward foreign exchange market, what of interest rate swaps? To understand the link with other instruments, let's go back to our circa 1985 example of an interest rate swap. At that time, all the rates were unique to the issuers, and the interest rates in the swap were negotiated. However, the core of the swap was simply a LIBOR-based rate and a fixed rate. To make a standardized product, suppose we fix both the floating and the fixed rates so that everyone knows what they are. Let's fix the floating rate at LIBOR and the fixed rate with reference to the government bond rate, with the choice of rate depending on whether it is a five-year, 10-year, or other maturity contract. Suppose the BBB bond issue was a five-year bond, so that we have a five-year interest

**TABLE 11.6**     **Percent Interest Rate Swap**

| | A | B |
|---|:---:|:---:|
| Quotes | (AAA) | (BBB) |
| Floating | LIBOR + 0.25 | LIBOR + 0.75 |
| Fixed | 10.8 | 12.0 |
| **Initial** | | |
| Floating | | −(LIBOR + 0.75) |
| Fixed | −10.8 | |
| Swap | B pays A fixed and<br>A pays B floating | |
| | +10.65 | −10.65 |
| | −LIBOR | +LIBOR |
| Net | −(LIBOR + 0.15) | −11.4 |
| Saving | 0.1% | 0.6% |

rate swap. Let's say the five-year government bond rate was 10.65 percent at the time. In this way, the swap could be quoted simply as 10.65 percent. In fact, this is how swaps are now quoted, and this rate is called the **swap rate**.

We revisit our previous example and assume the swap rate was 10.65 percent at the time. This transaction is depicted in **Table 11.6**.

In this case, unlike our original example, the 0.7-percent difference in spreads has been allocated as 0.1 percent to company A and 0.6 percent to company B. This generally has been the trend over time, as the gains to the higher-rated AAA are relatively small, given that it has good access to most markets. In contrast, it is the lower-rated issuers that sometimes face very large spread differences across different markets. Further, the AAA-rated firm is often a bank, and banks now make money trading swaps rather than acting as counterparties. In the above example, the swap rate of 10.65 percent would actually be the mid-point of an "ask" or "bid" rate of 10.63 percent and an "offer" rate of 10.67 percent. If a company wants to swap floating for fixed, it would pay the 10.67-percent fixed (offer) rate, but if it wanted to swap fixed for floating, it would receive the 10.63-percent fixed (ask) rate from the bank. The spread of 0.04 percent between these two rates rewards the bank for trading swaps.

Interest rate swaps are now standard around the world. **Table 11.7** provides the "ask or offer" swap rates for the euro, U.S. dollar, and pound sterling on June 3, 2019.

**swap rate**   the rate of the fixed portion of a swap used for quoting swap prices

**TABLE 11.7**     **Interest Rate Swap Quotes**

| Fixed Rate | Euro(€) | US($) | UK(£) |
|---|---|---|---|
| 1 year | −0.1680 | 2.1771 | 0.9951 |
| 2 year | −0.2760 | 1.9382 | 0.8514 |
| 3 year | −0.2367 | 1.8655 | 0.8672 |
| 5 year | −0.1000 | 1.8891 | 0.9228 |
| 7 year | 0.0725 | 1.9575 | 0.9811 |
| 10 year | 0.3256 | 2.0662 | 1.0735 |
| 15 year | 0.6500 | 2.1925 | 1.1816 |
| 30 year | 0.8965 | 2.2770 | 1.2475 |

**Source:** Data from Bloomberg, intraday quotes on June 3, 2019

Notice that the swap rates follow the full spectrum of the yield curve out to 30 years, so interest rate swaps are very useful for managing interest rate exposure.[14] This also provides the link to other interest rate products. The link in this case is to forward rate agreements (FRAs), which are discussed in Appendix 11A. Appendix 11A notes that by selling a one-year bond and investing in a two-year bond, a bank can create forward contracts on the one-year interest rate for the next year. In the same way, it can sell a six-month bond and invest in a one-year bond to create a six-month interest rate forward for hedging LIBOR. Doing the same thing at six-month intervals creates an FRA. The FRA can be seen as a series of forward interest rates equivalent to an interest rate swap. What this means is that the two core products in the swap market, the interest rate and currency swaps, are simply combinations of forward contracts—either on interest rates or on exchange rates. Creating swaps is therefore a key component of the skill set of all the major banks.

The integration of swap markets with the forward market has allowed an enormous expansion of the market. If a company has a banking relationship with an outstanding line of credit, we have already seen that a company can call and buy and sell forward foreign exchange contracts. The same thing now happens in the swap market. If a company wants to change a floating rate liability into a fixed rate liability, it calls the bank and executes an interest rate swap. More than 80 percent of swap transactions are now worth around $10 million as secondary market transactions executed against a bank line of credit.

---

### Concept Review Questions

1. Explain how plain vanilla interest rate swaps are structured and what purposes they serve.
2. Explain how currency swaps are structured and how they can be used for hedging purposes.
3. Why does it make sense that interest rate swaps involve an exchange of net payments, while currency swaps exchange all cash flows?

---

## 11.4 The Financial Crisis and the Credit Default Swap Market

**LEARNING OBJECTIVE 11.4**
Explain how the credit default swap market contributed to the financial crisis.

**total return swap**   an exchange of an interest rate return for the total return on an equity index, plus or minus a spread

Interest rate and currency swaps were the main focus of the previous section because they are the major vehicles for managing interest rate and currency exposure. However, there are more applications for swaps. If an investor doesn't like what's happening in the bond market and wants to increase exposure to the equity market, that investor could sell bonds and buy equities. The downside is that the bond market is not very liquid and the transaction costs are high. The investor could instead turn to the swap market and enter into a **total return swap**. This can be accomplished by first entering into an interest rate swap to convert the fixed rate bond payments into payments that vary with a floating rate, such as LIBOR, because almost all swaps go through LIBOR. The investor would then enter into a total return swap, paying LIBOR and receiving the total return from an equity index, such as the S&P 500 Index or the S&P/TSX 60 Index, plus or minus some spread. The existence of futures contracts on stock market indexes—on the S&P/TSX 60 Index on the Montreal Exchange, for example, or the S&P 500 Index on the CME—allows the equity market exposure to be hedged. These types of swaps are not for the small investor, as the notional principal amount involved is usually $100 million.

---

[14]In the Eurozone, swap rates are quoted out to 50 years.

What the total return swap does indicate is how swaps have emerged as a major vehicle for managing exposure to any traded commodity that can be hedged. The result is a huge proliferation of specialized swap contracts and a huge transfer of risk, since, for example, if someone is to receive the return on the S&P 500 Index, then someone else has to pay it. This dramatically increases counterparty or credit risk because some of the newer swaps are for highly volatile underlying securities. It is for this reason that Warren Buffett, one of the world's greatest investors, termed derivatives in general "financial weapons of mass destruction." His warning was ignored, but in the summer of 2007 his words came back to haunt policy-makers around the world as credit default swaps began to self-destruct and threw the world into its first genuine global economic crisis.

A **credit default swap (CDS)** is just like any other swap. In this case, the agreement is essentially to swap the payments on a risk-free government bond in return for the proceeds of a default risky bond. Consider, for example, a default risky corporate bond paying 10-percent interest. The investor does not like the risk but for some reason is unable to sell the bond. They can enter into a CDS in which they pay the difference between the bond's 10-percent interest and, say, the 4-percent interest on the government bond; in this way, the investor's interest receipts are reduced to the level of a risk-free bond. In return for these payments, the counterparty gives the investor the right to receive the par value of the bond should it default. In this way, a CDS is essentially the same as buying default insurance on the risky corporate bond, where the buyer pays for the default protection and the seller sells the protection.

**credit default swap (CDS)** an agreement in which one party makes a series of interest payments and then is compensated by the counterparty in the event of default on the bond; it is essentially default insurance on the bond

However, there are two big differences between a CDS and insurance. First, the risk attached to regular insurance, such as house or car insurance, is essentially random since the risk depends on factors unique to an individual. As a result, by pooling a lot of these unique risks, the insurer's exposure becomes predictable. In contrast, for a CDS, the underlying risk depends on the economy, as defaults tend to be clustered during a slowdown or recession, when individuals and companies are more likely to reorganize or go bankrupt. As a result, CDS contracts have market risk.

The second problem is that the CDS market is simply part of the swap market, and, as an OTC market, everything depends on the two counterparties fulfilling their promise. A heavily regulated insurance company is required to keep reserves to ensure it can fulfill its promises. In the swap market, in contrast, this risk is mitigated by restricting counterparty risk to large, stable financial companies, such as American International Group (AIG), and requiring them to put up "margin" or other collateral should their financial health decline. However, in 2007–8 these measures proved inadequate simply because of the size of the market and the limited number of major participants. **Table 11.8** displays data compiled by the Bank for International Settlements that includes aggregate global data for OTC and exchange-listed derivatives.

| **TABLE 11.8** | **Global Derivatives Market Notional Value Outstanding, Billions of U.S. Dollars, Data as of December 2018** | |
|---|---|---|
| **Contract Type** | **Over the Counter (OTC)** | **Exchange Traded** |
| Futures: | | |
| Interest rate | — | 37,345 |
| Foreign exchange | — | 257 |
| Options: | | |
| Interest rate | — | 68,141 |
| Foreign exchange | — | 142 |
| Foreign exchange | 90,662 | — |
| Interest rate | 436,837 | — |
| Equity-linked | 6,417 | — |
| Commodity | 1,898 | — |
| Credit default swaps | 8,143 | — |
| Total exposure | 544,386* | 105,885 |

*This total includes US$429 billion of unallocated derivatives of non-reporting institutions.
**Source:** Data from BIS.org Quarterly Review, June 2019

As long as these markets were small and the underlying products were clearly understood, they could flourish. However, by the end of 2007 the CDS market was worth US$58 trillion or nearly four times the value of the U.S. stock market (it has since declined to just over US$8 trillion in notional value). Even worse than the increased size of the CDS market was the fact that many of the newer CDS contracts were on securities tied to the U.S. sub-prime mortgage market. As the sub-prime market grew, many of the banks generating the risky mortgages bought CDS contracts to swap out of the risk. Essentially, they bought insurance against the possibility of the risky mortgages defaulting. The protection sellers of these CDS contracts varied, but by 2007, AIG alone had written "protection" on US$440 billion worth of mortgage-backed securities, or about a third of the entire U.S. sub-prime market. From AIG's point of view, it was receiving the insurance premiums on underlying securities with a very low risk of default, since most of these mortgage-backed securities were rated AAA. However, as the sub-prime market in the United States collapsed in 2007 and into 2008, AIG was increasingly called on to make good on these CDS contracts until the very solvency of AIG became questionable. As AIG faced the prospect of posting collateral or margin to make sure it fulfilled its CDS contracts, it simply ran out of cash and was forced to turn to the U.S. government for help.

The U.S. government eventually pumped $180 billion into AIG to save it from bankruptcy. This money was part of the Troubled Asset Relief Program (TARP), which was designed to save the U.S. banking system from collapse. To avoid similar problems in the future, the U.S. government passed the *Dodd-Frank Wall Street Reform and Consumer Protection Act* on July 21, 2010. This act represents the most extensive overhaul of the regulation of the U.S. financial services industry in history, most of it aimed at the banking system. However, one key component is an attempt to move derivatives trading away from OTC markets onto exchanges, where trades would attract margin. Similar regulatory changes are in the works in Canada and have been pushed by the International Monetary Fund.

As the data in Table 11.8 show, the OTC market is more than five times bigger than the exchange-traded market; by December 2018, the notional amounts covered by all OTC derivatives was US$544 trillion (a decline of over 13 percent in five years) versus "only" about US$106 trillion for exchange-traded derivatives. By moving more of the OTC market onto organized exchanges, the hope is that a company like AIG will never again be able to place such large bets that it imperils the stability of the financial system. Instead, by posting margin, as on any futures exchange, all market participants will be aware of each participant's position and their ability to fulfill their commitments. This planned shift has not yet materialized, and there remains significant credit exposure that could potentially lead to another global crisis. On November 25, 2011, the Canadian Securities Administrators issued a consultation paper (91-403) that concluded: "It is the view of the Committee that effective surveillance and monitoring, harmonized market conduct rules and consistent enforcement will bring about greater transparency in the OTC derivatives markets, combat improper market conduct, and help support Canada's G20 commitments." However, its first recommendation was for "further study," its second to obtain data, and a final recommendation was to obtain legislative authority for new rules if "such rules are determined to be appropriate." The problem, as the committee noted, is that the majority of transactions entered into by Canadian participants involve foreign counterparties. As a result, Canada has to wait until major markets like those in New York and London have implemented specific policies on trading derivatives.

## Lessons to Be Learned

There is an old adage "If it sounds too good to be true, it probably is." Nowhere is this more relevant than in the derivatives market. Derivatives are not inherently bad, but then neither are guns. In both cases, it is a question of how they are used. The collapse of AIG has shown that many derivative products pose systemic risk—that is, they pose risks to the entire financial system—even when their use is restricted to highly trained professionals and large, sophisticated companies. The essence of derivatives is that they enable risk to be transferred in the same way that insurance contracts transfer risk from the insured to the insurer. The financial system has functioned very efficiently with heavily regulated insurance companies for many decades, but the swap market allowed these functions to be carried out in an unregulated market. The resulting meltdown has ensured that we will now see more heavily regulated derivatives markets as we relearn the lessons our grandparents learned decades ago: *plus ça change, plus c'est la même chose. . .*

## APPENDIX 11A   Forward Interest Rates and Forward Rate Agreements (FRAs)

**LEARNING OBJECTIVE 11.5**
Explain how the general principles of forward contracts can be applied to fixed income securities.

## Forward Interest Rates

Interest rate parity is a special example of forward pricing simply because the cost of carry is the ratio of one plus the interest rates in both countries. In other words, for IRP,

$$(1 + c) = \frac{(1 + k_{domestic})}{(1 + k_{foreign})}$$

For our synthetic forward example in this chapter, the cost of carry is the cost of borrowing in Canadian dollars relative to the investment income earned in U.S. dollars. If the Canadian one-year interest rate is 10 percent and the U.S. interest rate is 5 percent, then the cost of synthetically creating the forward rate is $1.1/1.05 - 1$, or 4.76 percent. The income lost because of the cost of borrowing in Canadian dollars is higher than the income earned on the U.S. investment. As a result, the cost of carry is positive, and the forward rate of Canadian dollars for U.S. dollars has to show a 4.76-percent depreciation in the Canadian dollar. That is, if the spot rate is 1.0, the forward rate has to be 1.0476. In this way, the income loss of 4.76 percent is offset by a 4.76-percent capital gain on the exchange rate. Alternatively, if the Canadian borrowing rate is 5 percent and the U.S. rate is 10 percent, the cost of carry is negative ($-4.55$ percent), and the forward rate has to show a 4.55-percent appreciation of the Canadian dollar to 0.95. In this way, the income gain from borrowing at 5 percent in Canada and investing at 10 percent in the United States—that is, a negative cost of carry—is offset by a capital loss from being in U.S. dollars.

Note that in the IRP condition, it is the ratio of one plus the interest rate in both countries that determines whether the forward rate exceeds or is less than the spot rate. However, in Table 11.1 there were forward foreign exchange rates for the Canadian dollar against the U.S. dollar extending two years into the future. This brings up another very important forward rate: the **forward interest rate**. In Chapter 6, we discussed the term structure of interest rates and the yield curve, and noted that the yield curve constantly shifts, based on the state of the economy and expectations about where interest rates are going. **Figure 11A.1** shows the average annual yield on 91-day T-bills issued by the Government of Canada and the average annual yield on a portfolio of long Canada bonds with an average maturity exceeding 10 years. The two yields represent the very short and very long end of the yield curve, respectively.

**forward interest rate**   an interest rate that is specified now for some time in the future

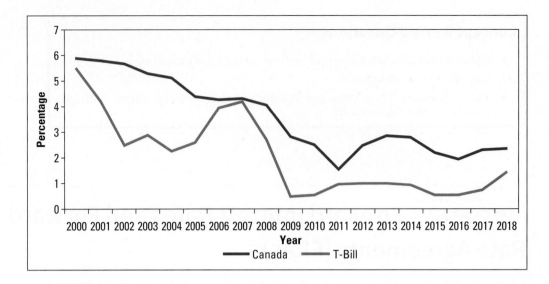

FIGURE 11A.1 Canadian Interest Rates

We can see that near the start of the period, in 2000, the yields on T-bills and on long Canada bonds were very similar; in fact, at the end of 2000, both yielded 5.6 percent. This was an example of a flat yield curve, in which interest rates were essentially the same across all maturities. Short-term interest rates then declined to around the 2-percent level, where they remained until the end of 2004, when the Bank of Canada started increasing interest rates again; they consistently increased to reach the same 4.2-percent level as the yields on long Canada bonds by mid-2006. T-bill yields actually exceeded those on long Canada bonds for the first few months of 2007, a situation referred to as an inverted yield curve, which usually implies a slowdown or recession. Sure enough, shortly afterward, T-bill yields started to fall, and by spring 2009 they were barely positive. Since then, T-bill yields have marginally increased and have been nearly constant at close to 1 percent for the past three years, while long Canada bond yields fell steadily until 2011 and have since risen to remain constant at just under 3 percent. T-bill yields were actually negative for a short time in the United States as central banks around the world tried to stimulate rapidly worsening economies. With the spread between T-bill yields and those on long Canada bonds at 1.8 percent from 2012 to 2014, the yield curve was upward or normally sloping.

However, for illustrative purposes, let's go back to mid-2004, when T-bill yields were close to 2 percent, and see what the yield curve indicated.

Suppose at that time that the yields on zero coupon bonds, which were discussed in Chapter 6, were as follows:

| One year | 2% | Four year | 3.65% |
|---|---|---|---|
| Two year | 2.75% | Five year | 4% |
| Three year | 3.25% | Ten year | 5% |

Remember that zero coupon bonds are discount bonds; they do not pay interest explicitly, so the return is earned by buying them at a discount and then selling them at maturity for their par value. Now, suppose an investor wanted to invest for two years. There are several ways to invest for two years, but let's look at two alternatives: an investor can either buy a two-year bond or buy a one-year bond and then invest in another one-year bond at whatever interest rate is available in one year. **Figure 11A.2** represents these choices schematically.

The two-year bond will earn the investor 2.75 percent compounded for two years or 5.576 percent in total (i.e., $(1.0275)^2 - 1$). Conversely, if the investor invests for one year only and gets 2 percent for the first year, they will have to reinvest the next year at an unknown rate

| | Year 1 | Year 2 |
|---|---|---|
| Two-year zero | | $(1 + 2.75\%)^2$ |
| One-year zero and reinvestment | $(1 + 2\%)$ | $(1 + 2\%)(1 + F_1)$ |

for a one-year bond. We can work out a break-even rate, denoted *F1*, which makes these two strategies equal, using the following equation:

$$(1 + 2.75\%)^2 = (1 + 2\%)(1 + F_1)$$

Solving, we find that $F_1 = 3.51$ percent, because $(1.0275)^2 = 1.05576 = (1.02)(1.0351)$. We have called this rate $F_1$ because this interest rate is also a forward rate. It is actually the forward rate for a one-year bond, one year in the future. In fact, embedded in the yield curve are a host of forward rates. For example, we could use the three-year and two-year zero coupon yields to calculate a forward rate for a one-year bond starting in two years, which would be:

$$(1 + 3.25\%)^3 = (1 + 2.75\%)^2 (1 + F_2)$$

which is 4.26 percent. Equivalently, we could calculate the forward rate for a one-year bond for time period 3 by using the yields on three- and four-year bonds, for time period 4 by using four- and five-year bonds, and so on. In the same way, we could also calculate the forward rate on a two-year bond by using the current yield on the one-year and three-year bonds.

These break-even interest rates are also forward rates because a bank can lock in the rate on a one-year bond for one year in the future. It does this by borrowing using the current one-year rate and then using the proceeds to simultaneously invest for two years at the two-year rate. In one year's time, the bank will owe $102 when it has to repay the one-year 2-percent loan. However, the proceeds from that loan will have been invested in the two-year bond, and the bank is still owed the $105.576 payoff from this bond in the next year. As far as the bank is concerned, this is the same as investing $102 next year in a one-year bond that pays $105.576 at the end of that year, or pays 3.51 percent. As a result, the 3.51-percent break-even rate is also the forward rate for a one-year bond, one year in the future.

Equation 11A.1 is the general formula for calculating forward interest rates ($F_t$) for the one-year bond:

$$F_t = \frac{(1 + R_t)^t}{(1 + R_{t-1})^{t-1}} - 1 \qquad [11A.1]$$

Equation 11A.1 says (1) find the future value of investing for *t* periods by investing in the *t* period discount bond, then (2) divide by the future value generated by investing for $t - 1$ periods by using the $t - 1$ bond, and (3) subtract 1. This gives the break-even rate as the forward rate for the one-period bond available at the start of time period $t - 1$.

---

**EXAMPLE 11A.1** | Estimating Forward Rates

Estimate the one-year forward rate for years 4 and 5, given that zero coupon bonds were yielding the following percentages: three-year, 3.25 percent; four-year, 3.65 percent; and five-year, 4 percent.

**Solution**

$$\text{Year 4 forward rate } F_4 = \frac{(1 + 0.0365)^4}{(1 + 0.0325)^3} - 1 = 0.0486 = 4.86\%$$

$$\text{Year 5 forward rate } F_5 = \frac{(1 + 0.0400)^5}{(1 + 0.0365)^4} - 1 = 0.0541 = 5.41\%$$

# Forward Rate Agreements (FRAs)

**forward rate agreement
(FRA)** an agreement that uses
forward rates to manage a firm's
exposure to interest rate risk; an
agreement to borrow or lend at a
specified future date at an interest
rate that is fixed today

Banks actually use these forward rates to offer a product called a **forward rate agreement
(FRA)** to manage a firm's exposure to interest rate risk. Suppose, for example, that a firm has
issued a floating rate bond for which it is required to pay the one-year T-bill yield plus a 0.5-percent
credit spread, and the rate adjusts annually with the one-year T-bill yield. The firm may have
issued this note in 2000, when it thought short-term interest rates would fall and it wanted to
avoid locking in at a higher fixed-term interest rate. But in 2004, suppose that it thinks interest
rates are going to increase and it wants protection against rising interest rates. This is the same
as saying that it wants to hedge the interest rate exposure from its floating rate note.

If the firm's floating rate note has two years left before it matures, the first year's interest
cost is fixed, so what it wants to do is fix next year's interest cost. Because this cost is based
on the one-year T-bill rate, the bank would offer an FRA based on the one-year forward rate
of 3.5 percent. If the T-bill yield is higher than 3.5 percent—say 4 percent—then the bank
would pay the firm the difference of 0.5 percent. If the T-bill yield is less than 3.5 percent—say
3 percent—the firm would pay the bank the difference of 0.5 percent. The cash flows
(expressed as percentage rates) as far as the firm is concerned are shown in **Table 11A.1**.

**TABLE 11A.1  Forward Rate Agreements**

| T-Bill Yield (%) | Spread (%) | FRA (%) | Total (%) |
|---|---|---|---|
| 3.0 | 0.5 | +0.5 | 4.0 |
| 3.5 | 0.5 | 0.0 | 4.0 |
| 4.0 | 0.5 | −0.5 | 4.0 |

Regardless of the T-bill yield, the firm has locked in an overall cost of 4 percent, which is
the forward rate for the one-year T-bill of 3.5 percent, plus the 0.5-percent credit spread.

In comparing this interest rate example with our foreign exchange example, we can see
that the FRA is a forward contract on the one-year T-bill yield. In this case, the firm starts out
with a series of short positions in the one-year T-bill because it is obligated to pay the one-year
T-bill yield plus 0.5 percent as long as its floating rate note is outstanding. To cover or hedge
this short exposure, it goes long by buying an interest rate forward contract or FRA, which
obligates it to pay the difference between the T-bill yield and the forward rate of 3.5 percent.

The example illustrates how banks offer FRAs to help firms manage their interest rate
exposure in the same way that they offer forward foreign exchange contracts to help them
manage their foreign exchange exposure. In practice, FRAs are more complex than the one in
our simple example. This is because most floating rate notes have interest rates that fluctuate
with LIBOR every three or six months, rather than with the T-bill yield every year. The second
major difference is that forward foreign exchange contracts are generally one-shot deals to
cover a single exposure. However, floating rate notes cover a series of future interest payments
extending to the note's maturity. As a result, FRAs are tailored to the maturity of the note and
are equivalent to a series of interest rate forward contracts. However, there is a basic similarity
between FRAs and forward contracts—they are both bank instruments designed to help manage a firm's exposure to interest rates and foreign exchange.

On July 16, 2015, the *Financial Post* gave the quotes for FRAs in U.S. and Canadian
dollars, as shown in **Table 11A.2**.

**TABLE 11A.2  Forward Rate Agreements in U.S. and
Canadian Dollars**

| | C$ | US$ |
|---|---|---|
| Three month | 0.97 | 0.35 |
| Six month | 0.98 | 0.50 |
| Nine month | 0.89 | 0.69 |

**Source:** Data from *Financial Post*, July 16, 2015

In each case, the FRAs in Table 11A.2 are for three-month rates for contracts ending three, six, and nine months in the future. Upward sloping U.S. FRA rates imply a recovery in the U.S. economy that will likely cause borrowing costs to rise. In Canada, these rates tell a different story. The six-month FRA is only 1 basis point higher than the three-month FRA, while the nine-month FRA is 9 basis points lower than the six-month FRA. The Canadian central bank cut short-term rates several times in 2015 and may cut them further to help stimulate a sluggish Canadian economy that is still heavily dependent on weak commodity demand and low oil prices.

---

### Concept Review Questions

1. Discuss three different strategies you can follow to invest in Canadian securities to obtain a return over a three-year period.
2. If the yield curve is upward (downward/inverted), where is the market expecting short-term interest rates to go?

---

# Review

## Summary

In this chapter, we learn how to diagnose long and short positions in foreign currency and how these positions can be hedged by using forward foreign currency contracts. Interest rate parity is discussed again and used to derive forward interest rates and to show how banks could derive synthetic securities. Futures contracts are then discussed, and we see that they can be viewed as the public market version of forward contracts. We then discuss swap markets and show how basic interest rate and currency swaps can be used to lower borrowing costs or to hedge interest rate or foreign currency exposures.

The forward, futures, and swap markets are all derived from the underlying asset, whether it is foreign exchange rates or interest rates. It is in this sense that these contracts are all derivatives. Market participants regularly use the futures market to offset positions in the swap market, the swap market to offset positions in the forward market, and the forward market to offset positions in the futures market. Moreover, they do this by making contracts with a variety of other market participants, creating a web of linkages, which means that defaults by one party can quickly affect other parties in the financial system, as the failure of AIG has reminded us.

## Summary of Learning Objectives

### 11.1 Describe forward contracts, including how they are used and priced.

Spot contracts are agreements for immediate exchange—the price is agreed now, and money and goods (or securities) are exchanged now. Forward contracts are agreements for exchange in the future— the price is agreed now, but money and goods (or securities) are exchanged at a future date. A long position with a spot contract means that you own something, whereas a long position with a forward contract means that you agree to buy the underlying asset in the future. A short position with a spot contract means that you have sold something, and a short position with a forward contract means that you agree to sell the underlying asset in the future. Investors in a long forward position make money when the underlying asset's price rises. Investors in a short forward position make money when the

underlying asset's price falls. Forwards (and futures) are instruments that can be used to hedge risk or to speculate on price movements. Hedgers with a short position in the underlying asset use long positions in forwards or futures to eliminate their price risk, and hedgers with a long position in the underlying asset use short positions in forwards or futures to eliminate their price risk. Forward prices are tied to spot prices through the cost-of-carry relationship. Forward prices are equal to the spot price plus the cost of carry.

### 11.2 Explain what futures contracts are and why they can be viewed as the public market version of forward contracts.

Futures contracts are standardized forward contracts that are traded on exchanges. Everything in a futures contract is fixed (by the exchange) except the price. Futures contracts feature a clearinghouse that guarantees counterparty performance—that is, it protects against counterparty default. An integral part of the clearinghouse system is the margin account and daily marking to market. These institutions help ensure counterparty performance. With daily marking to market, daily profits and losses are added to (subtracted from) each counterparty's account.

### 11.3  Describe the mechanics of simple swap structures, including interest rate swaps and currency swaps.

A plain vanilla interest rate swap involves one party borrowing at a fixed rate and another borrowing at a floating rate. The two parties then swap interest payments. In addition to interest rates, swaps can also involve different currencies. The mechanics are the same.

### 11.4  Explain how the credit default swap market contributed to the financial crisis.

By 2007, the CDS market was worth US$58 trillion, or about four times the value of the U.S. stock market. Even more critical than the increased size of the market was the fact that many of the newer CDS contracts were on securities tied to the U.S. sub-prime mortgage market. As the sub-prime market grew, many of the banks generating the risky mortgages bought CDS contracts to hedge their risk. Essentially, they bought insurance against the risky mortgages defaulting. The

protection offered by the sellers of these CDS contracts varied, but by 2007, AIG alone had written "protection" on US$440 billion worth of mortgage-backed securities or about a third of the entire U.S. sub-prime market. As the sub-prime market in the United States collapsed in 2007 and into 2008, AIG was increasingly called on to make good on these CDS contracts until the very solvency of AIG was at risk. Eventually, AIG was forced to turn to the U.S. government for help. The failure of AIG precipitated fears that other financial institutions would also fail, so banks began conserving cash to ride out the storm. Also, since CDS contracts were with so many different parties, it was difficult for regulators to estimate the extent of the problem and to address it.

### 11.5  Explain how the general principles of forward contracts can be applied to fixed income securities.

The Canadian government bond market contains a rich array of securities in terms of differing maturities. One can invest for three years, for example, by buying a three-year bond, or by buying a two-year bond and then reinvesting in a one-year bond in two years' time. We can then define the forward rate for a one-year bond in time period 2 that would make these two strategies equal. Assuming the market is indifferent to any risk differences between these strategies provides a free market interest rate forecast. It also provides the banks with a way to provide simple hedging instruments (forward rate agreements or FRAs) that allow companies to manage their interest rate risk.

## Key Terms

basis risk, p. 11-16
clearing corporation, p. 11-11
commodity, p. 11-8
comparative advantage, p. 11-18
contango, p. 11-9
convenience yield, p. 11-9
cost of carry, p. 11-9
counterparties, p. 11-18
covering, p. 11-5
credit (counterparty) risk, p. 11-4
credit default swap (CDS), p. 11-25
currency swap, p. 11-21
daily resettlement, p. 11-11
exposure, p. 11-4

forward contract, p. 11-1
forward interest rate, p. 11-27
forward rate agreement (FRA), p. 11-30
futures contract, p. 11-11
hedging, p. 11-4
initial margin, p. 11-11
interest rate swap, p. 11-18
London inter-bank offered rate (LIBOR), p. 11-8
long, p. 11-3
maintenance margin, p. 11-11
margin, p. 11-11
margin call, p. 11-11
naked position, p. 11-3
net payments, p. 11-20

notional amount, p. 11-11
offsetting, p. 11-12
open interest, p. 11-15
plain vanilla interest rate swap, p. 11-19
settlement price, p. 11-11
short, p. 11-3
speculate, p. 11-3
spot contract, p. 11-1
storage costs, p. 11-9
swap, p. 11-18
swap rate, p. 11-23
total return swap, p. 11-24
underlying asset, p. 11-3
variation margin, p. 11-11

## Equations

| Equation | Description | Formula | Page |
|---|---|---|---|
| [11.1] | Profit (Loss) from Long Position | Profit (loss) from long position $= (S_T - F) \times n$ | p. 11-3 |
| [11.2] | Profit (Loss) from Short Position | Profit (loss) from short position $= (F - S_T) \times n$ | p. 11-5 |
| [11.3] | Forward Premium or Discount | $\dfrac{F}{S} = \dfrac{(1 + k_{domestic})}{(1 + k_{foreign})}$ | p. 11-7 |

*(continued)*

| Equation | Description | Formula | Page |
|----------|-------------|---------|------|
| **[11.4]** | Forward Exchange Rate | $F = S \times \dfrac{(1 + k_{domestic})}{(1 + k_{foreign})}$ | p. 11-8 |
| **[11.5]** | Forward Rate for Storable Commodities | $F = (1 + c) \times S$ | p. 11-10 |
| **[11.6]** | Payment on an Interest Rate Swap | Payment (fixed rate payee) $= NP \times (Fixed - FR) \times \frac{1}{2}$ | p. 11-20 |
| **[11A.1]** | Forward Interest Rate | $F_t = \dfrac{(1 + R_t)^t}{(1 + R_{t-1})^{t-1}} - 1$ | p. 11.29 |

# Questions and Practice Problems

## Multiple Choice Questions

**1. (LO 11.1)** Which of the following statements is *false*?

  **a.** A spot price is a price today for immediate delivery.

  **b.** If a Canadian firm has to pay U.S. dollars in the future, it worries about the potential depreciation of the U.S. dollar.

  **c.** The forward price is a price today for future delivery.

  **d.** We say long Canadian dollar and short U.S. dollar when you buy Canadian dollars and sell U.S. dollars.

**2. (LO 11.1)** What is the one-year forward rate if the spot rate is 0.6£/C$ and the one-year interest rates are 5 percent in Canada and 6 percent in Britain?

  **a.** 0.616£/C$

  **b.** 0.606£/C$

  **c.** 0.609£/C$

  **d.** 0.611£/C$

**3 (LO 11.1)** Which of the following statements is *false*?

  **a.** Removing a naked position is called hedging.

  **b.** To hedge, you take a long position in a U.S. dollar forward contract if you have a long position in U.S. dollars.

  **c.** There is no initial cash outlay for a forward contract.

  **d.** Forward contracts could be used to hedge against exchange rate changes.

**4. (LO 11.1)** Assuming interest rates in Canada and the United States are 5 percent and 4 percent, respectively, what is the cost of carry of synthetically creating a forward rate by borrowing in Canadian dollars and investing in U.S. dollars?

  **a.** 1.24 percent

  **b.** 0.86 percent

  **c.** 0.96 percent

  **d.** 1.05 percent

**5. (LO 11.1)** Which of the following statements is *false*?

  **a.** Cost of carry could be either positive or negative.

  **b.** The forward rate will change if the spot rate changes.

  **c.** An income loss is offset by a capital gain on the exchange rate if IRP holds.

  **d.** The spot rate is the forward rate multiplied by + (1 + cost-of-carry percentage).

**6. (LO 11.1)** Which of the following statements about forward contracts is *false*?

  **a.** In a naked position, the investor is exposed to changes in the value of the underlying asset.

  **b.** When an investor has agreed to buy U.S. dollars and sell Canadian dollars forward, they are long U.S. dollars and short Canadian dollars.

  **c.** Long means investors own something.

  **d.** Short means investors own something.

**7. (LO 11.1)** Which of the following statements about the profit (loss) from a forward contract is *false*?

  **a.** Profit from a long position is negatively affected by the spot price.

  **b.** Profit from a long position is the difference between the spot price and strike price, multiplied by the number of contracts.

  **c.** Profit from a short position is negatively affected by the spot price.

  **d.** Profit from a short position is the difference between the strike price and spot price, multiplied by the number of contracts.

**8. (LO 11.2)** Which of the following is *false* concerning forward contracts and futures contracts?

  **a.** Futures contracts involve more credit risk than forward contracts do.

  **b.** The Canadian Derivatives Clearing Corporation (CDCC) takes responsibility for reducing credit risk.

  **c.** The higher the credit risk, the higher the margin.

  **d.** Futures contracts are marked to market every day.

**9. (LO 11.2)** Suppose a futures contract is for 1,000 units of a certain asset and the starting price is $30. The initial margin is 5 percent and the price closed on the first day at $45. Which of the following statements is *true*?

  **a.** Only the buyer puts down a $1,500 deposit when entering into the contract; the seller does not put down an initial deposit.

  **b.** The futures contract is worth $15,000 to the seller at the end of the first day.

  **c.** The buyer's commitment is to buy 1,000 units of the asset at $30 on a certain date.

  **d.** At the end of the first day, the seller's equity increased by $45,000.

10. **(LO 11.2)** Which of the following statements concerning futures contracts is *false*?

    a. The initial value of the futures contract is zero.

    b. The values of the buyer and the seller of the futures contract offset each other.

    c. If the seller gains, the clearinghouse will transfer the gained value from the seller's account to the buyer's account.

    d. If an investor's account falls below the maintenance margin, they receive a margin call.

11. **(LO 11.2)** In practice, most futures contracts are closed out

    a. with an offsetting transaction before the final day of trading.

    b. by actual deliveries of the underlying assets.

    c. by leaving the contracts to expire.

    d. by cash settlement.

12. **(LO 11.2)** Which of the following statements concerning Government of Canada bond futures is *false*?

    a. The contract price is quoted per $100.

    b. A maximum position limit is set to prevent a single dominant holding.

    c. Basis risk exists when the underlying asset to be hedged is not identical to the asset used as the hedge.

    d. To hedge, an investor should short a Government of Canada bond futures contract when they need to buy the same bonds in the future.

13. **(LO 11.2)** Which of the following statements about the mechanics of futures contracts is *false*?

    a. All futures contracts are made with a futures exchange, not with an individual.

    b. Investor A might buy a futures contract and investor B might sell one, but instead of one contract between A and B, there are two contracts involving each individual and the exchange.

    c. The riskier the asset, the higher the margin.

    d. All futures contracts are marked to market each month, as the value of the contract changes.

14. **(LO 11.2)** Which of the following statements about hedging with futures contracts is *false*?

    a. Futures have less basis risk than forwards.

    b. Basis risk is the risk associated with a hedged position that is attributable to the fact that the asset to be hedged is not identical to the asset used as the hedge.

    c. One of the advantages of forward contracts is that they can be structured to minimize (or even eliminate) basis risk.

    d. Unlike futures contracts, forwards are not standardized and can therefore be tailor-made with respect to underlying assets and maturity dates.

15. **(LO 11.2)** What are *not* traded on the Montreal Exchange?

    a. Futures on the bankers' acceptances futures contracts (BAX)

    b. Futures on two-year and 10-year Government of Canada bonds

    c. Futures on S&P/TSX 60 Index (SXF)

    d. Futures on S&P 500 Index

16. **(LO 11.2)** Which of the following statements about forwards and futures is *true*?

    a. Forwards are customized and futures are standardized.

    b. Forwards are traded on exchanges while futures are traded on the dealer or OTC markets.

    c. Credit risk is less important for forwards because they are guaranteed by the clearinghouse.

    d. Forwards are marked to market daily.

17. **(LO 11.3)** Suppose ABC Inc. pays a fixed rate of 9.5 percent and DEF Inc. pays a floating rate of LIBOR + 1.5 percent. They enter into a swap in which ABC Inc. agrees to pay LIBOR to DEF Inc. and DEF Inc. agrees to pay 9.5 percent to ABC Inc. What is the net paying interest rate for ABC Inc.?

    a. LIBOR + 1 percent

    b. LIBOR

    c. 12 percent

    d. LIBOR + 0.5 percent

18. **(LO 11.3)** Suppose ABC Inc. borrows at a fixed rate of 9.5 percent or a floating rate of LIBOR + 1 percent. DEF Inc. borrows at a fixed rate of 12 percent or a floating rate of LIBOR + 1.5 percent. Currently, ABC Inc. borrows at its fixed rate and DEF Inc. borrows at its floating rate. They enter into a swap in which ABC Inc. agrees to pay LIBOR to DEF Inc. and DEF Inc. agrees to pay 9.5 percent to ABC Inc. How much, in percentage, could ABC Inc. and DEF Inc. save through the swap, respectively?

    a. 1 percent and 1 percent

    b. 0.5 percent and 1.5 percent

    c. 1.5 percent and 0.5 percent

    d. 2 percent and 0 percent

19. **(LO 11.3)** Which of the following statements about interest rate swaps is *false*?

    a. Credit risk exists in interest rate swaps.

    b. The actual cash flows depend on the notional value of the swap.

    c. Net cash settlement increases the credit risk of the interest rate swap.

    d. Interest rate swaps are settled by paying a net amount between the two parties.

20. **(LO 11.3)** Which of the following statements about currency swaps is *false*?

    a. The swap rate for currency swaps is the exchange rate.

    b. The swap rate for currency swaps is the interest rate.

    c. The notional amounts of the currency swap are exchanged at the beginning and end of the swap only.

    d. Usually, one party pays a fixed rate, while a counterparty pays a floating rate.

21. **(LO 11.3)** Which of the following statements are *true*?

    a. A currency swap allows a firm to borrow in their local market where they have the best access to capital, and then "swap" the interest/coupon and principal payments to whichever currency they would prefer to make payments.

    b. Firms employ swaps to make investments and raise funds in the most attractive geographic locations/currencies while mitigating exchange rate risk exposure between their assets and liabilities.

    c. The correlation between a firm's free cash flows and spot exchange rates is a typical identifier of the presence of exchange rate risk.

    d. All of the above.

**22. (LO 11.3)** Which of the following statements about plain vanilla interest swaps is *false*?

    **a.** It is a "fixed for floating" interest rate swap denominated in one currency.

    **b.** Counterparties exchange payments representing the difference between the fixed and floating rates.

    **c.** The semi-annual payment from the fixed rate payee is the notional amount multiplied by the difference between the fixed rate and the floating rate, and divided by two.

    **d.** The semi-annual payment from the floating rate payee is exactly the same as that from the fixed rate payee.

**23. (LO 11.4)** Which of the following are traded over the counter?

    **a.** Equities

    **b.** Bonds

    **c.** Futures

    **d.** Credit default swaps

**24. (LO 11.5)** Which of the following statements is *false*?

    **a.** FRAs are normally based on six-month LIBOR.

    **b.** FRAs are designed to hedge against exchange rates only.

    **c.** FRAs are tailored to match the maturities of floating rate notes.

    **d.** FRAs could be viewed as a series of interest rate forward contracts.

## Practice Problems

### Basic

**25. (LO 11.2)** Describe the process of marking to market for futures contracts.

**26. (LO 11.2)** Describe open interest with respect to futures contracts.

**27. (LO 11.3)** Explain why two counterparties would enter into an interest rate swap even when one has an absolute financing advantage in both the fixed and the floating rate markets.

**28. (LO 11.4)** Describe how total return swaps work.

**29. (LO 11.2)** If the trading volume of a futures contract has been increasing over the past 5 days, does this mean that the open interest has also been increasing?

### Intermediate

**30. (LO 11.1)** Simon manages a large bond portfolio and wishes to hedge against interest rate risk. His portfolio includes Government of Canada bonds and high-grade Canadian corporate bonds. The correlation between the returns on his fund and the Government of Canada 6-percent, 10-year bond is 1.00.

    **a.** Describe how Simon can hedge against changes in interest rates.

    **b.** Your analysis has just shown that the actual correlation between the returns on Simon's portfolio and the 6-percent, 10-year Government of Canada bond is only 0.65. What are the implications for the hedge described in part a?

    **c.** Simon strongly believes that interest rates will fall in the near future. Describe how he can speculate on that belief. What risks are inherent in that position (i.e., what happens if interest rates rise)?

**31. (LO 11.1)** You have received the following incomplete information about a set of currency forwards. All the forwards are for C$1,000 in one year. Complete the following table.

| | | | **Today** | | | **In One Year** | |
| | | | | | | | |
| | Number | Spot | Cost | | Spot | | Profit |
| | of | (C$/ | Today | Forward | (C$/ | Payoff | (Loss) |
| Position | Contracts | US$) | (C$) | (C$/US$) | US$) | (C$) | (C$) |
|---|---|---|---|---|---|---|---|
| A Long | 1 | 1.15 | $0 | 1.20 | 1.40 | | |
| B Short | 1 | 1.15 | | 1.20 | 1.40 | | |
| C Long | 2 | 0.80 | $0 | | 0.65 | $100 | |
| D | 3 | 1.05 | | 1.30 | 1.20 | | $(300) |
| E Long | 5 | 1.10 | $0 | 1.25 | | | $800 |
| F | | 1.00 | | 1.05 | 1.30 | | $(2,500) |

**32. (LO 11.1)** Complete the following table. The underlying asset is ounces of gold. Assume no arbitrage.

| | Spot | Cost of Carry | 1-Year Forward Price | 1-Year Interest Rate | Annual Storage Cost |
|---|---|---|---|---|---|
| A | $200 | | | 8% | 4% of spot |
| B | $235 | | $285 | | 2% of spot |
| C | | | $300 | 7% | 3% of spot |
| D | $350 | | $400 | 4% | |
| E | $200 | | | 9% | $20 per ounce |
| F | | | $300 | 3% | $5 per ounce |
| G | $250 | | $285 | | $15 per ounce |

**33. (LO 11.1)** The Health Bracelet Company will need 1,000 kilograms of copper in one year and is trying to decide between buying the copper on the spot market or using a forward contract. The spot price of copper is $15 per kilogram. The forward price is $19 per kilogram. Health Bracelet will need to rent a warehouse space to store the copper at a cost of $100 per month. Health Bracelet is able to borrow and lend at 4 percent per year. Should Health Bracelet buy its copper using the spot market or the forward market? Explain.

**34. (LO 11.1)** Suppose the spot exchange rate is C$1.4665 per euro, while the six-month forward rate is C$1.50 per euro. What will be the profit for an investor who assumes a €100,000 long position in the forward contract if the spot rate in six months equals the following amounts?

    **a.** C$1.40 per euro

    **b.** C$1.60 per euro

**35. (LO 11.1)** Assume an investor takes a €100,000 short position in the six-month euro forward contract with forward rate of C$1.50 per euro. Determine the investor's profit (loss) if the spot rate in six months equals the following amounts:

    **a.** C$1.40 per euro

    **b.** C$1.60 per euro

**36. (LO 11.1)** The spot exchange rate is C$1.4665 per euro, while the six-month forward rate is C$1.50 per euro. Suppose a firm has to pay a foreign supplier €100,000 in six months and decides to eliminate its foreign exchange exposure by entering into a six-month forward contract.

    **a.** Should it enter into a short or a long forward position, and if so, for how much?

    **b.** Assuming it enters into the appropriate forward position, determine the cost in Canadian dollars for the following future spot rates:

        **i.** C$1.40 per euro

        **ii.** C$1.60 per euro

**37. (LO 11.1)** The spot exchange rate is C$1.4665 per euro, while the six-month forward rate is C$1.50 per euro. Suppose a firm expects to receive €100,000 in six months from a foreign customer and decides to eliminate its foreign exchange exposure by entering into a six-month forward contract.

a. Should it enter into a short or a long forward position, and if so, for how much?

b. Assuming it enters into the appropriate forward position, determine the proceeds in Canadian dollars for the following future spot rates:

   i. C$1.40 per euro

   ii. C$1.60 per euro

**38. (LO 11.1)** CanComp has a contract to deliver a large computer system to a South African company in one year and would like to hedge the currency risk. CanComp will receive payment of R3.5 million (the currency of South Africa is the rand) in one year for the computer system. CanComp can borrow and lend in Canada at 3 percent per annum and can borrow and lend in South Africa at 7 percent per annum. Assume the borrowing and lending is risk free. The current spot exchange rate is C$/Rand 0.35 and there is no one-year forward exchange rate. Describe how CanComp can hedge the currency risk by creating a synthetic forward contract. Demonstrate that your synthetic forward contract hedges the currency risk. Assume all investments are risk free.

**39. (LO 11.2)** Explain the difference between forwards and futures.

**40. (LO 11.2)** Explain basis risk and the advantage of forward contracts over future contracts in minimizing basis risk.

**41. (LO 11.2)** Ethel and Egbert have decided to invest in the futures market. Both entered into 1,000 futures contracts, which required a $30,000 initial margin. The maintenance margin for each investor is $22,500. Ethel and Egbert disagree about the future so Ethel went long while Egbert went short. Estimate each investor's daily profit (loss) and equity position (assuming no cash deposits or withdrawals).

| | | Ethel | | Egbert | |
|---|---|---|---|---|---|
| | | | Equity | | Equity |
| | | Daily | Position | Daily | Position |
| | Spot | Profit | (Margin | Profit | (Margin |
| Day | Price | (Loss) | Balance) | (Loss) | Balance) |
| 0 | $100 | | $30,000 | | $30,000 |
| 1 | $95 | | | | |
| 2 | $80 | | | | |
| 3 | $85 | | | | |
| 4 | $100 | | | | |
| 5 | $110 | | | | |

**42. (LO 11.2)** An investor enters into a long position in 50,000 futures contracts that require a $50,000 initial margin and have a maintenance margin that is 75 percent of this amount. The futures price associated with the contracts is $20. Assume the spot price of the underlying asset closes at the following prices for the next five days: $20.50, $20.75, $21.00, $19.75, and $19.25. Estimate the daily profit (loss) for this investor, as well as the equity position, assuming no cash deposits or withdrawals are made from the account.

**43. (LO 11.2)** An investor enters into a short position in 50,000 futures contracts that require a $50,000 initial margin and have a maintenance margin that is 75 percent of this amount. The futures price associated with the contracts is $20. Assume the spot price of the underlying asset closes at the following prices for the next five days: $20.50, $20.75, $21.00, $19.75, and $19.25. Estimate the daily profit (loss) for this investor, as well as the equity position, assuming no cash deposits or withdrawals from the account.

**44. (LO 11.2)** Ethel decided to invest in the futures market. She entered a long position in 1,000 futures contracts that require a $30,000 initial margin. The maintenance margin is $22,500. Assume that Ethel deposits the minimum amount of cash required to satisfy any margin calls and makes no cash withdrawals. Assume also that the cash earns no interest. At the end of day 5, Ethel closed her position.

Complete the following table.

| Day | Spot Price | Daily Profit (Loss) | Equity Position before Cash Deposit | Margin Call? | Cash Deposit | Equity Position (Margin Balance) |
|---|---|---|---|---|---|---|
| 0 | $100 | | $0 | | $30,000 | $30,000 |
| 1 | $92 | −$8,000 | $22,000 | Yes | $500 | $22,500 |
| 2 | $95 | | | | | |
| 3 | $103 | | | | | |
| 4 | $90 | | | | | |
| 5 | $100 | | | | | |

**45. (LO 11.3)** Aqua Boat Company recently issued floating rate debt. The rate is LIBOR + 3 percent, reset semi-annually. Compost Earth Company has recently issued fixed rate debt. The rate is 5 percent per year. Aqua and Compost have entered into a two-year interest rate swap with a notional value of $1 million. Aqua agrees to pay 6 percent fixed; Compost agrees to pay LIBOR + 2 percent. Payments are exchanged every six months based on LIBOR at the beginning of the six-month period. Determine the interest rate swap net payments for Aqua.

| Start of Period | Libor % | Floating Pay % | Fixed Pay % | Net Pay % | Net Pay $ |
|---|---|---|---|---|---|
| 1 | 4% | | | | |
| 2 | 5% | | | | |
| 3 | 3% | | | | |
| 4 | 1% | | | | |

**46. (LO 11.4)** David says, "CDS is essentially the same as buying default insurance on the risky corporate bond, where the buyer pays for the default protection and the seller sells the protection." Thus he concludes that CDS is the same as other insurance. Comment on David's conclusion.

**47. (LO 11.5)** You are in the process of developing forecasts of short-term interest rates. In order to determine a bond trading strategy, you want to determine the market's short-term (one-year) interest forecasts for different future periods. You have obtained the following data on traded Government of Canada zero coupon bonds of different maturities. Determine the implied one-year forward rates.

| Maturity | Observed YTM% |
|---|---|
| 1 year | 3% |
| 2 years | 5% |
| 3 years | 7% |
| 4 years | 6% |
| 5 years | 5% |

| 1-Year Forward Rate Expected in | Implied 1-Year Forward Rate % |
|---|---|
| 1 year | |
| 2 years | |
| 3 years | |
| 4 years | |
| 5 years | |

**48. (LO 11.5)** Calculate the $F_1$, $F_2$, $F_3$ given the following interest rates on zero coupon bonds:

| | | | |
|---|---|---|---|
| One year | 2.1% | Four year | 3.75% |
| Two year | 2.65% | Five year | 4.05% |
| Three year | 3.25% | | |

**49. (LO 11.2)** On a given day, a new futures contract starts to trade. There are five participants in the market labelled as investors V, W, X, Y, and Z. Four sets of trades for the day were as follows:

Investor V buys 10 contracts from X and buys 5 contracts from Z.

Investor W buys 8 contracts from Y and buys 3 contracts from Z.

Investor X buys 7 contracts from W and buys 1 contract from Y.

Investor Y buys 2 contracts from V and buys 6 contracts from Z.

What is the open interest at the end of the day?

**50. (LO 11.2)** A certain group of futures traders may be interested only in the financial exposure of the underlying asset. If this is the case, do you think the open interest will increase or decrease as the futures contract gets closer to maturity?

## Challenging

**51. (LO 11.1)** CanComp, a Canadian computer manufacturer, will be delivering a large computer system to a German firm in six months. CanComp expects to receive payment of US$1.5 million at that time. Currently the spot rate is C$1.15 per US$ and the six-month forward rate is C$1.25 per US$.

**a.** What risks does CanComp face with the sale of the computer system?

**b.** Describe how CanComp can hedge the currency risk.

**c.** Determine CanComp's profit or loss on the hedge if the actual spot rate in six months is:

**i.** C$0.75 per $US

**ii.** C$1.50 per $US

**d.** Given your answers to parts a and b, should CanComp hedge? *Hint:* Remember ex ante versus ex post.

**52. (LO 11.1)** Bert, the business reporter for the *Sidney Driftwood*, a small newspaper, has contacted you for information about the oil market. Provide responses to his questions below with arbitrage opportunities.

**a.** "I understand supply and demand and the difference between the spot and the forward market. I understand that there will be an effect on the forward price of oil if an oil field in Iraq, which is expected to go into production in one year, does not go into production. There will be a decrease in the expected supply so it makes sense that the price expected in the future (the forward price) will increase. What I don't understand is why this causes a change in the spot price. After all, the supply of oil today hasn't changed, so why would today's price change?"

**b.** "The second thing that puzzled me was the effect of Hurricane Katrina on the forward price of oil. The area around New Orleans is a major storage depot for oil in the United States and there was extensive damage to the storage facilities in the hurricane. Consequently, there would have been a decrease in the amount of oil available today and, logically, the spot price would have gone up. What I don't understand is why the forward price also rose—future oil production doesn't depend on the availability of storage facilities today."

**53. (LO 11.3)** Joyce and Anthony are in the process of renewing their mortgages. Each mortgage is an interest-only mortgage (i.e., the borrower pays only interest and has a balloon payment at the end) for $100,000. Anthony, having an excellent credit history, is offered the choice between a fixed rate mortgage at 3 percent and a floating rate mortgage at prime + 1 percent ("prime" rate is the domestic version of LIBOR). Joyce is offered the choice between a fixed rate mortgage at 7 percent and a floating rate mortgage at prime + 3 percent. The current prime rate is 3 percent. Floating rate mortgages are reset at the start of each year.

Anthony and Joyce have both recently retired—Anthony's future income is closely tied to market interest rates (he has his retirement funds invested in bonds) while Joyce has a fixed retirement income (the Canada Pension Plan).

**a.** Ignoring interest costs, which mortgage would Anthony prefer—fixed or floating? Why? Which mortgage would Joyce prefer—fixed or floating? Why?

**b.** Assume that Anthony chose a fixed rate mortgage and Joyce chose a floating rate mortgage.

**i.** Design a swap agreement between Anthony and Joyce that will make them both better off.

**ii.** What is this type of swap called and what are the risks associated with it?

**iii.** If the prime rate for the next four years is 3 percent, 5 percent, 4 percent, and 2 percent, respectively:

**1.** Show the cash flows between Anthony and Joyce.

**2.** Demonstrate that the swap will make Anthony and Joyce better off.

**54. (LO 11.3)** Suppose ABC Inc. can borrow at a fixed rate of 9.5 percent or a floating rate of LIBOR + 1 percent. DEF Inc. can borrow at a fixed rate of 12 percent or a floating rate of LIBOR + 1.5 percent. Supposing they engage in an interest rate swap in which both companies can mutually benefit, explain how the spreads can be shared between the two parties, and describe the absolute advantage and comparative advantage in the swap.

**55. (LO 11.3)** CanGold Mining Company borrowed €100 million in France at an annual interest rate of 3.5 percent. The principal plus interest is due in one year. CanGold used the funds to purchase machine parts in Germany for use in its Indonesian gold mine. In one year, the mine is expected to produce 1 million ounces of gold. Gold is sold on the world market in U.S. dollars. CanGold would like to hedge its currency and commodity risk. The CFO of CanGold has been quoted the following forward contracts:

**i.** One-year C$/euro forward exchange rate: 1.60

**ii.** One-year C$/US$ forward exchange rate: 1.05

**iii.** One-year US$/euro forward exchange rate: 1.10

**iv.** One-year gold forward contract: US$250 per ounce

Design two hedging strategies for CanGold so that CanGold has profit in C$. Which strategy is better? *Hint:* Are there any arbitrage opportunities?

**56. (LO 11.3)** Angela, a new investor, has contacted you with a question about the swap market. Provide a response to her question: "A swap agreement allows two companies to swap payments. Presumably, both parties believe that this agreement will make them better off. If the markets are efficient, how can a swap make both participants better off?" Answer this with respect to both interest rate and currency swaps.

**57. (LO 11.5)** At the end of the current year, you observe the following data about Government of Canada pure discount bonds (zero coupon bonds):

| | | |
|---|---|---|
| Bond issue: A | Years to maturity: 1 | YTM%: 5 |
| Bond issue: B | Years to maturity: 2 | YTM%: 7 |
| Bond issue: C | Years to maturity: 3 | YTM%: 10 |

a. What price do you expect bond C to sell for at the end of year 2?

b. The Government of Canada is considering issuing a coupon bond. The bond will pay a 7-percent coupon, paid annually. The face value of the bond will be $1,000. What price would you expect the bond to sell for today?

**58. (LO 11.2)** Over a given day, there were 10,000 trades made for corn futures (i.e., 10,000 buyers and 10,000 sellers). A total of 2,000 of these trades were by buyers entering into new positions and 9,000 of these trades were by sellers entering into new positions. Did the open interest increase, decrease, or stay the same? Quantify the impact to the open interest if any.

# Options

---

**LEARNING OBJECTIVES**

After studying this chapter, you should be able to:

**12.1** Describe the basic nature of call options and the factors that influence their value.

**12.2** Describe the basic nature of put options and the payoffs associated with long and short positions in put options.

**12.3** Explain how to use put-call parity to estimate call and put prices, and explain how it can be used to synthetically create call, put, and underlying positions.

**12.4** Explain how to use the Black-Scholes option pricing model to price call options.

**12.5** Explain how options are traded and what is meant by implied volatility.

**12.6** Explain, using the simplest option pricing model, what factors affect the value of a call option.

---

In Chapter 11, we discussed linear derivative contracts, in which the payoffs directly reflect the behaviour of the underlying asset, so both gains and losses are generated. In this chapter, we discuss contracts that produce non-linear payoffs and that may be limited in some way through a maximum gain, loss, or both. The most basic contract is a call option, for which the payoff is limited on the downside, so losses are restricted. Working out the value of an asset that in some cases can generate only positive payoffs led to a Nobel Prize for the development of the celebrated Black-Scholes option pricing model (OPM). We show why the OPM is such a powerful model and how it can be derived by creating a risk-free asset. You will learn what determines the value of options, how to use the OPM on the Montreal Exchange's website, and what all those Greek letters mean. This chapter introduces ideas that are often used in business finance, as you will see in Chapter 19, for example, when you learn how options have been used to design innovative new financing instruments.

---

## 12.1 | Call Options

---

**LEARNING OBJECTIVE 12.1**
Describe the basic nature of call options and the factors that influence their value.

---

## Call Option Basics

We begin by considering the characteristics of the basic **call option**, which is defined as the *right, but not the obligation,* to *buy* an underlying asset at a fixed price for a specified time. The price at which an investor can buy the underlying asset is called the

**call option** the right, but not the obligation, to buy an underlying asset at a fixed price for a specified time

**exercise price** or **strike price** the price at which an investor can buy the underlying asset

**exercise** to implement the rights of options by buying (in the case of call options) or selling (in the case of put options)

**expiration date** the last date on which options can be converted or exercised

**payoff** the proceeds that would be generated from the option if today was the expiration date

**exercise price** or **strike price**, and the last date at which the option can be converted or **exercised** is called the **expiration date**.

We begin our discussion with a simple example in which the forward price on an underlying asset is $50. We assume a call option is available on that asset with an exercise price ($X$) of $50. We set the exercise price equal to the forward price to simplify some of the discussion; however, it is not a necessary assumption. For now, we will not specify the expiration date of the option. The **payoff** for the buyer (holder) of this call (i.e., a long call position) for various underlying asset prices is depicted in **Figure 12.1**. The payoff refers to the proceeds that would be generated from the call option if today was the expiration date and the option holder had to decide whether to exercise the option or not. It does not exactly reflect the investor's profits, because it does not account for the purchase price of the option, which we will discuss later. We have also included the payoff from a long position in the underlying asset (i.e., from holding it) in Figure 12.1.

First, think about a long position in the underlying asset. In this case, the payoff is a 45-degree line going through the origin, because the value varies one to one with the price of the underlying asset. In other words, the underlying asset is worth (or pays off) $1 if the price goes to $1, $2 if it goes to $2, $50 if the price goes to $50, and so on. Now let's shift the 45-degree line over so it cuts the horizontal axis at the strike price, which in this case is the forward price of $50. The result is the payoff from a forward contract, as discussed in Chapter 11. If an investor buys the asset forward, then they have a long position; if the asset price exceeds the forward price, the investor has a profit, and if the asset price is less than the forward price, the investor has a loss. The fact that the payoff on the forward contract is a straight line (which happens to be 45 degrees) is the reason that we previously referred to it as a linear payoff.

Now think about the call with the strike price equal to the forward price of $50. If at expiration the underlying asset's price is above $50, say $55, the investor exercises the call. This means that they pay $50 and "call" the asset away from the counterparty—that is, the person who has sold the call. The investor could then obtain a payoff of $5 by selling the asset for $55 in the open market, exactly as we discussed with respect to the forward contract. In this case, we say the call is **in the money**. Conversely, if the underlying asset's price is below $50, the call is worthless and would not be exercised. No one would pay the strike price to call the asset away from its owner for $50 when it can be bought for less in the open market. This is the crucial fact about options: they give the owner the *right*, but not the *obligation*, to do something. In contrast to the long position in the forward contract, the investor doesn't incur losses in a long call position when the price of the underlying asset is below the strike price, which we

**in the money** the option would generate a positive payoff if exercised today

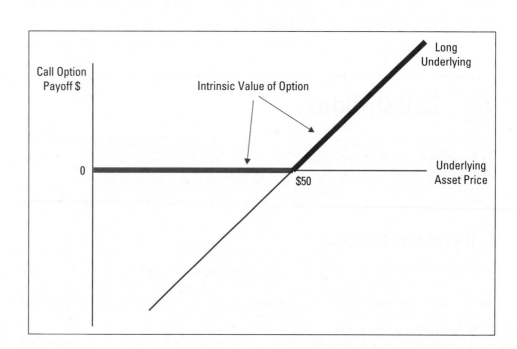

**FIGURE 12.1** **Call Holder's Payoff**

refer to as being **out of the money**.[1] As a result, the investor gets the payoff from the forward contract above the strike price and gets zero below. For this reason, options are examples of securities with non-linear payoffs.[2]

**out of the money**  the option would generate a negative payoff if exercised today

---

**EXAMPLE 12.1** | Call Holder's Payoffs

Complete the following table, giving the payoffs for various underlying asset prices for a call option buyer who buys a call option with a strike price of $50.

| Asset price ($) | 30 | 40 | 50 | 55 | 60 | 70 |
|---|---|---|---|---|---|---|
| Call holder's payoff ($) | | | | | | |

**Solution**

| Asset price ($) | 30 | 40 | 50 | 55 | 60 | 70 |
|---|---|---|---|---|---|---|
| Call holder's payoff ($) | 0 | 0 | 0 | 5 | 10 | 20 |
| | | | | $(55 - 50)$ | $(60 - 50)$ | $(70 - 50)$ |

Notice that the payoff is zero for all prices at or below the strike price of $50. Beyond $50, the payoff increases by $1 for every $1 increase in the underlying asset price.

---

The previous discussion leaves out one important detail—namely, the seller from whom investors are buying the option. The contracts we are examining in this chapter are secondary market options, which means that the supply and trading of these options has no impact on the underlying asset. When investors buy a call option, they buy it from some other market participant unrelated to the underlying asset. Until 35 years ago, investment bankers arranged option contracts directly between two parties, so there was significant credit risk attached to the counterparty. In other words, when investors exercised the call, they could not be certain that the counterparty would deliver it. In this way, option markets were similar to the original swap and forward markets. Today, as with the swap markets, option markets consist of unique over-the-counter (OTC) options that are still arranged between two parties with credit risk. However, there are a significant number of exchange-traded options, similar to futures, that have been designed to remove credit risk. In fact, traded options markets are tightly integrated with futures markets. For now, we will ignore credit risk and consider the payoff for the person who sells a call option; such a person is called an **option writer**, because they have written the call option that is purchased by someone else. It is common to say that option writers have assumed a **short position** in the option.

**option writer**  the person who sells an option

**short position**  the position taken by the option writer

If someone sells a call option, the payoff is the mirror image of that received by the person who buys it, just as the payoff to a short forward position is the mirror image of that of a long forward position. For example, we have already looked at the payoff to the $50 call holder and noted that, as the asset price increases—say to $55—the payoff on the call also increases—in this case to $5. This $5 payoff occurs as the asset is called away from the option writer for $50 and sold for $55. The payoff to the call option writer is the opposite, as they have to go into the market and buy this asset for $55, then surrender it for only $50, losing $5. Conversely, when a call expires out of the money and is not exercised, the option writer doesn't lose anything. The payoff of this $50 call for the option writer is depicted in **Figure 12.2**.

Notice that the payoff from writing the call is the mirror image of that from buying the call. It is the payoff from buying the call "folded" downward at the exercise price.

---

[1]An option is said to be "at the money" when the market price of the underlying asset equals the strike price.
[2]Strictly speaking, the payoffs are piecewise linear.

**FIGURE 12.2** **Call Option Writer's Payoff**

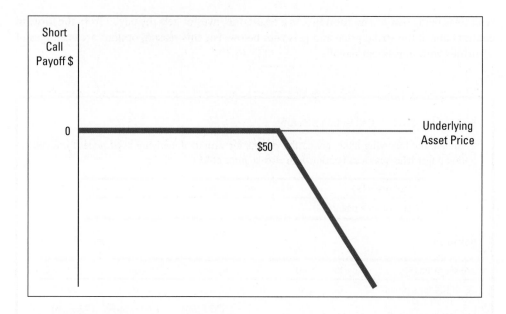

**EXAMPLE 12.2** | Option Writer's Payoffs

Complete the following table, depicting the payoffs for various underlying asset prices for an option writer who sells a call option with a strike price of $50.

| Asset price ($) | | | 30 | 40 | 50 | 55 | 60 | 70 |
|---|---|---|---|---|---|---|---|---|
| Option writer's payoff ($) | | | | | | | | |

**Solution**

| Asset price ($) | 30 | 40 | 50 | 55 | 60 | 70 |
|---|---|---|---|---|---|---|
| Option writer's payoff ($) | 0 | 0 | 0 | −5 | −10 | −20 |
| | | | | (50 − 55) | (50 − 60) | (50 − 70) |

Notice that the payoff is zero for all prices at or below the strike price of $50. Beyond $50, the payoff decreases by $1 for every $1 increase in the underlying asset price, because the option writer has agreed to sell the asset for $50.

## Call Option Values

**intrinsic value (IV)** the value of an option at expiration; it is positive when the option is in the money and zero when it is at or out of the money

So what is the value of a call option? At expiration, when the call is in the money, the value of the option is the asset price (*S*) minus the exercise price (*X*). When it is out of the money, the value is zero. This is called the **intrinsic value (IV)** and is depicted by the bold line in Figure 12.1. Equation 12.1 shows how we can determine the intrinsic value of a call option.

$$IV\,(Call) = Max\,(S - X, 0)$$ [12.1]

Equation 12.1 states that the IV of a call equals *S* − *X* when the call is in the money and equals 0 otherwise.

The IV is the value of an option on the expiration date. However, before expiration, the value of a call will exceed its intrinsic value because of the option's **time value (TV)**. The market value of the option, commonly known as the **option premium**, is the sum of its IV and its TV. This relationship is given in Equation 12.2.

**time value (TV)** the difference between the option premium and the intrinsic value

**option premium** the market value of the option; the sum of an option's IV and TV

$$Option\ premium = IV + TV$$ [12.2]

We can rearrange this equation to solve for the time value, as shown in Equation 12.3.

$$\boxed{\text{TV} = \text{Option premium} - \text{IV}}$$ [12.3]

---

**EXAMPLE 12.3** | Estimating Call Option Intrinsic and Time Values

Assume the $50 call option referred to in examples 12.1 and 12.2 is selling for $3 in the market. Determine the intrinsic value and time value of this call option, assuming the following prices for the underlying asset:

**a.** $48

**b.** $50

**c.** $52

**Solution**

**a.** IV = Max(48 − 50, 0) = 0; TV = 3 − 0 = $3

**b.** IV = Max(50 − 50, 0) = 0; TV = 3 − 0 = $3

**c.** IV = Max(52 − 50, 0) = 2; TV = 3 − 2 = $1

---

It has long been known that the option value depends on the price of the underlying asset, as indicated in Figure 12.1. However, it was not until Fischer Black and Myron Scholes, two finance professors from the University of Chicago, came up with the Black-Scholes option pricing model that the relationship was clearly understood.[3] We discuss this option pricing model later in the chapter; for now, let's step back and think intuitively about what drives option values.

The option value is influenced by the ratio of the price of the underlying asset to the strike price. Because $X$ is fixed for each call, this essentially means that as $S$ falls far below $X$, not only is the IV of the option zero, but so is the TV because there is less chance of the price of the underlying asset recovering to exceed the strike price. At the other extreme, when the price of the underlying asset is far above the strike price, the time value gets smaller, as discussed below. This means that **deep** in the money and deep out of the money calls are easier to value, because their values get closer to their intrinsic values as their time values get smaller.

**deep** describes options that are so far in (out of) the money that they are almost certain (not) to be exercised

For example, suppose over the next period it is equally likely that the price of the underlying asset will increase or decrease by $5. If the asset price is currently $10 and the strike price $50, the call is deep out of the money. With a decrease in the asset price to $5, the call remains deep out of the money. Even with an increase in the asset price to $15, it is still deep out of the money. With deep out of the money calls, the investor needs a sequence of very positive returns on the underlying asset to generate any value. This makes the time value very small.

Now take the opposite situation, in which the asset price is $100. This means the intrinsic value of the call is $50, so it is deep in the money. When the price changes by $5, the intrinsic value of the call also changes by close to $5. If the time value is zero, then the change in the value of the call is exactly the same as the underlying asset. In the extreme case of a call on an asset with a strike price of $0, then the call is deep in the money and exactly the same as the underlying asset.[4]

The impact of the underlying asset's price on the call's value means that a curve connects the intrinsic value of the option when it is deep in and deep out of the money. This relationship is illustrated in **Figure 12.3**, and it means that the call value is related in a non-linear way to the underlying asset price.

---

[3]Robert Merton was also a pioneer in option pricing. He and Myron Scholes (from Timmins, Ontario) shared the 1997 Nobel Prize in economics for their work. Unfortunately, Fischer Black died in 1995, before he could be similarly honoured.

[4]This assumes that the value of the asset, like that of a common share, cannot become negative.

**FIGURE 12.3** The Value of a
Call Option

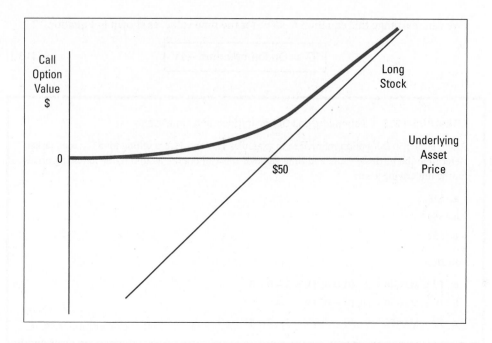

The fact that deep in and out of the money call options are relatively easy to value means that the most difficult options to value are those for which the price of the asset is close to the strike price. For options that are at the money (i.e., where $S = X$), the TV is at its largest and, by definition, the IV is zero. Unfortunately, most options start out with the strike price set close to the price of the underlying asset, so they have lots of time value and little intrinsic value. This factor is what makes option valuation complicated.

The discussion above directs our attention to the most important component of the option value, which is the *risk* of the underlying asset. In most areas of finance, risk is estimated as the variability or standard deviation of an asset's return. However, this is closely related to the range of possible outcomes, and it was the *range* that we used when we said the outcomes could be plus or minus $5, or a range of $10. Now suppose we are valuing two at the money calls on different assets that both have the same $50 strike price. The first call is on an asset with two equally likely outcomes of plus or minus $5 for a price range of $10, while the second is on a riskier asset with two equally likely outcomes of plus or minus $10 or a range of $20. Which call is more valuable?

First, consider what happens when the price of the underlying asset falls below $X$. We know that we are not going to exercise the call and will let it expire worthless, so whether the asset price is $5 or $10 below the strike price does not matter. Conversely, the amount by which the asset price exceeds $X$ does matter. The call on the low-risk asset will now have an intrinsic value of $5, whereas that on the riskier asset will have an intrinsic value of $10. An important aspect of option pricing is the fact that call options on riskier assets are worth more than those on low-risk assets. This is because the call protects you from "downside" risk, so how far down you go doesn't matter since the payoff is still zero. All that matters is the upside or how far above the strike price the asset price can get. Anything that expands the range of outcomes or risk of the underlying asset makes a call on the asset more valuable.

Now consider *time*. Risk itself is important, but option values also depend critically on how much time is left until expiration. No matter how risky an underlying asset, if a deep out of the money call is close to expiration—say a day away—it will not be worth much. A deep out of the money call on a risky asset with a long time to expiration may be very valuable. Take our previous example of a plus or minus $5 change in the price of an underlying asset currently worth $10. If this is the possible weekly change, then a one-week call at $50 is worthless, because it is not possible for the price of the underlying asset to exceed $50. However, if the same call has nine weeks left, it is possible that the price of the underlying asset can increase by $5 each week and go from $10 to $55, thereby giving the call value.

Over long periods, all sorts of things can happen to give value to the underlying asset and, therefore, to a call on that asset. For example, in 2001, the value of the Canadian dollar was barely US$0.65, the price of a barrel of oil was $20, and the price of one share of Nortel Networks Corporation, a major Canadian telecom company, was $122. In 2012, the Canadian exchange rate was at parity with the U.S. dollar; oil was consistently over US$100 a barrel; and Nortel had gone into bankruptcy protection, rendering its shares almost worthless. Such dramatic price movements illustrate why call options on risky assets with a long time to expiration are very valuable.

We will discuss the impact of risk and time more formally when we discuss a model of option pricing, but for now it's important to remember that risk compounds through time, causing the range of outcomes to increase. This compounding or magnification is greater for high-risk stocks than it is for low-risk stocks, which makes long-dated call options on risky assets more valuable than options on short-dated low-risk assets. For any given call option, if everything else is constant, its value will *decrease* over time. For example, an at the money call starts out with maximum time value and no intrinsic value. If nothing else changes, and it is still at the money at expiration, then it is worthless. Generally, the time value decreases at an increasing rate as the call gets closer to expiration.

We should also consider the factors driving the underlying asset's price. For example, from Chapter 7, we know that the value of a common share is the present value of a stream of dividends, so call options on equities depend on these dividend payments. We will discuss dividend policy in Chapter 22, but suppose a resource company has very large profits because natural resource prices are at an all-time high, which is not expected to continue. As a result, a company's stock price is $38, consisting of a $26 value for its continuing operations and $12 for its cash. If the firm decides to pay out this cash as a dividend, the stock price will drop by $12, reducing the value of a call on the stock.

Generally, options are not protected from any dividend payments made by the underlying asset, so options on high-dividend-paying stocks or assets with large cash distributions are worth less than those on non-dividend-paying stocks. In 1989, Inco Ltd., one of the largest nickel producers in the world, was in the situation described in the preceding paragraph and unexpectedly paid out a US$10 dividend, which was worth about C$12 at the time, causing a dramatic drop in its stock price. This illustrates how important it is to pay attention to the dividend payments of the underlying asset, because they can affect the price of both the underlying asset and the option.

The final factor that affects option prices is the *risk-free interest rate*. Normally, when interest rates go up, the values of securities go down. For example, bond prices always go down when interest rates rise, as discussed in Chapter 6, but equity prices also tend to go down, because the equity discount rate may go up. However, option prices behave differently, because the main effect of increasing interest rates is to decrease the present value of the strike price. An increase in the interest rate has a similar effect on a call price as decreasing the strike price. As a result, call options tend to increase with increases in interest rates.

To summarize our discussion, call option prices display the following characteristics:

- They approach their intrinsic value for deep in and deep out of the money calls.
- They increase with the price of the underlying asset.
- They decrease with a higher strike price.
- They increase if the underlying asset is riskier.
- They increase as the time to expiration increases.
- They decrease as the dividend payments of the underlying asset increase.
- They increase as interest rates increase.

That's a lot of factors to consider in a pricing model, and it is important to remember that we considered each of them in isolation, looking at the impact of a change in only one factor at a time. In reality, of course, many of these factors are changing all the time, and they affect one another. For example, an increase in interest rates or a change in risk may have a negative effect on option prices if the indirect effect on the asset price is greater than the *direct* effects discussed above. However, before we consider how to incorporate these factors into a pricing model, we can bracket the value of the call option by considering the characteristics of put options.

*Finance in the News 12.1* presents some option trading strategies open to investors in the wake of sharp declines in Boeing stock prices following recent tragic flight disasters.

## 12.1 Finance in the News  Boeing Stock's Fall Turns Some Options Traders Into Bulls

Boeing Co.'s struggling shares have unleashed a frenzy of options trading on its stock, with some trades positioned for a rebound.

The aerospace and defense company's shares are down 11% this week. One of Boeing's models, the 737 MAX jet, has been in two crashes over the past five months, raising questions about the plane's flight-control system. The latest occurred in Ethiopia over the weekend, killing 157 people.

Options volumes on Tuesday hit at least a two-year high, with some traders looking at a 7% advance in its shares from that day's closing price. Activity stayed elevated on Wednesday. Some of the most popular contracts this week were bullish calls that pay out if the shares jumped to $400 or $410, according to data provider Trade Alert. Boeing shares closed at $377.14 Wednesday.

Calls give traders the right to buy shares at a given price, known as a strike, later in time. Puts confer the right to sell stock. Traders can use options to make directional bets on a stock or hedge their positions.

The thinking is, "this is temporary news, and we could rally right back," said JJ Kinahan, chief market strategist at TD Ameritrade.

Mr. Kinahan said he also noticed some traders selling bearish put options to take advantage of how volatile the shares were. Options prices tend to surge when a stock records bigger swings and traders can sell options to collect premiums from the contracts. This can be a risky strategy if the stock falls, the options are exercised and the put seller is then forced to buy the shares from someone else.

Some investors may have sold their Boeing stock and bought options instead, analysts said. This would enable them to profit from a rebound in the shares, while protecting holdings from a deeper dive.

Prior instances show that though such air accidents are tragic, they don't leave a meaningful dent in stock prices. The Federal Aviation Administration halted all flights by another Boeing model in 2013 after emergency landings stemming from the plane's faulty batteries. The company's shares trailed the broader market for a few months before outperforming the S&P 500 in 2013, The Wall Street Journal reported.

Since the weekend, countries around the world have sought to ground Boeing's model. Moody's Corp. analysts said Tuesday that one risk to Boeing is that airlines ... would seek compensation from the company for lost revenue or [defer] their orders for new planes. The 737 MAX aircraft involved in the crash is a lucrative model for Boeing. But, they said, accidents generally don't lead to sweeping changes to airlines' fleet plans.

"We believe the MAX program will overcome the near-term challenges it now faces because of the two accidents," they wrote.

Some were bracing for big moves for the company's shares in either direction, including a drastic fall. Other actively traded options on Wednesday were bearish puts that pay out if Boeing hit $350 and $360, up to a roughly 7% drop from that day's close, Trade Alert data show.

And many expect the volatility in Boeing shares to persist. A measure of expected swings for the stock is near a yearlong high, Trade Alert data show.

"The market is more concerned about immediate price movement" than the stock's longer-term trajectory, said Mark Sebastian, managing partner at Option Pit.

**Source:** Banerji, Gunjan, "Boeing Stock's Fall Turns Some Options Traders Into Bulls." *The Wall Street Journal,* March 14, 2019. Copyright 2019 Dow Jones & Company, Inc. All rights reserved. Reprinted by permission.

**Rush to Bet**

Boeing's stock decline has triggered a flurry of options activity on its shares.

**Daily options volume**  ■ Bearish puts  ■ Bullish calls

**Source:** Data from Trade Alert

**Concept Review Questions**

1. Explain why the payoff from a call option is non-linear.
2. Explain how to estimate the intrinsic value and time value for a call option.
3. Briefly describe the main factors that affect a call option's value and how they affect the value.

---

## 12.2 Put Options

> **LEARNING OBJECTIVE 12.2**
>
> Describe the basic nature of put options and the payoffs associated with long and short positions in put options.

## Put Option Payoffs

A **put option** is the opposite of a call option: it gives the owner the *right, but not the obligation,* to *sell* an underlying asset at a fixed price for a specified time. Consider the value of a put on an underlying asset with a strike price equal to the forward price of $50. The payoff for the holder of a put is depicted in **Figure 12.4**.

In considering the behaviour of a call option, we first examined a long position in the asset. Because a put is the opposite of a call, we start with the opposite of a long position in the underlying asset, which is a short position. When the underlying asset is sold forward and its price exceeds the forward price at $55, the investor loses $5. This occurs because they have to go into the market and pay $55 to buy the asset to deliver against the forward contract, for which they get only $50. Conversely, if the asset price falls to $45, the investor generates a $5 profit. They buy the asset for $45 and then deliver it to meet the forward commitment and receive the $50 forward price. Graphically, the short position is a 45-degree line going through the forward price of $50, as depicted in Figure 12.4. Notice that this is the mirror image of the long position.

Now consider the payoff on the put option. If the asset price increases, the investor does not exercise the put option, because there is no reason to sell the asset for $50 when the investor can sell it in the open market for, say, $55. Conversely, if the asset price drops to $45, the investor exercises the put. It is better to use the put contract and sell it to the counterparty for $50 than to sell it in the open market for $45. The result is the opposite of the call option; put options pay

**put option** the right, but not the obligation, to sell an underlying asset at a fixed price for a specified time

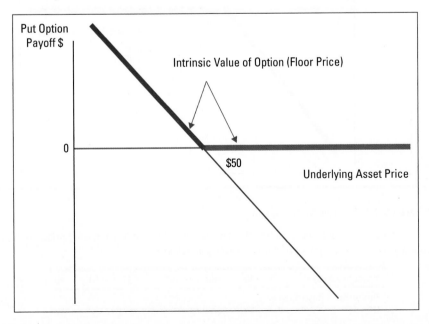

**FIGURE 12.4** Put Holder's Payoff

off when the asset price drops below the strike price, and they are worthless when the asset price is above the strike price. The put allows an investor to take advantage of the downside risk attached to an asset, just as the call allows an investor to benefit from an upside move in price.

---

**EXAMPLE 12.4** | Put Holder's Payoffs

Complete the following table, depicting the payoffs for various underlying asset prices for an investor who buys a put option with a strike price of $50.

| Asset price ($) | 30 | 40 | 50 | 55 | 60 | 70 |
|---|---|---|---|---|---|---|
| Put holder's payoff ($) | | | | | | |

**Solution**

| Asset price ($) | 30 | 40 | 50 | 55 | 60 | 70 |
|---|---|---|---|---|---|---|
| Put holder's payoff ($) | 20 | 10 | 0 | 0 | 0 | 0 |
| | (50 − 30) | (50 − 40) | | | | |

   Notice that the payoff is zero for all prices at or above the strike price of $50. Below $50, the payoff increases by $1 for every $1 decrease in the underlying asset price.

---

Now we consider the payoff for the put writer, who has assumed what is commonly called a short position in the put. We know that when the asset price increases above the strike price, the put expires worthless, so the payoff to both the put owner and writer is zero. When the asset price drops below the strike price, say to $45, then the owner of the put buys the asset for $45 in the open market and sells it to the put writer for $50, making a $5 profit. The put writer's payoff is the opposite of the put holder's, because they have to pay $50 for an asset that can be sold for only $45, thereby incurring a $5 loss. The payoff for the put writer is given in **Figure 12.5**.

   Notice that it is the mirror image of the put holder's payoff, or the put holder's payoff folded downward.

**FIGURE 12.5** **Put Writer's Payoff**

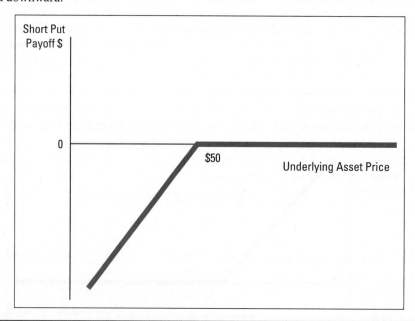

---

**EXAMPLE 12.5** | Put Writer's Payoffs

Complete the following table, depicting the payoffs for various underlying asset prices for a put option writer who sells a put option with a strike price of $50.

| Asset price ($) | 30 | 40 | 50 | 55 | 60 | 70 |
|---|---|---|---|---|---|---|
| Put writer's payoff ($) | | | | | | |

**Solution**

| Asset price ($) | 30 | 40 | 50 | 55 | 60 | 70 |
|---|---|---|---|---|---|---|
| Put writer's payoff ($) | −20 | −10 | 0 | 0 | 0 | 0 |
| | (30 − 50) | (40 − 50) | | | | |

Notice that the payoff is zero for all prices at or above the strike price of $50. Below $50, the payoff decreases by $1 for every $1 decrease in the underlying asset price, because the put writer has agreed to buy the asset for $50.

## Put Option Values

Equation 12.4 shows how we can estimate the intrinsic value of a put option.

$$\text{IV (Put)} = \text{Max} \, (X - S, \, 0) \qquad [12.4]$$

Equation 12.4 states that the IV of a put equals $X - S$ when the put is in the money, and equals 0 otherwise. Equations 12.2 and 12.3, regarding the option premium and time value of an option, apply to puts in the same way as they did for calls.

---

**EXAMPLE 12.6** | Estimating Put Option Intrinsic and Time Values

Assume the $50 put option referred in examples 12.4 and 12.5 is selling for $2.25 in the market. Determine the intrinsic value and time value of this put option, assuming the following prices for the underlying asset:

**a.** $48

**b.** $50

**c.** $52

**Solution**

**a.** IV = Max(50 − 48, 0) = 2; TV = 2.25 − 2 = $0.25

**b.** IV = Max(50 − 50, 0) = 0; TV = 2.25 − 0 = $2.25

**c.** IV = Max(50 − 52, 0) = 0; TV = 2.25 − 0 = $2.25

---

The factors that drive put prices are the same factors that affect call prices. However, the effects are usually in the opposite direction. When the asset price is significantly above the strike price, the put is deep out of the money, so the price approaches its intrinsic value of zero. Conversely, when the asset price drops and is well below the strike price, the put is deep in the money, and again the put's price approaches its intrinsic value. This is opposite to the call but, like the call, the put's maximum time value occurs at the strike price, when its intrinsic value is zero. In contrast to the call, an increase in the asset price will decrease the put price, while a higher strike price will increase its value. However, an increase in either the expiration date or the risk (uncertainty) in the underlying asset will increase the put price in the same manner as it would a call price. A decrease in interest rates or an increase in cash dividend payments will increase the put price.

All of the effects discussed above are predictable, given the intuitive understanding of these factors' impact on call prices. However, there is a major difference between puts and calls when it comes to whether or not an investor can exercise the option before the expiration date. Note that **European options** can be exercised only at maturity, whereas **American options** can be exercised at any time up to and including the expiration date. This distinction is no longer geographic, as the names imply, because European options are traded in North America and vice versa. For call options on non-dividend-paying assets, the distinction is not important; as long as the option can be sold, it should never be exercised before maturity, because there is always some time value.[5] However, the distinction is important for put options. Consider what happens

**European options** options that can be exercised only at maturity

**American options** options that can be exercised at any time up to and including the expiration date

---

[5]For interest- or dividend-paying assets, early exercise may occur in the case of a very large payment that significantly reduces the value of the underlying asset.

**TABLE 12.1** Factors Affecting Option Prices[6]

|  | Call Prices | Put Prices |
|---|---|---|
| Higher asset price ($S$) | ↑ | ↓ |
| Higher exercise price ($X$) | ↓ | ↑ |
| Longer expiration ($t$) | ↑ | ↑ |
| Increased volatility ($\sigma$) | ↑ | ↑ |
| Higher interest rates ($r$) | ↑ | ↓ |
| Higher dividends ($D$) | ↓ | ↑ |

if the underlying asset price goes to zero, perhaps because it is a common share and the firm goes bankrupt. Because the underlying asset can never go below zero, the put reaches its maximum value. In this case, all American options would be exercised, because the put holder gets the maximum payoff immediately, and that cash can then be reinvested elsewhere.

We summarize the impact of these basic factors on option prices in **Table 12.1**.

**Concept Review Questions**

1. Contrast the payoff from a put option with that from a call option.
2. Explain how to estimate the intrinsic value and time value for a put option.
3. Briefly describe the main factors that affect a put or a call option's value, and explain how they affect the value of each.

## 12.3 | Put-Call Parity

**LEARNING OBJECTIVE 12.3**

Explain how to use put-call parity to estimate call and put prices, and explain how it can be used to synthetically create call, put, and underlying positions.

### The Four Basic Option Positions

The four basic option positions are (1) long call, (2) short call, (3) long put, and (4) short put. These positions were diagrammed in figures 12.1, 12.2, 12.4, and 12.5. We will consider these four positions again, only this time we will put them all in one figure. Note that if we combine a long call and a short put, we have a 45-degree line going through the strike price, which in our example is also the forward price of $50. This is a long forward contract with gains and losses around the strike price. Similarly, if we combine a long put and a short call, we have a 45-degree line going through the forward price. This is a short forward contract with losses and gains around the strike price. The payoffs on these contracts are depicted in **Figure 12.6**.

---

[6]The table shows how the indicated change in each factor will affect the value of a call or put, positively or negatively, all other factors remaining constant. These price changes are collectively referred to as the "comparative statics" of each option. Strictly speaking, the price changes in the table hold for American options. They mostly hold for European options as well, but in the case of time to maturity, having more time may not be beneficial for European calls and puts, depending on the timing and magnitude of subsequent dividend payments. Therefore, the direction of the price change, while mainly positive for longer-lived European options, is deemed to be uncertain.

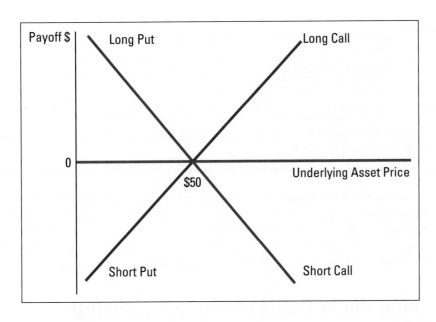

**FIGURE 12.6** Combining Option Positions

It is now obvious why we started with puts and calls with a strike price equal to the forward price. In this special case, the long call and short put are the equivalent of a forward contract, and the long put and short call are the equivalent of a short forward contract. Examples 12.7 and 12.8 demonstrate.

---

**EXAMPLE 12.7** | Long Call Plus Short Put Payoffs

Complete the following table depicting the payoffs for various underlying asset prices for an investor who simultaneously buys a call and sells a put, each with a strike price of $50.

| Asset price ($) | 30 | 40 | 50 | 55 | 60 | 70 |
|---|---|---|---|---|---|---|
| Long call payoff ($) | | | | | | |
| Short put payoff ($) | | | | | | |
| Net payoff ($) | | | | | | |

**Solution**

| Asset price ($) | 30 | 40 | 50 | 55 | 60 | 70 |
|---|---|---|---|---|---|---|
| Long call payoff ($) | 0 | 0 | 0 | 5 | 10 | 20 |
| Short put payoff ($) | −20 | −10 | 0 | 0 | 0 | 0 |
| Net payoff ($) | −20 | −10 | 0 | 5 | 10 | 20 |

Notice that the payoff for the net position is exactly the same as that from a long forward position at a forward price of $50.

---

**EXAMPLE 12.8** | Short Call Plus Long Put Payoffs

Complete the following table depicting the payoffs for various underlying asset prices for an investor who simultaneously sells a call and buys a put, each with a strike price of $50.

| Asset price ($) | 30 | 40 | 50 | 55 | 60 | 70 |
|---|---|---|---|---|---|---|
| Short call payoff ($) | | | | | | |
| Long put payoff ($) | | | | | | |
| Net payoff ($) | | | | | | |

**Solution**

| Asset price ($) | 30 | 40 | 50 | 55 | 60 | 70 |
|---|---|---|---|---|---|---|
| Short call payoff ($) | 0 | 0 | 0 | −5 | −10 | −20 |
| Long put payoff ($) | 20 | 10 | 0 | 0 | 0 | 0 |
| Net payoff ($) | 20 | 10 | 0 | −5 | −10 | −20 |

Notice that the payoff for the net position is exactly the same as that from a short forward position at a forward price of $50.

If an investor simultaneously established all four basic option positions, the net position would be zero, because in aggregate the four contracts are a "zero sum game": wealth is neither created nor destroyed. This is shown in examples 12.7 and 12.8, because the investor would be combining the two net payoff positions, which add to zero for any underlying asset price. With secondary market options, wealth is simply rearranged among market participants.[7]

# Deriving the Put-Call Parity Relationship

**put-call parity**   the relationship between the price of a call option and a put option that have the same strike price and expiry dates; assumes that the options are not exercised before their expiration

Understanding how these four contracts end up looking like long and short forward contracts is the key to understanding **put-call parity**. Consider two portfolios. The first, portfolio A, consists of buying a put ($P$) with $X = \$50$ and simultaneously purchasing the underlying asset ($S$). The second, portfolio B, consists of buying a call ($C$) with $X = \$50$ and investing the present value of the exercise price, $PV(X)$, in a risk-free asset paying interest at the risk-free rate ($RF$), so that the investor has $50 available to exercise the call option. We assume the options are European so that they can be exercised only at maturity. We also assume the underlying asset provides no dividends or other income. **Table 12.2** shows the payoffs from these two portfolios, assuming the underlying asset price can be either $45 or $55.

Notice that the payoff from either strategy is the same, whether the ending share price is $45 or $55. In fact, it is easy to demonstrate that the payoffs for these two portfolios will always be the same, as depicted in **Table 12.3**.

The payoff from either strategy is the same no matter what the ending share price is. Because early exercise is not possible, and the payoffs at the expiration date ($T$) will always be the same, the *cost* of constructing each portfolio must be the same. Denoting the cost of the put as $P$, the cost of the call as $C$, and the price of the underlying asset as $S$, we get Equation 12.5, which states that

$$P + S = C + PV(X)$$

[12.5]

| TABLE 12.2 | Payoff from Combining Calls, Puts, and Underlying Asset Positions | |
|---|---|---|
| **Underlying Price** | **$55** | **$45** |
| **Portfolio A** | | |
| Long put payoff | 0 | +$5 |
| Long asset payoff | +$55 | +$45 |
| Total payoff for A | $55 | $50 |
| **Portfolio B** | | |
| Long call payoff | +$5 | 0 |
| Invest present value of $50 at *RF* | +$50 | +$50 |
| Total payoff for B | $55 | $50 |

---

[7]This ignores the option prices, the fees charged by brokers, and the exchange to make the market. This is why many experts argue that, in aggregate, options waste scarce resources in the economy.

| TABLE 12.3 | Payoff from Combining Calls, Puts, and Underlying Asset Positions: The General Case | |
| --- | --- | --- |
| **Underlying Price at Expiration Date ($S_T$)** | $S_T > X$ | $S_T < X$ |
| **Portfolio A** | | |
| Long put payoff | 0 | $X - S_T$ |
| Long asset payoff | $S_T$ | $S_T$ |
| Total payoff for A | $S_T$ | $X$ |
| **Portfolio B** | | |
| Long call payoff | $S_T - X$ | 0 |
| Invest PV of $X$ | $+X$ | $+X$ |
| Total payoff for B | $S_T$ | $X$ |

Rearranging Equation 12.5, we get the basic put-call relationship:

$$C - P = S - PV(X) \qquad [12.6]$$

It is important to recognize that this relationship holds for European options on non-dividend-paying assets. It is also important to recognize that we can solve this equation to determine the call option price, given $P$, $S$, $X$, and $RF$, and we can also determine the put option price given $C$, $S$, $X$, and $RF$. Both of these equations are shown below.

$$C = P + S - PV(X) \qquad [12.7]$$

$$P = C - S + PV(X) \qquad [12.8]$$

Although put-call parity doesn't help us to price the call unless we know the price of the put and vice versa, it does demonstrate again that these contracts are all derivative—that is, not original. There is evidence that the basic properties of put-call parity have been known for centuries. We demonstrate how to apply put-call parity in examples 12.9 and 12.10.

---

**EXAMPLE 12.9** | Finding a Call Price by Using Put-Call Parity

A company's common shares are selling for $20, and a one-year European put option on those shares, with a $20 strike price, is selling for $0.50. If the risk-free rate is 5 percent, find the value of a one-year European call on the same stock with a $20 exercise price.

**Solution**

$$C = P + S - PV(X) = \$0.50 + \$20 - \$20/(1.05) = \$20.50 - \$19.05 = \$1.45$$

---

**EXAMPLE 12.10** | Finding a Put Price by Using Put-Call Parity

A company's common shares are selling for $20, and a six-month European call option on those shares, with a $20 strike price, is selling for $0.90. If the risk-free rate is 5 percent, find the value of a six-month European put on the same stock with a $20 exercise price.

**Solution**   Six-month discount rate = $5\%/2 = 2.50\%$

$$P = C - S + PV(X) = \$0.90 - \$20 + \$20/(1.025) = -\$19.10 + \$19.51 = \$0.41$$

The put-call parity equation can also be solved for *S*, as shown in Equation 12.9.

$$S = C - P + PV(X)$$
[12.9]

Equation 12.9 shows that a long position in the underlying asset is equivalent to a long position in a call, a short position in a put on the same underlying asset with the same strike price and time to maturity, and an investment of *PV(X)* in a risk-free asset. If we multiply this equation by −1, we can see that a short position in the underlying asset is equivalent to a short position in a call, a long position in a put on the same underlying asset with the same strike price and time to maturity, and borrowing *PV(X)* at the risk-free rate.

## Creating Synthetic Positions by Using Put-Call Parity

The put-call parity relationships are particularly important for hedging purposes. Applying our discussion of how to create synthetic positions by using forward contracts from Chapter 11, we can see how we could use equations 12.7 through 12.9 to synthetically create long or short positions in puts, calls, or the underlying asset. For our present purposes, we ignore the *PV(X)* term, which involves borrowing or lending at *RF*, because it does not affect the shape of the net payoff diagram.

We begin by considering a long position in the underlying asset; for example, assume that the asset is U.S. dollars receivable, as we discussed in Chapter 11. We already showed that an investor can sell U.S. dollars at the forward rate (*F*) to remove the exposure completely, but perhaps the investor thinks the Canadian dollar is going to weaken and wants the possibility of getting more Canadian dollars for those U.S. dollars. In other words, the investor wants downside-risk protection if the Canadian dollar strengthens and wants to maintain upside potential if it weakens. Suppose the contract is priced so that if the Canadian dollar appreciates to $0.90 per U.S. dollar, the investor will break even, but below this, they lose money. In this case, the investor might not want to risk a depreciation of the U.S. dollar below C$0.90, so they buy a put option to sell U.S. dollars at C$0.90 to fix the minimum Canadian dollars they will get out of the contract.

**protective put** the purchase of a put option to protect a long position in an underlying asset

Buying a put option to protect a long position in an underlying asset is generally referred to as entering into a **protective put**. In this case, the purchase of the put option gives the right to sell the U.S. dollar at a fixed price for Canadian dollars, which insures the long position against losing money. The net payoff from this overall position resembles that of a long call position, as predicted by put-call parity in Equation 12.7 and as depicted by the solid bolded line in **Figure 12.7**.

The 45-degree line indicates the long position in U.S. dollars from the contract; the green dotted line indicates the long put position we discussed earlier. If the value of the U.S. dollar is

**FIGURE 12.7** **A Protective Put**

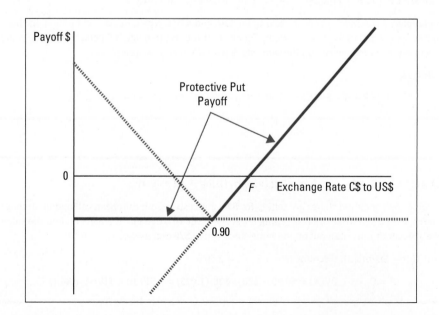

above C$0.90, the investor does not exercise the put and exchanges U.S. dollars at the spot rate. However, as the U.S. dollar depreciates below C$0.90—say to C$0.80—the investor exercises the put and exchanges the depreciating U.S. dollar for C$0.90 instead of taking the spot rate. The combination is depicted by the bold line in Figure 12.7, which looks like a long call, as predicted by put-call parity. This example indicates a very important result: although buying puts and calls "naked" is regarded as risky, it is not risky when the investor already has the asset. In that case, the combination of being long in puts and in the underlying asset is equivalent to being long in a call option, so the put acts like insurance.

The insurance argument has been used extensively to sell put options. Consider basic house insurance. If homeowners don't have insurance, either nothing happens or they suffer a loss when, for example, their house burns down. Buying insurance removes the loss at the cost of the insurance premium. If nothing happens, homeowners are out the insurance premium, but if the house burns down, they sell the ashes to the insurance company in return for a new house. Car insurance works the same way: if drivers don't have an accident, nothing happens, but if drivers do have an accident, they transfer the loss—that is, vehicle damage and other personal liability—to the insurance company. In both cases, insurance is just a put option, where the buyer has paid for the right to transfer the loss to the insurance company.

---

**EXAMPLE 12.11** | A Protective Put

Complete the following table, depicting the payoffs for an investor who buys an underlying asset for $50 and simultaneously buys a put with a strike price of $50.

| Asset price ($) | 30 | 40 | 50 | 55 | 60 | 70 |
|---|---|---|---|---|---|---|
| Long asset payoff ($) | | | | | | |
| Long put payoff ($) | | | | | | |
| Net payoff ($) | | | | | | |

**Solution**

| Asset price ($) | 30 | 40 | 50 | 55 | 60 | 70 |
|---|---|---|---|---|---|---|
| Long asset payoff ($) | −20 | −10 | 0 | 5 | 10 | 20 |
| Long put payoff ($) | 20 | 10 | 0 | 0 | 0 | 0 |
| Net payoff ($) | 0 | 0 | 0 | 5 | 10 | 20 |

Notice that the payoff for the net position is exactly the same as that for buying a call at a strike price of $50.

---

Let's consider another situation where the investor is long the asset but doesn't think the asset is going to increase in value. Normally, they would sell the asset. However, suppose the investor is a large pension fund and the asset is a stock market portfolio of $20 billion. In practice, it is difficult to sell that much without causing the price to drop. The investor can sell call options, because they don't think the price is going to increase to make the calls valuable. (The payoff from this strategy is explained below.) This is called a **covered call writing** strategy, because the investor has sold a call but owns the underlying asset. As **Figure 12.8** indicates, the net payoff position resembles a short put position, which is what put-call parity (i.e., Equation 12.8) predicts.

**covered call writing**  selling call options while owning the underlying asset

The long position in Figure 12.8 is the 45-degree line; the short call position is the dotted green line; and the combined position is the bold blue line. If the asset value increases above the call price, it is called away from the investor, so all they get is the strike price, which is set above the forward price. However, below the strike price, the call expires worthless and the investor gets the full value of the long position. Essentially, by selling a call, the investor has sold away some of the upside in the value of the underlying asset. This makes sense if they don't think there is much upside. Covered call writing can be considered an income-producing strategy if the belief is that the value of the underlying is not likely to increase during the life of the option. If in fact the value of the underlying increases and the call buyer exercises the option, the call writer can reduce the downside by holding stock that can be sold to the holder of the call, albeit at a loss compared with the higher prevailing market price.

**FIGURE 12.8** **Covered Call Writing**

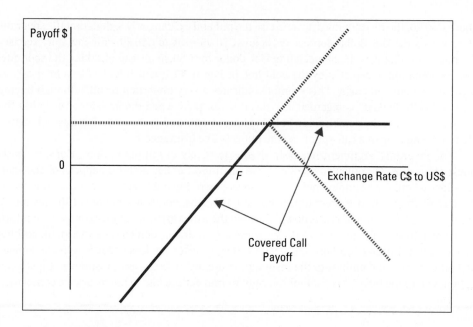

EXAMPLE 12.12 | A Covered Call

Complete the following table depicting the payoffs for an investor who buys an underlying asset for $50 and simultaneously writes a call with a strike price of $50.

| Asset price ($) | 30 | 40 | 50 | 55 | 60 | 70 |
|---|---|---|---|---|---|---|
| Long asset payoff ($) | | | | | | |
| Short call payoff ($) | | | | | | |
| Net payoff ($) | | | | | | |

**Solution**

| Asset price ($) | 30 | 40 | 50 | 55 | 60 | 70 |
|---|---|---|---|---|---|---|
| Long asset payoff ($) | −20 | −10 | 0 | 5 | 10 | 20 |
| Short call payoff ($) | 0 | 0 | 0 | −5 | −10 | −20 |
| Net payoff ($) | −20 | −10 | 0 | 0 | 0 | 0 |

Notice that the payoff for the net position is exactly the same as that for writing a put at a strike price of $50.

If an investor is long the asset, then buying a put places a floor under how much they can lose, whereas selling a call places a ceiling on how much they can earn. So far, we have not talked about how much these options are worth, but clearly they are very valuable, as anyone pricing car insurance (i.e., puts) knows! So buying a put and insuring your asset is costly; one way of financing this is to sell a call, as in **Figure 12.9**.

Notice that if the asset price goes above $S_2$, the strike price in the call, the asset is called away, so this is a ceiling price. Below $S_1$, the strike price in the put, the put is exercised, so it is a floor price. In between $S_1$ and $S_2$ is the payoff from a long position in the underlying asset. The net position is the bold line, and is generically called a **collar**, because the put and call options provide a collar for the price range. In foreign exchange, such contracts have been called flexible forwards or range forwards, while in financing cases they are referred to as floor-ceiling loans.

**collar** a position between the floor and ceiling price

We have discussed the most basic option strategies, which in practice are limited only by an investor's imagination. For example, an investor could have a long position and sell two options instead of one, or could buy both puts and calls at different exercise prices or expiration dates. However, in order to make sense of such strategies, we need to discuss how much these options are worth.

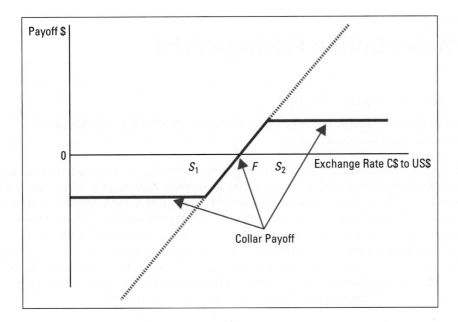

**FIGURE 12.9** **A Collar**

---

**EXAMPLE 12.13** | A Collar

Complete the following table, depicting the payoffs for an investor who buys an underlying asset for $50 and simultaneously buys a put with a strike price of $45 and sells a call with a strike price of $55.

| Asset price ($) | 30 | 40 | 50 | 55 | 60 | 70 |
|---|---|---|---|---|---|---|
| Long asset payoff ($) | | | | | | |
| Long $45 put payoff ($) | | | | | | |
| Short $55 call payoff ($) | | | | | | |
| Net payoff ($) | | | | | | |

**Solution**

| Asset price ($) | 30 | 40 | 50 | 55 | 60 | 70 |
|---|---|---|---|---|---|---|
| Long asset payoff ($) | −20 | −10 | 0 | 5 | 10 | 20 |
| Long $45 put payoff ($) | 15 | 5 | 0 | 0 | 0 | 0 |
| Short $55 call payoff ($) | 0 | 0 | 0 | 0 | −5 | −15 |
| Net payoff ($) | −5 | −5 | 0 | 5 | 5 | 5 |

The payoff for the net position equals −$5 for all prices below $45 (the put's strike price), equals +$5 for all prices above $55 (the call's strike price), and increases by $1 for each $1 increase in the underlying asset price between $45 and $55.

---

## Concept Review Questions

1. Illustrate how to combine the four basic option positions to create a variety of net payoff positions.

2. Explain why the put-call parity relationship should hold if markets are efficient.

3. Explain how to synthetically create long and short positions in calls, puts, and the underlying assets by using put-call parity.

## 12.4 | The Black-Scholes Option Pricing Model

> **LEARNING OBJECTIVE 12.4**
>
> Explain how to use the Black-Scholes option pricing model to price call options.

Appendix 12A discusses the binomial option pricing model, which can be used to value complicated securities. That model is based on the assumption that the price of the underlying asset can go either up or down to some value over a given period. Although this assumption may seem simplistic, so far we haven't specified the period involved. We can shorten the period from a month to a week, a day, a minute, or a second, and the model still holds. We can then think of a whole sequence of up and down movements representing the possible movement in the asset price, and use numerical procedures,[8] similar to those above, to calculate the option price. Although this is possible, it ignores one of the advantages of the Black-Scholes formula, which reduces to a simple "plug-in" formula, shown in Equation 12.10.

$$C = SN(d_1) - Xe^{-rt}N(d_2)$$ [12.10]

where

$$d_1 = \frac{Ln(S/X) + (r + \sigma^2/2)t}{\sigma\sqrt{t}}$$

$$d_2 = d_1 - \sigma\sqrt{t}$$

Technically, Equation 12.10 applies to European call options on non-dividend-paying stocks; however, variations of this equation exist for calls on dividend-paying stocks and for puts.[9]

It might be difficult to think of this as a plug-in formula, but it is. First, some of the numbers are straightforward, such as $S$, which is the current asset price, and $X$, which is the strike price. The term $e^{-rt}$ is the present value factor when we are discounting in continuous time, so just think of $Xe^{-rt}$ as the present value of the strike price, where $r$ is the risk-free rate and $t$ is the time to the expiration of the option. If we set $N(d_1)$ and $N(d_2)$ equal to one for now, the Black-Scholes formula says the value of a call is the value of the asset minus the present value of the exercise price. If the asset increases in value at the risk-free rate, then it is in or out of the money at expiration.

The key to option pricing is understanding the $N(d_1)$ and $N(d_2)$ terms—the cumulative standard normal density functions for the values $d_1$ and $d_2$—because we need to know the cumulative probability that the asset price will exceed the strike price at expiration. To estimate this probability, Black and Scholes assumed that the underlying asset followed a lognormal distribution.[10] This means that the natural logarithm (Ln) of the asset price $S$ is normally distributed, which explains why the term $Ln(S/X)$ is in the equation. To simplify, assume that the call is issued at the strike price, so this is the natural logarithm of 1.0, which is zero. We can also simplify by assuming that this is a single-period call option and the risk-free rate is zero, so $r = 0$ and $t = 1$. This leaves a formula for $d_1 = \sigma/2$. Because we are looking for the value of

---

[8]See Hull, John, *Options, Futures and Other Derivatives*, 10th ed. (New York: Pearson Education, 2018).

[9]You can readily obtain the Black-Scholes formula to value a European put by starting with the Black-Scholes call formula and using the continuous time version of put-call parity. You should end up with $P = Xe^{-rt}N(-d_2) - SN(-d_1)$.

[10]The lognormal distribution has the desirable feature that it is bounded from below by zero; i.e., it cannot take on negative values, just like a share of common stock.

$N(\sigma/2)$, we need the cumulative probability of being half a standard deviation above the mean of the normal distribution. We can look at a table for the standard normal distribution or use Excel and find this value as 0.69. Similarly, $d_2 = -\sigma/2$, which is the cumulative probability of being half a standard deviation below the mean of the distribution, which is 0.31.

To understand $d_1$, think of it as the number of standard deviations that the call is expected to be in the money, so we will call this the expected "moneyness" of the call. The value for $N(d_1)$ is then the cumulative probability of being in the money. The larger the risk of the underlying asset, the larger $N(d_1)$ and the moneyness of the call will be. This reiterates that the more volatile the underlying asset, the more valuable the call. All we are doing is shifting this estimate of the call's expected moneyness. For example, if the asset price is currently above the strike price, $Ln(S/X)$ is no longer zero; instead, it is positive, and moneyness increases. Similarly, a higher risk-free rate simply increases the expected moneyness of the call. Finally, the time to expiration of the call increases both the risk-free rate and the standard deviation, so it compounds both, thereby increasing the call's moneyness. We illustrate all this in Example 12.14.

---

**EXAMPLE 12.14** | Using Black-Scholes I

Assume that an asset is selling for $50 and an investor wants to price a call with an exercise price of $55. The expiration date is 182 days or 182/365 of a year, the risk-free rate is 6 percent, and the standard deviation of the return on the underlying asset is 30 percent. What's the value of the call?

**Solution**   First, we calculate the present value of the strike price:

$$PV(X) = Xe^{-rt} \text{ or } \frac{X}{(1+r)^t}$$

We can use either continuous compounding or approximate with discrete compounding. Let's approximate and discount back at 3 percent to get $53.425. With continuous compounding, we would get $53.379.

Next, we calculate $d_1$ as

$$d_1 = \frac{Ln(\$50/\$55) + (0.06 + 0.30^2/2) \times 182/365}{0.30 \times \sqrt{182/365}} = -0.2028$$

and $d_2 = -0.4146$. Inserting these results into the cumulative normal density function, we get $N(d_1) = 0.4197$ and $N(d_2) = 0.3392$. The call is worth $2.876.

---

$N(d_1)$ and $N(d_2)$ can be calculated from standard statistical tables. **Table 12.4** includes a portion of such a table.

We can also determine $N(d_1)$ by using a spreadsheet, such as Excel. In Excel, the "NORM.S.DIST" function calculates the probability for the cumulative (between $-\infty$ and $d_1$) standard normal distribution function (i.e., mean = 0, standard deviation = 1). Entering the following:

$$N(d_1) = NORM.S.DIST \ (z = d_1, TRUE)$$

returns the value for $N(d_1)$.[11] The values to enter are, $z$, which is the spreadsheet cell entry for the value $d_1$ and the value, "true," which indicates the cumulative normal distribution; "false" would indicate the individual point estimate of the probability. Calculating the Black-Scholes value for a call option is then straightforward in Excel, since the only part of Equation 12.10 that is difficult is the $N(d)$ function.

---

[11]NORM.S.DIST (z, TRUE) works for Excel versions after 2007. For Excel versions 2007 and earlier, NORMSDIST (z) gives the cumulative standard normal probability.

**TABLE 12.4** The Cumulative Probabilities for a Standard Normal Distribution

| d | N(d) | d | N(d) | d | N(d) | d | N(d) | d | N(d) |
|---|------|---|------|---|------|---|------|---|------|
| −0.50 | .3085 | −0.48 | .3156 | −0.46 | .3228 | −0.44 | .3300 | −0.42 | .3373 |
| −0.40 | .3446 | −0.38 | .3520 | −0.36 | .3594 | −0.34 | .3669 | −0.32 | .3745 |
| −0.30 | .3821 | −0.28 | .3897 | −0.26 | .3974 | −0.24 | .4052 | −0.22 | .4129 |
| −0.20 | .4207 | −0.18 | .4286 | −0.16 | .4365 | −0.14 | .4443 | −0.12 | .4523 |
| −0.10 | .4602 | −0.08 | .4681 | −0.06 | .4761 | −0.04 | .4841 | −0.02 | .4920 |
| 0.00 | .5000 | 0.02 | .5080 | 0.04 | .5160 | 0.06 | .5239 | 0.08 | .5319 |
| 0.10 | .5398 | 0.12 | .5478 | 0.14 | .5557 | 0.16 | .5636 | 0.18 | .5714 |
| 0.20 | .5793 | 0.22 | .5871 | 0.24 | .5948 | 0.26 | .6026 | 0.28 | .6103 |
| 0.30 | .6179 | 0.32 | .6255 | 0.34 | .6331 | 0.36 | .6406 | 0.38 | .6480 |
| 0.40 | .6556 | 0.42 | .6628 | 0.44 | .6700 | 0.46 | .6773 | 0.48 | .6844 |
| ... | ... | ... | ... | ... | ... | ... | ... | ... | ... |
| 2.00 | .9772 | 2.10 | .9821 | 2.20 | .9861 | 2.30 | .9893 | 2.40 | .9918 |
| 2.50 | .9938 | 2.60 | .9953 | 2.70 | .9965 | 2.80 | .9974 | 2.90 | .9981 |
| 3.00 | .9986 | – | – | – | – | – | – | – | – |

Rather than using a spreadsheet, we can use one of several calculators that are available on the Internet. The Montreal Exchange (MX) has an online option pricing calculator at www.m-x.ca/marc_options_calc_en.php. By using the MX option pricing model and entering the values for our example, the model produces the output shown in **figures 12.10A** and **B.**

**FIGURE 12.10A** **Pricing a Call Option**

Source: Options Calculator, Montreal Exchange, June 2019, available at m-x.ca. 2019 Montreal Exchange Inc.

**FIGURE 12.10B**  **Pricing a Put Option**

```
┌─ Option Calculator ──────────────────────────────────────────────┐
│ Inputs                                                            │
│         American*◉  European* ○      Underlying Price ($)* [50.00]│
│   Type of Underlying* [Stock/ETF ▽]     Volatility (%)*   [30.00] │
│          Option Type* [Put ▽]         Interest Rate (%)   [6.00]  │
│     Expiration Date* [09/12/2019]    Dividend Amount ($)  [0.00]  │
│    Days to Expiration* [182]         Dividend Frequency [Annual ▽]│
│       Strike Price ($)* [55.00]      Expected Dividend Date [N/A] │
│                                                                   │
│             No of steps (max 100) [100]                           │
│                                                                   │
│ * Modifying any of these fields will unlink the selected option   │
│                                               APPLY CHANGES       │
│ ┌──────────┬─────────┬────────┬────────┬─────────┬─────────┐     │
│ │ $6.58    │ −0.6272 │ 0.0433 │ 0.1316 │ −0.0071 │ −0.1085 │     │
│ │THEOR PRICE│ DELTA  │ GAMMA  │ VEGA   │ THETA   │ RHO     │     │
│ └──────────┴─────────┴────────┴────────┴─────────┴─────────┘     │
│ Implied Volatility                                                │
│   Option Price ($) [Enter Value]   Implied Volatility (%) [Enter Value]│
└───────────────────────────────────────────────────────────────────┘
```

**Source:** Options Calculator, Montreal Exchange, June 2019, available at m-x.ca. 2019 Montreal Exchange Inc.

MX's value for the option is also $2.88. The calculator gives the price of a $55 put on the same asset as $6.58.[12] It also provides some other values, which we will discuss in the next section.

**EXAMPLE 12.15** | Using Black-Scholes II

Find the value of a three-month call option with a $20 strike price if the price of the non-dividend-paying underlying asset is $20.50 and its standard deviation is 25 percent. Assume the risk-free rate is 5 percent.

**Solution**

$$S = \$20.50; X = \$20; r = 5\%; t = 3/12 = 0.25; \sigma = 25\%$$

$$d_1 = \frac{Ln(S/X) + (r + \sigma^2/2)t}{\sigma\sqrt{t}} = \frac{Ln(\$20.50/\$20) + (0.05 + (0.25)^2/2)(0.25)}{(0.25)\sqrt{0.25}}$$

$$= \frac{0.02469 + 0.0203}{0.125} = \frac{0.0450}{0.125} = 0.3600$$

$$d_2 = d_1 - \sigma\sqrt{t} = 0.3600 - 0.25\sqrt{0.25} = 0.2350$$

Using the MX's online option pricing calculator or Excel, we can find

$$N(d_1) = 0.6406 \text{ and } N(d_2) = 0.5929$$

$$So, C = SN(d_1) - Xe^{-rt}N(d_2) = (\$20.50)(0.6406) - (\$20)e^{-(0.05)(0.25)}(0.5929)$$
$$= \$13.13 - \$11.71 = \$1.42$$

[12]The numbers provided in the output are for American options, based on more complicated variations of Black-Scholes equations, which technically apply only to European options. In any event, because the underlying asset in this example does not pay any dividends, the value of a European call option will equal that of an American call option. Conversely, the corresponding European put option would be worth $6.25, approximately $0.33 less than the American put. The maximum number of steps (100) were specified in the binomial calculation. The options calculator is programmed to value American options by stepping back through the binomial tree and verifying at each node in the tree whether or not early exercise is optimal. If it is, then the theoretical option value calculated at the node is replaced by the intrinsic value and the step-by-step calculations continue until the current value of the option is obtained.

## The "Greeks"

The other values provided by the MX in figures 12.10A and B—delta, gamma, theta, rho, and vega—indicate the sensitivity of the option price to changes in the underlying parameters. The first four are Greek letters and are commonly referred to as **the Greeks** in option pricing (though vega is not a Greek letter).

**the Greeks** the values—delta ($\Delta$), gamma ($\Gamma$), theta ($\theta$), rho ($\rho$), and vega—that indicate the sensitivity of the option price to changes in the underlying parameters

**delta** the change in the price of the option for a given change in the price of the underlying asset

**theta** the change in the option value with time

**gamma** the change in delta with respect to a change in the underlying asset

**rho** the change in the option value with respect to a change in the interest rate

**vega** the change in the option value with respect to a change in the volatility of the underlying asset

- As the stock price increases, so does the call value. The change in the price of the option for a given change in the price of the underlying asset is referred to as **delta**. In our example, if the stock price increases to $50.10, when we use the MX website to recalculate the value of the call, it shows an increase to $2.92 (from $2.88), for a change of $0.042. This change is consistent with the 0.4192 delta provided by the MX, which means the call will increase in value by about $0.42 for every $1 increase in the price of the underlying asset.

- **Theta** is the change in the option value with time. If we move forward one day so that the call has 181 days to expiration, its value drops to $2.87, a loss of about $0.014 per day. The theta reported by the MX is approximately this number ($-0.0144$).

- **Gamma** is the change in delta with respect to a change in the underlying asset.[13] This is important for hedging, but we don't include a full discussion of gamma here as it is beyond the scope of this text.

- **Rho** is the change in the option value with respect to a change in the interest rate. For example, if the interest rate in our example increases from 6 percent to 7 percent, the option value increases to $2.97, a rise of $0.09, so a 1-percent change in the interest rate causes a $0.09 change in the option value, consistent with the rho reported by the MX (0.0902).

- **Vega** is the change in the option value with respect to a change in the volatility of the underlying asset. If the standard deviation in our example increases by 1 percent to 31 percent, the option value increases to $3.02. Thus, a 1-percent increase in volatility increases the option value by about $0.14, consistent with the vega reported by the MX ($0.1412).

Running the numbers through our Black-Scholes calculator indicates that the call option price behaves the way that it should: it goes up with increases in volatility, the risk-free rate, and the price of the underlying asset, and it falls as time passes.

Finally, what about the extremes? If the current asset price is deep out of the money at $30, to two decimal places, the value of the call is $0.01; at $25, it is $0.00. This shows why deep out of the money calls are essentially worthless. Similarly, if the asset price is $100, so that it is deep in the money, the call option is worth $46.63, where $45 is the intrinsic value. So the value of a call mainly reflects its intrinsic value.

---

### Concept Review Questions

1. How can the Black-Scholes equation be used to price options?
2. What is measured by each of the five Greeks discussed in this section?

---

## 12.5 Options Markets

**LEARNING OBJECTIVE 12.5**

Explain how options are traded and what is meant by implied volatility.

Like swaps, options are either traded over the counter, mainly with the major banks, or on organized exchanges. In Canada, options trading is focused on the MX, which has a standard

---

[13]In the language of calculus, gamma is the second derivative of the call or put value with respect to the underlying asset; i.e., $\partial^2 C/\partial S^2$ or $\partial^2 P/\partial S^2$. It turns out that the gamma of a call is equal to the gamma of a put.

**TABLE 12.5    Aurora Cannabis Inc. Options Quotes, June 11, 2019**

| Date | Strike | Bid | Ask | Last | Volume |
|---|---|---|---|---|---|
| July 2019 | 11c | 0.30 | 0.40 | 0.30 | 13 |
|  | 11p | 1.10 | 1.20 | 1.20 | 0 |
| January 2021 | 11c | 2.50 | 2.70 | 2.55 | 11 |
|  | 11p | 2.65 | 3.00 | 2.90 | 0 |

**Source:** Data from The Montreal Exchange <https://www.m-x.ca/accueil_en.php>

practice of listing options on all the constituents of the S&P/TSX 60 Index, as well as on the S&P/TSX MidCap Index. Each option class has to have the interest of two market makers who stand ready to buy and sell the options to create an orderly market. These options follow a short expiration cycle based on the next two months, and there is a minimum daily volume of 40 contracts. If the volume exceeds 80, then longer-dated options are introduced based on months in the next quarterly cycle, and if there is enough interest, long-dated options are introduced with a January expiration date.

For greater clarity, let's consider two relatively well-known MX options on Aurora Cannabis Inc. (ACB) and Bell Canada Enterprises Inc. (BCE). By 1 pm, Montreal time, June 11, 2019, ACB had trading volume of 296 contracts and BCE had trading volume of 339 contracts. Each contract was for 100 shares, meaning that ACB traded contracts representing 29,600 shares of stock while BCE option trading volume represented 33,900 shares of stock. The total number of contracts outstanding at the time was 98,687 for ACB calls and 70,354 for ACB puts. Similarly, open interest in BCE calls and puts was 83,015 and 65,995, respectively.

The ACB stock price in the afternoon of June 11, 2019, was $10.34, and **Table 12.5** shows four options out of the dozens that were listed: two calls (c) and two puts (p), with two different expiration dates—short-dated options expiring in July 2019 and longer-dated options expiring in January 2021. Both of these had an $11 strike price. At the time, the July call was out of the money by $0.66 and the time value was $0.30 if investors were to sell it back to the market maker at the price the market maker was willing to buy it for (i.e., the bid price). The time value was $0.40 if investors bought it from the market maker at the price the market maker was willing to sell it for (i.e., the ask price).

For the January 2021 call option, the ask price increased from $0.40 to $2.70, even though the exercise price was the same, $11; the additional $2.30 represents more time value, since the option had 19 more months to run from the initial date. Also, note that the MX provides the last trade price, which for the January 2021 $11 call was $2.55. However, since trades for many of these options are so infrequent, this price could have been established days earlier and is not as useful a reference point as the last price is for common shares.

In contrast to the call option, the July 2019 $11 put option was in the money by $0.66, since the exercise price of $11 was above the current market price. Further, it was close to expiration, and the bid price quoted by the market maker for this option was $1.10, while the market maker was willing to sell the put for $1.20. The time values in this case were $0.44 and $0.54, respectively. The January 2021 put options had even more time value at $1.99 for the bid (quoted at $2.65) and $2.34 for the ask (quoted at $3.00). There were no put options traded with an expiration of January 2021 on June 11, 2019.

For option prices, most of the data are objective and verifiable, such as the strike price, the current price of the underlying asset, the risk-free rate, and the expiration date. The only "soft" number is the volatility of the underlying asset's price. However, once we know the price of the option, we can work back and find the volatility that matches this price. For ACB's $11 July 2019 call option, we can use the average of the bid-ask price and ACB's current dividend per share (0.00) with the Black-Scholes option pricing model to estimate this volatility by trial and error or by simply checking for the value on the MX website. It turns out to be quite high, at 44.6 percent. This number is the **implied volatility** of the option. In actual practice, the MX calculates this number for options when there are enough trades, and it also reports the 30-day historic volatility, which in the case of ACB was very high at 48.4 percent.

**implied volatility**  an estimate of the price volatility of the underlying asset based on observed option prices

**FIGURE 12.11** Implied Volatilities for the S&P/TSX 60 Index

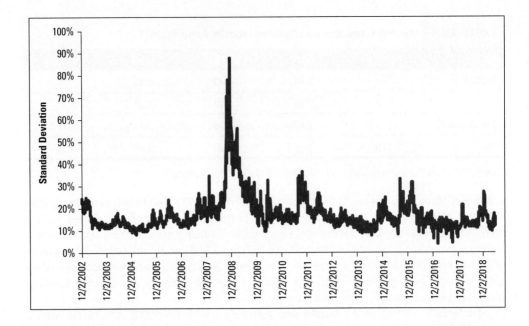

Implied volatilities provide useful information. Remember from our discussion of the capital asset pricing model in Chapter 9 that the volatility of the market portfolio is a key number in deriving expected rates of return. The MX trades options on the S&P/TSX 60 Index, which reflects the biggest and most valuable companies in Canada. Every minute of every trading day, the MX calculates the implied volatility of the S&P/TSX 60 Index from a cross section of option prices. These are then used to estimate the 30-day implied volatility for the Canadian market. Calculations used to create the MX volatility index (VIXC) are analogous to those used to create the Chicago Board of Exchange (CBOE) Volatility Index (VIX) for the U.S. market.

The graph in **Figure 12.11** shows the implied volatilities for the MX index from December 2, 2002, until May 2019.[14] Note that volatility changes over time. In early 2003, it was just less than 25 percent before falling to around 15 percent, where it remained until late 2005, after which it began increasing and reached the 25-percent level again. By June 2006, the options markets were indicating increased volatility, but this was just the beginning as the implied volatility increased until it peaked at 88 percent on November 11, 2008, during the worst of the financial crisis. Since then the VIXC has gradually receded to more normal levels.

Remember that the volatility of the S&P/TSX 60 is the volatility of a market portfolio of securities. This is always much lower than the volatility of an individual security due to the fact that the returns on individual companies are not perfectly correlated. This puts the volatility of ACB in perspective. We can see that the volatility of an individual stock will often be substantially higher than that of an index such as the S&P/TSX 60.

## Lessons to Be Learned

The key insight from option pricing theory is that "flexibility" is valuable. Remember, a call option is the right to be able to do something but is not an obligation, which means there is flexibility. Think about all the call options you experience in everyday life. For example, consider course grading, where some instructors give students the option of having their mid-term exam count as their final grade if it is higher than their final exam grade. Is this a valuable option, and if so, is it more valuable in the winter, where the chance of being "under the weather" is higher than in the summer? This is an example of a real option rather than a financial option. We will discuss real options at various points in the text, but the absence of options or flexibility can dramatically increase risk and be very dangerous.

---

[14]Data prior to October 2009 are from an earlier, slightly different, MX volatility index.

## Concept Review Questions

1. Where are options traded?

2. How are implied volatilities calculated? What information do they provide?

3. What real options have you been given over the past year, and how valuable were they? What factors do you think influenced your valuation of them?

---

**APPENDIX 12A** # Binomial Option Pricing and Risk-Neutral Probabilities

### LEARNING OBJECTIVE 12.6
Explain, using the simplest option pricing model, what factors affect the value of a call option.

## Binomial Option Pricing

In the chapter, we discussed the Black-Scholes option pricing model, but here we consider a simpler model. Previously, we used an example of an asset selling for $50 with an equal proba-bility of the price going up or down by $5. Now let's give the price a 60-percent chance of going up to $55, and a 40-percent chance of going down to $45. We do this to set the expected value on the asset at $51 (i.e., [0.6 × $55] + [0.4 × $45]), for a 2-percent expected rate of return. For simplicity, let's assume that this refers to a one-month period and that the monthly risk-free rate is 1 percent. This is an example of what is termed the **binomial model** (i.e., two num-bers), because the asset price can only go up or down.

> **binomial model**   an option pricing model that uses two numbers, assuming the asset price can only go up or down

Now let's consider a one-period call option on this asset with a strike price of $50. In this case, when the asset price is $55, the investor exercises the option and realizes a $5 payoff, but when the asset price is $45, the option expires worthless. The payoffs on the asset and the call are provided in **Figure 12A.1**.

In the figure, $S_0$ and $S_1$ represent the asset prices at times 0 and 1, respectively; $C$ is the payoff on the call, and $P$ is the probability of a given price occurring. To understand how to price the call, we take advantage of the fact that it is a derivative and its payoff depends on the underlying asset value. This is the motivation for the central insight of Black and Scholes, which is that although we may not know how to value the call directly, we do know how to

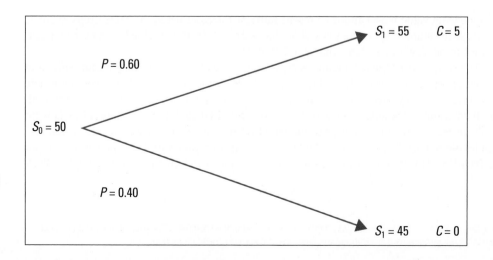

**FIGURE 12A.1**   **Binomial Prices**

value a risk-free asset. Thus, we can derive the value of the call indirectly if we create a portfolio of the asset and the call, which generates the same payoff regardless of the price of the underlying asset. If the payoff of the portfolio is the same, regardless of whether the price of the asset goes up or down, then by definition it is risk-free, and we can value it by discounting at the risk-free rate.

When the price of the asset goes down to $45, the value of the call is zero. So if an investor builds a portfolio of the asset and the call, it doesn't matter how many calls they have, the value of the portfolio is still $45. To create a risk-free payoff, we have to think about a portfolio of the asset and the call that generates a payoff of $45 when the price of the asset is $55. For example, suppose the investor has a portfolio of the asset and sells one call—that is, the investor is long the asset and short the call. When the asset is worth $55, the call is exercised against the investor and they get $50 for the asset, which is the payoff from the portfolio. Clearly, this is too high. Suppose the investor sells two calls against the asset. Now when the asset price goes to $55, two calls are exercised against the investor, but they have one underlying asset to deliver against two calls, so they have to go and buy another one. The payoff to the portfolio is $45, the same as if the asset value dropped to $45.

What we have discovered is that a portfolio that is long the asset and short two calls gives a payoff of $45 regardless of the price of the underlying asset. This means we have the following:

$$S - 2C = \frac{\$45}{1 + r} = \$44.55$$

A portfolio long the asset and short two calls has a payoff of $45, which, given the 1-percent risk-free rate, is worth $44.55 today. However, we know that the asset is worth $50 today, so rearranging we get

$$C = \tfrac{1}{2}(\$50 - \$44.55) = \$2.725$$

The call is worth $2.725.

To provide the solution for the general case, we denote the increased price for the asset as *PU* (price up) and the decreased price as *PD*. The number of calls that an investor needs to sell to establish the same payoff whether the asset price goes up or down is called the **hedge ratio (h)**, which we can estimate as $PU - h(PU - X) = PD$.

This can be solved to give the following:

**hedge ratio (h)** the number of calls the investor needs to sell to hedge a long position in the underlying asset

$$h = \frac{PU - PD}{PU - X} \qquad\qquad \text{[12A.1]}$$

In our example, the price can go to either $45 or $55, which means the hedge ratio is $(55 - 45)/(55 - 50)$, or 2, so two calls have to be sold for every long position in the asset. The value of the call is then estimated by solving the following equation:

$$C = \frac{1}{h}\left(S - \frac{PD}{(1 + r)}\right) \qquad\qquad \text{[12A.2]}$$

The asset value is $50 and the present value of the asset when the price drops to $45 is $44.55, so the amount in brackets is $5.45—that is, $50 - 45/1.01$. With the hedge ratio of 2, that means the call is worth $2.725—that is, $1/2 \times \$5.45$.

The simplicity of the calculation is deceiving: some of the best minds in economics and finance spent decades trying to find the correct formula for valuing a call and could not. The reason was that they tried to value it *directly* by estimating the expected cash flow on the call and then using a risk-adjusted discount rate to value that cash flow. Although this is what we do in most areas of finance, no one could derive the correct discount rate. Black and Scholes did not use this approach,[15] and they came up with the central idea of valuing the call *indirectly* by valuing something we knew how to value: a risk-free payoff. Essentially, Black

---

[15]See Cox, J., Ross, S., and Rubinstein, M., "Option Pricing: A Simplified Approach." *Journal of Financial Economics* 7, no. 3 (1979), pp. 229–63. The arbitrage argument has also been credited to Robert Merton.

and Scholes took advantage of the central insight of option pricing, which is that the option is a derivative.

The use of a hedge to generate a risk-free payoff is the central idea of option pricing. With our example, a financial institution selling two calls has to go long the underlying asset to remove or hedge its risk. This is the central reason that the use of derivatives has exploded: rather than selling calls and creating risk for themselves, financial institutions now know how to hedge that exposure. They simply need to calculate the hedge ratio required to create a risk-free payoff. In our example, this hedge ratio is two: two calls have to be sold to hedge a long position in the asset.

Note also the factors that determine the value of the call in the general formula. The critical three factors are the hedge ratio, the asset value, and the present value of the down payoff on the asset. We will consider the second two first, as the hedge ratio is more complex. So, with our numbers, we have

$$C = \frac{1}{h}\left(\$50 - \frac{\$45}{1.01}\right)$$

We make the following observations:

- First, the call is clearly worth more as the asset price goes up. If the current price is $50.25, the call price increases to $2.85.

- Second, the call is worth more as the risk-free rate goes up. Because the present value gets smaller when the price of the asset goes down, less is subtracted from the current asset value. With a 1.5-percent risk-free rate, the call is worth $2.83.

- Third, the call price goes up as the risk of the asset increases. As the range of possible outcomes increases, the asset value falls when the price goes down, making the call worth more. If the range increases to $20, lowering the payoff when the asset goes down to $40, the value of the call increases to $5.20.

- Fourth, as the strike price increases, the denominator in the hedge ratio (Equation 12A.1) gets smaller, so the investor has to sell more calls, which reduces the value of the call. At a strike price of $54, the hedge ratio increases to 10 and the call price drops to $0.545.

- Fifth, the call price increases if the up price increases, and the call price decreases if the up price decreases. For example, at $54 the hedge ratio increases to 2.25 and the call price drops to $2.42. We can think of a decrease in the up price as the impact of a dividend payment. Consider two firms. One pays a dividend and the other does not. In good economic conditions, the dividend-paying firm increases its dividend by $1, so its stock price drops to only $54, whereas the stock price of the non-dividend-paying firm goes to $55.[16]

These five observations are consistent with the intuitive results that we discussed in the chapter. The time to expiration can't be applied to this example, however, because this is a single-period binomial model. We also have not discussed the expected return on the asset as a factor in the option price. Nor have we discussed any of the factors that directly affect the market price of risk discussed in the CAPM earlier. In fact, the problem that bedevilled the pricing of options for many decades—determining the correct discount rate to value the option's payoff—is absent completely. In this case, we have an amazing result: we can behave as if the investor is risk neutral and value the option accordingly.

## Risk-Neutral Probabilities

Let's go back to our simple example in which the payoff is either $55, with a probability of 60 percent, or $45, with a probability of 40 percent, so the expected rate of return is 2 percent—that is, $0.60 \times (55 - 50) + 0.40 \times (45 - 50) = 0.60 \times 10\% + 0.40 \times (-10\%)$. This 2-percent expected rate of return exceeds the risk-free rate of 1 percent because investors are risk averse. However, because the option price does not depend on risk aversion, we will keep things

---

[16]We discuss dividend policy in Chapter 22, but the main point to recognize here is that stock prices tend to fall after payment of a dividend.

**risk neutral** the state of ignoring the risk involved in determining expected rates of return

simple and assume the investor is **risk neutral**. In this case, we can calculate the probabilities that will earn a risk-neutral investor the same 1-percent rate of return as the risk-free rate does. We can do this because this is what risk neutrality means: investors ignore the risk involved in determining expected rates of return.

We can calculate the probabilities that will generate a 1-percent return on the asset given the two possible payoffs of $55 and $45. Because a 1-percent return means that the price of the asset has to be $50.50 in the next period, we use the formula of an expected value to get

$$\$50(1.01) = \$55P + \$45(1 - P)$$

$$P = \frac{\$50.50 - \$45}{\$10} = 0.55$$

If instead of a 60-percent chance of going up to $55, there is only a 55-percent chance, then the expected rate of return is 1 percent, the same as the risk-free rate. We can value the option directly as the payoff is still $5 when the asset price is $55. The only difference is that now we use the probability of 55 percent, so the expected payoff is $2.75, while there is a 45-percent chance of getting zero. If this expected cash flow of $2.75 is discounted back one period at the risk-free rate, the result is the option price of $2.72.

As we indicated before, this is an amazing result, but to get it we have derived new probabilities that ensure the asset price goes up with the risk-free rate, instead of dealing with the actual probabilities of the asset going up and down. These probabilities are called the **risk-neutral probabilities**. They are the probabilities that would exist if the investor were risk neutral; of course, they are not the true probabilities, because investors are not risk neutral. However, because the call option can be valued as if the investor were risk neutral, we can use these risk-neutral probabilities to determine the expected payoff on the call and value it directly. This insight has generated a huge industry in option pricing, where complicated securities are valued in a risk-neutral world, as if the underlying asset always earned the risk-free rate. It has proven to be an incredibly useful construct in solving complex problems and comes directly from the Black-Scholes and binomial option pricing models.

**risk-neutral probabilities** derived probabilities that ensure the asset price goes up with the risk-free rate; the probabilities that would exist if the investor were risk neutral

---

## Concept Review Questions

1. Explain how to create a risk-free portfolio from the stock and the option's payoff.
2. What is a hedge ratio?
3. Why don't the probabilities of going up and down affect the option's value?
4. What are risk-neutral probabilities?

---

# Review

## Summary

This chapter discusses the Nobel Prize–winning ideas of Fischer Black, Myron Scholes, and Robert Merton. Continuing our discussion from Chapter 11, in which we looked at derivatives with linear payoffs, in this chapter we look at non-linear payoffs, where either the gains or the losses are truncated or changed at some points. We discuss the payoffs from call and put options and look at how the value of these options are determined by the underlying asset's price and volatility, the strike price and time to expiration

of the option, and the conditions in the economy in terms of the risk-free rate. We go on to discuss put-call parity and how options can be used for hedging. We also show how options can be valued using the Black-Scholes option pricing model and then discuss how options are traded. Finally, we discuss the very important topic of real options and why the central ideas of option pricing have dramatically changed the way we look at a variety of finance and management topics.

## Summary of Learning Objectives

### 12.1   Describe the basic nature of call options and the factors that influence their value.

A call option is the right, but not the obligation, to buy an underlying asset at a fixed price for a specified time. The value of a call option

- increases with the price of the underlying asset
- decreases with a higher strike price
- increases if the underlying asset is riskier
- increases as the time to expiration increases
- decreases as the dividend payments of the underlying asset increase
- increases as interest rates increase
- approaches its intrinsic value for deep in and deep out of the money calls

### 12.2   Describe the basic nature of put options and the payoffs associated with long and short positions in put options.

A put option is the opposite of a call option: it gives the owner the right, but not the obligation, to *sell* an underlying asset at a fixed price for a specified time. The value of a put option

- decreases with the price of the underlying asset
- increases with a higher strike price
- increases if the underlying asset is riskier
- increases as the time to expiration increases
- increases as the dividend payments of the underlying asset increase
- decreases as interest rates increase

### 12.3   Explain how to use put-call parity to estimate call and put prices, and explain how it can be used to synthetically create call, put, and underlying positions.

Put-call parity is the relationship between the price of a call option and the price of a put option that have the same strike price and expiry date; it assumes that the options are not exercised before their expiration. See $P + S = C + PV(X)$.

- You can create a synthetic call option by longing a put and the underlying stock and shorting cash. See $C = P + S - PV(X)$.
- You can create a synthetic put option by longing a call and cash and shorting the underlying stock. See $P = C - S + PV(X)$.
- You can create the underlying positions by longing a call and cash and shorting a put. See $S = C - P + PV(X)$.

### 12.4   Explain how to use the Black-Scholes option pricing model to price call options.

The Black-Scholes option pricing model provides a formula to calculate the premium for European call options. (Put prices can be solved using the put-call parity condition.) The Black-Scholes model shows that the option premium is a function of the underlying asset's price, the option strike price, the volatility of the underlying asset's price, the risk-free interest rate, and the time remaining to maturity. The Black-Scholes option pricing model can be used to calculate the "Greeks": delta, gamma, theta, rho, and vega. The "Greeks" measure the sensitivity of the option premium to changes in the model parameters, except for gamma, which measures the sensitivity of delta to changes in the underlying asset's price.

### 12.5   Explain how options are traded and what is meant by implied volatility.

Options are traded over the counter and on exchanges. In Canada, options are traded on the Montreal Exchange (in the United States, options are traded on the CBOT [Chicago Board of Trade], the Chicago Mercantile Exchange, and the Philadelphia Exchange, to name three). Implied volatility is solved from the Black-Scholes option pricing model using the market price of the option and solving for the level of volatility, which yields the market price.

### 12.6   Explain, using the simplest option pricing model, what factors affect the value of a call option.

The binomial option pricing model shows how the intuitive factors discussed in sections 12.1 and 12.2 actually affect option prices.

## Key Terms

## Equations

| Equation | Description | Formula | Page |
|----------|-------------|---------|------|
| **[12.1]** | Intrinsic Value (IV) of a Call | $IV\ (Call) = Max\ (S - X, 0)$ | p. 12-4 |
| **[12.2]** | Option Premium | $Option\ premium = IV + TV$ | p. 12-4 |
| **[12.3]** | Time Value (TV) | $TV = Option\ premium - IV$ | p. 12-5 |
| **[12.4]** | Intrinsic Value (IV) of a Put | $IV\ (Put) = Max\ (X - S, 0)$ | p. 12-11 |
| **[12.5]** | Put-Call Parity | $P + S = C + PV(X)$ | p. 12-14 |
| **[12.6]** | Put-Call Relationship | $C - P = S - PV(X)$ | p. 12-15 |
| **[12.7]** | Call Option Price | $C = P + S - PV(X)$ | p. 12-15 |
| **[12.8]** | Put Option Price | $P = C - S + PV(X)$ | p. 12-15 |
| **[12.9]** | Underlying Asset Price | $S = C - P + PV(X)$ | p. 12-16 |
| **[12.10]** | Black-Scholes Option Pricing Model | $C = SN(d_1) - Xe^{-rt}N(d_2)$ | p. 12-20 |
| **[12A.1]** | Hedge Ratio | $h = \dfrac{PU - PD}{PU - X}$ | p. 12-28 |
| **[12A.2]** | Binomial Call Price | $C = \dfrac{1}{h}\left(S - \dfrac{PD}{(1 + r)}\right)$ | p. 12-28 |

# Questions and Practice Problems

## Multiple Choice Questions

**1. (LO 12.1)** Which of the following statements about a call option is *false*?

  **a.** A call option is the right, not the obligation, to buy the underlying asset.

  **b.** A call option is in the money if the asset price is less than the strike price.

  **c.** A call option is at the money if the asset price is the same as the strike price.

  **d.** On the expiration date, a call option has no time value.

**2. (LO 12.1)** Before the expiration of a call option, if its intrinsic value is $13 and the market value of the option is $19, what is the time value of the option? What do we call the market value of the option?

  **a.** $32; option premium

  **b.** $6; option premium

  **c.** $32; option price

  **d.** $6; option price

**3. (LO 12.1)** Which of the following *increases* the value of a call option?

  **a.** The price of the underlying asset decreases.

  **b.** The volatility of the price of the underlying asset decreases.

  **c.** The remaining time to expiration of the call option increases.

  **d.** The underlying stock increases its dividend payment.

**4. (LO 12.2)** Which of the following *decreases* the value of a put option?

  **a.** The price of the underlying asset decreases.

  **b.** The underlying asset becomes riskier.

  **c.** The interest rate decreases.

  **d.** The strike price decreases.

**5. (LO 12.3)** Which of the following may create a synthetic loan?

  **a.** Long a put, short the stock, and long a call.

  **b.** Long a put, long the stock, and long a call.

  **c.** Short a put, long the stock, and long a call.

  **d.** Long a put, long the stock, and short a call.

**6. (LO 12.1, 12.2)** What is the intrinsic value (IV) of a put if the underlying asset price (*S*) is $40 and the strike price (*X*) is $45? What is the IV if it is a call?

  **a.** $0, $5

  **b.** $5, $0

  **c.** $5, $5

  **d.** $0, $0

**7. (LO 12.1, 12.2)** Which of the following positions is the most risky?

  **a.** Long a call

  **b.** Short a call

  **c.** Long a put

  **d.** Short a put

8. **(LO 12.4)** Which of the following statements about the Black-Scholes model is *false*?

  **a.** It uses a continuously compounded risk-free rate.

  **b.** $d_1$ can be thought of as the expected moneyness of the call.

  **c.** $N(d_1)$ is the cumulative probability of being out of the money.

  **d.** The model assumes that the underlying asset price follows a lognormal distribution.

9. **(LO 12.1, 12.5)** Which of the following statements is *correct*, given the following information?

| January 2022 | Strike | Bid | Ask | Last |
|---|---|---|---|---|
| Call A | 25 | 1.85 | 2.05 | 1.85 |
| Put B | 36 | 1.10 | 1.35 | 1.15 |
| Call C | 30.75 | 1.50 | 1.75 | 1.60 |

  **a.** The market maker's profit of call A is 0.25.

  **b.** If the market price of the underlying asset is 35, then the time value of put B is 0.1.

  **c.** The time value for a put is usually higher than that for a call.

  **d.** By using the market price of an option, we can calculate the implied volatility of the option.

10. **(LO 12.6)** What is the hedge ratio ($h$) for a call if PU is $52, PD is $45, and the strike price ($S$) is $48?

  **a.** 1.33

  **b.** 2.05

  **c.** 1.75

  **d.** 2.33

11. **(LO 12.6)** Which of the following is the correct meaning of a hedge ratio of 1/3?

  **a.** Short one call to hedge a long position of three units of the underlying asset.

  **b.** Short three calls to hedge a long position of the underlying asset.

  **c.** Long one call to hedge a long position of three units of the underlying asset.

  **d.** Long three calls to hedge a long position of the underlying asset.

12. **(LO 12.6)** Which of the following statements about risk-neutral probabilities is *false*?

  **a.** Risk-neutral probabilities are probabilities that exist if investors are risk neutral.

  **b.** Risk-neutral probabilities are the actual probabilities of the asset price going up and down.

  **c.** Risk-neutral probabilities are the probabilities that ensure the asset price goes up with the risk-free rate.

  **d.** Risk-neutral probabilities assume the underlying asset earns the risk-free rate.

## Practice Problems

### Basic

13. **(LO 12.4)** Briefly explain "the Greeks" (delta, theta, vega, and rho) in option pricing.

14. **(LO 12.1)** In practice problem 30, if the time value is $5, calculate the intrinsic value.

15. **(LO 12.3)** FinCorp Inc. has both a call option and a put option with exercise prices of $50. Both expire in one year. The call is currently selling for $10 per share, while the put is currently selling for $2 per share. If the risk-free rate is 5 percent per year, what should the stock price be so that there is no arbitrage opportunity?

### Intermediate

16. **(LO 12.1, 12.2)** You are in the process of interviewing for a promotion at FinCorp Inc. and have to identify the type of security based on the payoff diagrams above. All options expire on January 15, 2022,

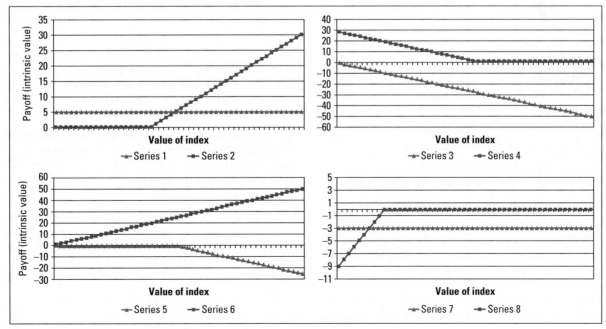

**Graphs Accompanying Question 16**

and the underlying asset is the index. Match the series from the diagrams to the appropriate security and position.

| | Position | Series |
|---|---|---|
| A | Long index | |
| B | Short index | |
| C | Long call | |
| D | Short call | |
| E | Long put | |
| F | Short put | |
| G | Long bond | |
| H | Short bond | |

**17. (LO 12.1, 12.2)** Richards & Co. Analysts has provided FinCorp Inc. with incomplete information, and it is your job to fill in the missing information in the table below.

| Long or Short | Call or Put | Strike Price | Value of Option Today | At Expiration Value of Underlying Asset | Payoff (Intrinsic Value) | Profit (Loss) |
|---|---|---|---|---|---|---|
| Long | Call | 130 | 5 | 155 | | |
| Short | Call | 130 | 5 | 155 | | |
| Long | Put | 130 | 5 | 100 | | |
| Short | Put | 130 | 5 | 100 | | |
| Long | Call | 155 | 5 | 130 | | |
| Short | Call | 155 | 5 | 130 | | |
| Long | Put | 155 | 5 | 175 | | |
| Short | Put | 155 | 5 | 175 | | |

**18. (LO 12.1, 12.2)** The following table contains option pricing data for company XYZ, whose shares are currently trading at $144. It is currently January. Assume all interest rates are greater than zero and ignore commissions.

| Expiration | Strike Price | Call Option Price | Put Option Price |
|---|---|---|---|
| February | $132.00 | $9.12 | $0.72 |
| March | $132.00 | $10.56 | $1.86 |
| May | $132.00 | $12.30 | $3.42 |
| August | $132.00 | $15.55 | $5.64 |

Using only the information provided, which two options appear to be mispriced? Explain your reasoning.

**19. (LO 12.1, 12.2)** Mr. Cabinet, your boss at FinCorp Inc., prefers to have his information presented visually. At his request, graph the payoffs (intrinsic values) and profits at expiration for the following option investments.

    **a.** long call, strike = $65, cost today = $10

    **b.** short call, strike = $65, cost today = $10

    **c.** long put, strike = $65, cost today = $10

    **d.** short put, strike = $65, cost today = $10

**20. (LO 12.1, 12.2)** Briefly state all the factors that affect the value of a call option and a put option.

**21. (LO 12.1)** Your boss has observed that the call options on XCT and BRG are trading at different prices. Both options have the same strike price and the same time to expiration. Provide two possible explanations for this observation.

**22. (LO 12.1, 12.2)** Mr. Cabinet is interested in the payoffs to combinations of options. Graph the intrinsic values of the following portfolios (all options expire on the same day and are written on the same non-dividend-paying asset).

    **a.** long one call, strike = $35; long one put, strike = $30

    **b.** short one call, strike = $35; long one put, strike = $25

    **c.** long one call, strike = $35; short one put, strike = $35

    **d.** long one call, strike = $35; short one share of underlying asset

    **e.** long one call, strike = $35; short one share; $35 in cash

    **f.** long one put, strike = $35; long one share; short $35 in cash (i.e., repay loan)

**23. (LO 12.1, 12.2)** You have observed that a very smart and successful investor has bought a call and a put on the S&P/TSX Index. The options have the same strike prices and expire on the same day. What does the smart investor think is going to happen to the S&P/TSX Index? (*Hint:* When will she make money on this investment?)

**24. (LO 12.1, 12.2)** You observe the following data on different options (all are European options with the same exercise date, and all are written on the same underlying security). What are the profits you would earn for every possible price of the underlying stock at the exercise date for each of the following strategies?

| Security | Current Price | Strike Price |
|---|---|---|
| IBL Stock | 60 | |
| Call | C1 | 70 |
| Call | C2 | 80 |
| Call | C3 | 50 |
| Call | C4 | 40 |

    **a.** Using arbitrage arguments, rank the prices of the calls.

    **b.** Buy one call with an exercise price of $50 and buy one share.

    **c.** Buy two calls with a strike price of $80 and short sell one share.

    **d.** Write two calls with a strike price of $40 and buy one share.

**25. (LO 12.1)** Compare the payoff of a call option and the underlying security. Show that the price of a call option must always be less than the value of the underlying security.

**26. (LO 12.2)** Ready Lumber is in the lumber business and has purchased a put option with an exercise price of $9.35 per tonne at a cost of $0.48 per tonne on 250,000 tonnes of lumber. What will be the net gain or loss when 240,000 tonnes are actually sold for $10.25 per tonne?

**27. (LO 12.3)** Richards & Co. Analysts have provided the following partially completed table of information about different securities. All options are written on XCT, a non-dividend-paying stock, and expire on the same day in one year. Fill in the missing information.

| | XCT Stock Price | Price of Call | Price of Put | Strike Price | Risk-Free Rate |
|---|---|---|---|---|---|
| A | 100 | | 6 | 85 | 5% |
| B | 130 | 30 | | 110 | 5% |
| C | | 3 | 2 | 16 | 6% |
| D | | 5 | 5 | 25 | 10% |
| E | 95 | 25 | 30 | 100 | |
| F | 140 | 25 | 20 | | 5% |

**28. (LO 12.4)** Fill in the missing information in the following table for a non-dividend-paying stock and European call options.

| | S | X | r | σ | T | $d_1$ | $d_2$ | $N(d_1)$ | $N(d_2)$ | $Xe^{-rt}$ | Call Value |
|---|---|---|---|---|---|---|---|---|---|---|---|
| A | 100 | 98 | 2% | 0.03 | 1 | | | | | | |
| B | 100 | 98 | 2% | 0.04 | 1 | | | | | | |
| C | 100 | 98 | 3% | 0.03 | 1 | | | | | | |
| D | 100 | 99 | 2% | 0.03 | 1 | | | | | | |
| E | 100 | 98 | 2% | 0.03 | 0.3 | | | | | | |
| F | 99 | 98 | 2% | 0.03 | 1 | | | | | | |

**29. (LO 12.4)** Does put-call parity hold for the following? Risk-free rate = 5%, $P_0 = \$13$, $C_0 = \$10$, stock price $(S) = \$30$, $t = 4$ years, strike price $(X) = \$33$. If not, what is the put price according to put-call parity, assuming the other figures are correct?

**30. (LO 12.4)** Determine the call price $(C)$, given the following information: stock price $(S) = \$36$, strike price $(X) = \$32$, risk-free rate $(r) = 5\%$, $t = 2$ years, $\sigma = 20\%$.

**31. (LO 12.3)** Calculate the put price $(P)$, according to put-call parity, given the information in practice problem 30.

**32. (LO 12.4)** What is the price of a put option with a strike price of $50 and six months to maturity when the stock price is currently trading at $45? Assume the stock-price variance is 0.5 and the risk-free rate is 5 percent.

**33. (LO 12.3)** QBV, a non-dividend-paying stock, is currently trading for $100 a share. There is a 25-percent chance that the stock will trade for $85 in one year, and a 75-percent chance that the price will increase to $135. The risk-free rate is 5 percent per year. All options expire in one year. You would like to purchase a call with a strike price of $125. Unfortunately, it is not available on the market, so you will have to create it synthetically. Design a portfolio to create a call with a strike price of $125 and demonstrate that it will give the same payoff as the desired call.

**34. (LO 12.3)** In most markets, you are not permitted to short sell if the stock price has fallen. That is, you can only short sell on an "uptick." Using put-call parity, show that you can replicate the cash flows of a short sale.

**35. (LO 12.3, 12.6)** QBV, a non-dividend-paying stock, is currently trading for $80 a share. There is a 25-percent chance that the stock will trade for $65 in one year, and a 75-percent chance that the price will increase to $105. The risk-free rate is 5 percent per year. All options expire in one year.

   **a.** A call option has a strike price of $100. Determine the hedge ratio.

   **b.** Use the binomial option pricing formula to determine the value of a call with a strike price of $100.

   **c.** Use put-call parity to determine the value of a put with a strike price of $100.

**36. (LO 12.6)** QBV, a non-dividend-paying stock, is currently trading for $100 a share. There is a 25-percent chance that the stock will trade for $85 in one year, and a 75-percent chance that the price will increase to $135. The risk-free rate is 5 percent per year. All options expire in one year.

   **a.** If the call option on QBV with a strike price of $115 is actually trading for $10, show that there is an arbitrage opportunity.

   **b.** If the put option on QBV with a strike price of $98 is actually trading for $0.50, show that there is an arbitrage opportunity.

**37. (LO 12.6)** DPG, a non-dividend-paying stock, is currently trading for $150 a share. There is a 30-percent chance that the stock will trade for $125 in one year, and a 70-percent chance that the price will increase to $175. The risk-free rate is 5 percent per year. There is a one-year call with a strike price of $165.

   **a.** What is the price of the call?

   **b.** What is the delta of the call? Define and calculate.

**38. (LO 12.6)** What is the strike price $(X)$ if PU is $50, PD is $42, and the hedge ratio $(h)$ is 2?

**39. (LO 12.6)** Assume stock XYZ does not pay dividends and has a market value of $98 per share. There is a 60-percent chance that the stock will trade for $130 in one year, and a 40-percent chance that it will trade for $55 in one year. What is the value of a put option with an exercise price of $90 if the risk-free rate is 5 percent per year?

## Challenging

**40. (LO 12.1, 12.2)** Complete the following table.

| | Long Call or Short Put | or Strike Price | Value of Option Today | Value of Underlying Asset | In/Out of the Money | Payoff (Intrinsic Value) | Profit (Loss) |
|---|---|---|---|---|---|---|---|
| A | Long Put | 90 | 0.05 | | | | −0.05 |
| B | Long Call | 90 | 2 | | | | −1 |
| C | Short Put | 90 | 0.05 | | | | −0.95 |
| D | Short Call | 90 | 0.05 | | | | −0.95 |
| E | Long Call | | 1 | 135 | | | 25 |
| F | Short Put | 134 | | 135 | | 0 | −2 |
| G | | 35 | 2 | 105 | | 0 | −2 |
| H | | 35 | 2 | 105 | | 70 | 68 |
| I | Call | 85 | | 100 | | | 2 |
| J | Put | 85 | | 100 | | | 2 |
| K | Call | 85 | 5 | 100 | | | −10 |
| L | Put | 85 | | 100 | | | −2 |
| M | Short Call | 110 | | | | 0 | 2 |
| N | Put | 80 | 3 | | | −25 | −22 |

**41. (LO 12.1, 12.2)** Mr. Kent, one of your clients, has been reading his daughter's finance textbook and has a question about options. He says: "If I buy a call option, I have the right to buy the asset at the strike price. If I buy a put option, I have the right to sell the asset at the strike price. And if I sell a put, I have to buy the asset at the strike price. Therefore, buying a call option is the same as selling a put. So if I observe that puts and calls have different prices, I can make money because they should have the same price!" Comment on Mr. Kent's statement. Is he correct?

**42. (LO 12.1, 12.2)** The current price of a stock is $107. You expect the price of the stock to be in the range of $105 to $115 in the next period. The call option with an exercise price of $115 is $1.30; the put option with an exercise price of $105 is $1.00. Both options expire in the next period. Using options only, explain how you can earn a profit.

**43. (LO 12.4)** You have just been appointed manager of the equity portfolio of a large pension plan. The portfolio has a current value of $100 billion and is well diversified; consequently, it has a beta close to one. The trustees of the pension plan are very risk averse, and in order to prevent you from taking on too much risk, they have structured your compensation as follows: if the value of the fund drops below $90 billion in one year, you will be fired with no severance pay.

If the fund is between $90 billion and $120 billion, you will be paid $2 million + 0.01 percent of the difference between the fund value and $90 billion (i.e., if the fund is worth $95 billion in one year, you will be paid $2 million + $500,000 = $2.5 million). If the fund is worth more than $120 billion, your salary will be capped at $5 million. You are allowed to invest in options on the S&P/TSX. The current value of the S&P/TSX is 1,000, and there are puts and calls traded that expire in one year. The puts and calls both have multipliers of $100. The standard deviation of returns on the S&P/TSX is 10 percent per year, and the risk-free rate is 3 percent per year. Assume that there are no dividends for either the portfolio or the S&P/TSX and that the options are European.

    **a.** Describe how you can best protect your personal interests.

    **b.** How much will these actions cost the portfolio?

**44. (LO 12.3)** In the next period, the economy can be in either state 1 or state 2, with a probability of 50 percent. You may trade any combination, including fractions of shares, of the following three securities:

| Security | Value Today | Value in Future | |
|---|---|---|---|
| | | State 1 | State 2 |
| MCD | 15 | 25 | 20 |
| SB | 5 | 10 | 25 |
| BK | 3 | 75 | 17.50 |

    **a.** Are these securities correctly priced? If not, why not? (*Hint:* Set up a portfolio with proper weight in MCD and SB so that the portfolio has the same payoff as security BK.)

    **b.** If there is an arbitrage opportunity, explain how you would exploit it.

    **c.** What is the maximum you would be willing to pay for SB? (*Hint:* The maximum I would be willing to pay for a share of SB is the cost of the portfolio that replicates one share of SB.)

**45. (LO 12.3)** The current price of TSY Inc. is $75. In one year, the price could be either $50 or $100. The risk-free rate is 5 percent per year. Construct a portfolio with the same payoff as a call option. What is the most you would pay for a call on TSY Inc. with a strike price of $90?

**46. (LO 12.6)** Xiang Zhu, a client of FinCorp Inc., has phoned you with a question. She has been reading a finance textbook and cannot understand how to use the binomial option pricing model to value a call option. The underlying stock is currently trading for $100. There is a 30-percent chance it will increase to $190 in one year, and a 70-percent chance it will fall to $85 in the same period. The risk-free rate is 10 percent. There is a call option with a strike price of $170, which according to the binomial model should have a value of $4.329. Xiang is confused because she calculates that if there is a 30-percent chance the call will be worth $20 and a 70-percent chance it will be worth zero, the expected value should be $6. Why is it only worth $4.329?

    **a.** Demonstrate that if the call was trading for $6, there would be an arbitrage opportunity.

    **b.** Calculate the risk-neutral probabilities.

    **c.** Calculate the expected present value of the call option using the risk-neutral probabilities.

    **d.** Why can we value options as if the investors are risk neutral?

**47. (LO 12.6)** HSA, a non-dividend paying stock, is currently trading at $42 a share. The stock is expected to be either up by 25 percent or down by 18 percent in six months. The annual continuously compounded risk-free rate is 4 percent. Suppose a call option on the stock with a six-month time to expiry and an exercise price of $42.50 exists.

    **a.** Determine the hedge ratio.

    **b.** Use the binomial option pricing formula to determine the value of the call option.

    **c.** Calculate the risk-neutral probabilities.

    **d.** Calculate the expected present value of the call option using the risk-neutral probabilities found in part (c).

# Capital Budgeting, Risk Considerations, and Other Special Issues

---

**LEARNING OBJECTIVES**

After studying this chapter, you should be able to:

**13.1** Describe the capital budgeting process and explain its importance to corporate strategy.

**13.2** Identify and apply the main tools used to evaluate investments.

**13.3** Analyze independent projects and explain how they differ from interdependent projects.

**13.4** Explain what capital rationing is and how it affects firms' investment criteria.

**13.5** Explain the importance of international foreign direct investment both inside and outside Canada.

**13.6** Explain how the modified internal rate of return (MIRR) is calculated and why this represents a conceptual improvement over the way the IRR is calculated.

---

Business investment plays a critical role in the productivity of the firm. In this chapter, we discuss long-term investment decisions made by companies, particularly decisions about investments in real assets, such as property, plant, and equipment. In previous chapters, we have seen that a firm's investment decisions are critical to firm value, because market values are based on the expected future growth in company earnings, dividends, and distributable cash flows. In this chapter, we will also revisit several concepts we discussed when describing how to value bonds and shares, and we will emphasize that the basic techniques are identical: we have to estimate future cash flows, determine appropriate discount rates, convert those expected future cash flows back into their corresponding present values, and compare them with their cost. The essential difference between valuing shares and valuing projects or companies is not in the approach but in the judgement necessary because of the differing "quality" of the inputs.

---

## 13.1 | Capital Expenditures

---

**LEARNING OBJECTIVE 13.1**

Describe the capital budgeting process and explain its importance to corporate strategy.

---

# The Importance of the Capital Expenditure Decision

**capital expenditures** a firm's investments in long-lived assets, which may be tangible or intangible

**Capital expenditures** are a firm's investments in long-lived assets, which may be tangible assets, such as property, plant, and equipment, or intangible assets, such as research and development (R&D), copyrights, brand names, and franchise agreements. Tangible assets are hard, physical assets, while intangible ones are more abstract; it is easier for a firm to borrow against tangible assets than against intangible ones.

These long-term investment decisions determine a company's future direction and could be viewed as the most important decisions a firm can make, because a firm's capital expenditures (capex) usually involve large amounts of money, and the decisions are frequently irrevocable. For example, TransCanada PipeLines Ltd. transmits natural gas from western Canada to central Canada and Chicago. Once its pipeline assets are in place, they are largely unique to that application and have very little alternative use. It is therefore important that any decision related to these capex investments is made on sound financial and economic grounds. The irrevocable and unique nature of real investments has its parallel in investments in intangible assets. The decision to bring out a new soft drink, for example, with the attendant new product development costs and marketing campaign, is also irrevocable. In this case, it is almost impossible to recover the investment costs of a failed new product launch.

The importance of capex decisions lies in their ability to affect the risk of the firm. In some cases, the very survival of the firm depends on the success of a new product produced from prior capex decisions. Ford, for example, was saved from extinction in the 1980s when it brought out the then revolutionary Ford Taurus, which went on to become the most popular family car in North America.

**capital budgeting** the process by which a firm makes capital expenditure decisions by (1) identifying investment alternatives, (2) evaluating these alternatives, (3) implementing the chosen investment decisions, and (4) monitoring and evaluating the implemented decisions

**Capital budgeting** refers to the process by which a firm makes capital expenditure decisions, as shown below.

| Identify investment alternatives | → | Evaluate these alternatives | → | Implement the chosen investment decisions | → | Monitor and evaluate the implemented decisions |
|---|---|---|---|---|---|---|

We will focus most of our discussion on the general framework that should be used to evaluate various investment alternatives, because the remaining decisions are firm-specific and covered in managerial accounting (which develops the firm's control and audit systems). First, we will briefly discuss some important factors in the investment process.

One of the factors contributing to improved productivity is increased investment in machinery and equipment. Conversely, one could surmise that if a firm does not invest effectively, it will find itself at a competitive disadvantage, which in the extreme will affect its long-term survival. In the short run, poor investment decisions will make a firm less attractive than those that have better prepared themselves for the future. This will show up in the market price of the firm's debt and equity securities, which will decline, and will hence increase its cost of capital.

Finance in the News 13.1 challenges our ability to accurately measure foreign direct investment in a world where asset value is seen as increasingly shifting from the tangible to the intangible. Talent and ideas are far more difficult to value compared with what we have traditionally considered as assets that are targeted for investment.

Michael Porter has written extensively on the notion that successful companies will create a "competitive strategy" for themselves. He identifies five critical factors that determine the attractiveness of an industry:

- entry barriers
- the threat of substitutes
- the bargaining power of buyers
- the bargaining power of suppliers
- rivalry among existing competitors

## 13.1 Finance in the News    It's Time for Canada to Capitalize on Its Ideas

There has been a Canadian consensus on the merits of foreign direct investment (FDI) for decades that cuts across sectors and partisan lines. In our traditional industries, it makes perfect sense. When foreign investors put up a hotel or finance resource development, there are obvious positive economic spillovers to the benefit of Canadians.

However, as the driver of wealth creation in the global economy shifts from tangible assets such as infrastructure to intangible assets such as algorithms, data sets and software-as-services, the national benefits of FDI into the domestic tech sector become opaque.

There are two foundational areas of global competition in the intangibles economy: talent and ideas. They are deeply intertwined. Foreign multinational tech behemoths such as Google and Amazon have been known to jurisdiction shop to find top talent at universities, largely engineers and data scientists, to drive their current commercialization and to generate new ideas to be commercialized. When such ideas and talent exist in a corporate structure, they often conduct early acquisitions, referred to as "acquihires," regardless of the economic fundamentals of such companies.

The talent and their ideas are portable with little tax or other implication. More precisely, an algorithm developed in Waterloo, Ont., can be transferred, intrafirm, to another jurisdiction, say California, to be commercialized by the parent company without oversight, despite the public investments in the creation of those assets.

This can create negative economic spillovers for a country such as Canada that subsidizes key services such as education and health care in addition to the incentives it offers for companies to conduct research and development and to create jobs. It's important to note that Canada has negative unemployment among data and computer scientists.

Such incentives create wage inflation for Canadian firms that require such talent for their growth, as well as creating nontechnical jobs such as sales and marketing, administration and operations roles.

This is not a theoretical argument. Canadians have been at the forefront of the development of the base artificial-intelligence (AI) algorithms at our universities. This has created much hype about Canada leading the global AI revolution.

This is true at the ideation phase, but when we look to who ultimately owns such ideas and can extract significant rents from them, look no further than the largest foreign multinational firms, which have acquired the intellectual property (IP) in exchange for what seems to be research funding to a university or a job for the faculty member.

This is the case with Geoffrey Hinton's groundbreaking AI research, often associated with the University of Toronto, which has been patented by Google. Such foundational technologies can generate billions of dollars of revenue both for the company and jurisdiction where they are commercialized. In 2017, Eric Schmidt, chairman of Google's parent company, speaking about Canadian research into AI, stated: "We now use it throughout our entire business and it's a major driver of our corporate success."

The company's revenue in 2017 was US$110-billion.

Google is not alone, as South Korean giant LG recently announced an AI research partnership with the University of Toronto.

Universities are becoming ever more important in the intangible economy given that they sit at the nexus of talent development and ideation.

In Canada, universities seem to be striking partnerships with foreign multinational tech companies at an increasing rate across the tech spectrum.

For example, Canadian researchers are among the pack in the race to 5G wireless technology, which is seen as another transformational platform technology.

The government of Canada announced it would spend $40-million to lure Finnish company, Nokia, to conduct research on 5G.

The government's approach doesn't seem to prescribe Canadian commercialization provisions, IP ownership or a royalty structure in exchange for the investment.

This will create negative economic spillovers if the technology is commercially successful.

Beyond the economic spillovers, there are also national-security considerations of such research partnerships. Given that such foundational technologies are developed at universities, governance of such research partnerships should be a primary consideration for administrators and funders.

However, a Globe and Mail investigation revealed that the National Research Council, a federal government funder of university research, was looking for academic reviewers of a pending 5G research partnership between Canadian universities and Huawei, the Chinese technology giant, while not letting geopolitical considerations come in to their evaluation. This is despite the fact that the Canadian government is considering blocking the company from our telecommunications infrastructure supply chain.

Leading U.S. research institutions such as the Massachusetts Institute of Technology have cut off Huawei from research partnerships.

Considering the economic spillovers of FDI into our innovation economy, asking for shrewder terms in exchange for publicly funded research partnerships with foreign companies or the consideration of geopolitical realities before striking such agreements is not economic nationalism. It's a pillar of a modern prosperity strategy and enlightened sovereignty.

Canadians, whether they ever step foot on a university campus, fuel research partnerships through their taxes. We're publicly funding research at one of the highest rates among member countries of the Organization for Economic Co-operation and Development, yet our productivity has plummeted compared with our competitors.

We deserve for those investments to create a virtuous feedback loop. One which sees a return on the public investments we make, including some Canadian companies growing to globally competitive scale through intellectual property created and commercialized in Canada that creates quality technical and nontechnical jobs, significant tax revenues to fund our health care, education and other essential services as well as new philanthropic resources.

If we don't awaken to these realities and act soon, Canada will have subsidized our own digital colonization.

**Source:** Desai, Neil, "It's Time for Canada to Capitalize on Its Ideas." *The Globe and Mail*, June 7, 2019. ©2019 The Globe and Mail Inc. All rights reserved. Reprinted by permission.

**five forces** the five critical factors that determine the attractiveness of an industry: entry barriers, the threat of substitutes, the bargaining power of buyers, the bargaining power of suppliers, and rivalry among existing competitors

These are often called the **five forces**.[1] Porter argues that, after inception, firms have little immediate control over the attractiveness of the industry they are in. This implies that industry structure will have a significant input into every firm's investment decisions. However, Porter points out, firms *do* exert control over the manner in which they strive to create a competitive advantage within their industry. Obviously, these decisions will also be closely related to a firm's long-term investment decisions, as discussed below.

Porter argues that firms can create competitive advantages for themselves by adopting one of the following strategies:

1. **Cost leadership: strive to be a low-cost producer.** This strategy is viable for firms that are able to take advantage of economies of scale, proprietary technology, or privileged or superior access to raw materials. Obviously, investment outlays should be made in accordance with a firm's potential advantage. For example, if economies of scale or technological advantages are possible, firms should invest in a manner that will enable them to exploit these opportunities.

2. **Differentiation: offer "differentiated" products.** Firms can provide products that are differentiated from others in several ways. The most obvious is to have a product that is itself unique by virtue of its physical or technological characteristics. However, firms can also differentiate their products by providing customers with unique delivery alternatives or by establishing a marketing approach that distinguishes their products from those of their potential competitors.

Either of these strategies can be applied with a broad (industry-wide) focus or with a narrow (industry-segment) focus, and both have their corollary in capex decisions. As we will discuss, cost leadership usually follows from *replacement* decisions, when firms are constantly striving to use the latest technology to lower the costs of production. Product differentiation usually follows from *new product development decisions,* such as the launch of a new flavoured soft drink or a new model of car.

Porter suggests that it is difficult to sustain a competitive advantage once one has been created. This is particularly true in industries where competition is heated or where barriers to entry are low or nonexistent. Therefore, companies must continually plan (and invest) strategically. This brings up the question: what is the relationship between corporate strategy and the capex decision?

A basic premise of finance suggests that when a senior executive justifies a project on non-financial grounds, either the analysis is not rigorous enough, with the advantages not fully developed, or it is a pet project and should not be pursued. Every project is amenable to the analytical techniques that we discuss in the sections that follow—the only difference is that the more qualitative the inputs, the more strategic the analysis. However, this does bring up a basic distinction—the difference between bottom-up and top-down analysis.

**bottom-up analysis** an investment strategy in which capex decisions are made in isolation, without considering general industry and economic trends or whether the firm should continue in this particular business

**Bottom-up analysis** is based on the idea that a firm is simply a set of capex decisions. Equipment replacement is a typical bottom-up analysis, in which an engineer estimates the savings that will be realized—in terms of labour hours, power, material costs, and so on—by replacing one piece of equipment with another. A financial analyst then translates these savings into financial parameters to determine whether the replacement savings are worth the cost of the equipment. However, at no point does the engineer or the financial analyst consider whether the firm should continue in this business. An analogy might be the engineer on the *Titanic* deciding to replace some equipment just after the ship struck the iceberg. In isolation it might be a good decision, but obviously it is irrelevant on a larger scale.

---

[1]Porter, M., "How Competitive Forces Shape Strategy." *Harvard Business Review,* (March–April 1979).

In contrast, **top-down analysis** focuses on strategic decisions about which industries or products the firm should be involved in. For example, Ford's F150 trucks were the best-selling vehicles in North America for several years, while its car division was losing money. Consequently, there was serious discussion about whether Ford should "do a Volvo" and sell its car business to someone or shut some plants and become a truck manufacturer. The strategic decision was whether Ford should produce passenger cars or focus solely on trucks, rather than the decision of which passenger cars should be developed. Of course, Ford didn't shut down its car division, and the car lines have been doing much better recently.

In looking at bottom-up versus top-down analysis, the capital budgeting framework is identical. What is different is the quality of the estimates. In replacement decisions, the analysis is one of risk, in which the analyst estimates the cost savings with clearly defined probabilities. It may be possible, for example, to estimate there is a 30-percent chance of saving $50,000 and a 70-percent chance of saving $100,000 per year. In this way, replacement decisions are similar to the evaluation of equity investments for which there is a long price history, and for which means, variances, and so on can be estimated to say there is a 50-percent chance of a share going up 15 percent in price and a 50-percent chance of its going down 5 percent. In contrast, top-down or strategic decisions often involve a situation of *uncertainty*, in which it is almost impossible to estimate probabilities for the possible outcomes. In these situations, as we will discuss later, it is important for the analysis to involve different scenarios, so the firm can respond to different situations. This flexibility in top-down decision-making is an application of the theory of option pricing to capex decisions and is called real option valuation (ROV). ROV is difficult to implement but is one of the hottest areas in financial management. We will discuss it in detail in Chapter 14.

In Chapter 2, we pointed out that the firm's goal should be to maximize shareholder wealth. In this chapter, we develop techniques for making capex decisions that are consistent with this overriding objective. These techniques are generally called **discounted cash flow (DCF) methodologies**. As their name suggests, they are the capex analogues to the valuation techniques discussed earlier. DCF valuation involves estimating future cash flows and comparing their discounted values with investment outlays required today. In this way, they are technically identical to the approaches used to evaluate bonds (see Chapter 6) and preferred and common shares (see Chapter 7).

The only practical difference is that whereas the cash flows are fixed when valuing bonds and shares (in the sense that the analyst cannot change them), when making capex decisions the analyst can affect the underlying cash flows by changing the structure of the project. For example, after the analysis, the firm can decide to defer a project for a year or change the form of a product. If the firm is developing a new car, it may decide some parts will become optional extras in order to hit a target price point, or a substitute sweetener may be used in a new soft drink. As a result, the application of DCF valuation techniques in capex decisions is, by its nature, more of an *iterative* process than a one-time decision.

In discussing DCF techniques, we defer our discussion of how to estimate cash flows until Chapter 14. In this chapter, we will focus on the application of the approaches themselves and discuss their relative advantages, assuming that we already know the expected cash flows. In this way, we first focus on the capital budgeting framework.

**top-down analysis** an investment strategy that focuses on strategic decisions, such as which industries or products the firm should be involved in, looking at the overall economic picture

**discounted cash flow (DCF) methodologies** techniques for making capex decisions that are consistent with the overriding objective of maximizing shareholder wealth; they involve estimating future cash flows and comparing their discounted values with investment outlays required today

## Concept Review Questions

1. What is the difference between a tangible asset and an intangible asset?

2. What are irrevocable investment decisions? Why are they important for capital budgeting?

3. Contrast top-down and bottom-up analysis.

4. In what ways is DCF capex analysis similar to valuing common shares, and in what ways is it different?

# Evaluating Investment Alternatives

### LEARNING OBJECTIVE 13.2
Identify and apply the main tools used to evaluate investments.

In a 2011 survey, Canadian chief financial officers (CFOs) were asked about their capital budgeting decisions (as well as financing issues).[2] Their responses regarding the capital budgeting criteria they used are reported in **Figure 13.1**. In this section we will cover in depth six of the nine techniques these CFOs said they used most frequently to evaluate investment opportunities: net present value (NPV) analysis, internal rate of return (IRR), payback period, discounted payback period, profitability index, and modified internal rate of return (in Appendix 13A). We will start with payback period and discounted payback period.

**FIGURE 13.1** **Survey Results of Capital Budgeting Techniques Used by Canadian Firms When Deciding Which Projects or Acquisitions to Pursue**

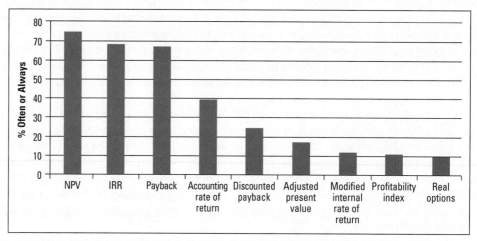

**Source:** Data from Baker, Kent H., Dutta, Shantanu, and Saadi, Samir, "Corporate Finance Practices in Canada: Where Do We Stand?" *Multinational Finance Journal* 15, no. 3/4 (September/December 2011), Table 3, p. 173.

## Payback Period and Discounted Payback Period

**payback period** the number of years required to fully recover the initial cash outlay associated with a capital expenditure

As shown in Figure 13.1, 67.2 percent of the CFOs surveyed said they used the payback period technique "often" or "always." The **payback period** is defined as the number of years required to fully recover the initial cash outlay associated with a capital expenditure. Shorter payback periods are better, and usually this decision criterion is implemented by choosing a cutoff date and rejecting projects whose payback period goes past the cutoff date. If we let the payback period $= T$, the estimated future after-tax incremental cash flow at time $t = CF_t$ and the estimated future after-tax incremental initial cash outlay $= CF_0$, then equation 13.1 can be written as:

$$CF_1 + CF_2 + CF_3 + \cdots + CF_T = CF_0 \text{ or } \sum_{t=1}^{T} CF_t = CF_0 \qquad [13.1]$$

Put another way, $T$ is the length of time required to recover the initial investment ($CF_0$).

[2]Baker, Kent H., Dutta, Shantanu, and Saadi, Samir, "Corporate Finance Practices in Canada: Where Do We Stand?" *Multinational Finance Journal* 15, no. 3/4 (September/December 2011), pp. 157–92. In a similar survey of the CFOs of major U.S. companies, Graham and Harvey produced results that were similar qualitatively, and very close in terms of the actual percentages, to those found by Baker, Dutta, and Saadi in Canada. See Graham, John R., and Harvey, Campbell R., "The Theory and Practice of Corporate Finance: Evidence from the Field." *Journal of Financial Economics* 60 (2001), pp. 187–243.

Example 13.1 illustrates how the payback period is calculated.

---

**EXAMPLE 13.1** | Calculating Payback Period

Suppose a company has an investment that requires an after-tax incremental cash outlay of $12,000 today. It estimates that the expected future after-tax cash flows associated with this investment will be $5,000 in years 1 and 2 and $8,000 in year 3. Calculate the payback period.

**Solution**

| Year | Cumulative CFs Recovered |
|------|--------------------------|
| 1 | $ 5,000 |
| 2 | $10,000 |
| 3 | $18,000 |

$$\text{Payback} = 2 + (\$2,000/\$8,000) = 2.25 \text{ years}$$

With a $12,000 cash outlay, $10,000 is recovered in two years, and the additional $2,000 is recovered a quarter of the way through the third year, assuming that the cash flows are evenly spaced throughout the year.

---

The payback period provides a useful intuitive measure of how long it takes to recover an investment and is sometimes used as an informal measure of project risk. This is because, in some sense, the quicker a firm recovers its investment outlay, the less risky the project is. However, the payback period has some important drawbacks. In particular, it disregards the time and risk value of money, because it treats a dollar of cash flow received in year 3 the same as those received in year 1, and so on. In addition, the payback period does not account for the cash flows received after the cutoff date, which could be substantial for some long-lived projects. Finally, the choice of the cutoff date is somewhat arbitrary and may vary from one firm to the next.

The **discounted payback period** alleviates the first shortcoming of the payback period by accounting for the time value of money. It is defined as the number of years required to fully recover the initial cash outlay in terms of *discounted* cash flows. Shorter periods are better, and projects with discounted payback periods before the cutoff date will be accepted. Unfortunately, as was the case for the payback period criterion, the discounted payback period ignores cash flows beyond the cutoff date, and the cutoff date is somewhat arbitrary. We calculate the discounted payback period using Equation 13.2.

**discounted payback period** the number of years required to fully recover the initial cash outlay associated with a capital expenditure in terms of discounted cash flows

$$\frac{CF_1}{(1+k)^1} + \frac{CF_2}{(1+k)^2} + \frac{CF_3}{(1+k)^3} + \cdots + \frac{CF_T}{(1+k)^T} = CF_0 \text{ or } \sum_{t=1}^{T} \frac{CF_t}{(1+k)^t} = CF_0 \quad [13.2]$$

where $k$ = the appropriate risk-adjusted after-tax discount rate (which is usually the firm's after-tax marginal cost of capital).

Example 13.2 shows how the discounted payback period is calculated.

---

**EXAMPLE 13.2** | Calculating Discounted Payback Period

Assuming a discount rate of 15 percent, revisit Example 13.1 and estimate the discounted payback period of the project under consideration.

**Solution**

| Year | Cumulative CFs Recovered | PV of Cumulative CFs Recovered |
|------|--------------------------|--------------------------------|
| 1 | $ 5,000 | $5,000/(1.15) = $4,348 |
| 2 | $10,000 | $4,348 + $5,000/(1.15)^2 = $8,129 |
| 3 | $18,000 | $8,129 + $8,000/(1.15)^3 = $13,389 |

$$\text{Discounted payback} = 2 + \left[ (\$12,000 - \$8,129)/(\$8,000/1.15^3) \right]$$

$$= 2 + [\$3,871/\$5,260] = 2.74 \text{ years}$$

---

In Example 13.2, the discounted payback period is longer than the simple payback period; the future cash flows are worth less because they have been discounted for time and risk. If a firm is going to use discounting, it might as well discount all the future cash flows and calculate the net present value (NPV), as we will see next. For this reason, the discounted payback period is a compromise between the payback period and the NPV, which is probably why it is not rated as highly as the NPV by CFOs.

# Net Present Value (NPV) Analysis

**net present value (NPV)** the sum of the present value of all future after-tax incremental cash flows generated by an initial cash outlay, minus the present value of the investment outlay; the present value of the expected cash flows net of the costs needed to generate them

The **net present value (NPV)** of a project is defined as the sum of the present value (PV) of all future after-tax incremental cash flows generated by an initial cash outlay, minus the present value of the investment outlays. In other words, the NPV is the present value of the expected cash flows net of the costs needed to generate them. This process is depicted graphically in **Figure 13.2**, where, for simplicity, there is a single outlay at time zero.

Usually we use the firm's after-tax marginal cost of capital as the appropriate discount rate for projects that are similar to the normal operations of the firm, because it should reflect the firm's normal financing costs. (We will revisit the reasonableness of using this discount rate later in this chapter.) The NPV of an $n$-year project can therefore be determined using Equation 13.3.

$$NPV = \frac{CF_1}{(1+k)^1} + \frac{CF_2}{(1+k)^2} + \frac{CF_3}{(1+k)^3} + \cdots - CF_0 = \sum_{t=1}^{n}\frac{CF_t}{(1+k)^t} - CF_0 \qquad [13.3]$$

**incremental** in capital budgeting, the change in revenues or costs resulting from the investment decision

Note that we described the cash flows as **incremental**, which means they change as a result of the decision. Cash flows that have already been incurred are referred to as "sunk" costs and are ignored, since they do not change as a result of the firm's investment decision. This type of thinking has led 46 percent of surveyed Canadians to conclude that renting is a waste of money even though buying a home in high-cost cities such as Toronto and Vancouver is unaffordable for many.[3]

We have discussed previously that the market value of any firm in an efficient market should equal the present value of its expected after-tax cash flows, discounted at an appropriate **risk-adjusted discount rate (RADR)**, which is set based on the overall riskiness of the project. Therefore, we can say that projects that have a *positive* NPV add value to the firm and should be accepted because, by definition, a positive NPV implies that the PV of the expected future cash flows will exceed the cash outlay today—that is, it increases the value of the firm. Because the firm's creditors have a fixed claim on the firm's income, regardless of the value of the project, this NPV drops down to the shareholders and increases the market value of the firm's common shares. In this way, accepting positive-NPV projects maximizes the firm's market value and creates shareholder value. In contrast, accepting *negative-NPV* projects destroys firm value, and such projects should be rejected because, by definition, the destruction of shareholder value is not in the best interests of the shareholders.

**risk-adjusted discount rate (RADR)** a discount rate that is set based on the overall riskiness of a project

We would expect positive NPVs to arise only in situations in which a company has a competitive advantage. Because of the competitive nature of today's business environment, we would not expect to see an abundance of such opportunities, nor would we expect them to persist for very long. Therefore, projects that produce an NPV of zero will be the norm where firms operate in competitive markets. These projects should be accepted, because they provide the appropriate return required to compensate for the financing costs (and risks) associated with the investment.

**FIGURE 13.2** **The Cash Flow Pattern for a Traditional Capital Expenditure**

[3]Warren, May, "Nearly Half of Canadians Think Paying Rent Is a Waste of Money, Survey Finds," *Toronto Star*, December 13, 2018.

**EXAMPLE 13.3** | Calculating NPV

Revisit Example 13.1 and estimate the project's NPV.

**Solution** Using a 15-percent discount rate as before:

$$NPV = \frac{CF_1}{(1+k)^1} + \frac{CF_2}{(1+k)^2} + \frac{CF_3}{(1+k)^3} + \cdots - CF_0$$

$$= \left[ \frac{\$5,000}{(1.15)^1} + \frac{\$5,000}{(1.15)^2} + \frac{\$8,000}{(1.15)^3} \right] - \$12,000 = \$13,388.67 - \$12,000 = +\$1,388.67$$

The project would be accepted, because it has a positive NPV and would increase firm value by $1,388.67.

---

**EXAMPLE 13.3** | Solution Using a Financial Calculator

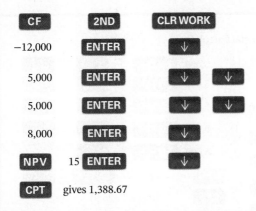

| CF | 2ND | CLR WORK |
|---|---|---|
| −12,000 | ENTER | ↓ |
| 5,000 | ENTER | ↓ ↓ |
| 5,000 | ENTER | ↓ ↓ |
| 8,000 | ENTER | ↓ |
| NPV | 15 ENTER | ↓ |
| CPT | gives 1,388.67 | |

---

**EXAMPLE 13.4** | Calculating NPV When Future CFs Represent an Annuity

A project that requires an initial investment of $30,000 is expected to generate after-tax cash flows of $5,000 per year for the next nine years, and then $6,000 in year 10. Estimate the NPV using a 12-percent discount rate.

**Solution** The "long version" of the solution, which involves discounting each of the nine future cash flows separately, is time-consuming and unnecessary. This is because the future CFs are all equal, at $5,000 (i.e., they form an annuity), except for the ending cash flow of $6,000, which we can view as another $5,000 payment, plus an additional one-time cash flow of $1,000. Therefore, we can solve the PV of the future cash flows by finding the sum of the PV of a 10-year annuity of $5,000 and the PV of a $1,000 cash flow, arriving at $t$ equals 10, as follows:

$$PV_0 = \$5,000 \left[ \frac{1 - \frac{1}{(1.12)^{10}}}{0.12} \right] + \frac{\$1,000}{(1.12)^{10}} = \$5,000(5.650223) + (\$1,000)(0.32197)$$

$$= \$28,251.12 + \$321.97 = \$28,573.09$$

So, NPV = $28,573.09 − $30,000 = −$1,426.91

The project should be rejected, because it has a negative NPV and would destroy firm value.

Example 13.4 is solved more easily using a calculator and using only the time value of money functions, as shown here.

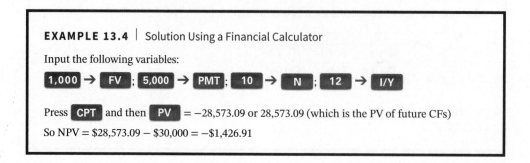

**EXAMPLE 13.4** │ Solution Using a Financial Calculator

Input the following variables:

1,000 → FV ; 5,000 → PMT ; 10 → N ; 12 → I/Y

Press CPT and then PV = −28,573.09 or 28,573.09 (which is the PV of future CFs)

So NPV = $28,573.09 − $30,000 = −$1,426.91

Of course, Example 13.4 can also be solved using the NPV function, as shown here.

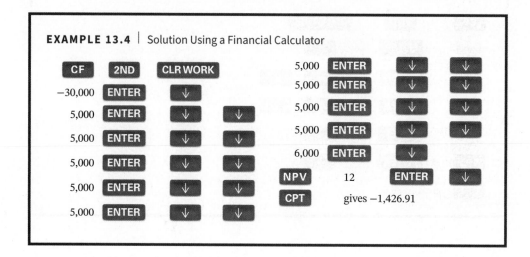

**EXAMPLE 13.4** │ Solution Using a Financial Calculator

CF   2ND   CLR WORK

−30,000 ENTER   ↓

5,000 ENTER   ↓   ↓

5,000 ENTER   ↓   ↓

5,000 ENTER   ↓   ↓

5,000 ENTER   ↓   ↓

5,000 ENTER   ↓   ↓

5,000 ENTER   ↓   ↓   ↓

5,000 ENTER   ↓   ↓

5,000 ENTER   ↓   ↓

5,000 ENTER   ↓   ↓

6,000 ENTER   ↓

NPV   12   ENTER   ↓

CPT   gives −1,426.91

In fact, we can use a shortcut when using the NPV function available on the TI BA II Plus calculator.

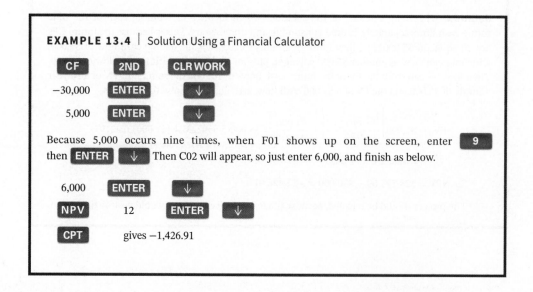

**EXAMPLE 13.4** │ Solution Using a Financial Calculator

CF   2ND   CLR WORK

−30,000 ENTER   ↓

5,000 ENTER   ↓

Because 5,000 occurs nine times, when F01 shows up on the screen, enter 9 then ENTER ↓ Then C02 will appear, so just enter 6,000, and finish as below.

6,000 ENTER   ↓

NPV   12   ENTER   ↓

CPT   gives −1,426.91

# The Internal Rate of Return (IRR)

The **internal rate of return (IRR)** is the same as the yield to maturity (YTM) for a bond, which we estimated earlier. In fact, the YTM is the IRR of a bond for a given purchase price. As we showed then, the IRR is the discount rate that makes the NPV equal to zero for a given set of cash flows. This implies that it is the discount rate that sets the PV of future CFs equal to the initial cash outlay. Thus, it is a rate of return that is internal to this particular set of cash flows; for this reason, it is often called the "economic rate of return" of a given project. We can rearrange Equation 13.3 to obtain Equation 13.4, which can be used to estimate the IRR.

**internal rate of return (IRR)**   the discount rate that makes the present value of future cash flows equal to the initial cash outlay

$$\frac{CF_1}{(1+IRR)^1} + \frac{CF_2}{(1+IRR)^2} + \frac{CF_3}{(1+IRR)^3} + \cdots = CF_0 \text{ or } \sum_{t=1}^{n}\frac{CF_t}{(1+IRR)^t} = CF_0 \qquad [13.4]$$

The general rule for IRR evaluation criteria is that a firm should accept a project whenever the IRR is greater than the appropriate risk-adjusted discount rate ($k$), which is usually the firm's cost of capital. Just like NPV, the IRR represents a discounted cash flow approach; in general, it will lead to the same accept/reject decisions as NPV does. However, note that in Equation 13.4 we could multiply through by $(1+IRR)^n$, and it then becomes clear that in finding the IRR, we are solving for the roots of an $n$th-degree polynomial. Unfortunately, every time the sign of the polynomial changes—that is, every time the cash flows change from positive to negative—there is a root (the polynomial curve crosses the $x$-axis), so for complex cash flow streams, we often find that there is more than one IRR or more than one root. (This is a common problem in evaluating leases, which we discuss in Chapter 16.)

Also note that in solving Equation 13.4, just as for the bond YTM case, there is no general closed-form solution for the IRR beyond the fourth degree.[4] What this means is that solving for the IRR requires a trial-and-error process similar to the one used to estimate the YTM for a bond. Fortunately, financial calculators or computer spreadsheets make this process manageable, but be warned that in the case of multiple roots, these procedures give the IRR closest to your starting guess. We didn't worry about this for the bond's YTM because there is only ever one change in cash flow sign: when we buy the bond and there is a cash outflow followed by a series of cash inflows. We illustrate the calculation process in Example 13.5.

---

**EXAMPLE 13.5** | Calculating the IRR

Revisit Example 13.1 and estimate the IRR of the project under consideration.

**Solution**   The IRR solves the following expression:

$$\left[\frac{\$5,000}{(1+IRR)^1} + \frac{\$5,000}{(1+IRR)^2} + \frac{\$8,000}{(1+IRR)^3}\right] = \$12,000$$

Solving by trial and error is very complicated, even for this simple three-period problem. We start by estimating the IRR and try IRR = 20 percent. Substituting this rate into the equation gives us a value on the left side of $12,268.52. Therefore, the IRR must be higher than this, because the PV amount is greater than the $12,000 initial outlay. So now we try IRR = 25 percent, which produces a corresponding value on the left side of $11,296. We can conclude that 25 percent is too high. Therefore, we know that the rate we are looking for is between 20 percent and 25 percent.

We can obtain a reasonable approximation by using linear interpolation, which was discussed in Chapter 6:

| Discount Rate | V(LHS) |
|---|---|
| 20% | $12,268.52 |
| IRR | $12,000 |
| 25% | $11,296 |

---

[4]This is known in mathematics as the Abel-Ruffini theorem, published in 1824.

We find the IRR as follows:

$$\frac{IRR - 20}{25 - 20} = \frac{\$12,000 - \$12,268.52}{\$11,296 - \$12,268.52}$$

$$\frac{IRR - 20}{5} = \frac{-\$268.52}{-\$972.52}$$

$$IRR - 20 = 5 \times \frac{-\$268.52}{-\$972.52} = 1.3805$$

So, IRR ≈ 21.38 percent.

This is one case for which it is worthwhile to use a financial calculator or Excel—and this is only a three-period project. Imagine if it were a 20-year project!

**EXAMPLE 13.5** | Solution Using a Financial Calculator

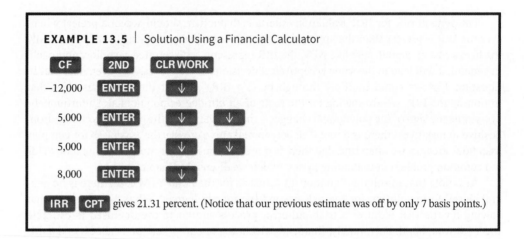

**IRR** **CPT** gives 21.31 percent. (Notice that our previous estimate was off by only 7 basis points.)

Notice in Example 13.5 that the IRR of 21.31 percent exceeds the firm's cost of capital of 15 percent, which implies that the project increases shareholder value and should be accepted. This will always be the case when the NPV is positive, as it was in this case (recall from Example 13.3 that the NPV for this project was +$1,388.67). In fact, this should be obvious when we look at equations 13.3 and 13.4, because the NPV will equal zero when the IRR equals $k$. Therefore, when IRR is greater than $k$, the NPV will be positive because the PV will be higher when we use a *lower* discount rate (i.e., $k$) than it will be when we use the *higher* discount rate (i.e., IRR). This is intuitive: a positive NPV implies that a project earns a return (IRR) that is higher than the cost of funds (which is reflected in $k$). Similarly, we can say that a negative NPV implies that IRR is less than $k$, and vice versa.

**EXAMPLE 13.6** | Calculating the IRR When Future CFs Represent an Annuity

Estimate the IRR for the project in Example 13.4.

**Solution**   We will skip the long trial-and-error version of the solution, because it is unnecessary here: the future CFs are equal at $5,000 (i.e., they form an annuity), except for the ending cash flow of $6,000, which we can view as another $5,000 payment plus an extra $1,000 that can be discounted separately. Therefore, we can solve the IRR using a financial calculator.

**EXAMPLE 13.6** | Solution Using a Financial Calculator

Input the following variables:

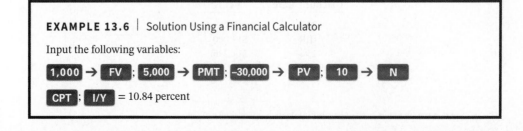

The problem can also be solved using the IRR function, as shown here.

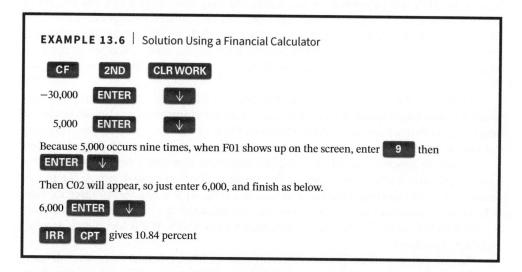

**EXAMPLE 13.6** | Solution Using a Financial Calculator

CF  2ND  CLR WORK

−30,000  ENTER  ↓

5,000  ENTER  ↓

Because 5,000 occurs nine times, when F01 shows up on the screen, enter 9 then
ENTER  ↓

Then C02 will appear, so just enter 6,000, and finish as below.

6,000  ENTER  ↓

IRR  CPT  gives 10.84 percent

## A Comparison of NPV and IRR

The relationship between the NPV and the IRR can be seen from an NPV profile diagram, such as the one shown in **Figure 13.3** for two separate projects. NPV profiles depict the NPV of a project for various discount rates.

Figure 13.3 graphs the NPV against the discount rate. It shows how the NPV depends critically on the appropriate discount rate—of course, this is obvious from the NPV equation (i.e., Equation 13.3). As the discount rate increases, the NPV decreases and eventually becomes negative for higher discount rates. By definition, we know that the IRR occurs at the discount rate that makes the NPV equal zero. This corresponds to the point at which the NPV curve crosses the $x$-axis in Figure 13.3. For project A, the IRR is 12 percent, while for project B, the IRR is 15 percent. The diagram shows that whenever the discount rate exceeds the IRR, we have a negative NPV, and whenever the discount rate is less than the IRR, we have a positive NPV. We have previously noted these relationships between NPV and IRR.

We can make several useful observations from Figure 13.3. We begin by noting that the decision to accept the project depends on the discount rate used ($k$). According to either

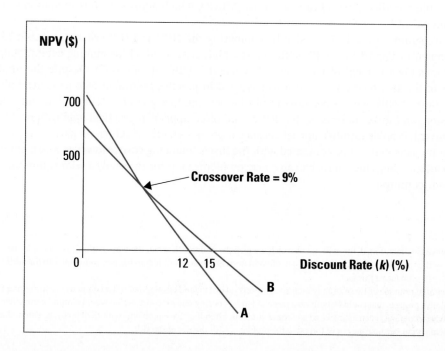

**FIGURE 13.3** **Two NPV Profiles**

the NPV or the IRR evaluation criteria, project A should be accepted if *k* is less than 12 percent, because the NPV will be positive for these discount rates and because IRR will be greater than *k*. Conversely, if *k* is greater than 12 percent, project A should be rejected, because the NPV will be negative and because IRR is less than *k*. Similarly, project B should be accepted if *k* is less than 15 percent, and it should be rejected if *k* is greater than 15 percent. So if we are independently evaluating a project using either the NPV or the IRR evaluation criteria, we should arrive at the same conclusion.[5]

Figure 13.3 also shows that we can rank projects differently when we use NPV than when we use IRR. Suppose, for example, these two were **mutually exclusive projects**, which means that a firm has to decide between them and can accept only one.[6] Because the IRR of project B is 15 percent, while the IRR of project A is only 12 percent, project B appears to be superior, according to the IRR approach. However, when we use the NPV approach, we arrive at different rankings depending on the firm's cost of capital (*k*). In this example, the NPV profiles cross over and have the same NPV at one special discount rate, which is the **crossover rate**. If *k* is greater than the crossover rate of 9 percent, then project B is preferable to project A, because it generates a higher NPV. If *k* is less than 9 percent, project A is preferred.

The two approaches rank projects differently, so which one is better? To answer this question, we have to understand why the slopes of the two NPV profiles differ. The slope reflects the change in the NPV as the discount rate changes. If a project has cash flows that are far in the future, then changes in the discount rate have a big impact on the NPV of the project. In this case, project A has cash flows that are further away, so at a high discount rate, these cash flows are valued less and the NPV falls by more than the NPV of project B. As a result, beyond the crossover point, B is preferred to A, because A's far-off cash flows are worth less, whereas at lower discount rates, the reverse happens and A is preferred to B.

The fact that the NPV decision depends on the discount rate, whereas the IRR decision does not, is important and relates to the different reinvestment rate assumptions of the two techniques. The NPV assumes that all cash flows are reinvested at one consistent discount rate (i.e., the cost of capital). The IRR assumes instead that all cash flows are reinvested at the IRR. If we remember that most projects will have low or zero NPV in a competitive market and that the discount rate reflects the opportunity cost or the all-in required return of the firm's investors, it is clear that the NPV assumption is more realistic. To put it another way, if an executive estimates an IRR of, say, 30 percent because they find a wonderful project, the executive is then implicitly assuming that the cash flows generated by this wonderful project can be reinvested in another similarly wonderful project. This means that the executive is assuming that they have many wonderful projects, which is not normally a very realistic assumption. In Appendix 13A, we discuss an adjustment to the traditional calculation of IRR, called the modified internal rate of return (MIRR), which adjusts for this limitation of the traditional IRR.

We summarize this discussion by comparing the NPV and IRR criteria in **Table 13.1**. As shown in Figure 13.1, NPV is the most widely used method for making capital budget decisions (74.6 percent of CFOs said they use it "often" or "always"). Despite the limitations of the IRR method, it is also widely used in practice (sitting at 68.4 percent), falling just short of NPV. This is because, in most cases, the IRR gives the "correct" accept/reject decision, and the criticisms of the IRR do not often appear in practical applications. More important, it holds intuitive appeal because it provides a rate of return on particular investment projects that can be compared with the firm's financing costs. However, as we pointed out earlier, using this approach can cause problems later for the analyst who is unaware of its shortcomings.[7]

**mutually exclusive projects** a situation in which the acceptance of one project precludes the acceptance of one or more alternative projects

**crossover rate** a special discount rate at which the net present value profiles of two projects cross (are equal)

[5]As previously mentioned, this will not be true if we pick the wrong IRR when there are multiple reversals in the signs of the cash flows. This does not happen often in normal projects, but it does happen sometimes, to the surprise of analysts who forget this fact.
[6]A common example of two mutually exclusive projects relates to land development. If a company is considering two alternative projects that could be built on a piece of land, choosing one for construction would eliminate the other.
[7]We have sometimes been approached by former students when they have problems with their analysis. Often, these problems occur because they have forgotten the problems with the use of the IRR.

**TABLE 13.1** NPV versus IRR

| Issue | NPV | IRR |
|---|---|---|
| **1.** Future cash flows change sign | NPV works the same way for both accept/reject and ranking decisions. | Multiple IRRs may result—in this case, the IRR cannot be used for either accept/reject or ranking decisions. |
| **2.** Ranking projects | Higher NPV implies greater contribution to firm wealth—it is an absolute measure of wealth. | The higher IRR project may have a lower NPV, and vice versa, depending on the appropriate discount rate and the size of the project. For example, would analysts prefer an IRR of 100 percent on $1,000 or 20 percent on $1 million? |
| **3.** Reinvestment rate assumed for future cash flows received | Assumes all future cash flows are reinvested at the discount rate. This is appropriate because it treats the reinvestment of all future cash flows consistently, and $k$ is the investor's opportunity cost. | Assumes cash flows from each project are reinvested at that project's IRR. This is inappropriate, particularly when the IRR is high. |

Finance in the News 13.2 discusses investing in the art world and the internal rate of return that is earned on this class of investment compared with a broad stock market index and the return on government-issued debt.

## 13.2 Finance in the News    Superrich Keep Spending on Art

Buyers paid about $2 billion for artworks this past week at auction houses Christie's, Sotheby's, and Phillips, as New York's spring art season kicked into gear. Art from Rashid Johnson and Francis Bacon set new artist records, as did blue-chip works such as a Claude Monet haystack painting and a Louise Bourgeois Spider sculpture.

Heading into 2019, confidence in the art market had taken a "U-turn" into anxiety, according to ArtTactic. Despite that, trade-war worries, and stock market volatility, these auctions show a pretty happy and healthy luxury market, full of superrich buyers as competitive as ever over precious works.

Christie's spring auctions sold a total of $1.1 billion; Sotheby's (ticker: BIG), more than $800 million; and Phillips, more than $134 million.

Evan Beard, who runs the National Art Services business at Bank of America's private bank, sees three main reasons for buyers' optimism in the face of disquieting news on global trade: Tariffs largely affect consumer cyclicals, such as technology; art and luxury goods are mostly manufactured in Europe; and art buyers can be economically irrational.

"The folks buying those works are doing it for reasons of cachet and status," Beard told Barron's.

If anything, they're more sensitive to interest rates, the opportunity cost of buying a work, he says, adding that "prevailing low interest rates is much more correlated to aggressive buying of art and luxury goods than tariffs brinkmanship between two large economies."

The trade conflict presents risks, however: For years, Chinese buyers have been seen as the great hope for growth. Worsening economic relations might create trouble for cross-border business. But "no one expects that," Beard said.

The art market can be slow to notice paradigm shifts, as it is far more "sentiment driven," he said. Sotheby's hosted a major auction the day Lehman Brothers collapsed in 2008, "and it had absolutely no impact—it was a successful sale," Beard added.

Setting the tone this past week, a painting by Paul Cézanne sold for $59.3 million on the first night of the auctions, above a high estimate of $40 million. Robert Rauschenberg's Buffalo II, forecast to fetch at least $50 million, sparked a 10-minute phone bidding war on Wednesday, before selling for $88.8 million.

The auctions were good to living artists, who present market risk, given that they may yet produce more work and dilute their existing catalogue. Jeff Koon's Rabbit sold for $91 million, an auction record for a living artist. The stainless-steel sculpture was bought by art dealer Bob Mnuchin, father of U.S. Treasury Secretary Steven Mnuchin. Bidding skyrocketed for paintings by Brooklyn's Dana Schutz and Los Angeles' Jonas Wood, which sold for four times their presale estimates, setting records.

Before the auctions began, risk takers signed up as "third-party guarantors," submitting "irrevocable bids" on at least 84 works for an estimated $611 million combined, The Wall Street Journal's Kelly Crow reported. [Guarantors take up to a third of the sellers' proceeds above the agreed-upon bid.]

Beard calculates that last fall's sales generated about a 5% **internal rate** of **return** for sellers, trailing the S&P 500 index's year-to-date **return**, but beating Treasuries'. He expects about the same this season. But, again, that's not really why people buy art. Big-ticket lots are "something two billionaires, maybe more, are going to wrestle over," he said.

No one bids hoping for a great IRR; that already has gone to whoever bought the work from the artist, for, say, $1 million, as with Koons' Rabbit.

Auction-buying is for status, he said, and is defined by "the tenacity and testosterone of a couple of bidders."

Of the other techniques mentioned in Figure 13.1, we will, as noted, discuss modified internal rate of return in Appendix 13A. We will also discuss real options in Chapter 14; however, this is not really an independent technique but, rather, a more sophisticated implementation of the techniques discussed earlier. While accounting rate of return is important to determine how a project will affect the firm's financial statements and is valuable for very large projects, it is not commonly used for small projects. Similarly, adjusted present value can be ignored for our purposes. It is a sophisticated technique that is very difficult to implement and rarely used. This leaves the last technique mentioned, the profitability index.

## Profitability Index (PI)

**profitability index (PI)**
another discounted cash flow approach used to evaluate capital expenditure decisions; defined as the ratio of a project's discounted net incremental after-tax cash inflows over the discounted cash outflows, which are usually the initial after-tax cash outlays

The **profitability index (PI)** is another DCF approach used to evaluate capital expenditure decisions. Like the IRR, the PI is a *relative* measure of project attractiveness. It is defined as the ratio of a project's discounted net incremental after-tax cash inflows divided by the discounted cash outflows, which are usually the initial after-tax cash outlays. Equation 13.5 shows how the PI is calculated.

$$PI = \frac{PV \text{ (cash inflows)}}{PV \text{ (cash outflows)}}$$
[13.5]

It should be obvious from Equation 13.5 that projects with ratios greater than one should be accepted because, by definition, they have positive NPVs; projects with ratios less than one should be rejected. It is also obvious that larger ratios are favoured because their NPVs are higher. The discount rate to be used is the same as the one used for calculating the NPV, which is usually the firm's cost of capital. Therefore, we observe the following relationship between NPV and PI: when the PI is greater than one, the NPV is greater than zero (and vice versa); when the PI is less than one, the NPV is less than zero, and vice versa.

---

**EXAMPLE 13.7** | Calculating the PI

Revisit Example 13.1 and estimate the PI of the project under consideration.

**Solution**　With a discount rate of 15 percent as before, we get:

$$PI = \frac{PV \text{ (cash inflows)}}{PV \text{ (cash outflows)}} = \frac{\frac{\$5,000}{(1.15)^1} + \frac{\$5,000}{(1.15)^2} + \frac{\$8,000}{(1.15)^3}}{\$12,000} = \frac{\$13,388.67}{\$12,000} = 1.116$$

Therefore, the project should be accepted because the PI is greater than 1. Of course, we knew this already, because we found that its NPV was greater than 0 in Example 13.3, and that its IRR was greater than $k$ in Example 13.5.

---

We could also have answered Example 13.7 by solving for the NPV (by long hand, by using a financial calculator, or by using Excel) and adding the NPV to the initial outlay of $12,000 to find the numerator of the equation in Example 13.7 (i.e., $1,388.67 + $12,000 = $13,388.67), and then proceeding as in Example 13.7.

---

**EXAMPLE 13.8** | Calculating the PI When Future CFs Represent an Annuity

Revisit Example 13.4 and estimate the PI of the project under consideration.

**Solution**

$$PI = \frac{\$5,000 \left[ \frac{1 - \frac{1}{(1.12)^{10}}}{0.12} \right] + \frac{\$1,000}{(1.12)^{10}}}{\$30,000} = \frac{\$28,573.09}{\$30,000} = 0.952$$

Therefore, this project should be rejected because its PI is less than 1.

As discussed in Example 13.7, the PI produces the same accept/reject decisions as do the NPV and, normally, the IRR. In addition, the PI does not suffer from two of the weaknesses of the IRR, because it uses one consistent and reasonable discount rate and because it works even when future cash flows change signs. Like the IRR, the PI is attractive because it can be expressed as a percentage, so rather than 1.116 in Example 13.7, we could have said the PI was 111.6 percent.

One weakness that the PI shares with IRR is that it is a relative measure and not an absolute measure of wealth, like NPV. Although it is useful as a starting point for ranking projects when some projects must be rejected, final decisions should be based on which projects maximize the total NPV for the firm. (We will elaborate on this point later in this chapter, when we discuss mutually exclusive projects and capital rationing.) In this case, the PI is often used when firms are constrained by their capital budget, as we will discuss.

---

### Concept Review Questions

1. Why is the payback period a poor evaluation technique?
2. What discount rate do we use to determine the NPV of a project and why?
3. Why do we sometimes get multiple IRRs for a project?
4. What are the reinvestment rate assumptions underlying NPV and IRR?
5. What is the crossover rate?
6. Is the PI rule consistent with the NPV rule?

---

## 13.3 | Independent and Interdependent Projects

### LEARNING OBJECTIVE 13.3

Analyze independent projects and explain how they differ from interdependent projects.

---

**Independent projects** have no relationship with one another. For example, a firm's decision to accept one project (e.g., purchase a new computerized accounting system) has no impact on the firm's decision to accept another project that is independent of the first one (e.g., replace an aging piece of machinery that is used in the production process). As long as there are no capital spending restrictions,[8] the decision rule is to accept projects that generate a positive NPV (or an IRR greater than $k$, or a PI greater than one), and reject those that don't. However, many projects do have relationships with one another. These types of projects are referred to as **interdependent projects**. We must take these relationships into account in our decision process, as discussed next.

Capital expenditures can represent **contingent projects**. A firm can implement investment A (e.g., purchase the newest accounting software package) only if it also undertakes investment B (e.g., change the operating system to Microsoft Windows). In other words, one project is feasible only if another project is undertaken either beforehand or simultaneously. For these types of investment projects, the rule is to estimate the total NPV of *all* contingent projects and accept them if this total NPV is positive. In such a situation, even if the initial project (e.g., the updating of an operating system) does not generate a positive NPV on its own, it can be accepted if the benefits provided by the contingent projects more than offset the losses it generates. In fact, this is often the case with operating systems.

**independent projects**   projects that have no relationship with one another; accepting one project has no impact on the decision to accept another project

**interdependent projects**   projects that are related such that accepting or rejecting one has an impact on the value of other projects under consideration

**contingent projects**   projects for which the acceptance of one requires the acceptance of another either beforehand or simultaneously

---

[8]We will elaborate on this point later in the chapter, when we discuss mutually exclusive projects and capital rationing.

Mutually exclusive projects, as defined earlier, require that a firm choose among two or more alternatives. In other words, if a firm is considering replacing an old computer system with either system A or system B, it would never buy both, even if the analysis suggested that they both generated positive NPVs.[9] In such a case, the firm must decide which project is best. Recall from our previous discussion of IRR versus NPV that whenever a firm has to rank projects, NPV is superior. The decision will be straightforward if the projects have identical time horizons, because the firm will choose the one that produces the highest NPV, assuming the NPV is positive. However, when the projects under consideration have different time horizons, the firm must take this into consideration in its analysis.

Projects with unequal lives can be compared by using two approaches, both of which assume that the project can be replicated at the end of its useful time horizon. The **chain replication approach** involves finding a time horizon into which all the project lives under consideration divide equally and then assuming each project is repeated until they all reach this horizon. For example, if a firm is comparing a three-year project with a four-year project, it would assume the three-year project could be replicated four times and that the four-year project could be replicated three times (for a total of 12 years each). It then finds the PV of all the replicated projects for each individual project and chooses the one that generates the highest NPV over the entire period, assuming the NPV is positive. This approach is demonstrated in Example 13.9.

**chain replication approach**
a way to compare projects with unequal lives by finding a time horizon into which all the project lives under consideration divide equally and then assuming each project repeats until it reaches this horizon

---

**EXAMPLE 13.9** | The Chain Replication Approach

A company is considering three separate, mutually exclusive projects, A, B, and C. Project A requires a $10,000 cash outlay today and is expected to generate after-tax cash flows of $7,000 in year 1 and $6,000 in year 2. Project B requires an $8,500 cash outlay today and is expected to generate after-tax cash flows of $4,000 in year 1 and $7,000 in year 2. Project C requires a $10,600 cash outlay today and is expected to generate after-tax cash flows of $5,000 for each of the next three years. Assume that 15 percent is the appropriate discount rate, and use the chain replication approach to determine which project the firm should choose.

**Solution**   Notice that projects A and B both have two-year time horizons, so we can calculate their respective NPVs and choose the one that generates the higher NPV, provided it is positive.

$$NPV_A = \left[\frac{\$7{,}000}{(1.15)^1} + \frac{\$6{,}000}{(1.15)^2}\right] - \$10{,}000 = \$10{,}623.82 - \$10{,}000 = +\$623.82$$

$$NPV_B = \left[\frac{\$4{,}000}{(1.15)^1} + \frac{\$7{,}000}{(1.15)^2}\right] - \$8{,}500 = \$8{,}771.27 - \$8{,}500 = +\$271.27$$

Therefore, the firm would choose project A over project B.
Now the firm would compare project A with project C, which has a three-year life. First, it would calculate the NPV for project C.

$$NPV_C = \left[\frac{\$5{,}000}{(1.15)^1} + \frac{\$5{,}000}{(1.15)^2} + \frac{\$5{,}000}{(1.15)^3}\right] - \$10{,}600 = \$11{,}416.13 - \$10{,}600 = +\$816.13$$

Project C is also attractive. Notice that it generates an NPV ($816.13) that is higher than the one A generates ($623.82) over a two-year period. If C produced an NPV that was lower than (or equal to) project A's NPV, which was generated over a shorter period, the firm would accept A over C. However, because this is not the case, the firm needs to determine the project that is best over a six-year period (because the projects have two- and three-year horizons).

The firm would now estimate the total NPV generated by projects A and C over a six-year time horizon, assuming A is replicated twice and C is replicated once.

Assuming A generates an NPV at time 0 of $623.82 (over years 1 and 2), the same NPV at time 2 (over years 3 and 4), and the same NPV at time 4 (over years 5 and 6), the total NPV at time 0 is as follows:

$$NPV_A = \left[\$623.82 + \frac{\$623.82}{(1.15)^2} + \frac{\$623.82}{(1.15)^4}\right] = \$623.82 + \$471.70 + \$356.67 = \$1{,}452.19$$

Similarly, for project C, the total NPV is as follows:

$$NPV_C = \left[\$816.13 + \frac{\$816.13}{(1.15)^3}\right] = \$816.13 + \$536.62 = \$1{,}352.75$$

Therefore, project A should be accepted instead of project C, because it would generate a higher total NPV over a six-year period than project C would, assuming both projects can be replicated.

---

[9]If A and B were *independent* projects that generated positive NPVs, a firm would accept both projects.

The chain replication approach is a reasonable method for solving Example 13.9, which had to extend to only six years to find a common time horizon for projects A and C. But what if we had to compare a five-year project with a seven-year project? This would force us to go out to 35 years, which would be cumbersome indeed! Fortunately, another approach leads to the same conclusions as the chain replication approach, but is much more computationally efficient. The **equivalent annual NPV (EANPV) approach** finds the NPVs of individual projects and then determines the amount of an annual annuity that is economically equivalent to the NPV generated by each project over its respective time horizon.[10] We then choose the project that generates the highest EANPV, which is defined in Equation 13.6.[11] Examples 13.10 and 13.11 demonstrate how the EANPV approach could be used.

**equivalent annual NPV (EANPV) approach** a way to compare projects by finding the net present value of the individual projects and then determining the amount of an annual annuity that is economically equivalent to the NPV generated by each project over its respective time horizon

$$\text{EANPV} = \frac{\text{Project NPV}}{\left[\dfrac{1 - \dfrac{1}{(1 + k)^n}}{k}\right]} \qquad [13.6]$$

where $n$ is the project's time horizon, and the denominator is the PV annuity factor for an $n$-year annuity, as discussed in Chapter 5.

---

**EXAMPLE 13.10** | The EANPV Approach

Redo Example 13.9 using the EANPV approach instead of the chain replication approach.

**Solution** We already solved for the NPVs of all three projects in the solution to Example 13.9, so we will not replicate those calculations here. The NPVs for A, B, and C were $623.82, $271.27, and $816.13, respectively, and that would rule out project B, because it has the same lifespan as A but has a lower NPV. Therefore, all we need to do is compare the EANPV of A with the one for C.

$$\text{EANPV}_A = \frac{\text{Project NPV}_A}{\left[\dfrac{1 - \dfrac{1}{(1 + k)^2}}{k}\right]} = \frac{\$623.82}{\left[\dfrac{1 - \dfrac{1}{(1.15)^2}}{0.15}\right]} = \frac{\$623.82}{1.625709} = \$383.72$$

$$\text{EANPV}_C = \frac{\text{Project NPV}_C}{\left[\dfrac{1 - \dfrac{1}{(1 + k)^3}}{k}\right]} = \frac{\$816.13}{\left[\dfrac{1 - \dfrac{1}{(1.15)^3}}{0.15}\right]} = \frac{\$816.13}{2.283225} = \$357.45$$

---

**EXAMPLE 13.10** | Solution Using a Financial Calculator

Project A: `0` → `FV` ; `623.82` → `PV` ; `2` → `N` ; `15` → `I/Y` ;

`CPT` → `PMT` $= -383.72$

Project C: `0` → `FV` ; `816.13` → `PV` ; `3` → `N` ; `15` → `I/Y` ;

`CPT` → `PMT` $= -357.45$

---

Therefore, the firm would choose project A over project C, just as we determined by using the chain replication approach. The EANPV approach shows that project A generates a higher NPV per year than does project C.

---

[10]This approach is sometimes referred to as the equivalent annual annuity (EAA) approach, since essentially what it involves is estimating an annual NPV annuity.

[11]It would be incorrect to take the NPV and divide by the number of years required to generate the NPV, because this would disregard the time value of money.

**EXAMPLE 13.11** | Applying the EANPV Approach

Assume you managed to obtain some data that would allow you to compare the long-term contract for Brad Richards of the NHL's New York Rangers (at the time) to the one that was previously "rejected" by the NHL for the New Jersey Devils' Ilya Kovalchuk. Kovalchuk's contract was rejected (and New Jersey was fined $3 million and otherwise penalized) because it was deemed to be structured in a manner to circumvent the "salary cap" that the NHL imposes on its teams (by, for example, calculating small—well, relatively small—continuing payments far into the future). The details are provided here.

| Year | Richards ($Million) | Kovalchuk ($Million) |
|------|---------------------|----------------------|
| 1 | 12 | 6 |
| 2 | 12 | 6 |
| 3 | 9 | 11.5 |
| 4 | 8.5 | 11.5 |
| 5 | 8.5 | 11.5 |
| 6 | 7 | 11.5 |
| 7 | 1 | 11.5 |
| 8 | 1 | 10.5 |
| 9 | 1 | 8.5 |
| 10 | 0 | 6.5 |
| 11 | 0 | 3.5 |
| 12 | 0 | 0.75 |
| 13 | 0 | 0.55 |
| 14 | 0 | 0.55 |
| 15 | 0 | 0.55 |
| 16 | 0 | 0.55 |
| 17 | 0 | 0.55 |

**Solution**   At first glance, you might be tempted to say that Kovalchuk's contract is superior—clearly the total payments are much higher ($102 million versus $60 million). Therefore, it is not surprising that the NPV is also much higher ($72.73 million versus $49.46 million). However, this ignores the fact that Richards' contract is only over 9 years, while Kovalchuk's spans 17 years, with some very small payments in the future. While Richards would be older after 9 years and perhaps not able to command as high a salary as he could early in his career, barring injuries he could probably sign another contract and earn much more than $0.55 million per year.

So how do you determine which contract is better given the "unequal lives"? One approach would be to determine the EANPV. It turns out that the EANPV is higher for Richards' contract ($7.27 million per year) than for Kovalchuk's ($6.94 million). For this situation, however, this might not be the "precise" answer because it assumes their contracts would be "replicated." This is unlikely since both players will age and market salary conditions will change. Nonetheless, it does provide a useful comparison of the two contracts.

## Concept Review Questions

1. What is the difference between independent and mutually exclusive projects?
2. How can we compare two choices, one involving a wooden bridge lasting 10 years and another involving a steel bridge lasting 25 years that costs more?

## 13.4 | Capital Rationing

**LEARNING OBJECTIVE 13.4**

Explain what capital rationing is and how it affects firms' investment criteria.

Theoretically, firms should accept all independent projects that generate positive NPVs, which will enhance firm value. However, in practice, firms often face capital budget constraints, which may force them to turn down attractive projects. Theoretically, this constraint should not exist in an efficient market because firms should always be able to source new financing to take advantage of investment opportunities that generate returns (i.e., IRRs) that exceed the cost of raising the required investment funds. However, these constraints may arise because of market inefficiencies, which restrict the firm's ability to raise funds in the capital markets, or because they are imposed internally (i.e., management may set certain budget limits that cannot be exceeded). When firms face capital budget constraints, it is common to say that **capital rationing** prevails—that is, investment capital must be rationed among available investment projects.

**Figure 13.4** depicts the cash flow situation for CP in fiscal 2018. With $2,712 million in cash flow from operations, and cash flows for investing of $1,458 million, CP had positive free cash flow and was the antithesis of a capital-constrained company. It could accept all the projects listed on its **investment opportunity schedule (IOS)** until the IRR equalled its weighted average cost of capital (WACC)[12]—or until the last project accepted had an NPV of zero—and still have money left over to pay a dividend or pay down debt. However, suppose CP had only $1,000 million of internal funds (most companies would envy this situation); in that case, it could not accept all its projects and would be capital rationed unless it raised new financing, which many firms are reluctant to do.

The important point about capital rationing is that the cost of capital is no longer the appropriate opportunity cost, since the firm no longer has sufficient funds to accept all the projects that it should. This means that now the cash flows generated by a project can be reinvested at a higher rate than assumed by the cost of capital, because the firm is leaving some positive-NPV projects on the table because of lack of financing. The reinvestment rate assumption underlying the IRR has more validity, because the firm can reinvest the cash flows from a project at the IRR of the marginal project, rather than at its cost of capital. The problem is that the IOS schedule is rarely the nice smooth downward-sloping function shown in Figure 13.4.

**capital rationing**   when the total amount of investment capital available is restricted and must be allocated among available investment projects

**investment opportunity schedule (IOS)**   the internal rate of return expected on each potential investment opportunity, ranked in descending order

**FIGURE 13.4**   Canadian Pacific's Investment and Internal Cash Flow (Optimal Investment), 2018

---

[12]We will discuss the WACC in detail in Chapter 20 and explain why we have defined it the way we have. At this stage, simply treat the WACC as the company's hurdle rate for evaluating investments.

When firms with limited funds have to choose among discrete, lumpy projects, they must consider the cost of the investment, because this is constrained by the capital budget. In this case, we can first estimate the NPVs and the IRRs, but we can't fully rely on either of them as a criterion, because they ignore the cost of the investment and the capital constraint. The PI is often a useful starting point because it gives the highest present value relative to the initial cash outlay, which is constrained. However, the final decision should be based on which combination of projects generates the highest total NPV while satisfying the capital budget constraint. This is because the PI, like the IRR, may lead to incorrect decisions because it is a relative measure. Example 13.12 shows the correct procedure for dealing with capital rationing.[13]

---

**EXAMPLE 13.12** | Capital Rationing

A firm is considering the following independent investments:

| Project | CF$_0$ (Initial Cash Outlay) | NPV | Project Life | PI |
|---------|------------------------------|-----|--------------|-----|
| A | $100,000 | $13,646 | 4 | 1.136 |
| B | $50,000 | −$3,342 | 6 | 0.933 |
| C | $80,000 | $10,558 | 3 | 1.132 |
| D | $60,000 | $4,320 | 7 | 1.072 |
| E | $75,000 | $10,825 | 5 | 1.144 |
| F | $90,000 | $7,225 | 6 | 1.080 |

a. In the absence of capital rationing, which projects should be selected? Determine the size, in total dollars, of the firm's capital budget under this scenario. What is the total NPV of all the projects selected?

b. Now suppose a capital budget constraint of $250,000 is placed on new investments. Determine which projects should be selected. What is the total NPV under this scenario? What is the loss to the company from the capital rationing constraint?

**Solution**

a. In the absence of capital rationing, the firm should select projects A, C, D, E, and F because they all have positive NPVs and are assumed to be independent.

Capital budget = $100,000 + $80,000 + $60,000 + $75,000 + $90,000 = $405,000

Total NPV = $13,646 + $10,558 + $4,320 + $10,825 + $7,225 = $46,574

b. The firm should take on the combination of positive-NPV projects that maximizes total NPV, within the given budget constraints.

| Combination | Total NPV | Capital Budget | Within Budget |
|-------------|-----------|----------------|---------------|
| A, C, D | $28,524 | $240,000 | Yes |
| A, D, E | $28,791 | $235,000 | Yes |
| C, E, F | $28,608 | $245,000 | Yes |
| A, C, E | $35,029 | $255,000 | No |

If the capital budget constraint is fixed, the firm should select projects A, D, and E.[14] The total NPV is now only $28,791 under capital rationing, and the "loss" to the company is $46,574 − $28,791 = $17,783. Notice that the loss of $17,783 equals the sum of the NPVs of the two forgone positive-NPV projects (i.e., C and F). This is detrimental to firm value as it is forced to turn down two "good" positive-NPV investments because the firm lacks the capital to proceed with them. The PI criterion indicates A, C, and E have the highest PIs, but unfortunately they cost more than the budget allows. Although the PIs are a good starting point, they rarely give the optimal solution.

Although we have come up with the maximum NPV given the budget constraint, in reality the firm would conduct further analysis. For example, the company would forecast its budget for the following year and look at the deferral possibilities. It may turn out, for example, that C can be deferred and it is better to go with A and E this year and roll over the excess in the budget to take on C and other projects next year.

---

[13]This problem can be solved using integer programming techniques, but rarely is the problem difficult enough to justify the analysis.
[14]If there was $5,000 "slack" in the constraint, the combination of A, C, and E would generate the highest NPV; however, it requires a $255,000 outlay, which exceeds the $250,000 constraint.

How relevant is a situation of capital rationing? Theoretically, financing should always be available for good (i.e., positive-NPV) projects, which by their nature should increase firm value. This belief underlies the justification for using the WACC as the discount rate and basing decisions on the NPV criterion. However, this does not always hold true in practice, as financing is often limited or is sometimes simply not available, as happened to many firms during the financial crisis of 2008–9. Consider, for example, Maple Leaf Foods Inc.'s decision in October 2011 to shut down six meat plants, upgrade others, and shed 1,500 jobs. Maple Leaf CEO Michael McCain suggested that part of the impetus for such a drastic decision was that Canadian factories were "starved for capital."[15]

# The Appropriate Discount Rate

As mentioned in the previous section, it is usually appropriate to use a firm's weighted average cost of capital (WACC) as the discount rate to evaluate long-term investment projects. **Figure 13.5** shows that this is, in fact, the case in practice. Baker, Dutta, and Saadi's survey of Canadian CFOs suggests that 63.6 percent of CFOs use the WACC often or always. The WACC represents the after-tax cost of the average dollar of long-term financing to the firm, and we assume that firms will finance long-term investments by using long-term financing. This is appropriate if the project under consideration is an "average" risk investment for the company—in other words, if it is a typical investment and will not substantially change the asset mix of the company.

However, if a company is considering a project that is "atypical" in the sense that it is either more or less risky than the average investment for that company, this fact should be reflected in the discount rate used to evaluate that project. For example, a company could be considering introducing a new product line that entails greater (or lower) risks than its traditional offerings. Under these circumstances, a higher discount rate should be used for projects that possess above-average risk, and a lower discount rate should be used for projects that possess below-average risk. If a firm does not adjust the discount rate under these circumstances and merely uses a constant WACC to select investment projects, it will make inappropriate decisions. In particular, this could lead the firm to reject positive-NPV low-risk projects that appear unattractive if evaluated using a discount rate that is too high. It could also lead the firm to accept negative-NPV high-risk projects that appear attractive if evaluated using a discount rate that is too low.

A good example of this problem is provided by Marathon Oil Corporation in the United States. For a time, the company was made up of two divisions: the original oil company and US Steel. Suppose that the oil company's WACC was 8 percent and the steel company's was 12 percent. If each division made up 50 percent of the overall company, the company WACC would be 10 percent. Applying the company WACC of 10 percent to capital projects would cause some of the steel division's bad projects, with IRRs of 11 percent, to be accepted, even if stand-alone steel companies were rejecting similar projects. Likewise, good oil projects earning 9 percent would be rejected, even if they were being accepted by equivalent oil companies. If Marathon Oil did this over time, it would gradually become a bad steel company, because it would be doing things that good steel companies weren't. Similarly, it would be rejecting many good opportunities that good oil companies would have accepted.

The common response to the Marathon Oil problem is to estimate risk-adjusted discount rates (RADRs) by adjusting the cost of capital up or down based on the risk level and

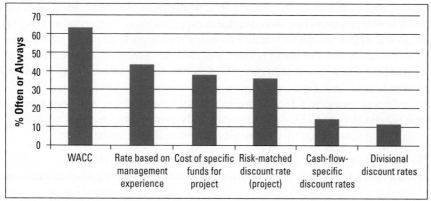

**FIGURE 13.5** Survey Results of Discount Rates Used by Canadian Firms When Evaluating a New Project

**Source:** Data from Baker, Kent H., Dutta, Shantanu, and Saadi, Samir, "Corporate Finance Practices in Canada: Where Do We Stand?" *Multinational Finance Journal* 15, no. 3/4 (September/December 2011), Table 5, p. 176.

[15]McNish, Jacquie, "Maple Leaf's Big Move." *The Globe and Mail*, October 20, 2011, p. B1/5.

**pure play approach** estimating betas and the risk associated with an investment and the optimal financing by estimating the WACC of firms in an industry associated with the project

financing of a specific project under consideration. For example, Marathon Oil would use a discount rate of 8 percent in its oil division and 12 percent in its steel division. Estimating these different discount rates involves estimating betas and the risk associated with the investment and the optimal financing. One method of doing this is the **pure play approach**, which involves estimating the WACC of firms in an industry associated with the project. Another approach is to estimate beta for the project by regressing the return on assets (ROA) of the project against the ROA of the market index. Similar techniques can be used to estimate the appropriate project cost of debt and then to estimate the appropriate overall cost of capital.

Several practical difficulties are associated with estimating RADRs. For example, it may be difficult to find an appropriate company to use in the pure play approach, and the regression of project ROA on an index ROA may lead to an inaccurate beta measure. In addition, intuitive adjustments made by managers are subjective in nature and prone to error—though they may be no more so than other techniques. However, despite the associated difficulties, estimating RADRs is preferable to blindly applying one constant discount rate to all projects, regardless of their individual risk characteristics.

---

### Concept Review Questions

1. What complications arise when firms are rationed in terms of their available capital budget?
2. Explain how firms should decide which projects to accept and which to reject when capital rationing exists.
3. How and why do we adjust the discount rate for multi-divisional firms?
4. What mistakes can occur if firms do not make the appropriate adjustments?

---

## 13.5 | International Considerations

**LEARNING OBJECTIVE 13.5**

Explain the importance of international foreign direct investment both inside and outside Canada.

**Figure 13.6** depicts foreign direct investment (FDI), which represents investment in real assets and companies by firms. All types of investments across national boundaries are increasing as the world becomes one giant marketplace. Figure 13.6 shows that both outbound FDI by Canadian firms and inbound FDI from foreign countries have increased through time. Figure 13.6 also shows that both outbound and inbound FDI move in similar fashion, although there was a noticeable spike in outbound FDI investing by Canadian firms in 2015. This implies they are affected by similar factors. In fact, their correlation over the 2010 to 2018 period was very high, at 0.98. Firms make these foreign investments for many reasons: they may want to take advantage of cheaper resources, whether labour or materials; they may want to enter new markets; or they may want to have access to new technology. To exploit such opportunities, many firms establish foreign subsidiaries or enter into joint ventures with firms that are in foreign countries.

Regardless of the motives, foreign investment is a capex decision, and firms have to apply the same criteria as they do for domestic projects. However, some practical difficulties arise when attempting to apply the NPV evaluation process to foreign investments:

- How do we account for the political risk of expropriation or insurrection, or the imposition of foreign exchange controls that prevent the firm's getting its investment back?[16]

---

[16]A survey of companies found that for foreign capital budgeting decisions in which there is substantial political risk, companies tend to use a method such as the payback period. In contrast, in cases where there is little political risk, companies tend to use the net present value method. **Source:** Holmen, Martin, and Pramborg, Bengt, "Capital Budgeting and Political Risk: Empirical Evidence." *Journal of International Financial Management and Accounting* 20, no. 2 (Summer 2009), pp. 105–34.

**FIGURE 13.6** Foreign Direct Investment In and Out of Canada (2010–2018) ($Billion)

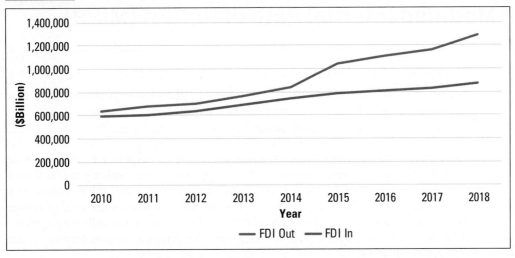

**Source:** Data from Statistics Canada website, Cansim 36-10-0008-01

- How do we account for other potential legal and regulatory issues where local competitors may have privileged access to cronies in the government?
- How do we adjust for foreign exchange risk because cash flows are denominated in a foreign currency?
- How do we adjust for the taxes paid in a foreign currency and the possibility that when they are paid back to Canada, they may be taxed again?
- How do we finance a foreign project if the local markets are poorly developed?

Many large Canadian firms are dealing more frequently with these important questions, which are covered in a multinational business finance course. The Export Development Corporation of Canada (EDC) also helps Canadian firms export and make FDI decisions. EDC is a branch of the Canadian government and offers extensive insurance programs to mitigate some of the risks of FDI. For example, EDC offers political risk insurance (PRI) against

- breach of contract risk
- conversion risk
- expropriation risk (including gradual or creeping expropriation)
- risk of non-payment by a sovereign obligor
- political violence risk
- repossession risk
- transfer risk

The terms of the PRI vary from one country to another depending on the risk, but in evaluating FDI, the PRI can, in part, be removed by charging the project with a 1-percent PRI fee based on the capital committed, which is the normal fee for comprehensive political risk insurance for a typical developing country.

The techniques developed in chapters 11 and 12 to manage financial risk are often used to manage foreign exchange risk. Canadian firms routinely use forwards to sell future foreign cash flows forward into Canadian dollars and may also issue foreign currency debt to hedge their investment. Therefore, FDI project analysis involves all the standard domestic problems, plus a variety of complex institutional problems that make it considerably more difficult than domestic project analysis.

## Concept Review Questions

1. What is so different about evaluating FDI compared with domestic projects?
2. Name some unique risks that can arise when evaluating FDI.

| APPENDIX 13A | # The Modified Internal Rate of Return (MIRR)

**LEARNING OBJECTIVE 13.6**

Explain how the modified internal rate of return (MIRR) is calculated and why this represents a conceptual improvement over the way the IRR is calculated.

**modified internal rate of return (MIRR)** a variation of the IRR that allows adjustments for the reinvestment rates on cash flows that are generated during the life of the project

The assumption, built into the internal rate of return mathematics, that all cash inflows are reinvested at the internal rate of return may be too aggressive a supposition to make. We can modify this assumption by calculating the return on the project with a more realistic view of the reinvestment of cash inflows. The result is the **modified internal rate of return (MIRR)**. The accept/reject criteria for the MIRR is similar to that of the IRR: if a project has a MIRR greater than its cost of capital, it is acceptable; if a project's MIRR is less than its cost of capital, it is not acceptable.

Let's start with a project, X, that has a project cost of capital of 10 percent and the following cash flows:

| Year | End-of-Year Cash Flow |
|------|----------------------|
| 0 | −$10,000 |
| 1 | 4,200 |
| 2 | 4,200 |
| 3 | 4,200 |

The IRR of project X is 12.51 percent, and the NPV is $444.78. The IRR of 12.51 percent assumes all cash flows are reinvested and earn a return of 12.51 percent, which is well above the firm's cost of capital. To illustrate the role of reinvestment, let's assume that the company has no other projects in which to reinvest any of these cash flows. We calculate the return on project X in this situation by comparing the investment of $10,000 with what is available at the end of the project. If each cash flow that comes in is deposited in an account that earns no interest, the company will have $12,600 at the end of three years.

Therefore,

$PV = \$10,000$

$FV = \$12,600$

$N = 3$

Solve for I/Y → I/Y = 8.01 percent

Given no other use of the cash, the company has a return, which is the MIRR, of 8.01 percent.

Under these circumstances, project X is not acceptable.

Now let's assume that the company has other investment opportunities available that earn 5 percent. We can represent this in a diagram, indicating the cash flows and how they "grow" when reinvested at 5 percent:

| Year | 0 | 1 | 2 | 3 |
|------|---|---|---|---|
| Cash Flow | −$10,000 | $4,200 | $4,200 | $ 4,200 |
| | | | $4,200 (1 + 0.05)$^1$ | 4,410 |
| | | | $4,200 (1 + 0.05)$^2$ | 4,630.50 |
| | | | | $13,240.50 |

In table form, we have:

| Year | End-of-Year Cash Flow | Future Value of Reinvested Cash Flows, End of Period 3 |
|------|----------------------|--------------------------------------------------------|
| 0    | −$10,000             |                                                        |
| 1    | 4,200                | $ 4,630.50                                             |
| 2    | 4,200                | 4,410.00                                               |
| 3    | 4,200                | 4,200.00                                               |
| Total |                     | $13,240.50                                             |

The future value of the reinvested cash flows, FV, is $13,240.50, and therefore the MIRR is 9.81 percent:

$PV = \$10,000$

$FV = \$13,240.50$

$N = 3$

Solve for $I/Y \rightarrow I/Y = 9.81$ percent

Again, the project is not acceptable because the return on the project is less than the project's cost of capital.

A common assumption for reinvestment opportunities uses the company's cost of capital, which is the return on the typical or average project of the company. The reasoning is simple: if the company has cash flows from a project, they will most likely be reinvested in a typical project for the company. Using the company's cost of capital of 10 percent, the MIRR becomes 11.61 percent.[17] In this case, the project is acceptable because the MIRR of 11.61 percent exceeds the project's cost of capital of 10 percent.

The MIRR is sensitive to the reinvestment assumption, as we show in **Figure 13A.1**, where we graph the MIRR against the reinvestment rate for project X; the better the reinvestment opportunities, the better the return on the project, as measured by MIRR.[18] In general, the "normal" assumption used in calculating MIRR is that funds will be reinvested at the firm's cost of capital, so if you see a reported MIRR and there is no explicit mention of the reinvestment rate used, it is reasonable to assume the firm used its cost of capital.

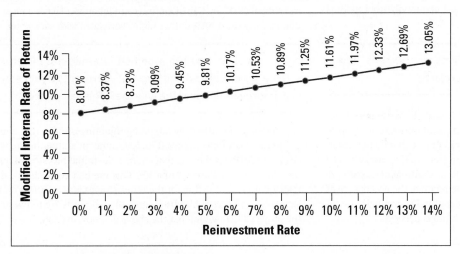

**FIGURE 13A.1** Modified Internal Rate of Return for Project X

## Concept Review Questions

1. What improvement does MIRR represent over traditional IRR?

2. When will a calculated MIRR be greater than a calculated IRR?

---

[17]If you are checking this calculation, the future value of the cash flows, considering reinvestment at 10 percent, is $13,902.
[18]Using Microsoft's Excel Solver function, we can solve for the reinvestment rate at which the MIRR is equal to the project's cost of capital. We do this by setting the goal of the MIRR equal to 10 percent and then solve for the reinvestment rate that is applied against the project's cash inflows. For project X, the project is acceptable as long as the return on reinvested cash flows is equal to or greater than 5.5329 percent.

# Review

## Summary

In this chapter, we discuss the capital budgeting process for companies. We focus most of our discussion on the criteria (payback period, discounted payback period, NPV, IRR, and profitability index) that are commonly used to evaluate capital expenditure decisions. We show why NPV is the preferred measure, although the other criteria also provide useful information. Finally, we consider three specific complexities: those caused by capital rationing, those caused by risk differences within multi-divisional firms, and those caused by FDI. In Chapter 14, we will show exactly how to calculate the cash flows and will work through more detailed examples. We will also delve further into the complex issue of deciding what "incremental" means in practice.

## Summary of Learning Objectives

### 13.1 Describe the capital budgeting process and explain its importance to corporate strategy.

Capital budgeting refers to the process by which a firm makes capital expenditure decisions by (1) identifying investment alternatives, (2) evaluating these alternatives, (3) implementing the chosen investment decisions, and (4) monitoring and evaluating the implemented decisions.

### 13.2 Identify and apply the main tools used to evaluate investments.

The main tools used to evaluate investments include payback period, discounted payback period, net present value (NPV) analysis, internal rate of return (IRR), and profitability index (PI). The most commonly used method is NPV and the second most commonly used method is IRR.

### 13.3 Analyze independent projects and explain how they differ from interdependent projects.

Independent projects are analyzed standing alone. As long as there are no capital spending restrictions, the decision rule is to accept projects that generate a positive NPV and reject those that do not. Interdependent projects are related to other projects. In this case, we need to consider the relationships among projects. Contingent projects are projects for which the acceptance of one requires the acceptance of another, either beforehand or simultaneously. For mutually exclusive projects, the firm must decide which project is best.

### 13.4 Explain what capital rationing is and how it affects firms' investment criteria.

Capital rationing occurs when the total amount of investment capital available is restricted and must be allocated among available investment projects. Projects are ranked on an investment opportunity schedule using NPV and are selected based on positive NPV from the highest to the lowest, until the maximum capital input is reached.

### 13.5 Explain the importance of international foreign direct investment both inside and outside Canada.

All types of investments across national boundaries are increasing as the world becomes one giant marketplace. Both outbound foreign direct investment (FDI) by Canadian firms and inbound FDI have increased dramatically since 2010 and are highly correlated with each other.

### 13.6 Explain how the modified internal rate of return (MIRR) is calculated and why this represents a conceptual improvement over the way the IRR is calculated.

We calculate the MIRR by adjusting the reinvestment rate applied to interim cash flows received to determine an ending future value (FV). The MIRR is the rate that equates the initial investment outlay (i.e., the PV) with this ending FV. This method represents a more realistic way of adjusting for the reinvestment rate assumed on projects, since we do not blindly assume that all funds are reinvested at the project's IRR, which may be above or below average.

## Key Terms

bottom-up analysis, p. 13-4
capital budgeting, p. 13-2
capital expenditures, p. 13-2
capital rationing, p. 13-21
chain replication approach, p. 13-18
contingent projects, p. 13-17
crossover rate, p. 13-14
discounted cash flow (DCF) methodologies, p. 13-5

discounted payback period, p. 13-7
equivalent annual NPV (EANPV) approach, p. 13-19
five forces, p. 13-4
incremental, p. 13-8
independent projects, p. 13-17
interdependent projects, p. 13-17
internal rate of return (IRR), p. 13-11
investment opportunity schedule (IOS), p. 13-21

modified internal rate of return (MIRR), p. 13-26
mutually exclusive projects, p. 13-14
net present value (NPV), p. 13-8
payback period, p. 13-6
profitability index (PI), p. 13-16
pure play approach, p. 13-24
risk-adjusted discount rate (RADR), p. 13-8
top-down analysis, p. 13-5

## Equations

| Equation | Description | Formula | Page |
|---|---|---|---|
| [13.1] | Payback Period | Find T such that: $CF_1 + CF_2 + CF_3 + \cdots + CF_T = CF_0$ or $\sum_{t=1}^{T} CF_t = CF_0$ | p. 13-6 |
| [13.2] | Discounted Payback Period | Find T such that: $\dfrac{CF_1}{(1+k)^1} + \dfrac{CF_2}{(1+k)^2} + \dfrac{CF_3}{(1+k)^3} + \cdots + \dfrac{CF_T}{(1+k)^T} = CF_0$ or $\sum_{t=1}^{T}\dfrac{CF_t}{(1+k)^t} = CF_0$ | p. 13-6 |
| [13.3] | Net Present Value | $NPV = \dfrac{CF_1}{(1+k)^1} + \dfrac{CF_2}{(1+k)^2} + \dfrac{CF_3}{(1+k)^3} + \cdots - CF_0 = \sum_{t=1}^{n}\dfrac{CF_t}{(1+k)^t} - CF_0$ | p. 13-8 |
| [13.4] | Internal Rate of Return | $\dfrac{CF_1}{(1+IRR)^1} + \dfrac{CF_2}{(1+IRR)^2} + \dfrac{CF_3}{(1+IRR)^3} + \cdots = CF_0$ or $\sum_{t=1}^{n}\dfrac{CF_t}{(1+IRR)^t} = CF_0$ | p. 13-11 |
| [13.5] | Profitability Index | $PI = \dfrac{PV\ (\text{cash inflows})}{PV\ (\text{cash outflows})}$ | p. 13-16 |
| [13.6] | Equivalent Annual NPV | $EANPV = \dfrac{\text{Project NPV}}{\left[\dfrac{1 - \dfrac{1}{(1+k)^n}}{k}\right]}$ | p. 13-19 |

# Questions and Practice Problems

## Multiple Choice Questions

1. **(LO 13.1)** What will probably happen if a firm does not invest effectively?

   **a.** The firm could still maintain its competitive advantage.

   **b.** The cost of capital of the firm will be unchanged.

   **c.** The long-term survival of the firm will be affected.

   **d.** The short-term performance will be unaffected.

2. **(LO 3.1)** Which of the following is *not* a critical factor that Porter identified in determining industry attractiveness?

   **a.** Bargaining power of suppliers

   **b.** Entry barriers

   **c.** Rivalry among competitors

   **d.** Bargaining power of government

3. **(LO 13.2)** What is the NPV for a project with an after-tax initial investment of $22,000 and five equal cash flows of $10,200 at the start of each year, beginning with the fourth year? The appropriate discount rate is 16 percent. Should it be accepted?

   **a.** −$603.45; reject

   **b.** $2,820.00; accept

   **c.** $6,791.20; accept

   **d.** $11,397.80; accept

4. **(LO 13.2)** When will NPV and IRR have different rankings when we evaluate two mutually exclusive projects? $IRR_A < IRR_B$.

   **a.** Discount rate $(k)$ < crossover rate

   **b.** Discount rate $(k)$ < $IRR_A$

   **c.** Discount rate $(k)$ > crossover rate

   **d.** Discount rate $(k)$ > $IRR_B$

5. **(LO 13.2)** Which project(s) should a firm choose when the projects are independent? When they are mutually exclusive? Suppose both are within the capital budget and $k$ is 12 percent for both projects.

   Project A: $CF_0 = -\$5,000$; $CF_1 = \$1,500$;
   $\qquad CF_2 = \$4,000$; $CF_3 = \$2,000$

   Project B: $CF_0 = -\$5,000$; $CF_1 = \$1,500$;
   $\qquad CF_2 = \$1,500$; $CF_3 = \$4,500$

   **a.** Both projects; project A

   **b.** Both projects; project B

   **c.** Project B; project B

   **d.** Neither project; neither project

6. **(LO 13.2)** What is the IRR of the following project? After-tax initial investment = $8,000; $CF_1 = \$2,000$; $CF_2 = \$3,000$; $CF_3 = \$4,000$; $CF_4 = \$5,000$. If $k = 18$ percent, should you accept the project?

   **a.** 16.25 percent; no

   **b.** 20.50 percent; yes

   **c.** 22.66 percent; yes

   **d.** 25.33 percent; yes

7. **(LO 13.2)** We should *reject* a project if:

   **a.** NPV > 0.

   **b.** IRR > required rate of return.

   **c.** discounted payback period < required period.

   **d.** PI < 1.

8. **(LO 13.3)** Which of the following statements about IRR and NPV is *incorrect*?

   a. NPV and IRR yield the same ranking when evaluating projects.

   b. NPV assumes that cash flows are reinvested at the cost of capital of the firm.

   c. A project may have multiple IRRs when the sign of the cash flow changes more than once.

   d. IRR is the discount rate that makes the NPV equal zero.

9. **(LO 13.4)** Which of the following would *not* happen if a firm uses WACC for all projects, regardless of the individual risks of the projects?

   a. Accept a high-risk project with negative NPV

   b. Reject a low-risk project with positive NPV

   c. Accept an average-risk project with positive NPV

   d. Reject a high-risk project with positive NPV

10. **(LO 13.4)** To estimate risk-adjusted discount rates, a firm could do all of the following, *except:*

   a. use the cost of capital ± risk premium method.

   b. regress the ROA of the project on the ROA of the whole firm.

   c. regress the ROA of the project on the ROA of the market index.

   d. use the pure play approach.

11. **(LO 13.5)** What is *true* about evaluating FDI compared with domestic projects?

   a. We cannot use the NPV rule to evaluate FDI.

   b. We cannot use IRR to evaluate FDI.

   c. FDI has some unique risks.

   d. FDI always has negative NPV.

12. **(LO 13.5)** Which is *not* the unique risk of FDI compared with domestic projects?

   a. Interest rate risk

   b. Political risk of expropriation or insurrection or the imposition of foreign exchange controls that prevent the firm getting its investment back

   c. Potential legal and regulatory issues where local competitors may have privileged access to cronies in the government

   d. Foreign exchange risk because cash flows are denominated in a foreign currency

13. **(LO 13.6)** What improvement does MIRR represent over traditional IRR?

   a. It calculates the NPV of a project.

   b. It relaxes the assumption that cash flows are reinvested at IRR.

   c. It always gives the same accept/reject decision as IRR.

   d. It always gives the same accept/reject decision as NPV.

14. **(LO 13.6)** In which of the following situations is MIRR likely to be greater than a calculated IRR?

   a. Reinvestment rate is the same as the cost of capital.

   b. Reinvestment rate is less than the cost of capital.

   c. Reinvestment rate is greater than IRR.

   d. A firm deposits cash flows in a zero-interest account.

## Practice Problems

### Basic

15. **(LO 13.2)** A farmer cultivates a certain crop. It costs $125,000 to buy the seeds, prepare the ground, and sow the crop. Harvesting the crop, which will happen in one year's time, will cost $55,000. If the crop can then be sold for $190,000 and assuming an interest rate of 8%, calculate the net present value (NPV) of this investment to the farmer.

16. **(LO 13.2)** Ada is in contract negotiations with a publisher for her upcoming fourth novel. The publisher has made her two offers: (1) receive $150,000 up front in addition to annual royalties expected to total $39,000 per annum at the end of each year for five years, or (2) receive $300,000 up front and no royalties. Which offer should Ada accept assuming a discount rate of 7.5%?

17. **(LO 13.2)** Bert has just been hired by your company as a summer co-op student and has been assigned to assist you. Bert is puzzled about why your company is calculating IRR and payback periods for investment projects. According to Bert's finance textbook, NPV gives the best measure of the impact of a project on shareholder wealth.

   a. Explain to Bert the advantages and disadvantages of payback and IRR.

   b. Which evaluation techniques are the most popular with companies (i.e., your company's clients)?

   c. Given the disadvantages and limitations of payback and IRR, why do you think so many CFOs continue to use them as criteria for evaluating projects?

18. **(LO 13.2)** State the drawbacks of the payback period and discounted payback period.

19. **(LO 13.2)** An investment has the following cash inflows: $2,500 at the end of the first year, $2,000 at the end of the second year, and $1,500 at the end of the third year. What is the discounted payback period if the discount rate is 0 percent and the initial cash outflow is $5,000?

20. **(LO 13.4)** Briefly explain the pure play method for estimating beta.

21. **(LO 13.4)** LargeCo has a capital budget of $100 million to invest in projects. It has evaluated six independent projects and the results of the analysis are summarized in the following table.

| Project | Initial Investment | NPV | Salvage Value |
|---|---|---|---|
| A | $10 million | $5 million | $3 million |
| B | $90 million | $15 million | $5 million |
| C | $25 million | $8 million | $2 million |
| D | $40 million | $7 million | $1 million |
| E | $25 million | $3 million | $5 million |
| F | $15 million | $2 million | $8 million |

   a. If the company was not capital constrained, which projects should it undertake?

   b. Given its capital constraint, which projects do you recommend that it undertake?

   c. How can the firm increase its capital budget?

### Intermediate

22. **(LO 13.1)** For the following decisions, indicate whether they are examples of a bottom-up analysis or a top-down analysis:

   a. Replacing the printing press at a newspaper

   b. A newspaper's decision to sell all its print services and move into online data services

   c. A pharmaceutical company's research investment in developing a cholesterol drug

   d. A car company's research investment in developing a cholesterol drug

   e. Your decision to take an English literature elective rather than a sociology elective this semester

   f. Your decision to do a degree in business rather than medicine

*Use the following information to answer practice problems 23 to 30 about BigCo Manufacturing Company.*

You have been hired as a consultant for BigCo Manufacturing Company. BigCo is considering several projects and has provided the forecasted annual after-tax cash flows in Table 1.

**TABLE 1** **Annual Cash Flows (All Amounts in $Million)**

|  | Project A | Project B | Project C | Project D | Project E | Project F | Project G |
|---|---|---|---|---|---|---|---|
| Year 0 | −1,200 | −2,400 | −8,500 | −5,100 | −5,300 | −11,000 | −3,200 |
| Year 1 | 500 | 1,500 | 2,000 | 4,800 | 2,500 | 3,000 | 1,500 |
| Year 2 | 1,000 | 1,200 | 2,000 | 1,000 | 3,000 | 2,000 | 1,200 |
| Year 3 | 1,200 | 300 | 8,000 | 6,000 | 5,000 | 1,000 | 500 |
| Year 4 | 2,500 | 500 | 2,000 | −3,000 | 1,000 | 2,000 | |
| Year 5 | 3,000 | 200 | 2,500 | −4,000 | 3,000 | 3,000 | |

**23. (LO 13.2)** Assume that BigCo's cost of capital for all the projects is 10 percent. Calculate the NPV, IRR, payback period, discounted payback, and profitability index for each project in Table 1. The firm requires a payback period of 2 years and a discounted payback period of 2.5 years.

| | Project A | Project B | Project C | Project D | Project E | Project F | Project G |
|---|---|---|---|---|---|---|---|
| NPV | | | | | | | |
| IRR | | | | | | | |
| Payback | | | | | | | |
| Discounted payback | | | | | | | |
| Profitability index | | | | | | | |

**24 (LO 13.2) a.** If the firm is not capital constrained and the projects in Table 1 are independent, which projects should the firm undertake using the following criteria?

    **i.** NPV

    **ii.** IRR

    **iii.** Payback period

    **iv.** Discounted payback period

**b.** Are any of your recommendations, based on the criteria in part a, contradictory? Explain how that would be possible.

**25. (LO 13.2) a.** If the firm is not capital constrained and the projects in Table 1 are mutually exclusive, which project should the firm undertake using the following criteria?

    **i.** NPV

    **ii.** IRR

    **iii.** Payback period

    **iv.** Discounted payback period

    **v.** Profitability index

**b.** Are any of your recommendations, based on the criteria in part a, contradictory? Explain how that would be possible.

**26. (LO 13.4)** Using projects A to F in Table 1, construct BigCo's investment opportunity schedule. If BigCo has $9,000 (millions) available for investment, which projects should it undertake (assume all projects are independent)? Justify your recommendations to the CEO of BigCo.

**27. (LO 13.2)** The CFO of BigCo is concerned about the sensitivity of his decisions to the choice of discount rate. For projects A, C, and E, plot the NPV profiles on the same graph. Does the NPV ranking of the three projects remain the same for every possible discount rate? Explain your observations.

**28. (LO 13.2)** Calculate the crossover rate for projects B and C from Table 1.

**29. (LO 13.4)** You have conducted an analysis of BigCo and have found that the firm is made up of two different divisions: Satellites-RUs (a satellite launching service) and a bank. Projects A to G are all related to satellite-launching technology. You have also examined the industry of each division and have found the following:

| Firm | Industry | Cost of Capital |
|---|---|---|
| Crash'n Burn | Satellite launching | 27% |
| Liddy's Launchers | Satellite launching | 20% |
| Reliable Bankers | Banking | 5% |
| Reliance Bank | Banking | 4% |
| VBigCo | Satellite launching and banking | 10% |

**a.** What is the appropriate discount rate for projects A to G? Describe your assumptions.

**b.** What will be the impact on the shareholder value of BigCo if the firm used 10 percent, the overall WACC, in the valuation of the satellite-launching projects (A to G)?

**30. (LO 13.2)** The CEO of BigCo has just bought a fancy financial calculator and calculated the IRR and NPV of Project D from Table 1. He is utterly confused. His calculator is telling him that the IRR is 20.72 percent, but when he uses a cost of capital of 1 percent, the NPV is negative. The CEO expects that if the IRR is greater than the cost of capital then the NPV should be positive. How are the CEO's observations possible? Hint: See the NPV profile of Project D.

**31. (LO 13.2)** Cutler Compacts will generate cash flows of $30,000 in year 1 and $65,000 in year 2. However, if it makes an immediate investment of $20,000, it can instead expect to have cash streams of $55,000 in total in year 1 and $63,000 in year 2. The appropriate discount rate is 9 percent.

**a.** Calculate the NPV of the proposed project.

**b.** Why would IRR be a poor choice in this situation?

**32. (LO 13.2)** Elaine is evaluating two investments—investment 1 has a profitability index (PI) of 2.4 while investment 2 has a PI of 1.2. As these investments are mutually exclusive, Elaine is recommending investment 1. The chair of the board of BigCo has asked for your comments on Elaine's recommendation.

**33. (LO 13.2)** Daria is evaluating two investments—investment 1 will produce cash flows for the next five years and has an NPV of $1,000. Investment 2 will produce cash flows for the next 15 years and has an NPV of $700. Based on this analysis, Daria recommends investment 1. Discuss whether this conclusion is appropriate.

**34. (LO 13.2)** What is the crossover rate ($r$) given the following?

Project A: $CF_0 = -\$25{,}000$; $CF_1 = \$6{,}600$; $CF_2 = \$10{,}200$; $CF_3 = \$19{,}800$

Project B: $CF_0 = -\$20{,}000$; $CF_1 = \$5{,}400$; $CF_2 = \$7{,}800$; $CF_3 = \$16{,}500$

**35. (LO 13.2)** If the NPV of a project is $5,360 and its after-tax initial investment is $12,050, what is its PI? Should the firm accept the project? Does the PI yield the same decision as the NPV? (Assume all the cash flows except for the initial investment are inflows.)

**36. (LO 13.2)** SK Inc. has two projects as follows:

| Project | Initial $CF$ | $CF_1$ | $CF_2$ | $CF_3$ | $CF_4$ |
|---------|------------|--------|--------|--------|--------|
| A | −$2,500 | $800 | $1,200 | $900 | $2,000 |
| B | −3,000 | 750 | 1,500 | 1,000 | 4,000 |

If SK set 2.6 years as a cut-off period for screening projects, which projects will be selected, using the payback period method?

**37. (LO 13.2)** Which project(s) will be selected if the company uses the discounted payback period method in practice problem 34 and the discount rate is 12 percent?

**38. (LO 13.2)** State the decision rules for NPV, IRR, PI, and the discounted payback period. List two possible consequences of using IRR.

**39. (LO 13.2)** SK Inc. has a project that requires a $60,000 after-tax initial investment and produces these after-tax cash flows at each year-end: $20,000; $22,000; −$8,000; $38,050; $55,000; and $16,000. The appropriate domestic discount rate is 16.6 percent. The project is in another developing country, where extra risk is assumed to be 3.8 percent. Calculate the project's NPV. Should SK Inc. accept or reject the project?

**40. (LO 13.2)** Calculate the NPV and IRR of the following project and check whether they produce the same decision. After-tax initial investment is $66,777; after-tax cash flows at each of the following six year-ends are $20,000. The year-end cash flow at year 7 is $40,000. Assume $k$ is 18 percent.

**41. (LO 13.2)** Your truck has a market value of $60,000. You can sell it to your brother, who agreed to buy it now and pay $75,000 three years from now, or you can sell it to your cousin who agreed to pay you $65,000 at the end of the year. To whom should you sell the truck if your cost of capital is 8 percent?

**42. (LO 13.2)** You are interested in an investment where the initial investment is $118,000 and your required cost of capital is 12 percent. Cash inflows from this project are expected to be $11,400 at the end of the first year and are expected to grow at 4 percent a year indefinitely. Calculate the NPV.

**43. (LO 13.2)** Name one condition under which the discounted payback period will be equal to the payback period.

**44. (LO 13.2)** You have two mutually exclusive projects:

| Year | Cash Flow (A) | Cash Flow (B) |
|------|---------------|---------------|
| 0 | −$160,000 | −$110,000 |
| 1 | 30,000 | 60,000 |
| 2 | 50,000 | 45,000 |
| 3 | 70,000 | 30,000 |
| 4 | 90,000 | 20,000 |

Irrespective of the project, the discount rate is 10 percent. Calculate the payback and discounted payback periods for the projects. Which one will you consider?

**45. (LO 13.2)** Using initial cost of $I_0$, and annual cash inflows of $R$ over $N$ period, express $R$ in terms of $I_0$ and $N$ such that the payback period is equal to its life.

**46. (LO 13.2)** Using NPV, should you invest in a project where the initial cash outflow is $24,000 and the cash inflow in the first year is $1,600 and "grows" at a rate of 3 percent thereafter? Assume cost of capital is 10 percent.

**47. (LO 13.2)** A bond is currently trading at par, which is $1,000. If the bond pays an annual coupon rate of 10 percent, calculate the IRR of this bond.

**48. (LO 13.3)** What are independent projects? What are mutually exclusive projects?

**49. (LO 13.3)** For each pair of investment opportunities, indicate if they are more likely to be mutually exclusive or independent projects. Explain your choices.

  **a.** Cruise line:

    **i.** Build a cruise ship to carry 10,000 passengers

    **ii.** Build two ships each carrying 5,000 passengers

  **b.** Mining company in northern Alberta:

    **i.** Use old open pit mine for waste disposal

    **ii.** Use old open pit mine for fishing and hunting lodge

  **c.** University:

    **i.** Use classroom for tutorials

    **ii.** Use classroom for faculty meetings

  **d.** You:

    **i.** Latte

    **ii.** Cappuccino

  **e.** You:

    **i.** Salad

    **ii.** Steak

**50. (LO 13.5)** What are the practical difficulties when attempting to apply the NPV evaluation process to foreign investments?

## Challenging

**51. (LO 13.3)** Refer to the information for BigCo Manufacturing Company in Table 1. BigCo is debating whether to invest in Project H (a three-year project) or Project D. Project H has cash flow of −$3,500, $1,800, $1,400, and $1,000 (all $million) in years 0, 1, 2, and 3. Determine which project is preferred (assuming that the appropriate cost of capital is 10 percent) using the

  **a.** chain replication approach.

  **b.** equivalent annual NPV approach.

**52. (LO 13.2)** Malcolm, a very junior reporter, has asked for your help with his first article for a major national newspaper. He has provided you with the following excerpt from his article and would like your comments:

> The BathGate Group, one of the few all-equity firms left in Canada, has recently built a widget-manufacturing plant in Whitby. The firm has invested $1 million and, according to our sources, the promised return on the investment (IRR) is over 27 percent! The shareholders of the firm must be ecstatic—they are currently only receiving a return of 10 percent. Just think—in 10 years the value of the plant is expected to be close to $11 million.

  **a.** What is Malcolm assuming about the reinvestment rate? Does it make sense?

  **b.** What is Malcolm assuming about the riskiness of the project? Are the shareholders necessarily happy with this decision?

**53. (LO 13.2)** Longlife Company is considering an investment in Ponce Leon Mineral Baths. The investment has the same risk characteristics as the firm. It is assumed that all cash flows are perpetuities and that there are no taxes. Currently the firm has cash flows of $1,000 a year with required debt payments of $300 per year. The current market value of the firm (debt plus equity) is $13,000. The firm is considering an investment of $5,000 in a project that will generate $610 a year forever. Assume that the firm can continue to borrow at 5 percent.

  **a.** Should the firm undertake the investment?

  **b.** Demonstrate that the investment will increase/decrease shareholder value (show the impact on cash flows to debt holders and equity holders).

**54. (LO 13.2)** The analysis of a two-division company (DV2) has indicated that the beta of the entire company is 1.35. The company is 100-percent equity funded. The company has two divisions: Major League TV (MLTV) and Minor League Shipping (MLS), which have very different risk characteristics. The beta of a pure play company comparable to MLTV is 1.85 while for MLS the beta of a comparable pure play company is only 0.75. The risk-free rate is 3.5 percent and the market risk premium is 6 percent. Assume all cash flows are perpetuities and the tax rate is zero.

  **a.** Calculate the cost of capital of the entire company.

  **b.** The company is evaluating a project that has the same type of risk as MLS. The project requires an initial investment of $10,000 and pays $880 per year forever. Should the company undertake this project? Why or why not?

**55. (LO 13.2)** Westlake Corp. has a capital structure that has 60-percent debt at a cost of 10 percent and 40-percent equity. Westlake's stock has a beta of 1.6, market risk premium of 7 percent, and risk-free rate of 3 percent. The firm has a potential project on hand that requires an initial investment of $125,000 and generates an annual year-end after-tax cash flow of $36,000 for five years. Calculate the IRR of this project. Decide if the project should be accepted or not, assuming the project is less risky for the firm; $T_c = 35$ percent.

**56. (LO 13.2)** A project has an NPV of $55,000. Calculate the cost of capital of this project if it generates the following cash flows for six years after an initial investment of $200,000:

| | |
|---|---|
| Year 1: $40,000 | Year 2: $60,000 |
| Year 3: $80,000 | Year 4: $70,000 |
| Year 5: $60,000 | Year 6: $50,000 |

**57. (LO 13.2)** Based on the cash flows given below, calculate the PI of a project that has a required rate of return of 15 percent. Also, indicate whether the project should be accepted.

| | |
|---|---|
| Year 0: −$90,000 | Year 1: $20,000 |
| Year 2: $40,000 | Year 3: −$15,000 |
| Year 4: $100,000 | |

**58. (LO 13.2)** GiS Inc. has the following four projects on hand:

| Project | Initial CF | Accum. $CF_1$ | Accum. $CF_2$ | Accum. $CF_3$ | Accum. $CF_4$ |
|---|---|---|---|---|---|
| 1 | −$15,067 | $3,385 | $8,965 | $14,078 | $21,495 |
| 2 | −14,543 | 2,578 | 6,865 | 12,095 | 19,067 |
| 3 | −8,565 | 3,097 | 5,674 | 9,883 | 15,688 |
| 4 | −6,500 | 2,955 | 4,985 | 4,985 | 12,000 |

Note the cash flow in the table is accumulative. Assume that $R_F =$ 5 percent, $ER_M = 12$ percent, firm beta = 1.2, after-tax cost of debt = 6.5 percent. The firm is financed by 40-percent debt and 60-percent equity. Projects 1, 2, and 3 have the same capital structure as the firm, while project 4 has a 1-percent risk premium. Calculate the cost of capital for the four projects using the following methods:

  **a.** The payback period for projects 1, 2, and 3: If the cut-off period for screening projects 1 and 2 is 3.5 years and for project 3 is 2.25 years, which project(s) should be rejected?

  **b.** The discounted payback period method for project 4: If the cut-off period for screening project 4 is 3.25 years, should it be accepted?

**59. (LO 13.2)** You are considering buying a machine that will cost you $15,000. There will be a maintenance cost of $1,200 at the beginning of each year, and the machine will generate cash flows of $5,750 over the next five years. After the five years, the machine will have no salvage value. What is the NPV of this machine if the cost of capital is 10 percent?

**60. (LO 13.3)** MedCo, a large manufacturing company, currently uses a large printing press in its operations and is considering two replacements: the PDX341 and PDW581. The PDX costs $400,000 and has annual maintenance costs of $10,000 for the first 5 years and $15,000 for the next 10 years. After 15 years, the PDX will be scrapped (salvage value is zero). In contrast, the PDW can be acquired for $100,000 and requires maintenance of $30,000 a year for its 10-year life. The salvage value of the PDW is expected to be zero in 10 years. Assuming that MedCo must replace its current printing press (it has stopped functioning), has an 8-percent cost of capital, and all cash flows are after tax, which replacement press is the most appropriate?

**61. (LO 13.3)** GiS Inc. now has the following two projects available:

| Project | Initial CF | After-Tax $CF_1$ | After-Tax $CF_2$ | After-Tax $CF_3$ |
|---|---|---|---|---|
| 1 | −$12,095 | $5,500 | $6,000 | $9,500 |
| 2 | −3,080 | 3,450 | 3,000 | |

Assume that $R_F = 4$ percent, risk premium = 8 percent, and beta = 1.25. Use the chain replication approach to determine which project GiS Inc. should choose if they are mutually exclusive.

**62. (LO 13.3)** Solve practice problem 61 using EANPV.

**63. (LO 13.3)** Stephenson Lawncare has learned that a rival has offered to supply a condominium complex with landscaping services for 10 years for $55,000 up front and a further $18,500 per year. Stephenson Lawncare is looking to make an offer to provide landscaping services for eight years for an upfront cost of $80,000 and a separate yearly payment. Assuming a discount rate of 5%, what would Stephenson's annual payment have to be so that their offer would be equivalent to their rival's offer".

**64. (LO 13.3)** A firm is considering two mutually exclusive projects, as follows. Determine which project should be accepted if the discount rate is 15 percent. Use the chain replication approach. Assume both projects can be replicated.

| Project | Initial CF | After-Tax $CF_1$ | After-Tax $CF_2$ | After-Tax $CF_3$ |
|---|---|---|---|---|
| 1 | −$5,000 | $2,500 | $4,050 | $0 |
| 2 | −3,000 | 750 | 1,750 | 2,000 |

**65. (LO 13.3)** Redo practice problem 64 using the EANPV approach.

**66. (LO 13.4)** Assume that SK Inc. has a capital budget of $250,000. In addition, it has the following projects for evaluation. Determine which project(s) should be chosen, assuming $k$ is 15 percent.

| Project | Initial CF | $CF_1$ | $CF_2$ | $CF_3$ |
|---|---|---|---|---|
| A | −$120,000 | $90,000 | $90,000 | $0 |
| B | −100,000 | 50,000 | 60,000 | 70,000 |
| C | −130,000 | 45,000 | 90,000 | 80,000 |

**67. (LO 13.6)** Project X has a cost of capital of 10 percent and the following cash flows: investment of $20,000 in year 0, cash inflows of $8,500, $6,400, and $11,200 in years 1, 2, and 3.

**a.** What is the IRR? What is the assumption of IRR on reinvesting cash?

**b.** Suppose the cash is deposited in an account with a 4-percent annual interest rate. What is the MIRR?

**c.** Suppose the cash is deposited in an account with a 10-percent annual interest rate. What is the MIRR?

**d.** Suppose the cash is deposited in an account with a 13.83-percent annual interest rate. What is the MIRR?

# Cases

### Case 13.1 | RoadPro's New Project

The Government of Ontario has offered your company, RoadPro Roadways Inc., a contract to transport 50,000 tonnes of asphalt each year for the next five years, as part of a provincial infrastructure project focusing on the province's northern roads. The busy season lasts for four months, beginning after the spring thaw and wrapping up in the fall. As a small transport company owner, this contract is desirable for you but you don't currently have any extra equipment available. To take the contract you would need to purchase three highway tractor units, three trailers, and a wheel loader. The loader and highway tractors could be purchased used, in good condition. However, it is difficult to find a good used asphalt trailer, so the trailers would be purchased new. Your administrative staff is capable of handling the new work without additional help. The contract specifies first right of refusal (a type of call option), meaning you are essentially guaranteed the full tonnage every year. Details, including estimates for cost, are listed in the table below.

**Equipment Costs and Salvage**

| | |
|---|---|
| Used highway tractors (price for one) | $75,000 |
| New asphalt trailers (price for one) | $25,000 |
| Used wheel loader | $65,000 |
| Total fixed asset expected salvage value | $120,000 |

**Expected Revenues and Expenses**

| | |
|---|---|
| Contract revenue | $7.00/tonne |
| Labour | $31,680/season |
| Fuel | $125,000/season |
| Maintenance | $35,000/season |
| Fixed costs* | $40,000/season |
| Initial additional net working capital (NWC) requirement | $25,000 |
| Discount rate | 15% |
| Corporate tax rate | 25% |
| CCA rate | 30% |

*Includes administration, permits, and licensing

The contract specifies that revenue will increase by 2.25 percent annually, to offset inflation. This is an excellent inclusion, but something that concerns you is the effect of inflation on your cost estimates. You estimate that the cost of fuel will increase at 2.5 percent per year while labour, maintenance, and fixed costs will probably increase at 1.5 percent per year. You expect to recover your NWC at the end of the project's life. You are the sole owner of RoadPro and want a 9 percent return after personal taxes from this project. Since you are in the highest tax bracket in Ontario, this means a 15 percent rate of return on the after-tax cash flows earned from the project.

**1.** Forecast the project's initial cash outflows

**2.** Forecast the annual after-tax cash inflows from sales from the contract for each of the next five years assuming the cash inflows occur at the end of each year. Initially assume the base case for capital cost allowances using a 50 percent allowance for the first year.

**3.** Forecast the terminal value for the contract at the end of the last year assuming that Roadpro has no other equipment in the same asset class.

**4.** Calculate the following project values:

**a.** NPV

**b.** IRR

**c.** Payback, in both full and partial years

**5.** Based on the values calculated in the previous question, should Roadpro go with the contract?

**6.** Assume, for this question only, that the NPV calculated earlier was exactly zero. How should this value be interpreted? For an investor, would an NPV of zero be undesirable? If so, explain why or why not.

**7.** Roadpro has to consider the risk involved in this contract. In terms of the NPV, calculate sequentially, not cumulatively, what would happen to the NPV of the project in the following cases:

**a.** The government changes the CCA rules to triple the first-year deduction to 150 percent of the calculated amount instead of 50 percent (as will be the case until 2024 or so).

**b.** You think you will still be working in five years' time, so although the equipment will still be sold, you estimate that the pool will not be wound down.

**c.** You discuss easing your daughter into the business and setting up a small business with her in charge to serve this contract. The company will then pay tax at 15 percent, instead of 25 percent, and she will use an 11 percent discount rate since she is in a much lower personal tax bracket.

**d.** You estimate that on termination you can only recapture 50 percent of the net working capital instead of 100 percent.

**8.** In discussing the contract around the dinner table with your family, a number of questions come up. Qualitatively, assess the importance of the following and discuss how they would affect the value of the project.

**a.** Your spouse indicates that you are going to spend a good part of the limited summer in Northern Ontario supervising your crew, but have not priced in the value of your time. She insists that you should look into hiring a part-time manager to do the job and separate the financial from the operating side of the business.

**b.** Your daughter suggests that a good performance in satisfying this contract will open up additional opportunities, since government contracts like this one come up all the time.

**c.** Your son indicates that you are only earning 9 percent if everything goes well, but you can earn 7 percent on preferred shares and almost that on some bank shares with very little risk.

# Cash Flow Estimation and Capital Budgeting Decisions

Chapter 13 illustrated the capital budgeting process and discussed the most important approaches used to evaluate investment opportunities. However, the inputs to the analysis were largely specified for you. These inputs, such as the size of estimated future cash flows, are critical. This chapter is hands-on, and you'll have many opportunities to practise your skills and estimate inputs yourself.

## 14.1 General Guidelines for Capital Expenditure Analysis

In Chapter 13, we discussed several capital budgeting evaluation criteria (i.e., payback period, discounted payback period, NPV, IRR, and profitability index). All of these methods require an estimate of the present cash outlay, as well as estimates of the future cash flows associated with the investment opportunity. In this chapter, we discuss how to estimate these important inputs into those evaluation procedures. We will need to draw on our discussions in chapters 3 and 4 regarding the firm's financial statements, as well as our knowledge of the capital cost allowance (CCA) system in Canada.

We begin by providing some general guidelines for estimating the cash flows associated with capital expenditure decisions:

1. Estimate all cash flows on an *after-tax* basis, because taxes can play an important role in any investment decision and because we use an after-tax cost of capital to discount these cash flows. As we will show, there are many ways to approach capital budgeting, but one of the most important principles is to compare like with like, which is why we use after-tax cash flows with an after-tax discount rate.

**marginal** or **incremental cash flows** the additional cash flows that result from capital budgeting decisions, generated by new projects

2. Use the appropriate cash flow estimates that represent the **marginal** or **incremental cash flows** arising from capital budgeting decisions, including the changes in existing flows that result from the firm's decisions. For example, suppose a firm is considering introducing a new product line that will generate $100,000 per year in additional after-tax cash flows. However, the introduction of this new product line will "cost" the firm $40,000 in after-tax cash flows as a result of lost sales for an existing product. This is called "cannibalization," and the marginal cash flows that should be used to evaluate the new product line are $60,000 per year (i.e., $100,000 − $40,000).

3. Do *not* include associated interest and dividend payments in estimated project cash flows; they should already be accounted for in the discount rate (i.e., the appropriate cost of capital). This is why we discount with the weighted average cost of capital (WACC), which captures all the financing costs in the discount rate. The WACC is discussed in detail in Chapter 20.

4. Adjust cash flows (particularly the initial cash outlay and the terminal cash flow at the end of the estimated project life) to reflect any additional working capital requirements that are associated with the project. For example, consider a firm that is evaluating a new production process. The process requires that the firm hold additional inventory on hand, which would tie up more funds and would be reflected in the firm's level of working capital (as defined in Chapter 3).[1] This represents a drain of cash that should be considered in the capital budgeting decision, because any funds that are tied up have an associated cost. Of course, a firm could also be considering a process that requires it to hold lower amounts of inventory on hand, which would represent a source of funds for the firm. This should also be considered when evaluating the implementation of that process. Further, we typically assume that any initial change in working capital is reversed at the end of a project's life.[2] This reversal assumption leads to working capital changes that net out to zero through a project's life, but it is important to recognize that the present value of these changes will not generally net out to zero!

**sunk costs** costs that have already been incurred, cannot be recovered, and should not influence current capital budgeting decisions

5. Treat **sunk costs** as irrelevant; we are concerned with future cash flows. Suppose a firm has spent $50,000 to get a project up and running. If something happens to make the project undesirable, the firm should not proceed any further; otherwise, it will simply be "throwing good money after bad." In other words, it should accept the $50,000 loss, which makes more sense than losing another $100,000 on the project. Obviously, this is easier said than done.

**opportunity costs** cash flows that must be forgone as the result of an investment decision

6. Although sunk costs are irrelevant, **opportunity costs** should be factored into cash flow estimates. Opportunity costs represent cash flows that must be forgone as the result of an investment decision. The following example shows the difference between sunk costs and opportunity costs. Consider a firm that purchased a piece of land several years ago for $150,000. Today, the firm is considering whether or not to use the land as the location for a new storage facility. In this situation, the original outlay of $150,000 is a sunk cost and should be ignored. However, the land cannot be considered "free," because the firm always has the option of using it for another purpose or selling it. Assuming the firm could sell this

---

[1]We use the term "working capital" interchangeably with "net working capital." Both terms refer to the difference between current assets and current liabilities.

[2]Recall from basic accounting that an increase in an asset account (inventory and accounts receivable are the assets we usually consider) represents a reduction in cash, whereas an increase in a liability account (accounts payable is the liability we are generally concerned with) represents an increase in cash.

land today at a market price of $200,000, this would represent the opportunity cost of using the land for the storage facility; as such, it should be included in the cost of the project.

7. Determine the appropriate time horizon for the project. We need to know how long a project is likely to continue before it is economical to finish or replace it. In this sense, "abandonment decisions" have to be considered, because projects are finished when it is economical to do so, not when the engineer says the assets are no longer functioning.

8. Ignore intangible considerations that cannot be measured in the financial analysis, unless their impact on cash flows can be estimated. Often, intangible benefits are used to justify poor projects. If there are spinoffs, they should be analyzed and incorporated into the analysis, however difficult it is to do so.

9. Ignore **externalities** in the calculations. Externalities are the consequences that often result from an investment that may benefit or harm unrelated third parties. As with intangible factors, although we do not account for these effects in the financial analysis, they could have a huge impact on the final investment decision.[3] An example is a project that generates employment in a depressed region: it is the government's job to assess the value of these externalities, not the firm's.

**externalities** the consequences that result from an investment that may benefit or harm unrelated third parties

10. Consider the effect of all project interdependencies on cash flow estimates. This issue was discussed in Chapter 13 in connection with mutually exclusive projects and contingent projects. Undertaking a project now could mean a negative NPV in the short term but might give the firm the option to do other things in the future that may generate value.

11. Treat inflation consistently. This harks back to comparing like with like: discount nominal cash flows with nominal discount rates, and real cash flows with real discount rates.

12. Undertake all social investments required by law. This may be obvious, but many social and infrastructure projects must be undertaken even though they have negative rates of return or no definable impact on the value of the firm.

---

## Concept Review Questions

1. How should we treat taxes and inflation when determining the present value of future cash flows?
2. What do we mean by incremental cash flows?
3. What are externalities and opportunity costs?
4. Why do we not deduct interest costs from the cash flows to be discounted?

---

## 14.2 | Estimating and Discounting Cash Flows

**LEARNING OBJECTIVE 14.2**

Estimate the future cash flows associated with potential investments.

Sometimes it is convenient to distinguish among three different categories of cash flows—initial after-tax cash flow, expected annual after-tax cash flow, and ending (or terminal) after-tax cash flow—and estimate each type separately. Each category of cash flow is discussed in this section.

---

[3]This is important to recognize, as we are not suggesting these be ignored. In many cases they could be the deciding factor. We are merely saying that we ignore them for "financial" analysis, which will be one part of the overall investment decision.

# The Initial After-Tax Cash Flow ($CF_0$)

**initial after-tax cash flow ($CF_0$)** the total cash outlay required to initiate an investment project, including the change in net working capital and associated opportunity costs

The **initial after-tax cash flow ($CF_0$)** refers to the total cash outlay that is required to initiate an investment project.[4] It includes additional cash flows, such as the change in net working capital (NWC) and associated opportunity costs, both of which were discussed in the previous section. These items may affect the firm's cash flow, but they cannot be expensed for tax purposes. $CF_0$ differs from the **capital cost ($C_0$)** of an investment, which includes all costs incurred to make an investment operational, such as machinery installation expenses, landclearing costs, and so on. These can be depreciated for tax purposes. The $CF_0$ can generally be estimated using Equation 14.1.

**capital cost ($C_0$)** all costs incurred to make an investment operational, such as machinery installation expenses, land-clearing costs, and so on; these can be depreciated for tax purposes

$$CF_0 = C_0 + \Delta NWC_0 + OC \qquad [14.1]$$

where

$C_0$ = the initial capital cost of the asset

$\Delta NWC_0$ = the change in net working capital requirements (as discussed in the previous section)

$OC$ = the opportunity costs associated with the project (as discussed in the previous section)

Example 14.1 illustrates how to estimate the $CF_0$.

---

**EXAMPLE 14.1** | Calculating $CF_0$

Brennan Co. is evaluating the proposed acquisition of a new milling machine. The machine's base price is $625,000, and it would cost another $25,000 to modify it for special use by the firm. To use the machine, the firm will need to maintain additional raw materials inventory of $100,000. Estimate the firm's associated after-tax cash outlay.

**Solution**

Capital cost = $C_0$ = $625,000 + $25,000 = $650,000

Initial cash outlay = $CF_0$ = $C_0 + \Delta NWC_0 + OC$ = $650,000 + $100,000 + $0 = $750,000

---

Note that, in Example 14.1, the cost of the capital asset is not just the $625,000 purchase price but also all other cash outlays that are needed to get the equipment operational. In this case, the $25,000 in modifications have to be capitalized and then depreciated over the life of the machine because, just like the equipment itself, they generate benefits over the life of the equipment. Generally, in any analysis, costs have to be divided into capitalized costs and expenses. The Canada Revenue Agency (CRA) requires anything that generates future benefits to be capitalized; the value is then expensed through depreciation over future periods. In contrast, costs that generate no future benefits can be expensed immediately and are immediately tax deductible.

**expected annual after-tax cash flows ($CF_t$)** the cash flows that are estimated to occur as a result of the investment decision, comprising the associated expected incremental increase in after-tax operating income and any incremental tax savings (or additional taxes paid) that result from the initial investment outlay

# Expected Annual After-Tax Cash Flows ($CF_t$)

The **expected annual after-tax cash flows ($CF_t$)** are those that are estimated to occur as a result of the investment decision. These cash flows comprise the associated expected incremental increase in after-tax operating income (i.e., the operating CFs), as well as any incremental tax savings (or additional taxes paid) that result from the initial investment outlay. The tax savings are associated with the additional depreciation expenses that may be

---

[4]In fact, this could involve a cash *inflow* rather than an outlay for some projects. For example, if a firm is considering selling a division, it will get the cash today (so $CF_0$ will be negative) and will forgo the future cash flows ($CF_t$) associated with that division, which will be recognized as *negative* cash flows for capital budgeting decision-making purposes. This is the type of analysis a company would have to undertake before deciding to sell off some existing assets and/or cancel future planned investments.

**TABLE 14.1** Common Asset Classes Established by Canada Revenue Agency

| Asset Class | Type of Assets | CCA Rate |
|---|---|---|
| Class 1 | Buildings | 4% |
| Class 8 | Office equipment | 20% |
| Class 10 | Computer hardware, system software | 30% |
| Class 43 | Manufacturing equipment | 30% |
| Class 50 | Computer/hardware | 55% |

charged for tax purposes as a result of the initial investment. Recall from our discussion in Chapter 3 that the amount of depreciation charged for tax purposes is called the capital cost allowance (CCA) and is prescribed by CRA according to the asset class associated with the cash outlay. Consistent with Table 3.3, several common asset classes are listed in **Table 14.1**.

Because CCA is a non-cash expense, and we are trying to estimate cash flows, we have two ways to deal with it. The first approach is to deduct CCA from operating income, then deduct the associated taxes payable, and finally add the amount of the CCA expense back (because it is a non-cash expense). The second approach is to recognize that CCA creates tax savings for the firm in the amount of the CCA expense multiplied by the company's effective tax rate ($T$), which is then added to the after-tax operating income, determined by deducting the taxes associated with the firm's before-tax operating income (before depreciation). These two approaches are shown in **Table 14.2** and illustrated in Example 14.2.

**TABLE 14.2** Two Ways to Determine Cash Flows after Capital Cost Allowance

| (1) Before-tax operating income (before depreciation) | (2) Before-tax operating income (before depreciation) |
|---|---|
| $-$ CCA | $-$ Taxes payable on operating income |
| $=$ Taxable income | $=$ After-tax operating income |
| $-$ Taxes payable | $+$ CCA tax savings |
| $=$ After-tax income | $=$ Net cash flow |
| $+$ CCA (non-cash expense) | |
| $=$ Net cash flow | |

**EXAMPLE 14.2** | Calculating Future Annual $CF_t$

With respect to the milling machine purchase that Brennan Co. was considering in Example 14.1, the firm's production department anticipates the machine will generate an additional $450,000 per year in annual operating revenue, while the associated annual operating expenses are projected to be $325,000 per year. The economic life of the machine is expected to be five years. This milling machine is in asset class 9, which has a CCA rate of 30 percent (declining balance method). Estimate the amount of the annual after-tax cash flow for each year, using both approaches described earlier.

**Solution** For all five years, operating income = operating revenue − operating expense = $450,000 − $325,000 = $125,000

Recall from Chapter 3 that the half-year rule applies in the first year an asset is acquired, which means that only half of the CCA rate is applied in year 1. Therefore, we can estimate CCA in year 1 as:

$$\text{CCA (year 1)} = C_0 \times \text{CCA rate} \times 1/2 = \$650{,}000 \times 0.3 \times 1/2 = \$97{,}500$$

Because the full CCA rate is applied to the undepreciated capital cost (UCC) of the asset in all years subsequent to the first year, we can estimate the CCA expense in years 2 through 5 as follows:

$$\text{UCC (beginning of year 2)} = \text{UCC (beginning of year 1)} - \text{CCA (year 1)}$$
$$= \$650,000 - \$97,500 = \$552,500$$
$$\text{CCA (year 2)} = \text{UCC} \times \text{CCA rate} = \$552,500 \times 0.3 = \$165,750$$
$$\text{UCC (beginning of year 3)} = \text{UCC (beginning of year 2)} - \text{CCA (year 2)}$$
$$= \$552,500 - \$165,750 = \$386,750$$
$$\text{CCA (year 3)} = \text{UCC} \times \text{CCA rate} = \$386,750 \times 0.3 = \$116,025$$
$$\text{UCC (beginning of year 4)} = \text{UCC (beginning of year 3)} - \text{CCA (year 3)}$$
$$= \$386,750 - \$116,025 = \$270,725$$
$$\text{CCA (year 4)} = \text{UCC} \times \text{CCA rate} = \$270,725 \times 0.3 = \$81,218$$
$$\text{UCC (beginning of year 5)} = \text{UCC (beginning of year 4)} - \text{CCA (year 4)}$$
$$= \$270,725 - \$81,218 = \$189,507$$
$$\text{CCA (year 5)} = \text{UCC} \times \text{CCA rate} = \$189,507 \times 0.3 = \$56,852$$
$$\text{UCC (end of year 5)} = \$189,507 - \$56,852 = \$132,655$$

Combining these estimates with the firm's tax rate of 45 percent, we can estimate $CF_t$ as follows:

**Approach 1**

| | Year 1 | Year 2 | Year 3 | Year 4 | Year 5 |
|---|---|---|---|---|---|
| Operating income | $ 125,000 | $ 125,000 | $ 125,000 | $ 125,000 | $ 125,000 |
| − CCA expense | −97,500 | −165,750 | −116,025 | −81,218 | −56,852 |
| Taxable income | 27,500 | (40,750) | 8,975 | 43,782 | 68,148 |
| − Taxes payable (@45%) | −12,375 | +18,338* | −4,039 | −19,702 | −30,667 |
| After-tax income | 15,125 | (22,412) | 4,936 | 24,080 | 37,481 |
| + CCA expense | +97,500 | +165,750 | +116,025 | +81,218 | +56,852 |
| Net cash flow | $ 112,625 | $ 143,338 | $ 120,961 | $ 105,298 | $ 94,333 |

**Approach 2**

| | Year 1 | Year 2 | Year 3 | Year 4 | Year 5 |
|---|---|---|---|---|---|
| Operating income | $ 125,000 | $ 125,000 | $ 125,000 | $ 125,000 | $ 125,000 |
| − Taxes payable on operating income (@45%) | −56,250 | −56,250 | −56,250 | −56,250 | −56,250 |
| After-tax operating income | 68,750 | 68,750 | 68,750 | 68,750 | 68,750 |
| + CCA tax savings (CCA × T) | +43,875 | +74,588 | +52,211 | +36,548 | +25,583 |
| Net cash flow | $ 112,625 | $ 143,338 | $ 120,961 | $ 105,298 | $ 94,333 |

*In year 2, we assume that the firm can refile the previous year's tax return and get a tax refund, so CRA sends the firm a cheque for $18,338. Alternatively, the assumption is that the firm has other taxable income that it can then shield from tax.

Notice the following points from Example 14.2:

1. Both approaches give the same result. Because it is relatively easy to calculate the amount of the associated CCA tax savings, we will use approach 2. This decision is important because the use of declining-balance CCA means that the tax deductions last forever and the asset is never fully depreciated. This makes it difficult to put all the cash flows into a spreadsheet unless we make some assumptions about the end of the project's life. As a result, we can estimate the annual operating cash flows by using Equation 14.2.

$$CF_t = CFBT_t(1 - T) + CCA_t(T)$$

[14.2]

where

$CFBT_t$ = cash flow before taxes (i.e., incremental pre-tax operating income)

$CCA_t$ = the CCA expense for year $t$

$T$ = the firm's marginal (or effective) tax rate

2. CCA expense is lower in year 1 because of the half-year rule, is highest in year 2, declines in year 3, and declines every year thereafter as the UCC continually declines.

3. After-tax operating income is the same for each of the five years in Example 14.2, and we could view these cash flows as an annuity. This becomes particularly important because there is a formula that determines the present value of the CCA tax shield associated with capital investments, which we will introduce shortly.

---

**EXAMPLE 14.3** | Estimating the PV of Future $CF_t$

Refer to Example 14.2, determine the present value of the cash flows from years 1 to 5, assuming the firm's cost of capital is 12 percent.

**Solution**[5]

$$PV (\text{Future } CF_t) = \frac{\$112,625}{(1.12)^1} + \frac{\$143,338}{(1.12)^2} + \frac{\$120,961}{(1.12)^3} + \frac{\$105,298}{(1.12)^4} + \frac{\$94,333}{(1.12)^5}$$

$$= \$100,558 + \$114,268 + \$86,098 + \$66,919 + \$53,527 = \$421,370$$

---

Examples 14.2 and 14.3 deal with future cash flows in which the CCA tax savings cash flows are determined without considering what happens to the machine at the end of its useful economic life. As discussed in Chapter 3, if this asset is sold at that time, its price may affect the CCA expense (and cash flow) in the terminal year of the project. Before proceeding to this issue, however, we will first deal with the issue of the ending (or terminal) cash flow.

# Ending (or Terminal) After-Tax Cash Flow ($ECF_n$)

The **ending (or terminal) after-tax cash flow** ($ECF_n$) is the total cash flow that is expected to be generated in the terminal year of a project, aside from that year's expected after-tax cash flow. It comprises the estimated selling or **salvage value** ($SV_n$) of the asset.

As discussed in Chapter 3, this selling price can have tax consequences. First, if the selling price is greater than the original capital cost, a capital gain arises, which is taxable. The converse is not true: depreciable capital assets do not generate tax-deductible capital losses when they are sold below their original purchase price, because this lower price is expected (i.e., because they are depreciable assets, they are expected to depreciate in value below their original cost).

Aside from capital gains, additional tax consequences can arise. In particular, CCA recapture or terminal losses may be generated by the sale of an asset (or assets) if the CCA asset class is terminated by selling the asset. This would occur only if no other assets were included in that asset class for the firm. Under this scenario, the firm would have to pay additional taxes on "excess" CCA charged against the asset (or assets) if the salvage value is greater than the ending UCC for the asset (or asset class). The amount by which the salvage value exceeds the

**ending (or terminal) after-tax cash flow ($ECF_n$)** the total cash flow that is expected to be generated in the terminal year of a project, aside from that year's expected after-tax cash flow; the estimated salvage value of the asset

**salvage value ($SV_n$)** the estimated sale price of an asset at the end of its useful life

---

[5]Note that the CCA tax savings are as risky as the firm's pre-tax income. Without any pre-tax income, the CCA tax shields are worthless, and CRA places restrictions on the transfer of CCA tax shields within different types of firms. For this reason, they are discounted at the firm's WACC. In the United States, where it is easier to file consolidated tax returns and transfer depreciation tax shields between firms, the tax shields are often discounted at the firm's borrowing cost. In practice, this adjustment usually makes little difference in the final DCF analysis.

UCC is referred to as "CCA recapture" and is fully taxable.[6] However, if the salvage value is less than the ending UCC, the amount by which the UCC exceeds the salvage value is called a terminal loss and is fully tax deductible.[7] Finally, CCA recapture may occur even if an asset class is not closed, if an asset (or assets) is sold for a price that exceeds the remaining UCC for that asset class.

In addition to the salvage value and all the associated tax implications, the working capital that was associated with the project will be recaptured at the end of the project, which represents a cash inflow. This means that the people to whom you have extended credit will pay off the debts once the project is finished, and all inventory on hand will be sold, so that the net amount after the firm has paid its suppliers is available to finance other projects.

We can estimate the ending cash flow with tax implications by using Equation 14.3. The second-last term of the equation is included only if a capital gain arises, and the last term is included only if a terminal loss or CCA recapture occurs.[8]

$$\text{ECF (with tax implications)}_n = SV_n + \Delta NWC_n - 0.5\left[(SV_n - C_0) \times T\right] - \left[(SV_n - UCC_n) \times T\right]$$

[14.3]

where

$ECF\text{(with tax implications)}_n$ = ending cash flow in year $n$ (i.e., at the end of the project life)

$SV_n$ = the estimated salvage value in year $n$ for the asset purchased

$\Delta NWC_n$ = the net working capital "released" upon termination of the project

$C_0$ = the original capital cost of the asset

$UCC_n$ = the asset (or asset class) ending UCC balance

$T$ = the firm's effective tax rate

Generally, capital gains are rare for depreciable capital assets since the market price of machinery, equipment, etc., tends to go down and not up due to normal wear and tear, as well as obsolescence. CCA recapture is also rare because most large firms will have several assets in a given CCA pool, and the pool will remain open after the asset is sold. As a result, the asset cost and UCC will usually be greater than the salvage value of any particular asset, so capital gains, terminal losses, and CCA recapture will not happen. In such situations, we can estimate the ending cash flow using Equation 14.4, which eliminates the last two terms of Equation 14.3.

$$\text{ECF}_n = SV_n + \Delta NWC_n$$

[14.4]

---

**EXAMPLE 14.4** | Calculating $ECF_n$

Regarding the project being considered by Brennan Co. in examples 14.1, 14.2, and 14.3, the production department estimated that the $100,000 in additional net working capital requirements will be released at the end of the economic life of the machine. Management estimates that at the end of five years, the milling machine can be sold for $132,655. Assume the asset class remains open after the milling machine is sold. Determine the ending cash flow and the present value of this ending cash flow.

---

[6]In other words, it is viewed as if the firm charged too much CCA (depreciation), because the asset is sold for more than its depreciated book value for tax purposes (UCC). Therefore, the firm must pay back the amount of tax it saved by charging too much CCA.

[7]In other words, the firm did not charge enough CCA, because the asset was sold below its book value for tax purposes (UCC). Therefore, it is permitted to depreciate the asset to its selling price and deduct this charge for tax purposes.

[8]Notice that the last term "self-adjusts" for terminal losses or CCA recapture, because it will be negative if CCA recapture occurs (i.e., because $SV_n$ is greater than $UCC_n$), and it will be positive if a terminal loss occurs (i.e., because $SV_n$ is less than $UCC_n$).

**Solution**  Notice in this example that no capital gains arise because $SV_n$ is less than $C_0$. Because the asset class is left open, a terminal loss is not possible. Because $SV_n$ equals $UCC_n$, there is no CCA recapture—we do not need to check against the UCC for the entire class. Therefore, we can use Equation 14.4, as follows:

$$\text{ECF}_n = \text{SV}_n + \Delta\text{NWC}_n = \$132{,}655 + \$100{,}000 = \$232{,}655$$

$$\text{PV(ECF}_n) = \frac{\$232{,}655}{(1.12)^5} = \$132{,}015$$

To reinforce the point made earlier, the net effect on the $\Delta NWC$ through the life of this project is zero since the company experienced an initial cash outflow of \$100,000 followed by a cash inflow of \$100,000 at the end. On the other hand, the $PV(\Delta NWC)$ is not equal to zero. We have:

$$\text{PV}(\Delta\text{NWC}) = -\$100{,}000 + \frac{\$100{,}000}{(1.12)^5} = -\$100{,}000 + \$56{,}742.69 = -\$43{,}257.31$$

# Putting It All Together

Recall from Chapter 13 that the NPV of an investment equals the present value of the future cash flows minus the initial cash outlay. This was expressed in Equation 13.3, which is replicated here:

$$\text{NPV} = \sum_{t=1}^{n}\frac{\text{CF}_t}{(1+k)^t} - \text{CF}_0 = \text{PV(Future CFs)} - \text{CF}_0$$

If we decompose the future $CF_t$ in the previous equation into annual CFs and the ending cash flow, as discussed earlier, we obtain Equation 14.5.

$$\boxed{\text{NPV} = \text{PV(Annual CFs)} + \text{PV(ECF}_n) - \text{CF}_0} \qquad\qquad [14.5]$$

Referring to examples 14.1 through 14.4, we can use Equation 14.5 along with the values we calculated to find the NPV of this project for Brennan Co. We do this in Example 14.5.

---

**EXAMPLE 14.5** | Estimating the NPV

Determine the NPV of the project being considered by Brennan Co., using the information in the solutions to examples 14.1 through 14.4. Should Brennan Co. accept or reject this project?

**Solution**

$$\text{NPV} = \text{PV(Operating CFs)} + \text{PV(ECF}_n) - \text{CF}_0$$

$$= \$421{,}370 + \$132{,}015 - \$750{,}000 = -\$196{,}615$$

Therefore, Brennan Co. should reject the project.

---

# Valuation by Components

Evaluating the project that was considered in examples 14.1 through 14.5 was relatively straightforward. However, it would take much longer to find the NPV if it were a 20-year project, because we would have to calculate cash flows for each year and then discount them back individually. Obviously, the use of a spreadsheet program, such as Excel, is one way to make the calculations. However, if using Excel is not an option, we can use formulas to simplify the calculations by separating the problem into its different components.

Whenever operating cash flows are assumed to be the same every year, as in Example 14.5, we can view these cash flows as an annuity and find their present value using the present value of an annuity formula, which was introduced in Chapter 5. This assumption is reasonable for most replacement decisions in which the cash savings are assumed to be the same each year. The example is depicted in Equation 14.6.

$$PV(\text{Operating Cash Flows}) = CFBT(1-T) \times \left[ \frac{1 - \frac{1}{(1+k)^n}}{k} \right] \qquad [14.6]$$

In addition to the annuity formula for the operating cash flows, we can also separately determine the present value of the tax shield created by the CCA expenses for the investment. The first equation can be used in most circumstances, because it applies when there is no CCA recapture or terminal loss. This situation occurs whenever an asset class is left open or when the salvage value is less than the UCC for an entire class, which is generally what happens for long-term capital expenditures.

$$PV(\text{CCA Tax Shield}) = \frac{(C_0)(d)(T)}{(d+k)} \times \frac{(1+0.5k)}{(1+k)} - \frac{(SV_n)(d)(T)}{(d+k)} \times \frac{1}{(1+k)^n} \qquad [14.7]$$

where $d$ = the applicable CCA rate

The first part of the first term of Equation 14.7 $\left[ \frac{(C_0)(d)(T)}{(d+k)} \right]$ is a variation of the dividend discount model (DDM), which was introduced in Chapter 7 as a method of finding the present value of a growing perpetuity (of dividends). However, in this situation, the starting cash flow in the numerator is the tax savings generated by the CCA expense, $[(C_0)(d)(T)]$, instead of $D_1$ as it is in the DDM. The denominator, $(d+k)$, is a variation of $k-g$ in the DDM, where $d$ is positive to reflect the fact that the amount of CCA charged actually declines (or displays negative growth) every year.[9] The second part of the first term in the equation reflects the impact of the half-year rule on the CCA tax savings in the first year. This first term, therefore, estimates the present value of CCA tax savings if the asset were held indefinitely. The second term in Equation 14.7 reflects the fact that the CCA tax savings do not, in fact, go on perpetually, because the asset is assumed to be sold at some estimated salvage value at the end of the project's estimated useful life. Therefore, we subtract the present value of this part of the CCA tax savings that the firm will not realize, because this portion would be generated only if the asset were held indefinitely.

Equation 14.7 applies when there are no terminal losses or CCA recapture. Whenever an asset class is terminated, the possibility exists that one of these items will arise. In those cases, we need to use Equation 14.8 to estimate the present value of CCA tax savings. Equation 14.8 would also apply if an asset class were left open and CCA recapture occurred, except that we would replace the UCC for the asset in question with the UCC for the entire asset class.

$$\begin{aligned} PV(\text{CCA Tax Shield}) = {} & \frac{(C_0)(d)(T)}{(d+k)} \times \frac{(1+0.5k)}{(1+k)} - \frac{(UCC_n)(d)(T)}{(d+k)} \times \frac{1}{(1+k)^n} \\ & - \frac{(SV_n - UCC_n)(T)}{(1+k)^n} \end{aligned} \qquad [14.8]$$

The last term in this equation reflects the present value of the cash flow impact of any terminal loss or CCA recapture that arises. Notice that it will be negative when CCA recapture occurs (i.e., when $SV_n$ is greater than $UCC_n$), and it will be positive if a terminal loss occurs (i.e., when $SV_n$ is less than $UCC_n$).

Finally, whenever capital gains occur, we must also estimate the present value of the cash flow implications arising from the taxable capital gain. We can do so by using Equation 14.9, which estimates the present value of the capital gain multiplied by the firm's tax rate and is

---

[9]In other words, it is the same as $k-g$, except that $g$ is negative.

based on the assumption that the firm pays taxes at the full marginal rate on its taxable gains, which may or may not always be the case.[10]

$$\text{PV(Capital Gains Taxes Paid)} = \frac{(SV_n - C_0)(T)}{(1 + k)^n}$$  [14.9]

We have already accounted for the tax implications at the end of the project, so we must therefore estimate the present value of the ending cash flow by using $ECF_n$, as defined in Equation 14.4. Combining all this information, we can express the NPV equation as follows:

$$\text{NPV} = \text{PV(Operating CFs)} + \text{PV(CCA Tax Shield)} + \text{PV(ECF}_n)$$
$$- \text{PV(Capital Gains Taxes Paid)} - CF_0$$  [14.10]

In this equation, the *PV(Operating CFs)* term can be estimated using Equation 14.6 if the operating cash flows are expected to be the same every year. The *PV(CCA Tax Shield)* can be estimated using equation 14.7 or 14.8, depending on whether or not terminal losses or CCA recapture arise, while the *PV(Capital Gains Taxes Paid)* term applies only if a capital gain arises. It can be estimated using Equation 14.9.

---

**EXAMPLE 14.6** | Finding the NPV Using the Valuation by Components Approach I

Use equations 14.6 through 14.10 (as applicable) to estimate the NPV of the Brennan Co. project that was solved using the longer approach in examples 14.1 through 14.5.

**Solution**

$$CF_0 = \$750,000$$

$$\text{PV(Operating Cash Flows)} = \text{CFBT}(1 - T) \times \left[ \frac{1 - \frac{1}{(1 + k)^n}}{k} \right]$$

$$= [\$125,000(1 - 0.45)] \times \left[ \frac{1 - \frac{1}{(1.12)^5}}{0.12} \right]$$

$$= (\$68,750) \times (3.604776) = \$247,828$$

Because there is no terminal loss or CCA recapture associated with the termination of this project, we use Equation 14.7 to estimate the present value of the CCA tax shield:

$$\text{PV(CCA Tax Shield)} = \frac{(C_0)(d)(T)}{(d + k)} \times \frac{(1 + 0.5k)}{(1 + k)} - \frac{(SV_n)(d)(T)}{(d + k)} \times \frac{1}{(1 + k)^n}$$

$$= \frac{(\$650,000)(0.30)(0.45)}{0.30 + 0.12} \times \frac{(1 + 0.5 \times 0.12)}{1 + 0.12} - \frac{(\$132,655)(0.30)(0.45)}{0.30 + 0.12} \times \frac{1}{(1.12)^5}$$

$$= \$197,736 - \$24,195 = \$173,541$$

$$\text{PV(ECF)} = \frac{\$232,655}{(1.12)^5} = \$132,015 \text{ (as calculated in Example 14.4)}$$

There are no capital gains, so this term is zero.
Now we can put these items together to determine the NPV of the project.

$$\text{NPV} = \text{PV (Operating CFs)} + \text{PV (CCA Tax Shield)} + \text{PV (ECF}_n) - \text{PV (Capital Gains Taxes Paid)} - CF_0$$

$$= \$247,828 + \$173,541 + \$132,015 - \$0 - \$750,000 = -\$196,616$$

This is the same answer we obtained when we solved the problem in examples 14.1 through 14.5. (The \$1 difference is due to rounding.)

---

[10]If the firm faces a different tax rate for capital gains ($T_{CG}$), we can simply substitute this rate for $T$ in the equation.

**EXAMPLE 14.7** | Finding the NPV Using the Valuation by Components Approach II

Redo Example 14.6, assuming that the asset class is now closed upon termination of the project and that the salvage value is

**a.** $100,000

**b.** $200,000

**Solution** Notice that changing the salvage value affects only the *PV(CCA Tax Savings)* and the *PV(ECF$_n$)* terms; therefore, we do not need to re-estimate the other terms.

$$CF_0 = \$750,000$$

$$PV(\text{Operating Cash Flows}) = \$247,828$$

Because there are no capital gains, that term is still zero.

In this example, because the asset class is closed at the termination of the project, we must use Equation 14.8, which accounts for a terminal loss or CCA recapture, to estimate the present value of the CCA tax shield.

**a.** $ECF_n = \$100,000 + \$100,000 = \$200,000$

$$PV(\text{CCA Tax Shield}) = \frac{(C_0)(d)(T)}{(d+k)} \times \frac{(1+0.5k)}{(1+k)} - \frac{(UCC_n)(d)(T)}{(d+k)} \times \frac{1}{(1+k)^n} - \frac{(SV_n - UCC_n)(T)}{(1+k)^n}$$

$$= \frac{(\$650,000)(0.30)(0.45)}{0.30+0.12} \times \frac{(1.06)}{(1.12)} - \frac{(\$132,655)(0.30)(0.45)}{0.30+0.12} \times \frac{1}{(1.12)^5}$$

$$- \frac{(\$100,000 - \$132,655)(0.45)}{(1.12)^5}$$

$$= \$197,736 - \$24,195 + \$8,338 = \$181,879$$

$$PV(ECF_n) = \frac{\$200,000}{(1.12)^5} = \$113,485$$

So,

$$NPV = PV(\text{Operating CFs}) + PV(\text{CCA Tax Shield}) + PV(ECF_n) - PV(\text{Capital Gains Taxes Paid}) - CF_0$$

$$= \$247,828 + \$181,879 + \$113,485 - \$0 - \$750,000 = -\$206,808$$

The project is even less attractive because of the lower salvage value, despite the increase in the CCA tax shield through the terminal loss of $32,655 (i.e., $132,655 UCC − $100,000 salvage value).

**b.** $ECF_n = \$200,000 + \$100,000 = \$300,000$

$$PV(\text{CCA Tax Shield}) = \frac{(C_0)(d)(T)}{(d+k)} \times \frac{(1+0.5k)}{(1+k)} - \frac{(UCC_n)(d)(T)}{(d+k)} \times \frac{1}{(1+k)^n} - \frac{(SV_n - UCC_n)(T)}{(1+k)^n}$$

$$= \frac{(\$650,000)(0.30)(0.45)}{0.30+0.12} \times \frac{(1.06)}{(1.12)} - \frac{(\$132,655)(0.30)(0.45)}{0.30+0.12} \times \frac{1}{(1.12)^5}$$

$$- \frac{(\$200,000 - \$132,655)(0.45)}{(1.12)^5}$$

$$= \$197,736 - \$24,195 - \$17,196 = \$156,345$$

$$PV(ECF_n) = \frac{\$300,000}{(1.12)^5} = \$170,228$$

So,

$$NPV = PV(\text{Operating CFs}) + PV(\text{CCA Tax Shield}) + PV(ECF_n) - PV(\text{Capital Gains Taxes Paid}) - CF_0$$

$$= \$247,828 + \$156,345 + \$170,228 - \$0 - \$750,000 = -\$175,599$$

The project will still be rejected—although it is more attractive because of the higher salvage value—despite the decrease in the CCA tax shield because of the taxable CCA recapture of $67,345 (i.e., $132,655 UCC − $200,000 SV).

# The Accelerated Investment Incentive

As first mentioned in Chapter 3, the Liberal government introduced new tax measures in November 2018 in an effort to offset the previous reduction in the U.S. corporate tax rate from 35 percent to 21 percent. An important part of these measures included an incentive to reward Canadian companies making capital investments.[11] The incentive took the form of a depreciation expense that could be claimed on tangible assets (as well as intangible assets like patents and goodwill) at a rate that is three times higher than the one that would normally apply assuming the half-year rule.[12]

This **accelerated depreciation** is short-term and can be fully applied only to eligible assets acquired from November 21, 2018, up to the end of 2023. Thereafter, a phase-out period will be in force until the end of 2027, when the incentive will end entirely. Finance in the News 14.1 provides some additional background information related to the economic statement.

**accelerated depreciation** a depreciation method that creates a higher depreciation expense in the earlier years and lower charges in the later periods

---

## 14.1 Finance in the News    Ottawa unveils $14B in tax savings for businesses

OTTAWA—Confident the Canadian federal coffers can weather global economic uncertainty, the Liberal government proposes a $14.4 billion package of tax measures to boost manufacturing and clean energy production, as well as a new fund to drive social and environmental investment and aid for struggling media outlets.

The fall economic blueprint, entitled "Investing in Middle Class Jobs," does not chart a path to a balanced budget, instead projecting an $18.1 billion deficit this year [2018].

However with an election now less than a year away, Wednesday's statement was as much a political as it was an economic document, as the Liberals reaffirmed their commitment to a carbon tax and poked critics who would "bury their heads in the sand" on climate change.

It delivers a key measure sought by business groups with tax changes to allow companies that invest in manufacturing or in "clean energy" to fully write off spending immediately on new equipment and machinery. Meanwhile other businesses of all sizes and in all sectors will be able to more quickly write off a greater portion, but not the full amount, of their capital spending.

Altogether, the three tax changes total $14.4 billion over five years in foregone revenue to federal tax coffers.

On top of that, Finance Minister Bill Morneau promised $1.4 billion over five years in spending to help explore new markets for Canadian exports, millions more to remove internal trade barriers and trim regulations, and an extra $800 million over five years will be injected into an existing business innovation fund. That means a total package of $16.48 billion in measures to keep Canadian businesses competitive, said Morneau.

Big business had urged Morneau to match the U.S. corporate tax rate after President Donald Trump slashed it from 35 per cent to 21 per cent. He portrayed that as an irresponsible course to pursue, saying it would cost tens of billions.

The pro-business measures, from a finance minister who last year angered Canada's business community with corporate tax changes, were only partially offset—from a political perspective—by new spending to boost socially conscious projects and, in Morneau's words, to boost democracy in Canada by allocating $595 million over five years to aid journalistic outlets.

A new $755-million 10-year "social finance fund," loosely modelled on the U.K.'s "Big Society" fund, will provide loans to non-profits or for-profit ventures to juice riskier, low-return investments in social housing, job training or environmental measures to improve Canada's long-term social health—moves that attempt to hew to the Trudeau government's "progressive" brand.

Conservative Leader Andrew Scheer was not in the Commons to deliver the Official Opposition response to the update.

But Conservative finance critic Pierre Poilievre slammed it, noting that the deficit is "three times the size the Liberal party promised in the last election."

The measures outlined in the update push the deficit to $18.1 billion in the current fiscal year, rising to $19.6 billion next year before starting downward, reaching a projected $11.4 billion in 2023–24.

New Democratic Party Leader Jagmeet Singh said the Liberals' "blanket giveaways" to corporations show they "are playing Santa Claus to the corporations but abandoning

---

[11]The full document is referred to as the *Fall Economic Statement 2018* and can be downloaded from https://www.budget.gc.ca/fes-eea/2018/docs/statement-enonce/toc-tdm-en.html.
[12]Note that equipment for manufacturing or processing of goods (class 53) as well as specified clean energy equipment (classes 43.1 and 43.2) may be fully expensed in the year of acquisition.

ordinary Canadians" who he said need more help with affordable housing and prescription drugs. He said the capital spending measures will allow corporations "to buy limousines and corporate jets."

In a speech to the Commons, Morneau talked up Canada's economic prospects even in the face of uncertainty from rising interest rates, debt-burdened consumers, slumping oil prices, and ongoing trade disputes with the country's biggest trading partner south of the border.

He said Canada's debt continues to decline as a function of the country's overall economic output, and he defended the choice not to move quickly to cut the yearly deficit, saying to do so would have entailed drastic spending cuts....

Craig Alexander, a partner and chief economist at Deloitte, said the update doesn't serve up the full tax break sought by some corporations but does reward new investment, a less costly move for the federal government at a time when it's trying to keep its deficit under control.

"If you're worried about investment leaving the country, this does address it," Alexander said.

After 10 years of economic good times, Alexander said he would have expected a balanced budget by now.

The Canadian Manufacturers and Exporters, the Business Council of Canada and the Canadian Electricity Association all welcomed the tax changes and other measures to diversify trade and cut red tape.

"However, we all need to recognize that Canada's competitiveness challenges go much deeper than any single tax measure," said Goldy Hyder, president of the Business Council. "We will continue to urge the government to adopt a comprehensive strategy to foster business confidence, attract investment and enable the creation of new, high-value jobs."

**Source:** MacCharles, Tonda, and Bruce Campion-Smith, "Ottawa Unveils $14B in Tax Savings for Businesses," *The Toronto Star*, November 21, 2018. Available at www.thestar.com. Copyright 2018. Reproduced with permission of Toronto Star Newspapers Ltd.

To adjust for accelerated depreciation, equations 14.7 and 14.8 need to be modified as follows:

$$PV(\text{CCA Tax Shield}) = \frac{(C_0)(d)(T)}{(d+k)} \times \frac{(1+1.5k)}{(1+k)} - \frac{(SV_n)(d)(T)}{(d+k)} \times \frac{1}{(1+k)^n} \quad [14.11]$$

$$PV(\text{CCA Tax Shield}) = \frac{(C_0)(d)(T)}{(d+k)} \times \frac{(1+1.5k)}{(1+k)} - \frac{(UCC_n)(d)(T)}{(d+k)} \times \frac{1}{(1+k)^n} - \frac{(SV_n - UCC_n)(T)}{(1+k)^n} \quad [14.12]$$

Notice that the half-year rule adjustment (the second term in each equation) has been altered to account for a tripling of CCA in the year of acquisition.

Due to its short-term effect, the Accelerated Investment Incentive will be treated as a special case of the usual CCA tax treatment that employs the half-year rule (see examples 14.8 and 14.12 for details).

**EXAMPLE 14.8** | Finding the NPV Using the Valuation by Components Approach III

Redo Example 14.6, assuming that the asset is purchased after November 20, 2018, and before the end of 2023 and is eligible for accelerated depreciation. Again, assume that the asset class is closed upon termination of the project and that the salvage value is

a. $50,000

b. $200,000

**Solution** As before: $CF_0 = \$750,000$

Now we adjust the CCA to account for accelerated depreciation.

Both the annual CCA and UCC are determined, since we need the ending UCC in particular to quantify the tax implications that result at the end of the project's life. Calculations are as follows:

$$\text{CCA (year 1)} = C_0 \times \text{CCA rate} \times 1.5 = \$650,000 \times 0.3 \times 1.5 = \$292,500$$

$$\text{UCC (beginning of year 2)} = \text{UCC (beginning of year 1)} - \text{CCA (year 1)}$$
$$= \$650,000 - \$292,500 = \$357,500$$

$$\text{CCA (year 2)} = \text{UCC} \times \text{CCA rate} = \$357,500 \times 0.3 = \$107,250$$

$$\text{UCC (beginning of year 3)} = \text{UCC (beginning of year 2)} - \text{CCA (year 2)}$$
$$= \$357,500 - \$107,250 = \$250,250$$

$$\text{CCA (year 3)} = \text{UCC} \times \text{CCA rate} = \$250,250 \times 0.3 = \$75,075$$

$$\text{UCC (beginning of year 4)} = \text{UCC (beginning of year 3)} - \text{CCA (year 3)}$$
$$= \$250,250 - \$75,075 = \$175,175$$

$$\text{CCA (year 4)} = \text{UCC} \times \text{CCA rate} = \$175,175 \times 0.3 = \$52,552.50$$

$$\text{UCC (beginning of year 5)} = \text{UCC (beginning of year 4)} - \text{CCA (year 4)}$$
$$= \$175,175 - \$52,552.50 = \$122,622.50$$

$$\text{CCA (year 5)} = \text{UCC} \times \text{CCA rate} = \$122,622.50 \times 0.3 = \$36,786.75$$

$$\text{UCC (end of year 5)} = \$122,622.50 - \$36,786.75 = \$85,835.75$$

As before, PV(Operating Cash Flows) = $247,828

Because there are no capital gains, that term is still zero.

As stated, the acquisition is eligible for accelerated depreciation, and since the asset class is closed at the termination of the project, we must use Equation 14.12, which adjusts for both the increased depreciation and a terminal loss (part a below) or CCA recapture (part b below).

**a.** $ECF_n = \$50,000 + \$100,000 = \$150,000$ and $PV(ECF_n) = \$150,000 \times \dfrac{1}{(1.12)^5} = \$85,114$

$$PV(\text{CCA Tax Shield}) = \frac{(C_0)(d)(T)}{(d+k)} \times \frac{(1+1.5k)}{(1+k)} - \frac{(UCC_n)(d)(T)}{(d+k)} \times \frac{1}{(1+k)^n} - \frac{(SV_n - UCC_n)(T)}{(1+k)^n}$$

$$= \frac{(\$650,000)(0.30)(0.45)}{(0.3+0.12)} \times \frac{(1.18)}{(1.12)} - \frac{(\$85,835.75)(0.3)(0.45)}{(0.30+0.12)} \times \frac{1}{(1.12)^5}$$

$$- \frac{(\$50,000 - \$85,835.75)(0.45)}{(1.12)^5}$$

$$= \$220,121 - \$15,655 + \$9,150 = \$213,616$$

So,

$$NPV = PV(\text{Operating CFs}) + PV(\text{CCA Tax Shield}) + PV(ECF_n) - PV(\text{Capital Gains Taxes Paid}) - CF_0$$

$$= \$247,828 + \$213,616 + \$85,114 - \$0 - \$750,000$$

$$= -\$203,442$$

Even with the accelerated depreciation and the terminal loss, the relatively low salvage value contributes to making the project financially unacceptable.

**b.** $ECF_n = \$200,000 + \$100,000 = \$300,000$ and $PV(ECF_n) = \$300,000 \times \dfrac{1}{(1.12)^5} = \$170,228$

$$PV(\text{CCA Tax Shield}) = \frac{(C_0)(d)(T)}{(d+k)} \times \frac{(1+1.5k)}{(1+k)} - \frac{(UCC_n)(d)(T)}{(d+k)} \times \frac{1}{(1+k)^n} - \frac{(SV_n - UCC_n)(T)}{(1+k)^n}$$

$$= \frac{(\$650,000)(0.30)(0.45)}{(0.3+0.12)} \times \frac{(1.18)}{(1.12)} - \frac{(\$85,835.75)(0.3)(0.45)}{(0.30+0.12)} \times \frac{1}{(1.12)^5}$$

$$- \frac{(\$200,000 - \$85,835.75)(0.45)}{(1.12)^5}$$

$$= \$220,121 - \$15,655 - \$29,151 = \$175,315$$

So,

$$NPV = PV(\text{Operating CFs}) + PV(\text{CCA Tax Shield}) + PV(ECF_n) - PV(\text{Capital Gains Taxes Paid}) - CF_0$$

$$= \$247,828 + \$175,315 + \$170,228 - \$0 - \$750,000$$

$$= -\$156,629$$

The PV(Operating CFs), PV(CCA Tax Shield), and PV(ECF_n) are not sufficient to overcome the relatively large $CF_0$ value. Hence, the project should be rejected.

**EXAMPLE 14.9** | Finding the NPV When $k$ Changes

Redo Example 14.6 by assuming, once again, that the asset class is left open, the salvage value is $132,655, and all else is as in the original example, except that the discount rate is 10 percent instead of 12 percent.

**Solution**    All of the terms, except for the initial cash outlay, will be affected by the change in the discount rate.

$$CF_0 = \$750,000$$

$$PV(\text{Operating Cash Flows}) = CFBT(1-T) \times \left[ \frac{1 - \frac{1}{(1+k)^n}}{k} \right]$$

$$= [\$125,000(1-0.45)] \times \left[ \frac{1 - \frac{1}{(1.10)^5}}{0.10} \right]$$

$$= (\$68,750) \times (3.79079) = \$260,617$$

Because no terminal loss or CCA recapture is associated with the termination of this project, we use Equation 14.7 to estimate the present value of the CCA tax shield:

$$PV(\text{CCA Tax Shield}) = \frac{(C_0)(d)(T)}{(d+k)} \times \frac{(1+0.5k)}{(1+k)} - \frac{(SV_n)(d)(T)}{(d+k)} \times \frac{1}{(1+k)^n}$$

$$= \frac{(\$650,000)(0.30)(0.45)}{0.30+0.10} \times \frac{(1+(0.5\times0.10))}{1+0.10} - \frac{(\$132,655)(0.30)(0.45)}{0.30+0.10} \times \frac{1}{(1.10)^5}$$

$$= \$209,403 - \$27,799 = \$181,604$$

$$PV(\text{ECF}_n) = \frac{\$232,655}{(1.10)^5} = \$144,460$$

So,

$$NPV = PV(\text{Operating CFs}) + PV(\text{CCA Tax Shield}) + PV(\text{ECF}_n) - PV(\text{Capital Gains Taxes Paid}) - CF_0$$

$$= \$260,617 + \$181,604 + \$144,460 - \$0 - \$750,000 = -\$163,319$$

The project would still be rejected, although the NPV is higher (less negative) because of the use of a lower discount rate, which increases the present value of the future cash flows.

---

**EXAMPLE 14.10** | Finding the NPV When Operating Cash Flows Are Higher

Redo Example 14.9 (again assuming $k = 10$ percent), but now assume that all of the annual operating cash flows are 10-percent higher than the original estimates.

**Solution**    The only term that is affected by this assumption is the present value of the operating cash flows.

$$CF_0 = \$750,000$$

$$CFBT_{New} = CFBT_{Old} \times 1.1 = \$125,000 \times 1.1 = \$137,500$$

$$PV(\text{Operating Cash Flows}) = CFBT(1-T) \times \left[ \frac{1 - \frac{1}{(1+k)^n}}{k} \right]$$

$$= [\$137,500(1-0.45)] \times \left[ \frac{1 - \frac{1}{(1.10)^5}}{0.10} \right]$$

$$= (\$75,625) \times (3.79079) = \$286,678$$

$$PV(\text{CCA Tax Shield}) = \$181,604 \text{ (as in Example 14.9)}$$

$$PV(\text{ECF}_n) = \$144,460 \text{ (as in Example 14.9)}$$

So,

$$NPV = PV(\text{Operating CFs}) + PV(\text{CCA Tax Shield}) + PV(\text{ECF}_n) - PV(\text{Capital Gains Taxes Paid}) - CF_0$$

$$= \$286,678 + \$181,604 + \$144,460 - \$0 - \$750,000 = -\$137,258$$

The project would still be rejected, although the NPV is higher (less negative) because of the increase in estimated operating cash flows.

### Concept Review Questions

1. Why does the initial cash outlay often exceed the purchase price of an asset?
2. How do taxes affect the annual cash flows and terminal cash flows of an investment project?
3. Explain why the valuation by components approach can save computational time and still lead to the correct answer.
4. When does accelerated depreciation apply and what is its impact on capital budgeting decisions?

## 14.3 | Replacement Decisions

### LEARNING OBJECTIVE 14.3
Explain how to make replacement decisions, and explain what is special about them.

Earlier in this chapter, we introduced 12 guidelines for estimating cash flows. Guideline 2 stated that we should focus on *marginal* or *incremental* cash flows that arise as a result of a capital budgeting decision. This refers to the additional cash flows that will be generated for the firm. So far, this has been relatively easy to deal with, because we have been considering **expansion projects**—that is, projects that would add something extra to the firm in terms of extra sales or cost savings. For these types of projects, the new cash flows that arise from the investment decision represent incremental cash flows.

   **Replacement projects**, as their name suggests, involve the replacement of an existing asset (or assets) with a new one. We deal with these types of decisions in the same manner as we deal with expansion problems, except that we must focus more on incremental cash flows. We demonstrate this point in Example 14.11.

**expansion projects**   projects that add something extra to the firm in terms of sales or cost savings; their new cash flows are incremental cash flows

**replacement projects**   projects that involve the replacement of an existing asset (or assets) with a new one

---

**EXAMPLE 14.11** | Evaluating Replacement Decisions

A firm is considering the purchase of a new machine priced at $350,000 to replace an existing machine. The present market value of the existing machine is $50,000, and it is expected to have a salvage value of $15,000 at the end of eight years. Management estimates that the company will benefit from the new machine by reducing annual operating expenses by $50,000 over the life of the project, which is expected to be eight years. This new machine is expected to have a salvage value of $100,000 at the end of eight years. The firm's marginal tax rate is 40 percent, and its marginal cost of capital is 15 percent. Both machines belong to class 10, which has a CCA rate of 30 percent, and the asset class will remain open. Estimate the NPV of replacement and decide whether or not replacement should occur.

**Solution**   We must first estimate the incremental capital cost ($\Delta C_0$), which is the difference between the purchase price of the new machine and the salvage price of the old machine. This will be the addition to the asset class and will determine the additional CCA tax savings generated by the new investment. The incremental capital cost also represents a component of the firm's incremental initial after-tax cash outlay ($CF_0$).

$$\Delta C_0 = C_0^{New} - C_0^{Old} = \$350,000 - \$50,000 = \$300,000$$

   In this example, there is no mention of opportunity costs arising or of additional working capital being tied up, so we can estimate the initial cash outlay as follows:

$$\Delta CF_0 = \Delta C_0 + \Delta NWC_0 + OC = \$300,000 + \$0 + \$0 = \$300,000$$

Now we need to estimate the present value of the annual incremental operating cash flows (*ΔOperating CFs*).

$$\Delta CFBT = \$50,000 \text{ per year in additional cost savings}$$

$$PV(\Delta \text{Operating CFs}) = (\Delta CFBT)(1 - T)\left[\frac{1 - \dfrac{1}{(1+k)^n}}{k}\right]$$

$$= (\$50,000)(1 - 0.40)\left[\frac{1 - \dfrac{1}{(1.15)^8}}{0.15}\right] = (\$50,000)(0.60)(4.487322)$$

$$= \$134,620$$

Now we estimate the present value of the incremental CCA tax savings generated by the replacement decision. Because the asset class is left open and there is no CCA recapture or terminal loss, we can use Equation 14.7, making sure to use the incremental capital cost ($\Delta C_0$) as estimated earlier, and also using the incremental salvage value ($\Delta SV_n$), which is estimated here:

$$\Delta SV_n = SV_{New} - SV_{Old} = \$100,000 - \$15,000 = \$85,000$$

$$PV(\Delta CCA \text{ Tax Shield}) = \frac{(\Delta C_0)(d)(T)}{(d+k)} \times \frac{(1+0.5k)}{(1+k)} - \frac{(\Delta SV_n)(d)(T)}{(d+k)} \times \frac{1}{(1+k)^n}$$

$$PV(\Delta CCA \text{ Tax Shield}) = \left[\frac{(\$300,000)(0.30)(0.40)}{0.30 + 0.15} \times \frac{(1+0.5(0.15))}{1+0.15}\right]$$

$$- \left[\frac{(\$85,000)(0.30)(0.40)}{0.30 + 0.15} \times \frac{1}{(1.15)^8}\right]$$

$$= \$67,373$$

Next, we need to estimate the present value of the incremental ending cash flow ($\Delta ECF_n$) associated with the replacement decision, as follows:

$$\Delta ECF_n = \Delta SV_n + \Delta NWC_n = \$85,000 + \$0 = \$85,000$$

$$PV(\Delta ECF_n) = \frac{\Delta ECF_n}{(1+k)^n} = \frac{\$85,000}{(1.15)^8} = \$27,787$$

We can combine the previous results to determine the NPV of the replacement decision, as follows:

$$NPV = PV(\Delta \text{Operating CFs}) + PV(\Delta CCA \text{ Tax Shield}) + PV(\Delta ECF_n) - \Delta CF_0$$

$$= \$134,620 + \$67,373 + \$27,787 - \$300,000 = -\$70,220$$

Therefore, the firm should not go ahead with this replacement project.

---

**EXAMPLE 14.12** | Evaluating Replacement Decisions Assuming Accelerated Depreciation

Redo Example 14.11 assuming that the machines referred to are both purchased after November 20, 2018, and before the end of 2023. Assume further that this asset class is eligible for accelerated depreciation.

**Solution** The incremental capital cost ($\Delta C_0$) and the initial cash outlay ($\Delta CF_0$) are the same as they were in Example 14.11. Therefore,

$$\Delta C_0 = \$300,000 \text{ and } \Delta CF_0 = \$300,000$$

The *PV(ΔOperating CFs)* and *ΔSV_n* are also the same as in the previous example. Therefore,

$$PV(\Delta \text{Operating CFs}) = \$134,620 \text{ and } \Delta SV_n = \$85,000$$

There is, however, a change in the *PV(ΔCCA Tax Shield)* owing to the November 2018 provision permitting accelerated depreciation. We have

$$PV(\Delta CCA \text{ Tax Shield}) = \frac{(\Delta C_0)(d)(T)}{(d+k)} \times \frac{(1+1.5k)}{(1+k)} - \frac{(\Delta SV_n)(d)(T)}{(d+k)} \times \frac{1}{(1+k)^n}$$

$$= \frac{(\$300,000)(0.3)(0.4)}{(0.3+0.15)} \times \frac{(1.225)}{(1.15)} - \frac{(\$85,000)(0.3)(0.4)}{(0.3+0.15)} \times \frac{1}{(1.15)^8}$$

$$= \$77,808$$

From Example 14.11, $\Delta ECF_n = \$85,000$ and $PV(\Delta ECF_n) = \$27,787$
Putting it all together:

$$NPV = PV(\Delta\text{Operating CFs}) + PV(\Delta\text{CCA Tax Shield}) + PV(\Delta ECF_n) - \Delta CF_0$$

$$= \$134,620 + \$77,808 + \$27,787 - \$300,000$$

$$= -\$59,785$$

With a negative NPV, the replacement cannot be justified on a financial basis.

## Concept Review Question

1. Discuss any differences in the evaluation of a replacement decision versus the evaluation of an expansion decision.

## 14.4 | Sensitivity to Inputs

### LEARNING OBJECTIVE 14.4

Conduct a sensitivity analysis to see how the value changes as key inputs vary, and determine what is a real option.

Examples 14.7 through 14.10 examine the impact of changing one or more of the inputs into the "base-case" (most likely) project estimates. We used them to illustrate the impact of various estimates on the resulting NPV, as well as to implement various forms of the equations introduced in the earlier sections. In practice, companies are dealing with estimates of future cash flows, discount rates, and so on. Because any estimate of the future is subject to error, it is often useful to examine the impact on the attractiveness of a project if one or more of the estimates is incorrect. In other words, firms may want to estimate the NPV (or IRR, profitability index, or payback period) of projects using a range of estimates in order to examine the "risks" in their estimates.

In this section, we briefly discuss some commonly used methods for analyzing risks, which are all included in the survey results in **Figure 14.1**. There isn't much to say about the number-one answer (judgement, used by 76.9 percent of firms), as all investment decisions are critical management decisions, which obviously involve some judgement. We discuss the others next.

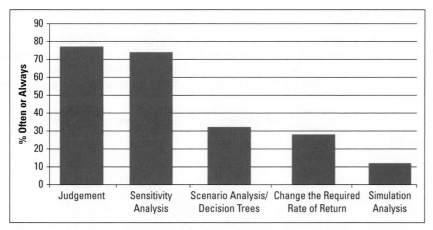

**FIGURE 14.1** Risk Analysis Techniques Used by Canadian Firms When Deciding Which Projects or Acquisitions to Pursue

**Source:** Baker, H. Kent, Dutta, Shantanu, and Saadi, Samir, "Corporate Finance Practices in Canada: Where Do We Stand?" *Multinational Finance Journal* 15, no. 3/4 (September/December 2011), Table 4, p. 174.

# Sensitivity Analysis and Scenario Analysis

**sensitivity analysis**   an examination of how an investment's NPV changes as the value of different inputs are changed, one input at a time

The second-most-commonly used method in Figure 14.1 (at 73.5 percent) is **sensitivity analysis**, which examines how an investment's NPV changes as we change the value of one input at a time, just as we did in examples 14.7 through 14.10. For instance, in Example 14.7, we varied the estimated salvage value and recalculated the NPV, which demonstrated how a change in this estimate could affect the attractiveness of a project. Similarly, in examples 14.9 and 14.10, we changed the value of the discount rate (i.e., the number-four answer in Figure 14.1) and then the operating cash flow estimates to isolate how sensitive the NPV is to these inputs. This type of analysis allows firms to determine which of their estimates are the most critical in the final decision. Obviously, the most critical estimates require the greatest amount of scrutiny from the firm.

**scenario analysis**   an examination of how an investment's NPV changes in response to varying scenarios in terms of one or more estimates, such as sales or costs

The third-most-common method in Figure 14.1, **scenario analysis**, examines how an investment's NPV changes in response to differing scenarios with respect to the values of one or more estimates, such as sales or costs. It is also informative to vary the discount rate used in the NPV calculations, because this variable is hard to estimate precisely and can change substantially through time as market, industry, and company conditions change. It often makes sense to vary more than one input variable at a time, because it allows us to account for interactions among the variables and for the fact that many of them can be related to external variables, such as the overall health of the economy or the company's industry. For example, if interest rates decline, it is reasonable to assume that a firm's discount rate may decline, and if the product it sells is sensitive to interest rates, it is also reasonable to assume that the operating cash flows associated with a particular capital expenditure could increase under this favourable scenario. Similarly, if the price of oil declines, this may reduce the expected operating cash flows from an investment for an oil producer. The decline in oil prices could also cause the market price of the oil producer's common shares to decline, which could increase its cost of capital.

It makes sense to view the impact on *all* variables of certain scenarios that might arise. Scenario analysis can provide important information, because we know that estimates will rarely be completely accurate and can often be well off the mark.

Scenario analysis is often conducted in the form of a "what if" analysis. For example, a company would typically estimate a base-case scenario. It would then make more optimistic and more pessimistic assumptions to produce, at minimum, an optimistic (or best case) scenario and a pessimistic (or worst case) scenario. In practice, it is common to produce a wide variety of what-if scenarios, which can easily be handled through the use of a spreadsheet program, such as Excel. As Figure 14.1 suggests, some companies will use "simulation analysis" to generate various scenarios using a mathematical or computerized simulation generation procedure. We provide a simple scenario in Example 14.13.

---

**EXAMPLE 14.13** | Scenario Analysis

A company has a project that requires an initial after-tax cash outlay of $100,000, which is also the amount for the capital cost of the assets that are purchased to get the project up and running. The asset class will be left open at the end of the project's useful life, and the applicable CCA rate is 20 percent. The firm's effective tax rate is 40 percent. It makes the following estimates:

|  | **Base Case** | **Best Case** | **Worst Case** |
|---|---|---|---|
| Project life | 12 years | 15 years | 9 years |
| Discount rate ($k$) | 12% | 10% | 14% |
| Salvage value | $50,000 | $60,000 | $30,000 |
| Annual operating after-tax cash flows | $12,000 | $15,000 | $9,000 |

Determine the NPV for each scenario.

**Solution**

$$CF_0 = \$100,000$$

Base case:

$$PV(\text{Operating Cash Flows}) = [\$12,000] \times \left[ \frac{1 - \frac{1}{(1.12)^{12}}}{0.12} \right]$$

$$= (\$12,000) \times (6.194374) = \$74,332$$

Because no terminal loss or CCA recapture is associated with the termination of this project, we use Equation 14.7 to estimate the present value of the CCA tax shield. There are no capital gains, so this term is zero.

$$PV(\text{CCA Tax Shield}) = \frac{(C_0)(d)(T)}{(d+k)} \times \frac{(1 + 0.5k)}{(1+k)} - \frac{(SV_n)(d)(T)}{(d+k)} \times \frac{1}{(1+k)^n}$$

$$= \frac{(\$100,000)(0.20)(0.40)}{0.20 + 0.12} \times \frac{(1 + (0.5 \times 0.12))}{1 + 0.12}$$

$$- \frac{(\$50,000)(0.20)(0.40)}{0.20 + 0.12} \times \frac{1}{(1.12)^{12}}$$

$$= \$23,661 - \$3,208 = \$20,453$$

$$PV(\text{ECF}_n) = \frac{\$50,000}{(1.12)^{12}} = \$12,834$$

$$NPV = PV(\text{Operating CFs}) + PV(\text{CCA Tax Shield}) + PV(\text{ECF}_n) - CF_0$$

$$= \$74,332 + \$20,453 + \$12,834 - \$0 - \$100,000 = +\$7,619$$

The base-case NPV suggests that the project should be accepted because it generates a positive NPV.

Best case:

$$PV(\text{Operating Cash Flows}) = [\$15,000] \times \left[ \frac{1 - \frac{1}{(1.10)^{15}}}{0.10} \right]$$

$$= (\$15,000) \times (7.60608) = \$114,091$$

$$PV(\text{CCA Tax Shield}) = \frac{(\$100,000)(0.20)(0.40)}{0.20 + 0.10} \times \frac{(1 + (0.5 \times 0.10))}{1 + 0.10}$$

$$- \frac{(\$60,000)(0.20)(0.40)}{0.20 + 0.10} \times \frac{1}{(1.10)^{15}}$$

$$= \$25,455 - \$3,830 = \$21,625$$

$$PV(\text{ECF}_n) = \frac{\$60,000}{(1.10)^{15}} = \$14,364$$

$$NPV = PV(\text{Operating CFs}) + PV(\text{CCA Tax Shield}) + PV(\text{ECF}_n) - CF_0$$

$$= \$114,091 + \$21,625 + \$14,364 - \$0 - \$100,000 = +\$50,080$$

The best-case NPV suggests that the project is extremely attractive and should be accepted.

Worst case:

$$PV(\text{Operating Cash Flows}) = [\$9,000] \times \left[ \frac{1 - \frac{1}{(1.14)^9}}{0.14} \right]$$

$$= (\$9,000) \times (4.94637) = \$44,517$$

$$PV(\text{CCA Tax Shield}) = \frac{(\$100,000)(0.20)(0.40)}{0.20 + 0.14} \times \frac{(1 + 0.5(0.14))}{1 + 0.14}$$

$$- \frac{(\$30,000)(0.20)(0.40)}{0.20 + 0.14} \times \frac{1}{(1.14)^9}$$

$$= \$22,085 - \$2,171 = \$19,914$$

$$PV(\text{ECF}_n) = \frac{\$30,000}{(1.14)^9} = \$9,225$$

$$\text{NPV} = \text{PV(Operating CFs)} + \text{PV(CCA Tax Shield)} + \text{PV(ECF}_n) - \text{CF}_0$$
$$= \$44{,}517 + \$19{,}914 + \$9{,}225 - \$0 - \$100{,}000 = -\$26{,}344$$

The worst-case NPV suggests that the project is extremely unattractive and should be rejected. Examining these three scenarios tells the company that although the project seems attractive and has significant upside, it could also turn out to be a losing proposition and is not without risk.

Once we conduct scenario analysis, a final step is to consider a what-if scenario analysis. In Example 14.13, we assumed that a variable changed, yet the firm did not change anything in response. In the extreme, we said that the project was extremely unattractive if the worst case materialized and the operating cash flows were only $9,000 a year for nine years, although the risk of the project increased and the salvage value dropped to $30,000. But a firm would not stand by and watch a project deteriorate without doing anything. In practice, firms respond to changing circumstances. **Real option valuation (ROV)**, discussed in the next subsection, recognizes that firms respond to different situations and change their operating characteristics accordingly.

**real option valuation (ROV)**
an assessment that recognizes that firms respond to different circumstances and change their operating characteristics

## Real Option Valuation (ROV)

Real option valuation (ROV) was listed as a capital budgeting approach in Figure 13.1, with 10 percent of CFOs saying they used it often or always. ROV places great weight on the flexibility involved in a firm's operations. The classic example of ROV is in mining. Suppose it costs $150 to put into operation a mine that lasts for one year and can produce 100 units of production at a fixed cost of $200 and a variable cost of $6. If the price of the ore is expected to be $10 and the discount rate is 12 percent, then the NPV is:

$$\text{NPV} = -\$150 + \frac{(\$10 - \$6) \times 100 - \$200}{1.12} = \$28.57$$

Clearly the mine is a go because it has a positive NPV. However, suppose the analyst then conducted a sensitivity analysis with respect to the most important factor, which is the ore price, to see what happens when there is an equal probability of the ore price being either $12 and $8, or $14 and $6, or $16 and $4. We might suppose that the mine becomes less valuable as the ore price volatility increases, yet this is not the case. **Table 14.3** shows the cash flow estimates under the three ore-price scenarios.

The expected cash flows are highest in scenario 3, in which the ore price variability is highest and the ore price is either $16 or $4. The reason is that the cash flow for the bad price scenario remains at −$200, which is the same as in scenario 2 because there is an explicit option available to the firm: to shut down. According to basic economics, a firm will operate only when the contribution margin is positive or, in other words, when the price exceeds the variable cost. In the case of the mine, when the ore price is at or below its $6 variable cost, the firm can't lose more than its fixed $200 costs or it will shut down. As a result, in the $16 ore price case it earns $800, while in the $4 case it loses only $200, so the expected cash flow is a 50-percent chance of $800 and a 50-percent chance of −$200 or $300. Therefore, the value of the mine goes up as the volatility of its ore price increases.

**TABLE 14.3**  **Real Options Example**

| | Scenario 1: Ore Price $12 or $8 | Scenario 2: Ore Price $14 or $6 | Scenario 3: Ore Price $16 or $4 |
|---|---|---|---|
| Good price ($p = 0.5$) | $12 | $14 | $16 |
| Cash flow | $400 | $600 | $800 |
| Bad price ($p = 0.5$) | $8 | $6 | $4 |
| Cash flow | $0 | −$200 | −$200 |
| Expected cash flow | $200 | $200 | $300 |

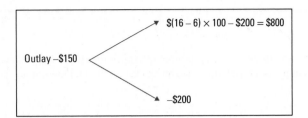

**FIGURE 14.2** Decision Tree on Two Possible Outcomes

We illustrate this with a **decision tree** in **Figure 14.2**, in which we map out two possibilities for scenario 3.

**decision tree** a schematic way to represent alternative decisions and the possible outcomes

For simplicity, we have assumed no taxes or CCA.

The firm loses the $200 fixed costs regardless of the ore price, because these costs are defined as fixed. However, its contribution depends on the ore price. When the ore price is above $6, there is a positive contribution; when it is below $6, the contribution is zero because the firm shuts down. Although we call this the shutdown option, it is, in fact, a 100-unit call option on the ore. If the ore price is above $6, the firm executes its option to go into business and produce ore; if the ore price is below $6, it throws the option away and does not open the mine.

We can use the binomial option pricing model discussed in Appendix 12A to value this option as long as we have the futures price for the ore. In fact, option pricing is used to value mines producing copper, gold, zinc, and other commodities when they are traded commodities and the cost structure of the mine is clearly defined, as it usually is.

ROV has been applied to other cases in which the firm has the option to defer or delay a project, abandon a project, or switch the use of an asset from producing one product to another. For example, we started out by saying capex decisions could possibly change the risk of the firm and were very important if they involved irrevocable unique assets. However, if the assets involved generic modern production equipment that could be used to do other things, then the flexibility available to close down an unprofitable project and use the assets elsewhere considerably reduces the project's risk. In such a case, scenario analysis combined with these event-changing parameters gives a more accurate NPV than assuming that nothing changes as critical values faced by the project change. As a result, ROV and decision-tree analysis have dramatically increased our understanding of corporate decision-making and the value of flexibility and of the strategic considerations raised by senior management.

ROV is much more difficult to apply than conventional capital budgeting, and you can use the binomial or Black-Scholes option pricing models only in highly restrictive circumstances. However, the following options almost always exist in a capital expenditure decision:

1. When do you undertake the investment, now or at some point in the future?
2. Will the acceptance of this project generate other projects—that is, are investment projects linked or interdependent?
3. Can you put the resources to alternative uses if things don't pan out?
4. Can you terminate the project if cash flows do not materialize?
5. Can you learn, from undertaking the project, how to lower expected cash costs?

## NPV Break-Even Analysis

Because the annual operating after-tax cash flows are so critical to the success or failure of many investment projects, firms may pay particular attention to how variations in these cash flows affect the viability of a project. Sometimes they will want to know what level of annual operating cash flow is required for a project to "break even" in the sense of producing an NPV of zero. We will denote this as the operating cash flow **NPV break-even point** of a project.[13] The break-even discount rate is the IRR of the project. In Example 14.14, we calculate the operating cash flow NPV break-even point for the project discussed in Example 14.13.

**NPV break-even point** the level of annual operating cash flow required for a project to produce an NPV of zero

---

[13]Firms pay attention to many other break-even points, such as the accounting break-even point, which occurs when the accounting profit equals zero and is typically measured in units of sales.

**EXAMPLE 14.14** | Scenario Analysis

Use the base-case estimates for all inputs other than operating after-tax cash flows for the project examined in Example 14.13. Determine the break-even amount for the annual operating after-tax cash flow.

**Solution**

$$CF_0 = \$100,000$$
$$PV(\text{CCA Tax Shield}) = \$20,453$$
$$PV(ECF_n) = \$12,834$$

We can set the NPV equal to 0 and solve for the required value of the PV of the operating CFs, as follows:

$$NPV = PV(\text{Operating CFs}) + PV(\text{CCA Tax Shield}) + PV(ECF_n) - CF_0$$

$$\$0 = PV(\text{Operating CFs}) + \$20,453 + \$12,834 - \$100,000$$

$$PV(\text{Operating CFs}) = \$66,713$$

Now we can solve for the annual after-tax CF that satisfies this equation, as follows:

$$PV(\text{Operating CFs}) = [\text{Break-Even Operating CF}] \times \left[ \frac{1 - \dfrac{1}{(1.12)^{12}}}{0.12} \right]$$

$$\$66,713 = (\text{Break-Even Operating CF}) \times (6.194374)$$

$$\text{Break-Even Operating CF} = \$10,770$$

Notice that this annual cash flow is less than the $12,000 estimate in the base case, which had produced a positive NPV.

## Concept Review Questions

1. What insights can be gained by using sensitivity analysis, scenario analysis, and NPV break-even analysis?

2. What limitations of scenario analysis does the real option valuation approach address?

---

## 14.5 Inflation and Capital Budgeting Decisions

**LEARNING OBJECTIVE 14.5**

Explain how mistakes can easily be made when dealing with inflation.

Capital expenditures typically involve the estimation of cash flows several years in the future. Inflation can play an important role in determining these estimates, because it will affect future levels of sales and expenses. In addition, inflation affects the level of interest rates and therefore the cost of capital, which could very well influence the decision to accept or reject a new investment opportunity.

Earlier in this chapter, we introduced guideline 11 for estimating cash flows, which said that we need to treat inflation *consistently*. So far, we have been estimating future cash flows on a nominal basis (i.e., estimating the actual cash flow that will result in year 2, etc., without making adjustments for inflation). As a result, we have been discounting these cash flows using nominal (or actual) discount rates. This approach treats inflation consistently. An alternative is to estimate future *real*, or inflation-adjusted, cash flows and discount these real cash flows using *real* discount rates, which have also been adjusted for inflation. One difficulty with this approach is that the CCA tax-savings estimates represent the actual amount of CCA that can be charged in a given year. Therefore, the easiest way to proceed is usually to estimate the nominal cash flows and discount them using nominal discount rates.

It is important for firms to consider the impact that inflation will have on both sales and expenses, as well as on the discount rate. Although it is often reasonable to assume that both items will be equally affected by inflation, this will not be the case for all firms or all situations. Much depends on the industry firms are in and on the products they sell. For example, sometimes inflation will have a greater impact on selling prices than it will on expenses, and sometimes it will be the opposite. Example 14.15 demonstrates the impact that such variations in the growth of sales and expenses can have on the NPV of a project.

---

**EXAMPLE 14.15** | The Impact of Inflation

A firm is considering a project with the following forecasts:

- The initial after-tax cash outflow will be $1,000,000; the entire outflow represents a capital cost of $1,000,000; and the appropriate CCA class is asset class 8 (CCA rate is 20 percent, declining balance method).
- There is no terminal loss or CCA recapture associated with the project.
- Revenues will be $350,000 in the first year and will grow at 5 percent per year after that.
- Costs will be $75,000 in the first year and will grow at 5 percent per year after that.
- The project will last 10 years, and the equipment has an estimated salvage value of $100,000 at that time.
- The firm's required return is 18 percent.
- The firm pays taxes at a marginal rate of 40 percent.

**a.** Calculate the NPV of this project.

**b.** Redo part a by assuming the first year's revenue is $350,000; however, there is no growth in revenue beyond that. In addition, costs turn out to be $100,000 the first year and grow at 7 percent per year thereafter.

**c.** Redo part a by assuming the first year's revenue turns out as expected, but revenue grows at a rate of 7 percent per year thereafter until year 10, while costs are $75,000 in the first year and rise at 3 percent per year thereafter until year 10.

**Solution**  This problem can be solved much more efficiently using a spreadsheet program, such as Excel, but we will proceed using formulas.

The present value of CCA tax savings and the present value of the ending cash flow will be the same for parts a, b, and c, so we solve for these items first.

$$C_0 = \$1,000,000$$

$$CF_0 = C_0 + \Delta NWC_0 + 0C = \$1,000,000 + \$0 + \$0 = \$1,000,000$$

$$PV(\text{CCA Tax Shield}) = \left[ \frac{(\$1,000,000)(0.20)(0.40)}{0.20 + 0.18} \times \frac{(1 + 0.5(0.18))}{1 + 0.18} \right]$$
$$- \left[ \frac{(\$100,000)(0.20)(0.40)}{0.20 + 0.18} \times \frac{1}{(1.18)^{10}} \right]$$

$$= \$194,469 - \$4,022 = \$190,447$$

$$ECF_n = SV_n + \Delta NWC_n = \$100,000 + \$0 = \$100,000$$

$$PV(ECF_n) = \frac{ECF_n}{(1 + k)^n} = \frac{\$100,000}{(1.18)^{10}} = \$19,106$$

**a.** The operating cash flows are expected to grow at a rate of 5 percent per year, because both revenue and expenses are expected to grow at 5 percent per year for 10 years. We *could* estimate all 10 operating cash flows separately and discount each of them. In fact, this would be the appropriate strategy if we were using a spreadsheet. However, when solving this with a calculator, a computationally more efficient method is to use a variation of the constant growth version of the DDM, which gives the present value of a "growing perpetuity." The cash flows in this example do not grow at 5 percent forever, but only for 10 years. We can adjust for this fact by subtracting the present value of the growing perpetuity of operating cash flows from years 11 to infinity from the present value of the perpetuity from time 0 to infinity. This leaves us with the PV of the 10-year annuity. In other words:

$$\text{PV(Operating CFs)} = \frac{\text{CFBT}_1(1-T)}{k-g} - \frac{\text{CFBT}_{11}(1-T)}{k-g} \times \frac{1}{(1+k)^{10}}$$

$$= \frac{(\$350,000 - \$75,000)(1-0.40)}{0.18-0.05}$$

$$- \frac{(\$350,000 - \$75,000)(1-0.40)(1.05)^{10}}{0.18-0.05} \times \frac{1}{(1+0.18)^{10}}$$

$$= \frac{\$165,000}{0.13} - \frac{(\$165,000)(1.628895)}{0.13} \times (0.1910645)$$

$$= \$1,269,231 - \$395,015 = \$874,216$$

Combining the previous results, we can find the NPV as follows:

$$\text{NPV} = \text{PV(Operating CFs)} + \text{PV(CCA Tax Shield)} + \text{PV(ECF}_n) - \text{CF}_0$$

$$= \$874,216 + \$190,447 + \$19,106 - \$1,000,000 = \$83,769$$

Strictly speaking, the firm should go ahead with the project (however, the NPV is not that high, relative to the $1-million required outlay).

**b.** Revenues display no growth and remain at $350,000 per year for 10 years. Expenses start at $100,000 (not $75,000) and grow at 7 percent per year thereafter.

The beginning cash flow, tax shield, and ending cash flow calculations are not affected; only the operating cash flows are, so we redo those here. Notice that revenues and expenses now grow at different rates, so we must consider each separately.

$$\text{PV(Operating Revenues)} = \frac{\text{Rev}_1(1-T)}{k-g} - \frac{\text{Rev}_{11}(1-T)}{k-g} \times \frac{1}{(1+k)^{10}}$$

$$= \frac{(\$350,000)(1-0.40)}{0.18-0} - \frac{(\$350,000)(1-0.40)(1.0)^{10}}{0.18-0} \times \frac{1}{(1+0.18)^{10}}$$

$$= \frac{\$210,000}{0.18} - \frac{(\$210,000)(1.0)}{0.18} \times (0.1910645)$$

$$= \$1,166,667 - \$222,909 = \$943,758$$

$$\text{PV(Operating Costs)} = \frac{\text{Cost}_1(1-T)}{k-g} - \frac{\text{Cost}_{11}(1-T)}{k-g} \times \frac{1}{(1+k)^{10}}$$

$$= \frac{(\$100,000)(1-0.40)}{0.18-0.07} - \frac{(\$100,000)(1-0.40)(1.07)^{10}}{0.18-0.07} \times \frac{1}{(1+0.18)^{10}}$$

$$= \frac{\$60,000}{0.11} - \frac{(\$60,000)(1.967151)}{0.11} \times (0.1910645)$$

$$= \$545,455 - \$205,011 = \$340,444$$

The PV(Operating CFs) = $943,758 - $340,444 = $603,314, which is well below the value of $874,216 calculated in part a under the previous assumptions.

The NPV can now be calculated as

$$\text{NPV} = \text{PV(Operating CFs)} + \text{PV(CCA Tax Shield)} + \text{PV(ECF}_n) - \text{CF}_0$$

$$= \$603,314 + \$190,447 + \$19,106 - \$1,000,000 = -\$187,133$$

Under this scenario, the project produces a negative NPV and would be unattractive.

**c.** Revenues grow at 7 percent instead of 5 percent for 10 years. Expenses start at $75,000 and grow at 3 percent per year thereafter. Once again, the beginning cash flow, the CCA tax shield, and the ending cash flow calculations are not affected. Notice that revenues and expenses again grow at different rates, so we must consider each separately.

$$\text{PV(Operating Revenues)} = \frac{\text{Rev}_1(1-T)}{k-g} - \frac{\text{Rev}_{11}(1-T)}{k-g} \times \frac{1}{(1+k)^{10}}$$

$$= \frac{(\$350,000)(1-0.40)}{0.18-0.07} - \frac{(\$350,000)(1-0.40)(1.07)^{10}}{0.18-0.07} \times \frac{1}{(1+0.18)^{10}}$$

$$= \frac{\$210,000}{0.11} - \frac{(\$210,000)(1.967151)}{0.11} \times (0.1910645)$$

$$= \$1,909,091 - \$717,537 = \$1,191,554$$

$$PV(\text{Operating Costs}) = \frac{\text{Cost}_1(1-T)}{k-g} - \frac{\text{Cost}_{11}(1-T)}{k-g} \times \frac{1}{(1+k)^{10}}$$

$$= \frac{(\$75,000)(1-0.40)}{0.18-0.03} - \frac{(\$75,000)(1-0.40)(1.03)^{10}}{0.18-0.03} \times \frac{1}{(1+0.18)^{10}}$$

$$= \frac{\$45,000}{0.15} - \frac{(\$45,000)(1.343916)}{0.15} \times (0.1910645)$$

$$= \$300,000 - \$77,032 = \$222,968$$

The PV (Operating CFs) = \$1,191,554 − \$222,968 = \$968,586, which is well above the \$874,216 that was calculated under the assumptions in part a.

$$NPV = PV(\text{Operating CFs}) + PV(\text{CCA Tax Shield}) + PV(\text{ECF}_n) - CF_0$$

$$= \$968,586 + \$190,447 + \$19,106 - \$1,000,000 = \$178,139$$

Under this scenario, the project would produce a much larger positive NPV and would be more attractive.

## Lessons to Be Learned

In this section we discussed how to adjust for inflation when making capital expenditure decisions. Generally speaking, the Bank of Canada's adherence to a target range of 1- to 3-percent inflation (with a 2-percent goal) since 1991 has made it much easier for companies and investors to forecast future inflation rates. On the other hand, the depth of the financial crisis in the United States was so great that it prompted the largest increase in the money supply and the largest increase in U.S. government spending since the end of World War II. In finance, we talk about "the law of unintended consequences." In responding to the worst downturn in 70 years, the United States injected so much stimulus into the economy, by lowering interest rates and by other means, that concerns abound that if it is not careful when it removes the stimulus as the economy recovers, it may overshoot into an inflationary environment. In 2015, much of the discussion in the U.S. did not centre on *if* interest rates would rise but rather *when* they would rise.

## Concept Review Questions

1. Why is it usually more precise to use nominal cash flows and nominal discount rates when evaluating projects?
2. Why might inflation affect cash inflows differently from the way it affects cash outflows?

# Review

## Summary

In this chapter, we demonstrate several approaches and guidelines for estimating the future cash flows associated with an investment. The chapter involves a lot of number crunching, because in capex evaluation there are alternative ways to solve many of the problems. We also introduce several equations that can be used to estimate the present value of future cash flows and differentiate between expansion and replacement decisions. We proceed to discuss how sensitivity analysis, scenario analysis, what-if decision-tree analysis, and NPV break-even analysis can be used to determine how variations in estimates might affect the attractiveness of project evaluations. We conclude by illustrating the impact that inflation can have on capital budgeting decisions.

## Summary of Learning Objectives

### 14.1 Outline the basic framework for capital expenditure analysis.

(1) Estimate all cash flows on an *after-tax* basis. (2) Use the appropriate cash flow estimates that represent the marginal or incremental cash flows arising from capital budgeting decisions. (3) Do *not* include associated interest and dividend payments in estimated project cash flows; they should already be accounted for in the discount rate (i.e., the appropriate cost of capital). (4) Adjust cash flows (particularly the initial cash outlay and the terminal cash flow at the end of the estimated project life) to reflect any additional working capital requirements that are associated with the project. (5) Treat sunk costs as irrelevant; what is of concern are *future* cash flows. (6) Although sunk costs are irrelevant, opportunity costs should be factored into cash flow estimates. (7) Determine the appropriate time horizon for the project. (8) Ignore intangible considerations. (9) Ignore externalities in the calculations. (10) Consider the effect of all project interdependencies on cash flow estimates. (11) Treat inflation consistently. This harks back to comparing like with like: discount nominal cash flows with nominal discount rates, and real cash flows with real discount rates. (12) Undertake all social investments required by law.

### 14.2 Estimate the future cash flows associated with potential investments.

The cash flows include three categories: initial cash flow, the expected annual after-tax cash flows, and the ending cash flow.
- Initial cash flow = Initial investment + Change in net working capital + Opportunity cost.
- Expected annual after-tax cash flows = (Sales − Cost) × (1 − $T$) + $T$ × CCA.

- Ending cash flow = Salvage value + Change in net working capital. It could get more complicated if a capital gain, CCA recapture, or terminal loss is incurred.

### 14.3 Explain how to make replacement decisions, and explain what is special about them.

Replacement projects, as their name suggests, involve the replacement of an existing asset (or assets) with a new one. What is special is that one must focus more on incremental cash flows.

### 14.4 Conduct a sensitivity analysis to see how the value changes as key inputs vary, and determine what is a real option.

Sensitivity analysis examines how an investment's net present value (NPV) changes as the value of one input is changed at a time. Scenario analysis examines how an investment's NPV changes in response to differing scenarios with respect to the values of one or more estimates. The real option valuation (ROV) approach places great weight on the flexibility involved in a firm's operations. Using a decision tree, the ROV approach considers alternative decisions and the possible outcomes.

### 14.5 Explain how mistakes can easily be made when dealing with inflation.

Inflation must be treated consistently. More specifically, nominal cash flow needs to be discounted by the nominal discount rate, and real cash flow by the real discount rate. Mistakes can easily be made if the consistency rule is not followed.

## Key Terms

accelerated depreciation, p. 14-13
capital cost ($C_0$), p. 14-4
decision tree, p. 14-23
ending (or terminal) after-tax cash flow ($ECF_n$), p. 14-7
expansion projects, p. 14-17
expected annual after-tax cash flows ($CF_t$), p. 14-4

externalities, p. 14-3
incremental cash flows, p. 14-2
initial after-tax cash flow ($CF_0$), p. 14-4
marginal cash flows, p. 14-2
NPV break-even point, p. 14-23
opportunity costs, p. 14-2

real option valuation (*ROV*), p. 14-22
replacement projects, p. 14-17
salvage value ($SV_n$), p. 14-7
scenario analysis, p. 14-20
sensitivity analysis, p. 14-20
sunk costs, p. 14-2

## Equations

| Equation | Description | Formula | Page |
|---|---|---|---|
| **[14.1]** | Initial Cash Outlay | $CF_0 = C_0 + \Delta NWC_0 + OC$ | p. 14-4 |
| **[14.2]** | Annual After-Tax Cash Flows | $CF_t = CFBT_t(1 - T) + CCA_t(T)$ | p. 14-6 |
| **[14.3]** | Ending Cash Flow (with tax implications) | $\text{ECF (with tax implications)}_n = SV_n + \Delta NWC_n - 0.5\,[(SV_n - C_0) \times T] - [(SV_n - UCC_n) \times T]$ | p. 14-8 |
| **[14.4]** | Ending Cash Flow (ignoring tax implications) | $ECF_n = SV_n + \Delta NWC_n$ | p. 14-8 |
| **[14.5]** | Net Present Value | $NPV = PV(\text{Annual CFs}) + PV(ECF_n) - CF_0$ | p. 14-9 |
| **[14.6]** | Present Value of Operating Cash Flows | $PV(\text{Operating Cash Flows}) = CFBT(1 - T) \times \left[\dfrac{1 - \dfrac{1}{(1 + k)^n}}{k}\right]$ | p. 14-10 |
| **[14.7]** | Present Value of CCA Tax Shield (ignoring CCA Recapture and Terminal Loss) | $PV(\text{CCA Tax Shield}) = \dfrac{(C_0)(d)(T)}{(d + k)} \times \dfrac{(1 + 0.5k)}{(1 + k)} - \dfrac{(SV_n)(d)(T)}{(d + k)} \times \dfrac{1}{(1 + k)^n}$ | p. 14-10 |
| **[14.8]** | Present Value of CCA Tax Shield (accounting for CCA Recapture or Terminal Loss) | $PV(\text{CCA Tax Shield}) = \dfrac{(C_0)(d)(T)}{(d + k)} \times \dfrac{(1 + 0.5k)}{(1 + k)} - \dfrac{(UCC_n)(d)(T)}{(d + k)} \times \dfrac{1}{(1 + k)^n} - \dfrac{(SV_n - UCC_n)(T)}{(1 + k)^n}$ | p. 14-10 |
| **[14.9]** | Present Value of Capital Gains Taxes Paid | $PV(\text{Capital Gains Taxes Paid}) = \dfrac{(SV_n - C_0)(T)}{(1 + k)^n}$ | p. 14-11 |
| **[14.10]** | Net Present Value (Components) | $NPV = PV(\text{Operating CFs}) + PV(\text{CCA Tax Shield}) + PV(ECF_n) - PV(\text{Capital Gains Taxes Paid}) - CF_0$ | p. 14-11 |
| **[14.11]** | Present Value of CCA Tax Shield Allowing for Accelerated Depreciation (ignoring CCA Recapture or Terminal Loss) | $PV(\text{CCA Tax Shield}) = \dfrac{(C_0)(d)(T)}{(d + k)} \times \dfrac{(1 + 1.5k)}{(1 + k)} - \dfrac{(SV_n)(d)(T)}{(d + k)} \times \dfrac{1}{(1 + k)^n}$ | p. 14-14 |
| **[14.12]** | Present Value of CCA Tax Shield Allowing for Accelerated Depreciation (accounting for CCA Recapture or Terminal Loss) | $PV(\text{CCA Tax Shield}) = \dfrac{(C_0)(d)(T)}{(d + k)} \times \dfrac{(1 + 1.5k)}{(1 + k)} - \dfrac{(UCC_n)(d)(T)}{(d + k)} \times \dfrac{1}{(1 + k)^n} - \dfrac{(SV_n - UCC_n)(T)}{(1 + k)^n}$ | p. 14-14 |

# Questions and Practice Problems

## Multiple Choice Questions

**1. (LO 14.1)** When making capital expenditure decisions, firms should *not* consider which of the following?

   **a.** After-tax incremental cash flows

   **b.** Additional working capital requirements

   **c.** Sunk costs

   **d.** Salvage value

**2. (LO 14.1)** Which of the following will yield the same capital expenditure decisions?

   **a.** Using nominal cash flows and a real discount rate versus using nominal cash flows and a nominal discount rate

   **b.** Using nominal cash flows and a nominal discount rate versus using real cash flows and a real discount rate

   **c.** Using real cash flows and a real discount rate versus using real cash flows and a nominal discount rate

d. Using nominal cash flows and a nominal discount rate versus using real cash flows and a nominal discount rate

**3. (LO 14.1)** When making capital budgeting decisions, firms should consider which of the following?

    **a.** After-tax incremental cash flows

    **b.** Sunk costs

    **c.** Associated interest and dividend payments

    **d.** Externalities

**4. (LO 14.1)** When making capital budgeting decisions, firms should *not* consider which of the following?

    **a.** Change of working capital

    **b.** Opportunity cost

    **c.** All project interdependencies

    **d.** Intangible considerations whose impact on cash flows cannot be estimated

**5. (LO 14.2)** What is the initial after-tax cash flow $(CF_0)$ of a project given the following information: initial cost = $435,050; R&D costs associated with the project = $12,000; associated opportunity costs = $81,000; decrease in inventory = $12,000; installation costs = $6,000.

    **a.** $480,050        **c.** $490,050

    **b.** $510,050        **d.** $530,050

**6. (LO 14.2)** Which of the following items is *not* included in the calculation of the ending (or terminal) cash flow $(ECF_n)$?

    **a.** Salvage value

    **b.** Change in inventory levels

    **c.** Change in accounts receivable levels

    **d.** Operating cash flows

**7. (LO 14.2)** A firm has a project that is expected to generate annual revenue of $48,000, while incurring an annual cost of $29,000. The CCA is $42,000 and the tax rate is 40 percent. What is the after-tax cash flow?

    **a.** $28,200        **c.** $37,600

    **b.** $19,400        **d.** $48,500

**8. (LO 14.2)** A firm's discount rate is 15 percent. Suppose annual revenue starts at $50,000; annual expenses start at $20,400; and both will grow at a rate of 5 percent from year 2 to year 15. The firm's tax rate is 40 percent. What is the present value of operating cash flows for all 15 years?

    **a.** $120,855        **c.** $132,225

    **b.** $115,635        **d.** $109,485

**9. (LO 14.2)** Which of the following will *not* decrease the present value of the CCA tax shield associated with an investment project?

    **a.** An increase in the discount rate

    **b.** A decrease in the corporate tax rate

    **c.** A decrease in the CCA rate

    **d.** A decrease in the discount rate

**10. (LO 14.2)** Which of the following statements is *false*?

    **a.** CCA recapture occurs when the salvage value is greater than the ending UCC for the asset or asset class.

    **b.** Capital gains occur when the salvage value is greater than the original cost of the asset.

    **c.** CCA recapture is taxable.

    **d.** A terminal loss occurs when the salvage value is greater than the ending UCC for the asset or asset class.

**11. (LO 14.2)** What is the terminal cash flow $(ECF_n)$ based on the following information? The release of additional inventory tied up = $2,500; salvage value = $11,500; UCC = $22,000; initial cost $(C_0)$ = $55,000; $T = 40$ percent. Assume the asset class will remain open.

    **a.** $12,000        **c.** $8,000

    **b.** $16,000        **d.** $14,000

**12. (LO 14.2)** Determine the present value of the ending cash flow using the following information: initial capital cost = $100,000; net working capital invested = $10,000; salvage value = $12,000; CCA rate = 30 percent; ending UCC = $20,408; tax rate = 35 percent, discount rate = 12 percent; project life = 5 years. Assume the asset class is closed on termination of the project.

    **a.** $12,483        **c.** $11,580

    **b.** $14,153        **d.** $17,254

**13. (LO 14.2)** Determine the present value of the ending cash flow using the following information: initial capital cost = $100,000; net working capital invested = $10,000; salvage value = $22,000; CCA rate = 30 percent; ending UCC = $20,408; tax rate = 35 percent, discount rate = 12 percent; project life = 5 years. Assume the asset class is closed on termination of the project.

    **a.** $17,254        **c.** $17,841

    **b.** $11,580        **d.** $18,158

**14. (LO 14.4)** Which of the following statements is *true* about sensitivity analysis and scenario analysis?

    **a.** Sensitivity analysis examines the impact of the change of one input at a time.

    **b.** Scenario analysis examines the impact of the change of one input at a time.

    **c.** Sensitivity analysis examines PV changes in response to differing scenarios.

    **d.** Sensitivity analysis usually includes a base-case scenario, a best-case scenario, and a worst-case scenario.

**15. (LO 14.3)** Oak Inc. is planning to purchase new, faster printers to replace its existing printers. The capital cost of the new printers = $250,000. The current market price of the old printers = $50,000. The applicable CCA rate $(d)$ = 30 percent; the tax rate = 40 percent; and $k$ = 20 percent. It is estimated that the new printers could last for 15 years. What is the second-year incremental CCA expense? (Include the half-year rule.)

    **a.** $46,000        **c.** $58,000

    **b.** $51,000        **d.** $63,000

**16. (LO 14.3)** Which of the following statements is *true* about replacement decisions?

    **a.** Incremental cash flow is used.

    **b.** Only the cash flow generated from the new machine is considered.

    **c.** The cash flow that would be generated from the old machine is irrelevant.

    **d.** The salvage value of the new machine is irrelevant.

**17. (LO 14.5)** Suppose the nominal cash flow is $1,050 in year 1, the nominal discount rate is 8.15 percent, the real discount rate is 5 percent, and the inflation rate is 3 percent. What is the PV of the cash flow?

    **a.** $952.38        **c.** $1,000

    **b.** $970.87        **d.** $950

## Practice Problems

### Basic

**18. (LO 14.1)** Firms A and B are competing for a project. The potential client has provided the following information on a hypothetical project: initial cost is $500,000; building renovation is $600,000; and the building cannot be rented due to the project (currently the building is vacant). Firm B has made the following statement to the board of directors:

> We have conducted an extensive analysis of the project and have concluded that your decision should consider the initial cost of $500,000 only. The $600,000 spent on renovations will not affect future cash flow; therefore we can ignore it. The potential rental revenue should be ignored also, as the building is currently empty and therefore is not a cost of this project.

The board of directors has asked for your comments on firm B's statement.

**19. (LO 14.1)** An investor has observed that BathGate Company, a shareholder wealth–maximizing company, has just made an investment that appears to have a negative NPV. The investor is very puzzled about why a company would undertake a negative NPV project. Assume that the NPV of the cash flows is in fact negative, and the project is actually shareholder wealth maximizing. What aspect of the project is the investor not considering?

**20. (LO 14.1)** Summarize all the cash flows that cannot be used in the capital budgeting process and explain the reasons.

**21. (LO 14.2)** Calculate the initial cash flows ($CF_0$) for the following projects. Which project has a larger $CF_0$?

  a. Project A: equipment purchase price = $195,000; installation cost = $4,500; extra working capital requirement = $30,500; opportunity cost = $18,000

  b. Project B: machine purchase price = $220,500; shipping cost = $10,000; decrease in working capital = $12,000; opportunity cost = $31,500

**22. (LO 14.2)** Describe how CCA recapture and CCA terminal losses occur and their tax treatment.

**23. (LO 14.4)** What is the difference between sensitivity analysis and scenario analysis?

**24. (LO 14.4)** Explain how real option valuation (ROV) is applied.

### Intermediate

**25. (LO 14.1)** Your boss is very puzzled by the finance courses in his MBA program. He has learned that "cash flow is king," but notices that the capital budgeting problems spend a lot of time and effort dealing with depreciation and CCA but not with interest expense. He knows that depreciation and CCA are non-cash expenses, and he knows that interest is definitely a cash expense. He would like an explanation of why he needs to bother with depreciation and CCA and not with interest expense.

**26. (LO 14.1)** Jensen's Juice Bar is considering purchasing a new blender. Indicate which of the following statements is a relevant consideration in the new-blender decision.

  a. Last year, Jensen's spent $500 on a new blender.

  b. Customers *would* prefer to have their juice made in the new blender and won't buy juice produced in the old one.

  c. The manager of the juice bar just got a raise.

  d. The juice bar's tax rate is 29 percent.

  e. The juice bar's monthly rent is $500.

  f. If Jensen's buys a blender, there will be no space for a coffee maker.

  g. The new blender is blue, and blue is your favourite colour.

  h. Jensen's Juice Bar spent $10,000 in renovations last year.

**27. (LO 14.2)** Complete the following table.

|   | Tax Rate | Annual Cash Flow before Taxes | Discount Rate | Project Life | PV(Future CFs) |
|---|---|---|---|---|---|
| A | 24% | $5,000 | 5% | 5 | |
| B | 43% | $3,000 | 10% | 6 | |
| C | 36% | $8,000 | 8% | 3 | |
| D | 50% | $15,000 | 15% | 4 | |
| E | 15% | $9,000 | 36% | 2 | |
| F | 30% | $20,000 | 12% | 7 | |

**28. (LO 14.2)** Prepare a schedule of the annual capital cost allowance for a major project. The initial investment is $80,000, the tax rate is 40 percent, and the CCA rate is 30 percent. Determine the amount of CCA allowed each year. Assume that the item will continue in use for more than four years. (Include the half-year rule.)

| Year | Opening UCC Balance | CCA | Closing UCC Balance |
|---|---|---|---|
| 1 | | | |
| 2 | | | |
| 3 | | | |
| 4 | | | |

**29. (LO 14.2)** Complete the following table. Assume that the asset class is left open, and/or the salvage value is less than the UCC for the entire class. (Include the half-year rule.)

|   | CCA Rate | Tax Rate | Discount Rate | Initial Investment | Salvage Value | Project Life (n) | PV (CCA Tax Shields) |
|---|---|---|---|---|---|---|---|
| A | 15% | 35% | 10% | $16,000 | $800 | 6 | |
| B | 20% | 40% | 14% | $12,000 | $1,000 | 5 | |
| C | 25% | 35% | 5% | $50,000 | $2,500 | 12 | |
| D | 40% | 45% | 12% | $30,000 | $1,200 | 8 | |
| E | 30% | 50% | 8% | $40,000 | $2,000 | 10 | |
| F | 20% | 35% | 15% | $15,000 | $600 | 9 | |
| G | 10% | 27% | 6% | $90,000 | $3,000 | 15 | |

**30. (LO 14.2)** In November 2018, the Liberal government introduced the Accelerated Investment Incentive, which essentially allowed companies to claim a depreciation expense for income tax purposes in the first year at a rate three times higher than they could have assuming the half-year rule applied. Re-do practice problem 29 adjusting for accelerated depreciation.

**31. (LO 14.2)** Complete the following table.

|   | CCA % | Tax % | k % | Project Life | NWC $C_0$ $ | NWC $ | SV $ | UCC $ | Asset Class | $ECF_n$ $ | ($ECF_n$) $ |
|---|---|---|---|---|---|---|---|---|---|---|---|
| A | 15 | 35 | 10 | 6 | 16,000 | 1,000 | 800 | 6,567 | Open | | |
| B | 20 | 40 | 14 | 5 | 12,000 | 800 | 1,000 | 4,424 | Closed | | |
| C | 25 | 35 | 5 | 12 | 50,000 | 2,000 | 2,500 | 1,848 | Closed | | |
| D | 20 | 45 | 12 | 8 | 30,000 | 1,500 | 1,200 | 5,662 | Open | | |
| E | 30 | 50 | 8 | 10 | 40,000 | 1,800 | 2,000 | 1,372 | Closed | | |
| F | 20 | 35 | 15 | 9 | 15,000 | 500 | 600 | 2,265 | Open | | |
| G | 10 | 27 | 6 | 15 | 90,000 | 2,500 | 3,000 | 19,560 | Closed | | |

**32. (LO 14.2)** Which of the following items, relating to working capital, would be considered a cash inflow or outflow when evaluating a project (and why)?

  a. Increase in inventory

  b. Increase in accounts payable

  c. Increase in accounts receivable

  d. Decrease in inventory

**33. (LO 14.2)** You are given the following information: $C_0 = \$300,000$; CCA rate $(d) = 0.3$; $T = 0.4$; $RF = 4.5$ percent; project beta $= 1.2$; market risk premium $= 10$ percent; $SV_n = \$35,000$; $UCC_n = \$55,000$. This project has a five year life. (Include the half-year rule.)

   **a.** Calculate the discount rate.

   **b.** Assuming that the asset class is terminated, calculate the present value of the CCA tax shield.

   **c.** Calculate the PV (CCA tax shield) if the asset class remains open.

**34. (LO 14.2)** You are given the following information: $CFBT = \$215,000$; $T = 40$ percent; this project will last for eight years. The project has a 2.5-percent extra risk premium compared with the firm's cost of capital. The firm has 40-percent debt at a cost of 6 percent and 40-percent common equity at a cost of 12 percent, and the remainder is preferred shares at 8 percent.

   **a.** What is the WACC?

   **b.** What is this firm's cost of capital?

   **c.** Calculate the present value of operating cash flows.

**35. (LO 14.2)** Calculate the present value of the operating cash flows if the revenue of a project grows at 5 percent, while expense grows at 4 percent, given that Revenue1 $= \$15,000$ and Expense 1 $= \$7,000$. Assume the firm is all-equity financed; $RF = 8$ percent; project beta $= 0.8$; the market risk premium $= 5.5$ percent; and $T = 40$ percent. The project is expected to last for eight years.

**36. (LO 14.2)**

   **a.** Describe how CCA expenses change through the life of a project. (Include the half-year rule.)

   **b.** Given $C_0 = \$250,000$; CCA rate $= 20$ percent; tax rate $= 40$ percent; and year 2 operating income $= \$150,000$, calculate the cash flow in year 2.

## Challenging

**37. (LO 14.2)** KRZ Company's tax rate is 40 percent and the appropriate discount rate is 10 percent. It is considering a project. Each asset class is large and continues after the project terminates. KRZ is not capital constrained. There is no change in net working capital at the beginning or at the termination of the project. The initial investment is $4,000; annual pre-tax operating cash flow is $2,000; salvage value is 0; the CCA rate is 30 percent; and the length of the project is three years. Should KRZ take this project? (Include the half-year rule.)

**38. (LO 14.2)** KRZ Company's tax rate is 40 percent and the appropriate discount rate is 8 percent. It is considering a project. Each asset class is large and continues after the project terminates. KRZ is not capital constrained. There is no change in net working capital at the beginning or at the termination of the project. The initial investment is $48,000; annual pre-tax operating cash flow is $8,500; salvage value is $2,500; the CCA rate is 30 percent; and the length of the project is 10 years. Should KRZ take this project? (Include the half-year rule.)

**39. (LO 14.2)** Java Cafe's tax rate is 45 percent and the appropriate discount rate is 8 percent. It is considering a project. Each asset class consists only of the project asset and will be terminated at the end of the project. Java Cafe is not capital constrained. The initial investment is $40,000; annual pre-tax operating cash flow is $15,000; salvage value is $30,000; the CCA rate is 10 percent; and the length of the project is three years. Should Java Cafe take this project? (Include the half-year rule.)

**40. (LO 14.2)** Java Cafe's tax rate is 45 percent and the appropriate discount rate is 8 percent. It is considering another project. Each asset class consists only of the project asset and will be terminated at the end of the project. Java Cafe is not capital constrained. The initial investment is $90,000; annual pre-tax operating cash flow is $20,000; salvage value is $50,000; the CCA rate is 30 percent; and the length of the project is five years. Should Java Cafe take this project? (Include the half-year rule.)

**41. (LO 14.2)** Java Cafe's tax rate is 40 percent and the appropriate discount rate is 12 percent. It is considering another project. Each asset class consists only of the project asset and will be terminated at the end of the project. Java Cafe is not capital constrained. The initial investment is $120,000; annual pre-tax operating cash flow is $27,500; salvage value is $25,000; the CCA rate is 30 percent; and the length of the project is ten years. Should Java Cafe take this project? (Include the half-year rule.)

**42. (LO 14.2)** KRZ Company has hired you to help evaluate several projects. The firm's tax rate is 40 percent and the appropriate discount rate is 10 percent. Each asset class is small and will be terminated at the end of each project. KRZ is not capital constrained. The initial investment is $4,000; annual pre-tax operating cash flow is $2,000; salvage value is $500; the CCA rate is 30 percent; and the length of the project is three years. Should KRZ take this project? (Include the half-year rule.)

**43. (LO 14.2)** KRZ Company has hired you to help evaluate several projects. The firm's tax rate is 40 percent and the appropriate discount rate is 15 percent. Each asset class is small and will be terminated at the end of each project. KRZ is not capital constrained. The initial investment is $16,500; annual pre-tax operating cash flow is $5,000; salvage value is $1,500; the CCA rate is 20 percent; and the length of the project is six years. Should KRZ take this project? (Include the half-year rule.)

**44. (LO 14.2)** You are trying to decide whether or not to go to graduate school. If you get a job right after you get your bachelor's degree, you expect to earn $40,000 a year, and you expect your salary to increase by 5 percent a year for the next 40 years. If you go to graduate school, you will spend four more years at school. The tuition and books are expected to cost $8,000 a year.

Assume living expenses are $15,000 a year. After graduate school, you expect to start at a higher salary that will increase by 7 percent a year. However, you will only be able to work for 36 years. Your savings earn 4 percent a year.

What is the minimum post-graduate school starting salary you will require to make going to graduate school a positive NPV project? (Note: do not consider the non-monetary benefits of a higher education.) Use Excel "solver" function.

**45. (LO 14.2)** You are trying to decide whether to continue renting an apartment or to buy a house. In 20 years, you plan on leaving Canada and moving to a warm tropical island and would like to have as much money as possible. You have just won $25,000 in the lottery and will be able to use that money for a down payment. At the moment, your rent is $700 a month and you expect it to increase by 1 percent a year. The long-term forecast for housing in your area is that house prices are expected to rise at a rate of 5 percent a year for the next 20 years. With $25,000 down, you are able to obtain a five-year, $250,000 mortgage at 7 percent, compounded monthly and amortized over 20 years (the value of the house you are considering is $275,000). Every five years you will have to renegotiate the mortgage, and you expect interest rates to increase by 50 basis points (half of a percentage point) each time. Assume zero taxes.

   **a.** If you expect to earn 10 percent on your investments, should you buy a house or continue to rent?

   (Suggestion: use a spreadsheet to solve this problem.)

   **b.** Would your answer change if you expected to earn only 4 percent on your investments?

**46. (LO 14.2)** Brigid Co. has the following potential project:

Machine price $= \$1,800,000$; additional inventory requirement $= \$150,000$. Cash flows will be generated at year end. $Rev_1 = \$400,000$ and grows at 5 percent each year for five years, while $Cost_1 = \$125,000$ and grows at 4 percent. At the end of the five-year project, the assets can be sold for $200,000, while the additional inventory that was tied up will be released. The applicable CCA rate is 30 percent. The tax rate $= 40$ percent, and $RF = 4.5$ percent; project beta $= 1.25$; $ERM = 9.5$ percent. The ending UCC $= \$367,353$.

Calculate the NPV of the project if the asset class remains open upon termination of the project. Decide whether or not Brigid Co. should accept the project. (Include the half-year rule.)

**47. (LO 14.4)** Calculate th1e NPV in practice problem 46 assuming a best case of the following: project life = 10 years; project beta = 0.8; $SV_n$ = $100,000; $Rev_1$ = $500,000. (Include the half-year rule.)

**48. (LO 14.2)** You have been hired as consultants to XrayGlasses Corporation (XGC). XGC is in the process of deciding whether to invest in a new production facility. The new facility will enable it to produce and sell X-ray machines to airports. The manufacturing and marketing process is not very different from their current line of business. The management of XGC has produced certain estimates about the new facility. Review the estimates to:

**a.** Calculate beginning UCC, CCA, and ending UCC each year. (Include the half-year rule.)

**b.** Calculate investment, opportunity cost, and changes in net working capital each year. Note that these items are not subject to tax.

**c.** Calculate revenue and cost of the X-ray machines project each year and the lost revenue and saved cost of X-ray glasses each year.

**d.** Calculate after-tax cash flows each year.

**e.** Determine the appropriate discount rate for the X-ray machines project.

**f.** Determine the NPV of this project to XrayGlasses Corporation. Make a recommendation, with supporting arguments, to the management of XrayGlasses about the project.

• Cost of the machinery: $45,000; installation costs: $15,000

• Life of the project: five years; the expected salvage value of the machine is $2,000

• An environmental assessment of the building site that is already paid: $200,000

• Charles LeCrook has offered XrayGlasses $150,000 for the building. XrayGlasses paid $45,000 for the building 10 years ago and spent $50,000 last month on renovations.

• The CCA rate on the machinery is 25 percent, and there are other assets in the pool. At the end of the project, the pool is not expected to be closed. The firm's tax rate is 35 percent.

• Currently work-in-progress inventory is $65,000. This is expected to increase by $2,000 immediately and to remain at that level for the life of the project. This inventory will be sold at the end of the project.

• Currently accounts receivable are $15,000. This is expected to increase by $3,000 by the end of year 1. The higher level of accounts receivable is expected to continue until the end of the project, at which time the accounts will be paid in full.

• Currently accounts payable are $25,000. This is expected to increase by $2,000 by the end of year 1. The higher level of accounts payable is expected to continue until the end of the project, at which time the accounts will be paid in full.

• XGC expects to sell 25 machines in year 1, 30 in year 2, and 40 machines per year for years 3 to 5.

• Variable costs are expected to be $5,000 per machine; the expected sales price is $50,000.

• Annual fixed costs for the firm are currently $900,000 per year and will rise to $930,000 during the project.

• Currently the firm sells 400 pairs of x-ray glasses to airport security guards each year. These sales are expected to disappear when the x-ray machines enter service. The price of a pair of glasses is $550 and the cost of production is $50.

• The company will have to borrow to finance the start-up of the project. The expected interest expense is $5,000 per year. Each year the firm will have to repay $3,000 of the principal of the loan. Overall, the firm expects to remain at its optimal capital structure.

• Currently the firm pays $25,000 in dividends. This is expected to increase to $28,000 during the life of the project.

• The yield to maturity of the firm's debt is 5 percent, the cost of equity is 14 percent, and the WACC is 10 percent.

**49. (LO 14.2)** GG Inc. has a project that requires purchases of capital assets costing $60,000 and additional raw material inventory of $3,000. Shipping and installation costs are $1,800. GG Inc. estimated that the project would generate an annual operating after-tax cash flow of $9,000 for six years at each year end. At the end of the project, the assets can be sold for $5,000, while the additional inventory that was tied up will be released. The assets are in asset class 9, which has a CCA rate of 30 percent. The tax rate = 40 percent, and $k$ = 12 percent. Calculate the NPV of the project assuming that the asset class is left open, and/or the salvage value is less than the UCC for the entire class. Also assume that that this scenario takes place in 2019 with the Liberal government's Accelerated Investment Incentive ("AAI") in full effect. Decide whether or not GG Inc. should accept the project. Did the AAI impact the decision outcome?

**50. (LO 14.2)** Repeat practice problem 49 assuming that the project would generate annual revenue of $68,000 and annual costs of $50,000 for six years. The ending UCC = $10,469. Did the AAI impact the decision outcome?

**51. (LO 14.2)** Repeat practice problem 49 assuming that the project would generate annual revenue of $70,000 and annual costs of $40,000 for six years. Also, the asset class will be closed at the end of six years.

**52. (LO 14.2)** Calculate the NPV of the project described in practice problem 50, but assume that the discount rate has changed based on the following information: $RF$ = 3.4 percent; project beta = 1.2; the market risk premium = 5.5 percent; and the firm is financed entirely by equity. Assume the asset class will remain open. What is the percentage change in the NPV because of the change in the discount rate? Decide whether or not the project should be accepted.

**53. (LO 14.4)** Calculate the after-tax operating cash flow NPV break-even point for the project described in practice problem 49 by using a 12-percent discount rate. The ending UCC = $10,469. Also, the asset class will be closed at the end of six years.

**54. (LO 14.4)** You are evaluating a project for a small manufacturing firm. The firm has provided the following data: the initial cost of the project is $2,500; the CCA rate is 10 percent; the tax rate is 25 percent; and the cash flow in the first year is $700. Cash flows are expected to increase at 5 percent a year for four years. At the end of the fourth year, the project will end and the machinery acquired to start the project will be scrapped (zero salvage). The asset class is large and will continue. The appropriate discount rate is 7 percent.

**a.** Calculate beginning UCC, CCA, ending CCA, and after-tax cash flow in each year. Calculate the NPV of this project. (Include the half-year rule.)

**b.** You have also obtained the following information about the best- and worst-case scenarios. In the best case, the cash flow in the first year will be $900 and will grow at 8 percent a year. In the worst case, the cash flow in the first year will be $300 and will grow at 2 percent a year. The base case was presented earlier. The probability of the worst case is 30 percent, best case is 15 percent, and base case is 55 percent. Calculate the expected NPV of the project.

**c.** You are not very confident about the growth rate assumption and the initial cash flow estimate. Do a sensitivity analysis to assess the impact of possible errors in those estimates. Assume that growth rates could be 3 percent, 5 percent, or 7 percent and the initial cash flow could be $400, $700, or $1,000.

**d.** Using the base case estimates, determine the NPV break-even initial cash flow.

**55. (LO 14.4)** AK Radio has hired a consultant to help in the assessment of a project to launch a satellite to deliver a 24/7 infomercial radio station to the world. The satellite costs $400 million and has a CCA rate of 30 percent. The satellite is expected to last 10 years and then burn up in the earth's atmosphere. AK does not expect to replace the satellite, and the asset class will terminate in 10 years. The launch is expected to take place in two years and will cost $5 million. Satellite launches are risky undertakings, and there is a 30-percent chance that the rocket taking the satellite into space will explode on take-off. If the launch fails, AK will close the business, as it will have only $50 million of cash left and will be unable to acquire another satellite.

**a.** Calculate the NPV of a terrestrial project. Assume it lasts 12 years. (Include the half-year rule.)

**b.** If the satellite launch project is successful, calculate beginning UCC, CCA, ending UCC, and after-tax cash flow every year. Calculate the present value of CCA terminal loss. Calculate the NPV of the satellite launch project if it is successful.

**c.** If the satellite launch project fails, calculate beginning UCC, CCA, ending UCC, and after-tax cash flow every year. Calculate the present value of CCA terminal loss. Calculate the NPV of the satellite launch project if it fails.

**d.** Calculate the NPV of the satellite launch project. Do you recommend that AK invest in the satellite launch project?

**e.** Describe how your analysis would change if the licensing restriction allowed AK to decide on terrestrial or space in two years.

**56. (LO 14.4)** The CFO of CanGold Company is considering investing in a gold mine in Mongolia. The mine will cost $200 million to get into production and will last for one year. At the end of one year, it is expected to produce 1 million ounces of gold. The price of gold is expected to be $500 an ounce in one year (the forward price). The current price of gold is $300 an ounce. Fixed costs of production are $50 million and variable costs are $250 per ounce. Assume no taxes or CCA. The appropriate discount rate for the mine is 15 percent. Risk-free borrowing and lending is available at a rate of 3 percent per year.

**a.** Based on NPV, should CanGold invest in the Mongolian gold mine?

**b.** If in one year, we know that the price of gold will be either $200 per ounce or $850 per ounce:

  **i.** Describe how having the choice of closing the mine can change the value of the asset.

  **ii.** Describe how the volatility of the price of gold could increase the value of the mine.

  **iii.** Draw the decision tree for this project.

  **iv.** Value the mine as a call option on gold. (Hint: use the arbitrage arguments behind the binomial option pricing model. Think of the mine as a financial security).

**57. (LO 14.3)** A consultant has presented the following statement to the board of directors of BigCo:

When comparing two mutually exclusive projects, we only need to consider the NPV. When the two projects have different lives, we recommend comparing the NPV/life (i.e., NPV divided by the number of years) ratios of the projects and choosing the project with the highest ratio. The NPV/life ratio reflects the average annual increase in shareholder value expected from the project.

The chair of the board is not convinced and has asked FinCorp Inc. to review this statement. Explain to the chair why the consultant's approach to dealing with projects of different lives is incorrect. Provide a numerical demonstration to support your arguments.

**58. (LO 14.3)** Consider the following scenario and calculate the beginning UCC, CCA, ending UCC, CCA tax shield, and after-tax incremental cash flow for each and every year of the project. Assume the asset class is closed on termination of the project. Decide whether a newspaper, *Weekday*, should replace its current printing press with the new one.

Currently *Weekday* has a printing press in its plant that costs $3,000 a year in maintenance. The maintenance costs are expected to increase by $500 a year for the next five years. At the end of the five years, the machine will be scrapped and the salvage value will be zero. The press was fully depreciated eight years ago. The current press has a unique capability to print very large certificates in addition to the regular printing. The revenue from the certificate business is expected to be $1,500 per year for the next five years.

A replacement machine is available at a cost of $25,000 with a life expectancy of five years. At the end of the five years, the salvage value is expected to be $5,000. The CCA rate for the machine is 20 percent. The new machine is expected to generate revenue of $6,000 per year for the next five years. Annual maintenance costs of the new machine are $500 per year.

The company is expected to be very profitable in the future. The real risk-free rate is 2 percent, inflation is expected to remain at 3 percent for the next five years, and the appropriate real discount rate for risky cash flows is 5 percent. The tax rate is 34 percent. (Include the half-year rule.)

**59. (LO 14.3)** GG Inc. is now considering replacing some old equipment. The market price of the old equipment is $50,000 and the salvage value at the end of five years is $15,000. The new equipment will cost $100,000 and could be sold at the end of five years for $35,000. An additional $4,000 in working capital is required and will be released at the end of five years. The new equipment is estimated to generate $10,000 in before-tax operating income, compared with $6,000 for the old one. Assume that $T = 40$ percent and $k = 15$ percent. Both the new and old equipment belong to class 10, which has a CCA rate of 30 percent, and the asset class will remain open at the end of five years. Calculate $PV(CCA\ Tax\ Shield)$ by formula. Estimate the NPV of the replacement decision and decide whether or not replacement should occur. (Include the half-year rule.)

**60. (LO 14.5)** BathGate Group has just completed its analysis of a project. The CFO has presented the following information to the board of directors:

The initial cost of the project is $15,000. Sales are expected to be 10,000 units in year 1 and are expected to grow by 5 percent per year forever. In year 1, we expect to sell units for $3 each and foresee no real change in unit price. Variable and fixed costs are zero.

The firm's required rate of return is 8 percent. The corporate tax rate is 30 percent. Assume the CCA rate is zero.

**a.** Calculate the NPV of this project if there is zero inflation forecasted.

**b.** Calculate the NPV of this project if inflation is forecasted to be 2 percent per year. Assume the required rate of return is nominal.

**c.** Calculate the NPV of this project if inflation is forecasted to be 2 percent per year, and the firm requires a real rate of return of 8 percent.

# Mergers and Acquisitions

---

**LEARNING OBJECTIVES**

After studying this chapter, you should be able to:

**15.1** Describe the different types of takeovers.

**15.2** Explain securities legislation as it applies to takeovers.

**15.3** Differentiate between friendly and hostile acquisitions and describe the process of a typical friendly acquisition.

**15.4** Explain the various motivations underlying mergers and acquisitions.

**15.5** Identify the valuation issues involved in assessing mergers and acquisitions.

**15.6** Identify the issues involved in accounting for mergers and acquisitions.

---

In chapters 13 and 14, we discussed the issues surrounding the typical capital expenditure decisions of firms. We focused on typical investments that would help the existing firm grow from within—this is often referred to as "organic growth." However, firms can also grow by acquiring other firms or by acquiring selected assets from other firms. Sometimes an entirely new entity is formed; at other times the acquiring firm simply becomes larger and the "target" firm ceases to exist. In this chapter, we illustrate how financial decisions about mergers and acquisitions can be evaluated using standard discounted cash flow valuation techniques.

---

## 15.1 | Types of Takeovers

---

**LEARNING OBJECTIVE 15.1**
Describe the different types of takeovers.

---

Few topics generate more interest from the financial media than the subject of corporate **takeovers**, which refers to the transfer of control from one ownership group to another. Global merger and acquisition (M&A) activity in 2018 was worth over US$3.5 trillion in terms of market values of companies involved.[1] In fact, these takeovers can occur in several manners, which are described in this section.

**takeover** the transfer of control from one ownership group to another

The terms "mergers," "acquisitions," and "takeovers" are often used interchangeably; however, their strict definitions differ. An **acquisition** occurs when one firm (the acquiring firm or bidder) completely absorbs another firm (the target firm). Under this arrangement, the acquiring firm retains its identity, while the acquired firm ceases to exist. An example is provided by the acquisition of Foster's, an Australian brewer, by SAB Miller of the United States for AUS$9.9 billion (US$10.2 billion) in December 2011. Immediately following approval of

**acquisition** the purchase of one firm by another

---

[1]Mergermarket, "Mergermarket Releases 2018 Global M&A Report with League Tables," https://www.mergermarket.com/info/mergermarket-releases-2018-global-ma-report-league-tables. Accessed May 8, 2019.

**merger** the combination of two firms into a new legal entity

the acquisition by shareholders and by the Supreme Court in the state of Victoria, Foster's ceased trading. This illustrates the key idea that, in an acquisition, the purchased company disappears as all senior management functions reside with the acquirer.

In contrast, a **merger** is usually the combination of two firms into a new legal entity. Such a situation notionally occurred in 2008, when the TSX Group Inc. and the Montreal Exchange Inc. combined to form the TMX Group Inc., which existed in that form until 2012. As discussed in Chapter 1, a new company called the TMX Group Ltd. was subsequently formed in 2012 with the acquisition of the Canadian Depository for Securities Ltd. (CDS) along with Alpha Trading Systems Inc. and Alpha Trading Systems Limited Partnership (collectively Alpha).

Some "mergers" run into issues over the intent to merge equals. Consider, for example, the proposed 2011 merger between the TMX Group Inc. and the London Stock Exchange (LSE) in the United Kingdom, which failed to materialize due to a lack of investor support. One of the key issues was that the deal called for a "merger of equals," yet LSE shareholders would receive 55 percent of the shares in the new entity, versus 45 percent for TMX shareholders. In addition, the board of directors would consist of eight LSE-appointed directors versus seven TMX-appointed ones.

In some cases, issues arise because after companies have announced their intention to merge as equals, events occur that take them down a different path. For example, on May 2, 1998, Daimler-Benz and Chrysler announced that they were combining as a "merger of equals" worth almost US$40 billion. The combination of the third-largest U.S. car company with the prestigious maker of Mercedes-Benz cars was obviously big news, and the fact that the new company's name was a hybrid of the merging firms' names suggested that it was an integration of the two companies, with neither dominant. For a time, it appeared as if nothing had changed, but in 2003 the *Detroit News* announced that the merger was in fact a takeover or acquisition of Chrysler by Daimler. This sparked multiple lawsuits, since it was clear that Chrysler was becoming a division of Daimler, and effective control and decision-making would take place in Germany.

These examples indicate the elasticity of the terms "merger," "acquisition," and "takeover." The proposed Miller takeover of Foster's was clearly an acquisition right from the start, with Foster's ceasing to exist, while the TMX Group Inc. was formed out of a merger of the TSX and the Montreal Exchange. The furor over Daimler's acquisition of Chrysler arose from the fact that it was announced as a merger, with the implication that the two companies would be integrated in the new entity, with shared responsibilities and management, when in reality it was an acquisition that left Daimler in charge. Shortly after, most of the senior Chrysler management left.

## Financing Takeovers

**cash transaction** the receipt of cash for shares by shareholders in a target company

One key consideration in classifying acquisitions and mergers is the means by which the deal is financed. Most acquisitions, such as the $1.25-billion offer by San Francisco–based URS Corp. in 2012 to acquire Calgary-based Flint Energy Services Ltd., are made through a **cash transaction**, with the shareholders in the target company receiving cash for their shares. In section 15.2, we will briefly discuss securities legislation as it applies to takeovers, but generally, when one company acquires another, the approval of the target company's shareholders is required, since they have to agree to sell their shares. The shareholders of the *acquiring* company do not normally have to give their approval. Buying another company is regarded as similar to buying a new piece of equipment or any other purchase. Only if there is some specific provision in the company's charter do the shareholders of the acquiring firm get to vote on whether or not the company should make the acquisition.

**share transaction** the offer by an acquiring company of shares or a combination of cash and shares to the target company's shareholders

The alternative to a cash transaction is a **share transaction**, in which the acquiring company offers shares or some combination of cash and shares to the target company's shareholders. For example, the 2012 all-share takeover bid by Glencore International PLC for Xstrata PLC provided 2.8 shares to Xstrata shareholders for each of their shares, valuing the deal at $30 billion.[2] In contrast to a cash transaction, a share transaction often does require the

[2]"Xstrata CEO Poised to Get $46-Million Retention Package." *The Globe and Mail*, May 31, 2012. Available at www.theglobeandmail.com.

approval of the acquiring firm's shareholders, depending on whether the firm has a limit on its authorized share capital. If the firm's authorized share capital is limited to, say, 3 million shares, and it wants to offer shares in excess of this limit, then shareholder approval is needed. To get around this, in recent years, most companies have sought and received shareholder approval to issue an unlimited number of shares. However, this does point to the most basic distinction between a merger and an acquisition.

# Amalgamations

In a merger, a new company is created, so both sets of shareholders have to agree to exchange their existing shares for shares in the new company. This means that, in a genuine merger, both sets of shareholders are required to approve the transaction. In Canada, this process is called an **amalgamation**. For example, the TSX–Montreal Exchange combination discussed earlier was referred to as an amalgamation, and the announcement began by stating that 99.6-percent approval had been obtained from the Montreal Exchange shareholders. The two companies approve an amalgamation agreement, and a special meeting of the shareholders is called to vote on the agreement. Under the *Canada Business Corporations Act* (*CBCA*), 21 days' notice is given for this special meeting, and since the shareholders have to vote, all the normal rules for proxy statements and other information are invoked. The basic rule is that two-thirds of the shareholders of both amalgamating firms have to approve the special resolution to amalgamate.[3] This can sometimes result in tense battles as dissident shareholders refuse to support an agreement crafted by the two sets of managers. An amalgamation also takes place when the acquirer has purchased all the shares in the target, but in this case, since the acquirer owns all the shares, the process is a formality.

> **amalgamation**  a genuine merger in which both sets of shareholders must approve the transaction

An amalgamation can also become a tense situation after a firm has partially completed a takeover. Sometimes the acquirer can end up with a majority of the shares, say 70 percent, so that it knows it can get the two-thirds majority to approve an amalgamation, yet there are still 30 percent of the shares outstanding and held by dissident shareholders who have not agreed to sell their shares. This is a special form of acquisition called a **going private transaction** or **issuer bid**.

> **going private transaction** or **issuer bid**  a special form of acquisition where the purchaser already owns a majority stake in the target company

These sorts of transactions have been common in Canada, because there were many Canadian companies with a majority of shares owned by another company and only a minority owned by Canadian shareholders. For example, Imperial Oil's majority owner is Exxon. Similarly, U.S. parent companies have owned the majority of shares for companies like DuPont Canada, Shell Oil Canada, Goodyear Canada, Ford Canada, and so on. In such cases, the minority of shares traded in the Canadian market were not the result of failed take-over bids but of U.S. companies' desire to keep a public "float" of the shares in the hands of Canadian shareholders. This motivation became less important after Canada signed the Free Trade Agreement (FTA) with the United States in the 1990s and the economies were more closely integrated. A side effect of the FTA was that U.S. multinationals wanted to integrate their companies in the two countries, and buying out the Canadian minority shareholders removed an obstacle to this.[4]

Regardless of how a public minority of shareholders is created, the issues and principles are the same. When a controlling shareholder seeks approval for an amalgamation, special rules kick in. The presumption is that the controlling shareholder has a much more accurate knowledge of the true value of the shares and will abuse this position unless safeguards are in place. The critical safeguards are that a majority of the minority shareholders approve the special resolution to amalgamate the two companies and that there be a **fairness opinion**. A fairness opinion is an independent expert's opinion about the value of a firm's shares, based on an external valuation. These valuations are particularly difficult given that, with a controlling shareholder, there is little possibility of any other party buying the shares.

> **fairness opinion**  an opinion provided by an independent expert regarding the true value of a firm's shares, based on an external valuation

---

[3]Note that this is two-thirds of all the shareholders, including groups that do not normally have the right to vote. Moreover, sometimes they have the right to vote as a class, so a small group can defeat an amalgamation proposal.
[4]Under the *CBCA*, directors of a Canadian company have to act in the best interests of the company as a whole, and not just the majority shareholder. This restricted the ability of the U.S. parents to integrate their Canadian subsidiaries into their North American operations.

A good example of this principle comes from Sears, Roebuck and Co., which on December 5, 2005, announced that it would make a bid for the 46 percent of Sears Canada that it did not own, paying $16.86 a share. Sears' initial aim was to buy enough shares that it would own 90 percent; under Ontario securities law, when minority shareholders hold less than 10 percent of a company's shares, they must accept the offer that has been accepted by the other shareholders. This rule prevents a "holdup" problem that might occur if the last shareholder asks for a ridiculously high price. However, since the offer was an insider bid, Sears Canada set up a committee of six independent members of the board of directors to evaluate the bid. They hired Genuity Capital Markets to do a fairness opinion, which came in at a range of $19 to $22.25 a share—well above the offer from Sears, Roebuck. On this basis, the independent directors unanimously rejected the offer from their own company's parent and also announced that they would not stand for re-election at the May 2006 annual general meeting. (Given the directors' decision, they probably would not have been nominated for re-election.)

In March 2006, Sears, Roebuck announced that it had received only 9.5 percent of the 46 percent of the Sears Canada shares it did not hold. It also announced that instead of trying to buy the shares directly, it would seek a statutory amalgamation at a special meeting of shareholders. In this case, all it needed to amalgamate Sears Canada with Sears, Roebuck was the two-thirds necessary for an amalgamation plus a majority of the minority shareholders. It also sweetened the price marginally to $18. However, a new valuation by Genuity Capital reiterated its valuation and judgements on both sides.

This situation deteriorated when it was discovered that Sears' Canadian financial advisors had entered into a "lock-up agreement" to sell shares they controlled to Sears, Roebuck without disclosing this. The Ontario Securities Commission (OSC) was asked to rule on this and decided that these shares could not be counted as part of the majority of the minority rule, a decision that was upheld by the Ontario Divisional Court.

---

## Concept Review Questions

1. What is the difference between an acquisition and a merger?
2. What is an amalgamation?
3. What is the majority of the minority rule?

---

# Securities Legislation and Takeovers

**LEARNING OBJECTIVE 15.2**
Explain securities legislation as it applies to takeovers.

## Concerns Regarding Takeovers

The previous discussion on takeovers highlights the role of securities legislation in determining what can be done and when. In fact, many takeovers are nullified by regulators, such as the proposed merger of the NYSE Euronext and the Deutsche Bourse, which was shot down by European regulators. Authorities can reject takeovers for a variety of reasons, including the following:

- concerns related to national security
- concerns about "sensitive" industries that are seen as critical to the nation (this is why there are foreign ownership restrictions for Canadian banks)
- anti-trust concerns in situations where an amalgamation of two or more businesses would create an entity that would too narrowly restrict competition

In Canada, as of 2019, regulators review foreign takeovers of private sector companies worth over $1.5 billion and subject them to the so-called net benefit rule, with a much lower threshold of $379 million for state-owned or -influenced enterprises.[5] Questions about how, precisely, this rule is implemented have been the cause of much concern in Canada, especially in light of the 2010 rejection of the Australian giant BHP Billiton's proposed takeover of Potash Corporation of Saskatchewan Inc.

# Critical Thresholds

In addition to takeovers that cause anti-trust and/or foreign ownership concerns, securities legislation is relevant for all potential takeovers because it governs the exchange of shares by the target company's shareholders and protects their right to receive full value for their shares. We will examine other aspects of securities law later, when discussing new issues of securities, but the main thing to remember is that this is a provincial responsibility, and there are slight differences between provinces. However, the *Ontario Securities Act*, administered by the OSC, contains many features that are common to all jurisdictions, and we will use it to illustrate some of the usual characteristics of securities legislation.

There are several critical shareholder percentages that investors have to be aware of:

1. 10 percent: early warning

2. 20 percent: takeover bid

3. 50.1 percent: control

4. 66.7 percent: amalgamation

5. 90 percent: minority squeeze-out

The 10-percent early warning threshold (which is set at 5 percent in the United States) refers to the level of shareholding by any one owner that requires a report to be sent to the OSC.[6] This lets the company know who owns its shares and whether a significant block has been bought by a potential acquirer. Once a shareholder holds 20 percent of shares, they cannot buy any more shares in the open market without making a takeover bid (we will discuss this in more detail later). The 50.1-percent ownership level gives a company control so that it can call a special meeting of the shareholders (5-percent ownership is required to attend the meeting) and change the membership of the board of directors (BOD). In Canada, but not in the United States, members of the BOD can be removed without cause, so the majority shareholder can change management and take control of the firm's affairs.[7]

As described, a firm can seek to hold a special meeting of shareholders to vote on an amalgamation, which needs support from owners of 66.7 percent of the shares, but the amalgamation can be disputed by a majority of the minority shareholders. Finally, following a takeover bid, if the firm owns 90 percent of the shares, it can force the minority of the shareholders to sell their shares at the takeover price. This prevents a small minority from frustrating a bid that has been accepted by the majority of shareholders. Otherwise, a few dissidents could wreak havoc by refusing to sell a small number of shares.

These share percentage milestones explain a lot of takeover behaviour. Initially, most firms will acquire less than the 10 percent of shares that trigger the early warning and then purchase up to the 20-percent level of the target's shares in the open market. This is referred to as "obtaining a toehold." Firms do this to acquire the shares at the market price without paying a premium. After acquiring 20 percent, buying any more shares requires a takeover

---

[5]Bodrug, John, Tingley, Charles, and Feldman, David, "*Investment Canada Act* Net Benefit Review Threshold Increased Again for Many Foreign Investors," September 21, 2017, https://www.dwpv.com/en/Insights/Publications/2017/Net-Benefit-Review-Thresholds-in-Investment-Canada-Act-Increase. Accessed May 8, 2019.

[6]Proposed regulation changes that would have reduced this threshold to 5 percent in Canada were abandoned in the fall of 2014 after the government received negative feedback from market participants.

[7]In the United States, directors have a fixed term and cannot be forcibly removed simply because of a change in ownership. By having directors serve non-concurrent terms, a firm can prevent a majority owner from immediately changing the board and senior management. As a result, it may take several years for a majority owner to change directors and senior managers.

bid, which is an offer to purchase outstanding voting shares that, together with the offeror's shares, equal 50 percent or more of the target's shares.

This definition of a takeover bid applies to individuals alone or "working in concert with others." Otherwise, a company could buy 20 percent itself and then get friendly parties or another subsidiary to buy two more blocks of 20 percent and thereby effect a takeover without making a takeover bid.

## Takeover Rules

Unless the purchase is exempt from the *Ontario Securities Act*, any further takeover bid must then follow strict rules. A takeover circular (similar to a prospectus) describing the bid, financing, and all relevant information must be sent to all shareholders for review. The target then has 15 days to circulate a letter indicating acceptance or rejection, and the bid has to be open for 105 days, which is typically reduced to 35 days if the target's board issues a new release to that effect. Shareholders then **tender** to the offer by signing the authorizations sent to them; in the event that another firm makes a competing offer, they can withdraw their acceptance. A competing bid automatically increases the takeover window by 10 days.

**tender**   to sign an authorization accepting a takeover bid made to target company shareholders

The takeover bid does not have to be for 100 percent of the shares. If the bid is for, say, 60 percent, and more shares are tendered, the acquirer prorates the shares tendered so everyone receives an equal proportion. That is, if 80 percent are tendered and 60 percent are bought, then everyone who has tendered gets to sell 75 percent (60/80) of the shares tendered. While the tender offer is outstanding, the acquirer can buy another 5 percent of shares through the facilities of the stock exchange as long as it announces that it intends to do so. Finally, the tender offer price cannot be for less than the average price of shares that the acquirer has bought in the previous 90 days. This is to prevent a coercive takeover bid, where the acquirer offers one price for the shares needed to get control and then a lower price once it has control. (This kind of bid is called a two-part tender offer and is illegal in Canada because it produces a rush to sell into the higher price at the first stage and "coerces" shareholders.[8])

The basic objective of these rules is to make sure that an acquirer treats all the shareholders fairly and everyone gets the same price. Otherwise there is an economic incentive to lock up shares early at a high price, so that an acquirer has control and can then offer a lower price, knowing that no one else can mount a competing bid. In this way, different classes of shareholders are treated differently, and the shares are sold below their true value. As the Sears, Roebuck example highlights, once you have control, no one else can bid and there is a temptation to try to buy the remaining shares cheaply.

As mentioned earlier, all takeovers have to abide by these rules unless they are exempt from the *Ontario Securities Act* for one of the following reasons:

- Where there is limited involvement by shareholders in Ontario—say a takeover of a Manitoba company in which there are very few Ontario shareholders—securities legislation in another province (in this case, Manitoba) will apply.

- Securities legislation is concerned with the involvement of the public, so takeovers of private firms are exempt.

- An acquirer can also buy shares from fewer than five shareholders as long as the premium over the market price is not more than 15 percent. This is to allow the sale of blocks of shares.

- Finally, and most importantly, a normal tender offer can be made through a stock exchange as long as no more than 5 percent of the shares are purchased through the exchange over a one-year period. This 5-percent rule allows for **creeping takeovers**, where a company acquires a target over a long period of time by slowly accumulating shares.

**creeping takeover**   the acquisition of a target company over time by the gradual accumulation of its shares

There are many other regulations that relate to takeovers. In fact, a "solvency" clause that was inserted by BCE Inc.'s lawyers to protect them from bondholder litigation proved

---

[8]Coercive two-part tender offers are allowed in the United States.

to be a "dagger" that ended the proposed $52-billion takeover of BCE Inc. by the Ontario Teachers' Pension Plan and a group of investors, as KPMG refused to sign off on the deal in November 2008.

---

### Concept Review Questions

1. What is a tender?
2. What is a takeover circular?
3. What is a creeping takeover?

---

## 15.3   Friendly versus Hostile Takeovers

### LEARNING OBJECTIVE 15.3

Differentiate between friendly and hostile acquisitions and describe the process of a typical friendly acquisition.

## Friendly Takeovers

With a knowledge of securities legislation, we can now consider whether an acquisition should be hostile or friendly and discuss how a deal is hammered out. To understand this, think first about the difficulty of valuing a company when an external party has access only to public sources of information. How do you value a small biotech company, for example, when you have no direct information on whether recent lab tests were positive or negative? Similarly, for an oil and gas company or mining firm, it may not be obvious how much potential is left in an oil and gas field or mineral reserve. The obvious thing to do, when faced with this uncertainty, is to go to the target company and ask whether it is interested in being acquired. In this situation, the acquirer hopes for a **friendly acquisition**. The URS-Flint takeover discussed previously was a friendly deal that resulted in a 70-percent premium offer. In contrast, the $1-billion friendly bid by Canadian-based Fortis Inc. for U.S.-based CH Energy Group Inc. in 2012 resulted in a premium offer of only 10.5 percent—so it is hard to make generalizations about the premiums offered based on the nature of the deal.

Friendly acquisitions also start out when the target voluntarily puts itself into play. This can occur for many reasons, but it often happens when the founder is no longer actively involved in the business, and it is time for the firm to leave the controlling owner and be sold to other interests. Such an incident occurred on July 12, 2006, when a deal was reached to sell CHUM Ltd. to Bell Globemedia for $1.7 billion. In this case, the estate of Allan Waters, the founder of CHUM Ltd., agreed to sell its controlling 88.6 percent of the voting shares to Bell Globemedia. If a firm decides to sell itself, it normally consults an investment bank to put together an **offering memorandum** that describes the most important features of the company to potential buyers. This offering memorandum is much like an abbreviated prospectus, which will be discussed in detail with respect to securities issues in Chapter 17. Regardless of whether it is the company that decides to sell itself, or an acquirer that approaches it, the company that is willing to be sold has to provide more information so that its fair value can be estimated.

The target firm can disclose more information by setting up a **data room**, where it keeps confidential information. When serious acquirers express interest, they can access the data room by signing a **confidentiality agreement**. Not all acquirers will want to sign a confidentiality agreement, since normally this restricts the acquirer's freedom of action. Typically, the acquirer is prohibited from using the information to damage the target—by hiring away

**friendly acquisition**   the acquisition of a target company that is willing to be taken over

**offering memorandum**   a document describing a target company's important features to potential buyers

**data room**   a place where a target company keeps confidential information about itself for serious potential buyers to consult

**confidentiality agreement**   a document signed by a potential buyer to guarantee the buyer will keep confidential any information about a target company that is available in the data room and will not use the data to harm the target company

**due diligence** the process of evaluating a target company by a potential buyer

**letter of intent** a letter signed by an acquiring company that sets out the terms of agreement of its acquisition, including legal terms

**no-shop clause** a clause in a letter of intent stating that the target agrees not to find another buyer, demonstrating its commitment to close the transaction

**break fee** a fee paid to an acquirer or target should the other party terminate the acquisition, often 2.5 percent of the value of the transaction

key employees, for example, or approaching key customers. There is also usually a time limit for these restrictions. The objective of the confidentiality agreement is to restrict access to important information to serious potential acquirers. This process of evaluating the target is called **due diligence** and is an important part of the acquisition process.

Once the confidential data have been evaluated, if the acquirer goes forward, it normally signs a **letter of intent**. This sets out the terms of an agreement and allows the acquirer to do the third stage of the due diligence process,[9] in which its legal team checks the title for property, terms of contracts, and so on, to make sure that all the claims in the data room documents are actually correct and the firm owns the assets that it says it owns. The letter of intent also usually contains a **no-shop clause**, which states the target agrees not to try to find another buyer. In this way, the target shows that it is committed to making the transaction work. There is also usually a termination or **break fee** of approximately 2.5 percent of the value of the transaction. In the case of the URS-Flint deal discussed previously, the break fee was $42 million (or 3.4 percent of the deal value), while for the Teachers'-BCE deal the break fee was $800 million (or 1.55 percent of the $51.7-billion deal value).

Break fees have become very controversial. The justification for the break fee is that once companies get into the final round of due diligence, the expectation is that a deal will be completed. However, despite a no-shop clause, sometimes a competing bid does come in. Faced with two alternative offers, a company's BOD has a fiduciary duty to act in the best interests of the shareholders and seek the best possible price. It may then be that the firm that started the process and has committed significant resources to negotiating an agreement finds itself the loser. The break fee is designed to compensate the original acquirer for these costs and to reward it for generating a competing bid and getting the target shareholders a better price.

Once the final due diligence phase has been completed and everything has worked out to the satisfaction of the acquirer, the final sale agreement is reached and ratified, or agreed to, by both parties. If it is a private company, that is the end of the story, but for a firm with public shareholders, the deal then goes to the shareholders for approval.

This typical process is illustrated in **Figure 15.1**.

With a friendly transaction, there is considerable scope for structuring the acquisition to the mutual benefit of both parties. The key areas usually involve careful tax planning, legal structuring to avoid certain liabilities, providing milestones for incentive agreements, and the possibility of "cherry picking" for certain more valuable assets. We will discuss each of these in turn.

Careful tax planning is important in any transaction. When an acquirer uses cash to purchase a company, that cash is always taxable in the hands of the target company

**FIGURE 15.1** **Friendly Acquisition**

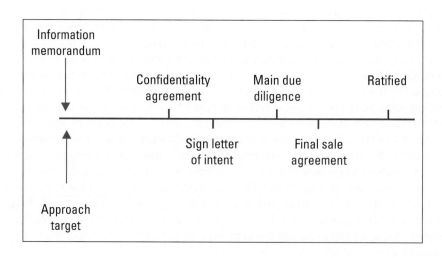

[9]The first phase is the examination of public information that is usually included in the offering memorandum; the second phase is the provision of confidential documents in the data room; the final phase is the serious verification process.

shareholders. If the share price has run up significantly, this could mean the shareholders must pay capital gains tax on the appreciation in the value of their shares. On the other hand, a share swap is usually non-taxable. This is why, in many smaller acquisitions, the target company's shares are swapped for preferred shares in the acquiring company. The target's shareholders, usually the founders, get a steady income from the preferred shares and are relieved of day-to-day concerns about their company. The acquiring firm can then integrate the target into its existing operations.

Tax concerns are also the reason a target company's assets, rather than its shares, are sold to the acquirer. In an **asset purchase**, the target firm receives the proceeds from the sale and uses these proceeds to pay off its debts. The target firm then has the option of either "reinventing itself" or liquidating itself and paying out the proceeds to the firm's shareholders. This approach may be attractive to the acquiring firm, since it can depreciate the assets at the value that it has paid for them; there are usually tax advantages from having a higher CCA value. In contrast, the target may be able to shield any potential tax payments with other losses.

> **asset purchase**   a purchase of the firm's assets rather than the firm itself

Also, sometimes the target firm has contingent liabilities that the acquirer does not wish to assume. For example, there may be potential warranty claims, which create a huge uncertainty surrounding the firm. Sometimes this warranty can be sidestepped by buying the assets. However, this potential is severely limited in some cases. For example, environmental claims generally follow the assets, so you can't dodge an environmental lawsuit from a polluting factory by selling the factory to someone else. In this case, the contingent liability stays with the asset, not the shareholders. Otherwise, legitimate claims could be avoided simply by reorganizing the firm.[10]

Deals often fall through because of fundamental disagreements concerning the target's value. Often the target's managers or founders are optimistic about the future prospects of the firm and value it based on a scenario in which everything goes right. In contrast, the acquirer may have experience with acquisitions that didn't go so well and may approach this one with a more cautious attitude. To bridge the valuation gap when the acquisition is small, "earn outs" are often used: the acquirer pays an upfront price and then makes future payments conditional on the performance of the target after it has been acquired. These future payments are usually based on divisional sales or other reasonably objective data that both parties agree on.

Of course, not all friendly acquisitions follow this process. Some legal experts tell their clients not to sign a letter of intent, because this is essentially a preliminary sale agreement and the acquirer could be held liable if it backs out of the deal.

## Hostile Takeovers

In practice, many deals, far from being friendly, are **hostile takeovers**. In a hostile deal, the target has no desire to be acquired, actively rebuffs the acquirer, and refuses to provide any confidential information. Usually, in such cases, the acquirer has already obtained a toehold and has 20 percent of the shares, so the target knows it is in for a fight.

> **hostile takeover**   a takeover in which the target has no desire to be acquired, actively rebuffs the acquirer, and refuses to provide any confidential information

In hostile bids there is usually a **tender offer**, in which the acquiring firm makes a public offer to purchase shares of the target firm from its existing shareholders. Typically, the bidder includes the provision that the offer is only good subject to the bidder being able to obtain a certain minimum percentage of the outstanding voting shares. The advantage of this approach to the bidder is that a formal vote by the target shareholders is not required, since they merely decide on their own whether or not they want to sell their shares to the acquiring firm.

> **tender offer**   a public offer in which the acquiring firm offers to purchase shares of the target firm from its existing shareholders

When a hostile tender offer is launched, external parties always look for certain clues. The most obvious is the behaviour of the market price relative to the offer price. If the market price immediately jumps above the offer price, the market is saying that a competing offer is likely or that the bid is too low, and the bidder will have to increase the offer price. Alternatively, if the market price stays close to the offer price, it indicates that the price is fair and the deal is likely to go through.

---

[10]Deliberately selling assets to evade legitimate claims on the firm could also open up both sets of shareholders to lawsuits based on fraudulent conveyance.

Professionals then look for the amount of trading in the target's shares. Very little trading is usually a bad sign for the acquirer because it means shareholders are sitting on the shares and are reluctant to sell. On the other hand, a large amount of trading indicates that shares are cycling from regular investors into the hands of specialists: people who specialize in predicting what happens in takeovers. These specialists are called **arbs**.[11] This is good for the acquirer, since arbs are only interested in selling as long as the price is right. However, the arbs buy the shares after the announcement, so they pay a premium and then expect to get a bigger premium when they sell. Their motivation is to extract the highest possible price.

The attempted takeover of Sears Canada, described in section 15.1, was rejected because the $18 offer price was below what the arbs wanted. They had bought the shares after the Sears, Roebuck announcement, hoping for an increase in the price, and then didn't see it happen. As a result, they pressured Sears, Roebuck to increase the offer price. At that time, 14.1 percent of Sears Canada's shares were owned by three New York hedge funds. These are professionally managed funds with managers who are experts in securities law and tactics designed to get the highest price for their shares. Most of the regular investors in Sears Canada sold out to these professional takeover speculators, so it became a battle of wits among experts in the area.

## Defensive Tactics against Takeovers

In the Sears Canada example, there is no question that the arbs would sell their shares—it was only a matter of when and at what price. In contrast, in hostile bids, the target doesn't want to be taken over at any price and resists the bid, often entering into anti-takeover tactics. What the target can do is restricted by securities laws, since the securities commissions in Ontario and elsewhere will take a dim view of any action on the part of the target firm that interferes with the fundamental right of shareholders to dispose of their shares at full market value. As a result, takeover defences that work in the United States, for example, do not work in Canada.

One of the most common **defensive tactics** used by some BODs is to implement a **shareholder rights plan**, also known as a **poison pill**. Under such a plan, in the event of a takeover, the non-acquiring company shareholders have the right to buy 50 percent more shares at a discounted price. This increase in the number of shares makes the acquisition much more expensive and, if everything else is constant, forces the acquirer to negotiate with the target company and make a friendly offer, since the BOD can then remove the poison pill through a vote.

Poison pills are also allowed in the United States. Moore Corporation, a large Canadian company, attempted a hostile takeover of Wallace Computer Services, which had a poison pill. Moore Corporation asked for and got a special meeting of shareholders, 78 percent of whom passed a resolution to nullify Wallace's poison pill. However, the Wallace BOD ignored the resolution and refused to nullify the poison pill, thereby making it prohibitively expensive for Moore to proceed. This decision was supported when Moore took Wallace to court; the U.S. court decided that it was up to the business judgement of the BOD.

In contrast, Canadian securities commissions take a completely different view. The acquirer will go to the securities commission directly to get the poison pill nullified. The securities commission then looks to three basic criteria:

- Is there a likelihood of another offer?
- Can the offer be withdrawn?
- Are the shareholders lobbying for the removal of the poison pill?

In Alberta, Saskatchewan, and Ontario, poison pills have been struck down when shareholders lobbied for their removal because they produced very little chance of a counter bid and a good chance that the existing bid would be withdrawn. In contrast, when MDC Corporation attempted to take over Regal Greetings and Gifts Inc. in September 1994, the OSC allowed the poison pill to remain for three weeks, since the target was actively seeking another bidder. The upshot is that, in Canada, poison pills can be used only as a delaying tactic; they cannot

---

**arbs** (short for arbitrageurs), specialists who predict what will happen in takeovers and buy and sell shares in target companies, with the possibility of earning a premium

**defensive tactic** a strategy used by a target company to stave off a takeover or to try to get the best deal for its shareholders

**shareholder rights plan** or **poison pill** a plan by a target company that allows its shareholders to buy 50 percent more shares at a discounted price in the event of a takeover, which makes the target company less attractive

---

[11] "Arbs" is short for "arbitrageurs," but technically these specialists are taking significant risks, and their positions are not arbitrage (riskless) positions, which involve buying and selling the same security at different prices.

be used to frustrate a bid the way they are in the United States. However, more recently, such plans are subject to enhanced scrutiny in the United States.

Other tactics involve making the target unattractive to the acquirer. There are many ways to do this. One tactic, called **selling the crown jewels**, involves selling the asset the acquirer is really interested in. For example, in 1979, Edper Equities made a hostile bid for Brascan Ltd. Brascan's major asset was $500 million in cash that it had just received from selling a Brazilian power plant, so Edper made a partial bid for Brascan. It was a partial bid because Edper needed only 50.1 percent to control 100 percent of the cash. Regardless, the day after Edper approached Brascan, Brascan responded by making a hostile bid for F.W. Woolworth Co., knowing that Edper wanted the cash, not Woolworth. The other major defence is to try to find a **white knight** to rescue the company and make a counter bid.

**Figure 15.2** shows the number of unsolicited bids in Canada over the 2005–14 period. The study underlying Figure 15.2 shows that there were 143 such bids over the entire period, with almost 55 percent of the initial bidders being successful. Combining these successful bids with those that resulted in acquisitions by white knights implies that over 70 percent of the targets were acquired once put in play.

An interesting example of a hostile bid that met with many forms of resistance occurred in December 2000, when Indigo Books and Music Inc. made a hostile $13-a-share offer for Chapters Inc., its main bookselling rival, in an attempt to consolidate the Canadian bookselling industry in the face of potential U.S. competition. Chapters fiercely resisted the hostile offer and first tried selling the crown jewels, offering to buy back the minority interest in its Chapters Online Internet bookstore for $3.40 a share (shares in the Internet bookstore had closed trading the previous day at $2.00). This got rid of cash and increased Chapters' ownership in something Indigo did not want. As Gerry Schwartz, who was bankrolling the Indigo bid, said, "Chapters has become virtually the only company in North America to offer cash to bail out the shareholders of a failing e-tailer."[12] When this tactic failed, Chapters paid Future Shop a break fee in order to get it to offer $16.80 a share as a white knight. This forced Indigo to raise its offer to $17.00, which was eventually successful.

Indigo was successful in its hostile bid for Chapters for several reasons. First, the business was straightforward and known to the acquirer, so little due diligence was needed; that is, there was no great uncertainty about the value of Chapters to Indigo. Second, there was no other strategic buyer that could generate similar value by acquiring Chapters. In this respect, a combination of a bookstore (Chapters) and an electronics seller (Future Shop) offered little retail logic—it was simply a mechanism to get Indigo to bid more. Finally, Indigo could afford a long, drawn-out takeover battle, since the value of Chapters was unaffected by the struggle. In contrast, sometimes the value of a target is dissipated as a result of lost contracts or key people leaving the company.

**selling the crown jewels**   the sale of a target company's key assets, which the acquiring company is most interested in, to make the target company less attractive for takeover

**white knight**   an entity that rescues a target company from a hostile takeover by making a counter bid

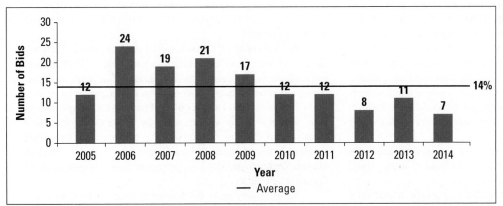

**FIGURE 15.2**   **Unsolicited Bids, 2005 to 2014**

**Source:** From Fasken Martineau DuMoulin LLP, "2015 Canadian Hostile TakeOver Bid Study," Harvard Law School Forum on Corporate Governance and Financial Regulation (blog), April 16, 2015 https://corpgov.law.harvard.edu/2015/04/16/2015-canadian-hostile-take-over-bid-study/. Copyright 2015. Reproduced with the permission of Fasken Martineau DuMoulin LLP.

---

[12]"Chapters Plots to Fend Off Indigo Takeover." *CBC News,* December 8, 2000. Accessed at http://www.cbc.ca/news/business/story/2000/12/08/chapters001208.html.

---

### Concept Review Questions

1. What goes into a confidentiality agreement and why do people sign them?
2. What is due diligence?
3. What is a shareholder rights plan?
4. What are some standard takeover defences?
5. When is it best to mount a hostile bid?

---

## 15.4 Motivations for Mergers and Acquisitions

> **LEARNING OBJECTIVE 15.4**
> Explain the various motivations underlying mergers and acquisitions.

### Classifications of Mergers and Acquisitions

Acquisitions are made because the acquirer thinks that the target company will enhance the firm's long-term value. The source of this value depends on the type of acquisition and the structural changes occurring in the economy at various times. The influence of economic conditions on merger activity is discussed in Finance in the News 15.1, which refers to potential detriments to M&A activity in early 2019, including trade uncertainty, weak oil and gas prices, and forecast interest rate increases.

---

**15.1 Finance in the News** Trade, Economic Uncertainties Threaten to Slow M&A Activity

Unpredictability on the trade and economic fronts threatens to temper Canadian merger and acquisition activity in 2019, as corporate buyers reassess the risks of making big deals.

The deal flow hit a record in the third quarter of 2018, and there is still keen interest in corporate purchases, with more than US$1-trillion in private capital seeking opportunities globally. However, some deal-making veterans question how much support public markets in Canada have for major transactions, in the form of putting up capital, after a year in which major stock indexes declined.

"M&A is driven by confidence and the greatest enemy of M&A is uncertainty," said Peter Buzzi, co-head of mergers and acquisitions at Royal Bank of Canada.

The S&P/TSX composite index fell 12 per cent in 2018 on a host of factors, including rising interest rates and concern over trade disputes between China and the United States, as well as tensions between Ottawa and Beijing. In addition, there has been a mass exodus from Canadian oil and gas shares due to weak prices and protracted regulatory and legal delays to pipeline projects. Meanwhile, U.S. economic data have recently shown cracks that indicate slower growth ahead.

"So I think people are starting to wonder if this is the beginning of the end of the long economic bull-market cycle we've been in," Mr. Buzzi said.

For much of 2018, Canadian markets dealt with uncertainty as talks toward a new North American trade deal dragged on amid warnings about potential negative effects on Canadian manufacturing and other sectors. There has also been no shortage of friction with China, after Ottawa quashed the $1.5-billion takeover of construction firm Aecon Group Inc. by China Communications Construction Co. Ltd., citing security concerns. In December, Canada's arrest of Meng Wanzhou, the chief financial officer of Huawei Technologies Co. Ltd., prompted tit-for-tat detentions of Canadians in China.

"We are a very trade and foreign investment-sensitive country and sometimes the political headwinds, trends, vicissitudes around us have an outsized impact on the M&A market," said Jake Bullen, a Toronto-based lawyer who specializes in deals and private equity at Cassels Brock & Blackwell LLP. "Even before the Huawei arrest, we were seeing a tail-off in Chinese investment." He noted that some of that had to do with factors taking place in China, including currency controls.

Still, deal activity was brisk for much of last year. In the third quarter of 2018, Canadian deal-making hit a record 881 announced transactions, according to advisory firm Crosbie & Co. The overall value declined by $6-billion from the previous quarter to $68-billion, owing to a drop in the number of very large takeovers. In the first nine months of the year, the number of deals totalled 2,541, a 15-per-cent increase from the same period in 2017.

Some sizable transactions included Brookfield Asset Management's US$6.8-billion acquisition of Cleveland-based Forest City Realty Trust and Barrick Gold Corp.'s US$6-billion takeover of Randgold Resources Ltd. In the fourth quarter, Ensign Energy Services Inc. won a $470-million hostile takeover bid for Trinidad Drilling Ltd.

Domestic mid-market-size deals were hot in 2018, and that should play out next year, Mr. Bullen noted. Despite the political and trade risks, Canada is still seen as a stable place for such activity, especially privately-held targets. "I think we've still got a lot of companies performing very well in their sectors, from tech to advanced manufacturing to consumer products. And I think the exchange rate continues to entice U.S. buyers," he said.

Energy and mining firms have been largely absent from raising capital in public markets over the past year owing to depressed commodity prices and lagging valuations, but Roman Dubczak, head of global investment banking for CIBC World Markets Inc., said the bank remains committed to the sectors.

For example, CIBC advised Nu-Vista Energy Ltd. on its $625-million acquisition of natural gas assets in northwestern Alberta from Cenovus Energy Inc.—a deal that took place under "really tough market conditions," Mr. Dubczak said.

"In the old days, that would have just been a phone call and a bought deal," he said. "Now, it required a bit of work. And the deal went well. Everyone was happy. But you really have to become an adviser to your clients and devote quite a bit of time and creativity to getting stuff done."

Companies with cash reserves, as well as private-equity buyers, will have good buying opportunities in 2019 as stock markets roil, said Geoff Barsky, head of M&A Canada & International at BMO Capital Markets. Another factor that may loom large is activist investors looking to boost value at lagging public companies, he said.

There are three broad classifications of mergers and acquisitions:

1. **Horizontal merger**: This occurs when two firms in the same industry combine. For example, in April 2019, Chevron announced a $33-billion cash and stock takeover of Andarko Petroleum Corp., which is in the same business. Chevron CEO Mike Wirth said that "the deal offers 'a compelling and unique fit' because the two operate in similar areas."[13]

**horizontal merger** a merger in which two firms in the same industry combine

2. **Vertical merger**: A firm can expand by acquiring a company that is closer to its existing customers ("going forward") or by acquiring a supplier that provides inputs into its production process ("going backward"). Bell Globemedia's acquisition of CHUM Ltd. is an example of going forward to create an integrated media company, adding CHUM's radio stations to Bell Globemedia's stable of television, print, and other media outlets. AOL's acquisition of Time-Warner—probably the most-storied failed merger in history—was an attempt by AOL to go backward by accessing both media content and a cable distribution system to create an integrated media company. In 2012, Glencore International made a $6.1-billion bid for Canadian firm Viterra Inc., one of the world's largest grain companies, which was subsequently approved by 99.8 percent of Viterra's shareholders. Glencore is a large Swiss commodities trading company, so this is an example of buying a key supplier, which is critical for most companies, especially a trading company. Curt Vossen, president of Winnipeg-based Richardson International, noted, "Your greatest fear would be in this global demand environment, can I continue to source the raw materials that I trade?"[14]

**vertical merger** a merger in which one firm acquires a supplier or another firm that is closer to its existing customers

3. **Conglomerate merger**: This occurs when two firms in unrelated businesses combine. The motivation to create a conglomerate is that the different businesses face different risks, which tend to cancel each other out, lowering the overall risk of the combined company. One classic example comes from November 1981, when the United States Steel Corp. bought control of Marathon Oil Corp. In this case, U.S. Steel was the white knight, bidding in response to a hostile bid for Marathon from Mobil Corp. However, the result was an oil company and a steel company with few economic reasons for the combination. A classic Canadian example of a failed expansion into unrelated business lines was the 1995

**conglomerate merger** a merger in which two firms in unrelated businesses combine

[13]Benny, John, and Hiller, Jennifer, "Chevron to Buy Anadarko in $33-Billion Deal." *The Globe and Mail Report on Business*, April 13, 2019, p. B3.

[14]Reguly, Eric, Waldie, Paul, and Erman, Boyd, "Glencore's Viterra Deal Spurs Grain Sector Shakeup." *The Globe and Mail*, March 20, 2012.

**FIGURE 15.3** Canadian Cross-Border M&A Activity, 2012 to November 2016

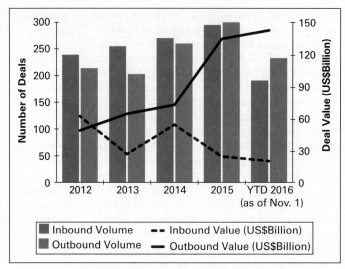

**Source:** From Mergermarket, "Crossing Over: Canadian Cross-Border Dealmaking," December 14, 2016, p. 1.https://www.mergermarket.com/info/crossing-over-canadi-an-cross-border-dealmaking. Accessed April 20, 2019. Copyright 2019. Reproduced with the permission of Mergermarket. "Mergermarket, an Acuris company".

acquisition of Universal Studios by Seagram's, a longstanding Canadian producer of whisky. This represented an ill-founded desire to branch out into the entertainment business. The business combination faced numerous challenges, and the company ceased to exist after its entertainment and beverage divisions were sold off separately in 2000, ending a legacy that went back to 1857.

**cross-border (international) M&A** a merger or acquisition involving a Canadian and a foreign firm as either the acquiring or target company

Acquisitions can also be classified as domestic or **cross-border (international) M&As**. Many Canadian companies have been involved, as both acquiring firms and as target firms, in high-profile cross-border mergers throughout the years. For example, we have already discussed a situation in which a Canadian company (Viterra) was the target, and another where a Canadian company (Fortis Inc.) was looking to expand into the U.S. **Figure 15.3** shows cross-border M&A activity in Canada from 2012 to November 2016. An examination of the reasons underlying this activity leads us to a discussion of some of the common motivations for M&As.

## M&A Activity

**Figure 15.4** shows Canadian M&A activity over the period from 1985 to April 2019 and demonstrates sharp declines in the volume of M&As following significant stock market declines in both 2001 and 2008. Much of the 2008 decline in activity was driven by limited availability of capital and a rapid deterioration in earnings. However, activity increased steadily from 2008 onwards, and by 2017, the number of M&As had surpassed the previous high in 2007. While the total deal value in 2017 exceeded 2005 levels, it was still below the higher values observed in 2006 and even higher ones in 2007. These high values in 2006–7 were driven by soaring M&A activity in the Canadian energy and commodity sectors, fuelled by high energy prices, high commodity prices, a strong currency, and a healthy economy.

That a wave of M&A activity ended during 2008 is nothing new. Dating to the turn of the nineteenth century, M&A activity has tended to occur in periodic waves of robust activity, as depicted in **Table 15.1**.

**synergy** value created from economies of integrating a target and acquiring company; the amount by which the value of the combined firm exceeds the sum value of the two individual firms

Theoretically, the primary motive for a merger or acquisition should be the creation of **synergy**, which causes the value of the combined firm to exceed the sum value of the two individual firms. Synergy is created due to economies of integration that are expected to occur for one reason or another. If $V_A$ is the pre-merger value of the acquiring firm, $V_T$ is the pre-merger value of the target firm, and $V_{A-T}$ is the value of the post-merger firm, we can say that synergy occurs whenever $V_{A-T} > V_A + V_T$. Synergy is the additional value created ($\Delta V$), as expressed in Equation 15.1:

$$\Delta V = V_{A-T} - (V_A + V_T)$$

[15.1]

**FIGURE 15.4**   Canadian M&A Statistics, 1985 to April 2019

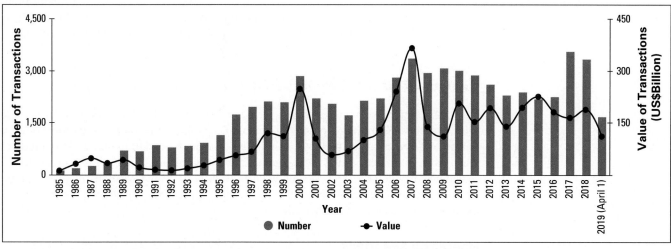

**Source:** IMAA, "Canada—M&A Statistics," https://imaa-institute.org/m-and-a-canada/. Accessed April 20, 2019. Copyright 2019. Reproduced with permission of the Institute for Mergers, Acquisitions and Alliances.

**TABLE 15.1**   M&A Activity in Canada

| Period | Major Characteristics of M&A Activity |
|---|---|
| 1895–1904 | • Driven by economic expansion, U.S. transcontinental railroad, and the development of national U.S. capital markets<br>• Characterized by horizontal M&As |
| 1922–29 | • 60 percent occurred in fragmented markets (chemical, food processing, mining)<br>• Driven by growth in transportation and merchandising, as well as by communications developments |
| 1940–47 | • Characterized by vertical integration<br>• Driven by evasion of price and quota controls |
| 1960s | • Characterized by conglomerate M&As<br>• Driven by aerospace industry<br>• Some firms merged to play the earnings-per-share "growth game" (discussed in section 15.5 under "The Effect of an Acquisition on Earnings per Share") |
| 1980s | • Characterized by leveraged buyouts and hostile takeovers |
| 1990s | • Many international M&As (e.g., Chrysler and Daimler-Benz, Seagram and Martell)<br>• Strategic motives were advanced (although the jury is still out on whether this was truly achieved) |
| 1999–2001 | • High technology/Internet M&As<br>• Many stock-financed takeovers, fuelled by inflated stock prices<br>• Many were unsuccessful and/or fell through as the Internet "bubble" burst |
| 2005–8 | • Resource-based/international M&A activity<br>• Fuelled by strong industry fundamentals, low financing costs, strong economic conditions |

**Source:** Adapted in part from Weston, J. Fred, Chung, Kwang S., and Hoag, Susan E., *Mergers, Restructuring, and Corporate Control* (Toronto: Prentice-Hall Canada, 1990).

If the target and acquirer have initial values of $50 million ($V_T$) and $100 million ($V_A$), respectively, and the combined firm is worth $200 million ($V_{A-T}$), then there are synergy values of $50 million. Of course, in this case, the key questions are where do these synergies come from and who gets them? If the acquirer pays $100 million for the target, then all the synergy value flows through to the target shareholders and none to the acquirer. On the other hand, at any value less than $100 million, the synergy gains are split between the acquiring and target firm shareholders. In this case, the acquisition has created value of $50 million.

# Value Creation Motivations for M&As

Most M&A announcements go to great lengths to describe the synergies, or total positive gains, associated with the proposed transaction. For example, the proposed takeover of Flint Energy by URS, discussed previously, indicated cost savings of $10 million to $15 million in year 1, with continued annual savings going forward. Sometimes these gains materialize and sometimes they don't. In this section, we list a variety of "value creation" motives that are often used to justify a merger or acquisition decision. Some of these justifications hold greater merit than others, as we discuss next.

## Operating Synergies

1. **Economies of Scale**

   Economies of scale arise whenever bigger is indeed better. Some potential benefits may arise from the following economies:

   - **Reducing capacity.** It may be, for example, that an industry has grown too big and there are too many firms operating in it. A merger or acquisition in this situation is often called an **over-capacity M&A**. For example, in 2003, Alcan, the major Canadian aluminum producer, purchased the French producer Pechiney, while the U.S. bank JPMorgan purchased another American bank, Chase.

   - **Spreading fixed costs.** Often, significant costs in a business are fixed, independent of scale. By increasing the company's size, these costs are spread over greater volumes, and the firm is more efficient. This was the ostensible motivation for the proposed Royal Bank–Bank of Montreal merger, which was stopped by the Government of Canada in 1998. The banks argued that the costs of information technology could be reduced through a merger since both banks were developing similar technology. The same arguments apply to spreading research and development costs.

   - **Geographic synergies.** Often an industry is fragmented and ripe for consolidation. A **geographic roll-up** occurs when a national firm is created out of a series of regional firms. The original Standard Oil in the United States was created when John D. Rockefeller consolidated the U.S. oil industry, which allowed common marketing and managerial overhead. Retailing has similarly been consolidated, with the creation of national chains from regional ones to gain economies in purchasing and an improvement in the distribution channel.

2. **Economies of Scope**

   An economy of scope occurs when the combination of two activities reduces costs. Such economies typically result when two products share similarities in their production process, which can be exploited. A classic example is a distribution system that can be used to sell two lines of product instead of one. On this basis, Seagram (think whisky) purchased Martell (think fine cognac) in 1988. Seagram's rationale was that it could sell Martell's cognac through its U.S. distribution system as easily as its own whisky, and thereby generate expanded sales at little extra cost.

   Another example occurred in the early 1980s. Until then, commercial banking (i.e., making corporate loans) was separated from investment banking (i.e., selling corporate securities). The Ontario Securities Commission held a series of hearings to determine whether the investment dealers—firms like Dominion Securities and Wood Gundy—should be allowed to convert from being partnerships to corporations, and whether they should be permitted to be acquired by the banks. The OSC approved the changes largely on the basis that there were efficiencies to be gained if investment banking and commercial banking were carried on by the same institution. However, regulators have so far resisted arguments that banks be allowed to use their distribution systems to sell insurance.

**over-capacity M&A** a merger or acquisition that occurs when an industry has too many firms operating in it

**geographic roll-up** the creation of a national firm from a series of regional ones

Two of the many other examples of economies of scope achieved by acquisitions are Coca-Cola's purchase of Gatorade to gain entry into the sport drinks market, and Quaker Oats buying Snapple Beverage Corporation.

### 3. Complementary Strengths

Complementary strengths occur if one firm is more efficient in one or more areas of operations than another. For example, a marketing-oriented firm may acquire a production-oriented firm if it feels the product line is not being sold efficiently. A classic example of this is Remington, the razor company. It was acquired by Victor Kiam, who immediately cut engineering and product development and marketed a smaller range of razors. He did this to great effect by advertising himself, saying, "I liked the razor so much I bought the company."

Another example can be seen in the 2008 acquisition of the American Stock Exchange (Amex) by NYSE Euronext. While Amex was a national stock exchange, it was very small in comparison to the NYSE. However, Amex traded a wider array of exchange-traded funds (ETFs) and options than the NYSE. Hence, it possessed some strengths that complemented those of NYSE Euronext. Of course, the acquisition also presented opportunities to cut costs associated with duplicated efforts, and the Amex trading floor was officially shut down during the summer of 2008.

Another example of complementary strengths is the **extension M&A**. Certain organizational cultures are good at doing certain things. The research part of research and development, for example, usually requires a creative organizational culture that encourages risk taking. The development part, on the other hand, often requires extensive managerial and production skills. As a result, big pharmaceutical companies, like Merck & Co. Inc., and Pfizer Inc., often buy small drug companies after they come up with a potential new drug, since often only the big companies can take the drug through the clinical trials it must pass before it is certified for use by consumers.

> **extension M&A**  a merger or acquisition that extends a firm's expertise

Similarly, many mineral finds have been made by small firms, often consisting of a few geologists. After a deposit is found, however, they sell the company to the major international companies that have the skills and resources to develop it. An example in Canada was the Voisey's Bay nickel deposits in Labrador, found by Diamond Fields Resources Inc. in 1994. This was the most significant mineral discovery in Canada in 40 years and sparked a furious bidding war for the rights to develop the deposits, which was eventually won by Inco Ltd. In this case, the M&A occurred because the exploration and development functions, as opposed to the R&D functions, were best carried out by separate entities.

## Efficiency Increases

Efficiency gains materialize whenever one or both of the firms involved have excess capacity—that is, they possess factors that are currently being underused. This is a common motivation for mergers, and, unfortunately for employees, some of the synergy that arises involves the elimination of jobs. Of course, efficiency gains do not always have to result in job losses; the excess capacity could exist in one or more of many factors, such as shipping, storage, and information technology. Another important source of increased efficiency could be improved company management—that is, the acquiring firm believes that its management team will operate more efficiently than the target firm's management team. It is in this sense that people often refer to the "market for corporate control" as a viable corporate governance mechanism, since inefficient management will pay the ultimate price.

## Financing Synergies

Financing synergies may arise for a number of reasons. The main ones discussed here are all variations on the theme that larger is better in accessing capital markets.

- **Reduced cash flow variability.**  Cash flow volatility tends to be lower for larger entities, especially if the cash flows from the two underlying businesses are not highly correlated. This may enable the company to reduce its need for external financing, since future financing needs can be forecast with greater certainty.

- **Increase in debt capacity.**   Debt capacity may rise due to the increase in size and/or reduction in cash flow volatility of the new company. Smaller, riskier firms generally cannot carry as much debt as larger firms, and the use of additional debt provides the firm with greater tax savings, as we will discuss in more detail in chapters 20 and 21.
- **Reduction in average issuing costs.**   Since most security issues occur in large increments, the average cost of floating new debt or equity will decrease as the firm issues larger amounts. Additionally, larger firms can access more sources of capital than smaller ones, resulting in cost savings.
- **Fewer information problems.**   Larger firms usually attract more external security analysts and have greater exposure in the media. The result is that they attract big institutional investors, which may lower their financing costs.

## Tax Benefits

Tax benefits occur when one firm has substantial operating loss credits that it cannot take advantage of because it is not operating profitably. These losses are valuable since they can be carried forward and used against future profits to reduce taxes. However, if the firm is unlikely to become profitable in the near term, these losses may expire worthless. On the other hand, if the firm combines with a profitable one in the same basic line of business, these losses can be used to offset the other firm's profits to reduce taxes. This was the case in the Kmart–Sears merger of 2004. At the time of the merger, Kmart had $509 million in tax-loss carryovers that were due to expire in the 2021–23 tax years. Kmart had little chance of using these losses unless it combined with a profitable company.[15] By combining with a profitable company, the net operating loss carryover could then be used as offsets against future taxable income, hence reducing taxes of the combined company.[16]

Tax benefits may also arise due to the depreciation of capital assets (i.e., current cost accounting tax shields) that can be claimed by the combined entity, and the increased use of debt financing with more interest tax shields, as discussed previously.

Finally, tax benefits can provide an incentive for M&A activity across different tax jurisdictions. This was one of the motivations for the acquisition of Canadian-based Tim Hortons Inc. by U.S.-based Burger King Worldwide in 2014.[17] Not only was the prevailing corporate tax rate lower in Canada (versus the U.S.) at that time, but by setting up headquarters in Canada, the company could avoid double taxation on foreign income, which represented a significant component of Burger King's income.

## Strategic Realignments

The acquisition of new managerial skills and new product/service line growth opportunities resulting from an M&A may allow the new entity to pursue strategies that were previously not feasible.

# Managerial Motivations for M&As

Creating value for shareholders may be the basic motivation for running a business, but, as we discussed previously, it is the managers who control the company. Therefore, we sometimes get managerial motives for M&As that are distinct from the shareholder motivation. Two of the more common motivations are described here.

1. **Increased firm size.**   This may or may not be a good thing, depending on whether any economic synergies are created. Unfortunately, in the past, some M&As have been advocated by managers who were equally concerned with the additional personal compensation

---

[15]Information from Kmart Holding Corporation 2004 fiscal year 10-K filing with the Securities and Exchange Commission, p. 49.

[16]Sears Holdings, the parent company after the acquisition, announced store closures at the end of 2011 because of poor holiday earnings, a sign that the company continued to struggle. If Sears Holdings does not generate taxable earnings to apply against those net operating losses, the losses may still expire worthless.

[17]The resulting company became a subsidiary of Restaurant Brands International (RBI), which was in turn owned by Brazilian mega-company 3G Capital.

and power they would realize as a result of the transaction. The classic example here is the 1998 attempted merger between Glaxo Wellcome and Smith Klein, two big British pharmaceutical companies. In February 1998, the proposed merger was called off because the two CEOs couldn't decide on the management team of the new company. With the announcement of the cancellation of the merger, £13 billion (about C$30 billion) was wiped out from the combined companies' market value. In this case, the personal egos of the senior managers destroyed value; normally value is destroyed by making bad acquisitions rather than cancelling potentially good ones.[18]

2. **Reduced firm risk through diversification.**  M&As may also be used to diversify a firm—geographically, across industries, or in its product mix—through conglomerate mergers, as discussed earlier. Unfortunately, the evidence suggests that diversification is generally a poor motive for a merger, often resulting in additional managerial complications and a lack of focus by managers running disparate businesses. The markets recognize this and are not willing to pay a premium for diversification, since it is easy to diversify a portfolio across the same industries and geographic borders. In fact, the evidence suggests quite the opposite: investors tend to pay a premium for "pure play" companies that are focused on one strategic plan.

## Gains Resulting from Mergers: Empirical Evidence

So what does the evidence on M&As tell us about the gains? There are numerous empirical studies that examine the gains from mergers. The evidence suggests that the target firm shareholders gain the most, with premiums over the prior stock market price in the 15- to 20-percent range for stock-financed takeovers, and from 25 to 30 percent for cash-financed takeovers. These gains consist of a one-third run-up in the stock price prior to the announcement, plus about a two-thirds gain after the announcement.

There is considerable disagreement about the source of the run-up prior to the announcement. On one hand, some people believe that information about an impending merger is leaked, resulting in insider trading, which is, of course, illegal. On the other hand, many believe that informed industry specialists can make reasonable predictions about takeover activity based on transactions elsewhere. For example, on February 12, 2007, *The Times of London* reported that BHP and Rio Tinto, two huge British-Australian mining companies, had drawn up plans for a $40-billion bid for New York–based aluminum producer Alcoa. In response, rival Alcan's stock price jumped $4 on speculation that if it didn't buy Alcoa, someone might buy Alcan.

Regardless of the source, it always pays for shareholders of the target firm to be taken over. Short-term gains of 20 to 40 percent are the reasons why the arbs, the M&A specialists discussed earlier, refused to let Sears, Roebuck buy Sears Canada cheaply. In their lexicon, Sears, Roebuck was not playing fair by refusing to let the arbs make a profit.

These takeover gains to the target can be even higher, especially if bidding wars develop, and they tend to be higher still when the deals are 100-percent cash, since the target shareholders usually have to pay capital gains tax. In contrast, the acquiring firm's shareholders, on average, see no change in their stock price. In fact, the stock price usually dips marginally on news of the bid. This implies that acquiring firms pay too much for target firms, acquire them for the wrong reasons, and/or overestimate the benefits resulting from the merger. Numerous studies concerning post-merger value indicate there is little or no increase in value; there are no synergistic gains to the acquirer, which are the supposed rationale for mergers.

In a recent study of mergers and acquisitions globally, researchers examining over 13,000 mergers in 89 different countries indicated that the gains to acquirers and targets were different in very competitive markets (e.g., the United States and United Kingdom) compared to other markets around the world.[19] They also found that acquirers in these competitive markets tended to underperform relative to acquirers in less competitive markets. The researchers observed that in acquisitions involving cash as a medium of exchange, the acquisition resulted in a shift of wealth from the acquiring shareholders to the target shareholders; in other words,

---

[18]The deal did eventually go through, as even managerial egos could not stand in the way of C$30 billion.

[19]Alexandridis, G., Petmezas, D., and Travlos, Nicholas G., "Gains from Mergers and Acquisitions around the World: New Evidence." *Financial Management* (Winter 2010), pp. 1671–95.

value was not created, merely shifted. In the case of the exchange of shares, the researchers observed synergistic gains only in non-competitive markets.

Consider a $2-billion company that wants to take over a company with a $1-billion value because it thinks there are $0.5 billion in synergies. If it gets into a bidding war and pays $1.5 billion in cash for the company and then finds that there are no synergies, it has lost the $0.5-billion premium it paid. In this case, it has 25 percent of its market value at risk in the acquisition ($0.5/$2). In contrast, if the acquiring company does a share swap at $1.5 billion, the original shareholders own only 57.14 percent of the new company ($2/$3.5) and will lose only this fraction of the lost $0.5 billion, or $286 million. The rest has been lost by the shareholders of the target, who accepted shares in the new company only to see them go down in value.[20]

This analysis is called "shareholder value at risk," or SVAR, in M&As. It illustrates the basic point that, when using cash, the acquirer bears all the risk, whereas when using share swaps, the risk is borne by the shareholders in both companies. For example, Nortel was a major Canadian technology company during the Internet bubble, and it made a large number of acquisitions, almost all of them using its own shares. Nortel used its high share price as an acquisition currency, and unless the target shareholders sold their shares immediately, they lost as much when the market crashed as did Nortel's original shareholders. Using share swaps for its acquisitions also meant that Nortel survived the crash, whereas if it had borrowed the money to make cash purchases, it could never have supported the debt load after the crash.

SVAR supports the argument that when firms make deals using cash, they are a lot more careful about the acquisition price than when they use their shares. One reason for this is that the managers have less interest in the financing of the deal than in getting it done in the first place.

---

### Concept Review Questions

1. What is the difference between vertical and horizontal mergers?
2. What is an extension M&A, an over-capacity M&A, and a geographic roll-up M&A?
3. What financial synergies are possible in an M&A transaction?
4. What tax benefits can occur in an M&A?
5. What is the empirical record on the success of M&As in the 1990s?
6. What is SVAR and why do managers prefer to finance with shares rather than cash?

---

## 15.5 | Valuation Issues

### LEARNING OBJECTIVE 15.5
Identify the valuation issues involved in assessing mergers and acquisitions.

## The Concept of Fair Market Value

So far we have discussed how to do an acquisition, different types of acquisitions, and the securities law surrounding acquisitions—almost everything about acquisitions except the critical question of how to value them. Since companies are always buying something, they have to know the basics of valuation, especially in a merger, where they must determine the share exchange ratio. In principle, this involves the same issues as valuing a project (discussed

---

[20]Rappaport, A., and Sirower, M., "Stock or Cash." *Harvard Business Review* (November/December 1999), pp. 147–58.

in earlier chapters) and valuing securities like bonds and shares. However, it is considerably more complex for a variety of reasons that we discuss next.

James Needham of Arthur Young and Company summed up some of the issues this way: "In pricing an acquisition, we can always agree on the numbers. What the value is tends to be more in the realm of poets than financial people."[21] In other words, value generically means a willingness to sell or to buy—that is, we are talking about supply and demand curves. The price, on the other hand, is the value at which a deal is consummated. When we look at most commodities that are bought and sold, there are many people in the market buying and selling, so the price is clearly derived. In this sense, it is an equilibrium price. For companies, on the other hand, while the shares may trade between many buyers and sellers, there is a limited market for the company as a whole, so we are dealing with only a few points on the demand and supply curves. This naturally leads to a wide range of possible deal prices.

We illustrate this point in **Figure 15.5**. Normally, in a basic economics course, we draw a supply and demand curve assuming multiple buyers and sellers so that the equilibrium price is P*. This may be the case if there are many steel companies, for example, and many potential buyers, but in reality what happens is that one company may be "put in play" at any point in time, and the seller may want a price of S1, which is its valuation of the company. There may be only one potential buyer, who places the value at B1. So rather than all the points on the demand and supply curve, we simply have two points. If these two parties can come to an agreement, the transaction price can be anywhere between these two prices. This is the crux of Needham's comment: we may have an idea of what P* should be, but if there are only two parties, their own valuations can be all over the place.

This concept underlies the definition of **fair market value (FMV)**, which is described as the highest price obtainable in an open and unrestricted market between knowledgeable, informed, and prudent parties acting at arm's length, with neither party being under any compulsion to transact. We often need to know the value of something for tax and other legal purposes, and FMV reflects this specific valuation, which is not necessarily a transaction price.

If we look at the definition of FMV, there are certain key words and phrases we must understand:

- **Open and unrestricted market:** there are no barriers and anyone can buy or sell.
- **Knowledgeable, informed, and prudent parties:** all the information is in the market, and the value is determined by people who know what they are doing.
- **Arm's length:** the value is determined by parties who do not know each other.
- **Neither party under any compulsion to transact:** it is not a panic sale, causing distressed valuations.

> **fair market value (FMV)** the highest price obtainable in an open and unrestricted market between knowledgeable, informed, and prudent parties acting at arm's length, with neither party being under any compulsion to transact

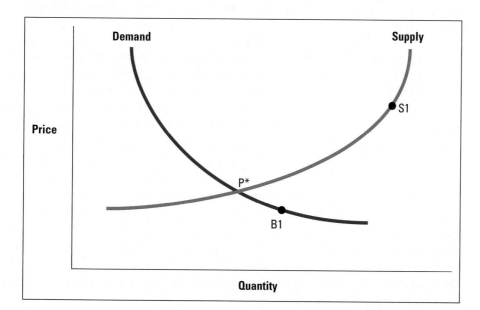

**FIGURE 15.5** Demand and Supply of Company Shares

[21]Needham, James, "The Leading Edge in Mergers and Acquisitions." *Mergers & Acquisitions* (November/December 1986).

The Canada Revenue Agency (CRA) adopts FMV as the standard definition of selling price, since otherwise a party wishing to avoid capital gains tax could sell an asset to a related party at a "knockdown" price. This is why the definition includes the "arm's length" provision. Indeed, if you look carefully at these four components, you will realize that this is a description of an ideal or perfect market, where everyone is reasonable and arrives at values in an objective, rational way. It is also why the courts have frequently thrown out actual transaction values when these conditions were not met.

The relevance of FMV is that it comes up all the time in valuing transactions, but the requirements for it highlight why transaction values frequently depart from FMV. In a hostile takeover, for example, the acquirer does not have access to a data room or confidential information and often *overbids* for a firm. Similarly, managers selling a single division of a firm or putting the whole firm up for sale on the death of the founder are frequently under a compulsion to act and are dealing in a restricted market.

To put these comments in perspective, we can think of purchasers as belonging to four different groups:

1. **Passive investors** value the firm based on estimated cash flows as they are at present, with only minor adjustments. Passive investors are mutual funds and any small investor that cannot change what the firm is doing.

2. **Strategic investors** value the firm based on estimated synergies and changes that may arise due to the integration of the firm's operations with their own. Over-capacity, extension, and roll-up mergers all fall into this category.

3. **Financials** value the firm based on how it can reorganize its operations by "juggling" the pieces and refinancing them. For example, these purchasers might consider the "break-up" value of the company and then sell off some pieces and refinance the rest. This strategy was common in the 1970s and 1980s as conglomerates were purchased and then reorganized.

**management buyouts (MBOs) or leveraged buyouts (LBOs)** buyouts in which the purchasers are a firm's managers; these buyouts usually involve high levels of debt financing

4. **Managers** value the firm based on their own job potential and their ability to motivate their staff and reorganize the firm's operations. Like financials, they usually involve significant amounts of debt financing and are referred to as **management buyouts (MBOs)** or **leveraged buyouts (LBOs)**.

Market pricing will reflect the influence of these different buyers and their importance at different stages of the business cycle. Regardless of which group is dominant, the same basic valuation methods are used all the time. We can break these methods into two extremes: *reactive* versus *proactive*. The basic **reactive methods** are based on multiples and liquidation or break-up values.

**reactive method** a valuation method based on general rules of thumb and examining the present pricing of similar securities

1. **Multiples or relative valuation.** This approach involves the use of ratios such as price-earnings (P/E), enterprise value to earnings before interest, taxes, depreciation, and amortization (EV/EBITDA), market-to-book (M/B), price-to-sales (P/S), and price-to-cash flow (P/CF). They are called "multiples" because we are arriving at a market value by using some multiple of an item in the firm's forecast financial statements. The relative valuation comes in because we arrive at these multiples by looking at comparable firms, known as "comps," and deciding what a reasonable multiple is. (We discussed these multiples in Chapter 7.) This approach is used extensively and can also be used as a first step in a proactive analysis. The justifiable multiples are often estimated based on historical trading values, "rules of thumb," "comparables" (such as industry averages or comparable companies), and/or precedent transactions (which refers to the multiples observed in previous takeovers of similar companies). This method provides a starting point for the valuation process by establishing the value in relation to historical values, rules of thumb, and similar companies. The basic multiples valuation approach is illustrated in **Figure 15.6** and in examples 15.1 to 15.3.

2. **Liquidation values.** This approach involves estimating the liquidation value of the company's assets at present market prices. For example, we know that cash is worth 100 percent,

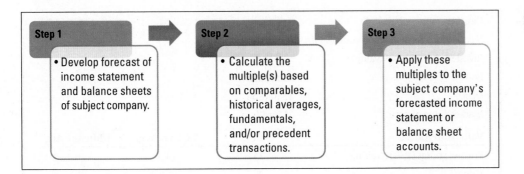

**FIGURE 15.6**  **Multiples Valuation**

and we can estimate accounts receivable at 85 percent; inventory at 75 percent; and property, plant, and equipment at 50 percent of their book values. This can be an especially important consideration if the acquiring firm plans on selling some of the target firm's assets to help pay off the debt financing associated with the purchase.

In contrast to reactive methods, which are reacting to general rules of thumb and the pricing of other securities, **proactive methods** work out what the value *should be,* based on future values of cash flow and earnings. The most common proactive method is the discounted cash flow (DCF) model.

**proactive method**   a valuation method to determine what a target firm's liquidation value should be, based on future values of cash flow and earnings

**Discounted cash flow (DCF) model.**   An approach that involves estimating the future cash flows associated with the new combined entity and discounting them back to the present to determine the fair market value. Sound familiar? This is exactly how we evaluated the traditional investment decisions in chapters 13 and 14 and individual securities in chapters 6 and 7. This simply reflects the fact that DCF valuation is the workhorse of finance.

## Multiples Valuation

The following three examples illustrate how multiples may be used to evaluate a company and highlight the difficulties that may arise from using this approach.

---

**EXAMPLE 15.1** | Valuation Using Multiples

Let's go back to the example we used in Appendix 7B of Chapter 7, where we have the following information about a target company (T1) that an acquiring firm (A) is considering buying.

**Sales and Income Statement Items**

| | | |
|---|---|---|
| Sales | | $10 million |
| | Volume 1 million | |
| | Price per unit $10 | |
| | | ($ million) |
| Costs | | 9.0 |
| | Variable costs | 5.0 |
| | Fixed cash costs | 1.7 |
| | Depreciation | 0.8 |
| | Interest | 0.5 |
| | Income tax | 1.0 |
| Net income | | 1.0 |
| Dividends | | 0.5 |

**Capital**

Number of common shares outstanding 0.5 million

Invested capital (book values)

| Equity | $5 million |
|---|---|
| Debt | $5 million |
| Market value of equity | $15 million |

| Valuation Ratios | T1 | T1 5-Yr. Avg. | Industry Avg. |
|---|---|---|---|
| Price-earnings (P/E) (trailing) | 15 | 14.5 | 16.5 |
| Value/EBIT | 8 | 5.5 | 7.5 |
| Value/EBITDA | 6.06 | 4.8 | 6 |
| Price/Sales (P/S) | 1.5 | 1.35 | 1.6 |
| Price/Book value (P/B) (equity) | 3 | 3 | 3.2 |
| Price per unit of output | $15 | $14.50 | $16 |
| Return on equity (ROE) | 20% | 16.5% | 17.5% |

Remember in these ratios that EBIT (earnings before interest and taxes) and EBITDA (earnings before interest, taxes, depreciation, and amortization) belong to all the security holders, not just the shareholders, so these multiples are based on the total market value of the firm—that is, the value of the equity plus the debt. In this case, to get the equity value, we then have to subtract the market value of the debt.[22]

Of course, the actual value ratios for T1 listed in the table are based on the current market price of T1's common shares, and we cannot use them to value T1 since they just give us back the current value. In order to use the multiples approach to estimate the true value of T1, we would need to estimate "justifiable" P/E ratios drawn from comparables or a bottom-up analysis, as discussed in Chapter 7.

Estimate the value of T1's equity

**a.** using the industry averages for the first five valuation ratios presented in the table.

**b.** using the five-year averages for T1 for the first five valuation ratios presented in the table.

**c.** using the forward P/E ratio that is calculated based on the assumptions that

    **i.** 9 percent is a reasonable cost of equity for T1,

    **ii.** T1 maintains its present dividend payout ratio, and

    **iii.** T1's dividends and earnings grow at an annual rate of 6 percent indefinitely.

**Solution**

**a.** Using P/E ratio: Value P/E × Net income = 16.5 × $1m = $16.5m

Using V/EBIT ratio: Value = V/EBIT × EBIT − Debt = 7.5 × $2.5m − $5m = $18.75m − $5m = $13.75m

Using V/EBITDA ratio: Value = V/EBITDA × EBITDA − Debt = 6 × $3.3m − $5m = $19.8m − $5m = $14.8m

Using P/S ratio: Value = P/S × Sales = 1.6 × $10m = $16m

Using P/B ratio: Value = P/B × BV = 3.2 × $5m = $16m

The industry average multiples indicate that T1's equity may be currently undervalued at $15 million, and it should be valued somewhere around $16 million, depending on which multiple is used.

**b.** Using P/E ratio: Value = P/E × Net income = 14.5 × $1m = $14.5m

Using V/EBIT ratio: Value = V/EBIT × EBIT − Debt = 5.5 × $2.5m − $5m = $13.75m − $5m = $8.75m

Using V/EBITDA ratio: Value = V/EBITDA × EBITDA − Debt = 4.8 × $3.3m − $5m = $15.84m − $5m = $10.84m

Using P/S ratio: Value = P/S × Sales = 1.35 × $10m = $13.5m

Using P/B ratio: Value = P/B × BV = 3 × $5m = $15m

---

[22]Often the price-to-sales ratio used may be the total firm market value-to-sales ratio.

The company's historical (five-year) average multiples indicate that T1's equity should be valued somewhere between $8.75 million and $15 million, depending on which multiple is used.

c. The justifiable forward P/E ratio for T1 based on these assumptions can be calculated as follows:

P/E (forward) = Payout/(k − g) = (0.5m/1m)/(0.09 − 0.06) = 0.5/0.03 = 16.67

Next year's earnings based on a 6-percent growth rate = ($1m)(1.06) = $1.06m

Value of T1's equity = (P/E)(E$_1$) = (16.67)($1.06m) = $17.67m

Example 15.1 demonstrates that various valuation models may be used to estimate justifiable multiples, which can then be used to evaluate a target firm. However, in practice, we cannot just passively use these ratios for several reasons. For one thing, the use of different accounting methods can affect many of the items used in the multiples approach. We illustrate how these differences can affect the ratios and the valuation process in Example 15.2.

---

**EXAMPLE 15.2** | Accounting Differences

Consider two companies, A and B, that are identical in sales and profitability. Both have 1 million common shares outstanding. However, their income statements differ significantly as a result of the accounting methods they choose. In particular, their accounting choices differ in the following ways:

a. Firm A uses LIFO to account for inventory, while firm B uses FIFO.[23]

b. Firm A uses an accelerated depreciation method, while firm B uses straight-line depreciation.

c. Firm A fully funds pension costs, while B reports an unfunded pension liability.

d. Firm B sells surplus property for a gain to beef up earnings, while A has similar unrealized gains available to it.

The differences in the income statements of A and B are illustrated here:

|  | A($) | B($) |
|---|---|---|
| Sales | 10,000,000 | 10,000,000 |
| Cost of goods sold | 6,000,000 | 6,000,000 |
| Selling and general | 1,500,000 | 1,500,000 |
| LIFO difference | 400,000 | 0 |
| Depreciation | 400,000 | 300,000 |
| Pension costs | 200,000 | 50,000 |
| Gain on property sale |  | 150,000 |
| Earnings before tax | 1,500,000 | 2,300,000 |
| Income tax expense @ 40% | 600,000 | 920,000 |
| Net income | 900,000 | 1,380,000 |
| Earnings per share | 0.90 | 1.38 |

Estimate the price of A's and B's shares using a P/E ratio of 15.

**Solution**

|  | A | B |
|---|---|---|
| Price using P/E ratio of 15x | $13.50 | $20.70 |
| Total equity value | $13.5m | $20.7m |

Notice that the "only" differences in the companies are their accounting choices, yet we get very different valuations if we blindly use a P/E multiple of 15. This implies the importance of taking such factors into consideration in the valuation process. It also explains why many analysts tend to focus on cash flow instead of earnings to mitigate the influence of accounting decisions.

---

[23]Canadian firms tend to use FIFO; U.S. firms tend to use FIFO or LIFO.

Example 15.2 illustrates how different accounting choices can affect income statement items. Of course, a firm's capital structure decisions will also affect valuation ratios, as illustrated in Example 15.3.

---

**EXAMPLE 15.3** | Differing Capital Structures

Consider two companies, C and D, that are identical in sales and operating profitability (as measured by EBIT), but have different capital structures, as shown in the following. Calculate the P/E ratio for both companies.

|  | C($) | D($) |
|---|---|---|
| EBIT | 2,000,000 | 2,000,000 |
| Interest | 500,000 | 0 |
| EBT | 1,500,000 | 2,000,000 |
| Income taxes (40%) | 600,000 | 800,000 |
| Net income | 900,000 | 1,200,000 |
| Debt (Book value) | 10,000,000 | 0 |
| Equity (Book value) | 10,000,000 | 20,000,000 |
| Equity (Market value) | 12,000,000 | 20,000,000 |

**Solution**

|  | C | D |
|---|---|---|
| P/E ratio | (12,000,000/900,000) | (20,000,000/1,200,000) |
|  | 13.333x | 16.667x |

Notice the significant difference in P/E ratios that is caused by the fact that C uses $10 million in debt financing while D is all equity financed. Obviously, capital structure decisions can have a big impact on valuation multiples, as we discuss in Chapter 21 when we consider the question of an optimal capital structure.

---

In order to avoid the problems associated with the multiples approach, we can make adjustments to the financial statements and/or to the multiples we use for valuation purposes. Alternatively, we can use a different valuation framework that avoids some of the problems associated with using multiples. But note that if we have to use a multiple, most corporate valuations focus on the EBITDA and EBIT multiples, since they remove the problem with capital structure and focus higher up the income statement, avoiding some of the accounting problems that result from firms focusing on the bottom line (i.e., net income).

## Liquidation Valuation

This approach can be implemented following a process such as the one here:

1. Estimate the liquidation value of current assets based on their "realizable value." For example, if a company's accounts receivable are with firms of good credit quality, and most of them are current, it might be reasonable to value them at 80 percent of their book value. This percentage could be lower for firms whose customers are of lower average credit quality, or if they have a large percentage of overdue receivables. Similarly, inventory could be valued according to its marketability, etc.

2. Estimate the present market value of tangible assets such as machinery, buildings, and land.

3. Subtract the value of the firm's liabilities from the total estimated liquidation value of all the firm's assets. This represents the liquidation value of the firm.

The liquidation value approach is useful, but it can involve several estimates that may be imprecise at best, especially when a company has a lot of assets. More importantly, it values companies based on existing assets and is not forward looking. Therefore, we will devote most of our attention to the discounted cash flow valuation approach, which is discussed next. This approach must also overcome several challenges, as we shall see.

## Discounted Cash Flow Analysis

The discounted cash flow (DCF) approach was applied to specific securities in chapters 7 and 8. Now we apply it to the valuation of a company. The first step in this process is to estimate the future after-tax cash flows associated with a company. This step is fraught with difficulties, as alluded to in Professor Finagle's three laws of information, quoted here:[24]

1. The information we have is not what we want.

2. The information we want is not what we need.

3. The information we need is not available.

Let's examine these three "laws" one at a time, modifying the last statement so that we have a viable way of approaching the issue.

1. **The information we have is not what we want.**
   What we *have* (i.e., what we can find from the company's financial statements) is accounting earnings, which represent the bottom line, are affected by accounting choices, and can be manipulated by accounting "trickery."
   What we *want* is cash flow. The typical solution is to add back non-cash items such as depreciation, amortization, and deferred taxes, which leaves us with the traditional cash flow.

2. **The information we want is not what we need.**
   What we *want,* or what analysts typically try to estimate, is cash flow from operations (CFO). Recall from Chapter 3 that CFO may be estimated as traditional cash flow minus the increase in accounts receivable and/or inventory, plus the increase in accounts payable and/or other accruals.
   Using CFO helps eliminate the issues involved with accounting differences, such as the use of different revenue recognition policies. However, CFO does not truly reflect what we need, which is discussed next.

3. **The information we need, we can have, if only we look.**
   What we really need is an estimate of the cash that can be withdrawn from a business after the firm has made all required investments to sustain its future growth. This is best described as the free cash flow of a firm, which was defined in Chapter 3 and can be estimated using the following formula:

   Free cash flow = CFO − "Normal" capital expenditure (capex) requirements

---

[24]Hunt, Pearson, "Funds Position: Keystone in Financial Planning." *Harvard Business Review* (May/June 1975).

This cash flow estimate not only adjusts for the accounting problems discussed in items 1 and 2, but also ensures the firm grows in the long term and does not "run down" its assets to sustain profitability in the short term.

To summarize, the cash flows we will use in the DCF valuation approach will be the company's free cash flows. These free cash flows, which are defined in Equation 15.2, are the free cash flows to equity holders, since they represent the cash flows left over after all obligations, including interest payments, have been paid.[25]

Free cash flow to equity = Net income +/− Non-cash items (amortization, deferred taxes, etc.) +/− Changes in net working capital (not including cash and marketable securities) − Net capital expenditures  [15.2]

The next step in DCF valuation is to discount all of the future cash flow estimates back to the present, as depicted in Equation 15.3. Notice that this is similar to Equation 7.5 from Chapter 7, which depicted the generalized version of the dividend discount model (DDM); the only difference is that we use cash flows in the numerator instead of dividends. Since we are using free cash flow to equity, the appropriate discount rate $(k)$ will be the risk-adjusted cost of equity for the target firm.

$$V_0 = \frac{CF_1}{(1+k)^1} + \frac{CF_2}{(1+k)^2} + \cdots + \frac{CF_\infty}{(1+k)^\infty} = \sum_{t=1}^{\infty} \frac{CF_t}{(1+k)^t}$$  [15.3]

Like the constant-growth version of the DDM, this equation can be simplified, as shown in Equation 15.4, if we assume that these cash flows grow at some constant annual rate $(g)$ to infinity.

$$V_0 = \frac{CF_1}{k - g}$$  [15.4]

In practice, it is common to refine this process so that we can focus on estimating cash flows that will arise in the short to medium term and then make some simplifying assumption about cash flows beyond some terminal date $(T)$. This process is depicted in **Figure 15.7**.

The final term in the equation in Figure 15.7 is the terminal value $(V_T)$. This is the present value of all future cash flows from time $T$ to infinity, and it is usually estimated assuming some reasonable sustainable annual growth rate in cash flows from some time $T$ forward.

**FIGURE 15.7** The DCF Valuation Framework

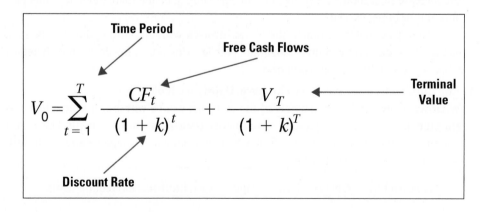

---

[25]This also assumes the firm does not issue any new debt, which would be added to the free cash flow amount. We ignore this component of free cash flow to equity for valuing takeover targets, since the new financing would presumably come from the acquiring firm going forward. The free cash flow to the firm (both equity and debt holders) would simply be the free cash flow to equity plus the after-tax amount of the interest payments (less any new debt issued that was added to determine free cash flow to equity).

Notice that this is the same approach we used when we applied the multiple-stage growth DDM in Chapter 7. For future reference, we number and present Equation 15.5 from Figure 15.7.

$$V_0 = \sum_{t=1}^{T} \frac{CF_t}{(1+k)^t} + \frac{V_T}{(1+k)^T} \qquad [15.5]$$

---

**EXAMPLE 15.4** | DCF Valuation I

We are given the following information about a potential takeover candidate firm (T2) for next year, based on what it is expected to contribute after it is acquired (i.e., with any arising synergies included): expected EBIT = $2 million; expected interest payments = $200,000; expected depreciation and amortization expense = $100,000; expected deferred taxes = $50,000; tax rate = 42 percent; expected increase in net working capital = $200,000; and expected net capital expenditures = $150,000.

  **a.** Estimate T2's free cash flow to equity next year.

  **b.** Estimate the value of T2's equity in total and on a per-share basis, assuming that next year's free cash flow increases annually at a 5-percent rate indefinitely. The firm has 500,000 shares outstanding. The appropriate beta is 1.2, the expected return on the market is 10 percent, and the risk-free rate is 4 percent.

**Solution**

  **a.** Net income = ($2,000,000 − $200,000) × (1 − 0.42) = $1,044,000
     Free cash flow to equity = Net income + Non-cash expenses − Increase in net working capital − Net capital expenditures = $1,044,000 + $100,000 + $50,000 − $200,000 − $150,000
     = $844,000

  **b.** Since we are assuming constant growth in the cash flows to infinity, we can use Equation 15.4.

$$k = 4 + (10 - 4)(1.2) = 11.2\%$$

$$CF_1 = \$844,000; \ g = 5\%$$

$$V_0 = \frac{CF_1}{k-g} = \frac{\$844,000}{0.112 - 0.05} = \$13,612,903$$

    Therefore, the per-share value = $13,612,903/500,000 = $27.23

---

**EXAMPLE 15.5** | DCF Valuation II

We are given the following information about a potential takeover candidate firm (T3) for the next three years.

| | Year 0 | Year 1 | Year 2 | Year 3 |
|---|---|---|---|---|
| Net income | $1,450 | $1,500 | $1,550 | $1,600 |
| Depreciation | 100 | 100 | 100 | 100 |
| Deferred taxes | 50 | 50 | 50 | 55 |
| Accounts receivable | 200 | 230 | 250 | 260 |
| Inventory | 150 | 160 | 180 | 190 |
| Accounts payable | 210 | 230 | 240 | 250 |
| Capital expenditures | 80 | 70 | 80 | 90 |
| Dividends | 150 | 150 | 160 | 160 |

After three years, free cash flow is expected to grow at 6 percent per year indefinitely. Estimate the value of T3's equity using DCF analysis, assuming the appropriate discount rate is 12 percent.

**Solution**

|  | Year 1 | Year 2 | Year 3 |
|---|---|---|---|
| Net income | $1,500 | $1,550 | $1,600 |
| + Depreciation | +100 | +100 | +100 |
| + Deferred taxes | +50 | +50 | +55 |
| − Increase in accounts receivable | −30 | −20 | −10 |
| − Increase in inventory | −10 | −20 | −10 |
| + Increase in accounts payable | +20 | +10 | +10 |
| − Capital expenditures | −70 | −80 | −90 |
| Free cash flow to equity | 1,560 | 1,590 | 1,655 |

$$k = 12\%;\ CF_1 = \$1,560;\ CF_2 = \$1,590;\ CF_3 = \$1,655$$

Since we are assuming constant growth after three years, we can use Equation 15.5.

$$V_0 = \sum_{t=1}^{T} \frac{CF_1}{(1 + k)^t} + \frac{V_T}{(1 + k)^T}$$

We can estimate the terminal value after three years using the constant growth version of the DCF formula, since $g = 6\%$ per year from year 3 to infinity.

$$V_T = \frac{CF_{T+1}}{k - g} = \frac{(\$1,655)(1.06)}{0.12 - 0.06} = \$29,238.33$$

Now we can estimate the value of T3 today:

$$V_0 = \frac{\$1,560}{(1.12)} + \frac{\$1,590}{(1.12)^2} + \frac{\$1,655}{(1.12)^3} + \frac{\$29,238.33}{(1.12)^3}$$

$$= \$1,392.86 + \$1,267.54 + \$1,178.00 + \$20,811.27 = \$24,649.67$$

# The Acquisition Decision

In the previous section, we discussed different methods of determining the value of a take-over candidate. This is a critical part of the takeover decision process, since an acquisition will make sense only if the target firm can be acquired for a price that is less than its value to the acquiring firm. For example, the acquiring firm in Example 15.5 should acquire firm T3 only if it can acquire T3 at a cost less than or equal to $24,650. Example 15.6 demonstrates that the cost of acquiring T3 depends on how the target firm is purchased, by cash or shares.

---

**EXAMPLE 15.6** | The Cost of an Acquisition

Firm A estimates that it can purchase firm T3 from Example 15.5 at a price of $24,650 in one of two ways: (1) by paying $24 per share in cash; or (2) by giving T3's shareholders two shares in the new combined firm, A-T3, for each share of T3.

Prior to the merger, T3 had 1,000 shares outstanding, which are trading at $20 per share, and A had 3,000 shares outstanding, trading at $12 per share.

Assuming that A is properly priced prior to the acquisition, should A acquire T3? If so, which method should it use to acquire T3?

**Solution** We estimate the cost under each method:

a. **Cash**: The cost is $24 × 1,000 = $24,000, which means that purchasing T3 by cash would generate an NPV of $24,650 − $24,000 = +$650.

b. **Stock:** Since A is giving T3's shareholders two of its shares (worth $12 each) for every share of T3, and since T3 has 1,000 shares outstanding, the cost appears to be 2,000 shares × $12 = $24,000; however, this is not correct since what A is really giving to T3's shareholders is 2,000 shares in the new company, A-T3, which is created from the merger.

To estimate the cost, we must therefore estimate the value of A-T3 after the merger:

Post-merger value of A-T3 = Value of A + Value of T3 to A = (3,000)($12) + $24,650 = $60,650

Since there will be 3,000 + 2,000 (new shares issued) = 5,000 shares outstanding in the new firm, each share will be worth $60,650/5,000 = $12.13.

So, the actual cost of giving T3's shareholders 2,000 shares equals:

Cost = (2,000 shares)($12.13 per share) = $24,260

Thus, the NPV under this scenario would be $24,650 − $24,260 = +$390.

Therefore, A would be better off to finance the deal using cash.

Example 15.6 highlights the SVAR analysis. Using cash lets the original shareholders keep the expected NPV, whereas using a share swap lets the target firm shareholders share in the NPV. Clearly, if the firm is very confident in the NPV, it should use cash, especially if cash is readily available. But if the NPV is highly uncertain, then a share swap reduces the risk to the original shareholders.

# The Effect of an Acquisition on Earnings per Share

Table 15.1 referred to the earnings per share (EPS) "growth game" as a motive for several M&As during the 1960s. An acquiring firm can increase its EPS if it acquires a firm that has a P/E ratio lower than its own, even if no synergies arise from the merger. This is illustrated in Example 15.7.

**EXAMPLE 15.7** | The EPS Effect

Firm A2 acquires firm T4 for cash at T4's present market value, and no synergies arise. The following pre-merger information is provided. What is the EPS of the new firm (A2-T4)?

|  | A2 | T4 |
|---|---|---|
| Total earnings | $10,000 | $3,000 |
| Number of common shares outstanding | 4,000 | 2,000 |
| EPS | $2.50 | $1.50 |
| Market price per share ($P_0$) | $20 | $9 |
| P/E ratio | 8 times | 6 times |
| Total market value of equity | $80,000 | $18,000 |

**Solution**   New firm A2-T4:

Total earnings = $10,000 + $3,000 = $13,000

Total shares outstanding = 4,000 (i.e., the number of shares A2 had outstanding)

Post-merger EPS = $13,000/4,000 = $3.25 (well above A2's pre-merger EPS of $2.50)

Notice that if the market were inefficient and the P/E ratio for A2 remained at 8, the value of A2-T4 would equal EPS × P/E ratio = $3.25 × 8 = $26.

Therefore, the market value of A2-T4 would equal $26 × 4,000 = $104,000.

> This is well above what it should be in an efficient market, since we know the combined market value should equal the market value of A2 plus the market value of T4, assuming no synergies were created. In other words, the combined market value of A2-T4 should equal $80,000 + $18,000 = $98,000. Total market value of A2 (after paying cash for T4) is $80,000. This implies that the P/E ratio should be $98,000/$13,000 = 7.54, and the share price for A2-T4 should be $3.25 × 7.54 = $24.50, not $26.

In an efficient market, the market value of the combined firm in Example 15.7 should be $98,000 and not $104,000. Given full disclosure, analysts are aware of the earnings multiplier game and see through such accounting gimmicks. This would mean that the accounting motivation for M&A is not significant. However, many firms do not seem to disclose the full extent of their acquisitions. For example, Tyco, the large U.S. conglomerate, was the target of much criticism for its disclosure of its M&A activity, with some suspicion that its earnings were in part from accounting and not organic growth. As a practical matter, many analysts and companies entering into M&As prefer those that are "accretive" to (i.e., increase) EPS.

## Concept Review Questions

1. What is the difference between value and price?
2. What is fair market value?
3. What key multiples are used in valuing companies?
4. Why do differing capital structures cause problems with using P/E multiples?
5. What is free cash flow?
6. When does EPS increase when using a share swap?

---

## 15.6 | Accounting for Acquisitions

**LEARNING OBJECTIVE 15.6**

Identify the issues involved in accounting for mergers and acquisitions.

**purchase method** a method of accounting for business combinations in which one firm assumes the fair market value of all the assets and liabilities of the other (target) firm and all operating results from the date of acquisition going forward

Historically, Canadian companies could use one of two methods to account for business combinations: the **purchase method** or the pooling-of-interests method. However, the Canadian Institute of Chartered Accountants (CICA) worked closely with the Financial Accounting Standards Board (FASB) of the United States to eliminate the pooling-of-interests method as of June 30, 2001. This caused fewer difficulties in Canada than in the United States, since the pooling method was permitted only in the rarest of circumstances in Canada. It had been used more frequently in the United States. The International Accounting Standards Board (IASB) also no longer permits the use of the pooling method. Given the conversion of Canadian GAAP to the IFRS standards in 2011, this means Canadian firms still have no choice and cannot use the pooling method. Since this method is no longer used, we will not elaborate on its application.

Under the purchase method, one firm basically assumes all of the assets and liabilities of the other (target) firm and all operating results from the date of acquisition going forward. No restatement of prior periods' results is necessary. At the time of the acquisition, all the assets and liabilities of the target firm are restated to reflect its FMV as of the acquisition date. Since we know that equity is defined as assets minus liabilities, this implies the difference between the FMV of the target firm's assets and liabilities is the FMV of its equity. If the purchase price exceeds the FMV of the target firm's equity, the excess amount is referred to as **goodwill**, which is reported on the asset side of the balance sheet for the new entity. Example 15.8 illustrates the purchase method of accounting for an acquisition.

**goodwill** the amount of a target firm's purchase price that exceeds the fair market value of its equity

**EXAMPLE 15.8** | The Purchase Method

Assume company A1 acquires company T5 for $1,250 in cash on June 30, 2022. The table that follows provides the balance sheets for A1 and T5 on that date, as well as the estimated market values for T5's assets and liabilities. Construct A1's balance sheet after the acquisition, using the purchase method.

| | A1 | T5 (Book Value) | T5 (FMV) |
|---|---|---|---|
| Current assets | $10,000 | $1,200 | $1,300 |
| Long-term assets | 6,000 | 800 | 900 |
| Goodwill | | | |
| Total | 16,000 | 2,000 | 2,200 |
| Current liabilities | 8,000 | 800 | 800 |
| Long-term debt | 2,000 | 200 | 250 |
| Common shares | 2,000 | 400 | 1,250 |
| Retained earnings | 4,000 | 600 | |
| Total | 16,000 | 2,000 | 2,300 |

**Solution**

| | A1 (Pre-Merger) | T5 (Book Value) | T5 (FMV) | A1 (Post-Merger) |
|---|---|---|---|---|
| Current assets | $10,000 | $1,200 | $1,300 | $11,300[1] |
| Long-term assets | 6,000 | 800 | 900 | 6,900[2] |
| Goodwill | | | | 100[3] |
| Total | 16,000 | 2,000 | 2,200 | 18,300 |
| Current liabilities | 8,000 | 800 | 800 | 8,800 |
| Long-term debt | 2,000 | 200 | 250 | 2,250 |
| Common shares | 2,000 | 400 | 1,250 | 3,250 |
| Retained earnings | 4,000 | 600 | | 4,000 |
| Total | 16,000 | 2,000 | 2,300 | 18,300 |

[1]$10,000 + $1,300 = $11,300
[2]$6,000 + $900 = $6,900
[3]Goodwill = $1,250 (Price paid) − MV (T5's equity) = $1,250 − [$2,200 MV(T5's assets) − $1,050 MV (T5's liabilities)] = $1,250 − $1,150 = $100

In addition to the accounting rule changes with respect to purchase versus pooling accounting, rules have also been implemented about the valuation of goodwill and intangibles. One of the most important rule changes is that the goodwill resulting from an acquisition may not be amortized. Prior to the rule change, amortization was mandatory. Instead, the market value of goodwill must be assessed annually, and it is written down and charged directly to earnings if the value is deemed to have been permanently "impaired." As a result of this treatment of goodwill, its fair value is subject to an annual impairment test. As discussed in this section, the value of goodwill on the balance sheet is what is left over after properly valuing everything else. This means companies are required to employ common valuation techniques, such as detailed discounted cash flow analysis, in order to determine fair value.

## Concept Review Questions

1. Explain how the purchase method gives rise to goodwill.
2. How is goodwill treated for accounting purposes in Canada and the United States?

# Review

## Summary

In this chapter, we discuss the various forms of business combinations, paying particular attention to mergers and acquisitions. We examine some of the most common motives that exist for takeovers, as well as some desirable characteristics of potential takeover "targets." We then demonstrate how to evaluate a potential takeover candidate using the multiples approach and using discounted cash flow analysis. We conclude with a discussion of how acquisitions should be accounted for in the financial statements, and we show the impact that acquisitions can have on earnings per share.

## Summary of Learning Objectives

### 15.1 Describe the different types of takeovers.

**Takeover:** the transfer of control from one ownership group to another

**Acquisition:** the purchase of one firm by another

**Merger:** the combination of two firms into a new legal entity

**Amalgamation:** a genuine merger in which both sets of shareholders must approve the transaction

**Going private transaction (issuer bid):** a special form of acquisition in which the purchaser already owns a majority stake in the target company

### 15.2 Explain securities legislation as it applies to takeovers.

Securities legislation governs the exchange of shares by the target firm's shareholders and protects the shareholders' right to receive full value for their shares. Securities legislation falls under provincial jurisdiction; therefore, there are differences between the provinces. The *Ontario Securities Act*, administered by the Ontario Securities Commission, contains many features that are common to all jurisdictions. Critical shareholder percentages are:

- 10 percent: early warning
- 20 percent: takeover bid
- 50.1 percent: control
- 66.7 percent: amalgamation
- 90 percent: minority squeeze-out

### 15.3 Differentiate between friendly and hostile acquisitions and describe the process of a typical friendly acquisition.

In a friendly acquisition, the management of the target company agrees to the takeover. In a hostile acquisition, the management of the target company resists the acquirer, so the acquirer makes a tender offer directly to the shareholders of the target.

The steps in a typical friendly acquisition process are:

1. The target issues an information memorandum.
2. The potential acquirers conduct due diligence.
3. The most interested acquirers sign letters of intent.
4. The winning acquirer makes a final agreement with the board of the target.
5. The offer is approved by the shareholders of the target company.

### 15.4 Explain the various motivations underlying mergers and acquisitions.

Mergers and acquisitions are most commonly motivated by the following benefits:

- Economies of scale: increased size produces benefits, such as reducing over-capacity in the industry
- Economies of scope: combined activities reduce costs
- Complementary strengths: one firm's strength benefits the other
- Efficiency increases: e.g., eliminating excess capacity increases efficiency
- Financing synergies: larger is better for accessing capital markets
- Tax benefits: e.g., one firm's losses can be used to offset the other firm's profits to reduce taxes
- Strategic realignments: e.g., the acquisition of new managerial skill and new product/service line growth opportunities

### 15.5 Identify the valuation issues involved in assessing mergers and acquisitions.

1. **Multiples or relative valuation** involves the use of ratios, such as price-earnings (P/E), enterprise value to earnings before interest, taxes, depreciation, and amortization (EV/EBITDA), market-to-book (M/B), price-to-sales (P/S), and price-to-cash flow (P/CF).
2. **Liquidation valuation** involves estimating the liquidation value of the firm's assets at present market prices.
3. **Discounted cash flow (DCF)** *analysis* involves estimating the future cash flows associated with the new combined entity and discounting them back to the present to determine the fair market value.

### 15.6 Identify the issues involved in accounting for mergers and acquisitions.

Under the purchase method, the assets of the target are restated to reflect their fair market value (FMV). The FMV of the assets is added to the assets of the acquiring firm. If the purchase price exceeds the FMV of the assets, then the difference is recorded as goodwill on the acquiring firm's balance sheet.

## Key Terms

acquisition, p. 15-1
amalgamation, p. 15-3
arbs, p. 15-10
asset purchase, p. 15-9
break fee, p. 15-8
cash transaction, p. 15-2
confidentiality agreement, p. 15-7
conglomerate merger, p. 15-13
creeping takeover, p. 15-6
cross-border (international) M&A, p. 15-14
data room, p. 15-7
defensive tactic, p. 15-10
due diligence, p. 15-8
extension M&A, p. 15-17
fair market value (FMV), p. 15-21

fairness opinion, p. 15-3
friendly acquisition, p. 15-7
geographic roll-up, p. 15-16
going private transaction, p. 15-3
goodwill, p. 15-32
horizontal merger, p. 15-13
hostile takeover, p. 15-9
issuer bid, p. 15-3
letter of intent, p. 15-8
leveraged buyouts (LBOs), p. 15-22
management buyouts (MBOs), p. 15-22
merger, p. 15-2
no-shop clause, p. 15-8
offering memorandum, p. 15-7
over-capacity M&A, p. 15-16

poison pill, p. 15-10
proactive method, p. 15-23
purchase method, p. 15-32
reactive method, p. 15-22
selling the crown jewels, p. 15-11
share transaction, p. 15-2
shareholder rights plan, p. 15-10
synergy, p. 15-14
takeover, p. 15-1
tender, p. 15-6
tender offer, p. 15-9
vertical merger, p. 15-13
white knight, p. 15-11

## Equations

| Equation | Description | Formula | Page |
|---|---|---|---|
| [15.1] | Synergy | $\Delta V = V_{A-T} - (V_A + V_T)$ | p. 15-14 |
| [15.2] | Free Cash Flow to Equity | Free cash flow to equity = Net income +/− Non-cash items (amortization, deferred taxes, etc.) +/− Changes in net working capital (not including cash and marketable securities) − Net capital expenditures | p. 15-28 |
| [15.3] | Firm Value (long version) | $V_0 = \dfrac{CF_1}{(1+k)^1} + \dfrac{CF_2}{(1+k)^2} + \cdots + \dfrac{CF_\infty}{(1+k)^\infty} = \sum_{t=1}^{\infty}\dfrac{CF_t}{(1+k)^t}$ | p. 15-28 |
| [15.4] | Firm Value (constant growth version) | $V_0 = \dfrac{CF_1}{k-g}$ | p. 15-28 |
| [15.5] | Firm Value (multi-stage growth version) | $V_0 = \sum_{t=1}^{T}\dfrac{CF_t}{(1+k)^t} + \dfrac{V_T}{(1+k)^T}$ | p. 15-29 |

# Questions and Practice Problems

## Multiple Choice Questions

1. **(LO 15.1)** Which of the following statements about takeovers is *false?*
   a. Mergers create a new firm, while acquisitions do not.
   b. Both mergers and acquisitions require two-thirds votes from both firms.
   c. In the tender offer, the acquiring firm makes a public offer to purchase shares of the target firm.
   d. Acquisition of assets is one of the types of takeover.

2. **(LO 15.1)** Which of the following firm structures is *least* likely to be the target for a bidder?
   a. Common shares are widely held.
   b. The stock is undervalued.
   c. It has a simple corporate structure.
   d. There are many legal problems.

3. **(LO 15.2)** Which of the following critical shareholder percentages is *false?*
   a. 10 percent: early warning
   b. 20 percent: takeover bid
   c. 50.1 percent: control
   d. 100 percent: minority squeeze-out

4. **(LO 15.3)** Which of the following statements about hostile takeovers is *false?*
   a. In hostile takeover bids, there is usually a tender offer.
   b. A formal vote by the target shareholders is required.
   c. The target has no desire to be acquired.
   d. The target actively rebuffs the acquiring firm and refuses to provide any confidential information.

**5. (LO 15.3)** Which of the following statements is *false* when the market price immediately jumps above the tender offer price in a hostile bid?

   **a.** A competing offer is likely.

   **b.** The bid is too low.

   **c.** The bidder will have to increase the offer price.

   **d.** The bid is too high.

**6. (LO 15.3)** Which of the following statements is *false* regarding a tender offer during hostile takeovers?

   **a.** If there is little trading, this is usually a bad sign for the acquiring firm, since shareholders are sitting on the shares and are reluctant to sell.

   **b.** A large amount of trading indicates that shares are cycling from regular investors into specialist hands.

   **c.** Arbitrageurs are only interested in selling as long as the price is right.

   **d.** The motivation of arbitrageurs is to take control of the target.

**7. (LO 15.3)** Which of the following is *not* a defensive tactic in a hostile takeover?

   **a.** A shareholder rights plan (a poison pill)

   **b.** Selling the crown jewels

   **c.** Finding a white knight

   **d.** Cooperating with the acquirer

**8. (LO 15.4)** Which of the following statements is *true*?

   **a.** The synergies of a merger, on average, add so much value to the combined firm, that the share price of both firms (target and acquirer) tends to increase substantially.

   **b.** When a bid is announced, on average, the share price of the target firm tends to drop.

   **c.** In order to entice the shareholders of a target firm to accept an offer, acquirers typically pay an acquisition premium for a target. When such a bid is announced, on average, the share price of the target tends to rise rapidly, while the price of the acquiring firm falls by a corresponding amount.

   **d.** Acquirers often justify paying a premium for a target firm by suggesting the transaction, through the elimination of redundancies, will result in significant efficiency gains.

**9. (LO 15.4)** Which of the following is *not* one of the three types of merger?

   **a.** Vertical M&A

   **b.** Horizontal M&A

   **c.** Proxy contest

   **d.** Conglomerate

**10. (LO 15.4)** Which of the following M&As is value enhancing?

   **a.** $V_{A-T} = \$400,000$; $V_A = \$200,000$; $V_T = \$205,000$

   **b.** $V_{A-T} = \$390,000$; $V_A = \$200,000$; $V_T = \$190,000$

   **c.** $V_{A-T} = \$410,000$; $V_A = \$200,000$; $V_T = \$190,000$

   **d.** $V_{A-T} = \$600,000$; $V_A = \$400,000$; $V_T = \$210,000$

**11. (LO 15.4)** Which of the following is a poor motive for M&As as suggested by evidence?

   **a.** Diversification

   **b.** Economies of scale

   **c.** Economies of scope

   **d.** Complementary strengths

**12. (LO 15.4)** Which of the following is *not* a reason for financial synergies?

   **a.** Fewer information problems

   **b.** Reduced average issuing costs

   **c.** Reduced cash flow volatility

   **d.** Increased need of external financing

**13. (LO 15.5)** What is the market value of the equity of a firm that has a trailing P/E ratio of 14.5 and expected earnings ($E_1$) of $550,000? The firm is expected to grow at 5 percent.

   **a.** $7,595,238.10

   **b.** $8,745,000.00

   **c.** $8,285,714.29

   **d.** $6,904,761.91

**14. (LO 15.5)** Which of the following cash flow measures should be used in the DCF valuation approach?

   **a.** Cash flow from operations (CFO)

   **b.** Free cash flow

   **c.** Cash flow from investing (CFI)

   **d.** Cash flow from financing (CFF)

**15. (LO 15.5)** Which of the following statements about liquidation valuation is *false*?

   **a.** Current accounts receivable with good credit firms should be realized at a relatively high percentage of book value.

   **b.** Liquidation value equals book value of current assets plus market value of tangible assets minus the value of the firm's liabilities from the total estimated liquidation value of all the firm's assets.

   **c.** Overdue accounts receivable with bad credit firms should be realized at a relatively low percentage of book value.

   **d.** The liquidation valuation approach is not forward-looking.

## Practice Problems

### Basic

**16. (LO 15.1)** Briefly describe the two types of takeovers.

**17. (LO 15.3)** The Bynum Private Equity group has just made a tender offer for, at most, 60 percent of Vendall Company. Vendall has 1,000 shares outstanding. Mr. VanDuun is a shareholder of Vendall and has tendered his shares. For each of the following situations, indicate the number of shares accepted by Bynum and how many of Mr. VanDuun's shares will be accepted by Bynum.

| | Total Shares Tendered by Vendall Shareholders | Mr. VanDuun's Tendered Shares | Total Number of Shares Accepted by Bynum | Number of Mr. VanDuun's Shares Accepted by Bynum |
|---|---|---|---|---|
| A | 1,000 | 400 | | |
| B | 1,000 | 300 | | |
| C | 500 | 400 | | |
| D | 500 | 300 | | |
| E | 500 | 100 | | |
| F | 500 | 200 | | |

**18. (LO 15.3)** Describe the process of a friendly acquisition.

**19. (LO 15.3)** Briefly describe three common defensive tactics against a takeover and the difference between U.S. and Canadian practice on poison pills.

**20. (LO 15.3)** Describe the possible market price change after a tender offer and the possible reasons.

21. **(LO 15.4)** Describe horizontal M&A, vertical M&A, and conglomerate.

22. **(LO 15.4)** Describe the economies of scale of M&A.

23. **(LO 15.4)** Describe the financing synergies of M&A.

24. **(LO 15.4)** Describe the empirical evidence on the actual gains or losses resulting from mergers.

25. **(LO 15.6)** Describe the purchase method in accounting for acquisitions.

### Intermediate

26. **(LO 15.2)** Marcel owns 12 percent of Steam Forge Company (SFC). SFC trades on the Toronto Stock Exchange and has been the subject of a takeover attempt by Iron Forge Company (IFC). Assuming that Marcel is the only minority shareholder who will not co-operate with IFC, determine the minimum level of ownership IFC needs in order to do the following. (Round your answer to one decimal.)

   a. Call a special meeting of the shareholders.

   b. Replace the board of directors.

   c. Replace the firm's management.

   d. Force Marcel to sell at the takeover price.

   e. Win a vote on amalgamation.

   f. Make a takeover bid.

27. **(LO 15.2, 15.4)** Julius is a shareholder in a public corporation that has recently acquired another company, and the consequences for the bidding firm have been catastrophic. Julius is suing the bidder's board of directors for breach of duty as he believes that they failed in their duties to the shareholders. The board of directors, in their response to the suit, said: "A board member is from British Columbia, and he knew about a timber company that was for sale and we could get it cheap. We saw that the profits of lumber companies had increased over the past two years, so we bought it. We did not waste time and money looking at other possible candidates because we had found a good deal. We knew the deal was good because the CEO of the target was the cousin of the board member from B.C." The bidding company, prior to the acquisition, was in the business of making sewing machines. The board of directors of the bidding firm has 12 members, 8 of whom are either current or former executives with the firm.

   Discuss at least four serious problems with the board's approach toward this acquisition.

28. **(LO 15.6)** A bidder paid $1,500 for a target. The target's market asset is $2,000 and market liability is $1,250. What is the goodwill created during the acquisition?

### Challenging

29. **(LO 15.4)** You are a risk arbitrageur and you observe the following information about a deal: the current price of the target is $22 per share and the current price of the bidder is $16 per share. The bidder is offering two bidder shares per target share, and you expect the deal to be completed in one year. Neither company is expected to pay dividends over the next year. Assume you can freely short sell and there are no margin requirements. You do not use any leverage.

   a.  i. Calculate the offer premium as a percentage.

      ii. Describe the transaction you will undertake to capture the premium.

      iii. Show how your transaction will make money.

   b. Is it possible that your actual return will be less than the expected return? Describe two situations that can cause the risk in risk arbitrage.

30. **(LO 15.3, 15.4, 15.5)** Carla is the CEO of Superior Sausage Company (a Canadian firm, listed on the Toronto Stock Exchange) and believes that the best way for the company to grow is through acquisitions. She has identified a likely target, Bunns & Bagels (B&B), which is also listed on the Toronto Stock Exchange.

   a. Describe two different motives for this acquisition.

   b. Carla is very uncertain about the value of B&B. Describe how she can structure the deal to reduce the risk to Superior Sausage.

   c. Carla has just publicly announced that she feels that the senior management of B&B is not only incompetent, but likely to have been committing fraud.

      i. Is a takeover by Superior Sausage more likely to be friendly or hostile? Why?

      ii. Is Superior more likely to use a tender offer or a merger offer? Why?

      iii. Describe three ways B&B could try to defend itself from Superior.

   d. Before the market opened on Monday, B&B announced that it had received a merger offer from Franks' Fine Franks. By the end of trading on Monday, B&B has earned a return of −2 percent (negative 2 percent). The return on the market that day was 4 percent, and the daily risk-free rate was close to zero. The beta for B&B is 2, with a standard deviation of the regression of 2 percent.

      i. What is the expected return for B&B on Monday based on CAPM?

      ii. What is the abnormal return for B&B on Monday?

      iii. Given the empirical evidence on mergers and acquisitions, is the market's reaction unusual? Why or why not?

*Use the following information to answer practice problems 31 to 35.*

| | |
|---|---:|
| Sales | $1,750,000 |
| Cost of goods sold | 450,000 |
| Depreciation | 400,000 |
| Interest | 150,000 |
| Income tax | 275,000 |
| Dividends | 300,000 |
| Common shares outstanding | 500,000 |
| P/EBITDA | 10x |

31. **(LO 15.5)** Calculate the market price of the firm's common shares using a relative valuation approach. (Round your answer to one decimal.)

32. **(LO 15.5)** Calculate the trailing and forward P/E ratios using the price calculated in practice problem 31. Assume a 6-percent earnings growth. (Round your answer to one decimal.)

33. **(LO 15.5)** Calculate the trailing and forward P/E ratios using the following assumptions: RF = 3.5 percent; $\beta$ = 1.12; market risk premium = 5 percent; dividends and earnings grow at 6 percent indefinitely; and the firm maintains its current dividend payout ratio. (Round your answer to one decimal.)

34. **(LO 15.5)** Calculate the market value of the firm given the following additional information: cost of equity is 8.25 percent; free cash flow to equity grows at 6 percent indefinitely; total debt outstanding = $1,000,000; increase in current assets = $400,000; increase in current liabilities = $300,000; and capital expenditures = $100,000. (Round your answer to the nearest dollar.)

35. **(LO 15.5)** In practice problem 34, if the free cash flow to equity grows at 8 percent for the first two years and then grows at 5 percent indefinitely, what is the market value of the firm now? (Round your answer to the nearest dollar.)

**36. (LO 15.5)** ABC Inc. is planning to purchase DEF Inc. in one of two ways: (1) by paying $24 per share in cash; or (2) by giving DEF's shareholders two shares in the new combined firm ABC-DEF for each share of DEF. Prior to the merger, DEF had 500,000 shares outstanding, trading at $22 per share. ABC had 600,000 shares outstanding, trading at $23 per share. Assume that ABC is properly priced prior to the acquisition. DEF is valued at $25,875,000 to ABC. Should ABC acquire DEF? If so, which method should it use to acquire DEF?

*Use the following information to answer practice problems 37 and 38:*
Large Corp. ("LC"), a manufacturing conglomerate, is considering acquiring Mini Industries ("MI") and they intend to pay for the transaction by issuing new shares. LC, with earnings per share (EPS) of $5, has 10 million shares outstanding that are trading at $50 each. The target, MI, has earnings per share (EPS) of $1.25 and 4 million shares outstanding that are trading at $25 each. LC will not pay a premium for MI and the transaction is not expected to yield any synergies.

**37. (LO 15.5)** What will Large Corp.'s earnings per share (EPS) be following the merger?

**38. (LO 15.5)** Calculate Large Corp.'s pre and post-merger price-to-earnings (P/E) ratio.

**39. (LO 15.5)** Calculate the post-merger EPS and market value of equity, assuming no synergies arise in the following acquisition settled in cash. Analyze the difference, if there is any. Further, calculate the new P/E ratio and share price for post-merger B-T. Additional information is given as follows:

| | Bidder | Target |
|---|---|---|
| Total earnings | $25,000 | $8,000 |
| Number of common shares outstanding | 8,000 | 4,000 |
| EPS | $3.125 | $2.00 |
| Market price per share (P$_0$) | $29.50 | $12.00 |
| P/E ratio | 9.44 times | 6 times |
| Total market value of equity | $236,000 | $48,000 |

**40. (LO 15.6)** The balance sheets of a bidder and target companies are as follows:

**Balance Sheet (Bidder) as at 31/12/2x**

| Tangible assets | $60,000 | | |
|---|---|---|---|
| Accumulated depreciation | $42,000 | Total debt | $15,000 |
| Net tangible assets | $18,000 | | |
| Goodwill | 3,000 | Equity | 6,000 |
| Total assets | $21,000 | Total claims | $21,000 |

**Balance Sheet (Target) as at 31/12/2x**

| Tangible assets | $36,000 | | |
|---|---|---|---|
| Accumulated depreciation | $15,000 | Total debt | $19,000 |
| Net tangible assets | $21,000 | | |
| Goodwill | 0 | Equity | 2,000 |
| Total assets | $21,000 | Total claims | $21,000 |

The tax rate for both companies is 25 percent. The acquisition will be accounted for using the purchase method. Prior to the acquisition, the bidding firm had 10,000 shares outstanding, with a share price of $20. The target had 5,000 shares outstanding, with a market price of $10. The bidder acquired the target by offering 0.8 bidder shares per target share.

After analyzing the target, the bidder has decided that the market value of the target's assets is $65,000, and the market value of the bidder's assets are $45,000.

**a.** How many shares will be outstanding for the combined firm, B-T?

**b.** What fraction of the combined company will be owned by the original bidder shareholders?

**c.** How much goodwill was created by this transaction?

**d.** How much are the net tangible assets for the combined firm?

**e.** Show the consolidated balance sheet for B-T (use the template provided).

**Combined Firm Balance Sheet as at 31/12/2x**

| Net tangible assets | Total debt |
|---|---|
| Goodwill | Equity |
| Total assets | Total claims |

**41. (LO 15.6)** Complete the following balance sheet for the post-merger firm B-T. The bidder acquired the target for $8,000 in cash.

| $ | Bidder | Target (Book Value) | Target (Fair Market Value) | B-T (Post-Merger) |
|---|---|---|---|---|
| Current assets | 25,000 | 4,500 | 4,900 | |
| Long-term assets | 10,000 | 2,000 | 2,300 | |
| Goodwill | | | | |
| Total assets | 35,000 | 6,500 | 7,200 | |
| Current liabilities | 11,000 | 1,500 | 1,500 | |
| Long-term debt | 5,000 | 1,200 | 1,200 | |
| Common shares | 15,000 | 2,400 | 4,500 | |
| Retained earnings | 4,000 | 1,400 | | |
| Total | 35,000 | 6,500 | 7,200 | |

# Leasing

This chapter discusses leasing arrangements, which may represent attractive alternatives for companies looking to finance both short- and long-term investments. The asset-based financing and leasing industry is the largest provider of debt financing to business customers and consumers in Canada after the traditional lenders (banks and credit unions). The Canadian Finance and Leasing Association (CFLA) estimates that the assets of the asset-based financing industry were worth just over $400 billion in Canada in 2017. This chapter deals with basic financial issues faced by Canadian individuals as well as firms. Think of this chapter the next time you decide to buy or lease a new car.

## 16.1 Leasing Arrangements

In earlier chapters, we considered the purchase of a piece of equipment separate from its financing, which will be discussed in later chapters. In **asset-based lending**, these two decisions are combined into one decision, with the financing tied directly to the particular asset being purchased. This is an example of **secured financing**, in which the financing is based on an underlying asset that serves as collateral in the event of a default. Examples of asset-based lending are secured loans, conditional sales contracts, and leases. We will discuss the differences between these types of asset-based financing in this chapter, but the main focus is on leases. While most textbooks discuss leasing as either a financing or investment decision, we have chosen to discuss it as a capital budgeting decision because it provides a further chance to develop basic valuation skills in discounting cash flows. Also, a firm may choose to lease rather than purchase one of the long-term assets considered in capital budgeting. **Figure 16.1** illustrates the level of asset-based financing in Canada.

**asset-based lending** financing that is tied directly to a particular asset

**secured financing** financing based on an underlying asset that serves as collateral in the event of a default

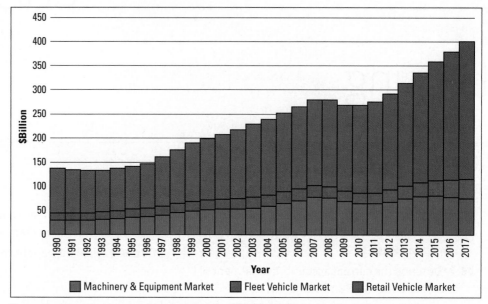

**Source**: From Canadian Finance and Leasing Association (CFLA), *2016/2017 Annual Report*, p. 10. Available at www.cfla-acfl.ca. Reproduced with permission from Canadian Finance and Leasing Association (CFLA).

The figure shows that this kind of financing exceeded $400 billion for the first time in 2017, and that it closely follows the pattern of business investment.

First let us step back and discuss the institutional framework for asset-based financing. The Canadian Finance and Leasing Association (CFLA) is the professional body that acts as the umbrella group for asset-based lenders in Canada. It has about 215 members representing three broad groups of financial companies. Independent asset-based finance companies, such as CIT, hold about 60 percent of the outstanding balances in Canada; the **captive finance companies** of the major manufacturers, such as IBM, hold about 25 to 30 percent of the outstanding balances; and the remainder is with the chartered banks. There are restrictions in the *Bank Act* that prevent the chartered banks from leasing consumer household property, vehicles (except for commercial transportation equipment), and real property (land and buildings). As a result, this is one major segment of the capital market where the banks are not as important as they are elsewhere.

Asset-based financing is always tied directly to some underlying asset and is split among three major categories—commercial equipment, fleet (commercial) vehicles, and retail vehicles. **Table 16.1** shows the volumes for new asset-based financing in 1990 and in 2017. We can see that in 2017, 74 percent of new asset-based financing was for retail vehicles, 10 percent for fleet vehicles, and 16 percent for machinery and equipment. The major assets financed in this way are broadly distributed between the different types of financial companies. The independents are mainly involved in machinery and equipment financing; approximately 20 to 25 percent of all machinery and equipment is leased, with 60 percent of their customers being **small and medium-sized enterprises (SMEs)**. Over 30 percent of the assets financed are either transportation equipment, such as buses, trucks, and trailers, or office equipment. As we will

**captive finance companies** finance companies that are divisions of major manufacturers and provide loans to purchase or lease their products

**small and medium-sized enterprises (SMEs)** businesses that generally have fewer than 50 employees

**TABLE 16.1** **Asset-Based Financing Market in Canada**

|  | 1990 | 2017 |
|---|---|---|
| **New Business Total ($Billion)** | 43 | 128 |
|  | **Percentages by Category** | |
| Commercial equipment | 22% | 16% |
| Fleet (commercial vehicles) | 11% | 10% |
| Retail vehicles | 67% | 74% |

**Source:** Data from Canadian Finance and Leasing Association (CFLA), 2013/2014 and 2017/18 annual reports. Available at www.cfla-acfl.ca.

discuss, this financing tends to be extremely flexible, is often tailored to meet the needs of the original manufacturers, and ranges across the whole spectrum of asset-based financing. Often an SME will approach a manufacturer for a piece of equipment and will be offered on-the-spot financing as a pre-arranged package with the asset-based financier.

In contrast, the captive finance companies are subsidiaries of the major manufacturing companies and finance the purchase of the equipment they sell. This sector is dominated by the big vehicle manufacturers like GM, Ford, and Toyota. It is estimated that about a third of all new vehicles are leased, a third paid for with cash, and a third paid for through borrowing. The final group of financial companies, the chartered banks, are much more restricted, since they primarily finance through capital leases, a direct alternative to a secured loan.

So what is a lease and how is it distinct from other asset-based forms of financing? The CFLA provides the following definition: "A lease contract is an agreement where the owner conveys to the user the right to use an asset in return for a number of specified payments over an agreed period of time. The owner of the asset is referred to as the **lessor**, the user the **lessee**."[1]

Leasing provides lessees with an alternative to purchasing an asset that they need.

As indicated previously, there are different types of asset-based financing, and, unfortunately, the definitions differ from one accountant, lawyer, and tax authority to another. As a result, some forms of asset-based financing are specifically structured to meet one interpretation for accounting and a different one for tax purposes. However, broadly speaking, we can differentiate between **operating leases** and **financial leases**, which are also commonly referred to as full payout or capital leases. Recent changes in accounting standards that are discussed in section 16.2 dictate that virtually all leases will be treated as financial leases under IFRS as of 2019, while U.S. GAAP will still allow leases to be treated as operating or financial leases (although the treatment of operating leases will change from the historical treatment).

## Types of Asset-Based Financing

In 1983, the Canada Revenue Agency (CRA) released an interpretation bulletin (IT-233R) spelling out when a lease should be considered a lease for tax purposes. In 2001, CRA repealed IT-233R, stating, "It is our view that the determination of whether a contract is a lease or sale is based on the legal relationship created by the terms of the agreement."[2] Although the bulletin was repealed, it is useful to take a look at its text to see how CRA formerly viewed a lease. IT-233R implied that CRA viewed a lease as a sale of equipment through a *conditional sales agreement* if one of the following occurred:

- The lessee automatically acquired ownership at some point.
- The lessee was required to buy the asset at some point or guarantee that the lessor got a certain value for it.
- The lessee had the right to buy the asset at some point for substantially less than the likely fair market value.
- The lessee had the right to buy the asset at a price that would cause a reasonable person to conclude that they would buy it.

The CRA concern was that if any of these conditions were satisfied, a reasonable person would conclude that the expectation was that ownership of the asset was being transferred to the user of the asset, even though that party had to make a series of future payments that "looked like" a loan or lease payment. CRA was interested in this because the owner of the asset had the right to claim capital cost allowance (CCA) for tax purposes. So if any of the conditions had been satisfied, CRA would have regarded the user—and not the party receiving the payments—as the party with the right to claim CCA.

The accounting profession's view of a financial lease has historically been that all the benefits of ownership transfer to the lessee. In this interpretation, the payments to the lessor are

**lessor**   the owner of the asset; the party in a lease agreement who conveys the right to use the asset in return for payment

**lessee**   the party in a lease agreement who pays to obtain the right to use the asset

**operating lease**   a lease in which some of the benefits of ownership do not transfer to the lessee but remain with the lessor

**financial lease**   a lease in which essentially all the benefits of ownership transfer to the lessee; also known as a capital or full payout lease

---

[1]Canadian Finance and Leasing Association (CFLA), "The Asset Based Financing, Equipment and Vehicle Leasing Industry." Backgrounder for the House of Commons Finance Committee, September 4, 1998.

[2]For information about the cancellation of IT-233R, see Canada Revenue Agency, *Income Tax Technical News*. No. 21, June 14, 2001.

compensation for the initial purchase of the equipment and provide the lessor with a financial return. In this case, the lease usually

- requires the lessee to carry out maintenance and insure the asset,
- provides the lessee with a fixed-purchase option,
- covers at least 75 percent of the economic life of the asset,
- is structured so that the present value of lease payments exceeds 90 percent of the cost, and
- involves fixed rental payments.

The lessee is assumed to own the asset and thus claims depreciation on the firm's income statement and records the value of the asset as an asset and the financing obligation as a liability on its balance sheet.

In contrast, the critical feature of an operating lease (which is still permissible under U.S. GAAP) is that some of the benefits of ownership do not transfer to the lessee but remain with the lessor. As a result, the conditions are the opposite of those for a financial lease. For example, operating leases are usually, though not always, *full-service* leases in which the lessor is responsible for maintaining the asset, providing any insurance, and paying property taxes on the asset (if the asset is land or a building).

When we compare financial leases with operating leases, we can see that the criteria for operating leases are all different ways of saying that the lessor maintains significant residual exposure to the value of the asset. In fact, under the *Bank Act*, chartered banks cannot write a lease if they have significant exposure to the residual value of the asset.

**sale and leaseback (SLB) agreement** an agreement in which the owner of an asset sells it to another party and then leases the asset back

Another type of leasing arrangement is a **sale and leaseback (SLB) agreement**. In an SLB, the owner of an asset sells it (usually to an insurance company or pension fund) and then signs an agreement to lease the asset back. Thus, the lessee retains the use of the asset and receives a large, one-time cash inflow at the time of the sale. At one time, this type of arrangement was particularly popular for organizations in very low tax brackets. Universities, for example, pay no tax. They are therefore unable to claim any tax deductions for depreciation on the assets that they own. A university could sell an asset to someone who did pay taxes and could use the depreciation deduction. When the university leased the asset back, part of the tax savings that the new owner was enjoying could be passed back to the university in the form of lower lease payments.

The 1989 federal budget changed the tax rules concerning SLB agreements so that the lessor could deduct depreciation on leased assets only from the income derived from leasing, which has made them less attractive from a tax minimization point of view. As a result of this legislation, the number of SLBs for non-profit organizations, such as universities and hospitals, has declined substantially.[3]

**leveraged lease** a three-way agreement between the lessee, lessor, and third-party lender(s) in which the lessor buys the asset with only a small down payment, and the lender supplies the remaining financing

A **leveraged lease**, which is depicted in **Figure 16.2**, is a popular financing vehicle in the United States. It is a three-way agreement between the lessee, the lessor, and one or more external lenders. As with other lease arrangements, the lessee uses the asset and makes regular lease payments, while the lessor purchases (or owns) the asset, delivers it to the lessee, and receives lease payments. However, the lessor puts up only a small portion (usually in the 20- to 50-percent range) of the purchase price of the asset, and lenders supply the remaining financing in return for interest payments from the lessor. The lenders are protected against default because they have a first lien on the leased asset and because the lease payments go directly to the lenders in the event of a loan default by the lessor.

The attractiveness of leveraged leases in the United States is that the lessor puts up only a portion of the asset purchase price but receives all of the tax benefits of ownership and has lease payments available to service the loan payments. Leveraged leases are not popular in Canada, because CRA restricts the use of CCA deductions to the party at risk, and the deductions cannot be carried over into other income. In the United States, however, they can be, and the lessee can realize a benefit in the form of lower lease payments whenever the lessor's costs are reduced.

---

[3]One prominent Canadian university sold its library and then leased it back. At the time, some observers could understand why the institution sold the library, but not why it leased it back.

**FIGURE 16.2** A Leveraged Lease

**Lender**
- Finances some of the lessor's purchase of asset
- Receives interest on loan from lessor

**Lessor**
- Borrows some of purchase price from lender
- Pays interest to lender
- Receives lease payments from lessee

**Lessee**
- Has use of asset in exchange for lease payments

---

## Concept Review Questions

1. What is the difference between an operating and a financial lease?
2. What type of leases do chartered banks normally make?
3. What is a sale and leaseback agreement (SLB)?

---

## 16.2 | Accounting for Leases

### LEARNING OBJECTIVE 16.2

Describe the current accounting treatment of leases under IFRS and U.S. GAAP.

While analysts have tended to use the broad definitions of operating and financial leases discussed in the previous section, accountants have used a more stringent definition of financial leases. For accounting purposes, leases are classified as financial leases under current U.S. GAAP[4] if *at least one* of the following criteria is met:

- The lease transfers ownership of the property to the lessee by the end of the lease term.
- The lessee can buy the asset at a price that is reasonably certain to be exercised (i.e., has a bargain purchase option) before or when the lease expires.
- The lease term is for the major part (i.e., more than 75 percent) of the estimated remaining economic life of the asset.
- The sum of the present value of remaining lease payments and any guaranteed residual amount by the lessee equals or exceeds substantially all of the fair value of the asset.
- The asset is specialized to the extent that it would have no alternative use to the lessor at the end of the lease term.

---

[4]These rules are very similar to those previously used to classify financial leases under IFRS, although IFRS now classifies all leases (greater than 12 months) as financial leases, as discussed in this section.

This classification was historically important under both IFRS and U.S. GAAP, because financial leases were included on the balance sheet of the lessee, while operating leases were not, with the lessor retaining the leased asset on its balance sheet. In particular, for a financial lease, the present value of all lease payments was entered as a liability along with debt on the right side of the lessee's balance sheet. The same amount was entered on the left side of the balance sheet as the value of the asset being leased.

As a result of this accounting treatment, operating leases represented an important example of **off-balance-sheet financing** (for the lessee) and were included only in the notes to the financial statements. This practice has long been a contentious issue for users of financial statements, since it reports an understated value of the company's true obligations. New accounting rules that apply as of January 1, 2019, address this concern, as discussed in Finance in the News 16.1, which states:

> At long last, a company's lease obligations—formerly buried in the back of the footnotes of the financial statements—*are moving front and center onto the balance sheet [emphasis added]*, as a new leasing standard goes into effect for both US GAAP and IFRS companies at the beginning of this year. CFA Institute has long advocated for recognition of lease obligations on the balance sheet.

While the balance sheet differences noted earlier no longer apply under the new accounting standards, the income statement is still affected by the classification of a lease as operating

**off-balance-sheet financing**
a financing arrangement that does not appear in a company's balance sheet but only in the notes to the financial statements

---

## 16.1 Finance in the News Leases: What Investors Need to Know about the New Standard: Top Ten Considerations for Investors

At long last, a company's lease obligations—formerly buried in the back of the footnotes of the financial statements—are moving front and center onto the balance sheet, as a new leasing standard goes into effect for both US GAAP and IFRS companies at the beginning of this year. CFA Institute has long advocated for recognition of lease obligations on the balance sheet, and while the measurement methodology does not incorporate our preferred method of reflecting current market conditions, we generally view this change in accounting as a positive development.

The new standard for leases is effective 1 January 2019, or just around the corner as the first quarter and half yearly results are being published. Because the vast majority of the change resulting from the leasing standard is related to lessee accounting, which has a broader impact for investors, this report focuses only on lessee accounting.

What's changing? The short answer is that previously invisible leverage from leasing activities will now become visible, as all lease obligations will be presented as a liability on the balance sheet, offset by a "right-of-use asset," representing the right to use the leased asset.

The longer answer is that analysts will need to do much more than look at the new lease liability on the balance sheet. Investors must understand the various methods of transition to the new standard, the fact that most companies won't restate prior periods, and the differing treatment of leases under US GAAP and IFRS. They will also have to understand the key assumptions underlying the new accounting, such as the discount rate selected, and how the changes in various financial statement captions will impact financial statement ratios and common non-GAAP measures.

......

Where the new standard gets messy for investors is the differing treatment of leases between US GAAP and IFRS. While both standards require the recognition of a right-of-use asset and a lease liability on the balance sheet, and will therefore have a significant impact on the balance sheet of many companies (particularly those in the retail, airline, telecom, and transportation industries), the income statement treatment and cash flow presentation differ.

Under US GAAP, many leases will be classified as "operating leases" and there will be little change to the income statement and cash flow statement. In contrast, all leases under IFRS will be classified as "finance leases"; the income statement treatment follows a pattern similar to that of the old model's capital leases, with interest expense recognized, and overall expense recognition higher in the earlier years of the lease. The bottom line is that in many situations, the exact same lease will be treated differently under US GAAP as compared to IFRS, thereby creating analytical challenges for investors.

And, while actual cash flows are not changing, the *presentation* of cash flows in the statement of cash flows will, in many instances, change. In addition, the recognition of interest expense for leases classified as finance leases will impact non-GAAP measures such as EBIT and EBITDA, as discussed in Section V, and will also impact profitability ratios such as net profit margin, operating profit margin, and pretax margin. Changes to balance sheet captions will significantly impact many other financial statement ratios, as discussed in Section VII. Because many companies are not expected to restate prior years, comparability and trend analysis in financial statement captions and ratios will be difficult.

This paper will help investors unpack the impact to these ratios and adjust as necessary to ensure results are truly comparable.

**Source:** Excerpted from Peters, Sandra J., and Ciesielski, Jack, "Leases: What Investors Need to Know about the New Standard: Top Ten Considerations for Investors," CFA Institute, April 1, 2019. Available at www.cfainstitute.org. Copyright 2019. Reproduced with permission of CFA Institute.

or financial under U.S. GAAP. For operating leases, the full amount of the lease payments is classified as a rental expense for the lessee and as rental income for the lessor, while the lessor charges depreciation expense against the asset.

For financial leases, the lease payments are broken down into interest expense and principal repayment. The latter is not an expense, but is reflected in the declining value of the liability reported on the balance sheet. As a result, for financial leases, the lessee's associated expenses will be in two forms: interest associated with the financing arrangement and depreciation expense associated with the asset. The lessor reports income in the form of a gain (or loss) on the asset at the time the lease arrangement (i.e., the sale) is initiated, and then it reports periodic interest income based on the interest portion of the lease payments it receives.

Under previous accounting standards, there were some potential benefits in the appearance of the balance sheet for firms when leases were classified as operating leases rather than financial leases. The new accounting regulations referred to previously will significantly affect these balance sheet impacts, as well as the general process of financial analysis of leases, as noted in Finance in the News 16.1.

Some of the major considerations for financial analysts arising from these accounting changes are noted by the CFA Institute in Finance in the News 16.1, which is excerpted from the executive summary of a comprehensive document that was prepared for investors. These include:

1. Leases formerly classified as operating leases that were not reported on the balance sheet will now be reported as a liability on the balance sheet, with an offsetting "right-of-use asset" that will be reported on the asset side. The exception is for leases with terms less than 12 months for both IFRS and U.S. GAAP, and for leases under $5,000 for IFRS.

2. The accounting treatment of leases will differ according to U.S. GAAP versus IFRS:

   - IFRS will now record previous operating leases as "financial leases," which will be treated similar to how financial leases have been treated in the past.
   - In contrast, U.S. GAAP will continue to report these leases as operating leases; however, they will now be recorded on the balance sheet.

3. The new standards came into effect January 1, 2019; however, most companies will not restate prior year's financial statements.

4. The changes will impact the calculation of several financial ratios, as well as the calculation of "non-GAAP" measures such as EBIT and EBITDA.

5. The new treatment will not change the actual cash flows to firms, but they will change the presentation of cash flow statements in many cases.

Table 16.2 distinguishes the accounting differences under new U.S. GAAP rules for the treatment of operating versus financial leases. As noted previously, under IFRS, all leases are classified as financial leases, so the general treatment of all leases under IFRS is as outlined in the last column of Table 16.2.

**TABLE 16.2   Operating versus Financial Leases for Lessees under U.S. GAAP**

| | Operating | Financial |
|---|---|---|
| Asset | Record on balance sheet (B/S) as a liability, with an offsetting "right-of-use-asset" | Record on B/S as a liability, with an offsetting "right-of-use-asset" |
| Lease payments | Expense the full amount as rental expense | Decompose into interest and principal repayment, and expense the interest portion |
| Depreciation expense (associated with leased asset) | Cannot claim | Claim |

# Financial Statement Effects of Lease Classification

Historically, the classification of a lease as operating or financial had a significant impact on a firm's financial statements, since operating leases were not reported on the balance sheet. The new rules have changed the significance of this distinction, since all leases will be classified as financial leases under IFRS, and even those classified as operating leases under U.S. GAAP will now be reported on the balance sheet. However, the income statement treatment of lease expenses differs for operating versus financial leases under U.S. GAAP. This will affect some of the ratios that analysts use to examine company performance (discussed in Chapter 4), as well as non-GAAP measures such as EBIT and EBITDA, and the presentation of the cash flow statements in many cases. The examples in this section illustrate some of the major differences that can arise.

Example 16.1 makes two things obvious:

1. Net income will generally be higher for operating leases in the early years, and it will generally be lower in the later years. This is because the interest expense charged for financial leases declines as the liability (lease obligation) is amortized by the lease payments. This means that the expense associated with a financial lease will decrease over time, since the depreciation expense usually is constant, whereas the lease expense for an operating lease remains constant through the years (i.e., it equals the amount of the lease payments).

2. The cash flow from operations (CFO) will be lower when a lease is classified as operating under U.S. GAAP, since the full lease payment will be subtracted from CFO. For financial leases, only the interest portion of these payments is subtracted. On the other hand, the cash flow from financing (CFF) will be higher for operating leases because, unlike financial leases, they have no principal repayment component. Even more important to note is that the overall effect on total cash flow will be the same as for financial leases. It is merely the classification of the cash flows that is affected.

---

**EXAMPLE 16.1** | Income Statement and Cash Flow Statement Effects

Assume a company leases an asset with a present fair market value of $317,000. The lease arrangement requires four annual payments of $100,000. The appropriate interest rate is 10 percent. Assume the asset has a zero salvage value at the end of its useful life of four years, and that it can be depreciated using straight-line depreciation. Contrast the income statement and cash flow statement impacts of classifying the lease as financial versus operating.

Assume the following are the firm's expected income and cash flow statements for the next four years, ignoring the effect of this lease arrangement:

|  | Year 1 | Year 2 | Year 3 | Year 4 |
|---|---|---|---|---|
| Revenue | $10 million | $10 million | $10 million | $10 million |
| Net income (excluding lease) | $500,000 | $500,000 | $500,000 | $500,000 |
| Cash flow from operations (CFO) | $600,000 | $600,000 | $600,000 | $600,000 |
| Cash flow from financing (CFF) | $100,000 | $100,000 | $100,000 | $100,000 |
| Cash flow from investing (CFI) | −$300,000 | −$300,000 | −$300,000 | −$300,000 |
| Net cash flows | $400,000 | $400,000 | $400,000 | $400,000 |

**Solution**

**Operating Lease (under U.S. GAAP)**

The annual charge to the income statement = Rental expense = $100,000

The annual effect on CFO = $100,000

The annual effect on total cash flow = $100,000

*Net Effects*

|  | Year 1 | Year 2 | Year 3 | Year 4 |
|---|---|---|---|---|
| Net income | $400,000 | $400,000 | $400,000 | $400,000 |
| CFO | $500,000 | $500,000 | $500,000 | $500,000 |
| CFF | $100,000 | $100,000 | $100,000 | $100,000 |
| CFI | −$300,000 | −$300,000 | −$300,000 | −$300,000 |
| Net cash flows | $300,000 | $300,000 | $300,000 | $300,000 |

**Financial Lease (under U.S. GAAP or IFRS)**

*Effect on Income Statement*

Annual depreciation expense = ($317,000 − 0)/4 = $79,250

Interest expense (year 1) = $317,000 × 0.1 = $31,700

Principal repayment (year 1) = $100,000 − $31,700 = $68,300

Principal outstanding (end of year 1) = $317,000 − $68,300 = $248,700

Interest expense (year 2) = $248,700 × 0.1 = $24,870

Principal repayment (year 2) = $100,000 − $24,870 = $75,130

Principal outstanding (end of year 2) = $248,700 − $75,130 = $173,570

Interest expense (year 3) = $173,570 × 0.1 = $17,357

Principal repayment (year 3) = $100,000 − $17,357 = $82,643

Principal outstanding (end of year 3) = $173,570 − $82,643 = $90,927

Interest expense (year 4) = $90,927 × 0.1 = $9,093

Principal repayment (year 4) = $90,927 (i.e., the total principal outstanding at the beginning of the year, which must be fully paid)

*Associated Expenses*

|  | Year 1 | Year 2 | Year 3 | Year 4 |
|---|---|---|---|---|
| Depreciation expense | −$79,250 | −$79,250 | −$79,250 | −$79,250 |
| Interest expense (@10%) | −$31,700 | −$24,870 | −$17,357 | −$9,093 |
| Charges on net income | −$110,950 | −$104,120 | −$96,607 | −$88,343 |

*Effect on Cash Flow Statement*

|  | Year 1 | Year 2 | Year 3 | Year 4 |
|---|---|---|---|---|
| CFO |  |  |  |  |
| Interest expense[5] | −$31,700 | −$24,870 | −$17,357 | −$9,093 |
| CFF |  |  |  |  |
| Principal repayment | −$68,300 | −$75,130 | −$82,643 | −$90,927 |
| Net effect on total cash flow | −$100,000 | −$100,000 | −$100,000 | −$100,020* |

*The extra $20 is required to fully amortize the purchase price.

|  | Year 1 | Year 2 | Year 3 | Year 4 |
|---|---|---|---|---|
| Net income | $389,050 | $395,880 | $403,393 | $411,657 |
| CFO | $568,300 | $575,130 | $582,643 | $590,907 |
| CFF | $31,700 | $24,870 | $17,357 | $9,073 |
| CFI | −$300,000 | −$300,000 | −$300,000 | −$300,000 |
| Net cash flows | $300,000 | $300,000 | $300,000 | $299,980* |

*As explained, the $20 difference is required to fully amortize the purchase price.

[5]This example assumes that interest expense is recorded under CFO for IFRS, which is an option. However, under IFRS, the interest expense might alternatively have been classified under CFF or CFI. For U.S. GAAP, the interest MUST be classified under CFO, as in the example.

Example 16.2 demonstrates that the firm will appear larger and will have more debt if a lease is reported on the balance sheet, as is now required by both IFRS and U.S. GAAP. This is important to understand, since it will impact the balance sheets of many companies as they must now transition to the new accounting rules and record on the balance sheet millions (and billions) of dollars in leases that were previously categorized as operating leases, and hence not reported on the balance sheet. For example, on page 24 of the CFA Institute document referenced in Finance in the News 16.1, Union Pacific Corporation stated: "The Company continues to evaluate the impact of this standard on our consolidated financial position, results of operations, and cash flows, and expects that the adoption will result in an increase in the Company's assets and liabilities of over $2 billion."

Example 16.3 shows the impact of the lease classification on some commonly used ratios that were discussed in Chapter 4.

Example 16.3 shows that there used to be a significant impact on a company's balance sheet ratios depending on whether a lease was classified as operating or financial. Under new accounting rules, such a classification is not permissible under IFRS, while the balance sheet ratio benefits no longer exist for classifying leases as operating under new U.S. GAAP rules, since the leases must still be recorded on the balance sheet. However, classifying a lease as operating still leads to higher profitability ratios under new U.S. GAAP rules due to the income statement treatment of the lease payments. Thus, while the incentives for managers to classify leases as operating have been greatly reduced, they still may exist in certain circumstances. However, all of this information is publicly available and, if markets are efficient, any attempt to fool readers should be a waste of time, since most analysts would see through this type of manipulation.

---

**EXAMPLE 16.2** | Balance Sheet Effects

Assume the company from Example 16.1 decides to lease the asset worth $317,000 considered in that example. The company's balance sheet, excluding the lease, is given here. Depict the firm's balance sheet after the lease arrangement has been entered into, assuming the lease is classified as (1) an operating lease under the "old" IFRS and U.S. GAAP rules, and (2) an operating lease under current U.S GAAP and/or as a financial lease (under current U.S. GAAP or IFRS).

| Current assets | $2,000,000 | Current liabilities | $1,000,000 |
|---|---|---|---|
| Long-term assets | 8,000,000 | Long-term debt | 6,000,000 |
| | | Equity | 3,000,000 |
| Total assets | $10,000,000 | Total liabilities and equity | $10,000,000 |

**Solution**

**Operating Lease (Old Rules—IFRS and U.S. GAAP)**

Under the old accounting rules, if the lease were classified as operating, the balance sheet would remain unchanged—it would be exactly the same as the previous one. The only difference is that the firm would have to disclose the lease in the footnotes to the financial statements.

**Operating Lease (New Rules—U.S. GAAP) or Financial Lease (New Rules—IFRS and U.S. GAAP)**

The new balance sheet would reflect the $317,000 on both sides.

The $317,000 on the liability side would be broken down into the current portion of the obligation (i.e., the first year's required principal repayment component of the lease payment) and the remaining part of the lease, which would be classified as long-term debt.

Addition to current liabilities = $68,300 (principal repayment as calculated in Example 16.1)

Long-term debt = $317,000 − $68,300 = $248,700

| Current assets | $2,000,000 | Current liabilities | $1,068,300 |
|---|---|---|---|
| Long-term assets | 8,317,000 | Long-term debt | 6,248,700 |
| | | Equity | 3,000,000 |
| Total assets | $10,317,000 | Total liabilities and equity | $10,317,000 |

---

**EXAMPLE 16.3** | Financial Ratio Effects

Calculate the following ratios for the company in examples 16.1 and 16.2 for year 1: current, debt, leverage, net income (NI) margin, asset turnover, return on assets (ROA), return on equity (ROE), price-earnings (P/E).

　　Use the balance sheet items from Example 16.2 and the income statement information from Example 16.1, assuming the lease in question is classified as (1) an operating lease under the "old" IFRS or U.S. GAAP rules, (2) an operating lease under the new U.S. GAAP rules, or (3) a financial lease (under the new IFRS or U.S. GAAP rules). Assume the firm has 1 million common shares outstanding and that its share price is $10 per share regardless of the method of accounting for the lease. Comment on any differences in the ratios.

**Solution**

| Ratio | (1) Operating ("Old" Rules) | (2) Operating (U.S. GAAP—"New" Rules) | (3) Financial (IFRS and U.S. GAAP) |
|---|---|---|---|
| Current (CA/CL) | $2,000,000/$1,000,000 = 2 | $2,000,000/$1,068,300 = 1.87 | $2,000,000/$1,068,300 = 1.87 |
| Debt (TL/TA) | $7,000,000/$10,000,000 = 0.7 | $7,317,000/$10,317,000 = 0.71 | $7,317,000/$10,317,000 = 0.71 |
| Leverage (TA/E) | $10,000,000/$3,000,000 = 3.33 | $10,317,000/$3,000,000 = 3.44 | $10,317,000/$3,000,000 = 3.44 |
| NI margin (NI/S) | $400,000/$10,000,000 = 4% | $400,000/$10,000,000 = 4% | $389,050/$10,000,000 = 3.89% |
| Asset turnover (S/TA) | $10,000,000/$10,000,000 = 1 | $10,000,000/$10,317,000 = 0.97 | $10,000,000/$10,317,000 = 0.97 |
| ROA (NI/TA) | $400,00/$10,000,000 = 4% | $400,000/$10,317,000 = 3.88% | $389,050/$10,317,000 = 3.77% |
| ROE (NI/E) | $400,000/$3,000,000 = 13.33% | $400,000/$3,000,000 = 13.33% | $389,050/$3,000,000 = 12.97% |
| P/E ($P_0$/EPS) | $10/$0.40 = 25 | $10/$0.40 = 25 | $10/$0.38905 = 25.7 |

　　There are several observations that are evident from these calculations. First, when all leases are reported on the balance sheet as they are under the new accounting rules, the firm will report lower current ratios, higher debt and leverage ratios, and lower asset turnover ratios than when they were not (i.e., as operating leases were not under the "old" rules). Under the current rules, these ratios will be the same whether the lease is classified as operating, which is still permitted under the new U.S. GAAP rules, or whether they are classified as financial leases under either U.S. GAAP or IFRS.

　　When a lease is classified as an operating lease under the new U.S. GAAP rules, it will report lower profitability ratios (at least in the early years), despite the fact they are now reported on the balance sheet. Since the classification of a lease has no impact on a firm's total cash flows, its price should be unaffected by the resulting higher EPS figure; therefore, the P/E ratios should be higher to reflect the lower earnings per share (EPS). However, note that if the P/E ratio remained at 25, rather than increasing to 25.7, the share price would be lower, reflecting the lower EPS. This is obviously inappropriate and should not happen in efficient markets.

---

**Concept Review Questions**

1. What are the cash flow from operations and the free cash flow implications of an operating lease versus a financial lease?

2. Which type of lease, operating or financial, gives a higher net income margin in the early years of a lease agreement?

---

| 16.3 | # Evaluating the Lease Decision |
|---|---|

**LEARNING OBJECTIVE 16.3**

Evaluate the lease decision using discounted cash flow valuation methods.

Leasing provides an alternative to buying an asset. This is a decision most of us face when we are deciding whether to lease or buy a car, and the same principles apply to companies considering leasing any asset. Finance in the News 16.2 offers some perspectives on the automobile buy-versus-lease decision.

---

**16.2 Finance in the News**    Leasing a Car Is the Worst Financial Option for Most

Canada's auto guru Dennis DesRosiers has a quick response to the question of whether it's best to lease or finance a new car: pay cash.

That's what he does, for the simple reason that it's the least expensive option.

But he realizes most Canadians can't just lay down tens of thousands of dollars at one go, or don't want to, so when asked about the remaining options, his response is more nuanced.

"It depends," he says, on what you expect out of your driving experience and whether you are more sensitive to the size of

Londoneye/Vetta/Getty Images

monthly payments or the end-of-use total cost of the purchase. And it depends whether owning a vehicle is important to you.

"The general rule of thumb is that if you are a consumer that changes vehicles every two, three, or four years, leasing is a highly attractive option in most cases, though not all. The longer you keep your vehicle the more attractive loans become."

First, if you are the type of person who is addicted to the new-car smell, lease if you can afford it, he says.

But if you are looking for the least costly option and don't mind hanging on to your car longer—the average length of first ownership on a new vehicle is 9.2 years—then leasing is likely the worst thing you can do, Mr. DesRosiers adds.

The funny thing is that it may not appear that way when negotiating a financing arrangement at the local car dealer.

Invariably, the monthly payments on a lease are lower than on loans even though the posted interest rate is almost always higher. And leasing appears so worry-free. Take a new car, drive it for three years, then return it and get another new car. Repeat the process.

"It's the voodoo of leasing," Mr. DesRosiers says. "Leasing is absolutely the highest cost of borrowing in the market place. Hands down, no exceptions, but it doesn't look that way."

Why is that? Monthly payments are comprised of two components—interest on the principal or cost of the vehicle, and paying down the principal. On a loan, the paying down the principal portion can be quite steep because the buyer is paying off the entire cost of the vehicle during the financing term. On a lease, depending on the end residual value, the consumer may be only paying down half the cost of the vehicle.

That's why monthly payments are usually lower, but at the end of the lease, the consumer doesn't own the vehicle and will have paid more in interest than on a loan.

"The embedded interest in a lease is typically about $100 a month higher than the interest on a loan," Mr. DesRosiers says.

As well, there are additional costs that could accrue on a lease, and they can be substantial. Leasing companies insist a vehicle be returned in good working order and with "normal wear and tear."

What that means is open to interpretation—with the consumer having little input—but it usually requires replacing tires, possibly a brake job, and body work for bumps and scrapes that may have occurred. The end-of-lease surprise can add up to hundreds and even thousands of dollars.

As well, Mr. DesRosiers says many consumers wind up paying hefty penalties if they put on more than 25,000 kilometres a year, not that unusual since the average driver in Toronto clocks in at over 30,000 annually.

"So leasing is a consumer beware item," he says.

That doesn't mean it's the worst choice, however. Silvana Aceto of the Canadian Automobile Association says her organization advises members to do the math, but also to consider their personal circumstances.

"Some people like the flexibility of a lease, they like to have a new car every two or three years, and they don't have to worry about maintenance because when the car is new, usually that's when repairs are the fewest," she says.

You may not own the car at the end of the lease term, but then you don't have the worries older cars can bring, including breakdowns and repair costs.

Ms. Aceto says the CAA does not pick sides, but advises members to "do the math" and consider carefully their preferences.

Mr. DesRosiers agrees. If he has one hard-and-fast rule, it's never get into an open-ended lease where the customer is responsible for assuming the residual value—what's left owing on the car at the end of the lease period.

"Residuals are extremely volatile and nearly impossible to predict. Billions have been lost in residual value [usually by auto companies] over the years," he says.

By Mr. DesRosiers' calculations, about 18 percent of Canadians leased their vehicle last year, while the vast majority financed. That's about right, he says.

"For 15 to 20 percent of customers, leasing is a viable option, but for the rest they would be better off financially with a loan," he says.

"The issue is not whether you would like a new vehicle every three years, it's whether you can afford a new vehicle every three years, and most consumers can't."

**Source:** Beltrame, Julian, "Leasing a Car Is the Worst Financial Option for Most." *The Globe and Mail*, March 2, 2012. Copyright © 2012 The Canadian Press. Reprinted by permission.

---

As suggested in Finance in the News 16.2, if a company needs an asset and has the opportunity to either lease or buy it, the company must compare the cash flows from leasing with the cash flows from buying in order to determine which is better. Under current CRA leasing regulations, lessees are required to expense the interest component of their lease payments and are permitted to charge CCA on the leased asset, so the tax consequences are exactly the same as if they borrowed the money and bought the asset (i.e., they are treated as financial leases, which is consistent with the current IFRS treatment of leases). Therefore, the only real difference between a standard financial lease and buying the asset using a loan is that the lease payments are made at the beginning of the period, while the loan payments are made at the end of the period.[6]

In Example 16.4, we consider how to evaluate a lease versus buy and borrow in Canada under current IFRS and CRA standards.

---

**EXAMPLE 16.4** | Entering into a Financial Lease versus Borrowing

A company is given the option of entering into a five-year, $100,000 financial lease arrangement that calls for monthly payments based on a 6-percent lease rate, or borrowing $100,000 through a five-year loan that calls for monthly payments based on a 6.12-percent lending rate. Which option should the firm choose?

---

[6]In reality, loans require some form of down payment, whereas leases may provide 100-percent financing. Note that when operating leases were permitted for tax purposes, there were four main differences in the cash flows for a company that leased an asset instead of buying it: (1) it did not have to pay for the asset up front; (2) if it was an operating lease or if title was not transferred through a financial lease, the company did not get to sell the asset when it was finished with it; (3) if the lease was an operating lease, the full amount of the lease payments was tax deductible; and (4) it did not get to depreciate the asset for tax purposes if it was an operating lease.

**Solution** Notice that we cannot blindly select the lease option just because 6 percent is less than 6.12 percent, because the lease involves beginning-of-month payments, while the loan involves end-of-month payments.

First, we calculate the monthly payments for each option.

**Lease**

$$\text{Monthly lease rate} = 6\%/12 = 0.5\%$$

$$\text{Number of monthly payments} = 5 \text{ years} \times 12 \text{ months} = 60$$

$$\text{Monthly lease payments} = \frac{\$100,000}{\left[\dfrac{1 - \dfrac{1}{(1.005)^{60}}}{0.005}\right](1.005)} = \$1,923.66$$

**Loan**

$$\text{Monthly loan rate} = 6.12\%/12 = 0.51\%$$

$$\text{Monthly loan payments} = \frac{\$100,000}{\left[\dfrac{1 - \dfrac{1}{(1.0051)^{60}}}{0.0051}\right]} = \$1,938.86$$

Now we need to find the PV of the payments under each option, but which discount rate should we use? It turns out it does not matter, but it makes the most sense to use the loan rate, since we are evaluating the lease option.

Trivially, the PV of the loan payments using the monthly loan rate = $100,000 (since that is the amount we used to determine the required payments).

Now we need to estimate the PV of the beginning-of-month lease payments using the loan rate.

$$\text{PV (Lease payments)} = \$1,923.66 \times \left[\frac{1 - \dfrac{1}{(1.0051)^{60}}}{0.0051}\right](1.0051) = \$99,721.78$$

This implies that the firm should enter into the lease arrangement, since the effective cost of the asset would be less than $100,000, which is the cost under the loan arrangement.[7] Notice that we could have come to the same conclusion if we had used the monthly lease rate to evaluate both options. We would have found that the PV of the lease payments was $100,000, while the PV of the loan payments was $100,288.88.

The solution to Example 16.4 may appear somewhat lengthy, but it is a useful framework because it accommodates other variations in the loan versus lease decision, such as differences in required down payments, any services provided through leasing arrangements, and any bargain purchase options.

Note that in Example 16.4, the lower PV of leasing payments tells you that leasing is better than buying, but not whether you should acquire the asset in the first place. This question should be answered based on the total NPV of the project, as discussed in chapters 13 and 14. To incorporate lease financing into an overall NPV problem, simply calculate the NPV of the project, assuming that you buy the asset, then adjust for the lower cost of acquiring the asset through leasing. This gives the NPV of the project, including the advantage of financing the asset through leasing.

## Concept Review Question

1. Explain how to calculate comparisons in the lease-versus-buy decision for leases in Canada under current IFRS and CRA standards.

---

[7]In fact, we could say the NPV of leasing versus borrowing = $100,000 − $99,721.78 = +$278.22.

## 16.4 | Motivation for Leasing

**LEARNING OBJECTIVE 16.4**

Explain the various motives for leasing.

In the previous section, we showed how leases could, under some circumstances, provide "cheaper" financing than typical loan arrangements. The attraction of leases in such cases is obvious; however, leases provide other benefits to lessees. Here, we provide a description of some of the most common reasons why firms enter into lease arrangements; some are better reasons than others.

1. **Cheaper financing.**   This used to be the case for operating leases because the entire lease payment was tax deductible. It still may be the case when lessees receive attractive leasing rates due to a variety of factors, including market conditions and competitive pressures.

2. **Reduce the risks of asset ownership.**   Leasing allows companies to acquire needed equipment without assuming the risk of having to resell the asset or of having it become obsolete. This is particularly important for assets whose technological capabilities are constantly changing, which is one reason many companies lease computers rather than purchasing them. Essentially, this means that the equipment manufacturer or other lessor, rather than the user, bears the risk of the salvage value of the asset at the end of the lease.

3. **Implicit interest rates.**   Leasing usually offers firms fixed-rate financing over the life of the lease, whereas small firms, in particular, are often forced to use variable-rate, prime-based lending when borrowing from banks.

4. **Maintenance.**   Under a full-service lease arrangement, the lessor will provide maintenance. Often, the lessor will be a specialist in this type of equipment and is therefore better able to provide maintenance than the lessee.

5. **Convenience.**   It is often more convenient to lease an asset than to purchase it, especially if it is only needed for a relatively short period of time and/or if it is a very specialized or illiquid asset that may be hard to sell in the future.

6. **Flexibility.**   Leases often offer more flexibility. For example, they often include the option to cancel the lease, which may be important when obsolescence is a possibility.

7. **Capital budget restrictions.**   Since leasing requires a very limited initial capital outlay (just the first lease payment plus any arrangement fees), managers may be able to circumvent capital budget constraints by leasing assets, rather than buying them. This is a dubious reason for leasing, since it allows division managers to circumvent broader-based company policies.

8. **Financial statement effects.**   As demonstrated in Example 16.3, the use of operating leases (under U.S. GAAP) can allow firms to report higher profitability ratios during the early years of a lease. However, this should not affect the firm's value in efficient markets, because it does not affect the level of its cash flows or the nature of the financial risks it faces. It merely changes the way these items are reported in the financial statements. Therefore, this is not a good reason for leasing.

## Concept Review Questions

1. Why are leases often more flexible than a borrow-purchase option?
2. Why do you think the major market for leasing is often SMEs, rather than large corporations?
3. If you were opening a copy centre, do you think you would lease or borrow to buy the equipment and why?

# Review

## Summary

In this chapter, we discuss leasing as a financing source. In a lease arrangement, the lessor retains ownership rights to an asset but makes the asset available for use by the lessee, who in turn agrees to make periodic lease payments to the lessor. We discuss the general differences between operating and financial (or capital) leases. We also discuss how leases are treated under IFRS and U.S. GAAP based on new rules that came into effect in 2019, which differ from their previous treatment. We proceed to show how firms can evaluate a potential lease decision using the discounted cash flow (DCF) analysis framework. We conclude by discussing various motivations that firms might have for entering into leasing arrangements, and we focus on the flexibility of lease contracts and the close relationship that exists between manufacturers and equipment-leasing firms.

## Summary of Learning Objectives

### 16.1 Identify the basic characteristics of leases and differentiate between operating and financial (or capital) leases.

A lease is an agreement where the owner conveys to the user the right to use an asset in exchange for a set of payments over a specified time period. Leasing an asset is an alternative to borrowing money and buying the asset. An operating lease is one in which some of the benefits of ownership do not transfer to the lessee but remain with the lessor—e.g., a short-term (i.e., less than 12 months) lease is an operating lease. A financial lease is a lease in which essentially all of the benefits of ownership transfer to the lessee.

### 16.2 Describe the current accounting treatment of leases under IFRS and U.S. GAAP.

Under current IFRS rules, all leases greater than 12 months and for more than $25,000 will be treated as capital leases, while U.S. GAAP still retains the operating lease classification for qualifying lease agreements. Both IFRS and U.S. GAAP now require the reporting of essentially all lease arrangements on the balance sheet, with the present value of the lease payments appearing as both an asset and a liability. With a financial lease, the lessee depreciates the asset for tax purposes and expenses the interest portion of the lease payments. With an operating lease, the lessee treats the full amount of lease payments as rental expense.

### 16.3 Evaluate the lease decision using discounted cash flow valuation methods.

A lease is an optimal form of financing (compared to borrowing and buying) if the present value of the incremental benefits exceeds the present value of the incremental costs. One benefit of a lease is the fact that the asset does not have to be purchased, and lessees can often obtain 100-percent financing for the asset, whereas most loans to purchase assets require substantial deposits (i.e., 10 percent or more). Another benefit of some leases is the after-tax maintenance expense savings. The cost of leases includes the after-tax payments and, in some cases, the forgone salvage value of the asset.

### 16.4 Explain the various motives for leasing.

- Leases can be a cheaper source of financing.
- Leases reduce the risk of ownership, because the asset can be returned at the end of the lease term.
- Leases provide a form of fixed-interest-rate financing (as opposed to variable rate).
- For some leases, the lessor provides maintenance of the asset.
- Leasing can be more convenient than buying, especially for items that are needed for a relatively short period, are very specialized, and may be hard to sell in future.
- Leases often provide flexibility through a cancellation option.
- Managers may be able to circumvent capital budget constraints by leasing assets, rather than buying them.
- Operating leases (which are still permissible under U.S. GAAP) can improve the appearance of the firm's profitability ratios during the early years of lease agreements.

## Key Terms

# Questions and Practice Problems

## Multiple Choice Questions

**1. (LO 16.1)** Which of the following statements about leveraged leases is *false*?

    **a.** The lease involves an external lender, lessor, and lessee.

    **b.** The lender receives interest payments from the lessee.

    **c.** The lessee can bargain for lower lease payments if the market is competitive.

    **d.** The lender has the first lien on the leased asset.

**2. (LO 16.2)** Given the following information, what is the asset/liability recognized on the lessee's balance sheet at the beginning of the lease? Salvage value = $0; minimum annual lease payment at the beginning of each year = $15,000; lease term = 5 years; appropriate discount rate = 5 percent.

    **a.** $68,189.26

    **b.** $64,942.15

    **c.** $58,764.46

    **d.** $75,000.00

**3. (LO 16.2)** Which of the following is *higher* under operating leases?

    **a.** NI and CFO

    **b.** NI in the early years and CFF

    **c.** Depreciation and NI

    **d.** Total cash flow and CFO

**4. (LO 16.2)** Which of the following financial figures is *changed* if a lease is classified as operating versus financial under U.S. GAAP?

    **a.** Leverage ratio

    **b.** P/E ratio

    **c.** Total cash flow

    **d.** Asset turnover

**5. (LO 16.2)** New accounting rules came into effect on January 1, 2019, regarding the classification of a lease as operating or financial. This change has a significant impact on a firm's financial statements, since operating leases previously were not reported on a firm's balance sheet. Which of the following statements about major impacts on firms is *false*?

    **a.** Firms will appear larger and will have more debt.

    **b.** Firms will report lower current ratios and higher debt and leverage ratios.

    **c.** Firms will report higher asset turnover ratios.

    **d.** Firms will report lower NI margins, ROA, and ROE in the early years.

## Practice Problems

### Basic

**6. (LO 16.4)** Briefly describe three motivations for leasing.

**7. (LO 16.4)** Charles Zhang, the owner of a small moving company, has decided that economic conditions are perfect for him to expand his business. Such an expansion will require him to buy five new moving trucks at a total cost of $275,000. Mr. Zhang's company has $8,000 in cash and a $45,000 line of credit at the bank. It is a small company, so it does not have the option of issuing public debt, and Mr. Zhang is not comfortable mortgaging his family home to buy the trucks. Describe two ways Mr. Zhang can acquire the trucks. Discuss the advantages and disadvantages of each.

### Intermediate

**8. (LO 16.1)** Financial statements for Canadian public corporations are available from corporate websites or from the System for Electronic Document Analysis and Retrieval (SEDAR) at www.sedar.com.

    **a.** Review a copy of Air Canada's annual report for fiscal year end December 31, 2018, and determine the portion of Air Canada's long-term debt and financial leases that was made up of financial leases.

    **b.** Obtain the same ratio for TELUS for 2018.

**9. (LO 16.3)** Nash Business School is considering whether to lease or buy shuttle buses for students travelling between its two campuses. The buses cost $2 million, with a CCA rate of 20 percent. The lease payments are $450,000 per year for the next five years, with payments made at the beginning of each year. There is no maintenance cost, and the expected market value of the buses after five years is zero. Assuming the cost of borrowing is 6 percent, should Nash Business School lease the buses or buy them? Note that universities do not pay tax.

### Challenging

**10. (LO 16.2)** A firm is deciding whether to enter into a lease agreement for an asset that can be purchased for $50,000. The lease term is five years. The annual lease payment is $12,000 at the beginning of each year, and the borrowing cost is 7 percent. Should the firm buy or lease the asset?

**11. (LO 16.3)** A firm plans to either lease a piece of equipment or purchase it. The upfront purchase price is $900,000, and it is depreciated at $90,000 per year for tax purposes. The equipment could be sold in nine years for $90,000. If the firm leases the equipment, it pays annual lease payments of $45,000 at the beginning of each of nine years. The firm's effective tax rate is 40 percent. Determine whether or not the firm should lease the equipment, assuming the before-tax cost of borrowing is 9 percent.

**12. (LO 16.3)** A firm plans to either purchase or lease a machine that costs $300,000 and is subject to a 20-percent CCA rate, using the declining balance method. The required lease payments are $35,000 at the beginning of each of four years. The lessor has agreed to provide maintenance as part of the lease contract, and the firm has estimated it would incur $25,000 per year in maintenance expense if it decided to purchase the machine. It estimates the asset could be sold for $138,240 after four years (the ending UCC at the end of year 4). The firm's before-tax borrowing rate is 9 percent, and its effective tax rate is 40 percent. Should it purchase or lease the machine, assuming the acquisition of the machine has a positive NPV? (Include the half-year rule.)

**13. (LO 16.3)** Suppose you are going to enter into a six-year, $25,000 financial lease that requires monthly payments based on a 9-percent lease rate. Alternatively, you could borrow $25,000 via a six-year loan that requires monthly payments based on an 8-percent lending rate. Which option should you choose?

**14. (LO 16.3)** Paolo, the CEO of Paola Bros Inc., wants to have a fleet of electric cars. These electric cars cost $1.5 million. For tax purposes, assume that these cars will depreciate at a rate of $160,000 per year.

In five years, the electric cars can be sold for $800,000. The electric cars could be leased on a five-year lease for $185,000 per year. The lease payment would be made at the beginning of the year. If the effective tax rate of Paolo Bros Inc. is 35 percent, and its before-tax cost of borrowing is 9 percent, should Paolo lease the electric cars or buy them?

**15. (LO 16.3)** In practice problem 14, what would the lease payment have to be for Paolo to be indifferent about whether the company buys or leases the electric cars?

**16. (LO 16.3)** A firm has the option of borrowing $2.5 million through a 12-year loan with monthly payments based on a 7.5-percent lending rate, or entering into a 12-year, $2.5-million financial lease arrangement with monthly payments based on a 7.5-percent lease rate. Which option is more advantageous to the firm?

**17. (LO 16.3)** A used car that currently costs $25,000 will have a market value of $8,000 in four years. As a student, you cannot afford to pay $25,000, but you want to have a car while you are going to university for the next four years. Your father agrees to lend you $25,000 on the condition that you pay him $300 at the end of every month for the next four years and $25,000 at the end of the four years. The car dealer provides financing facilities, and you are qualified to get a lease for which you will have to make monthly, end-of-month payments of $650 for 48 months. Which option will leave you better off, assuming your opportunity cost is 6 percent?

**18. (LO 16.3)** Emma operates a small bakery and needs a new commercial oven. The model she needs costs $90,000, or she can lease it for five years for $2,100 per month, with payments due at the beginning of each month. The cost of borrowing is 7 percent, compounded monthly. Assuming that the oven's useful life is five years (the entire lease term), should Emma buy or lease the oven?

# Investment Banking and Securities Law

---

**LEARNING OBJECTIVES**

After studying this chapter, you should be able to:

**17.1** Explain what is meant by "information asymmetries" and how these affect the raising of capital.

**17.2** Explain the purpose of securities laws and regulations in the financial markets.

**17.3** Explain what a prospectus is, what it contains, and why it is critical for initial public offerings (IPOs).

**17.4** Outline the basic stages in taking a firm public through an initial public offering (IPO) of securities.

**17.5** Explain why continuous disclosure requirements are important for investors and how they affect secondary offerings.

---

In any market, it is important that purchasers understand what they are buying. This is particularly true in financial markets, since the purchased security involves the expectation of earning income and being paid back over long periods of time. This requires that the purchaser has information about the possibility of gains and losses that is similar to the information the seller has. This ideal state is referred to as a situation of *symmetric* information. However, it might seem obvious that when firms raise money from investors (purchasers of securities), they have more and better information about their firm's future prospects than do the investors. This is referred to as a situation of *asymmetric* information. At its most basic, securities law is designed to minimize these asymmetries so that purchasers can be confident they know what they are buying. Without that confidence, as we will show, markets can fail.

In Chapter 17, to understand these issues, we start with the most egregious form of information asymmetry, which is outright fraud, where the seller knows that the securities being sold are not worth the money being asked for them. We then discuss some major financial scandals in which investors lost millions or billions of dollars. After illustrating the problem of information asymmetry with recent and classic frauds, we discuss how securities regulation is designed to ameliorate the problem and why all those legal requirements exist. We then discuss the process of taking a firm public, when equity securities are first issued to the general public, since this is where information problems are most acute. We discuss the experience of raising capital through both initial public offerings (IPOs) and subsequent seasoned equity offerings (SEOs).

17.1 # Conflicts Between Issuers and Investors

> **LEARNING OBJECTIVE 17.1**
> Explain what is meant by "information asymmetries" and how these affect the raising of capital.

## The Basic Problem of Asymmetric Information

**asymmetric information**
information that one party in a deal has and the other doesn't; an extreme example is someone knowingly selling worthless securities that the investor doesn't know are worthless

We start with the most extreme case, where investors are buying what, unknown to them, is a deliberate fraud. This is an extreme example of **asymmetric information**, or information that one side has and the other doesn't. This is an extreme case because one side, the sellers, knows that the securities being offered are worthless—that is, they are completely fraudulent—while the investors think they are being offered a legitimate business opportunity. In Chapter 1, we introduced Bernard Madoff, who committed arguably the biggest fraud in history. However, as the stock market crashed in 2008, more and more frauds came to light as investors tried to cash in their investments and retreat from the market, only to find that they had invested in a Ponzi scheme and their money had disappeared. This has reinforced the importance of securities legislation and what we referred to as due diligence, which is, simply, not accepting things at face value but doing basic background checks.

In chapters 6 and 7, we discussed the valuation of bonds and common stocks (equities) and developed discounted cash flow valuation formulas. In all cases, there is an initial outflow to buy the security and then a series of expected future cash inflows. These future inflows are discounted back to the present to estimate the present value of a security. However, think about an initial issue of securities from the issuer's perspective. The issuer receives an immediate cash inflow based on the assumption that it will, in turn, pay a series of expected future cash flows. If both the investor and issuer agree on the expected stream of future cash flows, the situation is *symmetric*: what the investor expects to receive is what the issuer expects to pay, so the investor's expected rate of return is equal to the issuer's cost of raising capital.

This is the basic approach of corporate finance: we look to the capital markets to get an indication of the cost of certain types of financing, which is the reason, in this textbook, we discussed the essentials of capital markets before discussing corporate financing. If the current interest rate on long-term debt is 6 percent, we say that the (before-tax) cost of long-term debt financing to the firm is 6 percent; if we estimate the capital asset pricing model (CAPM) required rate of return on equity is 12 percent, we say the cost of common equity financing is 12 percent. We will deal with some of the nuances later, but the principal assumption is that the investor and the issuer agree on the value of the expected stream of cash flows and come up with the same estimate. The problem, however, is that capital markets exhibit information asymmetries, which is a fancy way of saying that people frequently have different information about the same future stream of cash flows, so they value the securities differently. In fact, they can disagree so much that a market may not exist, and a firm that cannot find anyone to buy its securities experiences a "financing gap."[1]

The classic example of market failure in the presence of information asymmetries was demonstrated by Professor George Akerlof, who formalized the notion of a market for lemons. Consider the most familiar "lemons market," which is that for used cars. Suppose that for a given make and year of used car, there are two types: good cars, which were driven by responsible drivers who regularly maintained them, and lemons, which were driven excessively by people who never properly maintained them. However, let's assume the lemon looks as good

---

[1]Governments are constantly worried about financing gaps and the fact that good companies cannot get financing on reasonable terms. Of course, people disagree profoundly on what constitutes reasonable terms.

as the good-quality car because the owner has turned the odometer back and put heavier oil in the transmission. Suppose the true value of the good car is $15,000, and that of the lemon is $10,000. If there are equal numbers of both types of car in the market, the average price for the car will be $12,500 or, more likely, less than this amount, taking into account the risk of buying a lemon. So let's say it is $11,000.

At a market price of $11,000, the owners of good cars will not offer them for sale. Instead, these owners will sell their cars privately to someone who trusts them, like a relative or close friend. After all, the owners know the true mileage and know they have completed the scheduled maintenance. As a result, they will not offer a $15,000 car for sale to the general public for $11,000, so the supply of good cars will go down. For the lemon, the situation is the opposite. Because their owners know they own a lemon and know the going market price exceeds its true value, they will put their cars up for sale. The result is that there will be an unequal supply of good cars and lemons; the market supply will consist entirely of lemons plus a few good cars sold by people with no friends or relatives. As a result, the overall market for cars fails.

This market for lemons is an example of "Gresham's law." Sir Thomas Gresham, who coined the phrase "bad money drives out good," observed that in 16th-century England, gold and silver coins circulated at their par value; for example, a one-shilling coin was valued at one shilling. However, the metallic value of the coins, based on their gold and silver content, would vary because some coins were "clipped." This was a practice in which people deliberately clipped or shaved off some of the coin and used the gold and silver for other purposes. As a result, if someone had two coins in hand—a new, fully valued silver coin and a clipped one—the owner would spend the clipped one and save (or clip) the fully valued coin. Hence, the bad money drives good money out of circulation. Gresham's law applies to any situation in which there is a single market price, yet the value of the commodity traded differs. Inevitably, it is the commodity of inferior value that is passed on, as is the case in Akerlof's car example, in which the car market becomes dominated by lemons.[2]

Of course, there are mechanisms to adjust for this market failure. In Gresham's time, people would weigh the coins and refuse to accept badly clipped ones at face value. Similarly, in Akerlof's example, one solution is to get a mechanic's report. However, a buyer may not have any faith in the seller's choice of mechanic, requiring that the buyer also get a mechanic's report, adding two layers of cost. Another solution is to buy from the dealer who originally sold and serviced the car, thus relying on the car dealer's reputation. In this case, the lemons would be sold at auction, where only the pros (mechanics and used-car dealers) buy. Failing that, a last solution is to buy a used car from someone who clearly has no friends or relatives! The point is that we get a richer set of markets with alternative market mechanisms. This is what happens in financial markets: much of the richness of financial markets is derived from arrangements developed to deal with these information asymmetries.

Let's return to our discussion of an investor who wants to buy a new issue of securities but doesn't realize the issue is fraudulent. From the issuer's perspective, this is a fantastic deal: for the initial cash received from selling the securities, the criminal promises to make a series of future payments. All they have to do for this cash is provide some "legal" documentation and a few certificates, essentially some paper. If the criminal can raise, say, $200 million from a group of investors, they only need to make a few payments before jumping on a plane to a jurisdiction that won't extradite them back to Canada. The criminal enjoys a $200-million inflow in return for printing up a few certificates.

## Real-World Examples of Fraudulent Activities

Historically, financial markets have been rife with fraud and abuse. A little more than 100 years ago, many of the securities sold to the general public were frauds. However, frauds occur at all levels and not just with the general public. For example, in 2004, William E. Lyons

---

[2]Gresham's law also explains why coins have traditionally been "milled" with a defined edge, so that everyone knows the coin has not been tampered with. This practice has continued, even though most coins now have little monetary value.

was accused of trying to sell US$200 million in fraudulently issued zero coupon bank guarantee notes to Bear Stearns Companies, Inc. (Bear Stearns). In the original SEC complaint, section 16 alleged that

> Lyons' efforts to market the bank guarantee offering to Bear Stearns were designed to persuade representatives of Bear Stearns to tender the $200 million payment for the purchase of a purported $220 million bank guarantee. Such a payment by Bear Stearns would have generated a total of approximately $1 million in compensation to SV Group and Lyons.

Lyons was a former broker at Bear Stearns, and the SEC complaint in section 13 further alleged that,

> had Lyons conducted an independent inquiry, he would have discovered that the purported bank guarantees that he was offering and their associated funding and issuing transactions had the hallmarks of a fraudulent prime bank securities scheme.

Bear Stearns rejected Lyons' proposal in December 2002, indicated that the transaction was probably fraudulent, and suggested he check the SEC website. However, Lyons then apparently tried to sell the securities to Merrill Lynch & Co., Inc. (Merrill Lynch), Goldman Sachs Group, Inc., and Chase Manhattan Bank, three other prominent U.S. financial institutions. This is when the SEC intervened.

Lyons settled the case with the SEC and agreed to a $25,000 fine and restrictions on his activities as a broker-dealer. However, the alleged actions illustrate that if a criminal wants to steal, they go where the money is: the major financial institutions. If Lyons had tried to sell these securities to the general public, it would have taken a lot more effort over a much longer period of time, with a lot more publicity. It is also interesting that he tried to sell non-interest-bearing (zero coupon) securities. If a fraudster sells regular interest-bearing securities, the lack of interest payments would have soon caused the purchasers to contact the SEC or police after missed interest payments. In contrast, zero coupon bonds offer no payments until maturity, so there is no tipoff that they are fraudulent until they are redeemed.

**bearer bonds** unregistered bonds that are payable to whomever holds them

Fraudsters like zero coupon bonds and bearer bonds. **Bearer bonds** are unregistered bonds; the owner is the person who has the bonds at a particular time. Bearer bonds are popular in Europe, where they are allegedly often used for tax evasion. This is because traditionally you "clipped" the coupon and sent it in to receive the interest, but often there was no record of who received the interest. However, in North America, almost all bonds are registered and maintained as (computer) book entries, and there are just a tiny number of bearer bonds. In contrast to bearer bonds, the interest payments and repayments of principal for registered bonds go to the individual who is the registered owner. This produces a paper trail for the cash that all can see, including the Canada Revenue Agency. For example, since 1995, all Government of Canada bonds have been sold in "global certificate form" directly to the Canadian Depository for Securities (CDS), and purchases and sales have to then go through a participant in the CDS debt clearing operation.[3]

One of the biggest frauds in England involved a fraudulent issue of 10-year zero coupon bonds that were sold into a small regional market, away from the major market in London where it would have quickly been noticed. The fraud became known only after the bonds were sold and the bearer bonds were warehoused. A lowly clerk happened to notice that the new bonds didn't seem to be as stiff as other bonds that he had previously catalogued and put away. On checking, he discovered they all had the same serial number! It turned out the bonds had been copied on reasonably sophisticated photocopiers, but the paper was different. *Zero Coupon* (1993), a popular novel by Paul Erdman, was loosely based on this real-life fraud.

---

[3]The Canadian Depository for Securities (CDS) is owned by the TMX Group, which owns the Toronto and Montreal Exchanges. In 2017 CDS handled 444 million transactions and provided custodial services for $5.4 trillion of securities (both debt and equity). Purchases and sales are made through computer entries at CDS, which is regulated by the Quebec, Ontario, and BC Securities Commissions and the Bank of Canada.

In advising investors, the SEC points to five major warning signs of fraud:

- Excessive guaranteed returns: 20 to 200 percent
- Fictitious financial instruments
- Extreme secrecy
- Exclusive opportunity
- Inordinate complexity

As we pointed out in Chapter 8, common equities average returns of only 10 to 11 percent, so to be offered a guaranteed—that is, risk-free—return in excess of 20 percent is a sure sign that something is wrong. If this opportunity is then dressed up as a complicated financial instrument that is only available to a small number of investors by "invitation," in a transaction that has to be "secret," and for which you have to sign a non-disclosure agreement, the best thing is to say you'll get back to them, and then contact the RCMP or appropriate securities regulator. However, frauds don't have to be that complicated.

For example, zero coupon bonds aren't needed for fraud; all that is needed is some mechanism for keeping investors happy while the fraudster tries to defraud more people. The classic way of doing this is to sell enough new fraudulent securities so that the cash inflow from their sale can make the interest payments on the earliest fraudulent bonds. This type of fraud is called a **Ponzi scheme**, after Carlo Ponzi, an Italian born in 1882, who immigrated to the United States. When dealing with a customer in Spain, Ponzi noticed that he received an international postal reply coupon that could be exchanged for U.S. stamps. What he also noticed was that he could buy these coupons in Spain and exchange them for U.S. stamps worth six times as much. In financial terms, we say that he recognized an *arbitrage* opportunity—he could buy something in one market (i.e., Spain and other countries) and resell it for more in another market (i.e., the United States). Technically, arbitrage implies the ability to earn a profit without assuming any risk. In any event, Ponzi subsequently discovered that the cost of the round-trip transaction involved so many administrative details that he could not make a profit. However, his idea was easily understood, and friends and relatives had wanted in on his investment before it occurred to him that it was not profitable. He took their money and issued them notes promising a 50-percent return in six months, ostensibly so he could buy more postal coupons. He then paid off the notes as they came due with the money from new investors as word of his genius spread. The more he bragged about his financial acumen, and the more satisfied customers he had, the more the money rolled in.

Several groups warned investors that something was wrong, but as long as Ponzi paid off the 50-percent interest-bearing notes, he had an army of satisfied investors who were vociferous in their support of his enterprise. His status was enhanced after he paid off a horde of investors who panicked and demanded their money back. It seemed that Ponzi could do no wrong. However, auditors looking at his books eventually declared that he was bankrupt, and the U.S. federal authorities arrested him on August 13, 1920. It turned out that in order to fulfill his scheme, he needed to buy 180 million postal certificates, and he had bought only two! He was sentenced to five years in jail by the U.S. government, and seven to nine in Massachusetts, but he skipped bail and was later found selling "underwater" building lots in Florida for $10, promising investors they could be resold for $5.3 million within two years.

Bernard Madoff's fraud was similar to Ponzi's, although much more sophisticated. One major difference is that Madoff was a prominent financier who at one time was chair of the board of directors of the National Association of Securities Dealers (NASD) in the United States. He owed this position to his company's role as a market maker, trading shares in small companies at very low spreads and undercutting the major companies. It is now known that this activity was increasingly a front or loss leader for his illegal activity, which was managing money for other institutional accounts. Madoff was very cunning; he did not sell any securities directly to the public and did not advertise, so he avoided the eyes of the watchdogs. Instead, feeder funds brought him money as he "earned" higher and higher rates of return, and his fame spread by word of mouth. However, like Ponzi, he did not really earn these rates of return; they were simply an illusion created as new money came in from new investors. When the stock market crashed in 2008 and investors wanted some of their money back, his whole scheme came tumbling down. On June 29, 2009, Madoff was sentenced to 150 years in prison. The actual size of his scam is difficult to determine—the high estimate of US$65 billion includes the impact of his promised high

**Ponzi scheme** a fraud that involves selling enough new fake securities so the cash inflow can be used to make the interest payments on the earliest fake securities rates of return—but even allowing for no income on the invested funds, it still appears to be at least a US$10-billion fraud.

The examples of Lyons and Madoff, and the classic case of Ponzi, illustrate the problems of information asymmetry in issuing securities. In all three cases, the issuers knew that what they were selling was not worth what investors were paying. These are extreme cases of information asymmetry, but in the face of any such fraudulent activity, financial markets cannot survive. As an example, take two possible issuers: one a fraudster, like Ponzi, and the other a legitimate company. If the investor cannot distinguish between them, then they have to bear this fraud risk, keeping in mind that every dollar invested in the fraudulent scheme will be lost. Increasing the interest rate to compensate for the risk of fraud might solve this problem, but such a solution is self-defeating.

Consider a simple case in which the market interest rate is 10 percent for non-fraudulent bonds. If one in five bonds in a given market is fraudulent, then introducing a "fraud premium" would put the "break-even" interest rate at 37.5 percent, based on a one-year investment horizon. This rate may be calculated as follows:

$$\$4 \times (1 + k) = \$5 \times (1.10)$$

$$k = 0.375$$

In other words, the investor wants 10 percent or $1.10 (principal plus interest) on each $5 invested but will get only $(1 + k)$ on the $4 invested in the legitimate businesses and will get $0 from the fraudster. As the amount of fraudulent activity in the market increases, so too does the market interest rate applied to all borrowers. Further, this is just the break-even rate; if the investor wants a risk premium, then the rate is even higher.

However, there is a problem with increasing the market interest rate, just as there was a problem with the market rate in Akerlof's market for lemons. We know that Ponzi was willing to pay 37.5 percent—after all, he actually paid 50 percent on six-month notes—but fraudsters usually have no intention of paying all the money back. As a result, they will *promise* to pay any market interest rate, because they don't expect to pay it at all. Conversely, legitimate businesses can't normally generate the profits required to pay 37.5 percent and will balk at paying such a high rate when they have no intention of committing fraud. Consequently, they will not issue securities to the general public, just as the owner of a good car doesn't sell to the public. Instead, legitimate businesses will rely on private financing, and the public markets will be left to the fraudsters and will inevitably dry up. In this case, an issuer's willingness to pay an exorbitant interest rate should be a tipoff to any sensible person not to lend them money.

This insight drives almost all securities law. Quite simply, if investors cannot distinguish good investments from lemons offered by fraudsters, they will not invest in the public markets. As the OSC points out, "The OSC mandate is set by statute: To provide protection to investors from unfair, improper, or fraudulent practices and to foster fair and efficient capital markets and confidence in capital markets."[4] Investors have to be confident that they are being treated fairly in the capital market; otherwise they will invest offshore, where they are treated fairly, or they will invest in real assets, such as houses and gold. There is then a social loss from the collapse of financial markets. This explains why there is a direct (positive) correlation between the existence of public capital markets and respect for the "rule of law." In countries where there is no confidence in the enforcement of laws against fraud, or where there is a belief that markets are rigged, financial transactions are done mostly through private placements in which the borrower and lender know each other. In these cases, there are also usually social enforcement costs to mitigate fraud. These generally involve either social costs, such as being excluded from the best "clubs,"[5] or draconian punishment for criminals.

---

[4]Ontario Securities Commission, "About the OSC." On the OSC website, http://www.osc.gov.on.ca/en/About_about_index.htm.

[5]Traditionally, in Canada, as in many other countries, the perpetrators of fraud were disciplined by being designated social outcasts and having their families excluded from the best schools, clubs, and so on. The loosening of social bonds has weakened the effectiveness of these types of constraints in Canada but not in more socially cohesive cultures.

## 17.1 Finance in the News   Largest Ponzi Scheme in Canadian History Exploited Boom Time Alberta

Alberta in the mid-2000s was fertile ground for promoters and salesmen like Gary Sorenson and Milowe Brost.

The price of crude was climbing toward $100 a barrel. A generation of Albertans had more spare cash than ever. Opportunity was everywhere.

On Saturday, a jury in Calgary found Mr. Sorenson, 71, and Mr. Brost, 61, guilty of fraud and theft in what the RCMP has characterized as the largest Ponzi scheme in Canadian history. Their crimes left behind a trail of shattered dreams and lost life savings. As many as 3,000 investors—a third of them Canadian—lost as much as $300 million in a series of affiliated mining and investment companies that prosecutors said were just fronts to channel cash to the two businessmen.

"Partly it's the culture in Alberta," Crown prosecutor Brian Holtby said in an interview. "There are times in Alberta when money is freely available, and they were able to take advantage of one of those times."

The case, one of the longest criminal trials in Calgary history, is part of a spate of Ponzi schemes in Canada and the United States that collapsed around the time of the Bernie Madoff scandal as investors tried to cash out during the financial crisis.

**Source:** Excerpted from McKenna, Barrie, "Largest Ponzi Scheme in Canadian History Exploited Boom Time Alberta." *The Globe and Mail*, February 15, 2015. Available at www.theglobeandmail.com. © The Globe and Mail Inc. All rights reserved. Reprinted by permission.

Finance in the News 17.1 discusses a case in Alberta, which the RCMP characterized as the largest Ponzi scheme ever in Canada. What is striking is the number of investors who were duped, over 3,000, some of whom lost their life savings. So what can regulators and individuals do?

As in the used-car market, alternative market mechanisms have evolved in the financial markets so that individuals can invest with some assurance that they are not buying lemons. The main mechanisms are basic research, securities legislation, and corporate law, which keep known criminals out of the markets, require those interacting with the public to be registered, and require that any securities offered to the public are checked to ensure they are legitimate. This overall process of checking securities offered to the public and providing basic information is called **due diligence**, and it can be very expensive and time consuming. It is as a result of fraud that so much checking and legal documentation is required. We will discuss some more Canadian cases of fraudulent activity in the next section.

**due diligence**   the process of checking securities offered to the public to ensure they are legitimate

## Some Canadian Examples of Fraudulent Activities

In 1908, Carlo Ponzi served 20 months in jail for a similar pyramid scam in Canada. If U.S. securities laws had been as tough in 1920 as they are now, he would never have been allowed to sell securities to the public, since his criminal background would have disqualified him from registration as a securities broker-dealer. Likewise, one of the charges the SEC levied against William Lyons was that he was not registered to sell financial securities. Keeping known criminals out of the business, and making sure that those in it understand the basics of the business and abide by professional standards, is a necessary, if insufficient, condition for minimizing fraud in the markets.

In her book *Contrepreneurs* (1988), Diane Francis details how Toronto used to be the "bucket shop" capital of the world. "Bucket shops" or "boiler rooms" were basically basements in large buildings with banks of dedicated telephones, where salespeople would call wealthy doctors and dentists in the United States, touting junior resource stocks on the Vancouver Stock Exchange (VSE).[6] The broker-dealers selling these "penny stocks" would often trade among themselves in "wash sales," in which the sum of the external sales activity was zero. By selling among themselves at ever higher prices, they generated the appearance of momentum, which attracted investors looking at the statistics in the newspaper. These securities were highlighted as emerging "growth" stocks, with great potential to attract investors looking for a quick profit. However, once the price had been artificially inflated to attract

---

[6]The Vancouver Stock Exchange no longer exists and has been replaced by the TSX Venture Exchange.

enough external investors, the insiders sold out, and the external investors discovered that there was no one else to sell to. This example of "pumping and dumping" illustrates the basic proposition that although it is easy to buy securities, they are often difficult to sell. If you don't want to read Diane Francis' book, watch *The Wolf of Wall Street*, a movie starring Leonardo DiCaprio, to get an idea of how a bucket shop works; it is based on the true story of Jordan Belfort and the firm he founded in the 1990s, Stratton Oakmont.[7]

A final Canadian example of outright fraud is Sino-Forest. Between 2007 and 2010, Sino-Forest raised almost $3.0 billion in Canada's debt and equity markets. Sino-Forest claimed to own timberland in China where it produced wood fibre for export. It produced audited financial statements showing total assets growing from $0.7 billion in 2004 to $5.7 billion in 2010. However, on June 2, 2011, an independent research report claimed Sino-Forest was fraudulently inflating its financial statements, and on August 26, 2011, the OSC suspended trading in its shares. In 2015 the firm's auditors, Ernst and Young, paid $117 million and others $38.5 million to settle investors' lawsuits. In 2017 the Ontario Superior Court awarded $2.65 billion to claimants against Sino-Forest's co-founder Allen Chan. Justice Penny declared that Chan abused his position to orchestrate an extremely large and complex fraud.[8]

If buying securities directly from a company or through a broker-dealer is considered risky, why not buy them through an asset manager selling mutual funds? Buying a mutual fund holding many securities is less risky—right? Not necessarily. In Quebec, Norbourg Asset Management Inc. (Norbourg) was closed down and its founder, Vincent Lacroix, was charged by Quebec's main regulator, the Autorité des marchés financiers (AMF), with misappropriating investor funds. The AMF claimed Lacroix stole $84 million from Norbourg and Evolution mutual funds, and claimed a further $10 million in punitive damages. The AMF froze Norbourg's assets in August 2005, and a later audit revealed that $130 million was missing. Luckily for the 9,200 investors in this case, they got almost all their money back as a result of legal claims against the regulators and others who should have been aware of what was going on.[9] Lacroix was found guilty on multiple criminal charges and sentenced to 12 years in jail.

Regulators and police try hard to stop criminal activity, but they can never shut it down completely. It's like trying to stop people from speeding—the laws are there, as is the enforcement, but the police can't be everywhere. Investors need to remember the old adage "If it sounds too good to be true, it probably is."

This warning may be obvious, but it is remarkable how gullible people can be. Moreover, the statistical evidence is that gullible investors tend to be of above-average intelligence and are workaholics who consider themselves to be financially literate. This is why doctors and dentists are prime candidates for fraudsters: they have lots of money and are eager to get more, while they are also clever enough to think they understand what's going on and don't need expert advice. It appears that the easiest person to defraud is someone who has a high opinion of themselves.

---

## Concept Review Questions

1. How does the existence of asymmetric information lead to market inefficiencies?
2. Why can increases in interest rates not be used to solve the "lemons problem" in financial markets?
3. Why are securities legislation and corporate laws essential for markets to perform properly?

---

[7]After four years in prison, Belfort repositioned himself as a motivational speaker and is now worth over US$100 million.

[8]Miller, Mathew, "Canadian Court Awards $2.6 Million in Sino-Forest Fraud Case." Reuters, March 15, 2018.

[9]See Marotte, Bernard, "Norbourg Investors Declare a Victory for Us." *The Globe and Mail*, January 31, 2011.

# Securities Legislation—Basic Responsibilities

**LEARNING OBJECTIVE 17.2**
Explain the purpose of securities laws and regulations in the financial markets.

When you consider markets, you might think that the securities market in Canada should be one market, with one regulator, since the Government of Canada has the power to regulate trade and commerce. However, this is not the case as the *Constitution Act*, formerly the *British North America Act*, gives responsibility to the provinces. For many years the Government of Canada has been campaigning for a federal securities regulator, and in 2009 it established the Canadian Securities Transition Office to lead and manage the transition to a national or federal securities regulator. However, in 2011 the Supreme Court of Canada determined that the draft regulations were constitutionally invalid, which shot the whole idea down. Today we continue to have a patchwork of provincial securities regulators, so that when securities are sold across Canada, each provincial regulator has to "clear" them to be sold to residents in their province.

The main regulators in Canada are the Ontario, British Columbia, and Quebec provincial securities commissions. With the failure of the Government of Canada's initiative, British Columbia, Ontario, and the federal government signed an agreement to move toward a co-operative capital markets regulatory system. Subsequently, New Brunswick, Saskatchewan, and Prince Edward Island have all signed on to develop common legislation and have also renewed their invitation to the other provinces to join. Whether this initiative results in meaningful change is still not obvious.

Securities regulation in the United States is a state responsibility, just as it is a provincial responsibility in Canada. However, since so many U.S. issues are national in scope and cross state lines, the U.S. **Securities and Exchange Commission (SEC)** is, in effect, a national securities regulator and has pre-empted state regulations. Issues can be sold within a state, though, if no out-of-state investors are involved. This raises the basic point that securities regulation is designed to protect investors in a specific jurisdiction, so the provincial and territorial authorities exert authority whenever their citizens are involved. For the same reason, a majority of Internet fraud now seems to come from Eastern Europe where regulation is lax and it is foreigners not locals being defrauded.

**Securities and Exchange Commission (SEC)**   a U.S. agency that is, in effect, a national securities regulator

In protecting local residents, provincial regulators in Canada rely on three main methods: registration, disclosure, and enforcement. Registration means that all securities firms and investment advisors need to be registered. Background checks to keep out criminals, and educational requirements—in particular, passing the Canadian Securities Course—are designed to increase professional standards. If a claim is then brought against disreputable people or institutions, they can be deregistered so they cannot practise in Canada, since the **Investment Industry Regulatory Organization of Canada (IIROC)** keeps a national register. Enforcement means that regulators monitor events continuously to check for market manipulation. First, however, we will discuss disclosure.

**Investment Industry Regulatory Organization of Canada (IIROC)**   the national self-regulatory organization of the Canadian securities industry

A security, according to the *Ontario Securities Act (OSA)*, includes "any document, investment, or writing commonly known as a security,"[10] such as bonds and common equities. The critical fact is that the list is not exhaustive. In practice, the OSC and other provincial and territorial securities commissions aim to protect investors not just from fraud but also from "the imposition of unsubstantial schemes"—that is, misleading and bad investments.

---

[10]See the OSC's current investigations and rules at its website, www.osc.gov.on.ca. This section is heavily based on Macintosh, Jeffrey, and Nicholls, Christopher, *Securities Law* (Toronto: Irwin Law, 2002); and Nicholls, Christopher, *Corporate Finance and Canadian Law* (Toronto: Carswell, 2000).

In determining whether a security exists, the OSC looks at several factors, including the following:

- whether the promoter raises money and leads the investor to expect a profit
- whether the investor has any control on how the money is spent
- whether there is risk involved

Other factors are also important, but these are the major ones, and taking a broad interpretation of these criteria implies that almost any document can be construed as a security. For example, securities have been found to exist when a half interest in a pair of royal chinchillas was sold, when warehouse receipts were sold to indicate ownership of casks of whiskey, and when leases were sold that gave drilling rights. The critical point seems to be the protection of the public interest, and courts have taken a broad view of what this interest is.

A classic case involved Pacific Coast Coin Exchange of Canada (PCCE), which sold silver on a 35-percent margin (that is, purchasers put up only 35 percent of the money for the silver). Purchasers could then sell the silver back to PCCE; pay interest on the loan, storage, and handling charges; and receive the difference (positive or negative) in the price of silver. PCCE promoted its business, emphasizing silver as a store of value during a highly inflationary period.[11] The OSC shut down PCCE's operations because it was in violation of the *OSA*, a decision that the Supreme Court of Canada confirmed. Although PCCE's operations did not technically meet the definition of a security as it then existed, the Supreme Court stated that the important point was the policy behind the legislation, and that "substance not form" dictated whether or not something was a security. All that is necessary for the OSC to claim jurisdiction is that a transaction has an effect on Ontario residents sufficient to prejudice the public interest.

This broad interpretation of what constitutes a security and where securities laws can be applied means that the OSC is involved in five major areas in which securities are transferred or traded:

- *primary market offerings* (where money is raised directly from investors by the company)
- *secondary market trading* (where existing securities are traded between investors)
- *activities of investment professionals* (where professionals are trading or advising on these securities and thereby affecting market prices)
- *insider trading* (where people who have privileged information about a company, not available to the general public, are buying or selling shares at prices that do not reflect their true value)
- *takeover bids* (where shareholders are being asked to sell their shares to a purchaser)

The broad definition of a trade is the *sale* of a security for valuable consideration. It also includes the activities of traders on an organized exchange, registrants who take orders to buy and sell securities, and any "act, advert, solicitation, conduct or negotiation to directly or indirectly further a trade." Traders and individuals registered to buy and sell securities (i.e., registrants) are regulated; however, given the broad scope of what constitutes a security, many individuals are traders and do not realize it. For example, lottery tickets sold at the corner store could be regarded as securities, with the storekeeper required to register with the OSC. However, the fact that lotteries are well known, with no public interest issues involved, means that, in practice, they are not treated as securities.[12]

---

## Concept Review Question

1. What are some of the more important issues arising from the fact that securities regulation is a provincial and territorial, not a federal, responsibility in Canada?

---

[11]The case was settled in 1978, and the 1970s saw inflation at double-digit levels.
[12]The fact that only about 35 percent of the gross proceeds from lotteries are returned as payouts should be a concern. In Ponzi's scheme, the eventual liquidation of his "business" resulted in about a 35-percent payout as well.

17.3 # Security Offerings

---

**LEARNING OBJECTIVE 17.3**

Explain what a prospectus is, what it contains, and why it is critical for initial public offerings (IPOs).

---

The other main implication of the definition of a trade is the promotion aspect. Anyone who phones someone to generate a sale is involved in trading, as is any website that promotes particular securities. Moreover, the OSC has broad powers to restrict such activity before a trade is effected, meaning that documents used to generate sales of securities are highly regulated. The most significant area involves **initial public offerings (IPOs)** of securities, because the assumption is that information asymmetry is greatest with IPOs. IPO trades are "primary offerings"—that is, they are a first-time distribution of securities. Most provinces in Canada, including Ontario, have a closed system for the distribution of securities. What this means is that any distribution of securities has to be accompanied by a **prospectus**, a formal summary of the security that describes the costs, investment objectives, and risks involved. It is illegal to distribute securities without delivering a prospectus to the purchaser. The system is "closed" because there are a limited number of *exemptions* from the prospectus requirement.

There are two types of prospectuses: long form and short form. For IPOs, a firm has to have a **long-form prospectus** that consists of many pages of dense discussion about the firm.[13] The overriding requirement is that the prospectus supply "full, true and plain disclosure of all material facts relating to the securities proposed to be distributed." This definition has important components. The "full, true and plain" means that it has to be understandable (not in "legalese") and it must correctly portray the situation of the firm. Further, every "material fact" has to be disclosed. A material fact is something that can reasonably be expected to affect the price of the securities being distributed. This also means that half-truths, even if they are technically correct, and omissions do not represent full, true, and plain disclosure. The prospectus has to be signed by both the chief executive officer (CEO) and the chief financial officer (CFO) on behalf of the issuing firm's board of directors (BOD), the investment dealer helping to sell the securities, and the accounting firm auditing the financial statements. This makes all signatories liable for damages in the event of misrepresentation.[14]

The possibility of a lawsuit is what ensures that the investment dealer and the issuing firm do a comprehensive job of explaining the firm's position. This involves performing their due diligence, defined earlier, and doing a reasonable investigation of the facts to ensure that there has been no material misrepresentation. The standard applied is "that required of a prudent person in the circumstances of the particular case." The investment dealers and the lawyers preparing the prospectus have to check and recheck the statements made by the issuing firm to assure themselves that the prospectus fairly represents the firm's position.[15]

The British Columbia Securities Commission (BCSC) has a 79-page document dictating what has to be included in a prospectus.[16] Broadly speaking, this document says that a prospectus must contain the following information:

- a description of the securities being issued and who can buy them
- the price of the securities, the fees to the investment dealer involved with the distribution, and the net proceeds
- the market for the securities—that is, whether they will be traded

**initial public offering (IPO)** the first sale of a security

**prospectus** a formal summary of a security that describes the costs, investment objectives, risks, and performance

**long-form prospectus** a long document, written in plain language, that supplies full, honest disclosure of all facts that can reasonably be expected to affect the price of the security; it must be signed by the chief executive officer and chief financial officer

---

[13] All legal documents in Canada can be retrieved from the OSC's System for Electronic Document Analysis and Retrieval (SEDAR) website at www.sedar.com. Investors can search for both long-form and short-form prospectuses.

[14] Before *Sarbanes-Oxley (SOX)*, discussed in Chapter 3, the standard advice was not to trust the annual report but, instead, look to the last prospectus, because an investor could sue for misrepresentation in the prospectus but not in the annual report. This is still true for Canadian companies that are not subject to *SOX*.

[15] This does not mean that the prospectus includes "full, true and plain disclosure of all material facts." If the firm deliberately wants to commit fraud, then even diligent work by the investment dealer and its lawyers may not uncover it.

[16] BC Securities Commission, *Form 41-101F1: Information Required in a Prospectus.* This form is on the commission's website at www.bcsc.bc.ca.

- the business of the issuer and its subsidiaries, with a discussion of the past three-year history
- risk factors involved with buying the securities
- summary financial information
- management's discussion and analysis

Under each of these general groupings are extensive lists of what needs to be discussed, as well as specific requirements for different types of distributions, such as those by mining firms or mutual funds. It is easy to understand, from reviewing the BCSC document, why the cost of preparing a prospectus is at least $500,000 for a $20-million offering. Despite the cost, a prospectus is required for all distributions.

## Types of Distributions

The OSC has determined that there are three types of distributions. The first is a distribution by an issuer. The assumption here is that the issuer is raising money in the primary market from investors and, by definition, knows more about the true value of the securities than the investors do. Hence, the prospectus is designed to remedy this information asymmetry. Imagine, for example, if Carlo Ponzi had had to describe his business with a "full, true and plain" disclosure, and an investment bank and legal firm had to sign off on his prospectus.

The second type of distribution is one being sold from a control block.[17] The assumption here is that someone owning a control block also has privileged access to the firm; as a result, there is an information asymmetry that the prospectus is designed to remedy. In this case, a prospectus has to be prepared even if the firm is raising no money; this is an example of a secondary market transaction rather than a primary market transaction. Again, the fact the firm has to bear this cost is not a factor. What is important is that investors buying the securities are protected.

The third type of distribution is one in which restricted shares are being sold to the public for the first time. Restricted shares are generally shares that have not been registered for sale to the general public. Usually, the firm issues them when it buys another firm, so that the firm's owner gets shares that cannot be immediately sold.

As indicated previously, a prospectus is required for most distributions of securities. In the process, the securities are registered, which means that a securities firm registered with the appropriate securities commission can trade in them. In Canada, the Canadian Depository for Securities (CDS) is normally the registered owner of the securities, and trades in the securities are effected by means of computer (book) entries. What this means is that the prospectus requirement goes hand in hand with the registration of the securities, which allows them to be subsequently bought and sold in the public markets. Without a prospectus, the securities are not registered and cannot be publicly traded. The market for non-registered securities is called the **exempt market**.

**exempt market** the unregulated market for non-registered securities that raise money from private investors

If a firm wants to raise a small amount of money, preparing a $500,000 prospectus and engaging an investment dealer to distribute the securities does not make much sense. As a result, there are exemptions from the prospectus requirement based on smaller issues, the sophistication of the potential investors, and the low-risk nature of the securities. To prevent securities that are sold in the exempt market from slipping into the public markets—what is called "backdoor underwriting"—the exempt purchasers can sell only to other exempt purchasers. Under certain circumstances, they can sell the securities in the public market after holding them for a certain time,[18] if the issuer has effectively met the prospectus requirements by becoming a "reporting issuer," which will be discussed later.

**offering memorandum** a document with the same objectives as a prospectus but that provides significantly less information, which lowers the cost of preparing it

For the exempt market, the issuer normally prepares an **offering memorandum**, rather than a prospectus. Although both of these documents have the same objective and have to be correct, the amount of information in an offering memorandum is significantly less, which lowers the cost of preparing it.[19]

---

[17]Control blocks are not defined in law. Clearly, 50.1 percent effects legal control, but a prospectus may also be required to distribute smaller blocks, even down to 5 percent, if there are grounds for believing that there is inside information.

[18]Normal hold periods are four months to two years, after which the securities are regarded as seasoned.

[19]In some cases, the *OSA* requires an offering memorandum, which is delivered to the OSC but is not publicly available. In other cases, the issuer decides, or the investment dealer insists, on the preparation of an offering memorandum to help market the issue.

The sophisticated purchasers of the exempt market are essentially individuals and institutions that can be expected to hire their own experts to conduct the necessary due diligence. For example, securities can be sold without a prospectus to accredited investors, such as banks, governments, wealthy investors (net assets of more than $1 million and $300,000 a year in family income), investment dealers, and individuals owning control blocks.

Similarly, government debt issues are exempt, as are the debt issues of many financial institutions. Finally, securities issued as part of a takeover or corporate reorganization are exempt because they are covered by corporate law requirements to provide proxy circulars and similar documents that substantially replicate the contents of a prospectus.

The other major exemption is for private firms, now called "closely held issuers." As long as no promotion is done and less than $3 million is raised, securities can be sold to no more than 35 individuals with the approval of the BOD. In this case, the issue has to be accompanied by an information statement containing basic information about the issuer. One might ask, how is this keeping up with the Internet's ability to reach millions of people? The answer is, on November 5, 2015, the major securities regulators agreed to a "crowdfunding exemption" to Canada's closed system,[20] by which small amounts of money can be raised from a large number of investors. The critical requirements are that the securities offered not be complex; each investor can then contribute no more than $2,500 and acknowledge they have read the issuing documents and are aware of the risk; and the issuer cannot raise more than $1.5 million a year and must issue an offering document and be liable for any misrepresentations.

Although securities regulations are comprehensive, they cannot prevent all possible abuses. One major area of concern involves situations where companies change their strategy and their operations. Although such changes are revealed through mandatory disclosures, it is possible, by taking over a firm that has reduced its operations, to bypass the IPO process and thereby avoid a long-form prospectus. Such a "reverse" takeover also means that a private firm can buy a publicly traded firm and thereby acquire a listing on the Toronto Stock Exchange (TSX). This is often called a "backdoor" listing—after the takeover, the name of the listed firm is usually changed and it enters a completely different line of business. This was how Sino-Forest acquired its TSX listing through a reverse takeover.

Securities legislation has come a long way since the days of Carlo Ponzi. The definition of a security is now so broad as to cover any attempt to sell an interest in something to someone with an expectation of making a profit. All such distributions must be accompanied by a prospectus, unless they are sold into the exempt market by means of what is referred to as a "private placement." The prospectus is designed to minimize problems of information asymmetry so that Ponzi schemes and other frauds are rare and so that investors will have confidence in the public markets. This confidence is encouraged by the breadth and depth of the information required in a prospectus and the fact that almost everyone involved in its production can be sued if there are material misrepresentations. The restrictions on "hyping" securities while they are being issued and the requirement that professionals involved in their subsequent trading be registered are both designed to enhance the confidence in secondary as well as primary markets.

However, the legal system is constantly having to react to the dynamic nature of financial markets. One particular change is that investors are increasingly diversifying internationally, and stock markets are also globalizing as they compete for listings and trading. Not too long ago, we had four "largish" stock exchanges in Canada, whereas now we have only one, and that one was almost taken over by the London Stock Exchange in 2011.[21] In response to this competition among exchanges, the Toronto Stock Exchange has tried to position itself as a resource-based exchange and has actively sought out non-Canadian firms to list. The Sino-Forest situation has alerted securities regulators to the problems arising from the fact that making these firms accessible to Canadian investors means they have to abide by the same disclosure and governance rules of Canadian firms. This can be difficult and expensive given that their operations are often thousands of kilometres away.

---

[20]Multilateral Instrument 45–108 Crowdfunding.

[21]The "merger" between the TSX and LSE was killed on June 29, 2011, when it failed to get enough shareholder approval in the face of a rival bid from a consortium of Canadian financial institutions.

## 17.2 Finance in the News    OSC Aims to Improve Compliance for Emerging Market Issuers

The Ontario Securities Commission (OSC) is proposing a series of recommendations for issuers, underwriters, and auditors aimed at improving compliance for companies that are largely based overseas, but are listed on Canadian markets.

The review, which the OSC launched in July 2011 following the revelation of apparent disclosure problems at China-based forestry firm, Sino-Forest Corp., examines a sample of 24 issuers listed on Canadian exchanges that have significant business operations in emerging markets. The regulator focused on the adequacy of issuer disclosure and corporate governance practices, as well as the roles played by auditors, underwriters and exchanges in bringing these issuers to market.

No specific policy actions are recommended as a result of the review. Instead, it identifies a variety of areas of regulatory concern, including issues related to the quality of emerging market issuer governance and disclosure, the adequacy of the audit function, the adequacy of the due diligence conducted by underwriters in these sorts of offerings, and the nature of the exchange listing approval process.

"One of our central concerns was the apparent 'form over substance' approach to compliance with applicable standards for disclosure, issuer governance, board oversight, audit practices and due diligence practices," the report says. "In our view, the level of rigor and independent-mindedness applied by boards, auditors and underwriters in doing their important jobs—management oversight, audit, due diligence on offerings—should have been more thorough."

One of the basic reasons that auditor and underwriter due diligence appears to be lacking is the fact that the core operations and assets of many of the issuers are located in emerging markets, and the firms have very little presence in Canada, it notes. A lack of understanding of local business practices, language barriers, and translation issues also contributed to these problems, it says.

The review found several areas of potential concern for auditors including a lack of professional skepticism, a lack of knowledge about local cultural and business practices, too much delegation to foreign auditors, difficulty in obtaining domestic auditor working papers, and language barriers.

Similarly, for underwriters, the review found wide variation in due diligence practices and documentation, and a lack of professional skepticism and rigor, among other things. "We noted several instances where 'red flags' should have prompted further probing or questions. Our review indicated little or no follow-up in these instances to either understand or analyze the concerns, or disclose them," it says.

In terms of exchanges, the review says that no particular form of listing, whether by IPO, reverse takeover, or direct listing, was specifically problematic. It did have concerns though, including whether additional listing requirements for emerging market issuers are necessary, a lack of transparency when exchanges waive certain listing requirements, and a heavy reliance on third parties in conducting due diligence.

The report says that the OSC will follow up with issuers, auditors, and underwriters in areas that it has identified for improvement, and that some issues uncovered in the review have been referred to enforcement. It also says that it will continue to work with the Canadian Public Accountability Board to address audit related concerns, with staff at the exchanges to address concerns related to the listing process, and with the Investment Industry Regulatory Organization of Canada on underwriting practices.

The report proposes a list of recommendations, which it says do not necessarily require the creation of new policies or rules, but instead involve the development of guidance, best practices or enhanced vigilance to improve compliance with current requirements.

For issuers, this includes guidance to improve corporate governance practices, clarifying the regulatory expectations of CEOs and CFOs in conducting reasonable due diligence, better disclosure of complex corporate structures, better risk disclosure, ensuring the maintenance of appropriate books and records in Canada, the possibility of imposing a minimum language competency component for board members in the firm's local language, and possible minimum Canadian director residency requirements.

For auditors, it calls for improved access to audit working papers; examining whether securities rules need to be enhanced to allow more information sharing for the oversight of audit firms, whether suitability standards for auditors should be developed, and whether auditors should be required to publicly disclose and explain their resignation from a file. It also calls for greater cooperation among securities regulators and audit oversight bodies.

For underwriters, the report recommends: establishing a consistent and transparent set of requirements for the conduct of due diligence, developing best practices for documenting due diligence, and best practices for due diligence calls and site visits.

Finally, it says that the exchanges will need to assess whether additional listing requirements are needed, provide greater transparency regarding waivers of any listing requirements, assess the extent of reliance on third parties in conducting due diligence and whether additional due diligence steps are warranted, and review the role of sponsors in bringing issuers to market, "to ensure that there is adequate accountability placed on the sponsor and if there is an appropriate level of transparency regarding the sponsor's due diligence work."

"The OSC expects issuers and gatekeepers to act in a manner that promotes investor protection and supports confidence in our capital markets," said Howard Wetston, chair and CEO of the OSC.

**Source:** Langton, James, "OSC Aims to Improve Compliance for Emerging Market Issuers." *Investment Executive* (March 20, 2012). Available at www.investmentexecutive.com. Reprinted by permission.

Finance in the News 17.2 discusses a review by the OSC, which stated that firms from emerging markets have to abide by Canadian securities laws if they are to list in Canada and sell shares to the Canadian public. The overriding objective of Canadian securities regulators is to protect Canadians and ensure that they have faith in any securities offered to them, whether they are from Canadian or non-Canadian firms. This means non-Canadian companies can't use reverse takeovers to bypass securities regulations and the due diligence process designed to protect Canadians. In the sections that follow, we will discuss the IPO process, where this due diligence is at its highest level; why firms choose to go public rather than sell securities through a private placement or the exempt market; and how ongoing supervision of firms is carried out after they have filed their initial long-form prospectus.

**Concept Review Questions**

1. Why are prospectuses so important for public market issues?
2. Explain how offering memorandums differ from prospectuses and how exempt markets differ from public markets.
3. What is a reverse takeover and a backdoor listing?

## 17.4  IPOs and Investment Banking

**LEARNING OBJECTIVE 17.4**
Outline the basic stages in taking a firm public through an initial public offering (IPO) of securities.

## The Motivation for IPOs

The principles that we have discussed apply to all public offerings of securities, whether they are debt or common equity securities and whether or not this is the first time such securities have been offered. In this section, we discuss a particularly important public offering of securities: namely, offering common shares to the public for the first time (i.e., an IPO). Although it is not strictly necessary, such public offerings are almost always listed on an organized exchange, such as the Toronto Stock Exchange (TSX) or TSX Venture Exchange, which allows these shares to be easily traded.

Most firms that "go public" have had this as a long-term goal for many years before they actually become a publicly traded company. The response to a Conference Board of Canada survey indicates that firms have several reasons for going public.[22] One of the most frequently cited reasons is the desire on the part of some investors to "cash out." Sometimes this is a way to pay off private equity investors and other venture capitalists who financed the firm in its earlier stages of development. At other times, the founders of the company might want to cash out if they are no longer actively involved in managing the company. As we discussed in Chapter 2, an *agency relationship* exists when people hire someone else to execute their wishes. In this respect, managers are agents for the owners of the firm. As a firm grows, it makes the switch from being an owner-managed firm to one that has a *separation* of ownership from control (which is what normally happens when a firm goes public). The managers then face the choice of either selling the company to someone else privately or going public and combining a sale of shares by the company with the sale of the founders' shares. In this situation, an important part of going public is the fact that a market price exists and shareholders can evaluate and liquidate their investment more easily.

Other firms go public because they want access to a more diversified set of financing options. In particular, two often-expressed motives are to escape dependence on bank lending and to increase the use of common equity as an acquisition currency. We discussed the closed system of securities regulation in the previous section, but if a firm wants to buy another firm through an exchange of shares, the purchasing firm's ability to exchange shares is restricted, unless it is publicly traded, because the shares are not registered and can be sold only to exempt purchasers and not to the general public. This lack of liquidity in the stock makes the firm's shares unattractive as a means of financing takeovers. As discussed in Chapter 15, any firm making extensive acquisitions will find it advantageous to have publicly traded shares.

It is also important to recognize that many private firms are extremely dependent on their bank for financing. Even if they have a good relationship with their bank, there is a

---

[22]For some case histories see Andrews, Michael, *Initial Public Offerings: The Experience of Eight Canadian Growth Companies* (Ottawa: Conference Board of Canada, 1995).

perception that this relationship improves after they go public. This may be due to the belief that being a "listed company" has significant value. The listing of a firm's shares on a major exchange, coupled with the prospectus requirement, dramatically increases the flow of information about the firm, which the bank may find comforting. Several respondents to the Conference Board of Canada study reported that the relationships with suppliers and customers did improve as a result of a public listing, which provides a kind of "seal of approval" that the firm has arrived.

The reasons participants in the Conference Board's eight case studies gave for these improved relationships are broadly consistent with the ideas advanced by Stewart Myers.[23] Myers also emphasizes the use of the stock price as an incentive mechanism to enhance managerial efficiency.

Suppose, for example, we divide a new firm's development into five stages:

1. technological experimentation
2. pilot studies and sales
3. improvement in production and scaling up manufacturing
4. full-scale marketing and production
5. expansion into other lines

These five stages roughly correspond to the product life cycle discussed in strategy classes. What Myers added is the need to provide incentive for the founders and reward them for their industry and innovation, which will vary across the product life cycle.

In Myers' view, the entrepreneur is essential at stages 1 and 2, valuable at stage 3, useful but replaceable at stage 4, and not needed at all at stage 5. So suppose at stages 1 and 2 the entrepreneur is willing to commit "sweat equity" and all their savings to the enterprise but needs some external finance. The company can't raise external equity at this stage, because the informational problems are too large. Instead, the firm raises **private equity** or **venture capital** from a partner. In this way, the funds are provided from the exempt market.

**private equity** or **venture capital**   money raised from private investors in the exempt market

The entrepreneur, as well as the partner, then needs a commitment to go public at either stage 3 or certainly by stage 4, as the proportion of intellectual or human capital versus real capital in the value of the firm goes down. Essentially, if the venture is successful after stage 2, then the entrepreneur's value has been validated by an increase in the value of the firm. Yet at this stage, significant external funds are needed to formalize the firm's business plan and buy real assets. This is the ideal point to take the firm public so the investment by the entrepreneur or founder and backers can be monetized. Otherwise, the value will be diluted by the new funds raised to take the firm to the next stage. Also at this stage, the entrepreneur is no longer as important to the firm as it moves into a classic production mode with a formal managerial culture, with less need to provide incentive on the creative side of the business.

**agency theory**   the study of relationships between shareholders and a company's managers and the costs of resolving conflicts between them and aligning their interests

Myers was writing at the time of the Internet bubble in the late 1990s and was clearly influenced by the large number of hi-tech firms going public at that time. The basic idea is consistent with **agency theory**—the study of relationships between shareholders and a company's managers and the costs of resolving conflicts between them and aligning their interests—and with the observation that private firms involve a higher proportion of "intellectual" capital. Such firms go public when the proportion of intellectual capital is less important and when they face increased financing needs. The corollary is that firms with little need to provide incentives for management have less need to go public. It is hardly surprising, for example, that utility firms, like the local water company, are often run under private (normally municipal) management; they often have less need to motivate management to be efficient and create value. However, even here private sector discipline can be important. On November 5, 2015, the Ontario government sold its first tranche of 81.1 million shares worth $1.66 billion in Hydro One Inc. Hydro One owns the bulk of the electricity grid in Ontario and distributes electricity to many communities; it is one of the largest utilities in Canada. By 2017, the Ontario government's ownership had dropped to 49 percent, but it still exerted effective control by dismissing the entire board of directors in July 2018 after a change in government following a provincial election.

---

[23]Myers, Stewart, "Financial Architecture." *European Financial Management* 5, no. 2 (1999), pp. 133–41.

Agency theory also explains why divisions are sometimes spun off from larger firms. Entrepreneurial activity cannot be properly rewarded within a large firm when there is little correspondence between the effort expended by entrepreneurial managers and the value they create. In contrast, entrepreneurial activity is often stimulated in a wave of innovation as a division is spun off from a bureaucratic parent company, and the managers start focusing on creating enough value to take the firm public.

Going public can thus be seen as a longer-term objective of many firms to monetize the value created by the founders when their value to the firm starts to wane, and the firm moves to stage 3 or 4. Even before this point, the firm will have been in constant contact with its investment dealer as it sought different sources of financing. It is also often a way to re-energize divisions within more bureaucratic organizations.

## The Stages of the IPO Process

A typical IPO involves four basic stages[24] and normally involves an investment dealer (or investment bank in the United States) that specializes in raising capital for firms and being their "eyes and ears" on the capital market. The first stage involves the initial discussion with the investment dealer, which then triggers the formal IPO process. The second stage consists of drafting an initial prospectus. The third stage, commonly called the waiting period, involves finalizing the prospectus and obtaining clearance from the securities commission. The final stage involves pricing and distributing the issue and providing after-market stabilization. The process is illustrated in **Figure 17.1**.

### The First Stage: Discussion

The Conference Board of Canada survey referred to earlier indicates that, in this first phase of going public, the firm will use its existing investment dealer but will frequently add other dealers to broaden the distribution of its shares and increase the number of analysts who will subsequently follow, and make recommendations on, the firm. At this early stage, the firm will also "clean up" its legal structure by removing different classes of shares, changing its bylaws and its board of directors, and generally making itself more marketable.

### The Second Stage: Preliminary Prospectus

The second phase involves preparing the **preliminary prospectus**, a document produced for prospective investors by an underwriter, with the understanding that it may be modified significantly before the final prospectus is published. This usually takes from three to five months to complete and is often called a "red herring" due to the bold red disclaimer on the first page, required by law, which indicates that it is not final. It is this stage that illustrates a Catch-22. The investment dealer would like to do some pre-marketing to gauge the amount of interest in the company. However, promoting and discussing the sale of shares is regarded as trading, and this cannot happen until a prospectus has been delivered. Consequently, the firm will normally sign a "letter of intent" with its investment dealer, indicating that the firm will

**preliminary prospectus**
a document produced for prospective investors by an underwriter, with the understanding that it may be modified significantly before the final prospectus is published

**FIGURE 17.1**  The Stages of an IPO

| Discussion triggers IPO | Preliminary prospectus: three to five months | Waiting period and road shows: one to two months | Pricing, distribution, and after-market stabilization: one month |

Initial filing: red herring

Final clearance

---

[24]See IIROC, *Equity Capital Markets New Issue Practices Handbook* (January 2010).

**best efforts offering** an offering in which an investment dealer signs an agency agreement to do its best to sell shares, but with no guarantee of success; investment dealers are paid a certain amount for each share they sell

**firm commitment offering** an offering in which the investment dealer buys the new securities from the issuer and guarantees the sale of a certain number

**bought deal** an offering in which the underwriter buys all the shares of a seasoned issue to resell later, even before the drafting of the preliminary prospectus

**standby** or **rights offering** an offering of common shares at a discount to investors who already own shares; can only be used with seasoned offerings

**spread** the difference between the price at which an investment dealer buys shares and the slightly higher price at which they are resold to the public

**underwrite** to assume risk by guaranteeing an offering

**lead investment dealer** a securities firm that manages the process of selling larger issues

**banking** (or **dealer**) **syndicate** a group formed temporarily to jointly underwrite and sell a new security offering

**selling group** everyone who works to sell an issue

**market** or **disaster "out" clause** a clause that gives the underwriter the right to cancel an issue if financial markets deteriorate so much that the underwriter cannot market the issue profitably

**overallotment** or **"green-shoe" option** a clause that gives the underwriter the option of buying more shares from the issuer if investor demand is strong

cover all out-of-pocket costs as the dealer helps it prepare a preliminary prospectus. During this period, the firm, its lawyers, and the investment dealer are not allowed to hype or promote the stock, and communications with the public have to remain unchanged. Further, the investment dealer has to restrict the flow of information.

It is at this stage that the firm and the investment dealer decide on the broad type and terms of the public offering. They can choose from four different types of public offerings: a **best efforts offering**, a **firm commitment offering**, a **bought deal**, or a **standby** or **rights offering**. The last two can be used only with seasoned offerings, and most IPOs are firm commitment offerings. In a best efforts offering, the investment dealer signs an agency agreement to do its best to sell the shares, with no guarantee of success. The investment dealer is rewarded on the basis of the shares that it sells—that is, it is paid a certain amount for each share it sells. Such offerings are rare, because firms do not like the uncertainty attached to the process. If this is the only option that is available to the firm after it contacts several investment dealers, it may be a warning sign that the firm should not go public. Occasionally, a firm commitment offering will be converted into a best efforts offering after the investment dealer discovers there is limited investor interest.

In a firm commitment offering, the investment dealer buys the new securities from the issuer and guarantees the sale of a certain number, while in a bought deal, the underwriter buys all the shares of a seasoned issue to resell later, even before the drafting of the preliminary prospectus. In a standby or rights offering, common shares are offered at a discount to investors who already own shares.

The standard IPO contract is a firm commitment arrangement in which the investment dealer buys the shares for a fixed price and resells them to the public at a slightly higher price, thus earning profits on this **spread** (i.e., the difference between the purchase and reselling price). In this case, the investment dealer **underwrites** or guarantees the offering, which is why investment dealers are commonly referred to as *underwriters*.[25] Larger issues will have a **lead investment dealer** that manages the whole process, and a **banking** (or **dealer**) **syndicate** that is formed temporarily to sell part of the issue. Both groups underwrite the issue and guarantee the proceeds to the firm. However, sometimes an investment dealer joins as part of the **selling group** on a best efforts basis, and any shares it cannot sell are returned to the banking syndicate.

The compensation to the investment dealer comes from the standard 4-percent underwriting fee, based on the gross proceeds of the issue,[26] and the difference between the price the dealer pays the issuer for the shares and the price at which the dealer sells them to the public. The IIROC enforces rule 29.2 on business conduct, which expressly prohibits selling securities at a price higher than that provided in the prospectus during the course of the distribution. As a result, the investment dealer cannot earn extra profits by marking up the securities' price if demand turns out to be very strong.

The underwriting agreement includes standard clauses that provide the issuer with the authority to issue the securities, require it to prepare a prospectus, prevent it from issuing any other securities while the underwriting is underway, and obligate it to pay the underwriter. The contract also stipulates when the securities will be transferred to the underwriter and when the underwriter will pay the issuer. This payment is normally conditional on a **market** or **disaster "out" clause**.[27] If the state of the financial markets deteriorates substantially so the underwriter cannot market the issue profitably, then the issue can be cancelled. This is clearly a huge safety net for the underwriter, but "deterioration" in the state of the market has not been clearly defined. The B.C. Supreme Court stated that the market out clause referred to the state of the issuing company's shares and not the market generally. Like many legal interpretations, this one has yet to be tested in other cases.

Another standard underwriting clause is an **overallotment** or **"green-shoe" option** that gives the underwriter the option of buying more shares from the issuer (usually 15 percent

---

[25]Canadian investment banks are often called investment dealers, as discussed in Chapter 2, because the use of the term "bank" was restricted under the *Bank Act* in Canada. Because most of the dealers are now owned by the chartered banks, the use of the American term "investment bank" is becoming more common, although we still use "investment dealer" throughout most of our discussion.

[26]In the United States, the fee is 7 percent, as there is less competition among the investment banks.

[27]The difference between the two is the extent of deterioration in the markets and the amount of margin that the investment dealer is allowed to post. All investment dealers finance their inventory of securities with borrowings, mainly from the chartered banks.

more) if investor demand is strong. Finally, many agreements also contain a **lock-up period** that prevents the founders of the company from selling their shares for a given time. Because cashing out the shares of the founding entrepreneur, or the shares of private equity investors, is a common motive for going public, as discussed previously, the last thing the investment dealer wants is a large number of shares being sold just as it is marketing the issue. For this reason, the investment dealer almost always negotiates a lock-up period so that these shares cannot be sold for six months. The actual lock-up period depends on the investment dealer's assessment of how many of the existing common shares are likely to flood the market. If the number of shares is large, the dealer might impose a *phased* period in which only a certain percentage of the shares can be sold over certain intervals.

**lock-up period**   a time during which the founders of the company are prohibited from selling their shares

### The Third Stage: Waiting Period

Once the preliminary prospectus has been drafted, it is sent to the securities commission to be examined for any deficiencies. This third phase is generally called the **waiting period**, as the investment dealer and the issuer wait for final clearance to sell the securities. This period usually lasts at least three weeks. It is longer for IPOs because there is less information already available for them than there is for seasoned offerings.[28] During the waiting period, the underwriter can market the issue and collect "expressions of interest." However, the final price has not been set, so the underwriter indicates a range of possible prices, usually $2 apart, because it is illegal to sell the securities until the prospectus is final.

**waiting period**   the time after the preliminary prospectus has been drafted and sent to the securities commission to be examined for deficiencies, during which the investment dealer and the issuer wait for final clearance to sell the securities

The marketing of the issue will involve "road shows" (or "dog and pony shows") to describe the issuer and the issue itself in the major financial cities where the issue will be marketed.[29] Typically, exempt purchasers (i.e., the major financial institutions) will be contacted by different members of the selling group and invited to these presentations by senior management and the lead underwriter. Because it is important for the underwriter to sell the issue as quickly as possible, the focus is on institutional clients that can buy large blocks of shares. Significant retail investors may also be invited to attend, although this is less common now than in the past.

It is important to note that at this stage the "expressions of interest" are not firm orders. In the case of major institutions, the expressions of interest are usually in the form of **limit orders**, in which they indicate that they are willing to buy so many shares at a certain price. For retail investors, expressions of interest generally take the form of **market orders**, which means they are for fixed amounts of shares at whatever the final price is. This interaction between the investment dealer and the market is useful for setting the final terms of the issue and confirming that the issue can be sold.

**limit orders**   expressions of interest that are not firm orders but indications from major institutions of how much they are willing to buy at a certain price

**market orders**   orders from retail investors for fixed amounts at whatever the final market price is

If the securities commission finds any deficiencies in the prospectus, the issuer has a minimum of 10 days to rectify them—although it may take longer if the deficiencies are significant. Once the revised prospectus has been accepted by the commission, it becomes a final prospectus. The securities regulator will then issue a receipt, and the prospectus will be sent for printing. It is at this stage that the issuer and the investment dealer finalize their underwriting contract and meet to set the final price and quantity of shares being issued. Normally, the price is set after the market closes early in the week so that the issue can be sold quickly. As a guideline, the underwriter sets the price assuming that the issue will be at least twice oversubscribed, based on the earlier expressions of interest. In this way, the underwriter hopes that the price will rise above the issue price on the first day of trading. The fact that the price is expected to rise and generate short-run profits to the purchasers is partly why IPOs tend to be oversubscribed. The practice of short-term trading by buying IPOs is referred to as "stagging" the new issue and can be very profitable when many attractive issues come to the market.

### The Fourth Stage: Distribution Period

Once the issue is cleared for sale by the securities regulator, the underwriters go into high gear to convert the expressions of interest into firm sales. This is the beginning of the fourth phase and is formally called the **distribution period**. Its length depends on the nature of the issue. Normally, the underwriter has to write a cheque to the issuer within three days or so of the issue as the issuer delivers the shares to the underwriter. The underwriter is under great pressure to sell the shares as quickly as possible to reduce their risk, while the issuer is under a continuing

**distribution period**   the period after the issue has been cleared for sale by the securities commission, when the underwriters convert the expressions of interest into firm sales

---

[28]It is no longer the practice of the OSC, as it has been in the past, to examine every prospectus in detail.
[29]The prospectus needs to be cleared in each province and territory in which the securities will be sold.

obligation to amend the prospectus if a material change occurs during the distribution period. This obligation continues after the issuer is paid by the underwriter and only finishes when the underwriter has informed the issuer that the shares have been sold. This distribution period usually lasts about a month. During that time, the underwriter is under special restrictions.

The first restriction is that this is the "quiet" period. Essentially, all the relevant information should have been included in the prospectus, so the underwriter and issuer are both prohibited from hyping the stock to help sell it. The investment dealer, in particular, cannot issue an analyst report recommending the shares. Also during this period, the underwriters as a group are normally restricted from reducing the price—otherwise, one member of the group could dump its shares if market conditions deteriorate. Finally, the lead underwriter has the right to trade in the shares to maintain an orderly market and help make the issue successful.[30]

The basic way in which an underwriter supports the share price during the distribution period is through the overallotment option. First, the underwriter will try to sell more shares than are issued and then will not have enough shares to sell if successful. In this case, the underwriter exercises its option and gets more shares from the company. However, under Canadian laws (and the laws of most other countries), investors have a two-day "cooling off" period and can renege on an offer to purchase the shares. Alternatively, if the issue appears to be having trouble, many of the expressions of interest may disappear, and even those investors that honour their commitments may dump the shares if they learn that the issue is in trouble or if they want to take short-term profits.

The underwriter will quickly realize if an issue is in trouble as it makes a market in the stock and sees the selling pressure. Because the underwriter is short the stock, it can buy it back in the open market. This constant buying by the underwriter is what supports the price during the distribution period if the issue is "cold" or if shares are being dumped for short-term profits. If this price support is ineffective, then, after supporting the price, the underwriter will give up and the price will drift (sometimes quickly) lower. The underwriter will then take a loss or try to exercise its *market out* clause at the cost of its reputation.

Remember that all the investment dealer has before it begins selling the shares are expressions of interest. Given the common knowledge that there is a first-day run-up in the share price for IPOs, many investors order more shares than they want to hold for the long term. As a result, the investment dealer faces the risk that these expressions of interest either do not materialize as actual purchases or are quickly sold into the market. To counter this risk, the investment dealer tries to place as much of the issue as possible in the friendly hands of investors that have demonstrated they will honour their commitments and not cut and run. A corollary is that for cold issues, when large-scale institutional purchases dry up, the banking group is forced to turn to the retail or ordinary investor to try to sell the issue. When an investor gets a call from a retail broker selling an IPO, it is often a signal that the issue is cold and institutions have already turned it down.

## IPO Underpricing

One controversial issue in the IPO process is the size of the first-day return earned by investors. If the investment dealer had a fiduciary duty to the issuer to get the best possible price for the issue, then nothing would happen on the issue day. However, the first-day return tends to be very high, meaning that the issuer could have sold at a higher price but, instead, "left money on the table." In other words, the IPO is priced at less than its market value, and the **underpricing** pricing an IPO at less than its market value; it is the difference between the initial offering price and the price on the first day of trading
price on the first day of trading is much higher. This is referred to as **underpricing**. Jay Ritter has surveyed the literature on first-day underpricing in North America versus other countries and reports the first-day returns, shown in **Table 17.1**.

The countries included here were chosen because their capital markets are very similar, based on external capital and English common law. What is of interest is that Canada's first-day return is by far the lowest, at 6.5 percent, and is nearly one-third of first-day returns in the United States. The first-day return of 6.5 percent is the lowest of any of the 52 countries sampled by Ritter except Argentina, Austria, and Russia, where sample sizes were very limited.

When investment dealers are asked why there is relatively little underpricing in Canada, they respond that there is too much competition for business in Canada, and Canadian firms do not

---

[30]This is also the reason that the other members can't sell below the stated price; otherwise, they would be selling to the lead underwriter.

**TABLE 17.1**   Evidence of IPO Underpricing

| Country | Sample | Period | Return (%) |
|---------|--------|--------|-----------|
| Canada | 720 | 1971–2013 | 6.5 |
| United Kingdom | 4,932 | 1959–2012 | 16.0 |
| United States | 12,702 | 1960–2014 | 16.9 |
| Australia | 1,562 | 1976–2011 | 21.8 |
| New Zealand | 242 | 1979–2013 | 18.6 |

**Source:** Adapted from Table 1 in Loughran, Tim, Ritter, Jay R., and Rydqvist, Kristian, "Initial Public Offerings: International Insight" from *Pacific-Basin Finance Journal*, 1994 Vol. 2, pp. 165–199, 2015 by Elsevier.

need to tolerate high underpricing because they want the best price for their shares. In contrast, a number of reasons have been given for the underpricing in the United States, none of them entirely convincing. The most obvious is that it lowers the risk that the underwriter will lose money on the issue. However, this implies that the U.S. investment banks are more powerful than their equivalents in Canada, and although there is anecdotal evidence of this, it is difficult to prove.

Another reason that has been advanced for the high level of underpricing in the United States is the litigious nature of the U.S. economy. If the share price falls, then the risk is high that someone will mount a class action suit against the underwriter for misleading the purchasers. In support of this is the observation that some U.S. law firms specialize in suing underwriters, and they do this routinely if the share price falls by 20 percent shortly after the IPO, which seems to be the magic number. However, these same law firms can sue Canadian firms as well, so this too is not entirely convincing.

It has also been suggested that a well-received public offering paves the way for subsequent offerings by the firm and builds momentum into the share price. However, the relative rarity of equity issues makes this rationale dubious.

Finally, **spinning** has been offered as a reason for high underpricing. In this process, the underwriter allocates IPOs to favoured clients, knowing that they will make a large profit on the first day, making some people very wealthy. Spinning was popular among investment dealers during the Internet bubble, when first-day returns on hot Internet stocks were often more than 100 percent. Allocating IPOs to favourite clients was then essentially a way of bribing them with millions of dollars to get future investment banking business. The bribe was paid at the expense of the issuing firm, which did not receive full value for its securities.

Spinning is obviously unethical. It was severely criticized after the stock market crashed in 2001 and investors became aware of the corruption in the marketing of Internet stocks in the United States during the 1990s. In April 2003, Eliot Spitzer, then the attorney general for New York, reached a global settlement with most of the major U.S. investment banks in which they agreed to pay US$1.4 billion in restitution. Most of the settlement was related to the biased nature of security analyst reports, which were used to pump up Internet and technology stock prices. However, part of the settlement was related to spinning, which became illegal and was banned. In May 2003, Spitzer reached a settlement with Philip Anschutz, former chair of Qwest Communications International, Inc. (Qwest), a major U.S. telecom company. As part of the settlement, Anschutz "disgorged" US$4.4 million in profits on IPO shares he received from Salomon Smith Barney, a major U.S. investment bank. According to Spitzer, the IPO allocations were awarded to Anschutz as a reward for investment banking business from Qwest and were never disclosed.

**spinning**   a process by which the underwriter allocates IPOs to favoured clients, knowing that they will make a large profit on the first day

## Concept Review Questions

1. Briefly discuss the possible motivation for firms to enter into IPOs, and relate these motivations to the five stages of firm development discussed by Myers (1999).

2. List and briefly describe the four basic stages of the IPO process.

3. List and briefly describe some possible reasons for the existence of IPO underpricing.

# Post-IPO Regulation and Seasoned Offerings

**LEARNING OBJECTIVE 17.5**

Explain why continuous disclosure requirements are important for investors and how they affect secondary offerings.

## The Post-IPO Market

After the quiet period has ended, the investment dealer's research analyst can initiate coverage on the company because it is assumed that by this time the prospectus no longer contains all relevant information, and the analyst may add value. In fact, promising analyst coverage of the firm's shares is a key part of the pitch that an investment dealer makes to win investment banking business. The analyst coverage, plus the investment dealer's agreement to make a market in the firm's shares, offers the firm the possibility of enhancing liquidity in its shares and increasing its recognition within the investment community.

Unfortunately, these practices were also taken to excess in the United States during the Internet bubble. In the settlement that Eliot Spitzer extracted from the major U.S. investment banks, he not only stopped the practice of spinning, but also revealed the depth to which research analysts were compromised in their pursuit of investment banking business. It was routine to reward analysts with a share of the investment banking business they brought in, in effect turning research analysts into promoters of the company's stock rather than providers of objective research.

In the settlement reached with Eliot Spitzer, two analysts, Jack Grubman of Salomon Brothers and Henry Blodget of Merrill Lynch, were charged with issuing fraudulent research reports and agreed to pay penalties of US$15 million and US$4 million, respectively. They were both also banned from the securities business for life. The SEC charged Credit Suisse First Boston (CSFB) with issuing fraudulent research on two stocks and producing misleading research on three others. Allegations were made that investment banks paid other investment banks to provide analyst research coverage to avoid the appearance that the "buy" recommendations were coming from within.

The excesses evident in the United States were not evident in Canada, and regulatory changes in the United States have made research analysts independent of investment banking. However, it is obviously difficult to win investment banking business from a company if a research analyst is trashing the stock. Hence, even when a formal separation exists between research and investment banking, it is sensible to discount recommendations from the company's investment dealer, which leaves investors reliant on analysis from the investment dealers who want to win the firm's business in the future and may not know as much about it!

The other holdover from the IPO is that the lock-up period usually lasts around six months. During the Internet boom, share prices tended to dip, sometimes as much as 20 percent, after six months, when the lock-ups expired and insiders sold some of their shares. This was particularly evident for technology and Internet stocks, because insiders usually continued to hold more than 80 percent of the shares—that is, the IPOs were so sought-after at the time that only 20 percent of the shares were sold on the IPO date. Consequently, insiders were under tremendous pressure to diversify their own portfolios by selling shares. To counter this tendency for prices to drop as the lock-ups expired, research coverage was often initiated with buy recommendations at about the six-month mark!

## Continuous Disclosure Requirements

IPOs are not as hot as they were in the late 1990s, so the fraction now held by insiders is usually much less than 80 percent. However, common advice is to be wary of IPOs when the founders are left with a high percentage of the shares, because the market will likely have to absorb some of this supply in the future. After the IPO, people who buy the shares in the secondary market do not get a copy of the prospectus. After all, the information in the prospectus rapidly becomes outdated, so it is of little value to secondary market investors. To remedy this, almost all issuers are required to become **reporting issuers** and provide **continuous disclosure**. The main components of continuous disclosure are the filing of quarterly and annual financial statements, annual information forms (AIFs), and proxy and information circulars.

Although firms normally include full financial statements in their annual report, in Ontario there is no requirement to include all the material normally contained in the AIF. Since 1982, the OSC has required larger firms (i.e., those with a market value greater than $75 million or sales of more than $10 million) to file an AIF complete with a comprehensive management discussion and analysis (MD&A) of its operations. The AIF and MD&A provide prospectus-type disclosure for all larger firms with securities traded in Ontario. Under corporate law, an annual proxy statement has to be filed for the annual general meeting in order to change the company's bylaws and elect members of the BOD, so this is regarded as part of continuous disclosure as well.[31]

Firms are also required to disclose any "material changes" in the affairs of a reporting issuer. Note that material *facts* are also required to be disclosed, but a material *change* is broader and encompasses more than a material fact. A material change can occur even when all the facts are already known. However, the exact definition of a material change is elusive; the interpretation seems to be that investors should know it when they see it.

The OSC requires that firms issue a press release and file a material change report in its System for Electronic Document Analysis and Retrieval (SEDAR), on the OSC's website, as soon as is practical and within 10 days of a material change. It is important that firms cannot selectively disclose facts, not even to industry professionals, such as security analysts. This first became important in the United States, where regulation FD, which stands for **fair disclosure**, mandated that information given to security analysts, such as earnings guidance, had to be made available to all. The result has been a surge in webcasts where analysts ask questions of the company—for example, about its quarterly earnings results. Ordinary investors can now listen to these webcasts and get the same information as the professionals. Checking the section of a company's website for investor relations usually reveals information about upcoming webcasts.

In Canada, selective disclosure became a hot issue in October 2000 after the CFO of Air Canada instructed staff to leave telephone messages on the answering machines at major investment dealers. The messages indicated that Air Canada's upcoming results would be worse than expected. The next day, it released most of this information in a press release, but by then the share price had already dropped. Air Canada paid both the Ontario and Quebec Securities Commissions $500,000 plus costs in restitution. In October 2001, the recommendations of the Crawford Committee on analyst standards led to the formal adoption of FD in Canada.

## Seasoned Offerings and Short-Form Prospectuses

The upshot of these requirements for continuous disclosure is that the preparation of a long-form prospectus for a seasoned equity issue by a reporting issuer is redundant, because the information should be available already. The result has been the development of the **short-form prospectus**. Essentially, any reporting issuer with an existing AIF can issue securities under a short-form prospectus, which indicates the nature and pricing of the securities, omits all corporate information, and incorporates existing documents by reference. As long as the securities are not "novel," they can be cleared by the OSC in a matter of days, so that issues can be brought to market very quickly.[32]

The short-form prospectus has changed the basic way firms raise both debt and equity capital, and it has led directly to the growth of the bought deal, in which the underwriting contract is signed even before the drafting of the preliminary prospectus. The OSC allows this because it knows that the prospectus now includes only details of the offering, rather than of the issuer, and that the prospectus will follow within two days. This allows the investment dealer to market the issue to major institutions and close the transaction usually within two to three days after the

**reporting issuers** issuers that are required to provide continuous information disclosure

**continuous disclosure** the filing of quarterly and annual financial statements, annual information forms, and proxy and information circulars

**fair disclosure** the requirement that all information given to security analysts, such as earnings guidance, be made available to everyone

**short-form prospectus** a document that indicates the nature and pricing of the securities, omits all corporate information, and incorporates existing documents by reference

---

[31]These requirements also explain why investing in small-cap stocks is so risky. The fact is that these companies do not provide the same level of disclosure as reporting issuers, and information asymmetry can be more acute.
[32]Examples of short-form prospectuses are available at www.sedar.com, but long-form prospectuses are now quite rare.

initial discussions with the issuer. Often the investment dealer directly approaches the issuer and tells the issuer that, based on its knowledge of the market, it can raise a certain amount of money. As a result, it is often the investment dealer that initiates the transaction and not the issuer.

To show how dynamic seasoned equity offerings have become, we consider the $180 million in common equity raised by BC Gas in October 2001. BC Gas (now FortisBC Energy Inc.) is primarily a local gas distribution company in the lower B.C. mainland. As a largely regulated utility, there is little unknown about its operations. In late 2001, it bought the gas distribution assets of another utility company on Vancouver Island from Westcoast Energy Inc. To pay for this acquisition on the closing of the deal, BC Gas invited bids from a series of investment dealers and then awarded the underwriting contract to RBC Dominion Securities Inc. (RBCDS) and Scotia Capital Inc. Apart from the standard 4-percent underwriting fee, the underwriters agreed to pay BC Gas $36.15 a share. The only snag was that the closing price for the BC Gas shares was $36.10. That is, the underwriters paid more than the market price for the shares.

The BC Gas financing deal shows how competitive the investment dealer business has become now that the prospectus requirements have been reduced in favour of continuous disclosure. It downplays the importance of the other skills provided by the investment dealer in favour of its raw trading and marketing power. In the BC Gas case, the market was so short of deals that both RBCDS and Scotia Capital were willing to incur a trading loss (because they knew the closing price) and eat into their 4-percent commission, simply to generate activity for their investment dealer teams. The example illustrates how seasoned offerings have developed in Canada to enable larger firms to rapidly access markets to raise capital at a very low cost.

## The Size of the Investment Banking Market

**Investment Industry Association of Canada (IIAC)**   a member-based, professional association that advances the growth and development of the Canadian investment industry

The **Investment Industry Association of Canada (IIAC)** is the organization that represents the 166 investment dealers of the securities industry in Canada. The IIAC raises the financing needed for new and existing businesses and polices the trading practices of its members so that investors can "trade with confidence in open and fair capital markets." IIAC also collects important information that helps investors understand the capital markets and freely distributes this information from its website at www.iiac.ca.

For example, in 2017 the Canadian securities industry raised $5.1 billion in IPOs, a further $77.1 billion in SEOs, and $108.1 billion in corporate bonds. We will discuss why firms issue these different types of securities in the next few chapters, but these data put some flesh on the discussion of the investment banking process. Also in 2017, the Canadian securities industry raised $203.8 billion for federal and provincial governments. Referring back to Chapter 1, this is almost $400 billion in capital that was transferred from lenders (investors) to issuers (borrowers) in 2017 through Canada's capital markets, indicating the vital role played by securities firms in Canada's economy.

### Lessons to Be Learned

During 2008 and 2009, we relearned some old lessons about the securities markets. One of the most fundamental is that, despite extensive securities regulations that intrude into almost all the operations of raising money and trading securities, there are still crooks in the capital market. The Madoff Ponzi scheme came as a shock to many, and the very size of it was a shock even to the U.S. Securities and Exchange Commission, which had actually investigated the firm on several occasions. The fact is that Madoff was part of the establishment and operated by word of mouth and personal recommendations. This very secrecy enhanced his reputation, especially when he did not solicit money himself but

obtained it through feeder funds, which many people invested in, unaware that the funds were actually going to Madoff.

Similarly in Canada, the push on the part of the TSX to gain a market niche as the premier market for resource stocks ran into snags with the Sino-Forest fraud, which to many had eerie similarities to the $6-billion Bre-X fraud of a decade earlier.[33] It is often said that a "rising tide lifts all boats," to which Warren Buffett replied, "You only find out who is swimming naked when the tide goes out." When the tide went out after the financial crisis and the stock market collapsed, more scams came to light than ever before.

[33]Bre-X was a Calgary firm that bought a gold mine in Indonesia in 1993 and by 1995 was announcing record levels of gold reserves. It moved its listing to the TSX, but a soaring stock price collapsed in 1997 when its ore samples were found to be fraudulent.

# Review

## Summary

A prerequisite for understanding corporate financing is understanding the basics of securities and corporate law. Investment bankers (dealers) who assist firms in raising capital must abide by these laws, which severely restrict what they can and cannot do.

In this chapter, we discuss how one of the core problems in raising capital is the existence of information asymmetry—some people have access to privileged information and have a clearer idea of the value of the securities being offered than others do. In the extreme case of fraud, there is a clear asymmetry of information. In fact, it was the existence of fraud in the financial markets that led to the creation of securities commissions and the tight regulation of the offering process. We show how broad the legal definition of a security is, what constitutes a prospectus, and why it takes so much time and effort to raise money through an IPO. In contrast, once the information is available in the capital markets, the requirement for continuous disclosure for larger firms means that secondary offerings (SEOs) and private placements can be accomplished incredibly quickly in today's markets, at very low cost.

## Summary of Learning Objectives

### 17.1 Explain what is meant by "information asymmetries" and how these affect the raising of capital.

The term "information asymmetry" is applied to transactions where the counterparties have differing private information about the asset/good/service being exchanged. Information asymmetry is a significant problem in new issues, since the issuer has much more information about the value of the security than the prospective investor. Information asymmetry can lead to outright fraud, such as when issuers sell worthless securities to investors.

### 17.2 Explain the purpose of securities laws and regulations in the financial markets.

Securities laws are designed to protect investors from being defrauded due to their informational disadvantage. Securities laws require firms to make full, true, and plain disclosure of all material facts—both at the IPO through the prospectus and through continuous disclosure. Securities laws also restrict corporate insiders from trading on the basis of undisclosed material information. These insider trading rules protect investors against information asymmetry.

### 17.3 Explain what a prospectus is, what it contains, and why it is critical for initial public offerings (IPOs).

A prospectus is a formal summary of a security that describes the costs, investment objectives, risks, and performance. There are two types: long form and short form. All material facts about the company must be included in the prospectus. For example, a description of the security being issued, the price of the security, underwriter fees, where the security will be traded, business history, historical financial statements, risk factors, and MD&A (management discussion and analysis). A long-form prospectus is required in all initial public offerings. The extra detail is required since there are no securities analysts writing reports on the company, and the information asymmetry is greatest at this point.

### 17.4 Outline the basic stages in taking a firm public through an initial public offering (IPO) of securities.

There are four basic steps in an IPO:

1. discussion
2. preparation of the preliminary prospectus (red herring)
3. waiting period and road show
4. pricing and distribution

Negotiation of deal type occurs during the preparation stage or during the waiting period.

### 17.5 Explain why continuous disclosure requirements are important for investors and how they affect secondary offerings.

The prospectus protects investors from asymmetric information during the IPO; however, the information becomes stale and does not help investors during subsequent secondary market trading. Continuous disclosure requires firms to file quarterly financial statements and information circulars. Thus, firms must continue to disclose all material information in a full, true, and plain manner. Reporting issuers (who make continuous disclosure) can issue new securities using a short-form prospectus instead of a regular prospectus—this makes the new issue process quicker and cheaper.

## Key Terms

agency theory, p. 17-16
asymmetric information, p. 17-2
banking syndicate, p. 17-18
bearer bonds, p. 17-4
best efforts offering, p. 17-18
bought deal, p. 17-18
continuous disclosure, p. 17-23
dealer syndicate, p. 17-18
disaster "out" clause, p. 17-18
distribution period, p. 17-19
due diligence, p. 17-7
exempt market, p. 17-12
fair disclosure, p. 17-23
firm commitment offering, p. 17-18
"green-shoe" option, p. 17-18

initial public offering (IPO), p. 17-11
Investment Industry Association of Canada (IIAC), p. 17-24
Investment Industry Regulatory Organization of Canada (IIROC), p. 17-9
lead investment dealer, p. 17-18
limit orders, p. 17-19
lock-up period, p. 17-19
long-form prospectus, p. 17-11
market orders, p. 17-19
market "out" clause, p. 17-18
offering memorandum, p. 17-12
overallotment, p. 17-18
Ponzi scheme, p. 17-5
preliminary prospectus, p. 17-17

private equity, p. 17-16
prospectus, p. 17-11
reporting issuers, p. 17-23
rights offering, p. 17-18
Securities and Exchange Commission (SEC), p. 17-9
selling group, p. 17-18
short-form prospectus, p. 17-23
spinning, p. 17-21
spread, p. 17-18
standby offering, p. 17-18
underpricing, p. 17-20
underwrite, p. 17-18
venture capital, p. 17-16
waiting period, p. 17-19

# Questions and Practice Problems

## Multiple Choice Questions

1. **(LO 17.1)** Which of the following statements about due diligence is *false*?

   a. It is designed to ensure the legitimacy of securities offered to the public.

   b. It is designed to ensure that there is no misleading information when companies issue shares.

   c. It is expensive to implement.

   d. There is no cost to implement it.

2. **(LO 17.1)** Which of the following statements about asymmetric information is *false*?

   a. There is asymmetric information between managers and investors.

   b. There is no asymmetric information in financial markets.

   c. A prospectus is designed to reduce information asymmetry in the capital market.

   d. Information asymmetry varies across corporations.

3. **(LO 17.1)** Which of the following statements about Ponzi schemes is *false*?

   a. Such schemes are named after Carlo Ponzi, an Italian born in 1882 who immigrated to the United States.

   b. Ponzi schemes are legal in Canada.

   c. There were cases of Ponzi schemes in the United States.

   d. There were cases of Ponzi schemes in Canada.

4. **(LO 17.2)** Which of these pieces of information is *not* required in an IPO prospectus by the British Columbia Securities Commission?

   a. A description of the securities being issued and who can buy them

   b. The price of the securities, the fees to the investment dealer involved with the distribution, and the net proceeds

   c. The market for the securities—that is, whether they will be traded

   d. The CEO's resume

5. **(LO 17.2)** Which of the following regulators does *not* exist in Canadian securities markets?

   a. Ontario Securities Commission

   b. British Columbia Securities Commission

   c. Federal Securities Commission

   d. Quebec Securities Commission

6. **(LO 17.3)** Which of the following statements is *false*?

   a. An IPO is assumed to have the least information asymmetry.

   b. An IPO is the distribution of securities from the corporation to the investors.

   c. An IPO is the first-time distribution of securities.

   d. "Full, true, and plain" means every material fact has to be disclosed.

7. **(LO 17.3)** The market for non-registered securities is called the:

   a. non-registered market.

   b. secondary market.

   c. primary market.

   d. exempt market.

8. **(LO 17.3)** Which of the following statements about the exempt market is *false*?

   a. "Backdoor underwriting" refers to the practice of slipping securities from the exempt market into the public market.

   b. In the exempt market, the issuer prepares a prospectus too.

**c.** Only if the issuer becomes a reporting issuer can the issuer sell securities in the public market.

**d.** The exemption from prospectus requirement is based on smaller issues, the sophistication of the potential investors, and the risk of the securities.

9. **(LO 17.3)** Which of the following issuers is *not* exempt?

**a.** Government debt issuers

**b.** Financial institution debt issuers

**c.** Securities issued as part of takeovers

**d.** Private firms issuing large amounts of shares

10. **(LO 17.4)** Which of the following statements about public offerings is *false*?

**a.** There are four types of offerings: a best efforts offering, a firm commitment offering, a bought deal, and a standby or rights offering.

**b.** Bought deal offerings and standby offerings are used only for seasoned offerings.

**c.** Most IPOs are best efforts offerings.

**d.** A lead investment dealer and a banking syndicate are involved in larger issues.

11. **(LO 17.4)** Which of the following statements regarding best efforts IPOs is *false*?

**a.** This is the basis under which underwriters commonly take on smaller IPOs.

**b.** The underwriter is on the hook if the entire issue doesn't sell out.

**c.** This type of offering is quite rare due to the uncertainty attached to the process and successful outcome.

**d.** A firm commitment offering might be converted into a best efforts offering based on limited investor interest.

12. **(LO 17.4)** Outline some of the benefits or motivations of a firm going public via an IPO.

13. **(LO 17.5)** Which of the following is *not* a main component of continuous disclosure?

**a.** Filing of quarterly financial statements

**b.** Filing of annual financial statements

**c.** Filing of proxy and information circulars

**d.** Filing of monthly financial statements

14. **(LO 17.5)** Which of the following statements about seasoned offerings is *false*?

**a.** A seasoned offering's prospectus has the same content as the prospectus for an IPO.

**b.** A seasoned offering has less information asymmetry than an IPO.

**c.** A seasoned offering allows the use of a short-form prospectus.

**d.** A seasoned offering is the offering after the firm goes public.

## Practice Problems

### Basic

15. **(LO 17.4)** What is the lock-up period in an IPO?

16. **(LO 17.4)** What is the waiting period in an IPO?

17. **(LO 17.4)** Winnipeg Water & Gas Co. recently issued a series of bonds; the gross proceeds were $25 million. The underwriting fees were 2.8 percent, and additional issuance costs were $150,000.

How much did the company actually receive from the sale? As a percentage of the gross proceeds, what were the total costs of the bond issue?

### Intermediate

18. **(LO 17.1)** In late 2006, Canada Post began issuing "permanent" stamps. Purchased at the current first-class letter rate these stamps may be used indefinitely even if the price of stamps increases. Arthur Ponzarelli (known to his friends as "Ponzi") is always looking to make a quick buck, and he thinks these stamps present a lucrative opportunity. In August 2019, the pre-tax rate on a first-class letter is $0.85. Expecting the price of postage to increase by $0.01 very soon, he decides to "invest" in 100,000 stamps.

**a.** If Canada Post raises the postal rate to $0.86 in September 2019, and Arthur resells his securities (the stamps) at the new price, how much profit will he make?

**b.** To avoid running afoul of securities laws, Arthur decides to sell his stamps to someone in another province and will have to pay $249 for shipping and insurance. Unfortunately, his reputation for shady deals has preceded him, so the purchaser is only willing to pay $0.8525 per stamp. Will Arthur still make a "quick buck"?

**c.** To avoid running afoul of securities laws, Arthur decides to sell his stamps to someone in another province and will have to pay $249 for shipping and insurance. He successfully sells the stamps at $0.86 each. How much money will he make?

19. **(LO 17.2)** State the five major areas in which the Ontario Securities Commission (OSC) is involved.

20. **(LO 17.2)** State three types of distributions of securities determined by the OSC.

21. **(LO 17.3)** Describe three major categories of exempt purchasers.

22. **(LO 17.4)** Describe the basic stages of IPOs.

23. **(LO 17.4)** Why are there no firm orders in a standard underwritten IPO?

24. **(LO 17.4)** What is the "quiet period"?

25. **(LO 17.4)** Describe four different types of public offerings.

26. **(LO 17.4)** Describe the market or disaster "out" clause.

27. **(LO 17.4)** Describe the overallotment or "green-shoe" option.

28. **(LO 17.4)** Why is the lead underwriter allowed to trade in the securities of the IPO firm?

29. **(LO 17.5)** What are continuous disclosure requirements?

30. **(LO 17.4)** Back in their college days, David and Douglas Finn started renting refrigerators to other students for use in their dormitory rooms. Over the years, Finns' Fridges has grown and financed its operations by retaining most of the profits it made. Now, however, the brothers would like to "cash out" by taking the company public through an IPO. Together, the brothers own 500,000 shares and will sell half of their holdings. In addition, the company will issue 250,000 new shares as part of the IPO to provide additional growth financing. What percentage of the firm's shares will the Finns own after the IPO?

31. **(LO 17.4)** If the IPO for Finns' Fridges (see practice problem 30) goes well, the contract with the investment bankers has a "green-shoe" clause that permits them to sell 15 percent more shares than originally planned. These additional shares would all be issued by the company, not sold by the Finn brothers themselves. How much of the firm will the brothers own if this overallotment option is taken up?

## Challenging

**32. (LO 17.4)** Niagara Vineyards and Winery needs to raise $4 million in new equity.

    **a.** If the costs of the share issue are estimated to be 6 percent of gross proceeds, how large does the offering need to be? How much will Niagara pay in flotation costs?

    **b.** If the underwriters give a discount and only charge 5 percent of gross proceeds, how large does the offering need to be? How much will Niagara save on flotation costs?

**33. (LO 17.1)** If the interest rate for non-fraudulent bonds is 8 percent, and chances are that one out of eight bonds is fraudulent, what is the interest rate based on a one-year investment and assuming the market does not require a risk premium?

**34. (LO 17.4)** Little Box Retailers has a market capitalization of $1.5 billion and 60 million shares outstanding selling at $25 a share. The management of Little Box is planning a rights offering to raise further capital to finance their growth. Each shareholder will receive one right for each share held, entitling them to buy one share at a price of $20.

    **a.** How much money will this raise if all shareholders exercise their rights?

    **b.** What will be the price of a share after the rights offering if all shareholders exercise their rights?

**35. (LO 17.4)** Why is IPO underpricing less severe in Canada than it is in the United States? What causes underpricing?

**36. (LO 17.4)** Lansdowne Ltd. needs to raise $20 million and intends to sell additional shares. The company's existing shares are trading on the Toronto Stock Exchange for $54. However, the investment dealer hired by Lansdowne has cited investors' concerns about information asymmetry to justify an offering price of $50 per share. Underwriting costs charged by the investment dealer are 4 percent of the issue price. How many shares must the firm sell to net $20 million? Why does the investment dealer suggest an offering price less than the trading price?

**37. (LO 17.4)** The little company you and your friend started in your parents' garage has grown so much that you are now ready to take the firm public. In your discussions with one of the top investment dealers, you have been given a choice between two alternatives:

Plan I: The investment dealer will underwrite the issue of 1 million shares at $11 per share. There will be an underwriting fee of 7 percent of the gross proceeds.

Plan II: The investment dealer will accept the 1 million shares on a "best efforts" basis. The price will be $12 per share, and it is believed that 95 percent of the shares will be sold. The investment dealer's fee will be $850,000.

What will the net proceeds be under each plan? What will the investment dealer charge under each plan? Which plan should you accept?

**38. (LO 17.4)** Pills4u.com and Drugs-R-Us Co. both sell prescription medications over the Internet. Each company has recently announced an IPO at $20 per share. At this price, one of the companies is undervalued by $3, while the other is overvalued by $2. Unfortunately, you have no way of knowing which is which, as you have no particular expertise in pharmaceuticals or Internet sales. Nonetheless, you plan to buy 1,000 shares of each company's share at the offer price.

    **a.** If you are allocated the full 1,000 shares of each new issue, how much profit will you make when the shares adjust to their true value?

    **b.** If an issue is undervalued, it will be rationed, and you will only get half your order. What profit do you expect in this situation?

    **c.** If an issue is undervalued, it will be rationed, and you will only get one-fifth of your order. What profit do you expect in this situation?

**39. (LO 17.4)** Sous-Chef Inc. is an employment agency that specializes in the restaurant industry. The company intends to sell 800,000 shares in its IPO and the investment dealers working on the issue have been seeking expressions of interest in the shares from various investors (pension plans, mutual funds, and so on). As the dealers sit down with the company's management to price the issue, the "order book" at different prices looks like this:

| Investor | Number of shares | Limit price |
| --- | --- | --- |
| A | 150,000 | $21.00 |
| B | 150,000 | $20.50 |
| C | 200,000 | $20.00 |
| D | 200,000 | $19.25 |
| E | 150,000 | $19.00 |
| F | 350,000 | $18.75 |
| G | 250,000 | $18.50 |
| H | 200,000 | $18.00 |
| I | 150,000 | $17.50 |
| J | 200,000 | $17.00 |

    **a.** What is the highest issue price that the shares can command if all the investors live up to their intentions as shown in the table?

    **b.** Suppose the investment dealers want to set the price so that the issue is two-times oversubscribed. That is, all the shares will sell even if the investors only purchase half the number of shares indicated in the table. At what price should the shares be issued?

    **c.** Assume the IPO was priced at $18.00 and will trade on the Toronto Stock Exchange. If the amount of underpricing is the same as the historical average for Canadian shares, what do you expect the price of the share to be at the end of its first day of trading? What would its price be if the first-day return is the same as what is typically seen in the United States?

# Debt Instruments

**LEARNING OBJECTIVES**

After studying this chapter, you should be able to:

**18.1** Define "debt" and identify the basic features that distinguish debt from equity financing.

**18.2** Identify and describe the different types of short-term debt issued in the money market.

**18.3** Describe the types of debt financing provided by banks.

**18.4** Identify the requirements that must typically be satisfied for public debt issues.

**18.5** Explain how debt ratings are determined, what they mean, and how useful they are in predicting default and recovery rates associated with public debt issues.

In Chapter 17, we described the steps involved in raising capital and the role of securities regulation in protecting the public through mandatory disclosure. However, no matter how much information is disclosed, investors will disagree on the interpretation of that information and will view the firm's prospects differently. Consequently, they will invest in different types of securities. In this chapter, we discuss the implications for debt securities, one of the two classic types of securities. In Chapter 19, we will discuss the implications for equity securities, the second classic type of security, and so-called hybrids, which are part debt and part equity.

## 18.1 What Is Debt?

**LEARNING OBJECTIVE 18.1**

Define "debt" and identify the basic features that distinguish debt from equity financing.

Debt is a contract between a lender and a borrower that stipulates the terms of repayment of the loan. As a contract, these terms are limited only by the imagination of the contracting parties. However, a critical component is that the interest on debt securities is fully deductible for tax purposes by the borrower (payer or issuer) and fully taxable for the lender (recipient or investor). As a result, one of the major factors determining whether or not a security is debt is its treatment by the Canada Revenue Agency (CRA). In this sense, debt is what the CRA accepts as debt for tax purposes. We will see that many factors determine whether a firm issues debt or equity securities or some form of hybrid, but tax consequences are always a factor.

It might seem obvious what debt is. After all, many of us have borrowed money from friends, relatives, or financial institutions. For example, you might borrow $1,000 at 10-percent interest and agree to pay the loan back in one year's time. In this case, you have to pay back $1,100 at the end of the year; 10-percent interest is the cost of "renting" the $1,000 in principal for the year. In this way, the 10-percent interest rate is the cost of borrowing money.

**fixed contractual commitments** contractual terms that commit the parties involved to adhere to specific requirements

All of this is straightforward, but it is important to point out that the interest cost and principal repayment are **fixed contractual commitments**, and failing to honour them has serious implications that we discuss later. The fact that the principal and interest payments are fixed contractual commitments is the essential difference between debt and equity. With equity, an investor is an owner, shares in the profits of the business, and has no "contractual" rights because equity is not a contract in the way that debt is. Instead, a shareholder owns a share in the business and, as an owner, has the rights allocated in the company's articles of incorporation and bylaws (discussed in Chapter 2) as well as in the general provisions of corporate and securities laws. However, shareholders do not have a specific contract that details the cash flows they can expect to receive from the investment. An owner is a "residual claimant," which means that they get what is left after all the firm's contractual commitments have been met.

The fact that payments on debt are a fixed contractual commitment puts them in the same category as the firm's rental payments on property, its wage bill to its workforce, and its other business expenses. They are legitimate costs of doing business and are tax deductible. In contrast, equity costs are not a cost of doing business in the same sense. Instead, they represent returns to the *owners* of the business after the company has paid all its legitimate expenses. As such, equity securities are treated differently for tax purposes. By investigating this difference, we can understand why and how debt and equity securities differ.

Suppose, for example, that a firm has $10 million in assets and expects to generate 10 percent of this amount (or $1 million) in earnings before interest and tax (EBIT). If the corporate tax rate is 30 percent, then the firm will pay $300,000 in tax, assuming it makes no interest payments. However, if the firm borrows $5 million at 7 percent, it will have a $350,000 interest expense deduction, reducing its taxable income to $650,000 and its tax bill to $195,000. The firm's tax bill drops by $105,000 because of its decision to finance part of its operations with debt instead of equity. The calculations are shown here.

|  | No Debt ($) | $5 Million in Debt ($) |
|---|---|---|
| EBIT | 1,000,000 | 1,000,000 |
| Interest | 0 | 350,000 |
| Taxable income | 1,000,000 | 650,000 |
| Tax (30%) | 300,000 | 195,000 |
| Net income | 700,000 | 455,000 |

Of the $350,000 in interest expense paid by the firm, only 70 percent, or $245,000, is actually paid by the owners of the firm; the other 30 percent, or $105,000, is paid through a reduction in income taxes remitted to the government. We can see this in the fact that net income has dropped by only $245,000 despite the increased interest payments of $350,000.

This simple example highlights a very important point: the firm's net cost for using debt is the after-tax cost. In our example, this was the 7-percent interest rate multiplied by one minus the tax rate $(1 - 0.3)$ or 70 percent. This gives the debt cost as 4.9 percent. Generally, we can use Equation 18.1 to determine this **after-tax cost of debt (k)**.

**after-tax cost of debt (k)** the net cost to the firm for using debt, calculated as the before-tax interest cost of the firm's debt multiplied by one minus the corporate tax rate

$$k = k_d(1 - T)$$ [18.1]

In Equation 18.1, $k_d$ is the before-tax interest cost of the firm's debt, and $T$ is the corporate tax rate.

We will generically use $k$ as the yield, or required return, that the investor wants on a security and indicate what type of security it is by using subscripts; in this case, the subscript is $d$, indicating debt.

This discussion illustrates a basic rule: if a business is taxable, it makes sense to correctly identify all legitimate costs of doing business, because these reduce the taxable income and thus the tax bill. For corporations, it means they legitimately try to ensure that their financing costs are tax deductible, because it reduces their income taxes. Conversely, the CRA has to make sure that the *Income Tax Act* is enforced and that firms take only legitimate deductions for genuine debt securities.

The CRA uses three basic tests to make sure that the interest on debt is tax deductible:

1. Interest is compensation for the use or retention of money owed to another.

2. Interest must be referable to a principal sum.

3. Interest accrues from day to day.

These criteria make sense. Using the example of a $1,000 loan again, the $1,000 is the principal sum, and the interest of 10 percent is referable back to that principal to get the $100 in interest. If the loan is paid off late, the borrower would expect to pay more than $100 in interest, because they have rented the principal for a longer time. This is the way in which the interest accrues as the loan is outstanding: the longer the loan is outstanding, the more interest is paid. However, as simple as this appears to be, a huge amount of litigation has been involved in deciding whether these three factors actually hold for a particular security.

For example, Stephen Richardson shows that the second requirement (i.e., that interest is referable to a principal sum) dates to a Supreme Court of Canada decision concerning the *Saskatchewan Farm Security Act* of 1944.[1] At that time, the Province of Saskatchewan wanted to reduce the debt burden faced by its farming community. It could not waive interest payments because they are a federal responsibility and are stipulated in the federal *Income Tax Act*. Therefore, the province passed a law reducing the principal value associated with the required interest payments but stipulated that the interest payments would not be reduced, even though the principal value was. Effectively, the reduction in principal payments was set so that it would offset the interest paid, thereby removing the burden of the interest payments and helping Saskatchewan farmers. However, the Supreme Court of Canada ruled that the interest payments could no longer be regarded as interest, because the principal sum was being reduced and the interest had to be tied back to this principal.

This is a typical pattern in finance. "Innovative" financing vehicles are created to exploit the wording in the *Income Tax Act* in an attempt to make things appear to be debt, and tax deductible, when they really are not. As the Saskatchewan example highlights, this isn't just a corporate or personal activity; governments do it as well.[2] It may take years for the CRA to dissect an income statement and challenge a deduction, but when it does respond, the matter often ends up in tax court. The courts rule on whether these securities comply with the definitions of interest and the intent of the *Income Tax Act*. If the deduction is disallowed, the loophole is then closed until clever financiers find another way to do the same thing. However, before we talk about some of the "grey area" securities between debt and equity, we will consider "plain vanilla" debt securities. First, we will discuss short-term debt.

---

## Concept Review Questions

1. Distinguish debt from equity.
2. Explain how to estimate the after-tax cost of debt.
3. What three characteristics does the CRA look for to determine whether interest payments are tax deductible?

---

[1]Richardson, Stephen, "New Financial Instruments: A Canadian Tax Perspective." In *New Financial Management* (Toronto: Canadian Tax Foundation, 1993).

[2]Another example of provincial activity was the sale and leaseback of Ontario's GO Transit rolling stock. The provincial government, as a non-taxable entity, cannot use any tax shields. However, by selling the rolling stock to a private enterprise that can use the tax shields, and then leasing the equipment back at a favourable rate, the province gained at the expense of the federal government.

# Short-Term Debt and the Money Market

---

**LEARNING OBJECTIVE 18.2**

Identify and describe the different types of short-term debt issued in the money market.

---

We will discuss different types of debt in this chapter, but two key features are the maturity of the debt—that is, how long until the debt has to be repaid—and whether the debt is marketable and can be traded in a secondary market. We start with the most debt-like of all debt securities, which is short-term debt, since the probability of being repaid in full without any loss in value is generally highest for this type of debt.

## Government Treasury Bills

**promissory note** a written promise to pay back a loan

The simplest sort of debt contract is one that most of us have made by lending friends a few dollars and telling them to pay us back next week. This is obviously a loan, but it is not backed by anything other than the friend's promise to repay in a week's time. If this promise is documented in a written contract that says, "I promise to pay $X to YYY on April 30," the contract is a security called a **promissory note**. The next time a friend borrows money from you, get them to sign such a note; you will have created the most basic type of financial security and will be on your way to becoming a financier!

**treasury bill (T-bill)** a promissory note issued by a government treasury department

Governments issue such short-term promissory notes, which are generically called **treasury bills (T-bills)**, because the promise is issued by the treasury department of the government. Generally, any debt instrument with a maturity of less than a year is called a "bill" or "paper"; if it matures in one to seven years it is called a "note," and if it has a maturity of more than seven years it is a "bond." All the bills and short-term paper outstanding are generically referred to as the money market.

As of the end of December 2018, the Government of Canada had issued $130 billion in T-bills. The standard reference point in the money market is the 91-day federal government T-bill. The implicit interest rate for this is commonly referred to as "the" T-bill yield. However, the Government of Canada sells T-bills of varying maturities up to one year, depending on its financing needs. It does this by auctioning off a stock of bills and requiring government securities dealers to place minimum bids on these securities.

The Bank of Canada acts as the Government of Canada's fiscal agent in selling these securities and maintaining an orderly auction market. It does this by requiring that all orders for T-bills be submitted through government securities distributors (GSDs) and by dividing orders into "competitive" and "non-competitive" bids. Competitive bids are orders to buy securities at a particular price at the auction, whereas non-competitive bids are orders to buy them at the average price determined in the auction. A special group of GSDs, the largest and most active dealers, are called "primary dealers" and are given preferential treatment because of their importance to the implementation of monetary policy.[3] These primary dealers then have to bid for a certain amount of T-bills at each auction. The Bank of Canada sets special limits on how much of the auction each dealer can buy to avoid market manipulation.[4]

As of December 2018, the primary dealers in the treasury bill market were the Bank of Montreal, Canadian Imperial Bank of Commerce, Desjardin Securities Inc., HSBC Bank

---

[3]The Bank of Canada controls interest rates by buying and selling treasury bills and moving government deposits around, and the dealers are important for these processes. At the end of December 2018, the Bank of Canada held just under $25 billion of the $130 billion in T-bills outstanding.

[4]These new procedures were introduced when the number of dealers declined in response to reduced government financing requirements. In particular, three major U.S. dealers withdrew from the Canadian auction in 2001 as there simply wasn't enough government borrowing.

Canada, Laurentian Bank Securities Inc., Merrill Lynch Canada Inc., National Bank Financial Inc., RBC Dominion Securities Inc., Scotia Capital Inc., and the Toronto-Dominion Bank. As is to be expected, this group is dominated by the Big Six integrated Canadian banks.[5]

As discussed in Chapter 6, T-bills, like most money market instruments, are normally sold on a discount basis. This means that the Bank of Canada might auction off $500 million in T-bills, but the bills do not pay a specific interest rate. Instead, they are sold at a discount to their par value, and the "interest" is earned by the investor being paid the full par value at the maturity date. For example, suppose that, in an auction, the winning bid for a $1,000 par value, 91-day T-bill is $990.099. The interest is the difference between the market price of $990.099 and the $1,000 paid back by the government in 91 days, or $9.901. This means the 91-day interest rate is 1 percent, which we can calculate as

$$990.099 = \frac{1,000}{(1 + k)}$$

We do not deal with T-bill yields and pricing in great detail here because we did so in Chapter 6; however, we can see that if we solve for $k$, it is 1 percent, because $1,000/(1.01) = $990.099. In order to establish interest rates, this 1 percent is converted to an annual rate by multiplying by the number of 91-day periods in a year, which means the rate would be quoted as 4.011 percent (i.e., 1% × 365/91).[6] Most money market issues are traded on a discount basis, but some commercial paper is issued in interest-bearing form.[7]

Although the federal government's T-bill auction plays a pivotal role in the money market, there are other T-bills outstanding. The larger provinces, particularly Ontario and Quebec, sell T-bills through the major investment dealers, as do some of the larger government enterprises and municipalities. As of the end of December 2018, there was approximately $60 billion in outstanding T-bills and their equivalents issued by the provinces and their enterprises.

## Commercial Paper

For corporate financing, companies can issue **commercial paper (CP)**, an instrument that is similar to T-bills. Unlike T-bills, however, CP is normally issued with maturities of 30 and 60 days, rather than 91 days. One major problem with CP is that corporations have credit risk: they may default on their obligation to pay investors back in 30 or 60 days. This is a major problem for all corporate debt obligations, but it is particularly acute for CP because it is almost always unsecured, which means the investor has no underlying assets to seize in the event of a default. Further, the dollar amounts involved are frequently very large, for reasons we will come to shortly.

To understand the importance of credit risk, consider a 30-day, interest-bearing CP issue (instead of a discount issue) of $100 million with the same interest rate as the T-bill yield of 6 percent (or approximately 0.5 percent per 30 days). However, now there is a 1-percent chance of the CP issuer defaulting. If it does, the investor gets nothing. We represent this in **Figure 18.1**.

Because money market instruments are quoted on an approximate interest rate basis, the 6-percent annual rate translates to 0.5 percent per month (i.e., 6%/12). On a $100-million investment, if the issuer does not default, the investor gets $100.5 million after one month; if the issuer defaults, the investor gets nothing. The investor has a 99-percent chance of getting $100.5 million and a 1-percent chance of getting $0; the average of these two, or the expected payoff, is $99.495 million (i.e., 0.99 × $100.5 + 0.01 × $0). If this expected payoff is discounted back for one month at 0.5 percent, the $100-million CP is worth only $99 million (i.e., $99.495 million/1.005).

**commercial paper (CP)** short-term debt instruments, usually unsecured, issued by companies

---

[5]The Bank of Canada's website, www.bankofcanada.ca, is the critical source of information on government debt markets.

[6]There are many quoting conventions. One of the most common in the United States is to treat each month as if it had 30 days. Thus, when the U.S. government issues 90-day treasury bills, not 91-day as in Canada, the annual rate is exactly four times the quarterly rate.

[7]For tax purposes, the CRA regards the increase from the purchase price to the par value as interest and not capital gains, because the "gain" is locked in at the time of purchase.

**FIGURE 18.1** Commercial
**Paper Payoffs**

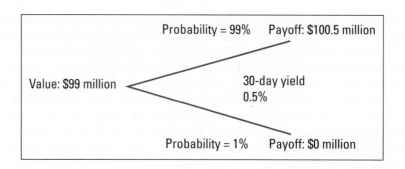

**promised yields** the quoted
interest rates received if the issuer
does not default and the investor
is paid off on time, as promised

This example illustrates an important point: the quoted interest rates are called **promised yields**. They are the rates investors would get if the issuer does not default and they are paid off on time, as promised. For Canadian government issues, where there is virtually no default or credit risk, these promised yields are also expected rates of return. However, for corporate issues, which have default risk, the expected rate of return is always *lower* than the promised yield because the promised yield is the maximum rate the investor can hope to earn by holding the security to maturity.

In our example, the company could not issue $100 million of CP at the T-bill yield of 6 percent, because if it did, the CP would be worth only $99 million. Instead, to raise the $100 million, the company would have to increase the promised yield higher than the default-free T-bill yield. The value of the 30-day CP issue can be found using Equation 18.2.

$$V = \frac{PAR(1+R)P + RECOVER(1-P)}{(1+k)}$$ [18.2]

In this equation, par or promised value (PAR) is $1,000, $R$ is the promised yield, $P$ is the probability of not defaulting, $(1-P)$ is the probability of defaulting, RECOVER is the recovery rate if the company defaults, and $k$ is the investor's required return.

In our example, we simplified this equation by setting RECOVER equal to zero and the investor's required rate of return equal to the T-bill yield. If we continue with these assumptions, we can find the promised yield necessary for the CP to be issued at PAR—that is, PAR = $V$:

$$R = \frac{(1+k_{TB})}{P} - 1$$ [18.3]

where $k_{TB}$ is the required return for investing in T-bills. In the absence of default risk ($P = 1$), the promised yield on CP would be the same as that on T-bills. However, with the 1-percent chance of default, the promised yield has to be 1.515 percent per month (i.e., 1.005/0.99 − 1) or 18.2 percent per year (i.e., 1.515% × 12).

**default** or **credit yield spread**
the difference between the yield
on a default-risky debt instrument
and the yield on an equivalent-
maturity Government of Canada
instrument

The difference between the promised yield on CP and the yield on the equivalent-maturity T-bill is called the **default** or **credit yield spread**. In this case, given a 1-percent chance of default, the yield spread is 12.2 percent (i.e., 18.2% to 6%). The 12.2-percent yield spread is compensation for the fact that if the CP defaults, the investor gets nothing. Obviously, as the probability of default goes up, $P$ goes down and the yield spread increases. The important point to note from this example is the huge impact that default risk has on promised yields. Even if the risk of default drops from 1 percent to 0.1 percent, the monthly promised yield for CP is still 0.6 percent (versus 0.5 percent) for a yield spread of 1.2 percent annually.

For reference purposes, as of December 31, 2018, the yields on three-month T-bills and "prime" CP were 1.64 percent and 2.21 percent, respectively, resulting in a yield spread of 0.57 percent. This indicates the extremely low default risk attached to prime CP in Canada.[8] This yield spread had a volatile ride during the financial crisis of 2008–9, for reasons we will

---

[8]Or it indicates the extremely high recovery rates in the event of default.

discuss shortly. However, it indicates that the actual risk of investing in CP is extremely low, so only the best companies can access the CP market. This is because assessing default risk requires time as well as analytic skills. This outlay may be worthwhile when investing for a long period, but few investors are inclined to do this analysis for an investment with a three-month maturity or less. In this sense, investors in the paper market are not so much investing as simply "parking" money for a short period of time. However, as we noted, default risk does have a huge impact on yields. To solve this problem, the market has developed alternative risk-assessment measures. Credit rating agencies have developed the most basic measure, which provides default or credit ratings to investors, thereby relieving investors of the need to do individual analyses.

The most important credit rating agency in Canada is the Dominion Bond Rating Service (DBRS). Two U.S. rating agencies, Moody's and Standard & Poor's (S&P), also provide ratings on Canadian firms, although they mainly provide ratings on longer-term issues, particularly those issued in the U.S. market, rather than money market instruments. However, S&P, in particular, has evolved into a major competitor to DBRS since it took over the Canadian Bond Rating Service (CBRS) in 2001.

DBRS rates CP, longer-term bonds, and preferred shares and has separate rating categories for each. Generally, the ratings are very similar, but sometimes the short-term risk of investing in CP is less than the longer-term risk of investing in the same company's long-term bonds, so the ratings may differ slightly.

For CP, DBRS has three basic rating categories:

R-1 Prime credit quality
R-2 Adequate credit quality
R-3 Speculative

Within these categories, DBRS adds sub-ratings of high, mid, and low, so R-1 (high) is the highest rating, while R-3 (low) is the lowest. In practice, these rating categories are moot to some extent, because as of April 2017, the bulk of CP is usually rated R-1 (mid) or above. In fact, the limited amount of R-2 (high) was a recent phenomena resulting from the strong Canadian economy, as in the previous year there had been none outstanding. The actual percentage distribution of CP by rating category is shown in **Table 18.1**.

The two rating groups are for CP issued by companies and CP issued as securitizations. We will discuss these latter issues later in this chapter and again when we talk about working capital management in Chapter 24. However, the important point is that relatively little CP has been issued in the Canadian market with other than a prime R-1 rating. This is important since even R-2 is rated adequate quality or "investment" grade.

The distribution of DBRS CP ratings confirms the fact that the CP market is accessible only to firms with the best credit ratings. However, even with these firms, investors are wary of investing in CP unless the companies have **liquidity support**, ensuring that money will be available to pay off the CP if the firms cannot roll it over by selling to new investors. Liquidity support is usually a dedicated backup line of credit from a bank. The firm can draw on the credit line to pay off the CP if needed when it comes due. The commitment fee to establish a bank line of credit for liquidity support is about 0.125 percent per year, but varies with credit market conditions, which adds to the overall cost for a company issuing CP. We will discuss these facilities shortly when we discuss bank financing.

CP is sold directly from the dealing rooms by the major investment banks. The trading or dealing room is a huge room with areas or desks allocated for selling different securities;

**liquidity support** money available to pay off a debt, often in the form of a dedicated backup line of credit from a bank, which ensures that companies have money to pay off the CP if the firms cannot roll it over by selling to new investors

| TABLE 18.1 | Distribution of CP by DBRS Rating Category |
|---|---|
| **Type** | **Total (%)** |
| R-1 (high) | 26.1 |
| R-1 (mid) | 15.4 |
| R-1 (low) | 49.7 |
| R-2 (high) | 8.8 |

each desk is flanked by a series of computer screens. The "money market desk" is an area in which traders sell CP. The traders call major institutional investors and sell them the CP that the bank has arranged to sell on behalf of its clients. Usually the bank charges 0.125 percent as a selling commission, but this is often bid down, depending on market conditions. CP is usually sold on the basis of its credit rating, and an investor will ask, "What do you have R-1 (low)?" This is why the credit ratings are so important because, to a large extent, all the R-1 (low) issues are interchangeable when you are investing for only a month or two.

## Bankers' Acceptances (BAs)

**bankers' acceptances (BAs)**
short-term paper sold by an issuer to a bank, which guarantees or accepts it, obligating the bank to pay off the debt instrument at maturity if the issuer defaults

If an issuer does not have a good enough credit rating to access the CP market, it is forced to rely more heavily on its bank for financing. One way of doing this is to have its bank guarantee or "accept" its commercial paper by selling the CP to the bank, which then stamps "accepted" on it and sells it from its own money market desk. These accepted CP issues are called **bankers' acceptances (BAs)**. If the issuer defaults, the bank will pay off the CP at maturity, thereby converting the instrument's credit status into that of the major bank that guarantees it.

In many countries, including the United States, BAs are created as a result of international trade. Typically, an exporter will receive a "bill of exchange" in return for the export of its goods. This bill of exchange is essentially a promissory note issued by the foreign importer, usually guaranteed by its local bank. The exporter will then have this note accepted by its own bank so the note can be sold for cash. This is how BAs are created in the United States and many other countries, but BAs in Canada have nothing to do with trade. They are a method by which lower-rated companies can issue short-term paper into the money market.

BAs trade as bank CP. Because most Canadian banks are rated R-1 (mid), BA yields are usually marginally lower than prime commercial paper, which is generally a mixture of R-1 (low) and R-1 (mid). However, this is not currently the case. As of December 31, 2018, yields on T-bills, BAs, and CP were as shown in Table 18.2.

As we can see, the yields on CP and BAs were very close, with prime commercial paper slightly lower than the yield on BAs. This is somewhat unusual, but reflected the large cash holdings of Canadian corporations, which were buying rather than selling commercial paper.

In terms of the cost to a firm, issuing CP involves the actual interest cost plus the bank fees. These fees typically include the issuing or dealing fee of 0.125 percent and the cost of a line of credit of 0.125 percent, so the total cost of issuing three-month CP as of December 31, 2018, would be about 2.21 percent plus typically 0.25 percent and any other incidental fees. These incidental fees consist of the costs of computer screens and data services, part of the time the firm devotes to managing the issue, and the administrative costs charged for registering and redeeming the securities. In total, the cost of a CP issue is usually the CP yield plus another 0.375 percent, but the cost varies with the state of the money market. In contrast, a firm's cost for issuing BAs is the yield on the BA plus the bank's stamping or acceptance fee. This fee is usually 0.5 to 0.75 percent, depending on the credit risk involved. So taking these fees into account, the total cost of financing with BAs or CP on December 31, 2018, was about 2.75 to 3.0 percent. CP tends to be significantly cheaper for the largest creditworthy companies that do not need 100-percent backup from a line of credit and that raise significant amounts of money.

| TABLE 18.2 | Yields on T-Bills, BAs, and CP (December 31, 2018) | |
|---|---|---|
| **Type** | **1-Month (%)** | **3-Month (%)** |
| T-bills | 1.63 | 1.64 |
| BAs | 2.25 | 2.24 |
| CP | 2.22 | 2.21 |

**TABLE 18.3**   **Canadian Money Market (June 2019)**

|  | $Billion |
|---|---|
| Corporate commercial paper | 31.2 |
| Securitizations | 33.0 |
| BAs | 95.1 |
| Provincial T-bills | 64.7 |
| Canada T-bills | 134.9 |
| Total | 358.9 |

Overall, as of June 2019, the Canadian money market consisted of the amounts outstanding shown in **Table 18.3**.

With $358.9 billion of securities, most with a maturity of one to three months, there is a huge amount of money turning over every day as most of the debt is simply renewed by issuing new securities. The money market is therefore a huge liquid market of short-term securities that are regarded as virtually default free and very safe. However, if that promise to repay becomes doubtful, the market evaporates in a hurry, which is what happened starting in July 2007. **Figure 18.2** shows the default yield spreads for both BAs and CP starting before the financial crisis developed. These spreads were at 15 basis points in January 2007, but jumped in August when the Canadian money market was rocked by the revelation that some commercial paper was backed by securities linked to U.S. sub-prime mortgages.

The financial crisis first became apparent in July 2007, when a prominent U.S. investment bank, Bear Stearns, revealed that two of its hedge funds were almost worthless because their underlying assets, tied to U.S. sub-prime mortgages, had lost significant value. These two failures initiated a hunt for U.S. sub-prime exposure in Canadian securities, and on August 13, 2007, Coventree, a major manager of asset-backed commercial paper (ABCP), was unable to refinance its maturing paper. In short order, the ABCP market in Canada "froze up" as investors refused to buy new securities to replace those maturing.

ABCP is an example of the "securitizations" that we mentioned previously. We will discuss how these are used in Chapter 24, but, in essence, ABCP consists of commercial paper issued not by a specific company but by a special-purpose vehicle (SPV), with the CP paid from the proceeds of the underlying assets in the SPV. Typically, the underlying assets are things

**FIGURE 18.2**   **Money Market Spreads in Basis Points (1/100 of a Percent)**

**Source:** Data from Bank of Canada, www.bankofcanada.ca/rates/interest-rates; CANSIM V121812, V121778, and V121775

like car loans, mortgages, or other short-term debts owed to companies. These loans are sold to the SPV, which finances their purchase by issuing CP. The advantage is that investors in the CP are not at risk from other corporate activities; they are simply at risk of the loans not being paid off. This risk is usually reduced by various credit enhancement techniques, so ABCP is given a high credit rating by DBRS and can easily be sold.

This changed on August 13, 2007, when Coventree indicated that a small percentage of the underlying assets of the ABCP it managed was backed by debt obligations linked to U.S. sub-prime mortgages. As indicated earlier, a mere hint of default is enough to cause promised yields on debt to increase dramatically. In this case, as the ABCP came due, investors demanded their money back and refused to finance new issues of ABCP. This meant Coventree and others were forced to pay off the ABCP, with no cash coming in from new issues. In this liquidity crisis, Coventree called on its banks to honour their liquidity agreements, but they refused, for reasons we will discuss shortly. The result was a freeze in the ABCP market, and $32 billion of ABCP instantly went from being liquid commercial paper to totally illiquid securities of questionable value as investors shied away from anything that could be linked to U.S. sub-prime debt.

Default spreads on CP and BAs remained high after August 2007 as, first, Bear Stearns was bailed out by the U.S. government in March 2008 when it verged on bankruptcy, and then Lehman Brothers was allowed to fail on September 14, 2008, when the U.S. government decided it could not bail out yet another investment bank. The failures of two major U.S. investment banks caused investors around the world to wonder who was next and to retreat from any form of risk. This forced drastic actions on the part of the U.S. government to calm the markets, and gradually money market spreads returned to normal, where they have been for the past several years. However, this shows that the money market is usually a very boring market punctuated by periods of extreme panic.

---

### Concept Review Questions

1. Explain how interest is received on most money market instruments.
2. Contrast treasury bills, commercial paper, and BAs in terms of who issues them, their basic structure and default risk, and the yields they provide.
3. Define yield spreads and explain how they arise.

---

## 18.3 Bank Financing

### LEARNING OBJECTIVE 18.3
Describe the types of debt financing provided by banks.

In short-term financing, the chartered banks are important. For example, when issuing CP, most firms are required to have a backup line of credit to ensure that, in the event of a disruption in the money market, funds are available to pay off the CP.[9] However, the line of credit is not generally available if the credit condition of the company or security deteriorates, and that credit condition is reviewed continually by the bank. This is why the banks refused to honour their liquidity support when Coventree called on them after announcing that its ABCP was backed in part by assets linked to U.S. sub-prime debt. In the banks' view, Coventree's problem

---

[9]Sometimes external factors, such as an unexpected major default, cause investors to stop buying CP, even though the credit status of an issuer is unchanged.

was not caused by external factors—that is, a market disruption—but by a deterioration in the credit quality of Coventree's ABCP.

Whether the banks were right in not honouring their liquidity support hinges on whether investor refusal to buy new issues of ABCP was due to a deterioration in credit quality or a general flight to quality that affected all of the CP market. This question was the subject of significant litigation, since hundreds of millions of dollars were frozen for many years, but the fact is that other areas of the CP market operated normally. However, the Coventree example reinforces the critical role of the banks in the money market. We have already seen that if a CP issuer wants an unconditional guarantee from a bank, the issuer can have the CP guaranteed so it becomes a BA. This costs 50 to 75 basis points, because the bank is then exposed to credit risk. The Office of the Superintendent of Financial Institutions (OSFI) requires that banks provide the right amount of capital when making such guarantees, since they are not costless.

However, the CP and BA markets are useful only for companies that have reasonably large and continuous financing needs because CP and BAs are sold in large amounts, usually at least $1 million. For smaller, irregular-sized financing requirements, firms rely more on traditional bank financing. These consist of term loans and lines of credit.

## Lines of Credit (LCs)

We have already mentioned **lines of credit (LC)** in our discussion of CP. The different types of LCs are a basic financing tool provided by banks. The standard type is an **operating** or **demand LC**. These are lending facilities that are made available by the bank for the firm's operating purposes—they generally cannot be used to back up a CP program. Technically, operating LCs are demand loans that can be cancelled at any time. However, in practice, banks are reluctant to do anything that might trigger financial problems for a firm, because this might leave them legally liable for damages. In structure, an LC is a loan for a maximum dollar amount that the firm can draw down by electronically transferring funds from the operating line to its chequing (or current) account.

The standard cost of the operating line is the **prime lending rate**. Prime is an example of a **floating interest rate** because it changes regularly, so the cost of a firm's demand loan will float with the bank's prime lending rate. This, in turn, is linked to the Bank of Canada's monetary policy and the overnight rate. As prime changes, the bank will inform the firm of the change in the cost of its loan for the upcoming month. Whereas CP costs just under 3.0 percent as of December 31, 2018, the prime rate at most Canadian banks was 3.70 percent, or significantly more. This is why the major banks will make loans available to their most creditworthy customers at rates below prime, particularly if they are large enough to access the money market, since otherwise this is what they will do, taking their business away from the banks. However, most small to medium-sized firms are "prime plus" borrowers, so borrowing rates are quoted as prime plus 0.5 percent, prime plus 1 percent, and so on.

The second type of bank line of credit adds more stability to the firm. This is the **term** or **revolving LC**. The term is usually at least 364 days and can be as long as five years, renewable every six months. Often a five-year "revolver" is renewed at the end of each year, making it an "evergreen" five-year line of credit. Because the revolver is a commitment of credit, the bank has to provide capital against these commitments to ensure the liquidity of the bank. These LCs are commonly for 364 days because more capital is required against a one-year or 365-day LC.

Revolving LCs are flexible financing tools for both the bank and the firm. In addition to being used to provide straight borrowings, they are also used to back up CP programs or other commitments, such as forward foreign currency contracts. However, banks have tightened up on the potential uses for these bank LCs, observing the general principle that lines of credit are for "liquidity" and not "credit enhancement" purposes. This means that the bank will withdraw or adjust the line of credit if a "material adverse change" occurs—that is, if the credit quality of the firm deteriorates. The LC provides the firm with liquidity that it can draw down only if its credit quality is constant. The Office of the Superintendent of Financial Institutions (OSFI), which regulates the banks, monitors lines of credit to make sure that they are used for liquidity purposes. What the OSFI is worried about is the possibility that a deterioration in credit quality could cause large numbers of firms with poor credit to suddenly draw down their lines of credit, thus endangering the stability of the banking system.

**line of credit (LC)** a basic financing tool provided by banks that establishes a loan with a specified limit to a firm based on its creditworthiness

**operating** or **demand LC** lending facilities that are made available by the bank for the firm's operating purposes and that generally cannot be used to back up a CP program; these demand loans can be cancelled at any time

**prime lending rate** the interest rate banks use to calculate their other interest rates; it is also the standard cost of an operating line of credit

**floating interest rate** an interest rate that changes regularly

**term** or **revolving LC** a line of credit extended by a bank to a firm for a specific amount that automatically adjusts as payments are made or received

Firms have to meet a variety of restrictions to maintain access to the funds in an LC. Typically, the maximum value of the LC is determined by using a standard formula—for example, that it cannot exceed 75 percent of a company's receivables plus 50 percent of its inventory. Normally, the firm must provide periodic abbreviated financial statements, sometimes monthly. The firm may then have to meet certain credit restrictions documented in clauses or **covenants** in the contract, such as maintaining the following:

**covenants** promises or restrictions in a contract

- a minimum current ratio of 1.4 or net working capital of $100 million
- net worth (shareholders' equity) in excess of $250 million
- a minimum interest coverage ratio (times interest earned) of 1.75
- an asset coverage ratio in excess of 2 and a debt ratio less than 0.75

The covenants in the revolving loan allow the bank to pull the loan (i.e., demand repayment) and/or prevent the firm from drawing the loan down beyond a certain amount as its credit quality deteriorates. However, the restrictions are only of limited effectiveness; firms usually have more than one bank account, and they know before the bank does whether they are going to violate the conditions. In that case, they can simply draw down the line of credit before informing the bank of the violations and can transfer the funds to another bank where they have full use of the money. Of course, this will damage their reputation, which could impede their ability to borrow in the future.

In addition to the interest costs, the banks normally charge a commitment fee of around 0.5 percent for setting up the LC, which is also charged on the unused balance. As with the operating line, most revolvers are based on prime, with less creditworthy firms paying higher spreads above prime. However, larger customers, who may be able to access the money market directly, are increasingly being offered lines that can be drawn down in either Canadian or U.S. dollars. The Canadian dollar funds are then based on BA plus 0.5 percent to 0.75 percent, while the U.S. rate is based on LIBOR. This is consistent with our discussion in Chapter 11, where we saw that the base borrowing rates for banks are the BA rate in Canadian dollars and LIBOR for U.S. dollars.

## Term Loans

The idea behind LCs is that the funds are used for working capital: financing receivables, inventory, and ongoing corporate activity, such as hedging by using swaps and forwards. In fact, some more traditional banks still require "cleanup" periods, in which the firm has a zero balance on its line of credit, to make sure that the bank is not providing "permanent" financing, which should be financed with longer-term funds. **Term loans** differ from lines of credit because they have a fixed maturity, require repayment to be made on a fixed schedule, and are meant to finance longer-term requirements such as equipment purchases.

**term loans** loans to finance longer-term requirements, such as equipment purchases; they have a fixed maturity and require repayment to be made on a fixed schedule

These loans are structured in a variety of ways. They are usually for a term of at least three years and may go out to 10 years or longer. Some involve "bullet" or "balloon" payments: only interest is paid until maturity, at which time the entire principal is due and payable. Such loans generally provide permanent financing of the firm's operations, rather than financing a particular asset. In contrast, amortizing loans are similar to conventional loans made to individuals, in which a monthly payment consists of both interest and principal payments. These are similar to a car loan or mortgage, which are valued as annuities, as discussed in Chapter 5.

Similar to other forms of bank financing, term loans may be based on the prime lending rate and thus float with the general level of interest rates. However, term loans are often offered with a fixed interest rate over the term of the loan. In addition, term loans are also offered by insurance companies and specialized business finance companies, often for longer periods than those offered by the chartered banks.

The big advantage of term loans to a borrowing company is that they are easy to arrange. All firms have banking relationships because they need chequing accounts to gain access to the payments system, and they also need banks for short-term financing and to arrange hedging contracts, such as swaps and forwards. Consequently, the firm's bank already has inside knowledge of its activities and can readily arrange a term loan if it judges the firm to be creditworthy. Further, the term loan can often be structured to fit with a firm's operating and revolving LCs. For example, sometimes a revolver is structured to switch into a term loan at the end of its five-year life.

---

**Concept Review Questions**

1. Briefly describe operating LCs, revolving LCs, and term loans.
2. Why do banks typically impose debt covenants on their borrowing customers?
3. Why is it reasonable to assume that most firms will have a banking relationship?

---

## 18.4 Long-Term Debt and the Money Market

**LEARNING OBJECTIVE 18.4**

Identify the requirements that must typically be satisfied for public debt issues.

Long-term financing generally refers to any debt issued with a term longer than one year. It is often called "funded" debt. This is because short-term debt is not regarded as permanent capital; therefore, when a firm accumulates "too much" short-term debt, it "funds" this debt by issuing long-term debt. As discussed in the previous section, banks provide medium-term financing through term loans, which are also provided by insurance companies and other specialized financial companies. These are examples of private financing, because the debt is not offered to the general public. For bank financing, the firm generally does not have to provide any extra information, because it already provides information in support of its existing bank relationship. For term loans from other entities, the firm will have to provide an offering memorandum. As described in Chapter 17, this document contains much the same type of information as a prospectus does, but in less detail.

The remaining forms of financing involve public financing, and here it is important to realize that securities legislation, with the requirement that a prospectus be filed, applies to debt as well as equity offerings. As discussed in Chapter 17, most financing in the capital markets is done by reporting issuers, who can raise capital, both debt and equity, through the issue of a short-form prospectus. These documents are filed with the provincial or territorial securities commissions and are publicly available. (For example, the documents filed with the Ontario Securities Commission are available on www.sedar.com.)

On November 21, 2001, BC Gas (now FortisBC Energy Inc.) filed a short-form prospectus to raise $500 million in medium-term note debentures (MTNs).[10] (The word "debenture" formerly meant "unsecured bonds" but now generically refers to any bond, so we refer to secured and unsecured debentures.) The prospectus indicated that the MTNs would be in either interest-bearing or discount form and would be registered for sale either in Canada or as global debentures. The interest rates were to be determined by the company, after consultation with its dealers, for an amount of up to $500 million for 25 months from the date of the prospectus, bringing the total MTN borrowing up to $1,400 million.

The short-form prospectus simply gave notice that BC Gas intended to raise $500 million in some form or another over the next two years. The exact terms of any issue would then be documented in a pricing supplement or "term sheet" negotiated between the company and its investment dealers, who would be canvassing major institutional purchasers to work out the most attractive issue at any point in time. As we discussed in Chapter 11, BC Gas could always use the swap market to convert the terms of a particular issue into something more attractive to it.

---

[10]The following discussion paraphrases the information in the prospectus.

Apart from the information included in the prospectus, the following was included "by reference":

- annual information form
- audited financial statements
- unaudited six-month statements
- any other information filed with the securities commission after the date of the prospectus but before the termination of the offering

Essentially, all the regular documents filed by BC Gas as a reporting issuer were part of the prospectus. The BC Gas short-form prospectus is an example of the new "continuous disclosure" practices that allow larger firms to access the capital markets on an almost continuous basis.

When firms issue securities to the general public, some basic mechanical problems have to be solved. For example, who keeps track of who owns the securities, makes sure they get their interest or dividends, and ensures that the company meets its obligations? Securities offered to the general public are normally held by the Canadian Depository for Securities (CDS). CDS physically holds the securities and maintains book entries regarding security ownership, but as we pointed out in Chapter 17, this is usually a major institution rather than the ultimate owner. A **transfer agent** looks after the day-to-day administration of the securities. For the BC Gas MTNs, CIBC Mellon Trust Company (CIBC Mellon) was the transfer agent and registrar. It maintained a record of the individuals who owned the MTNs and who therefore expected to receive interest and principal payments. Payment of interest, for example, could be made by electronic funds transfer or by cheque (dated on the interest date) to the owner in CIBC Mellon's records.

The transfer agent also makes sure that the legal documentation is satisfied. For example, the BC Gas MTNs were issued under a 1977 indenture between CIBC Mellon and a predecessor company (Inland Gas and Oil, Ltd.). This indenture had been updated many times since, but it stipulated the rights of the MTN holders. For example, it stipulated that BC Gas could issue an unlimited amount of MTNs, but the bonds would rank equally with all other unsecured and unsubordinated debt of the company. What does this mean?

First, it means that the MTNs ranked behind any secured debt outstanding in the event of default—that is, the secured debt holders had first claim on the particular underlying assets in the event of default. In the case of BC Gas, two different types of secured bonds technically ranked ahead of the MTNs. The first were BC Gas's "first mortgage bonds." Mortgage bonds are similar to residential mortgage arrangements, in which the lender has registered a claim on the underlying real property that is financed. For BC Gas, this real property largely consisted of small-diameter pipelines used for distributing natural gas to customers in British Columbia. These were "first" mortgage bonds because they had first claim on the underlying assets, whereas "second" bonds would rank behind them.

BC Gas also had $275 million in **purchase-money mortgages** outstanding. These are mortgages that constitute all or part of the compensation received for the sale of property and are used when the seller is also the lender. These were issued for the purchase of the gas-distribution assets of another B.C. company.

For BC Gas, the impact of these secured bonds was moot because none of the first mortgage bonds were still outstanding, while the purchase-money mortgages were specialized financing tools. Generally, mortgage bonds have been declining in popularity because, as with a regular mortgage, the claim of the lender has to be registered, which involves significant legal costs, particularly for companies with assets across Canada. Furthermore, what is a creditor going to do if it has to seize kilometres and kilometres of underground gas mains?[11] The problem is that many underlying assets are specific to the firm; if it does go bankrupt, forcing the lender to seize the assets, they have little value. So, de facto, there were few claims above BC Gas's MTNs.

The term **unsubordinated debt** means that no other unsecured debt ranked ahead of these MTNs in terms of either receiving interest or getting paid should BC Gas go into bankruptcy. BC Gas did not have any subordinated debt outstanding at the time, but if it did, it would simply mean that this class of unsecured debt ranked behind the MTNs. If BC Gas had "junior" subordinated

**transfer agent** a company that handles the day-to-day administration of securities and maintains records, including purchases, sales, and account balances

**purchase-money mortgages** mortgages that constitute all or part of the compensation received for the sale of property; used when the seller is also the lender

**unsubordinated debt** unsecured debt that ranks first with the company; no other unsecured debt ranks ahead of it

---

[11]The alternative uses for small-diameter natural gas pipes are rather limited.

debt, it would mean that this debt ranked even further behind. This ranking has the same interpretation as the terms "first" and "second" when used in reference to mortgage bonds.

The BC Gas indenture also indicated the actions of the company that could trigger default:

1. nonpayment of principal when due

2. nonpayment of interest after 30 days

3. an order for the winding up or liquidation of the firm

4. issuance of a general assignment of debts or declaration of bankruptcy

5. nonpayment after 45 days of any execution enforced against the property of the company to the extent that it had not been challenged

6. default on its first mortgage bonds or purchase-money mortgages

7. violation of a covenant provision and failure to make good on such a violation in 60 days

The first two clauses are clear: failing to make a contractual payment of principal or interest causes default. Clause 6 indicates that default on its other long-term obligations also constitutes default on the MTNs; this is referred to as a **cross-default clause**. Under clause 5, if someone goes to court and is allowed to claim any of the assets of BC Gas, and this claim has not been settled in 30 to 45 days (depending on the type of asset), this also causes default. This clause is similar to the cross-default clause in that it indicates an inability to pay a court order. Clauses 3 and 4 indicate that even if the company has not defaulted on any of its obligations, if it initiates procedures to wind down its business or go into bankruptcy, this constitutes default.

**cross-default clause**   a clause that indicates that default on one obligation also constitutes default on another

All these actions constitute "default," so how does this happen? It is the job of the trustee, CIBC Mellon, to monitor BC Gas's situation and, at its discretion or on the direction of the holders of 25 percent of the outstanding value of the MTN bonds, inform BC Gas that all of the outstanding MTN debt and accrued interest are due immediately. If BC Gas fails to pay on demand the full principal and interest owed, CIBC Mellon, at its discretion or again at the request of holders of 25 percent of the value of the outstanding MTNs, proceeds to get a court order to enforce payment. It is this movement to enforce payment that usually triggers the defaulting firm to go into bankruptcy protection.

Clause 7 refers to violations of the covenant provisions in the BC Gas MTN indenture, which restrict what BC Gas can do. These particular MTNs were relatively "clean" in that they had few restrictions. The major covenants were as follows:

1. BC Gas will not "mortgage, pledge, charge, or otherwise encumber" any of its assets unless the MTNs are given the same security. The only exception is the existing first mortgage bonds and purchase-money mortgages.

2. BC Gas will not guarantee any debt that is not necessary for carrying on its existing business.

3. The company will not issue any additional debt unless its earnings in 12 of the past 23 months satisfy a 2.0 times interest coverage ratio after the new debt has been issued and other debt retired.

4. The company will maintain its facilities for the supply of gas to enable it to carry on its business and will not sell shares that cause certain designated subsidiaries to cease to be subsidiaries.

The first covenant is a standard **negative pledge** clause. It means that BC Gas cannot create higher-priority debt that ranks above the MTNs without giving the MTN holders the same security. All BC Gas can do is issue more debt under its two existing secured debt indentures. The idea behind the negative pledge is simply to prevent the company from issuing large amounts of senior debt that ranks above the MTNs, thereby making them riskier. The second covenant prevents BC Gas from issuing guarantees. The reason for this restriction is that BC Gas is part of a holding company, and the bondholders are worried that its parent might make the company guarantee other assets of the company. If the guarantee were then called, it would endanger the credit of the company, making the MTNs riskier. The fourth covenant ensures that BC Gas remains a utility that distributes natural gas.

**negative pledge**   a clause that stipulates that a borrower may not create higher-priority debt without giving the other debt holders the same security

The most interesting covenant provision is the third one, which is standard to most gas-distribution utilities. This is the interest coverage restriction (ICR). Although the company could issue an unlimited amount of MTNs under the indenture, the ICR restricts such issues to make sure they do not make the existing MTNs riskier. As we discussed in Chapter 4, the interest coverage ratio is determined by taking the earnings before interest and tax (EBIT) and dividing this figure by the interest payments. The ICR ensures the firm does not issue so much debt that this ratio drops below 2.0. In doing this, it allows the company to "smooth" its earnings a bit by taking the best 12 out of 23 months. The interest on the new debt is then added to the existing interest costs, and the interest on any retired debt is subtracted. The focus on the ICR is common for utilities because their earnings are stable. For other firms, the restriction is more often in terms of the debt ratio.

An ICR of 2.0 would be very low for a typical firm, but utilities have low business risk because they are regulated and provide an essential service. The result is that utility debt is also low risk. A critical element in the prospectus for the MTNs was the fact that BC Gas debt was rated A by DBRS and, in the opinion of BC Gas's legal counsel, was an eligible investment under most of the legislation governing prudent investments for major financial institutions.[12] These rules are often referred to as "legal for life" rules and mean that the BC Gas MTNs could be sold to the widest possible group of investors.

This discussion of an actual bond issue by a major Canadian company is important because it emphasizes that bonds are a contractual obligation. The bond contract is exactly that—a contract—and the company cannot violate its terms without the trustee taking them to court or at least forcing them to negotiate. In Chapter 17 we discussed Sino-Forest in connection with securities regulation. Following a securities analyst's devastating critique of the company in June 2011 and the collapse in its share price, Sino-Forest was investigated and forced to suspend the release of its 2011 Q3 financial results. This violated a covenant in its bond contract and meant that the bondholders could seek court action to protect their interest. However, they didn't; instead, they pressured Sino-Forest to make major changes to address the serious concerns raised by the securities analyst and pay a "waiver fee" of 1 percent of the outstanding debt as compensation for the bondholders waiving their right to force Sino-Forest into bankruptcy. In the interim, the Ontario Securities Commission suspended trading in Sino-Forest's common shares because there was so much uncertainty about the true state of the company.

---

### Concept Review Questions

1. Define mortgage bonds, secured debentures, unsecured debentures, and subordinated debt.
2. Discuss the rationale for including debt covenants in a public issue.
3. Briefly describe negative pledge and cross-default clauses.

---

## 18.5 | Bond Ratings

**LEARNING OBJECTIVE 18.5**

Explain how debt ratings are determined, what they mean, and how useful they are in predicting default and recovery rates associated with public debt issues.

### Interpreting Debt Ratings

We have already seen that DBRS rates commercial paper and that a rating is essential to access the CP market. When investments have such a short maturity, it makes credit analysis expensive. For longer-term debt issues, most purchasers, like the major institutions mentioned

---

[12]These regulations include, for example, the *Insurance Companies Act*, the *Trust and Loan Companies Act*, and the *Pension Benefits Standards Act (Canada)*.

| **TABLE 18.4** | **DBRS's Rating Structure for Long-Term Debt** |
|---|---|
| AAA | Highest credit quality |
| AA | Superior credit quality |
| A | Satisfactory credit quality |
| BBB | Adequate credit quality |
| BB | Speculative |
| B | Highly speculative |
| CCC/CC/C | Very highly speculative |

earlier, do their own credit analysis. However, bond ratings are still important. In Chapter 6, we listed Standard & Poor's (S&P) debt-rating categories; in **Table 18.4** we show DBRS's rating structure for long-term debt.

In addition, each rating may be modified with a high or low rating. The lowest **investment-grade** bond rating is BBB (low); below this the bonds are regarded as speculative—that is, non-investment grade and commonly referred to as **junk bonds**, although they are more politely referred to as "high-yield bonds."

The long-term bond ratings are similar in meaning to the CP ratings we discussed earlier. In fact, normally there is a direct correspondence, with R-1 (high) being equivalent to AAA, R-1 (mid) to AA, and R-1 (low) to A.

We previously noted that there is currently little R-2-rated CP outstanding in the Canadian money market, where R-2 is equivalent to a BBB long-term bond rating and is still regarded as investment-grade debt. Similarly, until recently there was little BBB-rated original issue long-term debt in Canada. The relatively few issues outstanding were either from smaller regulated utilities or from issuers that started out as some form of A and were subsequently downgraded—the so-called fallen angels. The rule of thumb is that non-investment-grade issuers, below BBB (low), generally raise debt in the U.S. high-yield market and then swap back into the Canadian market, because there are more investors willing to invest in original issue high-yield debt in the United States.

The most common DBRS rating is A, which DBRS defines in the following way:

Long-term debt rated "A" is of satisfactory credit quality. Protection of interest and principal is still substantial, but the degree of strength is less than that of AA-rated entities. While "A" is a respectable rating, entities in this category are considered to be more susceptible to adverse economic conditions and have greater cyclical tendencies than higher-rated securities.[13]

## Determining Bond Ratings

DBRS determines a bond rating after extensive consultation with the company—which includes a site visit in which the company can state its view of its business and future prospects—and after examining at least five years of financial statements. The rating agency also usually has prior knowledge of the company from its extensive industry surveys. DBRS will issue a draft report to the company so it can check for any analytic or data errors before the agency issues a final rating. In determining its rating, DBRS is guided by two basic principles: the stable rating philosophy and the hierarchy principle.

The **stable rating philosophy** is founded on the idea that the rating is based on structural and not cyclical factors. The fortunes of most companies will fluctuate with the business cycle: when the economy is hot, most companies will make money; conversely, when it is in recession, most companies will struggle. Holders of 20- or 30-year debt can expect the company

**investment grade**   a bond rating that means the issuer is likely to meet payment obligations

**junk bonds**   speculative bonds with ratings below investment grade; often called "high-yield bonds"

**stable rating philosophy**   the idea that ratings are based on structural and not cyclical factors; changes in ratings are not made in response to temporary changes in the economy but only when there are clear structural changes in a company's credit

[13]Dominion Bond Rating Service, "Bonds, Long Term Debt and Preferred Share Ratings." DBRS press release, January 2000.

to operate through many ups and downs of the business cycle. DBRS aims to see through these predictable effects and change ratings only when a clear structural change occurs in the company's credit. For this reason some rating agencies refer to it as "rating through the (business) cycle." This sounds easier than it is because, in practice, it can be difficult to maintain ratings when the economy is in deep recession, even though the company is responding to that recession in a predictable manner. This is the stage when many rating agencies put companies on **credit watch**, rather than cutting the rating.

**credit watch** a status applied to a firm by a rating agency when it is monitoring the firm

**hierarchy principle** a principle based on the fact that rating agencies rate debt issues and not companies; rating agencies rate each class of debt lower than the previous class, unless there is little of the higher-ranked debt outstanding

The **hierarchy principle** is based on the fact that DBRS rates particular debt issues as well as the company itself. The rating on the company is referred to as an issuer rating. Some companies will ask for an issuer rating even if they have no debt outstanding, since it is often useful in contracting for other services. DBRS then also rates individual issues of debt that the firm has outstanding. Generally DBRS takes off a level in the bond rating for each class of debt. So the first mortgage bonds of a company might be rated as A (high), unsecured MTNs one level or "notch" lower at A, and junior subordinated bonds two notches lower at A (low). DBRS departs from this rule when there is little of the higher-ranked debt outstanding, in which case the next class of debt assumes the rating of the more senior debt. The reason for the hierarchy principle is simply that if a firm defaults, generally it defaults on all its obligations from mortgage bonds to MTNs to junior subordinated debentures. However, the amount that is recovered or paid out on each of these instruments in bankruptcy or reorganization will differ depending on their priority. For example, the proceeds from selling the property secured by the mortgage bonds can't generally be given to the junior unsecured debenture holders until the mortgage bonds have been paid in full. With a higher expected recovery rate for the mortgage bonds than the junior subordinated debentures, DBRS would rate the mortgage bonds higher.

In determining its rating, DBRS looks at six basic factors:

1. *Core profitability:* This is an assessment based on standard profit measures, such as the return on equity, return on assets, the "quality" of a firm's earnings, its cost structure (i.e., whether it is a low-cost producer, etc.), its growth opportunities, and its pricing structure.

2. *Asset quality:* Assets are made up of many different types, so DBRS looks at the importance of intangibles (for example, how valuable is the goodwill on the firm's balance sheet), the market value of the firm's assets, and its use of derivatives and risk management to see whether it is managing its operational and market risks effectively.

3. *Strategy and management strength:* Ultimately, a firm comprises assets and management, so the capabilities of the senior management group are vitally important to an assessment of a firm's credit risk. This is particularly important if the firm is actively involved in mergers and acquisitions, where a clear strategic approach and skills at integrating acquired companies are valuable.

4. *Balance sheet strength:* If the lenders have to initiate bankruptcy proceedings, it is important that they know where they stand in the overall liabilities of the firm, so awareness of standard debt ratios, coverage tests, and the amount of financial flexibility available to the firm is important. The latter includes an assessment of the firm's reliance on short-term debt, its commitment to a capital expenditure program that cannot be easily stopped, and the support potentially available from other parties, such as affiliated companies. Size is important because larger firms are usually less risky and have more market power.

5. *Business strength:* This category looks at standard factors, including market share; key intangibles, such as the quality of the work force; industry issues, such as the degree of unionization and competition; growth prospects for the industry; and issues specific to the company, such as its implementation of a defensible base of diversified operations and up-to-date management information systems.

6. *Miscellaneous issues:* This is a "catch-all" category, including such issues as the quality of the firm's financial statements and whether there have been frequent restatements, the structure of the bond indenture, and the importance of the firm and industry to the province or territory or to Canada.

DBRS Ltd. has downgraded its ratings on CI Financial Corp. and its subsidiary, CI Investments Inc., to BBB (high) from A (low), with a negative trend, on concerns about the wealth-management company's financial flexibility, rating agency announced Friday.

. . .

The downgrades stem from the rating agency's concern that rising debt levels at CI "have led to deterioration in the company's financial flexibility as indicated by its leverage and fixed-charge coverage ratios," DBRS says in a news release.

. . .

"Although the company is currently able to comfortably cover its debt-servicing payments due to good market performance overall, there is the risk that a stressed market environment leading to a decline in assets under management (AUM) may result in declining revenues," DBRS says.

**Source:** Excerpted from Langton, James, "DBRS Downgrades Ratings for CI." *IE Investment Executive*, August 17, 2018. Accessed at https://www.investmentexecutive.com/news/research-andmarkets/dbrs-downgrades-ratings-for-ci/.

Overall, the DBRS approach combines standard financial analysis, based on the ratios discussed in Chapter 4, with a broader firm and industry analysis. The result is a mixture of quantitative and qualitative factors. Finance in the News 18.1 discusses the decision of DBRS to downgrade CI Financial Corporation and two of its subsidiaries on August 17, 2018. CI is a major manager of mutual funds, which have come under increasing competitive pressures from low-cost exchange traded funds (ETFs). This has led to a decline in assets under management and lower revenues from fees.

## Empirical Evidence Regarding Debt Ratings

We can assess the quality of the DBRS ratings by looking at how accurately they correlate with future default rates. In April 2005, DBRS assessed the default experience in Canada by using what is termed a static pool analysis.[14] What this amounts to is looking at the ratings for all the firms, then tracking the default rates for these classes in the future, ignoring any subsequent changes in rating. The basic results, based on averages in the number of companies (and not on the dollar amounts outstanding) after 5, 10, and 20 years, are shown in **Table 18.5**.

The DBRS analysis makes several important points. First, the default rates clearly increase as the DBRS rating goes down, so the ratings provide a good indicator of credit risk. Second, for the investment-grade bond ratings, we can see why BBB is the cutoff point between the

**TABLE 18.5** Average Default Rates (%) in Canada

| DBRS Rating | Number of Years Examined | | |
| --- | --- | --- | --- |
| | 5 | 10 | 20 |
| AAA | 0.00 | 0.00 | 0.00 |
| AA | 0.56 | 0.63 | 0.63 |
| A | 0.95 | 1.60 | 2.33 |
| BBB | 2.34 | 3.82 | 5.03 |
| BB | 6.37 | 8.99 | 10.11 |
| B | 28.33 | 28.33 | 28.33 |
| CCC | 33.33 | 33.33 | 33.33 |

[14]Dominion Bond Rating Service, *DBRS Corporate Default Study* (Toronto: DBRS, April 2005).

investment and non-investment-grade ratings. For the AAA, AA, and A ratings, the default rates are low, with no AAA-rated issuers actually defaulting, and only 0.63 percent of the AAs defaulting. However, there is an exponential increase as credit quality deteriorates, with 2.33 percent of the As defaulting after 20 years, 5.03 percent of the BBBs, 10.11 percent of the BBs, and 28.33 percent of the Bs. From this, we can understand why many major institutional investors restrict their bond portfolio holdings to debt with a minimum rating of A, or utilities with BBB. Finally, for the really risky low-rated debt—B and CCC—default either happens quite early or doesn't happen at all, because the default rates are essentially stable beyond five years.

Of course, DBRS does not leave its ratings unchanged when structural changes affect the underlying credit risk. As a result, ratings migrate as the credit quality of a firm deteriorates. DBRS gives the example of Trizec Properties Inc., formerly a major Canadian property developer. Three years before bankruptcy it was rated AA (low); two years before bankruptcy it was rated BBB (low); one year before bankruptcy it was B rated; and three months before bankruptcy it was CCC.

The DBRS study is rather limited simply because defaults generally occur during recessions, when firms experience cash flow problems, so just because there are no defaults does not mean there is no risk. There are also relatively few firms in each industry in Canada with which to assess industry default levels. In the United States, S&P has a larger sample of default rates because the U.S. economy is approximately 11 times bigger than Canada's. In **Figure 18.3**, a graph from S&P shows the weighted average default rates, with the defaults weighted by the issuer base of debt outstanding at the start of the year. There are clear differences in default rates across different industries. The lowest default rates are generally in regulated industries, with insurance the lowest risk. The highest default rates occur in more competitive industries that are more sensitive to the business cycle, with leisure time and media at the top of the list.

Of course, defaulting is only part of the story, because investors want to know how much they are likely to recover in the event of a default. Information on recovery rates is difficult to gather because it depends on the industry the firm is in and the nature of the underlying assets. However, in a December 2003 review, Altman et al. gave the market

E&NR–Energy and natural resources. Forest–Forest and building products and homebuilders. High tech–High technology, computers, and office equipment. Leisure–Leisure time and media. AACGM–Aerospace, auto, capital goods, and metals. Health–Health care and chemicals. Sources: S&P Global Fixed Income Research and S&P Global Market Intelligence's CreditPro®. Copyright ©2018 by Standard & Poor's Financial Services LLC. All rights reserved.

**FIGURE 18.3** **Global Corporate Default Study and Rating Transitions (2017)**

**TABLE 18.6**   Default Recovery Rates

| Bond Seniority | No. of Issues | Median Price (%) | Average Price (%) | Weighted Price (%) | Standard Deviation (%) |
|---|---|---|---|---|---|
| **Senior secured** | | | | | |
| Investment grade | 89 | 50.50 | 54.50 | 56.39 | 24.42 |
| Non-investment grade | 283 | 33.50 | 36.63 | 31.91 | 26.04 |
| **Senior unsecured** | | | | | |
| Investment grade | 299 | 42.75 | 46.37 | 44.05 | 23.57 |
| Non-investment grade | 598 | 30.00 | 33.41 | 31.83 | 23.65 |
| **Senior subordinated** | | | | | |
| Investment grade | 11 | 27.31 | 39.54 | 42.04 | 24.23 |
| Non-investment grade | 411 | 26.50 | 31.48 | 28.99 | 24.30 |
| **Subordinated** | | | | | |
| Investment grade | 12 | 35.69 | 35.64 | 23.55 | 23.83 |
| Non-investment grade | 238 | 28.00 | 30.91 | 28.66 | 21.98 |
| **Discount** | | | | | |
| Investment grade | – | – | – | – | – |
| Non-investment grade | 113 | 16.00 | 20.69 | 21.24 | 17.23 |
| **Total sample** | **2,054** | **30.04** | **34.76** | **30.78** | **24.38** |

values for different types of debt shortly after a firm defaulted.[15] **Table 18.6** shows these market values, which reflect the recovery rates on different types of debt securities. The data indicate that after going into default, the average ratio of market price to face value was only 34.76 percent—that is, the expected recovery rate was only 34.76 percent. However, this rate clearly declines with the ranking of the debt, because senior secured debt formerly rated investment grade traded for 54.5 percent of face value, while subordinated debt traded for only 35.6 percent of face value. Interestingly, the drop was not as great for bonds that were not investment grade before default. This is the hierarchy principle that DBRS uses when it rates individual *issues* of debt rather than the overall *issuer* rating. So if a firm had all these types of debt outstanding, its senior secured debt would have a higher rating than its senior unsecured, which would in turn be higher than its senior subordinated debt, and so on.

Standard & Poor's uses a slightly different approach. Rather than relying on a hierarchical approach, it allocates issues into five "buckets" based on their expected recovery rates. For example, if the expected recovery rate is 90 to 100 percent, then even in the event of a default the investors would recover most of their investment. In this case, the rating on this particular *issue* would be rated two levels higher than the company's overall *issuer* rating, say A (high) rather than A (low). This might be the case if this issue is secured, for example, by a mortgage on real property. In contrast, if the recovery rate is expected to be only 0 to 10 percent, then the rating on this issue of securities from the same issuer would be two levels lower than the company's issuer rating, say BBB rather than A (low).

The data on default and recovery rates indicate what we would expect: high-risk bonds have both a higher probability of defaulting and a lower expected recovery rate. **Figure 18.4** shows the yield spreads between different bond ratings, which captures both of these components of risk to the investor. In each case, the bond yield is from an index of long-term bonds with similar bond ratings that was maintained initially by Scotia Capital Markets; the spread is the difference between the yield on the index and the yield on an

---

[15]Altman, E., Resti, A., and Sironi, A., "Default Recovery Rates in Credit Risk Modelling: A Review of the Literature and Empirical Evidence." *Economic Notes* 33, no. 2 (July 2004), pp. 183–321.

FIGURE 18.4 Canada Bond Yield Spreads in Basis Points (1/100 of a Percent)

**Source:** Data from Datastream series SCM3BLG, SCM1ALG, SCM2ALG, SCMCLNG

index of long Canada bonds. The spreads are weekly values from December 1979 until January 2019, but in the earlier period, only monthly values are available. For the overall period, the average AA spread over long Canada bonds was 0.83 percent, the A spread was 1.17 percent, and the BBB spread was 1.87 percent. Unfortunately, there are no longer enough AAA-rated bonds outstanding in Canada to make up an index. What the data in Figure 18.4 show, for example, is that, "on average," an AA-rated issuer pays 0.83 percent more for long-term debt than does the Government of Canada. However, averages are deceptive. What also matters is the variability. In this case, the standard deviation of the spreads is 0.46 percent (AA), 0.48 percent (A), and 0.77 percent (BBB), indicating that the spreads are not only higher with the lower-rated debt, but also much more variable. We can see this during the slowdown experienced in the Canadian economy during the early 1990s and again after the stock market peaked in October 2000. Each time, the BBB spreads reached over 3 percent, whereas the spreads on A and AA bonds were much more stable. In contrast, during the financial crisis of 2008–9, it was not just the BBB spreads, but also the A and AA spreads that dramatically increased, with the latter reaching record highs.

The spread experience indicates that during economic slowdowns there is a "flight to quality"; investors are reluctant to invest in riskier securities, and they invest more heavily in low-risk investments, like Canada treasury bills and, to a lesser extent, long Canada bonds. As they sell corporate bonds they drive their yield up, and as they buy long Canada bonds they drive their yield down. As a result, there is an increase in the "default" spread between corporate and government bonds. During these recessionary or slowdown periods, some firms experience financing problems and discover that they cannot access long-term funds on what they regard as reasonable terms. In fact, these spreads are on **seasoned bond issues** (or actively traded bond issues), and they do not indicate whether new funds are available on those terms. For this reason, during these periods, lower-rated companies usually have to finance with shorter-term debt or rely on bank borrowings.

**seasoned bond issues** actively traded bond issues that have been outstanding for some time

## Concept Review Questions

1. Differentiate investment-grade debt from junk debt.
2. Briefly describe the main factors DBRS considers in determining its debt ratings.
3. Briefly summarize the evidence regarding how well debt ratings work.

# Review

## Summary

In this chapter, we discuss the basic features of debt financing. Debt is a fixed contractual commitment. In order to be tax deductible, debt payments have to represent compensation for money owed, be referable back to a principal sum, and accrue from day to day. We then distinguish between short-term funds in the money market and long-term funds in the capital market. Money market securities are normally traded on a discount basis and are referred to as paper or bills. The biggest component of the money market is the treasury bill market, but commercial paper and bankers' acceptances are also important. Firms also use bank borrowings in the form of lines of credit and term loans.

Longer-term debt must be issued under a prospectus when sold to the general public. Most large companies in Canada are now reporting issuers and so can issue using a short-form prospectus. The information in the prospectus includes the type of debt and the major covenant provisions that restrict what the firm can do. The critical clauses are usually cross-default clauses, negative pledge clauses, and interest coverage restrictions. The bonds will then need a bond rating in order to be sold to major institutional purchasers. DBRS is the major bond-rating agency in Canada for both CP and long-term issues. Bond ratings run from AAA down to C, but, in practice, most Canadian bonds are rated A or higher, just as there is currently little CP rated lower than R-1 (low) outstanding. These ratings are highly correlated with actual default rates and the recovery rates that investors can expect in case of default.

## Summary of Learning Objectives

### 18.1   Define "debt" and identify the basic features that distinguish debt from equity financing.

Debt is a contract between a lender and a borrower that stipulates the terms of repayment of the loan. Three basic features distinguish debt from equity financing:

- With debt, interest cost and principal repayment are fixed contractual commitments; with equity, an investor is an owner, shares in the profits of the business, and has no contractual rights, because equity is not a contract in the way that debt is.
- Debt costs are legitimate costs of doing business and are tax deductible. In contrast, equity costs are not a cost of doing business in the same sense.
- Interest on debt is paid before corporate tax, but dividends on stocks are paid after tax.

### 18.2   Identify and describe the different types of short-term debt issued in the money market.

The short-term debt issued in the money market includes government treasury bills, commercial paper (CP), and bankers' acceptances (BAs). Treasury bills are promissory notes issued by a government treasury department. CP are short-term debt instruments, usually unsecured, that are issued by companies. BAs are short-term paper sold by an issuer to a bank, which guarantees or accepts it, obligating the bank to pay off the debt instrument at maturity if the issuer defaults.

### 18.3   Describe the types of debt financing provided by banks.

Banks provide a backup line of credit in CP and provide support in the BA market. However, the CP and BA markets are useful only for companies that have reasonably large and continuous financing needs because CP and BAs are sold in large amounts, usually at least $1 million. For smaller, irregular-sized financing requirements, firms rely more on traditional bank financing. This consists of term loans and lines of credit.

### 18.4   Identify the requirements that must typically be satisfied for public debt issues.

The company must offer a prospectus. The following items are incorporated in the prospectus by reference: annual information form, audited financial statements, unaudited interim statements, and any other information filed with the securities commission after the date of the prospectus but before the termination of the offering.

### 18.5   Explain how debt ratings are determined, what they mean, and how useful they are in predicting default and recovery rates associated with public debt issues.

In determining its rating, the Dominion Bond Rating Service looks at six basic factors: core profitability, asset quality, strategy and management strength, balance sheet strength, business strength, and miscellaneous issues. The ratings are AAA for highest credit quality, AA for superior credit quality, A for satisfactory credit quality, BBB for adequate credit quality, BB for speculative, B for highly speculative, and CCC/CC/C for very highly speculative. Bond rating is very important for investors making investment decisions. It indicates the credit quality of a bond (i.e., the likelihood that it will default).

## Key Terms

after-tax cost of debt ($k$), p. 18-2
bankers' acceptances (BAs), p. 18-8
commercial paper (CP), p. 18-5
covenants, p. 18-12
credit watch, p. 18-18
credit yield spread, p. 18-6
cross-default clause, p. 18-15
default yield spread, p. 18-6
demand LC, p. 18-11
fixed contractual commitments, p. 18-2

floating interest rate, p. 18-11
hierarchy principle, p. 18-18
investment grade, p. 18-17
junk bonds, p. 18-17
line of credit (LC), p. 18-11
liquidity support, p. 18-7
negative pledge, p. 18-15
operating LC, p. 18-11
prime lending rate, p. 18-11
promised yields, p. 18-6

promissory note, p. 18-4
purchase-money mortgages, p. 18-14
revolving LC, p. 18-11
seasoned bond issues, p. 18-22
stable rating philosophy, p. 18-17
term loans, p. 18-12
term LC, p. 18-11
transfer agent, p. 18-14
treasury bill (T-bill), p. 18-4
unsubordinated debt, p. 18-14

## Equations

| Equation | Description | Formula | Page |
|---|---|---|---|
| [18.1] | After-Tax Cost of Debt | $k = k_d(1 - T)$ | p. 18-2 |
| [18.2] | Commercial Paper Issue | $V = \dfrac{PAR(1 + R)P + RECOVER(1 - P)}{(1 + k)}$ | p. 18-6 |
| [18.3] | Promised Yield to Issue at PAR | $R = \dfrac{(1 + k_{TB})}{P} - 1$ | p. 18-6 |

# Questions and Practice Problems

## Multiple Choice Questions

1. **(LO 18.1)** Which of the following statements about debt is *incorrect?*

   a. Interest payments and principal payments are fixed commitments.

   b. Interest payments are not tax deductible.

   c. Bond holders are paid a series of fixed periodic amounts before the maturity date.

   d. A debt indenture is a legal document, specifying payment requirements.

2. **(LO 18.1)** What is the after-tax cost of debt, assuming $T = 40$ percent and before-tax cost of debt = 6 percent?

   a. 2.4 percent          c. 4.2 percent

   b. 3.6 percent          d. 6.0 percent

3. **(LO 18.2)** What is the promised yield to issue at par, assuming a zero recovery rate, a required return on T-bills of 1 percent, and a 2-percent chance of default?

   a. 0.60 percent          c. 2.02 percent

   b. 1.00 percent          d. 3.06 percent

4. **(LO 18.2)** What is the yield spread, if the promised yield on 30-day CP is 5 percent, the yield on the 91-day T-bill is 2 percent, and the yield on the 30-day T-bill is 1 percent?

   a. 2 percent          c. 4 percent

   b. 3 percent          d. 5 percent

5. **(LO 18.2)** Which of the following money market instruments could a firm without a very sound credit rating use when seeking financing?

   a. Commercial paper

   b. Bankers' acceptance

   c. Bill of exchange

   d. Both A and B

6. **(LO 18.2)** Which of the following investments is considered to be the safest?

   a. Commercial paper

   b. Corporate bonds

   c. Treasury bills

   d. Treasury bonds

7. **(LO 18.2)** Which of the following sources of financing is likely to provide the most favourable rates for large, highly rated firms seeking short-term financing?

   a. Selling commercial paper

   b. Selling secured long-term debt

   c. Getting an unsecured line of credit from a bank

   d. Selling bankers' acceptances

8. **(LO 18.3)** Which of the following statements about bond covenants is *true?*

   a. Covenants in a bond contract restrict the actions that management can take that, at the expense of the equity holders, would benefit the debt holders.

**b.** The presence of restrictive bond covenants, all else equal, tends to increase an issuer's borrowing costs.

**c.** If an issuer fails to adhere to any covenant, they immediately go into bankruptcy.

**d.** Bond indentures often contain covenants that restrict the ability of management to pay dividends.

**9. (LO 18.3)** Parts of the indenture that limit certain actions a company takes during the term of the loan to protect the lender's interests are called

    **a.** debentures.

    **b.** negative pledge clauses.

    **c.** bond ratings.

    **d.** covenants.

**10. (LO 18.3)** Which of the following reflects the negative pledge clause?

    **a.** The issuing firm must make its interest payments.

    **b.** The issuing firm must fulfill its supplies to promised customers.

    **c.** The issuing firm has to maintain a current ratio of more than 2.5.

    **d.** The issuing firm must not issue any new debt with existing assets as collateral.

**11. (LO 18.3)** Which of the following statements about lines of credit is *false*?

    **a.** An operating or demand line of credit is the standard type.

    **b.** A revolver has less stability than an operating line of credit.

    **c.** Prime is the cost base of an operating line of credit and is a floating rate.

    **d.** A revolver is usually at least 364 days.

**12. (LO 18.5)** Which of the following ratings is the lowest?

    **a.** A                  **c.** AA

    **b.** B                  **d.** BB

## Practice Problems

### Basic

**13. (LO 18.1)** State the three basic tests the CRA uses to ensure interest payments are tax deductible.

**14. (LO 18.2)** Determine the selling price of a Government of Canada treasury bill that has a quoted annual interest rate of 1.2 percent and will mature in 90 days. Assume a par value of $1,000.

**15. (LO 18.2)** Collingwood Corp.'s 60-day commercial paper has a promised yield of 10 percent per year, but the expected yield is just 1.5 percent due to the risk of default. If the current 60-day T-bill yield is 1 percent, what is the yield spread on this commercial paper?

**16. (LO 18.2)** As the newly appointed treasurer for Collingwood Corp., you have to decide how to raise $25 million in short-term financing. You believe you could issue commercial paper with a promised yield of 10 percent. However, your bank will charge a commitment fee of 0.125 percent on the line of credit to back up this paper, as well as 0.125 percent as a selling commission. As an alternative, the bank suggests using bankers' acceptances that would have a lower yield of 9.75 percent. The bank's "stamping" fee for these BAs is 0.325 percent. Which financing alternative should you choose?

**17. (LO 18.3)** Collingwood Corp. has a revolving line of credit on which it owes $25 million. One of the restrictions imposed with this financing arrangement is that the company must maintain a minimum interest coverage ratio of 2. If this is the only borrowing, and the annual interest rate is 10.75 percent, how much does the company have to earn to live up to the covenant?

### Intermediate

**18. (LO 18.2)** On a one-year loan of $10,000, a bank charges interest at 8 percent. The bank also charges an application fee of $75 to cover processing expenses. What is the effective interest cost (annual rate) being paid by the borrower?

**19. (LO 18.2)** Calculate the price of a 91-day T-bill if the face value is $1 million and the quoted interest rate is 3.8 percent. Round to the nearest dollar.

**20. (LO 18.2)** Calculate the value of the one-month CP given the following: par value is $2 million, promised yield is 4 percent, probability of not defaulting is 97 percent, recovery rate is zero, and required return is 14 percent. Round to the nearest dollar.

**21. (LO 18.2)** Discuss the important characteristics of money market debt instruments. How are these characteristics important to money market participants?

**22. (LO 18.2)** Jackie would like to borrow $125,000 to expand her small business, but needs to understand the impact of the 6-percent interest payments. Last year, her company did not pay any interest and had total earnings before tax of $143,500. The tax rate was 30 percent. Determine the company's net income for the year. Assuming that EBIT and the rate of taxation will not change, calculate how much the net income figure will change if Jackie proceeds with the loan. Explain to Jackie why her company's net income does not fall by the full amount of the interest payments.

**23. (LO 18.2)** The cost (interest rate) of the loan Jackie needs for her business is 6 percent per year. Given that the company's net income will fall by less than the amount of interest paid (see practice problem 22), is Jackie correct to think that the after-tax cost of the loan is lower than 6 percent? With a tax rate of 30 percent, what is the after-tax cost of this loan?

**24. (LO 18.3)** In your job as treasurer of Collingwood Corp., you have to arrange a line of credit for the firm. The following is taken from the company's balance sheet.

| **Current assets** | |
| --- | --- |
| Cash | $ 1,271,987 |
| Accounts receivable | 8,536,000 |
| Inventory | 80,196,000 |
| | 90,003,987 |
| Property and equipment (net) | 126,323,000 |
| Goodwill | 46,888,000 |
| Total assets | $263,214,987 |

The bank will provide credit up to the sum of 75 percent of the value of receivables and 50 percent of the inventory value. What is the maximum credit limit that Collingwood can obtain?

**25. (LO 18.4)** Briefly define what is meant by a bond's seniority.

**26. (LO 18.4)** Why do corporations issue long-term bonds, knowing that interest rate risk is higher for longer-term bonds?

**27. (LO 18.4)** Collingwood Corp.'s bank is willing to provide it with a 10-year term loan for $25 million. The annual payments on this loan will be $2.65 million, and there is a "bullet" payment of $25 million at maturity. What is the interest rate being charged by the bank? Does it make sense that this loan would have a higher cost than the alternatives presented in practice problem 16?

**28. (LO 18.5)** List and briefly describe the six basic factors used to determine a DBRS rating.

## Challenging

**29. (LO 18.2)** Michael M. specializes in buying high-risk commercial paper; his required return on these investments is 14 percent per year. He is considering buying some 60-day paper from Collingwood Corp. with a promised yield of 10 percent per year. However, Michael believes there is a 1-percent chance that Collingwood will default on this debt, in which case he would recover only 75 percent of the face value. How much will Michael be willing to pay for each $1,000 par value of this paper?

**30. (LO 18.2)** Collingwood Corp. is able to issue its 60-day commercial paper at par with a promised yield of 10 percent per year. The current T-bill yield is 6 percent per year (or 1 percent for the 60-day period). The expected return on the commercial paper is 1.5 percent, as there is some risk of default. If Collingwood were to default, investors would recover 75 percent of the face value of the debt. Based on this information, what is the probability that Collingwood will default on its commercial paper? Round to two decimals.

**31. (LO 18.2)** When Collingwood Corp. issued its 60-day commercial paper, the promised yield was 10 percent, whereas the 60-day T-bill yield was 6 percent. There is a 1-percent chance that Collingwood will default on this debt. If investors were willing to pay the full par-value amount ($1,000) to purchase the paper, how much do they expect to recover in the event of a default?

**32. (LO 18.5)** Rather than take a term loan from the bank, Collingwood Corp. has decided to issue $25 million of 10-year bonds. DBRS has assigned a rating of "BB" to this bond issue.

a. Determine the probability that no default occurs during the life of these bonds, based on historical average default rates provided in Table 18.5.

b. Valuing long-term bonds with default risk is quite difficult. For simplicity, assume that the bonds mature in one year and can be valued in the same manner as commercial paper (Equation 18.2). Collingwood Corp. will pay coupon interest (the promised yield) of 9 percent, whereas the current yield on treasury bonds is 6 percent. Use the estimated default rate from part a to determine the value of the bonds. You may assume that the bonds are worthless in the event of a default.

**33. (LO 18.5)** Sometimes, bonds are completely worthless when a company defaults on payments. However, in practice, bonds typically have some market value (recovery rate) even after a default. Collingwood's bonds are unsecured, but are senior to any other debt. Use the information in Table 18.6 and the information in practice problem 32 to determine the value of the bonds.

**34. (LO 18.5)** Assume two bonds in the market—bond A and bond B—have the same rating and the same YTM. Discuss three reasons that might make one bond preferable to the other.

**35. (LO 18.5)** Great White North Co. has the following: EBIT of $130 million, EBITDA of $214 million, a $500 million outstanding 10-year bond paying a coupon of 5%, and shareholders' equity of $970 million.

Given the following information, what is Dominion Bond Rating Service's likely credit rating?

| Ratio/Rating | AAA | AA | A | BBB | BB |
|---|---|---|---|---|---|
| **Pretax Interest Coverage** [EBIT/Interest Expense] | 15x | 10x | 8x | 5x | 2x |
| **EBITDA Interest Coverage** [EBITDA/Interest Expense] | 20x | 15x | 12x | 8x | 3x |
| **LT Debt to Capitalization** [Debt/Debt + Equity] | 15% | 20% | 35% | 40% | 60% |
| **Total Debt/EBITDA** | 0.5x | 1x | 1.7x | 2.5x | 3.7x |

# Equity and Hybrid Instruments

---

**LEARNING OBJECTIVES**

After studying this chapter, you should be able to:

**19.1** Explain the basic rights associated with share ownership.

**19.2** Describe the various classes of shares and the shareholders' rights associated with each.

**19.3** Describe preferred shares and outline the various features associated with them.

**19.4** Explain how combining warrants with debt issues, or issuing convertible bonds or debentures, can provide firms with attractive financing options.

**19.5** Describe the various hybrid financing options available to firms, and explain how they are constructed.

---

In Chapter 18, we discussed debt and how one of the major factors determining whether or not a security is debt is its treatment by the Canada Revenue Agency (CRA) for tax purposes. In this chapter, we consider non-debt securities, beginning with equity, both common shares and preferred shares, which are part of shareholders' equity. We show that the basic rights provided to common shareholders can be distributed among different classes of common shares. As a result, all common shares are not equal. In particular, some of them have voting rights, others don't, and some of them have larger dividends than others do. Preferred shares in Canada come in a wide variety of forms because of the way dividends are taxed. This means some preferred shares are similar to commercial paper (CP), mid-term notes, or long-term financing, with the major difference being that preferred shares pay dividends rather than interest. We then show how conversion features in warrants and convertibles make convertible bonds part common equity and part debt, depending on the structure of the conversion feature. We also look at the non-tax features of different securities and how they are treated by the major rating agencies. A good understanding of the material in this chapter is necessary to comprehend the range of corporate financing activities undertaken by firms and the ways firms can mix them in an attempt to lower their overall financing cost, which will be discussed in Chapter 20.

In Chapter 7, we defined "equity securities" as ownership interests in an underlying entity, usually a corporation. We defined "common shares" as certificates of this ownership so that common shareholders represent the true "owners" of the corporation. Finally, we defined "preferred shares" as shares that provide the owners with a preferential claim to a fixed amount of equity or dividends that are both established when the shares are first issued. However, Macintosh and Nicholls point out that the terms "common share" and "preferred share" have no statutory definition in Canada; they are used only to describe different classes of securities within shareholders' equity.[1] Our discussion in this chapter distinguishes between the two forms of equity and examines the implications for investors and for the underlying business.

---

[1]Macintosh, Jeffrey, and Nicholls, Christopher, *Securities Law* (Toronto: Irwin Law, 2002). Also see the Government of Canada website, https://www.ic.gc.ca/eic/site/cd-dgc.nsf/eng/cs06644.html.

# 19.1 Shareholder Rights

---

**LEARNING OBJECTIVE 19.1**

Explain the basic rights associated with share ownership.

---

In Chapter 18, we saw that the basic definition of debt flows from what the CRA determines to be a fixed contractual commitment, such that the interest is a cost of renting capital and doing business, similar to the cost of office rent; wages; heat, light, and other utilities; etc. This is why interest is tax deductible. In contrast, equity, representing the interests of the owners, cannot have a fixed contractual commitment; instead it gets whatever is left over after all the fixed commitments are paid. In this sense, the equity owners are the "residual" claimants on the firm's assets and income, and equity can be regarded as a security for which the payments are not tax deductible.

The *Canada Business Corporations Act* (*CBCA*) 24(3) provides that

> Where a corporation has only one class of shares, the rights of the holders thereof are equal in all respects and include the rights
>
> **(a)** to vote at any meeting of shareholders of the corporation;
>
> **(b)** to receive any dividend declared by the corporation; and
>
> **(c)** to receive the remaining property of the corporation on dissolution.

Provincially incorporated companies operate under provincial laws with similar provisions. These three provisions define the basic rights of common shareholders.

## The Right to Vote

The most basic right of common shareholders is the right to vote. Because they own a "share" of the business, shareholders have the right to make important decisions at the annual general meeting. These include the right to elect the members of the board of directors (BOD) that determine the company's strategy and appoint the senior managers; the right to appoint the auditors of the firm; the right to make changes in the articles of incorporation and bylaws of the company; and the right to vote on major changes in the firm's operations. What constitutes a major or fundamental change in the firm's operations is difficult to define, but it normally includes the acquisition of another firm through an exchange of shares or the disposition of major assets. As corporations have got ever larger, the "distance" between the firm and its owners has become greater, making it more difficult for shareholders to enforce their rights. However, ensuring that shareholders can in fact exercise these rights is an important issue called corporate governance.

## The Pre-Emptive Right

**pre-emptive right** the right of shareholders to maintain proportional ownership in a company when new shares are issued

One example of how these rights have become restricted is provided by the **pre-emptive right**, which is the right to maintain your proportional ownership in a company. For example, if a firm that gives shareholders a pre-emptive right were to issue 50-percent more shares in a seasoned equity offering, then all shareholders would have the right to buy 50 percent more shares and so maintain their proportional interest or share in the company. If there is no pre-emptive right, it means that the company can sell shares to "new" shareholders and dilute or reduce the ownership interest of existing shareholders. In this way, voting control can pass from one group to another.

Historically, the pre-emptive right meant that most new issues of shares were made by means of a "rights offering" to existing shareholders. Starting in the early 1950s, Canadian companies changed their corporate structure, removing the pre-emptive right so they could sell shares more quickly and cheaply to new, principally institutional, investors. We saw in Chapter 17, for example, that bought deals can be accomplished very quickly by having an investment bank buy shares directly from a company and then immediately resell them into the market. This is only possible if the shares can be sold to major institutions like pension funds, mutual funds, and insurance companies. In the process, the ordinary retail investor is largely cut out and forced to buy the shares once they enter the market. As a result, very few rights offerings are now made in Canada, and shareholders cannot prevent their ownership share from being diluted by the sale of new shares to other investors.[2] Essentially the "need" to raise new equity cheaply from big institutions has removed one of the basic rights of shareholders.

The loss of the pre-emptive right has been exacerbated by the fact that most companies now have authorized an unlimited number of common shares or have increased the authorized capital so that they no longer need shareholder approval to issue more common shares. Again, for reporting issuers, this means that firms can sell new shares very quickly by means of a bought deal. However, while a firm can raise capital more cheaply, it also means it no longer needs shareholder approval for the new share issue or, most of the time, no longer has to explain what it intends to do with the financing. The result has been a significant reduction in oversight of corporate activities by the firm's owners, the shareholders, and increased power for its senior management.

An interesting angle to this loss of corporate control was the recent suit by Maurice "Hank" Greenberg, former CEO of American International Group (AIG), against the United States government.[3] AIG was a major piece of the 2008–9 financial crisis, since it guaranteed many sub-prime debt issues and eventually teetered on bankruptcy when it had to make good on these guarantees. To avoid a disastrous collapse, the Federal Reserve (the U.S. central bank) indirectly took an 80-percent interest in AIG. However, it couldn't buy the shares needed to "rescue"—that is, control—AIG, since the authorized number of shares was not large enough. This restriction was circumvented by a 1 for 20 reverse stock split. What this meant was that for every 20 existing shares, each shareholder received one new AIG share. On its own this made little difference, but with the authorized number of shares unchanged it allowed the Federal Reserve to buy enough new shares directly from AIG to exercise control. In the process, Hank Greenberg, who was AIG's largest shareholder, saw his holdings and control of AIG diluted—that is, his ownership share of AIG was dramatically reduced—so he sued the U.S. government. The U.S. Supreme Court decided the actions were legal, but the Federal Reserve broke the law since it is not allowed to buy common shares. However, since the actions of the Federal Reserve saved the U.S. financial system, they were justified!

**Table 19.1** lists the largest rights issues in the world as of November 24, 2009, compiled by Reuters. What is striking about the companies listed is not who is there, but who is not. For example, we might expect to see no Canadian companies, but it is surprising that there are no American companies. This is despite the fact that the World Bank lists the pre-emptive right as a basic shareholder right. Instead, the list is dominated by European, principally British, companies and by financial institutions like HSBC, which reflects the enormous fundraising efforts they had to quickly make in the aftermath of the financial crisis. If a firm has to scramble to raise cash, a rights issue is an easy way to force shareholders to contribute more cash, so we see this in Canada as well. On July 25, 2017, Redknee Solutions (now Optiva) announced a rights issue at a 40-percent discount to the prevailing share price. It urgently needed the cash to fund a restructuring of its business and got 92.6-percent shareholder approval. If existing shareholders didn't want to buy in at this hugely discounted share price, they could sell these rights to others who would.

---

[2]In fact, a standard takeover defence is to sell shares to a friendly investor, thereby reducing the stake of a potentially hostile acquirer. "Poison pills," discussed in Chapter 15, are another example of how the lack of the pre-emptive right dilutes shareholders' stake in a firm.

[3]See Myers, Adrian, "U.S. Broke the Law—for the Greater Good." *Globe and Mail Report on Business*, June 18, 2015.

**TABLE 19.1** Top 10 Rights Issues as of November 2009

| Issuer | Date | US$Billion at Current Foreign Exchange | Billion in Local Currency | US$Billion at Historic Foreign Exchange |
|---|---|---|---|---|
| 1. Lloyds Banking Group | Nov 09 | 22.3 | £13.5 | 22.1 |
| 2. HSBC | Apr 09 | 21.8 | £13.2 | 19.4 |
| 3. RBS | Jun 08 | 20.4 | £12.3 | 24.4 |
| 4. Fortis | Oct 07 | 20.3 | €13.6 | 19.3 |
| 5. UBS | May 08 | 15.8 | 16.0 Swiss francs | 15.4 |
| 6. Rio Tinto | Jul 09 | 12.4 | £7.5 | 12.3 |
| 7. Enel | Jun 09 | 11.9 | €8.0 | 11.1 |
| 8. Santander | Nov 08 | 10.7 | €7.2 | 9.3 |
| 9. Sberbank Rossii | Feb 07 | 10.0 | €6.7 | 8.8 |
| 10. Imperial Tobacco | Jun 08 | 8.3 | £5.0 | 9.9 |

**Source:** Data from Thomson Reuters.

## Other Rights

The shareholders' two remaining rights—to receive a dividend and to receive any remaining property on the dissolution of the corporation—reflect the equity shareholders' rights as the **residual owners**. For example, the equity holders have no right to a dividend until it is declared by the company's BOD. Legally, the shareholders cannot force a company to pay a dividend—this decision is the prerogative of the BOD. Furthermore, there are extensive legal restrictions on when the company can declare a dividend; the major one is that the firm has to have the resources to pay the dividend without impairing its ability to meet its fixed contractual commitments. Otherwise, a company going bankrupt could simply strip out all its cash through a dividend prior to declaring bankruptcy. In this sense, payment of a dividend reflects the fact that the equity holders are last in line after all other claims on the firm's earnings stream have been met. In the same way, if the firm is liquidated, all other claimants on the firm's assets have to be paid before the equity holders receive any payment.

A right not explicit in the *CBCA* description, although fundamental to the *CBCA* itself, is the right to limited liability, which was discussed in Chapter 2. The equity holders commit initial financing to the firm by buying shares, but they are legally protected from being forced to put more money into the firm. As a result, if the firm cannot meet its fixed commitments to pay interest and so on, the equity holders do not have to inject more money into the firm so it can meet these commitments. If the creditors then force the firm into bankruptcy, and there is not enough money to pay off all the claims on the firm, the equity holders are still not required to invest more money in the firm. Limited liability ensures that the shareholders can only lose their initial investment. This means their *downside* risk is limited, while they have unlimited *upside* potential. In this sense, common shares have some of the characteristics of call options, discussed in Chapter 12. We will use this insight later when discussing financial strategy.

**residual owners** equity owners who receive any remaining cash flows or property (on the dissolution of the corporation) after all other commitments have been satisfied

---

### Concept Review Question

1. What are the basic rights associated with equity securities? How do these differ across different categories or classes of equities?

## 19.2 | Different Classes of Shares

> **LEARNING OBJECTIVE 19.2**
> Describe the various classes of shares and the shareholders' rights associated with each.

The *CBCA* definition qualifies the three rights of the common shareholders by stating these rights apply "where a corporation has only one class of shares." When a company has more than one class of shares, it must indicate in its articles of incorporation[4] how these rights are allocated among the various classes of shares. The only legal requirement is that each of these three rights has to be attached to a class of shares so that all these rights are clearly defined.

For example, the following share structure could be set up:

### Class A Shares

- no voting rights as long as dividend payments are made
- a $0.05 dividend in addition to any dividend paid to class B shares, but only if class C dividends are not in arrears
- an equal share with class B shares in any residual receipts on the winding up of the company

### Class B Shares

- full voting rights
- no dividends if dividends on class C shares are in arrears
- an equal share with class A shares in any residual receipts on the winding up of the company

### Class C Shares

- no voting rights unless dividends are in arrears for two years, after which each share gets one vote
- a dividend of $0.30 per share every quarter when declared by the BOD; no dividends on class A and B shares can be paid if these dividends are in arrears
- payment of $25 par value before any payments to class A and B shares on the winding up of the company

This is a loose description of a relatively simple share structure that meets the *CBCA* requirements. The voting rights rest with the class B shares, and all shares have clearly specified rights in the event of a dividend payment or the winding up of the company. In this case, the class B shares would be regarded as common shares. The class A shares have no voting rights but have a slight preferential dividend and would commonly be referred to as **non-voting** or **limited voting shares**. The class C shares are preference or preferred shares because they have a preferred dividend over both the A and B shares. Note that only the preferred shares need have a par value, since the common and limited voting shares share equally in what is left over in a bankruptcy or windup of the company after the holders of preferred shares get their par value.

There are no limitations on the share structure a company can set up as long as these three shareholder rights are clearly articulated. This example of two classes of common shares and one class of preferred shares is common for Canadian firms. However, it raises the problem of allocating voting rights.

**non-voting** or **limited voting shares**  common shares that have no voting rights but a slight preferential dividend

---

[4]It costs about $600 to do a simple incorporation listing the owner, number of shares issued, etc., and registering with the CRA for tax purposes.

# Voting and Non-Voting Shares

Voting rights give shareholders control and the ability to choose the BOD and, through it, senior management and the strategic direction of the company. In the event of a takeover, voting shares are more valuable than non-voting shares because of this control value. A company wishing to take over another can do so only by buying the voting shares. A good example of the importance of voting shares is provided by Bell Globemedia Inc.'s takeover offer for CHUM Ltd. on July 12, 2006.

CHUM had a dual-class share structure, which means that it had A and B shares similar to those described previously.. In CHUM's case, 90 percent of the class A shares were held by the Waters family, descendants of CHUM's founder, Allan Waters. These shares had normal voting rights. The family also owned 10 percent of the class B non-voting shares, which were otherwise widely held—that is, they were mainly held by retail and institutional investors. Bell Globemedia offered $52.50 for the class A shares and $47.50 for the class B shares. In both cases, the offer price was about a 60-percent premium over the average price for CHUM's shares immediately before the offer, so it was a "good" deal. However, the fact that the A shares received a $5 per share premium rankled many big institutional shareholders. If the same offer had been made to both classes of shares, the price would have been $48.50. As a portfolio manager at AIC said, "The overall price is not the issue. It's the difference and discrimination, if you will, that's fairly large."[5]

The offer price difference in the CHUM bid was relatively minimal compared with previous cases. For example, in 1988, holders of the voting shares in Canadian Tire Corporation, Ltd., received a takeover premium; those holding non-voting shares did not. To prevent this from happening again, the Toronto Stock Exchange (TSX) changed its rules after the Canadian Tire case, creating "coattail" provisions so that both classes of shares have to be purchased; the non-voting shares ride the coattails of the voting shares, which the acquirer needs to get control. However, the rules apply only to new listings, and CHUM, like many companies, was grandfathered because its shares were already outstanding.

The decision to establish or maintain classes of shares with different voting rights is common to many family-run businesses in which the founder needs external capital but wants to maintain control. A classic example was Four Seasons Hotels Inc., a chain founded by Isadore Sharpe, whose family controlled 67 percent of the votes through multiple voting shares.[6] In September 1996, Four Seasons proposed to reorganize its two main classes of shares. The subordinated voting shares were to be renamed limited voting shares, and the multiple voting shares owned by Sharpe family members, who already had 12 votes each, were to be renamed variable voting shares. The plan was to increase the voting power of these shares to keep the Sharpe family at 67 percent of the votes as more limited voting shares were issued. In essence, without putting up any more money, the Sharpe family would always control the company through these variable voting shares. Many institutional investors refuse to invest in limited or non-voting shares, but on the day the Four Seasons plan was announced, the stock price went up 55 cents and reached a 52-week high.

What both the CHUM and the Four Seasons examples highlight is the role of the founder of the company. When the voting rights are concentrated in the hands of a visionary leader who has built the company, investors are often only too happy to see control concentrated in their hands because the company *is* the senior management. For this reason, many institutional investors were relatively indifferent to the Four Seasons' plan. The problems arise when the bloodline "thins out," and the second and third generations of the family do not have the managerial skills evident in the original founder, or when the firm is sold. This was the case with CHUM: when control passed out of the hands of the founder, there was no clear strategic direction for the company. CHUM became a takeover target, and investors were upset by the price differential between the voting and non-voting shares.

The value of these voting rights depends on who has control of the company and whether it is good or bad for shareholder value creation. Empirical studies estimating the value of these voting rights have produced mixed results, as have studies of the stock market's reaction when firms recapitalize their share structure to create or remove voting differentials. The problem is that differential voting rights may not affect value when the founder runs the company, but

---

[5]Sethi, Chanakya, "CHUM Investors Criticize Dual-Class Discount." *The Globe and Mail*, July 13, 2006, p. B4.
[6]Shecter, Barbara, "Four Seasons Plan Assailed." *Financial Post*, September 27, 1996.

they do when that founder ceases to be involved and the bloodline thins. Regardless, the limited or non-voting shares usually offer a slight premium in the form of the right to a dividend to offset the lost value of control.

## Family Trusts

Another well-known example of a method for maintaining the founding family's control is provided by Ford Motor Company, in which 71 million B shares, with 40 percent of the voting rights, are in a **family trust** with an agreement that if anyone wants to sell, their shares are first offered to other family members. Trusts solve the problem of what happens after the founder ceases to be involved and the wealth gradually disperses over succeeding generations. Trusts are a standard way of separating ownership from control. For example, when an inheritance goes to an heir under the age of majority, the wealth is typically put into a trust. The minor receives the income from the inheritance but cannot control it until they reach a given age, normally 25. In similar fashion, the shares in the Ford family trust ensure that income flows through to the hundreds of individuals descended from Henry Ford, but all the votes are held by the trustees. In this way, control remains with the family even though they own only 2 percent of the company.

**family trust**  a trust that ensures income flows to the people descended from the company founder while all the votes are held by the trustees

Family members installed Clay Ford, great-grandson of Henry Ford, as president and CEO of Ford in 2001. In the next decade, Ford's stock price fell from just over $20 in 2001 to less than $2 in November 2008, and things became so desperate that Ford hired investment bankers to see how the company could be reorganized or broken up. One extreme option considered was to sell off Ford's assets except its truck division, which continued to make record profits. Luckily for Ford's external shareholders, Clay Ford had the good sense to pull back, becoming Ford's executive chairman, and to install Alan Mullaly in his place as CEO. Mullaly pledged Ford's assets and raised a significant amount of money just before the stock market collapse in 2008 and the subsequent recession. If he had not taken this route, Ford could easily have followed General Motors and Chrysler into bankruptcy. Ford's share price has recovered since then and shareholder resolutions to change Ford's share structure have been defeated each of the past several years, but each year the number of votes in favour of a change tends to increase.

This discussion of shareholder rights indicates that not all shares are created equal due to the existence of supervoting shares and family trusts. Although the differences between shares are not as great as the contractual differences between different classes of bonds, it is still important to be aware of the rights associated with each class of shares. It is also interesting to see that, as the Canadian economy has matured, the importance of founders and different classes of shares has decreased. **Figure 19.1**, taken from research by professors at

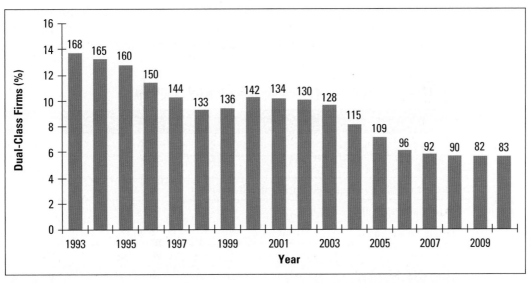

**Source:** Amoako-Adu, Ben, Smith, Brian F., and Baulkaran, Vishaal, "Assessing the Cost of Parting with Stronach and Dual-Class Shares." *Canadian Investment Review*, January 18, 2012. Accessed at www.investmentreview.com/analysis-research/magna-the-true-cost-of-share-unification-5694. Reprinted with the permission of *Canadian Investment Review*.

**FIGURE 19.1**  **Decline of Dual-Class Shares on the TSX**

## 19.1 Finance in the News Alphabet Shareholders Want More Voting Rights but Larry and Sergey Don't Want It That Way

Alphabet's shareholder meeting last week resulted in a predictable outcome: All stockholder proposals were voted down. Stockholder proposals tend to fail at any company. Management votes against them and larger investors with more shares typically vote with management.

At Alphabet, the parent company of Google, voting power is even more concentrated because of a limited supply of supervoting shares belonging mostly to Google co-founders Larry Page and Sergey Brin. Basically, it's a founders' company with the founders controlling the outcome of the vote.

One proposal this year in particular demonstrates just how much control Page and Brin have because of their special voting powers, and it's a proposal that deals with that very issue. Shareholders proposed that each shareholder get a vote equal to the number of shares they own without any super votes. Here's how the tally came down:

- For: 191.7 million
- Against: 472.6 million

Page and Brin have about 393 million votes between them because of their supervoting powers. We're assuming they voted against this proposal though we don't have a breakdown from Google. Without their supervote powers, their share of the "against" tally would be reduced to 39.3 million. Then it looks like this:

- For: 191.7 million
- Against: 118.9 million

Clearly, shareholders are interested in having more power over the direction of Alphabet and are not in agreement with top management.

**Source:** Excerpted from Townsend, Tess, "Alphabet Shareholders Want More Voting Rights But Larry and Sergey Don't Want It That Way." *Recode*, June 12, 2017. Available at recode.net. All rights reserved. Reprinted by permission of Vox Media, Inc.

Wilfrid Laurier University and the University of Lethbridge, shows the persistent decline in the importance of dual-class shares on the Toronto Stock Exchange (TSX). In contrast, Finance in the News 19.1 indicates this is a significant problem in the tech industry in the U.S., where founders are of critical importance. For example, the founders of Google, Sergey Brin and Larry Page, continue to control Google's parent, Alphabet, with 51 percent of the votes through their ownership of supervoting shares, and they are not willing to give up that control.

## Calculating Share Value and Dividend Yield

We now return to our previous example of Canadian Pacific (CP), where we calculated many key ratios and discussed its financial statements in chapters 3 and 4. Its shareholders' equity figures for the fiscal year ends of December 31, 2017, and December 31, 2018, are presented in **Table 19.2**.

Notice that CP had no preferred shares outstanding, just common shares. Its 2018 common equity figure consisted of $2,044 million contributed by shareholders through public offerings, and adjustments to shareholders' equity through net retained earnings (earnings

**TABLE 19.2** **Canadian Pacific Shareholders' Equity ($Million)**

|  | 2017 | 2018 |
|---|---|---|
| Preferred stock | 0 | 0 |
| Capital stock | 2,075 | 2,044 |
| Retained earnings and accumulated other comprehensive loss | 4,362 | 4,592 |
| Total shareholders' equity | 6,437 | 6,636 |
| Total liabilities and equity | 20,135 | 21,254 |
| Shares outstanding at year end (million) | 144.9 | 140.5 |
| Book value per share ($) | 44.42 | 47.23 |
| Diluted earnings per common share ($) | 16.44 | 13.61 |
| Common dividend per share ($) | 2.1875 | 2.5125 |

retained within the firm after dividends), share repurchases, and accumulated other comprehensive loss totalling $4,592 million.

As of its December 31, 2018, year end, CP had 140.5 million shares outstanding, so each common share had a book value per share (BVPS) of $47.23, calculated as

$$\text{BVPS} = \frac{\text{Common equity}}{\text{Number of shares}} = \frac{\$6,636}{140.5} = \$47.23$$

CP's BVPS indicates the net amount of money that CP shareholders have invested in the firm, either directly or through net earnings retained in the business. As we discussed in Chapter 4, CP is currently profitable, and its market price reflects the current and future expected profits. As a result, the market price ($P$) of its shares at year end was $242.24, compared with a BVPS of $47.23, which translates into a market-to-book ratio (M/B) of 5.13, calculated as

$$\frac{M}{B} = \frac{\text{Price}}{\text{BVPS}} = \frac{\$242.24}{\$47.23} = 5.13$$

Partly due to this high market-to-book ratio, CP would generally be regarded as a growth company. In 2018, it paid a dividend of $2.5125 ending as a quarterly dividend of $0.65, so its dividend yield at the end of 2018 using its annualized dividend per share of $2.60 divided by its year-end market price of $242.24, or 1.07 percent,[7] calculated as

$$\text{Dividend yield} = \frac{\text{Dividend per share}}{\text{Price}} = \frac{\$2.60}{\$242.24} = 1.07\%$$

Interestingly, CP has been increasing this dividend per share over the past couple of years as well as repurchasing its shares. We will discuss this under dividend policy in Chapter 22.

A dividend yield of 1.1 percent on its own would be regarded as low for a stable company like CP. **Figure 19.2** plots the dividend yield on the S&P/TSX Composite Index since January 1956, which is the longest period available. The dividend yield has averaged just above 3 percent over this period, but there has been considerable volatility because the dividend yield decreases as market prices increase as well as when the dividend per share is reduced. We can clearly see the significant increase in the dividend yield on the S&P/TSX index during the 1970s, when high levels of inflation hurt the stock market, forcing prices down and dividend yields up. We can also see the impact of the financial crisis starting in the fall of 2008, as the stock market crashed and the dividend yield popped up. However, since the markets recovered, the dividend yield has stayed about 2.75 percent, or a little above the long-run inflation rate. Dividends are

**FIGURE 19.2**  **TSX Dividend Yield since 1956**

---

[7]For the dividend yield we use the current quarterly dividend per share times four. Alternatively, we could have used the past four quarterly dividends; this is called the trailing dividend. They differ when a company, like CP, increases its dividend rate during the year.

very attractive for corporations and individuals in Canada for tax reasons. As we discussed in Chapter 3, dividends received by one Canadian corporation from another Canadian corporation are not taxed. This is in order to avoid double taxation of income at the corporate level.[8] In contrast, interest income paid by one corporation to another is taxable because, as we discussed before, interest expense is tax deductible. In this way, tax law is symmetrical.

Dividend income is attractive for individuals because of the dividend tax credit available for Canadian investors in Canadian companies. Traditionally, this system was structured so that the effective tax rate paid by owners of small private corporations was the same whether they withdrew their compensation as dividends or as salary. These dividends are classified as "ineligible" dividends and are taxed at a slightly higher rate than "eligible" dividends from large corporations due to the preferential tax rate Canada allows small business owners. In contrast, dividends from foreign shares are taxed the same as interest income, making foreign shares less attractive for tax reasons.

For federal income tax purposes, eligible Canadian-sourced dividend income is "grossed up" by 38 percent.[9] This means that for every dollar of dividends, you have to include $1.38 in your taxable income. The federal government then allows a dividend tax credit of 20.73 percent of the actual dividend applied against the federal tax. Further, each province allows a provincial dividend tax credit to partially offset against provincial taxes. The result is that the combined tax rate on eligible dividend income for an Ontario resident in the top tax bracket is 39.34 percent, compared with 53.53 percent for interest income and 26.76 percent for capital gains income. For "ineligible" dividends from a private small business, the tax rate is 47.40 percent. The tax rate on both eligible and ineligible dividends has been increasing as the corporate tax rate has declined. In this way, the overall tax rate on equity income is roughly the same as on other sources of income. All these tax rates change periodically with new budgets, but it is unlikely that the relative tax preference for dividend income by retail (personal) investors will change, since it reflects the fact that, unlike interest income, dividends are paid out of after-tax income and have already borne the effect of corporate income taxes. The result is that every investor in Canada has a tax preference to receive dividend rather than interest income, while in many provinces, low-income tax filers pay no tax on dividend income at all.[10]

---

### Concept Review Questions

1. Why do voting rights affect the prices of some common shares and not others?
2. Why is dividend income preferred by both corporations and individual investors?

---

## 19.3 | Preferred Shares

### LEARNING OBJECTIVE 19.3
Describe preferred shares and outline the various features associated with them.

The fact that interest income and dividend income are taxed differently is well known in the capital market. BMO Capital Markets, the investment dealer arm of the Bank of Montreal, produces a monthly preferred share statistics report that tracks the performance of the preferred share market. The April 30, 2015, issue of *Preferred Share Statistics* provided the yields on various instruments. **Table 19.3** reports the yields on three different

---

[8]Of course, the income is eventually taxed twice in total because individual investors pay taxes on any dividends received. However, eliminating the tax on dividends paid to other corporations avoids having the same dollar of income taxed three times—twice at the corporate level and once again when received by individual investors.

[9]"Eligible" essentially means Canadian source income from a corporation that has paid tax at the full corporate tax rate.

[10]See the current tax calculators provided by Ernst & Young on its website, http://www.ey.com/CA/en/Services/Tax/Tax-Calculators-2019-Personal-Tax.

**TABLE 19.3**  Preferred Share Yields, April 30, 2015

| Straight Preferreds | (%) |
|---|---|
| Dividend yield | 4.81 |
| Long Canada yield | 2.18 |
| After-tax spread yield for corporate at 30% | 3.28 |
| After-tax for individual at top tax rate | 2.08 |
| **Retractable Preferreds** | **(%)** |
| Dividend yield | 3.80 |
| Mid Canada yield | 0.98 |
| After-tax spread yield for corporate at 30% | 3.11 |
| After-tax spread for individual at top tax rate | 2.02 |
| **Floating Rate Preferred Shares** | **(%)** |
| Dividend yield | 3.63 |
| BA (3-month) | 0.93 |
| After-tax yield for corporate at 30% | 2.98 |
| After-tax yield for individual at top tax rate | 1.93 |

**Source:** Data from BMO, *Preferred Share Statistics* (May 2015)

types of preferred shares, which we discuss next. Because of the favourable tax treatment accorded dividends in Canada, a variety of types of preferred shares exist in the capital market. Many of these issues are designed to mimic different types of bonds and appeal to bond investors who want the more favourable tax treatment. This is why BMO reports the after-tax yields to both corporate investors and ordinary or retail investors: some of these preferred shares are specifically designed for corporate investors, while others are for the traditional retail market. Remember that although preferred shares are a type of equity and the dividends are not legally an obligation until they are declared, for low-risk companies their payment is virtually assured.

## Types of Preferred Shares

### Straight Preferred Shares

The first type of preferred share reported in Table 19.3 is the traditional **straight preferred share**. These are preferred shares that have no maturity date and pay a fixed dividend at regular intervals (usually quarterly). As discussed in Chapter 7, these can be viewed as perpetuities and are valued accordingly. These were the most common type of preferreds in the Canadian market until the 1970s. In Table 19.3, the straight preferred yields are 4.81 percent, compared with a yield of 2.18 percent for long Canada bonds, implying a positive yield spread or difference between the two of 2.63 percent.

There are several reasons for this difference in yields. The most obvious is that bonds issued by the Government of Canada are clearly a lower risk than preferred shares issued by a firm that may default. In addition, straight preferred shares that have no maturity date have a longer life than even the longest-term government bonds, so they will have greater maturity risk, as discussed in Chapter 6. These risks, particularly the default risk, are reflected in this yield spread, even before we take taxes into account.

The 2.63-percent spread is based on before-tax yields, so it does not take into account the **tax value of money**: the fact that dividends are taxed more favourably than interest income and so are more valuable than interest income. To account for the tax differences, BMO

**straight preferred share**
a preferred share that has no maturity date and pays a fixed dividend at regular intervals, usually quarterly

**tax value of money**  the fact that some sources of income like dividends are taxed at preferential rates and are thus more valuable than other sources of income like interest income

Capital Markets also estimates the after-tax yields, which are based on the dividends being in the hands of a corporate investor in the 30-percent tax bracket, for whom the dividend income is non-taxable, and in the hands of a private investor in the highest tax bracket, where BMO assumed a top rate in 2015 on dividend income of 33.82 percent, versus 49.53 percent on interest income. As a result, the after-tax spread is reported by BMO as 3.28 percent for a corporate investor, and 2.08 percent for a personal investor.

How did BMO get these rates? Well, the dividend is non-taxable for the corporate investor, so the after-tax yield is the same as the before-tax yield, or 4.81 percent. In contrast, interest is tax deductible when paid by a corporation, and is thus taxable when received—that is, the tax code is symmetrical. As a result, the after-tax yield on the long Canada bonds is the 2.18 percent multiplied by (1 – 0.3) or 1.53 percent. So the after-tax spread thus increases from the pre-tax spread of 2.63 percent to 3.28 percent. The same calculations for the individual using the 33.82-percent top rate for dividends and 49.53 percent for interest results in an after-tax spread of 2.08 percent.

## Retractable Preferred Shares

**retractable preferred share**
a share that gives the investor the right to sell it back to the issuer, thus creating an early maturity date

The second type of preferred share presented in Table 19.3 is the **retractable preferred share**. Retraction means that the investor has the right to sell the shares back to the issuer at a date prior to maturity. Retractable preferred shares permit early retirement, with the typical retraction date being set at five years. Therefore, even though the preferred shares may end up being outstanding for longer periods, they are valued as if the maturity is five years. For this reason, BMO Capital Markets compares the yields on retractable preferreds with those on mid-term bonds. On April 30, 2015, the retractable preferred shares yielded 3.8 percent, while the mid-term Canada bonds yielded 0.98 percent, producing a before-tax spread of 2.82 percent in favour of the riskier preferred shares. The after-tax spread BMO then calculates as 3.11 percent for the corporate investor and 2.02 percent for the individual investor.

## Floating Rate Preferred Shares

**floating rate preferred share**
a share that has a long maturity date but that has its dividend reset by an auction mechanism every three or six months so that the dividend yield is in line with market interest rates

The final type of preferred share reported in Table 19.3 is the **floating rate preferred share**. These shares generally have a long maturity date, but every three or six months, their dividend is reset by an auction mechanism so that the dividend yield will be in line with current market interest rates. Alternatively, many of the floating rate preferred shares issued by the major banks have their dividend rate float with 75 percent of the prime rate, usually to some maximum rate. The result is that they always sell close to their par value because their dividend rate is always close to the current market interest rate. In Table 19.3, the yield on these "floaters" is compared with the yield on three-month bankers' acceptances (BAs), which represent an alternative short-term fixed income investment. The yield on the floaters was 3.63 percent compared to the 0.93-percent yield on the BAs, producing a pre-tax spread of 2.7 percent. The after-tax spread was 2.98 percent for corporate investors and 1.93 percent for individual investors.

Three important points about the yield data emerge. First, although the time and risk value of money are important, so too is the tax value of money, since this is the money that investors actually receive after the government takes its share. Second, the capital market is creative in its ability to design securities that meet investor demand. The BMO data match the preferred shares with similar Government of Canada bonds, where the main distinguishing feature is the tax treatment of the income.[11] Finally, the comparisons are never perfect because preferred shares are unambiguously riskier than Government of Canada securities, even those of the same maturity, due to both the default risk and also generally the fact that preferred shares are less liquid. Generally, the after-tax spreads are smallest for the shorter-term securities, where the risk differences are the lowest, and largest for the perpetual straight preferred shares, when compared with long-term Canada bonds.[12]

---

[11]At one point in the 1980s, there was an attempt to issue 30-day preferred shares to directly mimic BAs. The CRA closed this down, which stimulated the growth of the floating rate preferred share market.

[12]Note the spreads increase from the floating rate to the retractable to the fixed rate preferred shares versus equivalent maturity bonds.

# Other Features of Preferred Shares

The basic risk attached to investing in preferred shares is that they have "equity risk" in addition to the investment risks attached to fixed income securities. As mentioned previously, equity securities do not provide a contractual right to anything except the residuals after all other claimants have been paid off. If, in any quarter, the BOD decides *not* to pay a dividend, the holders of preferred shares cannot seek legal action to force payment. This legal principle gives a firm some flexibility if it runs into serious financial trouble, because it can conserve cash by suspending the dividend payments, whereas it cannot unilaterally suspend interest payments.

However, because they don't carry a right to receive a dividend, most preferred shares do have a **cumulative provision**, which states that no dividends can be paid on common shares until preferred share dividends, both current and arrears, are paid in full. This ensures that the common shareholders, who have voting rights, don't suspend payment on the preferred share dividends while continuing to pay dividends on the common shares. Some preferred shares also get limited voting rights as the arrears accumulate, which allows the preferred shareholders to exercise some control over the company. However, these rights depend on the structure of the preferred shares.[13]

**cumulative provision** a stipulation that no dividends can be paid on common shares until preferred share dividends, both current and arrears, are paid in full

Commonly, firms experiencing financial trouble will suspend dividend payments on all classes of shares, including preferred shares, to conserve cash. If the firm then recovers, it must make significant cash payments to clear off the preferred dividend arrears. In practice, what often happens in these situations is that the arrears are paid through the issue of common shares or some combination of cash and shares. This allows the firm to clean up its balance sheet and start fresh.

An example of a traditional straight preferred issue is the series G preferred shares issued by Great-West Lifeco Inc. Great-West Lifeco has several series of preferred shares outstanding, each with slightly different features. As with other classes of shares, Great-West Lifeco's authorized capital allows it to issue more of these shares if it wants, or it can start another series. As of February 2019, there was $300 million of the G series outstanding, each with a par value of $25. Unlike common shares, preferred shares have a par value so their value is known in the event of bankruptcy. In addition, as is the case for bonds, the amount of the dividend payment is sometimes expressed as a percentage of par. In the case of these particular preferred shares, the dividend is $1.30 and they trade on the TSX under the symbol "GWO.PR.G," similar to common shares. On February 14, 2019, the G preferred shares sold at a discount to their par value of $23.07 to yield 5.60 percent. An interesting feature of Great-West Lifeco's preferred shares is that the series G through P do not have dividends that cumulate, and it has now redeemed its preferred share series A through F, which did have cumulative dividends.

Also similar to bonds, and like many other preferred share issues, this series is "callable" by Great-West Lifeco. The shares were callable at $26 in December 2010, with the call price dropping by $0.25 every December until 2013, after which they could be redeemed at par ($25). This means that at Great-West Lifeco's option, it can call the preferred shares away from their owners by paying the fixed call price. Since these preferred shares were selling at a discount in 2019, there was no incentive for Great West Lifeco to redeem them.

From this description of Great-West Lifeco's preferred shares, we can see that they have many of the characteristics of bonds. Like bonds, they have different features that require that each series of preferred shares be evaluated separately. We have discussed retraction features and call features, but some preferred shares (convertibles) can be converted into other securities, usually common shares, which we will discuss shortly. Other preferred shares have "purchase funds," which act like sinking funds for debt securities (discussed in Chapter 6). Like sinking funds, purchase funds require the company to buy back a certain number of shares each year, creating a "two-edged" sword: in the short run, this increases the number of purchasers and ensures a ready market for the shares; in the long run, however, as the number of shares goes down, it has the opposite effect.

---

[13]Note that many of the short-term preferred shares, particularly those issued by the banks, do not have this cumulative feature, because the risk of non-payment is very low.

Just like bonds and commercial paper, preferred shares are rated by the rating agencies, such as Dominion Bond Rating Service (DBRS). However, because preferred shares are riskier than either bonds or CP, the rating structure is more limited. Pfd-1 is equivalent to both AAA- and AA-rated bonds, Pfd-2 to A-rated bonds, Pfd-3 to more highly rated BBB bonds, Pfd-4 to lower-rated BBB and BB-rated bonds, and Pfd-5 to B- or lower-rated bonds. The Great West Lifeco preferred shares are all rated Pfd-1 (low) by DBRS.

We have discussed preferred shares in the context of shareholders' equity because, legally, they are equity securities; they simply have a different allocation of the rights under the *CBCA*. However, as the discussion here demonstrates, they share many characteristics with debt and are commonly regarded as a **hybrid security**, part debt and part equity. In fact, there is a continuum of financial securities that run the full range from common shares to what people typically think of as debt. Some of the hybrids can be very important for corporate financing, and we will discuss them in the following sections.

**hybrid security** a security that is part debt and part equity

---

### Concept Review Questions

1. Briefly describe the following types of preferred shares: straight, retractable, and floating rate.
2. Briefly describe the following features that may be associated with preferred shares: cumulative provision, callable feature, and purchase funds.
3. Why are preferred shares sometimes called hybrid securities?
4. Why would you want a cumulative feature when purchasing preferred shares?

---

## 19.4 | Warrants and Convertible Securities

### LEARNING OBJECTIVE 19.4
Explain how combining warrants with debt issues, or issuing convertible bonds or debentures, can provide firms with attractive financing options.

We now consider the last major class of securities issued by companies, which includes warrants, convertible bonds, and convertible preferred shares.

### Warrants

**warrants** the corporate finance equivalent of call options, issued by firms to raise capital; when they are exercised, more shares are created; they usually have long maturities, which make them more valuable

**Warrants** are the corporate finance equivalent of call options, so they are affected by the same factors as those that affect call options, as discussed in Chapter 12. However, there are two major differences.

- First, call options are transactions between two external investors; what one investor gains, the other loses, but there is no impact on the firm. Warrants are issued by firms to raise capital; when they are exercised, more shares are created—that is, they are exercised against the company.
- Second, call options are usually issued with very short maturities because they are standardized. Warrants almost always have longer maturities, which makes them more valuable.

**Table 19.4** lists the data on five warrants outstanding on the Toronto Stock Exchange on February 19, 2019. The data come from Canadianwarrants.com.

Many of the warrants in Canada are for mining firms or other resource companies. In fact, most warrants are issued by junior firms looking for equity financing. The company receives initial financing by issuing the warrants; then, if events turn out well (for example, if a drilling operation is successful), the stock price rises and the firm sees a further infusion of

**TABLE 19.4**   **Warrant Listings, February 19, 2019**

| Company | Stock Close | Stock Exchange | Ticker | Exercise Price | Recent Close | Intrinsic Value | Time Value | Days Left | Expiry Date |
|---|---|---|---|---|---|---|---|---|---|
| Aurora Cannabis | 9.30 | TSX | ACB.WT | 4.00 | 5.56 | 5.30 | 0.26 | 622 | 2-Nov-20 |
| Canada Jetlines | 0.56 | TSXV | JET.WT | 0.50 | 0.04 | 0.06 | 0.02 | 9 | 28-Feb-19 |
| Kootenay Silver | 0.13 | TSXV | KTN.WT | 0.55 | 0.05 | −0.42 | 0.47 | 792 | 21-April-21 |
| TAG Oil | 0.38 | TSX | TAO.WT | 0.90 | 0.01 | −0.52 | 0.53 | 29 | 20-Mar-19 |
| Yellow Pages | 5.80 | TSX | Y.WT | 28.16 | 0.46 | −22.36 | 22.82 | 1,400 | 20-Dec-22 |

**Source:** Data from Canadianwarrants.com, accessed February 19, 2019.

equity as the warrants are exercised. In contrast to the situation with calls, when the warrants are exercised, the warrant holder pays the exercise price to the company in return for shares. Warrants thus provide *primary* financing because the issuing company raises capital from their sale and, if the company is successful, receives a further infusion of cash on conversion. Warrant financing is very attractive for junior or start-up companies with uncertain prospects.

Canadianwarrants.com provides all the standard data needed to price warrants as call options. The first warrants listed, for example, were issued by Aurora Cannabis with an exercise price of $4.00, and on February 19, 2019, they had 622 days until their maturity date of November 2, 2020, which is slightly longer than standard secondary market call options. These warrant holders had done well, as legal changes in Canada regarding the recreational use of cannabis in 2017 had increased the underlying value of Aurora Cannabis shares more than threefold. On February 19, 2019, Aurora Cannabis's stock price was $9.30, meaning that they could be exercised immediately to earn $5.30, which was their intrinsic value. However, as they were selling for $5.56, the warrants still had a time value of $0.26 since they still had 622 days until maturity.

The second warrant was issued by Canada Jetlines, which through a backdoor underwriting (see Chapter 17) is listed on the Toronto Venture Exchange. This is an interesting situation, since Canada Jetlines plans to offer ultra-low-cost carrier service across Canada and the U.S. with a home base in Vancouver. The warrants were priced at $0.04 with an exercise price of $0.50, while the stock price was only $0.56 with 9 days left to expiration. The intrinsic value of $0.06 was less than the warrant price, meaning that it was cheaper to buy the stock by buying the warrants and then exercising them. In this case, the warrants were part of the start-up financing of a new airline.

The final three warrants all had negative intrinsic value, but for different reasons. Kootenay Silver and TAG Oil warrants are typical Canadian resource stocks that have suffered with the decline in commodity prices. For Kootenay Silver, the exercise price was $0.42 above the stock price, but as a junior exploration company with two years remaining on the warrant life, there was still a chance they would be exercised. For TAG Oil, however, the warrants had only 29 days left before maturity, and even at a price of $0.01 were regarded as overvalued, since the probability that the stock price could increase from $0.38 to the $0.90 exercise price was remote. The final warrants on Yellow Pages have been in previous editions of this book, since they are very long-dated warrants that still had 1,400 days left to maturity as of February 19, 2019. However, in the 4th edition the options were worth $4.68 with an exercise price of $28.16; now their value has dropped to $0.46 as the underlying stock price for Yellow Pages has continued to drop. In effect, the Internet has destroyed Yellow Pages' underlying business model.

The prior discussion presents some of the standard factors needed for pricing call options. However, the fact that the number of shares outstanding increases when warrants are exercised means that warrants have to be valued by using a variant of the standard option pricing model. We denote the existing number of shares as $n$ and the number of shares issued on exercise of the warrants, at an exercise price of $X$, as $m$. If the value of the firm, without taking into account the warrants, is $V$, then the payoff if the warrants are exercised can be expressed as shown in Equation 19.1:

$$\text{Payoff to warrant holders} = \frac{m}{n+m}(V + mX) - mX \qquad [19.1]$$

Equation 19.1 indicates that after the warrants are exercised, the value of the firm must be the value without the warrants ($V$) plus the proceeds to the firm from the exercise of the warrants ($mX$), for a total value of $V + mX$. Of this total value, the percentage owned by the warrant holders is $m/(n + m)$, whereas the cost to them is the exercise value of $mX$. As a result, the payoff to the warrant holders is the difference between these two values. If we multiply the exercise value $mX$ by $(n + m)/(n + m)$ and simplify, the payoff reduces to Equation 19.2:

$$\text{Payoff to warrant holders} = \frac{m}{n+m}(V - nX) \qquad [19.2]$$

In Equation 19.2, $V - nX$ can be viewed as the standard payoff to $n$ secondary market calls with the same strike price of $X$—in other words, if we divide both of these terms by $n$, the first term is the share price (i.e., $V/n$), and the second term is the exercise price ($X$). The first term, $m/(n + m)$, is the **dilution factor**, which results from the additional shares that are created as the warrants are exercised. Consequently, however the value of a secondary market call is determined, the value of the warrant is this amount multiplied by the dilution factor. This result holds whether we use the Black-Scholes or the binomial option pricing models discussed in Chapter 12 and Appendix 12A, respectively. The equation also indicates the importance of the dilution factor, particularly as many of these warrants are issued by junior resource firms where it is usually very significant.

**dilution factor** the amount by which ownership is reduced when additional shares are issued

---

**EXAMPLE 19.1** | Estimating Payoffs to Warrants

A company has 10 million shares outstanding that are trading at $20 per share. The company has 1 million warrants outstanding that have an exercise price of $18 each. What is the payoff to the warrant holders of exercising them?

**Solution**

$$m = 1 \text{ million}$$
$$n = 10 \text{ million}$$
$$V = \$20 \times 10 \text{ million} = \$200 \text{ million}$$
$$X = \$18$$

By using Equation 19.2, we can estimate the payoff as

$$\text{Payoff} = \frac{m}{n + m}(V - nX) = 1/(10 + 1) \times (\$200 - (10)(\$18)) = (1/11) \times (\$20) = \$1.818 \text{ million}$$

---

Because they are valuable, warrants are frequently used as "sweeteners" to make issues more attractive and thereby access financing that would not otherwise be available. For example, junior mines often have significant capital expenditures and limited cash flow to meet interest payments on financing. If they approach a venture capitalist for debt financing, they may be asked to pay a very high interest rate, given the risks involved. This compounds the problem of a lack of cash flow to make the interest payments. In these circumstances, the combination of a low-cost loan and warrants may allow the firms to raise debt. The low interest rate helps alleviate a firm's cash flow problems, while the warrants make new equity financing available if the firm is successful. Investors may be willing to buy these warrants, which might provide a significant payoff if the firm does well and its share price increases.

Furthermore, the very risk that makes debt financing expensive also makes the warrants valuable. Recall from our discussion in Chapter 12 that call options are more valuable when the underlying asset price is volatile. This is also true for warrants, which are simply corporate-issued call options. As a general rule, we often see warrants and convertibles (which are discussed next) being issued by firms that face significant uncertainty and possess correspondingly low bond ratings. They have difficulty raising debt capital without resorting to the use of some form of sweetener. For these firms, using warrants or adding convertible features reduces the cash outlay for interest payments, thus lowering the risk of financial distress.[14]

---

[14]A basic problem of debt financing is that increasing the interest rate for risky borrowers makes the borrowers even riskier.

For similar reasons, warrants are often part of staged financing by a company. If the company is successful, the stock price will go up, so by issuing warrants that include the right to buy further warrants, a company can generate an automatic sequence of financing. The warrants in this kind of financing strategy are often referred to as "bunny warrants," for obvious reasons. If the warrants are "detachable," the institution providing the debt may sell the warrants to other investors. If they are not detachable, issuing bonds plus warrants is similar to issuing convertible bonds.

## Convertible Securities

In this section we focus on the conversion feature attached to both convertible bonds and convertible preferred shares. Although the underlying security is different, the conversion features operate in an identical manner, and for convenience we will discuss convertible bonds. Note that due to their similarity, both convertible bonds and preferred shares are traded on the Toronto Stock Exchange. As described in Chapter 6, convertible bonds are bonds that can be converted into a specified number of common shares at the option of the bondholder. In many ways, they are similar to bonds with warrants. The key difference is that when convertibles are converted, the bonds or preferred shares are exchanged for common shares and are no longer outstanding, whereas for debt with warrants attached, the debt remains outstanding and the exercise price is paid in cash. This means that the firm does not get any new financing when convertibles are converted; all that happens is that the debt is converted into common shares. In contrast, with warrants the firm gets new financing from the sale of new shares at the exercise price. However, even though they get no additional financing, firms issue convertibles because the conversion does change the firm's capital structure by increasing the amount of common equity and reducing either debt or preferred shares. As we will discuss in Chapter 21, this increases the firm's financial flexibility and allows it to issue more debt in the future.

On June 3, 2015, the *Financial Post* reported the data shown in **Table 19.5** for three convertible bonds outstanding in Canada. Like companies offering warrants, companies that issue convertible bonds tend to be high risk. The first company listed in Table 19.5 is 5N Plus Inc., which is a small specialty metals company headquartered in Montreal with a market value of barely $100 million. 5N Plus has a convertible bond with a 5.75-percent coupon selling for $85. These bonds have just four years to maturity, and a yield to maturity of 10.36 percent, since they are selling at a $15 discount to their par value. The *Financial Post* reported a **conversion ratio (CR)** of 14.81 for these bonds. This means that each bond could be converted into approximately 14.81 5N Plus common shares. Remember that bonds have a $1,000 par value but are always quoted as $100, so if we divide the 14.81 into $100, we can say that the **conversion price (CP)** is $6.75 (i.e., $100/14.81), as reported in the listing. 5N Plus is effectively selling common shares for $6.75 if the bonds are converted. We depict this relationship in Equation 19.3.

**conversion ratio (CR)**   the number of shares for which a convertible security can be exchanged

**conversion price (CP)**   the price at which a convertible security can be converted into common shares based on its conversion ratio

$$CP = \frac{Par}{CR}$$   [19.3]

**TABLE 19.5**   **Convertible Bond Listings, June 3, 2015**

| Issuer | Coupon | Maturity | Last Price | Parity | Yield to Maturity | Premium | Conversion Ratio | Conversion Price | Share Price |
|---|---|---|---|---|---|---|---|---|---|
| 5N Plus | 5.75% | 30-Jun-19 | 85 | 18.52 | 10.36% | 359.00% | 14.81 | 6.75 | 1.25 |
| Altus Group | 6.75% | 30-Jun-17 | 187.19 | 186.9 | −23.49% | −0.01% | 10 | 10 | 18.72 |
| Atrium Mortgage | 5.25% | 30-Sep-21 | 100 | 80.27 | 5.50% | 24.57% | 6.83 | 14.65 | 11.76 |

**Source:** Data from *Financial Post*, http://www.financialpost.com/markets/data/bonds-debentures.html

**conversion value (CV)**   the value of a convertible security if it is immediately converted into common shares

At the time, however, the market price ($P$) of 5N Plus's common shares was only $1.25, so the **conversion value (CV)** for these convertibles, denoted as "Parity" in the listing, was 14.81 times the current share price, or $18.52. The conversion value is the value of the bonds if they are immediately converted into common shares, as expressed in Equation 19.4.

$$CV = CR \times P \qquad [19.4]$$

Because the last price for these bonds was $85, and their value if immediately converted into common shares was only $18.52, the bonds were selling for a premium over their conversion value of 359 percent (i.e., (85 − 18.52)/18.52). Equation 19.5 calculates this conversion premium.

$$\text{Conversion premium} = \frac{(\text{Market value} - CV)}{CV} \qquad [19.5]$$

We can view this 359-percent premium as the percentage by which the 5N Plus share price has to increase before it will make sense to convert the bonds into common shares. Recall from Chapter 12 that when the stock price is less than the exercise price for call options, we say the option is "out of the money" and has an intrinsic value of zero; no one would exercise the call. Similarly, with the 5N Plus convertibles, when the conversion value is less than the bond's market value, no one will voluntarily convert the bonds into common shares.

The 5N Plus bonds are an example of an out-of-the-money call option since the conversion value or parity is such a small proportion of the bond's current market value. Because the bonds are deep out of the money, it is unlikely that they will be converted into common shares in the time left before they mature on June 30, 2019. In this case, the convertible is largely selling on its **straight bond value (SBV)**. The SBV can be determined by using the standard bond pricing equation that was introduced in Chapter 6, using the yield on similar non-callable bonds as the market rate ($k_b$). Using Equation 6.1, we can calculate SBV.

**straight bond value (SBV)** the price that a convertible bond would sell for if it could not be converted into common stock

$$SBV = I \times \left[ \frac{1 - \dfrac{1}{(1 + k_b)^n}}{k_b} \right] + F \times \frac{1}{(1 + k_b)^n} \qquad [19.6]$$

In Equation 19.6,

$SBV =$ the straight bond value

$I =$ interest (or coupon) payments

$k_b =$ the yield on similar non-callable bonds

$n =$ the term to maturity

$F =$ the face (par) value of the bond

In Table 19.5, the *Financial Post* simply reversed the bond-pricing Equation 19.6, using the current market price to calculate the yield to maturity on the convertible bond of 10.36 percent. With four-year Canada bonds selling on yields of 0.7 percent at that time, a spread of 9.66 percent for these bonds indicates the market regards them as junk with a high default probability or limited recovery.

**floor value (FV)**   the lowest price a convertible bond will sell for, which is equal to the larger of its straight bond value or its conversion value

Every convertible bond has a **floor value (FV)**, because it will always sell *for no less than* the larger of its straight bond value or its conversion value. This is logical because even if the company's shares are trading at a price well below the conversion price, so that the value of the conversion feature is negligible, the bond would still be held by investors and valued as a straight bond, as seems to be the case for the 5N Plus bond. Therefore, it will never trade below the SBV. Similarly, a convertible bond would never sell below its conversion value because if it did, arbitrageurs would buy the bond, convert it into common stock, and sell the shares, thus earning riskless profits.

If we look at the Altus Group convertible bond, included in the *Financial Post* table, its conversion value (parity) is $186.90, which is essentially its current market price. In this case, the recorded yield is −23.49 percent, since if it were held for the two years to maturity, these bonds would be redeemed at $100 for a capital loss. As we can see, the convertible for 5N Plus is selling essentially at its straight bond value, while that for Altus is selling at its conversion value. This confirms that we can estimate the FV of a convertible using Equation 19.7.

$$FV = \text{Max (SBV,CV)}$$

[19.7]

Of course, in practice, convertibles usually sell at prices higher than their minimum value because of the time value of the conversion option, in the same way that warrants and calls sell above their intrinsic value. However, for 5N Plus the option is deep out of the money, while for Altus it is deep in the money.

---

**EXAMPLE 19.2** | Convertible Bond Values

A 10-percent coupon bond has 10 years to maturity when market rates on similar non-convertible bonds are 8 percent. It is convertible into 50 common shares and has a $1,000 par value. Estimate the following for this convertible:

  **a.** conversion price
  **b.** straight bond value (SBV), assuming it pays annual coupons
  **c.** conversion value (CV), if the shares are trading at $25 per share
  **d.** floor value (FV)
  **e.** conversion premium, if it was trading at $1,350

**Solution**

  **a.** $CP = Par/CR = \$1,000/50 = \$20$
  **b.** $Par = \$1,000; I = \text{coupon rate} \times F = 0.1 \times \$1,000 = \$100; n = 10; k_b = 0.08$

  With this information, we can use Equation 19.6 to find the price, or we can solve it using a financial calculator.

  $$SBV = \$100 \times \left[ \frac{1 - \dfrac{1}{(1.08)^{10}}}{0.08} \right] + \$1,000 \times \frac{1}{(1 + 0.08)^{10}} = \$1,134.20$$

  **c.** $CV = CR \times P = 50 \text{ shares/bond} \times \$25/\text{share} = \$1,250$
  **d.** Floor value $(FV) = \text{Max(SBV,CV)} = \text{Max}(\$1,134.20, \$1,250) = \$1,250$

  The convertible *cannot* trade below this.
  **e.** Conversion premium $= (\$1,350 - \$1,250)/\$1,250 = 8\%$

---

**EXAMPLE 19.2** | Solution Using a Financial Calculator

$-100 \rightarrow$ **PMT** $; 10 \rightarrow$ **N** $; -1,000 \rightarrow$ **FV** $; 8\% \rightarrow$ **I/Y** $;$ **CPT** **PV** $= \$1,134.20$

---

Conceptually, we can view a convertible bond as a straight bond plus the option to convert the bond into common shares. The convertibles are thus a hybrid. This hybrid characteristic can be illustrated by thinking about what happens at maturity, when the purchaser can surrender the bond for its par value. Essentially, there are two alternatives: either the share price goes higher than the conversion price or it does not. If the price goes higher, then investors will convert the bonds into the common shares, because the conversion value will exceed the bond value of the convertible. To make sure that conversion occurs, most convertible

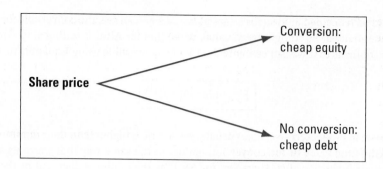

**FIGURE 19.3** **Convertible Scenarios**

bonds are also callable by the issuer. Therefore, if the conversion value exceeds the par value, the company can state its intention to buy them back at par, thereby forcing conversion by the investors because they will get a higher price by converting than by selling them back at par.

If the company did not have the right to buy the bonds at $100 plus accrued interest, investors would continue to hold the bonds and would not convert them into common shares because there would still be time value attached to the option to convert. If, on the other hand, the share price is less than the conversion value at the maturity date, the holders will simply demand their par value of $100 for the bond, and the conversion privilege will expire worthless, just like an out-of-the-money call option. These two scenarios are illustrated in **Figure 19.3**.

When convertibles are issued, the conversion price is normally set so that the share price has to increase by 25 percent before the bonds will be converted. Look, for example, at the third convertible bond, issued by Atrium Mortgage. This bond is selling exactly at par, so the coupon is approximately the same as the yield to maturity. However, its conversion value (parity) is $80.27, meaning the bond is selling at a 24.57-percent premium over its conversion value. This is typical for convertibles: when they are issued they are priced assuming at least a 25-percent increase in the share price over a five- to six-year time horizon.

So let's look at our two other bonds, recognizing that when they were issued, investors received a lower interest rate in return for an expected capital gain through the share price. In the case of Altus Group, the share price had increased by much more than 25 percent and was 87.2 percent more than the conversion price. In this case, an even better strategy, in retrospect, would have been to finance with straight debt and then issue shares for $18.72 rather than the conversion price. The after-the-fact best financing choices would have been, in order, debt, convertibles, and common shares. However, firms (or investors) do not have the luxury of perfect foresight.

Now consider what happened to 5N Plus. In this situation, the company will be forced to redeem the bonds at par value if it can, but it will have had the benefit of debt that cost only 5.75 percent, when similar straight debt would have cost much more. As a result, 5N Plus will have ended up with cheaper debt financing. However, at the issue date, the expectation was that the stock price would increase by at least 25 percent, so that the holders of the convertible bonds would convert them into common shares. The fact that the shares have instead dropped to $1.25 means that the shareholders have received an inadequate rate of return. The best scenario, in retrospect, would have been for 5N Plus to sell common shares rather than convertibles on the issue date. After the fact, the best financing choices for 5N Plus were common shares, convertibles, and debt. The fact they effectively sold cheaper debt hides the fact they could have sold expensive equity.

This what-if scenario analysis indicates that convertibles are rarely the "right" decision, but they are never the "wrong" decision, because the firm gets either cheaper debt or cheaper equity financing. It is this compromise that makes convertibles popular for many high-risk junior companies that have trouble accessing debt markets because of the high interest rate. Convertibles are also popular when a company's management is reluctant to issue more common shares because it believes its share price is undervalued.

This discussion has emphasized that convertibles are hybrids: they are part equity and part debt. When 5N Plus and Altus issued their convertibles, straight debt financing would have been expensive. However, issuing convertibles did not mean they got cheap debt, since on the issue date they were both partly debt and partly equity. The low interest rate is compensation for also selling the implicit call option. How much they were of each depends on the terms of the convertible and the option value, but the fact they were hybrids means we cannot consider them to be either debt or equity in isolation.

As we look at the other convertibles, we note that what the *Financial Post* lists as the "premium" is the market price minus the conversion value, divided by the conversion value. This will always be positive because the convertibles will always sell for more than the higher of their conversion value or bond value due to their option value.

---

### Concept Review Questions

1. Explain why issuing debt or preferred shares with warrants attached, or issuing convertible bonds or convertible preferred shares, may represent attractive sources of financing for higher-risk firms.

2. Define and explain how to determine the following for a convertible: conversion price, conversion value, straight bond value, floor value, and convertible premium.

---

## 19.5 | Other Hybrids

**LEARNING OBJECTIVE 19.5**

Describe the various hybrid financing options available to firms, and explain how they are constructed.

Warrants, convertible bonds, and convertible preferred shares are the most obvious types of hybrids. However, there has been enormous innovation in corporate financing aimed at creating hybrids that satisfy multiple objectives.

## Categorizing Hybrids

Our focus on hybrids so far has been on the CRA's definition of interest for tax purposes. However, there is also the question of how these securities are categorized on the firm's financial statements—are they treated as debt or equity?—and by the rating agencies. The financial criteria for viewing hybrids as debt, equity, or some mix of the two are different from the CRA's criteria. DBRS, for example, looks at four factors to determine whether a security is debt or equity: the permanence factor, the subordination factor, the legal factor, and the subjective factor.

The **permanence factor** relates to whether or not the security will be outstanding for a long period. Common shares are the gold standard because they have no maturity date and no requirement to redeem them at any point. Commercial paper (CP), conversely, is the ultimate debt instrument because it has a very limited life, 30 or 60 days, after which it is expected to be redeemed. The **subordination factor** refers to the priority of the claim on the firm's assets and income stream. Again, common shares are the gold standard and CP is obvious debt because it has an absolute claim to be paid off in 30 or 60 days. The **legal factor** refers to the legal rights of the investors—that is, do they have a contractual right to receive income or is it in some way discretionary, such as the declaration of a dividend by the BOD? Finally, the **subjective factor** is the intention of the company when it issues the securities.

Standard & Poor's (S&P), one of the two major U.S. bond-rating agencies, has gone into the issue of hybrids in more detail because there are more outstanding in the U.S. market. S&P has four criteria that are similar to those of DBRS.[15]

**permanence factor** the length of time for which the security will be outstanding; a major factor in determining whether a security is debt or equity

**subordination factor** the priority of the security's claim on the firm's assets and income stream; a major factor in determining whether a security is debt or equity

**legal factor** the rights, contractual or discretionary, of investors to receive income; a major factor in determining whether a security is debt or equity

**subjective factor** the intention of the company when it issues securities; a major factor in determining whether a security is debt or equity

---

[15]Standard & Poor's, *Corporate Equity Criteria—Equity Credit* (October 28, 2004).

1. Does it have ongoing payments that could lead to default?
2. Does it have a maturity or repayment requirement?
3. Does it provide a "cushion" for creditors in case of distress?
4. Is it expected to remain in the capital structure?

Clearly, S&P's first criterion is the same as DBRS's factor 3, which is the contractual commitment to pay interest, where failure leads to default. S&P 2 is the same as DBRS 1, which is the question of permanence versus a maturity date. S&P 3 is similar to DBRS 2, where the deeper the subordination, the more "cushion" is provided to senior bondholders. Finally, S&P 4 is similar to DBRS 4, which involves the intention of the company and whether the security is expected to remain part of the firm's long-term financing or its capital structure.

## Creative Hybrids: Some Examples

### Hard and Soft Retractable Shares

An example illustrating the DBRS and S&P criteria might help. In our discussion of preferred shares, we noted that there are different types of preferred shares that mimic debt but attract the tax treatment of dividends. One class of these preferred shares was retractable preferred shares, which BMO Capital Markets compared with five-year Government of Canada bonds. What we didn't discuss was what these preferred shares were retractable into—that is, when the holders ask for their money back, what do they get?

**hard retraction**  the requirement that preferred shares be paid off in cash

**soft retraction**  the allowance for preferred shares to be paid off with common shares or other preferred shares

A **hard retraction** requires that the preferred shares be paid off in cash. In effect, this makes them very bond-like, because apart from getting dividends for five years instead of interest at the end of five years, the investor gets cash back. A **soft retraction** allows the preferred shares to be paid off with common shares or other preferred shares. In this case, the firm has no commitment to pay cash; it simply issues more shares with no cash outlay.

In terms of the S&P/DBRS criteria, preferred shares with a hard retraction are very debt-like because they are not permanent, have a fixed contractual commitment to pay off at maturity with cash, and are not a permanent part of the firm's capital structure. The soft retractables have no fixed contractual commitments, have no maturity (because they are simply replaced with other types of equity), and are more likely to be a permanent part of the firm's capital structure. Hence, they are more like equity. DBRS and S&P would give them greater equity weight because they do not strain the firm's cash flow.

### Income Bonds

**income bonds**  bonds issued after a reorganization, with interest tied to some cash flow level for the firm and with long maturity dates

**cash flow bonds**  bonds sold in the United States that have the same objectives as income bonds in Canada

Another security that looks like debt but is closer to equity is an **income bond**. These bonds are generally issued after a reorganization, so the "interest" is tied to some cash flow level for the firm. **Cash flow bonds** are now sold in the United States with the same objective. In both cases, the maturity dates are long, usually at least 30 years, and the fact that the "interest" payments are conditional on the firm meeting certain thresholds reduces the contractual commitment to pay interest. As a result, income bonds are given significant equity weight. In fact, in Canada, the payments are not tax deductible and are classified as dividends. This reduces their attractiveness as far as the company is concerned, which is why they have mainly been a "desperation play" after a major reorganization (when the company has lots of tax-loss carry forwards and little use for tax shields).

### Indexed Bonds

**commodity bond**  a bond whose interest or principal is tied to the price of an underlying commodity such as gold

Some firms achieve the same type of objective with the **commodity bond**. Suppose a gold producer has fixed mine costs to produce gold but faces uncertain revenues because they are tied to the price of gold. One way to manage this gold-price risk is through the use of derivatives that are tied to the price of gold, such as those discussed in Chapter 11, or through long-term fixed-price contracting. However, an alternative is to tie the bond payments to the price of gold. This can be done in two ways: either the interest payment or the principal is tied to the price of gold. If the principal is tied to the price of gold, then as the gold price increases, so too does the principal; because interest is expressed as a percentage of the principal, the investor receives more interest. If the bond payments are structured carefully, CRA criteria are met and the interest is tax deductible, but the bonds are less risky to the firm because the interest payments are tied to its major risk, which is the price of gold.

Commodity bonds, in which the principal is tied to some external index, are an example of indexed bonds. The most common of these are the Real Return Bonds issued by the Government of Canada (discussed in Chapter 6). In this case, the principal is tied to the consumer price index (CPI). As the CPI increases, the principal increases, and the interest is expressed as a percentage of this increasing principal. In this way, the investor's income increases with inflation, thereby preserving a real rate of return. As of February 15, 2019, the yield on the Real Return Bond, equivalent to the regular 30-year fixed-rate Canada bond, was a paltry 0.70 percent. In this instance, the investor could choose between the Real Return Bond, yielding 0.70 percent, and the regular long-term Canada bond, yielding 2.15 percent. The difference is that with the regular bond, the investor runs the risk that inflation will erode the real purchasing power of both the income and the maturity value of the bond. The difference between these two yields (1.45 percent) is below the middle of the Bank of Canada's target inflation band of 1 percent to 3 percent. However, on a simple comparison basis, if investors are worried about inflation or think the rate of inflation will be greater than this break-even rate of 1.45 percent, they should buy the Real Return Bond even at this very low yield.

The problem with the Real Return Bond is that the increase in the value of the principal is regarded by the CRA as income and is taxed as such even though it is simply compensating for inflation. Further, ordinary investors holding these bonds are taxed on this "income" even if they do not receive any cash. This makes the bonds unattractive for many investors unless they can hold them in tax-preferred savings plans, like Registered Retirement Savings Plans (RRSPs). For the same reason, these bonds are popular with institutional investors, such as pension plans, that do not pay tax but have fixed commitments indexed to the rate of inflation.

## Original Issue Discount Bonds and Low-Yield Notes

Real Return Bonds are not generally issued by corporations, but they do have one attractive property: the immediate interest payments are much lower than those from regular fixed-income bonds. Note, for example, that the yield on the Real Return Bond was 0.70 percent versus 2.15 percent for the regular bond. The offset is that, at maturity, the firm has to pay back a much larger principal to the investor, as the nominal $100 will have increased with the CPI. For firms that are short of immediate cash but have good long-run prospects, this type of indexing is an attractive proposition because it minimizes immediate cash payments, deferring them to a period when, it is hoped, the firm will be more valuable. Corporations achieve a result similar to that achieved by Real Return Bonds by issuing **original issue discount bonds (OIDs)** or **low-yield notes** that similarly sell at a discount.

**original issue discount bonds (OIDs)** or **low-yield notes** bonds that sell at a discount from par value when issued by firms

Table 19.6 shows the time path of the cash payments on two bonds: a 10-year regular interest bond with a 10-percent annual yield versus an OID with a 10-percent yield but a zero coupon. The principal for both bonds is set at $42.40 (for reasons we will come to in a minute).

**TABLE 19.6** OID versus Regular Bond Payments

| Year | Regular Bond | OID Bond Principal | OID Bond "Interest" |
|---|---|---|---|
| 2 | $4.24 | $46.65 | $4.24 |
| 3 | 4.24 | 51.32 | 4.67 |
| 4 | 4.24 | 56.45 | 5.13 |
| 5 | 4.24 | 62.09 | 5.64 |
| 6 | 4.24 | 68.30 | 6.21 |
| 7 | 4.24 | 75.13 | 6.83 |
| 8 | 4.24 | 82.64 | 7.51 |
| 9 | 4.24 | 90.91 | 8.26 |
| 10 | 46.65 | 100.00 | 9.09 |

The regular bond has annual cash outflows of $4.24 and, in year 10, a bullet payment of the principal of $42.40. The OID has no annual interest payments; instead, the 10-percent yield is earned by paying $42.40 today and receiving $100 at maturity in 10 years. As a result, the principal increases each year from $42.40 in year 1, to $46.65 in year 2, and so on, until it reaches $100 at the end of year 10. This increase each year is in the column marked "interest."

From the company's point of view, the discount bond involves no annual payments but a much larger payment at maturity. This time pattern of cash flows is useful for many cash-poor, opportunity-rich companies. However, from a tax point of view, the CRA regards the discount bond as locking in interest in the same way an issue of treasury bills on a discount basis does. The CRA has several ways of determining interest, but the correct way is to compound the $42.40 forward to the $100 maturity value. This provides the series of "interest" payments in the fourth column, which the CRA allows the company to deduct. Although this cash is not paid, investors have to pay tax on this imputed interest, just as they do with the interest from the Real Return Bond.

This zero coupon bond is an example of an "off-market" interest rate that causes the market value to deviate from par. Another variant is a low-yield note, in which the coupon is not zero but is less than the going market interest rate. This means that the cash flow pattern falls between the two extremes documented previously. In some cases, these low-yield notes are combined with a convertible feature, in which case they are called **liquid yield option notes (LYONs)**. LYONs are accretive convertibles, because the principal accretes or increases over time. Rogers Communications Inc. issued LYONs when it needed to conserve cash while building its cable network.

## Adjustable Rate Convertible Subordinated Securities

Another way to address the problem of tying interest payments to cash flow is to make the interest payments conditional on prior dividend payments. **Adjustable rate convertible subordinated securities (ARCS)** do just this. They have fixed principal and maturity, and the interest normally comprises two parts: a fixed interest rate, and some function of the dividend paid in the prior six months. These securities are almost all convertible into common shares, so the dividend is expressed as a percentage of the conversion price. If the conversion price is $50 and the dividend per share is $1, it would be expressed as 2 percent. The ARCS would then pay 5 percent plus twice this 2-percent dividend rate, or 9 percent in total. The ARCS are then subordinated—that is, junior—to the firm's senior debt.

ARCS combine debt and equity features. Because the interest is represented as a percentage, is tied to the principal value, and legally accrues, it is tax deductible. However, as a deeply subordinated debt issue in which the interest could drop to 5 percent if the dividend is not declared in the prior six-month period, it has some equity-like features.

## Preferred Securities

Another debt-versus-equity variant is **preferred securities**. Note that these are not preferred shares, because the payments are tax deductible. Texaco Inc. was the first to issue tax-deductible preferred securities in 1991. They have grown in popularity since then. Texaco set up a 100-percent-owned subsidiary in the Turks and Caicos Islands (a tax haven) to issue preferred securities. The proceeds were then loaned to the parent, for whom the interest paid was tax deductible. The interest flowed to the subsidiary, where it was not taxed, and all of it was used to make the dividend payments. The key provision was that Texaco would not let a 100-percent-owned subsidiary be forced into bankruptcy if it failed to make the interest payments. In turn, the preferred securities were sold with a five-year deferral of dividend payments, a 30-year life, and deep subordination.

Subsequently, trusts have been used to sell preferred securities; these are commonly called "trust preferred securities" and have been very popular with Canadian companies. Typically, they are rated BBB or lower and have been sold into the U.S. market, as there is little appetite in the Canadian market for any type of high-yield debt.

## Canadian Optional Interest Notes

Finally, there are **Canadian optional interest notes (COINs)**, often referred to as **prepaid bonds**. With COINs, a firm issues 99-year bonds with a par value of $100 and an interest rate of, say, 10 percent, which sell at par. After the bonds are issued, the firm immediately prepays the interest from years 11 to 99 ($38.546), leaving it with a net inflow of $61.454. This

---

**liquid yield option notes (LYONs)** low-yield notes that are combined with a convertible feature and are accretive convertibles because the principal accretes or increases over time

**adjustable rate convertible subordinated securities (ARCS)** securities that have fixed principal and maturity, and interest that normally comprises a fixed interest rate and some function of the dividend paid in the previous six months; typically convertible into common shares

**preferred securities** securities generated by a company by creating a 100-percent-owned subsidiary that issues the shares and then loans the proceeds to the parent company, for whom the interest is tax deductible; interest flows to the subsidiary, where it is not taxed, and is used to make dividend payments

**Canadian optional interest notes (COINs)** or **prepaid bonds** 99-year bonds that are sold at their par value of $100; the firm immediately prepays the interest from years 11 to 99, leaving the firm with a net inflow and allowing it to continue to deduct annual interest payments on $100, even though it has effectively borrowed less is why COINs are also called prepaid bonds. The firm has met all the legal requirements to continue deducting annual interest payments on $100, even though it has only effectively borrowed $61.454, not $100. Remember that this $100 represents the present value of each interest payment, as well as the $100 par value in 99 years. However, the discounting process means that the current value of the $100 par value in 99 years at 10 percent is only $0.008—that is,

$$\$0.007982 = \frac{\$100}{1.10^{99}}$$

By the same process, the present value of the interest payments from years 11 to 99 is $38.546, and that for years 1 to 10 is $61.446. The market value of $100 is the sum of these three components.

Some European companies using COINs reportedly wrote off the prepaid interest of $38.546 immediately, but the CRA has now limited the deduction of interest on these prepaid bonds to the imputed interest—that is, 10 percent of the actual amount raised, or $61.454. The speedy reaction of the CRA represents the dynamic interplay between innovative financing instruments and the tax authorities protecting their tax revenues.

## A Financing Hierarchy

S&P has ranked many types of hybrids according to their debt-equity mix, and **Table 19.7** shows a synopsis of the main securities that we have discussed.[16] They range from common shares, which are rated at 100 percent, to commercial paper, which is rated at –100 percent, because it is the most debt-like form of security.

As the S&P equity weighting scheme indicates, the risk of these instruments differs according to how much equity weight they have. At one extreme, common shares, as the riskiest security, are the most expensive, because investors require the highest rate of return to compensate them for the risk. At the other extreme, commercial paper (CP) has the least equity weight and is the most debt-like security. As such it has the lowest risk and required rate of return. The costs of the various securities fall between these extremes. A typical hierarchy of financing cost for a firm is shown in **Figure 19.4**, but much depends on exactly how they are structured.

In practice, the actual rates depend on the level of interest rates and the state of the economy, but common equity is the most expensive, and the cost decreases as the equity share falls and the debt share gets larger.

**TABLE 19.7**    **S&P Financing Rankings**

| | Equity Share (%) |
|---|---|
| Common shares | 100 |
| Mandatory convertible preferred shares* | 90 |
| Straight preferred shares | 50 |
| Trust preferred shares | 40 |
| Convertible preferred shares | 20 |
| Re-marketed preferred shares† | −10 |
| Normal convertible debt | −50 |
| Accreting convertible bonds (LYONs) | −60 |
| Very long-term bonds | −70 |
| Medium-term bonds | −80 |
| Auction preferred shares | −60 |
| Commercial paper | −100 |

*Preferred shares for which conversion into common shares is structured to be automatic.

†Preferred shares that are repriced and resold after five to seven years.

[16]Table 19.7 is our interpretation of the S&P rankings based on Canadian issues.

**FIGURE 19.4** Financing Hierarchy Costs

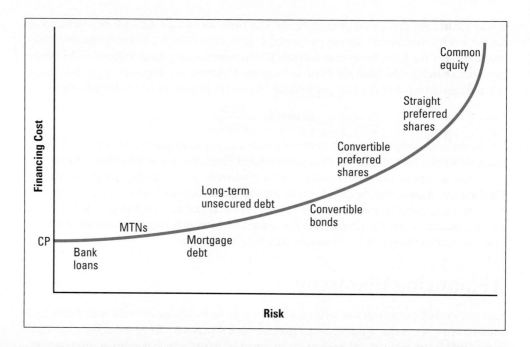

---

## 19.1 Ethics and Corporate Governance   Ontario Teachers Pension Plan Halts Lending of Shares to Short Sellers

The Ontario Teachers Pension Plan has taken the rare step of halting the lending of shares to short sellers and plans to set up a new internal lending operation, arguing it wants to maintain tighter control over its voting rights as an investor.

Teachers senior vice-president Brian Gibson said the pension plan halted its lending late last year after two companies in which it held stakes called for shareholder voting on closely contested matters, but Teachers couldn't vote shares that had been borrowed by short sellers.

Mr. Gibson said Teachers had standard arrangements with its securities custodian to allow it to recall shares when necessary, but found the system didn't work well, and the shares could not be retrieved in time for votes.

When shares are lent by an investor for short selling, the voting rights transfer to the borrower. The situation has led some major U.S. companies to criticize the power of hedge funds to sway corporate votes using shares they have only borrowed and do not actually own.

It's not clear that any Canadian votes have been decided by hedge funds using borrowed shares. Mr. Gibson wouldn't identify the cases Teachers encountered, but said that in the end, the missing votes were not needed to clinch a vote. Teachers' move comes as corporate governance experts are increasingly urging institutional investors to get more closely involved in voting their shares and make more in-house decisions about how to vote on key issues.

David Beatty, managing director of the Canadian Coalition for Good Governance, which represents institutional investors, said institutional investors have a fiduciary responsibility to their beneficiaries to ensure the priority is to manage their voting.

In the United States, proposals have been floated to toughen rules on voting borrowed shares, or to require companies to announce the issues that will be up for a vote at a future shareholder meeting when they set the record date for voting. That would allow institutions to see if there are important issues on the ballot and recall their shares before the record date passes.

There has been little public debate of the issue in Canada, where activity has been confined to the internal steps taken by institutional shareholders to control their votes.

Peter Chapman, executive director of the Vancouver-based Shareholder Association for Research and Education, says some investors try to control lending during voting periods. "Some institutions don't track it, so they lose their votes. The better practice would be not to lend during the windows when you lose your voting rights."

Doug Pearce, chief executive officer of the B.C. Investment Management Corp., which manages investments for the B.C. government and public sector pension plans, said his fund rarely needs to recall shares for voting. "It is an issue, but we make sure that we secure our vote first, and lending will be secondary to that."

An official at the Ontario Municipal Employees Retirement System said OMERS hasn't had any occasion to recall shares in recent years for voting purposes and has made no changes to its lending practices.

But Mr. Gibson said Teachers has found the system not only works imperfectly, but has not been economically worthwhile. He said Teachers was earning little income from its lending because most of the proceeds went to the custodian who administered the program.

"Losing votes costs us a lot more economically than the little bit we were making on lending."

He said Teachers has decided to develop an in-house lending program so it can maintain close control over the process.

The extra cost of managing its own lending will be offset by the additional income Teachers will receive by not sharing the revenue with a custodian, Mr. Gibson said.

**Discussion Questions**

1. **One share equals one vote, so when shares are lent to someone to sell, the new holder gets to vote. Who do you think should get to vote the shares: the underlying**

owner, such as Teachers, or the institution to whom it has lent the shares? Why?

2. Large institutions like Teachers have a lot of influence with their large shareholdings and actively intervene

to improve corporate governance. Is Teachers giving up its fiduciary duty to its pensioners by lending its shares and giving up the right to vote?

## Concept Review Questions

1. Name and discuss the four criteria used by DBRS to classify a security as debt versus equity.
2. Define the following types of hybrids: income bonds, commodity bonds, Real Return Bonds, original issue discount bonds, LYONs, ARCS, preferred securities, and COINs.
3. Relate the costs of various financing options to their equity-like characteristics.

# Review

## Summary

This chapter discusses equity and hybrid securities. Securities are financial contracts, and their level of risk depends on the design of the contract—specifically, how they are treated for tax purposes, and how much equity weight they have, which determines the risk they impose on the firm. Common shares impose the least risk because, according to S&P's criteria, they are a permanent part of the firm's capital structure, impose no commitments that might cause the firm to default, provide a cushion to senior debt that the firm can issue, and have no maturity date. CP and BAs are the opposite in that they have fixed payments, short maturities, a higher priority charge, and a lack of permanency. However, the interest on CP and BAs is tax deductible, whereas the dividends on common shares are not.

Between these two extremes are all the securities that firms issue. Conventional fixed rate preferred shares, retractable preferred shares, and floating rate preferred shares take advantage of the fact that dividends in Canada attract the dividend tax credit and are non-taxable between corporations. Convertible securities and warrants are the most equity-like securities, particularly if they are structured so that conversion is mandatory. They also have the advantage of deferred equity financing or cheap debt financing, depending on what happens to the firm's share price.

This chapter describes the menu of corporate financing opportunities available. How firms choose between them is the topic of chapters 20 and 22.

## Summary of Learning Objectives

### 19.1  Explain the basic rights associated with share ownership.

- (Some) equity holders can vote at shareholder meetings.
- Equity holders are entitled to dividends as declared by the corporation.
- Equity holders are residual claimants to the company's assets on dissolution.

### 19.2  Describe the various classes of shares and the shareholders' rights associated with each.

The differentiating features across classes are voting rights, rights in the event of a dividend payment, and rights in the event of terminating the company. An example of a share structure:

- Class A shares: referred to as non-voting shares or limited voting shares and have no voting rights as long as dividends are paid;

in the event of the winding up of the company, these shares are equal to class B shares.

- Class B shares: regarded as common shares and have full voting rights; there are no dividends paid if class C shares are in arrears, and these shares are equal with class A shares on the winding up of the company.
- Class C shares: have no voting rights unless dividends are in arrears for two years; no dividends can be paid on class A and B shares if class C shares are in arrears; for class C shares, there is a payment of $25 par value before any payments to class A and B shares on the winding up of the company.

### 19.3  Describe preferred shares and outline the various features associated with them.

Dividends for preferred shares can be skipped (unlike those for bond coupons) because, unlike interest, there is no contractual right to receive a dividend, as it has to be declared by the board of directors.

To protect the preferred shareholders, most preferred shares have a cumulative feature that requires skipped dividends to be made up at some future date before the common shareholders may receive a dividend. Preferred shareholders have a more senior claim to the company's assets than common shareholders in the event of dissolution, but the claim is limited to their par value (and to dividends in arrears). Straight preferred shares have no maturity date. Retractable preferred shares give the holder the right to redeem the share for the par value.

Some preferred shares pay a variable dividend rather than a fixed dividend. The dividend varies with a benchmark interest rate.

---

**19.4 Explain how combining warrants with debt issues, or issuing convertible bonds or debentures, can provide firms with attractive financing options.**

---

Risky companies with low bond ratings (e.g., young or start-up companies) can have difficulty borrowing money through the issue of debt. Warrants or convertibles can act as sweeteners to help raise capital. The option portion of the security (warrant or convertible) gives the holder some advantage if, as a result of the company's success, the stock price increases. In this case, if the company is successful, it

automatically gets some equity financing. Since this option is valuable, the company can issue debt at a lower interest rate, so if it is not successful it ends up with "cheap" debt. In this way, the convertible feature reduces the cash outlay for interest and lowers the risk of financial distress.

---

**19.5 Describe the various hybrid financing options available to firms, and explain how they are constructed.**

---

- Warrants are call options issued by the firm. When the options are exercised, the company acts as the writer and sells new shares in the company. The number of shares outstanding rises after warrant exercise, and the company raises new equity financing.

- Convertible bonds combine a coupon bond with a warrant. If the company is successful and the share price increases, the holder surrenders the bond in exchange for shares in the company. In this way, the firm's common equity increases and its debt decreases, opening up the ability to raise more debt.

- Convertible preferred shares combine a preferred share with a warrant and have the same impact as convertible debt.

## Key Terms

## Equations

| Equation | Description | Formula | Page |
|---|---|---|---|
| [19.1] | Payoff to Warrant Holders | $\text{Payoff to warrant holders} = \frac{m}{n+m}(V + mX) - mX$ | p. 19-15 |
| [19.2] | Payoff to Warrant Holders II | $\text{Payoff to warrant holders} = \frac{m}{n+m}(V - nX)$ | p. 19-16 |
| [19.3] | Conversion Price | $CP = \frac{Par}{CR}$ | p. 19-17 |
| [19.4] | Conversion Value | $CV = CR \times P$ | p. 19-18 |
| [19.5] | Conversion Premium | $\text{Conversion premium} = \frac{\text{Market value} - CV}{CV}$ | p. 19-18 |
| [19.6] | Straight Bond Value | $SBV = I \times \left[ \dfrac{1 - \dfrac{1}{(1+k_b)^n}}{k_b} \right] + F \times \dfrac{1}{(1+k_b)^n}$ | p. 19-18 |
| [19.7] | Floor Value | $FV = \text{Max}(SBV, CV)$ | p. 19-19 |

# Questions and Practice Problems

## Multiple Choice Questions

**1. (LO 19.1)** Which of the following does *not* appear in the share structure of a firm?

   **a.** Preferred shares     **c.** Limited voting shares

   **b.** Common shares      **d.** None of the above

**2. (LO 19.3)** Which of the following statements about preferred shares is *false*?

   **a.** Retractable preferred shares allow the shareholders to bring forward the maturity date.

   **b.** The most common preferred shares in Canada are straight preferred shares.

   **c.** Preferred shareholders can force bankruptcy if the firm defaults on the dividend payment.

   **d.** Floating rate preferred share dividends are reset periodically.

**3. (LO 19.4)** A(n)_____is a bond that may be exchanged for the common shares of the same corporation.

   **a.** exchangeable bond    **c.** convertible bond

   **b.** retractable bond      **d.** warrant

**4. (LO 19.4)** Which of the following statements is *true*?

   **a.** Bonds are exchanged for common shares when convertibles are converted.

   **b.** The current market price is paid in cash when warrants are exercised.

   **c.** Debt is exchanged for common shares when its attached warrant is exercised.

   **d.** A conversion ratio is not specified in convertibles.

**5. (LO 19.4)** Which of the following statements in the case of convertible bonds is *false*?

   **a.** Convertible bonds are bonds that can be converted into a specific number of common shares at the option of the bondholder.

   **b** A convertible bond will always sell for at least the larger of its straight bond value (SBV) or its conversion value (CV).

   **c.** The issuer of the convertible bond gets new financing when such bonds are converted.

   **d.** If simultaneously a company were to issue both a straight bond and a convertible bond, then the convertible bond would have a lower interest rate.

**6. (LO 19.2, 19.4)** Which of the following is a *correct* ranking of after-the-fact best financing choices, assuming that the share price increases beyond the conversion price?

   **a.** Debt, convertibles, common shares, and preferred shares

   **b.** Preferred shares, common shares, debt, and convertibles

   **c.** Preferred shares, common shares, convertibles, and debt

   **d.** Debt, convertibles, preferred shares, and common shares

**7. (LO 19.4)** Assume a warrant carries a right to buy two common shares at $20 per share. If the market price of a share is $30, what is the theoretical (intrinsic) value of the warrant?

   **a.** $20        **c.** $5

   **b.** $10       **d.** $0

**8. (LO 19.4)** A convertible bond selling for $1,000 can be converted to 20 common shares that are currently selling for $55 per share. What is most likely to happen?

   **a.** The bondholder will choose not to convert because the bond is worth more than the common shares.

   **b.** The bondholder will choose to convert.

   **c.** The stock price will go down to $50.

   **d.** It is impossible to predict using only the information provided.

**9. (LO 19.4)** A company has just issued convertible bonds with a face value of $1,000 and a conversion ratio of 50. Which of the following is most likely to be the current price per share of the company's common shares?

   **a.** Under $20      **c.** Between $20 and $40

   **b.** $20           **d.** Above $40

**10. (LO 19.5)** Which of the following is *not* one of the factors used to judge whether a security is debt or equity?

   **a.** Subordination

   **b.** Legal

   **c.** Subjective

   **d.** Coupon payment

**11. (LO 19.5)** Which of the following statements is *false*?

   **a.** A hard retractable means preferred shares must be paid off in cash.

   **b.** Commodity bonds help commodity producers to control the commodity price risks.

   **c.** Real Return Bonds are tied to the CPI.

   **d.** Preferred securities are another name for preferred shares.

**12. (LO 19.5)** What is the correct ranking of cost from the highest to the lowest?

   **a.** Common shares, convertible preferred shares, straight preferred shares

   **b.** Convertible preferred shares, convertible bonds, straight preferred shares

   **c.** Medium-term note debentures, bank loans, mortgage debt

   **d.** Common shares, long-term unsecured debt, mortgage debt

## Practice Problems

### Basic

**13. (LO 19.1)** State the three basic rights of common shareholders.

**14. (19.3, 19.4)** A firm has just issued convertible preferred shares with a $100 par value. The conversion price for these shares is $20 (per common share). What is the conversion ratio?

**15. (19.2, 19.4)** A firm has just issued convertible preferred shares with a call feature that permits the firm to repurchase the shares at par value (or, in effect, force the conversion into common shares). Usually, the common shares will be trading at least 20 percent above the conversion price before the call feature is invoked. Assuming the conversion price is $10, at what price of its common shares will the firm consider calling the preferred shares?

## Intermediate

**16. (LO 19.3)** Discuss three reasons why firms issue preferred shares.

**17. (LO 19.1)** A firm has just filed for bankruptcy and is likely to be liquidated. The creditors, such as equipment suppliers and employees, are owed $1.5 million.

   **a.** Determine how much the equity holders will receive if, when liquidated, the firm's assets are worth the following:

      **i.** $1.7 million

      **ii.** $1.2 million

   **b.** Suppose that equity holders did not have limited liability. How much would they receive for each asset value above?

**18. (LO 19.1)** With the savings from your summer job you were able to buy 500 shares of a hot new Internet company last year. A few months after your purchase, the company was low on cash and needed to raise more equity capital. The company's charter provided a pre-emptive right to shareholders, so you were offered the chance to buy one additional share for each five owned.

   **a.** What percentage of the firm's equity will you own after your initial purchase if there are one million shares outstanding?

   **b.** What percentage of the firm's equity will you own if you buy the extra shares offered?

   **c.** If you decline to buy the additional shares (but they are sold to other investors), how much of the firm's equity will you own?

**19. (LO 19.1)** When a firm needed to raise capital to expand, the founder was concerned about losing control of the firm if he sold too many shares. The solution devised by his investment banker was to create two different classes of shares. The founding member would retain 250,000 class A shares, which are entitled to two votes apiece; 750,000 common shares with one vote would be sold to the IPO investors. What percentage of the company's equity will the founder own? How much control (percentage of the votes) will the founder maintain?

**20. (LO 19.1, 19.3)** A firm has 50 million common shares outstanding, on which it pays a quarterly dividend of $0.25 per share. The firm's capital structure also includes 2 million cumulative preferred shares with a $50 par value that yield 8 percent per year (or 2 percent per quarter). After making some bad loans in the sub-prime mortgage market, the firm suffered a big loss and suspended its dividend payments on all forms of equity. Six months later, the company is once again in the black having earned $7 million (after tax), which it intends to pay as dividends. How much will the common shareholders receive per share?

**21. (LO 19.2)** Collingwood Corp. has decided to invest some of its excess cash in straight preferred shares issued by other companies. It will earn a yield of 4.5 percent on the $10-million investment. How much net income will Collingwood earn if its corporate tax rate is 25 percent?

**22. (LO 19.2)** The common shares of a firm are currently trading at $15, while its preferred shares trade at par (see practice problem 14). Calculate the conversion premium on the preferred shares. What does this premium mean?

**23. (LO 19.4)** What are the differences between call options and warrants?

**24. (LO 19.4)** Compare and contrast convertible bonds to bonds with warrants.

**25 (LO 19.4)** Oshawa Industries Corp. ("OIC") convertible bondholders have the following option:

   "Prior to the close of business on December 31, 2022 (maturity date), bondholders may convert their bonds into OIC common shares at a rate of 56.9 shares per $1,000 of par value. Cash will be paid in lieu of fractional shares."

Suppose that on December 31, 2022, OIC shares are trading at $18.52.

Calculate the conversion price and conversion value for these bonds.

**26. (LO 19.4)** Calculate the conversion price and conversion value of the convertible bonds given the following: selling price $102; each bond is convertible into five common shares; current common share price $18. Will the convertible bonds be converted?

**27. (LO 19.5)** Jack and Jill Inc. very nearly tumbled into bankruptcy last year. To refinance the firm, the firm issued $30 million worth of 30-year income bonds. These bonds have an 8-percent coupon that is payable only if the firm achieves earnings before interest and tax (EBIT) of $4 million. Suppose the firm exactly achieves its target and pays out the full coupon interest amount. Determine the company's net income if the tax rate is 30 percent.

## Challenging

**28. (LO 19.4)** In December 2022, Collingwood Corp. decided to issue 100,000 convertible bonds, maturing in December 2032. The bonds have a face value of $1,000 and promise an annual coupon payment of 5.75 percent. The conversion ratio of these bonds is 25.32, and it is known that Collingwood Corp.'s common shares were trading at $34 in December 2022. These bonds are rated A–, and straight bonds from similar companies with similar maturity yield 9 percent. The current market price of these bonds is $1,051. Calculate the conversion price, conversion value, SBV, floor value, and conversion premium for these bonds.

**29. (LO 19.4)** Calculate the payoff of fully exercising warrants given the following: 950,000 existing shares are outstanding; 150,000 warrants are outstanding and are exercisable at $10. The firm is valued at $10 million before the warrants are exercised. Calculate the payoff to warrant holders and the dilution factor.

**30. (LO 19.4)** Orion's Belt Mining Co. has 12 million common shares outstanding, which are currently trading for $5. In addition, the company has issued 2 million share purchase warrants with a strike price of $4.25 that are just about to expire.

   **a.** Determine the equity value of the firm before the warrants are exercised.

   **b.** What is the total cost to the warrant holders to purchase the new shares?

   **c.** Calculate the value of the shares that the holders of the warrants will own after they are exercised.

   **d.** What is the payoff to warrant holders? How much would you be willing to pay for each warrant?

**31. (LO 19.4)** A firm's common shares currently trade at $20 per share. The firm has warrants outstanding that entitle the holder to purchase two shares at an exercise price of $18 per share. The expiry date is two years from today.

   **a.** Calculate the minimum value (floor value) for the warrants.

   **b.** Show that the warrants cannot trade at a price that is below this floor value.

   **c.** Show the percentage change in the floor value of the warrants given a 10-percent change in the market price of the shares.

**32. (LO 19.4)** Straight preferred shares issued by a firm have a discount rate of 8 percent per year, whereas these shares are yielding 4 percent on the $25 par value. The conversion value of these shares is calculated to be $15. Determine the straight preferred value (SPV) and the floor value for the convertible preferred shares. Assume the shares have no maturity and can therefore be valued as a perpetuity.

# Cost of Capital

In chapters 17 to 19, we discussed securities legislation; the differences between debt, equity, and hybrid securities; and how securities are issued. We finished by describing a risk hierarchy that essentially corresponds to a particular security's resemblance to debt or equity. As we move from types of security that are 100-percent debt, such as commercial paper, to those that are 100-percent equity, they become riskier. This risk hierarchy corresponds to a cost hierarchy for a firm, because investors require compensation for additional risk, which translates into higher costs for the firm. In this chapter, we discuss how firms synthesize this information as they determine their overall cost of funds, called "the cost of capital."

The cost of capital is the most basic piece of information a firm needs, since it determines how the firm is valued and is often the appropriate "hurdle rate" to be used for making corporate investment decisions. (As noted in Chapter 13, the firm's cost of capital is the appropriate discount rate for evaluating projects that possess "average" risk for the company.) In this chapter, you will learn what the cost of capital means, how to calculate it, and how to avoid some basic yet common mistakes in corporate financing. During the process, we will discuss some of the problems that result when using the discounted cash flow models described in Chapter 7 (for valuing equities) and the capital asset pricing model (CAPM) described in Chapter 9. These two models are the "workhorses" of corporate finance for estimating the cost of capital.

After you master the material on the cost of capital, you will learn, in Chapter 21, how firms determine their financing decisions.

# Financing Sources

**LEARNING OBJECTIVE 20.1**
Explain how the three major problem areas in finance—valuation, cost of capital, and determining cash flows—are related.

## Capital Structure

We begin by returning to the balance sheet to review the major accounts, as depicted in **Table 20.1**.

On the asset side, we have current (short-term) assets consisting of cash and marketable securities, accounts receivable, inventory, and, usually, some accounting items, such as prepaid expenses. When the current assets are added to the net fixed assets (i.e., gross fixed assets less accumulated depreciation), we have total assets. We call the method of financing total assets the "**financial structure** decision," which reflects all of the firm's liabilities, including invested capital.

**financial structure** how a firm finances its total assets

For our purposes, it is useful to distinguish between debt and other types of liabilities that do not represent debt contracts in the strictest sense. In particular, many accruals are strictly accounting items required to prepare the statements according to International Financial Reporting Standards (IFRS) as well as generally accepted accounting principles (GAAP). As such, they do not represent a decision on the part of an investor or creditor to finance the firm. For example, the authors are paid by their universities with a one-month lag, which would show up as wages payable on their universities' balance sheets. However, none of us would consider this delay in getting paid as a financial investment on our part in the university. Instead, because the university does not pay us on a daily cash basis, the accountant accrues a liability. Similarly, as long as a firm's credit is good, accounts payable arise as the result of a telephone or computerized order, where the invoice arrives with the order. Again, in most cases the supplier is not explicitly thinking of the value of its shipment as an investment in the company.[1] It is simply the way business is done between companies. In this sense, the only current liability items that do reflect a creditor investing in the company are bank debt, other short-term debt, and the current portion of any long-term debt that is due within a year.

When it comes to long-term liabilities, the basic distinction is again between accounting items and money that has been invested in the firm. On the simple balance sheet presented in Table 20.1, all the liabilities are invested capital because we do not have any headings that are strictly accounting items. However, firms often report the value of benefits owing to workers as a liability, since they customarily pay health benefits after retirement, even when they are made on a "pay-as-you-go" basis. There are also often deferred income taxes, as discussed in

**TABLE 20.1** **Main Balance Sheet Accounts**

| | |
|---|---|
| Cash and marketable securities | Accruals |
| Accounts receivable | Accounts payable |
| Inventory | Short-term debt |
| Prepaid expenses | Current liabilities |
| Current assets | Long-term debt |
| Net fixed assets | Shareholders' equity |
| Total assets | Total liabilities and shareholders' equity |

[1]Note that this is not always the case. For firms in serious financial trouble, a shipment from a supplier may be seen as an investment with an explicit interest charge. We will discuss this in chapters 23 and 24.

**TABLE 20.2** **A Simplified Balance Sheet**

| | | | |
|---|---|---|---|
| Cash and marketable securities | 50 | Accruals | 100 |
| Accounts receivable | 200 | Accounts payable | 200 |
| Inventory | 250 | Short-term debt | 50 |
| Prepaid expenses | 0 | Current liabilities | 350 |
| Current assets | 500 | Long-term debt | 650 |
| Net fixed assets | 1,500 | Shareholders' equity | 1,000 |
| Total assets | 2,000 | Total liabilities and shareholders' equity | 2,000 |

Chapter 3, as well as other accounting items that do not reflect invested capital. In almost all cases, these "non-debt" accounting items are ignored when it comes to estimating firm capital. Apart from explicit debt and the shareholders' equity accounts, the only other item that is included as capital is minority interest, since this reflects the amount of shareholders' equity in a subsidiary that is not owned by the shareholders of the parent firm.[2] Decisions about the **capital structure** of the firm involve questions of how this invested capital is financed, including what proportion will be financed through debt and what proportion through equity. How the firm arrives at these decisions is the focus of Chapter 21.

> **capital structure** how a firm finances its invested capital

The simplified balance sheet in **Table 20.2** gives an example of one firm's capital structure.

The financial structure is $2,000, which is the firm's total assets, while the capital structure components total $1,700, consisting of $1,000 in shareholders' equity and total interest-bearing debt of $700 (i.e., $50 + $650), producing a **debt-to-equity ratio** of 0.7 (i.e., $700/$1,000). This hypothetical capital structure has a bit less debt than is typical of Canadian firms. **Figure 20.1** shows the average debt-to-equity ratio for Canadian firms from 1988 until September 2018. The ratio hovered around 1.15 in the early 1990s but has declined since then and has averaged 0.93 since 2000.

> **debt-to-equity ratio** the ratio of interest-bearing debt to shareholders' equity plus minority interest

**FIGURE 20.1** **Debt-to-Equity Ratio (Quarterly Data)**

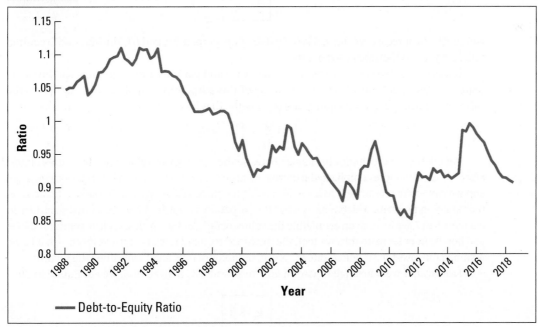

**Source:** Data from Statistics Canada CANSIM series V63465

[2]Minority interest arises when a firm reports consolidated financial statements. GAAP requires consolidated statements when a subsidiary is not 100-percent owned, but is controlled. (This usually means more than 50-percent ownership.) As a result, all of the subsidiary's debt and assets are included on the consolidated statements, and the portion of the subsidiary's equity that is not owned is shown as minority interest.

market-to-book (M/B) ratio the market price per share divided by the book value per share

The hypothetical numbers in Table 20.2 would come from the firm's financial statements and represent historical book values. For our purposes, we can convert them to market values. For simplicity, we can assume that the book and market values of the firm's debt are very close. This is usually the case, but as interest rates have declined it has caused the market value of the firm's debt to increase. In an actual calculation we would use the current market values. However, suppose that the firm's equity is selling for 2.5 times its book value, so that its **market-to-book (M/B) ratio**, defined in Chapter 4, is 2.5. For the example in Table 20.2, the total market value of the equity would be $2,500 (i.e., $1,000 × 2.5), and the total market value of the firm would be $3,200 (i.e., $700 + $2,500). Therefore, the firm's "market valued" debt-to-equity ratio would be 0.28 (i.e., $700/$2,500), which again is fairly typical of Canadian non-financial firms.

We introduce the firm's financial and capital structures to understand how the chief financial officer (CFO) can increase the firm's equity market value. Remember from our earlier discussion in Chapter 2 that the CFO should act in the best interests of the owners of the firm—that is, the shareholders. In order to do this, the CFO has to know what the shareholders want from their investment, which is the overall required rate of return or what we call in this chapter the cost of capital. Thus the two key issues in corporate financing are to attempt to increase the firm's equity market value by changing the mix of debt and equity, and to determine the minimum rate of return necessary to maintain this market value.

## Three Ways of Using the Valuation Equation

Before addressing these key issues, let's review the most basic implication of the simple perpetuity valuation problem, discussed in Chapter 5. Recall that the present value of a perpetuity is found by dividing the amount of the regular payment by the appropriate discount rate. For our purposes, let's assume the perpetuity is future estimated earnings, which are expected to remain at the same level indefinitely, thus experiencing no growth. We can discount these earnings using the investors' required rate of return to find the present value of those future earnings, as shown in Equation 20.1.

$$S = \frac{X}{k_e}$$ [20.1]

where $X$ is the forecast earnings, $S$ is the value of the perpetuity, and $k$ is the investors' required rate of return, subscripted $e$ for equity.

If a firm's common shares are expected to earn and pay out $1 in perpetuity, and investors require a 10-percent rate of return, the value of this perpetuity (which in this example is the value of the firm's common equity) is simply $10—that is:

$$S = \frac{X}{k_e} = \frac{\$1}{0.1} = \$10$$

We often use perpetuities in finance because they are easy to value, and the results almost always hold with more complicated patterns of earnings. However, note that this is one equation, and we can easily rearrange it to solve for any of the three values. We just happened to focus on the valuation problem, which tells us what the perpetuity is worth. When we valued securities in chapters 5 to 7, we focused on estimating the values of different securities, such as common shares and bonds. In order to do this, we took the investors' required rate of return as given—that is, we assumed the investors' required rate of return, or discount rate, and then valued the security.

However, if we rearrange Equation 20.1 to solve for $k_e$ instead of $S$, we get Equation 20.2.

$$k_e = \frac{X}{S}$$ [20.2]

Given a $10 market price and forecast perpetual earnings of $1 per year, we can estimate the investors' required rate of return as:

$$k_e = \frac{X}{S} = \frac{\$1}{\$10} = 10\%$$

This estimate of the investors' required rate of return, or the cost of equity capital to the firm, is called the **earnings yield**, because it is the forecast earnings divided by the market price, similar to the dividend yield.[3] The earnings yield is not often used as an estimate of $k_e$ for most firms, since there is usually some expectation for growth, either real or inflationary. As a result, the stock price reflects these growth opportunities as well as the current earnings. However, the earnings yield was commonly used in the 1950s when inflation and growth expectations were minimal and similar to today. It is the simplest method of estimating the discount rate, which is the term given to the rate that sets the forecast stream of earnings or cash equal to the current price. As such, it is the most basic of the discounted cash flow (DCF) methods for estimating the cost of equity capital, which we discuss later in this chapter. For now, recognize that this way of rearranging the valuation equation addresses the need to estimate what return investors require. In this example, we estimate that investors require a 10-percent return for holding this perpetuity.

> **earnings yield**   the estimate of the investors' required rate of return, which is also the cost of equity capital to the firm

Finally, we can rearrange the same equation and solve for the forecast earnings, as shown in Equation 20.3.

$$X = k_e \times S \qquad\qquad\qquad [20.3]$$

If the security is worth $10, and the investor requires a 10-percent rate of return, the firm must generate forecast earnings of $1, as shown here:

$$X = k_e \times S = 0.1 \times \$10 = \$1$$

This explicitly tells the firm's managers what their earnings targets must be to support the current valuation. This information is crucial for regulated industries, like utilities, which can only earn a set amount of profit. The regulator determines what prices utility companies can charge to realize this return, and in setting these prices, regulators use this last version of the valuation equation. In other words, the concepts and processes described in this chapter are used to set your telephone, water, gas, and electric bills as well as in basic corporate finance applications.

The same equation can therefore be used in three different ways. To illustrate the concept of the cost of capital, we will use this third approach. For the time being, let's assume that our example firm's earnings are a perpetuity, and the required rates of return are known: the yield on the firm's debt is 6 percent, and equity holders require a rate of return of 12 percent. We already know that the debt is worth $700 and the equity is worth $2,500, so with these data we can estimate the following:

$$\text{Interest for the bond holders} = k_d \times D = 0.06 \times \$700 = \$42$$

$$\text{Return to the shareholders} = k_e \times S = 0.12 \times \$2,500 = \$300$$

What this tells us is that with a $700 market value for the debt ($D$) and a 6-percent yield or required return on debt ($k_d$), the firm has to earn $42 to pay the bondholders their interest. Similarly, with the firm's common shares worth $2,500 ($S$), and the shareholders requiring a 12-percent return ($k_e$), the firm has to earn $300 to meet these expectations. So in total, with this mix of debt and equity and a $3,200 current market value, the firm has to earn $342. If it cannot expect to earn $342 in perpetuity, it cannot meet its investors' expectations and its market value will fall.

## Deriving the *Required* Income Statement

Once we have this information, we can work "up" the firm's income statement. Suppose, for example, that the firm has a 25-percent corporate income tax rate, and its operating costs are $558, composed of $300 of variable costs and $258 of fixed or period costs. The forecast income statement in this case is presented in **Table 20.3**.

---

[3]Notice that it is also the reciprocal of the firm's forward price-earnings (P/E) ratio, which was discussed at length in chapters 4 and 7.

**TABLE 20.3  A Forecast Income Statement**

| | |
|---|---|
| Sales | $1,000 |
| Variable costs | 300 |
| Fixed costs | 258 |
| EBIT | 442 |
| Interest | 42 |
| Tax (25%) | 100 |
| Net income | 300 |

If the firm has 1,000 shares outstanding, its earnings per share (EPS) are $0.30 (i.e., $300/1,000).

Note that rather than starting with sales and working down the income statement, we have done the opposite. This is exactly what regulators do in setting prices. They first start with a fair return to the common shareholders and then add in these other forecast costs to establish the firm's revenue or sales requirement, from which they set individual prices. This approach is common in all "rate of return regulated" industries, with the exception that they use book values for invested capital instead of market values.[4] Since regulated industries are capital intensive, and individual firms tend to have relatively high amounts of debt, these financial costs are a very important part of their cost structure.

We now have a lot of information about the firm. Given its total market value and investor return requirements, the firm has to have sales of $1,000. We also note that the firm's total assets are $2,000, so its **asset turnover ratio**, defined in Chapter 4 as sales divided by total assets, has to be 0.5 (i.e., $1,000/$2,000), and its **return on assets (ROA)**, defined in Chapter 4 as net income (NI) divided by total assets, is 15 percent (i.e., $300/$2,000). The book value of its invested capital is $1,700, and its EBIT is $442, so its **return on invested capital (ROIC)**, defined as EBIT divided by the book value of invested capital (IC), is 26 percent. ROIC, often referred to simply as ROI, can also be expressed on an after-tax basis by multiplying the ROI by $(1 - T)$, which in our case is 0.75, producing an after-tax ROI of 19.5 percent. The firm's **return on equity (ROE)**, defined as net income divided by the book value of equity, is $300 divided by $1,000, or 30 percent, which is very high.

The very high ROE explains the firm's M/B ratio of 2.5. Remember that the earnings per share equals the ROE times the book value per share (BVPS), as shown here:

$$EPS = \frac{NI}{Number\ of\ shares} = \frac{NI}{Equity} \times \frac{Equity}{Number\ of\ shares} = ROE \times BVPS$$

For our example, the BVPS is $1 ($1,000 shareholders' equity divided by 1,000 shares), and the EPS equals this $1 times the 30-percent ROE, or $0.30.

Since we are dealing with a perpetuity, the price per share can be expressed as shown in Equation 20.4.

$$P = \frac{EPS}{k_e} = \frac{ROE \times BVPS}{k_e} \qquad [20.4]$$

Using the numbers given, the share price is just the $0.30 EPS discounted in perpetuity at 12 percent, the investors' required rate of return or cost of equity capital.

$$P = \frac{EPS}{k_e} = \frac{ROE \times BVPS}{k_e} = \frac{0.30 \times \$1}{0.12} = \$2.50$$

**asset turnover ratio** sales divided by total assets

**return on assets (ROA)** net income divided by total assets

**return on invested capital (ROIC)** earnings before interest and taxes divided by the book value of invested capital

**return on equity (ROE)** net income divided by the book value of equity

[4]Regulators use book values based on the rationale that investors require a fair return on the money they have invested in the utility.

If we divide both sides of Equation 20.4 by the BVPS, we get the basic relationship that drives the M/B ratio:

$$\frac{P}{\text{BVPS}} = \frac{\text{ROE}}{k_e} \qquad\qquad [20.5]$$

For the numbers in this example, we get

$$\frac{P}{\text{BVPS}} = \frac{\text{ROE}}{k_e} = \frac{0.30}{0.12} = 2.50$$

Equation 20.5 simply says that if what the firm earns (ROE) exceeds what investors require ($k_e$), then investors are happy and they bid up the share price above the book value of the investment. This is a basic relationship in finance: if you exceed investor expectations, prices go up! Remember that in Chapter 6 we discussed the pricing of bonds and how, when interest rates increase, the price of bonds goes down, and vice versa. Further, we indicated that if the current interest rate exceeds the coupon rate on a bond, that bond sells at a discount from par value. However, if the interest rate is less than the coupon rate, the bond sells at a premium. The current interest rate is analogous to the investors' required return for investing in bonds. As a result, saying that bonds sell at a discount (or a premium) when required returns exceed (or are less than) the coupon rate is another way of saying their M/B ratio is less than (or greater than) 1.0. Similarly, in our example, the equity M/B ratio exceeds 1 because the ROE of 30 percent significantly exceeds the investors' required rate of return on equity of 12 percent.

Now that we have drawn the link between book values and market values, we will discuss the concept of the cost of capital.

---

## Concept Review Questions

1. Why is the earnings yield not usually an adequate measure of the investors' required return on equity?
2. How are the ROE and $k_e$ related to a firm's growth opportunities and its M/B ratio?

---

## 20.2  The Cost of Capital

### LEARNING OBJECTIVE 20.2
Calculate the weighted average cost of capital (WACC) and explain its significance.

## Determining the Weighted Average Cost of Capital (WACC)

So far we have considered only the equity market value, but now let's look at the overall market value of the firm—that is, the value of the debt plus the value of the equity ($D + S$), which for our example is $3,200. (This is often referred to as the **total enterprise value** ($V$).) We also know that the firm's after-tax ROI on its $1,700 book value is 19.5 percent, based on EBIT$(1 - T)$ of $331.50 or $442(1 - 0.25)$. This is an important number because EBIT$(1 - T)$ indicates the net income of the firm if it is financed 100 percent with equity— that is, if there is no deduction for interest payments on the firm's debt. It is also equal to a firm's net operating income if there are no items such as income from investments or capital gains and losses.

**total enterprise value ($V$)** the market value of invested capital— that is, all interest-bearing debt plus equity

We now have two of the three numbers needed in a valuation equation. We know the overall firm value is $3,200 and the EBIT$(1 - T)$ is $331.50, so we can find the discount rate that sets them equal. First we rewrite EBIT minus taxes as ROI × IC and re-express the valuation equation, as shown in Equation 20.6.

$$V = \frac{\text{ROI} \times \text{IC}}{k_a} \qquad [20.6]$$

Here we are still using the perpetuity equation, but have simply replaced $S$ (the value of the firm's equity) with $V$, which stands for the total enterprise value of the firm, and have denoted the required return as $k_a$, indicating it is the average, or overall, required rate of return. For the numbers in this example, ROI × IC = 0.195 × $1,700 = $331.50, so we get

$$V = \frac{\text{ROI} \times \text{IC}}{k_a} = \frac{\$331.5}{k_a} = \$3,200$$

Just as we did with the earnings yield previously, we can rearrange to find the overall required rate of return, which is given here:

$$k_a = \frac{\text{ROI} \times \text{IC}}{V} \qquad [20.7]$$

For the numbers in this example, we get

$$k_a = \frac{\text{ROI} \times \text{IC}}{V} = \frac{\$331.5}{\$3,200} = 10.36\%$$

So if we discount the EBIT minus taxes figure using this average required rate of return, we get the overall market value of the firm.

This is obviously a very important number. To understand where it comes from, remember that the total amount needed for the equity holders is $300, or $k_e \times S$, whereas the total amount needed for the bondholders is $42, or $k_d \times D$. This exceeds the amount the firm has to earn ($331.50) by $10.50. This $10.50 is the reduction in the firm's corporate income taxes due to the fact that interest is tax deductible. The exact amount needed to pay the bondholders is $k_d(1 - T) \times D$ or 0.06 × 0.75 × $700 = $31.50. It is this $31.50 that gives us the EBIT minus taxes of $331.50 when we add it to the required earnings for the equity holders. If we substitute these definitions into the equation for the average required return, we get Equation 20.8.

$$k_a = \frac{\text{ROI} \times \text{IC}}{V} = \frac{k_e S + k_d(1 - T)D}{V} = k_e \frac{S}{V} + k_d(1 - T)\frac{D}{V} \qquad [20.8]$$

**weighted average cost of capital (WACC) or cost of capital** an estimate of a firm's average cost for $1 of financing

In this equation, the average required rate of return is a **weighted average cost of capital (WACC)**, commonly referred to as the **cost of capital**. In this context, the cost of capital reflects the average rate of return required by all the investors who have contributed or invested capital to the firm.

Estimating the cost of capital is a way of calculating the overall required rate of return needed to meet investor expectations. There are three steps involved in estimating the WACC:

1. Estimate market values for the firm's sources of capital.

2. Estimate the current required rates of return for these various sources of capital invested in the firm.

3. Weight the costs of all sources of capital on the same corporate tax basis, recognizing that interest on debt is tax deductible, whereas the return to the equity holders is not.

For our example firm, we have a market-valued debt ratio of 21.875 percent ($700/$3,200) and a market-valued equity ratio of 78.125 percent (i.e., $2,500/$3,200). We assumed a required return on equity of 12 percent and on debt of 6 percent. Finally, the interest cost is tax deductible, so on an after-tax basis, with a corporate income tax rate of 25 percent, it is 4.5 percent (or 6% × [1 − 0.25]). Putting this all together we get

$$k_a = k_e\frac{S}{V} + k_d(1 - T)\frac{D}{V} = 0.12 \times 0.78125 + 0.06 \times (1 - 0.25) \times 0.21875 = 0.1036 = 10.36\%$$

The key result is that the cost of capital is just a *weighted average* of the after-tax costs of the different sources of capital, where the weights are the proportion of each in the total market value of the firm.

Before we proceed, we should note that Equation 20.8 is incomplete when a firm uses preferred share financing. In this case, we also replace the term $k_d(1 - T)$ with $k_i$ to denote the after-tax cost of debt, as shown in Equation 20.9.

$$\text{WACC} = k_e \frac{S}{V} + k_p \frac{P}{V} + k_i \frac{D}{V} \qquad [20.9]$$

$P$ is the market value of the firm's preferred shares, $k_p$ is the cost of preferred shares, and the value of the firm, $V$, now equals $S + P + D$. Notice that we do not need to adjust $k_p$ for taxes, since preferred shares pay dividends out of after-tax income, just like common shares.

## Estimating Market Values

Estimating the market value of a firm's common equity ($S$) is straightforward whenever a firm has shares that are traded publicly. We simply multiply the firm's market price per common share ($P_0$) by the number of shares outstanding ($n$), as shown in Equation 20.10.[5]

$$S = P_0 \times n \qquad [20.10]$$

Estimating the market value of a firm's preferred shares is also straightforward if it has preferred shares outstanding that are publicly traded, in which case we can simply use Equation 20.10, replacing the common share information with the market price of the preferred shares ($P_p$), multiplied by the number of preferred shares outstanding. In the event that the firm's preferred shares are not actively traded, we can estimate the market value of each of its preferred shares using Equation 20.11, which was first introduced in Chapter 7 for valuing straight perpetual preferred shares.

$$P_p = \frac{D_p}{k_p} \qquad [20.11]$$

Estimating the market value of a firm's debt can be somewhat more complicated, particularly if its debt is not publicly traded, as it also is for non-traditional (straight perpetual) preferred shares. As mentioned earlier, if interest rates have not changed much since the debt was first issued by the firm, then the book value of the firm's long-term debt is close to its market value, so we can use the book value. Otherwise, we can value the debt using the following bond valuation equation, introduced in Chapter 6, where the discount rate is derived from similarly rated traded bonds.

$$B = I \times \left[ \frac{1 - \frac{1}{(1 + k_b)^n}}{k_b} \right] + F \times \frac{1}{(1 + k_b)^n} \qquad [20.12]$$

where
   $B$ = the bond price
   $I$ = interest (or coupon) payments
   $k_b$ = the bond discount rate (or market rate)
   $n$ = the term to maturity
   $F$ = the face (par) value of the bond

---

[5]Notice that in deriving the market value of the equity we could have also multiplied the firm's book value of common equity figure by its M/B ratio.

If the firm has more than one series of bonds or other types of long-term debt issues outstanding, we can repeat this process and add up all the calculated market values to determine the total market value of the firm's outstanding debt.

Example 20.1 illustrates how to combine these concepts.

---

**EXAMPLE 20.1** | Estimating Market Values

Suppose firm ABC has the following balance sheet figures:

|  | **Book Value** |
|---|---|
| Debt: 8% coupon rate, annual coupons 10 years to maturity | $1 million |
| Preferred shares: 10% dividend rate ($D_p$) | $1 million |
| Common equity: | |
| Common shares: 100,000 shares (originally issued at $15/share) | $1.5 million |
| Retained earnings | $0.5 million |
| | Total $4 million |

Assume the marginal tax rate ($T$) is 40 percent.
The present market conditions are the following:

Debt: The present market rate on similar risk (same bond rating) 10-year bonds is 6 percent.
Preferred shares: Similar risk preferred shares are providing yields of 8 percent.
Common equity: Common share price is currently $25.

Find the market value proportions of these components, assuming the firm wants to raise new funds in order to maintain its present capital structure based on these market value proportions.

**Solution**
Long-term debt ($D$):

$$D = \$80,000 \times \left[\frac{1 - \frac{1}{(1+0.06)^{10}}}{0.06}\right] + \$1 \text{ million} \times \left[\frac{1}{(1+0.06)^{10}}\right] = \$1,147,202$$

Preferred shares:

$$P = \frac{D_p}{k_p} = \frac{(\$1m)(0.10)}{0.08} = \frac{\$100,000}{0.08} = \$1,250,000$$

Common equity:

$$S = P_0 \times n = (\$25)(100,000 \text{ shares}) = \$2,500,000$$

So, according to the "market" value of the firm's balance sheet, we obtain the solution:

$$V = D + P + S = \$1,147,202 + \$1,250,000 + \$2,500,000 = \$4,897,202$$

and $\frac{D}{V} = 0.234$, $\frac{P}{V} = 0.255$, and $\frac{S}{V} = 0.511$.

---

## Concept Review Questions

1. Why is the weighted average cost of capital (WACC) so important?
2. What are the steps involved in estimating a firm's WACC?
3. How can we estimate the market value of common equity, preferred equity, and long-term debt?

# Estimating the Non-Equity Component Costs

**LEARNING OBJECTIVE 20.3**

Estimate the cost of capital and its non-equity components.

## Flotation Costs and the Marginal Cost of Capital (MCC)

To derive the cost of capital in the previous section, we were given the cost of equity, as well as the before-tax cost of debt. In this section, we show how we can calculate the cost of debt and preferred equity if we do not have this information. In the following sections, we discuss estimating the cost of common equity.

One complication that arises with respect to all sources of capital, except for internally generated funds, is that the firm incurs **issuing** or **flotation costs** when it issues new securities. These include any fees paid to the investment dealer and/or any discounts provided to investors to entice them to purchase the securities. As a result, the cost of issuing new securities will be *higher* than the return required by investors, since the net proceeds to the firm from any security issue will be lower than what investors have actually paid.

**issuing** or **flotation costs**   costs incurred by a firm when it issues new securities

It is especially important to be aware of this fact when we consider the cost of common equity to the firm. In particular, remember that there are two sources of common equity financing: reinvested earnings, which show up on the firm's balance sheet in the retained earnings figure, and new common share issues. When the common equity portion of financing comes entirely from reinvested earnings, the firm's cost of equity will equal the return required by its shareholders, as discussed previously. However, when the firm is forced into issuing new common shares, it must pay flotation costs for issuing these shares, so the cost to the firm is higher than the cost of using internally generated funds.

At this point, it is useful to introduce the concept of the **marginal cost of capital (MCC)**, which may be defined as the weighted average cost of the "next dollar" of financing to be raised. Sometimes the terms WACC and MCC are used interchangeably, although they are not really the same, since the WACC represents the weighted average cost of each dollar raised in total. The two tend to be the same for most levels of financing. However, they will differ when, at some financing level, the firm's cost of raising new money increases, causing the MCC to exceed the WACC. Given the earlier discussion, it's clear the most common cause of this increase in the MCC occurs when the firm cannot supply all of its required common equity financing from reinvested earnings (i.e., internal funds). Therefore, it must issue new common shares and bear the brunt of issuing costs, in addition to providing common shareholders with their required rate of return. This causes the cost of common equity to increase, meaning the MCC increases. The reason MCC and WACC are often identical is that many firms restrict their investment outlays so that all of the common equity finance portion can be provided by internal funds. (Recall from Chapter 13 that this procedure is referred to as capital rationing.)

**marginal cost of capital (MCC)**   the weighted average cost of the next dollar of financing to be raised

In short, the MCC often exceeds the WACC due to the costs of raising additional funds. Changes in securities regulation have led to a drop in these issuing costs, so for large firms, like CP, they are relatively minor; bought deals, for example, mean that equity can be raised at a very low cost, since for reporting issuers, the legal requirements have largely been met. However, for small firms, these issue costs can be significant, causing the MCC to jump dramatically.

Issuing costs are approximately as shown in **Table 20.4** but differ from one firm to another based on their size and the frequency with which they access the capital market, as well as market conditions. Sometimes capital is simply not available at any reasonable price.

**TABLE 20.4**   **Average Issuing Costs**

| | |
|---|---|
| Commercial paper | 0.125% |
| Medium-term notes | 1% |
| Long-term debt | 2% |
| Equity (large) | 5% |
| Equity (small) | 5% to 10% |
| Equity (private) | 10% and up |

These issuing costs represent a "financing wedge" between what the investor pays and what the firm receives, the difference being the money that is lost to these issue costs. This means that when a firm makes investments, it has to earn enough to cover both the cost of the equity it receives and the issue costs it pays.

# Debt

We can determine the cost of debt to the firm by using a variation of Equation 20.12, in which we replace the bond price with the net proceeds (*NP*) the firm receives when it issues new bonds after paying its flotation costs. We would note here that flotation costs are tax deductible immediately. (On the other hand, when debt securities are issued at a discount from their face value, this cost will be amortized over the life of the debt.) We must make one more adjustment to Equation 20.12 to reflect the fact that the interest payments are tax deductible, whereas the principal repayment (i.e., the face value) is not. After making these substitutions, we merely solve for the firm's after-tax cost of debt ($k_i$) in the same manner by which we solved for the yield to maturity (YTM) in Chapter 6. This equation is given here.

$$NP = I \times (1 - T) \times \left[ \frac{1 - \frac{1}{(1 + k_i)^n}}{k_i} \right] + F \times \frac{1}{(1 + k_i)^n} \qquad [20.13]$$

---

**EXAMPLE 20.2** | Determining the Cost of Debt

Suppose firm ABC from Example 20.1 can issue new 10-year bonds at par value. The bonds pay 6-percent annual coupons. The before-tax issuing costs are 2.5 percent of par. Estimate the firm's before- and after-tax cost of debt.

**Solution**   Using $100 par value, we get the following values that can be substituted into Equation 20.13:

$$NP = \$100 - \$100(0.025)(1 - 0.4) = \$100 - \$1.50 = \$98.50$$
$$I = (0.06)(\$100) = \$6$$

So we have:

$$\$98.50 = \$6 \times (1 - 0.4) \left[ \frac{1 - \frac{1}{(1 + k_i)^{10}}}{k_i} \right] + \$100 \times \frac{1}{(1 + k_i)^{10}}$$

Solving for $k_i$ using a financial calculator,[6] as shown in Chapter 6, we get the solution shown next.

---

[6]Students who have not yet mastered the financial calculator can solve using the trial-and-error method illustrated in Chapter 6.

**EXAMPLE 20.2** | Solution Using a Financial Calculator

Then **CPT** **I/Y** will give 3.78 percent.

So the firm's after-tax cost of debt is 3.78 percent. This is slightly higher than the 3.6 percent that we get from the 6-percent yield and 40-percent tax rate, since we have taken into account the fact that the firm is not receiving all of the $1,000 market value of the bonds. Instead, there is $15 of after-tax issuing costs.

## Preferred Shares

The cost of preferred shares can also be determined by accounting for flotation costs. In Equation 20.11, replace $P_p$ with $NP$ and then solve the equation for $k_p$, as shown in Equation 20.14.

$$k_p = \frac{D_p}{NP}$$   [20.14]

**EXAMPLE 20.3** | Determining the Cost of Preferred Equity

Suppose firm ABC from Example 20.1 can issue new preferred shares at par value of $100, which pay annual dividends at an 8-percent rate. The net after-tax flotation costs are 2 percent of par. Estimate the firm's after-tax cost of preferred equity.

**Solution**   Based on their $100 par value, we get the following values, which can be substituted into Equation 20.14:

$$NP = \$100(1 - 0.02) = \$98; D_p = (0.08)(\$100) = \$8$$

So we have:

$$k_p = \frac{D_p}{NP} = \frac{\$8}{\$98} = 8.16\%$$

## Canadian Pacific Financing

Now that we have discussed how to estimate the cost of debt and preferred equity, let's see how we can apply the principles to CP. First, CP does not have any preferred equity, so it is simply a question of estimating its debt costs. **Figure 20.2** presents note 17 of CP's 2018 annual report, which is the basic starting place for our discussion. There are several very interesting points that reflect the historic importance of CP to the Canadian economy.

First, and most obvious, is that CP has a lot of debt, which is just the flip side to its underlying business. As the operator of several railway lines, it has a huge amount of fixed assets. As of year-end 2018, CP had total assets of $21,254 million, of which $18,418 million were its properties, primarily $13,363 mainly for track and roadways and $2,854 mainly for rolling stock. The remaining properties were buildings and the capitalized value of its information system. With such a heavy investment in net fixed assets, CP has to be able to access financial markets regularly, which means an investment-grade bond rating. DBRS raised CP's issuer and medium term note rating to BBB (high) on December 20, 2018. Since it has such a large amount of US$ denominated debt outstanding, it is also rated by S&P (BBB+) and Moody's (Baaa1).

| (in millions of Canadian dollars except percentages) | | | Maturity | Currency in which payable | 2018 | 2017 |
|---|---|---|---|---|---|---|
| 6.500% | 10-year Notes | (A) | May 2018 | U.S.$ | $ — | $ 345 |
| 6.250% | 10-year Medium Term Notes | (A) | Jun 2018 | CDN$ | — | 375 |
| 7.250% | 10-year Notes | (A) | May 2019 | U.S.$ | 477 | 439 |
| 9.450% | 30-year Debentures | (A) | Aug 2021 | U.S.$ | 341 | 314 |
| 5.100% | 10-year Medium Term Notes | (A) | Jan 2022 | CDN$ | 125 | 125 |
| 4.500% | 10-year Notes | (A) | Jan 2022 | U.S.$ | 339 | 311 |
| 4.450% | 12.5-year Notes | (A) | Mar 2023 | U.S.$ | 477 | 438 |
| 2.900% | 10-year Notes | (A) | Feb 2025 | U.S.$ | 955 | 878 |
| 3.700% | 10.5-year Notes | (A) | Feb 2026 | U.S.$ | 340 | 313 |
| 4.000% | 10-year Notes | (A) | Jun 2028 | U.S.$ | 682 | — |
| 7.125% | 30-year Debentures | (A) | Oct 2031 | U.S.$ | 477 | 439 |
| 5.750% | 30-year Debentures | (A) | Mar 2033 | U.S.$ | 334 | 307 |
| 4.800% | 20-year Notes | (A) | Sep 2035 | U.S.$ | 408 | 375 |
| 5.950% | 30-year Notes | (A) | May 2037 | U.S.$ | 607 | 558 |
| 6.450% | 30-year Notes | (A) | Nov 2039 | CDN$ | 400 | 400 |
| 5.750% | 30-year Notes | (A) | Jan 2042 | U.S.$ | 336 | 308 |
| 4.800% | 30-year Notes | (A) | Aug 2045 | U.S.$ | 748 | 687 |
| 6.125% | 100-year Notes | (A) | Sep 2115 | U.S.$ | 1,228 | 1,129 |
| 5.41% | Senior Secured Notes | (B) | Mar 2024 | U.S.$ | 113 | 111 |
| 6.91% | Secured Equipment Notes | (C) | Oct 2024 | CDN$ | 106 | 120 |
| 7.49% | Equipment Trust Certificates | (D) | Jan 2021 | U.S.$ | 57 | 52 |
| Obligations under capital leases | | | | | | |
| 6.99% | | (E) | Mar 2022 | U.S.$ | 104 | 96 |
| 6.57% | | (E) | Dec 2026 | U.S.$ | 52 | 52 |
| 12.77% | | (E) | Jan 2031 | CDN$ | 4 | 3 |
| | | | | | 8,710 | 8,175 |
| Perpetual 4% Consolidated Debenture Stock | | (F) | | U.S.$ | 41 | 38 |
| Perpetual 4% Consolidated Debenture Stock | | (F) | | G.B.£ | 6 | 6 |
| | | | | | 8,757 | 8,219 |
| Less: Unamortized fees on long-term debt | | | | | 61 | 60 |
| | | | | | 8,696 | 8,159 |
| Less: Long-term debt maturing within one year | | | | | 506 | 746 |
| | | | | | $8,190 | $7,413 |

At December 31, 2018, the gross amount of long-term debt denominated in U.S. dollars was U.S. $5,970 million (2017 – U.S. $5,755 million).

**Source:** Data from *Canadian Pacific Annual Report 2018*, Notes to Consolidated Financial Statements

**FIGURE 20.2** **Canadian Pacific Debt ($Million)**

Remember that the lowest investment-grade rating is BBB (low), and the issuer rating is for the overall company and not a particular debt issue. As CP has noted,

> A mid investment grade credit rating is an important measure in assessing the Company's ability to maintain access to public financing and to minimize cost of capital. It also affects the ability of the Company to engage in certain collateralized business activities on a cost effective basis.

"Collateralized" simply means activities where a company has to put up assets (collateral) as security.

Second, since CP regularly raises money to finance its operations, it has lots of different debt issues outstanding. The major ones are:

1. **Debt issues marked with (A).**  These are unsecured debt listed as notes, medium-term notes, or debentures, with maturities running from 10 years out to 100 years. You have to be very low risk for investors to buy notes with a 100-year maturity.

2. **Equipment financing listed as secured equipment loans marked (B), (C), and (D).**  These are either loans, usually with rolling stock as the underlying security, or some U.S. "Equipment Trust Certificates," where the ownership of the rolling stock resides in a trust until the debt is paid off.

3. **Capital lease obligations marked (E).**  In Chapter 16 we discussed leasing as an alternative to borrowing to buy, and distinguished between financial and operating leases. CP's capital leases are financial leases where ownership of the rolling stock has essentially been transferred to CP, but it makes lease payments to the lessor instead of interest payments.

4. **Perpetuities marked (F).**  CP is one of the few Canadian companies that has issued perpetual debt, which, as we discussed in Chapter 6, is debt that has no maturity date. This debt was issued in both pounds sterling (UK) and U.S. dollars and was originally thought to have a maturity date of 1953, but a close examination of the prospectus indicates it actually said "after 1953," and some of this debt is still outstanding. This debt was authorized by an act of Parliament in 1889.

5. **Commercial paper.**  CP initiated a U.S. commercial paper program in the last quarter of 2014, with a maximum issue of US$1,000 million backed by a committed credit facility from a series of major banks. As of December 2018, the facility was undrawn and no commercial paper was outstanding.

So what is the cost of all this debt? We could simply take a weighted average of all CP's debt to calculate an average debt cost, but that simply reflects the cost of the debt already raised and not its current cost. We also have to remember that we are estimating the cost of capital to reflect what investors want *now*, not what they wanted in the past, when the capital was originally raised. To answer this question we have to look at how the money will be invested, and here it is important to note, as we did earlier, that the vast bulk of CP's assets are long-term property investments in track and rolling stock. The *matching principle* (introduced in Chapter 3) states that we should match the term of the financing to the approximate term of the investment. In other words, we should not finance long-term assets with short-term funds.

The upshot of this discussion is that when calculating the weighted average cost of capital, we have to remember that it is used to evaluate the attractiveness of long-term investments. For this reason, we use the current cost of financing for CP in the weighted average cost of capital. As of February 21, 2019, there was only one issue of CP debt available in the Canadian market, which was the 6.45-percent 2039 medium-term notes. With $400 million outstanding, these are reasonably liquid and had a yield of 3.838 percent. At the same time, the cost of 30-year Government of Canada debt was 2.14 percent, and average yield on A-rated bonds was slightly less at 3.675 percent. This would be consistent with CP's BBB (high) bond rating. Adding in flotation costs would mean a pre-tax cost of 4 percent for long-term debt. CP uses an effective tax rate of 26 percent in its financial forecasts, so we would estimate the after-tax cost of CP's long-term debt at 2.96 percent. Given that some of CP's debt is 100-year debt while some comes due much earlier, an overall after-tax debt cost for use in the WACC of 3 percent is reasonable.

Estimating the cost of common equity is more complicated, and we elaborate on various approaches in the following sections.

---

**Concept Review Questions**

1. How do flotation costs affect the cost of capital sources for a firm?
2. Explain how to estimate the cost of debt and preferred equity for a firm.

---

**20.4** # The Effects of Operating and Financial Leverage

**LEARNING OBJECTIVE 20.4**
Explain how operating leverage and financial leverage affect a firm's risk.

## Sales Changes and Leverage

Before we formally consider how to estimate a firm's cost of common equity, we return to the firm from Table 20.3, which had to generate sales of $1,000 to cover its operating and financing costs. Suppose that the firm issued a report stating that sales potential had increased and it now expected to sell 20-percent more widgets; as a result, sales revenues were expected to be $1,200, all else remaining constant (**Table 20.5**).

In this example, the firm's variable costs increase by the same 20 percent that sales increase, rising to $360, but EBIT increases by 31.7 percent, to $582. This is because some of the firm's operating costs are fixed and do not increase with sales, a circumstance referred to as **operating leverage**. In addition to the fixed operating costs, the firm's interest costs of $42 are also fixed. As a result, the firm's net income increases by 35 percent, from $300 to $405. If this $405 is viewed as a perpetuity, as before, and is discounted back at the 12-percent cost of equity, the market value of the equity also increases by 35 percent, to $3,375 from $2,500.

We might also ask what happens to the market value of the firm's debt. One way to determine this is to go back and look at the times interest earned (TIE) or coverage ratio, which was defined in Chapter 4 as EBIT divided by interest expense. At sales of $1,000, if we divided the EBIT of $442 by the interest expense of $42, the TIE ratio was 10.52, which is very

**operating leverage** the increased volatility in operating income caused by fixed operating costs

| **TABLE 20.5** | **Forecast Income Statement after a 20-Percent Sales Increase** |
|---|---|
| Sales | $1,200 |
| Variable costs | 360 |
| Fixed costs | 258 |
| EBIT | 582 |
| Interest | 42 |
| Tax (25%) | 135 |
| Net income | 405 |

high. This means that there was $10.52 of EBIT available for every dollar of interest payments, so the firm's EBIT could drop precipitously and still be able to cover the interest payments. At the new sales and EBIT levels, the coverage ratio increases to 13.86 (i.e., $582/$42), which means the debt is even safer.

This might mean that the debt is marginally less risky, but as we discussed earlier, debt is normally issued under a trust indenture that indicates how much the firm can issue. For example, under the BC Gas indenture discussed in Chapter 18, BC Gas could issue as much debt as it wanted, provided it satisfied a specified interest coverage ratio test. As a result, with a higher coverage ratio, the bondholders would expect the firm to issue more debt so that the required return on the debt would stay the same and all the increased value would "drop through" to the common shareholders.[7] So with a constant market value for the example firm's debt, the overall firm value increases from $3,200 to $4,075.

Now let's consider what happens if sales drop by 20 percent, to $800. Table 20.6 illustrates how the income statement would appear in this case.

Now the effect of fixed operating and financial costs works in reverse. With fixed operating costs of $258, the firm's EBIT drops by 31.7 percent, to $302; with fixed interest costs, the net income drops by 35 percent, to $195. If this net income is expected to continue in perpetuity, then discounting it at 12 percent gives an equity market value of $1,625, which is also a drop of 35 percent.

With the lower sales level, the TIE ratio drops from 10.52 to 7.19. This is still very high, so the sales drop would not unduly concern the firm's bondholders, and the market value of the debt might stay the same. The result is that the overall firm value drops from $3,200 to $2,325 and is again fully borne by the shareholders.

This example illustrates the basic proposition that risk "drops down" through the income statement. The first claim on the firm's sales is the variable costs. Remember from microeconomics that the firm will not produce anything unless it covers its variable costs; otherwise, it is increasing its losses as it produces more. The next claim is the fixed operating costs, such as space rentals or leases on cars and equipment. These costs are not tied to the level of sales and are incurred regardless of the level of sales. Once the EBIT is determined, the first financial claim is that of the debt holders, since debt is a fixed contractual commitment. The last and residual claim is that of the equity holders. When times are good and sales increase, net income increases proportionately more than sales, depending on the size of the firm's fixed operational and financial commitments. This sensitivity was referred to in Chapter 4 as the degree of total leverage (DTL), which was defined as the contribution margin divided by the earnings before tax. In our example, the contribution margin at a sales level of $1,000 is $700 (sales minus variable costs), so the degree of total leverage is this divided by the earnings before tax of $400, which gives us 1.75. This indicates that for every 1-percent variation in sales, net income varied by 1.75 percent (i.e., a 20-percent change in sales produces a 35-percent change in net income).

| TABLE 20.6 | Forecast Income Statement after a 20-Percent Sales Decrease |
|---|---|
| Sales | $800 |
| Variable costs | 240 |
| Fixed costs | 258 |
| EBIT | 302 |
| Interest | 42 |
| Tax (25%) | 65 |
| Net income | 195 |

---

[7]Note that some of the increased value drops through to the government, because with a proportional corporate income tax, the government is a compulsory shareholder in all private-sector activity.

The example also indicates the residual nature of the common shareholders and the fact that they are last in line. As the firm's sales drop, everyone has a higher-priority claim than the common shareholders do, so they see much greater volatility in their return than either the debt holders or others with a stake in the firm's operations. It also explains why the stock market is so sensitive to sales and earnings announcements, given the great difficulty in forecasting future profit levels.

---

**Concept Review Questions**

1. Distinguish between operating and financial leverage.
2. Why do we say that equity holders bear the brunt of the effects of leverage?

---

## 20.5 | Growth Models and the Cost of Common Equity

**LEARNING OBJECTIVE 20.5**
Use the discounted cash flow model to estimate the cost of equity.

### The Importance of Adjusting for Growth

So far we have been talking about perpetuities, but very few firms expect to have constant earnings in perpetuity; they expect some growth whether from inflation or real activity. So we need to adjust for growth in our valuation. One way to assess a firm's growth prospects is to look at the stock market's time horizon, estimate the value of the firm's current dividend when viewed as a perpetuity, and then compare this value with the stock price. If the values are significantly different, it means that the stock market is valuing something other than the firm's current earnings and dividends. Table 20.7 breaks down the stock price for a number of stocks into this no-growth perpetuity value and the remaining percentage of the stock price, which is attributed to future growth opportunities.

**TABLE 20.7** Stock Prices and Growth Prospects

| Company | Price ($) | DPS ($) | Dividend Yield (%) | Perpetuity ($) | Growth Value (%) |
|---|---|---|---|---|---|
| AGF | 25.75 | 0.283 | 1.1 | 5.66 | 78 |
| BC Gas | 30.60 | 1.13 | 3.7 | 22.60 | 26 |
| CAE | 11.50 | 0.161 | 1.4 | 3.22 | 72 |
| Dennings | 3.50 | 0.102 | 2.9 | 2.04 | 42 |
| EL Financial | 285 | 0.570 | 0.2 | 11.40 | 96 |
| GSW(A) | 26.75 | 0.428 | 1.6 | 8.56 | 68 |
| Hammersen | 14.05 | 0.197 | 1.4 | 3.94 | 72 |
| Intrawest | 6.95 | 0.292 | 4.2 | 5.84 | 16 |
| Jannock | 29.60 | 0.148 | 0.5 | 2.96 | 90 |
| Average | | | 1.89 | | 62.22 |

**Source:** Data from Booth, Laurence, "What Drives Shareholder Value." *Financial Intelligence* IV-6 (Spring 1999), Table 1.

The firms in Table 20.7 were chosen randomly as the first firm in each alphabetical group that paid a dividend, according to the stock market pages of the *Financial Post*. The first column gives the share price, the second the dividend per share (DPS), and the third the dividend yield. The fourth column gives the perpetuity value of the dividend, using the yield on conventional preferred shares (which was 5 percent at the time) to value each firm's dividend. This is the value of the shares if nothing changes and the firm pays this dividend forever. The final column gives the proportion of the share price not explained by the dividend, which by definition is the value attributed to the firm's growth prospects. Overall, an average of 62.22 percent of the market value of this sample of firms could be attributed to growth opportunities, with the remaining 37.78 percent attributed to the present value of the current dividend. However, there is huge variation, from a low of only 16 percent attributed to growth for Intrawest, which was a property developer, to a high for EL Financial, with 96 percent of the share price attributed to growth. Some of this growth value is due to inflationary—that is, not real—growth. However, the important point of the data in the table is that the simple perpetuity model only works for firms with no growth prospects, and the data show that this is a valid assumption for only a limited number of firms, if any.[8]

In Chapter 7, we discussed how to value common shares when the earnings were not expected to be constant in perpetuity. The general principle was that the value of a common share was equal to the present value of its dividends. In order to make this equation practical, we had to impose some assumptions; otherwise, we would be forced to discount dividends to infinity, since common shares have no maturity date. One of the most important models we discussed in that chapter was the constant growth version of the dividend discount model (DDM), as expressed in Equation 7.7, which determines the present value of a growing perpetuity. We discuss this model in the next subsection.

## The Constant Growth Model

The constant growth DDM is commonly referred to as the Gordon model, after the late Professor Myron Gordon of the University of Toronto. The basic valuation equation was introduced in Chapter 7 and is reproduced here as Equation 20.15.

$$P_0 = \frac{D_1}{k_e - g}$$

[20.15]

where the price of a share ($P_0$) equals the expected dividend ($D_1$) divided by the required return by common share investors ($k_e$), minus the forecast long-run growth rate ($g$) in dividends and earnings.

As discussed in Chapter 7, we can rearrange this equation to estimate the common equity investors' discount rate or required rate of return. This process is called the discounted cash flow (DCF) method for estimating the investors' required rate of return. Equation 20.16 is the DCF equation.

$$k_e = \frac{D_1}{P_0} + g$$

[20.16]

In this equation, the required rate of return is composed of the expected dividend yield ($D_1/P_0$) plus the expected long-run growth rate ($g$). The long-run growth rate is then the estimate of the increase in the share price and the investors' capital gain. As discussed previously, this is the appropriate cost of equity capital for the firm when the firm can raise the required funds internally (i.e., when it uses reinvested profits). Example 20.4 illustrates how to use this equation.

---

[8]Note that the data also show why the stock market reacts so quickly to news about a firm's future prospects. With so much of the value of most firms' share price coming from future growth, small changes in these future prospects have a huge impact on the share price. The data also indicate how "far-sighted" the stock market is.

---

**EXAMPLE 20.4** | Determining the Cost of Common Equity Internal Funds

Let's revisit firm ABC from examples 20.1 through 20.3, and assume the firm paid a dividend per share last year of $1, which is expected to grow at 5 percent per year indefinitely. Recall that its share price is $25. Estimate the cost of common equity using internal funds.

**Solution**   First, we need to find $D_1$:

$$D_1 = D_0(1 + g) = \$1(1.05) = \$1.05$$

Now we can use Equation 20.16 to estimate $k_e$:

$$k_e = \frac{D_1}{P_0} + g = \frac{\$1.05}{\$25} + 0.05 = 0.042 + 0.05 = 0.092 = 9.2\%$$

---

Example 20.4 shows how we can estimate the cost of common equity for a firm if it does not need to issue new common equity, since it is simply the return required by common equity investors. However, what if a company needs to raise new common equity financing through a share issue? In this case, we need to account for the share issuance costs, as discussed previously. Equation 20.17 shows that the necessary adjustment to Equation 20.16 is straightforward. We simply replace the share price ($P_0$) with the net proceeds ($NP$) received by the firm. This accounts for the fact that the firm does not receive the full share price that investors are willing to pay, since a portion of these funds goes to pay for issuing costs. We provide Equation 20.17 here, denoting the cost of issuing new common equity as $k_{ne}$.

$$k_{ne} = \frac{D_1}{NP} + g \qquad\qquad [20.17]$$

---

**EXAMPLE 20.5** | Determining the Cost of Common Equity—New Issues

We revisit firm ABC from Example 20.4 and assume the firm can issue new shares with net after-tax flotation costs of 5 percent of the share price. Estimate the cost of new common equity to the firm.

**Solution**   First, we need to find $NP$:

$$NP = P_0(1 - 0.05) = \$25(0.95) = \$23.75$$

Now we can use Equation 20.17 to estimate $k_{ne}$:

$$k_{ne} = \frac{D_1}{NP} + g = \frac{\$1.05}{\$23.75} + 0.05 = 0.0442 + 0.05 = 0.0942 = 9.42\%$$

We can see that the firm's cost of equity is 0.22-percent higher for new share issues than when it uses internal funds.

---

Before we proceed further, it is important to note that equations 20.15 and 20.16 are the same; therefore, if Equation 20.15 does not hold, then neither does Equation 20.16 nor Equation 20.17. We mention this because equations 20.16 and 20.17 are commonly used to estimate the cost of equity capital, but the assumptions used to derive them are often forgotten. As a result, it is easy to misuse them.

Consider the case of a firm that pays no dividends and is growing at 20 percent per year, a growth rate that is expected to continue for the foreseeable future. A simple application of Equation 20.16 would suggest the cost of equity capital (internal funds) is 20 percent. Yet if we go back to Equation 20.15 and plug in 20 percent as a growth rate for a firm paying no dividends, we get results that make no sense. The reason for this is that 20 percent *cannot* be a long-run growth rate; in deriving Equation 20.15, we assume that the growth rate is constant forever and that the dividends start from a positive amount. If nominal GDP is growing at 5 to 6 percent a year, a firm that is growing at 20 percent will be capturing an ever bigger share of GDP. In fact, it is easy to show that such a firm would eventually be bigger than the whole economy. In this case, the assumption of constant growth used to derive Equation 20.15 is implausible, so using Equation 20.16 or 20.17 to estimate the cost of equity capital is *wrong*.

Unfortunately, people often try to squeeze the data used in equations 20.16 and 20.17 in an attempt to make them work; for example, they assume a small dividend and then reduce the short-run growth forecast to bring it more in line with what is possible in the long run. However, you cannot torture a model that doesn't fit the assumptions of a particular firm. Instead, you need to use a model that better fits the firm, such as the multi-stage growth models that were discussed in Chapter 7. Before discussing how to use these models, let's explore the constant growth model a bit more.

## Growth and ROE

In Chapter 7, we pointed out that one way to estimate growth was the sustainable growth method, in which the growth rate is the product of the firm's retention rate ($b$), defined as one minus the firm's payout ratio, multiplied by its forecast ROE, as shown in Equation 20.18.

$$g = b \times ROE$$  [20.18]

This equation makes it obvious that even if the firm retains all of its profits and reinvests them in the firm, it is not plausible that it could earn a 20-percent ROE on this investment forever. Such an assumption would imply that no other firm can enter the industry and compete with the firm for these high ROEs. If other firms can enter the market, which will normally be the case, these high ROEs will be reduced to normal levels due to competitive pressures.

We have to remember that Professor Myron Gordon developed the constant growth model for use in public utility regulation, where the allowed ROEs should be reasonable and where the problem of rapid growth rates does not exist. Further, a result of regulation is that all common equity earns virtually the same regulated ROE. In this case, the average and marginal ROE are exactly the same, and every dollar the firm retains earns the same ROE. In contrast, many extremely profitable firms cannot reinvest at the same ROE because they cannot find opportunities as good as their existing ones. In determining the growth rate, the ROE is the return on incremental investment, which may be greater or smaller than what the firm is currently earning.

However, for the time being let's return to the constant growth DDM with the assumption of a constant ROE. Substituting the sustainable growth rate, as expressed in Equation 20.18 (i.e., $b \times ROE$), into the constant growth DDM in place of $g$, we get Equation 20.19.

$$P_0 = \frac{D_1}{k_e - b \times ROE}$$  [20.19]

Further, we then recognize that the expected dividend per share ($D_1$) is the expected earnings per share ($X_1$) times the dividend payout rate (i.e., one minus the retention rate), since a dollar can either be paid out or retained and reinvested in the firm. Making this substitution for $D_1$, we get Equation 20.20.

$$P_0 = \frac{X_1(1 - b)}{k_e - b \times ROE}$$  [20.20]

This equation shows that the price per share is determined by the firm's forecast earnings per share, its dividend payout ($1 - b$), its ROE, and the return required by common equity shareholders ($k_e$).

One important use of Equation 20.20 is to see how growth and the firm's ROE affect its share price. Suppose, for example, that the firm's retention rate is 50 percent, its cost of equity capital is 12 percent, and its forecast earnings per share figure is $2. If the firm's ROE is 12 percent, then the forecast growth rate is 6 percent (i.e., 12% × 0.5), and the forecast dividend per share is $1, using the 50-percent payout ratio. In this case, the shares are worth $16.67—that is, $1 divided by 6 percent (i.e., $k_e - g = 12\% - 6\%$). Now suppose instead of a 12-percent ROE, the firm is expected to earn 10 percent or 14 percent. At a 10-percent ROE, the firm's forecast growth rate drops to 5 percent and its share price is only $14.29, whereas at a 14-percent ROE, the firm's growth rate is 7 percent and its shares are worth $20.

What this example illustrates is that the higher the growth rate, the higher the share price, since investors will forecast larger future dividends and earnings. If we rearrange Equation 20.20, we get the following variation of the constant growth DDM:

$$k_e = \frac{D_1}{P_0} + g = \frac{X_1(1-b)}{P_0} + b \times ROE \qquad [20.21]$$

In this equation, the first term is the forecast dividend yield, and the second is the sustainable growth rate. However, note what happens when we use this equation to estimate the cost of equity capital (internal) for our three growth scenarios, as depicted in **Table 20.8**.

Since the shares were valued using a constant 12-percent discount rate, when we "reverse engineer" from the share price, we get the same 12 percent back as the estimate of the cost of equity capital. In this case, the higher forecast growth rate leads to a higher market price and a lower dividend yield. Generally, firms with high dividend yields have lower forecast growth rates and vice versa. The only exception to this general rule is when a firm is under a lot of stress and is about to cut its dividend. However, there is no reason for the cost of equity capital to be the same, since the composition of the return between dividends and growth changes. This is a question of the firm's dividend policy, which will be discussed in detail in Chapter 22.

However, note that the firm's retention rate, and thus its dividend payout ratio, is reflected in the constant growth DDM as "b." **Table 20.9** gives the share price if this retention rate changes under the three scenarios in which the firm's ROE is 10, 12, or 14 percent.

Let's look first at the last column in the table, where the ROE is 10 percent. We already saw that at a 50-percent retention rate, the firm's share price was $14.29, but now we see that its share price *decreases* as the firm retains more money and reinvests it in the firm. In contrast, when the ROE is 14 percent, the share price increases as the firm retains more, while for the 12-percent ROE, the share price is independent of the retention rate.

The reason for these results is that when the firm's ROE is 10 percent, it is less than the investors' required rate of return of 12 percent. So as the firm invests more by increasing its retention rate, the shareholders are unhappy. Why would investors who require a 12-percent return be happy about a firm that reinvests at 10 percent? In this case, the share valuation model is telling the firm's management to reduce investment and return the funds saved as a larger dividend. The shareholders can then take these funds and invest them elsewhere to earn their 12-percent required rate of return. Conversely, when the firm is expected to earn 14 percent, the shareholders are saying the opposite: "Don't give us a dividend. We can earn only 12 percent elsewhere, so please reinvest more and earn 14 percent." As a result, the share price increases as the firm invests more. Finally, for the 12-percent ROE case, the shareholders are saying: "We don't care what you do, since you are not doing anything for us if you invest or give us a dividend." As a result, there is no impact on the share price.

**TABLE 20.8**  Growth and $k_e$

| ROE | $P_e$ | Expected Dividend Yield | Sustainable Growth Rate | $k_e$ |
|-----|-------|-------------------------|-------------------------|-------|
| 10% | 14.29 | 7% | 5% | 12% |
| 12% | 16.67 | 6% | 6% | 12% |
| 14% | 20.00 | 5% | 7% | 12% |

**TABLE 20.9**   **Retention Rates, ROE, and Share Prices**

| | ROE | | |
|---|---|---|---|
| *b* | **0.14** | **0.12** | **0.10** |
| 0.4 | 18.75 | 16.67 | 15.00 |
| 0.41 | 18.85 | 16.67 | 14.94 |
| 0.42 | 18.95 | 16.67 | 14.87 |
| 0.43 | 19.06 | 16.67 | 14.81 |
| 0.44 | 19.18 | 16.67 | 14.74 |
| 0.45 | 19.30 | 16.67 | 14.67 |
| 0.46 | 19.42 | 16.67 | 14.59 |
| 0.47 | 19.56 | 16.67 | 14.52 |
| 0.48 | 19.70 | 16.67 | 14.44 |
| 0.49 | 19.84 | 16.67 | 14.37 |
| 0.5 | 20.00 | 16.67 | 14.29 |
| 0.51 | 20.16 | 16.67 | 14.20 |
| 0.52 | 20.34 | 16.67 | 14.12 |
| 0.53 | 20.52 | 16.67 | 14.03 |
| 0.54 | 20.72 | 16.67 | 13.94 |
| 0.55 | 20.93 | 16.67 | 13.85 |
| 0.56 | 21.15 | 16.67 | 13.75 |
| 0.57 | 21.39 | 16.67 | 13.65 |
| 0.58 | 21.65 | 16.67 | 13.55 |
| 0.59 | 21.93 | 16.67 | 13.44 |
| 0.6 | 22.22 | 16.67 | 13.33 |

The example in Table 20.9 is very important in finance. For a long time it was felt that this result was due to the firm's dividend policy, because the firm's retention rate and dividend payout were changing. However, this is not the case. What is really changing is the amount of investment the firm is making, and the stock market is valuing whether the firm is creating or destroying value. When ROE is more than $k_e$, the firm is creating value when it reinvests; when ROE is less than $k_e$, it is destroying value. This result is independent of how much the firm decides to pay out as a dividend, since it can always raise money to pay a dividend. This points to another aspect of the cost of capital: not only is it important to value the firm's shares, but it is also a **hurdle rate** for making investment decisions. This is the meaning of the phrase "required return": unless an investment jumps this hurdle, it destroys value and should not be undertaken. We will discuss this more at the end of the chapter.

> **hurdle rate**   the return on an investment required to create value; below this rate an investment would destroy value

The example with the different ROEs and different retention rates also emphasizes another key point in finance: there is a big difference between a *growing* firm and a *growth* firm. When the ROE equals $k_e$, the cost of internal equity, the share price is independent of how much the firm reinvests. If the firm pays out all its earnings and does not grow at all ($b = 0$), the share price is $16.67, whereas if it reinvests all its earnings ($b = 1$) and grows at 12 percent per year, the share price is still $16.67. (This ignores taxes, which were discussed in Chapter 18.) This is an example of a growing firm that, because it simply reinvests at its cost of capital, is "not doing anything" for the shareholders; as a result, they don't care whether it is growing or not. Note also that the earnings yield for this growing firm at a 50-percent retention rate is 12 percent, which equals its forecast earnings per share divided by its stock price (i.e., $2/$16.67). So for growing firms, the earnings yield is a good estimate of their cost of equity capital.

On the other hand, when ROE is greater than $k_e$, the firm is doing something that the shareholders cannot do, which is reinvest at 14 percent. We call these firms "growth firms" and say they have "growth opportunities." In this case, note that the earnings yield is $2 divided by $20, or 10 percent, which underestimates the return required by common shareholders.

Finally, there are some firms that destroy shareholder value by investing where ROE is less than $k_e$. For these firms, the earnings yield is $2 divided by $14.29, or 14 percent, which overestimates their cost of internal equity. These results confirm that the earnings yield is not generally a good estimate of a firm's cost of internal equity capital. Dividends or earnings may be growing, but the crucial piece of information is whether the firm is investing at rates of return greater or less than its cost of equity capital—that is, whether growth opportunities exist. We can consider these cases by looking again at multiple-stage growth models.

## Multiple-Stage Growth Models

**multiple-stage growth DDM** a version of the DDM that accounts for different levels of growth in earnings and dividends

Another version of the DCF model to consider is the **multiple-stage growth DDM**, which was also discussed in Chapter 7. In practice, there is no limit to the extent of the growth stages, but let's consider a very simple case in which the firm has some investment today, which we assume equals the firm's book value per share (BVPS), which is earning a return ($ROE_1$) in perpetuity. The firm is expected to invest a similar amount next year (Inv), which will again earn a return ($ROE_2$) in perpetuity. This particular version of the multiple-stage model is expressed in Equation 20.22.

$$P_0 = \frac{ROE_1 \times BVPS}{k_e} + \frac{Inv}{(1 + k_e)}\left[\frac{(ROE_2 - k_e)}{k_e}\right]$$ [20.22]

The first term in this equation equals the perpetuity value of the current earnings, as discussed previously, where the firm is expected to earn an ROE equal to $ROE_1$. The second term represents further investment (Inv), which we assume is invested at $ROE_2$ and is discounted back one period, since it is one period further off in the future. However, it adds a perpetual amount, represented by the difference between the firm's ROE on this future investment of $ROE_2$ minus $k_e$. As before, if $ROE_2$ equals $k_e$, this future investment adds nothing to the value of the firm, since it does not create value, and the second term will equal zero. However, if $ROE_2$ is greater than $k_e$, this future investment adds value, with the amount of value depending on the amount of investment (Inv) that can be invested at this rate, and on how much $ROE_2$ exceeds $k$. Equation 20.22 is a simple approach to valuation that breaks out the value of shares into the **present value of existing opportunities (PVEO)**, the first term, and the **present value of growth opportunities (PVGO)**, as a result of investment in the future, the second term. Note that although we conventionally refer to the second term as PVGO, it is actually the *net* present value (NPV), since we have to subtract the future cost of the investments.

**present value of existing opportunities (PVEO)** the value of the firm's current operations assuming no new investment

**present value of growth opportunities (PVGO)** the net present value (NPV) today of the firm's future investments

We apply this equation by setting the investment amount arbitrarily at $20 for both the current book value and the next period's investment, and use a discount rate of 12 percent to value this stock. We now consider four scenarios:

A. In this scenario, PVEO is high, with $ROE_1$ of 20 percent and BVPS of $20, so PVEO is $33.33. The ROE for the next period is expected to remain high, at 20 percent, so PVGO is $11.90. Thus, the share price would be $45.23. Note in this case that the PVGO of $11.90 is less than the PVEO of $33.33, since it is actually the NPV of these future growth opportunities.

B. In this scenario, $ROE_2$ is less than or equal to 12 percent, so the firm has no PVGO and does not make any future investments, but we assume it has the same high ROE for current earnings of 20 percent, so its share price would be $33.33.

C. In this scenario, the firm has very poor current earnings, with $ROE_1$ of 2 percent, but it has the same great future prospects as it does in scenario A. Thus, its PVEO equals $3.33, and its PVGO would be $11.90, translating into a share price of $15.23.

D. In the final scenario, the firm has the same poor current prospects as in scenario C, so its PVEO would be $3.33. On top of that, it is destroying value by reinvesting in the future at an $ROE_2$ of 10 percent, so PVGO is −$2.98, and its share price would be a trivial $0.35 (i.e., $3.33 − $2.98)!

If we classify these four cases as types of firms, we have the following:

**A.** High PVEO and high PVGO

**B.** High PVEO and low (zero) PVGO

**C.** Low PVEO and high PVGO

**D.** Low PVEO and low PVGO

We can put them into a two-by-two matrix and classify them according to a conventional corporate description pioneered by the Boston Consulting Group, as shown in **Figure 20.3**.

Firm A would be classified as a **star** in Figure 20.3, having everything going for it—both very good PVEO and excellent PVGO. Firm B would be the **cash cow**, generating significant cash flows from its current opportunities and thus possessing a high PVEO, but with no good investment opportunities, so its PVGO is zero. Firm C is the **turnaround** candidate; its current operations are a drag on performance so PVEO is low, but everything is about the future, so its PVGO is high. Finally, Firm D is the **dog**, with poor current operations so its PVEO is low. On top of that, it has been investing in projects that provide returns lower than its cost of internal equity, so it possesses a negative PVGO.

We developed these four stylistic views of firm valuation to show that for every firm, there is a "story" that has to match its valuation. If you can understand this, then estimating each firm's cost of equity capital becomes easier as you know the biases in using DCF estimates. For example, A has the highest market price because both PVEO and PVGO are high. This could be a large capitalization stock (large cap) such as Apple, where everything is going right. The cash cow would be a utility like TransCanada Pipelines Ltd., with an excellent profitable core business but limited growth prospects. The cash cow might also be called a value stock, depending on its price. The turnaround company could be a pure growth stock, with very limited current value but great growth potential, such as an early-stage pharmaceutical company. Classic examples of such growth stocks would be the Internet and tech stocks of the late 1990s, where investors were paying a huge premium for the PVGO.[9] Finally, dogs *should* be scarce, since they are candidates for hostile takeovers. Regardless of the poor quality of their current operations (low PVEO), their value could be increased just by stopping them from throwing good money after bad by investing at less than their equity cost.

Note that we valued these four firms using the same 12-percent discount rate, so the cost of equity capital is exactly the same. However, the market-to-book ratio and earnings yield are different for each, as shown in **Table 20.10**.

**star**   a firm with high PVEO and high PVGO

**cash cow**   a firm with high PVEO but low PVGO

**turnaround**   a firm with low PVEO and high PVGO

**dog**   a firm with low PVEO and low PVGO

**FIGURE 20.3**  **Growth Opportunities and Firm Type**

Djurovic/iStockphoto

[9]A current example would by Alnylam, traded on Nasdaq as ALNY, with a US$8.2-billion market value but only $75 million in revenues. This is because its drugs are in clinical trials in the United States, and they are being "touted" not just as a cancer cure but also as something that could prolong life!

**TABLE 20.10** **The Impact of Growth Opportunities on Share Prices**

| | Earnings Yield (%) | Market-to-Book |
|---|---|---|
| Star | 8.84 | 2.26 |
| Cash cow | 12.00 | 1.67 |
| Turnaround | 2.63 | 0.76 |
| Dog | 114.29 | 0.02 |

The actual numbers are not that important, but the critical feature is that the star and the turnaround have very low earnings yields (or high price-earnings ratios). Both of these types of companies would be regarded as growth firms, since much of the value comes from PVGO. In the case of the turnaround company, its PVEO actually depresses its stock price. For both of these types of companies, DCF estimation methods are unreliable due to the importance of PVGO. The cash cow gives back the true discount rate, since there is no PVGO, and it may be viewed as a perpetuity. For the dog, the earnings yield is very high, exceeding 100 percent, because it is forecast to lose value from its future investments, which depresses the share price and thus increases the earnings yield.

The point of these examples is to show that you have to understand the type of firm before mechanically applying the DCF formulas; otherwise, it is very easy to make mistakes. The DCF models work best for non-growth firms and for the market as a whole, where growth opportunities are moderate and easiest to estimate. A good example of the latter use for the economy as a whole is the U.S. Federal Reserve System's application of the constant growth model in what is known as the "Fed model," discussed next.

# The Fed Model

The Fed model[10] was used to estimate whether the stock market was over- or undervalued and whether the U.S. Fed should "talk down" market values that might be excessive and cause problems if they collapsed. The exact equation used was:

$$\frac{V_{actual}}{V_{Fed}} = \frac{V_{actual}}{Exp(EPS)/(k_{TBond} - 1\%)} \qquad [20.23]$$

In this equation, $V_{actual}$ was the actual value for the U.S. stock market, and $V_{Fed}$ was the estimate from the Fed's model, which was the expected earnings per share on Standard & Poor's 500 Index (Exp(EPS)), as reported by security market analysts, divided by the yield on the long-term U.S. treasury bond ($k_{TBond}$) minus 1 percent. That is,

$$V_{Fed} = \frac{Exp(EPS)}{k_{TBond} - 1\%} \qquad [20.24]$$

Valuation is easier when you aggregate across all securities, since you remove the "nonsystematic risk" attached to individual securities. (This was discussed in chapters 8 and 9.) In the case of the market as a whole, after-tax earnings should grow at approximately the long-run real growth rate of GDP plus inflation, while the cost of equity for the market as a whole should be the treasury bond yield plus a market risk premium. So the Fed model implies that for fair valuation, the market risk premium is 1 percent less than the growth rate in nominal GDP.

Denoting Exp(EPS) as $X$, we can see that if the Fed model is rearranged, it also indicates that the market is fairly valued when the following condition exists:

$$\frac{X}{P_{S\&P500}} = k_{TBond} - 1\% \qquad [20.25]$$

---

[10]This discussion follows that in Yardeni, Edward, "US Stock Valuation Models." Deutsche Bank, October 4, 2000.

This equation says that "fair valuation" means that the expected earnings yield on the S&P 500 should be equal to the long-term treasury bond yield minus 1 percent. As discussed previously, the earnings yield is the appropriate discount rate for the no-growth case (i.e., for perpetuities), whereas we would expect the market as a whole to grow at the nominal GDP growth rate. So if this nominal GDP growth rate is 5 percent, another way of interpreting the Fed model is to say that the required return on the equity market as a whole averages the long-term treasury bond yield plus a 4-percent risk premium (i.e., the 5-percent nominal GDP growth rate minus 1 percent). With long-term U.S. treasury bonds yielding 1.8 percent in December 2019, this would indicate an overall equity cost for the U.S. market of less than 6 percent, which is very low. The actual "performance" of the Fed model since 1981 is illustrated in **Figure 20.4**, which comes from the Royal Bank of Canada's *Investment Strategy Playbook* of January 2016.

The Royal Bank of Canada (RBC) implemented the Fed model as the expected earnings yield versus the ten-year US Treasury yield. We can see that the model tracked the U.S. equity market quite well for much of the period until the late 1990s, when actual market values deviated significantly from the values implied by the Fed, that is the earnings yield dropped significantly below the US Treasury Yield. This was the period when the Governor of the US Fed was warning of "irrational exuberance" in the stock market. However, note that since the early 2000s the US Treasury yield has dropped significantly below the earnings yield. We could say this period has been marked by "irrational pessimism" or more likely the market risk premium in the US has jumped from 4% to a higher level due to the abnormally low U.S. government bond yields.

**FIGURE 20.4** **Earnings Yield vs. 10-Year Treasury**

**Source:** From "Investment Strategy Playbook", p.53, January 04, 2016. Copyright 2016. Reproduced with permission of RBC Capital Markets.

## Concept Review Questions

1. Explain how we can use the constant growth DDM to estimate the cost of firms' internal common equity, as well as the cost of new common share issues.

2. Explain the relationship between ROE, retention rates, and firm growth.

3. How can we relate the existence of multiple growth stages to four commonly used firm classifications?

4. Describe the Fed model and how it may be used to estimate the required rate of return of the market as a whole.

## 20.6 | Risk-Based Models and the Cost of Common Equity

> **LEARNING OBJECTIVE 20.6**
> Estimate the cost of equity using risk-based models and describe the advantages and limitations of these models.

### Using the CAPM to Estimate the Cost of Common Equity

In the previous section, we saw that the DCF model could be rearranged to estimate the investors' required return on a firm's common shares. We also discussed how the model performs poorly when applied to growth stocks, which pay low dividends and/or display high growth rates. In these situations, it makes sense to rely more heavily on **risk-based models**. The most important risk-based model is the **capital asset pricing model (CAPM)**, which was discussed in detail in Chapter 9.

**risk-based models** models that estimate costs based on the associated risks

**capital asset pricing model (CAPM)** a pricing model that uses one factor, beta, to relate expected returns to risk

Equation 20.26 represents the central equation of the CAPM, the security market line (SML).

$$k_e = R_F + MRP \times \beta_e \qquad [20.26]$$

In this equation, the return required by common shareholders ($k_e$) is composed of three terms:

**risk-free rate of return ($R_F$)** compensation for the time value of money

**market risk premium (MRP)** compensation for assuming the risk of the market portfolio

**beta coefficient** a measure of a firm's systematic or market risk

1. The **risk-free rate of return ($R_F$)**, which represents compensation for the time value of money
2. The **market risk premium (MRP)**, which is compensation for assuming the risk of the market portfolio and is defined as $ER_M - R_F$, where $ER_M$ is the expected return on the market
3. The **beta coefficient** ($\beta_e$) for the firm's common shares, which measures the firm's systematic or market risk and represents the contribution that this security makes to the risk of a well-diversified portfolio

The CAPM is derived as a single-period model, but just what is meant by a single period is unresolved, since investment horizons differ from investor to investor. In testing the CAPM, it is common to use a 30-day time horizon, yet such a short time horizon is rarely useful in making corporate finance decisions. In fact, when we talked about common equity in Chapter 19, one of the most important characteristics was the absence of a maturity date. While individual investors may invest for only 30 days, at that time they will sell the shares to other investors, so the security is still outstanding. In addition, as we will see when we discuss corporate investment decisions, the cost of capital or WACC is used to evaluate long-term investment decisions made by the firm. For this reason, the risk-free rate used in *corporate* applications of the CAPM is usually the yield on the longest-maturity Government of Canada bond, which is currently the 30-year bond. This is consistent with survey data reported by Professor Fernandez and his colleagues of IESE Business School in Spain: they found that the average respondent to a survey of financial executives and professionals used a risk-free rate higher than that of the 10-year government bond rate.[11]

In order to estimate the MRP, we generally use long-run averages supplemented by knowledge of the prevailing economic scenario. The basic idea is that over long periods of time, what people expect to happen should on average occur—that is, they are biased in forming their

---

[11]See Fernandez, Pablo, Pershin, Vitaly, and Acín, Isabel F., "Market Risk Premium and Risk-Free Rate Used for 59 Countries in 2018: A Survey." Working paper (April 4, 2018), University of Navarra, IESE Business School.

**TABLE 20.11** **Returns on the S&P/TSX Composite Index**

| | Returns (%) |
|---|---|
| 2012 | 7.19 |
| 2013 | 13.0 |
| 2014 | 10.55 |
| 2015 | −8.32 |
| 2016 | 21.08 |
| 2017 | 9.10 |
| 2018 | −8.89 |

**Sources:** Data from the Canadian Institute of Actuaries and from Datastream

expectations if they consistently over- or under-predict returns. In contrast, over short periods of time, expectations are unlikely to be realized. It's like tossing a die: you may get three consecutive 1s, but if you throw it enough times, eventually you will get 1s one-sixth of the time, 2s one-sixth of the time, and so on. Let's keep this in mind as we consider the performance of the S&P/TSX Composite Index over the 2012 to 2018 period, as reported in **Table 20.11**.

Clearly, it is difficult to argue that in any one particular year the performance of the S&P/TSX Composite Index was what was expected at the time. For example, nobody would have held shares in 2015 or 2018 if they expected the stock market to decline the way it did! Similarly, the performance in 2016 was exceptional; indeed, if you consistently earned returns of more than 20 percent, you would become very rich very quickly. In both cases, it is like observing three consecutive 1s when throwing a die; it can happen but is not what was expected.

In Chapter 8 we discussed the history of annual rates of return on the Canadian equity market and government bonds since 1938, when the Bank of Canada was established as a public institution. Over this long period of time, the average annual return on Canadian equities was 10.99 percent, while that on long-term Canadian government bonds was 6.09 percent. The difference between the average return on common equities and the average return on bonds in Canada was just under 5 percent—that is, $10.99 - 6.09 = 4.90$ percent—which would represent one estimate of our long-term MRP.[12] This MRP has fallen over the past few years due to the collapse in long-term government bond yields, which has generated great bond market returns and relatively weak equity markets. It is only representative of the expected MRP if events of the past almost 80 years are expected to repeat themselves in the future. The average estimate for the market risk premium from the Fernandez et al. survey (footnote 11) was 5.8 percent, where the participants used an average long Canada bond yield of 2.9 percent. Adding these two together, survey participants expected to earn about 8.7 percent annually over a long horizon.

In 2012, TD Economics came up with forward-looking estimates, presented in **Table 20.12**. The Dex Universe Bond Index mentioned in the table is a portfolio of long-term bonds originally maintained by Scotiabank. It is riskier than the long Canada bond, since some of the portfolio's holdings are corporate bonds with default risk, so the TD Economics estimate of the MRP is at least 4 percent over the long Canada bond yield. However, remember the discussion in Chapter 8 of arithmetic mean (AM) versus geometric mean (GM) returns, where we indicated that arithmetic mean returns (or simple averages) are always higher than geometric mean (or compound) returns, and that this difference increases with the variability in the arithmetic returns. In fact, the approximate relationship is expressed in this equation:

$$AM = GM + \frac{\sigma^2}{2}$$

[12]Notice that this figure differs from the market risk premium for treasury bills, alluded to in Chapter 9. Treasury bill yields are only appropriate as a risk-free rate for very short-term, 91-day, investments. For the cost of capital, we use long-term bond yields, since they better reflect the risk-free rate for long-term investments.

**TABLE 20.12** **Long-Run Financial Projections**

| Financial Forecasts | Average Annual Percent Return |
|---|---|
| Cash: 3-month T-bills | 2 |
| Income: Dex Universe Bond Index | 3 |
| Canadian equities: S&P/TSX Composite Index | 7 |
| U.S. equities: S&P 500 Index | 7 |
| International non-U.S. equities: MSCI EAFE Index | 7 |

**Source:** Data from TD Economics, "An Economic Perspective on Canadian Long-Term Financial Returns." October 19, 2012.

With annual stock market returns having a standard deviation of about 16 percent, as half of their variance is 1.3 percent, so the long-run MRP estimated by TD Economics is consistent with an arithmetic MRP of at least 5.3 percent (i.e., 4 percent + 1.3 percent). This figure is higher than that obtained using the long-run average MRP since 1938 due to the current low yield of the long Canada bond, but it probably still underestimates the current market risk premium. Balancing survey evidence with the historic experience indicates that the market risk premium is in the range of 5 to 6 percent.

## Estimating Betas

The beta coefficient is the final piece of information needed in order to use the CAPM to estimate required returns. The beta coefficient adjusts the risk of the market to the risk of an individual security, so it is an absolute number like 0.5 for a low-risk security and 1.5 for a high-risk security. It measures the degree to which securities move in relation to market movements: the more they move together, the fewer diversification gains there are and the riskier the security. Betas are normally estimated using the prior five years' monthly return data, but it is important to realize that if nothing happened during this period, this will be reflected in the estimate. Conversely, if something special happened during this period, the beta will reflect that. In other words, beta estimates, particularly those for individual stocks, tend to be sensitive to the chosen estimation period. For this reason, we tend to go back over long periods of time and analyze what happened during the estimation period.

**Figure 20.5** gives the beta coefficients estimated for three major sub-indexes of the S&P/TSX Composite Index, using the prior five years of monthly data. The data start in 1987, when the TSX overhauled its indexes, so the first beta observation is from 1988 and runs until the end of 1992. Each month a new value is added to the 60-month estimation window and the oldest one is dropped. In this way, we can see how the betas evolve over time right up until the end of 2018. The three major sub-indexes selected are industrials (IND), since CP is a part of this sub-index; consumer staples (CONS), which is a "low risk" sector; and information technologies (IT), for reasons we will shortly discuss.

What is striking about the beta estimates is the huge "bulge" from 2000 to 2006, with the IT sub-index beta jumping to peak beta at almost 3, whereas the consumer staples sub-index beta drops and is actually negative for a period, indicating that it moved in the opposite direction to the stock market as a whole and reduced the risk of a diversified portfolio.

As discussed in Chapter 9, if we sum up all the beta coefficients, their value-weighted average has to equal 1, which is the beta of the market as a whole. What these estimates indicate is that the IT sub-index was very important during this period, and as it increased, by definition, the other betas *had* to decrease on average. In fact, the beta estimates during this period are somewhat anomalous, since they reflect the Internet bubble of the late 1990s and its subsequent burst in the 2000s. **Figure 20.6** summarizes this phenomenon, showing the stock price of Nortel Networks Corporation until the end of 2005, which is the period of this beta "bulge."

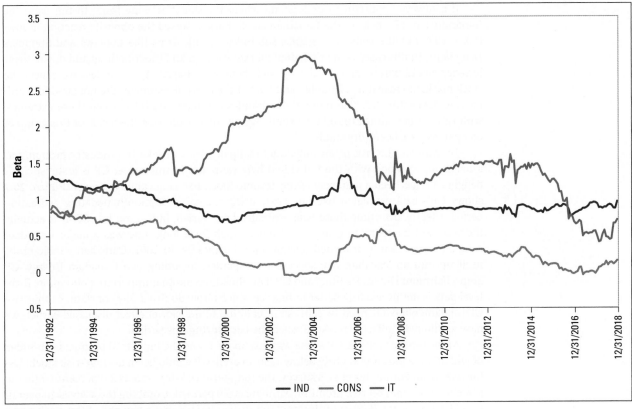

**Source:** Data from the Canadian Financial Markets Research Centre (CFMRC) Stock Return Data

**FIGURE 20.5**   **Estimated Betas for Major Sub-Indexes of the S&P/TSX Composite Index**

Nortel was originally a telecommunications manufacturer controlled by BCE Inc. However, during the Internet mania of the late 1990s, investor interest shifted to companies making the equipment for the backbone of the Internet. Two Canadian companies, Nortel and JDS Uniphase, attracted a huge amount of interest. As can be seen from Figure 20.6, Nortel's stock price jumped from the $20 to $40 range to peak at over $170 before collapsing to the penny stock range. The prices of JDS and other IT companies followed similar patterns over this time. At one point, Nortel and JDS combined to make up more than one-third of the market value of the S&P/TSX Composite Index; they pushed the value up along with them when they soared and dragged it back down again when they crashed. This is why the IT sub-index beta increased so dramatically: it was essentially dictating the major market movements and *was* the market.

**FIGURE 20.6**   **Nortel Stock Price (1987–2005)**

It is always important to understand where the statistics came from. In this case, the importance of IT stocks to the Canadian stock market caused the opposite reaction in low-risk stocks, like the consumer staples sub-index—think firms like Loblaws and Shoppers Drug Mart. In this case, as the Canadian market went on an IT tear both up and down, these low-risk stocks barely moved, causing their betas to collapse. Again, unless we expect the stock market to repeat its IT bubble and bust, these low-risk estimates are not good forward-looking beta estimates. The industrial sub-index estimates are in between these extremes, with values fluctuating around the overall average of 1. Moreover, the betas for this group of companies have been very stable.

To estimate the risk of an individual company, we can take the industry grouping as a major input, along with the individual beta estimate. In this sense, CP is a statistician's delight as it has been a mainstay of the Toronto Stock Exchange almost forever. **Figure 20.7** shows CP's beta estimated back to 1961, using the same 60-month updating estimation period. Clearly, over time these beta estimates have varied, but so too has CP. It is actually the successor company to Canadian Pacific, which for a long time was a major Canadian conglomerate—that is, it owned several other businesses. In 2001, Canadian Pacific broke itself up into no less than five successor companies, including Pan Canadian Energy, CP Ships, Fairmont Hotels, Fording, and CP. This illustrates another important point: more firm-level data is not necessarily better in finance, since rarely do firms stay constant. In this case CP fundamentally changed in 2001, so in addition to the Nortel effect discussed earlier, we have a unique CP effect that also affected the beta during this period.

At the time of writing, CP's beta was just above 1, and the industrial products sub-index of which it is a part was slightly below 1, so, overall, CP would be an average-risk stock. Using data from Fernandez et al.'s survey, the long-term risk-free rate is 2.9 percent while the low end of our market risk premium estimate is 5.0 percent. Combing these gives an overall CAPM estimate of CP's cost of (internal) equity capital using the low end of the market risk premium as

$$k_e = 2.9\% + 1 \times 5.0\% = 7.9\%$$

If instead we use the high end of our market risk premium of 6 percent, CP's cost of (internal) equity capital is

$$k_e = 2.9\% + 1 \times 6.0\% = 8.9\%$$

This range of 7.9 to 8.9 percent is based on both the low and high ends of the market risk premium. In this way, we acknowledge that estimating the cost of equity financing involves less precision than estimating the cost of debt. This range would be consistent with the recent Fernandez survey evidence that puts the Canadian market return at 8.7 percent, which with a beta of 1 would be CP's cost of equity capital as well.

If we use 7.9 to 8.9 percent as the cost of equity for CP, and 3.0 percent mentioned previously as its after-tax cost of debt, all we now need are the equity and debt weights. We already know that the book value of CP's debt was $8,696 million at year-end, and from Chapter 19 we know there were 140.5 million shares outstanding, at a year-end stock price of $242.24, so

**FIGURE 20.7** CP's Beta, 1961–2018

the equity market capitalization was $34,035 million. If we take the book value as an approximation for market value, CP's total market value would be $42,731 million, and the debt ratio $8,696/$42,731 or 20.4 percent.

The assumption that book equals market value is only correct for CP's recently issued and shorter-term debt. Much of CP's debt should be selling above book value. For example, earlier we used the yield on CP's 30-year Canadian bonds of 3.84 percent, but what we did not say was that they were selling for 37 percent over their par value, since the coupon of 6.45 percent far exceeds current interest rates. CP has in fact been refinancing as much of its debt as possible at currently much lower interest rates. Overall, CP's debt is at a premium of just over 10 percent to its book value, meaning that the market value of its debt was $9,639 and its market-valued debt ratio was 22.6 percent.[13] CP's debt ratio lies between these two extremes of 20.4 and 22.6 percent, which is a relatively small range. Given CP's depressed stock price at year-end, we will use a debt ratio of 21 percent.

What this means is that the equity weight in CP's capital structure was approximately 79 percent at year end 2018 and the debt weight only 21 percent despite its very large outstanding debt issues. Combining these capital structure weights with the higher after-tax cost estimates, we get the following estimate of the company's weighted average cost of capital.

$$\text{WACC} = 0.79 \times 8.9\% + 0.21 \times 3.0\% = 7.66\%$$

Notice two things about CP's WACC: first, the company uses relatively little debt. With an equity market value of over $31 billion, even more than $9 billion of debt is relatively "minor," so whether we use book or market values for the debt is not that important. The corollary of this is that the WACC is driven by CP's equity cost. Second, the overall cost looks quite low, at 7.3 percent, but not that low when we consider that inflation is below 2 percent and Government of Canada long-term debt is selling at yields only barely over 2.0 percent.

We conclude this section by revisiting firm ABC from examples 20.1 through 20.5 and determining its cost of internal and external common equity, as well as its WACC.

---

**EXAMPLE 20.6** | Determining the Cost of Internal Common Equity Using CAPM

Assume the beta for firm ABC from examples 20.1 through 20.5 is 1.15 and that the risk-free rate is 4.5 percent, while the MRP is 4.5 percent. Estimate the firm's cost of equity for internal funds using CAPM.

**Solution**

$$k_e = 4.50\% + 1.15 \times 4.5\% = 9.68\%$$

---

Notice that with the CAPM approach, the equity share price is not explicitly considered, which adds a complication if we want to estimate the cost of new common equity to the firm. There are two ways to deal with this issue. The first is to take the premium over the cost of internal funds that was estimated using the constant growth DDM approach, which does include the price. For this company, the premium was 0.22 percent, since the cost of internal equity was estimated at 9.2 percent, while the cost of new common equity was estimated to be 9.42 percent. However, this will not work when we are unable to use the DDM, which is exactly when we will want to use a risk-based approach such as the CAPM, as discussed previously. In this case, we can merely "scale" our estimate of $k_e$ by the following factor, which relates the share price to the net proceeds after

---

[13]In note 18 to its 13-502F1 filing, CP listed its Canadian debt as selling at a fair market value of $9,639 million at year end. At the time, CP's share price was depressed along with the whole Canadian equity market.

flotation costs: $P_0/NP$. This adjustment leads to the following estimate of the cost of new common equity ($k_{ne}$):

$$k_{ne} = k_e \times \frac{P_0}{NP}$$  [20.27]

Example 20.7 applies both approaches.

---

**EXAMPLE 20.7** | Determining the Cost of External Common Equity Using CAPM

Use the estimate of internal common equity for firm ABC, obtained in Example 20.6, to estimate the firm's cost of external equity.

**Solution**
**Approach #1**
Use the premium determined using the DDM approach, which equals:

$$k_{ne} - k_e = 9.42 - 9.2 = 0.22\%$$

Adding this premium to the estimated $k_e$ of 9.68 percent, we get

$$k_{ne} = k_e + 0.22 = 9.68 + 0.22 = 9.9\%$$

**Approach #2**
Adjust $k_e$:

$$k_{ne} = k_e \times \frac{P_0}{NP} = 9.68\left(\frac{\$25}{\$23.75}\right) = 10.19\%$$

Using this approach, we get a much larger premium of 0.29 percent.

---

**EXAMPLE 20.8** | Determining the WACC

Use the estimates for firm ABC determined in examples 20.1 through 20.7. Assume that, based on your analysis, you decide to use the common equity costs as determined using the constant growth DDM.

a. Estimate ABC's WACC and MCC, assuming it has more than sufficient internal funds to provide the required common equity financing.

b. Estimate ABC's MCC if it needs to issue new common shares to provide the required amount of financing.

**Solution**

a. Since the firm raises all its common equity internally, we can assume that its WACC equals its MCC.

$$\text{WACC} = \text{MCC} = k_e\frac{S}{V} + k_p\frac{P}{V} + k_i\frac{D}{V} = (9.2)(0.511) + (8.16)(0.255) + (3.78)(0.234) = 7.67\%$$

b. If the firm has to raise new common equity financing, its cost of common equity will rise, as will its MCC.

$$\text{MCC} = (9.42)(0.511) + (8.16)(0.255) + (3.78)(0.234) = 7.78\%$$

---

## Concept Review Questions

1. Explain how we can use the CAPM to estimate the cost of common equity.
2. Explain why beta estimates are "period specific," and outline the potential problems that may arise. Allude to problems with recent beta estimates.

| 20.7 | # The Cost of Capital and Investment |
| --- | --- |

**LEARNING OBJECTIVE 20.7**

Explain how WACC interacts with the investment decision framework introduced in chapters 13 to 17.

If investors in CP want an overall cost of capital of 7.66 percent, as calculated in the previous section, CP should not reinvest funds in its operations, which earn a rate of return less than this hurdle rate. This is because it can always earn 7.66 percent by retiring debt and buying back its own shares. This suggests that the WACC is not just a valuation tool—it is also used going forward as a tool to evaluate investments. A stylized version of this investment decision is shown in **Figure 20.8**.

We discussed how to evaluate firm investment decisions in chapters 13 and 14. Recall that the firm can look at its investments and rank them from highest to lowest profitability according to the rate of return they are expected to earn. This provides us with the downward-sloping line in Figure 20.8, indicating the firm's **investment opportunities schedule (IOS)**. This curve represents the firm's demand curve for funds. Corresponding to this is the firm's supply curve for funds, which is initially represented assuming all common equity is supplied by internal funds.

Remember from Chapter 3 that traditional cash flow is net income plus amortizations and deferred taxes (i.e., net income plus the non-cash items in the firm's income stream). In 2018, CP reported cash flow from operations of $2,712 million before making any dividend payments, refinancing its debt, or capital expenditures. This is the amount of money that CP had to invest at its WACC. It is indicated by the horizontal line in Figure 20.8. In 2018, CP actually had $1,458 million in capital expenditures, which is shown on the graph. CP's situation is depicted by the spot where CP's IOS intersects its WACC for the optimal investment.[14] In 2018 CP's cash flow from investing was significantly below the amount of internal cash flow it generated. The difference of $1,254 million is referred to as CP's free cash flow. It is "free" in the sense that it is available to refinance debt, pay dividends, or buy back shares. CP actually paid out $348 million in dividends and bought back $1,103 million in shares as well as refinancing some of its debt. How it distributes cash to shareholders as dividends and share buy-backs will be discussed in Chapter 22.

**investment opportunities schedule (IOS)**   the ranking of a firm's investments from highest to lowest profitability according to the rate of return they are expected to earn

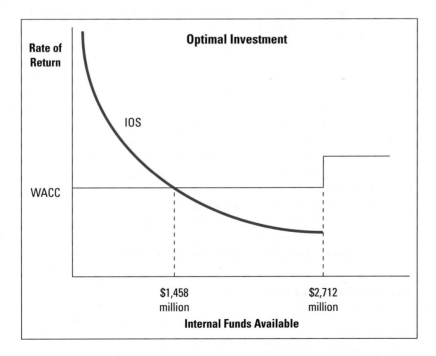

**FIGURE 20.8**   CP's Investment Opportunities Schedule (2018)

[14]The WACC estimates are not provided by CP; only the free cash flow and investment numbers are provided.

**TABLE 20.13** Survey Results on Estimating the Discount Rate

| Discount Rate | Percentage of Answers Saying "Often" or "Always" |
|---|---|
| 1. The company's WACC | 63.6 |
| 2. A rate based on management experience | 43.5 |
| 3. The cost of specific funds of the project | 38.2 |
| 4. A risk-matched discount rate for the project | 36.6 |
| 5. A different discount rate for each cash flow | 14.1 |
| 6. A divisional discount rate | 11.3 |

If CP's IOS shifted to the right (very far to the right!), so that its internal demand for funds outstripped its supply of funds, then it would have to raise additional capital. In this case, its MCC would increase above its WACC. This is indicated by the vertical jump in its supply of funds schedule. As discussed, in this scenario, the MCC would be above the WACC, simply due to the cost of raising additional funds.

So how does this discussion of what firms should do accord with what they actually do? In the spring of 2006, Kent Baker, Shantanu Dutta, and Samir Saadi surveyed Canadian firms to determine the answer to that question.[15] In particular, they asked firms what discount rate they used when evaluating a new project. The answers are in **Table 20.13**.

Overwhelmingly, the most popular discount rate was the WACC, followed by experience—but then, you would hope that all companies take into account the experience of their senior executives. What is more important are the final four answers. In deriving our WACC, we explicitly looked at what investors required for investing in the firm's shares and debt, so the WACC is an overall cost of capital for the firm. However, what if the firm itself is composed of many different lines of business? TransCanada Corporation, for example, owns the Mainline natural gas pipeline that runs from western Canada east to central Canada; this has traditionally been the core of the company. However, it also has an interest in nuclear power generation in Ontario, an oil pipeline that it hopes will take heavy Canadian crude down to the Gulf of Mexico, and U.S. and Canadian power operations. TransCanada Corporation's WACC reflects the average risk of all these businesses and is probably not reflective of any particular one of them.

To solve the problem of evaluating a company with multiple lines of business, the WACC should be adjusted to reflect a risk-based WACC appropriate for each individual business. This is what the last four answers essentially do. A divisional discount rate (answer 6) simply indicates that TransCanada should adjust its overall WACC up or down, depending on whether it is applied to its nuclear power operations or the Mainline. This divisional discount rate should reflect the different risks involved in the different divisions (answer 5) and the different financing of each (answer 3). From this perspective, answers 3, 5, and 6 are simply more sophisticated applications of the WACC to multi-divisional firms.

Answer 4 is the most sophisticated, since in any project there are, in fact, different cash flows. We discussed this in Chapter 14, where we described it as valuation by components. For example, as soon as a project is undertaken, the investment gives rise to future capital cost allowances and tax shields, which are largely independent of the other project cash flows. Technically, these different components of the future cash flow stream should be discounted at different discount rates. Table 20.13 indicates that some firms actually use this more sophisticated approach to capital budgeting, which affects their choice of the discount rate. In the future, this more sophisticated approach may generate more interest on the part of Canadian companies.

## Concept Review Questions

1. Explain the importance of using the WACC as a hurdle rate for making investment decisions.
2. Why does the MCC suddenly jump up and become expensive?

---

[15]Baker, H. Kent, Dutta, Shantanu, and Saadi, Samir, "Corporate Financial Practices in Canada: Where Do We Stand?" *Multinational Finance Journal* 15, no. 3 (2011): pp. 157–92.

# Review

## Summary

In this chapter, we synthesize information on the types of securities a firm may issue to finance its operations. In Chapter 19, we pointed out that these different types of securities differ in their degree of "equity-ness," so they all have different required rates of return. However, the firm as a whole has to earn enough money to pay the investors their required rate of return. Taking into account these different securities and their associated required rates of return and market values, we can determine how much the firm has to earn to meet these commitments. This is the basis for the weighted average cost of capital (WACC), which is the overall cost of the capital invested in the firm.

The WACC is a market-value-weighted average of the after-tax costs of all these securities. If the firm earns its WACC, then its present market values are supported, but if it is expected to earn less (more) than its WACC, its market value will fall (increase). In most cases, this change in market value drops through to the common shareholders, who are the residual claimants; as a result, they hold the riskiest of all the securities issued by the firm. In this sense, risk increases as we drop down the income statement.

We then show that the most difficult and the most important estimate in the WACC is determining the cost of common equity capital. In estimating this, we discuss the discounted cash flow (DCF)

model, which "reverse engineers" the valuation equation to use the current market price in order to estimate the discount rate used by the investor. In doing so, we emphasize that since there are many different types of DCF models, there are also many different ways to estimate the cost of common equity. While the constant growth DDM is by far the most popular model, it also leads to serious errors for high-growth companies. To illustrate which model to use in different situations, we discuss a simple characterization of types of firms based on the present value of existing and growth opportunities.

Alternatively, rather than using DCF models, the capital asset pricing model (CAPM) can be used to minimize estimation errors. We know that the market risk premium is currently between 5 and 6 percent, so the discount rate on the stock market as a whole is currently in the 7.9- to 8.9-percent range using a 2.9-percent long-term risk-free rate. In adjusting for the risk of individual securities, we show how beta estimates are critically dependent on the time period over which they are estimated. We show that if we don't make appropriate adjustments for what has happened in the stock market over the past 10 years, recent beta estimates are seriously misleading. As with the DCF model, use of the CAPM requires judgement, common sense, and an understanding of recent financial history.

## Summary of Learning Objectives

### 20.1 Explain how the three major problem areas in finance—valuation, cost of capital, and determining cash flows—are related.

Valuation of any securities is the sum of the discounted future cash flow. To do valuation, estimated cash flow and cost of capital (discount rate) are necessary inputs.

### 20.2 Calculate the weighted average cost of capital (WACC) and explain its significance.

The weighted average cost of capital (WACC) formula is given in Equation 20.8, in which WACC is the weighted average cost of equity and the after-tax cost of debt. It is significant because it is used in the valuation of projects.

### 20.3 Estimate the cost of capital and its non-equity components.

Cost of capital is the weighted average cost of equity and the after-tax cost of debt. Its non-equity component is the after-tax cost of debt.

### 20.4 Explain how operating leverage and financial leverage affect a firm's risk.

Operating leverage is generated by fixed costs. Companies with a greater proportion of fixed costs have a higher break-even sales level than firms with a lower proportion of fixed costs. As a result, they are riskier (because there is a higher variability in operating income). Financial leverage is generated by borrowing. Firms with debt have a higher variability of earnings per share but also have higher average return on equity than equivalent unlevered firms.

### 20.5 Use the discounted cash flow model to estimate the cost of equity.

Equations 20.16 and 20.17 show how to apply the discounted cash flow model to estimate the equity cost. The method is easy to use. However, it depends on assumptions, which may lead to misuse. For example, it assumes that dividends grow at a constant rate.

### 20.6 Estimate the cost of equity using risk-based models and describe the advantages and limitations of these models.

Equation 20.26 shows that cost of equity equals the risk-free rate plus market risk premium multiplied by beta. It is derived from the capital asset pricing model and is easy to understand. However, empirically, it is difficult to estimate market risk premium and beta, and even the proxy of the risk-free rate is highly debatable.

**20.7  Explain how WACC interacts with the investment decision framework introduced in chapters 13 to 17.**

Chapters 13 and 14 are about investment decisions and focus on the method and estimation of cash flow. Cash flow and the cost of capital are the two most important factors in capital expenditure. Thus, Chapter 20 completes the discussion on capital investment. Chapters 15 and 16 cover two specific examples of investment: mergers and acquisitions, and leasing, respectively. Chapter 17 covers how to raise cash flows for investment purposes and discusses securities law. They are important parts of capital investment as well.

## Key Terms

asset turnover ratio, p. 20-6
beta coefficient, p. 20-28
capital asset pricing model (CAPM), p. 20-28
capital structure, p. 20-3
cash cow, p. 20-25
cost of capital, p. 20-8
debt-to-equity ratio, p. 20-3
dog, p. 20-25
earnings yield, p. 20-5
financial structure, p. 20-2
flotation costs, p. 20-11

hurdle rate, p. 20-23
investment opportunities schedule (IOS), p. 20-35
issuing costs, p. 20-11
marginal cost of capital (MCC), p. 20-11
market risk premium (MRP), p. 20-28
market-to-book (M/B) ratio, p. 20-4
multiple-stage growth DDM, p. 20-24
operating leverage, p. 20-16
present value of existing opportunities (PVEO), p. 20-24

present value of growth opportunities (PVGO), p. 20-24
return on assets (ROA), p. 20-6
return on equity (ROE), p. 20-6
return on invested capital (ROIC), p. 20-6
risk-based models, p. 20-28
risk-free rate of return ($R_F$), p. 20-28
star, p. 20-25
total enterprise value ($V$), p. 20-7
turnaround, p. 20-25
weighted average cost of capital (WACC), p. 20-8

## Equations

| Equation | Description | Formula | Page |
|----------|-------------|---------|------|
| **[20.1]** | Perpetuity Valuation Formula | $S = \dfrac{X}{k_e}$ | p. 20-4 |
| **[20.2]** | Earnings Yield | $k_e = \dfrac{X}{S}$ | p. 20-4 |
| **[20.3]** | Required Earnings | $X = k_e \times S$ | p. 20-5 |
| **[20.4]** | Price per Share | $P = \dfrac{EPS}{k_e} = \dfrac{ROE \times BVPS}{k_e}$ | p. 20-6 |
| **[20.5]** | Price to Book for Perpetuity | $\dfrac{P}{BVPS} = \dfrac{ROE}{k_e}$ | p. 20-7 |
| **[20.6]** | Total Enterprise Value (TEV) | $V = \dfrac{ROI \times IC}{k_a}$ | p. 20-8 |
| **[20.7]** | TEV Discount Rate | $k_a = \dfrac{ROI \times IC}{V}$ | p. 20-8 |
| **[20.8]** | Weighted Average Cost of Capital (WACC) | $k_a = \dfrac{ROI \times IC}{V} = \dfrac{k_e S + k_d(1-T)D}{V} = k_e\dfrac{S}{V} + k_d(1-T)\dfrac{D}{V}$ | p. 20-8 |
| **[20.9]** | WACC with Preferred Shares | $WACC = k_e\dfrac{S}{V} + k_p\dfrac{P}{V} + k_i\dfrac{D}{V}$ | p. 20-9 |
| **[20.10]** | Equity Market Value | $S = P_0 \times n$ | p. 20-9 |
| **[20.11]** | Perpetuity Preferred Share Value | $P_p = \dfrac{D_p}{k_p}$ | p. 20-9 |
| **[20.12]** | Bond Valuation Formula | $B = I \times \left[\dfrac{1 - \dfrac{1}{(1+k_b)^n}}{k_b}\right] + F \times \dfrac{1}{(1+k_b)^n}$ | p. 20-9 |
| **[20.13]** | Net Bond Proceeds | $NP = I \times (1-T) \times \left[\dfrac{1 - \dfrac{1}{(1+k_i)^n}}{k_i}\right] + F \times \dfrac{1}{(1+k_i)^n}$ | p. 20-12 |

*(continued)*

| Equation | Description | Formula | Page |
|---|---|---|---|
| [20.14] | Cost of Perpetuity Preferreds | $k_p = \dfrac{D_p}{NP}$ | p. 20-13 |
| [20.15] | Constant Growth Model (CGM) | $P_0 = \dfrac{D_1}{k_e - g}$ | p. 20-19 |
| [20.16] | Equity Cost from the CGM | $k_e = \dfrac{D_1}{P_0} + g$ | p. 20-19 |
| [20.17] | Cost of New Equity (after Issue Costs) | $k_{ne} = \dfrac{D_1}{NP} + g$ | p. 20-20 |
| [20.18] | Sustainable Growth Rate | $g = b \times ROE$ | p. 20-21 |
| [20.19] | CGM with Sustainable Growth | $P_0 = \dfrac{D_1}{k_e - b \times ROE}$ | p. 20-21 |
| [20.20] | CGM with the Payout Ratio | $P_0 = \dfrac{X_1(1 - b)}{k_e - b \times ROE}$ | p. 20-21 |
| [20.21] | CGM with Equity Cost | $k_e = \dfrac{D_1}{P_0} + g = \dfrac{X_1(1 - b)}{P_0} + b \times ROE$ | p. 20-22 |
| [20.22] | Two ROE Model | $P_0 = \dfrac{ROE_1 \times BVPS}{k_e} + \dfrac{Inv}{(1 + k_e)}\left[\dfrac{(ROE_2 - k_e)}{k_e}\right]$ | p. 20-24 |
| [20.23] | Fed Model | $\dfrac{V_{actual}}{V_{Fed}} = \dfrac{V_{actual}}{Exp(EPS)/(k_{TBond} - 1\%)}$ | p. 20-26 |
| [20.24] | Fed's CGM | $V_{Fed} = \dfrac{Exp(EPS)}{k_{TBond} - 1\%}$ | p. 20-26 |
| [20.25] | S&P Earnings Yield | $\dfrac{X}{P_{S\&P500}} = k_{TBond} - 1\%$ | p. 20-27 |
| [20.26] | CAPM | $k_e = R_F + MRP \times \beta_e$ | p. 20-28 |
| [20.27] | Cost of New Equity | $k_{ne} = k_e \times \dfrac{P_0}{NP}$ | p. 20-34 |

# Questions and Practice Problems

## Multiple Choice Questions

1. **(LO 20.1)** Which of the following statements is *false*?

   **a.** Financing total assets is called the financial structure decision.

   **b.** Capital structure is how invested capital is financed.

   **c.** The financial structure is $34,000 if the total assets are $34,000.

   **d.** The invested capital is $50,000 if the total assets are $50,000.

2. **(LO 20.1)** If an all-equity firm is expected to earn and pay out a $2.25 dividend forever (in perpetuity), what is the value of the firm's stock given a cost of equity of 10 percent?

   **a.** $25.00          **c.** $12.50

   **b.** $25.50          **d.** $22.50

3. **(LO 20.1)** What is the earnings yield given a $55,000 earnings figure, a $20 market price per share, and 10,000 shares outstanding?

   **a.** 0.625          **c.** 0.4

   **b.** 0.375          **d.** 0.275

4. **(LO 20.1)** What does a firm have to earn given the following? MV of debt = $50,000; MV of equity = $115,000; $k_e$ = 10 percent; $k_d$ = 5 percent

   **a.** $17,000          **c.** $14,000

   **b.** $3,000           **d.** $13,000

5. **(LO 20.1)** Which of the following statements is *true*?

   **a.** When ROE < $k_e$, management is adding value to the firm.

   **b.** When ROE > $k_e$, management is decreasing the firm's value.

   **c.** When ROE > $k_e$, the market price goes above the book value of the investment.

   **d.** When ROE = $k_e$, the market price goes above the book value of the investment.

6. **(LO 20.2)** Which of the following is *not* an input in the calculation of WACC?

   **a.** Book values of equity and debt

   **b.** Market values of equity and debt

   **c.** Cost of equity

   **d.** Corporate tax rate

**7. (LO 20.5)** To increase the stock price of a firm that is assumed to grow at a constant rate g,

    **a.** increase the cost of equity.

    **b.** increase the constant growth rate.

    **c.** decrease the dividend payout ratio.

    **d.** increase the retention rate.

**8. (LO 20.5)** Northern Star Ltd. just paid a $3.60 dividend, which is expected to grow at a constant rate. Recent EPS is $6 and net income is $450,000. Total equity is $1.8 million and the cost of equity is 12 percent. What is the share market price?

    **a.** $165

    **b.** $150

    **c.** $198

    **d.** $300

**9. (LO 20.5)** Which of the following firms is a growth firm?

    **a.** $ROE > k_e$

    **b.** $ROE < k_e$

    **c.** $ROE = k_e$

    **d.** Net income $= k_e$

**10. (LO 20.5)** Which of the following statements is *false*?

    **a.** Star firms have both high PVGO and PVEO.

    **b.** Google and Yahoo are examples of turnarounds.

    **c.** Cash cows could be called growth stocks as well.

    **d.** Utility firms are examples of cash cows.

## Practice Problems

### Intermediate

*Use the information here to answer practice problems 11 to 13.*

### Balance Sheet

| | | | |
|---|---|---|---|
| Cash | $160,000 | Accounts payable | 240,000 |
| Marketable securities | 220,000 | Wages payable | 90,000 |
| Accounts receivable | 60,000 | Short-term debt | 210,000 |
| Inventory | 900,000 | Long-term debt | 780,000 |
| | | **Total liabilities** | **$1,320,000** |
| Fixed assets | 1,200,000 | Common shares | 1,040,000 |
| | | Retained earnings | 180,000 |
| **Total assets** | **$2,540,000** | **Total equity and liabilities** | **$2,540,000** |

### Income Statement

| | |
|---|---|
| Sales | $2,500,000 |
| CGS | $800,000 |
| Amortization | $125,000 |
| Interest | $66,400 |
| EBT | $1,508,600 |
| Taxes | $452,580 |
| NI | $1,056,020 |
| Shares outstanding | 500,000 |

**11. (LO 20.6)** What is the cost of equity ($k_e$) given $R_F = 3$ percent, beta ($\beta$) = 1.4, expected market return ($ER_M$) = 10 percent?

**12. (LO 20.5)** What is the market price and market-to-book ratio, assuming the firm's stock is a perpetuity and all earnings are paid out as cash dividends (i.e., the retention rate is zero)?

**13. (LO 20.1)** Calculate invested capital and before-tax ROI.

**14. (LO 20.3)** Provide two reasons why the cost of a security to a company differs from its required return in capital markets.

**15. (LO 20.2)** A firm has preferred shares outstanding with a current price of $90 (par value of $100) and an annual dividend of $8 per share. What is the implied cost of preferred shares?

**16. (LO 20.2)** A firm's market values of equity and debt are $12,500,000 and $7,500,000, respectively. The before-tax cost of debt is 5 percent; $R_F = 3.5$ percent; beta ($\beta$) = 1.5; the market risk premium = 8 percent; and the tax rate = 30 percent. Calculate the firm's WACC (weighted average cost of capital).

**17. (LO 20.2)** A firm's market values of equity and debt are $750,000 and $250,000, respectively. The before-tax cost of debt is 6 percent; $R_F = 3$ percent; beta ($\beta$) = 1.08; the market risk premium = 8 percent; and the tax rate = 25 percent. Calculate the firm's WACC (weighted average cost of capital).

**18. (LO 20.5)** What is $V_{Fed}$ if the expected earnings per share on the S&P 500 is $23.50 and the long-term U.S. bond rate is 4.75 percent?

**19. (LO 20.5)** Rocky Mountain Depot just announced its EPS of $5. Retention rate ($b$) = 0.4. The earnings are expected to grow at 10 percent for one year and then at 5 percent indefinitely. Given that $k_e = 16$ percent, what is the market price?

**20. (LO 20.5)** Calculate the cost of issuing new equity for a firm, assuming issue costs are 6 percent of the share price after taxes; market price per share = $50; current dividend = $3.75; and the constant growth rate in dividends is 4 percent.

**21. (LO 20.5)** A firm has common shares outstanding with a discount rate of 10.5 percent. The current market price is $25. The company just paid a dividend of $1.20 per share. What is the per-share implied growth rate?

**22. (LO 20.5)** A firm's earnings and dividends are expected to grow at a constant rate indefinitely, and it is expected to pay a dividend of $9 per share next year. Expected EPS and BVPS next year are $12 and $50, respectively. The cost of equity is 13.5 percent and there are 15,000 shares outstanding. Calculate the firm's value, assuming that the retention rate stays the same and the market value of debt is $600,000.

**23. (LO 20.5)** Calculate the cost of equity using the constant growth DDM given the following: current dividend = $3; payout ratio = 0.5 (assume it is not changing); ROE = 12 percent; and the current market price of the stock = $24. Is the current management adding to or reducing the shareholders' value?

**24. (LO 20.5)** Calculate PVGO, PVEO, and $P_0$ given the following information: $ROE_1 = 15$ percent; $ROE_2 = 20$ percent; further investment (Inv) = $200; BVPS = $25; and $k_e = 12$ percent. Is this firm a star? If not, what is it according to Boston Consulting Group?

**25. (LO 20.7)** A firm is going to finance a new project 100 percent with debt, through a new bond issue. Since the firm is using only debt to finance the project, the NPV of the project should be calculated using the cost of debt as the discount rate. Is this statement true, false, or uncertain? Explain.

**26. (LO 20.7)** Montreal Brokers, a small brokerage firm, and PEI Tech, a software development company, are both separately considering developing and marketing a new software package. Neither party is aware that the other is considering this project, and it is not at any point going to become a joint venture. These new software packages will organize mutual fund data into a new type of database and then run a series of complicated algorithms on that new database. The beta of the brokerage firm is 0.9 and the beta of the software firm is 2.3. The risk-free rate is 2 percent and the market risk premium is 10 percent. The NPV of the project, using an 11-percent discount rate, is +$1 million. However, using a 19-percent discount rate, the project has a negative $500,000 NPV. Should either or both parties go ahead with the project?

27. **(LO 20.7)** Suppose a firm uses a constant WACC to calculate the NPV of all of its capital budgeting projects, rather than adjusting for the risk of the individual projects. What errors will the firm make in its capital budgeting decisions?

## Challenging

28. **(LO 20.5, 20.6, 20.7)** A firm has the following capital structure based on market values: equity 60 percent and debt 40 percent.

The current yield on government T-bills is 3 percent, the expected return on the market portfolio is 10 percent, and the firm's beta is approximated at 2.15. The firm's common shares are trading at $30, and the current dividend level of $4 per share is expected to grow at an annual rate of 5 percent. The firm can issue debt at a 3-percent premium over the current risk-free rate. The firm's tax rate is 30 percent, and the firm is considering a project to be funded out of internally generated funds that will not alter the firm's overall risk. This project requires an initial investment of $15 million and promises to generate net annual after-tax cash flows of $2.25 million perpetually. Should this project be undertaken?

29. **(LO 20.5, 20.6, 20.7)** A firm has the following balance sheet items:

| | |
|---|---|
| Common shares: 400,000 shares at $8 each | $3,200,000 |
| Retained earnings | 1,200,000 |
| Debt: 8 percent coupon, 15 years to maturity | 2,000,000 |
| Preferred shares: 6 percent dividend | 1,500,000 |

The before-tax interest cost on new 15-year debt would be 7 percent, and each $1,000 bond would net the firm $972 after issuing costs. Common shares could be sold to net the firm $10 per share, a 12-percent discount from the current market price. Current shareholders expect a 16-percent return on their investment. Preferred shares could be sold at par to provide a yield of 5.5 percent, with after-tax issuing and underwriting expenses amounting to 5 percent of par value. The firm's tax rate is 30 percent, and internally generated funds are insufficient to finance anticipated new capital projects. Calculate the firm's marginal cost of capital.

30. **(LO 20.5, 20.6, 20.7)** AOK Ventures Inc. ("AOKVI") currently has the following on its balance sheet:

| Item | Book Value ($) |
|---|---|
| Debt – 15-year, 8 percent annual coupon, 10 years remaining | 4,000,000 |
| Common shares – 2,000,000 issued at $2 per share | 4,000,000 |
| Retained earnings | 500,000 |
| Total | 8,500,000 |

AOKVI has a 34 percent tax rate.

Present market conditions are as follows:

- Debt – similar risk, 10-year bonds could be issued at par with a yield to maturity at 6.5 percent and flotation costs of 2 percent.
- Common shares – currently trading at $3.14 per share

a. Calculate the market value weights of each source of capital.

b. Assume AOKVI is considering undertaking a capital project for which they have sufficient internal capital, i.e., only debt would have to be issued. What discount rate would AOKVI use to evaluate this project, assuming it had similar risk to the risk of the firm itself. Assume a cost of equity capital of 9.75%.

c. Assume internal capital is equal to the $500,000 specified as "Retained earnings" above. What is the maximum-sized project they could consider before having to raise common equity?

31. **(LO 20.5, 20.6, 20.7)** A company can issue new 20-year bonds at par that pay 6-percent annual coupons. The net proceeds to the firm (after taxes) will be 96 percent of par value. They estimate that new preferred shares providing a $2 annual dividend could be issued to investors at $25 per share to "net" the firm $23.50 per share issued (after taxes). The company has a beta of 1.18, and present market conditions are such that the risk-free rate is 3 percent, while the expected return on the market index is 10 percent. The firm's common shares trade for $30, and they estimate the net proceeds from a new common share issue would be $27 per share (after tax considerations). The firm's tax rate is 30 percent.

a. Determine the firm's cost of long-term debt, preferred shares, and common equity financing (internal and external sources) under the conditions given.

b. What is the firm's weighted average cost of capital, assuming that it has a "target" capital structure consisting of 30-percent debt, 20-percent preferred equity, and 50-percent common equity? Assume that it has $3 million in internal funds available for reinvestment and requires $5 million in total financing.

c. Suppose everything remains as given, except that the company decides it needs $8 million in total financing. Calculate the firm's marginal cost of capital.

32. **(LO 20.5, 20.6, 20.7)**

a. Kitchener Consumer Products plans to issue 25-year bonds with a 7-percent coupon rate, with coupons paid semiannually and a par value of $1,000. After-tax flotation costs (issuing and underwriting costs) amount to 3.5 percent of par value. The firm's tax rate is 30 percent. Determine the firm's effective annual after-tax cost of debt.

b. Kitchener Consumer Products plans to issue $50 par preferred shares (P/S) with annual dividends of $4 (i.e., an 8-percent dividend yield). It estimates flotation costs to be $2.50 per share after taxes. Find the firm's cost of P/S.

c. Kitchener Consumer Products wishes to make a new issue of common shares (C/S). The current market price ($P_0$) is $32, $D_1 = $2$ (expected dividend at the end of this year), while $g = 4$ percent per year indefinitely. Flotation costs and discounts amount to $3 per share after taxes. Find the firm's cost of issuing new common shares

i. using the dividend valuation approach.

ii. using CAPM, given that the risk-free rate is 4 percent, the expected return on the market is 12 percent, and the beta for Kitchener Consumer Products is 0.95.

d. Suppose everything remains as in part c; find the cost of internally generated common equity

i. using the dividend model approach.

ii. using the CAPM approach.

**33. (LO 20.7)** A firm wishes to raise funds in the following proportions: 20-percent debt, 20-percent preferred shares, and 60-percent CE (common equity). Assume the cost of internally generated funds is 15 percent. Annual after-tax cost of debt is 5.86 percent. Cost of preferred equity is 6.12 percent. It believes all of the CE component can be raised using internally generated funds.

a. Find the WACC.

b. Now suppose the firm wants to raise $10 million for investment purposes, and it has only $4 million of internally

generated funds available. Determine the "break point" of the CE component. Break point is the maximum investment in which all targeted equity can be financed internally.

c. Determine the marginal cost of capital (MCC) if the firm must raise funds beyond the break point. Assume the cost of new common equity issues is 20 percent.

# Cases

## Case 20.1  Clearview Security Technologies

Based in Winnipeg, Manitoba, Clearview Security Technologies Inc. (Clearview) was founded to provide security systems, facilities controls, and related services. Clearview established a solid reputation for quality and the business grew, thanks to strong relationships with large long-term customers in Canada and the United States. Clearview has experienced little competitive pressure in its core market and the company's offerings are standardized, enabled by significant technological and financial barriers to entry.

The Research and Innovation Group (RIG) is the development side of the company. Where Clearview's primary lines are standardized, the RIG is all over the map. Clearview uses this smaller division to provide contract software and consulting to a wide range of business types.

The RIG is considering a new contract that will strain resources for not only the RIG, but the entire company. The project involves new technology, a new customer, and a new geographic area. The director of operations has warned you that it will be substantially more risky than anything Clearview does in its core business. With an upfront cost of C$8.5 million, managers want to develop an understanding of expected financing costs. The director of finance explained that understanding cost of capital will be a key part of maintaining and improving Clearview's competitive edge. RIG managers have noticed competing bids for the contract and it is expected that margins will be pushed down.

You have been asked to calculate the company's weighted average cost of capital (WACC), based on the following information. Over the past five years the firm's stock price and earnings have both grown at approximately 5 percent a year. Clearview recently paid a dividend of $1.25 a share on earnings per share of $2.50 and the common shares trade at $45 per share with 250,000 shares outstanding. There are no preferred shares. You check the Bank of Canada's web page and the current 91-day T-bill yield is 1.25 percent and the long Canada bond yield is 2.5 percent. On your desk is a series of reports by major investment banks that indicate a long-run return on the Canadian equity market of 8 percent to 9 percent a year, and a note that Clearview's stock beta has been about 0.90. Clearview also has 25-year bonds outstanding with a $1,000 face value, 6.5 percent semi-annual coupon, and 20 years to maturity. The bonds currently trade at 115. The initial bond offering raised $15,500,000 and sold at par. The firm's marginal tax rate is 30 percent.

1. The cost of equity and debt

a. Calculate Clearview's cost of equity using the constant growth model approach and the CAPM approach. Take the arithmetic average of the two results.

b. Determine Clearview's after-tax cost of debt. Solving for the cost of debt is best done with a financial calculator, although

trial and error will also yield the correct result. The bond valuation formula is required in this approach, substituting values for $k_b$ until the bond value is determined. A third method for determining the cost of debt is an approximation formula:

$k_b$ approx. = ((annual coupon + (face − price))/years remaining)/((face + price)/2). The trial and error approach can be completed much faster if the approximation method is used first, to narrow the trial and error range.

2. The weight of equity and debt

a. Calculate the weights of equity and debt in Clearview's capital structure.

b. Determine Clearview's WACC.

3. The company will use its current capital structure to set target weights for debt and equity, with flotation costs of 2 percent for long-term debt and 7.5 percent for equity. How much capital must Clearview raise in order to cover the project cost and all flotation charges?

4. Determining the NPV

a. The RIG project is expected to generate revenues of $1,400,000 per year before tax, in each of the next 10 years. The PV (CCA tax shield) method for depreciation is appropriate using the half-year rule. The applicable CCA rate is 30%, salvage value will be zero, and net working capital considerations are minimal. Determine the NPV of the project using the WACC calculated earlier as the discount rate.

b. Rework the analysis in part a using a discount rate of 10%. What is the revised NPV of the project?

**The RIG Project Decision**

The director of finance asked you to discount the expected future cash flows for the RIG project using Clearview's WACC and to determine the NPV of the project. The director remains confident that using Clearview's WACC is appropriate because the WACC considers many key aspects of the business's finances.

5. a. How should you respond?

b. What would be the justification for using a higher discount rate, as introduced in question 4 b?

c. Describe a situation where using a lower discount rate than a firm's current WACC might be appropriate.

d. In considering the project's value, should the CCA tax shields be valued using the same discount rate as the firm's after-tax net revenues?

# Capital Structure Decisions

In Chapter 20, we discussed how a firm can estimate the cost of each source of funds and average them to estimate its weighted average cost of capital (WACC). In this chapter, we discuss how the firm may attempt to minimize its WACC through its financing choices. Just as a firm can increase its value by lowering its production costs, it can also increase its value by lowering its capital costs as measured by its WACC. This is much more difficult than lowering production costs and involves sophisticated concepts that are still debated after almost 60 years. As we explore these concepts, we will learn how to assess the limits placed on a firm's ability to issue debt, as creditors and bond-rating agencies calculate the risk attached to corporate debt issues, and will learn how this qualitative assessment conflicts with the celebrated Modigliani and Miller (M&M) proposition that the capital structure decision does not affect firm value. We will look at the tax advantages to issuing debt up to the point where the associated risks of financial distress and bankruptcy outweigh these gains. The result is the static trade-off model, which indicates the general determinants of a firm's target or optimal debt ratio. Firms may depart from this target by using a pecking order, issuing equity only when they are forced to do so or when the markets are particularly receptive.

## 21.1 | Financial Leverage

**LEARNING OBJECTIVE 21.1**

Explain how business and financial risk affect a firm's ROE and EPS, and identify the financial break-even points.

# Risk and Leverage

**invested capital (IC)** a firm's capital structure, consisting of shareholders' equity and short- and long-term debt

**return on invested capital (ROI)** the return on all the capital provided by investors; EBIT minus taxes, divided by invested capital

**return on equity (ROE)** the return earned by equity holders on their investment in the company; net income divided by shareholders' equity

**financial leverage** the effect of using debt as a source of capital

We begin by returning to the example we used in Chapter 20, where the firm had a capital structure of $1,700, composed of $1,000 of shareholders' equity and $700 of short- and long-term debt. This capital structure represented the firm's **invested capital (IC)**. We used this example to illustrate a discussion of the cost of capital, but we also worked out the required income statement, which is shown in **Table 21.1**.

Based on these data, we indicated that the firm's **return on invested capital (ROI)** equalled its EBIT-minus-taxes figure of $331.50, where we ignore the interest charge, divided by the invested capital of $1,700, or 19.5 percent. Its **return on equity (ROE)** equalled its net income of $300 divided by shareholders' equity of $1,000, or 30 percent. The manner in which this ROE varies with changes in ROI is due to the firm's **financial leverage**.

To understand how financial leverage works, consider the equation for ROE:

$$\text{ROE} = \frac{(\text{EBIT} - R_D B)(1 - T)}{\text{SE}} \qquad [21.1]$$

This simply says we work down the income statement from EBIT. First we subtract the interest expense, which is the interest cost of the firm's debt ($R_D$) times the book value of the firm's debt. As before, we use $R$ to indicate actual costs, and now, since we are looking at book values, we use $B$ to represent the book value of the firm's debt (bonds or $B$).[1] We then pay taxes, so $(1 - T)$[2] flows through to the common shareholders, where we represent the book value of equity using *SE* for shareholders' equity.

We now use the definition of ROI from Chapter 20, which is shown in Equation 21.2.

$$\text{ROI} = \frac{\text{EBIT}(1 - T)}{\text{SE} + B} \qquad [21.2]$$

If we re-express Equation 21.2 in terms of EBIT$(1 - T)$ and substitute into Equation 21.1, we get Equation 21.3, the financial leverage equation.

$$\text{ROE} = \text{ROI} + (\text{ROI} - R_D(1 - T))\frac{B}{\text{SE}} \qquad [21.3]$$

The importance of the financial leverage equation is that ROI measures the return the firm earns from its operations and does not explicitly consider how the firm is financed,

**TABLE 21.1** Example Income Statement

| | |
|---|---|
| Sales | $1,000 |
| Variable costs | 300 |
| Fixed costs | 258 |
| EBIT | 442 |
| Interest | 42 |
| Taxable income | 400 |
| Tax (25%) | 100 |
| Net income | 300 |

[1]Notice the difference from Chapter 20, where we used $D$ to denote the market value of the firm's debt and $S$ for the market value of its equity.

[2]In the chapter, "$T$" represents the corporate tax rate since we are dealing with only one tax rate. In Appendix 21A where we also have personal tax rates, we will subscript it "$c$" to avoid confusion.

because it uses EBIT minus taxes in the numerator and the *total* invested capital in the denominator. This is why we think of the firm's ROI as a reflection of its **business risk**, which was discussed in Chapter 20, while the ROE reflects business risk as well as **financial risk**. The financial leverage equation shows how these two risk factors in combination affect the ROE—that is, they show how much of the risk is due to the firm's operations and how much is due to the way the firm is financed.

**business risk** the variability of a firm's operating income (EBIT) caused by its operations

**financial risk** the variability of a firm's net income caused by the use of financial leverage

Consider again our example, in which we found that ROI = 19.5 percent. In this case, the interest cost was 6 percent, which is 4.5 percent after tax (i.e., $6 \times (1 - 0.25)$), and the book debt-equity (D/E) ratio was \$700/\$1,000 or 0.7. Substituting these numbers into Equation 21.3, we get:

$$ROE = 19.5 + (19.5 - 4.5) \times 0.7 = 30\%$$

This is exactly what we calculated directly from the firm's net income and the shareholders' equity (i.e., \$300/\$1,000). If we get the same answer, you might ask why we went to the trouble of calculating the ROE through this roundabout method. The answer is that doing so allows us to examine the impact of how the firm is financed.

Remember that each dollar invested in the firm earns the same ROI—that is, for investment purposes, a dollar is a dollar. There is no such thing as an equity dollar or a debt dollar. It is the corporate financing or capital structure decision that allocates the ROI to different claimants and causes differences in the returns to equity and debt holders. In our example, the debt holders want a fixed 6-percent return; because this cost is tax deductible, it costs the firm's shareholders only 4.5 percent after taxes. So each dollar borrowed from the debt holders earns the firm an ROI of 19.5 percent at a cost of 4.5 percent, and the spread of 15 percent drops through to the common shareholders. The only question is how many dollars of debt are carried by each dollar of equity, and this is answered by the debt-equity ratio of 0.7.

What is happening is that each dollar of equity earns 19.5 percent directly, but in addition, each dollar of equity also supports \$0.70 of debt, which earns the spread of 15 percent, which also goes to the common shareholders. So, indirectly, the shareholders earn another 10.5 percent, which is the spread of 15 percent times 0.7. The ROE of 30 percent is the direct return from investing at the ROI of 19.5 percent, plus the indirect return of 10.5 percent by "trading on the equity" and borrowing money at an after-tax cost of 4.5 percent while investing it at 19.5 percent. Previously, we used the term "OPM" to refer to the option pricing model. However, historically, OPM referred to this process of using "other people's money," or financial leverage.

In our example, financial leverage is extremely favourable for the firm because it adds another 10.5 percent to the common shareholders' ROE. However, remember that the cost of the debt is a fixed contractual commitment of 6 percent before tax, whereas the ROI reflects the business risk of the firm and can vary. If we rearrange Equation 21.3 to group the terms involving the ROI, we get:

$$ROE = ROI\left(1 + \frac{B}{SE}\right) - R_D(1 - T)\frac{B}{SE} \qquad [21.4]$$

We express the financial leverage equation in this way to show that the second term in Equation 21.4 is fixed, whereas the first term depends on the firm's uncertain ROI. This means we can graph the ROE against the firm's ROI as a straight line. This is what we do in **Figure 21.1**, with ROE plotted along the *y*-axis, and ROI plotted along the *x*-axis.

Figure 21.1 maps out the ROE that results from different levels of ROI for two financing strategies. The first strategy, labelled 0%, is to simply finance using 100-percent equity and not use any debt. In this case, the financial leverage equation indicates that ROI = ROE. The second strategy is the one employed by our example firm, where the firm's debt-equity ratio is 70 percent, which is labelled 70%. We will refer to the 70-percent strategy in our further discussion.

## The Rules of Financial Leverage

To understand Figure 21.1, you must work through several important points. Since the graph is a straight line, there are two break-even points. The first is where each financial strategy cuts the vertical axis. For the 100-percent equity financing strategy, which we label "0%" for a

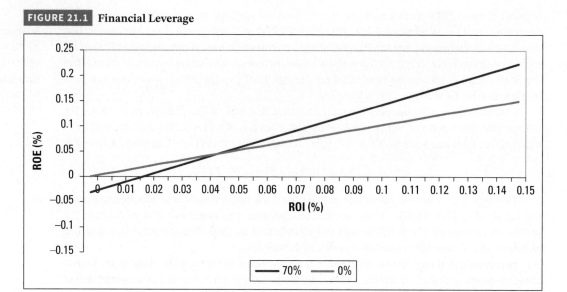

**FIGURE 21.1** Financial Leverage

zero debt-equity ratio, this point occurs where the ROI and ROE are zero. This is because if the firm's ROI is zero, so too is its ROE. However, in the case of the 70-percent strategy, which we label "70%," when the ROI is zero, the ROE is −3.15 percent, which is where the zero ROI cuts the vertical axis. This 3.15 percent is the product of the 0.7 debt-equity ratio multiplied by the 4.5-percent after-tax debt cost. The reason for this is that even if the ROI is zero, the firm still has to pay the debt holders their 6-percent interest rate, so with a 70-percent debt-equity ratio, each dollar of equity loses 4.2 percent. Assuming that the firm can use this loss to recapture previous income taxes paid, the after-tax cost is 3.15 percent.[3] If the firm cannot go back and reclaim previous taxes paid, the loss will be 4.2 percent. These break-even points are often called the **financial break-even points**.

**financial break-even points**
points at which a firm's ROE is zero

As the firm's ROI increases, we can see, using Equation 21.4, that the ROE for the firm without any debt increases in an identical manner. However, for the firm using the 70-percent strategy, the ROE increases by 1.7 times the increase in the ROI. This is the slope of the line in Figure 21.1. The 70-percent firm breaks even when its ROI is 1.85 percent. This is the point on the horizontal axis where the ROE is equal to zero, and it can be determined using Equation 21.4 by first calculating the second term, which is the after-tax debt cost times the debt-equity ratio (3.15 percent), and then dividing by one plus the debt-equity ratio of 1.7. Due to the steeper slope of the 70-percent line, it catches up with the 0-percent line at the second break-even point.

**indifference point** point at which two financing strategies produce the same ROE

The second break-even point is where the two financing strategies give the same ROE. This point is also often called the **indifference point**, because at this point the ROE is the same regardless of how the firm is financed. We can calculate this point by setting the two ROEs to be the same using Equation 21.3. For the 100-percent equity strategy, this point is where the ROI equals the after-tax debt cost of 4.5 percent, since at this point the ROE must equal 4.5 percent regardless of how the firm finances its operations.[4]

This result shows that using OPM tends to increase the ROE because the firm only has to earn more than the after-tax cost of debt. This should be easy for any firm! Remember from our discussion of the cost of capital that the firm should make investments only where it expects to earn more than its WACC, which is the weighted average of this after-tax debt cost and the cost of equity. Given that equity is almost always the most expensive form of capital, it follows that the WACC *is always* higher than the after-tax cost of debt. So the first "rule" of financial leverage is: *for value-maximizing firms, the use of debt increases the expected ROE, so shareholders expect to be better off by using debt financing, rather than equity financing.*

[3]Remember from our discussion of corporate income tax in Chapter 3 that the firm can carry back losses from the current year to recapture previous income taxes paid. If it has not paid taxes in the past few years, it can carry this loss forward and hope to offset future profits.

[4]Generally, the indifference point is close to the after-tax cost of debt. It will differ depending on the firm's historical financing rates (i.e., the costs of debt).

**TABLE 21.2**   **Varying ROI Values**

| | 70% Debt Equity | 0% Debt Equity |
|---|---|---|
| **ROI (%)** | **ROE (%)** | |
| 10 | 13.85 | 10 |
| 30 | 47.85 | 30 |
| Range | 34 | 20 |

In this situation, the firm expects to be to the right of the indifference point; the farther to the right the firm expects to be, the greater the value of using debt financing.

This is an important result, but it can also be misleading because it implies that the firm should always finance with debt, as the WACC is always higher than the after-tax cost of debt. We must consider what we are ignoring, since we have a result that says we must always make the same decision, when, in practice, firms make multiple decisions. This leads us to consider the second principle of finance, which is the **risk value of money**.

Remember that the behaviour of the ROI reflects the business risk of the firm. The expected ROI can be represented by a point estimate, such as 19.5 percent in our example. However, we have to take into account the business risk of the firm, which is the variability in the ROI. Suppose, for example, the forecast ROI was expected to be between 10 and 30 percent. Would this affect the judgement that debt financing increases the ROE? We can examine this by looking at the ROE for the two strategies in **Table 21.2** at the 10-percent and 30-percent ROI levels.

At an ROI of 10 percent or 30 percent, the 100-percent equity strategy produces ROEs equal to the ROIs, generating a range of 20 percent. In contrast, the 70-percent strategy leads to ROE values of 13.85 percent and 47.85 percent, for a range of 34 percent. This greater range for the 70-percent strategy is simply the ROE range multiplied by one plus the debt-equity ratio of 1.7. This demonstrates the fact that financing with more debt and increasing the debt-equity ratio to 0.7 increases the variability of the ROE—that is, it increases shareholders' risk.

Would this increase in risk affect the firm's shareholders? In this example, the answer is no, since the minimum ROI of 10 percent exceeds the indifference point of 4.5 percent. As a result, at all forecast levels of ROI, the firm's ROE is higher with the use of debt financing. However, the important point is that the variability of the ROE increases as the firm finances with more debt. This is because there are fixed financial charges—that is, the fixed interest costs—that the firm has to pay, which are independent of the firm's ROI. If we increase the range of ROI possibilities from −10 to 40 percent, we get the ROE values shown in **Table 21.3**.

With this wider range in ROI values, the ROE for the 70-percent strategy is −20.15 percent on the low end, which is much lower than the ROE for the strategy with no debt. As before, the range of ROE values is much higher for the leveraged position.

This leads to the second rule of financial leverage: *financing with debt increases the variability of the firm's ROE, which usually increases the risk to the common shareholders.*

As the previous examples illustrate, the range of ROE values always increases with debt financing, but, depending on the numbers, this does not necessarily mean that risk increases.

**risk value of money**   the principle that future cash flows (money) involving different amounts of risk have different present values

**TABLE 21.3**   **Varying ROI Values**

| | 70% Debt Equity | 0% Debt Equity |
|---|---|---|
| **ROI (%)** | **ROE (%)** | |
| −10 | −20.15 | −10 |
| 40 | 64.85 | 40 |
| Range | 85 | 50 |

Sometimes, as in the first example, the firm is better off at all ROI levels with debt financing regardless of the greater variability in the ROE. In this case, it simply says that the firm is not using enough debt, as it could raise more debt and unambiguously increase the ROE to the common shareholders. This means that the increased variability from using debt does not always mean increased risk; it all depends on how risky the firm's ROI is.[5] There are lots of very low-risk utility-type investments where the use of debt has very little impact on shareholder risk.

Since the range of ROE values increases with debt financing, the firm has to find the cash to cover the fixed interest payments. In the earlier worst-case scenario, where the firm has an ROI of −10 percent, it still has to cover the 4.5-percent after-tax and 6-percent before-tax interest payments. If the firm's underlying health remains sound, it will be able to borrow from the bank (as long as the bank continues to lend to the firm!) or use up some of its cash reserves to make these payments. However, sometimes a series of poor operating results can cause serious financial problems for a highly indebted firm. This situation can compound, as the firm's owners might change their operating procedures if there is a significant risk of financial distress or bankruptcy. We will discuss such a situation in more detail later in the chapter, but at this point we simply note the third rule of financial leverage: ***financing with debt increases the likelihood of the firm running into financial distress and possibly even bankruptcy.*** Figure 21.2 illustrates this proposition using actual data from the use of debt by individuals.

Figure 21.2 graphs the annual returns from investing in the S&P/TSX Composite Index using two different financing strategies. The first (denoted TSX) is simply the annual return generated from investing in the S&P/TSX Composite Index. This would be a "long-only" equity-investing strategy. The second (denoted Leveraged) assumes that investors borrow 50 percent on margin for a 100-percent debt-to-equity ratio[6]—that is, they put up $1 for every $1 borrowed. For this leverage strategy, we assume the investor pays the treasury bill rate plus 2.5 percent per year on their margin debt, which approximates the cost of borrowing using the equity securities as collateral. This is commonly referred to as margin investing. For convenience, we will ignore taxes. The graphs are generated simply by plugging the actual TSX returns and the actual treasury bill yields each year since 1936 into Equation 21.4.

**FIGURE 21.2**  **Investing Using Leverage**

[5]In more advanced finance courses, you will learn that this is a case of stochastic dominance.
[6]Margin loans are debt provided by a broker to finance the purchase of securities. The amount of margin debt a bank will provide varies with the price of the security and its risk; 50 percent is a reasonable margin only for low-risk securities like those included in the TSX 60. In Canada the prime is usually 2 percent over the treasury bill rate and margin debt usually attracts a 0.50-percent premium to prime.

You should notice two things about the graph. The first is the increased variability in the return from the leverage strategy, which is predicted by the second rule of financial leverage. As before, we can see this by simply looking at the range of the outcomes, which always increases with leverage. The second is that on some occasions the return from the highly leveraged strategy drops to disastrous levels, with losses sometimes reaching 60 to 80 percent. During the 2008 financial crisis, the leverage strategy meant a very bad TSX loss of 33 percent was turned into a leveraged loss of 71.74 percent! In fact, the data used for the graph are annual data, and during October 2008 the TSX lost much more than 33 percent, so the leveraged losses would have been even greater! Long before these horrendous losses would have occurred, the investor would have received a margin call from their bank, insisting they put up more capital. If they didn't, their investments would have been sold with no ability to recover if the market rebounded, as it did in 2009.

The graph in Figure 21.2 is real, since it reflects the actual returns on the Toronto Stock Exchange and the approximate cost of borrowing on margin. Is margin investing a good idea? On average, the return on the TSX over this 83-year period was 10.75 percent, and the average treasury bill yield plus a 2.5-percent spread was 6.93 percent. This means that by using the 100-percent margin strategy, you would have earned an average spread of 3.83 percent or an average return of 14.59 percent. This sounds pretty good, but statisticians like to joke that you can drown in a river with an average depth of one metre.[7] Stock market returns are the same: on average you make money using financial leverage, but you can also get financially killed in the process. This is because margin debt is a demand loan, and the bank can cancel its loan and sell you out during a financial crisis when the stock market is collapsing. Finance in the News 21.1 indicates that margin debt is currently at an all-time record high as Canadians take advantage of very low interest rates to buy houses and invest in the stock market as we have just described.

---

## 21.1 Finance in the News    Canadians Find New Way to Binge on Debt as Borrowing to Buy Stocks Hit Record Levels

Dennis Colpitts could pay down the mortgage on his house in western Canada early if he wanted. He's investing in the stock market instead—and in some cases borrowing to do so.

With a mortgage rate of 2.35%, Colpitts said it makes more sense to put his money into stocks or other investments that hold the potential for higher gains. He primarily invests in exchange-traded funds, including through a margin account, which allows him to borrow money from his broker to buy securities.

"I could liquidate all my stocks and ETFs and put them into my mortgage, but I don't," said Colpitts, 39, a technology consultant who lives with his wife and two children in Calgary. "I keep them with the hope of getting my 6 or 7% return."

Canadians like Colpitts are borrowing to invest at the highest level since at least 2000, racking up more than $19 billion on margin in January. That's helped fuel a 37% surge in mutual-fund assets in the past two years and a 41% rise in ETF assets. The figures illustrate Canada's rock-bottom interest rates aren't only fuelling house prices and consumer debt to record highs, they're enticing people to leverage in financial markets.

"There is some strategic borrowing going on by Canadians," Doug Porter, chief economist at Bank of Montreal, said in a phone interview from Toronto. "Some folks have relatively low-rate mortgages and are looking at the solid gains in equity markets,

generous dividends and making a conscious decision to not pay down their debt when they could and instead using the funds to invest. Some are even borrowing to invest."

### Resurgent Trading

Canadians borrowed $19.2 billion against their brokerage accounts in January, near a peak of $19.4 billion in September, according to figures from the Investment Industry Regulatory Organization of Canada. Investors surpassed the previous 2008 peak in 2013 and have been steadily increasing margin borrowing since.

"Over the last two years you've seen a resurgence in stock trading and investment and an increase in margin loans extended by dealers to clients to buy equity," Ian Russell, president of the Investment Industry Association of Canada, said in a phone interview.

Mutual-fund assets under management reached $1.22 trillion in the two years to February, up from $891.8 billion in February 2013, according to data from the Investment Funds Institute of Canada. ETF assets rose to $81.4 billion over the same period, figures from the Canadian ETF Association show.

**Source:** Lam, Eric, "Canadians Find New Way to Binge on Debt as Borrowing to Buy Stocks Hit Record Levels." *Bloomberg News*, April 1, 2015. Copyright 2015. Reproduced with permission of Bloomberg News.

---

[7]This is because rivers don't have the same depth throughout their run or at all times during the year.

Figure 21.2 shows that the effects of financial leverage are not confined to corporations. In fact, they apply to any economic entity, whether a firm, an individual, or a government.[8] Financial leverage tends to increase returns, but it also increases the variability of returns and financial distress. Consequently, the amount of debt a firm or an individual can carry very much depends on the underlying business risk of the asset being financed. As we saw in Figure 21.2, financing an investment in the stock market with a 100-percent debt-equity ratio or 50-percent debt strategy is very risky. In contrast, Canadians are happy to finance their house purchase with 80-percent debt. Indeed, with high-ratio mortgages, the amount of debt financing is frequently as high as 95 percent. In this case, the asset being financed is perceived to be lower risk than the stock market, so people are comfortable financing it with more debt. However, even here there have been times when 80-percent mortgage financing has been risky.[9]

## Indifference Analysis

Before leaving our discussion of financial leverage, we will examine one more set of financial leverage charts, which relate to the firm's earnings per share (EPS). We noted in Chapter 20 that the example firm has 1,000 shares outstanding, so the EPS in relation to the firm's EBIT can be defined using Equation 21.5.

$$EPS = \frac{(EBIT - R_DB)(1 - T)}{\#}$$ [21.5]

This is identical to the ROE-ROI relationship, except that instead of the book value of equity in the denominator, we now have the number of shares (#). As a result, we can rearrange the equation and show how EPS varies with the EBIT.

$$EPS = \frac{-R_DB(1 - T)}{\#} + \frac{EBIT(1 - T)}{\#}$$ [21.6]

Note that this is also a simple linear relationship; we plot the impact of EBIT (horizontal line) on EPS (vertical line) in **Figure 21.3**. If the firm has no debt, the first term is zero and the EPS is simply the EBIT minus taxes divided by the number of shares, which is the EPS for a firm financed 100 percent by equity, denoted as EPS (0%). If the firm finances with debt, it incurs the after-tax fixed-interest expense per share and then has fewer shares outstanding. The result is that the EPS-EBIT line pivots and gets steeper as more debt is used—denoted as EPS (70%). In this case, the same increase in the EBIT causes a bigger impact on the EPS. This is illustrated in Figure 21.3, where the firm is assumed to have 1,280 shares outstanding in the no-debt situation.

Note that, as in the ROE-ROI chart, the 0-percent debt-equity line has a lower intercept (because there are no after-tax fixed-interest payments to make) and is not as steep as the other line. In the EPS-EBIT chart, the 70-percent debt-equity line is steeper since there are fewer shares outstanding, whereas in the ROE-ROI chart it was steeper because of the higher debt-equity ratio. Either way, the result is the same: as the firm finances with more debt, its EPS and ROE are more sensitive to its operating results—that is, to its EBIT and ROI. All firms look at the impact of financing on their ROE and EPS, and the charts they create for this analysis are often called **profit planning charts**.

Like the ROE indifference point, discussed in connection with Figure 21.1, the **EPS indifference point** is the point in Figure 21.3 where the two lines intersect. We can solve for this indifference point in terms of EBIT by setting the EPS, as expressed in Equation 21.5,

**profit planning charts** charts showing ROE-ROI and EPS-EBIT that allow firms to analyze the impact of financing on their profits

**EPS indifference point** the EBIT level at which two financing alternatives generate the same EPS

---

[8]Ask Greece about the use of financial leverage. We hope that by the time you read this chapter, Greece's financial woes will have been solved.

[9]Below 80-percent financing, a mortgage is a prime mortgage; above 80 percent it is sub-prime. When U.S. house prices dropped in some areas by over 40 percent from 2007 to 2009, even prime mortgages became risky, which was the basic cause of the U.S. financial crisis in 2007–9.

**FIGURE 21.3**  EPS-EBIT Charts

equal for two alternative financing plans under consideration. Then we merely solve for the EBIT level at which the two financing alternatives generate the same EPS, which we denote as EBIT*. This will give the firm some useful direction when it comes to choosing between financing alternatives, because firms generally want to maximize their bottom line, as measured by EPS, and they usually have an estimate of their expected EBIT. Example 21.1 illustrates this process.

---

**EXAMPLE 21.1**  |  EPS Indifference Analysis

Calculate the EPS indifference point, EBIT*, for the firm discussed previously, assuming it maintains its present 70-percent D/E ratio, and then assuming it uses all equity financing. Its pre-tax cost of debt is 6 percent under the present structure, and there are 1,000 common shares outstanding. Further, assume that under the all-equity plan, the firm has 1,280 shares outstanding.[10] Which plan is preferable at the current level of sales and EBIT?

**Solution**

$$\text{EPS (70\%)} = \frac{(\text{EBIT} - 0.06 \times 700)(1 - 0.25)}{1{,}000} = \frac{0.75 \times \text{EBIT} - 31.5}{1{,}000}$$

$$\text{EPS (0\%)} = \frac{0.75 \times \text{EBIT}}{1{,}280}$$

Setting the two EPS equations together and solving for EBIT* will give us the indifference EBIT, as shown here:

$$750\ \text{EBIT*} = 960\ \text{EBIT*} - 40{,}320$$
$$210\ \text{EBIT*} = 40{,}320$$
$$\text{EBIT*} = \$192$$

Notice that this is the point where the two lines intersect in Figure 21.3. Beyond this EBIT level, the 70-percent debt-equity option is preferred because it produces a higher EPS; below this EBIT level, the all-equity option is preferred. Therefore, at the current EBIT level of $442, which is well above $192, the more leveraged financing option (i.e., the 70-percent debt-equity option) gives a significantly higher EPS and generally would be preferred.

---

Conducting EPS-EBIT indifference analysis is a useful beginning point for firms trying to evaluate potential financing plans. We will discuss some of the additional issues, which are considerable, in the following sections.

[10]We "guesstimate" this figure by assuming the firm can retire the $700 worth of debt by issuing 280 shares at $2.50 (i.e., $700/$2.50 = 280), using the market share price for this firm that was provided in Chapter 20.

## Concept Review Questions

1. Define business risk and financial risk.
2. How does financial leverage affect the relationship between ROI and ROE?
3. What are the three rules of leverage?
4. Describe how we determine the ROE and EPS indifference points for a firm based on various financing alternatives, and explain why this analysis provides the firm with useful information.

## 21.2 | Determining Capital Structure

**LEARNING OBJECTIVE 21.2**

Identify the factors that influence capital structure.

In 1990, the Conference Board surveyed 119 U.S. companies to determine how they set their capital structures. The results of the survey are presented in **Table 21.4**.

We will present some more recent survey results later in the chapter, but the Conference Board survey is useful because it reflects a professional focus. For example, it is clear that firms will consult with their advisors (#2) and look at other firms in their industry (#5) to check on what is reasonable. However, neither of these are primary methods of deciding on capital structure because they do not indicate how their advisors or other firms determine their capital structure. The three primary determinants are impact on profits (#4), risk (#3), and analysis of cash flows (#1). The profit planning charts discussed in the previous section are the basic way to assess the impact on profits. By varying EBIT and ROI, they can also be used to assess the impact of risk. What is left to discuss is cash flow.

However, let's first consider some standard, commonly used financial ratios. We can think of these as stock or flow ratios. *Stock* ratios are measures like the debt-equity and debt ratios. They measure the stock of outstanding debt relative to the total capital structure of the firm or the amount of equity. In contrast, *flow* variables measure the flow of income over a period, such as EBIT, and the flow of payments the firm is required to make, such as interest. Stock ratios are clearly useful: bond-rating agencies and others use them to do a quick check on the firm's financing, and they are also often used to limit the amount of debt the firm can raise through its trust indenture, as we discussed in Chapter 18. However, we must consider just how useful these ratios really are.

In Chapter 18, we discussed some of the features of different types of debt. For example, we noted that bankers' acceptances had a maturity of 30 days, whereas long-term bond

| **TABLE 21.4** | Determinants of Capital Structure |
|---|---|
| 1. Analysis of cash flows | 23.0% |
| 2. Consultations | 18.3% |
| 3. Risk considerations | 16.5% |
| 4. Impact on profits | 14.0% |
| 5. Industry comparisons | 12.0% |
| 6. Other | 3.4% |

**Source:** Conference Board, 1990

issues typically had a life of 20 or 30 years. It obviously matters a great deal to a firm if its debt has a 30-day versus a 30-year maturity. For one thing, if the firm has to "roll over" its debt—that is, renew it or borrow it back every 30 days—it must be confident that it has the cash to pay off this debt if the lenders refuse to renew it. Similarly, if the debt has sinking fund payments, where the firm is contractually obliged to pay off a certain amount of debt each year, this increases the firm's commitments to the debt holders and requires that it have the cash ready to fulfill this commitment. In both cases, it is not the stock of debt outstanding that matters so much as the maturity of the debt. That is why this information must be provided in the notes to the firm's financial statements. Further, it suggests that the stock ratios are not completely adequate, since they ignore some of the cash flow commitments attached to debt.[11]

In the same way, consider the great emphasis we placed in Chapter 18 on the interest coverage ratio, defined as EBIT divided by interest expense. This is a flow variable, since it is the ratio of the flow of EBIT to the flow of interest payments. Remember that there is often a clause in the trust indenture that states the firm cannot issue any more debt unless it has an interest coverage ratio of 2.0 or more. However, this also does not include all of the firm's commitments. The most basic limitation is that interest payments are made from cash and not from accounting earnings. Further, similar to the problems with the stock ratios, the interest coverage ratio does not show the impact of any sinking fund payments or other commitments, such as dividends to the preferred shareholders.

We can get around some of these problems by modifying the interest coverage ratio to include these other commitments. One way is to estimate the **fixed burden coverage ratio**, which is defined in Equation 21.7.

$$\text{Fixed burden coverage} = \frac{\text{EBITDA}}{\text{I} + (\text{Pref. Div.} + \text{SF})/(1 - \text{T})} \qquad [21.7]$$

**fixed burden coverage ratio** an expanded interest coverage ratio that looks at a broader measure of both income and the expenditures associated with debt; EBITDA divided by a firm's fixed financing payment requirements

In the numerator, instead of EBIT, we have EBITDA, which is EBIT before subtracting the non-cash deductions for depreciation and amortization. As such, it is a "better" estimate of the firm's cash flow.[12] In the denominator, along with interest, we have added the firm's commitment to make sinking fund payments (*SF*) on its debt and its preferred share dividends (*Pref. Div.*). Since both dividends and sinking fund payments are paid out of after-tax income, we "gross them up" by dividing by one minus the corporate tax rate (1 − *T*) to determine their pre-tax equivalent, which is then comparable to the interest payments. We ignore the common share dividends since these can be cut more easily than the dividends to the preferred shareholders.

Another way to modify the flow and stock variables is to combine them. One key ratio that does this is the **cash flow-to-debt ratio (CFTD)**, which directly measures the cash flow available over a period to cover the firm's stock of outstanding debt. This ratio may be calculated using Equation 21.8.

**cash flow-to-debt ratio (CFTD)** a direct measure of the cash flow available over a period to cover a firm's stock of outstanding debt

$$\text{CFTD} = \frac{\text{EBITDA}}{\text{Debt}} \qquad [21.8]$$

Again, as with many ratios, cash flow is measured either as net income plus non-cash charges like depreciation, or simply as EBITDA.

These last two ratios are very important. In Chapter 19, we discussed CP's financing. The company had to meet certain covenant provisions for its medium-term notes and its revolving line of credit, and the two most important ones were a fixed burden coverage ratio, similar to Equation 21.7, and a debt-to-cash flow ratio, which is the inverse of Equation 21.8. In both cases, the actual ratios and the method of calculating them were spelled out in some detail so CP could not make accounting changes to alter their values.

---

[11]This also indicates why margin debt is so risky, as the bank can always demand its money back on an even shorter term than is provided for bankers' acceptances.

[12]Some analysts simply add depreciation to net income.

As the financial ratios depart more and more from standard definitions, they become more analyst specific, but the general point is simply that there are serious drawbacks to using either stock or flow variables based on the firm's financial statements to measure how much debt a firm can handle. The best procedure is for the firm to generate its own forecast of expected cash flows over a short- to medium-term horizon, and then calculate internally what level of fixed commitments the firm can handle without exposing it to serious harm. This "scenario-based" approach to determining capital structure was pioneered by Gordon Donaldson.[13] However, the key question is whether lenders will lend to the firm based on its internal scenario-based assessment of how much debt it can carry. This requires that sensitive information be divulged to lenders and that the lenders believe the data. Consequently, there is still heavy reliance on standard ratios.

## Financial Ratios and Credit Ratings

Moody's is the third of the important rating firms in Canada, alongside DBRS and S&P, and it periodically provides data on the most commonly used credit ratios and how they correlate to Moody's credit ratings. (See the data provided in Table 21.5.) Moody's defines these ratios in its own way, but they broadly conform to the ratios described previously. The simple average of investment-grade (IG) companies—firms with at least a BBB bond rating—has higher coverage, less debt (leverage), a larger cash flow-to-debt ratio, less liquidity (cash plus marketable securities as a percentage of total assets), higher profit margins, and a higher return on assets (ROA) than the simple average of firms with non-investment-grade (non-IG) bond ratings. IG firms also tend to have more stable sales and are growing faster than non-IG firms, with greater capital expenditures to depreciation (asset growth).

All of these ratios make sense. Firms with better credit ratings tend to be larger and more profitable, generate more cash, and have more stable sales, meaning lower business risk. They also tend to have better investment opportunities so are reinvesting at a higher rate than firms with inferior credit ratings. Moody's looks at other ratios in addition to these and also adjusts these ratios across industries to reflect differences in business risk. As a result, the final credit rating is based on both quantitative and qualitative assessments.

**TABLE 21.5**    **Moody's Average Credit Ratios**

|  | IG | Non-IG |
|---|---|---|
| Coverage | 11.4 | 1.7 |
| Leverage (%) | 36.1 | 76 |
| Cash flow-to-debt (%) | 63 | 11.8 |
| Profit margin (%) | 16.9 | 7.1 |
| Return on assets (%) | 15.1 | 6.4 |
| Sales stability | 15.1 | 17.2 |
| Asset growth | 1.3 | 1 |
| Altman Z score* | 2.17 | 1.62 |

*From Moody's Investor Services, "The Distribution of Common Financial Ratios by Rating and Industry for North American Non-Financial Corporations," December 2004.

**Source**: Calculated using *Moody's Financial Metrics: Key Ratios by Rating and Industry for North American Non-Financial Corporations: 2008* (January 2009).

[13]Donaldson, Gordon, "New Framework for Corporate Debt Policy." *Harvard Business Review* (September/October 1978), pp. 149–64.

The final value in Moody's set of ratios is the Altman Z score. This is a weighted average of several key ratios that Professor Ed Altman found were useful for predicting a firm's probability of bankruptcy.[14] Equation 21.9 is his prediction equation.

$$Z = 1.2X_1 + 1.4X_2 + 3.3X_3 + 0.6X_4 + 0.999X_5$$ [21.9]

where

$X_1$ = working capital divided by total assets
$X_2$ = retained earnings divided by total assets
$X_3$ = EBIT divided by total assets
$X_4$ = market value of total equity divided by non-equity book liabilities
$X_5$ = sales divided by total assets

Note that most of the variables are scaled by total assets to standardize them, so we will refer to them by the numerator. However, they all have simple intuitive meanings.

If a firm has high amounts of working capital, it generally has more receivables and inventory as well, which are usually more liquid than fixed assets. The existence of retained earnings generally means that the firm has earned money in the past, and therefore it proxies for age and past profitability, among other things. EBIT is a measure of operating profitability. The market value of equity divided by non-equity book liabilities is another way to calculate a market-valued debt ratio. Finally, sales divided by assets is the turnover ratio, so it measures how productively the firm is using its assets.

The Altman Z score was the first of many such measures that attempt to summarize a large number of financial ratios into a simple score. In the case of the Z score, the larger the better. Altman estimated it using a sample of 66 U.S. manufacturing firms, equally divided between firms that did and did not go bankrupt. His bankrupt firms had an average Z score of about 1.5. What is interesting is that even though Altman estimated this function more than 50 years ago, Moody's (and many other debt analysis reports) still reported it. Further, it is still working in the sense that the IG firms have higher Z scores than the non-IG firms.

In terms of capital structure, we know that firms pay a lot of attention to the impact that issuing debt will have on their future profit levels and risk, so assessing their underlying business risk is very important. As firms issue more debt, most of their key ratios covered by Moody's deteriorate. As a result, their credit rating weakens, they pay higher interest charges, and they have to submit to more trust indenture provisions to lessen the risk involved. Consequently, it is vital that we understand how issuing debt affects the firm's credit rating.

However, a key question not raised by the results of the Conference Board survey is: does issuing debt increase or decrease the firm's market value? So far, our discussion has simply addressed the question of whether a firm can issue debt or not, and on what terms. It involves important factors like taxes and financial flexibility, but it does not answer the question of whether the firm should issue debt. This question is addressed in one of the most famous papers in finance, which is discussed in the next section. Surprisingly, the authors initially answered the question by saying that capital structure is irrelevant!

## Concept Review Questions

1. What are the main determinants of capital structure?
2. Explain how ratios may be used to assess a company's ability to assume more debt.
3. What is Altman's Z score and what does it measure?

---

[14]Altman, E., "Financial Ratios, Discriminant Analysis and the Prediction of Corporate Bankruptcy." *Journal of Finance* 23, no. 4 (September 1968), pp. 589–609.

**21.3** # The Modigliani and Miller (M&M) Irrelevance Theorem

> ### LEARNING OBJECTIVE 21.3
> Explain how Modigliani and Miller (M&M) "proved" their irrelevance conclusion that the use of debt does not change the value of the firm.

## M&M and Firm Value

**Franco Modigliani** and **Merton Miller (M&M)**   economists who devised a proposition stating that, under some simplifying assumptions, the capital structure decision does not affect firm value

In this section, we will discuss a theorem—a proposition based on a series of assumptions about how financial markets should work. It is, in fact, a very powerful theorem for which (in part) the authors, **Franco Modigliani** and **Merton Miller** (also known as M&M), won the Nobel Prize in economics.[15] Unfortunately, the "M&M results" are only as good as their assumptions, and most of them have been shown to reflect the "real" world rather poorly. However, their research pointed the way for many of the significant developments in corporate finance theory and practice over the past 60 years, as later researchers examined how M&M's assumptions affected their result.

The following are M&M's key assumptions:

- There exist two firms in the same "risk class" with different levels of debt.
- The earnings of both firms are perpetuities.
- Markets are perfect in the sense that there are no transactions costs or asymmetric information problems.
- There are no taxes.
- There is no risk of costly bankruptcy or associated financial distress.

Of these five assumptions, two are modelling assumptions and three are assumptions about the real world. In 1958, relatively little was known about the pricing of risk. M&M finessed this by assuming two firms with the same business risk. We could get M&M's result now by using the capital asset pricing model (CAPM) or some other risk-adjustment model to adjust for risk, so this is a simple modelling assumption. Similarly, we have already seen that assuming perpetuities makes valuation easy, since we just divide the expected cash flows by the required rate of return. Again, we can get the M&M results if we assume some growth in the underlying earnings, but this introduces needless complexity. The critical assumptions are the last three: markets are perfect, with no transaction costs and perfect information availability; there are no taxes; and there is no costly bankruptcy or financial distress risk. Later in the chapter we will discuss what it means to relax these assumptions, but right now we will discuss the basic M&M model.

M&M proved their proposition by means of an "arbitrage argument." As we discussed, with respect to the option pricing model, arbitrage arguments are the strongest in finance since they rely on two assumptions: there is no such thing as "free money," and investors prefer more money to less. Let's think about what this means to two firms with the same business risk but different levels of debt. We assume the first firm, which we will refer to as the unlevered firm (U), has no debt; the second firm, the levered firm (L), does have debt because it uses financial leverage. If we buy some arbitrary percentage ($\alpha$) of the unlevered firm, we simply get this percentage of the firm's earnings, which is paid out as a dividend. Since there is no interest paid by an unlevered firm, and since M&M assumed there were no taxes, the firm's EBIT is also its net income. Therefore, our share of the firm's earnings and dividends equals $\alpha$EBIT, which we have assumed will be paid out as a perpetuity.

[15]Modigliani, Franco, and Miller, Merton, "The Cost of Capital, Corporation Finance and the Theory of Investment." *American Economic Review* 48, no. 3 (June 1958), pp. 261–97.

**TABLE 21.6**   **M&M Arbitrage Table I**

| Portfolios (Actions) | Cost | Payoff |
|---|---|---|
| Portfolio A: Buy $\alpha$ of unlevered firm | $\alpha V_U$ | $\alpha$EBIT |
| Portfolio B: Buy $\alpha$ of levered firm's equity | $\alpha S_L$ | $\alpha$(EBIT − $k_D$D) |
| Buy $\alpha$ of levered firm's debt | $\alpha$D | $\alpha k_D$D |
| Total portfolio B | $\alpha(S_L + D)$ | $\alpha$EBIT |

If we buy the same share of the equity of the levered firm, we have to subtract the interest payments, so we receive a smaller amount as a dividend. In this case, our share is $\alpha$EBIT − $k_D$D, where the interest cost is the market value of the debt multiplied by the required return on debt. The values for the "payoff" from buying the equity of either firm are identical except for the interest charges, since we assumed that the two firms were in the same risk class. In other words, it would be like buying shares in two very similar steel companies or two drug companies.

M&M then asked the following question: if the levered firm sold at a discount to the unlevered firm (i.e., if investors did not like the effects of financial leverage), what could an investor do? To answer this question, they drew up the M&M arbitrage table depicted in **Table 21.6**.

The first row, Portfolio A, is the cost of, and payoff from, investing in the unlevered firm. The next two rows are the cost of, and payoff from, buying the same proportion of the equity and debt of the levered firm, where the levered firm's equity is subscripted "$L$" for levered ($\alpha S_L$). The final row is the cost of, and payoff from, this Portfolio B, which is composed of buying the same percentage of the levered firm's debt and equity. Note that what the levered firm pays as interest goes to the investors, because they have bought the levered firm's debt. Therefore, a portfolio of debt and equity in the levered firm ends up with the same amount of EBIT (i.e., $\alpha$EBIT) as if we had invested in the unlevered firm. Notice that the share of the levered and unlevered firm that you buy makes no difference, as $\alpha$ can be any number.

This is a powerful result. If you don't like the negative effects of financial leverage (e.g., the increased variability of returns), you can remove them by effectively "unlevering" the levered firm's equity by buying some of the firm's debt. This is where the arbitrage comes in: if the payoff is exactly the same, these two sets of cash flows must sell for exactly the same value, so their cost must be the same. That is:

$$V_U = S_L + D = V_L \qquad [21.10]$$

This equation says that the value of the levered firm ($V_L$) is the value of its debt plus the value of its equity ($S_L + D$), and this must equal the value of the unlevered firm ($V_U$). What this proof says is that, under M&M's assumptions, adding debt cannot destroy value, since the investor can undo the negative effects.[16]

If debt cannot destroy value, the next logical question is whether it can create value. Suppose the levered equity sells at a premium because of the favourable effects of financial leverage—what can the investor do then? M&M's answer to this was that an investor can create the effects of corporate leverage through the use of personal leverage. Remember that the effects of leverage are the same whether it is a firm, an individual, or a government borrowing money. In each case, it is simply the effect of using other people's money. So M&M came up with the arbitrage table shown in **Table 21.7**.

----

[16]This result underpinned the income trust market, where the trust owned both the equity and the debt of the operating company. If you are both the creditor and the debtor, the amount of debt clearly does not matter. The government changed the tax rules to eliminate this arbitrage on October 31, 2006, for fear of significant tax losses.

**TABLE 21.7** M&M Arbitrage Table II

| Portfolios (Actions) | Cost | Payoff |
| --- | --- | --- |
| Portfolio C: Buy $\alpha$ of levered firm's equity | $\alpha S_L$ | $\alpha(\text{EBIT} - k_D D)$ |
| Portfolio D: Buy $\alpha$ of unlevered firm | $\alpha V_U$ | $\alpha \text{EBIT}$ |
| Borrow $\alpha$ of levered firm's debt | $\alpha D$ | $-\alpha k_D D$ |
| Total portfolio D | $\alpha(V_U - D)$ | $\alpha(\text{EBIT} - k_D D)$ |

The strategy for Portfolio C is to buy the levered firm's equity at a cost of $\alpha S_L$, with a payoff of $\alpha(\text{EBIT} - k_D D)$. In Portfolio D, the individual replicates this payoff to see whether it can be bought more cheaply. First, the payoff from the unlevered firm at a cost of $\alpha V_U$ is $\alpha \text{EBIT}$. As before, the only difference is the absence of interest payments, and this is one thing everyone knows how to create: all you have to do is borrow money. So the individual borrows enough to pay the same interest payments of $-\alpha k_D D$ (the negative sign indicates that these are an outflow—i.e., a payment). This is where the perfect market assumption comes in, since M&M assume that the individual pays the same interest rate when borrowing against the unlevered firm's assets as the levered firm pays. In this case, the cost of generating these interest payments is the same as the cost of money borrowed by the levered firm (i.e., $-D$).

The cost to the portfolio that replicates the payoff from the levered firm's equity is therefore $V_U - D$, which has to equal the levered firm's equity value, $S_L$. Rearranging Equation 21.10, we get the same result as before: the levered firm's total value, equity plus debt, equals that of the unlevered firm. Therefore, the capital structure decision has no value. So now we have M&M's second proof. If you like the effects of financial leverage, you don't have to pay for them, because you can create the same effect through personal leverage. This is often referred to as M&M's **homemade leverage** result.

**homemade leverage** creating the effect of a firm's financial leverage through the use of personal leverage

In proving this result, M&M made use of our recognition that the effects of financial leverage are the same whether the debt is issued by a company, an individual, or a government. In fact, M&M took this a step further: with their assumptions, the effects are not only the same but identical since with the perfect markets assumption, individuals and corporations face the same financial market opportunities! This means homemade leverage and corporate leverage are perfect substitutes.

M&M's two results suggest that you can undo the effects of financial leverage if you don't like them, and you can create them if you do like these effects. These results rely heavily on the assumption that capital markets are perfect. They assume that individuals can buy both the debt and the equity of the levered firm to undo the effects, and that they can borrow on margin to create homemade leverage. Further, they assume that the interest rate investors pay for the debt is the same as that paid by the firm. However, nowhere is the investor defined or described. It could be a large financial institution or a hedge fund facing the same type of transaction costs faced by the firm. For this reason, most of the focus of the academic literature has been on the key assumptions of no taxes, no costly bankruptcy or financial distress costs, and no asymmetric information or agency costs. Before considering these assumptions, we should first work through what the initial M&M irrelevancy result means for the cost of capital.

## M&M and the Cost of Capital

The M&M results assume that the firm's earnings represent a perpetuity, so we can value the firm's equity as the present value of these earnings, as shown in Equation 21.11.

$$S_L = \frac{(\text{EBIT} - k_D D)}{k_e}$$

[21.11]

In this case, the cost of equity capital is the earnings yield, as we discussed in Chapter 20. As a result, we can estimate the equity cost using Equation 21.12, which divides the perpetual earnings (dividends) by the market value of the common shares ($S_L$).

$$k_e = \frac{(EBIT - k_D D)}{S_L}$$ [21.12]

Since M&M proved that the value of the firm is unchanged by leverage, we can define the unlevered value ($V_U$) by discounting the firm's expected EBIT by its unlevered equity cost ($k_U$), as shown in Equation 21.13.

$$V_U = \frac{EBIT}{k_U} = S_L + D = V_L$$ [21.13]

---

**EXAMPLE 21.2** | M&M's First Model and Firm Value

**a.** An unlevered firm (U) has an EBIT of $2 million, which is expected to remain constant indefinitely. Its cost of capital is 10 percent. What is the market value of this firm?

**b.** An identical risk-levered firm (L) has $5 million in debt outstanding. What is the value of this firm, and what is the value of its equity?

**Solution**

**a.** $V_U = \frac{EBIT}{k_U} = \frac{\$2 \text{ million}}{0.1} = \$20 \text{ million}$

**b.** $V_L = V_U = \$20$ million

$S_L = V_L - D = \$20$ million $- \$5$ million $= \$15$ million

---

Returning to Equation 21.13, we can solve for EBIT, substitute it for the EBIT in the leveraged equity cost equation (Equation 21.12), and rearrange to determine how the equity cost varies with the debt-equity ratio.[17] This is shown in Equation 21.14.

$$k_e = k_U + (k_U - k_D)\frac{D}{S_L}$$ [21.14]

This is referred to as the **M&M equity cost equation**. It states that if the firm has no debt in its capital structure, the investor requires a cost of equity of $k_U$, which is referred to as the cost of unlevered equity. This cost reflects the business risk of the firm and will depend on the risk class of the firm. As the firm uses debt, the equity cost increases due to the **financial leverage risk premium**, which is the difference between the unlevered equity cost and the cost of debt, multiplied by the D/E ratio.

Note that M&M's equity cost equation is not the same as the financial leverage equation (Equation 21.3). The financial leverage equation is based on book values, and in every case the sum of the debt plus equity equals the invested capital. However, the M&M equation holds because, according to their assumptions, the sum of the market value of debt plus equity equals the unlevered firm value. As we will see later, this is not the case when we relax M&M's assumptions. What this means is that M&M's equity cost equation (Equation 21.14) is a corollary of their constant value result (Equation 21.10).

**M&M equity cost equation** an equation used to determine how the equity cost varies with the debt-equity ratio

**financial leverage risk premium** the difference between the unlevered equity cost and the cost of debt, multiplied by the D/E ratio

---

[17]Using Equation 21.13, we can find EBIT $= k_U(S_L + D)$, which we substitute into Equation 21.12 to get:
$k_e = [k_U(S_L + D) - k_D D]/S_L = k_U + (k_U - k_D)D/S_L$.

A final implication of the M&M result applies to the cost of capital. If value is independent of financial leverage, we can ignore it and simply discount the EBIT cash flows with the unlevered equity cost. The problem is how to estimate this discount rate, because if the firm uses debt, all we observe is the levered equity cost ($k_e$). The solution is to go back to Equation 21.14 and rearrange it to solve for $k_U$.[18] If we do this, we get:

$$k_U = k_e \frac{S}{V} + k_D \frac{D}{V}$$

[21.15]

This is, of course, the weighted average cost of capital (WACC), as discussed in Chapter 20. However, there is one difference from the equation we provided there: in Equation 21.15, we have not adjusted $k_D$ for taxes, since in this ideal M&M world there are no taxes.

---

**EXAMPLE 21.3** | M&M's First Model and the Cost of Capital

Estimate the cost of equity and the WACC for the levered firm in Example 21.2, assuming that its cost of debt is 6 percent.

**Solution**

$$k_e = k_U + (k_U - k_D)\frac{D}{S_L} = 10 + (10 - 6)\frac{\$5}{\$15} = 11.33\%$$

$$WACC = \frac{\$15}{\$20}(11.33) + \frac{\$5}{\$20}(6) = 10\%$$

---

So M&M's results are really quite simple. The value of the firm is unaffected by the use of debt. This means that as the firm uses debt, the equity cost increases—by enough to exactly offset the advantage of using "cheap" debt. The result is that the firm's WACC is constant. This is illustrated in **Figure 21.4**.

**FIGURE 21.4** **M&M and the Cost of Capital**

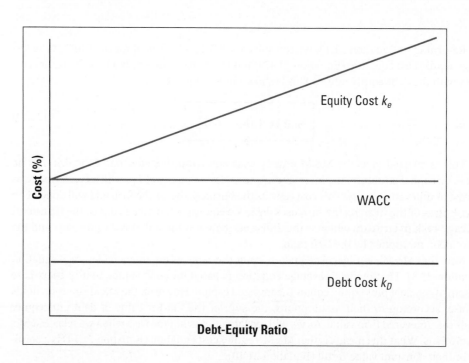

---

[18]Dropping the "L" subscripts and rearranging Equation 21.14 to group the unlevered equity cost terms, we get $k_U + k_U(D/S) = k_e + k_D/(D/S)$, or $k_U(1 + D/S) = k_e + k_D(D/S)$. Substituting S/S into the left-hand side for 1, we have $k_U[(S + D)/S]$ on the left, which can also be expressed as $k_U(V/S)$, since $V = S + D$. This leaves us with $k_U(V/S) = k_e + k_D(D/S)$. Multiplying both sides by S/V leaves $k_U = k_e(S/V) + k_D(D/V)$.

This is a very important figure. M&M were the first to logically analyze the capital structure decision and derive the relationship between the WACC and the firm's financing decision. Previously, people had speculated about it without imposing any logical structure. Even now, when first confronted with the M&M argument, people say that the firm's WACC must fall if the unlevered equity cost is, say, 10 percent and debt costs only 6 percent. Obviously 6 percent is less than 10 percent, so the WACC must fall! The error in this logic is that these people overlook the fact that the equity becomes riskier due to the financial leverage risk premium. With the M&M argument, the equity cost rises by exactly enough to offset the cheap debt, leaving the WACC unchanged. What M&M really suggest is that there is no free lunch in financial markets: even using a little bit of other people's money at a concessionary interest rate increases the risk enough to offset the expected gains.[19]

Other people go back to the financial leverage equation and say that the EPS must increase as long as the ROI exceeds the cost of debt, so that is the correct cut-off rate for evaluating investments, not the firm's WACC. This argument is also faulty, because the use of debt financing will increase the equity cost, which means the value of the shares may fall, even if the expected EPS goes up. Further, it is the firm's objective to maximize market values, not EPS.

Consider an unlevered firm with an expected EBIT of $10 million and an unlevered equity cost ($k_U$) of 10 percent. This means that its value is $100 million (i.e., $10 million/0.1). If it has 10 million shares outstanding, the share price is $10. Now suppose the firm finds a $10-million project with an ROI of 8 percent. Clearly, with a 10-percent equity cost, this project should not be accepted. However, suppose someone says, "We can borrow debt at a cost of 6 percent, so let's accept it, since the expected EPS will go up." This statement is partly true; we can work out the new higher expected EPS using the following equation:

$$\text{EPS} = \frac{\$10 + 0.08 \times \$10 - 0.06 \times \$10}{10} = \$1.02$$

This is higher than the original EPS of $1.00 (i.e., $10 million/10 million shares). The new EPS reflects the existing $10-million EBIT plus the EBIT from the new project of $0.8 million (8 percent × $10 million) minus the new interest charges of $0.6 million (6 percent × $10 million).

However, the critical value is what happens to the share price, and for this we need to determine the new equity cost. We can first find the net present value (NPV) of the new project using the 10-percent discount rate.

$$\text{NPV} = \frac{0.08 \times \$10}{0.1} - \$10 = -\$2$$

The present value of the project's earnings is $8 million, but since its cost is $10 million, the net present value is −$2 million. So after taking this project, the firm's equity market value will drop from $100 million to $98 million. We can then estimate the new equity cost using Equation 21.14.

$$k_e = 0.1 + (0.1 - 0.06)\frac{\$10}{\$98} = 10.41\%$$

Thus, the use of $10 million in debt has increased the variability in the EPS and ROE, causing the equity cost to increase from 10 to 10.41 percent.

The new equity price is then the new expected EPS in perpetuity, discounted at the new equity cost.

$$P = \frac{\$1.02}{0.1041} = \$9.80$$

Just as the value of the equity drops by $2 million, so the share price drops by $0.20, despite the increase in the expected EPS.

Remember that financial leverage has three effects: increased expected ROE, increased ROE variability, and increased risk of financial distress and bankruptcy. M&M's assumptions rule out

---

[19]This same argument was repeated ad nauseam after the 2008 financial crisis to suggest that bank capital structures do not matter so they should hold more equity. Those who made this argument failed to recognize that finance moved on from the M&M propositions decades ago. As John Maynard Keynes pointed out, the ideas of economists often influence policy long after they are dead.

the third effect, so we are left with one favourable and one unfavourable effect. In this example, the favourable increase in expected EPS is outweighed by the unfavourable effect of increased financial leverage. As a result, financing an 8-percent project with 6-percent debt increases the expected EPS, but when the WACC is 10 percent, the stock price still falls due to the higher financial leverage. *Only if the expected* ROI *of a project exceeds the* WACC *will the share price go up.*

---

### Concept Review Questions

1. State the assumptions underlying the M&M irrelevance theory.
2. Explain the importance of this theory.
3. What is the basic argument that M&M use to arrive at the irrelevancy result?
4. In this ideal M&M world, what will affect firm value?

---

## 21.4 The Impact of Taxes on Capital Structure

**LEARNING OBJECTIVE 21.4**
Explain how the introduction of corporate taxes affects M&M's irrelevance result.

### Introducing Corporate Taxes

Even back in 1958 there were taxes, and the impact of government on corporate investment and financing decisions still existed. Unfortunately, tax is amazingly complex, and a full discussion is beyond the scope of this text. However, one key feature we emphasized in Chapter 18 is that the interest on debt is tax deductible. This has a profound impact on the M&M results, since debt is favoured for tax reasons in Canada.[20] We will incorporate taxes into our discussion simply by making all the payments to the equity holders after corporate income taxes in the M&M arbitrage table. What this means is that we multiply all values by $(1 - T)$, as shown next.

The first thing to note is that the value of any firm will be reduced as taxes are introduced, since this reduces the earnings available to the shareholders. For example, the value of the unlevered firm, assuming perpetual EBIT, reduces to:

$$V_U = \frac{\text{EBIT}\,(1 - T)}{k_U} \qquad [21.16]$$

Notice that for the same level of EBIT, the firm value (as reflected in the numerator of this equation) is reduced as taxes are introduced. Further, the higher the tax rate, the lower the firm value, all else being equal.

We now focus on the value of the levered equity, since this is what decreases in value for the levered firm when we consider corporate income taxes.

In **Table 21.8**, everything is as in Table 21.7 except now buying the levered equity results in an after-tax net income and dividend of $\alpha(\text{EBIT} - k_D D)(1 - T)$; similarly the payoff to the unlevered equity is $\alpha\text{EBIT}(1 - T)$. Under this scenario, getting the same payoff for the home-made leverage portfolio formed by borrowing to invest in the unlevered equity requires interest payments of $\alpha k_D D(1-T)$. If these interest payments are discounted at the cost of debt, then

---

[20]Debt is not as much favoured in Canada as it is in the United States, as we shall see when we discuss the dividend tax credit system in Chapter 22.

**TABLE 21.8**   **M&M with Taxes**

| Portfolios (Actions) | Cost | Payoff |
|---|---|---|
| Portfolio C: Buy $\alpha$ of levered firm's equity | $\alpha S_L$ | $\alpha(EBIT - k_D D)(1 - T)$ |
| Portfolio D: Buy $\alpha$ of unlevered firm | $\alpha V_U$ | $\alpha EBIT(1 - T)$ |
| Borrow $\alpha$ of levered firm's debt | $\alpha D(1 - T)$ | $-\alpha k_D D(1 - T)$ |
| Total portfolio D | $\alpha[V_U - D(1 - T)]$ | $\alpha(EBIT - k_D D)(1 - T)$ |

the investor has to borrow $-\alpha D(1 - T)$ in order to generate these interest payments.[21] As a result, to avoid arbitrage, the value of the firm must equal $V_U - D(1 - T) = S_L$. Noting that $V_L = S_L + D$, we can rearrange the previous equation to get the following:

$$V_L = V_U + DT \qquad\qquad [21.17]$$

Equation 21.17 is M&M's valuation equation (Equation 21.10) extended to recognize that interest payments are tax deductible by the corporation. It is sometimes referred to as M&M's second model. The value of the firm *with* leverage is the value without leverage plus the **corporate debt tax shield** from debt financing.

Remember that interest is tax deductible, so in our cost-of-capital example, where the interest rate was 6 percent and the corporate tax rate 25 percent, the after-tax cost to the firm was only 4.5 percent. This means that 25 percent of the cost of the interest was paid for by a reduction in the firm's tax bill. If the firm is a perpetuity, this debt is outstanding forever; discounting this reduction in the interest cost to perpetuity gives the tax shield value $DT$. This is the implication of the M&M arbitrage argument.

Another way of thinking about this is to remember that the value of the firm is the value of the equity and the value of the debt. If the firm has no debt outstanding, the value is split between the government in tax revenues and the equity market value, since the taxes are proportional to the firm's taxable income. If the corporate income tax rate is 25 percent, then the government is getting 25 percent of the overall value, and the shareholders are getting 75 percent. However, if the firm raises debt, the government share of the pie falls as its tax revenue falls. Consequently, the value of the debt plus the equity goes up. This is illustrated in **Figure 21.5**.

**corporate debt tax shield**
the value added when a firm uses debt that is attributable to the associated tax benefits

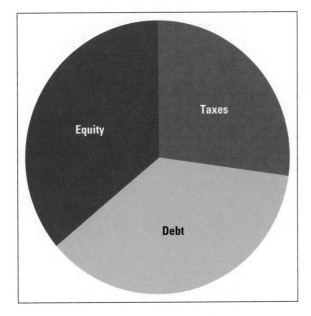

**FIGURE 21.5**   **Firm Value with Corporate Taxes**

---

[21]In this example we ignore personal taxes and whether the individual borrowing the money gets a tax deduction.

**FIGURE 21.6** **M&M with Corporate Taxes**

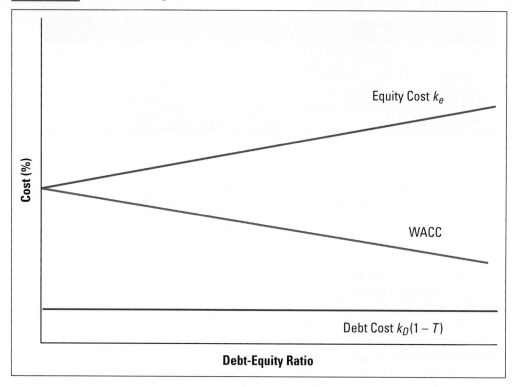

Also note that if there are no taxes, it makes no difference how you slice up the pie between debt and equity holders.

The tax subsidy for using debt explains why so many of the corporate financing vehicles described in Chapter 18 are designed with the intention of making the associated payments tax deductible as interest.

If the use of debt makes the value of the firm go up, the WACC must go down as the firm generates a bigger tax shield value and reduces the government share of the value of private enterprise. To see how this works, we can substitute the M&M tax value (Equation 21.17) into the earnings yield and get the new tax-corrected value of Equation 21.14. This is shown in Equation 21.18.

$$k_e = k_U + (k_U - k_D)(1 - T)\frac{D}{S_L}$$  [21.18]

In this case, the financial leverage risk premium is reduced by $(1 - T)$. If the government pays for 25 percent of the debt through a reduction in taxes, then the effective debt-equity ratio is only $(1 - T)D/S_L$. As a result, the equity cost does not increase by the same amount it would if there were no taxes paid. This is illustrated in **Figure 21.6**.

The key differences between Figure 21.6 and Figure 21.4 are that the interest cost and the financial leverage risk premium on the equity cost are both reduced by $(1 - T)$. As a result, as more debt is used, the cost of equity does not increase enough to offset the use of the cheaper debt. Therefore, the WACC declines continuously with the use of debt financing. Notice also that the equation to determine the WACC must be adjusted to reflect taxes and would now be the same as the WACC equation introduced in Chapter 20 (ignoring preferred shares). This is shown in Equation 21.19.

$$WACC = \frac{S}{V}k_e + \frac{D}{V}k_D(1 - T)$$  [21.19]

**EXAMPLE 21.4** | M&M with Corporate Taxes

Let's revisit the firms in Example 21.2 and assume that they both face a corporate tax rate of 30 percent, and they still generate an expected EBIT of $2 million perpetually.

**a.** Find the value of the unlevered firm (U), assuming its cost of capital is 10 percent.

**b.** Find the value of the identical risk-levered firm (L), which has $5 million in debt outstanding.

**c.** Find the cost of L's equity and its WACC.

**Solution**

**a.** $V_U = \dfrac{\text{EBIT}(1 - T)}{k_U} = \dfrac{\$2 \text{ million}(1 - 0.3)}{0.1} = \$14 \text{ million}$

Notice the decline of $6 million in U's market value. This is the present value of the future tax payments made to the government.

**b.** $V_L = V_U + DT = \$14 \text{ million} + (0.3)(\$5) = \$15.5 \text{ million}$

$S_L = V_L - D = \$15.5 \text{ million} - \$5 \text{ million} = \$10.5 \text{ million}$

Notice that L is worth $1.5 million more than U due to the tax shield value of debt ($DT$).

**c.** $k_e = k_U + (k_U - k_D)(1 - T)D/S_L = 10 + (10 - 6)(1 - 0.3)(\$5/\$10.5) = 11.33\%$

$\text{WACC}_L = (\$10.5/\$15.5)(11.33) + (\$5/\$15.5)(6)(1 - 0.3) = 9.03\%$

This explains why $V_L > V_U$, since L's WACC of 9.03 percent is below U's WACC of 10 percent (which equals its cost of equity because it is all equity financed).

---

Historically, the tax-extended M&M equity cost equation was often used in corporate finance because it captures one of the key features of corporate financing: the tax deductibility of interest payments. However, the M&M equity cost equations are rarely used anymore because there are now models—in particular the capital asset pricing model (CAPM)—that can adjust for risk. Assuming that the CAPM holds, the "beta" version of Equation 21.18 is

$$k_e = R_F + \text{MRP} \times \beta_U \left[ 1 + (1 - T)\dfrac{D}{S_L} \right] \qquad [21.20]$$

The equity cost without any debt is the risk-free rate plus the market risk premium (MRP) multiplied by the unlevered beta coefficient. With debt financing but ignoring corporate taxes, we get the financial leverage effect, and the unlevered beta is multiplied by one plus the debt-equity ratio. However, with corporate income taxes, as before, we multiply the debt by $(1 - T)$ to reflect that not all of the debt costs are paid by the shareholders.

Given the importance of the CAPM in estimating the equity cost, Equation 21.20 is used more often than the M&M equations from which it is derived.[22] Given the simplicity of the adjustment, it is relatively easy to unlever betas to get the unleveraged equity cost, and then relever them to account for changes in the firm's financial leverage. Although this is common practice, it contains a crucial flaw: the adjustment is based on the M&M equation, which implies that 100-percent debt financing is optimal—since there is always more tax shield value to using more debt, why stop? While it seems obvious on an intuitive level that firms should not finance with 100-percent debt, we can address the question more formally by relaxing M&M's assumptions that there are no costs related to the risk of financial distress or bankruptcy. We discuss these issues in detail in the next section.

---

[22]Hamada, R., "The Effect of the Firm's Capital Structure on the Systematic Risk of Common Stocks." *Journal of Finance* 27, no. 2 (May 1972), pp. 435–52.

The conclusion that 100-percent debt is optimal in the presence of corporate taxes also ignores the impact of personal taxes. We discuss the impact of personal taxes on M&M's conclusions regarding capital structure in Appendix 21A.

---

**Concept Review Questions**

1. How do taxes affect the M&M argument?
2. What are the practical difficulties associated with the implications of M&M's corporate tax model?

---

## 21.5 Financial Distress, Bankruptcy, and Agency Costs

**LEARNING OBJECTIVE 21.5**
Describe how financial distress and bankruptcy costs lead to the static trade-off theory of capital structure.

The problem with M&M's corporate tax model is that it recognizes the benefits of using debt (i.e., the tax shield $DT$), but disregards the associated risks, which include the increased risk of financial distress or bankruptcy. The important thing about financial distress and bankruptcy costs is that they produce a flow of value away from both the debt holders and the equity holders. In the simple M&M world, anyone can buy both the firm's debt and equity, and what the equity holder loses, the debt holder gains. This is an example of a "zero-sum game." All that is happening is value is being rearranged, but none is being destroyed. The key feature of bankruptcy and financial distress is that value is destroyed. So while the use of debt creates value by reducing the government's share of taxes, it also destroys value by causing increased risk of financial distress and bankruptcy. Before we go on, we must first explain what we mean by distress and bankruptcy.

### Bankruptcy and Financial Distress

**bankruptcy** a state of insolvency that occurs when a firm commits an act of bankruptcy, such as the non-payment of interest, and creditors enforce their legal rights to recoup money, or when a firm voluntarily declares bankruptcy in an effort to gain protection while it reorganizes so it can become solvent again

**Bankruptcy** is a legal state. It can occur in two ways: (1) when the firm commits an act of bankruptcy, such as the non-payment of interest, and creditors enforce their legal rights as a result; or (2) when the firm voluntarily declares bankruptcy. Under either scenario, in Canada, the firm is reorganized under the *Companies' Creditors Arrangements Act* (*CCAA*) or the *Bankruptcy and Insolvency Act* (*BIA*).

The *CCAA* is primarily for larger, more complicated firms (the debt must exceed $5 million) and is exceedingly flexible. Essentially, the court appoints a monitor, normally a trustee in bankruptcy working for one of the larger accounting firms, who then reports back to the court. The monitor has considerable flexibility to prevent creditors from exercising their claims against the firm, to restructure contracts, and to allow the management of the firm to develop a plan to reorganize in the hope of continuing operations. During this period, the firm is allowed to raise new financing, called debtor-in-possession (DIP) financing, with a higher priority over existing unsecured claims. It is this financing that gives the firm some breathing space to reorganize and present a plan to all creditors, which the court can impose, providing enough of the creditors agree.

The *BIA* is much more rigid. There is very limited scope for preventing creditors from seizing assets, the firm cannot raise DIP financing, and there is no provision for imposing a settlement on all creditors, even if a significant majority agree to it. If a restructuring plan is rejected, creditors can seize the assets and the firm is liquidated. Anything left after the secured creditors are paid is proportionally allocated to the unsecured creditors. The *BIA* is much simpler and more predictable than the *CCAA* and is used mainly by smaller companies, where the major creditor is a commercial bank. As a result, it is a lot easier to negotiate a settlement. In contrast, the *CCAA* is mainly used for large companies with many creditors, where a "stay" or breathing space is needed to sort things out.

## Costs of Bankruptcy

A reorganization is expensive, particularly under the *CCAA*, where there are much more significant legal, accounting, and court fees.[23] All of these fees represent an outflow of value that goes to neither the debt holders nor the equity holders. If the firm is actually wound up and liquidated, there are even more costs, as the major asset of a failing firm is usually a history of tax losses. These losses can be carried forward and used against future profits and are thus valuable to the firm. However, if the firm is wound up, these losses disappear and the major beneficiary is the government. In addition, the process of winding up a firm usually results in sales of assets to third parties at "bargain" prices that are less than their value in place, so again there is a value loss to the firm.

Firms try hard to reorganize prior to a formal bankruptcy and liquidation because of these deadweight losses to liquidation from reduced asset prices in distress sales, the loss of tax losses, and the costs of legal and accounting fees associated with a liquidation. These costs are often referred to as the **direct costs of bankruptcy**.

While the direct costs can be substantial, even greater losses in value may occur before the firm deteriorates into a bankruptcy situation. These latter losses are often referred to as the **indirect costs of bankruptcy** or, more simply, **financial distress costs**. Financial distress is a situation in which the firm has yet to commit the act of bankruptcy, although it knows that unless something dramatic happens, it will likely go bankrupt. Suppose, for example, the firm still has $10 million in cash, but its business is failing, it is worth only $20 million, and it has a $50-million loan coming due in a year. Clearly, if the firm doesn't do anything, in a year's time its creditors will insist on payment, and the $20-million business and the $10 million in cash will belong to the creditors. Ignoring any fees and other associated costs, the creditors will get $0.60 on the dollar for their debt, and the shareholders will lose everything. This is a situation of **financial distress**.

During periods of financial distress, there is an increase in the **agency costs** due to the growing divergence of the interests of equity holders and debt holders. In the example discussed in the previous paragraph, the debt holders have a chance to get back $0.60 on the dollar, while the equity holders' stake in the firm is zero. Therefore, the equity holders (who get to vote) may try to implement measures in an attempt to get something for themselves, at the expense of the debt holders. For example, the shareholders might vote to pay out the $10 million in cash as a dividend. This will give them some cash now, and in a year's time the creditors will get only $20 million instead of $30 million when they seize the firm's assets. However, this is illegal as well as being unethical.

The responsibility of the board of directors (BOD) is to act in the best interests of the company. For a solvent company, this means pursuing the best interests of the shareholders. However, for an insolvent company, the responsibility of the BOD shifts to all the stakeholders in the firm, including the creditors. In particular, once the firm is reorganized under the *CCAA* or *BIA*, all the dividend decisions of the previous year, and sometimes of the previous three years, are reviewed to see whether they were prudent and reasonable at the time. A sudden cash dividend of $10 million shortly before a firm goes bankrupt would immediately make the board members at the time the dividend was declared personally liable, and would cause the court to order the payments reversed.[24]

**direct costs of bankruptcy** costs incurred as a direct result of bankruptcy, including liquidation of assets, the loss of tax losses, and legal and accounting fees

**indirect costs of bankruptcy** or **financial distress costs** losses to a firm before it declares bankruptcy

**financial distress** a state of business failing where bankruptcy seems imminent if dramatic action is not taken

**agency costs** the costs associated with agency problems arising from the divergence of interests among managers, shareholders, and creditors, as discussed in Chapter 2

---

[23]We discussed Nortel earlier in Chapter 20. At that company's bankruptcy proceedings, lawyers and other professionals presented a $1,300-million bill for professional services. The Ontario Superior Court judge hearing the Canadian proceedings called the bill "shocking," but the Nortel situation is not an isolated incident. See Gray, Jeff, "Billion Dollar Nortel Tab Boosts Pressure over Runaway Legal Costs." *The Globe and Mail*, May 14, 2014.

[24]Note that this is also why directors usually resign as the firm gets into serious financial trouble. There have been times when all the directors have tried to resign, but the *Canada Business Corporations Act* requires at least one director.

However, just because something is illegal doesn't mean there is no way to achieve the same result. Funny things happen in failing firms: assets are sometimes sold to related companies owned by the shareholders at "knock down" prices, or the firm pays for joint venture activities that seem, on the surface, to offer little benefit. In all cases, these are simply more sophisticated ways to try to strip cash out of the company before it goes bankrupt, since these assets will belong to the creditors and not the shareholders when it does go bankrupt. Part of the expense of reorganizing or liquidating a company is simply working out what has happened in the previous few years and determining whether any assets have been fraudulently stripped out of the company.

## Shareholders' and Creditors' Reactions to Bankruptcy

A more subtle issue than outright fraud is the recognition that the shareholders essentially have a one-year call option on the underlying firm; the exercise price is the value of the debt. In one year's time, the value of the firm described previously will either exceed $50 million or it won't. If it exceeds $50 million, the firm can refinance and pay off its creditors, and the shareholders will have some residual value. On the other hand, if the value of the firm is less than $50 million, the shareholders are protected by limited liability and can simply walk away and hand the firm over to the creditors. The existence of limited liability, and the fact that shareholders are only exposed up to the value of their investment, create this call option. The shareholders' value is depicted in **Figure 21.7**.

If there is no limited liability, the shareholders have to pay off the $50 million in debt regardless, so they gain (lose) if the underlying firm value (the unlevered value) is greater (less) than the face value of the debt. However, with limited liability, they can't be forced to make up the losses if the value of the firm is less than the face value of the debt that is due. As a result, the value of the equity behaves like a call option, with the minimum value represented by the heavy intrinsic value line in Figure 21.7. The important thing to understand about the change in the characteristics of the shares in a firm in financial distress is that options react differently than ordinary common shares. For example, two major factors increasing the value of a call option are time and risk—both of which increase the option value. So with $10 million in cash, the shareholders can possibly increase the risk of the firm and extend the time until they go bankrupt.

 **The Firm as a Call Option for Shareholders**

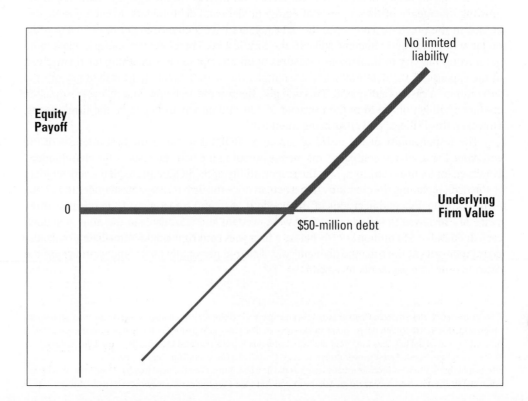

Whether or not they can extend the time period will depend on the type of debt that they have outstanding. In this example, all $50 million is due the next year. But if, instead, it were long-term debt with only the interest payments due in a year, the firm could continue to make the interest payments until all $10 million in cash was used up. During this period, the firm could devote all its time and energy to survival. It would skip normal maintenance, not replace machines, stop advertising and R&D, and generally allow the operations to run down. In this case, the shareholders would be hoping that something might happen to give value to the firm, while the worst that could happen is a delayed bankruptcy. For the creditors, this is a nightmare scenario because they are seeing the value of the operations, as well as the $10 million in cash, go down period by period until, by the time they can finally force bankruptcy, they don't get $30 million—they get much less.

The second major problem is that there is an incentive for the shareholders to gamble, since they are gambling with the debt holders' wealth. They might make risky investments that they would not otherwise make, because if the investments pay off, they could get the firm out of bankruptcy. If they don't pay off, it doesn't matter to the shareholders because they are essentially bankrupt anyway. This attitude often shows up in the form of poorly researched new product introductions, where the product hasn't been properly tested and the proper research and development has not been carried out. Unfortunately, the opposite scenario also occurs: if the firm is going bankrupt, the equity holders have no incentive to put in new money for minor projects, even if they are very profitable, since all this does is create more value for the creditors, not the shareholders.

All these examples illustrate the fact that the incentives for shareholders and the firm change once there is significant bankruptcy risk. Instead of making positive NPV decisions, where the equity holders bear the risk, they face a situation where it is the creditors who bear the risk. This is because the firm really belongs to the creditors, yet they cannot alter what the firm is doing until it commits the act of bankruptcy by non-payment of interest or principal.

During this period of financial distress, the underlying operations of the firm are often poorly managed due to this change in incentive structure. What this means in terms of the M&M argument is that if the firm raises too much debt, the underlying EBIT of the levered firm will change as poor projects are accepted, good ones ignored, operations neglected, and cash stripped out of the company. Again, as with direct bankruptcy costs, there is a value loss that is not being fully captured by either the debt holders or the equity holders.

Creditors are well aware that distressed firms may take these types of actions, which is why they take offsetting measures. One standard approach is not to make long-term loans to risky firms. Instead, debt is short term or includes sinking fund payments that create a continuous cash payment to the creditors, thereby reducing the maturity of the call option. This also explains all the stipulations in the BC Gas trust indenture we discussed in Chapter 18, in which the firm agrees to insure its assets, maintain them in good order, not sell them unless it meets certain tests, not exceed a particular debt ratio, and maintain certain levels of working capital. In all cases, the lender is simply trying to reduce the value of this call option and gain greater control over the affairs of the firm.

## The Static Trade-Off Theory

As discussed, there are significant costs attached to raising too much debt, since too much debt increases the risks of financial distress and bankruptcy, and the associated value outflows to third parties. This leads to a theory referred to as the **static trade-off**, which says a firm will use debt to maximize its tax advantages up to the point where these benefits are outweighed by the associated estimated costs of financial distress and bankruptcy. The model is illustrated in **Figure 21.8**.

The straight line in Figure 21.8 is the M&M value of the levered firm, taking into account the existence of corporate taxes. In other words, it is the value of the unlevered firm plus the tax shield value, where the slope of the line is determined by the tax rate, $T$, since value increases with debt by the corporate tax rate. The curved line is the expected value loss from financial distress and bankruptcy. Notice that the slope of this line increases with the debt ratio. This is because there is little risk of distress or bankruptcy at low levels of debt, but this risk and its consequences increase with the debt level. The optimal level of debt occurs where the slope of the financial distress curve is the same as that of the tax-corrected value line, because at this point the

**static trade-off** a theory that states a firm uses debt to maximize its tax advantages up to the point where these benefits are outweighed by the associated estimated costs of financial distress and bankruptcy

**FIGURE 21.8** Firm Value and
Financial Distress Costs

**FIGURE 21.8** Firm Value and
Financial Distress Costs

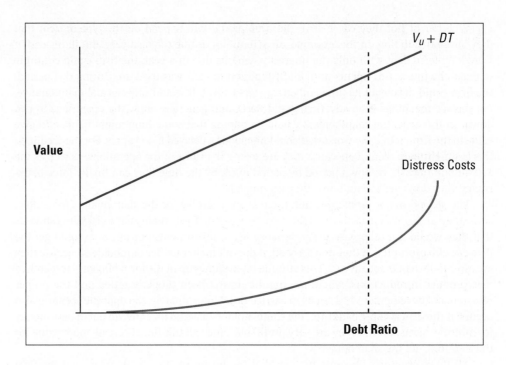

marginal tax shield benefit equals the marginal cost of financial distress and bankruptcy. In this
way, the tax advantages of debt are traded off against the distress and bankruptcy disadvantages.

The conclusions of the static trade-off model are depicted in **Figure 21.9**. The top diagram
shows that the cost of equity increases throughout as more debt is added, as expected. Initially,
the effect of this increase on the WACC is more than offset by the use of the cheaper debt. As
a result, the WACC initially declines as more debt is added. However, beyond a certain point,

**FIGURE 21.9** The Static
Trade-Off Model

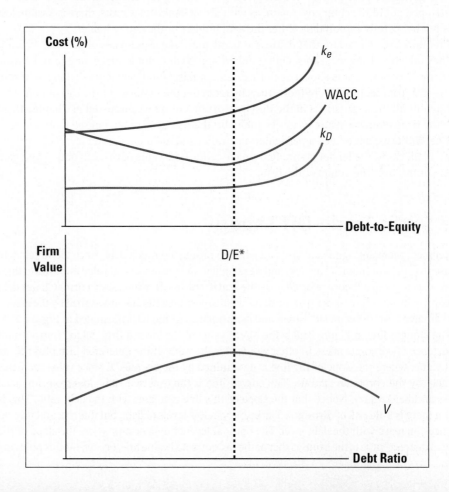

---

## 21.2 Finance in the News    Oilexco Financing Update: Subsidiary Faces Insolvency

Oilexco Incorporated announced today that its wholly owned subsidiary, Oilexco North Sea Limited ("ONSL"), intends to file petitions for administration ("Administration") in the High Court in the United Kingdom as soon as reasonably practicable but likely as early as next week. Oilexco Incorporated is considering its options in light of this development but at this time remains solvent and committed to the strategic review process that was previously announced.

As the Company previously announced on December 17, 2008, incremental funding was necessary in addition to the bridge funding announced that day, although no assurances were given that such funding would become available. Today, the Company was advised by The Royal Bank of Scotland plc on behalf of the syndicate of lenders that they are not prepared to advance any further funding to ONSL. Oilexco does not have any other source of funding at this time and has therefore concluded that an Administration must be pursued. Oilexco has been advised that funding for an Administration is in the process of being arranged by its senior secured lenders, subject to settlement of terms with the prospective administrators and counsel. Accordingly, all parties expect that safe and orderly operations will continue throughout this period.

As also announced on December 17, 2008, Morgan Stanley & Co. Limited and Merrill Lynch International have been retained by Oilexco in a strategic review process to seek alternative funding or the sale of the Company or some of its assets. Several parties have indicated significant interest in acquiring ONSL or all or substantially all of its assets. Oilexco understands that it is the intention of the proposed administrators to continue this process, with the intention of selling ONSL or all or substantially all of its assets in such a way as to maximize the value of the assets for all stakeholders, and maintain the business, its employees and systems as a going concern. However, there can be no certainty that any binding offers will be received or accepted or that any transaction will be completed or, if it is completed, that there will be any equity value for Oilexco shareholders. The shares of ONSL comprise substantially all of the assets of the Company.

**Source:** "Oilexco Financing Update: Subsidiary Faces Insolvency." Oilexco press release, December 31, 2008. Accessed at www.oilexco.com.

---

depicted as D/E*, the WACC begins to increase, reflecting the higher costs of both debt and equity in response to the increased risk of financial distress and bankruptcy. So the WACC is minimized at D/E*. As a result, as can be seen in the bottom diagram in Figure 21.9, the value of the firm is maximized at this same point. This point, D/E*, represents the optimal capital structure according to the static trade-off model.

How significant are these financial distress and bankruptcy costs? As we discussed earlier, a firm with too much debt and no financial flexibility cannot react to changing market conditions. A classic example of this is Oilexco, which was (note the tense) a Calgary-based oil and gas exploration company whose major activities were in the North Sea, through its British subsidiary. It had excellent technical know-how in extracting oil from fields that were felt to be dry, but at a relatively high cost. It became a darling of the stock market: as the price of crude oil hit $147 a barrel, its stock price went to $19.50, giving the company a value of $4.5 billion. However, it financed this activity through two series of bank loans syndicated through the Royal Bank of Scotland (RBS). When the financial crisis hit, RBS lost 28 billion pounds sterling (about $50 billion) and pulled the plug on all manner of risky loans. Remember that most bank loans are demand loans. Finance in the News 21.2 is a reprint of the Oilexco news release that explains what happened when the price of oil dropped below $50 a barrel.

Eventually, Oilexco's UK subsidiary was sold for less than the value of its debt of about $600 million. Unfortunately, Oilexco had guaranteed its subsidiary's debt. On July 16, 2009, Oilexco was forced to liquidate its remaining assets to make good on the guarantee. The result was that Oilexco went from a $4.5-billion market value to zero in the space of a year because it had no financial flexibility and could not access capital. Prior to the financial crisis of 2008, Oilexco could have raised financing with oil prices at $50, but in the middle of the crisis no one was willing to extend any credit. In recessions, "cash is king," and those without it run the risk of going bankrupt, like Oilexco.

---

## Concept Review Questions

1. Explain the impact of financial distress and agency costs on M&M's conclusions regarding capital structure.

2. Why can the firm's debt be viewed as the exercise price to the shareholders' option to purchase the firm?

3. Explain the static trade-off theory.

# Other Factors Affecting Capital Structure

**LEARNING OBJECTIVE 21.6**
Explain how information asymmetries and agency problems lead firms to follow a pecking-order approach to financing.

How well does the static trade-off model explain capital structures? It certainly captures the main effects. However, it ignores two important issues:

1. **Information asymmetry problems:** the effect of informational differences among shareholders, creditors, and management
2. **Agency problems:** the fact that managers make decisions on behalf of the shareholders but have their own interests at stake as well

First let's consider the impact of information differences. Suppose a firm has a market value of $20 million and, after careful consideration, decides to undertake a new project that costs $5 million and has a $5-million NPV. The firm has 1 million shares outstanding, so the share price prior to undertaking the new project is $20. What should it do and how should it finance this project? Theoretically, the CEO should call a news conference and announce this great new investment, the media and security analysts in attendance should clap their hands, the market value of the firm should go up by $5 million to $25 million, and the stock price should rise to $25. The firm should then issue 200,000 shares at $25 each to finance the project, spending the $5 million so the total value increases to $30 million and the stock price remains at $25 (i.e., $30m/1.2m).

However, the real world does not react like this. Investors will yawn, bombard the CEO with questions, and generally be extremely critical, since they have heard this story before and cannot distinguish between good firms telling the truth and poor firms spinning a story to boost the stock price. What is more likely to happen, therefore, is the stock price will stay at $20, forcing the firm to issue 250,000 shares at $20 to finance the project. Then, when the truth is revealed and the project does add value, the firm's value will increase to $30 million. So the firm value still gets to $30 million, but with 1.25 million shares outstanding and a stock price that only reaches $24.

The situation may be even worse than this, since stock prices often drop when firms announce a new share issue. This is because investors suspect that management thinks the stock price is overvalued and is therefore trying to issue common shares while they are trading at inflated prices. Suppose, for example, that the stock price drops to $18 on the announcement of the share issue. In that case, the firm will have to issue 277,778 shares to raise the $5 million, and even if the market value ultimately rises to $30 million, the stock price will only rise to $23.48. In both of these cases, the ownership of this positive NPV project is being shared by the existing shareholders and the new shareholders who are buying in at below "true" market price.

How can the firm handle this problem of information asymmetry? The obvious answer is to raise $5 million in debt. In this case, when the value of the firm rises to $30 million after the profits flow from the new investment, the equity will be worth $25 million and the debt $5 million, but there will still be only 1 million shares outstanding, and the stock price will rise to $25.

This suggests that firms should issue equity only as a last resort. Instead, they should finance using internal cash flow, then debt, and, finally, common equity, in what Stewart Myers refers to as a **pecking order**.[25]

**pecking order** the order in which firms prefer to raise financing, starting with internal cash flow, then debt, and finally common equity

Myers' argument that firms follow a pecking order is based on divulging information. If firms use internal cash flow, they do not need anyone's permission. Even the shareholders can't force the firm to pay a dividend. Similarly, the firm can talk to a bank and divulge privileged information to secure a loan. However, when it issues new common shares, as we have seen, the firm has to file a prospectus and reveal all material facts that affect the share price. In the process, the firm has to be careful not to reveal facts to a competitor that may give it a jump-start and allow it to compete away the NPV benefits of the project.

[25]Myers, S., "The Capital Structure Puzzle." *Journal of Finance* 39, no. 3 (July 1984), pp. 574–92.

The pecking order was discussed in a different context by Gordon Donaldson, who justified the pecking order through what we would now call "agency arguments."[26] He showed that managers' commitment to the firm is a result of their human capital, in contrast to the "short-term" financial commitment of shareholders. As a result, managers are more concerned about the long-term survival of the firm and less inclined to take risks. For these agency reasons, he argued that managers had a preference for financing by using internal cash flow (retained earnings), then debt, and finally by issuing new common equity. In an agency model, this financing hierarchy imposes the least risk on the firm and requires the least justification by managers.

Regardless of whether it is for agency reasons, information problems, or some combination of the two, we do see firms using the pecking order. Profitable firms tend to have the least debt simply because they don't need it and have more than enough internal funds. Leveraged recapitalizations involve issuing debt and using the funds to buy back shares. These tend to address the lack of debt over time, but only with a significant lag. The real puzzle is that there are some firms that simply don't use much debt, even though they could. Microsoft, for example, is relatively low risk, is hugely profitable, and has relatively little debt. Although it has $85 billion in debt outstanding, which seems to be huge, its equity market value is $858 billion, for a debt-equity ratio using market values of 0.10. Microsoft's return on equity is almost 40 percent and it could pay off most of its debt in a couple of years. It could undoubtedly lower its tax bill further by using more debt financing and buying back shares, but it hasn't done so.

---

### Concept Review Question

1. Explain how the existence of information asymmetries and agency problems may lead firms to follow a pecking order to financing.

---

## 21.7 | Capital Structure in Practice

### LEARNING OBJECTIVE 21.7
Describe other factors that can affect a firm's capital structure in practice.

So what do we make of all these factors? First we can say that the static trade-off theory suggests you should take advantage of the tax shields from debt, so the first question is: **Is the firm profitable?**

If the firm has no profits, it can't use the tax shields from debt. In this case, it might as well finance with equity. More to the point, it has no ability to make interest payments.

The second question deals with whether or not the firm can issue debt. As we saw, lenders make credit evaluations and won't lend if they fear financial distress. In particular, if firms have hard tangible assets that can be sold elsewhere, lenders may lend to them even if they are worried about the survival prospects of the firm. This is because they can always seize the assets, sell them, and recover most of their principal. This leads to the second question: **What type of assets does the firm have?** If they are tangible assets that can be used elsewhere, they can be used as collateral for a secured loan.

If the firm's assets are not good collateral, the lender has to look to the firm's cash flow rather than its assets for security. In this case, the lender will be concerned about the firm's business risk and the variability of its operations. This leads to the third question: **How risky is the firm's underlying business?**

It is a basic law of finance, illustrated by our discussion of financial leverage, that you do not layer significant financial risk on top of significant business risk.

---

[26]Donaldson, G., "Financial Goals: Management versus Stockholders." *Harvard Business Review* (May/June 1963).

Generally, financial markets are size constrained. This means that, because preparing a prospectus and other necessary documents is time-consuming and costly, only larger firms access the public markets. Further, larger firms tend to have more diversified operations and more market power. This is not an absolute, but larger firms tend to be less risky than smaller firms, so the fourth question is: ***How big is the firm?***

Finally, there is the basic question of whether the firm needs the money, which is very much a function of its profitability and growth rate. Growing firms need cash, whereas profitable firms generally spin off cash, so we ask: ***What is the firm's growth rate, and how profitable is it?***

These five questions go a long way to determining how much debt a firm can carry and what its optimal debt ratio will be. Of course, firms deviate from their target capital structure when they are offered a good deal. Like everyone else, we may do something we didn't intend to if someone offers us a good deal. In terms of financing, this means that if the firm can obtain attractive interest rates, it might lean more heavily on debt financing.

If a firm's share price is very high and increasing, and the firm believes the stock is overvalued, it may decide to take advantage of this window of opportunity to issue common shares. This is why we observe more equity financing in a strong equity market than a weak one. (In fact, firms often issue equity when they think it is overvalued. This opportunistic financing causes significant departures from their long-run target debt ratios.) Therefore, one other question we might ask is: ***How high is the stock price, how much has it appreciated over the last year, and how cheap is it to borrow?***

These are the basic questions that are asked in determining a firm's financing decisions. Let's finish with a survey carried out by Deutsche Bank. **Figure 21.10** presents results from the survey, in which companies were asked to rate the importance of the factors listed in determining an appropriate level of debt—from "not important" (0) to "very important" (5).

There were many more factors presented here than in the survey conducted by the Conference Board, which we discussed earlier in the chapter, but the implications are similar. The number-one factor mentioned is credit rating: firms often take drastic measures simply to maintain their A or BBB rating. Other factors consistent with our discussion are number 3, the tax shield value of debt, which reflects the tax deductibility of interest; and numbers 2 and 4, which reflect risk, since firms do not want to be put in a position where they have to restrict investments or cut their dividends. After that, the factors tend to be technical, such as who is willing to buy the debt (capacity), what costs are involved in issuing it, and the old standby: what do other companies do?

**Figure 21.11** presents results from the same Deutsche Bank survey. Firms were asked whether they have a target or optimal capital structure. If M&M are correct, the answer should

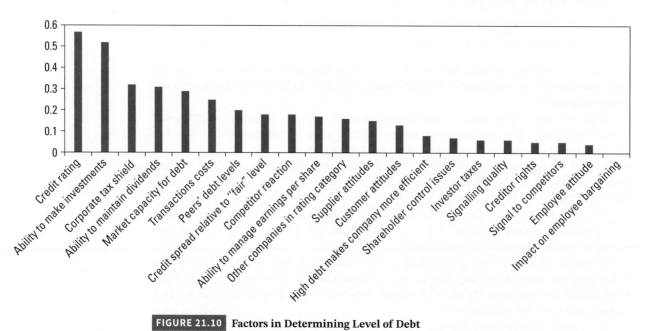

**FIGURE 21.10**  **Factors in Determining Level of Debt**

**Source:** Adapted from Servaes, Henri, and Tufano, Peter, Figure 21: Factors in Determining Level of Debt. In *The Theory and Practice of Corporate Capital Structure* (London, Deutsche Bank, January 2006), p. 42.

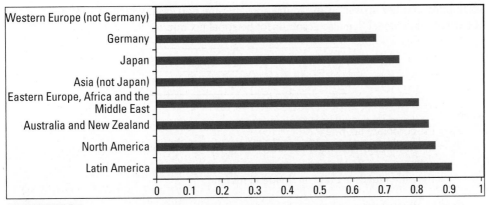

**FIGURE 21.11**  **Proportion of Firms with a Target Capital Structure by Region**

**Source:** Adapted from Servaes, Henri, and Tufano, Peter, Figure 18: Proportion of Firms with a Target Capital Structure by Region. In *The Theory and Practice of Corporate Capital Structure* (London, Deutsche Bank, January 2006), p. 37.

be "No, we don't care." However, 90 percent of companies domiciled in Latin America and 85 percent in North America have a target capital structure. The number is slightly less in Germany and the rest of Western Europe, but it turns out their tax systems do not give the same level of subsidy to interest payments as the systems in North America. Overall, the survey data provided by Deutsche Bank confirm the idea that we have been discussing: firms have an optimal capital structure, and it tends to be a trade-off between tax advantages and the loss of financial flexibility.

---

**Concept Review Question**

1. Explain four of the most important factors influencing capital structure decisions, as indicated in the survey results, and how they relate to the conceptual discussion of an optimal capital structure.

---

## APPENDIX 21A  |  Personal Taxes and Capital Structure

**LEARNING OBJECTIVE 21.8**

Explain how the introduction of personal taxes on investment income affects the corporate tax advantage to using debt.

Recall from our discussion of taxation in Chapter 3 that dividend income and interest income are taxed differently at the personal level, with dividends receiving preferential tax treatment. Since investors will base their valuations of securities on the after-tax cash flows they expect to receive from them, it is reasonable to assume that individual taxes may affect firm value and thus capital structure decisions.

One popular model dealing with personal taxes was introduced by Merton Miller (one of the Ms of M&M).[27] He argued that a firm should strive to minimize all taxes, both corporate and personal, paid on corporate income. By doing so, the firm maximizes total cash flows available to security holders after corporate and personal taxes. Based on a number of technical

---

[27]Miller, M., "Debt and Taxes." *Journal of Finance* 32, no. 2 (May 1977), pp. 261–75.

assumptions, Miller arrived at the following valuation equation, which is a variation of the M&M valuation model that also accounts for personal tax rates:

$$V_L = V_U + D\left[1 - \frac{(1-T_C)(1-T_D)}{(1-T_P)}\right]$$ [21A.1]

where

$T_C$ = the corporate tax rate
$T_P$ = the individual's personal tax rate on ordinary income (which also applies to interest income)
$T_D$ = the individual's tax rate on dividend income

Technically, we can note several things from this equation.

1. If $(1-T_P) = (1-T_C)(1-T_D)$, then $V_L = V_U$, and we get the M&M irrelevancy proposition. This is referred to as an integrated tax system and has historically been the tax system in use in Western Europe, where individuals get a tax credit for the corporate taxes paid on their behalf. Obviously, in this case there are no tax advantages to using debt.

2. If $(1-T_P) < (1-T_C)(1-T_D)$, then $V_L < V_U$, which suggests the firm loses value by issuing debt. In this case, there is an incentive for individuals, rather than the firm, to borrow money since they generate larger tax shields.

3. If $(1-T_P) > (1-T_C)(1-T_D)$, then $V_L > V_U$, which suggests the firm enhances value by issuing debt, since there are more debt tax shields at the corporate level than the personal level. This is the system we have in Canada and is referred to as a partially integrated tax system.

4. If the personal tax rate on dividends $(T_D)$ equals the tax rate on interest income $(T_P)$, then we have what is referred to as a classic tax system, in which all personal income is taxed at the same rate. This is historically the system in place in the United States. The ratio $(1-T_D)/(1-T_P)$ equals one, and the M&M corporate tax shield holds even with personal taxes—that is, $V_L = V_U + T_C D$.

Generally, the third case tends to hold—that is $(1-T_P) > (1-T_C)(1-T_D)$, so that $V_L > V_U$. It is the case in Canada that $T_D < T_P$, so the amount by which $V_L$ exceeds $V_U$ is less than the $T_C D$ term included in M&M's corporate tax model. In other words, there are usually gains to firm value associated with the use of debt, but the gains are not as great as that predicted by M&M's corporate tax valuation model.

For example, based on 2019 federal and provincial tax rate estimates, the combined federal and provincial corporate tax rate for a company operating in Ontario that does not qualify for the small business tax deduction is 26.5 percent. This is a significant drop as Canada has attempted to reduce corporate tax rates to attract new investment. Further, assume an Ontario individual in the highest federal and provincial tax brackets has a personal tax rate of 53.53 percent on personal income and 39.34 percent on eligible dividend income.[28]

Using these rates, we have the following:

$$(1-T_P) > (1-T_C)(1-T_D)$$
$$(1-0.5353) > (1-0.265)(1-0.3934)$$
$$0.4647 > 0.4459$$

What these numbers indicate is that if the firm pays out interest, this is deductible to the corporation but fully taxable to the investor, so with current tax rates the individual gets 46.47 cents on the dollar and the government 53.53 cents. On the other hand if the firm pays out dividends, first it has to pay corporate taxes of 26.5 percent, so it pays out 73.5 cents on which the investor then pays 39.34 percent in dividend taxes, leaving them with 44.59 cents on the

[28]A good site for determining current tax rates is the tax calculator provided on the Ernst & Young website at www.ey.com/CA/en/Services/Tax/Tax-Calculators.

dollar with the government taking 55.41 cents. These numbers imply the following gains to using corporate debt in Canada:

$$V_L = V_U + D \times \left(1 - \frac{0.4459}{0.4647}\right) \text{ or } V_L = V_U + D \times 0.04$$

Notice that the last term $(0.04 \times D)$ in this expression is much lower than that suggested by M&M's second model, which would be $0.265D$ based only on the corporate tax rate. Further, at these rates the combined tax on income earned through a large corporation is almost the same as that earned directly on interest income, implying a very low value for corporate leverage. This has been a major change in Canada due to the progressive reduction in the corporate tax rate and the significant increase in personal tax rates. In particular, despite the reduction in corporate tax rates, the overall tax burden in Canada has increased significantly since 2015.

While these results might appear useful at first glance, the model itself is based on several assumptions and is subject to several difficulties. First, as we have discussed several times throughout the text, the financial markets, and hence securities prices, are heavily influenced by the investing behaviour of institutional investors such as pension funds, insurance companies, and mutual funds, and most of these are not subject to tax. Second, individual investors face a variety of different marginal tax rates on both ordinary income and dividend income. As a result, the estimates of the tax advantages of using debt are a lower bound (a lower limit on the value). In fact, the dividend tax credit system was originally set up to fully integrate the tax system for small businesses based on their lower tax rate. This is because they have considerable discretion in paying out funds either as dividends or interest or salary, and the government wanted to remove any incentive for them to do one thing rather than another. However, if the system is neutral for a small business, it can't also be neutral for a larger business facing a higher corporate tax rate.

What we can say is that the Canadian tax system marginally favours corporate debt financing, and firms get a corporate tax shield from using debt. When we consider personal taxes, the advantage is not as large as that predicted from the corporate tax shield alone, since the government has set personal tax rates to reduce the double taxation of equity income in Canada. As a result, the tax advantages to using debt are between the value implied using personal taxes of 4.0 percent and that assuming no differential taxes at the individual level of 26.5 percent.

# Review

## Summary

In this chapter, we discuss some of the most important issues in finance. Long before OPM stood for the option pricing model, it stood for "other people's money" and was at the heart of financing activities. We show the three effects of financial leverage: expected ROE tends to increase, the variability of the ROE increases, and the risk of financial distress increases. These principles apply to the use of OPM regardless of who the borrower is: they are simply the effects of financial leverage. However, this text is concerned with corporate decisions, and the Conference Board shows that the major determinants of a firm's capital structure decision are that structure's impact on profits, risk, and cash flows. These impacts can be assessed by profit planning charts or financial break-even (indifference) analysis, as well as by the use of standard ratios calculated by the major rating agencies. However, these tools do not indicate how the use of debt creates value.

The classic M&M arguments assess whether the capital structure decision creates value. Their startling conclusion was that under some simplifying assumptions, issuing debt does not create value. This is because the firm is not doing anything that others can't do just as well—that is, borrow money. In essence, the M&M argument is that firms should stick to doing things where they have a comparative advantage, and it is difficult to see how borrowing money is such an activity, since

we can all do it. However, what this means is that the WACC is independent of the debt ratio, and simple statements like "debt is cheaper than equity" and "using debt lowers the WACC" are fundamentally wrong.

However, once we introduce the fact that interest on debt is tax deductible, whereas dividends to the common shareholders are not, we see that there is a tax shield value to raising debt. At a 26.5-percent tax rate, the fact that interest is tax deductible as a cost of doing business means that, for a profitable firm, 26.5 percent of the value of the debt is effectively being paid by the government in reduced taxes. Hence, there is a transfer of wealth to the private sector from the government as the firm finances with debt. This tax incentive to using debt is offset by the resulting financial distress and bankruptcy costs, as discussed in the static trade-off model.

As its name implies, the static trade-off model does not take into account dynamic effects. The pecking-order theory, on the other hand, does account for these dynamic effects, as firms tend to use internal cash flow first and then debt, and will only raise new common equity as a last resort. The result is that firms depart from the static trade-off optimal debt ratio over time, and then refinance to bring their debt ratio back in line with their target ratio. Therefore, actual capital structures are constantly changing as firms take advantage of market conditions.

# Summary of Learning Objectives

### 21.1 Explain how business and financial risk affect a firm's ROE and EPS, and identify the financial break-even points.

Business risk is the variability in operating income caused by operational risk. Business risk can be thought of as the factors that cause variation in EBIT (e.g., operating leverage). Financial risk is the variability in net income (EPS) caused by leverage. The expected EPS and ROE rise as more debt is added as long as the firm earns more than the interest cost, but they also become more volatile. At low levels of EBIT, ROE/EPS is lower for a leveraged firm than for an all-equity firm, and the firm can run into financial difficulty because of the interest payments. At high levels of EBIT, ROE/EPS is higher for a leveraged firm than for an all-equity firm.

### 21.2 Identify the factors that influence capital structure.

A firm's use of debt is a trade-off between the tax advantages of debt (since the interest payments are tax deductible) and the loss in financial flexibility (since in a recession the firm may not have the ability to make the interest payments). In the case of a recession, the firm may end up bankrupt or in severe distress, or at the very least may find itself making sub-optimal decisions just to survive. In the latter case, the firm may have to defer capital expenditures, curtail dividends, and devote all corporate resources to paying off creditors at a time when better-financed competitors can take advantage of its situation. Firms also take advantage of market opportunities and deviate from their optimal financing mix. For example, firms may not use their full debt capacity if the equity markets are buoyant, and they feel that it is cheaper to issue equity. Conversely, they will use as much debt as possible if they feel their equity is undervalued.

### 21.3 Explain how Modigliani and Miller (M&M) "proved" their irrelevance conclusion that the use of debt does not change the value of the firm.

The key assumptions underlying M&M's irrelevance argument are: perfect markets (no transaction costs and no asymmetric information), no taxes, no costs associated with financial distress, all earnings paid out as dividends, and individuals borrowing and lending at the same rate as companies. M&M showed that under these conditions, without taxes, firm value and WACC are completely unaffected by leverage. The irrelevance argument makes an analogy between firm value and a pie—how the pie is sliced does not affect the size of the pie. Similarly, how the firm structures the right-hand side of its balance sheet does not affect overall firm value. The irrelevance argument shows that investors can use leverage in their own account (homemade leverage) to offset corporate leverage.

### 21.4 Explain how the introduction of corporate taxes affects M&M's irrelevance result.

Corporate taxes change the M&M irrelevance conclusion. With taxes, a firm's value increases (and WACC decreases) with increased leverage due to the tax deductibility of interest. However, whether this remains true once we consider personal taxes is controversial, since individuals can also deduct the interest payments when they borrow money to buy shares.

### 21.5 Describe how financial distress and bankruptcy costs lead to the static trade-off theory of capital structure.

M&M assume costless bankruptcy and financial distress. However, bankruptcy includes costs, such as administrative, legal, and accounting costs as well as the loss of value due to distress sales. Financial distress includes costs too, such as customers buying elsewhere for fear that warranties will not be honoured, suppliers demanding cash payments for inputs they fear may not be paid otherwise, and agency costs. The present value of these expected costs reduces slightly the benefits of the interest tax shield. Under the static trade-off theory, companies use debt to maximize their tax advantages up to the point where these benefits are outweighed by the associated costs of financial distress and bankruptcy.

### 21.6 Explain how information asymmetries and agency problems lead firms to follow a pecking-order approach to financing.

Information asymmetry is a significant problem for new equity issues, since the issuer has much more information about the value of the security than the prospective investor. The asymmetry leaves investors vulnerable to buying overpriced securities. To compensate for this risk, most new issues are underpriced, which makes issuing new equity unattractive for companies. Companies prefer internal equity first, debt second, and new equity last. Agency costs refer to costs incurred when managers do not act in the best interest of shareholders. If managers are self-interested, they prefer little oversight so they can use company resources for their own purposes. The desire to avoid scrutiny leads to a preference for internal cash over debt or equity, since capital markets and lenders place restrictions on management's actions.

### 21.7 Describe other factors that can affect a firm's capital structure in practice.

In practice, firms are restricted in the amount of debt they can issue since they are the "supply" side, but there is also a "demand" side to the debt markets. During the financial crisis of 2008, we saw many well-run businesses shut out of the debt markets and unable to raise money; some even went bankrupt. Consequently, many firms follow a policy of maintaining an investment-grade bond rating or spare debt capacity. This is why the rating agencies are so important. By downgrading a firm's rating to junk or less than BBB, they restrict the firm's financing flexibility. In response, firms only use as much debt as they can issue and stay within the covenant provisions of their bond contract so they will maintain a BBB or higher rating.

## 21.8 Explain how the introduction of personal taxes on investment income affects the corporate tax advantage to using debt.

The Government of Canada has recognized that equity income is double taxed, being taxed at both the corporate and personal level. This is why there is the dividend tax credit system, where the credit is designed to offset the corporate income tax so that the overall taxation of interest and dividend income is similar. If the firm recognizes this, the tax advantage to using debt in Canada is much reduced. Whether it is reduced is complicated by the fact that much of the equity is owned either directly or indirectly by institutions or tax-preferred retirement vehicles so that, in practice, it remains an open question whether personal taxes affect capital structures for widely owned corporations.

## Key Terms

agency costs, p. 21-25
bankruptcy, p. 21-24
business risk, p. 21-3
cash flow-to-debt ratio (CFTD), p. 21-11
corporate debt tax shield, p. 21-21
direct costs of bankruptcy, p. 21-25
EPS indifference point, p. 21-8
financial break-even points, p. 21-4
financial distress, p. 21-25
financial distress costs, p. 21-25

financial leverage, p. 21-2
financial leverage risk premium, p. 21-17
financial risk, p. 21-3
fixed burden coverage ratio, p. 21-11
Franco Modigliani and Merton Miller (M&M), p. 21-14
homemade leverage, p. 21-16
indifference point, p. 21-4
indirect costs of bankruptcy, p. 21-25
invested capital (IC), p. 21-2

M&M equity cost equation, p. 21-17
Merton Miller, p. 21-14
pecking order, p. 21-30
profit planning charts, p. 21-8
return on equity (ROE), p. 21-2
return on invested capital (ROI), p. 21-2
risk value of money, p. 21-5
static trade-off, p. 21-27

## Equations

| Equation | Description | Formula | Page |
|---|---|---|---|
| **[21.1]** | Return on Equity | $ROE = \frac{(EBIT - R_DB)(1-T)}{SE}$ | p. 21-2 |
| **[21.2]** | Return on Investment | $ROI = \frac{EBIT(1-T)}{SE+B}$ | p. 21-2 |
| **[21.3]** | Return on Equity | $ROE = ROI + (ROI - R_D(1-T))\frac{B}{SE}$ | p. 21-2 |
| **[21.4]** | Return on Equity | $ROE = ROI\left(1+\frac{B}{SE}\right) - R_D(1-T)\frac{B}{SE}$ | p. 21-3 |
| **[21.5]** | Earnings per Share | $EPS = \frac{(EBIT - R_DB)(1-T)}{\#}$ | p. 21-8 |
| **[21.6]** | Earnings per Share | $EPS = \frac{-R_DB(1-T)}{\#} + \frac{EBIT(1-T)}{\#}$ | p. 21-8 |
| **[21.7]** | Fixed Burden Coverage Ratio | $Fixed\ burden\ coverage = \frac{EBITDA}{I + (Pref.\ Div. + SF)/(1-T)}$ | p. 21-11 |
| **[21.8]** | Cash Flow-to-Debt Ratio | $CFTD = \frac{EBITDA}{Debt}$ | p. 21-11 |
| **[21.9]** | Altman Z Score | $Z = 1.2X_1 + 1.4X_2 + 3.3X_3 + 0.6X_4 + 0.999X_5$ | p. 21-13 |
| **[21.10]** | Value of Unlevered Firm | $V_U = S_L + D = V_L$ | p. 21-15 |
| **[21.11]** | Equity Value of Levered Firm | $S_L = \frac{(EBIT - k_DD)}{k_e}$ | p. 21-16 |
| **[21.12]** | Cost of Equity | $k_e = \frac{(EBIT - k_DD)}{S_L}$ | p. 21-17 |
| **[21.13]** | Unlevered Value | $V_U = \frac{EBIT}{k_U} = S_L + D = V_L$ | p. 21-17 |
| **[21.14]** | M&M Equity Cost Equation | $k_e = k_U + (k_U - k_D)\frac{D}{S_L}$ | p. 21-17 |

*(continued)*

| Equation | Description | Formula | Page |
|---|---|---|---|
| [21.15] | Cost of Unlevered Equity | $k_U = k_e \dfrac{S}{V} + k_D \dfrac{D}{V}$ | p. 21-18 |
| [21.16] | Value of Unlevered Firm, Assuming Perpetual EBIT | $V_U = \dfrac{EBIT\,(1-T)}{k_U}$ | p. 21-20 |
| [21.17] | Value of Firm with Leverage | $V_L = V_U + DT$ | p. 21-21 |
| [21.18] | M&M Equity Cost | $k_e = k_U + (k_U - k_D)\,(1-T)\dfrac{D}{S_L}$ | p. 21-22 |
| [21.19] | Weighted Average Cost of Capital | $WACC = \dfrac{S}{V}k_e + \dfrac{D}{V}k_D(1-T)$ | p. 21-22 |
| [21.20] | CAPM Version of the Equity Cost Equation | $k_e = R_F + MRP \times \beta_U\left[1 + (1-T)\dfrac{D}{S_L}\right]$ | p. 21-23 |
| [21A.1] | Value of the Firm with Debt and Both Corporate and Personal Income Taxes | $V_L = V_U + D\left[1 - \dfrac{(1-T_C)(1-T_D)}{(1-T_P)}\right]$ | p. 21-34 |

# Questions and Practice Problems

## Multiple Choice Questions

**1. (LO 21.1)** What is the invested capital given the following? Accounts receivable = $50,000; current assets = $200,000; total assets = $700,000; shareholders' equity = $450,000; accounts payable = $10,000; short-term debt = $90,000; and long-term debt = $200,000.

   **a.** $700,000        **c.** $690,000

   **b.** $740,000        **d.** $590,000

**2. (LO 21.1)** Which of the following statements is *true*?

   **a.** Equity dollars are different from debt dollars.

   **b.** ROI is not affected by business risk.

   **c.** Each new dollar invested in a firm earns an incremental and different ROI.

   **d.** ROE is affected by financial risk.

**3. (LO 21.1)** Which of the following statements is *false*?

   **a.** The slope of the financial leverage line is (1 + debt-equity ratio).

   **b.** ROE = ROI if a firm is 100 percent financed by debt.

   **c.** The intercept of the financial leverage line is the debt-equity ratio times the after-tax cost of debt.

   **d.** One of the break-even points is when two financial strategies have the same ROE.

**4. (LO 21.1)** Which of the following statements of rules of financial leverage is *false*?

   **a.** The use of debt normally decreases the expected ROE.

   **b.** The higher the debt-equity ratio, the steeper the financial leverage line.

   **c.** Debt financing increases the risk to common shareholders.

   **d.** Debt financing increases the chances of financial distress.

**5. (LO 21.1)** The EPS-EBIT line

   **a.** is steeper if there are more shares outstanding.

   **b.** has a slope equal to EBIT$(1 - T)/\#$.

   **c.** has an intercept equal to $R_D B(1 - T)/\#$.

   **d.** indicates that if EBIT = 0, EPS $= -R_D B(1 - T)/\#$.

**6. (LO 21.1)** Which of the following is *not* an assumption of M&M's irrelevance theorem?

   **a.** Two firms exist with different levels of debt.

   **b.** There is no tax.

   **c.** Transaction costs are minimal.

   **d.** There is no risk of costly bankruptcy.

**7. (LO 21.2)** Which of the following will result in a *decrease* in the weighted average cost of capital (WACC)?

   **a.** A decrease in $T_C$

   **b.** An increase in the cost of debt

   **c.** An increase in the cost of equity

   **d.** A decrease in the weight of equity

**8. (LO 21.4)** In the M&M irrelevance world, which of the following is *false*?

   **a.** The cost of equity increases as the debt-equity ratio increases.

   **b.** If the expected ROI of a project is greater than the WACC, the share price will go up.

   **c.** The firm's objective is to increase the market value of the share price, not EPS.

   **d.** The WACC always increases as the debt-equity ratio increases.

**9. (LO 21.4)** What is the cost of equity for a levered firm given the following? $k_U = 10$ percent; $k_D = 6$ percent; $T = 25$ percent; and $D/S_L = 0.5$.

   **a.** 11.5 percent        **c.** 12.4 percent

   **b.** 10.6 percent        **d.** 14.8 percent

**10. (LO 21.5)** Any firm that takes on leverage trades off the tax shield on interest payments against the potential costs of financial distress. Which of the following are examples of distress costs:

   **a.** Difficulty retaining existing talent and/or attracting new talent.

   **b.** Increased agency costs.

**c.** Creditors/suppliers tighten access to capital.

**d.** All of the above.

**11. (LO 21.7)** Which of the following firms is the most likely to raise debt in the capital market?

**a.** A profitable firm that has a risky underlying business

**b.** A large and profitable firm with stable earnings and cash from operations

**c.** A less profitable firm that has a non-risky business and cyclical cash flows

**d.** A small firm that has seen its share price decrease in the past

## Practice Problems

### Basic

**12. (LO 21.1)** State the two rules of financial leverage.

**13. (LO 21.3)** In order for the M&M irrelevance theorem to hold, what key assumptions must be met?

**14. (LO 21.5)** Explain how the static trade-off model can be used to find an optimal capital structure.

**15. (LO 21.6)** What is the pecking order according to Myers' argument?

**16. (LO 21.7)** Summarize the main factors you need to consider if the CFO of your firm asks you to evaluate your firm's capital structure.

### Intermediate

**17. (LO 21.1)** Calculate ROE and ROI given the following.

| | | | |
|---|---|---|---|
| Sales | $480,000 | Taxes | $66,000 |
| Cost of goods sold | $100,000 | $R_D$ | 9% |
| Depreciation | $55,000 | SE | $800,000 |
| Selling, general, and | | Book value of | |
| administrative expenses | $60,000 | debt (B) | $500,000 |

**18. (LO 21.1)** Calculate ROE if ROI = 15 percent, $R_D$ = 10 percent, $B$ = $300,000, $SE$ = $500,000, and $T$ = 30 percent. Identify the business risk and financial risk.

**19. (LO 21.1)** What is the intercept and slope of the financial leverage (ROE-ROI) line in practice problem 18? Explain the meaning of the slope.

**20. (LO 21.1)** What is the ROE indifference point of these two financing strategies of Arctic Inc.: Strategy 1: debt-equity ratio = 0.6. Strategy 2: debt-equity ratio = 1.5? Arctic Inc.'s tax rate is 25 percent and its pre-tax cost of debt is 8 percent.

**21. (LO 21.1)** Use two different methods to calculate ROI given the following information for Brandon Corp.: sales = $400,000; cost of goods sold = $120,000; interest cost = $20,000; $T_C$ = 25 percent. The firm's debt ($B$ = $250,000) accounts for 25 percent of the invested capital. After-tax cost of debt is 6 percent.

**22. (LO 21.2)** Calculate the fixed burden coverage and cash flow-to-debt ratio given the following: EBIT = $680,000; depreciation and amortization = $66,000; preferred dividend = $40,000; sinking fund payments = $15,000; tax rate = 30 percent; debt = $220,000. Why do analysts use EBITDA more often than EBIT?

**23. (LO 21.2)** Calculate Altman's Z score for The Home Depot, Inc. in fiscal year 2019 (as at February 3, 2019) and then compare it with Moody's rating chart. Is this company an IG or non-IG? All numbers are in US millions.

| | | | Non-equity | | |
|---|---|---|---|---|---|
| Current assets | CA | $18,529 | book liability | BL | $ 45,881 |
| Retained | | | Market value | | |
| earnings | RE | $46,423 | of equity | MVE | $328,547 |
| Current | | | | | |
| liabilities | CL | $16,716 | Total assets | TA | $ 44,003 |
| EBIT | EBIT | $15,530 | Sales | S | $108,203 |

**24. (LO 21.2)** Explain the elements of Altman's Z score as used in practice problem 23.

**25. (LO 21.2)** Calculate the EPS indifference EBIT* level given the following information. The corporate tax rate is 20 percent. Under a 75-percent D/E ratio, the number of common shares outstanding is 30,000; pre-tax cost of debt is 10 percent; and outstanding debt is $675,000. Under a 30-percent D/E ratio, the number of common shares outstanding is 65,000; pre-tax cost of debt is 6 percent; and outstanding debt is $420,000. Discuss the implication of the indifference EBIT* and indicate which option is better, given an EBIT of $125,000.

**26. (LO 21.3)** In the M&M no-tax world, calculate the value of the levered firm ($V_L$). Cost of unlevered equity ($k_U$) = 16 percent; cost of debt ($k_D$) = 8 percent; debt ($D$) = $500,000; and NI = $480,000. What is the cost of levered equity?

**27. (LO 21.3)** With reference to the M&M irrelevance theorem, calculate the market value of an unlevered firm (U) and an identical risk-levered firm (L). The expected EBIT of U = $2.1 million, which will remain constant indefinitely. The cost of capital is 15 percent. If L has $5-million debt outstanding, what is the market value of the equity?

**28. (LO 21.4)** In the M&M tax world, what is the value of the levered firm ($V_L$) in practice problem 26 if the tax rate is 30 percent? What is the cost of levered equity? What is the market risk premium (MRP) given $\beta_U$ = 1.2 and $R_F$ = 3 percent?

**29. (LO 21.4)** In the M&M tax world, calculate the value of the unlevered firm (U) and the identical risk-levered firm (L). Corporate tax rate = 30 percent; perpetual EBIT for U and L = $3 million; cost of capital of U = 16 percent; L's outstanding debt = $5 million; pre-tax cost of debt = 8 percent. What is the WACC of L?

**30. (LO 21.5)** What important issues does the static trade-off model ignore?

**31. (LO 21.5)** Describe the factors that can affect a firm's capital structure in practice.

**32. (LO 21.5)** State the two possible ways bankruptcy can occur. What is the role of a monitor appointed by the court under the *Companies' Creditors Arrangement Act (CCAA)*? Compare the difference of recognizing firm bankruptcy under the *CCAA* and the *Business Insolvency Act*.

**33. (LO 21.5)** Describe the relationship between the debt ratio and firm value when we consider the existence of bankruptcy costs. How do you view the agency costs when bankruptcy occurs?

**34. (LO 21.7)** Gus Fitzgerald, a local shipping tycoon, is very confused. He has issued shares to finance a positive NPV investment. He expected the share price to rise, as positive NPV projects are supposed to increase shareholder value. However, the stock price fell! Explain how this is possible in an efficient market.

**35. (LO 21.8)** Your cousin has just started his MBA and is confused. He understands that without taxes, capital structure is irrelevant. He also understands that with taxes, firms should use 100-percent debt. However, his professor is saying that with taxes, there are times the investor will prefer an unlevered firm. How is this possible? Assume that there is no bankruptcy cost, information asymmetry, or agency problems. Assume that there is personal tax.

## Challenging

**36. (LO 21.3)** In the M&M no-tax world, an unlevered firm has a cost of equity of 12 percent and expected EBIT of $480,000. The firm decided to issue $3 million of debt at a cost of 8 percent to finance a project, which has an ROI of 18 percent. It has 200,000 shares outstanding.

    **a.** Calculate the value of the firm and price per share before issuing the debt.

    **b.** Calculate the firm's new earnings per share after issuing the debt.

    **c.** Calculate the value of the firm and the value of equity after the firm issues the debt.

    **d.** Calculate the cost of equity after the firm issues the debt.

    **e.** Calculate the new share price of the firm after it issues the debt.

**37. (LO 21.4)** Susan and Celia are twins but have very different attitudes toward debt. Susan believes that firms should have a D/E ratio of 0.2 while Celia believes that the D/E ratio should be 1.1. Both sisters have agreed that Okanagan Produce Inc. (OPI) is an excellent investment. However, the D/E of 0.5 is not quite right. OPI has an EBIT of $750,000 per year and pays interest of $100,000 per year. The cost of debt is 10 percent, and the twins can also borrow and lend at that rate. All cash flows are permanent and there are zero taxes.

    **a.** Determine what the cash flows from OPI would be if the firm had the desired D/E ratio in the table here:

| | OPI with D/E = 0.5 | Desired by Susan OPI with D/E = 0.2 | Desired by Celia OPI with D/E = 1.1 |
|---|---|---|---|
| Value of firm | $3,000,000 | | |
| Value of debt | $1,000,000 | | |
| Value of equity | $2,000,000 | | |
| EBIT | $750,000 | | |
| Interest | $100,000 | | |
| Cash flows to equity | $650,000 | | |

    **b.** Show the sisters how they can invest in OPI and still obtain their desired cash flows through borrowing and lending.

**38. (LO 21.4)** The Saskatchewan Botanicals Company expects a free cash flow of $1.08 million every year forever. Saskatchewan Botanicals currently has no debt, and its cost of equity is 18 percent. The corporate tax rate is 30 percent. The firm can borrow at 8 percent. All cash flows are perpetual. Saskatchewan Botanicals has 1 million shares outstanding.

    **a.** What is the value of Saskatchewan Botanicals with zero debt?

    **b.** If Saskatchewan Botanicals issues $3 million of debt and uses the proceeds to repurchase shares, determine the number of shares outstanding and the price per share after the repurchase.

    **c.** What is Saskatchewan Botanicals' cost of equity after the debt issue?

    **d.** Value Saskatchewan Botanicals' equity using the cost of equity. What is the cash flow to equity?

**39. (LO 21.4)** Athabascan Drilling is currently unlevered and is valued at $10 million. The company is considering including debt in its capital structure and wants to know the likely impact on its value and cost of capital. The current cost of equity is 20 percent. The firm is considering offering $4 million of new debt with an interest rate

of 12 percent. Athabascan Drilling will use the proceeds of the debt issue to repurchase shares. There are currently 1 million shares outstanding, and the marginal tax rate is 30 percent.

    **a.** What is the new value of Athabascan Drilling?

    **b.** What is the new WACC for Athabascan Drilling?

**40. (LO 21.4)** Straightforward Theatre Company has an EBIT of $1.2 million per year. The WACC of the firm is 10 percent and the before-tax cost of debt is 5 percent. The debt is risk free and all cash flows are perpetual. The current D/E ratio is 2/3. The corporate tax rate is 30 percent. The new CEO of Straightforward believes that the D/E ratio is too high and would like to reduce it to 1/3. She will issue shares to repay the debt.

    **a.** What is the impact on the EPS of Straightforward Theatre with this change in the D/E ratio?

    **b.** What is the impact on the cost of equity for Straightforward Theatre?

**41. (LO 21.4)** A friend of yours who works at a private equity firm recently approached you about participating in an acquisition they are considering. The firm, Hush Capital, is considering acquiring Silent Night Corp. ("SNC"), a chain of sleep apnea clinics, and is looking for a couple of high net worth individuals to contribute some capital to the deal. After hearing your friend's initial pitch, you consider investing $250,000 ($C_0$). Hush Capital believes this investment has an IRR of at least 15.2%.

Your accountant, being mindful of the tax deductibility of interest payments, has suggested that you make your investment via a personal holding company. This holding company can arrange debt financing at a pre-tax rate of 7% ($k_D$) and would pay a 20% tax rate ($T_C$) on any profits it generates. Assume the holding company has no constraints on the amount of debt it could assume.

You plan to use a mixture of debt and equity for the $250,000 investment. If you require an 18.5% return on your personal capital ($k_U$), what is the minimum amount of debt that you need to borrow? Remember that for this investment to have a positive NPV, the WACC must be ≤ IRR. Are you surprised by how much debt your holding company would need to take on to make the investment worthwhile?

**42. (LO 21.4)** FF Enterprises ("FFE") has an EBIT of $4 million per year. The WACC of the firm is 10 percent and the before-tax cost of debt is 4%. Assume that all cash flows are perpetual and that the debt is risk-free. FFE currently has a debt-to-equity ratio of 2/3 and faces a 25% tax rate. FFE's CEO feels that the company's capital structure might be causing some of their recent financial hardships and has asked you for help. As a background, calculate the following:

    **a.** What is the value of the firm currently ($V_L$)?

    **b.** Given the firm's debt-to-equity ratio, what is the value of debt and what is value of equity?

    **c.** Using M&M's second model with taxes, calculate how much value was created by adding debt to the firm.

After spending some time researching FFE's industry, you find that most firms in the business have minimal leverage. You recommend to the firm to work toward reducing the debt-to-equity ratio to 1/4. This capital structure closely matches the industry average.

    **d.** What would the value of the new levered firm be with a debt-to-equity ratio of 1/4?

    **e.** How much debt would have to be repaid to achieve this desired capital structure?

# Dividend Policy

**LEARNING OBJECTIVES**

After studying this chapter, you should be able to:

**22.1** Explain what a cash dividend payment is, how dividend payments are made, and why dividend payments are different from interest payments.

**22.2** Describe historical dividend payouts and explain the importance of dividends.

**22.3** Explain how Modigliani and Miller proved that dividend payments are irrelevant, due to the existence of homemade dividends, and therefore have no impact on market value.

**22.4** Explain why dividend payments generally reflect the business risk of the firm.

**22.5** Explain why firms are reluctant to cut their dividends and why they smooth their dividends.

**22.6** Explain why dividends are not a residual, as implied by M&M.

**22.7** Describe what a share repurchase program is and explain how it can substitute for dividend payments.

In Chapter 21, we discussed how a firm decides on its capital structure—that is, the mix between debt and equity securities. The second major topic in corporate financing is how to decide on a payout policy: how much of a firm's earnings to pay out to common shareholders and how to do this. Payout policy is more commonly referred to as dividend policy, but there are several ways to pay out cash to the shareholders apart from paying a cash dividend; one way is to repurchase shares. We have previously discussed how to value common shares by discounting the expected future dividends, so it might seem obvious that dividends matter. Yet it turns out this may not necessarily be true. Having challenged conventional wisdom in terms of capital structure, Modigliani and Miller (M&M) went on to challenge the notion that dividends matter and derived their second irrelevance theorem: given certain assumptions, how much a firm pays out in dividends is completely irrelevant.

In this chapter, you will learn why dividends may be irrelevant and what critical assumptions are needed to reach this conclusion. In the process, you will understand what "realities" M&M assumed away and how they can affect dividend policy. We will show how dividends are paid out, what types of dividends there are, and why a share repurchase is sometimes seen as a substitute for a regular cash dividend.

## 22.1 | Forms of Dividend Payments

**LEARNING OBJECTIVE 22.1**

Explain what a cash dividend payment is, how dividend payments are made, and why dividend payments are different from interest payments.

# The Mechanics of Cash Dividend Payments

As we discussed in connection with common shares in Chapter 7, there is no legal obligation for firms to pay common shareholders a dividend. A dividend has to be declared by the board of directors (BOD), after which it is announced and then becomes a contractual commitment. However, shareholders cannot force the members of the BOD to declare a dividend. Further, there are legal restrictions on whether or not the firm can declare a dividend. As we discussed in connection with bankruptcy in Chapter 21, the BOD cannot declare a dividend if by doing so it causes financial distress and makes the firm unable to fulfill its contractual commitments. If the BOD declares a dividend anyway, the members of the BOD can be held personally liable for damages. The *Canada Business Corporations Act* (*CBCA*) also expressly states that after the dividend payment, the value of the firm's assets has to exceed the total of its liabilities plus stated share capital. This is another way of saying that the dividend cannot be used to strip cash out of a firm in a period of financial distress.

On May 10, 2018, Canadian Pacific (CP) issued a press release announcing that "the board declared a quarterly dividend of $0.65, an increase of 15.5% to the previous dividend of $0.5625 per share. The dividend is payable on July 30, 2018 to holders of record at the close of business on June 29, 2018 and is an 'eligible' dividend for the purposes of the Income Tax Act (Canada) and any similar provincial/territorial legislation."

**declaration date** the date on which the board of directors decides that the firm will pay a dividend

**holder of record** person who officially owns a share or shares on a given date

In this case, May 10, 2018, is the **declaration date**; after this declaration, CP is legally obliged to pay a dividend of $0.65 per share. At this point in the firm's accounting system, the amount of the dividend is transferred from retained earnings to an accrued liability (dividends payable) in the financial statements. The press release also indicates the **holder of record** date, which is June 29, 2018. This means whoever is the owner "of record" of CP shares on June 29, 2018, will be entitled to receive the dividend. The dividend will then be paid on July 30, 2018, to all those owners.

One obvious question is "When can I buy the shares and get the dividend?" Or alternatively, "When can I sell the shares and not receive the dividend?" The answer is that on most exchanges, common share transactions are now settled two business days after the trade. For this reason, most exchanges, as well as most investment dealers for the over-the-counter market, establish an **ex-dividend date** two business days prior to the holder of record date, and they now email clients reminding them of that date. From this date on, the shares trade without the right to receive the dividend (i.e., ex-dividend). So for CP, the ex-dividend date would be June 27, 2018: if you sold the shares on June 26, 2018, you would not receive the dividend, since the shares would be registered to the new owner by June 29, 2018, and you would not be the shareholder of record. However, if you sold them on June 27, 2018, you would receive the dividend, since you would still be the holder of record on June 29, 2018.

**ex-dividend date** date after which shares trade without the right of the purchaser to receive a dividend

Also right up there with the press release is tax information. In this case, CP is telling investors that the dividend is an eligible dividend for Canadian tax purposes. What this means is that residents of Canada are entitled to the dividend tax credit on the grossed-up dividend, resulting in a lower tax rate than would otherwise be payable. As we saw in chapters 19 and 21, and will discuss again later in this chapter, in Canada, dividend income is taxed at a lower rate than interest income to offset the prior payment of corporate income taxes.

We look at Canadian Pacific not just because it is our example company throughout the text, but also because as a major Canadian company it pays a regular cash dividend and has a long history of doing so. **Figure 22.1** shows CP's quarterly dividend per share history since 2002. We can see that in September 2003, CP paid a quarterly dividend per share of $0.128, which was increased in September 2004 to $0.133, and then by a few cents every year until 2008, when it reached $0.248. This level was then maintained for two years—that is, CP did not increase it in 2009 as it waited out the effects of the 2008–9 financial crisis. This behaviour is typical of major corporations; the dividend per share is usually set once a year and maintained for the next four quarters unless something dramatic happens. Of note is that in 2012, CP's dividend reached $0.35, and was then constant for four years before dramatically increasing to $0.50 in 2016 and $0.65, where it was at the end of 2018.[1] This is a compound growth rate of almost 10 percent and is extremely high.

[1]The dividend per share information for CP comes directly from the company's website, https://investor.cpr.ca/stock/default.aspx.

**FIGURE 22.1**  Canadian Pacific Dividend per Share (DPS) History

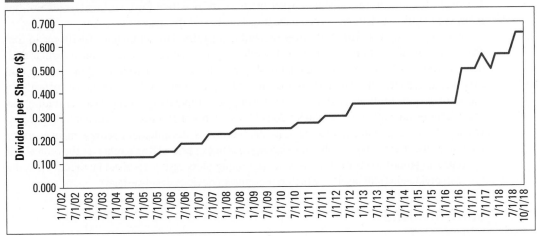

We have been discussing the dividend history of CP's regular dividend. In addition, firms often pay out a **special dividend**. Finance in the News 22.1 is an abridged press release from Kinder Morgan Canada Limited (KML). KML owned the Trans Mountain Pipeline, which moves western Canadian oil to a terminal in Burnaby, BC. The National Energy Board approved an expansion of this pipeline since there is not enough take-away capacity out of Canada, with the result that the price of Canadian oil was selling at a huge discount to similar oil. However, activists including the BC government threw up road block after road block, forcing the Government of Canada to buy the pipeline for $4.5 billion. This left KML with a huge cash pile and little to spend it on. The result was a special dividend with a twist: the amount was so great that it could not be paid out of retained earnings; instead, it consisted of a return of capital. After the distribution the adjusted stock price dropped by two-thirds.

**special dividend**  a dividend over and above a firm's normal dividend that the BOD indicates is not likely to be repeated

## Other Forms of Dividends

### Dividend Reinvestment Plans (DRIPs)

If the investor does not want to receive a dividend, many Canadian firms offer the option of using the cash dividend proceeds to buy new shares by way of a **dividend reinvestment plan (DRIP)**.[2] These shares are then issued by the company without any brokerage fees or transactions costs. Generally, DRIPs will buy as many shares as the cash dividend allows, with

**dividend reinvestment plan (DRIP)**  a plan that allows investors to use dividends to buy new shares

---

**22.1  Finance in the News**  Special Dividend: Return of Capital

The KML board also confirmed today the reduction in stated capital of the restricted voting shares by an aggregate amount equal to $1.45 billion, and declared a return of capital in the amount of $11.40 per restricted voting share. The return of capital is payable out of KML's portion of the net proceeds (after capital gains taxes, repayment of indebtedness and customary purchase price adjustments) from its sale of the Trans Mountain pipeline system and related expansion project completed on August 31, 2018. The return of capital is scheduled to be paid on January 3, 2019 to restricted voting shareholders of record as of the close of business on December 14, 2018. Subject to confirmation from the Toronto Stock Exchange (TSX), KML expects restricted voting

shares to commence trading on a "due bill" basis at the opening on December 13, 2018, and to commence trading "ex-distribution" on January 4, 2019. Concurrently with the payment of the return of capital on the restricted voting shares, Kinder Morgan Canada Limited Partnership will make a distribution payment of $11.40 per Class B limited partnership indirectly to Kinder Morgan, Inc.

**Source:** Excerpted from "Shareholders Vote to Approve Reduction in Stated Capital and Share Consolidation." Kinder Morgan press release, November 29, 2018. Available at https://www.prnewswire.com/news-releases/shareholders-vote-to-approve-reduction-in-stated-capital-and-share-consolidation-300757867.html

---

[2]Canadian investment dealers also reinvest dividends on behalf of investors, just as a company does.

the residual deposited as cash. At one time, firms allowed the shares to be purchased at a 5-percent discount to the closing market price as an incentive for investors to reinvest, but many companies, such as BCE Inc., have now phased out the discount.

DRIPs are popular with both investors and companies. For companies, DRIPs mean that shares are issued continuously at no cost, while they are also seen to be paying a regular dividend. DRIPs foster a more ongoing relationship with investors, who often end up holding **odd lots** of shares, so that their total shareholdings are in odd numbers, like 123 shares, instead of a round lot of some multiple of 100. This has become less important in recent years as trading has become more efficient and is no longer done in round lots of 100 shares each. For long-term investors who are not reliant on income from their portfolios, the automatic reinvestment averages their investment, since they are buying shares at a range of prices. It also removes the problem of accumulating funds to reinvest. However, even though less cash is received by the investor, the full cash dividend is still taxable, which represents an obvious disadvantage.

**odd lots** groups of shares that are purchased in odd-numbered lots instead of in multiples of 100

## Stock Dividends

**stock dividend** a dividend paid in additional shares rather than cash

A cash dividend along with a DRIP is similar to a **stock dividend**. In this case, rather than giving the investor cash and then giving them the choice of giving back the cash for shares, the company simply gives everyone more shares. A stock dividend is defined as any share distribution in which the number of shares issued is less than 25 percent of the outstanding shares. So a company may give a 10-percent stock dividend in which each investor gets 10 percent more shares. In terms of accounting, it is treated like a regular cash dividend, so the value of the shares issued is transferred from retained earnings into the capital stock account. As a result, stock dividends are limited by the amount of retained earnings available.

However, there is one significant difference between a cash dividend plus DRIP and a stock dividend. With the cash dividend plus DRIP, the cash is distributed first, and it is up to the investors to decide whether they want to buy more shares. Regardless of the investors' decisions, the firm has to have the cash to make the distribution. With the stock dividend, on the other hand, firms often do not have the cash and simply issue a stock dividend to give the investor "something." Whether the investors pay attention when they get more pieces of paper is another question, since all that is happening is the value of the common shares is being divided among more shares, which will cause the stock price to fall. In addition, the amount of the stock dividend is fully taxable, despite the fact that no cash is received. Finally, the fact that retained earnings have decreased reduces the firm's ability to pay subsequent cash dividends, which also have to be paid out of retained earnings.

## Stock Splits

**stock split** a greater-than-25-percent increase in the number of shares outstanding

An extreme version of a stock dividend is a **stock split**. In this case, there is a greater-than-25-percent increase in the number of shares outstanding. For example, a 50-percent increase in the shares outstanding would be referred to as a "three for two" stock split rather than a 50-percent stock dividend. This simply means that investors get three shares for every two they already hold, or 50-percent more. There are some accounting advantages to this because the retained earnings account is not altered, but the number of shares outstanding is simply increased (in this example, by 50 percent). In addition, in contrast to the case with stock dividends, investors face no tax implications arising from a stock split, except that the average purchase price for shares will be adjusted downward to reflect the split.

# Reasons for Stock Dividends and Stock Splits

Both stock dividends and stock splits simply divide the value of the common shares among more shares and, all else remaining constant, reduce the price per share. Why firms do this is something of a mystery, since there is no underlying change in the firm. One reason often advanced is that by increasing the number of shares, the price per share falls, which may be useful if there is an optimal trading range for the share price. This allows the shares to be traded in round lots at a reasonable value. For example, 100 shares at a price of $30 each means a $3,000 trade, but if the share price is $300, it means a $30,000 trade, which may be too big for small investors.

This argument had some validity when there were significant costs attached to trading shares, and round lots of 100 shares meant something. However, trading costs are now deregulated, and odd lots of, say, 50 shares can be traded without excessive transactions costs. Further, if the share price gets too high, what constitutes a round lot changes. For example, shares of Berkshire Hathaway (whose largest shareholder and CEO is Warren Buffett, one of the richest people in the world) closed at $303,605 a share on February 25, 2019. That sounds like a lot but was actually slightly down from the all-time high of $335,900 a share. These shares trade in round lots of one share and have no trouble attracting investors. However, to attract other investors without that kind of cash there are B shares (Berk-b) that closed at only $202.36 each.

On the other hand, foreign securities are often repackaged into bundles of shares known as American Depository Receipts (ADRs) to get their U.S. dollar price in New York into a "proper" trading range. UK stocks are routinely repackaged for the U.S. market, for example, because they trade in the United Kingdom in pence and would be regarded as "penny" stocks in New York if they weren't bundled. The Royal Bank of Scotland (RBS) was the largest bank in the world by assets in 2007, and on February 25, 2019, closed in London at the equivalent of US$3.37. To facilitate trading, the Bank of New York issues receipts (ADRs) backed by two London shares of RBS, so they traded at US$6.74 on the same day in New York. There are some advantages to getting the stock price above $5 in North America. However, Lloyds, the biggest bank in the UK with an almost $80-billion market value, does not see it, as their U.S. ADRs closed at US$3.10.

It is difficult to know whether these strategies have any economic significance, but exchanges do have rules for shares trading under $2 that are different from the rules for shares trading above $2. These rules affect the requirements for listing status as well as brokerage commission rates. Securities regulations in North America also often make it difficult to sell, or get margin to buy, stocks when they are priced under $5. In practice, Canadian and U.S. firms with large market capitalizations like to have their stock price trade well above $5. This became a problem for Nortel Networks Corporation when its stock price collapsed from US$122 down to the $2 range and then bounced around the $2 level for over two years. It was an embarrassment for Canada's premier technology company to be regarded as a penny stock. In response, at the company's annual shareholder meeting on June 29, 2006, the shares were consolidated in a "1-for-10" reverse split. Nortel explained that "the transaction was implemented to increase investors' visibility into the Company's profitability on a per share basis, reduce share transaction fees for investors and certain administrative costs for Nortel, and broaden interest to institutional investors and investment funds."[3]

If investors hadn't been paying attention, they might have thought the Nortel stock price boom of the 1990s had happened all over again; once the consolidation took place on December 1, 2006, Nortel's stock price was miraculously above $30 for the first time in six years. However, all that had happened was the number of Nortel shares they owned had been cut by 90 percent. Moreover, it didn't help Nortel much as the stock continued to drift down and is now bankrupt.

To emphasize: with stock splits and stock dividends, the firm's value is being divided by a greater number of shares, which means the share price should fall. (With a reverse split, the price should rise.) If there is an optimal trading range, a stock split or stock dividend might not cause the share price to decrease proportionally with the greater number of shares. This is easy to test. In a pioneering study, Fama et al. examined 940 stock splits in the United States from 1927 to 1959 and found no significant wealth change in the month of each split.[4] However, there were two important results. First, the researchers found that firms that split their stock did so after exceptionally good stock market performance. Consistent with the optimal trading range idea, they split their stock in order to bring the stock price back to a "normal" range. Second, they found that two-thirds of the firms in their sample increased their aggregate dividend payments; for those firms, the shares performed better in the next year. In contrast, for the one-third of the sample that kept their aggregate dividend constant, the share price underperformed the market.

---

[3]The information is available in Nortel's filings with the Ontario Securities Commission at www.sedar.com; this quote was taken from the Nortel website at www.nortel.com/corporate/investor/faq.html, but has since been removed.
[4]Fama, E., Fisher, L., Jensen, M., and Roll, R., "The Adjustment of Stock Prices to New Information." *International Economic Review* 10, no. 1 (February 1969), pp. 1–21.

The Fama study has been repeated several times since, and the basic message is the same. North American firms like to keep their share prices in a "normal" trading range and use stock dividends and stock splits to accomplish this. If the price run-up that causes the split results in higher dividends, the stock price continues to outperform the market; if there is no change, the share price slips back. This leads to the conclusion that it is not the stock split or dividend itself that is causing the price behaviour, but a signal of management expectations about the firm's future performance. Investors in Apple would agree: in June 2014 it split its stock 7 for 1, causing the price to decline from $645.57 on the Friday before the split to about $94 on the Monday after. In a survey of retail investors, CNN found that the majority of respondents took the split to be a positive thing. As of February 25, 2019, Apple closed at US$174.23, so the investors were right.

We will discuss this "signalling role" for dividends in more detail after we consider some data on dividends. However, whereas the stock split is a positive signal when firms maintain their dividend per share, a reverse stock split is rarely a good signal because such firms hardly ever pay a dividend in the face of a falling stock price. For example, the reverse stock split did nothing for Nortel, and its stock price continued to deteriorate because cutting the number of shares outstanding did nothing for its underlying business operations. Nortel then entered bankruptcy protection and is now dead.

---

### Concept Review Questions

1. Define four important dates that arise with respect to dividend payments.
2. Explain the similarities and differences of DRIPs, stock dividends, and stock splits.

---

## 22.2 | Historical Dividend Data

**LEARNING OBJECTIVE 22.2**
Describe historical dividend payouts and explain the importance of dividends.

We can look at dividends from both macro- and micro-level perspectives. The micro-level data deal with individual company dividend payouts, which we will discuss later. At the macro level, dividends are income, and data about them are collected on tax returns. These data end up in the National Income Accounts and are included as part of the gross domestic product (GDP). **Figure 22.2** shows the after-tax profit and dividends paid by corporate Canada divided by GDP, since 1961. We divide by GDP simply to standardize the dollar numbers and because, as income, the figures are also part of gross national income.

The graph shows that after-tax profits generally run at about 6 percent of GDP but are highly variable because they reflect all the uncertainty in the business cycle. During recessions, when GDP weakens, firms lose money because, while their sales decline, their fixed operating and financing costs do not drop proportionally. We can see the impact of the recessions in the early 1980s and early 1990s, when after-tax profits dropped to just below 3 percent and then barely 1 percent of GDP. We can also see the dramatic drop in 2009 as weaker commodity prices hit Canada very hard. The recession in the early 1990s was particularly painful due to the adjustment to the Free Trade Agreement (FTA) with the United States, when corporate Canada had to learn how to compete against larger, more competitive U.S. firms. Finally, we can see the surge in profits earned by corporate Canada in the early to mid-2000s as natural resource prices hit record levels. In recent years, after-tax profits have remained at historically high levels.

In contrast to the volatility in after-tax profits, dividends have remained relatively stable. Note that while dividends roughly tracked after-tax profits from 1961 to 1980, they were

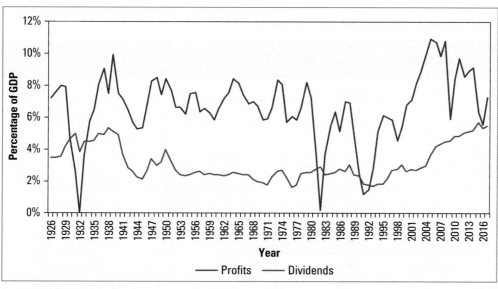

**FIGURE 22.2** Aggregate Dividends and After-Tax Profits as a Percentage of GDP

**Source:** Data from Statistics Canada

not cut during the recession of 1981–82 or during the deeper recession of 1991–93. Further, since 2000 we have seen a large increase in after-tax profits, which until recently has not been matched by an equivalent increase in dividends. However, since 2010 dividends have increased to the level they were at in the 1930s, at 5.5 percent of GDP in 2017.

We can see these effects more clearly when we look at the aggregate dividend payout, which is aggregate dividends divided by aggregate after-tax profits. **Figure 22.3** indicates that the median or typical payout is 42 percent of after-tax profits, but it increased to over 100 percent during the two recessions when profits dropped dramatically but dividends remained relatively stable. More importantly, with weaker commodity prices we have seen the payout trending upward; it was 75 percent in 2017.

Looking at the aggregate dividend and profits data naturally raises the first of two important questions:

1. **Why are dividends smoothed and not matched to profits?**

   Another way of asking this is: why don't firms just pay a constant proportion of profits out as dividends and cut them when their profits and cash flows drop, as they usually do during recessions? We saw, for example, in Figure 22.2 that the aggregate dividend payments across all Canadian firms remained remarkably consistent even through the financial crisis and recession of 2008–9.

   It is also interesting to look at the micro level—that is, the dividends paid by individual companies. **Table 22.1** contains the dividend per share and **dividend yield** (defined in chapters 4 and 7 as the trailing annual dividend per share divided by the

**dividend yield** annual dividend per share divided by the share price

**FIGURE 22.3** Payout Based on Aggregate Profits and Dividends (Median Payout 42 Percent)

**Source:** Data from Statistics Canada

**TABLE 22.1    S&P/TSX 60 Index Dividend Yields, as of February 25, 2019**

| | Ticker | MKT CAP ($Billion) | PE | EPS | DPS | Payout | Yield |
|---|---|---|---|---|---|---|---|
| Royal Bank of Canada | RY | 148 | 12.48 | 8.5 | 3.84 | 45.18% | 3.84% |
| Toronto-Dominion Bank | TD | 141 | 12.99 | 6.01 | 2.61 | 43.43% | 3.50% |
| Enbridge Inc. | ENB | 99 | 33.61 | 1.46 | 2.68 | 183.56% | 5.48% |
| Bank of Nova Scotia | BNS | 89 | 10.68 | 6.82 | 3.28 | 48.09% | 4.48% |
| Canadian National Railways | CNR | 83 | 19.44 | 5.87 | 1.82 | 31.01% | 1.60% |
| Suncor Energy Inc. | SU | 72 | 22.5 | 2.02 | 1.44 | 71.29% | 3.21% |
| Bank of Montreal | BMO | 66 | 12.57 | 8.17 | 3.78 | 46.27% | 3.72% |
| BCE Inc. | BCE | 52 | 18.83 | 3.1 | 3.02 | 97.42% | 5.17% |
| Brookfield Asset Management Inc. | BAM.A | 56 | 17.28 | 3.4 | 0.6 | 17.65% | 1.02% |
| Canadian Imperial Bank of Commerce | CM | 51 | 9.84 | 11.65 | 5.32 | 45.67% | 4.69% |
| TransCanada Corp. | TRP | 54 | 15.03 | 3.92 | 2.76 | 70.41% | 4.66% |
| Canadian Natural Resources Ltd. | CNQ | 45 | 12.24 | 3.07 | 1.28 | 41.69% | 3.44% |
| Nutrien Ltd. | NTR | 46 | 12.78 | 5.72 | 1.63 | 28.50% | 2.25% |
| Manulife Financial Corporation | MFC | 44 | 9.64 | 2.33 | 0.91 | 39.06% | 4.04% |
| Canadian Pacific Railway Ltd. | CP | 38 | 20.16 | 13.61 | 2.51 | 18.44% | 0.09% |
| Alimentation Couche-Tard Inc. | ATD.B | 42 | 23.53 | 3.19 | 0.3 | 9.40% | 0.40% |
| Sun Life Financial Inc. | SLF | 31 | 12.33 | 4.14 | 1.9 | 45.89% | 3.77% |
| TELUS Corp. | T | 29 | 17.88 | 2.68 | 2.1 | 78.36% | 4.55% |
| Waste Connections Inc. | WCN | 29 | 53.26 | 2.07 | 0.58 | 28.02% | 0.53% |
| Rogers Communications Inc. | RCI.B | 38 | 18.27 | 3.99 | 1.925 | 48.25% | 2.64% |
| Barrick Gold Corp. | ABX | 29 | NA | −1.32 | 0.16 | −12.12% | 0.96% |
| CGI Group Inc. | GIB.A | 24 | 21.77 | 4.08 | NA | NA | NA |
| Pembina Pipeline Corporation | PPL | 25 | 21.23 | 2.27 | 2.24 | 98.68% | 4.66% |
| Fortis Inc. | FTS | 20 | 18.2 | 2.59 | 1.73 | 66.80% | 3.66% |
| Magna International Inc. | MG | 23 | 10.53 | 6.61 | 1.36 | 20.57% | 1.93% |
| National Bank of Canada | NA | 21 | 10.46 | 5.94 | 2.44 | 41.08% | 3.90% |
| Restaurant Brands International Inc. | QSR | 39 | 34.06 | 2.42 | 1.8 | 74.38% | 2.18% |
| Franco-Nevada Corp. | FNV | 19 | 86.7 | 1.14 | 0.94 | 82.46% | 0.93% |
| Constellation Software Inc. | CSU | 24 | 62.28 | 17.9 | 4 | 22.35% | 0.36% |
| Teck Resources Ltd. | TECK.B | 17 | 5.63 | 5.34 | 0.2 | 3.75% | 0.65% |
| Agnico Eagle Mines Ltd. | AEM | 13 | NA | −1.4 | 0.44 | −31.43% | 0.77% |
| Thomson Reuters Corporation | TRI | 36 | 40.75 | 1.74 | 1.52 | 87.36% | 2.12% |
| Open Text Corp. | OTEX | 16 | 52.04 | 0.97 | 0.59 | 60.82% | 1.17% |
| Wheaton Precious Metals Corp. | WPM | 13 | 45.31 | 0.64 | 0.36 | 56.25% | 0.01% |
| Goldcorp Inc. | G | 11 | NA | −4.77 | 0.08 | −1.68% | 0.56% |
| Metro Inc. | MRU | 13 | 19.63 | 2.52 | 0.74 | 29.37% | 1.49% |
| Loblaw Companies Ltd. | L | 34 | 32.92 | 1.99 | 1.15 | 57.79% | 1.77% |
| Shaw Communications Inc. | SJR.B | 14 | 110.86 | 0.24 | 1.18 | 491.67% | 4.37% |

*(continued)*

**TABLE 22.1**    S&P/TSX 60 Index Dividend Yields, as of February 25, 2019 (*continued*)

| | Ticker | MKT CAP ($Billion) | PE | EPS | DPS | Payout | Yield |
|---|---|---|---|---|---|---|---|
| Emera Inc. | EMA | 11 | 15.26 | 3.04 | 2.28 | 75.00% | 4.91% |
| Cenovus Energy Inc. | CVE | 15 | NA | −2.17 | 0.2 | −9.22% | 1.65% |
| Dollarama Inc. | DOL | 11 | 22.42 | 1.62 | 0.16 | 9.88% | 0.44% |
| Power Corporation of Canada | POW | 13 | 10.31 | 2.71 | 1.48 | 54.61% | 5.32% |
| Saputo Inc. | SAP | 17 | 22.08 | 1.94 | 0.65 | 33.51% | 1.53% |
| Canadian Tire Corporation Ltd. | CTC.A | 9 | 13.76 | 10.64 | 3.74 | 35.15% | 2.56% |
| Gildan Activewear Inc. | GIL | 10 | 28.38 | 1.66 | 0.47 | 28.31% | 1.00% |
| Imperial Oil Ltd. | IMO | 28 | 12.57 | 2.86 | 0.73 | 25.52% | 2.05% |
| SNC-Lavalin Group Inc. | SNC | 7 | NA | −7.5 | 0.96 | −12.80% | 2.60% |
| Bausch Health Companies Inc. | BHC | 11 | NA | −11.81 | NA | NA | NA |
| Inter Pipeline Ltd. | IPL | 9 | 13.87 | 1.53 | 1.68 | 109.80% | 5.69% |
| First Quantum Minerals Ltd. | FM | 11 | 24.16 | 0.64 | 0.01 | 1.56% | 0.04% |
| Encana Corp. | ECA | 13 | NA | −0.2 | 0.06 | −30.00% | 0.65% |
| CCL Industries Inc. | CCL.B | 10 | 21 | 2.61 | 0.52 | 19.92% | 0.94% |
| George Weston Ltd. | WN | 14 | 23.33 | 3.99 | 1.89 | 47.37% | 2.05% |
| Cameco Corp. | CCO | 6 | 37.21 | 0.42 | 0.08 | 19.05% | 0.51% |
| Kinross Gold Corp. | K | 6 | NA | −0.02 | NA | NA | NA |
| BlackBerry Ltd. | BB | 6 | NA | −0.11 | NA | NA | NA |
| Bombardier Inc. | BBD.B | 6 | 29.22 | 0.09 | 0.03 | 33.33% | 1.23% |
| Husky Energy Inc. | HSE | 15 | 10.58 | 1.4 | 0.4 | 28.57% | 2.71% |
| ARC Resources Ltd. | ARX | 4 | 17.23 | 0.6 | 0.6 | 100.00% | 5.82% |
| Crescent Point Energy Corp. | CPG | 2 | NA | −0.52 | 0.36 | −69.23% | 8.53% |

**Sources:** Data from TSX eReview, December 2018, and Yahoo Finance Canada, February 27, 2019

share price) for the firms in the S&P/TSX 60 Index as of February 25, 2019. This is the cream of corporate Canada and the firms that most large institutional investors view as core holdings. However, this is a large range, with a total market value (MKT CAP) for Canada's most valuable firm, the Royal Bank of Canada, of $148 billion, to $2 billion for Crescent Point Energy, an oil and gas exploration firm.

Looking at the dividend yields, we see that they range from a low of zero for several firms, including BlackBerry (BB) and several resource-based firms like Kinross Gold, to a high of 8.53 percent for Crescent Point Energy. However, these yields are based on the dividends paid over the previous year; that is what trailing means. These are not necessarily what is expected. Crescent Point, in particular, cut its dividend to a nominal 1 cent due to poor profits. We also see most of the Canadian banks with dividend yields around 4 percent even though they only pay out less than 50 percent of their earnings as dividends. Further, even some serious loss-making firms, like Agnico Eagle Mines, continue to pay a dividend, while other profitable firms, like CGI Group, do not pay out a dividend even though they are profitable. This raises the other important question:

2. **Why is there such a substantial difference in dividend yields (and payouts) across major Canadian companies? Why do some firms have very high dividends and some very low or non-existent dividends?**

To answer this question, we consider the second major contribution of Modigliani and Miller and consider what value is created by paying a dividend.

**Concept Review Questions**

1. What obvious question arises when we examine historical patterns in aggregate dividend payouts?

2. What obvious question arises when we examine cross-sectional patterns in the dividend payouts of individual companies?

---

## 22.3 | Modigliani and Miller's Dividend Irrelevance Theorem

**LEARNING OBJECTIVE 22.3**

Explain how Modigliani and Miller proved that dividend payments are irrelevant, due to the existence of homemade dividends, and therefore have no impact on market value.

### M&M, Dividends, and Firm Value

After "proving" in 1958 that, under certain circumstances, a firm's capital structure did not matter, Franco Modigliani and Merton Miller (M&M) went on in 1961 to "prove" that dividend policy did not matter either,[5] thereby showing that two of the major activities of corporate finance were irrelevant. Needless to say, this position was highly controversial then and remains so today. However, the importance of the M&M argument is not that it is actually correct, but that it points the way to discovering where value can be created with dividend policy and why.

It might seem obvious that dividends matter; after all, one of the most basic equations used to value common shares is Equation 22.1.

$$P_0 = \frac{D_1 + P_1}{(1 + k_e)}$$ [22.1]

The price of a share today ($P_0$) is the present (discounted) value of next period's expected dividend per share ($D_1$) and price per share ($P_1$). The dividend per share is part of the valuation equation, so dividends must be important. However, M&M showed that all is not what it seems.

**equity market capitalization ($V_0$)** total common equity market value

To understand the M&M proof, first multiply the price per share by the current number of shares outstanding ($m$). This simply converts the price-per-share equation into an equation that values the total amount of common equity, or the **equity market capitalization ($V_0$)**.

$$mP_0 = V_0 = \frac{m(D_1 + P_1)}{(1 + k_e)}$$ [22.2]

As they did for their capital structure argument, M&M then made some very important assumptions:

1. There are no taxes.

2. Markets are perfect.

3. All firms maximize value.

4. There is no debt.

---

[5]Miller, M., and Modigliani, F., "Dividend Policy, Growth, and the Valuation of Shares." *Journal of Business* 34, no. 4 (October 1961), pp. 411–33.

The last assumption is there simply because they proved in 1958 that debt is irrelevant, so in this paper they could concentrate on dividend policy; it also helps simplify their use of the sources and uses of funds constraint. Remember from accounting that the cash flow statement, like all financial statements, always balances. Therefore, without any debt, the sources and uses of funds identity (i.e., sources = uses) can be expressed as:

$$X_1 + nP_1 = I_1 + mD_1 \qquad [22.3]$$

Here, $X$ represents cash flow from operations and $I$ represents investment, so $X - I$ is what we termed **free cash flow** in Chapter 3. This free cash flow can either be paid out as a dividend to the current shareholders ($mD_1$), or new funds can be raised by selling new shares ($n$) to investors next period at the price $P_1$.

**free cash flow** the result of subtracting the capital expenditures from the cash flow from operations

It is important to realize that Equation 22.3 is not an assumption; it is just a constraint indicating that the sources and uses of funds have to balance given the absence of debt financing. Consequently, we can solve for the dividends paid out ($mD_1$) to get:

$$mD_1 = X_1 + nP_1 - I_1$$

Notice that this relationship implies that if the firm pays out dividends that exceed its free cash ($X - I$), it must issue new common shares to pay for these dividends. When we substitute this term into the valuation equation (Equation 22.2) for $mD_1$, we get the following:

$$V_0 = \frac{X_1 - I_1 + [(m + n)P_1 = V_1]}{(1 + k)} \qquad [22.4]$$

So the value of the firm is simply the value of next period's free cash flow ($X_1 - I_1$) plus next period's equity market value ($V_1$, which equals ($m + n$) $P_1$). By repeatedly substituting this to find the value of the firm at all future points in time, we get the fundamental equity valuation formula, Equation 22.5. This is the basic equation we use to determine the total market value of the firm's equity as opposed to the price per share. It says that firm value is determined as the present value of the free cash flows to the equity holders.

$$V_0 = \sum_{t=1}^{\infty} \frac{X_t - I_t}{(1 + k)^t} \qquad [22.5]$$

It is important to realize that Equation 22.1 says that in order to value a share of common stock, we simply discount all the future expected dividends, since this is the cash received by the investor. Yet Equation 22.5 says that to value the aggregate of all the shares (i.e., the total market value of equity), we value the free cash flows to all the equity holders. Obviously these two approaches must give exactly the same value, which implies that the dividend is equal to the free cash flow each period. In this view, the dividend is the residual that remains after the firm has taken care of all its investment requirements, so we call this the **residual theory of dividends**.

**residual theory of dividends** the theory that the dividends paid out should be the residual cash flow that remains after the firm has taken care of all its investment requirements

So what does all this mean? To answer, let's return to the investment opportunities schedule (IOS) for CP for 2018, previously depicted in Chapter 20 and reproduced in **Figure 22.4**.

In this figure, we see CP's 2018 cash flow of $2,712 million and investment of $1,458 million. In the case of CP we have to use an approximation

$$X - I = \$1,254 \text{ million}$$

As we discussed in Chapter 20, CP has been making significant operational improvements that have generated significant surplus cash. If it could generate this level of surplus cash indefinitely, we would regard it as a **cash cow**. Or we could say that the residual theory of dividends suggests that CP should pay a higher dividend, but it does not. In Chapter 19, we showed that CP's dividend yield at the 2018 year end was only 1.07 percent. The dividend yield fluctuates with market prices and so is constantly changing, but CP's dividend yield is not very high. So where does the rest of its excess cash go? On October 17, 2018, CP announced that it would be repurchasing up to 5,680,000 common shares.

**cash cow** a firm with a high present value of existing opportunities but a low present value of growth opportunities

**FIGURE 22.4** CP's Internal Funds, Investment, and Dividends

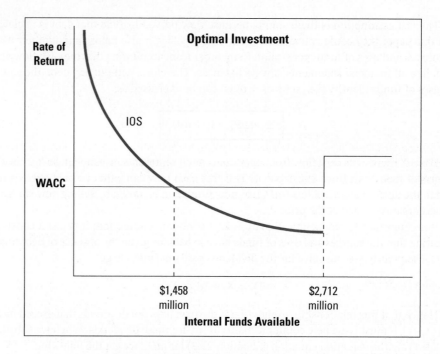

At the year-end share price of $242.24, that amounted to a possible expenditure of over $1.375 billion, dwarfing the annual dividend payment of about $230 million.

As M&M's theory showed, paying cash dividends or repurchasing common shares accomplishes the same purpose. Both actions return cash to the shareholders. If these numbers were reversed CP would be classified as a growth stock. In this case, the residual theory of dividends would indicate that it should not pay out a dividend since it would have to raise equity through new share issues to finance its investment.

The key insight from the M&M argument is that the firm always accepts the optimal amount of investment, so investment is independent of the firm's dividend policy. The main assumptions that generate this conclusion are that firms maximize value and markets are perfect. This means firms can always raise the necessary capital to undertake all positive net present value (NPV) projects, so they are not financially constrained. If firms are financially constrained, the idea that dividend policy is irrelevant falls apart, as we will show shortly.

With investment fixed and cash flow from operations determined by the firm's real operations, it is clear from the sources and uses of funds constraint, Equation 22.3, that new share issues and dividend payments are the opposite of each other. If all else is constant, an increase in cash dividends paid means the firm has to raise more cash by selling new shares.

---

**EXAMPLE 22.1** | Dividends and Free Cash Flow

A firm has cash flow from operations of $100 million and needs $90 million for investment purposes, leaving $10 million of free cash flow. Assume the firm has 10 million shares outstanding and its shares are presently trading at $20 per share. How many new shares must be issued if it plans to pay out a dividend per share of $2?

**Solution**

$$nP_1 = mD_1 - (X_1 - I_1) = (10)(\$2) - (\$100 - \$90) = \$10 \text{ million}$$

New proceeds required = $10 million.

Since its share price is $20, with 10 million shares outstanding, we can say that the value of the firm's equity is $20 × 10 million = $200 million.

When it issues new shares, this $200 million must be divided among the new shareholders ($n$) as well as the existing shareholders ($m$), so the new share price at time 1 will be:

$$P_1 = \frac{V}{m+n} = \frac{\$200}{10+n}$$

This reduces to: $10P_1 + nP_1 = \$200$

Since we know that $nP_1 = \$10$ million, we know that

$$10P_1 = \$200 - \$10 = \$190$$

So the new $P_1 = \$190/10 = \$19$

This implies the firm will need to issue the following number ($n$) of new shares:

$$n = 10 \text{ million}/\$19 = 526{,}316 \text{ shares}$$

Notice that the firm value remains the same, at \$200 million, in M&M's world, since it is simply the present value of the firm's future free cash flows to infinity. There are simply more shares outstanding (10,526,316), which are each worth \$19.

---

**EXAMPLE 22.2** | Residual Dividend Policy

Consider the firm from Example 22.1.

  a. How much would it pay out in dividends per share if it was all equity financed and the firm followed a strict residual dividend policy?

  b. Redo part a, but assume the firm plans to finance its future investments, including this year's total investment outlay of \$90 million, using 30-percent debt financing.

**Solution**

  a. Dividends per share = Free cash flow per share = \$10 million/10 million shares = \$1

  b. In this case, only \$63 million of the required investment is from operations (i.e., 70 percent of the \$90 million in total investments), since the other \$27 million (i.e., 30 percent of \$90 million) will be financed using debt. Therefore:

Dividends per share = Free cash flow per share = (\$100 million − \$63 million)/10 million = \$3.70

---

# M&M's Homemade Dividend Argument

M&M's argument is often illustrated using the concept of **homemade dividends**. This refers to the ability of individuals to create (or eliminate) dividends through their own behaviour in a perfect M&M world, with no taxes, transactions costs, or other market imperfections. In essence, according to M&M's assumptions, investors will buy shares regardless of the firm's underlying dividend policy, since they can create any dividend policy they want, as illustrated by Example 22.3.

**homemade dividends**
dividends created or eliminated by investors through their own behaviour

---

**EXAMPLE 22.3** | Homemade Dividends in an M&M World

Consider a no-growth company (NG) whose shares are presently trading at \$10 per share. The company has just announced that it plans to pay out all of its free cash flow of \$1 per share in the form of a \$1 dividend per share at the end of the year, and these dividends will be maintained indefinitely.

  a. Estimate the expected value of the company's shares after one year ($P_1$), assuming investors require a 10-percent return on these shares.

  b. Investor A holds 1,000 NG shares and does not want to receive any dividends next year, but then wishes to sell all her shares and collect all her investment income from NG. Explain what she can do and show how much she will receive after two years.

  c. Investor B also holds 1,000 NG shares but wishes to receive \$6,000 in income from his shares at the end of this year and collect his remaining investment income at the end of the second year, at which time he wishes to sell all his shares. Explain what he can do and show how much he will receive after two years.

  d. Explain why the amount of income received by the two investors differs.

**Solution**

**a.** $P_1 = \$1/0.1 = \$10$ per share

**b.** Investor A can take the $1,000 in dividends she receives (i.e., $1 × 1,000 shares) and buy new shares in NG at the end of the year. Assuming the shares are trading at $10 per share, as calculated in part a, the investor can purchase an additional 100 shares (i.e., $1,000/$10 per share) with the $1,000 in dividends she receives. At the end of two years, assuming the $1 free cash flow per share and the 10-percent discount rate remain constant, the shares will still be trading at $10 per share. Therefore, she will receive $11,000 for selling her 1,100 shares at $10 a piece, plus $1,100 in dividends, for a total of $12,100.

**c.** Investor B can take the $1,000 in dividends he receives and sell an additional 500 shares at $10 each to generate an additional $5,000 in investment income, for a total of $6,000. At the end of two years, assuming the $1 free cash flow per share and the 10-percent discount rate remain constant, the shares will still be trading at $10 per share. Therefore, he will receive $5,000 for selling his remaining 500 shares, plus $500 in dividends (i.e., 500 shares × $1 per share), for a total of $5,500.

**d.** Investor A receives a total of $12,100 at the end of year 2. Notice that investor B receives $6,000 at the end of year 1 and $5,500 at the end of year 2, for a total of only $11,500. The difference of $600 represents the forgone return of 10 percent on the $6,000 that investor B withdraws at the end of year 1, which investor A leaves invested in firm NG. Recall that our share price calculations are based on the assumption that the firm's shares provide investors with a 10-percent return.

Example 22.3 shows how investors can buy or sell shares in an underlying company to create their own cash flow patterns or simulated dividend streams. In fact, when you answered part b in the example, you were simply using a homemade dividend reinvestment plan or DRIP, which we discussed earlier. Investors who don't like dividends can sign up for a DRIP and undo the effects of a firm's dividend policy. Conversely, in answering part c, you saw an investor creating a cash flow from the firm simply by selling some or all of his shares.

What the example illustrates is that, given the M&M assumptions, the investor is indifferent to a firm's dividend policy. However, in the real world there are several practicalities to consider, such as transactions costs, risk, taxes, and other market imperfections. We will elaborate on these matters in the following sections.

### Concept Review Questions

1. Explain how, and under what assumptions, M&M show that dividends are irrelevant.
2. Explain the relationship between M&M's argument and the use of a residual dividend policy.
3. Briefly describe the notion of homemade dividends as it relates to M&M's irrelevancy argument.

## 22.4 The "Bird in the Hand" Argument

### LEARNING OBJECTIVE 22.4
Explain why dividend payments generally reflect the business risk of the firm.

M&M's dividend irrelevance proposition was as controversial in 1961 as it remains today, since it seems to conflict with the intuition that firms paying cash dividends are less risky than ones where the investors' return comes by way of a capital gain. It would seem to follow that firms that do not pay a cash dividend are riskier because this causes the cost of equity capital to increase and the stock price to fall. This idea is called the **"bird in the hand" argument** on the basis that a "bird in the hand" (cash dividend) is worth more than "two in the bush" (twice as much in capital gains).

**"bird in the hand" argument**
the notion that a cash dividend is worth more than an equivalent capital gain

In thinking through this argument, remember that in Chapter 20, we used the version of the two-stage growth model that is expressed in Equation 22.6.

$$P_0 = \frac{\text{ROE}_1 \times \text{BVPS}}{k_e} + \frac{\text{Inv}}{(1 + k_e)}\left(\frac{\text{ROE}_2 - k_e}{k_e}\right) \qquad [22.6]$$

This model drove a discussion about the value of a firm being split between the present value of existing opportunities (PVEO), as measured by the first term in Equation 22.6, and the present value of growth opportunities (PVGO), as measured by the second term. We then used this to discuss four stereotypes of firms: the cash cow, the star, the dog, and the turnaround. These different stereotypes are usually perceived to have varying risk, since PVEO is generally regarded as less risky than PVGO.

Think for a moment about where PVGO comes from: it requires that the firm earn a return on equity (ROE) that exceeds its cost of equity capital ($k_e$), so in the second term of Equation 22.6 we are adding the present value of all these future net present values. However, from basic economics we know that there will be new entrants to a market when firms earn more than a normal level of profits, where "normal" is defined as a fair rate of return on the funds invested or the cost of equity capital. As a result, if PVGO is high, we can expect other firms to try to enter the market and compete for these excess profits. This makes the PVGO part of the firm's market value extremely vulnerable, as future competition could see it diminish, if not disappear completely.

Of course, PVEO can also be vulnerable to market entry and competition if it, too, is partly derived from excess profits. However, for PVEO there is more information about potential entry and new competition for existing operations than there is for PVGO, which may stretch far into the future. Further, there is more information about the stability of PVEO, since the firm has an earnings history and has actually generated the PVEO. For these basic reasons, capital gains, or expected increases in the share price, are generally regarded as riskier than current dividends. This is the basic idea that the "bird in the hand" argument captures: that investors value current dividends more highly than future capital gains. The implication is that investors perceive non-dividend-paying firms to be riskier, and they apply a higher discount rate to value them, causing share prices to fall. The "answer" then seems to be for these firms to pay a dividend.

The "dividends-are-better" theory is normally associated with Myron Gordon, developer of the Gordon growth model.[6] It captures the notion that dividends are more stable than capital gains and, as a result, are more highly valued. It is commonly accepted that cash cows such as utilities and banks are less risky than high-tech firms such as Blackberry. Further, if you look at the dividend yields listed in Table 22.1 and ignore the income trusts, you will see that low-risk utilities and banks do indeed have high dividend yields, while cyclical resource stocks and high-risk tech firms rarely pay a dividend—and when they do, it tends to be very low. So, intuitively, the dividends-are-better argument seems to make sense. In addition, in practice, the share prices of high-dividend-paying stocks have tended to perform as well as, or better than, stocks with low dividend payouts, which indicates that investors need not sacrifice growth for income.

**Figure 22.5** illustrates the difference between the M&M and Gordon arguments. The M&M argument is that dividends and capital gains are perfect substitutes. If investors want a 10-percent rate of return, they can get this as a 10-percent dividend yield ($D_1/P_0$), or they can cut the dividend and reinvest more, which they receive as a capital gain ($(P_1 - P_0)/P_0$). The slope of the line as they cut the dividend is then −1, indicating that the investors' required rate of return or discount rate is constant. Gordon, on the other hand, argues that if investors want a 10-percent return from a 10-percent dividend yield, they will want an ever higher required rate of return as the dividend payout is cut, due to the increase in risk. As a result, they might

---

[6]Gordon, M., "Optimal Investment and Financing Policy." *Journal of Finance* 18, no. 2 (May 1963), pp. 264–72.

**FIGURE 22.5** M&M versus Gordon's "Bird in the Hand" Argument

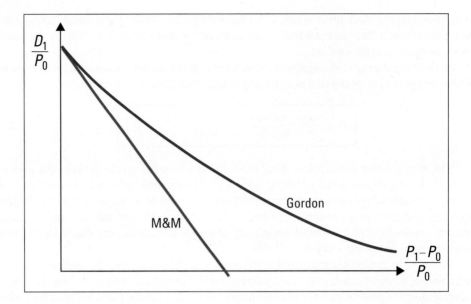

want a 15-percent required return if there is no dividend, because all of the return is coming from risky capital gains.

So how do we balance the obvious intuition of the "bird in the hand" argument against the formal "proof" offered by M&M? The easiest way is to work through an example. Suppose that a firm has a market value of $50 million and has $5 million in cash flow that equals its required investment level. Using Equation 22.4, we can see that this firm has zero residual cash and generally should not pay a cash dividend according to the residual theory of dividends. Further, if the discount rate is 10 percent, the market value of its equity is $45.45 million, as shown here.

$$\$45.45 = \frac{\$50 + \$5 - \$5}{(1.1)}$$

If we further assume there are 1 million shares currently outstanding ($m$), the price per share is $45.45. In this case, the investor expects to get a zero dividend and a 10-percent capital gain ($4.55/$45.45).

Now suppose the firm pays out the $5 million in a $5 per share cash dividend. In this case, M&M assume that the firm still has to find $5 million to pay for the required level of investment, since value creation requires that all positive NPV projects are undertaken.

As a result, the firm will have to issue more shares next period at the then-market price ($P_1$). We can designate these new shares as $n$, so the price per share is

$$P_0 = \frac{\$5m + \dfrac{\$50m}{1+n}}{(1.1)}$$

The price today is the dividend of $5 per share that will be paid to the existing owners. They will also have the new share price, which is the $50 million in market value divided by the current shares outstanding of 1 million, plus the new shares that will have to be issued ($n$). Note that the assumption of value creation means that all positive NPV projects are undertaken and the total market value next period of $50 million is the same regardless of the firm's dividend policy.

To find the number of shares that have to be issued, we can solve the following equation.

$$n\left[P_1 = \frac{\$50}{1+n}\right] = \$5 \text{ million}$$

This means that the number of shares ($n$) issued, multiplied by the price next period ($P_1$), is equal to the proceeds of the share issue, which is $5 million. Solving, we find that the firm has to issue 111,111 shares at $45 a share. The price per share is then

$$P_0 = \frac{\$5 + \$50/1.1111}{1.1} = \$45.45$$

Notice that this is the same as in the no-cash-dividend case.

In this case, the shareholders will get an expected dividend yield of 11 percent ($5/$45.45), but due to the extra shares being issued, their ownership in the firm will be diluted and they will actually suffer a capital loss of 1 percent as the share price declines from $45.45 to $45. Therefore, they obtain a 10-percent return. By varying the cash dividend amount, we can come up with different numbers for the expected dividend yield and capital gain (loss), but under the M&M assumptions, the investors' return stays the same.

Now that we see that the M&M argument "works," we can also see how to reconcile it with Gordon's argument. First, note that the capital gain in our M&M example is not far off in the future as it is with risky high-tech stocks—it is immediate, when the dividend is paid. As soon as the $5 million in cash is paid out as a dividend, the firm has to issue 111,111 shares at $45 per share to fund its investment. As a result, the capital gain—or in this case, loss—is like a stock split. Second, with the M&M assumptions, the underlying operations of the firm are unaffected by the dividend—this is the significance of the constant value of $50 million next period. What it means is that by changing from a firm with a zero-percent dividend yield to a firm with an 11-percent dividend yield, as in our example, the firm is not, going back to Table 22.1, changing itself from a growth stock like BlackBerry or Gildan Activewear or Constellation Software into a Royal Bank. The firm stays exactly the same. What is important to recognize is that these firms are *riskier than the Royal Bank due to their business risk, not because of its lack of a dividend*. In other words, the dividend policy of the firm should follow the business risk of the firm, and changing that dividend policy cannot change the risk of the firm.

Gordon is right in arguing that the dividend yield does indicate the risk of the firm, and firms that pay large amounts of dividends tend to be less risky than non-dividend-paying firms. However, M&M are also right, because changing the dividend cannot change the underlying risk of the firm; this comes from its underlying operations. In this sense, the dividend should reflect the firm's operations through the residual value of dividends, and the firm should not be able to change these underlying operational characteristics by merely changing the dividend. This reconciliation also leads to some implications as to why the stock market reacts to changes in a firm's dividend policy.

### Concept Review Questions

1. Explain the "bird in the hand" argument about dividends.
2. Reconcile the predictions of M&M with Gordon's arguments about dividend policy.

## 22.5 | Dividend Policy in Practice

### LEARNING OBJECTIVE 22.5
Explain why firms are reluctant to cut their dividends and why they smooth their dividends.

Accepting the M&M argument as a valid description of the real world leads to some problems. One is that if dividend policy doesn't matter, why is it we see such stability in dividend policy? The M&M proof indicates that the firm is valued based on the residual or free cash flows, so paying a dividend just means more share issues and lower capital gains. If this is true, the firm can cut the dividend if it is short of cash and increase it when it has surplus cash. In this way, the dividend is a residual and as volatile as the firm's free cash flow. However, we saw in

Figure 22.2 that aggregate dividends are much more stable than earnings (and cash flow), so firms smooth their dividends. But there is nothing in M&M's proof that indicates there is any value to dividend smoothing. Further, M&M's concern was with dividend policy in general, and they indicate no difference between a regular and a special dividend, or a cash dividend versus a share repurchase. So why is it that firms declare both regular and special dividends or buy back shares as well as pay a dividend?

The standard explanation for this observed dividend behaviour suggests that firms smooth their dividends over time as they move toward a new target level of dividends. The original work in this area was done by John Lintner, who suggested using the partial adjustment model specified in Equation 22.7.[7]

$$\Delta D_t = \beta(D^*_t - D_{t-1})$$  [22.7]

This equation simply says that the change in the dividend at time $t$ ($\Delta D_t$) is equal to an adjustment factor ($\beta$) times the difference between the target dividend for the period ($D^*_t$) and the dividend for the prior period ($D_{t-1}$). If the firm adjusts immediately to the target dividend, then the adjustment coefficient ($\beta$) is equal to 1, and the cash dividend is always optimal. If it doesn't adjust at all, then the dividend is constant and $\beta$ is equal to zero.

Lintner took the target dividend ($D^*_t$) to be a function of the firm's optimal payout rate of the firm's underlying earnings ($E_t$), which leads to the model in Equation 22.8.

$$D_t = a + (1 - b)D_{t-1} + cE_1$$  [22.8]

This equation suggests that dividends are a function of the previous period's dividends and current earnings. Lintner estimated the coefficient on lagged dividends to be 0.7, indicating an adjustment speed ($b$) coefficient of 0.3. He also estimated the coefficient on current earnings ($c$) to be 0.15. When the adjustment to the target dividend is complete, Lintner's estimates imply an optimal payout ratio for U.S. companies of 50 percent ($b/c$). This is consistent with the aggregate evidence that U.S. companies do pay out about 50 percent of their earnings as dividends, which is slightly higher than the median payout in Canada of about 40 percent. Lintner's results have been replicated many times, and their importance is twofold. First, the speed of adjustment is only 30 percent, which means that, during each period, the average firm moves only 30 percent of the way toward its target dividend. Alternatively, this means firms are reluctant to fully adjust, so their dividends are "sticky." Second, the coefficient on earnings is only 15 percent, so firms do not follow a policy of paying out a constant proportion of earnings as dividends.

The fact that actual dividend policy does not accord with the irrelevance theorem of M&M means, obviously (and not surprisingly), that some of their assumptions are not realistic. The critical suspect assumptions are that markets are perfect and there are no taxes. Finance in the News 22.2 describes the Bank of Montreal's very long history (188 years as of 2017) of paying a dividend. Consistent with the data in Table 22.1, the Canadian banks target a dividend payout of just under 50 percent and have some of the highest dividend yields in the TSX 60. In the next section, we will discuss why a bank would pay out so much.

## Concept Review Question

1. What does real-world evidence imply about how firms manage their dividend payments?

---

[7]Lintner, J., "Distribution of Incomes of Corporations among Dividends, Retained Earnings and Taxes." *American Economic Review* 46, no. 2 (1956), pp. 97–113.

## 22.6   Relaxing the M&M Assumptions: Welcome to the Real World!

**LEARNING OBJECTIVE 22.6**

Explain why dividends are not a residual, as implied by M&M.

The perfect markets assumption contains a number of unrealistic aspects, the most important of which are the absence of transactions costs and the belief that all information is freely available and understood.

## Transactions Costs

Transactions costs are important because it is assumed, in the M&M model, that the firm can pay a dividend and then issue shares to raise the money needed to make the required level of investment.[8] Let's take an extreme situation in which transactions costs are very high and the firm cannot raise new capital. In this case, the payment of the cash dividend reduces the amount of money available to invest and causes the firm to forgo positive NPV projects. The value of the firm would then go down faced with this loss in value.

Faced with significant costs attached to raising new money, cash-poor growth firms have little incentive to pay a dividend, since all they are doing is compounding their financing problems. Similarly, firms with volatile earnings, whose cash flow fluctuates significantly from year to year, will attempt to "store" cash from one period to another. As a result, they will conservatively maintain their dividend payments at a level that minimizes the need to constantly access the capital markets.

How important are these concerns? It turns out they are very important. In Chapter 21, Figure 21.10 listed the most important concerns for firms when making their capital structure

---

[8]Alternatively, it is assumed that investors can create homemade dividends by buying or selling shares without cost to generate any desired cash flows, which makes the firm's dividend decision irrelevant.

decision: the first two factors were their credit rating and their ability to continue to make investments, while the fourth was their ability to continue to make dividend payments. Overall, we regard this as "financial flexibility." To illustrate this concept, we saw in Chapter 21 that Oilexco went from being a $4-billion market capitalization firm to bankrupt in eight months when what should have been routine financing became unavailable during the financial crisis. The result is that firms are reluctant to "stretch" and put themselves at the mercy of capital markets by paying out "surplus" cash as a dividend. Similarly, they are reluctant to issue new shares to finance a dividend payment; instead, they would rather cut or defer investments. In Baker et al.'s survey of Canadian firms, fully 40 percent of the time the respondents considered themselves constrained in terms of capital.[9] The upshot is that dividends are not a residual, a result consistent with Lintner's empirical work.

This brings us to a second unrealistic aspect of the perfect markets assumption, which is that everyone has the same amount of information.

## Dividends and Signalling

The M&M model assumes perfect markets in which all participants have access to the same information. In practice, however, capital markets are rife with information asymmetries, with some parties knowing more than others. Even though the main focus of securities regulation is to ensure all material facts are public information, agents in the capital market often have widely different views about a firm's future prospects and value—that is, they interpret the same information differently.

For example, management usually knows more than external investors, so the firm has to have some way of signalling to investors that its press releases can be believed. As we discussed in Chapter 21, investors tend to view such information with a great deal of scepticism, so one way to signal a firm's credibility is to increase the dividend only when the firm believes it will not have to reduce future payouts. The fact that paying the cash dividend reduces the funds available to the firm and its financial flexibility means the firm will make the payment only when it thinks its internal funds are increasing and are enough to support the dividend payment.[10] Otherwise, as we just discussed, paying a dividend will impose more transactions costs on the firm when it has to raise more funds in the future. This "signalling model" explains why share prices tend to increase when dividends are initiated or increased unexpectedly. In both cases, the dividend increase indicates good news because it suggests that management believes it can support the dividend out of future earnings and those earnings have increased.

Another explanation for the favourable stock market reaction associated with dividend increases is provided by **agency theory**. Many investors are wary of senior management because managers tend to view the firm as "their" firm and not as something belonging to the shareholders. Investors fear that senior management may waste corporate resources over-investing in poor (negative NPV) projects, since it is not "their" money but the money of the shareholders that they are using. This view is supported by the argument put forward by Gordon Donaldson (discussed in Chapter 2 and again in Chapter 21): for agency reasons, senior management follows a pecking order when raising capital. This means, for example, that managers prefer to finance projects using internal cash flow (retained earnings), then debt, and finally by issuing new common equity. Shareholders, on the other hand, would prefer that cash be disgorged as a dividend, with management then explaining why it needs the money back by filing a prospectus and issuing new common shares.[11] From an agency perspective, paying a large dividend and forcing the firm to justify future expenditures creates value by controlling management. However, while an agency perspective justifies

**agency theory** the recognition of conflicts of interest in which managerial decision-making may not be in the best interests of shareholders

[9]Baker, H. Kent, Dutta, Shantanu, and Saadi, Samir, "Corporate Finance Practices in Canada: Where Do We Stand?" *Multinational Finance Journal* 15, no. 3/4 (2011), pp. 157–92.

[10]This also means that it is expensive for poor-quality firms to mimic this cash dividend payment.

[11]The economist Milton Friedman is famous for suggesting that firms should pay out 100 percent of earnings and then bid in the open market to get the funds back. Most CEOs shudder at the thought, as do many activists who view the firm through a social lens as creating jobs and doing good deeds. Both downplay the reality that firms have owners.

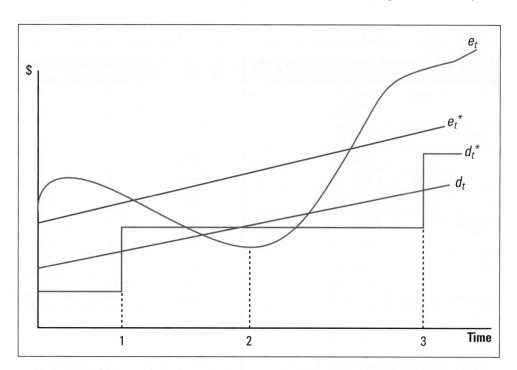

**FIGURE 22.6** The Signalling Model

the stock market's reaction to dividends, it cannot explain the phenomenon of dividend smoothing.

**Figure 22.6** helps explain the signalling model. The starred values in Figure 22.6 represent management's view of the underlying or permanent earnings ($e_t^*$) and dividends ($d_t^*$) per share, whereas the unstarred values are the actual values. Note that the underlying earnings and dividends are increasing through time, so the firm has some long-run target payout. However, actual earnings vary with "predictable" factors such as the state of the economy or the inflation rate. So when the actual earnings increase in line with underlying earnings, the firm increases the dividend per share as at time 1. However, when there are poor earnings at time 2, the firm does not cut its dividend, since to do so would signal to the market that these poor earnings are not temporary, but permanent. At this point in time, the firm cannot cover its dividend from its earnings, but it signals to investors that this earnings drop is expected to be temporary by maintaining the dividend.

Figure 22.2 shows that this is what many Canadian companies did during the recessions in the early 1980s, the 1990s, and 2008–9. During these recessions, dividends in aggregate were maintained even in the face of cyclically low earnings as managers signalled that this was cyclical and not fundamental. At time 3, the firm increases its dividend again to signal that the earnings increase this time is in line with the firm's underlying earnings increase. Ultimately if the earnings decline is perceived to be permanent, the dividend will be cut or reduced to a nominal amount. As we can see from Table 22.1, weak oil and gas prices have caused huge losses for major Canadian producers like Cenovus Energy and Encana, resulting in nominal dividend payments and significantly reduced market value compared to a few years ago.

This signalling model indicates that dividend changes have "information content," which provides an important role for dividend policy. The signalling model, when combined with the residual theory of dividends, provides the major theories that explain actual dividend policy. The residual theory of dividends explains generally which types of firms should pay a dividend and the general level of their payout. The signalling model explains how these dividends should be paid out as a slowly adapting dividend per share, as modelled by Lintner.

## Taxes

The final imperfection that affects all financial policy is the impact of taxes. Working out how taxes affect financial policy is difficult because different classes of investors have different tax brackets. With taxes, the general rule is that "one size does not fit all." As discussed in Chapter 19,

**TABLE 22.2** Marginal Individual Tax Rates (%) on Dividends and Capital Gains for 2019

| | Income Level | $25,000 | $50,000 | $75,000 | $200,000 |
|---|---|---|---|---|---|
| British Columbia | Dividends | 0 | 7.56 | 7.56 | 25.92 |
| | Capital gains | 11.81 | 14.10 | 14.10 | 22.9 |
| Alberta | Dividends | 0 | 7.56 | 7.56 | 23.43 |
| | Capital gains | 12.5 | 15.25 | 15.25 | 21.0 |
| Ontario | Dividends | 0 | 7.56 | 7.56 | 31.67 |
| | Capital gains | 10.0 | 14.83 | 14.83 | 23.98 |
| Quebec | Dividends | 0 | 17.66 | 17.66 | 35.39 |
| | Capital gains | 13.77 | 18.56 | 18.56 | 24.99 |
| Nova Scotia | Dividends | 0 | 15.98 | 18.35 | 36.06 |
| | Capital gains | 11.9 | 17.73 | 18.58 | 25.0 |

**Source:** Data from Ernst & Young Tax Calculator, www.ey.com/CA/en/Services/Tax/Tax-Calculators-2019-Personal-Tax

corporations pay no tax on dividend income if it is received from another Canadian corporation. This is because it is taxed when paid out to an individual; to do otherwise would result in a cascading tax, where the rate could end up greater than 100 percent.[12] As a result, there is a corporate preference for receiving dividend income. Individuals, on the other hand, might prefer either dividend or capital gains income depending on their province of residence and their income level.[13] **Table 22.2** provides the 2019 marginal tax rates for dividend and capital gains income in five provinces for different levels of taxable income, as reported by Ernst & Young.

As a general rule, marginal tax rates are lower on dividend income than on capital gains income because the capital gains tax rate is half the marginal tax rate, whereas dividend income attracts the dividend tax rate. This differential narrows as the amount of taxable income increases due to the progressive nature of our tax system, but the system still gives rise to **tax clienteles**. Stocks with a high dividend yield are often referred to as "widows and orphans stocks," since they are often held by investors in lower tax brackets (often retirees), who rely on the dividends for income. In contrast, stocks with a low dividend yield tend to be held by younger investors, who have longer-term horizons and are intent on holding for a long time to defer taxes. So although the payment of a dividend may not have an impact on the general level of share prices, it will have a major influence on the type of investors a firm attracts. The general advice that flows from this is not to drastically change dividend policy, because that upsets the existing ownership base.

**tax clienteles** a phenomenon reflecting the fact that investors in different tax brackets face different marginal tax rates on dividends versus capital gains income and thus have different preferences for receiving dividend income

## Repackaging Dividend-Paying Securities

The tax clienteles identified earlier are interested in different parts of the return generated by the firm. The problem is that the return comes packaged in one security, so each group gets part of what it wants and part of what it doesn't want. This has led to some interesting security repackaging products and **income stripping**.

Stripping is common in finance and is entirely respectable. It refers to the process of repackaging securities to provide different types of income based on different parts of the return. Take BCE Inc., for example, whose major asset is Bell Canada, which has a history of being a reasonably stable firm paying a high dividend. However, the telecommunications

**income stripping** the process of repackaging securities to provide different types of income based on different parts of the return

---

[12]This is because tax would be paid every time a dividend passed between different companies.

[13]There are substantial tax differences in how provinces tax investment income: Alberta and BC are much more investor friendly than Ontario, Quebec, and Nova Scotia given that most people do not earn investment income until middle age, when they are in a higher tax bracket.

revolution of the past 20 years has provided BCE with growth prospects. As a result, it attracts both growth investors and dividend yield investors, but they both have to buy the same package of returns from BCE. McLeod Young Weir (MYW), a company that is now owned by the Bank of Nova Scotia, found a way around this problem in 1986.

MYW bought $454 million in BCE common shares and repackaged them. The shares were placed in a trust company named "B" Corporation, which raised the $454 million by issuing two classes of securities backed by the BCE shares. One class of securities was special preferred shares. Investors buying these securities had the right to receive all the dividends on these shares for six years. At the end of six years, they got either the minimum of $30 or the BCE share price minus $1. MYW sold these preferred shares for $330 million. The second class of securities was referred to as "instalment receipts" (IR) and provided investors with the right to purchase the BCE shares at the end of six years by paying the minimum of $30 or the BCE share price minus $1. MYW sold these securities for $143 million.

The pattern of the securities is illustrated in **Figure 22.7**, but the upshot is that $454 million of BCE shares were repackaged and sold for $473 million, and MYW pocketed $19 million in fees to cover expenses.

The top box in Figure 22.7 is the valuation of the BCE shares at $454 million. This is the present value of six years of dividends plus the share price at the end of the six years. The bottom two boxes are the values of the preferred shares and IRs. Note that if you add the payoffs from the two securities together, they equal the payoff from the BCE shares. So MYW is just stripping the BCE shares into two new securities.

One interesting feature of these shares is the instalment receipts. Whenever you see minimums or maximums, you should think options, as in Chapter 12. In this case, the IR holders will pay only $30 to buy the BCE shares if the share price is above $30, so this is a straight call option. If the BCE share price is less than $30, they will pay $1 less than the shares are worth. Either way, the IR holders end up owning the shares at the end of six years, and the preferred shareholders simply receive the dividends on all the shares for the previous five years and either $30 or the BCE share price minus $1. Effectively, the IRs are long-term "in the money" call options on BCE common shares.

So instead of holding BCE shares and getting a package of dividends and capital gains, investors can buy the preferred shares and get more dividends than they can buy directly for $330 million, or they can buy the IRs and get all capital gains through a long-term call option. The fact that MYW made $19 million in fees indicates that the parts were worth more than the whole and that investors would prefer to own a pure dividend or pure capital gains stream of cash flows. In turn, this implies that tax clienteles do exist.

"B" Corporation was the first dividend strip of common shares in Canada. Since then there have been many examples of what are now termed **split shares**. The Bank of Nova Scotia now has the largest split share mutual fund, where instead of stripping the income on one company, such as BCE, they split it on a pool of companies. Allbanc Split Corporation II has a market value of approximately $43 million and splits the dividends and capital gains from a portfolio of bank shares, which, like BCE, have high dividends. The investor can either buy the preferred

**split shares**   shares sold as the dividends and capital gains parts of a security

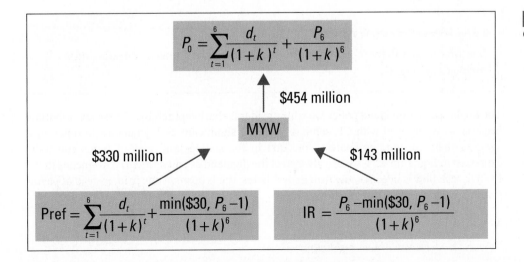

**FIGURE 22.7**   **MYW's "B" Corporation Shares**

shares, which have a fixed dividend of $1.22 (ALB.PR.C), or buy the capital shares, which receive any increase in dividends plus the capital appreciation (ALB). The shares are issued in the ratio of two capital shares for one preferred share as a unit, but they trade separately.

On its website, Scotia described the two classes of shares as follows:

> Allbanc Split Corp. II was created to hold a portfolio (the "Portfolio Shares") of common shares of Bank of Montreal, Canadian Imperial Bank of Commerce, National Bank of Canada, The Bank of Nova Scotia, Royal Bank of Canada and The Toronto-Dominion Bank in order to generate dividend income for the holders of the Company's Preferred Shares and to enable the holders of the Company's Capital Shares to participate in any capital appreciation in the Portfolio shares and to benefit from any increase in the dividends payable on the Portfolio Shares.[14]

The popularity of split shares has two major implications. First, there are investor dividend clienteles, and dividends do matter to some investors. This emphasizes that companies need to consider dramatic dividend changes as a serious event, not to be taken lightly. Second, the capital shares are marketed as a leveraged investment and can be considered an application of the homemade leverage theorem advanced by M&M. In this case, given investor preference for leverage and dislike of dividends, they can buy, for example, the Allbanc capital shares. The result is that the financial policies of the six banks in the Allbanc portfolio are being changed to the benefit of the capital shareholders in exactly the way suggested by M&M.

There are now almost 40 families of split shares traded on the TSX. These firms strip the dividends from the capital gains for a wide class of common shares ranging from bank and utility stocks to global telecom stocks. The existence of these families of split shares is an example of the M&M theorems in action, as well as an example of the efficiency with which financial markets adapt to "imperfections" that provide an opportunity to create value. Although M&M's work has had limited impact on corporate dividend policy, it has had a major impact on secondary market activity through the implications of their arbitrage argument.

---

## Concept Review Questions

1. Explain why dividend policy will be relevant in the presence of transactions costs, informational asymmetry and agency problems, and taxes.

2. Describe split shares and explain what their popularity implies about investor preferences for dividends in the real world.

---

## 22.7 | Share Repurchases

---

### LEARNING OBJECTIVE 22.7
Describe what a share repurchase program is and explain how it can substitute for dividend payments.

---

The final aspect of dividend policy we will consider is share repurchases. These are important because, as we noticed with CP, some firms make significant cash payments to repurchase some of their outstanding shares. Note that in the sources and uses of funds constraint expressed in Equation 22.3, we can always set the dividend as equal to zero. This means that if the free cash flow is negative, the firm issues shares; if it is positive, the firm, instead of paying a cash dividend, repurchases shares.

---

[14]Scotiabank website, www.scotiamanagedcompanies.com.

Let's return to our example of the firm with a $50-million value in the next period and 1 million shares outstanding. Further assume that it has an expected free cash flow of $5 million in the next period. So its value, with a $5 per share cash dividend, is now $50, as shown here:

$$P_0 = \frac{\$5m + \$50m}{(1 + 0.10)}/1,000,000 = \$50$$

However, if the firm used the $5 million in free cash flow generated during the year to buy back 90,909 shares at $55 each at the end of the year, in the next period the market value of the shares would be:

$$P_1 = \frac{\$50m}{909,090} = \$55$$

Therefore, the present value of $55 today, using the 10-percent discount rate, is once again $50.

This example shows that the firm can use the $5 million in cash to either pay a cash dividend or repurchase shares. Either way, with perfect capital markets, the shares are worth $50 today. The example also illustrates how share repurchase is simply another form of payout policy. It is an alternative to a cash dividend, where the objective is to increase the price per share rather than paying a dividend and forcing the shareholders to immediately pay tax on the dividend.

Of course, in this example the firm has to buy back the shares at $55, which is the ongoing value of the firm ($50) plus the $5 million in cash on hand, divided by the current 1 million shares outstanding. If it offers to buy the shares at $60, all the shareholders should tender their shares, as they are worth only $55. Similarly, if it offers $50 a share, no one should tender them. The advantage for the shareholders is that they can either hold their shares and receive a larger capital gain in the future or sell out now. Such a persistent policy of share repurchase is technically illegal, since there are rules against the improper accumulation of funds within the firm.[15] Consequently, firms sometimes adopt a policy of large, infrequent, share repurchase programs. At these points, insiders often hold on to their shares so that they defer any capital gains and associated taxes.

To return to CP. In its May 10, 2018, press release announcing its cash dividend, CP also stated:

> The company also announced that it has completed its normal course issuer bid announced on May 10, 2017. CP purchased 4,384,062 common shares at a weighted average price of $214.31. In total CP has repurchased 35.32 million of its common shares since 2014. This represents approximately 25 percent of its public float, as at March 31, 2018.

By "issuer bid" CP simply means that it bought the shares on a public stock exchange after announcing its intentions to do so in May 2017. This explains why the number of CP shares outstanding has been declining as indicated in Table 19.2. However, in buying back 25 percent of its outstanding shares, CP is behaving in a similar fashion to many U.S. companies that have recently been severely criticized by Senator Elizabeth Warren and other activist commentators who would prefer that the money be spent increasing employee wages and investing for growth. Ethics and Governance 22.1 is an extract expressing such a viewpoint, which is likely to be a major plank in the U.S. 2020 elections.

This example illustrates how a share repurchase program can act like a cash dividend by providing a payout of funds to the shareholders. However, unlike a dividend, share repurchases can be motivated by several other factors, so it is easy to think that it is part of a payout policy when in fact it is not. Some of the other factors motivating share repurchases are listed here:

- **Offset the exercise of executive stock options (ESOs).**   ESOs are call options granted to senior executives. When exercised, they result in more shares outstanding. Firms frequently repurchase shares to meet these exercise requirements, thereby leaving the number of shares outstanding constant.

---

[15]Until the late 1940s, the U.S. Treasury, for example, investigated for improper accumulation of funds any firm that did not pay out 70 percent of its earnings as dividends. The onus was on the firm to justify a reinvestment rate above 30 percent of earnings.

- **Carry out a leveraged recapitalization.** Often debt is raised and the proceeds used to repurchase shares to move the firm back to its optimal capital structure.

- **Send a signal.** Management often repurchases shares to signal to the market that it thinks the stock is undervalued.

- **Repurchase dissident shares.** If there is substantial disagreement among shareholders about the future of the firm, a share repurchase program gives the dissidents an opportunity to sell their shares without depressing the market price, thereby removing an "overhang" of shares.

- **Remove cash without generating expectations for future distributions.** A large share repurchase can return cash to the shareholders without generating expectations about receiving such distributions in the future, similar to a special dividend payout.

- **Take the firm private.** A share repurchase to buy all the firm's outstanding shares takes the firm out of the public markets.

---

## 22.1 Ethics and Corporate Governance  "The American Disease": Canadian Companies Pouring Cash into Stock Buybacks as Backlash Grows Abroad

Companies have continued to pour cash into buybacks, albeit with some recent signs of a slowdown. Last year alone, they announced they were repurchasing more than US$1-trillion worth of their own shares, spurred on by tax changes ushered in under President Donald Trump.

But the rising tide of repurchases in the U.S. has now inspired critics in Congress and on the presidential campaign trail who have drawn on [economist William] Lazonick's work. So much so, The New Yorker recently dubbed him as "The Economist Who Put Stock Buybacks in Washington's Crosshairs."

For example, Democratic Senator Tammy Baldwin released a staff report in March blasting buybacks for suppressing wages, driving inequality and decreasing investment. It was acknowledged the report "would not be possible without the help of William Lazonick," among others.

The pushback has mostly come from Democrats, including presidential candidate Elizabeth Warren, but a recent report by Republican Senator Marco Rubio questioned the theory that drives businesses to obsess over returning value to shareholders, saying it is, "as William Lazonick has called it, an ideology."

Such criticism has yet to take off in the same way in Lazonick's native land. Notwithstanding a stay in Montreal in the late 1980s, the academic says he has mostly lived in the U.S. since graduating from the University of Toronto in 1968.

. . .

Buybacks offer other perks as well, a recent report by CIBC World Markets noted. This includes rewarding investors while allowing them to defer tax payments until after the shares are sold, unlike dividends.

They are also not "long-term commitments," as dividends are, the report said, and they offer another use for extra cash lying around in a business, which "should result in additional capital discipline, ensuring that spending on any and all projects does not get unbridled support."

Repurchasing shares can demonstrate confidence in a stock, or simply look like a safer bet to an executive at a company facing trade-related uncertainty. For instance, Canadian oil and gas companies in 2018 announced and then followed up on buyback plans amid low stock prices and difficulties in getting their product to market.

"Whatever the reason, buyback investment strategies remain attractive," said Ian de Verteuil, head of portfolio strategy at CIBC World Markets, in the June report.

. . .

Repurchases of common and preferred shares among the TSX 60 companies rose approximately 101 per cent from 2015 to 2018, led by blue-chip stocks such as Royal Bank of Canada, Toronto-Dominion Bank and Thomson-Reuters Corp.

As a dollar figure, TSX 60 buybacks were nearly $58 billion in 2018, up from $36.6 billion in 2017, $26.1 billion in 2016 and $28.8 billion in 2015, when a drop in oil prices sideswiped Canadian energy producers. FactSet data show 2018 had the highest level of buybacks by historical members of the TSX 60 (which may not necessarily be today's members) since at least 2001—and by a good deal.

Meanwhile, capital expenditures among those companies were up approximately 9.5 per cent, to about $96.7 billion in 2018 from nearly $88.4 billion in 2015. Common dividends grew to $52.3 billion last year, a 31.3-per-cent increase over 2015.

**Discussion Questions**

1. Is the firm acting in the best interests of its shareholders if it fails to invest when it is profitable to do so and instead pays out cash as a dividend or through a share buyback? (What does Figure 22.4 have to say about this?)

2. If firms paid out higher dividends, rather than share buybacks, would William Lazonick's critique still hold? What is Mr. Lazonick's essential argument?

3. Mr. Lazonick takes a stakeholder view of corporate governance: that a corporation should not be run in the interests of its owners but instead meet social needs such as those of its employees and the economy in general. If you started a business that was successful, do you think external commentators are playing fair to criticize you for not making excessive investments or paying excessive wages that destroy part of the value you have created?

4. The CIBC report notes that share buybacks are not long-term commitments. In fact, buybacks have largely replaced "special dividends," which are now quite rare. Would Mr. Lazonick's critique still apply if firms paid

special dividends rather than use surplus cash to buy back shares?

5. Buybacks used to be severely circumscribed until the Securities and Exchange Commission (SEC) in the U.S. clarified the procedures that firms had to follow to avoid any suspicion they were manipulating share prices. These are the procedures that CP follows in its issuer bids. Would it be acceptable for there to be no restriction on share buybacks so firms could buy back shares without the public markets being aware of who they were selling to?

**Source:** Excerpted from Zochodne, Geoff, "'The American Disease': Canadian Companies Pouring Cash into Stock Buybacks as Backlash Grows Abroad." *Financial Post*, August 21, 2019. Available at business.financialpost. com. © Financial Post. All rights reserved. Reprinted by permission.

---

### Concept Review Questions

1. Why can share repurchases be viewed as an alternative to paying a cash dividend?
2. What factors may influence a firm's decision to enter into share repurchases?

---

# Review

## Summary

In this chapter, we look at different types of dividends, including regular and special cash dividends, stock dividends, and stock splits, as well as share repurchases. As in our discussion of capital structure theory, we present the major argument of M&M, which suggests that in a perfect market, the payment of a cash dividend should not affect the value of the firm. According to the M&M assumptions, this is because the value of the firm is determined by real factors such as the firm's free cash flow. Therefore, all a dividend does is create a greater financing need that has to be met by selling more common shares. This leads us to look at the role of M&M's assumptions.

One common argument that justifies the importance of dividends is that they create value because they are safer than capital gains. However, we see that while dividend-paying firms are generally lower risk than capital-gains-oriented ones, this tends to reflect the risk of their basic operations, as well as the residual theory of dividends. A more substantial critique is that transactions costs make it difficult for firms to follow the residual dividend policy implicit in the M&M argument, since it is expensive to raise capital.

The existence of transactions costs also leads firms to increase or initiate dividend payments to signal a higher level of earnings. As a result, dividends have information content, and the unexpected payment of a dividend generally causes stock prices to increase. Agency theory predicts the same results but cannot explain the most salient feature of actual dividend policy, which is that firms tend to smooth their dividends over time.

Finally, we recognize the existence of tax clienteles, since investors' preference for dividends versus capital gains depends on their tax bracket and level of income. This provides a tax motivation for firms to use share repurchases as a means of payout policy, because a repurchase leads to an increase in share prices and capital gains rather than dividends. However, we see that there are many other reasons why firms might want to repurchase their shares.

## Summary of Learning Objectives

**22.1   Explain what a cash dividend payment is, how dividend payments are made, and why dividend payments are different from interest payments.**

A cash dividend is the cash payment that shareholders receive periodically. A dividend has to be declared by the board of directors (BOD), after which it is announced and becomes a contractual commitment. However, shareholders cannot force the members of the BOD to declare a dividend. An interest payment is different in that it is a legal obligation.

**22.2   Describe historical dividend payouts and explain the importance of dividends.**

Typical dividend payouts are around 40 percent, but increase to over 100 percent during recessions. They trend downwards in booms. Dividends are an important source of holding period return.

**22.3   Explain how Modigliani and Miller proved that dividend payments are irrelevant, due to the existence of homemade dividends, and therefore have no impact on market value.**

Modigliani and Miller argue that dividend policy is irrelevant under certain assumptions: there are no taxes and there is a perfect market. Investors can create homemade dividends by selling off a small part of the stock that has appreciated in value, or they can also undo dividends by reinvesting the dividend cash. M&M show that a dividend with off-setting new issue is irrelevant—the same as doing nothing.

**22.4 Explain why dividend payments generally reflect the business risk of the firm.**

Firms that do not pay dividends are typically growth firms that need to retain cash to finance new projects. Growth firms have little residual cash flow to pay out. Low-growth firms have no new projects or investments and so have high residual cash flow—low-growth firms can pay high dividends. The "bird in the hand" argument stems from the belief that firms that do not pay a cash dividend are riskier because this causes the cost of equity capital to increase and the stock price to fall; therefore, a cash dividend ("bird in the hand") is worth more (twice as much—"two in the bush") than capital gains. The fallacy is that firms that pay dividends are perceived to be safer—to have a lower cost of equity and a higher stock price. Conversely, firms that do not pay dividends are perceived to be riskier and to have a higher cost of equity and a lower stock price.

**22.5 Explain why firms are reluctant to cut their dividends and why they smooth their dividends.**

Firms are reluctant to cut their dividends because it signals that the value of a firm's asset in place has decreased and causes the share price to drop. Firms smooth dividends for the following reasons: first, the transactions costs of raising new equity are so high that changing dividends will compound financing problems. Second, thanks to the signalling function of dividends, smoothing dividends creates a reputation that the firm's performance is stable and less risky. Third, drastically changing dividend policy upsets the existing ownership base, so smoothing dividends appeals to a firm's tax clientele.

**22.6 Explain why dividends are not a residual, as implied by M&M.**

M&M's perfect markets assumption contains a number of unrealistic aspects, the most important of which are the absence of transactions costs and the belief that all information is freely available and understood. (1) Transactions costs: faced with significant costs attached to raising new money, cash-poor growth firms have little incentive to pay a dividend, since all they are doing is compounding their financing problems. Similarly, firms with volatile earnings, whose cash flow fluctuates significantly from year to year, will attempt to "store" cash from one period to another. (2) Dividends and signalling: the fact that paying the cash dividend reduces the funds available to the firm means the firm will make the payment only when it thinks its internal funds are increasing and are enough to support the dividend payment. (3) Taxes: the general advice that flows from tax clienteles is not to drastically change dividend policy because that upsets the existing ownership base.

**22.7 Describe what a share repurchase program is and explain how it can substitute for dividend payments.**

In a share repurchase, a company buys back its own shares on the open market. A share repurchase reduces shares outstanding but it also reduces corporate resources. If a company repurchases its shares at a fair price, then its stock price is unchanged by the repurchase. If a company repurchases shares, then shareholders can sell the same proportion of shares as are repurchased and so receive some cash without changing their proportionate control of the company. In this way, repurchases are an alternative means of distributing cash to shareholders.

## Key Terms

agency theory, p. 22-20
"bird in the hand" argument, p. 22-15
cash cow, p. 22-11
declaration date, p. 22-2
dividend reinvestment plan (DRIP), p. 22-3
dividend yield, p. 22-7

equity market capitalization ($V_0$), p. 22-10
ex-dividend date, p. 22-2
free cash flow, p. 22-11
holder of record, p. 22-2
homemade dividends, p. 22-13
income stripping, p. 22-22

odd lots, p. 22-4
residual theory of dividends, p. 22-11
special dividend, p. 22-3
split shares, p. 22-23
stock dividend, p. 22-4
stock split, p. 22-4
tax clienteles, p. 22-22

## Equations

| Equation | Description | Formula | Page |
|---|---|---|---|
| [22.1] | Single Period Valuation Model | $P_0 = \dfrac{D_1 + P_1}{(1 + k_e)}$ | p. 22-10 |
| [22.2] | Required New Share Issue | $mP_0 = V_0 = \dfrac{m(D_1 + P_1)}{(1 + k_e)}$ | p. 22-10 |

*(continued)*

| Equation | Description | Formula | Page |
|---|---|---|---|
| **[22.3]** | Cash Flow Constraint | $X_1 + nP_1 = I_1 + mD_1$ | p. 22-11 |
| **[22.4]** | Single Period Free Cash Flow | $V_0 = \dfrac{X_1 - I_1 + [(m+n)P_1 = V_1]}{(1+k)}$ | p. 22-11 |
| **[22.5]** | Free Cash Flow Valuation | $V_0 = \sum_{t=1}^{\infty} \dfrac{X_t - I_t}{(1+k)^t}$ | p. 22-11 |
| **[22.6]** | Existing and Growth Opportunities Valuation | $P_0 = \dfrac{ROE_1 \times BVPS}{k_e} + \dfrac{Inv}{(1+k_e)}\left(\dfrac{ROE_2 - k_e}{k_e}\right)$ | p. 22-15 |
| **[22.7]** | Adaptive Dividend Model | $\Delta D_t = \beta(D^*_t - D_{t-1})$ | p. 22-18 |
| **[22.8]** | Lintner Equation | $D_t = a + (1-b)D_{t-1} + cE_1$ | p. 22-18 |

# Questions and Practice Problems

## Multiple Choice Questions

1. **(LO 22.3)** Dividend-payout ratio is defined as:
   a. the dividend yield plus the capital gains yield.
   b. dividends per share divided by earnings per share.
   c. dividends per share divided by income per share.
   d. dividends per share divided by current price per share.

2. **(LO 22.1)** Which of the following statements about stock splits is *incorrect*?
   a. Market price per share is reduced after the split.
   b. The number of outstanding shares is increased.
   c. Retained earnings are changed.
   d. Proportional ownership is unchanged.

3. **(LO 22.1)** When is the ex-dividend date if the holder of record date is March 23, 2022?
   a. March 20
   b. March 21
   c. March 25
   d. March 26

4. **(LO 22.1)** On January 7, a firm declared a $0.25-per-share quarterly dividend payable March 3 to shareholders of record on Monday, February 8. What is the latest date by which you could purchase the stock and still receive the recently declared dividend?
   a. February 4
   b. February 5
   c. February 28
   d. March 1

5. **(LO 22.2)** Which of the following has a negative impact on the share price?
   a. Unexpected dividend increase
   b. Unexpected dividend initiation
   c. Unexpected dividend decrease
   d. None of the above

6. **(LO 22.3)** Which of the following is an M&M assumption?
   a. There are personal taxes.
   b. All firms maximize value.
   c. There is debt.
   d. Markets are imperfect.

7. **(LO 22.3)** What is the market value of equity if next period's cash flow from operations, investment, and equity market value are $400,000, $200,000, and $1,200,000, respectively, and $k = 15$ percent?
   a. $1,173,913
   b. $1,347,826
   c. $1,217,391
   d. $1,359,499

8. **(LO 22.5)** A firm's target dividend is $4.50 and the prior-period dividend is $3.75. What is the change in dividends if the adjustment coefficient ($\beta$) is equal to 1?
   a. 0
   b. −$1.50
   c. $0.75
   d. $1.50

9. **(LO 22.5)** Suppose that the pre-tax holding period returns on two stocks are the same. Stock A has a low dividend payout policy and stock B has a high dividend payout policy. If you are an individual in a high marginal tax bracket and do not intend to sell the stocks during the holding period, which stock should you purchase?
   a. A because it will have a higher after-tax return than stock B
   b. B because it will have a higher after-tax return than stock A
   c. A or B (indifferent) because the after-tax returns on stocks A and B will be the same
   d. It is impossible to determine which stock to purchase given the information available.

10. **(LO 22.6)** Which of the following arguments supports the relevance of dividends?
   a. Informational release
   b. Reduction of uncertainty

c. Some investors' preference for current income

d. All of the above

**11. (LO 22.7)** Which of the following statements regarding motivation for a stock repurchase is *incorrect*?

a. Firms could be privatized using stock repurchases.

b. Investors consider a firm's stock undervalued when a stock repurchase occurs.

c. Firms use stock repurchases to move capital structure back to some optimum level.

d. None of the above.

**12. (LO 22.7)** If a firm repurchased 50 percent of its outstanding common shares, the result would be

a. a decline in EPS.

b. an increase in retained earnings.

c. a decrease in total assets.

d. a decrease in the number of shareholders by 50 percent.

**13. (LO 22.1, 22.5, 22.6, 22.7)** Which of the following four statements are *true*?

a. If dividends are taxed at a higher personal tax rate than capital gains, shareholders will generally prefer dividends to share repurchases.

b. When a firm repurchases their shares, the shares become more valuable and their price will rise.

c. Empirical evidence suggests that firms do not smooth repurchase activity; however, they do smooth regular dividend payments.

d. As dividends are seen as an implicit ongoing commitment from a firm to its shareholders, they send a weak signal of financial strength to shareholders.

## Practice Problems

### Basic

**14. (LO 22.1)** Describe the difference between a stock dividend and a cash dividend plus a DRIP.

**15. (LO 22.3)** Explain the implications of M&M's homemade dividend argument.

**16. (LO 22.4)** Discuss the "bird in the hand" argument in support of dividend payments.

**17. (LO 22.5)** According to John Lintner, what is the adjustment factor β? Interpret the calculated adjustment factor.

**18. (LO 22.6)** How do personal taxes affect preference for high versus low dividend yields?

**19. (LO 22.6)** Describe the implication of releasing the assumptions of no transactions costs.

### Intermediate

**20. (LO 22.2)** A firm has a dividend yield of 3.8 percent and a payout ratio of 36 percent. If its earnings are $22 million and there are 6 million shares outstanding, what is the price per share?

**21. (LO 22.3)** What is the market price per share if the next period's dividend = $2.50, $P_1$ = $30, and $k$ = 16 percent?

**22. (LO 22.3)** According to equity market capitalization, what is the cost of capital for the stock of the following firm? Current market

value of the equity is $1.8 million with 150,000 shares outstanding. The stock price is expected to grow 6 percent in a year, and the firm is expected to pay out a $1.80 dividend per share at the end of the first year.

**23. (LO 22.3)** Currently a firm has an operating cash flow of $42 million and there is a promising project available, which costs $30 million. There are 5 million shares outstanding with a current price of $64 per share. The firm is expected to pay out a dividend of $5 per share to existing shareholders. It will raise the money needed through issuing new shares.

a. What amount of new proceeds is required?

b. What is the new share price? Hint: the firm's equity market value is not changed.

c. How many new shares does the firm have to issue?

**24 (LO 23.4)** Which of the following statements are *true*:

I. A firm's operating cycle would be identical to their cash conversion cycle if they paid cash on delivery for their inventory purchases.

II. All else equal, the longer a firm's cash conversion cycle, the more cash it needs to run their day-to-day operations.

III. A firm's cash conversion cycle is equal to the average length of time between when a firm pays cash to purchase its initial inventory and when it receives cash from the sale of the product.

IV. A manufacturer of specialized large-sized construction vehicles (e.g., excavator, hauler) that maintains high levels of inventory and has long manufacturing and sales cycles, would be expected to need high levels of cash/working capital to conduct its daily operations.

a. I, II, and IV

b. I, III, and IV

c. II, III, and IV

d. All of the above.

Use the following information to answer practice problem 25:

*On August 5, 2015, Toronto-based Barrick Gold Corp cut its dividend as it attempted to reduce debt in a weak gold price environment. From 2012 to 2015, Barrick, one of the world's biggest gold producers, took active measures to reduce costs and divest assets. In July 2015, gold plunged below US$1,100 an ounce for the first time since early 2010, limiting the company's free cash flow. This prompted Barrick to cut its quarterly dividend by 60 percent to USD$0.02 a share. This move resulted in savings of almost USD $140 million a year. This was not the first time that Barrick had slashed dividends. In 2013, Barrick had implemented a 75% dividend cut. The August 5, 2015 slash in dividends resulted in the share price of the mining company going up 6.46% in midday trading on the news to $9.23.*

**25. (LO 22.4 and 22.5)** Comment as to how/why the share price of the security may have risen in response to the above outlined events and whether it is consistent with your expectations.

**26. (LO 22.5)** A firm follows a strict residual dividend policy. This firm will have profits of $800,000 this year. After screening all available investment projects, the firm has decided to take three out of the 10 projects and those three will cost $600,000. The current equity market value of this firm is $5,600,000 and the current market price of its shares is $32. Estimate the current year dividend per share. What is the shortcoming of this policy?

**27. (LO 22.5)** Explain why firms do not simply pay out dividends as a fixed portion of their profits. What do most firms do in terms of dividend policy?

**28. (LO 22.6)** Investor A's personal tax rate is 30 percent while Investor B's is 22 percent. Investor A owns 1,000 shares of SNS Company and receives an annual dividend of $1.75 per share. Investor B owns 1,000 shares of CGC Company and receives an annual dividend of $1.60 per share. Which investor receives the larger after-tax dividend amount?

**29. (LO 22.6)** Describe possible reactions from the market of the following dividend payout changes.

    **a.** Dividend initiation

    **b.** Dividend increase

    **c.** Dividend decrease

**30. (LO 22.6)** A company has announced an increase in its quarterly dividend from $0.30 to $0.42 per share. If an investor who owns 1,500 shares is in the 25-percent tax bracket, calculate the amount by which the investor's tax would increase annually due to the dividend.

**31. (LO 22.7)** List the main reasons why firms repurchase shares.

### Challenging

**32. (LO 22.3)** CGC Company is considering its dividend policy. Currently CGC pays no dividends, has cash flows from operations of $10 million per year (perpetual), and needs $8 million for capital expenditures. The firm has no debt and there is no tax. The firm has 2 million shares outstanding, which are currently trading at $50 per share. George, the majority owner of CGC (he owns 60 percent), would like to take $20 million out of the company to fund his various charities. You have been hired by CGC to consider different alternatives.

    **i.** George could sell stock to the market to raise the $20 million he requires. What are the advantages and disadvantages of this strategy (i.e., the impact on the value of CGC and George's control)?

    **ii.** CGC could pay a dividend so that George receives the $20 million.

    **a.** Describe how the company can issue stock to create the dividend.

    **b.** What is the effect on the value of CGC and on George's control of the firm?

**33. (LO 22.3)** A firm has 1 million shares outstanding. After-tax earnings have been constant at $8 per share. The firm pays out all earnings in dividends at the end of each year. The shareholders' required rate of return is 15 percent.

    **a.** Calculate the current share price.

    **b.** The firm considers a one-time retention of all earnings for the current year. It will revert to a zero retention policy from next year. Assume the new investment promises a return of 10 percent, 15 percent, or 20 percent in perpetuity. Calculate the new share price in each separate case.

    **c.** Is it reasonable for the firm to claim that it would always find enough positive NPV opportunities yielding at least 20 percent, and therefore, it will never pay dividends?

**34. (LO 22.3)** Assume that the shareholders of a firm pay a net tax of 30 percent on cash dividends received. After-tax earnings have been constant at $10 per share. The firm pays out all earnings in dividends at the end of each year. The market requires a 15-percent rate of return, which implies that shareholders require an after-tax return of $(1 - 0.3) \times 0.15 = 10.5$ percent.

    **a.** Calculate the share price if the firm pays out all earnings as dividends.

    **b.** Calculate the share price if the firm retains the current year earnings and reinvests it at 15 percent. Starting next year, the firm reverts to a zero retention policy. What is the capital gain? Do shareholders prefer dividends or capital gains?

**35. (LO 22.3)** A firm's next-period market value of equity is $3 million and there are 100,000 shares outstanding, with $k = 12$ percent.

    **a.** What is the current stock price if the firm pays $600,000 in cash dividends?

    **b.** What is the number of shares outstanding if a firm spends its extra $600,000 to buy back shares at $36 per share instead of paying $600,000 in cash dividends?

    **c.** What is the current stock price if a firm spends its extra $600,000 to buy back shares at $36 per share instead of paying $600,000 in cash dividends?

**36. (LO 22.3)** MCC Corporation currently has cash flow from operations of $10 million, capital expenditures of $8 million, and pays a dividend of $2 million (all are perpetuities). The firm has no growth prospects or debt, and shareholders expect an annual return of 5 percent. The total number of shares outstanding is 1,000. For the following investors, describe how they can achieve their desired cash flow patterns and the value of their strategy (future value) at the end of the second year. Each investor owns 10 percent of the firm and there are no taxes or transactions costs.

    **a.** Marie lives in a very high-cost city and would like to receive a dividend of $400,000 at the end of year 1. She needs this money to finance her lifestyle.

    **b.** Charlie has found another investment opportunity that will cost $400,000 at the end of year 1, pay him 15 percent, and pay back his initial investment of $400,000 at the end of year 2.

    **c.** Radha is very frugal and would rather not receive dividends at the end of year 1.

**37. (LO 22.4)** A dividend-paying company has a current dividend yield of 8 percent and a stock price of $100. The company has paid the same dividend for the past 15 years and it is not expected to change. Alice believes that the company is an excellent investment opportunity for her clients and has been contacting them. Here are some of the responses she has received:

Client A: I need income, I don't trust capital gains—they aren't real, just paper. I'm not interested in this stock; I'd rather just have a bond and get a nice fixed income.

Client B: Who cares about dividends? I pay more taxes on the dividends so I want capital gains where I can control the timing of the tax bill. The dividend is too high, and I will pay too much tax so I'm not interested in the stock.

    **a.** Which statement is consistent with the "bird in the hand" argument about dividends?

    **b.** Describe how income stripping would allow Alice to satisfy the needs of both clients.

**38. (LO 22.6)** The current stock price of Abacus is $50. For the past 20 years, the firm has paid an annual dividend of $5. On July 26, it announced a dividend of $6 payable on September 10 to shareholders of record at the close of business on September 1.

    **a.** What do you expect to happen to the price of Abacus stock on July 26?

    **b.** If the shareholders of Abacus pay no taxes on dividends, what do you expect to happen to the price of Abacus on the ex-dividend date?

    **c.** If the shareholders of Abacus pay taxes on dividends, do you expect the stock price reaction on the ex-dividend date to be greater, the same, or less than in part b?

**39. (LO 22.6)** Kumar expected his firm to earn $1,000 per year forever, with no growth. Given a cost of capital of 10 percent, the value of the firm is $10,000. Kumar identified a new project, which costs $1,000 but would earn 11 percent per year forever. To invest in this project, Kumar cancelled this year's dividend. Given that he is investing in a positive NPV project, he expected his stock to rise. However, it fell dramatically. Explain what happened. Does this mean that investors do not like positive NPV projects?

# Working Capital Management: General Issues

---

**LEARNING OBJECTIVES**

After studying this chapter, you should be able to:

**23.1** Explain why the management of net working capital is critical for the survival of a firm.

**23.2** Explain how managing receivables, inventory, and payables is related in an integrated approach to net working capital management.

**23.3** Explain how financing and current asset investment decisions interact to determine a company's overall working capital position.

**23.4** Describe some common ways to analyze a firm's management of its net working capital.

---

Well-run companies must consider day-to-day operating needs and this chapter highlights several important issues in dealing with the management of working capital. Companies that focus primarily on profitability at the exclusion of working capital requirements may quickly find themselves at odds with their customers and suppliers. Effective working capital management practices depend upon managing the respective asset and liability accounts, namely accounts receivable, inventory, and accounts payable. Failure to do so will inevitably lead to cash shortages necessitating additional short-term financing, which will negatively impact the profitability of the firm and may eventually reduce its share value. A series of working capital ratios will be examined in an effort to quantify working capital components relative to established industry norms.

In Chapter 4, we defined working capital as the sum of the firm's current assets. In Chapter 3, we talked about net working capital (NWC) as the difference between a firm's current assets and its current liabilities. Working capital management refers to the way in which a firm manages both its current assets (i.e., cash and marketable securities, accounts receivable, and inventories) and its current liabilities (i.e., accounts payable, notes payable, and short-term borrowing arrangements).

---

## 23.1 | The Importance of Working Capital Management

---

**LEARNING OBJECTIVE 23.1**

Explain why the management of net working capital is critical for the survival of a firm.

---

Effective **working capital management** is critical to both the short-term and the long-term viability of any firm. In fact, working capital *mismanagement* often causes liquidity problems, which, in extreme cases, can force a firm into bankruptcy. Some years ago, American Airlines

**working capital management** the way in which a firm manages both its current assets (i.e., cash and marketable securities, accounts receivable, and inventories) and its current liabilities (i.e., accounts payable, notes payable, and short-term borrowing arrangements) was struggling to raise funds as its liquidity deteriorated. The company's efforts to improve its working capital situation were largely unsuccessful, and American Airlines went into voluntary bankruptcy protection. Its situation highlights the difference between illiquidity and insolvency.

**illiquidity**  the inability of an entity to raise funds on reasonable terms, unrelated to its creditworthiness

**insolvency**  the inability of an entity to meet its financial obligations as they come due, leading to a default

**Illiquidity** is the inability of an entity to raise funds on reasonable terms, unrelated to its creditworthiness. **Insolvency**, on the other hand, is the inability of an entity to meet its financial obligations as they come due, leading to a default.[1] Clearly the two concepts are closely related. However, financing relies on both the supply of securities (that is, the demand for cash) and the demand to purchase those securities (the supply of cash), so illiquidity can come about simply because the lender decides not to buy the securities. Consequently, the firm can be "short of cash" or illiquid even if its creditworthiness has not changed. If the firm can find no other source of cash, this illiquidity may lead the firm to default on its obligations and become insolvent. Conversely, a firm may be liquid but still default or seek bankruptcy protection, which is what happened to American Airlines.

Just a month before American Airlines went into bankruptcy, a Standard & Poor's analyst had noted that the company's "Liquidity is adequate, but we expect cash to continue to decline . . . We forecast year-end cash in the $3.5 billion–$4 billion range . . . but above our $3 billion potential downgrade trigger. In reviewing any possible downgrade, we would also consider expected future cash generation, financing activities, and cash uses."[2] And JPMorgan had described a voluntary bankruptcy filing as highly unlikely because "the company has approximately $4.1 billion in unrestricted cash and short-term investments . . . [which] is anticipated to be more than sufficient to assure that its vendors, suppliers and other business partners will be paid timely and in full." On November 29, after the bankruptcy filing, an analyst at JPMorgan was reported as saying, "We were wrong," adding, "this WASN'T about liquidity (liquidity is about 18 percent of LTM revenue)." In JPMorgan's view, the filing by American Airlines was all about reducing costs and achieving a more viable competitive position in the long run for the airline, rather than signalling an inability to meet its commitments.[3]

Although this textbook is about corporate finance, it was a series of government financial problems, particularly those facing the United States and countries in the Eurozone, that dominated the headlines in 2011 and 2012. Countries need to finance their expenditures, just as corporations do, and they similarly have to rely on the willingness of others to buy their securities. If this willingness disappears, a country or a corporation can face a liquidity crisis, which simply confirms the critical importance of managing working capital.

Many entry-level jobs for finance graduates are in the field of working capital management. This is because every firm has to manage its working capital day-to-day, whereas decisions regarding capital structure, dividend policy, and capital budgeting are made infrequently. Consequently, this chapter covers "bread-and-butter" topics that anyone working in a finance capacity in a non-financial company must be familiar with.

What constitutes good working capital management? The answer is complicated; however, we can say that good working capital management is characterized by

1. the maintenance of optimal cash balances;

2. the investment of any excess liquid funds in marketable securities that provide the best return possible, considering any liquidity or default-risk constraints;

3. the proper management of accounts receivable;

4. an efficient inventory management system; and

5. the maintenance of an appropriate level of short-term financing in the least expensive and most flexible manner possible.

We deal with these points in Chapter 24. In this chapter, we address the concept of working capital management in general. However, before we discuss this concept, read the excerpt from *Business Week* of April 28, 1956, in Finance in the News 23.1. This topic is fundamental to sound corporate decision-making and is as important now as it was then.

---

[1]Technically, a company is insolvent if the value of its liabilities exceeds the value of its assets.
[2]Standard & Poor's Rating Service on American Airlines as reported in the *Dallas Morning News,* October 20, 2011. Reprinted with permission of *The Dallas Morning News.*
[3]Grocer, Stephen, "Analysts React to American's Bankruptcy Filing: 'This WASN'T about Liquidity'" (blog). *Wall Street Journal, Deal Journal,* November 29, 2011, http://blogs.wsj.com.

> ## 23.1 Finance in the News    How to Go Broke . . . While Making a Profit
>
> As the year started, Mr. Jones of the ABC Co. was in fine shape. His company made widgets—just what the customer wanted. He made them for $0.75 each, sold them for $1. He kept a 30-day supply in inventory, paid his bills promptly, and billed his customers 30 days net. Sales were right on target, with the sales manager predicting a steady increase. It felt like his lucky year, and it began this way:
>
> ### Jan. 1 Cash $1,000 Inventory $750 Receivables $1,000
>
> In January, he sold 1,000 widgets; shipped them at a cost of $750; collected his receivables—winding up with a tidy $250 profit.
>
> ### Feb. 1 Cash $1,250 Inventory $750 Receivables $1,000
>
> This month sales jumped, as predicted, to $1,500. With a corresponding step-up in production to maintain his 30-day inventory, he made 2,000 units at a cost of $1,500. All receivables from January sales were collected. Profit so far: $625.
>
> ### Mar. 1 Cash $750 Inventory $1,125 Receivables $1,500
>
> March sales were even better: 2,000 units.
>
> Collections: On time. Production to adhere to his inventory policy: 2,500 units. Operating result for the month: $500 profit. Profit to date: $1,125.
>
> ### Apr. 1 Cash $375 Inventory $1,500 Receivables $2,000
>
> In April, sales jumped another 500 units to 2,500—and Jones patted his sales manager on the back. His customers were paying right on time. Production was pushed to 3,000 units, and the month's business netted him $625 for a profit to date of $1,750. He took off for Florida before he saw the accountant's report.
>
> ### May 1 Cash $125 Inventory $1,875 Receivables $2,500
>
> May saw Jones' company really hitting a stride—sales of 3,000 widgets, production of 3,500, and a five-month profit of $2,500. But suddenly he got a phone call from his treasurer: "Come home! We need money!" His books had caught up with him.
>
> ### June 1 Cash $000 Inventory $2,250 Receivables $3,000
>
> He came home—and hollered for his banker.
>

---

## Concept Review Question

1. Why are liquidity and solvency issues important to every company?

---

## 23.2 | An Integrated Approach to Net Working Capital (NWC) Management

### LEARNING OBJECTIVE 23.2

Explain how managing receivables, inventory, and payables is related in an integrated approach to net working capital management.

## A Classic Working Capital Problem

The *Business Week* article in Finance in the News 23.1 is a classic because it highlights a basic problem: profits are not cash, and a firm can only pay its bills with cash. In this example, Mr. Jones' "books caught up with him" and he had to come home from his Florida vacation after getting a phone call from his accountant/treasurer. ABC's rapid growth was causing cash flow problems even though it was very profitable. Let's analyze what went wrong—or more accurately, what was going right and what the treasurer should have done to head off an entirely predictable problem.

First, look at the cash flow statement as of June 1, shown in **Table 23.1**, to find out what happened. Recall from Chapter 3 that firms produce three statements: the income statement, the balance sheet, and the cash flow statement. Of the three, financial analysts tend to look at the cash flow statement the most, because the other two frequently have accounting adjustments that make it difficult to find the firm's problems. The ABC example helps us contrast the usefulness of the income statement with that of the cash flow statement.

We know that Mr. Jones was running a profitable company. When we add up the sales from January to May, we see that he sold $1,000 worth of widgets in January and $500 more each month, so by the end of May he had cumulative sales of $10,000. These widgets had a $0.75 cost, so he had $7,500 in cost of goods sold. The operating profit was $2,500. We have not included any depreciation charge for wear and tear on his machines, and even if we had, we would just add it back to get operating cash flow, because depreciation is a non-cash charge. So if ABC had cash flow of $2,500, why the telephone call telling Mr. Jones to hurry back?

**trade credit** a form of credit in which a customer orders a product or service and the firm delivers it, along with an invoice indicating the terms of payment

The problem was the change in ABC's working capital. Mr. Jones sold his widgets on credit; his customers paid him, but with a 30-day delay. This is typical of **trade credit**, in which a customer orders ABC's widgets and the firm ships them out, along with an invoice indicating the terms of payment, which in this case is 30 days. By June 1, ABC's accounts receivable had risen from $1,000 to $3,000, an increased investment in receivables of $2,000. The reason for the increase was the increased sales level, from $1,000 in January to $3,000 in May, which meant that more credit was being granted to ABC's customers, even though ABC's credit policy had not changed.

Similarly, ABC had an inventory policy of keeping a 30-day supply on hand, so when customers placed an order, it could be boxed and sent out immediately. In January, Mr. Jones had $750 worth of widgets on hand; by June 1, this had increased to $2,250 worth of widgets as ABC's sales level rose. Again, the reason for the increased inventory was the increase in sales level from $1,000 to $3,000. ABC required a similar increase in inventory of $2,000 worth of widgets, because the firm's policy was to keep one month's sales on hand. However, the widgets were carried in inventory at the "lower of cost and market," so the inventory investment was the $0.75 cost rather than the $1 selling price. ABC had an increased inventory investment of $1,500.

ABC paid its bills immediately, so there were no accounts payable. The change in net working capital was the increase in receivables plus inventory minus the change in payables: −$3,500.

**TABLE 23.1**   **ABC: Sources and Uses of Funds**

| Cash Flow Statement | January–June 1 |
| --- | --- |
| Sales | $10,000 |
| Cost of goods sold | 7,500 |
| Profit | 2,500 |
| Operating cash flow | 2,500 |
| (No depreciation) | |
| Increase in accounts receivable | (2,000) |
| Increase in inventory | (1,500) |
| Change in working capital | (3,500) |
| Change in cash | −1,000 |

When the change in NWC was added to the operating cash flow, ABC had cash flow from operations of −$1,000. ABC started with $1,000 cash in the bank, but by the end of May the cash had been depleted and ABC had no cash to finance its operations. At that point, ABC's cheques would bounce.

Finance in the News 23.2 alludes to the vital importance of strong working capital management policies. Generating profit is critical for the long-term health of any company, but working capital considers the day-to-day needs of a company and cannot be ignored without disastrous effects.

---

**23.2 Finance in the News**   As SNC CEO Eyes Options for Turnaround, Key Rival Already Holds Playbook

As SNC-Lavalin Group Inc. interim chief executive Ian Edwards starts meeting stakeholders in his review of the company's strategic direction, he could look to a key rival for inspiration on how to execute a turnaround.

Some 2,400 kilometres south in Dallas lies the headquarters of Jacobs Engineering Group Inc., a company that has generated one of the sector's most successful corporate reversals in the past five years, says Canaccord Genuity analyst Yuri Lynk.

The key: Exit the highest-risk businesses and reorganize to become a more pure-play engineer consulting-services company, even if it's at the expense of revenue growth.

"SNC is burning hundreds of millions of dollars a year in cash through poorly executed lump-sum, turnkey contracts," Mr. Lynk said in a research note.

"While SNC is in a much tougher spot than Jacobs was, we believe similar bold moves are necessary [to those that Jacobs took] to turn the company around."

Calls for SNC to take dramatic action underscore the expectations that Mr. Edwards faces from most investors to deliver a blueprint for substantive change.

Although the CEO is working with valuable assets—such as a stake in Ontario's Highway 407 toll road—and SNC enjoys an investment-grade credit rating, it also has some troubled divisions.

His predecessor, Neil Bruce, made a big bet on oil and gas by buying Kentz Corp. for $2.1-billion in 2014 before the sector declined. SNC has also struggled with problematic loss-making contracts with clients such as Chilean miner Codelco and continues to suffer reputational damage from bribery and fraud charges related to its past business dealings in Libya.

Many shareholders, such as David Taylor of Toronto-based Taylor Asset Management, have their own prescriptions for the path SNC should take. The company has to be far more predictable and get out of volatile and competitive business lines that require a lot of capital. The large shareholders, including the Caisse de dépôt et placement du Québec and Royal Bank of Canada, have to get that message to the board and help dictate strategy, he said in an interview.

"Just stop bidding on [these infrastructure and resource] projects and wind these businesses down," Mr. Taylor said. "They absolutely suck cash."

SNC says Mr. Edwards, who replaced Mr. Bruce in a move Tuesday that set off a 7-per-cent rally in the shares, is being asked to develop a plan that will deliver "sustainable success" by lowering risk, simplifying the business model and generating consistent earnings and cash flow. The company did not provide answers to several questions put to it by The Globe and Mail Wednesday about the circumstances surrounding Mr. Edwards's appointment and what strategic options would be considered.

Jacobs, an engineering and construction company like SNC, struggled to meet its earnings guidance for years because of project writeoffs and other issues before shifting its focus to engineering services and digital capability, according to Mr. Lynk.

In remaking itself, Jacobs shocked many observers in 2018 by selling its energy, chemicals and resources unit, which had been a central element of its strategy for decades, he said.

Jacobs also bought CH2M Hill, a leading professional-services company to bulk up in consulting.

SNC-Lavalin already has a key consulting asset to build on: The British-based Atkins business it bought in 2017. Atkins is winning projects on work such as transit, roads and airports and is expected to generate an 11.7-per-cent margin on earnings before interest, taxes, depreciation and amortization (EBITDA) both this year and next, according to National Bank of Canada equity analyst Maxim Sytchev. Atkins maintained its margins—although sales decreased—during the past financial crisis, he said in a report this month.

"The biggest risk to Atkins operations is not Brexit but engineering talent leaving for greener pastures," Mr. Sytchev said.

The analyst offers another option for SNC, however: a go-private transaction. In a report—titled The Level of Apathy is Palpable. Why Stay Public?—he estimates enough SNC shareholders could be persuaded to tender their stock to a possible white knight, such as the Caisse or another investor, at a price of $38.37 a share for a deal to go through.

Mr. Taylor, however, isn't convinced that SNC shareholders would bite at that price.

He said all the net asset value analysis he's examined shows SNC can climb to $50 to $55 a share.

"Let's wait and see what the strategy is," he said. "Because if the strategy is the proper strategy, we can get $50."

It is important to note that cash flow from operations is the correct measure of the cash-generating ability of the firm. All finance instructors emphasize that depreciation and amortization are non-cash charges and need to be added to net income to get cash flow, but this is only part of the story; other cash items need to be considered in determining cash flow. If ABC had a cash-only sales policy and did not extend credit, the firm would receive $10,000 in cash with the same level of sales. However, the fact that sales were on credit with a 30-day payment period meant that ABC did not get any cash from the $3,000 of sales in May. When firms sell on credit, they have to make sure that they are actually collecting the cash from those sales. Similarly, the income statement includes only the cost of producing items that are sold. If production is unsold, it goes into inventory, but the firm has still paid to produce it, so there is still a cash outflow. The increased receivables and inventory, net of payables, are the most important net working capital items.

## The Cash Budget

**cash budget** a cash flow statement for each month

If Mr. Jones had estimated ABC's cash flow statement for May, he would have realized that he had a cash flow problem. However, he would need to do a cash flow statement for every month to know exactly *when* this problem would become acute. Firms do project a **cash budget**, which is essentially a cash flow statement for each month.

So let's think through ABC's problem. The sales level was $1,000, and Mr. Jones was forecasting a $500 increase every month. We can start the sales at $1,000 for month 1 and then increase by $500 for every future month. Mr. Jones could forecast the cash inflow from these sales, which for ABC, with a 30-day credit policy, meant that each month the firm would receive as an inflow the previous month's credit sales. (In practice, things are slightly more complicated, as we will discuss later.)

Remember that the only source of cash from operations was from sales; all the other items were uses of cash. ABC spent $0.75 producing every widget. Two types of widgets were produced: those that were sold and those that were held in inventory. For each month, ABC had a cash outflow for the cost of the widgets produced and sold, which for month 1 was $750, for month 2 was $1,000, and so on. However, in month 2, in addition to production for sales, there was an additional $375 outflow for the 500 widgets produced for inventory, because sales had increased by 500 units and ABC had an inventory policy of keeping a one-month supply on hand. In reality, for month 2, at a sales level of $1,500, ABC was receiving only the $1,000 from the previous month's sales, while it was paying $1,125 to produce for the current month's sales and an additional $375 to increase inventory, translating into a net cash outflow of $500.

The cash inflows and outflows record the change in the cash budget each month. ABC started with $1,000 in cash, which increased to $1,250 after month 1 and then decreased to $750 after month 2. If Mr. Jones had decided that ABC needed 20 percent of sales in cash "just in case," then the excess cash in month 1 would have been $1,050. This excess cash could have been invested for a month. However, by month 2 the drop in cash flow from operations meant that the excess cash had dropped precipitously, to $450. By month 3, the cash budget would have indicated to Mr. Jones that ABC had no excess cash and was now below its desired holding of cash. This was two months *before* ABC actually ran out of cash, which would have given Mr. Jones plenty of time to talk to the bank about arranging some short-term credit. Table 23.2 provides ABC's cash budget for six months.

The important thing about the cash budget is that it forecasts cash inflows and outflows over a forecast horizon and their cumulative impact on the firm's cash balances. All the problems we discuss in this chapter and Chapter 24 revolve around the cash budget. Typically, firms prepare a cash budget for at least the upcoming year on a monthly (and sometimes even a weekly or daily) basis. These cash budgets are important planning tools for the firm. For example, they indicate when and for how long a firm can expect to have excess cash balances that can be invested in marketable securities. For ABC, this was the first two months of the year. Cash budgets also show when and for how long a firm may need to arrange some short-term borrowing to cover any cash shortfalls.

Banks often require a cash budget as part of the documentation for a loan application, because they need to see whether the loan is necessary for a short period or is, in fact, permanent financing. The cash budget will indicate this and help the bank structure an operating line of credit or longer-term financing. A careful look at Table 23.2 indicates that the operating cash flow

**TABLE 23.2**   ABC's Six-Month Cash Budget

| $ | 1 | 2 | 3 | 4 | 5 | 6 |
|---|---|---|---|---|---|---|
| Sales | 1,000 | 1,500 | 2,000 | 2,500 | 3,000 | 3,500 |
| Cash inflow | 1,000 | 1,000 | 1,500 | 2,000 | 2,500 | 3,000 |
| Cash outflow | | | | | | |
| Current sales | 750 | 1,125 | 1,500 | 1,875 | 2,250 | 2,625 |
| Inventory | 0 | 375 | 375 | 375 | 375 | 375 |
| Operating cash | 250 | −500 | −375 | −250 | −125 | 0 |
| Start cash | 1,000 | 1,250 | 750 | 375 | 125 | 0 |
| End cash | 1,250 | 750 | 375 | 125 | 0 | 0 |
| Required cash | 200 | 300 | 400 | 500 | 600 | 700 |
| Surplus/deficit | 1,050 | 450 | (25) | (375) | (600) | (700) |

shortfall is declining: it peaks at $500 and declines to $0 by month 6. If Mr. Jones had presented this cash flow forecast to the bank at the beginning of the year, the lending officer would have requested he complete it for the whole year instead of just the first six months. This 12-month budget is presented in Table 23.3.

By completing the cash budget for the whole year, it becomes apparent that with the $500 increase in sales each month, ABC's cash flow problems peak in months 5 and 6 (May/June) and then correct themselves. By month 7 (July), operating cash flow is positive, at $125, and from then on the operating cash flow increases every month. By month 10, ABC has surplus funds again and can start to invest the excess in marketable securities.

Mr. Jones would not have enhanced his reputation with the people at the bank if he went to see them in May, saying, "Please help me. I am out of cash." At the least, it would have indicated poor cash management, and the lending officer would have paid close attention to any loans made to ABC. If Mr. Jones had, instead, completed the cash budget at the beginning of the year and explained that he needed to set up a facility whereby he could invest surplus funds at the start and end of the year, and that he needed some short-term borrowing in the middle months, the bank could have designed a borrowing and lending facility for ABC. Establishing a good reputation with the bank lending officer is critical, especially for small firms, and the tool for doing this is the cash budget, because it enhances an understanding of the cash inflows and outflows through the firm.

**TABLE 23.3**   ABC's 12-Month Cash Budget

| $ | 1 | 2 | 3 | 4 | 5 | 6 | 7 | 8 | 9 | 10 | 11 | 12 |
|---|---|---|---|---|---|---|---|---|---|---|---|---|
| Sales | 1,000 | 1,500 | 2,000 | 2,500 | 3,000 | 3,500 | 4,000 | 4,500 | 5,000 | 5,500 | 6,000 | 6,500 |
| Cash inflow | 1,000 | 1,000 | 1,500 | 2,000 | 2,500 | 3,000 | 3,500 | 4,000 | 4,500 | 5,000 | 5,500 | 6,000 |
| Cash outflow | | | | | | | | | | | | |
| Current sales | 750 | 1,125 | 1,500 | 1,875 | 2,250 | 2,625 | 3,000 | 3,375 | 3,750 | 4,125 | 4,500 | 4,875 |
| Inventory | 0 | 375 | 375 | 375 | 375 | 375 | 375 | 375 | 375 | 375 | 375 | 375 |
| Operating cash | 250 | −500 | −375 | −250 | −125 | 0 | 125 | 250 | 375 | 500 | 625 | 750 |
| Start cash | 1,000 | 1,250 | 750 | 375 | 125 | 0 | 0 | 125 | 375 | 750 | 1,250 | 1,875 |
| End cash | 1,250 | 750 | 375 | 125 | 0 | 0 | 125 | 375 | 750 | 1,250 | 1,875 | 2,625 |
| Required cash | 200 | 300 | 400 | 500 | 600 | 700 | 800 | 900 | 1,000 | 1,100 | 1,200 | 1,300 |
| Surplus/deficit | 1,050 | 450 | (25) | (375) | (600) | (700) | (675) | (525) | (250) | 150 | 675 | 1,325 |

The key components of a cash budget are sales forecasts, estimated production schedules, and estimates of the size and timing of any other major inflows (e.g., from the sale of an asset) or outflows (e.g., capital expenditures, dividend payments) that the firm expects. Example 23.1 provides a simplified exercise in constructing a cash budget.

---

**EXAMPLE 23.1** | Cash Budget

A firm has estimated its sales, purchases from suppliers, and wages and miscellaneous operating cash outlays for the first four months of next year as follows:

| Month | Sales | Purchases | Wages and Miscellaneous |
|---|---|---|---|
| January | $10,000 | $6,000 | $3,000 |
| February | $12,000 | $7,500 | $3,500 |
| March | $15,000 | $5,500 | $4,000 |
| April | $11,000 | $5,000 | $3,000 |

The firm estimates that 50 percent of its sales will be for cash and that 80 percent of its credit sales will be collected one month after the sale, with the remainder being collected in the following month. It also estimates that 50 percent of its purchases will be paid 30 days from the purchase date, while the remaining 50 percent will be paid in 60 days. Assume that sales and purchases were the same in November and December as they are estimated to be in January. Finally, the firm plans to pay dividends of $3,000 in March and expects to receive $1,500 in January from the sale of a used truck. The beginning cash balance is $1,000, which is the minimum cash balance the firm wants to maintain. Estimate the firm's cash budget for the first four months of next year.

**Solution**

| | January | February | March | April |
|---|---|---|---|---|
| **Cash inflows ($)** | | | | |
| Sales | | | | |
| Current month's sales | 5,000 | 6,000 | 7,500 | 5,500 |
| Previous month's sales | 4,000 | 4,000 | 4,800 | 6,000 |
| Sales from two months ago | 1,000 | 1,000 | 1,000 | 1,200 |
| Total sales receipts | 10,000 | 11,000 | 13,300 | 12,700 |
| Other cash inflows | 1,500* | | | |
| Total cash inflows | 11,500 | 11,000 | 13,300 | 12,700 |
| **Cash outflows ($)** | | | | |
| Purchases | | | | |
| Previous month | 3,000 | 3,000 | 3,750 | 2,750 |
| Two months ago | 3,000 | 3,000 | 3,000 | 3,750 |
| Total purchase outflows | 6,000 | 6,000 | 6,750 | 6,500 |
| Wages and miscellaneous | 3,000 | 3,500 | 4,000 | 3,000 |
| Other cash outflows | | | 3,000$^{\dagger}$ | |
| Total cash outflows | 9,000 | 9,500 | 13,750 | 9,500 |
| **Net cash flow** | 2,500 | 1,500 | (450) | 3,200 |
| Beginning cash | 1,000 | 3,500 | 5,000 | 4,550 |
| Ending cash | 3,500 | 5,000 | 4,550 | 7,750 |

\* From sale of truck
† Dividend payment

---

The firm's cash balance is expected to climb to $3,500 in January and not go below that figure any time before April. In fact, cash is expected to increase to $7,750 by the end of April. This implies that the firm could invest as much as $2,500 for at least three months in marketable securities and still maintain the $1,000 minimum amount in cash. In fact, if the surplus cash position was expected to last longer, the excess funds could be invested in other assets. We could just as easily have constructed an example in which a firm forecast a deficit cash position in a future month or months. In that case, the amount of the expected deficit would provide the firm with a starting estimate of how much short-term borrowing it needed to arrange—in practice, the firm would probably arrange to borrow an amount that exceeded the projected cash deficit, just to be cautious.

---

### Concept Review Questions

1. What is the difference between profit and cash flow from operations?
2. Why should all firms prepare a cash budget?

---

## 23.3 | Analyzing Cash Inflows and Outflows

### LEARNING OBJECTIVE 23.3

Explain how financing and current asset investment decisions interact to determine a company's overall working capital position.

## Cash Changes and Sales Growth

The cash budget is the basic tool for forecasting the cash inflows and outflows through a firm. Unfortunately, although it helps to identify key items, it does not explain the exact cause of the problem. Let's look at the problem faced by ABC in more detail. ABC's sales in the previous month can be represented as $S_{t-1}$, because it receives its cash with a one-month delay due to its collection policy. In this example, ABC is selling 500 units for $1 each. ABC's cash outflows are then $0.75 for production for current sales and $0.75 for inventory to support the increased sales. Algebraically, we can represent the change in cash ($\Delta$Cash) as

$$\Delta Cash = S_{t-1} - bS_t - b(S_t - S_{t-1})$$

The change in cash equals last month's sales minus the cost of production for this month ($bS_t$) and the cost of producing goods for inventory ($b[S_t - S_{t-1}]$), where $b$ is the $0.75 cash production cost or, conversely, $1 - 0.75$ (i.e., $0.25) is the contribution margin. If we define $g$ as the monthly sales growth rate, so that $S_t = S_{t-1} \times (1 + g)$, we get Equation 23.1.

$$\Delta Cash = S_{t-1}[1 - b(1 + 2g)] \qquad [23.1]$$

Finance professors love equations like Equation 23.1 because the change in cash is linear with the growth rate in sales—that is, if we graph the change in cash against the monthly sales growth rate, we get a straight line. We will do this shortly with a more general problem, but note that with ABC's problem, $b = 0.75$, so if we divide both sides by last period's sales, the equation reduces to

$$\frac{\Delta Cash}{S_{t-1}} = 0.25 - 1.5g$$

We have divided by last period's sales to standardize the problem and focus on the critical issues. Think about the equation. If the sales growth rate is zero, then last period's sales are the same as this period's sales, so with a 30-day credit policy, ABC's cash inflow is the same as this month's sales. Further, there is no production for inventory, so the cash outflow is the $0.75 production cost. As a result, with $g = 0$, ABC makes $0.25 on every dollar of sales, and its cash inflow is the 25-percent contribution margin for each sale (i.e., $\Delta\text{Cash} = \$0.25\,S_{t-1}$). So what about the $g$ coefficient?

Given ABC's credit policy, this month's sales increase has no impact on cash inflows, because these were fixed last month; all that a sales increase does is increase cash outflows. For ABC, there is increased cash outflow for production for the incremental sales and incremental inventory. With a "current monthly sales in inventory policy," this means that for every unit increase in sales, there is a cash outflow to produce two units: one for sales and one for inventory. As a result, the coefficient on the sales growth rate is twice the cost of production. Clearly, ABC's credit and inventory policies mean that the cash flow from operations is very sensitive to the sales growth rate. In fact, we can set the left side equal to zero and find the **break-even sales growth rate** at which the monthly cash flow from operations is zero. For ABC, this is 1/6 or 16.67 percent (i.e., $0.25 - 1.5g = 0$; so $g = 0.25/1.5 = 1/6$). This means that as long as ABC's monthly sales growth rate is less than 16.67 percent, it generates cash; above that rate, it needs cash.

Returning to the annual cash budget for ABC, we can see why ABC changes from needing cash to generating cash. The key is that Mr. Jones assumed a $500 increase in sales each month. For month 1, there was no increase, so ABC generated 0.25 times the $1,000 sales level or $250. For month 2, the sales increase was 50 percent, well above the 16.67-percent break-even rate, so ABC needed cash. In fact, using the above equation, we can see that the cash changed by $0.25 - (1.5 \times 0.5)$, or −50 percent of the previous month's sales of $1,000 (i.e., −$500), which is exactly what happened. This need for cash changed in month 6, when sales increased by $500 from the $3,000 level of the previous month, or by exactly 16.67 percent, so the change in cash was zero. After that, the constant $500 sales increase on ever-larger previous month's sales figures caused the growth rate to drop below the 16.67-percent break-even rate, so ABC generated cash.

The importance of the growth rate on cash flow from operations—specifically, whether that cash flow is positive or negative—is equivalent to our discussion in Chapter 4 on the importance of the sustainable growth rate. In both cases, a higher sales growth rate creates an external financing need. In Chapter 4, we were concerned with the overall financing needs of the firm over a long period and how it should raise long-term capital. In this chapter, the concern is for the firm's financing needs over a shorter horizon, and we are mainly concerned with NWC management. However, the fundamentals are the same: for most firms, the structure of their financial and operating policies means that higher growth rates generate a need for financing. Now we can see how NWC management policies interact in a more general way.

## Credit, Inventory, and Payables

We can define the firm's credit policy with $\alpha$ as the percentage of sales collected this month and the balance $(1 - \alpha)$ collected with a one-month delay. In practice, sales can be collected after two or more months, but the important thing is that by varying $\alpha$, we are changing the firm's credit policy to see how this affects its cash flow from operations. $\beta$ is the proportion of this month's production costs that are paid this month, and $(1 - \beta)$ is the proportion paid next month. In this way, we can have the firm pay for some of its current production costs with a one-month delay, reflecting credit provided to it by suppliers and the firm's workforce.[4] Finally, $\gamma$ is the percentage of the firm's monthly sales tied up in inventory, so $1/\gamma$ is the monthly inventory turnover ratio.

With these assumptions and the same notation as before, the change in cash each month is as shown in Equation 23.2.

$$\Delta\text{Cash} = \alpha S_t + (1 - \alpha)S_{t-1} - b\beta S_t - b(1 - \beta)S_{t-1} - b\gamma(S_t - S_{t-1}) \qquad [23.2]$$

[4]Workers generally are paid at the end of the week or month, so implicitly they finance some of the firm's operations.

Equation 23.2 looks cumbersome, but all that has changed is that cash inflows come from this month's and last month's sales; cash outflows for current sales also occur this month and the following month; and production for inventory depends on the inventory policy ($\gamma$). In ABC's case, $\alpha = 0$, because it collects all this month's sales the following month; $\beta = 1$, because it pays all this month's expenses this month; $b = \$0.75$; and $\gamma = 1$, because it tries to maintain the next month's projected sales in inventory. So for ABC, the equation reduces to the equation shown previously:

$$\Delta\text{Cash} = 0 + (1)S_{t-1} - (\$0.75)(1)S_t - \$0.75(0)S_{t-1} - (\$0.75)(1)(S_t - S_{t-1})$$
$$= S_{t-1} - \$0.75S_t - \$0.75(S_t - S_{t-1})$$

If we again remove the different sales levels by including the sales growth rate, $S_t = (1+g)S_{t-1}$, in Equation 23.2 and simplify, we get Equation 23.3:

$$\boxed{\frac{\Delta\text{Cash}}{S_{t-1}} = (1 - b) + [\alpha - b(\beta + \gamma)]g} \qquad [23.3]$$

As before, with no sales growth, we get the contribution margin of $(1 - b)$, and the firm generates cash. However, this time the coefficient on the growth rate is more complex, as we are allowing the firm's policies regarding receivables, payables, and inventory to change. For example, previously we assumed cash inflows were from the previous month's sales, so $\alpha = 0$. Similarly, we assumed that all bills were paid immediately, so $\beta = 1$, and the firm kept 100 percent of monthly sales in inventory, so $\gamma = 1$. The coefficient on the sales growth rate was 1.5. Now we allow this coefficient to change with the firm's working capital policy.

First, however, in **Figure 23.1**, we graph the change in cash against the sales growth rate.

We can now see several things. First, as before, growth normally causes cash flow problems as the investment in NWC soaks up cash more quickly than the incremental sales generate cash: this is generally referred to as the firm's **burn rate**. (This is also the reason why slow-growing profitable firms are referred to as "cash cows.") Fast-growing firms need to have more liquidity or external financing to offset this higher burn rate. Second, we can see what affects this burn rate. What the firm would like to do is flatten the slope of the line so that it reduces the amount of cash needed to finance the firm's growth—that is, it would like to lower its burn rate.

**burn rate**   the rate at which a firm uses up its cash reserves; it is synonymous with monthly cash flow deficits

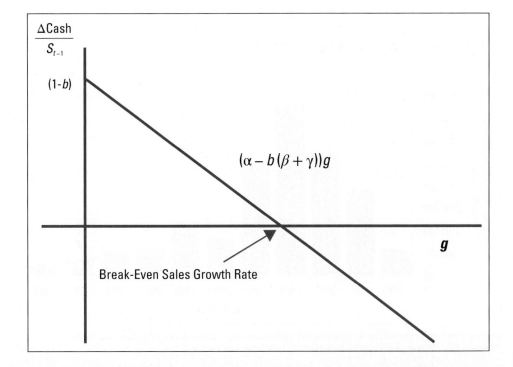

**FIGURE 23.1**   **Change in Cash and Sales Growth**

In the example of ABC Company, its burn rate was rapidly decreasing as its growth rate was declining, so if it held on long enough, its problem would reverse. However, this is not the case for companies suffering financial distress. Companies in financial distress worry about their *cash burn rate*, which refers to a company's cash on hand and the rate that cash is used in operations due to negative operating cash flows. The burn rate then indicates how long a company can operate before it has to raise funds, either by issuing stock or borrowing. For example, Ford burned through $4.7 billion of cash in the first six months of 2009, but was able to slow that burn with a significant positive cash flow in the fourth quarter of 2009, burning just $300 million for the entire year of 2009. The fate of Ford depended on its ability to slow the cash burn, which it did.

Many companies suffer from cash burn leading up to bankruptcy, including United Airlines and Consolidated Freightways in 2002. Consider Borders Group, a U.S. retail bookstore chain that filed for bankruptcy in 2011. Borders burned through cash as it approached bankruptcy (**Figure 23.2**).

A more recent example of a cash management problem is outlined in Finance in the News 23.3, which explains some of the challenges that automobile manufacturer Tesla Inc. has experienced in its efforts to ramp up production of its new Model 3.

One way to lower the burn rate is to increase $\alpha$ and hope that it changes the slope of the line from negative to positive. Increasing $\alpha$ essentially means collecting receivables more quickly. This changes the firm's **credit policy**. Alternatively, we can reduce $\beta$ and $\gamma$; $b$ has to remain positive as it is the firm's production cost. Reducing $\beta$ means delaying paying the bills; the greater $\beta$ is, the higher the percentage of bills paid in the current month. This changes the firm's **payment policy**. Finally, reducing $\gamma$ means having less inventory, which in turn means increasing the turnover ratio and changing the firm's **inventory policy**. For a given sales growth rate, the firm's main levers for growing faster are to collect its invoices more quickly, delay paying its bills, and reduce its stock of inventory. These policy changes may slow the growth rate, as we will see in Chapter 24. If the firm can't change these policies, another alternative is to increase its prices and slow its growth rate that way, which has the added advantage of increasing its contribution margin and lowering $b$.

As before, we can work out the monthly sales growth rate the firm can achieve without needing or generating cash. Equation 23.4 shows the extended example case.

$$g = \frac{(1 - b)}{[b(\beta + \gamma) - \alpha]} \qquad [23.4]$$

As can be seen from Equation 23.4, the firm can grow faster if it has a higher gross margin $(1 - b)$, has lower production costs $(b)$, collects its receivables more quickly (higher $\alpha$), pays its bills more slowly (lower $\beta$), and has less inventory (lower $\gamma$).

---

**credit policy** decisions on how a firm grants, monitors, and collects payment for outstanding accounts receivable

**payment policy** decisions on how quickly the firm pays its bills

**inventory policy** decisions on the levels of inventory the firm holds

---

**FIGURE 23.2** **Borders Group's Cash Burn**

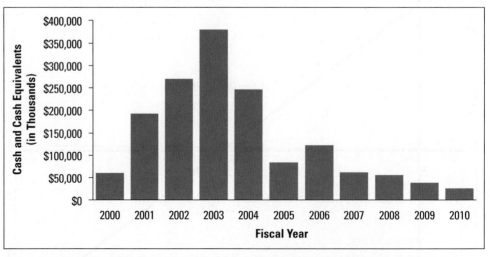

**Sources:** Data from Rouse, William B., *Enterprise Transformation: Understanding and Enabling Fundamental Change* (Hoboken, NJ: John Wiley & Sons, 2006); Borders Group 10-K filings, various years.

## 23.3 Finance in the News   Musk Gets Last Laugh as Firm Seems to Have Exceeded Dark Expectations

It was only a few months ago that Wall Street was bashing Elon Musk's Tesla Inc. One analyst called the stock "no longer investable," citing Musk's erratic behaviour in tweets and taunts. A short seller bet on a dramatic drop, saying it's "more and more apparent that Tesla is having difficulties paying their bills."

But an unexpected thing happened along the way: The company found its footing as an electric-car manufacturer, an achievement masked by Musk's bluster. Its stunning third-quarter profit picture, boosted by its ability to ramp up production of Model 3 sedans, surprised naysayers, and marked the beginning of a turn in market sentiment.

Tesla's stock is, somewhat improbably, right back near the highs it reached on the day of that infamous "funding secured" tweet that caused a furious rally before landing Musk in trouble with the U.S. Securities and Exchange Commission.

And so after a year of stomach churning swings that saw the stock post half-a-dozen rallies or sell-offs of 20 per cent or more, it is up nearly 18 per cent. Not bad at all when you consider that the S&P 500 is down 1.4 per cent on the year.

All of this, of course, could easily shift again at almost any moment, given Musk's penchant for impolitic remarks and the many operational challenges. But for now at least, Wall Street is bullish once again, expecting Tesla to be profitable and have positive free cash flow in the fourth quarter–accomplishments that would show the company has finally figured out how to produce cars at a stable pace and make money while doing it.

"Was the third-quarter a fluke? Time will tell," said Roth Capital Partners analyst Craig Irwin. "But the reality is that when you produce 50,000 cars a quarter, that is a big milestone, and you can see these guys are here for the long run. Tesla is squarely on its own two feet now, and learning and well-prepared to keep learning."

Tesla's stock has always been priced for perfection, and Musk's Twitter habits weren't the only roadblocks that investors faced in 2018. As it frantically tried to boost production of the Model 3, Tesla was burning cash at a rapid pace–as much as US$8,000 a minute as it entered the year, according to Bloomberg calculations. Musk acknowledged how dire the problem was in an interview last month, saying the company's earlier cash bleed had left it just a couple of months away from collapse.

Tesla's fundamentals are now improving, helped by increasingly efficient manufacturing, strong prices of its cars, and the "slow and disappointing" competition in the electric-vehicle market, Oppenheimer analyst Colin Rusch wrote in a note published on Wednesday. "We believe as TSLA delivers steady cash flow, a new group of investors will begin taking positions, helping drive shares higher." Tesla shares jumped as much as 1.4 per cent in New York.

Plenty of reasons for skepticism remain. Tesla is still highly levered up and 2019 is going to be an "uphill battle," Cowen analyst Jeffrey Osborne said. He cited the expiration of electric-vehicle tax credits and the lack of pent-up demand for electric cars that helped Tesla in 2018, among other things.

And despite the corporate governance reforms in Tesla's settlement with the SEC, the company is still at the mercy of Musk to control his behaviour as its public face and chief decision-maker. He responded to an exodus of top executives this year by assuming some of their responsibilities himself, and he bristled in a 60 Minutes interview at the idea that he now has a babysitter supervising him.

But Tesla's premium valuation today reflects its leadership in electric cars, far ahead of potential competitors. Analysts said they weren't impressed by two would be electric rivals unveiled this year by Audi and Mercedes-Benz.

General Motors, which is expected to sell about 4.7 million vehicles globally this year, had a market capitalization of US$49 billion through Tuesday. Tesla's is nearly US$63 billion though it's likely to sell only 256,000 vehicles.

"It is incredible to me, at the end of 2018, that the major automakers still haven't figured out how to respond competitively to Tesla," JMP Securities analyst Joseph Osha said. "Tesla plausibly can grow at eight to 10 per cent for a really long time, so it should be valued a lot more highly than companies growing at one or two per cent, which is what the rest of the auto business is growing at."

---

**EXAMPLE 23.2** | Break-Even Sales Growth Rates

A firm collects 10 percent of its monthly sales immediately and the rest a month later. Its production costs are 80 percent of sales. It holds two months' worth of sales in inventory, and it pays half its bills immediately and half after 30 days.

**a.** What is its break-even sales growth rate?

**b.** What happens to this rate if the firm reduces its inventory to one month's sales and speeds up its collection of receivables to 50 percent immediately and 50 percent after 30 days?

**Solution**

**a.** $\alpha = 0.1$; $b = 0.8$; $\beta = 0.5$; and $\gamma = 2$

Plugging these values into Equation 23.4, we get

$$g = \frac{(1-b)}{[b(\beta+\gamma)-\alpha]} = \frac{(1-0.8)}{[0.8(0.5+2)-0.1]} = 0.1053 = 10.53\%$$

**b.** With the new policy, $\gamma = 1$ and $\alpha = 0.5$, so the growth rate increases to

$$g = \frac{(1 - 0.8)}{[0.8(0.5 + 1) - 0.5]} = 0.2857 = 28.57\%$$

By reducing its inventory investment and speeding up the collection of its receivables, the firm can grow faster.

Another way of looking at the information in Figure 23.1 is to consider something called the "cash conversion cycle," which is a measure of how many days of financing are required. This topic is addressed in the next section.

## Concept Review Questions

1. What is the relationship between the break-even sales growth rate and a firm's collection policy, payables policy, and inventory policy?
2. Why does cash flow from operations increase if the firm speeds up the collection of receivables, delays paying its bills, or increases its inventory turnover ratio?

# 23.4 | Working Capital Management in Practice

**LEARNING OBJECTIVE 23.4**

Describe some common ways to analyze a firm's management of its net working capital.

We have discussed what characterizes good working capital management and how such decisions can be integrated. We now discuss some common ways to assess or summarize a firm's working capital management.

## Working Capital Ratios

We defined two common measures of firm liquidity in Chapter 4: the current ratio and the quick (or acid test) ratio. We repeat those definitions below:

$$\text{Current ratio} = \frac{\text{Current assets (CA)}}{\text{Current liabilities (CL)}} \qquad [23.5]$$

$$\text{Quick ratio} = \frac{\text{Cash (C) + Marketable securities (MS) + Accounts receivable (AR)}}{\text{CL}} \qquad [23.6]$$

Recall that the current ratio measures a firm's ability to repay current obligations from current assets. The quick ratio is a more conservative estimate of liquidity that reflects the fact that inventory is generally not as liquid as other current assets, while prepaid expenses are virtually worthless in the event of firm liquidation. There are no general rules setting out what are "good" values for these ratios, and optimal ratios vary by industry. For both of these ratios, higher values indicate that a firm has more liquidity. However, this does not necessarily mean that the firm is practising effective working capital management. In fact, it could indicate quite the opposite—that is, perhaps the firm is being too conservative and maintaining *excessive* liquidity, or perhaps it has high ratios because its credit policy is too lenient, which has left it with high levels of receivables outstanding.[5]

Although the current and quick ratios are useful summary statistics, they do not tell the whole story of working capital management. To gain better insight into a company's strengths and weaknesses, we need to look at how it arrived at these levels of CA and CL. We can again turn to Chapter 4, in which we introduced several efficiency ratios that are specifically related to working capital items. We begin by looking at two ratios that are related to accounts receivable:

$$\text{Receivables turnover (RT)} = \frac{\text{Rev}}{\text{AR}} \qquad [23.7]$$

$$\text{Average collection period (ACP)} = \frac{\text{AR}}{\text{Average daily revenue (ADR)}} = \frac{365}{\text{RT}} \qquad [23.8]$$

The receivables turnover (RT) ratio measures the revenues (Rev) that are generated for each dollar that is tied up in receivables, while the average collection period (ACP) measures how long it takes the average customer to pay their account. The ACP is 365 divided by the receivables turnover—that is, if accounts receivable turn over 10 times per year, the ACP is 36.5 days (365/10). Technically, both of these ratios should be calculated using credit revenues and not total revenues; however, because most companies do not break out revenues into cash and credit revenues, it is common to use the total revenues figures.

In Chapter 4, we also introduced some efficiency ratios that are related to inventory. One of these, the inventory turnover (IT) ratio, is defined in Equation 23.9.

$$\text{Inventory turnover (IT)} = \frac{\text{Cost of goods sold (CGS)}}{\text{Inventory}} \qquad [23.9]$$

The numerator of this ratio will be the CGS because when inventory is sold, it is expensed through this account. However, in practice, because of accounting differences, the CGS figure is not always reliable nor always comparable across firms. As a result, CGS is often replaced by revenues in the IT ratio, which is then defined as shown in Equation 23.10.

$$\text{Inventory turnover (IT)} = \frac{\text{Rev}}{\text{Inventory}} \qquad [23.10]$$

We will use this definition of IT for the remaining discussion.

Similar to our derivation of the ACP in Equation 23.8, we can divide 365 days by the IT ratio to find the average days of revenues in inventory (ADRI), which is given in Equation 23.11.

$$\text{Average days revenues in inventory (ADRI)} = \frac{\text{Inventory}}{\text{ADR}} = \frac{365}{\text{IT}} \qquad [23.11]$$

Notice that higher receivables turnover and higher inventory turnover are generally indicative of more efficient management of these current assets. However, they would cause a firm's current ratio (and its quick ratio, in the case of receivables turnover) to decline, all else being equal. This in itself demonstrates why current and quick ratios, when viewed in isolation, are insufficient measures of working capital management.

Finally, we focus on the current liability side of the working capital management issue by introducing the following two ratios that are related to a firm's management of its accounts payable:

$$\text{Payables turnover (PT)} = \frac{\text{Rev}}{\text{Accounts payable}} \qquad [23.12]$$

---

[5]The same could be said with respect to the current ratio if the firm maintains excess inventory. This would obviously not affect the quick ratio.

$$\text{Average days of revenues in payables (ADRP)} = \frac{\text{Accounts payable}}{\text{ADR}} = \frac{365}{\text{PT}} \qquad [23.13]$$

The payables turnover (PT) ratio shows how many times a year a firm pays off its suppliers, on average. The average days of revenues in payables (ADRP) ratio represents how long a firm defers payments to its suppliers, on average.[6]

## Operating and Cash Conversion Cycles

**operating cycle (OC)** the average time required for a firm to acquire inventory, sell it, and collect the sales proceeds

Two additional summary measures of working capital management deal specifically with the amount of time a firm must wait for cash to be generated from its sales and how much financing it will require. The **operating cycle (OC)** represents the average time required for a firm to acquire inventory, sell it, and collect the sale proceeds. As such, the OC can be estimated as the sum of the average days of revenues in inventory (ADRI) and the average collection period (ACP), as expressed in Equation 23.14.

$$\text{Operating cycle (OC)} = \text{ADRI} + \text{ACP} \qquad [23.14]$$

The OC measures the average number of days a firm holds items in inventory before they are sold, plus the average time it takes to collect on sales. Large OC figures indicate that a firm has a long operating cycle that requires large average investments in receivables or inventory. However, to estimate the amount of financing a firm requires, we must also consider how long it is able to delay making payments to suppliers. This can be measured by using the firm's average days of revenues in payables (ADRP) ratio, which measures how long it defers paying payables on average.

**cash conversion cycle (CCC)** an estimate of the average time between when a firm pays cash for its inventory purchases and when it receives cash for its sales; the average number of days of revenues that a firm must finance outside the use of trade credit

The **cash conversion cycle (CCC)** takes the payable deferral period into account and provides an estimate of the average time between when a firm pays cash for its inventory purchases and when it receives cash for its sales. In essence, the CCC represents the average number of days of revenues that a firm must finance outside the use of trade credit. As such, it is an important ratio that firms and their creditors consider when arranging financing. It can be broken into two components: the OC and the ADRP, as shown in Equation 23.15.

$$\text{Cash conversion cycle (CCC)} = \text{OC} - \text{ADRP} \text{ or } \text{CCC} = (\text{ADRI} + \text{ACP}) - \text{ADRP} \qquad [23.15]$$

We now return to our discussion of Mr. Jones' ABC Company. ABC had a policy of keeping one month's revenues in inventory, allowing 30 days of credit, and paying bills immediately. Therefore, ABC's ADRI was 30 days, as was its ACP, while its ADRP was zero. This translates into an OC of 60 days and a CCC of 60 days. If ABC immediately pays its bills for its widgets, it then has to finance them for 30 days while they sit in inventory and for another 30 days before the firm receives payment for them after they are sold. In other words, ABC has to finance 60 days' worth of revenues.

The CCC is clearly related to Figure 23.1. If the firm speeds up its collection policy, it gets its cash earlier, and the number of days in receivables goes down. Similarly, if it increases its inventory turnover ratio, it needs less inventory and the number of days of revenues that are tied up in inventory goes down. Finally, if it delays paying its bills, it has larger accounts payable. As a result of undertaking any of these actions, the firm can grow at a faster rate without needing cash, and the cash conversion cycle gets shorter.

---

[6]Technically, we should use the CGS instead of revenues in each of these ratios, because these payments represent costs that would be included in the CGS. However, for the same reasons we cited with respect to the use of revenues to calculate inventory turnover, it is common to use revenues.

> **EXAMPLE 23.3** | Cash Conversion Cycle
>
> Use the data provided for the company in Example 23.2 to calculate its cash conversion cycle under the policies outlined in parts a and b of that example.
>
> **Solution**
>
> **a.** The average days in receivables is 27, because 10 percent are collected immediately and 90 percent after 30 days; that is, days $= \alpha \times 0 + (1 - \alpha) \times 30$. The average days in inventory is 60, because the inventory is $\gamma \times 30$, while the average days in payables is 15, which is $\beta \times 0 + (1 - \beta) \times 30$. So the cash conversion cycle is 72 days (i.e., $27 + 60 - 15$). The company has to finance its widgets while they sit in inventory for 60 days and then for another 27 days until the company gets paid, which is partially offset by the 15-day trade credit the company gets by paying its bills with a delay.
>
> **b.** With the higher inventory turnover rate, as $\gamma$ is reduced from 2 to 1, the average days in inventory goes down to 30, while the quicker collection of receivables, as $\beta$ increases to 0.5, reduces the collection period to 15 days. Overall, the cash conversion cycle drops from 72 to 30 days (i.e., $15 + 30 - 15$). With a shorter cash conversion cycle, the firm's break-even growth rate goes up.

## Industry "Norms"

What are the practical implications when you are looking at a company's financial statements and trying to decide what to do when it comes to managing working capital? One approach is to compare one company to others in the same industry. Capital IQ (a division of Standard & Poor's), an extensive, widely used database containing corporate information that dates back to 1950, provides key business ratios that can be used for comparisons. Within this database, there is a sub-index of the S&P 500 Index made up of large U.S. railroad companies. Key ratios and other statistics are reported for 2017 and 2018 in **Table 23.4**.

Here we use averages of the data for major railroads operating in the U.S. in 2017 and 2018.

## An Illustrative Example

We now return to the financial statements for CP, which were analyzed in chapters 3 and 4, to demonstrate how to calculate and interpret the ratios discussed above. CP's balance sheets and income statements for 2017 and 2018 were presented in figures 3.4 and 3.5 of Chapter 3.

We begin by calculating CP's current and quick ratios for 2018 as follows:

$$\text{Current ratio} = \frac{\text{CA}}{\text{CL}} = \frac{\$1,117}{\$1,955} = 0.57$$

$$\text{Quick ratio} = \frac{\text{C} + \text{MS} + \text{AR}}{\text{CL}} = \frac{\$61 + \$0 + \$815}{\$1,955} = 0.45$$

The current ratio of 0.57 indicates that CP has $0.57 in CA for every dollar in CL, while its quick ratio is nearly 79 percent of its current ratio.

**TABLE 23.4   Capital IQ Key Business Ratios**

|  | 2017 | 2018 |
|---|---|---|
| Quick ratio | 0.68 | 0.73 |
| Current ratio | 0.94 | 0.96 |
| Collection period (days) | 27.52 | 27.83 |
| Inventory turnover | 15.23 | 16.69 |

Now we move on to calculate the various efficiency ratios, beginning with those related to receivables.

$$\text{Receivables turnover} = \frac{\text{Rev}}{\text{AR}} = \frac{\$7,316}{\$815} = 8.98$$

$$\text{ACP} = \frac{365}{\text{Receivables turnover}} = \frac{365}{8.98} = 40.65 \text{ days}$$

The receivables turnover ratio indicates that for every dollar invested in receivables, CP generated \$8.98 in revenues. The ACP indicates that if CP's revenues were all on credit, its customers were paying, on average, 40.65 days after purchase.

Next, we examine the company's ratios related to inventory management. We use revenues instead of cost of goods sold in our calculations, for the reasons discussed above. As mentioned in Chapter 4, CP is primarily a service company and does not have inventory in the usual sense, but the company does maintain an asset account labelled "Materials and Supplies," which we take as being equivalent to inventory.

$$\text{Inventory turnover} = \frac{\text{Rev}}{\text{Inv}} = \frac{\$7,316}{\$173} = 42.29$$

$$\text{ADRI} = \frac{365}{\text{Inventory turnover}} = \frac{365}{42.29} = 8.63 \text{ days}$$

The high inventory turnover (or low ADRI) reflects the nature of CP's service, which must be sold quickly in a competitive industry. So CP has only 8.63 days of revenues tied up in inventory and 40.65 in receivables. This translates into an operating cycle of 49.28 days:

$$\text{OC} = \text{ADRI} + \text{ACP} = 8.63 + 40.65 = 49.28 \text{ days}$$

We know that CP does not have to finance all 49.28 days of revenues because it can lean on its suppliers to a certain extent. We can measure its payables policy during 2018 by using the following two ratios:

$$\text{Payables turnover (PT)} = \frac{\text{Rev}}{\text{Accounts payable}} = \frac{\$7,316}{\$1,449} = 5.05$$

$$\text{Average days of revenues in payables (ADRP)} = \frac{365}{\text{PT}} = \frac{365}{5.05} = 72.28 \text{ days}$$

We can use this information to estimate CP's cash conversion cycle:

$$\text{CCC} = \text{OC} - \text{ADRP} = 49.28 - 72.28 = -23 \text{ days}$$

On average, CP does not have to finance its revenues since, in effect, its suppliers are doing this for CP. This is not unusual for a service firm such as CP, which does not have to order and store a lot of inventory to maintain its operations.

---

### Concept Review Questions

1. What are the limitations of the current ratio and the quick ratio as measures of working capital management?

2. What are the operating cycle and the cash conversion cycle, and how are they related to working capital policy?

---

## 23.1 Ethics and Corporate Governance    Bristol-Myers Squibb Company

The Securities and Exchange Commission today announced that it filed an enforcement action against Bristol-Myers Squibb Company, a New York-based company whose largest division, the U.S. Medicines Group, is based in New Jersey. The Commission's complaint, filed today in the United States District Court for the District of New Jersey, alleges that Bristol-Myers perpetrated a fraudulent earnings management scheme by, among other things, selling excessive amounts of pharmaceutical products to its wholesalers ahead of demand, improperly recognizing revenue from \$1.5 billion of such sales to its two largest wholesalers and using "cookie jar" reserves to meet its internal sales and earnings targets and analysts' earnings estimates.

In settling the Commission's action, Bristol-Myers agreed to an order requiring it to pay $150 million and perform numerous remedial undertakings, including the appointment of an independent adviser to review and monitor its accounting practices, financial reporting and internal controls.

Stephen M. Cutler, Director of the SEC's Division of Enforcement, said, "Bristol-Myers' earnings management scheme distorted the true performance of the company and its medicines business on a massive scale and caused significant harm to the company's shareholders. The company's conduct warrants a stiff civil sanction. As our investigation continues, we will be focusing on, among other things, those individuals responsible for the company's failures."

Timothy L. Warren, Associate Regional Director of the SEC's Midwest Regional Office, added, "For two years Bristol-Myers deceived the market into believing that it was meeting its financial projections and market expectations, when, in fact, the company was making its numbers primarily through channel-stuffing and manipulative accounting devices. Severe sanctions are necessary to hold Bristol-Myers accountable for its violative conduct, and deter Bristol-Myers and other public companies from engaging in similar schemes."

Specifically, the Commission's complaint alleges, among other things, that:

> From the first quarter of 2000 through the fourth quarter of 2001, Bristol-Myers engaged in a fraudulent scheme to inflate its sales and earnings in order to create the false appearance that the company had met or exceeded its internal sales and earnings targets and Wall Street analysts' earnings estimates.
>
> Bristol-Myers inflated its results primarily by (1) stuffing its distribution channels with excess inventory near the end of every quarter in amounts sufficient to meet its targets by making pharmaceutical sales to its wholesalers ahead of demand; and (2) improperly recognizing $1.5 billion in revenue from such pharmaceutical sales to its two biggest wholesalers. In connection with the $1.5 billion in revenue, Bristol-Myers covered these wholesalers' carrying costs and guaranteed them a return on investment until they sold the products. When Bristol-Myers recognized the $1.5 billion in revenue upon shipment, it did so contrary to generally accepted accounting principles.
>
> When Bristol-Myers' results still fell short of the Street's earnings estimates, the company tapped improperly created divestiture reserves and reversed

portions of those reserves into income to further inflate its earnings.

> At no time during 2000 or 2001 did Bristol-Myers disclose that (1) it was artificially inflating its results through channel-stuffing and improper accounting; (2) channel-stuffing was contributing to a buildup in excess wholesaler inventory levels; or (3) excess wholesaler inventory posed a material risk to the company's future sales and earnings.
>
> In addition, as a result of its channel-stuffing, Bristol-Myers materially understated its accruals for rebates due to Medicaid and certain of its prime vendors, customers of its wholesalers that purchased large quantities of pharmaceutical products from those wholesalers.

Bristol-Myers has agreed, without admitting or denying the allegations in the Commission's complaint, to the following relief:

- a permanent injunction against future violations of certain antifraud, reporting, books and records and internal controls provisions of the federal securities laws;

- disgorgement of $1;

- a civil penalty of $100 million;

- an additional $50 million payment into a fund for the benefit of shareholders;

- various remedial undertakings, including the appointment of an independent adviser to review, assess and monitor Bristol-Myers' accounting practices, financial reporting and disclosure processes and internal control systems.

**Discussion Questions**

1. **Bristol-Myers Squibb (BMS) was accused of channel-stuffing. What is channel-stuffing?**

2. **When does GAAP recognize a sale as occurring, and did a sale occur if BMS covered its distributors' costs and guaranteed them a return on their purchase of BMS products?**

3. **How did BMS's channel-stuffing affect its sales and cash flow? How could an analyst have picked up on BMS's channel-stuffing?**

**Source:** "Bristol-Myers Squibb Company Agrees to Pay $150 Million to Settle Fraud Charges." Securities and Exchange Commission press release, August 4, 2004. Available at www.sec.gov/news/press/2004-105.htm.

## Lessons to Be Learned

The importance of maintaining adequate liquidity has been highlighted over the past 15 years, as we have witnessed numerous dramatic corporate bankruptcies and an ongoing euro crisis resulting from a lack of liquidity that has negatively affected several countries, most notably Greece. This lesson was also learned by many individuals. The number of individuals declaring bankruptcy, particularly in the United States, has soared as consumers also borrowed too much and were not prepared to weather the economic storms that were experienced during the 2008–9 financial crisis. The lesson is that it is important to maintain adequate liquidity or financial reserves and not to leverage yourself with too much debt, particularly short-term debt that forces you to rely on someone else to continue to finance you. When times are tough it is difficult to distinguish between illiquidity and insolvency, and financing may be withdrawn even if you believe that you are solvent.

# Review

## Summary

In this chapter, we discuss the importance of effective net working capital management and demonstrate the classic cash flow problem faced by growing firms. We present an integrative approach to working capital management that focuses on the importance of the sales growth rate and demonstrates the usefulness of cash budgets, which allow firms to forecast their cash requirements. We conclude by showing how to use some common ratios to assess a firm's overall approach to working capital management.

## Summary of Learning Objectives

**23.1 Explain why the management of net working capital is critical for the survival of a firm.**

Sales growth may create a cash shortage, as increased inventory and accounts receivable consume cash. While sales growth also increases payables, the increase usually does not offset inventory and receivables. This cash shortage can lead to insolvency—for a growing firm! Even in a firm without growth, cash is used in production before it is collected from sales. This gap can lead to cash shortages, which can lead to a firm's insolvency if it does not plan for those shortages and accommodate them through short-term financing.

**23.2 Explain how managing receivables, inventory, and payables is related in an integrated approach to net working capital management.**

Net working capital is the difference between current assets and current liabilities. Current assets usually include cash, receivables, and inventory. Current liabilities include payables. Thus, net working capital = cash + receivables + inventory − payables. This is why receivables, inventory, and payables must be managed as part of the integrated approach to net working capital management.

**23.3 Explain how financing and current asset investment decisions interact to determine a company's overall working capital position.**

For most firms, the structure of their financial and operating policies means that higher growth rates generate a need for short-term financing. If current assets are less than current liabilities, net working capital becomes negative, which generates a need for outside financing. A company's overall working capital can also be affected by its policies concerning collection of receivables, payment of bills, and inventory management.

**23.4 Describe some common ways to analyze a firm's management of its net working capital.**

*Current ratio*: restates working capital as a ratio of current assets over current liabilities

*Operating cycle*: the amount of time between when inputs are purchased and when cash is collected from the sale of a finished product; the sum of days in inventory and the average collection period

*Cash conversion cycle*: the amount of time between when inputs are paid for and when cash is collected from the sale of a finished product; equal to the operating cycle less days in payables.

## Key Terms

break-even sales growth rate, p. 23-10
burn rate, p. 23-11
cash budget, p. 23-6
cash conversion cycle (CCC), p. 23-16

credit policy, p. 23-12
illiquidity, p. 23-2
insolvency, p. 23-2
inventory policy, p. 23-12

operating cycle (OC), p. 23-16
payment policy, p. 23-12
trade credit, p. 23-4
working capital management, p. 23-1

## Equations

| Equation | Description | Formula | Page |
|---|---|---|---|
| **[23.1]** | Change in Cash | $\Delta \text{Cash} = S_{t-1}[1 - b(1 + 2g)]$ | p. 23-9 |
| **[23.2]** | Change in Cash (general working capital) | $\Delta \text{Cash} = \alpha S_t + (1 - \alpha)S_{t-1} - b\beta S_t - b(1 - \beta)S_{t-1} - b\gamma(S_t - S_{t-1})$ | p. 23-10 |
| **[23.3]** | Change in Cash Percentage of Sales | $\dfrac{\Delta \text{Cash}}{S_{t-1}} = (1 - b) + [\alpha - b(\beta + \gamma)]g$ | p. 23-11 |
| **[23.4]** | Break-Even Sales Growth Rate | $g = \dfrac{(1 - b)}{[b(\beta + \gamma) - \alpha]}$ | p. 23-12 |
| **[23.5]** | Current Ratio | $\text{Current ratio} = \dfrac{\text{Current assets (CA)}}{\text{Current liabilities (CL)}}$ | p. 23-14 |
| **[23.6]** | Quick Ratio | $\text{Quick ratio} = \dfrac{\text{Cash (C)} + \text{Marketable securities (MS)} + \text{Accounts receivable (AR)}}{\text{CL}}$ | p. 23-14 |
| **[23.7]** | Receivables Turnover (RT) | $\text{Receivables turnover (RT)} = \dfrac{\text{Rev}}{\text{AR}}$ | p. 23-15 |
| **[23.8]** | Average Collection Period (ACP) | $\text{Average collection period (ACP)} = \dfrac{\text{AR}}{\text{Average daily revenue (ADR)}} = \dfrac{365}{\text{RT}}$ | p. 23-15 |
| **[23.9]** | Inventory Turnover (IT) | $\text{Inventory turnover (IT)} = \dfrac{\text{Cost of goods sold (CGS)}}{\text{Inventory}}$ | p. 23-15 |
| **[23.10]** | Inventory Turnover (IT) | $\text{Inventory turnover (IT)} = \dfrac{\text{Rev}}{\text{Inventory}}$ | p. 23-15 |
| **[23.11]** | Average Days of Revenues in Inventory | $\text{Average days revenues in inventory (ADRI)} = \dfrac{\text{Inventory}}{\text{ADR}} = \dfrac{365}{\text{IT}}$ | p. 23-15 |
| **[23.12]** | Payables Turnover (PT) | $\text{Payables turnover (PT)} = \dfrac{\text{Rev}}{\text{Accounts payable}}$ | p. 23-15 |
| **[23.13]** | Average Days of Revenues in Payables (ADRP) | $\text{Average days of revenues in payables (ADRP)} = \dfrac{\text{Accounts payable}}{\text{ADR}} = \dfrac{365}{\text{PT}}$ | p. 23-16 |
| **[23.14]** | Operating Cycle (OC) | $\text{Operating cycle (OC)} = \text{ADRI} + \text{ACP}$ | p. 23-16 |
| **[23.15]** | Cash Conversion Cycle (CCC) | $\text{Cash conversion cycle (CCC)} = \text{OC} - \text{ADRP or CCC} = (\text{ADRI} + \text{ACP}) - \text{ADRP}$ | p. 23-16 |

# Questions and Practice Problems

## Multiple Choice Questions

1. **(LO 23.1)** Which of the following is not a warning sign of potential liquidity problems?

   a. Declines in working capital and daily cash flows

   b. Increases in accounts receivable and longer collection periods

   c. Decreases in debt and debt ratios

   d. A buildup of inventory and declining inventory turnover

2. **(LO 23.2)** Which of the following is *true*?

   a. Cash budgets should not be prepared with uncertain numbers.

   b. Cash budgeting is a one-time process.

   c. It is helpful to prepare separate cash budgets for alternative forecasts of key variables.

   d. Cash budgets should not be used to evaluate the impact of different scenarios.

3. **(LO 23.2)** Which of the following usually does *not* increase as sales increase?

   a. Cash

   b. Accounts receivable

   c. Trade credit

   d. Short-term debt

*Use the following information to answer questions 4 to 6 and practice problem 16.*

| | |
|---|---|
| Cash | $ 500,000 |
| Marketable securities | 800,500 |
| Accounts receivable | 700,000 |
| Inventory | 1,003,000 |
| Short-term loans | 100,000 |
| Accounts payable | 800,000 |
| Sales | 1,287,555 |
| Cost of goods sold | 550,000 |

**4. (LO 23.4)** What are the current ratio and quick ratio?

   **a.** 4.57; 2.86

   **b.** 3.34; 2.86

   **c.** 3.34; 2.22

   **d.** 2.22; 3.34

**5. (LO 23.4)** What is the average collection period (ACP)? Round to the nearest day.

   **a.** 227 days

   **b.** 142 days

   **c.** 150 days

   **d.** 198 days

**6. (LO 23.4)** Calculate the operating cycle (OC) using CGS to calculate the inventory turnover ratio. Round to the nearest day.

   **a.** 1,025 days

   **b.** 539 days

   **c.** 864 days

   **d.** 940 days

**7. (LO 23.4)** What is the period of time between the outflow of cash from buying raw materials and the collection of cash from selling finished goods?

   **a.** Collection period

   **b.** Inventory period

   **c.** Cash conversion cycle

   **d.** Operating cycle

**8. (LO 23.4)** The period of time between the purchase of raw materials and the sale of the finished goods produced from the raw materials is called the

   **a.** collection period.

   **b.** inventory period.

   **c.** cash conversion cycle.

   **d.** operating cycle.

**9. (LO 23.4)** The period of time between the sale of finished goods on credit and the collection of the cash is called the

   **a.** collection period.

   **b.** inventory period.

   **c.** net financing period.

   **d.** operating cycle.

**10. (LO 23.4)** What changes will occur if an inventory policy change causes a firm to hold less inventory?

   **a.** The current ratio and the quick ratio will both decrease.

   **b.** The current ratio will decrease but the quick ratio will be unchanged.

   **c.** The inventory turnover ratio will decrease.

   **d.** The average days revenues in inventory (ADRI) will increase.

**11. (LO 23.4)** What changes will occur if a payment policy change causes a firm to pay its suppliers faster?

   **a.** The current ratio and the quick ratio will both decrease.

   **b.** The current ratio will increase, but the quick ratio will be unchanged.

   **c.** The payables turnover ratio will decrease.

   **d.** The average days of revenues in payables (ADRP) will decrease.

**12. (LO 23.4)** What changes will occur if a credit policy change causes a firm to allow its customers more time to pay their invoices?

   **a.** The current ratio and the quick ratio will not change as accounts receivable changes to cash.

   **b.** The current ratio will increase but the quick ratio will be unchanged.

   **c.** The receivables turnover ratio will increase.

   **d.** The average collection period (ACP) will decrease.

**13. (LO 23.4)** Which of the following four statements are *true*:

   **i.** A firm's operating cycle would be identical to its cash conversion cycle if it paid cash on delivery for its inventory purchases.

   **ii.** All else equal, the longer a firm's cash conversion cycle, the more cash it needs to run its day-to-day operations.

   **iii.** A firm's cash conversion cycle is equal to the average length of time between when a firm pays cash to purchase its initial inventory and when it receives cash from the sale of the product.

   **iv.** A manufacturer of specialized large-sized construction vehicles (e.g., excavator or hauler) that maintains high levels of inventory and has long manufacturing and sales cycles would be expected to need high levels of cash/working capital to conduct its daily operations.

   **a.** I, II, and IV

   **b.** I, III, and IV

   **c.** II, III, and IV

   **d.** All of the above.

## Practice Problems

### Basic

**14. (LO 23.1)** State the characteristics of sound net working capital management.

**15. (LO 23.1)** How is net working capital calculated?

**16. (LO 23.4)** Calculate the cash conversion cycle (CCC) for the company examined in questions 4 to 6. Round to the nearest day.

### Intermediate

**17. (LO 23.1)** Explain how trade credit allows firms to use their suppliers as sources of short-term funds.

**18. (LO 23.1)** Why is the efficient utilization of net working capital important?

**19. (LO 23.2)** Describe the types of cash inflows and outflows in a cash budget.

**20. (LO 23.2)** What is the connection between cash budgets and pro forma financial statements?

**21. (LO 23.2)** A properly prepared cash budget allows firms to better understand the timing, magnitude, and duration of cash flow surpluses and deficits. Explain why knowing this information in advance would be beneficial to a company.

**22. (LO 23.2)** For 2022, Ontario Manufacturing Company provided the following accounting information:

| | |
|---|---|
| Net operating income | $60,000 |
| Depreciation on equipment and building | 10,000 |
| Sale of land | 25,000 |
| Purchase of equipment | 15,000 |
| Retirement of long-term debt | 30,000 |
| Dividends paid | 15,000 |
| Purchase of long-term investments | 10,000 |

**a.** Which of the above are sources of funds?

**b.** Which of the above are uses of funds?

**c.** What is the overall increase or decrease in cash?

**23. (LO 23.2)** Calculate the ending cash balance of the current month for the following opening cash balance and current month's cash flows:

| | |
|---|---|
| Beginning cash | $ 20,000 |
| Prior month sales | 50,000 |
| Current month sales | 100,000 |
| Current purchases | 35,000 |
| Prior month purchases | 20,000 |
| Sale of old equipment | 70,000 |
| Dividend payment | 80,000 |
| Wages and others | 35,000 |

**24. (LO 23.3)** Would each of the following changes increase or decrease the break-even sales growth rate?

**a.** An increase in the amount of inventory held

**b.** An increase in the proportion of invoices that are paid immediately

**c.** A decrease in the amount of inventory held

**d.** A decrease in the proportion of invoices that are paid immediately

**e.** An increase in the proportion of sales for cash

**f.** An increase in the proportion of sales collected after the end of one month

**25. (LO 23.1, 23.3)** Many early-stage companies are short on liquidity and cash flow. What could happen if such a firm has plans to increase their sustainable sales growth rate by extending the average age of their accounts payable?

**26. (LO 23.3) a.** What can you conclude if a firm's planned sales growth exceeds its break-even sales growth rate?

**b.** What can you conclude if a firm's planned sales growth is less than its break-even sales growth rate?

**27. (LO 23.4)** Explain the difference between the receivables turnover ratio and the average collection period (ACP).

**28. (LO 23.3)** Discuss measures businesses can implement to improve working capital management.

**29. (LO 23.4)** Explain the difference between the operating cycle (OC) and the cash conversion cycle (CCC).

**30. (LO 23.4)** Explain the difference between the quick ratio and the current ratio.

**31. (LO 23.4)** Great Northern Manufacturing presently has net working capital of $100,000 and sales of $125,000. It is considering entering into a new project that would increase next year's sales by $15,000.

The project would result in a decrease in the average collection period of receivables (or days receivables) by two days (from 32 days to 30 days), but would have no impact on the other working capital items. Estimate the accounts receivable before and after the firm undertakes the project. Estimate the change in net working capital that will result for this firm if it undertakes the project.

**32. (LO 23.4)** Manitoba Services is considering undertaking a new order that would cause its average days of revenues in payables (ADRP) to decrease from 58 days to 48 days, while its average collection period (ACP) will remain at 90 days and its average days revenues in inventory (ADRI) will fall from 98 days to 82 days. What will be the effect on its operating cycle and cash conversion cycle if these estimates are correct?

**33. (LO 23.4)** Determine the operating cycle and cash conversion cycle for a company with inventory turnover of 6.25 times per year, receivables turnover of 8 times per year, and an average days of revenues in payables (ADRP) of 40 days.

**34. (LO 23.4)** Use the information in the financial statements below to answer the following.

| Balance Sheet | | Income Statement | |
|---|---|---|---|
| Cash and equivalents | $ 250 | Revenue | $2,000 |
| Accounts receivable | 150 | Cost of goods sold | 800 |
| Inventory | 300 | Operating expenses | 300 |
| Net fixed assets | 500 | Depreciation | 50 |
| Total assets | $1,200 | Interest | 50 |
| Accounts payable | $ 250 | Earnings before tax | 800 |
| Accrued expenses | 100 | Taxes | 250 |
| Long-term debt | 200 | Net income | $550 |
| Equity | 650 | Dividends | $ 25 |
| Total claims | $1,200 | | |

**a.** Calculate the current ratio, quick ratio, and net working capital.

**b.** Calculate the inventory turnover (using revenues), receivables turnover, and payables turnover.

**c.** Calculate the average days of revenues in inventory, average collection period, and average days of revenues in payables.

**d.** Calculate the operating cycle and cash conversion cycle.

## Challenging

**35. (LO 23.2)** Christmas Inc. is a wholesaler of Christmas decorations and wrapping paper. It is a seasonal business and, due to the timing of cash inflows and outflows, it frequently experiences a cash shortfall in the fourth quarter of the year, before it can liquidate its current assets. Christmas Inc. has a cash balance as of October 1 of $43,000. Cash receipts for October, November, and December are expected to be $20,000, $30,000, and $85,000, respectively. Fixed-cash operating expenses are $40,000 per month, and variable-cash operating expenses are generally 40 percent of the cash receipts for that month. If the line of credit is paid off the month after it is used, there is no interest charged. Prepare a cash budget for Christmas Inc., and determine whether Christmas Inc. will need to make use of its $10,000 credit line.

**36. (LO 23.2)** A firm has estimated its sales, purchases from suppliers, and wages and miscellaneous operating cash outlays for the first four months of next year as follows:

| Month | Sales | Purchases | Wages & Misc. |
|---|---|---|---|
| January | $100,000 | $60,000 | $20,000 |
| February | $102,000 | $70,000 | $30,000 |
| March | $105,000 | $55,000 | $35,000 |
| April | $110,000 | $50,000 | $25,000 |

It estimates that 50 percent of its sales will be for cash, and that it will receive the remaining portion in two equal amounts at the end of the subsequent two months. It plans to pay for all of its purchases two months after the purchase date.

The firm is scheduled to pay dividends of $40,000 in January, and to pay $20,000 for new equipment in March. Its beginning cash balance is $30,000, and the firm wishes to maintain a minimum balance of $10,000. Wages and miscellaneous must be paid monthly without delay. Estimate the firm's cash budget for the first four months of next year. Assume that the sales and purchases were the same in November and December as they are estimated to be in January.

**37. (LO 23.3)** A firm collects 60 percent of its monthly sales immediately and the rest a month later; its production costs are 80 percent of sales, and it holds two months of sales in inventory. It pays 40 percent of its bills immediately and the remainder after 30 days.

    **a.** What is its break-even sales growth rate?

    **b.** What happens to this rate if it increases its inventory to three months' sales and offers more lenient credit terms that result in only 40 percent of its sales being for cash, with the remainder being collected after 30 days?

**38. (LO 23.3)** Atlantic Transport collects 75 percent of its monthly sales immediately and the rest at the end of the month; has production costs that are 60 percent of sales; pays 50 percent of its bills immediately and the rest at the end of the month; and has four months of sales in inventory.

    **a.** Calculate the break-even sales growth rate.

    **b.** Suppose that Atlantic Transport adopts a more efficient inventory policy that reduces the size of its inventory to three months of sales. Atlantic Transport also reduces its production costs to 55 percent of sales. What is the new break-even sales growth rate?

**39. (LO 23.4)** MB Corporation has a receivables turnover of 10, an inventory turnover of 15, and a payables turnover of 5. Calculate its cash conversion cycle. What does a negative cash conversion cycle tell you about MB Corporation's business?

# Working Capital Management: Current Assets and Current Liabilities

---

**LEARNING OBJECTIVES**

After studying this chapter, you should be able to:

**24.1** Explain the motivation for holding cash and the methods used to implement effective cash management techniques.

**24.2** Describe how accounts receivable are managed.

**24.3** Describe how inventory is managed.

**24.4** Describe the major sources of short-term financing.

---

In Chapter 23, we discussed the importance of net working capital management to the firm, as well as ways to assess a firm's working capital position. In Chapter 24, we discuss the management of the individual working capital components. We begin by considering the decisions firms make with respect to their investments in current assets, and then we discuss the short-term financing decisions made by firms.

---

## 24.1 Cash and Marketable Securities

**LEARNING OBJECTIVE 24.1**

Explain the motivation for holding cash and the methods used to implement effective cash management techniques.

### Reasons for Holding Cash

Why do firms hold cash? Basically, they hold cash for the same reasons we do: to handle day-to-day spending requirements; to take care of emergencies; to finance any major outlays, such as tax instalments; and sometimes to buy a bargain that requires cash. Following this logic, we can break down the firm's motives for holding cash into the following categories.

**transactions motive** one of the reasons firms hold cash: to pay for normal operations, such as paying bills

**precautionary motive** one of the reasons firms hold cash: to take care of unanticipated required outlays of cash, such as unexpected repairs on equipment

**finance motive** one of the reasons firms hold cash: in anticipation of major outlays, such as lump-sum loan repayments and dividend payments

**speculative motive** one of the reasons firms hold cash: to take advantage of "bargains," such as the opportunity to purchase raw materials very cheaply

1. **Transactions motive**: This refers to the cash that is required for a firm's normal operations. For some companies, such as manufacturing firms, the actual "cash" portion required will be minimal, but they will require money in their chequing account (which is called a "current account" for companies) to handle bill payments and so on. Other firms, such as retail stores or restaurants, will need to have actual cash on hand, as well as money in their current account to cover cheques.

2. **Precautionary motive**: This refers to the cash that firms keep on hand to take care of unanticipated required outlays of cash, such as unexpected repairs on equipment.

3. **Finance motive**: This refers to the cash that firms will accumulate in anticipation of any major outlays, such as lump-sum loan repayments, dividend payments, and so on.

4. **Speculative motive**: Firms may keep extra cash available to take advantage of unexpected "bargains," such as the opportunity to purchase raw materials very cheaply.

This review of the motives for holding cash highlights the fact that when we speak of "cash," we really mean "cash on hand," money in the firm's current account and money in short-term marketable securities. This is because when we refer to "cash" in the previous definitions, what we are really talking about is the need to have funds available almost instantaneously. Such items as investments in short-term marketable securities are often referred to as "near-cash" or "cash equivalents" and include all items that can be quickly and inexpensively converted into cash. These items are typically short-term marketable securities such as treasury bills, bankers' acceptances, commercial paper, and so on. These money market instruments were discussed in detail in Chapter 18, so we will not elaborate on them here.

How much a firm holds in cash and cash equivalents is also partly determined by its ability to borrow on an operating line of credit or to run an overdraft. In fact, most firms will hold more liquidity in borrowing facilities than they will in cash and equivalents because the cost of standby lending facilities is relatively cheap compared with the opportunity cost of raising capital from the firm's shareholders to invest in marketable securities. In particular, motives 2 through 4 can all be satisfied by using near-cash items, such as investments in marketable securities, and by maintaining additional short-term borrowing capacity.

As individuals, we are certainly familiar with the concept of the importance of near-cash as a substitute for cash in our pockets. We can purchase almost anything using debit or credit cards, which have greatly reduced the need to carry actual cash. In addition, writing cheques is becoming outdated, as most of us pay our bills via automatic debit from our accounts or by using the Internet or automated banking machines (ABMs). From now on, for exposition purposes, when we refer to cash, we are talking about both cash and near-cash, unless we make the distinction clear.

## Determining the Optimal Cash Balance

Finance in the News 24.1 suggests that "the faster a business expands, the more cash it will need for working capital and investment," which we also demonstrated in Chapter 23. Finance in the News 24.1 goes on to discuss the working capital cycle and the importance of dealing with the various components, which are discussed in this chapter, before concluding with an important message: "More businesses fail for lack of cash than for want of profit." On that note, we turn to the question of how to determine the optimal amount of cash to maintain on hand. Like most decisions in finance, it comes down to a classic trade-off between risk and expected return. In general, cash and near-cash provide very low returns relative to investments in other assets; however, by definition, they provide the ultimate in liquidity and usually have minimal additional risks (i.e., usually cash and near-cash items are virtually default free). So it is appropriate to assume that cash is low risk, low expected return.

A firm can always take a conservative approach and choose to maintain a large amount of its assets in cash and near-cash. This will minimize the risk of the firm being unable to satisfy its liquidity requirements. Unfortunately, this approach sacrifices potential returns, which may not be optimal. (In addition, it may make the firm an attractive takeover candidate, because the acquiring firm can use some of this cash to pay down its takeover financing.) Another firm may choose to take an aggressive approach to cash management and maintain

## 24.1 Finance in the News   Working Capital Cycle

Cash flows in a cycle into, around and out of a business. It is the business's life blood and every manager's primary task is to help keep it flowing and to use the cash flow to generate profits. If a business is operating profitably, then it should, in theory, generate cash surpluses. If it doesn't generate surpluses, the business will eventually run out of cash and expire.

The faster a business expands, the more cash it will need for working capital and investment. The cheapest and best sources of cash exist as working capital right within business. Good management of working capital will generate cash, will help improve profits and reduce risks. Bear in mind that the cost of providing credit to customers and holding stocks can represent a substantial proportion of a firm's total profits.

There are two elements in the business cycle that absorb cash—*inventory* (stocks and work-in-progress) and *receivables* (debtors owing you money). The main sources of cash are *payables* (your creditors) and *equity* and *loans*.

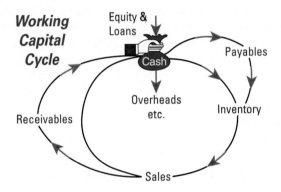

Each component of working capital (namely inventory, receivables and payables) has two dimensions: time and money. When it comes to managing working capital—time is money. If

you can get money to move faster around the cycle (e.g., collect monies due from debtors more quickly) or reduce the amount of money tied up (e.g., reduce inventory levels relative to sales), the business will generate more cash or it will need to borrow less money to fund working capital. As a consequence, you could reduce the cost of bank interest or you'll have additional *free* money available to support additional sales growth or investment. Similarly, if you can negotiate improved terms with suppliers, (e.g., get longer credit or an increased credit limit) you effectively create *free* finance to help fund future sales.

| If you....... | Then....... |
|---|---|
| Collect receivables (debtors) faster | You release cash from the cycle |
| Collect receivables (debtors) slower | Your receivables soak up cash |
| Get better credit (in terms of duration or amount) from suppliers | You increase your cash resources |
| Shift inventory (stocks) faster | You free up cash |
| Move inventory (stocks) slower | You consume more cash |

It can be tempting to pay cash, if available, for fixed assets (e.g., computers, plant, vehicles). If you do pay cash, remember that this is no longer available for working capital. Therefore, if cash is tight, consider other ways of financing capital investment—loans, equity, leasing etc. Similarly, if you pay dividends or increase drawings, these are cash outflows and, like water flowing down a plug hole, they remove liquidity from the business.

More businesses fail for lack of cash than for want of profit.

**Source:** PlanWare, "Managing Working Capital: Working Capital Cycle." Retrieved August 9, 2019, from www.planware.org/workingcapital.htm. Reprinted by permission.

---

minimal balances. This approach might produce higher returns; however, it also increases the risk of the firm becoming illiquid and having to generate liquidity in a hurry. Creating liquidity quickly is often very expensive, because the firm may have to negotiate short-term loans with higher borrowing rates. In more extreme situations, the firm may be forced to sell less-liquid assets, such as inventory or even fixed assets, at discounted prices.

Given our discussion here, it is reasonable to conclude that the **optimal cash balance** is one that balances the risks of illiquidity against the sacrifice of expected returns that is associated with maintaining cash. Therefore, the optimal cash balance as a percentage of total assets, for example, will differ substantially across firms; some firms have lower and more predictable cash requirements than others—these firms will require proportionately lower amounts of cash. Other firms with higher cash requirements for transaction purposes, or with less predictable cash flows (and therefore a greater need for precautionary liquidity), will hold higher levels of cash.

Near-cash items provide a method for alleviating the problem of the low returns associated with holding cash without sacrificing too much in the way of liquidity. For example, a firm can create excess borrowing capacity in the form of an operating line of credit. However, borrowers usually have to pay fees on the unused portion of these credit lines, which may offset the firm's advantage from holding less in cash. In addition, firms often maintain a large portion of their liquidity requirements in money market instruments, which provide a higher return than cash held in a traditional bank account. The level of investment in marketable securities is dictated to a large extent by the firm's liquidity urgency and by how accurately it is able to forecast its future

**optimal cash balance** the amount of cash that balances the risks of illiquidity against the sacrifice of expected returns that is associated with maintaining cash

cash requirements. The latter will be a function partly of the volatility of the firm's cash flows and partly of the firm's ability to design an efficient cash budgeting system. Firms that have well-developed cash management systems and more predictable cash flows will be able to maintain a higher portion of their liquidity in marketable securities and less in cash.

## Cash Management Techniques

The general approach to good cash management is to speed up inflows *as much as possible* and delay outflows *as much as possible*. We discussed this in Chapter 23 in terms of increasing $\alpha$ in the cash budget and decreasing $\beta$. The qualifier "as much as possible" is important because firms always face constraints that will delay inflows and prevent them from delaying outflows too much. For example, a firm can always speed up its inflows from sales by refusing to give credit to customers, but this will likely have a large impact on its sales, so it may not be a viable strategy. Similarly, a firm may delay making payments to suppliers; however, if the firm is perpetually late in making payments, it will develop a poor relationship with the suppliers. In extreme cases, suppliers may end up selling to the firm on a "cash only" basis, which would, in fact, speed up cash outflows rather than delaying them.

An important part of speeding up inflows is the establishment of an efficient credit policy, which specifies the policies for collecting receivables from customers. We will discuss this later in this chapter. Once the payment procedures for customers have been specified, it is important that firms process the payments as efficiently as possible. One objective at this stage should be to minimize **float** time, which can be defined as the time that elapses between the date the paying firm initiates payment—for example, mails the cheque—and the date the funds are available for use by the receiving firm. During this float period, the receiving firm does not have the funds available for use.

There are three major sources of float:

1. the time it takes the cheque to reach the firm after it is mailed by the customer
2. the time it takes the receiving firm to process the cheque and deposit it in an account
3. the time it takes the cheque to clear through the banking system so that the funds are available to the firm

Historically, the first source of float time has been the longest. Of course, firms can always obtain postdated cheques or stipulate that they require payment by a certain date, both of which minimize the float associated with mail and processing times. However, over the past decade in particular, firms have made great strides in eliminating float time by providing payment options that eliminate the need to mail cheques and making them available to (or mandatory for) customers. Today, most retailers accept debit cards, which automatically debit the customers' accounts. This eliminates the problems associated with accepting cheques (i.e., checking for identification, risking the account not having sufficient funds, taking the time to process and deposit the cheque). Many firms also make use of preauthorized payments, which automatically debit customer accounts on the payment date. Other companies use more advanced electronic collection systems, such as electronic funds transfer (EFT) and electronic data interchange (EDI) systems.

Although many advances have occurred, many firms still do things the "old-fashioned way": they bill their customers, and their customers pay by cheque. However, even these firms can take steps to speed up the process and reduce float time. Many firms establish centralized or "concentrated" banking arrangements. Under these arrangements, local offices receive customer payments and deposit them into a local bank account, which is combined with similar local accounts into one central account. This minimizes mail float. A similar strategy, which can be used concurrently with the concentrated bank account option, is to establish "lock box" banking arrangements. This involves setting up local post office boxes, to which customers mail their payments, and authorizing the local bank to empty these boxes and deposit the cheques into the company's account.

Although float works to a firm's disadvantage with respect to collections, it works to the firm's benefit with respect to disbursements. However, it is reasonable to assume that many of the firm's suppliers will employ the same strategies to minimize *their* float, which implies

**float** the time that elapses between the time the paying firm initiates payment and the time the funds are available for use by the receiving firm there is little benefit in trying to maximize disbursement float. In addition, as discussed previously, trying to delay payments may cause poor relations with suppliers. Even so, firms can still take steps to improve the efficiency of their cash outflows and minimize the cash they need to maintain on hand for required disbursements. Just as it makes sense for firms to have a centralized system to monitor collections, it makes sense to have a similar centralization for payments. This will ensure that payments are made on time, but not early (or late), to the greatest extent possible. In addition, most firms establish "zero-balance accounts," which are centralized accounts that combine the cash balances of many individual accounts into one central account. Under this system, funds are transferred from the central account to cover cheques written against the individual accounts as required. This system reduces the need for cash at the aggregate firm level, because it effectively transfers funds from individual accounts that have excess cash to those that need it. In addition, firms usually tie their operating loans to this central account, reducing the total amount of borrowing required by the firm.

Firms can use these methods to speed up cash inflows and slow down outflows to the greatest extent possible. However, another critical component in any cash management system is the actual tracking of cash requirements through time. This can be especially important for planning and for assessing short-term financing requirements. As demonstrated in Chapter 23, firms use the cash budget to forecast cash balances and borrowing requirements. This important planning tool will let firms know when, and for how long, they can expect to have excess cash balances that can be invested in marketable securities. It also shows firms how much they may require in excess borrowing capacity to cover any shortfalls, and the firms can arrange their short-term lending facilities accordingly. In fact, banks often require a cash budget as part of any loan application package.

# The Cash Balance "Puzzle"

This discussion of cash management techniques, which shows how firms have become more efficient at reducing their cash holdings, is primarily related to the transactions motive for holding cash. Finance in the News 24.2 highlights the attractiveness of investing in traditionally staid utility companies. These companies tempt many investors as long as interest rates are stable or declining. Although they usually fail to provide sizeable capital gains, the reliability of their cash flows is appealing to would-be investors.

## 24.2 Finance in the News    Why Investors Are Flooding Back into Boring Old Utilities Stocks

They were mostly abandoned by investors while central banks were hiking interest rates, but now that confidence in continued hikes has waned, utility stocks aren't just looking like a safe, defensive play — they're widely outpacing the TSX.

Since the beginning of January, the Solactive Equal Weight Canada Utilities Index has grown by more than 18 per cent to 201.15 points from 170.20. The growth was led by companies such as Emera Inc., Canadian Utilities Ltd., AltaGas Ltd and TransCanada Corp., which soared more than 16 per cent each. Toronto-based Crius Energy Trust was one of the biggest movers, climbing 88 per cent, but much of that activity came after an announcement that it would be acquired by Texas-based Vistra Energy Corp. By comparison, the S&P/TSX Index has risen 12.35 per cent in the same time frame.

The sector's performance isn't just simply tied to the TSX's recovery after a rough end to 2018.

The last time KJ Harrison Investors CEO and portfolio manager Joel Clark spoke with the *Financial Post* was in December when he suggested investors head into utilities companies such as

Enbridge Inc., which has grown by 13 per cent, and TransCanada because interest rates would drop.

"Now wasn't that a good call?" said Clark, answering his phone with a hearty laugh.

Since then, Canada's yield curve has inverted, meaning that 10-year government bonds are yielding less than those with a three-month duration. And while interest rates have not been cut, some economists are forecasting that the Bank of Canada will go that route as it's faced with a slowing economy. It's in this environment that utility stocks excel, Clark said, because with bonds becoming less tempting, conservative investors further value receiving a guaranteed payout from the dividends they pay.

"There's no growth in utilities — it's a cap rate play," said Clark. "So as rates go down, that income is worth more."

Yes, investors are making a play on interest rates plunging in the future, said Veritas Investment Research analyst Darryl McCoubrey, and that's helped return the sector to prominence, but such a recovery would not have been possible had several companies not spent the majority of 2018 attempting to vindicate themselves.

Years of lower interest rates following the financial crisis in 2008 fuelled one "paradigm-shifting deal" after another, McCoubrey said. Being saddled with high debt is already the norm for most major utilities companies that have to deal with costs of building and maintaining the infrastructure needed to continue to supply energy.

In 2016, three major deals rocked the sector: TransCanada acquired Columbia Pipeline Group for US$13 billion; Fortis Inc. acquired ITC Holdings Corp for $11.3 billion and Emera bought TECO Energy for US$10.4 billion.

"The vast majority of funding was coming from more debt that really strained the balance sheets," said McCoubrey, adding that U.S. tax reform had a negative impact on three acquisitions "and so debt became even more of a pronounced issue."

Companies like Emera, Fortis and AltaGas spent 2018 cleaning their balance sheets. Emera had a funding gap of approximately $2 billion, according to McCoubrey, while Fortis was in an $800 million hole. Between October 2017 and 2018, its stock fell by 20 per cent and due to its funding issues, investors began to question the safety of their dividends. Moody's had even threatened to drop Emera's credit to non-investment grade, he said. The company simply could not allow that to happen and had no choice but to sell off several assets to build $2 billion in equity.

The move has quieted Moody's for now, but McCoubrey said the company will likely need to issue $300 million in preference shares and go back to the equity market for another $400 million within the next 18 months.

As Emera and its competitors continue to eliminate debt in a bid to prove that they're self-funded utilities, they'll be "back to being the boring, slow-moving, dividend-growing utilities, for the most part," McCoubrey said.

Enbridge could still offer a few surprises though, he admits. Even if the Bank of Canada surprises investors and hikes rates, McCoubrey still believes Enbridge will have value because of the potential for it to be boosted by a powerful catalyst: the Line 3 pipeline replacement. Construction is not expected to begin until the second-half of 2020, but when it does, McCoubrey expects the stock to bounce.

Otherwise, investors may be too late to cash in, Clark said. Investors can still buy the stocks to take advantage of the dividend should interest rates fall, he said, but expecting further growth in the 10 to 15 per cent range may be illogical. He's holding on to his shares, he said, but not buying any more.

"I think you still want to be long [on] safe income going forward but don't expect the returns you received to be the same going ... forward," Clark said. "They have to be much more modest."

**Source:** Ferreira, Victor, "Why Investors Are Flooding Back into Boring Old Utilities Stocks," *Financial Post*, April 1, 2019. Available at https://business.financialpost.com. Copyright 2019, Financial Post, a division of Postmedia Network Inc. All rights reserved.

### Concept Review Questions

1. Why do firms hold cash?
2. What is float and why is it important to the firm?

## 24.2 | Accounts Receivable

**LEARNING OBJECTIVE 24.2**
Describe how accounts receivable are managed.

As soon as a firm decides to extend credit to its customers, it has consciously made a decision to allow some of its funds to be tied up in accounts receivable. This decision should be based on a cost-benefit analysis, just as the decision to have funds tied up in cash—or in any other asset, for that matter—should be. The expected benefits of extending credit are expanded sales and perhaps even improved relationships with customers. The costs may include losses, due to an increase in non-payment by customers, as well as the cost of financing the receivables, which is associated with the time the firm has to do without the cash payment for goods that have already been sold and whose production costs have already been paid (or at least partially paid, depending on the firm's ability to delay paying its suppliers and employees).

Although it is technically true that all firms face the decision of whether or not to provide credit for their customers, as a practical matter many firms really do not have much choice.

For example, it is hard to imagine a furniture retailer or car dealer remaining competitive within its industry if it did not provide customers with financing options. However, these types of companies typically provide financing for their customers through a finance subsidiary of the parent company or through arrangements made with one or more banks or financial institutions. Many companies extend credit to their customers by providing them with additional time to make payment on purchases. For these companies, the first decision they need to make is whether to extend credit at all. The second decision is to decide which customers will be granted credit. Next, the firms must determine the credit terms to be offered to customers (which may vary from customer to customer). Finally, they must decide on the details of the collection process.

## The Credit Decision

For most companies, the decision of whether or not to extend credit—the "trade credit decision"—will be largely determined by the nature of the product they sell, the industry they are in, and the prevailing policy of competitors. Assuming the firm decides to extend credit, it must then determine which of its customers will qualify for it. This decision is often based on a formal **credit analysis** process, which is designed to assess the risk of non-payment by potential customers. The process involves collecting information about their credit history; their ability to make payments, as reflected in their expected cash flows (which is closely related to income); and their overall financial stability (as reflected in their net worth and their level of existing debt obligations).

> **credit analysis**   a process designed to assess the risk of non-payment by potential customers, which involves collecting information about their credit history, their ability to make payments (as reflected in their expected cash flows), and their overall financial stability

Before considering how firms make these decisions, it is important to note that a firm's decision to extend trade credit is subtly different from a bank's decision to extend a loan. Suppose, for example, a firm is considering a $10,000 order for widgets. The customer promises to pay in 60 days. If the cost of trade credit is 12 percent per year, the firm might sell the widgets for $10,200, due in 60 days. We will talk about trade credit terms later, but this is similar to a bank lending the customer $10,000 to buy the widgets for cash, then charging 2-percent interest on the loan so that the customer pays $10,200 in 60 days. In both cases, the purchaser owes $10,200, either to the company or to the bank. The bank's profit from the loan is limited to the interest rate,[1] and if the customer defaults, the bank could be out the full $10,000 loan. However, the firm is in a slightly different position.

First, the firm's cost is not the $10,000 it charges for the widgets, because it has to factor a profit margin into the calculation. If the firm's profit margin is 10 percent, and if it can't sell the widgets to other customers, then its decision involves a potential loss of $9,000 if the customer does not pay, rather than the $10,000 the bank would lose. Further, if the customer does pay, it may become an established customer that makes further purchases, generating further profit margins for the firm. The fact that the firm thinks in terms of future profit margins from developing a good customer and loses only its production cost in the case of default means that trade credit is granted to customers who could not secure credit from a bank on the same terms.

This discussion also explains why some firms grant credit, whereas others do not. For example, eating-and-drinking establishments generally have very low collection periods; that is, they generally do not give credit. This is because they tend to be low-margin, high-volume businesses, for whom an additional sale is not very valuable and may not generate many future sales. Instead, purchases are made on bank credit cards rather than store cards, and they tend to use loyalty cards or gift cards to generate repeat business. In contrast, high-margin low-volume businesses, such as automobile and equipment manufacturers, do have in-house credit facilities to finance sales of their products. It is for these higher-margin businesses that the corporate credit decision is more important.

---

[1] More likely, in this situation, the bank would let the company advance the trade credit to the customer and then buy the receivable for $9,803.92. The bank would make its 2-percent interest when the customer paid off the $10,000 debt. This is called factoring.

## Sources of Credit Information

In making these decisions, firms can use a number of sources of information to assess the creditworthiness of a particular customer. Usually, firms begin by turning to professional credit agencies, such as Dun & Bradstreet (D&B) Canada Ltd., which provide credit ratings and comprehensive credit reports on companies. Unlike the major bond rating agencies, such as Dominion Bond Rating Service, Moody's, and Standard & Poor's, D&B rates private companies that do not access the public markets. These reports are based on available financial data, the firm's competitive position, and the company's credit history. In many cases, this report will provide sufficient information to make a credit decision; however, for larger accounts or for arrangements that are expected to last for a long time, the firm may decide to do some additional investigation. An important source of information can be the company's financial statements. Firms may also ask the company to provide a letter from its main banker. Finally, firms can always look for information regarding a company's past credit relationships from a variety of sources, such as trade associations, other firms that have had prior dealings with the company, and so on.

The evaluation of the credit information that has been gathered can vary significantly from one company to the next. Some companies will have very detailed and mechanical evaluation systems, while others will rely more on judgement. In either case, the key issue potential creditors are assessing is the likelihood of the customer paying the bills as they come due. There are two sides to this coin.

## Evaluation of Credit Information

**capacity** the customer's ability to pay

The first side is the potential customer's *ability* to pay. This is often referred to as the firm's **capacity**. As discussed in chapters 3 and 4, two of the most important factors affecting a firm's ability to meet future obligations are the amount of cash flow it expects to generate and the number of other obligations it has to satisfy. Thus, it is important to examine a firm's expected future profitability as well as its level of debt and the amount of debt payments it has accumulated. In addition, because most, if not all, trade credit is of a short-term nature, potential creditors are particularly interested in a potential customer's liquidity. As a last resort, creditors can always turn to the assets pledged as security for a loan. In this way, a firm's ability to offer collateral enhances its ability to secure credit. In many cases, items are sold on an **open account** basis, which means that the collateral is simply the assets sold to the customer. In such situations, the creditor must be wary because some assets do not hold their value. In addition, creditors may have difficulty getting the assets from the customer if it defaults on its obligation.

**open account** credit in which the collateral is the assets sold to the customer

**character** the customer's willingness to pay; its reliability and trustworthiness

This leads us to the other side of the coin referred to previously—how *willing* the firm is to pay. This is often referred to as the **character** of the firm. In other words, how reliable and trustworthy is the firm? This is an important question, because even if a firm is *able* to make the required payments, this makes little difference if it chooses not to. Creditors look for clues to the character of the customer's management team by examining, among other things, its payment history and details of the customer's past dealings.

**conditions** the state of the economy

These two sides to the credit decision are often referred to as the "two C's of credit," with collateral representing the third C. In addition, both capacity and character can be affected by the state of the economy. In a recession, the firm's capacity to pay is tested as cash flow dries up and finances are under pressure. So economic **conditions** affect the credit decision, and analysts include it as the fourth C of credit: capacity, character, collateral, and conditions. All four are interrelated.

Because the process of checking creditworthiness can be lengthy and costly, firms tend to prioritize the amount of time and effort devoted to the analysis. For example, all else being equal, larger orders require more scrutiny than do smaller ones.

## Credit Policies

**terms of credit** the due date and the discount date and discount amount, where applicable, offered to customers

Once a firm has decided to grant credit, it then chooses what **terms of credit** to offer its customers, such as the due date and the discount date and discount amount, where applicable. In practice, the terms a firm offers can vary from one customer to the next, based on credit analysis and on the importance of the account. In other words, key accounts with an impeccable credit rating will likely demand, and receive, better credit terms than smaller accounts or those with weaker credit ratings. For ease of exposition in our discussion, we will assume that most customers receive the same credit terms.

Credit terms of "2/20 net 45" offer customers a 2-percent discount if they pay the full amount due by day 20, with the full amount being due by day 45. Terms of "net 30" require full payment by day 30 and provide no discount options. We use these credit terms to work out how much taking trade credit costs. For example, 2/10 net 45 means that the customer pays either 98 percent after 10 days or 100 percent after 45 days. The cost is 2/98 for getting an extra 35 days to pay, so the effective annual interest rate for not paying on time is

$$k = \left(1 + \frac{2}{98}\right)^{\frac{365}{35}} - 1 = 23.45\%$$

We express the 2-percent discount in terms of a simple interest rate (2/98 or 2.04 percent) and then express it on an annual basis by working out how many 35-day periods are in a year.

In this example, the real cost is 98 percent of the quoted price if the customer pays immediately on receipt of the widgets, during the 10-day grace period. After that, the invoice has to be paid by 45 days, and the cost of getting this extra 35 days' credit is 23.45 percent. Most firms can borrow from their banks more cheaply than this, so, as a basic rule, firms should always take those discounts. If a customer doesn't take the discount, the full 100 percent comes due. It is best to pay by 45 days and avoid the payment reminder telephone calls. Paying on time lowers the effective cost to a more reasonable level.

Generally, when firms decide to extend more lenient credit terms, they expect revenues to increase because they will increase the number of units sold and, possibly, because they will charge higher prices. The costs include the increase in financing costs and the increased risk of non-payment by customers. Conversely, when firms adopt a more restrictive policy, it results in collections being accelerated, at the possible expense of sales. Firms can evaluate such decisions by using the now-familiar net present value (NPV) framework, as given in Equation 24.1.

$$\boxed{NPV = PV(\text{Future CFs}) - CF_0} \qquad [24.1]$$

The future cash flows (CFs) will generally be positive when firms loosen their credit terms and will be negative when they tighten them. $CF_0$ will represent an outlay when the credit terms are loosened, because that requires an additional investment in receivables; it will represent an inflow when the terms are tightened, because that will reduce the level of receivables. The after-tax cost of short-term debt is usually the appropriate discount rate to use, because receivables are low risk and are generally financed by using short-term debt (and the operating line of credit, in particular). Example 24.1 demonstrates how this framework can be used.

---

**EXAMPLE 24.1** | The NPV of Extending Additional Credit

Suppose a firm that currently does not grant credit is considering adopting a credit policy that permits its customers to pay the full price for purchases (with no penalties) within 40 days of the purchase (i.e., the credit terms are net 40). The firm estimates that it can increase the price of the product by $1 per unit as a result of the new policy, which results in a new price per unit of $111. The firm expects that unit sales will increase by 1,000 units per year (to 11,000 units) and that variable costs will remain at $99 per unit. It also estimates that bad debt losses will amount to $6,000 per year. The firm will finance the additional investment in receivables by using its line of credit, which charges 6-percent interest. The firm's tax rate is 40 percent. Should the firm begin extending credit under the terms described?

**Solution**   Because the firm did not previously have any receivables, the initial investment ($CF_0$) can be viewed as the amount of additional funds that will be tied up in receivables, which equals the number of days that sales must be financed, multiplied by the estimated sales per day:

40 days × Sales per day = 40 × [($111 × 11,000 units)/365 days]

= 40 days × $3,345.21/day = $133,808

Now we need to estimate the *PV(Future CFs)*, which equals the present value of the incremental after-tax cash flows generated by extending credit.

Incremental before-tax annual CFs = (1,000 extra units sold) × [($111 − $99) profit per unit]
+ (10,000 units sold) × ($1 increase in price per unit sold) − ($6,000 in bad debt losses)
= (1,000)($12) + (10,000)($1) − $6,000 = $12,000 + $10,000 − $6,000 = $16,000

The appropriate after-tax discount rate is

$$6\% \times (1 - 0.4) = 3.6\%$$

If we assume the firm reaps the benefits of this change in policy indefinitely, we can find the present value of the future benefits by viewing the incremental after-tax annual CFs as a perpetuity:

$$PV(\text{Future CFs}) = \text{Annual after-tax incremental CFs}/k$$
$$= [\$16,000 \times (1 - 0.4)]/0.036 = \$266,667$$
$$NPV = PV(\text{Future CFs}) - CF_0 = \$266,667 - \$133,808 = \$132,859$$

Thus, the firm should begin extending credit under the terms previously described.

In Example 24.1, we considered a firm that decided to extend credit, thus adopting a more lenient credit policy. Of course, firms can always choose to adopt a more stringent credit policy. In this case, the firm will free up cash by reducing the amount of receivables it has outstanding, and the cost will be the forgone additional future cash flows that may result if the firm loses sales or has to reduce its selling price, as Example 24.2 demonstrates.

---

**EXAMPLE 24.2** | Adopting a More Stringent Credit Policy

Suppose the firm from Example 24.1 adopts the net 40 credit policy, but one year later considers changing the terms to net 30. The firm estimates that it can maintain the same price for the product (i.e., $111 per unit) but that unit sales will decline by 500 units per year (to 10,500 units). Variable costs will remain at $99 per unit. The firm estimates that bad debt losses will be reduced by $2,000 per year (to $4,000) as a result of the new policy. As in Example 24.1, the appropriate after-tax discount rate is 3.6 percent and the tax rate is 40 percent. Should the firm switch to the new policy?

**Solution** The initial investment ($CF_0$) in this case can be viewed as the reduction in the amount of accounts receivable (AR) that need to be financed:

AR(new) − AR(old) = {30 days × [($111 × 10,500 units)/365 days]} − {40 days
× [($111 × 11,000 units)/365 days]} = [30 days × $3,193.15/day] − [40 days
× $3,345.21/day] = $95,795 − $133,808 = −$38,013

Now we need to estimate the *PV(Future CFs)*, which equals the present value of the incremental after-tax cash flows generated by changing the credit policy. In this case, it will be negative because the firm *loses* future cash flows as a result of tightening its credit policy.

Incremental before-tax annual CFs = (500 fewer units sold) × ($111 − $99 profit per unit)
+ ($2,000 reduction in bad debt losses) = (−500)($12) + $2,000 = −$4,000

If we assume the firm reaps the benefits of this change in policy indefinitely, we can find the present value of the future CFs (forgone CFs, in this case) by viewing the incremental after-tax annual CFs as a perpetuity:

$$PV(\text{Future CFs}) = \text{Annual after-tax incremental CFs}/k$$
$$= [-\$4,000 \times (1 - 0.4)]/0.036 = -\$66,667$$
$$NPV = PV(\text{Future CFs}) - CF_0 = -\$66,667 + \$38,013 = -\$28,654$$

Thus, the firm should not switch from its existing credit policy to the new one.

When firms offer discounts to customers, two things happen: (1) they lose profits when customers take advantage of the discounts; and (2) they receive payment sooner, so less money is tied up in receivables. The decision to offer discounts (or eliminate them) can be evaluated by using the NPV framework, as Example 24.3 demonstrates.

---

**EXAMPLE 24.3** | Offering a Discount

Suppose the firm from examples 24.1 and 24.2 is maintaining the net 40 credit policy evaluated in Example 24.1 but is now considering adopting a new policy that would involve a discount. In particular, it is considering adopting a 2/10 net 40 policy. The firm estimates that 60 percent of customers will take advantage of the discount, while the remaining 40 percent will pay on day 40. The firm expects that it can maintain the same price for the product (i.e., $111 per unit); unit sales will remain at 11,000 per year; variable costs will remain at $99 per unit; and bad debt losses will not be affected. As in Example 24.1, the after-tax discount rate is 3.6 percent and the tax rate is 40 percent. Should the firm switch to the new policy?

**Solution**   The initial investment ($CF_0$), in this case, can be viewed as the reduction in the amount of accounts receivable (AR) that need to be financed.

The average collection period (ACP) under the new policy will be reduced to [0.6 × 10 days + 0.4 × 40 days] = 22 days. The old ACP was assumed to be the net date (i.e., 40 days). The change (reduction) in receivables is

$$(22 - 40) \times [(\$111 \times 11{,}000 \text{ units})/365 \text{ days}] = (-18 \text{ days}) \times (\$3{,}345.21/\text{day})$$

$$= -\$60{,}214$$

Now we need to estimate the *PV(Future CFs)*, which equals the present value of the incremental after-tax cash flows generated by changing the credit terms. In this case, it will be negative because the firm loses future cash flows as a result of customers taking advantage of the discount.

$$\text{Incremental after-tax annual CFs} = (\text{Number of units sold at a discount})$$
$$\times (\text{Discount amount per unit}) \times (1 - \text{tax rate}) = (60 \text{ percent of customers taking discount}$$
$$\times 11{,}000 \text{ annual sales in units}) \times (0.02 \text{ discount amount} \times \$111 \text{ per unit}) \times (1 - 0.4)$$
$$= (6{,}600 \text{ units}) \times (\$2.22) \times (0.6) = \$8{,}791.20$$
$$\text{PV(Future CFs)} = \text{Annual after-tax incremental CFs}/k$$
$$= -\$8{,}791.20/0.036 = -\$244{,}200$$
$$\text{NPV} = \text{PV(Future CFs)} - CF_0 = -\$244{,}200 + \$60{,}214 = -\$183{,}986$$

Thus, the firm should not offer the discount.

---

## The Collection Process

Firms have many options when deciding how their customers will pay for their purchases. As discussed, several electronic methods are available, such as automatic debit of customers' bank accounts or the use of EFT or EDI systems. These approaches not only reduce payment processing time but also reduce (or eliminate) the risk of late payment and obviously represent attractive collection systems for many firms. However, some firms still invoice their customers at the time of sale and then collect and deposit cheques as they are received.

When firms are forced to wait for payments from customers, several issues arise. First, they must closely monitor their collections and receivables to avoid having many late payments or, worse yet, non-payments. Second, they must determine what to do when late payments occur. Usually, firms establish a systematic process to deal with such accounts. As a start, most firms will charge interest on overdue accounts as a deterrent. After a predetermined interval, companies will usually notify the customer that the account is in arrears and ask the customer to "settle up." This notification can be done by mail, e-mail, or phone. If payment is still not received, firms will generally issue a follow-up reminder (or two). Eventually, if they still have not received payment from the customer, firms must decide what to do next. One of the first things they will do, if they have not already done so, is not allow that customer to make any more purchases on credit. They must then decide whether to hand the bill over to a collection

**factoring arrangements** the sale of a firm's receivables, at a discount, to a financial company called a "factor," which specializes in collections; the outsourcing of the collections to a factor

agency or take legal action against the customer. Both of these options can be costly, so in many cases, firms will just write off the debt and inform the credit agency. This decision will be influenced by the amount that is due, among other things.

Sometimes firms avoid the collection process by entering into **factoring arrangements**, whereby they sell their receivables at a discount to a financial company called a "factor," which specializes in collections. Alternatively, many factors do not actually purchase the receivables but agree to handle the collections, for a fee of course.

It can be difficult to assess how well a firm manages its accounts receivable. In Chapter 4, we identified some common ratios that do provide useful insight into this issue: the average collection period (ACP) and the receivables turnover ratio. All else being equal, it is preferable to have a lower ACP and higher receivables turnover. However, firms can always make improvements in these ratios by sacrificing sales growth and/or profit margins, so it is not as simple as merely examining these ratios. In addition, these ratios do not tell us a great deal about the *quality* of a firm's receivables.

One tool that is useful for this purpose is the aged accounts receivable report, which categorizes the balances in receivables according to how long they have been outstanding. For example, a firm might provide a list that shows how much of its receivables are outstanding before the due date, after the due date, a month after the due date, and so on. Generally, receivables that have not been outstanding very long are regarded as higher quality than those that have been outstanding well beyond their due date. In fact, banks often require that borrowing firms provide them with this list each month to support any financing the banks provide in support of receivables. However, this report also has its limitations. For example, it would be preferable to have many receivables due from high-quality customers (such as government agencies) that are 30 days late than it would be to have many 10-day-old receivables from customers with low-quality credit. In fact, to accurately assess the quality of a company's receivables, it would help to have a list of the customers underlying the receivables and perhaps even a credit analysis of these customers, at least for the larger accounts.

Despite these limitations, aging of receivables is a very valuable tool. In fact, it applies to all debts and payments. The U.S. economy has safely exited the financial crisis of 2008 and is on fairly strong footing. In particular, Freddie Mac, in its June 2019 forecast, pointed to low mortgage rates and a buoyant labour market that will likely lead to modest growth through to the end of 2020. Long-term interest rates are trending lower due to global growth concerns and continuing trade disputes.[2]

While "old" receivables clearly indicate that the debt is of less than sterling quality, current receivables are not necessarily that much better: paying on time is sometimes an indication that the purchaser does not want to be examined too closely and is actually a crook. General Motors Acceptance Corporation (GMAC), at the time the financing arm of GM, found this out the hard way. In the 1980s and 1990s, John McNamara, a Buick-Pontiac dealer in the United States, operated a Ponzi scheme and defrauded GMAC of US$1 billion through fraudulent loans for thousands of vans that were never actually purchased. He claimed to be buying the vans for conversion and export and faked invoices for GMAC to finance. By paying GMAC invoices on time, he developed a reputation as a very good customer and was actively courted by GMAC and given more favourable terms than other purchasers, when in actuality he was simply paying off his old loans with new ones. His fraud came to light when internal auditors at GMAC could not find evidence for the matching purchases.[3]

### Concept Review Questions

1. Why is trade credit different from bank credit?
2. What are the four C's of credit?
3. What does 2/10 net 30 mean, and what is the implicit interest cost?
4. What is an aged accounts receivable report?

[2]See "Housing Market Expected to Realize Impacts of Low Mortgage Rates in 2019," available at FreddieMac.com.
[3]McQuiston, John T., "Car Dealer Admits Fraud of Billions." *The New York Times*, September 10, 1992.

24.3 # Inventory

---

**LEARNING OBJECTIVE 24.3**

Describe how inventory is managed.

---

A firm's decision about the level of inventory it will hold is based on a trade-off between benefits and costs, similar to the decisions about investments in cash, marketable securities, and accounts receivable. One reason firms hold large amounts of inventory is that they may have received discounts on large-volume purchases. However, the more important benefits of holding inventory are that having sufficient levels of raw materials minimizes disruptions in the production process, while maintaining adequate levels of finished goods on hand helps minimize lost sales (and lost customer goodwill) because of shortages.

The benefits of holding inventory do not come without significant costs. Aside from the obvious cost of financing the funds tied up in inventory, a number of other costs are important, including storage, handling, insurance, spoilage, and the risk of obsolescence. Thus, inventory decisions are critical to a firm's performance. In fact, the field of operations management devotes a great deal of attention to modelling efficient inventory control systems. We provide a brief discussion of some of the more common approaches to inventory management, but we do not elaborate on the technical details.

## Inventory Management Approaches

Most inventory control systems used by large companies employ highly automated computerized systems that can easily track all kinds of inventory items as they flow into and out of the company. These systems control inventory levels by relating them to the production process, which in turn is related to the firm's projected sales levels.

Any approach to inventory management must balance the benefits of holding inventory and the costs, as discussed previously. We will briefly describe four of these approaches.

1. The **ABC approach**: This approach divides inventory into several categories based on the value of the inventory items, their overall level of importance to the firm's operations, and their profitability. The higher the priority of the inventory item, the more time and effort will be devoted to its management.

2. The **economic order quantity (EOQ) model**: The EOQ model defines (and determines) the optimal inventory level as the one that minimizes the total of "shortage costs" and "carrying costs." As such, it determines the inventory level that balances the benefits (e.g., reduced shortage costs) against the carrying costs (e.g., financing, storage, insurance, spoilage, obsolescence). The model shows that, under certain assumptions, the minimum total cost occurs at the point at which carrying costs equal shortage costs. The EOQ model has three key assumptions: demand is uniform throughout the year; carrying costs are constant; ordering costs are constant. Uncertainty of demand can be addressed by increasing the inventory held (usually referred to as "safety stock"), but there are additional costs that would need to be accounted for in the analysis and weighed against the benefits of delaying shipments due to inventory shortages.

3. **Materials requirement planning (MRP)**: MRP is a detailed computerized system that orders inventory in conjunction with production schedules. The central idea is to determine the exact level of raw materials and work-in-process that must be on hand to meet finished-goods demand. With this capability and good sales forecasts, a company can run on extremely low levels of inventory.

**ABC approach** an inventory management approach that divides inventory into categories based on the value of the inventory items, their overall level of importance to the firm's operations, and their profitability, to determine the time and effort to devote to their management

**economic order quantity (EOQ) model** an inventory management approach that defines and determines the optimal inventory level as the one that minimizes the total of shortage costs and carrying costs; it determines the inventory level that balances the benefits (reduced shortage costs) against the carrying costs (financing, storage, insurance, spoilage, obsolescence)

**materials requirement planning (MRP)** an inventory management approach that uses a detailed computerized system to order inventory in conjunction with production schedules; managers determine the level of raw materials and work-in-process that must be on hand to meet finished-goods demand

**just-in-time (JIT) inventory systems** an inventory management approach that fine-tunes the receipt of raw materials so they arrive exactly when they are required in the production process, thereby reducing inventory to its lowest possible level

4. **Just-in-time (JIT) inventory systems**: JIT systems fine-tune the receipt of raw materials so they arrive exactly when they are required in the production process. The objective is to reduce inventory to its lowest possible level. JIT systems require close relationships with suppliers in order to work properly.

## Evaluating Inventory Management

Although effective inventory management is critical to the success of most firms, it is, like accounts receivable management, difficult to evaluate. In Chapter 4, we introduced two ratios—the inventory turnover ratio and the average days in inventory ratio—that outsiders commonly use to evaluate inventory management. Generally, high inventory turnover is recognized as a good sign, while lower or declining turnover is a warning sign. In particular, a declining inventory turnover ratio indicates that sales are declining, inventory levels are accumulating, or both. The greater the inventory buildup, the greater the financing, storage, spoilage, and insurance costs, and the greater the risk of obsolescence.

Although the inventory turnover ratio is a useful indicator, it is far from comprehensive. For example, it does not measure shortage costs or explicitly measure financing costs. As discussed previously, these are critical considerations in the implementation (and evaluation) of any inventory management system. In addition, turnover ratios cannot be compared across companies that use different methods of accounting for inventory (e.g., FIFO, average cost), because the reported inventory levels will differ substantially. Finally, inventory turnover says nothing about the breakdown of inventory in terms of raw materials, work-in-process inventory, and finished goods, which can make a big difference in establishing the market value of inventory.

### Concept Review Questions

1. Identify the costs and benefits of holding inventory.
2. What are the drawbacks to using the turnover ratio to measure inventory policy?

---

## 24.4 Short-Term Financing Considerations

### LEARNING OBJECTIVE 24.4
Describe the major sources of short-term financing.

A common trait of investments in current assets, such as cash, accounts receivable, and inventory, is that they all tend to increase automatically as sales increase. The same cannot be said for short-term financing, with the exception of trade credit. Therefore, it is critical that firms forecast their short-term financing requirements as accurately as possible and ensure they have adequate financing in place.

Because there are many potential sources of short-term financing, firms need to assess the cost effectiveness of alternative financing mechanisms. We use the following variation of Equation 5.13, which was introduced in Chapter 5, to estimate the annual effective rate of return or cost ($k$) associated with any financing alternative:

$$k = \left(1 + \frac{\text{n-day financing cost}}{\text{Purchase price}}\right)^{\frac{365}{n}} - 1$$ [24.2]

Firms also need to consider any additional benefits or risks associated with these alternatives. We will now discuss below the most common short-term financing options available to firms.

# Trade Credit

Trade credit is usually one of a firm's most important sources of short-term financing. Many firms finance their purchases through the credit terms offered to them by their suppliers, which permits them to delay payments to the supplier. In essence, a firm is *borrowing* from its suppliers when it purchases materials on account. This is the only form of short-term financing that automatically increases with sales, and, as such, it is often referred to as a "spontaneous" source of funds.[4] Trade credit provides firms with many advantages: it is generally readily available, convenient, and flexible, and it usually does not entail any restrictive covenants or pledges of security. In addition, it is usually inexpensive. It can, however, be expensive to forgo discounts, as demonstrated in Example 24.4.

---

**EXAMPLE 24.4** | Trade Credit and Discounts

A firm is considering the purchase of one of its inputs from supplier A. The selling price is $1,200 and the credit terms are 2/10 net 40.

   **a.** What is the effective annual cost of forgoing the discount?

   **b.** Another supplier (B) offers the same product for a price of $1,205 on credit terms of net 60. What is the effective annual cost of this option?

   **c.** If the firm can finance these purchases by using a loan that has an effective annual cost of 8 percent, should it take the credit terms or the loan?

**Solution**

   **a.** We need to recognize that forgoing the discount costs 2 percent of the $1,200 purchase price, or $24. In essence, the "true" price = $1,200 − $24 = $1,176, and the $24 is the 30-day financing cost. So we can estimate the cost of forgoing the discount by using Equation 24.2.

$$k = \left(1 + \frac{\text{n-day financing cost}}{\text{Purchase price}}\right)^{\frac{365}{n}} - 1 = (1.02040816)^{12.166667} - 1$$

$$= 0.2786 = 27.86\%$$

We could also solve this by replacing the discount percentage 2/98 for the actual dollar amounts of $24/$1,176, because the two ratios must be equal. In other words,

$$k = \left(1 + \frac{2}{98}\right)^{\frac{365}{30}} - 1 = 0.2786 = 27.86\%$$

Forgoing the cash discount is an expensive decision.

   **b.** Because we know from Example 24.4a that the "true" cost is $1,176, we can see that supplier B is charging $29 (i.e., $1,205 − $1,176) in financing charges for 60 days of financing. We can estimate the effective annual cost of this option as

$$k = \left(1 + \frac{29}{1,176}\right)^{\frac{365}{60}} - 1 = 0.1597 = 15.97\%$$

This option is less expensive than forgoing the discount but is still not cheap.

   **c.** We know what the firm should not do—that is, it should not choose supplier A and forgo the discount, because this costs 27.86 percent.

      This leaves us with two purchase/financing options: (1) buy through supplier A and pay on day 10, using the 8-percent loan to take advantage of the discount, or (2) buy through supplier B.

      We have already calculated that the cost of using supplier B would be 15.97 percent. The cost of going with supplier A and paying the amount due on day 10 to take advantage of the discount is 8 percent, because the firm can use a loan with a cost of 8 percent to finance the purchase.

      Therefore, the preferred option is to buy through supplier A and pay on day 10 to take advantage of the discount by using a loan at 8 percent.

---

[4]Although it is true that the amount borrowed on an operating line of credit will increase with the borrowing requirement (which tends to rise with sales), the credit limit on these lending facilities does not automatically increase with sales—they have to be renegotiated. Therefore, they do not represent a truly spontaneous source of funds.

## Lessons to Be Learned

In today's economy, credit is vital, whether it is consumer credit to allow the purchase of household items or corporate credit to allow companies to buy from each other. Corporate credit is a competitive market, with the major banks competing against specialist institutions as well as the 100-percent-owned captive financial companies of major "heavy goods" manufacturers such as John Deere, Caterpillar, and General Electric Credit Corporation. When the financial crisis broke and damaged the capital of many of these financial institutions, firms were left to fill the financing gap themselves. Having a strong balance sheet (including a lot of cash) is a competitive weapon that allows firms to finance their sales when other sources of finance dry up. This is a common occurrence for many companies as the economy moves through the business cycle.

# Bank Loans

Several short-term loan arrangements are available through financial institutions. Generally, they are variable rate (or prime-based) loans that are tied to the prime lending rate (the rate offered to the bank's best customers). The most common arrangement for businesses is to establish operating loans or lines of credit. As discussed previously, these loans are usually linked to the firm's current account (i.e., its chequing account), and they enable the business to borrow up to a predetermined amount to finance temporary cash deficits. Operating loans are generally set up so that the firm makes "interest only" payments. The amount of borrowing can be reduced at the firm's discretion, and many companies will have the bank automatically "revolve" the loan for them (for a fee). This involves paying down the amount of the loan whenever there is sufficient cash in the current account, or increasing the borrowing level when there is insufficient cash. Having the bank revolve the loan reduces unnecessary interest costs, because the loan will be paid down whenever the firm has sufficient funds available.

As discussed in Chapter 23, cash budgets can be used to estimate the amount of borrowing that should be arranged. This is important, because firms do not want to have to go back to the bank to arrange additional financing when the need for funds is urgent. Therefore, firms will try to have the necessary amount of funds available and maintain a little extra cushion. However, firms also want to avoid arranging unnecessary borrowing capacity, because banks normally charge a commitment fee against the unused portion of credit.

Operating loans are typically secured by accounts receivable and inventory, because these are the assets they are usually intended to finance. The standard procedure is for banks to offer an operating line for an amount that does not exceed 70 to 75 percent of the firm's good accounts receivable under 90 days plus up to 50 percent of the firm's inventory value.

Operating loans provide firms with an opportunity to develop a solid banking relationship, which can be important. They also offer a fair degree of flexibility, and the costs are usually quite low. Examples 24.5 and 24.6 illustrate how to estimate the costs associated with operating loans.

---

**EXAMPLE 24.5** | Bank Loans

A firm is offered a one-year variable rate loan at a rate of prime plus 1 percent at a time when the bank's prime lending rate is 2.85 percent. The loan is to be repaid in monthly instalments. Assuming there are no other fees associated with this loan, what is the effective annual cost of this loan?

**Solution** The annual quoted rate is prime (2.85 percent) plus 1 percent, so it is 3.85 percent.

Now we need to estimate the effective annual rate associated with this arrangement. We can use Equation 5-13 from Chapter 5.

$$k = \left(1 + \frac{\text{Quoted rate}}{m}\right)^m - 1 = \left(1 + \frac{0.0385}{12}\right)^{12} - 1 = 0.0392 = 3.92\%$$

Alternatively, we could estimate the one-month interest cost on a $1,000 loan.

$$\text{One-month interest cost} = (1/12) \times (0.0385) \times (\$1,000) = \$3.21$$

Then we could use a monthly (rather than daily) variation of Equation 24.2 to estimate the cost as

$$k = \left(1 + \frac{\text{n-month financing cost}}{\text{Purchase price}}\right)^{\frac{12}{n}} - 1 = \left(1 + \frac{3.21}{1,000}\right)^{\frac{12}{1}} - 1 = 0.0392 = 3.92\%$$

---

**EXAMPLE 24.6** | Operating Line of Credit

A firm arranges a one-year $800,000 operating line of credit, which carries a 5-percent quoted interest rate and a 0.5-percent commitment fee on the unused portion of the line. The loan calls for monthly payments. The firm uses the line to borrow $600,000 in the first seven months of the year, and then reduces the loan amount to $400,000 for the remainder of the year. What is the effective annual cost (rate) of this loan arrangement?

**Solution**   First, we determine the effective monthly rate.

$$0.05/12 = 0.0041667 = 0.41667\%$$

Now we can determine the total interest paid over the first seven months and over the remaining five months.

$$\text{Interest (months 1 to 7)} = \$600,000 \times 0.0041667 \times 7 = \$17,500.14$$
$$\text{Interest (months 8 to 12)} = \$400,000 \times 0.0041667 \times 5 = \$8,333.40$$
$$\text{Total interest} = \$17,500.14 + \$8,333.40 = \$25,833.54$$

We then need to estimate the commitment fees throughout the year.

$$\text{Commitment fee (months 1 to 7)} = (\$800,000 - \$600,000) \times 0.0050 \times 7 = \$7,000$$
$$\text{Commitment fee (months 8 to 12)} = (\$800,000 - \$400,000) \times 0.0050 \times 5 = \$10,000$$
$$\text{Total commitment fees} = \$7,000 + \$10,000 = \$17,000$$
$$\text{Total costs} = \$25,833.54 + \$17,000 = \$42,833.54$$

We then estimate the average amount of financing throughout the year, which can be related to the total annual costs. Notice that we need to take a weighted average to determine the appropriate figure.

$$\text{Average net financing} = [(7/12) \times \$600,000] + [(5/12) \times \$400,000] = \$516,667$$

Now we can use Equation 24.2 to estimate the effective annual cost.

$$k = \left(1 + \frac{\$42,833.54}{\$516,667}\right)^{1} - 1 = 0.0829 = 8.29\%$$

Notice that the exponent is 1 because we are using annual costs and annual average financing amounts (i.e., if we were using 30-day figures, then the exponent would be 365/30).

---

# Factor Arrangements

As described earlier, a "factor" is an independent company that acts as an outside credit department for its clients. It checks the credit of new customers, authorizes credit, handles collections and bookkeeping, and sometimes will purchase a firm's receivables (at a discount). In practice, various arrangements are possible, with factors providing different combinations of these services. Factors provide the ultimate in convenience; however, as with most things, there is a cost, and the costs are typically high. Example 24.7 demonstrates how we can estimate the costs associated with a particular type of factoring arrangement.

---

**EXAMPLE 24.7** | Factor Arrangement

A company has daily credit sales of $40,000 and an average collection period (ACP) of 45 days. A factor offers a 45-day accounts receivable (AR) loan equal to 75 percent of accounts receivable. The quoted interest rate is 8 percent and there is a commission fee of 1 percent of accounts receivable. The firm estimates that it will save $2,000 in collection costs and will experience a 0.5-percent reduction in bad debt losses (as a percentage of sales) as a result of the factoring arrangement. What is the effective annual cost of the arrangement?

**Solution**

$$\text{Accounts receivable (AR)} = \text{ACP} \times \text{Daily credit sales} = 45 \times \$40,000 = \$1.8 \text{ million}$$
$$\text{Loan amount} = 0.75 \times \text{AR} = 0.75 \times \$1.8 \text{ million} = \$1.35 \text{ million}$$
$$\text{Commission} = 0.01 \times \text{AR} = 0.01 \times \$1.8 \text{ million} = \$18,000$$
$$\text{Interest} = 0.08 \times 45/365 \times \$1.35 \text{ million} = \$13,315.07$$
$$\text{Savings} = \$2,000 + (0.005 \times 45 \text{ days} \times \$40,000/\text{day}) = \$2,000 + \$9,000 = \$11,000$$
$$\text{Net cost} = \$18,000 + \$13,315.07 - \$11,000 = \$20,315.07$$

$$k = \left(1 + \frac{\$20,315.07}{\$1,350,000}\right)^{\frac{365}{45}} - 1 = 12.88\%$$

---

# Money Market Instruments

Larger firms with good credit ratings that require large amounts of short-term financing may be able to issue money market instruments. These securities provide the firm with a cost advantage over other short-term financing options; however, the conditions may be somewhat restrictive. Firms generally have two major types of money market instruments available to them: commercial paper (CP) and bankers' acceptances (BAs).

As discussed in Chapter 18, commercial paper is essentially a short-term promissory note issued by firms, which is rated by external debt agencies in a similar fashion to bonds. Only large firms with top-notch credit ratings can issue CP. It is usually issued at a discount from face value, providing purchasers with an implicit yield. CP is issued in large amounts (usually more than $100,000), and the most common maturity dates are 30, 60, and 90 days. Usually, CP is backed by a bank line of credit.

Bankers' acceptances are similar to CP in many regards—they are issued at a discount from face value in large denominations, with common maturity dates of 30, 60, and 90 days. They differ from CP because they are "stamped" by a bank as accepted in return for a fee that is usually 0.25 percent to 1 percent of the face value of the BAs. In return, the bank guarantees the payments associated with these instruments. Therefore, BAs carry the credit risk of the bank that stamps them and not the company that borrows by using them. Most of the companies that issue BAs are large, well-known firms with excellent credit ratings. However, because of the bank guarantee, some firms that are not able to issue CP may be able to borrow by using BAs—provided they can find a bank that is willing to guarantee their payments.

However, while CP and BAs are generally a cheap source of financing for the firm, they have to be constantly "rolled over" or sold to new purchasers every 30, 60, or 90 days, with

## Lessons to Be Learned

During the 2008 financial crisis, the market for short-term financing through commercial paper and bankers' acceptances virtually "dried up." Unfortunately, many businesses were ill-prepared for this. When they approached the banks for additional short-term financing, they discovered that the banks were not lending freely either, and many firms faced a severe liquidity crisis, from which many of them never recovered. In fact, due to the critical nature of this market as a source of short-term business funding, the U.S. Federal Reserve established the Commercial Paper Funding Facility (CPFF) on October 27, 2008, in order to provide liquidity for this market; the Bank of Canada did likewise in Canada. The lesson for businesses and individuals alike is that it is prudent to maintain some excess liquidity, or excess borrowing power, in order to be prepared for emergencies.

no guarantee that the rate that will be charged in the future will remain competitive. As the financial crisis showed only too vividly, in a flight to quality, the cost is sometimes very high, and some firms may not be able to refinance at any price as investors cannot distinguish between good, stable firms and firms that might fail. In 2010, there was $26 billion in CP outstanding and $45 billion in BAs; by the end of 2018, these amounts increased to $59 billion and $86 billion, respectively. The significant increase was due in large part to a strong Canadian economy with an increased demand for low-cost financing.

The yield on CP and BAs is usually quoted based on an approximate annual yield, which is calculated using Equation 24.3.

$$\text{Approximate annual yield} = \frac{\text{Discount}}{\text{Market price}} \times \frac{365}{\text{Days to maturity}} \qquad [24.3]$$

To estimate the effective annual cost to the firm, we can use Equation 24.2, as we did for the other financing options, with the discount amount representing the major part of the financing cost. Examples 24.8 and 24.9 demonstrate how a firm estimates the cost associated with borrowing by using CP or BAs.

---

**EXAMPLE 24.8** | Commercial Paper

**a.** Estimate the effective annual cost to a firm of issuing 90-day commercial paper with a $10-million face value, for net proceeds of $9.90 million. The firm must maintain a $10-million credit line, on which it must pay a standby fee of 0.1 percent.

**b.** Determine the quoted yield for the commercial paper.

**Solution**

**a.** Discount = $10 million − $9.90 million = $0.10 million

Standby fee = 0.001 × $10 million = $10,000 = $0.01 million

Total financing cost = $0.10 million + $0.01 million = $0.11 million

$$k = \left(1 + \frac{\text{n-day financing cost}}{\text{Purchase price}}\right)^{\frac{365}{n}} - 1 = \left(1 + \frac{\$0.11 \text{ million}}{\$9.90 \text{ million}}\right)^{\frac{365}{90}} - 1 = 4.58\%$$

**b.** Approximate annual (quoted) yield

$$\text{Approximate annual (quoted) yield} = \frac{\text{Discount}}{\text{Market price}} \times \frac{365}{\text{Days to maturity}}$$

$$= \frac{\$0.10 \text{ million}}{\$9.90 \text{ million}} \times \frac{365}{90} = 0.0410 \text{ or } 4.10 \text{ percent}$$

---

**EXAMPLE 24.9** | Bankers' Acceptances

Estimate the effective annual cost to a firm that issues $100 million (face value) of 90-day BAs at a quoted rate of 4.25 percent, if the bank charges a 0.3-percent stamping fee.

**Solution**  We estimate the selling price of the BAs by rearranging Equation 24.3:

$$4.25\% = \frac{\text{Discount}}{\text{Market price}} \times \frac{365}{\text{Days to maturity}} = \frac{\text{Face} - \text{Price}}{\text{Price}} \times \frac{365}{90}$$

$$0.0425 \times 90/365 = (\$100 \text{ million} - \text{Price})/\text{Price}$$
$$0.010479 = (\$100 \text{ million} - \text{Price})/\text{Price}$$
$$0.010479 \times \text{Price} = \$100 \text{ million} - \text{Price}$$
$$1.010479 \times \text{Price} = \$100 \text{ million}$$
$$\text{Price} = \$100 \text{ million}/1.010479 = \$98.962967 \text{ million}$$

$$\text{Discount} = \$100 \text{ million} - \$98.962967 \text{ million} = \$1.037033 \text{ million}$$
$$\text{Stamping fee} = 0.003 \times \$100 \text{ million} = \$300,000 = \$0.3 \text{ million}$$
$$\text{Total financing cost} = \$1.037033 \text{ million} + \$0.3 \text{ million} = \$1.337033 \text{ million}$$

$$k = \left(1 + \frac{\text{n-day financing cost}}{\text{Purchase price}}\right)^{\frac{365}{n}} - 1 = \left(1 + \frac{\$1.337033 \text{ million}}{\$98.962967 \text{ million}}\right)^{\frac{365}{90}} - 1 = 5.59\%$$

# Securitizations

**special purpose vehicles (SPVs)** conduits for packaging portfolios of receivables and selling them to investors in the money market; a recent innovation in financing trade credit

A more recent innovation in financing trade credit is the use of **special purpose vehicles (SPVs)**. SPVs are conduits for packaging portfolios of receivables and selling them to investors in the money market. In this way, the purchaser relies on the credit of the SPV rather than the credit of the company selling the receivables. For example, Ford Motor Co. of Canada finances the purchase of its vehicles. It can do this by using any of the previously mentioned instruments. It can take out a bank loan or issue commercial paper or bankers' acceptances and then use the proceeds to finance car loans. However, such is the volume of car financing that Ford's balance sheet would quickly look like that of a financial institution, with large amounts of short-term borrowing financing short-term car loans. To avoid this, Ford can sell its car loans directly to the capital market through an SPV so that neither the loans nor the financing appear on its balance sheet. This process is called **securitization**.

**securitization** the process of packaging loans and/or receivables together to create new securities

The essence of securitization is that the credit risk of the seller of the receivables or loans is not directly involved. For example, when Ford packages its car loans, the buyers of these loans look primarily to the loans held in the SPV and evaluate their credit, rather than looking to Ford's credit, which is what would happen if Ford issued commercial paper to finance its car loans. However, as we saw in Chapter 18, the money market is highly credit conscious because investments are short term and, in practice, any money market instrument has to be of investment grade. This poses a problem because, as we have seen earlier, many firms will extend credit in situations where a bank would not. This occurs because the firm makes a profit margin on the sale and is anticipating a long-term relationship involving future sales and future profits. If a portfolio of receivables or loans is simply sold to investors, in all likelihood the credit quality would not be high enough to get an investment-grade rating. As a result, **credit enhancements** have to be made, such as requiring collateral, insurance, or other agreements, to reduce credit risk.

**credit enhancements** actions taken to reduce credit risk, such as requiring collateral, insurance, or other agreements

To access the Canadian money market, a Dominion Bond Rating Service (DBRS) credit rating is required. In generating its credit ratings, DBRS looks to the seller, the collateral, and the structure of the securitization. Although the primary credit concern involves the pool of receivables or loans, the financial health of the seller is still important for several reasons. The most obvious one is that the seller may sell poor-quality loans into the SPV so that, over time, the quality of the SPV deteriorates. (There is also a slim possibility of fraud.) As well, the seller still services the loans; when the creditor makes payments on the loan or someone pays off the receivable, it is the seller who has to service those payments and pass them to the SPV to be distributed to investors.

The collateral in the SPV depends on the particular issue. In the case of Ford, the underlying asset is car loans. Other securitizations have been made by Deere & Company (John Deere) and Bombardier Inc. with equipment loans, while Receivables Acquisition and Management Corporation and its clones have been used by Canadian Imperial Bank of Commerce (CIBC) to package receivables from a number of Canadian companies. In each

**prepayment** the payment of a debt before its due date

case, DBRS looks at the historical default rates on the loans and the history of **prepayments**, because frequently loans are paid off early. By pooling a large number of loans in an SPV, these financial characteristics are fairly stable, but DBRS will stress-test the effect of changing historical rates to see how it affects the ability of the SPV to pay off its securities. For example, the annual default rate for Ford car loans is about 1 percent and tends to be highest in the first two years, so the credit quality can be improved by taking more seasoned loans that have been outstanding longer. However, the problem then is that they are more likely to be prepaid.

The most important aspect of an SPV is usually the credit enhancements because, as mentioned earlier, the credit quality of the underlying assets often needs to be enhanced to get an AAA credit rating. For the sale of the loans to be taken off the seller's balance sheet, accounting standards require that the SPV can go back to the seller for no more than 10 percent of the assets. As a result, there are usually external as well as seller credit enhancements. These credit enhancements take several forms:

- The seller may absorb 5 percent of the losses—this is often referred to as over-collateralization.
- A third party, such as a major bank, like the Union Bank of Switzerland, may absorb the next 10 percent of losses on trade receivables.
- Subordinated debt may be issued by the seller to absorb further defaults on termination of the SPV.
- Different classes of securities may be created or issued so that the prepayment risks are allocated to different securities, as is often the case with mortgage SPVs.

Securitization has been an important part of the Canadian financial landscape for more than two decades. At the end of March 2019, the Canadian securitization market totalled nearly $96 billion. This is down from the peak year of 2006, when this form of financing reached $106 billion. It is dominated by credit card receivables, which make up nearly 38 percent of the market. Auto-related transactions follow next at over 26 percent of the total.[5]

In practice, firms use some combination of the short-term financing options mentioned to provide them with the desired mix of flexibility and cost effectiveness. Usually, trade credit and bank loans are the predominant sources of short-term financing, especially for smaller firms that do not have the option of accessing the money market.

## Concept Review Questions

1. What is the cost of 3/15 net 60 trade credit?
2. What is the difference between a bank operating line of credit and a traditional loan?
3. What additional services does a factor provide over a bank?
4. What is the difference between a BA and commercial paper?
5. Why do securitizations require credit enhancements?

---

[5]Data from DBRS, "Canadian Securitization Market Overview." Securitization Servicer Report, March 2019.

# Review

## Summary

In the first part of this chapter, we demonstrate that the optimal level of investment in cash, receivables, and inventory occurs when the benefits balance the costs. In the case of cash, the benefit is the reduced risk of insolvency, while the cost is the opportunity costs of having funds tied up in assets that provide a relatively low return. For receivables, the benefits tend to be increased sales and profitability, while the costs include the financing costs and the increased risk of non-payment by customers. Finally, for inventory, the benefits may be improved production processes or reduced risk of stock-outs, which result in forgone revenue and can also damage customer goodwill. The costs include financing, storage, spoilage, obsolescence, and insurance. Successful companies employ effective systems to maximize the benefits of these assets while minimizing the costs.

In the second part of this chapter, we examine the most common short-term financing options available to companies—namely, trade credit, bank loans, factoring arrangements, and money market instruments. We discuss the benefits and disadvantages of each method and show how we can estimate the associated effective annual costs.

## Summary of Learning Objectives

### 24.1 Explain the motivation for holding cash and the methods used to implement effective cash management techniques.

The motivations for holding cash include the transaction motive, the precautionary motive, the finance motive, and the speculative motive. The general approach to good cash management is to speed up inflows as much as possible and delay outflows as much as possible.

### 24.2 Describe how accounts receivable are managed.

The decision to extend credit is often based on a formal credit analysis process, which is designed to assess the risk of non-payment by potential customers. The process involves collecting information about customers' credit history, their ability to make payments as reflected in their expected cash flows (which is closely related to income), and their overall financial stability (as reflected in their net worth and their level of existing debt obligations).

### 24.3 Describe how inventory is managed.

There are four inventory management approaches: the ABC approach, the economic order quantity (EOQ) model, materials requirement planning (MRP), and just-in-time (JIT) inventory systems.

### 24.4 Describe the major sources of short-term financing.

- *Trade credit:* A firm purchases its supplies on account and, based on its credit terms, can delay payments to suppliers—essentially "borrowing." This is generally a convenient and inexpensive form of short-term financing; however, it can become expensive as firms often have to forgo discounts.
- *Bank loans (lines of credit):* A firm borrows up to a predetermined amount to finance temporary cash deficits; the firm has the ability to control the principal of the loan, increasing or decreasing it throughout the term.
- *Factor arrangements:* A firm hires an independent institution that collects accounts receivable for a fee or acts as an outside credit department.
- *Money market instruments (commercial paper and bankers' acceptances):* Larger firms with good credit ratings may be able to issue money market instruments; these securities provide a cost advantage over other short-term financing, but the conditions may be more restrictive.
- *Securitizations:* Special purpose vehicles are conduits for packaging portfolios of receivables and selling them to investors in the money market.

## Key Terms

## Equations

| Equation | Description | Formula | Page |
|---|---|---|---|
| **[24.1]** | Net Present Value | $\text{NPV} = \text{PV(Future CFs)} - \text{CF}_0$ | p. 24-9 |
| **[24.2]** | Annual Percentage Cost of Trade Credit | $k = \left(1 + \dfrac{\text{n-day financing cost}}{\text{Purchase price}}\right)^{\frac{365}{n}} - 1$ | p. 24-14 |
| **[24.3]** | Approximate Annual Yield on a Money Market Security | $\text{Approximate annual yield} = \dfrac{\text{Discount}}{\text{Market price}} \times \dfrac{365}{\text{Days to maturity}}$ | p. 24-19 |

# Questions and Practice Problems

## Multiple Choice Questions

1. **(LO 24.1)** Which of the following is *not* near-cash?

   **a.** T-bills

   **b.** Commercial paper

   **c.** Bankers' acceptances

   **d.** Long-term debt

2. **(LO 24.1)** Which of the following descriptions about near-cash is *false*?

   **a.** Low returns

   **b.** Great liquidity

   **c.** Minimal additional risk

   **d.** No credit risk

3. **(LO 24.2)** Which of the following statements about float time is *false*?

   **a.** Historically, mailing time is the shortest.

   **b.** An efficient credit policy speeds up inflows.

   **c.** Cheque-processing time is one source of float.

   **d.** Using preauthorized payment is one way to shorten float time.

4. **(LO 24.2)** A supplier offers a firm credit terms of 2/30 net 45. The sales price of the products is $1,000. What is the effective annual cost of forgoing the discount?

   **a.** 63 percent        **c.** 28 percent

   **b.** 18 percent        **d.** 62 percent

5. **(LO 24.2)** A firm's credit terms specify 1/10 net 30 and the accounts receivable days outstanding is 37 days. Which of the following can be concluded on the basis of this information?

   **a)** All customers pay within 37 days of purchase.

   **b)** Most customers pay for their invoices on time.

   **c)** All customers pay late.

   **d)** The average customer pays 7 days late.

6. **(LO 24.2)** Which of the following statements regarding a firm stretching their accounts payable is *false*?

   **a)** A firm's credit rating might be negatively impacted by frequent delays in paying suppliers.

   **b)** The supplier might demand COD (Cash on Delivery) or CBD (Cash before Delivery) going forward.

   **c)** The supplier might choose to discontinue their relationship with the firm if they viewed them as a delinquent customer and if they had doubts as to whether they would receive payment.

   **d)** The cost of credit, in some circumstances, would increase as payments are delayed.

7. **(LO 24.2)** Which of the following statements about factor arrangements is *false*?

   **a.** A factor is an independent company.

   **b.** A factor often checks the credit of new customers.

   **c.** Factor arrangements can be costly.

   **d.** A factor does not purchase accounts receivable from its clients.

8. **(LO 24.3)** Which of the following is a weakness of the inventory turnover ratio?

   **a.** It does not measure costs incurred due to a shortage of inventory.

   **b.** It does not explicitly measure financing costs.

   **c.** It cannot be used to compare companies that use different methods to account for inventory.

   **d.** All of the above

9. **(LO 24.4)** Which of the following statements about bank loans is *false*?

   **a.** The rate is normally variable.

   **b.** Lines of credit usually link to the firm's chequing account.

   **c.** Operating loans are usually secured by accounts receivable and inventory.

   **d.** The cost of operating loans is quite high.

10. **(LO 24.4)** Suppose a firm is offered a two-year variable rate monthly pay loan at prime plus 1 percent, with a prime rate of 5 percent. What is the effective annual cost of the loan regardless of other fees?

    **a.** 5.12 percent

    **b.** 12.68 percent

    **c.** 6.17 percent

    **d.** 12.72 percent

11. **(LO 24.4)** Which of the following statements about money market instruments is *false*?

    **a.** They provide large amounts of short-term financing for firms with good credit ratings.

    **b.** Two main types available are commercial paper and bankers' acceptances.

    **c.** They are similar to bonds.

    **d.** CP can be issued by any firm that needs large amounts of short-term financing.

## Practice Problems

### Basic

12. **(LO 24.2)** What are three major sources of float? What are some common methods that address float?

13. **(LO 24.2)** Explain the function of a factor in working capital management.

14. **(LO 24.2)** What is the purpose of credit analysis and how is it accomplished?

15. **(LO 24.2)** When a firm is deciding whether or not to extend credit to an applicant, what two things need to be established about the applicant?

16. **(LO 24.4)** Habitant Maple Syrup Sweets Company just issued $25 million of 180-day commercial paper for net proceeds of $24.5 million. What is the commercial paper's quoted yield?

### Intermediate

17. **(LO 24.1)** Explain the transactions motive.

18. **(LO 24.1)** State the principle of the optimal cash balance.

19. **(LO 24.1)** State four main motives firms have to hold cash.

20. **(LO 24.2)** Should trade credit always be used when it is offered?

21. **(LO 24.2)** What are captive finance companies?

**22. (LO 24.3)** What are some of the advantages of carrying inventories?

**23. (LO 24.3)** What are some of the disadvantages of carrying inventories?

**24. (LO 24.3)** Describe the four inventory management approaches.

**25. (LO 24.4)** Explain how commercial paper differs from bankers' acceptances.

**26. (LO 24.4)** Montreal Brewers is going to issue $100 million of 90-day commercial paper for net proceeds of $99 million. Montreal Brewers must maintain a $100-million credit line, on which it must pay a standby fee of 0.15 percent. What is the commercial paper's effective annual cost?

**27. (LO 24.4)**

    **a.** Calculate the effective annual cost of forgoing the discount from credit terms of 2/15 net 60. The selling price is $800.

    **b.** Another supplier offers $820 on credit terms of net 90. If you could finance the purchase by using loans at an effective annual cost of 10 percent for part a, which option should you choose?

**28. (LO 24.4)** What are special purpose vehicles (SPVs)? What is the main advantage of SPVs? List a few forms of credit enhancement that are critical to SPVs.

**29. (LO 24.4)** Suppose Sio Inc. has 45 days of accounts receivable (AR) of $900,000 on its books. A factor offers a 45-day AR loan equal to 90 percent of AR. The quoted interest rate is 6 percent, and there is a commission fee of 0.5 percent. The factoring will result in a reduction of $8,000 in bad debt losses. What is the effective annual cost?

**30. (LO 24.4)** What is the effective annual cost if a firm issues $5 million face value of 90-day commercial paper for net proceeds of $4.85 million? The firm pays a standby fee of 0.1 percent on the face value.

**31. (LO 24.2, 24.4)** There are two suppliers of one input for a factory. Supplier A offers a selling price of $1,000 with terms of 1/10 net 30, while Supplier B offers $1,100 with 3/10 net 60. Which supplier offers the lower effective annual cost?

## Challenging

**32. (LO 24.1)** A company receives an average of $100,000 in cheques per day from its customers. It takes the company an average of five days to receive and deposit these cheques. The company is considering a lockbox arrangement that would reduce its collection float time by two days, and cost it $100 per month. If its opportunity cost of funds tied up in float is 2 percent, should it adopt the new system?

**33. (LO 24.2)** ABC Inc. currently grants no credit, but it is considering offering new credit terms of net 30. As a result, the price of its product will increase by $2 per unit. The original price per unit is $50. Expected sales will increase by 1,000 units per year. The original sales are 10,000 units. Variable costs will remain at $25 per unit and bad debt losses will amount to $3,000 per year. The firm will finance the additional investment in receivables by using a line of credit, which charges 5-percent interest. The firm's tax rate is 20 percent. Should the firm begin extending credit under the terms described? (Assume ABC benefits from the credit policy change indefinitely.)

**34. (LO 24.2)** Suppose that ABC Inc. (see practice problem 33) switches to 3/10 net 30 from net 30. It is estimated that 80 percent of customers will take advantage of the discount, while the remaining 20 percent will pay on day 30. The price will increase from $52 to $53 per unit; unit sales will remain at 11,000 per year; and variable costs will remain at $25 per unit. Bad debt losses will not be affected. Assume a 40-percent tax rate and a 5-percent discount rate. Should the firm switch to the new policy?

**35. (LO 24.2)** EastShore Inc. has an ACP of 60 days and daily credit sales of $75,000. A factor offers a 60-day accounts receivable loan equal to 90 percent of accounts receivable. The quoted interest rate is 10 percent and the commission fee is 1.5 percent of accounts receivable of the firm. As a result, the firm will save $3,000 and have a 1-percent reduction in bad debt losses, which are $500,000. What is the effective annual cost of the factor arrangement?

**36. (LO 24.2)** ABC Inc. grants credit terms of net 25. It is considering a new policy that involves more stringent credit terms: net 20. As a result, the price of its product will stay the same at $45. The expected sales will decrease by 2,000 per year to 10,000 units. Variable costs will remain at $37 per unit and bad debt losses can be reduced by $1,000 per year to $2,000. ABC Inc. will finance the additional investment in receivables using its line of credit, which charges 5-percent interest after tax, and its tax rate is 30 percent. Should ABC Inc. switch to the new policy?

**37. (LO 24.4)** Calculate the effective annual cost of issuing 270-day BAs at a quoted rate of 5 percent with a face value of $10 million. The bank charges a 0.6-percent stamping fee.

**38. (LO 24.4)** A firm engaged a one-year, monthly pay, $100,000 line of credit at 9 percent plus a 0.25-percent commitment fee on the unused portion of the line. The firm used 75 percent of the line for the first half year and reduced the loan amount to 60 percent for the rest of the year. What is the effective annual rate of the loan?

**39. (LO 24.4)** Calculate the effective annual cost of a one-year $2-million operating line of credit. The firm borrowed $1.2 million for the first four months of the year and reduced the loan amount to $500,000 for the rest of the year. The quoted interest rate is 6 percent, and there is a 0.8-percent commitment fee on the unused portion.

**40. (LO 24.4)** What is the effective annual cost if a firm issues $10 million of 180-day BAs at a quoted rate of 5.5 percent, and the bank charges it a 0.4-percent stamping fee? Compare the effective annual cost of 180-day commercial paper issued at $10 million face value for a price of $9,748,000, while the firm must maintain a $10 million credit line and pay a standby fee of 0.4 percent.

**TABLE A.1**   Cumulative Normal Distribution Table

| d | N(d) | d | N(d) | d | N(d) | d | N(d) | d | N(d) | d | N(d) |
|---|---|---|---|---|---|---|---|---|---|---|---|
| −3.00 | .0013 | −1.58 | .0571 | −0.76 | .2236 | 0.06 | .5239 | 0.86 | .8051 | 1.66 | .9515 |
| −2.95 | .0016 | −1.56 | .0594 | −0.74 | .2297 | 0.08 | .5319 | 0.88 | .8106 | 1.68 | .9535 |
| −2.90 | .0019 | −1.54 | .0618 | −0.72 | .2358 | 0.10 | .5398 | 0.90 | .8159 | 1.70 | .9554 |
| −2.85 | .0022 | −1.52 | .0643 | −0.70 | .2420 | 0.12 | .5478 | 0.92 | .8212 | 1.72 | .9573 |
| −2.80 | .0026 | −1.50 | .0668 | −0.68 | .2483 | 0.14 | .5557 | 0.94 | .8264 | 1.74 | .9591 |
| −2.75 | .0030 | −1.48 | .0694 | −0.66 | .2546 | 0.16 | .5636 | 0.96 | .8315 | 1.76 | .9608 |
| −2.70 | .0035 | −1.46 | .0721 | −0.64 | .2611 | 0.18 | .5714 | 0.98 | .8365 | 1.78 | .9625 |
| −2.65 | .0040 | −1.44 | .0749 | −0.62 | .2676 | 0.20 | .5793 | 1.00 | .8414 | 1.80 | .9641 |
| −2.60 | .0047 | −1.42 | .0778 | −0.60 | .2743 | 0.22 | .5871 | 1.02 | .8461 | 1.82 | .9556 |
| −2.55 | .0054 | −1.40 | .0808 | −0.58 | .2810 | 0.24 | .5948 | 1.04 | .8508 | 1.84 | .9671 |
| −2.50 | .0062 | −1.38 | .0838 | −0.56 | .2877 | 0.26 | .6026 | 1.06 | .8554 | 1.86 | .9686 |
| −2.45 | .0071 | −1.36 | .0869 | −0.54 | .2946 | 0.28 | .6103 | 1.08 | .8599 | 1.88 | .9699 |
| −2.40 | .0082 | −1.34 | .0901 | −0.52 | .3015 | 0.30 | .6179 | 1.10 | .8643 | 1.90 | .9713 |
| −2.35 | .0094 | −1.32 | .0934 | −0.50 | .3085 | 0.32 | .6255 | 1.12 | .8686 | 1.92 | .9726 |
| −2.30 | .0107 | −1.30 | .0968 | −0.48 | .3156 | 0.34 | .6331 | 1.14 | .8729 | 1.94 | .9738 |
| −2.25 | .0122 | −1.28 | .1003 | −0.46 | .3228 | 0.36 | .6406 | 1.16 | .8770 | 1.96 | .9750 |
| −2.20 | .0139 | −1.26 | .1038 | −0.44 | .3300 | 0.38 | .6480 | 1.18 | .8810 | 1.98 | .9761 |
| −2.15 | .0158 | −1.24 | .1075 | −0.42 | .3373 | 0.40 | .6556 | 1.20 | .8849 | 2.00 | .9772 |
| −2.10 | .0179 | −1.22 | .1112 | −0.40 | .3446 | 0.42 | .6628 | 1.22 | .8888 | 2.05 | .9798 |
| −2.05 | .0202 | −1.20 | .1151 | −0.38 | .3520 | 0.44 | .6700 | 1.24 | .8925 | 2.10 | .9821 |
| −2.00 | .0228 | −1.18 | .1190 | −0.36 | .3594 | 0.46 | .6773 | 1.26 | .8962 | 2.15 | .9842 |
| −1.98 | .0239 | −1.16 | .1230 | −0.34 | .3669 | 0.48 | .6844 | 1.28 | .8997 | 2.20 | .9861 |
| −1.96 | .0250 | −1.14 | .1271 | −0.32 | .3745 | 0.50 | .6915 | 1.30 | .9032 | 2.25 | .9878 |
| −1.94 | .0262 | −1.12 | .1314 | −0.30 | .3821 | 0.52 | .6985 | 1.32 | .9066 | 2.30 | .9893 |
| −1.92 | .0274 | −1.10 | .1357 | −0.28 | .3897 | 0.54 | .7054 | 1.34 | .9099 | 2.35 | .9906 |
| −1.90 | .0287 | −1.08 | .1401 | −0.26 | .3974 | 0.56 | .7123 | 1.36 | .9131 | 2.40 | .9918 |
| −1.88 | .0301 | −1.06 | .1446 | −0.24 | .4052 | 0.58 | .7191 | 1.38 | .9162 | 2.45 | .9929 |
| −1.86 | .0314 | −1.04 | .1492 | −0.22 | .4129 | 0.60 | .7258 | 1.40 | .9192 | 2.50 | .9938 |
| −1.84 | .0329 | −1.02 | .1539 | −0.20 | .4207 | 0.62 | .7324 | 1.42 | .9222 | 2.55 | .9946 |
| −1.82 | .0344 | −1.00 | .1587 | −0.18 | .4286 | 0.64 | .7389 | 1.44 | .9251 | 2.60 | .9953 |
| −1.80 | .0359 | −0.98 | .1635 | −0.16 | .4365 | 0.66 | .7454 | 1.46 | .9279 | 2.65 | .9960 |
| −1.78 | .0375 | −0.96 | .1685 | −0.14 | .4443 | 0.68 | .7518 | 1.48 | .9306 | 2.70 | .9965 |
| −1.76 | .0392 | −0.94 | .1736 | −0.12 | .4523 | 0.70 | .7580 | 1.50 | .9332 | 2.75 | .9970 |
| −1.74 | .0409 | −0.92 | .1788 | −0.10 | .4602 | 0.72 | .7642 | 1.52 | .9357 | 2.80 | .9974 |
| −1.72 | .0427 | −0.90 | .1841 | −0.08 | .4681 | 0.74 | .7704 | 1.54 | .9382 | 2.85 | .9978 |
| −1.70 | .0446 | −0.88 | .1894 | −0.06 | .4761 | 0.76 | .7764 | 1.56 | .9406 | 2.90 | .9981 |
| −1.68 | .0465 | −0.86 | .1949 | −0.04 | .4841 | 0.78 | .7823 | 1.58 | .9429 | 2.95 | .9984 |
| −1.66 | .0485 | −0.84 | .2005 | −0.02 | .4920 | 0.80 | .7882 | 1.60 | .9452 | 3.00 | .9986 |
| −1.64 | .0505 | −0.82 | .2061 | 0.00 | .5000 | 0.82 | .7939 | 1.62 | .9474 | 3.05 | .9989 |
| −1.62 | .0526 | −0.80 | .2119 | 0.02 | .5080 | 0.84 | .7996 | 1.64 | .9495 | | |
| −1.60 | .0548 | −0.78 | .2117 | 0.04 | .5160 | | | | | | |

# Index

Note: Page references followed by "f" refer to figures, page references followed by "t" refer to tables, and page references followed by "n" refer to footnotes.